Measured
going 1

I can't im
least on

шен знешес
— Cape Argus

No wine producing country has such a dominant and all-embracing wine annual
— Jancis Robinson

A trusted and helpful companion
— Sowetan

An invaluable aide to the winelands for local wine lovers and foreign tourists alike
— Financial Mail

If you know absolutely nothing whatsoever about wine, this book will single-handedly save your blushes in so-called sophisticated company
— The Citizen

The bottom line is that if you like wine you should keep Platter close to hand
— The Witness

Platter's
SOUTH AFRICAN
WINES
2 0 0 8

THE GUIDE TO CELLARS, VINEYARDS

WINEMAKERS, RESTAURANTS

AND ACCOMMODATION

The John Platter SA Wine Guide (Pty) Ltd
www.platteronline.com

Publisher
Andrew McDowall

Editor
Philip van Zyl

Associate editors
Tim James, Jos Baker, Cathy van Zyl, Lindsaye McGregor & Ina Smith

Tasters
Michael Fridjhon, Angela Lloyd; Master of Wine Cathy van Zyl; Cape Wine Masters Tim James, Christine Rudman, Irina von Holdt & Meryl Weaver; Dave Swingler, Dave Biggs, Jabulani Ntshangase, Mzokhona Mvemve, Ingrid Motteux, Roland Peens, James Pietersen & Jörg Pfützner. 2007 edition: Dave Hughes & Clive Torr

Contributors
Lindsaye McGregor, Lynne Kloot, Wendy Toerien, Pippa de Bruyn, Ingrid Motteux, Joanne Simon, Jean-Pierre Rossouw, Tracey Hawthorne, Clifford Roberts; Cape Wine Masters Ginette de Fleuriot & Meryl Weaver

Co-ordinators
Anneke Potgieter, Kim Dicksen Greeff & Ina de Villiers

Database
Sean de Kock

Design
Aline Balayer

Maps & typesetting
Gawie du Toit

Photography
Dennis Gordon

Advertising
Linda Ransome   T 021-438-6161
Young Media   T 011-648-3869

Sales
Alison Worrall   T 083-530-9761

© The John Platter SA Wine Guide (Pty) Ltd 2008
PO Box 1466 Hermanus 7200
Tel: 082-490-1820 • Fax: 028-312-1395
winebook@mweb.co.za
www.platteronline.com

ISBN 9780-958-450-669

CONTENTS

Photo Gallery: A Toast to Mother Earth

On the eve of its 350th anniversary, South African wine marches in step with — and often in advance of — global trends regarding environmental conservation, sustainability and responsible eco-citizenship. In our annual visual round-up, we feature some of the individuals and organisations who contribute to not only a greener future but also more wholesome and enjoyable wine in our glass today.

Ratings & descriptions illustrative; refer to A-Z entry for current information

Diemersdal Estate 🍴 🍷 ☕ 🏛 📷
T 021-808 7911 • F 021-883 2603

Durbanville • Est 1698 • 1stB 1990 • Tasting & sales Mon-Fri 9-5 Sat 9-3 • Closed Easter Fri/
Sun, Dec 25 & Jan 1 • Tours by appt • Restaurant or BYO picnics • Walks • Owner Tienie Louw •
Winemakers Tienie & Thys Louw • Viticulturist Div van Niekerk (1980) • 172 ha (cab, merlot,
pinotage, shiraz, chard, sauvignon) • 1 730 tons 15 000 cs own label 79% red 21% white • PO
Box 27 Durbanville 7551 • wines@diemersdal.co.za

Representing the sixth generation of his family, Thys Louw has taken over from Johan Kruger
(see Sterhuis) as winemaker after completing his 'tutorship with Hermann Kirschbaum at
Buitenverwachting. 'With the arrival of the new generation, many things are happening,' says
father Tienie. 'The labels are changing, a new tasting room is being established and new
wines are seeing the light of day.' It was also Louw Jnr's idea to host a harvest picnic at full
moon, which proved such a success it will now become an annual event

★★★★ Shiraz Modern, accessible style with a hint of the classics. 04 (★★★★) more open, affable, than pvs; sweet fleshy fruit with smoky vanilla nuance, but no great dimension,
complexity. Unlike 03, which has many varietal & oak-derived layers. These 14% alc,
12-15 mths Fr oak.

★★★★ Chardonnay Reserve Opulent aromatics the keynote here, partly through new oak

Matys ☺ ★★★ Pronounced Mah-tace, gently wooded equal blend cab, merlot, shiraz,
with 10% pinotage; now 🍾 05 honest, well-made quaffer, lively & plumy. **Blanc de
Blanc ☺ ★★★** Pvs 4-way blend halved to just sauvignon, chard in 06, but pleasure's
doubled: delicious fresh-sliced pear tone; racy, lightish (13% alc); 🍾 for convenience.

Cabernet Sauvignon ★★★★ 04 rated by Tienie L as his best ever. Certainly shows potential – tightly packed ripe fruit, serious oaking (15 mths Fr), structure for keeping – but
needs time to develop. **Merlot** NEW **★★★★** A little gem. Truly ripe fruit, supportive oaking
(16 mths Fr); fine savoury spiciness to 04's raspberry/cherry flavours. **Pinotage ★★★★**
Hallmark charm & grace (rather than the variety's more usual power) on 04, dark fruit &
dried banana whiffs, pleasantly understated oak (14 mths Fr), usual not overpowering 14.
5% alc. **Private Collection ★★★★** 'Vintage' red, blend make-up varies from yr to yr. Bdx
line-up of cab, merlot, cab f (60/30/10) in 04; fairly juicy, with undaunting tannins but
seems embryonic mid-2006, has more to give – cellar yr/3. Fr oak, 2 yrs. – CR

ABBREVIATIONS

% alc	Percentage alcohol by volume	g/ℓ	Grams per litre
1stB	First bottled vintage	IPW	Integrated Production of Wine
BEE	Black Economic Empowerment	IWC	International Wine Challenge
BWI	Biodiversity & Wine Initiative	IWSC	International Wine & Spirit
BYO	Bring your own (wine, picnic)		Competition
Bdx	Bordeaux	JCWCA	Juliet Cullinan Wine
Cs	Cases		Connoisseur's Award
CWG	Cape Winemakers Guild	LBV	Late Bottled Vintage
CWT	Classic Wine Trophy	Malo	Malolactic fermentation
Est	Date established	MCC	Méthode cap classique
EW	Estate wine	MIWA	Michelangelo Int. Wine Awards

SYMBOLS

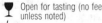

Bottles own wine on property	Other tourist attractions/amenities on the property
Open for tasting (no fee unless noted)	Bring your own (BYO) picnic
Restaurant/refreshments	Child friendly
Accommodation	Wheelchair friendly

Visitable wineries in the A-Z are open on public holidays unless noted

Case = 12 x 750ml bottles

T = Telephone number
F = Fax number

All wines dry unless noted

 ☺ Exceptionally drinkable and well priced

🍾 Screwcapped   **NEW** New wine
✓ Good Value   🌿 Organic

cabernet/cab = cabernet sauvignon
pinot = pinot noir
chenin = chenin blanc
sauvignon/sauv = sauvignon blanc
riesling = Rhine/weisser riesling
touriga = touriga nacional
tinta = tinta barocca
tinta r = tinta roriz
tinta f = tinta franca

Unless noted, red wines wooded (in 225/300ℓ French oak barrels);
Fr = French, Am = American oak;
whites unoaked

Taster's initials

OUR TRACK RECORD-BASED RATING SYSTEM

All wines rated 4 stars or more are set in red type

General rating | ★★★★ **Shiraz** Modern, accessible

For 4-star or better wines, we give the track record over two or more vintages

---

Vintage-specific rating **04** (★★★★) more open

Any differences from the general rating noted in brackets beside the particular vintage

---

★★★★★ Superlative. A Cape classic
★★★★★ Outstanding
★★★★ Excellent
★★★★ Very good/promising
★★★ Characterful, appealing
★★★ Good everyday drinking
★★ Pleasant drinking
★★ Casual quaffing
★ Plain and simple
★ Very ordinary
No star Somewhat less than ordinary

NE	Non-estate wine	Veritas	SA National Bottled Wine Show
NLH	Noble Late Harvest	VG	Veritas gold medal
NV	Non-vintage. Year of harvest not stated on label	VDG	Veritas double-gold medal
		WIETA	Wine Industry Ethical Trade Association
RS	Residual sugar		
SAA	South African Airways (selected for First or Premium Class)	Wine	Wine magazine
		WO	Wine of Origin
SAYWS	SA Young Wine Show	WOM	Wine of the Month Club
SLH	Special Late Harvest	WS	Wine Spectator
Swiss	Swiss Int. Air Lines Wine Awards		
TWS	Trophy Wine Show		

FOREWORD

I believe the vision for the South African wine industry should be '6 to 9'. The average yearly intake of wine in South Africa is more or less 6ℓ per person. How can we get this to 9ℓ? Theoretically, if we take only the rising black market of some 40-million people, and if they consume 3ℓ of wine per head yearly, there will be a shortage of wine soon.

Much is said about generic marketing of SA wines and I believe we can all be a part of this — it makes no difference whether you are a consumer, marketer, viticulturist or winemaker. My good friend Jan 'Ysterarms' Coetzee once shared a quote by well-known American author Louis L'Amour with me: 'Trail dust is thicker than blood.' I took it to mean that colleagues who have travelled together, shared in each other's trials and tribulations, and belong to the same wine industry, maybe even the same winegrowing area, will forever believe in each other, back one another up and be closer than family. We can all start by being positive about the SA wine industry and by not trampling on each other to get a better place in the wine sun.

We are all quick to criticise producers for monopolising winelists, paying for space on shelves, or putting up branded umbrellas. I wonder what the soft drink companies pay to put up their branding but I never hear anything negative about that. We are also quick to criticise the big players about a lot of things but who has thanked, say, Nederburg for having that huge advert on the walls of the OR Tambo International Airport? Or Namaqua Wines for branding UK taxis so that people start to think about SA wine and end up buying a bottle? Be part of the generic SA wine campaign by talking, hearing, writing and being positive about our wines.

A frequently asked question is: how are we going to get wine to the people? Last year, I had the opportunity to tour across the country with the ABSA Top 10 Pinotages and met many white, black and brown people between the ages of 22 and 25. One thing that impressed me was their passion for, and pride in, being part of SA, and their determination to succeed, not in the UK or the US but in our own land. These youngsters happened to all be musicians but there are sportspeople, bankers, lawyers and chefs who love wine and also have passion, pride and determination. Team up with them, and ultimately who do you think will drink only pinotage? (Sorry, I'm back on my favourite subject again …)

We can sometimes go way over the head of the average consumer when we talk about our wines. The pH, TA and VA should be on your fact sheet, not in your speech. Last week I met a black school teacher in the new Bottelary Wine Centre and he said that because of me he drinks only red wine now. Years ago, at a tasting, I told him about the positive effect red wine has on health, that it contains resveratrol which is 12 times stronger than any other antioxidant and, if you drink a glass or two a day, it increases the antioxidants working in your bloodstream by 75% for 15 hours, and that red wine per bottle is the cheapest medicine. I skipped the pH, TA and VA — and now he is sold on wine forever.

Let's ditch the jargon and start being more down-to-earth when talking about wine. Let's work together and co-operate rather than criticise. And let's support those with a passion for wine so that they become our brand ambassadors. If we achieve this, what seems an impossibly ambitious target of 9ℓ of (responsibly consumed) wine per person per year might turn out to be positively conservative!

Beyers Truter
Co-owner/winemaker of Beyerskloof, chairman of the Pinotage Association

EDITOR'S NOTE

As we put this book to bed, we were thrilled and buoyed by the news that the previous edition had been judged by the esteemed Louis Roederer International Wine Writers' Awards panel to be the best annual wine guide of 2007. Welcome recognition indeed for a publishing venture now in its 28th year and, more than ever, a team effort involving many talented, hard-working people. We gratefully share this honour with them, and with the SA wine industry, without whose support the book could not be produced.

For the present edition, our aim and approach remain the same: to taste, rate and describe as many SA-made wines available during the currency of the book, both locally and overseas, as possible. Much as we'd like to, the sheer number of individual wines (over 6 000) precludes us from re-tasting and re-rating vintages which have been submitted previously yet will still be available for sale during the book's currency. Only wines which last year were reviewed as tank or barrel samples, and thus rated provisionally (or considered too young and unformed to rate), are revisited for the current book. New and previously untasted vintages are, of course, reviewed as normal.

While the numbers of brands and producers burgeon unabated, wine prices continue to increase much less swiftly, and as a result we have adjusted the past few years' value-for-money parameters only slightly. Consumers therefore remain assured that wines flagged in the guide with either the good-value symbol (✓), indicating wines of 3½-star quality or better, or the easy-quaffing icon (☺), identifying best buys at 3 stars and below, continue to represent outstanding value in the present market.

New in this edition are a number of design elements, including bolder headlines and vertical section-identifiers, intended to make the book friendlier and easier to user. Readers of previous editions will also note the inclusion of two new icons: one highlighting wines fitted with that increasingly popular form of closure, the screwcap, the other identifying wines officially certified as being organically grown.

Not entirely new, but echoing a feature of some earlier guides, in which then editors John and Erica Platter paid tribute to a Winemaker of the Year, we give recognition this year to a producer who, in our personal opinion, epitomises all that is great and good in SA winemaking today. The Winery of the Year for 2008 is Cape Point Vineyards, a small but dynamic house which combines most if not all of the latest winegrowing buzzwords (a cool climate, 'extreme' viticultural sites, youthful enthusiasm and passion, and more) with virtues recognised and prized by winelovers everywhere, including value, authenticity and that elusive but vital 'wow' factor. And of course quality, more than amply illustrated by their trio of five-star ratings in the current edition.

Talking ratings, it bears repeating that the rankings reflected in the book are the result of a process beginning towards the end of June, when we mobilise our team of tasters to assess the SA-grown wines on sale locally and overseas. (Unavoidably examples slip past us, and of course we try to incorporate these and any new releases in the next edition.) The results of their tastings are reflected in the A-Z section, along with news about the wineries and winemakers, general information about products, vinification facilities, vineyards, amenities available to visitors and more. (Scores for all wines in the A-Z are also listed separately for convenience in the section named 'The Ratings Summarised'.)

In line with heightened international interest in SA wine, we continue to highlight names of brands and alternative labels used by local producers for overseas markets (these are also cross-referenced). Also featured in the A-Z are general style indicators and technical details (note that alcohol, acid, sugar levels, time in wood etc are provided only where they are useful in giving clues to the character of the wine).

For visitors in search of wine-route information, the maps have again been fully updated, along with accompanying quick-lookup tables which furnish key visitor information about the wineries of a particular region, such as whether or not they are open on weekends and public holidays, offer meals or refreshments, specifically cater for children, and are friendly to individuals with reduced mobility.

Still on the subject of accessibility, we are pleased that our initiative to provide professionally conducted audits of winetasting areas, cellar tours and other visitor facilities in the winelands, continues in conjunction with our original partner in this regard, accessibility specialist Guy Davies. Launched in 2001, the programme went into abeyance for practical reasons but is now very much on track. See under 'Disabled Access in SA Wineries' for more details.

Also of interest to tourists and wine-ramblers is the Eat-out and Stay-over sections, featuring hotels, B&Bs, restaurants, delis and a plethora of other fine-dining and unwinding venues among the vines. Well-qualified Jos Baker edits these sections.

Our wine ranking system remains the same as last year. We cover the full spectrum, from wines we consider 'somewhat less than ordinary' (and award 0 stars) to 'superlative Cape classics', worthy of a full 5 stars. Wines rated ★★★★ or higher are usually listed first in each entry, and set in red type. Vintages deviating from the general rating are individually starred in the text. Very good/promising wines and more modest examples (★★★☆ or fewer) are included in the 'run-on' listings at the end of entries. For easy identification, the quaffing best-buys are both boxed together and individually labelled with the wallet-cordial ☺ sign. See also the above-mentioned sections 'How to Use the Guide' and 'How to Use the A–Z'.

Because of deadlines, many wines in the guide are tasted freshly bottled or as works-in-progress; any considered unrateable as a result are noted as such in the text. It's worth mentioning that we taste from the end of June to early August. Except for the bottlings assessed for five stars (see the preamble to the Wines of the Year), all wines are tasted 'sighted' (with labels exposed). Because of the subjective element associated with wine assessment, we strongly recommend you view our rankings as adjuncts to the tasting notes rather than as oracular pronouncements. For this purpose we include the results of other professional tastings and competitions in both the A–Z and the Top Performers table.

Wines featured in the guide were assessed by a slightly enlarged team, whose professionalism and unflagging enthusiasm we again gratefully acknowledge. Their names and potted biographies appear in the Credits section on page 3 and the end-paper at the back of the book. Note that tasters' initials appear below the wines they tasted.

Warm thanks to the rest of the splendid and much enlarged team (see Credits). Specially to wine coordinators Anneke Potgieter, Kim Dicksen Greeff and their teams; the super-efficient Inas, Smith and de Villiers; Lara Philp and Johan Rademan of Vineyard Connection for the use of their excellent facilities; Aline Balayer for the new design; Sean de Kock for continuing IT wizardry; Mark Whyte and XtraSmile Couriers; Hanneli Smit & co at VinLAB; Ryk Taljaard for the WO mini-maps; the ever helpful SAWIS; Michael Bucholz for the calibration samples. And pinotage potentate Beyers Truter for his inspiring foreword.

Loving thanks to indefatigable wife Cathy, turning into something of a globetrotter in her expanding role as Master of Wine, and cricket-crazy son Luke, looking forward at press time to the 20/20 World Champs in South Africa.

And the usual invitation to visit our website, www.platteronline.com, for interactive versions of this and many previous editions of the guide.

wines of the YEAR

In the course of tasting and rating more than 6 000 wines for this edition, the members of our team individually identified a limited number of bottlings showing exceptional quality. These were entered into a second round of tasting, open only to finished/bottled wines, available during the currency of the book. The short-listed wines were retasted 'blind' (without sight of the label) by an assembled panel, and those regarded as superlative in an SA context awarded the guide's highest grading – five stars. These stand-outs are listed below under the heading 'Five Stars'. The highest scoring five-star wines were subjected to a further evaluation to determine the overall top scorer. The wine which emerged from this stringent selection represents the pinnacle of SA winemaking and is the recipient of the guide's highest accolade: Wine of the Year.

The wines which did not make the five-star selection, but which are extremely fine and collectible in their own right, are listed immediately below the Five Stars under the heading 'Highly Recommended'. Implicit in wines of this calibre is the potential to improve with further bottle-maturation – say 8-10 years, perhaps more, in the case of the reds and fortifieds, and around 6-8 years for the whites. (Proper storage is, of course, vital for sound maturation.) During the cycle of tasting, our tasters identified a number of bottlings, over and above the candidate five-stars, which show particular potential for cellaring. These ageworthy wines are listed separately under the heading 'Buy Now, Drink Later'.

Also listed is a selection of entry-level wines offering exceptional drinkability at budget prices. The 'Superquaffer of the Year' provides the best overall value and quaffability in this category.

This year we introduce a prestigious new 'super award', Winery of the Year, in recognition of a winegrowing team who, in the opinion of the editor, are ambassadors par excellence for South African wine.

Further details about all releases listed in this section will be found under the names of the relevant producers in the A-Z directory. The five-star tasting is audited by PKF (Cpt) Inc.

Winery of the Year

Cape Point Vineyards

Even before they impressed us with a hat trick of five-star wines in this edition, Cape Point Vineyards were the editor's choice for the inaugural Winery of the Year because of their ability to consistently produce delicious, exciting, site-revealing wines of stellar quality, with enthusiasm, care and a refreshing degree of modesty.

Platter's
SOUTH AFRICAN
WINE GUIDE
WINERY OF THE
YEAR

Wine of the Year

Pinot Noir

Bouchard Finlayson Tête de Cuvée Galpin Peak 2005

Platter's
SOUTH AFRICAN
WINE GUIDE
WINE OF THE
YEAR

Five Stars

Cabernet Sauvignon
- Edgebaston-Finlayson Family Vineyards CWG Auction Reserve 'GS' 2005
- Kanonkop Estate 2003

Shiraz
- De Trafford Wines 2005

Red Blends
- Beyerskloof Field Blend 2003
- Hartenberg Estate The Mackenzie 2005
- The Winery of Good Hope Radford Dale Gravity 2005

Chenin Blanc
- Ken Forrester Wines The FMC 2005

Sauvignon Blanc
- Cape Point Vineyards (Woolworths) Limited Release 2007

Semillon
- Cape Point Vineyards 2006

White Blends
- Cape Point Vineyards Isliedh 2006
- Sequillo Cellars White 2006

- Steenberg Vineyards Magna Carta 2007
- Vergelegen White 2006

Dessert Wine, Unfortified
- Fleur du Cap Noble Late Harvest 2006
- Paul Cluver Estate Weisser Riesling Noble Late Harvest 2006

Port
- Axe Hill Cape Vintage 2005
- Boplaas Family Vineyards Cape Tawny NV
- Boplaas Family Vineyards Vintage Reserve 2005
- De Krans Vintage Reserve 2005
- JP Bredell Wines Bredell's Cape Vintage 2003

Highly Recommended

Cabernet Sauvignon
- Boekenhoutskloof 2005
- Glen Carlou Gravel Quarry 2005
- Meerlust Estate 2004
- Vergelegen V 2004

Merlot
- Veenwouden Private Cellar 2004

Pinot Noir
- Hamilton Russell Vineyards 2006

Pinotage
- Simonsig Estate Redhill 2005

Shiraz
- Avondale Les Pleurs Syrah 2005
- Boekenhoutskloof Reserve Syrah 2005
- Boekenhoutskloof Syrah 2005
- Bon Courage Estate Inkará 2005
- Boschendal Wines Cecil John Reserve 2004
- Hartenberg Estate CWG Auction Reserve Gravel Hill 2004
- La Motte Pierneef Collection Shiraz-Viognier 2005
- Quoin Rock Syrah 2005
- Raka Biography 2005

- Rudi Schultz Wines Reserve Syrah 2005
- Saxenburg Private Collection 2004
- The Foundry Syrah 2004
- Vins d'Orrance Syrah Cuvée Ameena 2005

Red Blends
- Boschendal Wines Grand Reserve 2004
- Buitenverwachting Christine 2003
- Ernie Els Wines 'Ernie Els' 2005
- L'Avenir Estate Stellenbosch Classic 2005
- Morgenster Estate 'Morgenster' 2004
- Muratie Estate Ansela van de Caab 2005
- Rustenberg Wines John X Merriman 2005
- Simonsig Estate Tiara 2005
- Tulbagh Mountain Vineyards (Woolworths) Reserve 'The W' 2005

Highly Recommended (continued)

- Vergenoegd Estate 'Vergenoegd' 2004
- Vilafonté Series C 2005
- Waterford Estate CWG Auction Reserve Red 2004
- Waterford Estate The Jem 2004
- Zorgvliet Wines Richelle 2005

Chardonnay

- Ataraxia Mountain Vineyards 2006
- Bouchard Finlayson Missionvale 2006
- Cape Chamonix Wine Farm Reserve 2006
- Glen Carlou Quartz Stone 2006
- Hamilton Russell Vineyards 2006
- Jordan Winery Nine Yards Reserve 2006
- Jordan Winery (Woolworths) Limited Release Sur Lie 2007
- Springfield Estate Méthode Ancienne 2005
- The Winery of Good Hope Radford Dale 2006
- Uva Mira Vineyards Vineyard Selection Single Vineyard 2006
- Waterford Estate 2006

Chenin Blanc

- Racetrack Damarakloof 2006
- Rudera Wines Robusto 2006

Sauvignon Blanc

- Cape Point Vineyards 2006
- De Grendel Wines Koetshuis 2007
- Diemersdal Estate 8 Rows 2007
- Diemersdal Estate MM Louw 2007
- Diemersdal Estate Single Vineyard 2007
- Fryer's Cove 2007

- La Motte Pierneef Collection (Organically Grown) 2007
- Steenberg Vineyards Reserve 2007
- Vergelegen Reserve 2006

Semillon

- Steenberg Vineyards 2007

White Blends

- Flagstone Winery CWG Auction Reserve Weather Girl 2006
- Sadie Family Palladius 2006
- Vergelegen Auction Reserve White 2006

Méthode Cap Classique

- Villiera Wines Brut Natural 2004

Dessert Wine, Unfortified

- De Trafford Wines Straw Wine 2005
- Fairview La Beryl Blanc 2006
- Joostenberg Wines Chenin Blanc Noble Late Harvest 2006
- Rudera Wines Chenin Blanc Noble Late Harvest 2006
- Villiera Wines Inspiration 2006

Dessert Wine, Fortified

- Alvi's Drift Private Cellar Muscat de Frontignan White 2006

Port

- Boplaas Family Vineyards CWG Auction Vintage Reserve 2005
- De Krans Cape Tawny NV
- De Krans Cape Vintage 2005

Buy Now, Drink Later

Cabernet Franc

- Raats Family Wines 2005

Cabernet Sauvignon

- Belfield 2005
- Delheim Grand Reserve 2004
- Le Riche Wines 2003
- Nederburg Wines Private Bin 2005
- Rudera Wines 2004

Merlot

- Bein Wine 2005
- Laibach Vineyards 2006

Pinotage

- DeWaal Wines CT de Waal 2005

Platter's
SOUTH AFRICAN
WINE GUIDE
BUY NOW,
DRINK LATER

Shiraz

- Darling Cellars (Woolworths) Groenekloof Reserve 2004
- Tulbagh Mountain Vineyards TMV Swartland Syrah 2006

Red Blends

- Bouchard Finlayson Hannibal 2006
- Capaia 'Capaia' 2006
- Jordan Winery Cobblers Hill 2004
- Klein Genot Country & Wine Estate Black Swan 2005

Buy Now, Drink Later (continued)

- Morgenhof Estate Première Sélection 2004
- Morgenster Estate Lourens River Valley 2004
- Mvemve Raats De Compostella 2005
- Remhoogte Estate Bonne Nouvelle 2004
- Reyneke Wines Reserve 2005
- Sadie Family Columella 2005
- Vuurberg Reserve 2005

Chardonnay
- Bouchard Finlayson Kaaimansgat 2006
- Diemersdal Estate Reserve 2006
- Rustenberg Wines Five Soldiers 2005

Chenin Blanc
- Beaumont Wines Hope Marguerite 2006
- Jean Daneel Wines Directors Signature 2006
- Katbakkies Wine 2006
- The Spice Route Winery 2006

Sauvignon Blanc
- Ataraxia Mountain Vineyards 2007
- Durbanville Hills Biesjes Craal 2007

White Blends
- Solms-Delta Amalie 2006

Méthode Cap Classique
- Villiera Wines Monro Brut 2001

Superquaffer of the Year

Chenin Blanc
- Simonsig Estate 2007

Exceptionally Drinkable & Well Priced

Merlot
- Du Toitskloof Winery 2006

Shiraz
- JP Bredell Wines Vineyard Collection Helderzicht 2004

Red Blends
- Cape Chamonix Wine Farm Rouge 2005
- Whalehaven Wines Old Harbour Red 2005

Rosé
- Bernheim Wines Pinotage 2007

Chenin Blanc
- Hazendal Bushvine 2006
- Zidela Wines 2007

White Blends
- Knorhoek Wines Two Cubs White Blend 2007

the**RATINGS** Summarised

Here we summarise the wines featured in the A–Z section, with their ratings, sorted first by wine style, in alphabetical order, and then by producer or brand. **NS** = no star; **NT** = not tasted; **NR** = tasted but not rated; **D** = discontinued. Where wineries produce more than one version of a particular style, the number of versions is indicated in brackets after the name. A number of wines were tasted as pre-bottling barrel or tank samples, and therefore ratings are provisional. Refer to the A–Z for details.

Barbera ★★★☆ Fairview
★★★ Altydgedacht, Riverstone
★★☆ Hofstraat

Blanc de noir ★★★☆ Mellasat
★★★ Buitenverwachting, Laborie, Neethlingshof, Slaley ★★☆ Aan de Doorns Co-operative, Boschendal, Diemersdal, Groot Constantia, Hazendal, Klein Parys, Landskroon, Lynx, Swartland, The Stables ★★ Boplaas Family, Culemborg, Goudini, Groot Eiland, Jonkheer, Klawer Co-operative, Kloovenburg, KWV Limited, Oude Kaap, Van Loveren Private (2), Woolworths ★☆ Lovane Boutique Wine, Oranjerivier Wine ★ Calitzdorp, Montpellier, Oude Wellington, Rietrivier **D** Du Toitskloof, Freedom Hill, Louiesenhof

Bukettraube ★★★ Cederberg Private, Du Toitskloof ★★☆ African Roots Wine Brands ★★ Simonsvlei International ★ Swartland **D** Bovlei

Cabernet franc ★★★★☆ Plaisir De Merle, Woolworths ★★★★ Hermanuspietersfontein, High Constantia, Neethlingshof, Raats Family, Rainbow's End, Warwick, Whalehaven, Zorgvliet ★★★☆ Eikendal, Franschhoek, Signal Hill ★★★ Avondale, Zorgvliet ★★★ Ridgemor Farm ★★ My Wyn, Spookfontein **D** Avondale, Avontuur, Bellingham, Lourensford, Môreson

Cabernet sauvignon ★★★★★ Edgebaston, Kanonkop ★★★★☆ Belfield, Boekenhoutskloof, Cederberg Private, Darling, De Trafford, Delaire, Glen Carlou, Grangehurst, Hartenberg, KWV Limited, Le Riche (3), Meerlust, Nederburg, Neil Ellis, Rudera, Rustenberg, South Hill, Springfield, Stark-Condé, Thelema Mountain (2), Vergelegen, Vriesenhof, Waterford ★★★★ Allesverloren, Alluvia Boutique & Guesthouse, Alto, Annandale Distillers & Vintners, Anura, Asara, Avondale, Bilton, Blaauwklippen Agricultural, Black Pearl, Bloemendal, Blue

Crane, Blue Creek, Boland Kelder, Bon Courage, Bonfoi, Boplaas Family, Boschendal, Buitenverwachting, Camberley, Cederberg Private, Clos Malverne, Crows Nest, Darling, Diemersfontein, Ernie Els, Fairview, Flagstone (2), Fleur du Cap, Glen Carlou, Goede Hoop, Goedverwacht, Golden Kaan, Graceland, Graham Beck, Grande Provence, Havana Hills, Hidden Valley, Hoopenburg, Jordan, JP Bredell, Kaapzicht (2), Katbakkies Wine, Klein Constantia, Kleine Zalze, Knorhoek, KWV Limited, L'Avenir, Laibach, Landskroon, Le Bonheur, Linton Park, Longridge, Lynx, Marklew Family, Mischa, Mooiplaas, Morgenhof, Mount Rozier, Nederburg (2), Neethlingshof, Neil Ellis, Newton Johnson, Olsen, Overgaauw, Paul Cluver, Plaisir De Merle, Rhebokskloof Private, Rietvallei, Rijk's Private, Roodezandt &, Rust en Vrede, Rustenberg, Rusticus Vintage, Saxenburg, Simonsvlei International, Spier (2), Stellekaya, Stellenzicht, Sterhuis, Stonewall, Stony Brook, Stormhoek, The Company of Wine People, The Goose, The of Good Hope, Thelema Mountain, Tokara, Uitkyk, Usana, Vergenoegd, Vruchtbaar Boutique, Waverley Hills Organic (Organic), Wine of the Month Club (3), Woolworths (2), Zevenwacht, Zorgvliet (2) ★★★☆ African Pride, AntHill, Arra, Babylon's Peak Private, Belbon Hills, Bergsig, Bernheim, Blue Crane, Bon Cap Organic (Organic), Bonnievale Wine, Boscheim, Boschkloof &, Bottelary, Bovlei, Cape Chamonix Wine Farm, Cape Hutton, Coleraine, De Meye, De Wetshof, Delheim, Devon Hill, Diemersdal, Dieu Donné, Domaine Brahms Wineries, Dormershire, Dornier, Du Toitskloof, Durbanville Hills, Eaglevlei, Eikendal, Elgin Vintners, Fleur du Cap, Fort Simon, Franschhoek, Fredine le Roux, Galleon (2), Golden Kaan, Graham Beck, Grangehurst, Groenland, Groot Constantia, Groupe LFE South Africa, Haut Espoir, Hildenbrand Wine & Olive,

Hillcrest, Hofstraat, Jacobsdal, Jacques Smit, Klein Genot Country & Wine, Kleine Zalze, Kloovenburg, KWV Limited, La Bri, La Couronne, La Motte, La Petite Ferme, Laibach, Lanzerac, Lindhorst, Linton Park, Lourensford (2), Lutzville Cape Diamond, MAN Vintners, Manley Private, Meerendal, Middelvlei, Miravel, Mischa, Mont Rochelle Hotel & Mountain, Mostertsdrift Noble, Mountain Ridge, Muratie, Nederburg (2), Nitida, Oewerzicht Private, Oracle, Origin Wine, Ormonde Private, Oude Compagnies Post, Peter Bayly, Peter Falke, Post House, Rainbow's End, Rickety Bridge, Ridgeback, Rietvallei, Robertson, Savanha (2), Seidelberg, Shoprite Checkers, Simonsig, Southern Sky, Spier, Springfield, Stark-Condé, Stellar, Stellenbosch Hills, Stellenrust, Stellenzicht, Stettyn, Swartland, Sylvanvale, The Company of Wine People, The Springtree Wine Company, Under Oaks, Upland, Van Loveren Private, Villiera, Webersburg, Windmeul Cooperative, Zorgvliet (3) ★★★ African Roots Wine Brands, African Terroir, Altydgedacht, Alvi's Drift Private, Arabella, Ashanti, Avontuur, Ayama, Backsberg, Beau Joubert &, Blaauwklippen Agricultural, Blue Cove, Boekenhoutskloof, Boland Kelder, Bon Courage, Boplaas Family, Bosman Family, Botha Wine, Bottelary, Buck's Ridge & Olives, Buitehof, Bushmanspad, Clovelly, Culemborg, David Frost, De Meye, Diemersfontein, Domein Doornkraal, Doolhof, Douglas Green, Du Preez, DuVon, Eagle's Cliff/New Cape, Eikehof, Ernst & Co, Excelsior, FirstCape, Golden Kaan, Groenland, High Constantia, Hildenbrand Wine & Olive, Janéza Private, Journey's End, Klein Parys, Kleine Zalze, Koningsrivier, Kranskop, Kumala/Constellation South Africa (2), La Kavayan, Laborie, Landzicht GWK, Langverwacht, Linde, Long Mountain Wine Company (2), Lyngrove, Marianne, McGregor, Meerhof, Mooi Bly, Moordenaarskop, Môreson, Napier, Neethlingshof, Nelson, Niel Joubert, Noble Hill, Nuy Wine, Opstal, Origin Wine, Oude Kaap, Pick's Pick, Pulpit Rock, Rico Suter, Robertson (2), Roodezandt &, Rooiberg, Ruitersvlei, Rusticus Vintage, Savanha, Schalk Burger & Sons, Ses'Fikile, Simonsvlei International (2), Slaley, Slanghoek, Slowine, Somersbosch, Stellendrift (2), Swartland, Table Mountain, Terroir of SA, The Company of Wine People (2), The Springtree

Wine Company, Tulbagh Wine, Upland, Viljoensdrift, Wamakersvallei, Welgegund Farm, Welgevallen, Yonder Hill Wine Farm, Zandvliet, Zonnebloem, Zorgvliet ★★★ African Pride, African Terroir, Ashton, Bergwater (2), Bovlei, Calitzdorp, Cloof, Conradie Family, De Krans, De Villiers, De Wet Co-op, Elberti, Eshkol Kosher (Kosher), Gentis Family, Goedvertrouw, Goudini, Groot Eiland, Hippo Creek, Kango, Klawer Cooperative, Klein Parys, Kleine Draken (Kosher), Kleine Zalze, Kumala/Constellation South Africa, La Providence, Le Grand Chasseur, Leopard's Leap, Libertas, Lindiwe, Linton Park, Lushof, Lutzville Cape Diamond, Mons Ruber (2), Mount Vernon Farm, Namaqua, Nuy Wine, Obikwa, Origin Wine, Oude Wellington, Paddagang, Prospect1870, Quest, Rooiberg, Saam Mountain, Schalkenbosch, Seidelberg (2), Shoprite Checkers, Stellar, Stormhoek, The Company of Wine People, Tulbagh Wine (2), Wamakersvallei, Welgeleë, Wellington Cooperative, Wildekrans, Wines of Cape Town (3), Woolworths (2) (Organic) ★★ African Terroir (2), Belbon Hills, Bo La Motte, Brandvlei, Clairvaux Private, Devonvale Golf & Wine, Drakensig, Drostdy-Hof, Ernst & Co, Groupe LFE South Africa, Jacaranda, Jason's Hill Private, Keukenhof, KWV Limited, Le Manoir de Brendel, Long Mountain Wine Company, Lutzville Cape Diamond, Montpellier, Moordenaarskop, Mountain River, Natte Valleij, Onderkloof Vines & Oranjerivier Wine, Org de Rac Domain, Overhex International, Pulpit Rock, Riverstone, Spookfontein, Stellar (Organic), TTT, Villiersdorp, Wandsbeck, Wellington Cooperative, Windmeul Cooperative, Woolworths ★★ African Terroir (Organic), De Zoete Inval, Du Toitskloof, Eshkol Kosher (Kosher), Excelsior, Hartswater Wine, Koelenhof, Oranjerivier Wine, Org de Rac Domain, Origin Wine, Peter Falke, Rosendal Private, Tall Horse, Terroir of SA, Tulbagh Wine, Vunani ★ Hildenbrand Wine & Olive, Landzicht GWK, Lateganskop, Montagu Wine, Vredenheim ★ Welvanpas

NT Drakensig, Hartswater Wine, Jonkheer, Journey's End (2), Rose Garden, Rudera, Southern Sky **NR** Dispore Kamma Boutique , Riebeek, Smit Family, Stony Brook, Thelema Mountain, Uitvlucht **D** Catherine Marshall, David Frost, Eaglevlei, Freedom Hill, Jonkheer, Longridge, Makro, Mellasat, Môreson, Morgenhof, My Wyn, lemhoogte, Robertson, Ruitersvlei, Signal Hill, Steenberg, Stellenrust, Warwick, Withington

Carignan ★★★★ Fairview ★★★ Welgegund Farm

Chardonnay unwooded
★★★★★ Woolworths (2) ★★★★ Bouchard Finlayson, Constantia Uitsig, Springfield, Thelema Mountain, Woolworths
★★★★ Backsberg (Organic), Dalla Cia Wine & Spirit Company, De Wetshof, Groot Parys, Groote Post, Jordan, Linton Park, Mooi Bly, Neethlingshof, Rietvallei, Rustenberg, Steenberg, Vriesenhof, Zandvliet
★★★ Asara, Beaumont, Bellpost, Cloverfield Private, Darling, De Krans, De Meye, De Wetshof, De Zoete Inval, Dieu Donné, Doolhof, Eikendal, Hillcrest, Hippo Creek, Kleine Zalze, Langverwacht, Lazanou Organic (Organic), Linde, Louisvale, Millstream, Origin Wine, Rosendal Private, Seidelberg, Ses'Fikile, Strandveld, The of Good Hope, Wamakersvallei, Zorgvliet
★★★ Avondale, Bon Courage, Cape, De Villiers, De Wetshof, Du Preez, GlenWood, Goudini, Johan van Zyl, Jonkheer, Juno Wine Company, Kleine Zalze, Kumala/Constellation South Africa, KWV Limited, La Couronne, Linton Park, Louiesenhof, McGregor, Mont Rochelle Hotel & Mountain, Mount Rozier (2), Mzoli's, Oranjerivier Wine, Robertson, Rooiberg, Shoprite Checkers, Two Oceans, Van Zylshof, Von Ortloff, Vukani, Woolworths ★★ Arum Lily, Boplaas Family, Cloof, Drostdy-Hof, Du Toitskloof, Eagle's Cliff/New Cape, Groot Eiland, Headbutt, Hildenbrand Wine & Olive, Landskroon, Long Mountain Wine Company (2), Lutzville Cape Diamond, Môreson, Olsen, Oude Kaap, Oude Wellington, Paddagang, Somersbosch, Tall Horse, Wines of Cape Town, Woolworths (2) ★★ African Terroir, Ashton, Bovlei, Brandvlei, Cape, Mons Ruber, Origin Wine, Vunani ★ African Terroir, Janéza Private, Kango (2), Montpellier, Tulbagh Wine **NT** Drakensig, Hartswater Wine, La Petite Ferme, Ladismith **NR** Woolworths **D** African Terroir (2), Cape Bay, Delaire, Dominion Wine Company, Graham Beck, Main Street, Rhebokskloof Private, Robertson, Tulbagh Wine, Villiersdorp, Zandvliet

Chardonnay wooded ★★★★★ Ataraxia Mountain, Avontuur, Bouchard Finlayson,

Buitenverwachting, Cape Chamonix Wine Farm, Edgebaston, Glen Carlou, GlenWood, Groote Post, Hamilton Russell, Hartenberg, Jordan (2), Journey's End, Oak Valley, Paul Cluver, Plaisir De Merle, Springfield, The of Good Hope, Thelema Mountain, Uva Mira, Veenwouden Private, Vergelegen, Waterford, Woolworths ★★★★ Amani (2), Arendsig Hand-Crafted, Asara, Backsberg, Beaumont, Bouchard Finlayson (2), Buitenverwachting, Cape Chamonix Wine Farm, Cellar-Vie, De Meye, De Wetshof, Delaire, Delheim, Diemersdal, Doolhof, Durbanville Hills, Eikendal, Fairview, Fleur du Cap, Fort Simon, Goedverwacht, Golden Kaan, Graham Beck, Grande Provence, Groot Constantia, Hartenberg, Haskell, Haut Espoir, Hoopenburg, Iona, Jonkheer (2), Jordan, Joubert-Tradauw Private, Julien Schaal, Kloovenburg, Koelfontein, KWV Limited (2), La Motte, La Petite Ferme, Lanzerac, Le Riche, Lorraine Private, Louisvale (2), MC Square, Meerlust, Mont Rochelle Hotel & Mountain, Môreson, Mountain Oaks (Organic), Mulderbosch (2), Muratie, Nederburg, Neil Ellis (3), Newton Johnson, Pick's Pick, Quoin Rock, Rietvallei, Rupert & Rothschild Vignerons, Rustenberg (2), Simonsig, Sterhuis, Sumaridge, The Springtree Wine Company, Thelema Mountain, Tokara (2), Van Loveren Private, Vergelegen, Vriesenhof, Warwick, Waterkloof (2), Weltevrede (3), Woolworths, Zandvliet ★★★★ Altydgedacht, Alvi's Drift Private, AntHill, Avondale (2), Badsberg Wine, Bergsig, Boland Kelder, Bon Cap Organic (Organic), Bon Courage, Bonfoi, Bonnievale Wine, Boschendal, Boschkloof , Cape Point, Conradie Family, Cordoba, De Wetshof (2), Diemersdal, Douglas Green, Eikehof, Ernst & Co, False Bay, Glen Carlou, Goede Hoop, Golden Kaan, Graham Beck, Groupe LFE South Africa, Havana Hills, Hildenbrand Wine & Olive, Hillcrest, Jack & Knox Winecraft (2), Kanu, Klein Constantia, Kleine Zalze, Kumala/Constellation South Africa, L'Avenir, La Bri, La Couronne, Le Bonheur, Long Beach, Longridge, Lyngrove (2), Marklew Family, Meerendal, Neethlingshof, Nelson, Nitida, Onderkloof Vines &, Origin Wine, Ormonde Private, Overgaauw, Robertson, Roodezandt &, Saronsberg, Savanha, Saxenburg, Seidelberg, Simonsig, Slaley, Spier, Stellenbosch Hills, StellenHills (2), Stony Brook, The Company of Wine People

(2), The Goats do Roam Wine Company, Viljoensdrift, Vins d'Orrance, Von Ortloff, Vrede en Lust Wine Farm, Whalehaven, William Everson ★★★ African Terroir, Amani, Anura, Ashton, Backsberg, Cape Classics, Coleraine, Delheim, Détendu, Die Huis van Anjé, Dieu Donné, Durbanville Hills, Eagle's Cliff/New Cape, Fat Bastard, Fleur du Cap, Four Paws, Galleon, Goedvertrouw, Goedverwacht, Groot Parys, Hazendal, Hill & Dale, Hoopenburg, Kholisa, Klein Parys, La Chaumiere, Laborie, Libertas, Long Mountain Wine Company, Lourensford, Lutzville Cape Diamond, Makro, MAN Vintners, Middelvlei, Napier, Nederburg, Nuy Wine, Oaklands Wine Exporters, Obikwa, Oracle, Ormonde Private, Pulpit Rock, Rhebokskloof Private, Rickety Bridge, Rijk's Private, Rooiberg, Ruitersvlei, Schalk Burger & Sons, Stellenzicht, Stonewall, Table Mountain, The Stables, Tukulu, Uitkyk, Von Ortloff, Weltevrede, Ziggurat ★★★ African Pride, Anthony Smook, Beau Joubert &, Bonnievale Wine, Clovelly, Daschbosch Wine, Douglas Green, Du Toitskloof, FirstCape, Graham Beck, Johan van Zyl, Le Grand Chasseur, Leopard's Leap, Lismore, Lutzville Cape Diamond, Lyngrove, Mostertsdrift Noble, Nelson, Origin Wine, Pulpit Rock, Riebeek, Savanha, Simonsvlei International, Southern Sky, Spier, Stellar (Organic), Swartland, The Company of Wine People (2), Uitvlucht, Van Zylshof, Vrede Wine Farm, WaverleyTBS/uniWines, Windmeul Cooperative, Wines of Cape Town, Woolworths (Organic), Zonnebloem ★★ African Terroir (2) (Organic), Ayama, Backsberg (Kosher), Boland Kelder, Cape (2), Clairvaux Private, Culemborg, Eshkol Kosher (Kosher), Excelsior, Groupe LFE South Africa, Jason's Hill Private, Kaapzicht, Klawer Co-operative, Klein Parys, Kleine Draken (Kosher), Koelenhof, Kumala/Constellation South Africa, KWV Limited, Landzicht GWK, Lindiwe, Niel Joubert, Tanagra Private, Thorntree, Van Loveren Private, Withington, Wolvendrift Private ★★ African Terroir (Organic), Ashanti, Bergwater, Calitzdorp, KWV Limited, Lushof, Meerhof, Origin Wine ★ De Wet Co-op, Mountain River, Slanghoek **NT** Crows Nest, Douglas Wine, Fort Simon, Jonkheer, Journey's End, Lourensford, McGregor, Montagu Wine, Mountain River, Wellington Cooperative **NR** Cloverfield

Private, Morgenhof, Rietvallei, Riverstone **D** Anthony Smook, Babylon's Peak Private, Bellingham, Constantia Uitsig, Dominion Wine Company (2), Eaglevlei, Glen Carlou, Goudini, Groot Constantia, Hoopenburg, Koelenhof, Kranskop, Laibach, Lievland, Mooiuitsig Wine, Neethlingshof, Rhebokskloof Private (2), Riebeek, Rose Garden, Ruitersvlei, Stettyn, Tulbagh Wine, Wildekrans, Woolworths, Zidela

Chenin blanc unwooded dry

★★★★ Mountain Oaks (Organic), Old Vines, Post House, The of Good Hope, Vrede en Lust Wine Farm ★★★★ Barton Farm, Blue Cove, Boschendal, Cederberg Private, Cloverfield Private, Fort Simon, Groote Post, Hartenberg, Kanu, Koopmanskloof, MAN Vintners, Mooiplaas, Môreson, Napier, Old Vines, Perdeberg, Raats Family, Spier, Teddy Hall, The Company of Wine People, Tierhoek ★★★ African Roots Wine Brands, Anura, Arabella, Ayama, Blue Crane, Cape Classics, De Meye, Dornier, False Bay, Hazendal, Kaapzicht, Kleine Zalze, L'Avenir, Laibach, Lazanou Organic (Organic), Mont Destin, Monterosso, Môreson, Mount Vernon Farm, Nuy Wine, Perdeberg, Pulpit Rock, Rietvallei, Schalk Burger & Sons, Ses'Fikile, Seven Oaks, Shoprite Checkers, Simonsig, Simonsvlei International, Somerbosch, Stellenrust, Swartland, The Company of Wine People, The Springtree Wine Company (2), The of Good Hope, Windmeul Cooperative, Zidela (2) ★★★ Aan de Doorns Co-operative, Alvi's Drift Private, Avondale, Babylon's Peak Private, Barry Gould Family, Bellevue, Boland Kelder, Bottelary, Bovlei, Brandvlei, De Krans, Douglas Green, Du Preez, Du Toitskloof, Ernst & Co, Eshkol Kosher (Kosher), FirstCape (2), Groot Parys, Jacques Smit, Jason's Hill Private, Jonkheer, JP Bredell, Kleine Zalze, KWV Limited (2), Leopard's Leap, Libertas, Long Mountain Wine Company, Mooi Bly, Mountain River, Niel Joubert, Oaklands Wine Exporters, Obikwa, Opstal, Origin Wine, Ormonde Private, Oude Kaap, Ridgemor Farm, Riebeek, Robertson (2), Ruitersvlei, Seidelberg, Skilpadvlei, Southern Sky, Stettyn, Swartland, Table Mountain, Tulbagh Wine, Van Zylshof, Viljoensdrift, Villiersdorp, Wellington Cooperative, Woolworths ★★ Ashton, Badsberg Wine, Belbon Hills, Boland Kelder, Cape Bay, Cloof, Daschbosch Wine, De Villiers,

, FirstCape (Light & low-alco-
dini, Groot Eiland (2), Jacaranda,
rys, Landskroon, Langverwacht,
we, Lutzville Cape Diamond, McGregor,
Mellasat, Montpellier, Mount Rozier,
Nieuwedrift, Oranjerivier Wine, Origin Wine
(2) (Light & low-alcohol), Rooiberg, Rose
Garden, Seidelberg, Spier, Stellar, The Com-
pany of Wine People, Uitvlucht, Van
Loveren Private, Vaughan Johnson's Wine &
Cigar Shop, Wamakersvallei,
WaverleyTBS/uniWines, Wildekrans, Wines
of Cape Town, Woolworths ★★ African
Terroir, Arum Lily, Bergsig (2), Brandvlei,
Conradie Family, Constantia, Culemborg, De
Wet Co-op, Douglas Wine, Fairvalley
Farmworkers Association, Hawksmoor at
Matjieskuil, Rhebokskloof Private, Rickety
Bridge, Ridder's Creek, Sentinel, Vunani,
Wines of Cape Town ★ Drostdy-Hof (Light &
low-alcohol), Klawer Co-operative, Maske,
Montagu Wine, Origin Wine, Slanghoek,
Tulbagh Wine ★ Kango, Welvanpas
NT Ashanti, Bouwland, Grundheim,
Hartswater Wine, KWV Limited, Ladismith,
Under Oaks **NR** Coleraine, Saltaré, Smit
Family, Swartland, Woolworths **D** Anura,
Du Toitskloof, Eaglevlei, La Couronne,
Longridge, Lourensford, Mostertsdrift
Noble, Robertson, Stellenbosch Hills,
Wamakersvallei, Wandsbeck, Woolworths

Chenin blanc unwooded off-dry/semi-
sweet ★★★★ Ken Forrester, Knorhoek,
M'hudi, Saam Mountain ★★★ Backsberg,
Glenview, Perdeberg, Sagila, Virgin Earth
★★★ Hazendal, KWV Limited, Landskroon,
Lutzville Cape Diamond, Mike's Kitchen,
Millstream, Mont du Bleu, Mountain River,
Old Vines, Wamakersvallei ★★ Ashton,
Boland Kelder, Bottelary, Die Huis van Anjé,
Grünberger, Simonsvlei International
★★ Eagle's Cliff/New Cape, Landzicht GWK,
Simonsvlei International, Zandvliet ★
Oranjerivier Wine **NT** Leopard's Leap,
McGregor

Chenin blanc wooded ★★★★★ Ken For-
rester ★★★★ Jean Daneel (2), Racetrack,
Rudera, Simonsig, Spier, Springfontein, The
Spice Route ★★★★ Beaumont (2),
Bellingham, Cederberg Private, De
Morgenzon, De Trafford, Diemersfontein,
Flagstone, Fleur du Cap, Groot Parys,
Hazendal, Katbakkies Wine, Ken Forrester,
Kleine Zalze, Lammershoek, Meerendal,
Morgenhof, Mountain Oaks (Organic), Old

Vines, Raats Family, Rudera, Sterhuis,
Tokara, Villiera, Woolworths ★★★★ Allée
Bleue, Altydgedacht, Buck's Ridge & Olives,
Domaine Brahms Wineries, Eikendal, Hid-
den Valley, Jordan, Kanu, Kumala/Constel-
lation South Africa, L'Avenir, Lazanou
Organic (Organic), Main Street,
Mulderbosch, Rijk's Private, Signal Hill,
Springfontein, Stormhoek, Swartland,
Tukulu, Villiera, Waterford ★★★ Alvi's Drift
Private, Angora, Arum Lily, Fort Simon,
Fredine le Roux, Hildenbrand Wine & Olive,
Ken Forrester, KWV Limited, Long Mountain
Wine Company, Nabygelegen Private, Ori-
gin Wine (2), Remhoogte, Riebeek, Schalk
Burger & Sons, Stormhoek, Sylvanvale, The
Stables, Tierhoek, WaverleyTBS/uniWines,
Zevenwacht ★★★ Cape, Darling, Groot
Parys, Klein Parys, Koelenhof, Onderkloof
Vines &, Pumlani, Stellenbosch Wine &
Country ★★ KWV Limited, The Company of
Wine People ★★ Wellington Cooperative
D Fort Simon, Mountain Ridge,
Somerbosch, Stormhoek, Tulbagh Wine,
Vuurberg

Cinsaut ★★★ Landskroon ★★ Mac's Hill
★ Culemborg **D** Perdeberg, Welgegund
Farm

Colombard ★★★ Nuy Wine ★★★ Bon Cour-
age, Goedverwacht, Langverwacht,
McGregor, Nuy Wine, Oranjerivier Wine (2),
Origin Wine ★★ Conradie Family, Goudini,
Oranjerivier Wine, Origin Wine, Robertson
★★ Aan de Doorns Co-operative, Ashton,
Groot Eiland, Mont du Bleu, Origin Wine
(Light & low-alcohol), Van Loveren Private
★ Montagu Wine **D** Stellar

Fernão pires ★★ Van Loveren Private
★ Swartland

Gamay noir ★★★ Kleine Zalze

Gewürztraminer ★★★★★ Paul Cluver
★★★★ Neethlingshof, Simonsig,
Woolworths, Zevenwacht
★★★★ Altydgedacht, Buitenverwachting,
Delheim, Robertson, Villiera, Weltevrede
★★★ Bergsig, Koelenhof ★★★ Woolworths
D Landzicht GWK

Grenache blanc ★★★★ Signal Hill

Grenache noir ★★★★ Signal Hill
★★★ Johan van Zyl ★★ Tierhoek

Hanepoot fortified ★★★★ Badsberg Wine,
Du Preez, Du Toitskloof, Kango

★★★★ Goudini, Groot Eiland, Ladismith, Landzicht GWK, Simonsvlei International, SoetKaroo, Vriesenhof ★★★ Aan de Doorns Co-operative, Boplaas Family, Bottelary, Calitzdorp, Kaapzicht, Koelenhof, Mooiuitsig Wine, Swartland, TTT, Villiersdorp ★★★ De Wet Co-op, Klawer Co-operative, Muratie, Oranjerivier Wine, Paddagang ★★ Montagu Wine, Opstal, Rietrivier, Slanghoek ★★ Mooiuitsig Wine, Smit Family **D** Namaqua, Rooiberg

Hanepoot unfortified ★★★ Belbon Hills ★★ Overhex International, Riebeek

Icewine D Signal Hill

Jerepigo red ★★★★ Laborie ★★★★ Asara, Badsberg Wine, Feiteiras, Graceland, Grundheim, Slanghoek, Swartland ★★★ Boplaas Family, Botha Wine, Camberley, Catherine Marshall, Domein Doornkraal, Herold, Kango, Lammershoek, Mons Ruber ★★★ Mons Ruber, Mooiuitsig Wine, Riebeek, Simonsvlei International ★★ Landzicht GWK, Oranjerivier Wine ★ Hartswater Wine **NT** Hartswater Wine **D** Douglas Wine, Rooiberg

Jerepigo white ★★★★ Domein Doornkraal ★★★★ Asara, Calitzdorp, Feiteiras, Mons Ruber ★★★★ Backsberg, Domein Doornkraal, Jacaranda, Mons Ruber, Wamakersvallei ★★★ Botha Wine, Grundheim, Hartswater Wine, Mooiuitsig Wine, Perdeberg, Wellington Cooperative ★★ Brandvlei, Kango, Mons Ruber, Ship Sherry, Swartland ★★ Dellrust, Koelenhof, Lateganskop, Oranjerivier Wine, Sedgwick's Old Brown Sherry

Kosher ★★★★ Tempel ★★★ Eshkol Kosher ★★★ Eshkol Kosher (6), Kleine Draken (2) ★★ Backsberg (2), Eshkol Kosher (3), Kleine Draken ★★ Eshkol Kosher (4), Kleine Draken (3) ★ Kleine Draken **NT** Backsberg, Kleine Draken

Late Harvest ★★★★ Thelema Mountain ★★★ Boplaas Family, Delheim, KWV Limited ★★★ Namaqua, Wellington Cooperative ★★ Drostdy-Hof, Klawer Co-operative, KWV Limited, Overmeer, Simonsvlei International ★★ Mooiuitsig Wine, Robertson, Villiersdorp, Woolworths, Zomerlust ★ De Doorns, Kellerprinz, Montagu Wine, Oranjerivier Wine, Rietrivier **NT** Grundheim **NR** Swartland **D** Ashton, Bonnievale Wine,

De Zoete Inval, Du Toitskloof, Ha Wine, Klawer Co-operative, McGre

Light & low-alcohol ★★★ De Wet cc Twee Jonge Gezellen/The House of Krone ★★ FirstCape, Fleur du Cap, Namaqua, Origin Wine (2) ★★ Origin Wine, Robertson, Villiersdorp, Woolworths ★ Drostdy-Hof, Namaqua, Robertson (2), Swartland, Van Loveren Private, Zomerlust ★ Oranjerivier Wine **NT** Bellingham, Bergsig, Simonsvlei International

Malbec ★★★★ Paul Wallace, Signal Hill, Woolworths ★★★★ Anura, Diemersfontein, Hildenbrand Wine & Olive, Nederburg, Spier, Umkhulu ★★★ Bellevue, Landskroon ★★ Cape **NT** Ashanti, High Constantia **D** Bellevue

Merlot ★★★★★ Bilton, Hartenberg, Laibach, Quoin Rock, Steenberg, Veenwouden Private, Yonder Hill Wine Farm ★★★★ Akkerdal, Amani, Anura, Asara, Bein Wine, Boland Kelder, Coleraine, Cordoba, De Grendel, De Trafford, Dornier, Durbanville Hills (2), Eikendal, Fleur du Cap (2), Groote Post, Hillcrest, Hoopenburg, Jordan, Journey's End, Kaapzicht, KWV Limited, Lanzerac, Linton Park, Longridge, Main Street, Meerendal, Meerlust, Meinert, Morgenhof, Nederburg, Org de Rac Domain, Pick's Pick, Raka, Ridgeback, Rust en Vrede, Saxenburg, Spier, Sumaridge, The Spice Route, The of Good Hope, Thelema Mountain, Villiera, Waterkloof, Woolworths (3) ★★★★ Altydgedacht, Anura, Audacia, Bellpost, Bloemendal, Boschkloof , Bottelary, Bovlep, Buitenverwachting, De Krans, Delheim, Devon Hill, DeWaal, Diemersdal, Diemersfontein, Du Preez, Elgin Vintners, Ernie Els, Fort Simon, Franschhoek, Graceland, Groot Constantia, Havana Hills, Hazendal, Herold, Hofstraat, JP Bredell, Ken Forrester, Kleine Zalze, Koelfontein, KWV Limited, L'Avenir, La Couronne, Lindhorst, Lynx, Makro, Manley Private, Marklew Family, Mischa, Mooiplaas, Môreson, Mount Rozier, Nederburg, Neil Ellis Meyer-Näkel, Noble Hill, Overgaauw, Plaisir De Merle, Post House, Ross Gower, Savanha, Seidelberg, Sentinel, Slaley, Spier, Stellekaya, Stellenrust, Sterhuis, Stormhoek, Thelema Mountain, Usana, Vergelegen, Vergenoegd, Von Ortloff, Waterkloof, Whalehaven, Wine of the Month Club, Withington, Woolworths,

Zevenwacht, Zonnebloem ★★★ Arabella, Ashanti, Avondale, Ayama, Backsberg, Beau Joubert &, Bein Wine, Bergwater, Blaauwklippen Agricultural, BLANKbottle, Blue Cove, Blue Crane, Blueberry Hill, Buekenhoutskloof, Bonfoi, Cape Classics, Darling, David Frost, De Villiers, Dellrust, Diemersfontein, Dieu Donné, Doolhof, Douglas Green, Drakensig, Du Toitskloof, Durbanville Hills, Eaglevlei, Eikehof, Elberti, Ernst & Co, Fairview, Fort Simon, Fraai Uitzicht 1798, Glenview, GlenWood, Golden Kaan, Goudini, Graham Beck, Groupe LFE South Africa, Havana Hills, Het Vlock Casteel, Jacaranda, Janéza Private, Jonkheer, Klein Dauphine, Klein Genot Country & Wine, Kumala/Constellation South Africa (2), KWV Limited (2), La Bri, La Petite Ferme, Laborie, Le Riche, Linton Park (2), Lomond, Lourensford, M'hudi, Meerhof, Mischa, Morgenhof, Muratie, Neethlingshof, Nelson, Nico van der Merwe, Nietvoorbij Wine, Obikwa, Origin Wine (2), Ormonde Private, Pulpit Rock, Rickety Bridge, Rijk's Private, Rooiberg, Rusticus Vintage, Savanha (2), Slowine, Spookfontein, Stark-Condé, Stellar, Stellenbosch Hills, Stellendrift (2), Stellenzicht, Swartland, Table Mountain, The Springtree Wine Company (2), Uitvlucht, Villiera, Wamakersvallei, Welgegund Farm, Yonder Hill Wine Farm ★★★ African Roots Wine Brands, African Terroir, Badsberg Wine, Barrydale, Bergwater, Blaauwklippen Agricultural, Boland Kelder, Boplaas Family, Bottelary, Bovlei, Bushmanspad, Culemborg, DeWaal, Die Huis van Anjé, Eaglevlei, Eshkol Kosher (Kosher), Excelsior, FirstCape, Groupe LFE South Africa, Klawer Co-operative, Kloovenburg, Koelenhof, Kranskop, Libertas, Linde, Liquor World, Lourensford, Lushof, Lutzville Cape Diamond (2), Marianne, Maske, Miravel, Mont Rochelle Hotel & Mountain, Niel Joubert, Org de Rac Domain, Origin Wine (2), Perdeberg, Quest, Rietrivier, Robertson (2), Rose Garden, Seidelberg (2), Shoprite Checkers, Simonsvlei International, Somersbosch, Spier, Tall Horse, The Company of Wine People (2), Tulbagh Wine, Van Loveren Private, Villiersdorp, Waverley-TBS/uniWines, Wines of Cape Town, Wonderfontein, Woolworths (3) ★★ African Terroir, Calitzdorp, Conradie Family, Dispore Kamma Boutique , Drostdy-Hof, Du Preez, Eshkol Kosher (Kosher), Flat Roof Manor, Goedverwacht, Groot Eiland, Hill & Dale, Hippo Creek, Kumala/Constellation South Africa, KWV Limited, Le Manoir de Brendel, Lyngrove, Namaqua, Natte Valleij, Oaklands Wine Exporters, Pulpit Rock, Riebeek, Rooiberg, Ruitersvlei, Schalk Burger & Sons, Slanghoek, Spier, Stettyn, Thorntree, Wamakersvallei, Wildekrans, Woolworths (Organic), Zidela ★★ Botha Wine, Domein Doornkraal, Douglas Green, Keukenhof, Mzoli's, Origin Wine, Rietrivier, Stellar (Organic), Tulbagh Wine, Vooruitsig, Vredenheim ★ African Terroir (3) (Organic), Botha Wine, Constantia, Du Toitskloof, Groot Eiland, Kango, Landzicht GWK, Origin Wine **NT** Backsberg (2) (Organic, Kosher), Cape Hutton, Drakensig, High Constantia, Jonkheer, Lindiwe, Mountain River, Oude Compagnies Post, Rose Garden, Wellington Cooperative, Windmeul Cooperative **NR** Rainbow's End, Stony Brook, Westbridge **D** Avontuur, Bellingham, Camberley, David Frost, De Wetshof, De Zoete Inval, DeWaal, Du Preez, Freedom Hill (2), Groot Constantia, Kanu, Longridge, McGregor, Morgenhof, Namaqua, Remhoogte, Rhebokskloof Private, Ruitersvlei

Morio Muscat fortified
★★★☆ Landskroon

Mourvèdre ★★★★ Beaumont ★★★☆ Long Mountain Wine Company, The Spice Route, Val de Vie Winelands Lifestyle ★★★ Fairview, Waterkloof ★★ Montpellier

Muscadel, red, fortified ★★★★☆ Boplaas Family, Nuy Wine, Rietvallei, Groot Constantia, Jonkheer (2), Kango, KWV Limited (2) ★★★★ Avondale, Du Toitskloof, Groot Constantia, Jonkheer (2), Kango, KWV Limited (2) ★★★★ Alvi's Drift Private, Badsberg Wine, Bon Courage, De Wet Co-op, Rietvallei, Roodezandt &, Slanghoek, Van Loveren Private, Weltevrede ★★★ Aan de Doorns Co-operative, De Doorns, Groot Constantia, Grundheim, Klawer Co-operative, McGregor, Montagu Wine, Oranjerivier Wine, Overhex International, Rietrivier, Rooiberg, Seidelberg, Wolvendrift Private, Wonderfontein ★★★ Boland Kelder, Klawer Co-operative, Ladismith, Landzicht GWK, Mooiuitsig Wine, Uitvlucht ★★ Ashton, Douglas Wine, Excelsior Vlakteplaas ★★ Mooiuitsig Wine (Sacramental wine), Wandsbeck **NT** KWV Limited **D** Mons Ruber, Namaqua

Muscadel, white, fortified ★★★★★ Alvi's Drift Private, Bon Courage, Jonkheer, Monis ★★★★ Boland Kelder, De Krans (2), KWV Limited, Nuy Wine ★★★★ Ashton, Boplaas Family, Calitzdorp, De Wet Co-op, De Wetshof, Graham Beck, Kango, Riverstone, Yonder Hill Wine Farm ★★★ Ashton, Avondale, Boplaas Family, BurCon, Landzicht GWK, Le Grand Chasseur, Lutzville Cape Diamond, McGregor, Mons Ruber, Montagu Wine, Robertson, Saronsberg, Uitvlucht, Weltevrede ★★★ Clairvaux Private, Klawer Co-operative, Mooiuitsig Wine, Oranjerivier Wine ★★ Excelsior Vlakteplaas, Grundheim, Overhex International, Rietrivier, Uitvlucht **NT** KWV Limited, Twee Jonge Gezellen/The House of Krone **NR** Thelema Mountain **D** Namaqua, Roodezandt &

Muscadel, white, unfortified
★★★★ Thelema Mountain ★★★ Micu Narunsky **NT** Montagu Wine **D** Jonkheer

Muscat de Hambourg fortified
★★★★ Stellenbosch Hills

Muscat Ottonel unfortified ★★★ Villiera

Organic ★★★★★ La Motte ★★★★ Bon Cap Organic, Laibach, Mountain Oaks (5), Tulbagh Mountain, Waverley Hills Organic ★★★★ African Terroir, Backsberg, Bon Cap Organic (5), Lazanou Organic, Stellar, Tulbagh Mountain, Waverley Hills Organic ★★★ Avondale, Lazanou Organic (2), Waverley Hills Organic (2) ★★★ African Terroir (2), Bon Cap Organic (4), Kumala/Constellation South Africa, Lord's, Mountain Oaks, Stellar, Woolworths (4) ★★ African Terroir (3), Bon Cap Organic, Kumala/Constellation South Africa, Stellar (5), Woolworths ★★ African Terroir (3), Stellar, Woolworths ★ African Terroir, Stellar **NT** Backsberg, Lazanou Organic, Waverley Hills Organic **NR** Woolworths **D** African Terroir, Stellar

Natural Sweet, red ★★ Van Loveren Private ★ Drostdy-Hof, Rooiberg **NT** Domein Doornkraal

Natural Sweet, rosé ★★★ Namaqua ★★ Robertson (2), Simonsvlei International, The Saints ★★ Arum Lily, Drostdy-Hof, Landzicht GWK, Mountain Ridge, Robertson (Light & low-alcohol), Tulbagh Wine, Van Loveren Private ★ Grünberger, Rietrivier, Rooiberg **NT** Jonkheer, Rose Garden

Natural Sweet, white ★★★★ Klein Constantia (2), Meerendal, Quoin Rock ★★★★ Delheim, Somersbosch, Stony Brook, Zevenwacht ★★★★ Buitenverwachting, Cloof, L'Avenir, Nabygelegen Private, Rustenberg, Steenberg ★★★ Bloemendal, Goudini, Kaapzicht, Theuniskraal, Weltevrede ★★★ De Krans, Ridgeback, Saxenburg ★★★ Robertson (2), The Saints ★★ Drostdy-Hof, Hartswater Wine, Landzicht GWK, Rooiberg, Van Loveren Private ★ Grünberger, Kango, Vredenheim **NT** Twee Jonge Gezellen/The House of Krone **NR** Laibach **D** Ashanti, Bon Courage, Lievland, Morgenhof

Nebbiolo ★★★★ Idiom

Noble Late Harvest ★★★★★ Fleur du Cap, Ken Forrester, Paul Cluver, Signal Hill ★★★★★ Asara, Boekenhoutskloof, Bon Courage, Darling, De Wetshof, Delheim, Hillcrest, Joostenberg, Kanu, Lourensford, Neethlingshof, Rudera (2), Simonsig (2), Springfontein, Villiera ★★★★ African Terroir, Beaumont, Boekenhoutskloof, Jordan, Klein Constantia, Mulderbosch, Nederburg (3), Robertson, Rustenberg, Signal Hill (3), Slaley, Slanghoek, Tokara, Van Loveren Private, Vergelegen, Villiera, Waterford, Woolworths ★★★★ Badsberg Wine, Dieu Donné, Eikendal, Fort Simon, Jason's Hill Private, L'illa, Morgenhof, Nuy Wine, Savanha, WaverleyTBS/uniWines ★★★ Diemersdal, Hildenbrand Wine & Olive **NT** Bergsig, Buitenverwachting, Cape Point, Twee Jonge Gezellen/The House of Krone **NR** Buitenverwachting, Stony Brook **D** Du Toitskloof, Robertson, Spier

Non-muscat, red, fortified
★★ Daschbosch Wine

Non-muscat, white, fortified
★★★★ Cabrière, Daschbosch Wine

Nouvelle ★★★ Boland Kelder ★★ Eagle's Cliff/New Cape

Perlé wines ★★★ De Wet Co-op ★★ Autumn Harvest Crackling, Conradie Family, Riebeek ★★ Ashton **NT** Bergsig (Light & low-alcohol), Jonkheer

Petit verdot ★★★★ Du Preez, Zorgvliet ★★★★ Bellevue, Franschhoek, Signal Hill, Spier ★★★ Anura ★★★ My Wyn ★★ Ashanti ★★ Montpellier **NT** Rico Suter

Pinot blanc **NR** Ses'Fikile

Pinot gris/grigio ★★★ FirstCape, L'Ormarins Private, Stormhoek ★★★ Flat Roof Manor ★★ Woolworths ★★ Van Loveren Private **NT** Louiesenhof

Pinot noir ★★★★★ Bouchard Finlayson ★★★★☆ Bouchard Finlayson, Cape Chamonix Wine Farm, Flagstone, Hamilton Russell, Oak Valley ★★★★ Cabrière, De Trafford, Newton Johnson, Paul Cluver, Ridgemor Farm, Vriesenhof, Whalehaven, Woolworths ★★★☆ Anura, Catherine Marshall, De Grendel, De Wetshof, Elgin Vintners, Fryer's Cove, Glen Carlou, Groote Post, Klein Constantia, Klein Optenhorst, Meerlust, Minke, Muratie, Signal Hill, Strandveld, The of Good Hope (2), Topaz Wine, Vriesenhof ★★★ Avontuur, Elgin Vintners, Herold, Hoopenburg, Robertson ★★★ Ashton, Schindler's Africa, The Company of Wine People ★★ Goedvertrouw, Rose Garden ★★ Sumaridge ★ Constantia, Montpellier **NT** Bon Courage, Makro, Rusticus Vintage **NR** Zorgvliet **D** Bellevue, Flagstone, Woolworths

Pinotage ★★★★★ Ashbourne, Bellevue, Beyerskloof, DeWaal (2), Diemersfontein, Fairview, Hidden Valley, Kaapzicht, Kanonkop, L'Avenir, Meerendal, Simonsig, Umkhulu ★★★★ Asara, Avontuur, Beaumont, Bellevue, Boplaas Family, Camberley, Clos Malverne, Conradie Family, Darling, Diemersfontein, Domaine Brahms Wineries, Dornier, Flagstone, Graham Beck, Grangehurst, Horse Mountain, Jacobsdal, Kaapzicht, KWV Limited, L'Auberge du Paysan, L'Avenir, Laibach, Longridge, Lyngrove, Manley Private, Môreson, Mountain Oaks (Organic), Mountain River, Nederburg, Neethlingshof, Neil Ellis, Perdeberg, Pick's Pick, Reyneke, Robertson, Saxenburg, Scali, Siyabonga, Southern Right, Spier, Springfontein (2), Stanford Hills, Stellenzicht, Stormhoek, Sylvanvale, The Spice Route, Tukulu, Westbridge, Zonnebloem ★★★★ Altydgedacht, Bergsig, Beyerskloof, Boland Kelder, Bon Cap Organic (Organic), Bon Courage, Borg Family, Bottelary, Darling, De Krans, Devon Hill, DeWaal, Diemersdal, Doolhof, Eaglevlei, Fairview, Fort Simon, Freedom Hill, Goede Hoop, Goudini, Groot Constantia, Hartenberg, Hazendal, Kautzenburg, Ken Forrester, Kleine Zalze, KWV Limited, Lindhorst, Long Mountain Wine Company, Meerendal, Middelvlei, Mooiplaas,

Mountain River, Nelson, Nietvoorbij Wine, Nitida, Onderkloof Vines &, Oracle, Oude Compagnies Post, Pulpit Rock, Raka, Rijk's Private, Rooiberg, Saam Mountain, Schalk Burger & Sons, Schonenberg, Seidelberg (2), Simonsig, Southern Sky, Spier, Stellar, Stellenzicht, Sylvanvale, Tempel (Kosher), The Company of Wine People, The Stables, The of Good Hope, Viljoensdrift, Vriesenhof, Warwick, Westbridge, Windmeul Cooperative, Woolworths, Zevenwacht ★★★ African Terroir, Allée Bleue, Anthony Smook, Anura (2), Bellevue, Cape (2), Cloof, Clos Malverne, Culemborg, De Villiers, Delheim, Détendu, Doolhof, Douglas Green, Du Toitskloof, Durbanville Hills, Eagle's Cliff/New Cape, False Bay, FirstCape, Fleur du Cap, Four Paws, Golden Kaan, Graham Beck, Jonkheer, Ken Forrester, Klein Parys, Kleine Zalze, Knorhoek, La Petite Ferme, Laborie, Ladismith, Lammershoek, Landskroon, Lanzerac, Lyngrove, M'hudi, MAN Vintners, Marianne, McGregor, Millstream, Môreson, Nederburg, Olsen, Oranjerivier Wine, Oude Kaap, Perdeberg, Rico Suter, Robertson, Rusticus Vintage, Savanha, Schalkenbosch, Schindler's Africa, Ses'Fikile, Shoprite Checkers, Simonsvlei International, Slaley, Slanghoek, Spier, Stellenbosch Hills, Swartland, The Company of Wine People (3), The Springtree Wine Company, The Stables, Tulbagh Wine, Uitvlucht, Villiera, Virgin Earth, Wamakersvallei, Waverley-TBS/uniWines, Wildekrans (2), Woolworths, Zonnebloem ★★★ Aan de Doorns Co-operative, African Terroir (2), Alvi's Drift Private, Avondale (2), Avontuur, Ayama, Backsberg, Bellevue, Bergheim, Bernheim, BLANKbottle, Bon Cap Organic (Organic), Boplaas Family, Cape Bay, Cape Chamonix Wine Farm, Cape Classics, Cloof, De Wet Co-op, Dieu Donné, Eshkol Kosher (Kosher), Graham Beck, Hill & Dale, Jason's Hill Private, Jonkheer, L'Avenir, Libertas, Long Mountain Wine Company, Louiesenhof, Lutzville Cape Diamond, Meerhof, Mooi Bly, Morgenhof, Namaqua, Nelson, Niel Joubert, Obikwa, Origin Wine, Rhebokskloof Private, Rooiberg, Ruitersvlei, Saam Mountain, Schalk Burger & Sons, Seidelberg, Sentinel, Simonsvlei International, Slaley, Somersbosch, Stormhoek, The Company of Wine People, Van Loveren Private (2), Vunani, Wamakersvallei, Woolworths ★★ African Terroir (Organic), Ashanti, Backsberg (Kosher), Botha Wine, Bottelary,

Bovlei, Daschbosch Wine, Devon Rocks, Dominion Wine Company, Drakensig, Drostdy-Hof, Du Toitskloof, Eshkol Kosher (Kosher), Hawksmoor at Matjieskuil, Johan van Zyl, Klein Parys, Koelenhof, Le Grand Chasseur, Liquor World, Morewag, Mount Rozier, Mountain River, Neethlingshof, Pulpit Rock, Pumlani, Rietrivier, Rose Garden, Stellar (Organic), Sumaridge, Tulbagh Wine (3), Two Oceans, Vredenheim, Woolworths ★★ African Terroir, Fairvalley Farmworkers Association, Groot Eiland, Hippo Creek, Kango, Kleine Draken (Kosher), Origin Wine, Stellendrift, Swartland, Sylvanvale, Wellington Cooperative, Windmeul Cooperative ★ African Terroir, Boland Kelder, Kango, Klawer Co-operative, Origin Wine ☆ Botha Wine, Landzicht GWK, Welvanpas **NT** Bottelary, De Zoete Inval, Drakensig, Fort Simon, Hawksmoor at Matjieskuil, Jason's Hill Private, KWV Limited, La Couronne, Lindiwe, Mountain River, Rose Garden, Sylvanvale, Wellington Cooperative, Wines of Cape Town **NR** Lanzerac, Riebeek (3), Stony Brook, Thelema Mountain **D** Bellingham, De Zoete Inval, Dellrust, Eaglevlei, Hazendal, Headbutt, Le Manoir de Brendel, Longridge, Lourensford, Main Street, Mellasat, Mountain Ridge, Signal Hill, Stettyn, Woolworths

Port, red ★★★★★ Axe Hill, Boplaas Family (3), De Krans, JP Bredell ★★★★ Allesverloren, Boplaas Family, De Krans (2), JP Bredell, Overgaauw ★★★★ Allesverloren, Bergsig (3), Boplaas Family (2), De Krans, Domein Doornkraal, JP Bredell, KWV Limited, Landskroon, Makro, Monis, Morgenhof, Peter Bayly, Pick's Pick ★★★ Annandale Distillers & Vintners, Backsberg, Beyerskloof, Boplaas Family, Calitzdorp, De Wet Co-op, Douglas Green, Flagstone, Goudini, Jonkheer, KWV Limited (2), L'Avenir, Louiesenhof, Muratie, Rooiberg, Vergenoegd, Viljoensdrift, Villiera, Windmeul Cooperative ★★★ Beaumont, Bon Courage, Botha Wine, Calitzdorp, Du Toitskloof, Groenland, Groot Constantia, Jean Daneel, KWV Limited, Landzicht GWK, Le Grand Chasseur, McGregor, Mons Ruber, Nietvoorbij Wine, Robertson, Rose Garden, Rustenberg, Swartland, Tulbagh Wine, Uitvlucht, Van Loveren Private ★★★ Grundheim, Muratie, Paddagang, Riebeek, Somerbosch, Uitvlucht, Wamakersvallei ★★ Aan de Doorns Co-operative, Ashton,

Badsberg Wine, Boland Kelder, Bonnievale Wine, Bovlei, De Zoete Inval, Franschhoek, Kango, Klawer Co-operative, Montpellier, Mooiuitsig Wine, Rietrivier, Slanghoek, Swartland, TTT, Tulbagh Wine ★★ Dellrust, Gentis Family, Koelenhof, Oranjerivier Wine, TTT, Upland ★ Clairvaux Private, Linton Park **NT** Grundheim, Hartswater Wine, Kango, KWV Limited (2), Riverstone, Wellington Cooperative **NR** The Stables, Villiersdorp **D** Domein Doornkraal, Ruitersvlei

Port, white ★★★★ Axe Hill ★★★ Boplaas Family, De Krans **D** Domein Doornkraal

Red blends, Cape bordeaux

★★★★★ Beyerskloof, Hartenberg ★★★★☆ Buitenverwachting, Camberley (2), Capaia, Cordoba, Dalla Cia Wine & Spirit Company, De Toren Private, Delheim, Diemersdal, Dornier, Durbanville Hills, Ernie Els, Fleur du Cap, Grangehurst, Havana Hills (2), High Constantia, Horse Mountain, Ingwe, Jordan (2), Kanonkop, Klein Gustrouw, L'Avenir, Meerlust, Meinert, Môreson, Morgenhof, Morgenster (2), Muratie, Nabygelegen Private, Overgaauw, Rupert & Rothschild Vignerons, Rustenberg, Simonsig, Stellekaya, Sterhuis, Stony Brook, Tokara, Vergelegen (2), Vergenoegd, Vilafonté (2), Villiera, Von Ortloff, Woolworths ★★★★ Adler, Alkmaar, Asara, Avontuur, Backsberg (2), Beaumont, Bellevue, Bilton, Bonfoi, Camberley, Cape Chamonix Wine Farm, Cloof, Clos Malverne, Constantia Uitsig, David Frost, De Toren Private, Delaire, Diemersdal, Eikendal, Elgin Vintners, Epicurean, Flagstone, Fryer's Cove, Glen Carlou, Goede Hoop, Graham Beck, Groot Constantia, Hermanuspietersfontein, Hillcrest, Idiom, Jean Daneel, Joostenberg, JP Bredell, Kanu, Klein Constantia, Klein Genot Country & Wine, La Motte, Laibach (2) (Organic), Lanzerac, Lyngrove, Lynx, Meerlust, Miles Mossop, Mooiplaas, Mountain Oaks (Organic), Mulderbosch (2), Mvemve Raats, Nederburg (2), Neil Ellis, Nelson, Nitida, Oak Valley, Old Vines, Raka, Ridgeback, Rijk's Private, Rupert & Rothschild Vignerons, Saronsberg (2), Saxenburg, Schalk Burger & Sons, Seidelberg, Sentinel, Siyabonga, Springfield, Stellenbosch Hills, Stonewall, Stony Brook, The Goats do Roam Wine Company, Veenwouden Private (2), Von Ortloff, Vrede en Lust Wine Farm (2), Vriesenhof, Vuurberg, Warwick (2),

Webersburg, Wedgeview, Welgemeend (2), Woolworths, Yonder Hill Wine Farm ★★★★ Allée Bleue, Amani, Asara, Audacia, Blaauwklippen Agricultural, Black Oystercatcher, Boschkloof , Bouwland (2), Buitenverwachting, Capaia, Cellar-Vie, Dalla Cia Wine & Spirit Company, De Wetshof, Douglas Wine, Gusto, Haskell, Hermanuspietersfontein, Iona, Jonkheer, Jordan, Joubert-Tradauw Private, JP le Hanie, Julien Schaal, Klein Constantia, Kloovenburg, Koningsrivier, La Bri, La Couronne, Laborie, Laibach, Leopard Frog, Lindhorst, Louiesenhof, Makro, Marianne, Mont du Toit Kelder, Mont Rochelle Hotel & Mountain, Monterosso, Môreson, Morgenster, Napier, Neil Ellis Meyer-Näkel, Nick & Forti's, Niel Joubert, Nitida, Noble Hill, Ormonde Private, Peter Andrew Signature Collection, Rainbow's End, Reyneke, Schalkenbosch, Shoprite Checkers, Simonsvlei International, Slaley, Spier, Stellenrust, The Company of Wine People, The High Road, Umkhulu (2), Vendôme, Vergelegen, Vondeling, Vriesenhof (2), Vuurberg, Wedderwill, Welgemeend, Wildekrans, Windmeul Cooperative, Woolworths (3), Ziggurat, Zonnebloem, Zorgvliet ★★★ Anthony Smook, Avontuur (2), Bellingham, Bonnievale Wine, Cape Bay, Clairvaux Private, Cloof, Clos Malverne, Cordoba, Craighall, Crows Nest, Détendu, Dominion Wine Company, Douglas Green, Feiteiras, FirstCape, Fort Simon, Goedverwacht, Graham Beck, Hazendal, Idiom, Jason's Hill Private, Jean Daneel, Jordan, Kaapzicht, KWV Limited, La Vigne (2), Louisvale, Makro (2), MolenVliet Wine & Guest, Mont du Bleu, Mont du Toit Kelder, Mount Rozier, Neethlingshof, Nico Vermeulen, Oude Kaap, Overhex International, Perdeberg, Romond, Ruitersvlei, Schalkenbosch, Seidelberg, Ses'Fikile, Seven Oaks, Springfontein, Stellendrift (2), Swartland, The Company of Wine People, The Stables, The of Good Hope, Two Oceans, Uva Mira, Van Zylshof, Villiersdorp, Vrede Wine Farm, Wolvendrift Private ★★★ Agterplaas, Anura, Beau Joubert &, Bon Courage, Cape, Creation, Daschbosch Wine, Domein Doornkraal, Hermanuspietersfontein, Horse Mountain, Jacaranda, JP le Hanie, Kleine Draken (Kosher), La Couronne, Leopard's Leap, Liquor World, Lourensford, Rhebokskloof Private, Rickety Bridge, Schalkenbosch, Seidelberg,

Simonsig, Skilpadvlei, Swartland, The Company of Wine People, The of Good Hope, Vaughan Johnson's Wine & Cigar Shop, Wildekrans, Wines of Cape Town, Woolworths (2), Zidela ★★ Ashanti, Ashton, Bellingham, Bernheim, Blouvlei, Bottelary, Eagle's Cliff/New Cape, Juno Wine Company, Main Street, Makro, McGregor, Mooiuitsig Wine, Mostertsdrift Noble, Origin Wine (2), Overgaauw, Rooiberg, Schalk Burger & Sons, Shoprite Checkers, Tanagra Private, Van Loveren Private, Wedgewood ★★ Ashton, Dominion Wine Company, Du Toitskloof, Nuy Wine, Origin Wine, WaverleyTBS/uniWines ★ Vunani **NT** Anura, Bergsig, Bottelary Hills, Doolhof, Mountain River, Overhex International, Rico Suter **NR** MolenVliet Wine & Guest, Racetrack, The Stables, Viljoensdrift, Vunani, Woolworths, Zoetendal, Zorgvliet **D** Anura, Camberley, David Frost, Freedom Hill, Haskell, Headbutt, Lyngrove, Makro, MAN Vintners, Meerendal, Namaqua, Ruitersvlei, Stellenzicht, Vendôme, Vergelegen, Woolworths

Red blends, other ★★★★★ Boschendal, Waterford ★★★★ Akkerdal, Ataraxia Mountain, Avondale, De Krans, Lammershoek, Mont du Toit Kelder, Stony Brook, The Observatory, Val de Vie Winelands Lifestyle, Waarburg ★★★★ African Pride, Boland Kelder, Boschendal, Du Preez (2), Landskroon (2), Lynx, Micu Narunsky, Perdeberg, Slaley, Val de Vie Winelands Lifestyle, Veenwouden Private, Vergenoegd, Wellington Cooperative ★★★ Avontuur, Bottelary, Cape, Clovelly, Cloverfield Private, Eshkol Kosher (Kosher), Goudini, Kaapzicht, Kango, KWV Limited, Landskroon, Millstream, Morgenhof, Origin Wine, Ridgemor Farm, Saxenburg, Simonsvlei International, Theuniskraal, Villiera, Vleiland, Whalehaven ★★★ Aan de Doorns Co-operative, Backsberg, Barry Gould Family, Barrydale, Blouvlei, Boland Kelder, Bonnievale Wine, Darling, Douglas Green, Du Preez, Eshkol Kosher (Kosher), Excelsior, Idiom, Jonkheer, KWV Limited, La Petite Ferme, Micu Narunsky, Origin Wine, Oude Kaap, Perdeberg, Robertson, Saronsberg, Southern Sky, The Saints, Woolworths, Zandvliet ★★ African Terroir, Arum Lily, Botha Wine, Bottelary, Culemborg, Douglas Green, Douglas Wine, Hartswater Wine, Kholisa, Klawer Co-operative, Leopard's Leap,

Meerhof, Mooiuitsig Wine, Oude Kaap, Overhex International, Pick 'n Pay, Ridder's Creek, Robertson (2), Roodezandt & Ruitersvlei (2), Slanghoek (2), Swartland, The Stables, Tulbagh Wine, Vaughan Johnson's Wine & Cigar Shop, Vrede Wine Farm, Woolworths ★★ De Zoete Inval, Dellrust, Grande Provence, Origin Wine (2), Overmeer, Schalkenbosch, Simonsvlei International ★ Bottelary Hills, Brandvlei, Skilpadvlei, Welvanpas ★ Montagu Wine **NT** Avondale, Doolhof, Fredine le Roux, Grundheim, Koelenhof, Montagu Wine, Mooiuitsig Wine, Saxenburg (2), Simonsvlei International, The Goose, Wellington Cooperative **NR** Swartland **D** Avondale, Boschendal, Dellrust, Le Grand Chasseur, Main Street, Makro, Perdeberg, Rose Garden, Signal Hill, Uitvlucht, Wamakersvallei, Woolworths

Red blends, other cabernet-based

★★★★★ Anwilka, De Trafford, Ernie Els, Flagstone, Ingwe, Nederburg, Plaisir De Merle, Waterford ★★★★ Boschkloof , Camberley, Cameradi, Conspirare, De Meye, Diemersfontein, Durbanville Hills, Ernie Els, Four Paws, Graceland, Heron Ridge, Joostenberg, KWV Limited, Lourensford, Mont Destin, Mont du Toit Kelder, Nabygelegen Private, Neethlingshof, Pick's Pick, Prospect1870, Rijk's Private, Rust en Vrede, Rusticus Vintage, The Goose, Uva Mira, Wine of the Month Club, Woolworths ★★★★ Allée Bleue, Annandale Distillers & Vintners, Avondale (2), BLANKbottle, Boplaas Family, Cape Bay, Cape Point, Cloof, Doolhof, Flagstone, Glen Carlou, Hartenberg, Havana Hills, Kaapzicht, KWV Limited, La Kavayan, Lushof, Nederburg, Paul Cluver, Robertson, Stormhoek, Uitkyk, Virgin Earth, Waterford, Westbridge, Woolworths ★★★ BLANKbottle (2), Bo La Motte, Boschheim, Cloof (2), Clos Malverne, De Meye, De Zoete Inval, Delheim, Dieu Donné, Goede Hoop, Groote Post, Hill & Dale, Koopmanskloof (2), Mont Destin, Mountain Ridge, Origin Wine (2), Seven Oaks, The Springtree Wine Company, Thelema Mountain, Vrede en Lust Wine Farm (2), Vunani ★★★ Blaauwklippen Agricultural (2), Bon Courage, Bonnievale Wine, Bovlei, Dominion Wine Company, Douglas Green, Groupe LFE South Africa, Janéza Private, Kumala/Constellation South Africa, KWV Limited, Lievland, Mac's Hill,

Mountain River, Opstal, Origin Wine, Rietvallei, Seven Oaks, Simonsig, The Company of Wine People, Van Loveren Private ★★ Chateau Libertas, Du Toitskloof, Olsen, Retief, Rosendal Private, Schalkenbosch, Skilpadvlei, Southern Sky, Stellendrift, Tassenberg, Women in Wine ★★ Bottelary, Constantia ★ Devonvale Golf & Wine **NT** Waverley Hills Organic **D** Fairview, Zandvliet

Red blends, shiraz/syrah-based

★★★★★ The of Good Hope ★★★★★ Bilton, Fairview, Grangehurst, La Motte, Nico van der Merwe, Nico Vermeulen, Sadie Family, Saronsberg, The Spice Route, The of Good Hope, Woolworths ★★★★ Bellingham, Black Pearl, Boekenhoutskloof, Boplaas Family, Boschkloof , Bovlei, Catherine Marshall, Diemersfontein, Ernie Els, Gilga, Groenland, Hazendal, Hermanuspietersfontein, Idiom, Joostenberg, Julien Schaal, Karusa, Ken Forrester, La Bri, Lammershoek, Luddite, Meerhof, Newton Johnson, Saxenburg, Sequillo, Solms-Delta, Somerbosch, Stony Brook, The Company of Wine People, The Goats do Roam Wine Company, The Stables, The of Good Hope (2), Tulbagh Mountain (2) (Organic), Wine of the Month Club ★★★★ Akkerdal, Anura, Barton Farm, Bellingham, Blyde, Boschendal, Boschheim, Doolhof, Freedom Hill, Graham Beck, Joostenberg, Ken Forrester (2), Klein Parys, Kleine Zalze, KWV Limited, Lindhorst, Long Mountain Wine Company, Lourensford (2), Makro, Overgaauw, Ridgeback, Rijk's Private, Saam Mountain, Spier, StellenHills, Stonehill, Stormhoek, Swartland, The Company of Wine People, Val de Vie Winelands Lifestyle, Wine of the Month Club, Woolworths (2), Zevenwacht, Zonnebloem ★★★ Ayama, Bellingham, BLANKbottle, Bon Cap Organic, Boschendal, Cape Rock, Flat Roof Manor, Graham Beck, Groenland, Herold, Kanu, KWV Limited, La Vierge, Mike's Kitchen, Noble Hill, Old Vines, Prospect1870, Retief, Rickety Bridge, Ridgeback, Rijk's Private, Schalkenbosch, Stellenrust, Swartland, The Company of Wine People (2), The Stables, The of Good Hope, Thokozani, Two Oceans, Vaughan Johnson's Wine & Cigar Shop, Villiera, Vondeling, Vukani, William Everson ★★★ Boekenhoutskloof, De Wet Co-op, Douglas Green, FirstCape, Klawer Co-operative, Kleine Zalze, Makro, Malan Family

Vintners, Mellasat, Muratie, Mystery Wine Corporation, Nederburg, Opstal, Oranjerivier Wine, Overhex International, Ridgemor Farm, Riebeek, Seidelberg, Van Loveren Private, Withington ★★ Bellingham, Elberti, Kumala/Constellation South Africa, Mac's Hill, Wedgewood, Woolworths, Zidela, Zomerlust ★☆ Abbottshill, Oaklands Wine Exporters, Origin Wine, Terroir of SA, Vredenheim **NT** Somersbosch **NR** Hidden Valley, Riebeek, Swartland **D** African Pride, Anura, Douglas Wine, Kumala/Constellation South Africa, Lutzville Cape Diamond, Riebeek, Yonder Hill Wine Farm

Red blends, with Italian varieties
★★★★ Backsberg, Bouchard Finlayson, The Goats do Roam Wine Company ★★★★ Leopard's Leap, Stellekaya (2) ★★★ Flat Roof Manor, Havana Hills **D** Fairview

Red blends, with merlot
★★★★☆ Le Bonheur ★★★★ Adoro, Alto, Post House, Steenberg ★★★★ Amani, Blue Crane, Dornier, Mount Rozier, Nico van der Merwe, Raka, Saxenburg, Signal Hill, Stony Brook, Viljoensdrift ★★★ Beaumont, Bellingham, Bergwater, Coleraine, Groot Constantia, Groot Eiland, Kumala/Constellation South Africa, Leopard Frog, Onderkloof Vines &, Retief, The Company of Wine People, Two Oceans, Weltevrede, Whalehaven ★★★ Bergsig, Bergwater, Hillcrest, Joubert-Tradauw Private, Kumala/Constellation South Africa, KWV Limited, Long Mountain Wine Company, Marianne, The Company of Wine People, Zevenwacht ★★ Groot Eiland, Groupe LFE South Africa, Middelvlei, Nelson, Origin Wine, Van Loveren Private, Woolworths ★☆ Eikendal, Welvanpas **D** Hartenberg, Lourensford, Stormhoek

Red blends, with pinotage
★★★★☆ Beyerskloof, Clos Malverne, DeWaal, Graham Beck, Grangehurst (2), Kaapzicht, Meinert, Middelvlei, Raka, Remhoogte ★★★★ Bon Cap Organic (Organic), Cloof, Croydon Vineyard Residential (2), Dellrust, Devon Hill, Flagstone, Glenelly, Kaapzicht, Le Riche, Neethlingshof, Oude Compagnies Post, Remhoogte, Shoprite Checkers, Simonsig, The Observatory, Vriesenhof, Warwick ★★★★ Alvi's Drift Private, Asara, Babylon's Peak Private, Beyerskloof, Bovlei, Cederberg Private, Clos Malverne, Darling, Devon Hill, Domaine Brahms Wineries, Eaglevlei, Fairview,

Idiom, Kanonkop, Knorhoek (2), La Chataigne, Lyngrove, Makro, Marklew Family, Middelvlei, Mont Rochelle Hotel & Mountain, Mountain River, Oude Compagnies Post, Post House, Quoin Rock, Remhoogte, Rustenberg, Saam Mountain, Schonenberg, Stellekaya, Stellenrust, Stellenzicht, Swartland, Sylvanvale, The Goats do Roam Wine Company (2), Umkhulu, Welgemeend ★★★ African Roots Wine Brands, Allée Bleue, Babylon's Peak Private, Bellevue (2), Bellingham, Borg Family, Cape Chamonix Wine Farm, Cloof (2), De Krans, DeWaal, Diemersdal, Domaine Brahms Wineries, Eagle's Cliff/New Cape, Elberti, FirstCape, Fort Simon (2), Freedom Hill, Goedvertrouw, Goudini, Groot Eiland, JP Bredell, KWV Limited (2), Lammershoek, Leopard's Leap, Lorraine Private, Origin Wine, Spier, Umkhulu, Viljoensdrift, Villiera, Vruchtbaar Boutique, Wildekrans ★★★ African Pride, African Terroir (Organic), Ashton, Boplaas Family, Cape Bay, De Krans, Hartswater Wine, Klein Parys, Koelenhof, Kumala/Constellation South Africa (3) (Organic), Mellasat, Mount Vernon Farm, Mountain River, Nederburg, Origin Wine (5), Overhex International, Paddagang, Slaley, Spier, Stellenbosch Hills, Stellendrift, Tulbagh Wine, Two Oceans, WaverleyTBS/uniWines ★★ African Pride, Diemersfontein, Douglas Green, Drostdy-Hof (2), Du Toitskloof (2), Klein Parys, Kumala/Constellation South Africa (2), KWV Limited, L'Avenir, Lateganskop, Mount Rozier, Mountain Ridge, Namaqua (2), Oranjerivier Wine, Origin Wine, Overhex International (3), Pumlani, Slaley, Thor, Tulbagh Wine, Woolworths ★☆ BurCon, Du Toitskloof, FirstCape, Headbutt, Kumala/Constellation South Africa, Mountain River, Origin Wine (4), Rietrivier (2), Rooiberg, The Company of Wine People ★ Origin Wine **NT** Bottelary Hills, Dragonridge, Sylvanvale **NR** Bellingham **D** African Terroir (Organic), Ashanti, Dominion Wine Company, Doolhof, Flagstone, Lourensford, Makro, Namaqua, Rhebokskloof Private, Umkhulu, Wines of Cape Town

Riesling (Cape)
★★★ Bon Courage, De Villiers, Theuniskraal ★★ Du Toitskloof, KWV Limited, Nederburg ★ Van Loveren Private

Riesling (Rhine/Weisser)
★★★★ Hartenberg, Klein Constantia, Paul Cluver, Woolworths

★★★☆ Buitenverwachting, De Wetshof, Jack & Knox Winecraft, Nederburg, Ross Gower, Thelema Mountain (2), Villiera ★★★ Bergsig, Jordan, Woolworths ★★☆ Meerhof, Rietvallei **D** Delheim, Lievland, Rhebokskloof Private, Rooiberg, Weltevrede

Rosé dry ★★★★ Solms-Delta

★★★☆ Beyerskloof, De Grendel, De Morgenzon, High Constantia, Klein Constantia, Rustenberg, Signal Hill, South Hill, The Goats do Roam Wine Company, Ziggurat ★★★ Allée Bleue, Asara, Beaumont, Bein Wine, Beyerskloof, Cabrière, De Meye, Delaire, Dornier, Fairview, Flagstone, Golden Kaan, Haut Espoir, Joostenberg, Jordan, L'Avenir, Longridge, Lynx, Mont Rochelle Hotel & Mountain, Newton Johnson, Niel Joubert, Origin Wine, Raka, Rietvallei (2), Ross Gower, Saxenburg, Stonehill, Van Zylshof, Villiera, Vrede en Lust Wine Farm, WaverleyTBS/uniWines, Whalehaven ★★☆ Andy Mitchell, Anura, Avondale, Backsberg, Beau Joubert &, Bellingham, Bergsig, Bon Cap Organic (Organic), De Krans, Dormershire, Dunstone, Fort Simon, Graham Beck, Hermanuspietersfontein, Hill & Dale, Kleine Zalze, L'Avenir, La Petite Ferme, Leopard's Leap, Lutzville Cape Diamond, Mont Destin, Mont du Bleu, Mostertsdrift Noble, Mount Vernon Farm, Nelson, Oaklands Wine Exporters, Origin Wine, Overhex International, Riebeek, Shoprite Checkers, Slowine, Stellenrust, Sylvanvale, The Company of Wine People (2), Welgegund Farm, Women in Wine, Zorgvliet ★★ African Terroir, Bloemendal, Cloof, De Villiers, Grangehurst, Juno Wine Company, La Vierge, Lammershoek, Millstream, Muratie, Org de Rac Domain, Origin Wine (4) (Light & low-alcohol), Rooiberg, Savanha, Sumaridge, The Company of Wine People, The Stables, Van Loveren Private, Wamakersvallei, Zandvliet ★☆ Groupe LFE South Africa (2), Koelenhof, Mitre's Edge, Môreson, Origin Wine (2), Oude Compagnies Post, Oude Kaap, Ridgemor Farm, Schalkenbosch, Woolworths ★ De Zoete Inval ☆ Blouvlei **NT** Bottelary, Douglas Wine, Flagstone, Louiesenhof, Meerhof **NR** L'Avenir, Stony Brook **D** African Terroir, Ashanti, Excelsior, Lourensford, Namaqua, Overhex International, Zorgvliet

Rosé off-dry/semi-sweet

★★★☆ Mulderbosch ★★★ Altydgedacht,

Boland Kelder, Goedverwacht, Herold, Hildenbrand Wine & Olive, Koelenhof, Koopmanskloof, Lorraine Private, Mooi Bly, Stormhoek (2), Sylvanvale, Zevenwacht ★★☆ Angora, Arum Lily, Avondale, Backsberg, Bergwater, Bernheim, Blue Cove, Boschendal, Cape Chamonix Wine Farm, Delheim, Douglas Green, Eaglevlei, Eikendal, Grande Provence, Knorhoek, L'Avenir, Lanzerac, Morgenhof, Nederburg, Nuy Wine, Pumlani, Roodezandt &, Saronsberg, The Springtree Wine Company, Two Oceans, Viljoensdrift, Woolworths ★★ African Roots Wine Brands, Ashton (2), Avondale, Badsberg Wine, Bellingham (2), Blaauwklippen Agricultural, Boland Kelder, Bon Courage, Boplaas Family, Culemborg, Darling, Dellrust, Dieu Donné, Du Toitskloof, Eagle's Cliff/New Cape, FirstCape (3), Graça, Horse Mountain, Kumala/Constellation South Africa, KWV Limited, La Chataigne, Lutzville Cape Diamond, Nietvoorbij Wine, Seidelberg, Simonsvlei International, Skilpadvlei, Slanghoek, Spier, Spookfontein, Stellenbosch Hills, Swartland, The Company of Wine People (2), Theuniskraal, Thokozani, Wines of Cape Town, Woolworths (2) ★★ Arabella, Cellar Cask, Darling, Die Huis van Anjé, Drostdy-Hof, Du Toitskloof, Eshkol Kosher (Kosher), Groot Eiland, Jason's Hill Private, Mont du Bleu, Overgaauw, Pick 'n Pay, Robertson, Seidelberg, Spier, Tall Horse, Villiersdorp (Light & low-alcohol), Vredenheim ★ Clairvaux Private, Klawer Co-operative, Ladismith, Mooiuitsig Wine, Mystery Wine Corporation, Namaqua, Oranjerivier Wine, Seven Oaks, Stellar, Tulbagh Wine, Zidela **NT** KWV Limited (3), Montagu Wine, Viljoensdrift, Wellington Cooperative **NR** Cape Hutton, Swartland, Woolworths **D** Bovlei, Craighall, Daschbosch Wine, Graham Beck, Le Grand Chasseur, Ruitersvlei, Uitvlucht

Roussanne ★★★★ Rustenberg

Ruby cabernet ★★★★ Goudini

★★★ Bellpost, Long Mountain Wine Company, Riverstone ★★☆ McGregor, Oranjerivier Wine, Robertson ★★ Ladismith, Langverwacht, Wandsbeck ★☆ Kango, Lutzville Cape Diamond, Robertson **NT** Lateganskop, McGregor **D** Hartswater Wine, Lutzville Cape Diamond, Oude Kaap, Rusticus Vintage, Zandvliet

Sacramental wine ★★ Eshkol Kosher (Kosher), Kleine Draken, Mooiuitsig Wine

Sangiovese ★★★☆ Anura, Fairview, Idiom, Klein Parys ★★★ Dragonridge, L'Ormarins Private, Monterosso, Raka ★★☆ Tukulu

Sauvignon blanc unwooded

★★★★★ Woolworths ★★★★☆ Ataraxia Mountain, Buitenverwachting, Cape Point, Constantia Glen, De Grendel (2), Diemersdal (3), Durbanville Hills, Fort Simon, Fryer's Cove, Groote Post, Hermanuspietersfontein (2), Iona, Klein Constantia, La Motte (Organic), Neil Ellis, Nitida, Oak Valley (2), Steenberg, The Company of Wine People, The Spice Route, Thelema Mountain, Vergelegen, Waterkloof, Woolworths (2) ★★★★ Adoro, Alluvia Boutique & Guesthouse, Amani, Backsberg, Benguela Cove, Black Oystercatcher, Bloemendal, Boplaas Family, Boschendal, Buitenverwachting, Cape Point, Cederberg Private, Clouds, Constantia Uitsig, Dalla Cia Wine & Spirit Company, Darling, Delaire, Domaine des Dieux, Durbanville Hills (2), Elgin Heights, Fairview, Flagstone (2), Fleur du Cap (2), Graham Beck, Groot Constantia, Groote Post, Hazendal, Hermanuspietersfontein, Herold, Hidden Valley (2), High Constantia, Hillcrest, Jordan, Klein Constantia, KWV Limited (2), L'Avenir, La Chataigne, La Motte, La Vierge, Laibach, Lomond, Longridge, Mont Rochelle Hotel & Mountain, Mulderbosch, Nederburg (3), Neethlingshof, Nitida, Noble Hill, Paul Cluver, Plaisir De Merle, Quando, Quoin Rock, Raka, Rietvallei, Ross Gower, Saronsberg, Saxenburg, Sir Lambert, South Hill, Southern Right, Springfield (2), Steenberg, Strandveld, Sumaridge, The Company of Wine People, Thelema Mountain, Tokara (3), Usana, Uva Mira, Vergelegen, Villiera, Warwick, Waterford, Weltevrede, Zoetendal ★★★☆ Allée Bleue, Altydgedacht (2), Amani, Bellevue, Blaauwklippen Agricultural, Blue Cove, Bonfoi, Boschendal (2), Bottelary Hills, Bouchard Finlayson, Cape Chamonix Wine Farm, Catherine Marshall, Clos Malverne, Delheim, Dellrust, Devon Hill, DeWaal, Die Huis van Anjé, Diemersdal, Doolhof, Durbanville Hills (2), Eagle's Cliff/New Cape, Eaglevlei, Eikendal, Elgin Vintners, Ernst & Co, Flagstone, Fleur du Cap, Goede Hoop, Golden Kaan, Graham Beck, Groenland, Hartenberg, Havana Hills,

Hillcrest, Kanu, Ken Forrester, Klein Constantia, Kleine Zalze (2), Knorhoek, Lanzerac, Lomond (2), Lourensford, Luddite, Lushof, Main Street, Makro, MAN Vintners, Miravel, Mischa, Mont Rochelle Hotel & Mountain, Mooiplaas, Môreson (2), Morgenhof, Mountain River, Nederburg (2), Onderkloof Vines &, Oracle, Ormonde Private, Perdeberg, Robertson, Rustenberg, Saam Mountain, Saronsberg, Simonsig, Simonsvlei International, Somerbosch, Spier (2), Stellenbosch Hills, Stellenrust, Sterhuis, Stony Brook, Strandveld, Uitkyk, Under Oaks, Villiera, Vrede en Lust Wine Farm, Vukani, Waterkloof, Wedderwill, Woolworths, Zevenwacht, Ziggurat, Zonnebloem, Zorgvliet ★★★ Adler, African Roots Wine Brands, Anatu, Anura, Arabella, Arendsig Hand-Crafted, Asara, Avondale, Avontuur, Barrydale, Barton Farm, Beau Joubert &, Beaumont, Belbon Hills, Blue Crane, Boekenhoutskloof, Bon Courage, Buitehof, Cape Bay, Cloverfield Private, Creation, Crios Bríde, Crows Nest, Darling, Douglas Wine, Drakensig, Du Toitskloof, DuVon, Eaglevlei, Elberti, Excelsior, False Bay, Four Paws, GlenWood, Grande Provence, Groot Eiland, Groupe LFE South Africa, Haut Espoir, Hermanuspietersfontein, Hill & Dale, Jason's Hill Private, Kaapzicht, Kanu, Ken Forrester, Klein Parys, Kloovenburg, Kumala/Constellation South Africa (2), KWV Limited, La Vierge, Lammershoek, Le Bonheur, Leopard's Leap, Libertas, Lievland, Lindhorst, Long Beach, Lorraine Private, Louiesenhof, M'hudi, Meerendal, Mount Rozier, Neethlingshof, Nelson, Nico Vermeulen, Nietvoorbij Wine, Obikwa, Old Vines, Ormonde Private, Peter Falke, Rietvallei, Sagila, Ses'Fikile, Shoprite Checkers, Stanford Hills, Stellenzicht, Table Mountain, The Company of Wine People (2), The Goose, The Springtree Wine Company, The of Good Hope, Villiersdorp, Virgin Earth, Vondeling, Vruchtbaar Boutique, Waterford, Waterkloof, WaverleyTBS/uniWines, Wine of the Month Club (2), Woolworths, Zonnebloem, Zorgvliet ★★★ African Terroir (Organic), Ayama, Backsberg, Boland Kelder, Bon Cap Organic (Organic), Bonnievale Wine, Boplaas Family, Bottelary, Brandvlei, Cape Bay, Cape Classics, Cape Hutton, Cape, Daschbosch Wine, De Vallei Boutique, De Wet Co-op, De Wetshof (2), Dieu Donné, Dormershire, Douglas Green, Fat Bastard,

FirstCape, Freedom Hill, Goedvertrouw, Goedverwacht, Golden Kaan, Goudini (2), Groupe LFE South Africa, Gusto, Jason's Hill Private, Klein Dassenberg, Koopmanskloof, Kumala/Constellation South Africa, Laborie, Landskroon, Linde, Linton Park, Lord's (2) (Organic), Lourensford, Lutzville Cape Diamond (2), Lyngrove, Marianne, Monterosso, Mount Rozier, Mountain Ridge, Nabygelegen Private, Nuy Wine, Origin Wine (2), Overgaauw, Rickety Bridge, Rijk's Private, Roodezandt &, Saam Mountain, Seidelberg, Simonsvlei International, Stettyn, Stormhoek, Swartland, The Stables, Thorntree, Tierhoek, Two Oceans, Viljoensdrift, Wamakersvallei, Weltevrede, Wildekrans, Windmeul Cooperative, Wonderfontein, Woolworths (2) (Organic), Zandvliet, Zidela (2) ★★ African Pride, African Terroir, Ashton, Badsberg Wine, Bergsig, Bergwater, Botha Wine, Clairvaux Private, Craighall, De Villiers, DeWaal, Dispore Kamma Boutique , Du Preez (2), Koelenhof, KWV Limited, La Couronne, La Petite Ferme, Lateganskop, Le Grand Chasseur, Lindiwe, Long Mountain Wine Company, Longbarn, Lourensford, Lutzville Cape Diamond, McGregor, Mount Rozier, Mountain River (2), Overhex International, Rhebokskloof Private, Ridgeback, Riebeek, Riverstone, Robertson, Rosendal Private, Ruitersvlei, Savanha, Schalkenbosch, Skilpadvlei, Spier, Stellar (2) (Organic), Swartland, Tall Horse, Tulbagh Wine (2), United Nations of Wine, Van Zylshof, Von Ortloff, Vrede Wine Farm, Wines of Cape Town, Wolvendrift Private, Woolworths (2) ★★ Aan de Doorns Cooperative, African Terroir (Organic), Bovlei, Conradie Family, Culemborg, De Doorns, Dominion Wine Company (2), Drostdy-Hof, Eagle's Cliff/New Cape, Fairvalley Farmworkers Association, Hippo Creek, Janéza Private, Juno Wine Company, Kango, Kleine Draken (Kosher), Koelenhof, Langverwacht, Long Mountain Wine Company, Niel Joubert, Opstal, Origin Wine (2), Paddagang, Robertson, Rooiberg, Seven Oaks, Stellendrift, Van Loveren Private, Wandsbeck, Wines of Cape Town ★ African Terroir (2), Calitzdorp, Eagle's Cliff/New Cape, Klawer Co-operative, KWV Limited, Le Manoir de Brendel, Mooiuitsig Wine, Mystery Wine Corporation, Origin Wine, Rietrivier, Slanghoek **NT** Alvi's Drift Private,

Fort Simon, Jonkheer, Kleine Draken (Kosher), Oaklands Wine Exporters, Overhex International, Southern Sky (2), Wellington Cooperative, Withington **NR** Grande Provence, Perdeberg, Reyneke, Savanha, Slaley, Spier, The Stables, Zorgvliet **D** African Pride, African Terroir, Bergwater, Bilton, Dominion Wine Company (2), Du Toitskloof, Haskell, Longridge, Manley Private, Meerendal, Mostertsdrift Noble (2), Namaqua, Noble Hill, The of Good Hope, Umkhulu, Zandvliet

Sauvignon blanc wooded ★★★★☆ Cape

Chamonix Wine Farm ★★★★ Bellingham, Hoopenburg, Jordan, Neil Ellis, Newton Johnson, Pick's Pick, Steenberg ★★★☆ Boland Kelder, Capaia, Flagstone, Meerendal, Reyneke ★★★ La Petite Ferme, Simonsig, Uitvlucht **D** Black Oystercatcher, De Wetshof, Fort Simon, McGregor

Semillon unwooded

★★★★ Buitenverwachting, Stellenzicht, Woolworths ★★★★ Zonnebloem ★★★ Vondeling ★★★ Zorgvliet ★★ WaverleyTBS/uniWines, William Everson **NT** Eikehof **D** Aan de Doorns Cooperative, Slanghoek, Van Loveren Private

Semillon wooded ★★★★★ Cape Point

★★★★☆ Constantia Uitsig, Rijk's Private, Steenberg ★★★★ Boekenhoutskloof, Cederberg Private, Eikendal, Fairview, Jack & Knox Winecraft, La Bourgogne Farm, Nitida, Stony Brook, Vergelegen ★★★☆ Flat Roof Manor, Fleur du Cap, Klein Constantia, Stony Brook, Stormhoek ★★★ Bloemendal, Franschhoek, Hildenbrand Wine & Olive, Landau du Val, Rickety Bridge ★★☆ Bergheim, Haut Espoir **NT** La Chataigne **D** Black Oystercatcher, La Petite Ferme, Wildekrans

Shiraz/syrah ★★★★★ De Trafford, Fairview,

Hartenberg, Saxenburg ★★★★☆ Anthony de Jager, Asara, Avondale, Boekenhoutskloof, Bon Courage, Boschendal (2), Boschkloof , Camberley, Cederberg Private, Delheim, DeWaal, Flagstone, Gilga, Graham Beck, Hartenberg (2), Kleine Zalze, KWV Limited, La Motte, Luddite, Quoin Rock, Raka, Reyneke, Rickety Bridge, Ridgeback, Robertson, Rudi Schultz (2), Rustenberg, Sanctum, Saxenburg, Signal Hill, Simonsig, Stark-Condé, Stellenzicht, Stoney Croft, Stony Brook, The Company of Wine People, The Foundry, The Observatory, Tulbagh

Mountain, Vins d'Orrance, Woolworths ★★★★ Akkerdal, Allesverloren, Alto, Anatu, Angora, Annandale Distillers & Vintners, Anthony Smook, Arendsig Hand-Crafted, Avondale, Babylon's Peak Private, Beaumont, Bellingham, Bilton, Boland Kelder (2), Bonfoi, Boplaas Family, Boschrivier, Catherine Marshall, Cederberg Private, Cloof, Coleraine, Darling (2), De Grendel, De Meye, De Trafford (2), Delheim, Diemersfontein, Domaine Brahms Wineries, Domaine Newman , Drakensig, Edgebaston, Ernie Els, Fairview (4), Flagstone, For My Friends, Glen Carlou, Grande Provence, Groote Post, Hazendal, Hildenbrand Wine & Olive, Horse Mountain, Jack & Knox Winecraft, Joubert-Tradauw Private, JP Bredell (2), Julien Schaal, Kaapzicht, Kanu, Katbakkies Wine, Kloovenburg, Koelfontein, KWV Limited, Laborie, Lammershoek, Lindhorst, Linton Park (2), Luddite, Lyngrove, Lynx, Main Street, Manley Private, Metzer (2), Middelvlei, Mischa, Mont Destin, Môreson, Muratie, Nederburg, Neil Ellis (2), Noble Hill, Pax Verbatim, Plaisir De Merle, Post House, Rainbow's End, Rico Suter, Ridgemor Farm, Rijk's Private, Robertson, Rudera, Rust en Vrede, Rustenberg, Saronsberg, Scali, Schonenberg, Simonsig, Slaley, Solms-Delta, Stark-Condé, Stellekaya, Stellenzicht, The Cheviot, The Mason's (2), The Spice Route (2), The of Good Hope, Thelema Mountain (2), Tokara, Topaz Wine, Tukulu, Uva Mira, Val de Vie Winelands Lifestyle, Veenwouden Private, Vergelegen, Vergenoegd, Waterford, Weltevrede, Zandvliet (2), Zevenwacht, Ziggurat, Zonnebloem ★★★★ Aeternitas, African Pride, Altydgedacht, Amani, AntHill, Anthony Smook, Anura, Ashton, Avontuur, Bellpost, Bergsig, Bernheim, Blaauwklippen Agricultural, Black Oystercatcher, Black Pearl (2), Bloemendal, Boekenhoutskloof, Bon Cap Organic (Organic), Bon Courage, Boschendal, Buck's Ridge & Olives, Cape Classics, Cloof, Clovelly, Crows Nest, David Frost, Devon Hill, Diemersdal, Diemersfontein, Dieu Donné, Dormershire, Du Toitskloof, Durbanville Hills, Eagles Nest Farm, Eaglevlei, Elgin Vintners, Ernie Els, Ernst & Co, Fat Bastard, Freedom Hill, GlenWood, Goede Hoop, Goedverwacht, Golden Kaan, Goudini, Graceland, Graham Beck (2), Groenendal Farm, Groenland (2), Groot Constantia, Groupe LFE South Africa, Haskell, Havana Hills (2), Heron Ridge, Hex River Crossing Private, Hidden Valley (2), Iona, Jacques Smit, Jordan (2), Katbakkies Wine, Keisseskraal, Klein Constantia (2), Klein Genot Country & Wine, Klein Parys, Kleine Zalze, Kleinood, Koelenhof, Koningsrivier, Kumala/Constellation South Africa, La Chaumiere (2), La Petite Ferme, Landskroon, Lanzerac, Lievland, Lomond, Lourensford, MAN Vintners, Marianne, Meerendal, Meerhof, Mellasat, Mischa, Mont Rochelle Hotel & Mountain, Mooiplaas, Morton, Mount Rozier, Mountain Ridge, Mulderbosch, Muratie, My Wyn (2), Naughton's Flight, Nederburg, Nelson (2), Nick & Forti's, Nico van der Merwe, Nitida, Oaklands Wine Exporters, Org de Rac Domain, Origin Wine, Oude Denneboom, Pella, Perdeberg, Rhebokskloof Private, Riebeek, Rietvallei, Rooiberg, Rose Garden, Ross Gower, Saam Mountain, Saltaré, Savanha, Ses'Fikile (2), Shoprite Checkers, Signal Hill, Simonsig, Slaley, Southern Sky, Spier (3), Steenberg, Stellenbosch Hills, Stellenrust, Stellenzicht, The Company of Wine People, The Springtree Wine Company, The Stables, Thelema Mountain, Tulbagh Mountain (Organic), Twee Jonge Gezellen/The House of Krone, Umkhulu, Van Loveren Private, Villiera, Vrede en Lust Wine Farm, Wedderwill, Wederom Boutique, Welgeleë (2), Wildekrans, Windmeul Cooperative, Wine of the Month Club, Woolworths (2), Zandvliet, Zoetendal, Zorgvliet ★★★ African Pride, African Terroir, Allée Bleue, Alvi's Drift Private, Andy Mitchell, Arabella, Arra, Audacia, Avondale (2) (Organic), Ayama, Backsberg, Bellevue, Blaauwklippen Agricultural, Blue Cove, Blue Crane, Bo La Motte, Boland Kelder, Boplaas Family, Borg Family, Bottelary, Bovlei, Buthelezi, Cape Rock, Cape, Cloverfield Private, Culemborg, De Meye, De Vallei Boutique, Détendu, Doolhof, Dormershire, Douglas Green (2), Douglas Wine, Drostdy-Hof, Dunstone, Eagle's Cliff/New Cape, Eaglevlei, Eikehof, Eikendal, FirstCape, Fleur du Cap, Fort Simon, Franschhoek, Galleon, Gentis Family, GlenWood, Golden Kaan, Herold, Het Vlock Casteel, Hidden Valley, Hofstraat, Hoopenburg, JP Bredell, Klein Parys, Knorhoek, Kranskop, Kumala/Constellation South Africa, KWV Limited, La Couronne, Laborie, Landskroon, Linde, Lomond, Long Mountain Wine Company, Lorraine Private, Lutzville Cape Diamond (2), Migliarina,

Mitre's Edge, Mount Rozier, Namaqua, Nederburg, Neethlingshof, Niel Joubert, Nuy Wine, Obikwa, Oracle, Org de Rac Domain, Origin Wine, Perdeberg, Pulpit Rock, Rietrivier, Rietvallei, Riverstone, Robertson (2), Roodezandt &, Rooiberg, Ruitersvlei (2), Saam Mountain, Saronsberg, Savanha (2), Schalkenbosch, Simonsvlei International (3), Somerbosch, Springfontein, Stellar, Stony Brook, Stormhoek, Strandveld, Sumaridge, Swartland (2), Sylvanvale, Terroir of SA, The Chase, The Company of Wine People, The Springtree Wine Company, Thorntree, Two Oceans, Under Oaks, United Nations of Wine, Vondeling, Vrede Wine Farm, Wamakersvallei, Waverley Hills Organic (Organic), Wederom Boutique, Weltevrede, Wine of the Month Club (2), Zidela, Zorgvliet (2) ★★★ African Terroir (3), Ashton, Bergheim, Bonnievale Wine (2), Botha Wine, Bushmanspad, Calitzdorp, De Villiers, Détendu, Eaglevlei, Eshkol Kosher (Kosher), Excelsior, False Bay, FirstCape, Groot Eiland, Groupe LFE South Africa, Hawksmoor at Matjieskuil, Jason's Hill Private, Journey's End, Juno Wine Company, Kango, KapVino, Klawer Co-operative, Kumala/Constellation South Africa, KWV Limited, Langverwacht, Le Fût, Le Manoir de Brendel, Leopard's Leap, Lourensford, Lushof, Lutzville Cape Diamond, Lyngrove, McGregor, Mountain River, Nieuwedrift, Onderkloof Vines &, Oranjerivier Wine, Origin Wine (2), Overhex International, Pick's Pick, Ridder's Creek, Rietrivier, Rusticus Vintage, Schalk Burger & Sons, Seidelberg (2), Shoprite Checkers, Slanghoek, Slowine, Stellendrift, Sylvanvale, Terroir of SA, The Company of Wine People (2), Tulbagh Wine (4), Vukani, Wellington Cooperative, Westbridge, Wines of Cape Town, Woolworths (3) (Organic), Yonder Hill Wine Farm, Zidela, Zorgvliet ★★ Abbottshill, African Terroir (Organic), Ashanti, Barrydale, Bergwater, BLANKbottle, Clairvaux Private, Daschbosch Wine, De Wet Co-op, Du Preez, Fort Simon, Groenendal Farm, Haut Espoir, Hippo Creek, Kango, Klein Dassenberg, KWV Limited, Ladismith, Le Grand Chasseur, Lindiwe, Linton Park, Meerendal, Meerhof, Mitre's Edge, Mountain River, Oude Compagnies Post, Pulpit Rock, Riebeek, Rose Garden, Seidelberg, Stettyn, Versailles, Viljoensdrift, Vredenheim, Wamakersvallei, Wellington Cooperative, Wines of Cape Town,

Woolworths ★★ Belbon Hills, Bergwater, Bottelary, Eagle's Cliff/New Cape, Haut Espoir, Landzicht GWK, Montpellier, Rosendal Private, Tall Horse, Villiersdorp, Windmeul Cooperative ★ Origin Wine (2), Rusticus Vintage, Stellar ☆ Kleine Draken (Kosher), Stellar, Wandsbeck **NT** Bottelary Hills, Drakensig, Du Preez, Jean Daneel, Journey's End (2), Lazanou Organic (Organic), Long Mountain Wine Company, Mountain River, Neethlingshof, Rose Garden **NR** Boekenhoutskloof, Dispore Kamma Boutique , Lismore, Strandveld, The Goose, Uitvlucht, Woolworths (Organic), Zandvliet **D** African Terroir (2) (Organic), Anura, Avondale, Clos Malverne, De Toren Private, De Zoete Inval, Devon Hill, DeWaal, Dominion Wine Company, Glenview, Haskell, Koelenhof, Longridge, Makro, MAN Vintners, Namaqua (2), Noble Hill, Robertson, Stellenrust, Zandvliet

Sparkling, Méthode cap classique, red
★★★☆ Camberley ★★★ Nitida

Sparkling, Méthode cap classique, rosé
★★★★ Ambeloui Wine, Cabrière, Graham Beck, Simonsig, Twee Jonge Gezellen/The House of Krone, Villiera ★★★☆ JC le Roux, Woolworths

Sparkling, Méthode cap classique, white
★★★★★ Ambeloui Wine, Graham Beck, Saltaré, Simonsig, Villiera ★★★★ Avondale, Bon Courage (2), Boschendal, Buitenverwachting, Cabrière (2), Cape Chamonix Wine Farm (2), Graham Beck, High Constantia, JC le Roux, Jean Daneel, Laborie, Longridge, Morgenhof, Old Vines, Ross Gower, Silverthorn, Simonsig (2), Twee Jonge Gezellen/The House of Krone, Villiera, Woolworths (3) ★★★☆ Cabrière (2), Dieu Donné, Du Preez, Franschhoek, Groot Constantia, Hazendal, JC le Roux (2), Môreson (2), Pongrácz, Steenberg, Tanzanite, Villiera (2), Weltevrede, Woolworths ★★★ De Zoete Inval, JC le Roux, Le Grand Chasseur, Long Mountain Wine Company, Pongrácz, Riebeek, Saxenburg, The Company of Wine People (2) ★★☆ Montpellier ★★ Bloemendal, Bramon, Rhebokskloof Private, Wildekrans ★ Constantia **NT** Anura, Avontuur, KWV Limited **NR** Saronsberg **D** Boschendal, JC le Roux, Ruitersvlei

Sparkling, Non-MCC, red ★★☆ JC le Roux, Le Grand Chasseur ★★ Van Loveren Private

Sparkling, Non-MCC, rosé, dry ★★★ Eikendal ★★☆ Boplaas Family ★★ Origin Wine **D** Namaqua

Sparkling, Non-MCC, rosé, off-dry/semi-sweet ★★★ Twee Jonge Gezellen/The House of Krone ★★ Bon Courage, Boplaas Family, Domein Doornkraal, Klawer Co-operative, Rooiberg, Woolworths ★☆ Aan de Doorns Co-operative, Ashton ★ Jason's Hill Private

Sparkling, Non-MCC, white, dry ★★★ Riverstone ★★☆ Dominion Wine Company, Du Toitskloof, Eikendal, Goudini, Headbutt, JC le Roux, Klein Parys, Nederburg, Swartland, Wamakersvallei ★★ Bergsig, Groot Eiland, KWV Limited, Overhex International, Riebeek, Van Loveren Private ★☆ Ashton, Bonnievale Wine, Makro, Oranjerivier Wine, Rooiberg, Woolworths ★ Slanghoek **NT** Wines of Cape Town **D** Mooiuitsig Wine, Namaqua (2), Uitvlucht

Sparkling, Non-MCC, white, off-dry/semi-sweet ★★★ Kango ★★☆ African Terroir, Makro, Nuy Wine, Overhex International, Rhebokskloof Private, Slanghoek ★★ African Terroir, Badsberg Wine, Bon Cap Organic (Organic), Calitzdorp, Cold Duck (5th Avenue), Goedverwacht, JC le Roux (2), Koelenhof, KWV Limited (3), Lindiwe, Mooiuitsig Wine, Namaqua (Light & low-alcohol), Rooiberg, Swartland, Van Loveren Private, Woolworths ★☆ De Zoete Inval, Grand Mousseux, Oranjerivier Wine, Vredenheim, Woolworths ★ De Doorns, Landzicht GWK, Rietrivier **NT** Daschbosch Wine, Hartswater Wine, Montagu Wine, Wines of Cape Town **D** Makro, Namaqua, Uitvlucht, Wamakersvallei

Special Late Harvest ★★★★ Backsberg ★★★☆ Bon Courage, Fairview, Nederburg ★★★ Bergsig, Du Toitskloof, Roodezandt &, Slanghoek ★★★ Badsberg Wine, Drostdy-Hof, Van Loveren Private ★★ De Wet Co-op ★☆ Ashton, Oranjerivier Wine **NT** Hartenberg **D** Hartswater Wine, Klawer Co-operative, Rhebokskloof Private

Sweet red ★★★★☆ Signal Hill ★★★ Fairview ★★☆ Boplaas Family, Goudini ★★ Louiesenhof, Namaqua, The Saints, Woolworths ★☆ Bottelary, Cellar Cask, Douglas Wine, Hartswater Wine, Robertson (2), Taverna Rouge ★ Robertson **NR** Woolworths

Sylvaner ★★★☆ Overgaauw

Tempranillo ★★★☆ De Krans

Tinta barocca ★★★☆ De Krans, Lammershoek ★★★ Allesverloren, Boplaas Family, Lammershoek, Landskroon, Louiesenhof ★★☆ Swartland ★★ Micu Narunsky **NR** Riebeek

Touriga nacional ★★★☆ De Krans ★★★ Allesverloren, Boplaas Family, Calitzdorp **NT** Bergsig **D** Axe Hill

Verdelho ★★★☆ Feiteiras

Vin de paille ★★★★☆ De Trafford, Fairview, Hazendal, Tulbagh Mountain ★★★★ Fairview, Rustenberg ★★★☆ Lammershoek, Stellar ★★★ Stettyn, Tierhoek ★★ Mellasat, Vondeling **NT** La Bourgogne Farm, Sylvanvale **NR** Signal Hill

Viognier ★★★★☆ The Foundry ★★★★ Avondale, Backsberg, Bellingham, Fairview, Fleur du Cap, Graham Beck, Hex River Crossing Private, Katbakkies Wine, Kleinood, Lammershoek, Nederburg, Riverstone, Rusticus Vintage, Simonsig, The Spice Route, The of Good Hope ★★★★ African Pride, African Terroir (Organic), Arra, Babylon's Peak Private, Bon Cap Organic (Organic), Borg Family, Coleraine, Diemersfontein, Eagle's Cliff/New Cape, Eagles Nest Farm, Haut Espoir, Idiom, Mischa, Noble Hill, Origin Wine, Ridgeback, Rudi Schultz, Rustenberg, Spier, Stormhoek, The Company of Wine People, Topaz Wine, Wamakersvallei, Woolworths, Zorgvliet ★★★ Blue Cove, Eagle's Cliff/New Cape, Laborie, Lourensford, Mountain River, Origin Wine, Robertson, Signal Hill, Val de Vie Winelands Lifestyle, Vrede en Lust Wine Farm, Zonnebloem ★★★ DeWaal, Opstal, Perdeberg, Seidelberg ★★ Adler, Arabella, Montpellier, Niel Joubert ★★ Anura **NT** Arendsig Hand-Crafted, High Constantia, Ladismith, My Wyn, Naughton's Flight **NR** Lismore, Lourensford, Niel Joubert **D** Excelsior, Schalkenbosch

White blends, chardonnay-based unwooded ★★★☆ Cape Chamonix Wine Farm, Woolworths ★★★ Cabrière, Flagstone, Ridgemor Farm, Woolworths

★★★ Bellingham, FirstCape, KWV Limited, Ladismith, Nelson, Origin Wine, Pumlani, Zandvliet ★★ Craighall, Domein Doornkraal, Kumala/Constellation South Africa, Namaqua, Origin Wine, Overhex International, Vunani, Women in Wine, Woolworths ★★ Boplaas Family, Mons Ruber, Woolworths ★ The Stables **D** Ashanti, Clairvaux Private, Noble Hill, Rhebokskloof Private (2), Riverstone, Seidelberg

White blends, chardonnay-based wooded ★★★★★ Flagstone

★★★★ Boschendal, Rijk's Private ★★★ Woolworths ★★★ Douglas Green, Drostdy-Hof ★★ Bellingham

White blends, chenin blanc-based, unwooded ★★★★ Mike's Kitchen, Old Vines, Onderkloof Vines & ★★★ Beau Joubert &, Beaumont, Boschendal, Cloof, Ernst & Co, Jean Daneel, Post House, Slanghoek, Slowine, The Company of Wine People ★★★ African Pride, Boland Kelder, Bon Courage, Groupe LFE South Africa, Jordan, Kumala/Constellation South Africa, KWV Limited, La Chataigne, Leopard's Leap, Mount Rozier, Mountain Oaks (Organic), Mystery Wine Corporation, Nabygelegen Private, Nederburg, Origin Wine, Saxenburg, Spier, The Company of Wine People (2), Two Oceans (2), Zonnebloem (2) ★★ Darling, Dominion Wine Company, Douglas Green, Fleur du Cap (Light & low-alcohol), Groupe LFE South Africa, Grünberger, Kupferberger Auslese, KWV Limited (2), Makro, Nelson, Oranjerivier Wine (2), Overgaauw, Overhex International, Stellar, Wildekrans, Woolworths ★★ African Pride, Bonnievale Wine, Capenheimer, Culemborg, Douglas Wine (2), Groot Eiland, Kumala/Constellation South Africa, Mountain Ridge, Mountain River, Origin Wine (2), Oude Kaap, Overhex International, Simonsvlei International ★ African Terroir ★ Oom Tas **NT** KWV Limited, Overhex International, Simonsvlei International **NR** Constantia (2), Swartland **D** African Pride, Dellrust, Namaqua (2)

White blends, chenin blanc-based, wooded ★★★★★ Adoro, Dornier ★★★★ The Observatory, The of Good Hope

★★★★ Quando, The of Good Hope, Vondeling ★★★ Origin Wine, Siyabonga,

Swartland ★★ Origin Wine ★★ Origin Wine **D** Tulbagh Wine

White blends, other, unwooded, dry
★★★★ Flagstone, Vuurberg, Zevenwacht ★★★ Bon Courage, Boschendal, Nederburg, Wine of the Month Club ★★★ Ashton, Eikendal, Kumala/Constellation South Africa, Pick 'n Pay, Robertson (2), Van Loveren Private, Zandvliet
★★ Blaauwklippen Agricultural, Blouvlei, Botha Wine, Cabrière, DeWaal, FirstCape, McGregor, Mooiuitsig Wine, Nuy Wine, Origin Wine, Perdeberg, Rietrivier, Roodezandt &, Ruitersvlei, Skilpadvlei, Stellar (Organic), Swartland, The Saints, Twee Jonge Gezellen/The House of Krone, Viljoensdrift, Villiersdorp, Woolworths (3) ★★ Ashton, Bottelary Hills, Clairvaux Private, De Villiers, Drostdy-Hof, Eshkol Kosher (Kosher), KWV Limited, La Petite Ferme, Mooiuitsig Wine, Origin Wine (2), Overmeer, Robertson, Rooiberg, Simonsvlei International, Stellenbosch Hills, Tulbagh Wine (2), Van Loveren Private (2), Vaughan Johnson's Wine & Cigar Shop, Woolworths ★ Arum Lily, Klawer Co-operative, Namaqua (2) (Light & low-alcohol), Oude Kaap, Robertson (2) (Light & low-alcohol), Van Loveren Private (Light & low-alcohol), Zomerlust **NT** Backsberg, Bellingham, Bonnievale Wine, Langverwacht, Makro, Saxenburg, Simonsvlei International **NR** Nederburg, Swartland (3) **D** De Wetshof, Domein Doornkraal, Goudini, Hartenberg, Hartswater Wine, Ladismith, Landzicht GWK, Lutzville Cape Diamond, Overhex International, Uitvlucht, Umkhulu

White blends, other, unwooded, off-dry/semi-sweet ★★★ Altydgedacht, Boschendal, Nederburg, Twee Jonge Gezellen/The House of Krone, Vergelegen ★★★ De Wet Co-op, Du Preez, Namaqua, Robertson (2), Simonsig (2), Spier, Twee Jonge Gezellen/The House of Krone (Light & low-alcohol), Woolworths (2), Zevenwacht ★★ Blaauwklippen Agricultural, Bottelary, Bovlei, Clairvaux Private, Drostdy-Hof, Grande Provence, Groot Eiland, Hartswater Wine, Namaqua, Pick 'n Pay, Rhebokskloof Private, Ridder's Creek, Rietrivier, Robertson (2), Seidelberg, Slanghoek, Stellar, The Saints, Tulbagh Wine, Wines of Cape Town, Zomerlust ★★ Darling, Ladismith, Legacy, Mooiuitsig Wine, Overmeer, Pick 'n Pay, Rooiberg, Seidelberg, Simonsvlei

If you think we have

a lot of beans.

You should see our selection of wine.

You've always known us for our wide variety of quality foods. Now is the time to acquaint yourself with our extensive selection of fine wines - from easy drinking table varieties to the more sophisticated blends.

www.wineline.co.za

WE'RE ON YOUR SIDE

International, Vunani, Wildekrans, Woolworths ★ Cellar Cask, Pick 'n Pay, Robertson (Light & low-alcohol), Zidela ★ Virginia **NT** Bellingham (Light & low-alcohol), Ruitersvlei **NR** L'Avenir, Riebeek, Swartland (2) **D** Cape Bay, Lutzville Cape Diamond (2), Mooiuitsig Wine, Namaqua, Zandvliet

White blends, other, wooded dry
★★★★ Avondale, Quoin Rock ★★★ Origin Wine ★★★ Barrydale ★★ Aan de Doorns Co-operative, Du Preez, Kumala/Constellation South Africa (Organic), Origin Wine (2) ★★ Oranjerivier Wine **D** Flagstone

White blends, other, wooded, off-dry/semi-sweet ★★★★ Solms-Delta

White blends, sauvignon blanc-based, unwooded ★★★★★ Flagstone, Ingwe ★★★★ Buitenverwachting, Nico van der Merwe, Nico Vermeulen, Raka, Vendôme, Zorgvliet ★★★ Allée Bleue, Bellingham (2), Bilton, Delheim, Diemersdal, Groote Post, Jordan, Kaapzicht, Knorhoek, Rietvallei, Simonsig, The Company of Wine People (2), Villiera (2), Weltevrede, Woolworths ★★★ Asara, Douglas Green, FirstCape, Graça, Kumala/Constellation South Africa, Malan Family Vintners, Morgenhof, Sentinel, Wedgewood, Woolworths ★★ African Terroir, Avondale, Douglas Green (2), Du Toitskloof, Horse Mountain, Kumala/Constellation South Africa, Origin Wine, Overhex International, Schalkenbosch (2), Vaughan Johnson's Wine & Cigar Shop ★★ Tulbagh Wine **NT** Lourensford **D** De Zoete Inval, Fort Simon, Headbutt, La Couronne

White blends, sauvignon blanc-based, wooded ★★★★★ Cape Point, Steenberg ★★★★★ Steenberg ★★★★ Ashbourne, Flagstone, Newton Johnson, Nitida, Tokara ★★★ Nederburg ★★★ Le Grand Chasseur **NR** Springfontein, Strandveld

White blends, semillon-based, unwooded ★★★★ Groot Constantia, Rijk's Private ★★★ Franschhoek, La Vigne, Theuniskraal, Waverley Hills Organic ★★★ Leopard's Leap, Origin Wine, Two Oceans ★★ Wine of the Month Club ★ Dellrust **NT** Somersbosch

White blends, semillon-based, wooded ★★★★★ Vergelegen ★★★★★ Constantia Uitsig, Klein Constantia, Vergelegen ★★★★ Allée Bleue, Black Oystercatcher ★★★ La Vigne, Waverley Hills Organic ★★★ Long Mountain Wine Company ★★ Origin Wine **D** Vergelegen

White blends, with viognier
★★★★★ Sequillo ★★★★ Miles Mossop, Sadie Family, Scali, Solms-Delta, Tulbagh Mountain ★★★★ Bellingham, De Grendel, Fleur du Cap, Joostenberg, Laibach, Lammershoek, Rustenberg, The Company of Wine People, Thokozani, Zevenwacht ★★★ Bouchard Finlayson, Dragonridge, Graham Beck, Hidden Valley, Joostenberg, Perdeberg, Pick's Pick, Quoin Rock, Spier, The Company of Wine People, The Goats do Roam Wine Company, Val de Vie Winelands Lifestyle, Veenwouden Private, Vondeling, Whalehaven ★★★ Akkerdal, Bellingham, FirstCape, Glen Carlou, Kumala/Constellation South Africa, Leopard's Leap, Lourensford, Nederburg, Niel Joubert, Ridgeback, Saxenburg, The Goats do Roam Wine Company, Tulbagh Wine, Woolworths ★★★ Akkerdal, Bon Cap Organic (Organic), Douglas Green, Drostdy-Hof, Jason's Hill Private **NT** Alvi's Drift Private **D** Thokozani

Zinfandel/Primitivo ★★★★ Glen Carlou, Zevenwacht ★★★★ Idiom ★★★ Blaauwklippen Agricultural ★★★ Lammershoek

top**PERFORMERS**

The following are SA's top wines as measured by their showing in selected wine competitions, challenges and professional tastings in 2006-7, as well as in the 2007 edition of this guide. The listing covers the following results (see also section on SA wine competitions for more details): Veritas 2006 — we indicate double-gold medals; Trophy Wine Show (TWS) 2007 — trophies & gold medals; Michelangelo International Wine Awards (MIWA) 2006 — trophies & double-gold medals (Grand d'Or); SA *Wine* magazine (www.winemag.co.za) — 4-5 stars Jun 2006-7; UK *Decanter* magazine (www.decanter.com) — World Wine Awards 2007 — trophies & gold medals; US *Wine Spectator* magazine (WS, www.winespectator.com) — 90-100 points Jun 2006-7; International Wine Challenge 2007 (IWC, www.wineint.com) — gold medals; and International Wine & Spirit Competition 2006 (IWSC, www.iwsc.net) — gold medals. Our own 4½ and 5 star ratings for the 2007 edition are also shown. Rankings in these and other local and international competitions may be included in the A-Z section under the relevant producers and brands. Be aware that some wineries do not enter competitions and might not be represented here.

	Vintage	Platter	Veritas	Wine	TWS	Michelangelo	Decanter	Wine Spectator	IWC	IWSC
Red										
Cabernet Franc										
Eikendal	03			4						
Raats Family	03			4						
Raats Family	04	4½		4						
Raats Family	05			4						
Warwick	04							90		
Cabernet Sauvignon										
Alto	04			4						
Asara	00	4½								
Blue Creek	04	4½								
Boekenhoutskloof	04	5						90		
Cederberg V Generations	04						T			
De Trafford	04	4½								
Ernie Els Guardian Peak Lapa	04			4						
Flagstone Music Room	04			4						
Glen Carlou Gravel Quarry	04	4½						90		
Grangehurst Reserve	03	4½								
Katbakkies	03	4½								
Kleine Zalze Family Reserve	05						G		G	
KWV Cathedral Cellar	02	4½								
Le Riche CWG Auction Reserve	03	4½								
Le Riche Reserve	03	4½								
Longridge	04				T					
Marklew	04								G	
Morgenhof Reserve	01	4½								
Nederburg Private Bin	04	4½		4						
Neil Ellis Vineyard Selection	04	5								
Ormonde Alexanderfontein	05						G			

	Vintage	Platter	Veritas	Wine	TWS	Michelangelo	Decanter	Wine Spectator	IWC	IWSC
Oude Compagnies Post Compagnies Wijn	04			4						
Post House	03			4						
Rudera CWG Auction Reserve	02	4½								
Rudera	03	5								
Rudera	04							90		
Rustenberg Brampton	04			4						
Rustenberg Peter Barlow	04	4½								
Rustenberg Brampton	05				G					
Saxenburg Private Collection	03									G
Spier Private Collection	04			4						
Springfield Méthode Ancienne	01	4½		4						
Springfield Whole Berry	04	4½								
Stark-Condé Condé	04	4½						90		
Thelema CWG Auction Reserve	03	4½								
Thelema The Mint	04	4½		4				90		
Thelema	04	4½								
Vergelegen	03									G
Vergelegen	04	4½		4						
Wamakersvallei La Cave	04			4						
Waterford	03	4½		4						
Welgegund	04			4						
Merlot										
Avondale Les Pleurs	00	4½								
Bilton Wines	04	4½								
Blaauwklippen Vineyard Selection	04			4						
Boland Winemakers Selection	04		DG							
Durbanville Hills Luipaardsberg	03		DG							
Hartenberg Merlot	04	4½								
Hillcrest	05				T					
Laibach	04			4						
Longridge	03	4½								
Marklew	04			4						
Meerlust	04				G					
Morgenhof Reserve	01	4½								
Quoin Rock	03	4½								
Rust en Vrede	04		DG							
Steenberg	04	4½	DG							
Thelema Reserve	04	4½		4						
Veenwouden	03	4½								
Vergelegen	04	4½								
Mourvèdre										
Val de Vie	04						DG			
Nebbiolo										
Steenberg	05			4						

	Vintage	Platter	Veritas	Wine	TWS	Michelangelo	Decanter	Wine Spectator	IWC	IWSC
Pinot Noir										
Bon Courage Bruére Gold Reserve	04			4½						
Bouchard Finlayson Galpin Peak	04	4½		4						
Bouchard Finlayson Tête de Cuvée Galpin Peak	03	5								
Cabrière	04	4½								
Cape Chamonix Pinot Noir	05	4½								
Hamilton Russell	04			4				90		
Hamilton Russell	05	4½		4				91		
Meerlust	00	4½								
Muratie	05			4						
Sumaridge	04			4						
Pinotage										
Allée Bleue	05			4						
Bellevue PK Morkel	04	4½								
Camberley	05	4½								
Deetlefs Oak Matured	05			4						
DeWaal Top of the Hill	04	4½								
Diemersfontein Carpe Diem	04	4½								
Fairview Primo	04	4½								
Groot Constantia	05			4						G
Hartenberg	04				T					
Hidden Valley	04			4		DG				
Kaapzicht Steytler	03	4½								
Kanonkop	04	4½	DG	4½				90		
Laibach	05		DG							
L'Avenir Grand Vin	04	4½								
Longridge	04		DG							
Nitida	05					DG				
Oude Compagnies Post Compagnies Wijn	05			4						
Pulpit Rock Brink Family	05			4						
Pulpit Rock	04					T				
Simonsig Redhill	04	4½								
Simonsig Redhill	05			4						
Southern Right	05			4				90		
Stormhoek	05									G
Umkhulu	04	4½								
Sangiovese										
Anura	04			4						
Idiom	04			4						
Shiraz										
Anthony de Jager Homtini	05	4½								
Avondale Les Pleurs Syrah	02	4½								
Avondale Syrah	03			4						
Bellpost	05			4						
Boekenhoutskloof CWG Auction Reserve Syrah	03	4½								

	Vintage	Platter	Veritas	Wine	TWS	Michelangelo	Decanter	Wine Spectator	IWC	IWSC
Boekenhoutskloof Syrah	97			4½						
Boekenhoutskloof Syrah	04	5		4½				91		
Bon Cap Syrah	04			4						
Bon Courage Inkará	04		DG							
Boschendal Cecil John Reserve Syrah	04						T			
Camberley	04	4½								
Cederberg CWG Auction Reserve Teen Die Hoog	04	4½								
Cederberg	05		DG							
Cloof Crucible	04	4½								
Cloof The Very Sexy Shiraz	04			4						
De Trafford	04	4½						92		
De Trafford Blueprint	04							90		
Delheim Vera Cruz Estate	04	4½								
DeWaal	04	4½								
Ernie Els Cirrus Syrah	03							90		
Ernie Els Cirrus Syrah	04							91		
Fairview Solitude	03			4						
Fairview Solitude	04	5		4				90		
Fairview The Beacon	04							90		G
Fairview Shiraz	05							90		
Gilga Syrah	04	4½								
Glen Carlou Syrah	05	4½								
Graham Beck The Ridge Syrah	02					T				
Graham Beck The Ridge Syrah	03	4½								
Grande Provence Shiraz	04		DG							
Groote Post	03			4						
Hartenberg CWG Auction Reserve Gravel Hill	03	4½								
Hartenberg	04	4½								
Hartenberg The Stork	03		DG							
Hartenberg The Stork	04	5								
Hofstraat Winery Renosterbos	05					T				
Horse Mountain	04	4½								
Kaapzicht	04					DG				
Kleine Zalze Family Reserve	04	4½								
Kloovenburg	04	4½								
Koelfontein	04		DG	4						
KWV Cathedral Cellar	02	4½								
La Motte Pierneef Shiraz-Viognier	04	4½								
La Motte Pierneef Shiraz-Viognier	05								G	
La Motte	04	4½		4						
Luddite	04	4½								
Marianne	04			4						
Meerendal Bin 159	05			4						
Mulderbosch	03							90		
Muratie	04	4½								

	Vintage	Platter	Veritas	Wine	TWS	Michelangelo	Decanter	Wine Spectator	IWC	IWSC
Neil Ellis Vineyard Selection Syrah	03	4½						91		
Neil Ellis Vineyard Selection Syrah	04	4½								
Neil Ellis	03							90		
Quoin Rock Syrah	04	4½								
Quoin Rock Syrah	05				T					
Raka Biography	04	5	DG	4						
Rickety Bridge	03	4½								
Ridgeback	04	4½								
Rijk's	02	4½								
Robertson Winery No 1 Constitution Road	04	4½								
Rudi Schultz Syrah	04	4½						92		
Rustenberg Syrah	04							92		
Sadie Family Columella	03	4½		4				93		
Sadie Family Columella	04	4½					T	92		
Sadie Family Columella	05							95		
Saxenburg Saxenburg Shiraz Select (SSS)	02						G			
Saxenburg Saxenburg Shiraz Select (SSS)	03	5		4½						
Saxenburg Private Collection	03	4½		4.5						
Signal Hill Clos d'Oranje	05	4½								
Simonsig CWG Auction Reserve	04	4½								
Simonsig Merindol Syrah	04	4½								
Spice Route Flagship Syrah	04							92		
Spier Private Collection	03									G
Stark-Condé Condé Syrah	03	4½						90		
Stellenzicht Syrah	02	4½								
The Company of Wine People Kumkani Triple J	04	4½								
The Foundry Syrah	04	4½								
The Observatory Syrah	04	4½								
Thelema	04							91		
Tulbagh Mntn Vineyards TMV Swartland Syrah	04	4½								
Vergelegen	04	4½								
Vierlanden	04			4						
Vins D'Orrance Cuvée Ameena	04							90		
Waterford Kevin Arnold	03	4½	DG							
Red Blends										
Alvi's Drift Cape Fusion	05		DG							
Anwilka 'Anwilka'	05	4½						90		
Ashbourne Ashbourne	04	4½								
Ataraxia Serenity	05							90		
Avondale Julia	03					DG				
Beyerskloof Field Blend	02	4½								
Bilton Matt Black	04	4½		4						
Boekenhoutskloof The Chocolate Block	05	4½					G			
Bowwood Cabernet Sauvignon-Merlot	04			4						
Buitenverwachting Christine	02	4½								
Buitenverwachting Christine	03			4						

	Vintage	Platter	Veritas	Wine	TWS	Michelangelo	Decanter	Wine Spectator	IWC	IWSC
Camberley Cabernet Sauvignon-Merlot	03		DG							
Camberley Philosopher's Stone	04	4½								
Capaia 'Capaia'	05	4½						91		
Cloof Cabernet Franc-Cabernet Sauvignon-Merlot	03			4						
Clos Malverne Auret Cape Blend	03	4½								
Clos Malverne Auret Cape Blend Limited Release	01	4½								
Cordoba Crescendo	03	4½								
Dalla Cia Giorgio	03	4½								
Darling Cellars Kroon	03	4½								
De Toren Fusion V	04	4½						91		
De Trafford Elevation 393	03							91		
De Trafford Elevation 393	04	4½								
DeWaal Cape Blend	03	4½								
Durbanville Hills Caapmans Cabernet-Merlot	01	4½								
Eikendal Cabernet Sauvignon-Merlot	03			4						
Eikendal Classique	03			4						
Elgin Vintners Agama	05					G				
Ernie Els Engelbrecht-Els Proprietor's Blend	04	4½	DG	4						
Ernie Els Ernie Els	03			4						
Ernie Els Ernie Els	04	5		4				91		
Flagstone CWG Auction Reserve Love Handles	04	4½								
Flagstone Mary Le Bow	04	4½								
Glen Carlou Grand Classique	03			4						
Graham Beck The William	03	4½								
Grangehurst Cabernet Sauvignon-Merlot	01	4½								
Grangehurst Nikela	01	4½								
Grangehurst Shiraz-Cabernet Sauvignon Reserve	03	4½								
Hartenberg The Mackenzie	03			4						G
Hartenberg The Mackenzie	04	4½								
Havana Hills Du Plessis Reserve Du Plessis	04	4½								
Havana Hills Kobus	03	4½								
High Constantia Sebastiaan	03	4½								
Horse Mountain Michele	04	4½								
Idiom Cabernet Sauvignon-Merlot-Cabernet Franc	04					DG				
Idiom Shiraz-Mourvèdre-Viognier	04			4						
Ingwe Ingwe	03	4½								
Jean Daneel Signature Cabernet Sauvignon-Merlot	01	4½								
Jordan Cobblers Hill	03			4						G
Jordan Sophia CWG Auction Reserve	04	4½								
Kaapzicht Steytler Vision	03	5								
Kanonkop Paul Sauer	97			5						
Kanonkop Paul Sauer	03	4½	DG	4						

	Vintage	Platter	Veritas	Wine	TWS	Michelangelo	Decanter	Wine Spectator	IWC	IWSC
Kanu Keystone	03			4						
Kanu Rockwood	05			4						
Ken Forrester Gypsy	03	4½								
Klein Gustrouw Cabernet Sauvignon-Merlot	04	4½								
KWV Cathedral Cellar Triptych	01	4½								
La Vigne Owners Selection	05			4						
Laibach The Ladybird	04					T				
Laibach The Ladybird	05			4						
Lanzerac Classic	02									G
L'Avenir Stellenbosch Classic	04	4½								
Leopard Frog Tantra	04			4						
Makro (Overgaauw) Touriga Nacional-Cabernet Sauvignon	03	4½								
Meerlust Rubicon	01									G
Meerlust Rubicon	03	4½								
Meinert Synchronicity	04	4½								
Mont Destin Passioné	04			4						
Montorosso Estate Cabernet Sauvignon-Merlot	03					DG				
Môreson Magia	03				T					
Morgenhof Première Sélection	01	4½								
Morgenster 'Morgenster'	03	4½		4						
Muratie Ansela van de Caab	04	4½								
Mvemve Raats De Compstella	04								93	
Nederburg Private Bin R103 Cabernet Sauvignon-Shiraz	04	4½		4						
Neethlingshof Lord Neethling Laurentius	01	4½								
Nico van der Merwe Mas Nicolas	03	4½								
Oak Valley The Oak Valley Blend	04						T			
Overgaauw Tria Corda	04	4½								
Post House Penny Black	04	4½								
Raka Figurehead	04	4½								
Raka Spliced	04			4						
Remhoogte Bonne Nouvelle	03			4						
Reyneke Reserve	04	4½								
Rupert & Rothschild Baron Edmund	03	4½								
Rust en Vrede Estate Wine	03		DG					G		
Rustenberg John X Merriman	03			4½						
Rustenberg John X Merriman	04	4½								
Saronsberg Full Circle	04			4						
Saronsberg Seismic	04		DG							
Seidelberg Un Deux Trois	04				G					
Spice Route Malabar	03	4½		4			G			
Spice Route Malabar	04						T			
Spier Vintage Selection Shiraz-Mourvèdre-Viognier	04		DG	4						
Springfield The Work of Time	02	4½								

	Vintage	Platter	Veritas	Wine	TWS	Michelangelo	Decanter	Wine Spectator	IWC	IWSC
Stellekaya Orion	04	4½								
Stony Brook Ghost Gum	03	4½								
Swartland Idelia	04			4						
The Goats do Roam Wine Company Goat-Roti	05							90		
The Observatory Carignan-Syrah	03	4½								
The Winery of Good Hope Black Rock Red	05	4½								
Tokara Red	04	4½								
Tulbagh Mountain Vineyards Syrah-Mourvèdre	04							90		
Veenwouden Classic	03	4½								
Vergelegen CWG Auction Reserve Vergelegen	02	4½								
Vergelegen Vergelegen	03	4½								G
Vergelegen Vergelegen V	03	4½								
Vergenoegd Vergenoegd	03	4½								
Vilafonté Series C	04	4½						90		
Vilafonté Series M	04	4½						91		
Von Ortloff Quintessence	00	4½								
Vriesenhof Kallista	03	4½								
Warwick Trilogy/Estate Reserve	03						T			
Warwick Trilogy/Estate Reserve	04	4½						90		
Waterford CWG Auction Reserve	04	4½								
Welgemeend Estate Reserve	02	4½								
Woolworths (De Wetshof) Danie De Wet Cabernet Sauvignon-Merlot	03			4						
Woolworths (Jordan) Cobblers Hill	03	4½								
Zonnebloem Lauréat	04									G
Zorgvliet Richelle	04	4½								

White

Chardonnay

	Vintage	Platter	Veritas	Wine	TWS	Michelangelo	Decanter	Wine Spectator	IWC	IWSC
Ataraxia	05	4½						93		
Ataraxia	06							92		
Avontuur Luna de Miel	04	4½								
Backsberg Babylons Toren	03				T					
Bouchard Finlayson Kaaimansgat	04							90		
Buitenverwachting	05							91		
Cape Chamonix Reserve	97				T					
Cape Chamonix Reserve	04	4½								
Cape Chamonix	05			4						
Cape Point	04			4				90		
De Wetshof Bateleur	03							90		
Diemersdal Reserve	05					DG				
Durbanville Hills Rhinofields	05	4½								
Glen Carlou	05			4						
Glen Carlou Quartz Stone	05	4½								
GlenWood Vigneron's Selection	05			4						
Hamilton Russell	05	5		4				91		
Hamilton Russell	06			4	G			92		

	Vintage	Platter	Veritas	Wine	TWS	Michelangelo	Decanter	Wine Spectator	IWC	IWSC
Haut Espoir Reserve	05			4						
Hoopenburg Integer	05								G	
Jordan	04									G
Jordan CWG Auction Reserve	05	4½								
Jordan Nine Yards Reserve	04							90		
Jordan Nine Yards Reserve	05	4½		4						
Julien Schaal	05			4						
Longridge	04			4						
Meerlust	05							92		
Mulderbosch Barrel Fermented	02			4						
Mulderbosch Barrel Fermented	05			4	G					
Nederburg Private Bin D270	05	4½								
Neethlingshof Lord Neethling	02	4½								
Neil Ellis Elgin	04							90		
Neil Ellis Elgin	05							92		
Oak Valley	05	4½								
Paul Cluver	05	4½		4						
Plaisir de Merle	05			4						
Robertson Winery Kings River	05		DG							
Rupert & Rothschild Baroness Nadine	05			4						
Rustenberg Stellenbosch	05							90		
Rustenberg Five Soldiers	04							91		
Sterhuis Barrel Selection	05			4						
Sumaridge	05	4½								
The Winery of Good Hope Radford Dale	05	4½		4						
Tokara Stellenbosch	05			4						
Uva Mira Vineyard Selection	04									G
Uva Mira Vineyard Selection	05	4½								
Van Loveren Reserve	06				G					
Veenwouden Special Reserve	04	4½								
Vergelegen Reserve	05	4½								
Waterford	05	5								
Waterford	06							90		
Waterkloof Circumstance	05						G			
Woolworths (De Wetshof)	03	4½								
Chenin Blanc										
Beaumont Hope Marguerite	05			4						
Bellingham The Maverick	04									G
Bellingham The Maverick	05			4½						
Cederberg V Generations	04		DG							
Cederberg V Generations	05			4						
De Morgenzon	05	5								
Fortress Hill Reserve	05			4						
Hazendal Wooded	05			4						
Jean Daneel Signature	05	4½								
Kanu Wooded	04			4						

	Vintage	Platter	Veritas	Wine	TWS	Michelangelo	Decanter	Wine Spectator	IWC	IWSC
Kanu Wooded	05			4						
Katbakkies	04	4½								
Ken Forrester The FMC	03									G
Ken Forrester The FMC	04	4½		5			T	91		
Kleine Zalze Barrel Fermented	05			4						
Kleine Zalze Bush Vines	05			4½						
KWV Val du Chêne	04			5						
Mulderbosch	05							90		
Mulderbosch Steen op Hout	06			4						
Perdeberg Reserve	06					G				
Post House	05	4½								
Raats Family	05							90		
Rijk's	02			4½						
Rijk's	05				T					
Rudera Robusto	01	4½								
Rudera Robusto	05	5		4						
Simonsig Avec Chêne	05			4						
Spice Route	05	4½								
Spier Private Collection	05	5								
Springfontein Jil's Dune	05	4½								
Colombard										
Nuy Colombar	06		DG							
Gewürztraminer										
Woolworths (Paul Cluver)	05	4½								
Neethlingshof	06			4						
Paul Cluver	05	4½								
Riesling										
Nederburg Rhine Riesling	05			4						
Sauvignon Blanc										
Ataraxia	06							91		
Bellingham The Maverick Wooded	05			4½						
Bloemendal Suider Terras	05			4½						
Bon Courage	06			4						
Boschendal Cecil John Reserve	06						G			
Buitenverwachting	06			4						
Cape Chamonix	05			4						
Cape Chamonix Reserve	05	4½								
Cape Point	05	4½		4			T	90		
Cape Point	06				T					
Cederberg	06			4½						
Constantia Glen	06	4½						90	G	
De Grendal	06			4						
Diemersdal Eight Rows	06			4						
Diemersdal Single Vineyard	06			4½						
Doolhof Signatures of Doolhof	06		DG	4						

	Vintage	Platter	Veritas	Wine	TWS	Michelangelo	Decanter	Wine Spectator	IWC	IWSC
Durbanville Hills Biesjes Craal	06	4½								
Durbanville Hills Inner Valley	06	4½								
Flagstone Free Run	06			4						
Flagstone The Berrio	06		DG							
Fleur du Cap Unfiltered Limited Release	06			4					G	
Fort Simon	05	4½								
Graham Beck Pheasants' Run	06			4½						
Hermanuspietersfontein Die Bartho	06	4½		4						
Iona	02			4½						
Iona	06	4½		4						
Jordan	06	4½								
Klein Constantia Perdeblokke	05	4½								
Kleine Zalze	05								G	
Kleine Zalze Family Reserve Sur Lie	05		DG	4						
La Motte Pierneef	06	4½								
L'Avenir	06			4						
Mountain River Estuary	05		DG							
Mulderbosch	06	4½						90		
Neethlingshof Special Release	06			4						
Neil Ellis Vineyard Selection	04	4½								
Neil Ellis Groenekloof	04							90		
Neil Ellis Groenekloof	06	4½								
Nitida Club Select	06	4½								
Oak Valley Mountain Reserve	05	4½								
Oak Valley	05	4½								
Overgaauw	06			4						
Perdeberg Reserve	06		DG							
Quoin Rock Oculus	05			4						
Robertson Winery Retreat	06	4½								
Rustenberg Brampton	06								G	
Spier Private Collection	06			4						
Springfield Special Cuvée	06	4½		4						
Steenberg Reserve	05									G
Steenberg Reserve	06	4½		4						
Strandveld First Sighting	06			4						
The Company of Wine People Kumkani Lanner Hill	05	4½						90		
The Company of Wine People Kumkani Lanner Hill	06			4		G				
The Company of Wine People Kumkani	06	4½								
Thelema Sutherland	06			4						
Tokara White	05	4½		4½						
Tokara Walker Bay	06			4						
Vergelegen Schaapenberg	05	4½								
Vergelegen Reserve	05			4½						
Warwick Professor Black	06							90		

	Vintage	Platter	Veritas	Wine	TWS	Michelangelo	Decanter	Wine Spectator	IWC	IWSC
Waterford	06							90		
Weltevrede River's Edge	06			4						
Woolworths (Cape Point) Limited Release	06	5	DG	4						
Woolworths (Groote Post) Reserve	06	4½								
Zorgvliet	06	4½								
Semillon										
Black Oystercatcher	05	4½		4						
Boekenhoutskloof	04	4½						90		
Cape Point	05	4½			T	DG				
Constantia Uitsig Reserve	04			4						
Constantia Uitsig Reserve	05	4½								
De Grendel CWG Auction Reserve Koetshuis	06			4						
Fleur du Cap Unfiltered	05					DG				
Jack & Knox Green on Green	04			4						
Rijk's	04			4						
Steenberg	02			4½						
Steenberg	06	4½								
Stellenzicht Reserve	03			4						
Viognier										
Fleur du Cap Unfiltered Limited Release	06								G	
The Foundry	06							90		
White blends										
Adoro Wines Naudé	06	4½								
Cape Point Isliedh	05	5		4½				91		
Constantia Uitsig Constantia White	04			4½						
Flagstone CWG Auction Reserve Weather Girl	06			4						
Flagstone Winery CWG Auction Reserve Month of Sundays	05	4½								
Fleur du Cap Unfiltered Limited Release Viognier-Chardonnay-Semillon-Sauvignon Blanc	05			4						
Ingwe Amehlo White	06	4½								
Jordan Chameleon Sauvignon Blanc-Chardonnay	06			4						
Klein Constantia Mme Marlbrook	05	4½		4½						
Miles Mossop Saskia	04			4						
Newton Johnson Pour Mes Amis	05			4						
Sadie Family Palladius	04			4½						
Sadie Family Palladius	05	4½								
Solms-Delta Amalie	05			4						
Steenberg CWG Auction Reserve Barrel Fermented Sauvignon Blanc-Semillon	05	4½								
The Company of Wine People Kumkani Chardonnay-Viognier	05	4½		4						
Vergelegen CWG Auction Reserve White	04	4½								
Vergelegen White	02			4½						
Vergelegen White	05	5		4	G					
Vergelegen White	06				T					

	Vintage	Platter	Veritas	Wine	TWS	Michelangelo	Decanter	Wine Spectator	IWC	IWSC
Méthode Cap Classique Sparkling										
Bon Courage Jacques Bruére Brut Reserve Blanc de Blanc	02			4						
Cabrière Pierre Jourdan Blanc de Blancs	NV	4½								
Cabrière Pierre Jourdan Cuvée Reserve	NV	4½								
Graham Beck Brut	94			4						
Graham Beck Brut Blanc de Blancs	01		DG	4						
Graham Beck Brut Blanc de Blancs	02	4½		4						
Graham Beck Brut	NV			4						
JC le Roux Pinot Noir	98	4½								
JC le Roux Scintilla	99			4						
JC le Roux Scintilla	01			4						
Pongrácz Desiderius	99			4						
Pongrácz Desiderius	01			4½						
Simonsig Cuvée Royale	99	4½								
Tanzanite	NV			4						
Villiera Brut Natural	03	4½								
Woolworths (Villiera) Vintage Reserve Brut	99			4	T					
Dessert, Unfortified										
Asara NLH	03	4½								
Boekenhoutskloof NLH	02	4½								
Darling Cellars NLH	02	4½								
De Trafford Straw Wine	04			4½				90		
De Trafford Straw Wine	05	4½								
De Wetshof Edeloes	00	5								
Fairview La Beryl Blanc	05	4½								
Fleur du Cap NLH	05			4						
Hazendal The Last Straw	04			4						
Hillcrest Chardonnay NLH	05	4½								
Joostenberg Chenin Blanc NLH	05	4½								
Kanu Kia-Ora NLH	04	4½						92		
Ken Forrester 'T' NLH Chenin Blanc	05	5								
Klein Constantia Vin de Constance	01	4½		4						
Meerendal Chenin Blanc Natural Sweet	06			T						
Nederburg Edelkeur	03		DG	4						
Nederburg Edelkeur	04			4						G
Nederburg Edelkeur	05				G					
Nederburg NLH	05					DG				G
Nederburg NLH	06								G	
Nederburg Private Bin S316 Weisser Riesling	04									G
Neethlingshof Lord Neethling Weisser Riesling NLH	05	4½								
Paul Cluver Weisser Riesling NLH	05	5								
Robertson Winery Bowen's Folly NLH Riesling	01								G	
Robertson Winery Wide River Reserve NLH	01	5								
Rudera Chenin Blanc NLH	05	4½								

	Vintage	Platter	Veritas	Wine	TWS	Michelangelo	Decanter	Wine Spectator	IWC	IWSC
Rudera CWG Auction Reserve Chenin Blanc NLH	03	4½								
Signal Hill Eszencia	NV	5								
Simonsig Vin de Liza	05	4½								
Slanghoek Crème de Chenin	05			4						
Tulbagh Mountain Vineyards Vin Pi One	NV	4½						93		
Wlwrths (Ken Forrester) Rsrv Chenin Blanc NLH	06			4						
Dessert, Fortified										
Alvi's Drift Muscat de Frontignan White	04	4½		4						
Badsberg Red Muscadel	05		DG	4						
Bon Courage Red Muskadel	02			4½						
Caroline's (KWV) White Muscadel	92			4						
Du Toitskloof Hanepoot Jerepigo	03			4						
Monis Muscadel	00	4½								
Nuy Red Muscadel	05		DG							
Nuy White Muscadel	05			4						
Nuy Red Muscadel	06			4						
Rietvallei Muscadel 1908	05	4½		4						
Rietvallei Red Muscadel	06			4						
Rooiberg Red Muscadel	04					DG				
Port										
Allesverloren	02	4½								
Axe Hill Cape Vintage	04	4½								
Beyerskloof Lagare Cape Vintage Port	04			4						
Bon Courage Vintage	04			4						
Boplaas Cape Tawny	NV			4						
Boplaas Vintner's Reserve Selection Cape Tawny	80	5	DG	4						
Boplaas Vintner's Reserve Selection Cape Tawny	NV			4						
Boplaas Cape Vintage	04			4						
Boplaas Vintage Reserve	04	5		4						
Boplaas Vintner's Reserve Selection Cape Vintage Reserve	04			4						
Boplaas Cape Vintage	05			4.5						
Boplaas Vintage Reserve	05			4						
Boplaas Vintner's Reserve Selection Cape Vintage Reserve	05			4						
Boplaas CWG Auction Vintage Reserve	03	4.5								
De Krans Cape Tawny	NV	4½		4.5	T					
De Krans Vintage Reserve	04	5								
JP Bredell Bredell's Cape Vintage	00				T					
JP Bredell Bredell's Cape Vintage Reserve	01	5								
JP Bredell Bredell's Late Bottled Vintage	02		DG							
JP Bredell CWG Auction Reserve	03	4½								
KWV Full Tawny	NV			4						
Overgaauw Cape Vintage	97	5								

the**INDUSTRY**

An Overview

South Africa in 2004 (latest available year) retained its ranking as the world's 9th largest wine producer, its ±928m litres representing 3.1% of global production. France, with 19.2%, and Italy, with 17.8%, again were 1 and 2. Newest official SA statistics (for 2006) show a continuing decline in grape growers, from 4 360 in 2004 to 4 185, and, after years of sustained rise, a slight drop in wine cellars crushing grapes (581 vs 576). There are now 494 private cellars, 65 co-operatives ('producer cellars' in officialese) and 17 producing wholesalers. Nearly half (some 49%) of all cellars crush fewer than 100 tons — further evidence of the importance of micro-wineries and *garagistes*.

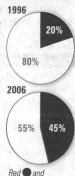

1996

20%

80%

2006

55%   45%

Red ● and white ○ grape varieties as % of total area

The vineyards

New white-wine planting continues to outstrip red, by 3 056 ha to 2 570 ha — a much smaller margin than in recent years. The grape most enthusiastically planted remains chenin (817 ha added), now closely followed by sauvignon (606 ha), with colombard 3rd (440 ha, mostly for brandy), then chardonnay (352 ha). Fashionable shiraz, 5th overall, is the most-planted of the reds (132 ha), now ahead of cab (92 ha), and — a real sign of the times — more viognier was planted (68 ha) than pinotage (57 ha). More chenin is uprooted than planted, in fact, but it still leads the total hectarage tables, with 18.1% of the total 102 146 ha. Cabernet, at 13.1%, is the leading red. The proportion of very young vines continues to decline: some 12.5% are under 4 years, while roughly 42% are 4-10 and 16.5% older than 20.

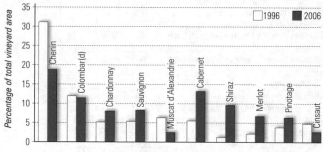

Top 5 white and top 5 red varieties

Exports

For various reasons, the volume of exported Cape wine declined in 2006 for the first time since the renaissance of 1994, notably in its largest markets, the UK and Netherlands. The latest (2006) data show by far the biggest drop in 'other white wine'; of the named varietal wines, pinotage and sauvignon were the only losers compared with the previous year.

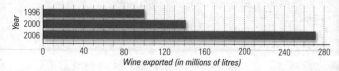

Wine exported (in millions of litres)

South African Wine Industry – Ten-year Overview

	1997	1998	1999	2000	2001	2002	2003	2004	2005	2006
Number of wineries	295	315	337	355	388	428	505	561	581	576
Total vine area (excl sultana) (hectares)	87 301	89 935	92 601	93 656	94 412	96 233	98 605	100 207	101 607	102 146
Producing area 4 yrs & older (excl sultana) (hectares)	76 025	76 895	75 892	74 335	76 071	79 073	82 719	85 331	87 284	89 426
Avg yield (tons/hectare)	14.74	13.54	15.46	14.77	12.85	13.66	14.91	15.38	13.42	14.55
Avg grape price – producer cellars/co-ops (R/ton) (2005/2006 est)	Not available	796	934	966	1 136	1 333	1 624	1 458	1 384	1 264
Avg grape price – excl producer cellars/co-ops (R/ton)	2 115	2 641	2 845	3 278	3 640	3 953	4 041	4 133	3 593	3 128
Grapes crushed (millions of tons)	1.12	1.04	1.17	1.10	0.98	1.08	1.23	1.31	1.17	1.30
Total production (millions of litres)	880.9	815.6	914.1	837.2	746.5	834.2	956.0	1015.7	905.2	1 013.0
Domestic sales (millions of litres)	401.6	384.6	390.9	389.2	390.2	388.4	348.7	350.9	345.0	345.2
Consumption per capita (litres SA wine)	9.8	9.2	9.2	9.0	9.0	8.9	7.9	7.7	7.4	7.3
Export volume (millions of litres)	110.6	118.4	129.1	141.0	177.3	217.7	239.4	267.7	281.8	271.6
Stock (millions of litres)	221.3	250.2	315.6	290.5	242.3	209.3	336.8	363.7	339.4	403.1
Stock : sales ratio	0.43:1	0.50:1	0.61:1	0.55:1	0.43:1	0.35:1	0.57:1	0.59:1	0.54:1	0.65:1

Chenin and chardonnay remain the most-exported varietal wines, followed by cabernet and sauvignon – but both the latter are outgunned by modish pink wines. The top five markets for SA wine are, in descending order, the UK, Germany, Netherlands, Sweden and Denmark (when it comes to bottled wine, The US and Canada replace the Scandinavian pair).

Local wine consumption

Adding to producers' concerns, domestic per-capita consumption remains only just above the 2005 new low of 7.37ℓ. Of natural wine sold locally, about 46% is in glass – a steadily rising proportion – and about 59% is in the standard 750ml bottle.

Note

Statistical data provided by SA Wine Industry Information & Systems (see below).

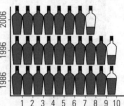
SA wine consumption per capita (litres)

Wine Industry Organisations

ARC Infruitec-Nietvoorbij Research & technology manager: Dr Johan van Zyl ▪ PR: Daleen Bosman ▪ **T 021-809-3018** ▪ F 021-809-3002 ▪ bosmand@arc.agric.za ▪ www. arc.agric.za
Internationally-regarded one-stop research institute, generating advanced technology for deciduous fruit- and grape-growers and related processors.

Biodiversity & Wine Initiative (BWI) Project Coordinator: Inge Kotze ▪ BWI Extension Officer: Joan Isham ▪ bwi@sawb.co.za ▪ www.bwi.co.za ▪ **T 021-886-8428** ▪ F 021-882-9510
Pioneering partnership between the wine industry and conservation sector to minimise loss of threatened natural vegetation and foster sustainable production through the implementation of biodiversity guidelines. Under BWI auspices, producers have set aside 60 000 ha of pristine natural vegetation for future generations. BWI is communicated through Wines of South Africa's variety is in our nature positioning, producers' biodiversity stories and the biodiversity wine routes. See also Integrated Production of Wine.

Cape Estate Wine Producers' Association (CEWPA) Chair: Braam van Velden ▪ **T 021-881-3815** ▪ F 021-881-3436 ▪ info@overgaauw.co.za

Cape Winemakers Guild (CWG) Chair: Philip Costandius ▪ General Manager: Kate Jonker ▪ **T 021-852-0408** ▪ F 021-852-0409 ▪ info@capewinemakersguild.com ▪ www. capewinemakersguild.com
Independent, invitation-only association, founded in 1982 to promote winemaking excellence among its members. Since 1985, the CWG has held a highly regarded annual public auction. A Development Trust, formed in 1999 with auction sponsor Nedbank, benefits disadvantaged communities living and working in the winegrowing regions.

Chenin Blanc Association (CBA) Chair: Francois Naudé ▪ **T 021-883-8469/ 072-200-5546** ▪ F 086-632-8690 ▪ info@winefix.co.za ▪ Manager: Wilmari Borel-Saladin **T 021-872-9779/082-770-8001** ▪ F 021-871-1619 ▪ wilmaribs@mweb.co.za ▪ www. chenin.co.za

Fair Trade South Africa Chair: Noel Oettle ▪ **T 027-218-1117/ 083-693-8676** ▪ F 027-218-1148 ▪ dryland@global.co.za ▪ Secretariat: Charles Starling ▪ **T 021-448-2871/084-581-9682** ▪ F 021-448-2225 ▪ charles@goldscarab.com ▪ www.fairtrade.org.za

Garagiste Movement Coordinator: Tanja Beutler ▪ **T 021-855-4275** ▪ F 021-855-5086 ▪ tanja@topazwines.co.za ▪ www.garagiste.co.za

Institute of Cape Wine Masters Chair: Margaret Fry ▪ **T 083-628-6511** ▪ F 086-611-7150 ▪ capewinemasters@gmail.com ▪ www.capewinemasters.co.za
Successful completion of examinations set since 1983 by the Cape Wine & Spirit Education Trust and, latterly, the Cape Wine Academy, have qualified 66 Cape Wine Masters. Their Institute holds seminars, runs tasting workshops, charts trends and names a Wine Personality of the Year.

Integrated Production of Wine (IPW) Manager: Jacques Rossouw ▪ jrossouw@ipw. co.za ▪ **T 021-809-3143** ▪ F 021-809-3113
Innovative, widely supported initiative aimed at producing wine in an environmentally sustainable, profitable way by means of guidelines for both farm and cellar, embracing all aspects of grape production, winemaking and, now, biodiversity conservation. See also Biodiversity & Wine Initiative.

Méthode Cap Classique Producers' Association Chair: Jeff Grier ▪ **T 021-865-2002** ▪ F 021-865-2314 ▪ wine@villiera.com

Muscadel Association Chair: Swepie le Roux ▪ **T 044-241-2556** ▪ F 044-241-2548 ▪ swepie@mweb.co.za ▪ Vice-chair: Henri Swiegers **T 023-344-3021** ▪ winemaker@ badsberg.co.za

Pinotage Association Chair: Beyers Truter ▪ **T 021-865-1235** ▪ F 021-865-2683 ▪ wine@beyerskloof.co.za ▪ Manager: Pierre Loubser **T 021-855-1128** ▪ F 086-502-9417 ▪ info@pinotage.co.za ▪ www.pinotage.co.za

Sauvignon Blanc Interest Group of South Africa (SBIG) Chair: JC Bekker ▪ **T 021-870-4200/082-447-4312** ▪ F 021-874-1531 ▪ jcb@dgb.co.za ▪ Secretariat: Pieter de Waal ▪ **T 021-976-3361/083-357-3864** ▪ F 021-948-3441 ▪ sbig@dw.co.za

Shiraz Association Chair: Jacques Borman ▪ **T 021-881-3268** ▪ F 021-881-3032 ▪ jborman@adept.co.za

South African Port Producers' Association (SAPPA) Chair: Carel Nel ▪ **T 044-213-3326** ▪ F 044-213-3750 ▪ boplaas@mweb.co.za

South African Society for Enology & Viticulture (SASEV) President: Ilse Trautmann ▪ **T 021-809-3123** ▪ F 021-809-6335 ▪ sasev@arc.agric.za
Disseminates the latest scientific knowledge and technology locally and world-wide, to improve the quality of grapes, wines and related products.

South African Black Vintners Alliance Chair: Vivian Kleynhans ▪ **T 082-764-0503** ▪ sabva@africanrootswines.com
Established to create an enabling environment for emerging black owned wineries.

South African Wine Industry Council CEO: Johan van Rooyen ▪ **T 021-886-8992** ▪ F 021-882-9510 ▪ johan@winecouncil.co.za; litta@winecouncil.co.za ▪ www. winecouncil.co.za
Non-profit body aimed at fast-tracking important issues (including transformation), promoting industry growth, and streamlining relations among all stakeholders to stimulate competitiveness and development locally and abroad.

South African Wine Industry Information & Systems (SAWIS) Executive manager: Yvette van der Merwe ▪ **T 021-807-5703** ▪ F 021-807-6000 ▪ info@sawis.co.za
Business unit of the South African Wine Industry Council responsible for the collection, processing and dissemination of industry information, and administers the Wine of Origin (WO) system.

South African Wine Industry Trust (SAWIT) Chair: Dr Thandi Ndlovu ▪ CEO: Charles Erasmus ▪ **T 021-889-8101** ▪ F 021-889-5900 ▪ info@sawit.co.za ▪ www.sawit.co.za
SAWIT aims to transform the wine industry, concentrating on education and training; research, development and technology transfer; generic local/export marketing; establishing new wine farmers from previously disadvantaged groups; support the upliftment of farm workers and communities and black economic empowerment within the wine industry.

Wine & Spirit Board Chair: Njabulo Nduli ▪ Secretary: Hugo van der Merwe ▪ **T 021-889-6555** ▪ F 021-889-5823 ▪ hugo@wsb.org.za
Mainly administers the Wine of Origin, estate brandy and Integrated Production of Wine (IPW) schemes.

Wine and Agricultural Industry Ethical Trade Association (WIETA) CEO: Peter Lewis ▪ **T 021-447-5660** ▪ F 021-447-5662 ▪ pete@wieta.org.za; anthea@wieta.org. za ▪ www.wieta.org.za
Non-profit, voluntary organisation established in 2002 to promote ethical trade in the wine industry. WIETA has adopted a code of labour standards for the industry, and its main task is to conduct ethical audits to assess members' compliance with the code.

Wines of South Africa (WOSA) Chair: Paul Cluver Snr ▪ **T/F 021-844-0605** ▪ drcluver@cluver.co.za ▪ CEO: Su Birch **T 021-883-3860** ▪ F 021-883-3861 ▪ info@wosa.co.za ▪ www.wosa.co.za; www.varietyisinournature.com
Generic marketing organisation, responsible for raising the profile of SA wine in key export markets. See also Biodiversity & Wine Initiative.

Wine Industry Network of Expertise & Technology (WINETECH) Executive manager: Jan Booysen ▪ **T 021-807-3324** ▪ F 021-807-3385 ▪ booysenj@winetech.co.za
Coordinates the research, training and technology transfer programmes of participating institutions and individuals, to improve the competitiveness of the wine industry.

Winegrowing Areas

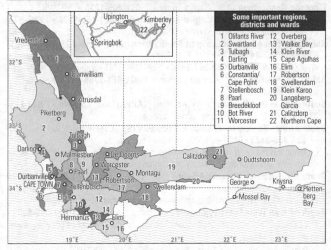

Some important regions, districts and wards		
1 Olifants River	12 Overberg	
2 Swartland	13 Walker Bay	
3 Tulbagh	14 Klein River	
4 Darling	15 Cape Agulhas	
5 Durbanville	16 Elim	
6 Constantia/ Cape Point	17 Robertson	
7 Stellenbosch	18 Swellendam	
8 Paarl	19 Klein Karoo	
9 Breedekloof	20 Langeberg-Garcia	
10 Bot River	21 Calitzdorp	
11 Worcester	22 Northern Cape	

From modest beginnings in the Dutch East India Company's gardens below Table Mountain, SA's vineyards now cover 102 146 ha and more than 80 official appellations. Recent changes to the Wine of Origin (WO) scheme of 1972/3 saw 'geographical units' incorporated into the WO classification alongside 'regions', 'districts' and 'wards' (the latter have the smallest footprint of the WO areas, following earlier amendments to the 'estate' legislation). Below are brief notes on the most important grape cultivation zones. Figures are supplied by SA Wine Industry Information & Systems (SAWIS), and reflect 2005 data for the WO areas. **Note:** Area maps are not to the same scale.

Cape Point Small (26ha), cool district on mainly western slopes of the Cape Peninsula. Recognised for sauvignon and semillon; the first red-wine vineyards recently came on-stream. Major varieties (ha): sauvignon (11), cab (6), shiraz (4) and chardonnay (3).

Constantia Premier viticultural ward on the eastern flank of the Cape Peninsula, summer-cooled by south-easterly sea breezes. Recognised for whites generally,

1 Constantia **2** Cape Point

notably sauvignon, semillon and muscat. Sauvignon (138), cab (60), chardonnay (60), merlot (45), shiraz (29).

Darling District around the eponymous town, best known for the wines from its higher-lying ward, Groenekloof, long the source of top-class sauvignon; also showing promise with reds such as shiraz. Groenekloof: cab (546), shiraz (347), sauvignon (248), pinotage (242), chenin (213).

Durbanville Ward within the Tygerberg district, with solid reputation for striking merlot and sauvignon. The latter (337) is now the dominant variety, followed by cab (305), merlot (228), shiraz (224) and pinotage (95).

Elgin Cool upland ward within the Overberg district, yielding exciting aromatic whites and elegant reds. Sauvignon (184), cab (61), merlot (47), shiraz (44), pinot (40).

Elim Small, promising maritime ward within the Cape Agulhas district, its 114 ha of vineyards are arrayed around the old mission village of Elim near Africa's most southerly point. Sauvignon (53), cab (16), shiraz (15), semillon (10), pinot (10).

Little Karoo Scrubby semi-arid region, ideal for ostrich farming but something of a challenge for viticulture, which is reliant on irrigation. Similarities (in climate, if not soil) with Portugal's Douro Valley have inspired some local growers, chiefly around Calitzdorp, to apply their talents to 'port', with results that impress even the Portuguese. Interesting stirrings in the tiny (47ha) Upper-Langkloof ward and newly declared Langeberg-Garcia district. Region also recognised for fortifieds generally. Calitzdorp district: hanepoot (110), colombard (44), cab (26), palomino (18), chardonnay (17). Tradouw ward: colombard (27), chardonnay (23) merlot (15), shiraz (12), cab (12).

Lower Orange This ward along the Orange River (Gariep) is a production zone within the Northern Cape Geographical Unit. Overwhelmingly a white-grape area but red plantings are increasing. Sultana (9 321), colombard (2 360), chenin (791), hanepoot (243), ruby cab (46), palomino (45).

Northern Cape See Lower Orange.

Olifants River Quality moves are afoot in this north-westerly Cape grape-growing region, particularly in the Bamboes Bay 'micro-ward' (just 6ha), new Lamberts Bay ward, and Lutzville Valley district nearer the coast, as well as the cool upland wards of Cederberg and Piekenierskloof. Further inland, a climate conducive to organic cultivation is now beginning to be exploited to that end. Koekenaap ward (Lutzville Valley): chenin (194),

1 Voor Paardeberg 4 Simonsberg-Paarl
2 Wellington 5 Franschhoek
3 Paarl

1 Polkadraai Hills 6 Simonsberg-
2 Bottelary   Stellenbosch
3 Devon Valley 7 Jonkershoek Valley
4 Papegaaiberg 8 Banghoek
5 Stellenbosch

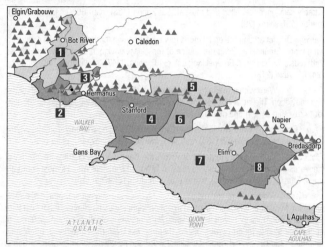

1 Bot River **3** Upper Hemel en Aarde **5** Kleinrivier **7** Cape Agulhas
2 Hemel en Aarde **4** Walker Bay **6** Sunday's Glen **8** Elim

colombard (166), sauvignon (111), cab (69), chardonnay (48). Cederberg: merlot (13), shiraz (12), chenin, pinotage & sauvignon (all 9). Piekenierskloof: palomino (84), cab (77), pinotage (66), chenin (55), sauvignon (45).

Paarl This district has many mesoclimates, soils and aspects, and thus succeeds with a variety of styles and grapes. Paarl proper is recognised for shiraz and, more recently, viognier and mourvèdre grown on warmer slopes. Chenin (1 708), cab (1 318), shiraz (946), cinsaut (556); pinotage (551). The following are all wards: Wellington shows promise, especially with shiraz and gutsy red blends generally. Chenin (1 127), cab (883),

1 Swartland **3** Philadelphia
2 Darling **4** Durbanville

1 Lutzville Valley **5** Citrusdal Mntn
2 Bamboes Bay **6** Citrusdal Valley
3 Lamberts Bay **7** Piekenierskloof
4 Olifants River

1 Eilandia   **3** Hoops River   **5** Agterkliphoogte   **7** Robertson   **9** Boesmans River
2 Vink River   **4** Klaasvoogds   **6** Le Chasseur   **8** McGregor   **10** Bonnievale

shiraz (495), cinsaut (440), merlot (366). Franschhoek, founded by 17th-century French Huguenots and now a millionaire's playground, recognised for cab and semillon. Sauvignon (220), cab (187), chardonnay (157), shiraz (141), merlot (137). Simonsberg-Paarl, on the warmer slopes of the Simonsberg, recognised for red blends, shiraz and chardonnay. Cab (349), chardonnay (222), shiraz (175), merlot (151), sauvignon (145). Voor Paardeberg, long an uncredited source of top-quality grapes, now becoming a star in own right. Cab (419), shiraz (282), chenin (227), merlot (212), pinotage (187).

Philadelphia A ward of Tygerberg, cooled by the Atlantic air and noted for cab, merlot and bordeaux-style reds. Cab (100), sauvignon (70), merlot (29), chardonnay (18), shiraz (15).

Robertson Traditionally a white-wine district, increasingly recognised for shiraz and cab. Chardonnay, sauvignon and sparkling remain stand-outs. Chardonnay (2 100), colombard (2 079), chenin (1 726), cab (1 423), sauvignon (1 095).

Stellenbosch To many, this intensively farmed district is the wine capital of SA. Key contributors to quality are the cooler mountain slopes, varied soil types and breezes off False Bay which moderate summer temperatures. Jonkershoek Valley, a ward east of Stellenbosch town, is recognised for cab and cab blends. Cab (63), merlot (27), chardonnay (20), sauvignon (20), shiraz (16). Simonsberg-Stellenbosch, in the south-western foothills of the Simonsberg mountain, is especially recognised for cab, cab blends, pinotage and reds generally. Cab (352), sauvignon (173), merlot (173), shiraz (151), chardonnay (118). North-west of Stellenbosch town are four adjoining wards: Papegaaiberg – chardonnay (25), sauvignon (23), chenin (23), cab (14), pinotage (13); Devon Valley, recognised mainly for red blends – merlot (187), cab (167), shiraz (111), sauvignon (93), pinotage (67); Bottelary, noted for pinotage, shiraz and warm-blooded blends – chenin (508), cab (420), sauvignon (343), shiraz (299), pinotage (260); and the newest and most westerly ward, Polkadraai Hills. Banghoek, the mountain amphitheatre above the village of Pniel – cab (91), shiraz (44), sauvignon (41), merlot (35), chardonnay (29). The remainder of the district, as yet unappellated, includes Stellenboschberg, Helderberg and Faure, recognised for red blends, chenin and sauvignon. Cab (2 186), shiraz (1 351), merlot (1 164), sauvignon (1 124), chenin (914).

Swartland Traditionally associated with beefy reds, especially pinotage and shiraz, this sunny district north of Cape Town has two wards, Malmesbury and Riebeekberg, plus a large appellated area. Riebeekberg: chenin (248), shiraz (183), cab (172), chardonnay (164), pinotage (158). Malmesbury: cab (781), chenin (616), shiraz (517), pinotage

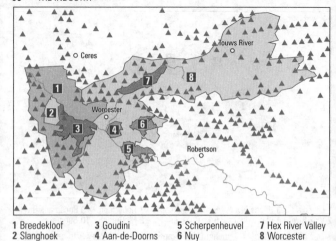

1 Breedekloof   3 Goudini   5 Scherpenheuvel   7 Hex River Valley
2 Slanghoek   4 Aan-de-Doorns   6 Nuy   8 Worcester

(436), merlot (287). 'Swartland': chenin (2 597), cab (939), pinotage (895), shiraz (756), chardonnay (410).

Tulbagh This inland district, traditionally known for sparkling and lightish whites, is rapidly moving towards quality reds. Major varieties: chenin (570), colombard (324), cab (192), shiraz (167), chardonnay (129).

Walker Bay Highly regarded maritime district south-east of Cape Town, recognised for pinot, pinotage, sauvignon and chardonnay. Sauvignon (92), shiraz (50), cab (49), chardonnay (46), merlot (42). The Sunday's Glen ward, dominated by sauvignon, is new.

Worcester Still the largest winegrowing district, measured by number of vines (more than 65m, over 20% of the total), producing chiefly for the brandy industry and merchant trade, but small quantities bottled under own labels often represent good quality/value. Recognised for everyday reds/whites and fortifieds. Chenin (4 107), colombard (2 461), chardonnay (1 591), cab (1 200), hanepoot (1 033). Worth noting is the tiny (185) new Hex River Valley ward, featuring cab and chenin.

Wine of Origin-defined production areas
(New appellations in **bold**.)

Region	District	Ward
Breede River Valley	Breedekloof	Goudini
		Slanghoek
	Robertson	Agterkliphoogte
		Boesmansrivier
		Bonnievale
		Eilandia
		Hoopsrivier
		Klaasvoogds
		Le Chasseur
		McGregor
		Vinkrivier
	Swellendam	Buffeljags
		Stormsvlei
	Worcester	Aan-de-Doorns
		Hex River Valley
		Nuy
		Scherpenheuvel

Region	District	Ward
Coastal	Cape Point	—
	—	Constantia
	Darling	Groenekloof
	Paarl	Franschhoek
		Simonsberg-Paarl
		Voor Paardeberg
		Wellington
	Tygerberg	Durbanville
		Philadelphia
	Stellenbosch	Banghoek
		Bottelary
		Devon Valley
		Jonkershoek Valley
		Papegaaiberg
		Polkadraai Hills
		Simonsberg-Stellenbosch
	Swartland	Malmesbury
		Riebeekberg
	Tulbagh	—
Klein Karoo	Calitzdorp	—
	Langeberg-Garcia	—
	—	Montagu
	—	Outeniqua
	—	Tradouw
	—	Upper Langkloof
Olifants River	—	Bamboes Bay
	Citrusdal Mountain	Piekenierskloof
	Citrusdal Valley	
	Lutzville Valley	Koekenaap
	—	Spruitdrift
	—	Vredendal
—	Bot River	—
—	Cape Agulhas	Elim
—	Douglas*	—
—	Overberg	Elgin
—		Klein River
—	Plettenberg Bay	—
—	Walker Bay	Upper Hemel-en-Aarde Valley
		Hemel-en-Aarde Valley
		Sunday's Glen
—	—	Cederberg
—	—	Ceres
—	—	Hartswater*
—	—	Herbertsdale
—	—	**Lamberts Bay**
—	—	Lower Orange*
—	—	Prince Albert Valley
—	—	Rietrivier (Free State)*
—	—	Ruiterbosch
—	—	Swartberg

Boberg (fortified wines from Paarl & Tulbagh)

*Production zones within the Northern Cape Geographical Unit (GU); all other areas above are part of the Western Cape GU. The third GU is KwaZulu-Natal.
Source: SAWIS

Grape Varieties

Though vines have been grown in SA for almost 350 years, Old World-style regional specialisation such as riesling in the Moselle Valley or nebbiolo in the Langhe Hills hardly exists here, and where it does, it is of fairly recent origin (Constantia muscat is a notable exception). Cabernet is acknowledged to do exceptionally well in the Simonsberg foothills, but it is also a feature of most other vineyard areas. Less forgiving varieties, such as merlot, are cultivated from Cape Point to the Kalahari. Recent years have brought a greater understanding of, and emphasis on, the importance of selecting the most suitable sites for any given variety, based on the evidence of scientific investigation and accumulated experience. International exposure has given the present generation of vinegrowers fresh perspectives and possibilities, suggesting that trial and experimentation with grapes and terroirs will continue to be a key feature of SA viticulture in the future. Below are brief notes on the main grape varieties in SA today, and their contribution to the national vineyard (statistics from SA Wine Industry Information & Systems — SAWIS). See under Winegrowing Areas for details of the most widely planted and best-performing varieties in the major vine cultivation zones.

Red-wine varieties

Cabernet sauvignon Adaptable and internationally planted black grape making some of the world's finest and longest-lasting wines. And retaining some of its inherent qualities even when overcropped in less suitable soils and climates. Can stand alone triumphantly, but frequently blended with a wide range of other varieties: traditionally, as in Bordeaux, with cab franc, merlot and a few minor others, but also in SA sometimes partnering varieties such as shiraz and pinotage. Number of different clones, with differing characteristics. A steady ±13% of total vineyard area.

Cabernet franc Like its descendant cabernet sauvignon, with which it is often partnered, a classic part of the Bordeaux blend, but in SA and elsewhere also used for varietal wines — particularly in the Loire. Tiny stable vineyard area (1%).

Carignan Hugely planted in the south of France, where it is not much respected. But there, as in SA, older, low-yielding vines can produce pleasant surprises. Insignificant vineyard area.

Cinsaut (noir) 'Cinsault' in France. Another of the mass, undistinguished plantings of southern France, which only occasionally comes up trumps. Used to be known locally as hermitage, the name reflected in its offspring (with pinot noir), pinotage. Less than 3% of vineyard area, decreasing.

Gamay noir Although it produces some serious long-lived wines in Beaujolais, its use for (mainly) early- and easy-drinking 'nouveau' wines there, often using carbonic maceration, is the model mostly copied in SA: Insignificant vineyard area.

Grenache (noir) The international (ie French) name for the Spanish grape garnacha. Widespread in Spain and southern France, generally used in blends (as in Rioja and Châteauneuf), but occasionally solo. A favourite for rosés. When vigour restrained, capable of greatness, but this is rare. Tiny plantings here. (White/pink versions also occur.)

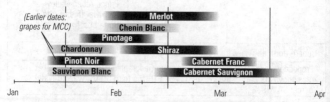

Approximate ripening dates in the Stellenbosch area for some important grape varieties

Malbec Once a significant part of Bordeaux's blend, now most important in Cahors in western France (where it is known as cot), and as Argentina's signature variety. In SA a few varietal and blended examples; very small plantings.

Merlot Classic blending partner (as in Bordeaux) for cabernet, fashionable around the world, where it tends to be seen as an 'easier' version of cab — although this is perhaps because it is often made in a less ambitious manner. Merlot varietal wines increasingly common in SA too. A steady ±7% of vineyard area.

Mourvèdre Internationally known by its French name, though originally Spanish (monastrell). In Australia and California also called mataro. Particularly successful in some serious southern French blends, and increasingly modish internationally. Minuscule plantings here.

Nebbiolo Perhaps the greatest red grape to have scarcely ventured from its home — Piedmont in this case, where it makes massive, tannic, long-lived wines. Minute plantings here.

Petit verdot Use of this excellent variety in the Médoc limited by its late ripening. Now appearing in some local blends, and a few varietals. Tiny but increasing quantities.

Pinotage A 1920s cross between pinot noir and cinsaut ('hermitage'). Made in a range of styles, from simply fruity to ambitious, well-oaked examples. 6.2% of vineyard area, decreasing (7.3% at zenith in 2001).

Pinot noir Notoriously difficult grape to succeed with outside its native Burgundy, but SA, along with the rest of the New World, now producing some excellent examples, especially as use of BK5 'champagne' clone wanes. Usually matured in wood; seldom at a bargain price. Still a relatively stable 0.6% of the vineyard.

Ruby cabernet US cross between cabernet sauvignon and carignan, designed for heat tolerance. Rather rustic, used mostly in cheaper blends. 2.5% of vineyard area.

Shiraz Better known as syrah outside SA and Australia (and on some local labels too). Internationally increasing in popularity, with northern Rhône and now also Australia as its major domiciles. Clearly happy in warmer climates, shiraz is seen by many as the great hope for SA wine. Made here in a variety of styles — generally wooded, often with American oak. 9.6% of vineyard area, slowly increasing.

Tinta barocca Elsewhere spelt 'barroca'. One of the important Portuguese port-making grapes, which is now its primary role in SA, usually blended. Also used for some varietal unfortified wines, and namelessly in some 'dry reds'. Insignificant vineyard area.

Touriga nacional Important Portuguese port-making grape, now usefully grown here for similar ends, along with tinta franca, tinta roriz (tempranillo) and souzão. Tiny plantings.

Zinfandel The quintessential Californian grape (of European origin, and the same as Italy's primitivo), used here in a small way for some big wines. Tiny plantings.

White wine varieties

Chardonnay In the Cape, as elsewhere, many new vineyards of this grape have come on-stream in recent years, with wines showing a wide range of styles, quality and price. Generally used varietally, but also in blends. Often heavily wooded in more ambitious wines. 8% of vineyard area, increasing slowly.

Chenin blanc SA has more chenin (locally also called steen) than even France's Loire Valley, the variety's home. Used here for everything from generic 'dry whites' to ambitious sweet wines, to brandy. Increasing numbers of table-wine successes in recent years, as well as inexpensive but flavoursome easy-drinkers. 18.7% of vineyard area, still declining.

Colombar(d) One of the mainstays of brandy production in the Cape, colombard (usually without the 'd' in SA) also used for numerous varietal and blended wines, ranging from dry to sweet — seldom wooded. 11.4% of vineyard area, still marginally inclining.

Gewürztraminer Readily identifiable from its rose-petal fragrance, best known in its Alsatian guise. In the Cape usually made in sweeter styles. Insignificant vineyard area.

Hanepoot Traditional Afrikaans name for muscat d'Alexandrie, the Cape's most planted muscat variety (see also muscadel below). 2.5% of vineyard area (some for raisins and table grapes), slowly declining.

Muscadel Name used here for both muscat de Frontignan and muscat blanc à petits grains (both red and white versions). The grape associated with the famous Constantia dessert wines of the 18th century today is used chiefly for dessert and fortified wines and for touching up blends. Red and white versions total ±1% of vineyard area.

Muscat See Hanepoot and Muscadel.

Riesling The name a source of confusion to consumers, and of distress to the producers of what is known in its great homeland, Germany, simply as riesling and here officially as Rhine or weisser riesling. In SA, standing alone, 'riesling' usually, and officially, refers to Cape riesling (sometimes called SA riesling), a much inferior grape properly known as crouchen blanc, mostly used here anonymously in blends, and sometimes varietally. Rhine/weisser riesling frequently in off-dry style here, in blends or varietally, some noteworthy botrytised dessert examples – and developing terpene character much earlier in SA than in cooler climates. Cape riesling: 1.1% of vineyard area, decreasing; Rhine: a minuscule 0.2%. Note: in this guide 'riesling' without qualification refers to the latter.

Sauvignon blanc Prestigious vine most associated with eastern Loire regions, Bordeaux and, increasingly, New Zealand – whose wines have helped restore fashionability to the grape. The Cape version no longer a poor relation of these. Usually dry, but some sweet wines; sometimes wooded, more often not (former sometimes called fumé blanc/blanc fumé). 8.2% of vineyard area, swiftly increasing.

Semillon Spelt sémillon in French. The present small hectarage devoted to semillon in SA is a far cry from the early 19th century, when the grape, also known as 'groen' (green), a reference to its bright foliage, represented 93% of all Cape vines. Now only ±1%. Sometimes heavily wooded.

Viognier Increasingly fashionable variety internationally, spreading out from its home in the northern Rhône, now showing promise here. Usually wooded. Still tiny plantings.

SA Wine Competitions, Challenges & Awards

An increasing number of wine competitions, awards and challenges are run by liquor industry bodies, independent companies, publishing houses and individuals. Below are the main national events:

ABSA Top Ten Pinotage Competition Run annually by the Pinotage Association and a major financial institution to help set international quality targets for growers of pinotage. Local/overseas judges. See under Industry Organisations for contact details.

Calyon Trophy Bordeaux Blend Challenge Competition lauding the best blends of at least two of the 'Bordeaux reds', cabernets sauvignon and franc, merlot, malbec and petit verdot. Local judges. ▪ alex@outsorceress.co.za ▪ **T 011-482-5936** ▪ F 011-482-2272

Classic Wine Trophy Staged under rules of the Office Internationale de la Vigne et du Vin (OIV), recognising ageworthy, classic SA wines. Overseas judges. ▪ Established since 1998 and run by Christophe Durand & Jean Vincent Ridon ▪ Contact: Sabrina **T 021-683-7479** ▪ F 021-683-7489 ▪ sabrina@vinum.co.za

Diners Club Winemaker of the Year Inaugurated 1981, this prestigious competition features a different category each year. Local panel with some overseas representation. ▪ celiag@rsp.co.za ▪ www.winemag.co.za ▪ **T 021-530-3145** ▪ F 021-531-2212

Juliet Cullinan Wine Connoisseur's Award National competition organised by local wine-entrepreneur Juliet Cullinan and judged by a panel of Cape Wine Masters. juliet@julietcullinan.co.za ▪ **T 011-447-1885/083-255-9430** ▪ F 011-219-7064

Landbouweekblad Woman Winemaker of the Year Launched 2004 to acknowledge the role and skills of women winemakers, and highlight the special qualities they bring to their craft. ▪ lorman@yebo.co.za ▪ www.sawinewoman.co.za ▪ **T 039-314-9913/5** or 082-556-8679; F 039-314-9914 ▪ Stellenbosch office: **T 021-865-2815** or T/F 021-865-2440

Old Mutual Trophy Wine Show See Trophy Wine Show

Michelangelo International Wine Awards Well-established event (1997) featuring hand-picked international panel and one local judge. Run under the international OIV rules. Aims to identify SA wines which will appeal to foreign palates. ▪ lorman@yebo.co.za ▪ www.michelangeloawards.com ▪ **T 039-314-9913/5** or 082-556-8679; F 039-314-9914 ▪ Stellenbosch office: **T 021-865-2815** or T/F 021-865-2440

Muscadel Award for Excellence Annual competition aimed at raising consumer awareness and recognising quality in the creation, packaging and promotion of SA's muscadel wines. Local judges. ▪ swepie@mweb.co.za ▪ **T 044-241-2556** ▪ F 044-241-2548

Peter Schulz Excellence Awards for Port Sponsored by importer-wholesaler NMK Schulz, and organised by the SA Port Producers' Association with the assistance of SA *Wine*, to select the best wine in each of the various port categories, and an overall winner. Local judges. ▪ boplaas@mweb.co.za ▪ www.sappa.co.za ▪ **T 044-213-3326** ▪ F 044-213-3750

South African Airways (SAA) Wine Awards Annual selection of wines to fly with the national carrier (drinkability in flight conditions an important consideration). The top red, white, bubbly and port each receive a trophy. Local & overseas palates. ▪ Mpho Omotola ▪ mphoomotola@flysaa.com ▪ www.flysaa.com ▪ **T 011-978-3311** ▪ F 011-978-3115

SA Terroir Wine Awards A new (2006) competition, rewarding the best wines from SA's officially recognised winegrowing areas. Local judges. ▪ mlab@iafrica.com ▪ www.novare.co.za ▪ **T 021-975-8166** ▪ F 021-979-0867

SA Young Wine Show Inaugurated 1975 to gauge the quality of embryo wines, prior to finishing and bottling, thereby also recognising wineries which sell their products in bulk. The grand champion receives the General Smuts Trophy. Local judges. ▪ ferreira@vinpro.co.za ▪ www.youngwineshow.co.za ▪ **T 021-807-3104** ▪ F 021-863-2079

Swiss International Air Lines Wine Awards Annual competition, judged by international/local wine buyers and Cape Wine Masters. Selected award winners fly with Swiss Business/1st Class. ▪ info@gourmetsa.com ▪ www.gourmetsa.com ▪ **T 021-797-4500** ▪ F 021-797-4179

Trophy Wine Show Launched in 2002 as Fairbairn Capital TWS, now sponsored by Old Mutual. Identifies the best wines in SA and awards trophies to the top wines in each of the major classes, as well as the top producer overall. Local and international judges. ▪ celiag@rsp.co.za ▪ www.trophywineshow.co.za ▪ **T 021-530-3145** ▪ F 021-531-2212

Veritas SA's biggest competition for market-ready wines, awarding double-gold, gold, silver and bronze medals across a wide range of categories. Local palates with some overseas input. ferreira@vinpro.co.za ▪ www.veritas.co.za ▪ **T 021-807-3104** ▪ F 021-863-2079

Wine Magazine Amorim Cork Cap Classique Challenge Annual competition to anoint SA's top bottle-fermented sparkling wines. Local judges. ▪ celiag@rsp.co.za ▪ www.winemag.co.za ▪ **T 021-530-3145** ▪ F 021-531-2212

Wine Magazine Value Awards SA judges gather annually to select the best value wines based on quality vs price. Results published in *Wine's Best Value Wine Guide*. ▪ celiag@rsp.co.za ▪ www.winemag.co.za ▪ **T 021-530-3145** ▪ F 021-531-2212

Wine Magazine FNB Private Clients Chenin Blanc Challenge Annual event in which wooded and unwooded chenins in the drier spectrum (max 20g/k sugar) are assessed by a mostly SA panel. ▪ celiag@rsp.co.za ▪ www.winemag.co.za ▪ **T 021-530-3145** ▪ F 021-531-2212

Wine Magazine Pick 'n Pay Shiraz Challenge Another SA *Wine*/Tops at Spar collaboration, uncovering benchmark SA wines made from shiraz/syrah. Local judges. ▪ celiag@rsp.co.za ▪ www.winemag.co.za ▪ **T 021-530-3145** ▪ F 021-531-2212

Winemakers' Choice Judged by selected panels of top winemakers, the prestigious Diamond Award goes to the winning wines, and a trophy to the best red and white on show. ▪ robyn@winemakerschoice.co.za or nan@winemakerschoice.co.za ▪ www.winemakerschoice.co.za ▪ **T 021-889-8479** ▪ F 021-889-8476

> **Note:** For a list of wines rated highest in selected professional tastings and competitions in the past year, plus our own 4½ and 5-star ratings, see Top Performers.

Wine Education

Cape Wine Academy Long-established (1979) general wine education body. Based in Stellenbosch and Johannesburg with satellites in Durban, Pretoria, Windhoek and Harare. Runs wine theory and tasting courses with examinations at several levels, from Introduction to SA Wine to Cape Wine Master, as well as skills workshops for front-of-house sales staff. The MD is Marilyn Cooper.
Stellenbosch ▪ www.capewineacademy.co.za ▪ **T 021-889-8844** ▪ F 021-889-7391 ▪ info@cwa.org.za ▪ Johannesburg T 011-783-4585 ▪ F 011-883-2356 ▪ busi.cwa@iafrica.com ▪ Durban T/F 031-564-5067

The Wine Ambassador thewineambassador@telkomsa.net ▪ www.thewineambassador.co.za ▪ **T 021-975-3906/ 084-499-6014**

Selected Wine Shops

The following retail outlets stock a wide range of fine-wines and/or provide specialised services to the wine-consuming public. 'Bricks-and-mortar' shops are listed first, by area, followed by on-line emporia.

Eastern Cape
Da Vino's (Port Elizabeth) ▪ T 041-583-2166 ▪ F 041-583-6220
Makro Port Elizabeth ▪ T 041-397-8000 ▪ F 041-397-8058
Picardi Rebel Port Elizabeth (Walmer) ▪ T 041-368-2840 ▪ F 041-368-2420
Picardi Rebel Port Elizabeth (Fig Tree Park) ▪ T/F 041-581-3177
Prestons (Walmer) ▪ T/F 041-581-1993
Spargs Liquor Mart (East London) ▪ T 043-748-1383 ▪ F 043-748-5059
Ultra Liquors East London ▪ T 043-743-5174/722-3476 ▪ F 043-743-4283
Ultra Liquors Newton Park ▪ T 041-364-1103 ▪ F 041-364-2277
Vintage Liquors (Port Alfred) ▪ T 046-624-3120 ▪ F 046-624-4419

Free State
Liquor World Bloemfontein T 051-434-1292 ▪ F 051-435-3074
Ultra Liquors Bloemfontein ▪ T 051-447-3328 ▪ F 051-447-3600

Garden Route
Picardi Rebel George ▪ T 044-887-0053 ▪ F 044-887-0054
Picardi Rebel Knysna ▪ T 044-382-3318 ▪ F 044-382-3319
Picardi Rebel Plettenberg Bay (Beacon Isle) ▪ T/F 044-533-1225
Picardi Rebel Plettenberg Bay (Main Str) ▪ T 044-533-1340 ▪ F 044-533-0574
The Lagoon Wine Shop (Plettenberg Bay) ▪ T 044-533-2440 ▪ F 044-533-2442
34° South Wine Shop (Knysna) ▪ T/ F 044-382-7331
Ultra Liquors George ▪ T 044-874-5514 ▪ F 044-874-5511

Gauteng
Alberts Liquors (Pretoria) ▪ T 012-543-0813
Alpha Liquor Store (Roodepoort) ▪ T 011-763-8740 ▪ F 011-763-8741
Bamboo-WINE+ (Melville) ▪ T 011-482-1020 ▪ F 011-482-5958
Bootleggers Liquor Specialist ▪ Booysens: T 011-493-2536 ▪ Fourways Crossing:
  T 011-465-9777 ▪ Glenanda: T 011-432-3570 ▪ Glenvista: T 011-432-3093 ▪ Irene:
  T 012-667-1907 ▪ Lombardy: T 011-882-6252
Cellar d'Or ▪ T 0861-235-527 ▪ F 011-465-9744
Central Liquors @ The Square (Boksburg) ▪ T 011-826-5070 ▪ F 011-826-7151
Glenfair Wine & Liquor (Pretoria) ▪ T 012-361-4509/4563 ▪ F 012-361-4509
John Wilson Sandton City ▪ T 011-783-7035 ▪ F 011-783-7036
Liquor Inn Heidelberg ▪ T 016-341-2343
Liquor World Camaro Square (Oakdene) ▪ T 011-436-1776
Liquor World Denver ▪ T 011-622-9494 ▪ F 011-622-4301
Liquor World East Rand (Boksburg) ▪ T 011-826-1420 ▪ F 011-826-1462
Liquor World Hillfox(Weltevreden Park) ▪ T 011-679-5670 ▪ F 011-475-5139
Liquor World Pretoria (Roseville) ▪ T 012-379-6050 ▪ F 012-379-7388
Liquor World Pretoria East ▪ T 012-809-0800 ▪ F 012-809-0985
Liquor World Springs ▪ T 011-817-1133 ▪ F 011-817-4702
Lynnridge Wine & Liquor (Lynnridge Mall) ▪ T/F 012-348-3456
Makro Centurion ▪ T 012-673-3734 ▪ F 012-665-1125
Makro Crown Mines ▪ T 011-309-1108 ▪ F 011-309-1089
Makro Germiston ▪ T 011-372-0313 ▪ F 011-453-1698
Makro Strubens Valley (Roodepoort) ▪ T 011-671-8422 ▪ F 011-671-8480
Makro Wonderboom (Annlin West) ▪ T 012-567-9158 ▪ F 012-567-9038
Makro Woodmead ▪ T 011-208-9152 ▪ F 011-208-9092
Manuka Wine Boutique Killarney Mall (Jhb) ▪ T 011-646-9600 ▪ F 011-646-9607
Manuka Wine Boutique Woodhill (Pretoria East) ▪ T 012-97-4669 ▪ F 012-997-1480
Morara Wines & Spirits Emporium (Soweto) ▪ T 011-982-2290 ▪ F 011-982-3734
Norman Goodfellow's Hyde Park ▪ T 011-325-6462 ▪ F 011-325-5450
Norman Goodfellow's (Johannesburg) ▪ T 011-788-4814 ▪ F 011-442-8868
Picardi Rebel Bedfordview ▪ T 011-615-9160 ▪ F 011-622-2475
Picardi Rebel Blackheath ▪ T 011-678-6817 ▪ F 011-678-5017
Picardi Rebel Fourways ▪ T 011-465-6921 ▪ F 011-465-6922
Picardi Rebel Honeydew ▪ T 011-475-4658 ▪ F 011-675 6404
Picardi Rebel Morning Glen (Gallo Manor) ▪ T 011-802-0964 ▪ F 011-802-0965
Picardi Rebel Northmead ▪ T 011-849-5392 ▪ F 011-849-7332
Picardi Rebel Sandton ▪ T 011-884-2151 ▪ F 011- 884-1067
Rivonia Cellars ▪ T 011-803-6121/2 ▪ F 011-803-7600
Solly Kramers Parkview ▪ T 011-486-2584 ▪ F 011-646-3663
Ultra Liquors Corlett Drive ▪ T 011-887-1001/2/3 ▪ F 011-887-4947
Ultra Liquors Eloffsdal (Pretoria) ▪ T 012-335-2780 ▪ F 012-335-5820
Ultra Liquors Hazelwood (Pretoria) ▪ T 012-460-6012 ▪ F 012-460-6831
Vintages-The Wine Seller (Sandton) ▪ T 011-784-8676/7 ▪ F 011-784-8674
Wine Direct (Midrand) ▪ T 011-315-3088 ▪ F 011-315-3098

KwaZulu-Natal
Blue Bottles Wine Cellar (Shelly Beach) ▪ T 039-315-1336
Buxtons La Cave Liquors ▪ F 031-572-2619 ▪ Umhlanga: T 031-561-6792 ▪ La Lucia
  Mall: T 031-572-6073
Liberty Liquors (Durban) ▪ T 031-303-9857 ▪ F 031-303-9864
Liquor World Durban ▪ T 031-902-8144/912-3730 ▪ F 031-912-3730
Liquor World Mt Edgecombe ▪ T 031-502-5380 ▪ F 031-502-6555
Makro Pietermaritzburg ▪ T 033-846-3600 ▪ F 033-386-8120
Makro Rossburgh ▪ T 031-480-7096 ▪ F 031-480-7060
Makro Springfield ▪ T 031-203-2827 ▪ F 031-203-5905

Marriot Gardens Liquor Store (Greyville) ▪ T 031-309-2079 ▪ F 031-309-2097
Parklane Cellars (Pietermaritzburg) ▪ T 033-342-3487 ▪ F 033-342-6413
The Village Vineyard (Kloof Village Mall) ▪ T -031-764-6679 ▪ F 031-764-7196
The Wine Cellar (Rosetta) ▪ T/F -033-267-7044
Ultra Liquors New Germany ▪ T 031-705-3777 ▪ F 031-705-6640
Ultra Liquors Tollgate (Mayville) ▪ T 031-261-2233/67 ▪ F 031-261-7980
Ultra Liquors Westville ▪ T 031-266-4364/60 ▪ F 031-266-4300

Limpopo
Liquor World Polokwane (Magnesiet Str) ▪ T 015-298-8800 ▪ F 015-298-8468
Liquor World Polokwane (Nikkel Str) ▪ T 015-292-2354 ▪ F 015-292-2352
Liquor World Tzaneen ▪ T 015-307-1254 ▪ F 015-307-1767

Mpumalanga
Big M Liquor Store (Delmas) ▪ T 013-665-2461
Hi-Octane Store (Secunda) ▪ T 017-634-7033
Liquor World Nelspruit ▪ T 013-753-2146 ▪ T 013-752-2915
Liquor World Hazyview ▪ T 013-737-6314 ▪ T 013-737-6315
Windmill Wine Shop (R536 between Hazyview & Sabie) ▪ T 013-737-8175 ▪ F 013-737-8966

Northern Cape
Liquor World Kimberley ▪ T 053-832-0878 ▪ T 053-832-0902
Zebrani Liquor City (Upington) ▪ T 054-331-2831 ▪ F 054-332-7928

North West
De Wijnwinkel & Deli (Wolmaransstad) ▪ T 083-262-0387 ▪ F 018-596-2890

Western Cape
Aroma Fine Wine Centres Constantia (Aroma Alphen Cellars): ▪ T 021-794-8693 ▪ Canal Walk: T 021-551-7511 ▪ Somerset West (Central): T 021-852-7551 ▪ Somerset West (Waterstone Village): T 021-850-0603
Bergkelder Vinoteque Wine Bank (Stellenbosch) ▪ T 021-809-8283 ▪ F 021-883-9533
Breede Valley Wines (Robertson) See A-Z section for details
Caroline's Fine Wine Cellar ▪ City Bowl: T 021-419-8984 ▪ F 021-419-8985 ▪ V&A Waterfront: T 021-425-5701 ▪ F 021-425-5702
Lisa's Little Wine Shop (pvsly Cellar in the City) (Kalk Bay, Cape Town) ▪ T 021-788-9116 ▪ M 072-431-4100
Chapmans Peak Wine & Spirits (Hout Bay, Cape Town) ▪ T 021-790-1088 ▪ F 021-790-1089
Darling Wine & Art Shop (Darling) ▪ T 022-492-3740 ▪ F 022-492-3524
De Oude Paarl Wijn Boutique (Paarl) ▪ T 021-872-1002 ▪ F 021-872-1003
De Wijngarten Boetiek (Bonnievale) ▪ T 023-616-2367 ▪ F 023-616-3160
Donvino, The Wine Merchant (Bellville) ▪ T 021-914-6952 ▪ F 086-684-7107
Grand World of Wines (Cape Town) ▪ T 021-412-9302 ▪ F 021-412-9305
Harbour Road Wines (Kleinmond) ▪ T 028-271-5151 ▪ F 086-620-5251
I Love Wine (Paarl) ▪ See A-Z section for details
La Cotte Inn Wine Sales (Franschhoek) ▪ T 021-876-3775 ▪ F 021-876-3036
La Vallée (Glencairn, Cape Town) ▪ T/F 021-782-7005
Liquor World Cape Town (Milnerton) ▪ T 021-551-9080 ▪ F 021-555-0223
Liquor World Cape Gate (Brackenfell) ▪ T 021-908-8000 ▪ F 021-981-0098
Liquor World George ▪ T 044-874-1370 ▪ F 044-874-1377
Main Ingredient (Cape Town) ▪ T 021-439 5169 ▪ F 021-439-5169
Makro Milnerton ▪ T 021-550-6348 ▪ F 021-550-6362
Makro Ottery ▪ T 021-703-6852 ▪ F 021-703-2508
Manuka Wine Boutique (Noordhoek) ▪ T 021-789-0898 ▪ F 086-684-2635
Manuka Wine Boutique (Somerset West) ▪ T 021-851-6060 ▪ F 021-851-9145
Manuka Wine Boutique (Stellenbosch) ▪ T 083-657-6958

Manuka Wines Boutique (Tokai) ▪ T 021-701-2046 ▪ F 021-701-0386
Manuka Wine Boutique (Tygervalley) ▪ T 021-914-7242 ▪ F 021-914-9561
Michelangelo Wine Company (Stellenbosch, see under Vrede Farm in A-Z section) ▪
T 021-865-2815 ▪ T/F 021-865-2440
Mooiberge (Stellenbosch) ▪ T/F 021-881-3222
Palmer Street Wine Merchants (Muizenberg Village) ▪ T 021-788-2507/082-851-
0494
Picardi Rebel Cape Town ▪ T 021-425-1639/425-1664 ▪ F 021-421-5841
Picardi Rebel Claremont (Main Rd) ▪ T 021-671-9918/671-9611 ▪ F 021-683-9025
Picardi Rebel Durbanville ▪ T 021-976-5318 ▪ F 021-976-5341
Picardi Rebel Longbeach Mall (Noordhoek) ▪ T 021-785-3323 ▪ F 021-785-3318
Picardi Rebel Parklands ▪ T 021-556-2675 ▪ F 021-556-2680
Picardi Rebel Rosmead (Claremont) ▪ T 021-683-1406 ▪ F 021-674-2094
Picardi Rebel Somerset West ▪ T 021-852-2580 ▪ F 021-852-3519
Picardi Rebel Sun Valley ▪ T 021-785-2149 ▪ F 021-785-2942
Picardi Rebel Tokai ▪ T 021-712-5082/712-5032 ▪ F 021-712-2536
Picardi Rebel Tygervalley ▪ T 021-914-1649/914-1650 ▪ F 021-914-2420
Riedel@Aroma (Constantia) ▪ T 021-794-8693 ▪ F 021-794-8694
Rubin's Liquors (Cape Town) ▪ T 021-425-4692 ▪ F 021-419-9405
Simon's Town Bottle Store (Cape Town) ▪ T 021-786-1438 ▪ F 021-786-1440
Spier Wine Centre (Stellenbosch) ▪ T 021-809-1143 ▪ F 021-809-1144
Stellenbosch Wine Export Centre ▪ T/F 021-883-3814
Steven Rom Wine Merchants & Exporters ▪ Cape Town: Sea Point T 021-439-6043 ▪
F 021-434-0401 ▪ Three Anchor Bay T 021-434-0001 ▪ Kloof Street T 021-424-8476 ▪
Stellenbosch (The Cape Grape & Wine Co): T 0860-10-30-34 / 021-905-0290 ▪ F 021-
905-0293
The Cape Grape & Wine Company See Steven Rom Wine Merchants & Exporters
The Noble Grape (Constantia) ▪ T/F 021-794-6899/082-331-1165
The Vineyard Connection (Muldersvlei) ▪ T 021-884-4360 ▪ F 021-884-4361
The Wine Shop at Constantia Uitsig (Constantia) ▪ T 021-794-1810 ▪ F 021-794-1812
Ultra Liquors Goodwood ▪ T 021-591-5581 ▪ F 021-591-8492
Ultra Liquors Greenpoint ▪ T 021-434-4847/4302/4838 ▪ F 021-434-7548
Ultra Liquors Parow ▪ T 021-930-2415/6 ▪ F 021-930-4007
Ultra Liquors Wynberg ▪ T 021-762-5885/1473 ▪ F 021-761-6005
Vaughan Johnson's Wine & Cigar Shop See A-Z section for details
Vino Pronto (Cape Town) ▪ T 021-424-5587 ▪ F 021-423-5707
Wine Cellar (incl insulated/secure maturation cellars; Cape Town) ▪ T 021-448-4105
Wine & Company (Hermanus) ▪ T 028-313-2047 ▪ F 028-312-4029
Wine Concepts ▪ Newlands: T 021-671-9030 ▪ F 021-671-9031 Gardens: T 021-426-
4401 ▪ F 021-426-4402
Wines@Oude Libertas (Stellenbosch) ▪ T 021-886-7404 ▪ F 021-886-7405
Wine Village Hermanus ▪ T 028-316-3988 ▪ F 028-316-3989

Online Wine Shops
Cape Wine Direct ▪ www.capewinedirect.co.za
Cybercellar.com ▪ www.cybercellar.com
eWine ▪ www.ewine.co.za
Getwine ▪ www.getwine.co.za
I Love Wine ▪ www.ilovewine.co.za
Manuka Wine Exports ▪ www.manuka.co.za
Meerlust Wine Shop ▪ http://shop.meerlust.com
Michelangelo Int. Wine Awards Wine Shop ▪ www.michelangeloawards.com
Morgenster Wine & Olive Product Shop ▪ http://shop.morgenster.co.za
The Wine Registry ▪ www.thewineregistry.co.za
Wine Cellar ▪ www.winecellar.co.za
Wine-Club ▪ www.wine-club.co.za

Wine Direct ▪ www.winedirectonline.co.za
WINEmag.co.za Online Auctions ▪ www.winemag.co.za/auction
Wine Village Hermanus ▪ www.wine-village.co.za
WineWeb ▪ www.wineweb.co.za

A-Code Numbers & Certification Codes

Many wines appear on the market under brand names, with, at first glance, no reference to their producers or purveyors. However, consumers need not buy 'blind', and may trace a wine's provenance by checking the official 'A-number' which appears on the bottle or pack. This identity code tells you either who has produced the wine, or who has acquired it. In the latter case, an enquiry to the purveyor should elicit the source. The list keeps growing and being revised, and is too lengthy to reproduce in this guide. It is administered by Marian Honing, Department of Agriculture, Directorate Plant Health & Quality, Pvt Bag X5015, Stellenbosch, 7599; marianh@nda.agric.za; T 021-809-1687; F 021-887-6396/2. Via the online SAWIS portal (**www.sawis.co.za**), it is possible to search the list of A-codes, as well as the certification codes issued for each wine by the Wine & Spirit Board, for details about the production area, variety and vintage. Navigate to Statistics, Searches, and see under Wine Seal and Label 'A' Number.

VINTAGES

Recent Cape Vintages

SA wines do not exhibit the major vintage variations seen in cooler northern climes. There are, nevertheless, perceptible differences from year to year. Dry, hot summers are the norm but a variety of factors make generalisations difficult and dangerous.

2007 Started hot and fast, ended with rain & lower temperatures. High hopes for elegant, structured whites, notably sauvignon; smaller red-grape berries resulted intense colour and fruit concentration, especially for cab and shiraz.

2006 Excellent and largely problem free (though complicated by Western Cape power cuts). Perhaps the best white-wine vintage in a decade — particularly expressive sauvignons and chenins. Fleshy, mild-tannined reds, with lower alcohols all round.

2005 Short, early and particularly challenging. Bone-dry winter followed by early-season rains, sparking disease and excessive plant vigour; then prolonged heatwaves. Concentrated if alcoholic reds; whites mostly average, some stellar exceptions.

2004 Long and late, bedevilled by uneven berry-set and an early aroma-stripping heatwave. Yet cooler dry conditions yielded healthy, elegant, often ageworthy wines with lower alcs and yielding tannins. Chardonnay, merlot and shiraz especially promising.

2003 Outstanding, especially for reds — concentrated and structured, and, on current evidence, slow to show their best. General euphoria tempered by some difficulties with late-ripening varieties in certain areas.

2002 Challenging and patchy, marred by disease and high harvest temperatures. Generally, individual producers' track record rather than variety or terroir should guide the purchase/cellaring decision.

2001 Hot, dry, largely disease-free vintage; some excellent reds — fruity and concentrated, possibly long-lived. White-wine producers who picked between heatwaves delivered flavourful if alcoholic wines.

2000 Another hot year with predictably powerful, concentrated reds, sometimes with big tannins. The best should keep very well. Whites, by contrast, generally less stellar and not for long ageing.

1999 Near-perfect ripening conditions meant fat, alcoholic reds with ripe fruit for earlier drinking. Some attractive, fruity chardonnay, semillon and chenin, but generally not too much excitement.

Older Vintages

1998 Excellent red vintage, enough fruit for extended cellaring; whites generally not for keeping. **1997** Among coolest, latest on record. Supple, elegant reds; some excellent, stylish whites. **1996** Generally awkward reds, not for keeping; whites, except for top NLHs, best drunk up. **1995** For many, vintage of the 90s. Concentrated reds, maturing spectacularly. **1994** Hottest, driest vintage in decades; variable quality; new-clone cabs, early ripening reds fared well. **1993** Without serious mishaps; some excellent sauvignons; above-average reds. **1992** Coolish, favouring whites, especially sauvignon; reds (especially pinotage) very good; **1991** Dry, warm to hot, favouring early to mid-season ripeners; some long-lasting reds. **1990** Uneven year, alternately cool, warm; average whites and reds. The **1980s**: even years (82, 84, 86) usually more favourable for reds; uneven years, marginally cooler, favoured whites, but 'white' years 87 and, especially, 89 produced remarkable reds. The **1970s**: again, even years generally favoured reds. Best was 74; but top wines from some other vintages still delicious. The **1960**s and earlier yielded some astonishingly long-lived wines, prompting a new look at the traditional 'dikvoet' winemaking style.

SA Wine Styles

Blanc de blancs White wine made from white grapes only; also used for champagne and méthode cap classique.

Blanc fumé or **fumé blanc** Dry white from sauvignon, not necessarily finished in wood (nor smoked, smoky).

Blanc de noir A pink wine (shades range from off-white through peach to pink) made from red grapes. May be labelled 'vin gris'.

Blend See Varietal wine and Cape blend

Brut See sugar or sweetness, sparkling wine.

Cap classique See Méthode cap classique.

Cape blend Evolving term, increasingly used to denote a (red) blend with pinotage, the 'local' grape making up 30%-70% of the assemblage; sometimes simply a blend showing a distinct 'Cape' character.

Carbonated See Sparkling wine.

Cultivar Grape variety (a contraction of 'cultivated variety').

Cuvée French term for the blend of a wine.

Demi-sec See Sugar or sweetness.

Dessert wine A sweet wine, often to accompany the dessert but sometimes pleasurably prior, as in the famous Sauternes/foie gras combo.

Dry to sweet See sugar or sweetness.

Estate wine Term now reserved for wine originating from an officially registered 'unit for the production of estate wine' (see under Industry Organisations for complete list). Fruit and, with some historical exceptions, vinification, maturation and bottling must from/on the 'estate' in question.

Fortified wines Increased in alcoholic strength by the addition of spirit, by SA law to minimum 15% alcohol by volume.

Grand cru See Premier Grand Cru

Jerepiko or **jerepigo** Red or white wine, produced without fermentation; grape juice is fortified with grape spirit, preventing fermentation; very sweet with considerable unfermented grape flavours.

Kosher See Winemaking terms section

Late Harvest Sweet wine from late -harvested and therefore sweeter grapes. See Sugar or sweetness.

Méthode cap classique (MCC) See Sparkling wine.

Noble Late Harvest (NLH) Sweet dessert wine (still, perlé or sparkling) exhibiting a noble rot (botrytis) character, from grapes infected by the *botrytis cinerea* fungus. This mould, in warm, misty autumn weather, attacks the skins of ripe grapes, causing much of the juice to evaporate. As the berries wither, their sweetness and flavour become powerfully concentrated. SA law dictates that grapes for NLH must be harvested at a minimum of 28° Balling and residual sugar must exceed 50g/ℓ.

Nouveau Term originated in Beaujolais for fruity young and light red, usually from gamay and made by the carbonic maceration method. Bottled a few weeks after vintage to capture the youthful, fresh flavour of fruit and yeasty fermentation.

Perlant, perlé, pétillant Lightly sparkling, carbonated wine.

Port Fortified dessert with improving quality record in Cape since late 1980s, partly through efforts of SA Port Producers' Association which recommends use of word 'Cape' to identify the local product. Following are SAPPA-defined styles: **Cape White**: non-muscat grapes, wood-aged min 6 mths, any size vessel; **Cape Ruby**: blended, fruity, components aged min 6 mths, up to 3 years depending on size of vessel. Average age min 1 year. **Cape Vintage**: fruit of one harvest; dark, full-bodied, vat-aged (any size); **Cape Vintage Reserve**: fruit of one harvest in year of 'recognised quality'. Preferably aged min 1 year, vats of any size, sold only in glass; **Cape Late Bottled Vintage** (LBV): fruit of single 'year of quality', full-bodied, slightly tawny colour, aged 3-6 years (of which min 2 years in oak); **Cape Tawny**: wood-matured, amber-orange (tawny) colour, smooth, slightly nutty taste (white grapes not permitted); **Cape Dated Tawny**: single-vintage tawny.

Premier Grand Cru Unlike in France, not a quality rating in SA – usually an austerely dry white.

Residual sugar See Sugar or sweetness.

Rosé Pink wine, made from red or a blend of red and white grapes. The red grape skins are removed before the wine takes up too much colouring.

Single vineyard wine A new classification for wines from officially registered vineyards, no larger than 6 ha in size and planted with a single variety.

Sparkling wine Bubbly, or 'champagne', usually white but sometimes rosé and even red, given its effervescence by carbon dioxide – allowed to escape in the normal wine-making process. **Champagne** undergoes its second fermentation in the bottle. Under an agreement with France, SA does not use the term which describes the sparkling wines from the Champagne area. Instead, **méthode cap classique** (MCC) is the SA term to describe sparkling wines made by the classic method. **Charmat** undergoes its second, bubble-forming fermentation in a tank and is bottled under pressure. **Carbonated** sparklers are made by the injection of carbon dioxide bubbles (as in fizzy soft drinks). See also Sugar or sweetness.

Special Late Harvest (SLH) SA designation for a lighter dessert style wine. There is no longer a legal stipulation for residual sugar content, but if the RS is below 20g/ℓ, the label must state 'extra dry', 'dry', 'semi-dry' or 'sweet', as the case may be. The minimum alcohol content has been raised from 10% to 11% by volume.

Stein Semi-sweet white wine, usually a blend and often confused with steen, a grape variety (chenin blanc), though most steins are made partly from steen grapes.

Sugar or sweetness In still wines: extra-dry or bone-dry wines have less than 2.5g/ℓ residual sugar, undetectable to the taster. A wine legally is dry up to 5g/ℓ. Taste buds will begin picking up a slight sweetness, or softness, in a wine – depending on its acidity – at about 6g/ℓ, when it is still off-dry. By about 8–9g/ℓ a definite sweetness can usually be noticed. However, an acidity of 8–9g/ℓ can render a sweet wine fairly crisp even with a sugar content of 20g/ℓ plus. Official sweetness levels in SA wine are:

Still wines	Sugar (g/ℓ)	Sparkling wines	Sugar (g/ℓ)
Extra dry	≤ 2.5	Extra dry/brut	≤ 15
Dry	≤ 5	Dry/sec	15–35
Semi-dry	5 ≤ 12	Semi-sweet/demi-sec	35–50
Semi-sweet	5 30	Sweet/doux	50
Late Harvest	≥ 20		
Special Late Harvest (SLH)	–		
Natural Sweet (or Sweet Natural)	20		
Noble Late Harvest	50		
Naturally dried grape wine (straw wine)	30		

Varietal wine From single variety of grape. Recently amended legislation requires the presence in the wine of 85% of the stated variety or vintage (previously 75% if for local market, 85% if exported). Blends may name component parts only if those components were vinified separately, prior to blending; then they are listed with the larger contributor(s) named first. If any one of the blend partners is less than 20%, percentages for all the varieties must be given. Proposed amendments will allow the blending of wines vinified separately in any recognised WO area (previously WO 'districts' only). Component areas may be named, as above (except the threshold is 30%).

Vintage In SA primarily used to denote year of harvest. Not a substantive quality classification (a 'vintage' port in Europe means one from an officially declared great port grape year).

Wine & Food

Perhaps one of the most stressful parts of eating out is choosing the most suitable wine to accompany the dish you have ordered. When pairing food and wine, try to balance and harmonise flavours, textures, intensity and taste. The old rule of thumb of red wine with meat and white with fish is a good guideline but inflexible when accommodating the multi-cultural taste influences of modern cuisine with its innovations in sauces and use of unusual ingredients.

As a general rule, serve dry before sweet, light-bodied before full-bodied and low-alcohol before high-alcohol wines. Think carefully about the 'star of the show': if this wine is complex and multi-layered then the food should be simple but of the same quality, so as not to compete on your palate. A carefully matured bordeaux-style blend from a good vintage matches a simple chateaubriand superbly but is wasted on a pepper steak with beetroot mousse and wasabi foam. When the food is the star, the reverse applies: the wine should step back and support the food.

When pairing food and wine, try to bring three qualities into harmony and balance: Firstly, match volatile components like aromas and flavours; then complement that which contributes to palate structure and taste (sweet, sour, bitter or salty); finally, address the tactile sensation arising from both the food and wine's weight and texture (eg alcohol and tannins).

There are two ways of achieving this. Either mirror and match the food, and succeed in reflecting the character and flavour intensity of the food with that of the wine. Both should reinforce each other as an intensely flavoured game dish reinforces a spicy and wild roaring shiraz/syrah. Or contrast the components: a spicy hot ostrich curry could be served with a low-alcohol fruity riesling, gewürztraminer or similar wine which gains its strength from the sweetness and the balancing acidity that is a hallmark of its style. The sweetness of the wine would counteract the spicy heat of the dish and the acidity would cleanse your palate and leave appetite for more.

The three harmonies

Flavour intensity and aroma Flavour intensity is different to weight. Cooked basmati rice is heavy in weight but almost neutral in flavour; freshly picked tomatoes are the opposite. So it is with wines; rieslings are light, intensely flavoured wines whereas chardonnays are often heavy wines that are lightly flavoured.

Frequently the dish's main ingredient is not the dominant flavour. With ox tongue in an oxtail sauce, focus on pairing the wine to the intense sauce, not the meat.

Weight Weight is very important, being the common denominator in your food and wine equation. In a wine, weight generally derives from its alcoholic strength and residual sugar.

The weight of a dish should be matched by the alcoholic strength and depth of the wine. Rich heavyweight foods, like red meat casseroles, need full-bodied wines, like a powerful red. Remember, the wine's weight, not its colour, is the most important consideration. So, if you are not a fan of full-bodied reds, a white equivalent will work just as well. For more delicate food, the same rule applies: do not drown a West Coast sole by partnering it with an overpowering heavyweight shiraz; rather float it on a delicate white or a slightly chilled, low-tannin, low-alcohol red.

Texture of food and wine Do not mistake texture in food for taste. Texture is a tactile sensation like the mouth-puckering astringency of tannins, the burning sensation of chilli or the sandy feeling of humus; it reacts differently with both taste sensation and alcohol.

Chilli gets amplified when served with high-alcohol wines. If you are unhappy with your in-laws, cook them a spicy hot red beef curry and serve it with a 15.5% alc zinfandel; I doubt you will ever have to cook for them again.

Tannins — derived from the grape's seeds and skins, and from oak barrel maturation — are, at tolerable levels, positive in wine. But they become coarse and mouth-puckering as your food's saltiness increases. Blunt the edginess of tannic wines like young pinotages or cabernets by pairing them with fatty foods like lamb or marbled beef.

The four taste components

Sweetness Perceived sweetness in wine should equal perceived sweetness in food. Try not to serve an ultra-dry acidic sauvignon with a dessert or some braised meats; the food's sweetness will expose the wine's worst side by making it taste bitter and tart. Sweetness in wine can also balance peppery or chilli hotness. One of my most unusual yet favourite combinations is steak with a very hot black pepper sauce served with young vintage port. And a classic food and wine pairing is an off-dry riesling with spicy hot Thai dishes, or try a rich, wooded chenin.

The acidity of most sweet wines makes them fantastic partners for rich foods like pâtés, cheeses, desserts and other indulgences.

Acidity Make acidity in a wine your friend: it cuts through layers of fat like a laser. Riesling makes the oily avocado dance over your palate and cleanses it afterwards; a crisp powerful chenin lifts heavily buttered crayfish effortlessly whereas a heavily oaked chardonnay would work well but leave you the after-effects of the combined richness.

Food and wine can both have acidity. With highly acidic food like tomatoes, citrus fruits and green apples, look for wines which can rise to the challenge. Cool-climate wines have more acidity than warm-climate ones and some grape varieties – such as sauvignon, chenin and riesling – have more acidity than others. Tart foods reduce the apparent acidity in wines by making them mellower and richer.

Saltiness When serving salty food, do not serve a tannic, high-alcohol red: it might spoil things. Rather go for a low-tannin, loosely structured wine: the salt in the food will keep the structure of the wine together. Salt is something that you normally do not taste in wine but salt from food magically transforms wine's tactile components by increasing the presence of tannins and alcohol.

If you are a salt lover, choose wines with higher acidity as this suppresses the saltiness of a dish. A dry, racy young riesling or sauvignon with salty canapés before dinner is a sure way to fire up your taste buds.

Sweetness can balance and enhance saltiness. A sauternes or a similar botrytis/Noble Late Harvest-style white famously provides the perfect match to intensely salty roquefort cheese.

Bitterness Bitter foods can be masked with a bit of residual sugar whereas the astringent feeling of harsh tannins tends to be enhanced by them.

Foods that challenge sommeliers

Artichokes are the ultimate test, as they contain a substance called cynarin; this changes the taste of the surrounding food and wine to sweet or bitter, depending on the taster. A matured fruity riesling, sauvignon, a dry rosé or perhaps pinot gris/grigio can work here. Fish with a lot of iodine – cod, haddock or mackerel – clash with red wines as their tannins make the wine taste rusty. Eggs coat the palate and kill flavours but he who quaffs wine with his breakfast of Eggs Benedict has bigger things to worry about.

Bon appetit!

Jörg Pfützner
Head sommelier, Aubergine Restaurant, Cape Town

words &
PHRASES

Winetasting Terms

Short of a ready description? Here are a few frequently-used words, phrases and explanations that may be helpful. See also Winemaking terms; SA wine styles.

Accessible, approachable Flavours and feel of the wine are harmonious, easily recognised; it is ready to drink.

Aftertaste The lingering flavours and impressions of a wine; its persistence — the longer, the better.

Alcoholic 'Hot' or, in excess, burning character caused by imbalanced or excessive alcohol. Also simply spiritous.

Astringent Mouth-puckering sensation in the mouth, associated with high tannin (and sometimes acid); also bitter, sharp.

Aroma Smells in the bouquet, or nose, especially the odours associated with the grape rather than the winemaking process.

Attack First sensations on palate/nose — pungent, aggressive, quiet etc.

Austere Usually meaning unyielding, sometimes harsh. Sometimes, more favourably, to imply a notable restraint/refinement.

Backbone The wine is well formed, firm, not flabby or insipid.

Baked 'Hot', earthy quality. Usually from scorched/shrivelled grapes which have been exposed too long to the sun, or from too warm a barrel fermentation, especially in some whites.

Balance Desirable attribute. The wine's chief constituents — alcohol, acid, tannin, fruit and wood (where used) — are in harmony.

Bead Bubbles in sparkling wine; a fine, long-lasting bead is the most desirable. See also Mousse.

Big Expansive in the mouth, weighty, full-bodied, as a result of high alcohol or fruit concentration.

Bite or **grip** Imparted by tannins and acids (and alcohol in fortified wines); important in young wines designed for ageing. If overdone can impart undesirable bitterness, harshness or spiry 'glow'.

Bitter Sensation perceived mainly on the back of the tongue, and in the finish of the wine. Usually unpleasant, though an accepted if not immediately admired character of certain Italian wines. Sometimes more positively associated with the taste of a specific fruit or nut, such as cherry-kernel or almond.

Body Fullness on the palate.

Botrytis/ed Exhibits a noble rot/botrytis character, from grapes infected by the *botrytis cinerea* fungus.

Bottle age Negative or positive, depending on context. Positively describes development of aromas/flavours (ie complexity) as wine moves from youth to maturity. Muchprized attribute in fine whites and reds. Negatively, bottle age results in a wine with stale, empty or even off odours.

Buttery Flavour and texture associated with barrel-fermented white wines, especially chardonnays; rich, creamy smoothness.

Charming Usually used in the context of lighter, simpler wines. Sometimes synonymous with 'sweet' (both as in 'sugary' and 'dear').

Claret Another name for a dry red bordeaux or bordeaux-like red

Classic Showing characteristics of the classics of Bordeaux, Burgundy etc; usually implying balance, elegance, subtlety.

Coarse Rough, unbalanced tannins, acid, alcohol or oak.

Complexity Strong recommendation. A complex wine has several layers of flavour, usually developing with age/maturation. See Bottle age.

Concentration See Intensity.

Confected Over-elaborately constructed, artificial, forced; also overly sweet.

Corked Wine is faulty; its flavours have been tainted by yeast, fungal or bacterial infections, often but not necessarily from the cork. It smells damp and mouldy in its worst stages – but sometimes it's barely detectable. In a restaurant, a corked wine should be rejected and returned immediately; producers are honour-bound to replace corked wine.

Creamy Not literally creamy, of course; more a silky, buttery feel and texture.

Crisp Refers to acidity. Positively, means fresh, clean; negatively, too tart, sharp.

Deep and depth Having many layers; intense; also descriptive of a serious wine.

Dense Well-padded texture, flavour-packed.

Deposits (also sediment or crust) Tasteless and harmless tartrates, acid crystals or tannin in older red wines. Evidence that wine has not been harshly fined, filtered or cold-stabilised.

Dried out Bereft of fruit, harder constituents remaining; tired.

Earthy Usually positive, wine showing its origins from soil, minerally, damp leaves, mushrooms etc.

Easy Undemanding (and hopefully inexpensive).

Elegant Stylish, refined, 'classic'.

Esters Scents and smells usually generated by alcohols and acids in wine. A wine may be 'estery' when these characteristics are prominent.

Extract An indication of the 'substance' of a wine, expressed as sugar-free or total extract (which would include some sugars). 18g/ℓ would be low, light; anything much above 23g/ℓ in whites is significant; the corresponding threshold for reds is around 30g/ℓ.

Fat Big, full, ample in the mouth.

Finesse Graceful, polished. Nothing excessive.

Finish The residual sensations – tastes and textures – after swallowing. Should be pleasant (crisp, lively) and enduring, not short, dull or flat. See also Length.

Firm Compact, has good backbone.

Flabby Usually, lacking backbone, especially acid.

Flat Characterless, unexciting, lacks acid. Or bubbly which has lost its fizz.

Fleshy Very positive, meaning a wine is well fleshed out with texture and grape flavours.

Flowery Floral, flower-like (i.e. the smell of rose, honeysuckle, jasmine etc). Distinct from 'fruity' (ie smell/taste of papaya, cantaloupe, grape! etc)

Forward rather than shy; advancing in age too; mature.

Fresh Lively, youthful, invigorating. Closely related to the amount of acid in the wine and absence of oxidative character: a big, intensely sweet dessert without a backbone of acidity will taste flat and sickly; enough acid and the taste is fresh and uncloying.

Fruity See Flowery.

Full High in alcohol and extract.

Gamey Overripe, decadent; not universally unattractive.

Gravel/ly With suggestions of minerally, earthy quality; also firm texture.

Green Usually unripe, sour; sometimes simply youthful.

Grip Often almost literally gripping, firm on palate, in finish. Acid, tannin, alcohol are contributors.

Heady Usually refers to the smell of a wine. High in alcohol; intense, high-toned.

Herbaceous Grassy, hay-like, heathery; can also indicate under-ripeness.

Hollow Lacking substance, flavours.

Honey or **honeyed** Sometimes literally a honey/beeswax taste or flavour; a sign of developing maturity in some varieties or more generally a sign of bottle age.

Hot Burning sensation of alcohol in finish.

Intensity No flab, plenty of driving flavour; also deep colour.

Lean Thin, mean, lacking charm of ample fruit; also, more positively, compact, sinewy.

Lees/leesy Taste-imparting dead yeast cells (with grape skins and other solid matter) remaining with wine in tank/barrel (or bottle in the case of *méthode champenoise* *e* sparkling wines) after fermentation. The longer the wine is 'on its lees' (sur lie) the more richness and flavour it should absorb.

Light/lite Officially wines under 10% alcohol by volume, also light in body (and often short on taste); a health-conscious trend in both reds and whites.

Lively Bouncy, fresh flavours.

Long or **length** Enduring; wine's flavours reverberate in the palate long after swallowing.

Maderised Oxidised and flat; colour is often brownish. Over-mature.

Meaty Sometimes suggesting a general savouriness; but also literally the aroma of meat – raw, smoked etc.

Mousse Fizz in sparkling wines; usually refers also to quality, size and effervescence of the bubbles. See also Bead.

Mouthfeel, mouthfilling Texture; feel; racy, crispness (fine with appropriate dishes) or generous, supple, smooth.

Neutral What it says, neither here nor there.

New World Generally implies accessible, bold, often extrovert (in terms of fruit and use of oak). **Old World** embraces terms like subtle, complex, less oaky, more varied and generally more vinous (than fruity). See also Classic.

Oaky Having exaggerated oak aromas/flavours (vanilla, spice, char, woodsmoke etc). Oak balanced by fruit in young wines may lessen with age, but over-oaked young wines (where fruit is not in balance) will become over-oaked old wines.

Palate Combination of flavour, taste and texture of a wine.

Pebbly See Gravelly.

Perfumed or **scented** Strong fragrances (fruity, flowery, animal etc)

Plump Well fleshed in a charming, cherubic way.

Porty Heavy, over-ripe, stewed; a negative in unfortified wine.

Rich Flavourful, intense, generous. Not necessarily sweet.

Robust Strapping, full-bodied (but not aggressive).

Rough Bull-in-a-china-shop wine, or throat sand-papering quality.

Round Well balanced, without gawkiness or jagged edges.

Sharp or **tart** All about acid, usually unbalanced. But occasionally sharpish, fresh wine is right for the occasion.

Short or **quick** Insubstantial wine, leaving little impression.

Simple One-dimensional or no flavour excitement.

Stalky Unripe, bitter, stemmy.

Stewed Over-ripe, cooked, soft, soggy fruit.

Structure Vague word, usually refers to the wine's make up (acid, tannin, alcohol) in relation to its ageing ability; if a wine is deemed to have 'the structure to age' it suggests these principal preservatives are in place.

Stylish Classy, distinguished; also voguish.

Supple Very desirable (not necessarily subtle), yielding, refined texture and flavours. See also Mouthfeel.

Tannic Tannins are prominent in the wine, imparting, positively, a mouth-puckering, grippy, tangy quality; negatively, a harsh, unyielding character.

Tension Racy, nervous fruity-acid play on the palate.

Terpene(s)/terpenoid Strong, floral compounds influencing the aromas of especially riesling, gewürztraminer and the muscats; with bottle-age, terpenes often develop a pungent resinous oiliness.

Texture Tactile 'feel' in the mouth: hard, acidic, coarse and alcoholic; or, smooth, velvety, 'warm'.

Toasty Often used for barrel-fermented and aged wines showing a pleasant biscuity, charry character.

Vegetal Grassy, leafy, herby – in contrast to fruity, flowery, oaky. Overdone, a no-no.

Yeasty Warm bakery smells, often evident in barrel-fermented whites and *méthode champenoise* sparkling wines, where yeasts stay in contact with the wine after fermentation.

Winemaking Terms

A few brief reference explanations. See also sections Winetasting terms, SA wine styles.

Acid and **acidity** The fresh — or, in excess, sharp or tart — taste of wine. Too little acid and the wine tastes dull and flat. In SA, winemakers are permitted to adjust acidity either by adding acid — at any stage before bottling — or by lowering the acid level with a de-acidifier. See also Volatile acid and Malolactic.

Alcohol Essential component of wine, providing fullness, richness and, at higher levels, sometimes an impression of sweetness. Also a preservative, helping keep wines in good condition. Produced by yeasts fermenting the sugars in the grape. Measured by volume of the total liquid. Most unfortified table wines in SA have between 11% and 14.5% alc by vol; fortifieds range from ±16% to 21%. A variation of up to 1% between the strength stated on the label and the laboratory analysis is permitted by local law. Various techniques (such as reverse osmosis and 'spinning cone', also the addition of water) exist to address the increasingly important issue of high alcohol levels in wine, and some have recently been legalised in SA (though not for export to, eg, Europe).

Barrels (barrel-aged; barrel-fermented) Wines are transferred into barrels to age, pick up oaky flavours etc. When must or fermenting must is put into barrels, the resulting wine is called barrel-fermented. A barrel or cask is generally a 225–500ℓ oak container; *barrique* is a French word for a 225ℓ barrel; a pipe, adapted from the Portuguese *pipa*, usually indicates a vessel of 530-630ℓ; vat is a term generally used for larger (2 000-5 000ℓ) wooden vessels.

Batonnage See Lees.

Biodynamic See Organic.

Blend A wine made from two or more different grape varieties, vintages, vineyards or containers. Some of the world's finest wines are blends.

Bottles While the 750ml (75cl) bottle is now the most widely used size of container for wine, it is by no means the only one. Smaller bottles (375 & 500ml) are popular with restaurants and airlines, and larger sizes are prized by collectors because of their novelty value and/or their tendency to promote slower wine ageing. The following are the larger bottle sizes (note: some no longer in production):

Capacity		Bordeaux	Champagne/Burgundy
litres	bottles		
1.5	2	Magnum	Magnum
3	4	Double magnum	Jéroboam
4.5	6	Jéroboam	Rehoboam
6	8	Impériale	Methuselah
9	12	–	Salmanazar
12	16	–	Balthazar
15	20	–	Nebuchadnezzar

Brettanomyces or **'brett'** Currently much-focused-on naturally occurring yeast, usually associated with red wine and regarded as a spoilage factor, because its growth triggers the formation of volatile acids, phenols and other compounds which, in sufficient concentration, impart a range of unpleasant characters, from barnyard to sweat to cheese.

Carbonic maceration or **maceration carbonique** Method of fermenting wine without first crushing the grapes. Whole clusters with stalks etc are put into closed vat; intracellular fermentation occurs within the grape berries, which then burst.

Chaptalisation Originally French term for the addition of sugar to grape must to raise the alcohol of a wine. Selectively legal in northern Europe, where acid adjustments are not allowed as they are in SA. Winemakers in both hemispheres bend the rules.

Charmat Method of making sparkling wine in a sealed tank (*cuvée close)* under pressure. Easier, cheaper than méthode champenoise.

Chips See Oak chips

Cold ferment 'Cold' is a relative term; applied to fermentation of mainly white wines in temperature-controlled tanks, it refers to a temperature around usually 13–16°C. The benefits, especially important in a warm country, include conserving the primary fruit aromas and ensuring fermentation is carried out steadily and thoroughly.

Cold soak or **cold maceration**. Red winemaking method carried out prior to fermentation. Skins and juice are held, usually for a few days, at a sufficiently cool temperature to prevent fermentation. The theory is that this extracts more favourable colour and aromas than after fermentation.

Cold stabilisation Keeping a wine at about –4°C for a week or more to precipitate tartaric acid and 'clean up' the wine, preventing later formation of (harmless) tartrate crystals in bottle. Some winemakers believe this process damages flavour and prefer to avoid it.

Disgorgement (*dégorgement* in French) Important stage in the production of traditionally fermented sparkling where accumulated sediment (or lees), which could cloud the finished wine, is removed from the neck of the bottle.

Dosage The sugar added to sparkling wine after the second fermentation.

Fermentation The conversion of sugar in grapes into alcohol and carbon dioxide, a function of enzymes secreted by yeasts. Wild yeasts occur in vineyards and wineries, but in modern Cape winemaking cultured yeasts are normally added to secure the process. Beyond about 15% of alcohol, yeasts are overwhelmed and fermentation ceases, although it usually is stopped (for instance by cooling, filtration or the addition of alcohol) before this stage. See also Malolactic.

Filtration Removes last impurities including **yeast** cells. Done excessively, can thin a wine. Some traditionalists bottle without cold- or protein-stabilisation or filtration.

Fining and **protein stabilisation** Fining is ridding wine of suspended particles by adding substances that attract and draw the particles from the wine.

Flash-pasteurisation See Kosher

Free run After grapes have been de-stalked and crushed, juice runs freely.

Garage wine Generic term for wine made in minuscule quantities, sometimes literally in a garage; grower of such wine sometimes called a *garagiste*.

Glycerol Minor product of alcoholic fermentation; from the Greek for sweet. Has an apparent sweetening effect on even dry wines and also gives a viscous, mouthfilling character.

Icewine Sweet, concentrated wine from grapes picked and pressed while frozen. Not a recognised category for SA wine production.

Kosher Wine made 'correctly', i.e. under rabbinical supervision, to be suitable for use by religious Jews. Vinification and any initial movement of the wine must be done by an observant Jew. Flash-pasteurisation, increasingly by means of new flavour-preserving processes such as Thermoflash, renders the resulting *meshuval* (literally 'boiled' or 'cooked') wine fit for handling by non-Jews.

Leafroll virus Virus (or complex of viruses), widespread throughout the winegrowing world, which causes the vine to perform below its potential and thereby produce wine which is lower in colour, body and flavour than that derived from virus-free or 'cleaned-up' plants.

Lees Spent yeast cells and other matter which collect at the bottom of any container in winemaking. Yeast autolysis, or decomposition, can impart richness and flavour to a wine, sometimes referred to as leesy. Lees stirring or *batonnage* involves mixing the bed of lees in a barrel or tank through the wine, which is said to be sur lie; it is employed primarily on barrel-fermented white wines. The main effects of mixing lees and wine are to prevent off-odours developing from lack of oxygen, to limit the amount of wood tannin and flavour extracted, and to increase flavour.

Malolactic fermentation (malo) Occurs when bacteria convert malic into lactic acids. This reduces the acidity of a wine, a normal and healthy process, especially in reds — provided, of course, it occurs before bottling.

Maturation Ageing properties are closely related to tannin and/or fixed acid content of a wine. A relatively full red wine with tannin has lasting power. With age, it may develop complexity, subtlety and smooth mellowness. Lighter wines with lower tannins are drinkable sooner but probably will not reach the same level of complexity. A number of Cape whites, especially chardonnays and rieslings, now mature well over several years, but most are best drunk in their fruity youth, up to 18 months.

Méthode champenoise Classic method of making champagne by inducing secondary fermentation in the bottle and producing fine bubbles. Due to French restrictions on terminology, Cape sparkling wines made in this way are called méthode cap classique (MCC).

Micro-oxygenation Relatively new (1990) technique enabling introduction of precise, controlled doses of oxygen to must/wine. Advocates claim softer tannins, more stable colours and other advantages.

Oak chips, either in older barrels or stainless steel tanks, are used increasingly in SA, as are oak **staves**. Still frowned on by some purists, the 'additives' approximate the flavour effects of a new barrel, far more cheaply, more easily handled.

Oak-matured See Barrels.

Organic viticulture/winemaking Increasingly popular alternative to 'conventional' or 'industrialised' winegrowing, emphasising natural and sustainable farming methods and cellar techniques. A variant is biodynamic viticulture, influenced by anthroposophy, focused on improving wine quality through harmony with nature and its rhythms.

Oxidation Change (usually for the worse) due to exposure to air, in whites often producing dark yellow or yellowish colour (called maderisation), altering, 'ageing' the taste. Controlled aeration is used to introduce acceptable and desirable development in wine.

Pasteurisation See Kosher

pH A chemical notation, used in winemaking and evaluation. The pH of a wine is its effective, active acidity — not in volume but by strength or degree. The reading provides a guide to a wine's keepability. The optimum pH in a wine is somewhere between 3.1 and 3.4 — which significantly improves a wine's protection from bacterial spoilage, so permitting it to mature and develop if properly stored.

Racking Drawing or pumping wine off from one cask or tank to another, to leave behind the deposit or lees.

Reductive Wine in an unevolved, unoxidised state is said to be 'reductive'; usually with a tight, sometimes unyielding character. The absence of air (in a bottled wine) or the presence of substantial sulphur dioxide (anti-oxidant) levels, will inhibit both oxidation and reduction processes, which are linked and complementary.

Reverse osmosis A specialised filtration technique, now permitted in SA for various purposes, including the removal of water from wine. See also Alcohol

Skin contact After crushing and de-stemming, white grapes may be left for a period with the juice, remaining in contact with skins (before being moved into the press, from which the grape juice is squeezed). Some winemakers believe the colours and flavours in and under the grape skins should be maximised in this way; others believe extended (or any) contact can lead to coarseness, even bitterness.

Spinning cone See Alcohol.

Sulphur dioxide (SO_2) Sterilising agent and preservative, near-ubiquitous in winemaking since antiquity, now strictly controlled. In SA, max total SO_2 levels for dry wines is 150-160mg/ℓ; for wines with 5+ g/ℓ sugar it is 200mg/ℓ; and botrytis-style wines 300 mg/ℓ. Any wine with more than 10mg/ℓ total SO_2 must carry the warning 'Contains sulphites' (or 'sulfites') on the label.

Sur lie See Lees.

Tannin Vital preservative in wine, which derives primarily from the grape skins. Necessary for a red wine's longevity. A young wine's raw tannin can give it a harshness, but no red wine matures into a great one without tannin, which itself undergoes change, combines with other substances and mellows. Tannin leaves a mouth-puckering dryness about the gums, gives 'grip' to a wine. A wooded wine will also contain some wood tannin. Various types or qualities of tannin are increasingly commented on.

Tartrates Harmless crystals formed by tartaric acid precipitating in non-cold-stabilised wine. Because of lack of public acceptance, usually avoided through cold stabilisation.

Terroir Important, controversial (and in SA over-used) French term embracing soil, climate, topography and other elements which constitute the natural environment of a vineyard site and give it a unique character.

Thermovinification/Thermoflash See Kosher.

Unfiltered See Filtration.

Virus or **virused** See Leafroll.

Volatile acid (VA) The part of the acidity which can become volatile. A high reading indicates a wine is prone to spoilage. Recognised at high levels by a sharp, 'hot', vinegary smell. In SA, most wines must by law be below 1.2g/ℓ of VA; in practice, the majority are well below 1g/ℓ.

Whole-bunch pressing or **cluster pressing** Some SA cellars use this age-old process of placing whole bunches directly in the press and gently squeezing. The more usual method is to de-stem and crush the grapes before pressing. Whole-bunch pressing is said to yield fresher, cleaner must, and wine lower in polyphenols which, in excess, tend to age wines faster and render them coarser.

Wood-fermented/matured See Barrels.

Yeasts Micro-organisms that secrete enzymes which convert or ferment sugar into alcohol. See fermentation.

Wine Routes, Trusts & Associations

For localised information about regional official wine routes and wineries, contact these organisations:

Breedekloof Wine and Tourism ▪ T 023·349·1791 ▪ F 023·349·1720
info@breedekloof.com ▪ www.breedekloof.com

Calitzdorp Wine Route ▪ T 044·213·3775 ▪ F 044·213·3302
calitzdorpinfo@kannaland.co.za ▪ www.calitzdorp.co.za

Constantia Wine Route ▪ T 021·794·5190 (Lars Maack) ▪ F 021·794·1351
lars@buitenverwachting.co.za

The Darling Wine & Art Experience ▪ T 022·492·3430 (Shaun Mc Laughlin) ▪
F 022·492·2935 ▪ mclaughlin@worldonline.co.za ▪ www.darlingtourism.co.za

Durbanville Wine Valley Association ▪ T 083·310·1228 ▪ F 021·976·1467 ▪ info@
durbanvillewine.co.za ▪ www.durbanvillewine.co.za

Elim Winegrowers ▪ T 082·551·2351 (Francis Pratt) ▪ fbpratt@telkomsa.net

Franschhoek See Vignerons de Franschhoek

Green Mountain Eco Route (Elgin/Bot River) ▪ T 021·859·4250 ▪ F 021·859·4230 ▪
info@greenmountain.co.za ▪ www.greenmountain.co.za

Helderberg See Stellenbosch

Klein Karoo Wine Route ▪ T/F 028·572·1284 (Ellen Marais)
info@kleinkaroowines.co.za ▪ www.kleinkaroowines.co.za

Northern Cape Wine Association ▪ T 054·337·8800 (Herman Cruywagen) ▪
F 054·332·4408 ▪ marketing@owk.co.za

Olifants River Vodacom Wine Route ▪ T/F 027·213·3126/082·611·3999
wineroute@matzikamamun.co.za ▪ www.olifantsriverwineroute.com

Orange River Wine Route See Northern Cape Wine Association

Outeniqua Wine Route ▪ T/F 044·873·4212/072·833·8223
harpie@xsinet.co.za

Paarl Vintners ▪ T 021·863·4886 ▪ F 021·863·4883 ▪ paarl@wine.co.za ▪ www.
paarlwine.co.za

Rawsonville Wine Route See Breedekloof Wine & Tourism

Robertson Wine Valley ▪ T 023·626·3167/083·701·5404 ▪ F 023·626·1054
. manager@robertsonwinevalley.com ▪ www.robertsonwinevalley.com

Stellenbosch American Express Wine Routes ▪ T 021·886·4310 ▪ F 021·886·4330
info@wineroute.co.za ▪ www.wineroute.co.za ▪ Helderberg office: T 021·852·6166 ▪
F 021·852·6168 ▪ hwr@mweb.co.za ▪ www.helderbergwineroute.co.za

Swartland Wine Route ▪ T 022·487·1133 ▪ F 022·487·2063
swartlandinfo@westc.co.za ▪ www.swartlandwineroute.co.za

Tulbagh Wine Route ▪ T/F 023·230·1348
tulbaghinfo@lando.co.za ▪ www.tulbaghtourism.org.za

Vignerons de Franschhoek ▪ T 021·876·3062 ▪ F 021·876·2964
franschhoek@wine.co.za ▪ www.franschhoekwines.co.za

Voor Paardeberg Visitors Centre ▪ T 021·869·8339 ▪ F 021·869·8732 ▪ taste@
voorpaardeberg.co.za ▪ www.voorpaardeberg.co.za

Walker Bay Wine Wander ▪ T 028·316·3988 ▪ F 028·316·3989
wine@hermanus.co.za

Wellington Wine Route ▪ T 021·873·4604 ▪ F 021·873·4607
welltour@mweb.co.za ▪ www.wellington.co.za

Worcester Winelands ▪ T 023·342·8710/20 ▪ F 023·342·2294
manager@worcesterwinelands.co.za ▪ www.worcesterwinelands.co.za

Winelands Tourism Offices

For additional accommodation options, brochures and local advice, contact the information offices and/or publicity associations of the wine areas you plan to visit.

Elgin Valley Tourism T 021·848·9838 ▪ F 086·660·6398 ▪ info@elginvalley.co.za ▪ www.elginvalley.co.za

Franschhoek Wine Valley Tourist Association ▪ T 021·876·3603 ▪ F 021·876·2768 info@franschhoek.org.za ▪ www.franschhoek.org.za

Helderberg Tourism ▪ T 021·851·4022 ▪ F 021·851·1497 info@helderbergtourism.co.za ▪ www.helderbergtourism.co.za

Hermanus Tourism Bureau ▪ T 028·312·2629 ▪ F 028·313·0305 infoburo@hermanus.co.za ▪ www.hermanus.co.za www.tourismhermanus.co.za

McGregor Tourism ▪ T 023·625·1954 ▪ F 086·612·9636 info@tourismmcgregor.co.za ▪ www.tourismmcgregor.co.za

Northern Cape Tourism ▪ T 053·832·2657 ▪ F 053·831·2937 tourism@northerncape.org.za ▪ www.northerncape.org.za

Paarl Tourism Association ▪ T 021·863·4937 ▪ F 021·863·4883 info@paarlonline.com ▪ www.paarlonline.com

Robertson Tourism Association ▪ T 023·626·4437 ▪ F 023·626·4290 info@robertson.org.za ▪ www.robertsonr62.com

Route 62 ▪ T 023·616·3563 ▪ F 023·616·3422 ▪ info@route62.co.za ▪ www.route62.co.za

Stellenbosch Tourism Info Bureau ▪ T 021·883·3584 ▪ F 021·883·8017 info@stellenboschtourism.co.za ▪ www.stellenboschtourism.co.za

Wellington Tourism Bureau ▪ T 021·873·4604 ▪ F 021·873·4607 welltour@mweb.co.za ▪ www.wellington.co.za

West Coast Peninsula Tourism Bureau ▪ T 022·714·2088 ▪ F 022·714·4240 bureau@kingsley.co.za

Worcester Tourism Bureau ▪ T 023·348·2795 ▪ F 023·342·2294 info@worcestertourism.com ▪ www.worcestertourism.com

Specialist Wine Tours

Adamastor & Bacchus ▪ English, Dutch, German, Norwegian ▪ johnford@iafrica.com ▪ T 021·439·5169/083·229·1172 ▪ F 021·439·5169

African Wonder Tours ▪ Afrikaans, English ▪ info@africanwonder.co.za ▪ www.africanwonder.co.za ▪ T 082·325·1485

Amber Wine Tours ▪ English ▪ ambertours@wol.co.za ▪ www.ambertours.co.za ▪ T 083·448·7016

Cape Floral Kingdom Vineyard Tours ▪ sbirch@iafrica.com ▪ www.CFKvineyardtours.co.za ▪ T 076·145·1996 ▪ F 021·847·1467

Double Gold Wineland Tours ▪ English ▪ kimdg@absamail.co.za ▪ T 021·785·5094/082·293·3176

Exclusively African Tours ▪ Dutch, English ▪ ian@exclusively-african.com ▪ www.exclusively-african.com ▪ T 021·852·0278/082·309·9991

Fusion Wine Tours ▪ Afrikaans, English ▪ fusion@oaklandswines.com ▪ 083·258·0952 / 082·853·9169 ▪ F 021·883·8722

Gourmet Wine Tours ▪ English ▪ sflesch@iafrica.com ▪ www.gourmetwinetours.co.za ▪ T 021·705·4317/083·229·3581 ▪ F 021·706·0766

Gudrun Grünewald ▪ English, German ▪ happyholiday@adept.co.za ▪ www.happyholiday.co.za ▪ T 082·699·3098

It Just Did! Wine Tourism ▪ English ▪ info@itjustdid.com ▪ www.itjustdid.com ▪ T 082·390·6092

Judy Krohn ▪ English, German ▪ judyk@zsd.co.za ▪ www.wineroutes.co.za ▪ T 084·500·1941/021·851·7009 ▪ F 021·851·7009

Ocean & Vine Tours ▪ English (translator on request) ▪ wayne@wine.co.za ▪ www.prowinetours.co.za T 021·559·6906/082·900·6999

Redwood Tours ▪ English ▪ rwt@adept.co.za ▪ www.redwoodtours.co.za ▪
T 021·886·8138/082·443·6480

Southern Destinations ▪ English ▪ info@southerndestinations.com ▪ www.
southerndestinations.com ▪ T 021·671·3090 ▪ F 021·674·7481

Tri Active Events Management (Green Mountain Eco Route) ▪ English ▪ info@
triactive.co.za ▪ www.triactive.co.za ▪ T 021·859·4250 ▪ F 021·859·4230

Vineyard Ventures ▪ English, Afrikaans, French, German ▪ vinven@iafrica.com ▪
www.vineyardventures.co.za ▪ T 021·434·8888/082·920·2825 ▪ F 021·434·9999

Vintage Cape Tours Paarl ▪ info@vintagecape.co.za ▪ www.vintagecape.co.za ▪
T 021·872·9252/082·553·8928/082·656·3994 ▪ F 021·862·1484

Vintour ▪ Afrikaans, English, German ▪ helmut@vintour.co.za ▪ www.vintour.co.za ▪
T/F 021·976·5709/083·626·0029

Walker Bay Wine Destination ▪ Afrikaans, English ▪ wine@hermanus.co.za ▪
T 028·316·3988

Wanderer Wines ▪ English, German ▪ wines@wanderer.co.za ▪ www.wanderer.co.za
▪ T·021·788·6850/082·878·1176

Wellington Wine Walk ▪ Afrikaans, English ▪ judy@winescapetours.co.za ▪
T 083·313·8383 ▪ F 021·461·5555

Window on Cape Wine ▪ English ▪ mvweaver@iafrica.com ▪
T/F 021·866·1002/082·782·5198

Wine Desk ▪ English, German (other languages on special request) ▪ winedesk@
tourcapetown.com; ligia@winedesk.co.za ▪ www.winedeskwaterfront.co.za ▪
T 021·405·4550/082·822·6127

Wine Walks ▪ info@winewalks.co.za ▪ www.winewalks.co.za ▪
T 021·851·2785/083·631·5944

Eat-outs in the Winelands and Cape Town

Below are some dining out options in Cape Town and the winelands. These are paid
entries. The venues supplied information on their cuisine, menus and attractions, which
was then edited for consistency of style. For more eat-outs among the vines, consult the
A-Z section of the guide for wineries which offer light lunches, picnics etc. Look for the 🍴
symbol beside the individual entries. Unless stated to the contrary, all allow you to bring
your own (BYO) wine – the corkage fee is indicated at the start of each entry. Should you
wish to know about wheelchair access, please discuss with the relevant restaurant.

Index of eat-outs

Listed alphabetically, with region.

Cape Town

Aubergine Restaurant 39 Barnet Street, Gardens, Cape Town ▪ Continental cuisine with Asian influence ▪ Lunch Wed-Fri from 12:00; 'Cinq à Sept' Mon-Sat 17:00-19:00 & dinner Mon-Sat 19:00-22:30 ▪ Closed Sun ▪ Booking advised ▪ Children welcome ▪ Major credit cards accepted ▪ Corkage R50 ▪ Owner Harald Bresselschmidt ▪ aubergin@mweb.co.za ▪ www.aubergine.co.za ▪ **T (021) 465-4909** ▪ F (021) 461-3781

The sleek revamp adds sophistication, complementing contemporary cuisine from an à la carte menu bursting with flavour, aroma and texture. Specialising in fish, seafood and prime matured SA meat (be tempted by four fish sushi with oriental vinaigrette; ginger ostrich with steamed aubergine; and Chai-spiced soufflé, plum compote and saffron ice-cream). Consult the sommelier about wine choice, both broad in variety and deep in vintage. *Dine* Top 10 special occasion; best restaurant in Rossouw's top category.

Balducci's Shop 6162, Victoria Wharf, V&A Waterfront, Cape Town ▪ International, Global cuisine & Royal Sushi Bar ▪ Open daily 09:00-23:00 ▪ Booking advised ▪ Children welcome ▪ Major credit cards accepted ▪ No BYO ▪ Owners Ian Halfon & Doron Duveen ▪ info@slickrestaurants.com ▪ www.balduccis.co.za ▪ **T (021) 421-6002/3** ▪ F (021) 421-6010

The place for crowd-watching over cocktails in the V&A Waterfront. Overlooking the harbour, the stylish, award-winning international café-restaurant is equally popular for luxury breakfasts, healthy or hearty lunches and dinners. The menu is wide (specialities are wood-fired pizzas, prime Karan beef steaks, Mozambique lobsters and imported shellfish). Helpings are generous and service attentive. Recipient of the 06 Diners Club and 07 *Wine Spectator* Winelist Awards. Sushi fans, do try the adjacent award-winning Balducci's Royal Sushi Bar.

Bascule Whisky Bar and Wine Cellar   Cape Grace, West Quay Road, V&A Waterfront, Cape Town ▪ Regional innovation cuisine ▪ Open daily 12:00-late ▪ Children welcome ▪ Major credit cards accepted ▪ Corkage R40 ▪ Owner Meikles Africa Hotels ▪ bascule@capegrace.com ▪ www.bascule.co.za ▪ **T (021) 410-7082** ▪ F (021) 419-7622

Deservedly popular spot for sundowners, below decks with access to the international private marina overlooking Signal Hill and Table Mountain. Vinotheque and extensive winelist with vintage wines, also the largest collection of whiskies south of the equator - over 400 at the last count - with a whisky club and sommelier to lead tastings for beginners upward. Plus a full range of international cigars. Best Bar & Tavern and Service with a Smile Awards, *V&A Waterfront Restaurant Guide* 2007; *Whisky Magazine's* Great Whisky Bar of the World 2006. (See also Stay-over section.)

Belthazar Restaurant & Wine Bar   Shop 153, Victoria Wharf, V&A Waterfront, Cape Town ▪ Grill; seafood & wine bar ▪ Open daily 12:00-23:00 ▪ Booking advised ▪ Major credit cards accepted ▪ No BYO ▪ Owners Ian Halfon, Doron Duveen & Jonathan Steyn ▪ info@slickrestaurants.com ▪ www.belthazar.co.za ▪ T (021) 421-3753/6 ▪ F (021) 421-3748

Indulge your palate at this multiple award-winning restaurant and world's biggest wine-by-the-glass bar, where sommeliers serve 250 of the Cape's finest wines by the glass and offer knowledgeable advice on a spoiled-for-choice 600-label winelist. Pair sought-after vintages with specialities ranging from prime cuts of aged and butter-tender Karan beef (cooked to order) to game and the freshest South African and imported Mozambican shellfish. Voted Best Steakhouse in South Africa 2005/06, Best Restaurant in the V&A Waterfront 2006/07 and recipient of the American Express Fine Dining Platinum Award 2007.

Café Bascule   Cape Grace, West Quay Road, V&A Waterfront, Cape Town ▪ Café cuisine ▪ Open daily 07:30-16:00 ▪ Children welcome ▪ Major credit cards accepted ▪ Corkage R40 ▪ Owner Meikles Africa Hotels ▪ bascule@capegrace.com ▪ www.bascule.co.za/cafebascule ▪ **T (021) 410-7082** ▪ F (021) 419-7622

Relish quality coffees (including an exclusive Bascule blend), teas (from green to a SA first: Red Espresso, a shot of filtered, refined Rooibos tea); breakfast, snacks and light lunches in an ambience encompassing the harbour, yachts and view of Table Mountain. Savour specialties like Bascule Benedict; or salmon and scrambled egg with crispy croissant and cream cheese, on the premises, or stylishly packed to go. (See also Stay-over section.)

Catharina's Restaurant   see under Constantia

Den Anker Restaurant   Pierhead, V&A Waterfront, Cape Town ▪ French/Belgian cuisine ▪ Open daily 11:00-16:00 & 18:00-22:30 (kitchen); 11:00-24:00 (bar) ▪ Booking advised ▪ Children welcome ▪ Major credit cards accepted ▪ No BYO ▪ Owner L De Visscher ▪ denanker@mweb.co.za ▪ www.denanker.com ▪ **T (021) 419-0249** ▪ F (021) 419-0251

Spectacular setting on the quayside of Cape Town's Victoria & Alfred Waterfront, where gulls swoop, seals bask, and passing yachts enhance the picture-postcard view of Table Mountain. Generous pots of mussels and *frites* are perennial, but be tempted by Cape specialities or gourmet *foie gras* brûlée, just-seared tuna, and sinful Belgian chocolate mousse. Attentive, informed serving staff, award-winning winelist and excellent selection of Belgian beers. Waterfront Top Service Award, *V &A Waterfront Restaurant Guide '07*.

Dine at the Andros   Andros Boutique Hotel, cnr Newlands & Phyllis Roads, Claremont, Cape Town ▪ French Country cuisine ▪ Open daily 07:00-23:00 ▪ Booking advised ▪ Children 12+ welcome ▪ Major credit cards accepted ▪ Corkage R30 ▪ Owners The Barrow Family ▪ info@andros.co.za ▪ www.andros.co.za ▪ **T (021) 797-9777** ▪ F (021) 797-0300

Intimate restaurant where chef Nicolene Barrow - who trained under Michel Roux Jr. at London's Le Gavroche - combines experience and love of local produce in a gutsy

French-style menu. Expect classics like beef fillet with marrow bone, braised shoulder of spring lamb, and poached pear brûlée. Cosy dining in front of a fire in winter and al fresco tables on the veranda in summer, overlooking park-like gardens. (See also Stay-over section.)

onewaterfront   Cape Grace, West Quay Road, V&A Waterfront, Cape Town ▪ Regional innovation cuisine ▪ Open daily for breakfast, lunch & dinner ▪ Booking advised ▪ Children welcome ▪ Major credit cards accepted ▪ Corkage R40 ▪ Owner Meikles Africa Limited ▪ onewaterfront@capegrace.com ▪ www.onewaterfront.co.za ▪ **T (021) 410-7080** ▪ F (021) 419-7622

Fusion - SA style. Menus marry the food of the Cape's West Coast to aromatic local Malay cuisine, creating innovative, inviting and confidently Cape dishes. Musts are Dim Sum (an irresistible intro to Cape Malay specialities); confit of duck bobotie; gourmand smoked duck and *foie gras* pizza. The ambience is sophisticated, the attentive service warm, and an award-wining wine list complements seasonal menus. Platinum American Express Fine Dining Award 2006 & '07; Best Hotels in the World Food Gold List '06. (See also Stay-over section.)

Savoy Cabbage Restaurant & Champagne Bar   101 Hout Street, Cape Town ▪ Contemporary cuisine ▪ Lunch Mon-Fri 12:00-14:30, dinner Mon-Sat 19:00-22:30 ▪ Closed Sun ▪ Booking essential ▪ Major credit cards accepted ▪ Air-conditioned ▪ Smoking section ▪ Secure night-time parking ▪ Corkage R20 ▪ Owner Caroline Bagley ▪ savoycab@iafrica. com ▪ **T (021) 424-2626** ▪ F (021) 424-3366

Lauded by the *New York Times* restaurant critic Frank Bruni, this consistently satisfying city-centre venue has garnered a string of accolades, including CNN's only 'Hot Spot' for Cape Town. Decor accents exposed brick and high ceilings; daily changing menus offer the freshest seasonal produce, offal and tempting vegetarian options. (Must-try dishes include warthog with sour fig sauce, and butter-sauced salmon and fresh crayfish). Boutique winelist.

Sundance Gourmet Food Company   59 Buitengracht Street; 25 Church Street & 18 Bay Road, Surrey Place, Mouille Point, Cape Town ▪ Exotic, funky & creative gourmet sandwiches ▪ Open daily – Buitengracht & Church open from 06:30-18:30; Mouille Point open from 06:30-20:30 ▪ Children welcome ▪ Major credit cards accepted ▪ Owner Conrad Gallagher ▪ info@conradgallagherfood.com ▪ www.sundancecoffeeco.com ▪ **T (021) 424-7590** ▪ F (021) 424-7593

Coffee culture goes cosmopolitan at this connoisseur must (which also offers office desk deliveries - though the aromatic in-store ambience is essential to Sundance style). Masterminded by Michelin star-rated chef Conrad Gallagher and wife Candice, gourmet sandwiches (on freshly baked designer bread and wraps) burst with exotic fillings; decadent cakes and exotic chocs ooze temptation; and selected coffees (beans roasted on-site) are poured by well-trained barristas.

The Nose Restaurant & Wine Bar   Cape Quarter, 72 Waterkant Street, Green Point, Cape Town ▪ Bistro-style, gastro-pub ▪ Open daily 09:00-late ▪ Closed Christmas, Boxing & New Year's days ▪ Booking advised ▪ Children welcome ▪ Major credit cards accepted ▪ No BYO ▪ Owners Kevin & Cathy Marston ▪ info@thenose.co.za ▪ www.thenose.co.za ▪ **T (021) 425-2200** ▪ F (021) 425-2210

Discover Cape wine by picking The Nose! This laidback, friendly venue on a piazza in trendy De Waterkant offers over 40 wines by the glass, many more by the bottle. First releases and unusual grape varieties marry signature Cape Malay curry, bangers 'n mash, springbok and stout pie, tasty finger food platters. Wine-tasting flights and full bar, plus introductory wine courses and food and wine-matching evenings. Diners Club Platinum Wine List of the Year 2007.

Theshowroom restaurant   10 Hospital Street, Harbour Edge, Green Point, Cape Town ▪ Modern flavours ▪ Lunch Tue-Fri 12:00-15:00, Dinner Mon-Sat 19:00-22:30 ▪ Closed Sun ▪ Booking essential ▪ Secure parking ▪ Major credit cards accepted ▪ Corkage R50 ▪ Chef/Owner Bruce Robertson ▪ reservations@theshowroomrestaurant.co.za ▪ www.

theshowroomrestaurant.co.za ▪ **T (021) 421-4682** ▪ F (021) 421-3858

Expect glass, class and panache; minimalist Melbournesque décor and a Lamborghini on the menu: this slick city restaurant adjoins the Bloomsbury showroom at Harbouredge. Unique mop-your-plate sauce selection, new savoury sundaes and informed wine pairing, by the bottle or glass. Owner Bruce Robertson has teamed up with head chef Phil Alcock and the award-winning team is on view 'live in action' in the open plan kitchen/restaurant.

Constantia

Buitenverwachting Restaurant & Café Petit Buitenverwachting, Klein Constantia Road, Constantia ▪ Contemporary continental cuisine with African touch ▪ Restaurant: Tue-Sat lunch 12:00-14:00 & dinner 19:00-21:30 (Apr-Oct); Mon-Sat lunch 12:00-15:00 & dinner 18:00-22:00 (Nov-Mar) ▪ Café Petit: lunch only Tue-Sat 12:00-15:00 (Apr-Oct) & Mon-Sat 12:00-16:30 (Nov-Mar) ▪ Closed Jul to mid-Aug ▪ Booking advised ▪ Children 12+ welcome ▪ Major credit cards accepted ▪ Corkage Restaurant R55 & Café Petit R35 ▪ Owners Mueller & Maack ▪ Chef & partner Edgar Osojnik ▪ restaurant@buitenverwachting.com ▪ www.buitenverwachting.com ▪ **T (021) 794-3522** ▪ F (021) 794-1351

Expect passion, enticing menus devised to match Buitenverwachting wines, friendly service and a mountain view to match. Chef Edgar Osojnik, now a partner after a decade of capturing custom, adds flavour-enhancing continental flair to prime local ingredients. Specials make the most of the season; even menu favourites – sophisticated seafood, butter-tender venison and a chocolate variation offering irresistible bite-sized temptations – evolve and change in presentation. (See also A-Z section.)

Catharina's The Restaurant @ Steenberg Steenberg Estate, Tokai ▪ Sophisticated contemporary South African cuisine ▪ Open daily 7:00-22:00 ▪ Booking advised ▪ Children welcome ▪ Major credit cards accepted ▪ Corkage R30 ▪ Owner Graham Beck ▪ info@steenberghotel.com ▪ www.steenberghotel.com ▪ **T (021) 713-2222** ▪ F (021) 713-2251

Named after Catharina, feisty first owner of the estate, this Cape-style restaurant occupies the original wine cellar, extending onto an oak-shaded patio. Host is Garth Almazan, Cape Town-born exec chef, who emerges from the kitchen to greet guests and discuss the menu. Tempting choices include signature dishes with a Cape slant: specialities are butter-tender venison and subtly flavoured seafood. American Express Platinum Award & Diners Club Award of Excellence 07. (See also Stay-over & A-Z sections.)

Constantia Uitsig Restaurant Constantia Uitsig, Spaanschemat River Road, Constantia ▪ Mediterranean with a strong Italian influence ▪ Open daily for lunch 12:30-14:30, dinner 19:30-21:30 ▪ Closed for lunch 31 Dec, New Year's day ▪ Booking advised ▪ Children welcome ▪ Major credit cards accepted ▪ Corkage R35 ▪ cureception@uitsig.co.za ▪ www.constantia-uitsig.com ▪ **T (021) 794-4480** ▪ F (021) 794-3105

A destination for those intent on Mediterranean cuisine that inclines towards Italy. Warmed by hospitality and housed in an original 19th century manor house flanked by vineyards, the restaurant is renowned for its evergreen specialities: beef carpaccio con rucola, abacchio alla Toscana, and sought-after veal sweetbreads. (Regulars don't bother with the extensive menu or list of daily specials). The excellent winelist showcases Constantia Uitsig award-winners. Consistently featured among SA's top ten restaurants. (See also Stay-over & A-Z sections.)

La Colombe Constantia Uitsig, Spaanschemat River Road, Constantia ▪ Classic & modern French cuisine with touches of Asia ▪ Open daily for lunch 12:30-14:30, dinner 19:30-21:30 ▪ Closed Sun eve (winter) & New Year's day lunch ▪ Booking advised ▪ Children welcome ▪ Major credit cards accepted ▪ Corkage R35 ▪ lc@uitsig.co.za ▪ www.constantia-uitsig.com ▪ **T (021) 794-2390** ▪ F (021) 794-7914

Chef Luke Dale-Roberts stepped seamlessly into the kitchen, maintaining the signature French-style fare. Menus are still chalked on blackboards: delights like springbok with celeriac purée, vintage port and black truffle reduction; figs poached in verjus and muscadel with cardamon ice-cream and pink pepper syrup. Linger over lunch in the stylish interior or sun-dappled courtyard; dine in a magical candlelit ambience. Extensive winelist, highlighting Constantia Uitsig award-winners. 28th Best Restaurant in the World and Best Restaurant in Africa and the Middle East 2006 (UK *Restaurant Magazine*). Top restaurant in South Africa for four consecutive years (*Business Day*). (See also Stay-over & A-Z sections.)

Pastis Bistro Brasserie   12 High Constantia Centre, Constantia Main Road, Constantia ▪ French bistro, Cape influences ▪ Kitchen open daily 08:30-22:00 (summer) & 09:00-22:00 (winter), drinks until midnight ▪ Booking advised ▪ Children welcome ▪ Major credit cards accepted ▪ No BYO ▪ Owner Derek Marshall ▪ pastis@mweb.co.za ▪ www. pastisbrasserie.co.za ▪ **T** (021) 794-8334 ▪ F (021) 794-8335

French fare is thriving in Constantia valley, cradle of SA winemaking. At this bustling Art Nouveau-style brasserie (complete with period posters and tablecloths from Brittany) breakfast on a croque monsieur; lunch on salad niçoise. Dinner delights with classics like bouillabaisse and fillet steak au poivre – adding local flavour with banana and mango tarte tatin. (For familiar favourites like burgers, ribs & chips, consult the bar menu).

The Cape Malay Restaurant   The Cellars-Hohenort Hotel, 93 Brommersvlei Road, Constantia ▪ Cape Malay cuisine ▪ Open Mon-Sat 19:00-21:30 ▪ Closed Mon (low season) & Sun ▪ Booking advised ▪ Children 12+ welcome ▪ Major credit cards accepted ▪ Corkage R50 ▪ Owner Liz McGrath ▪ reservations@collectionmcgrath.com ▪ www. collectionmcgrath.com ▪ **T** (021) 794-2137 ▪ F (021) 794-2149

Introduce your palate to authentic Cape Malay food, unique to the Western Cape. Chef Martha Williams' menu includes traditional taste treats like *smoorsnoek,* beef *bobotie,* tomato *bredie* and her legendary Malva pudding, complemented by an extensive, carefully chosen winelist. Spicy hued decor creates an Eastern ambience and friendly staff enrich the experience by sharing their knowledge of the food, life and culture of this colourful community. (See also Stay-over section.)

The Greenhouse Restaurant   The Cellars-Hohenort Hotel, 93 Brommersvlei Road, Constantia ▪ Contemporary French cuisine ▪ Open daily for breakfast 7:00-10:30, lunch 12:00-14:30 & dinner 19:00-21:30 ▪ Booking advised ▪ Children 12+ welcome ▪ Major credit cards accepted ▪ Corkage R50 ▪ Owner Liz McGrath ▪ reservations@ collectionmcgrath.com ▪ www.collectionmcgrath.com ▪ **T** (021) 794-2137 ▪ F (021) 794-2149

Award-winning, airy restaurant with garden vistas from both light-filled interior and sun-warmed terrace. Menus infuse contemporary French cuisine with flavours of Africa; signature dishes include home-smoked salmon, slow-roasted crispy duck, and deliciously classic orange and Grand Marnier soufflé. Friendly, attentive service, informed sommelier and extensive winelist. Sip pre-prandial drinks at The Martini, a sophisticated cocktail bar that boasts one of the world's largest martini menus. (See also Stay-over section.)

The River Café   Constantia Uitsig, Spaanschemat River Road, Constantia ▪ Healthy and wholesome cuisine ▪ Open daily 8:30-17:00 ▪ Closed Good Friday, Christmas, Boxing & New Year's days ▪ Booking advised ▪ Children welcome ▪ Major credit cards accepted ▪ Corkage R25 ▪ therivercafe@uitsig.co.za ▪ www.constantia-uitsig.com ▪ **T** (021) 794-3010 ▪ F (021) 794-2920

A byword for hearty breakfasts and country-fresh, appetising and organic lunches, this relaxed, welcoming al fresco venue is set against a mountain backdrop, overlooking vines. Regulars (including ladies who lunch) rave about the eggs Benedict, oversized organic salads and orgasmic chocolate brownies. Next to the Constantia Uitsig Wine Shop, which specializes in Constantia Uitsig wines, backed by a well-chosen selection from other areas. (See also Stay-over & A-Z sections.)

Darling

Hilda's Kitchen – The Restaurant at Groote Post   Groote Post Farm, Darling Hills Road, Darling ▪ Modern country cuisine ▪ Open for lunch Mon, Wed-Sun ▪ Closed July ▪ Booking advised ▪ Children welcome ▪ Major credit cards accepted (excl Amex) ▪ No BYO ▪

Owner Shaun Mc Laughlin ▪ mclaughlin@worldonline.co.za ▪ www.grootepost.com ▪
T (022) 492-2825 ▪ F (022) 492-2693

Savour a slice of history. Hilda's Kitchen, housed in a historic homestead, pays homage to Hildagonda Duckitt, doyenne of South African cookbook writers, who was born and raised at Groote Post. Her legacy lingers in the ambience, fresh produce and Debbie McLaughlin's modern country cooking, from homemade tarts and pies to tasty casseroles. For the full farm experience match your lunch to award-winning Groote Post wines. (See also Stay-over section for Trinity Lodge and A-Z section for Groote Post.)

Durbanville

The Hills Restaurant Durbanville Hills, M13, Durbanville ▪ Contemporary cuisine ▪ Lunch Tue-Sun 12:00-15:00; dinner Wed-Sat 19:00-22:00 (Aug-Apr) ▪ Closed Mon, Tue eve, religious & public holidays ▪ Booking advised ▪ Children welcome ▪ Wheelchair-friendly ▪ Major credit cards accepted ▪ No BYO ▪ Owners Natasha Jewaskiewitz, Marike Roggen & Marleen Brynard ▪ info@durbanvillehills.co.za ▪ www.durbanvillehills.co.za ▪ **T (021) 558-1300** ▪ F (021) 559-8169

The ambience is relaxed; the view is a sweeping panorama of Table Bay, Table Mountain, the Atlantic Ocean and Durbanville Hills vineyards. Match it to regional food (biltong and blue cheese soup; slow roasted neck of lamb), lightened with Mediterranean nuances, and presented in seasonal menus designed to complement the cellar's award-winning wines. Sunday lunch is a generous three-course buffet, popular with families. (See also A-Z section.)

Meerendal Restaurants Meerendal Wine Estate, Vissershok Road, Durbanville ▪ Bistro, deli & fine dining cuisine ▪ **Wheatfields** lunch & dinner Tue-Sat; **The Deli & Bistro** breakfast & lunch daily 08:00-17:00; **The Barn & Lawn** Sun lunch 'The Cape Table' from 12:30 ▪ Children welcome ▪ Wheelchair-friendly ▪ Booking advised for Wheatfields ▪ Major credit cards accepted ▪ Corkage R30 ▪ info@meerendal.co.za ▪ www.meerendal.co.za ▪ **T/F (021) 975-1655/072-856-6298**

A spectrum of eating options on a historic wine estate. Though venues differ in ambience, style (and price) priorities remain constant: menus change to highlight fresh ingredients, and all are created to complement Meerendal wines. The **Deli & Bistro** provides satisfying breakfasts, hearty lunches, scones, cakes, coffees and teas. The view-rich **Barn & Lawn** presents an appetising 'Cape Table' Sunday lunch buffet. (With a lawn where a marquee can accommodate up to 600, it's also a great venue for weddings and corporate functions). At **Wheatfields**, in the Meerendal manor house, Stephan Fraser, who worked with David Higgs, has stepped into his shoes as executive chef. Emphasis remains on fine dining, seafood and game. Who's for cognac-sauced crayfish and chive risotto with *foie gras*, or pastry-encased springbok, sweet potato and honey? (See also A-Z section.)

Franschhoek & Environs

Backsberg Restaurant Backsberg Estate Cellars, Simondium Road, Klapmuts ▪ South African cuisine ▪ Open daily 11:00-15:30, lunch served from 12:00 ▪ Booking advised ▪ Children welcome ▪ Wheelchair-friendly ▪ Visa & MasterCard accepted ▪ No BYO ▪ Owner Backsberg Estate Cellars ▪ restaurant@backsberg.co.za ▪ www.backsberg.co.za ▪ **T (021) 875-5952** ▪ F (021) 875-5144

Family friendly venue that makes fine wine and food an everyday pleasure. Beautiful mountain views and large lawns for relaxed al fresco lunching; a warming fire indoors on cold days. Lamb on the spit daily with Backsberg's signature roast potatoes; platters of meats and cheeses, and chocolate *roulade* as dessert speciality. To enjoy with Backsberg wines by the bottle or glass. Live music on Sundays. (See also A-Z section.)

Bread & Wine Restaurant - Farm Grocer Môreson Farm, Happy Valley Road, Franschhoek ▪ Rustic Mediterranean ▪ Open daily 12:00-15:00 ▪ Booking advised ▪ Children welcome ▪ Major credit cards accepted ▪ No BYO ▪ Owner Richard Friedman ▪ breadandwine@moreson.co.za ▪ www.moreson.co.za ▪ **T (021) 876-3692** ▪ F (021) 876-3105

The perfect pit stop for wine routers intent on a rustic taste of the Winelands. Court-yard seating under umbrellas provides a relaxed setting for appetizing, freshly baked moreish breads and hand-crafted charcuterie. Innovative dishes, beautifully presented, highlight chef/artisan Neil Jewell's culinary talent; highly rated Môreson wines are served by the glass or bottle. *Dine* Top 100 Restaurants; *Eat Out* Johnnie Walker Top 10 Restaurants 2007. (See also Le Quartier Français – 'iCi', Le Quartier Français 'The Tasting Room' & A-Z section for Môreson.)

Chamonix Restaurant Chamonix Wine Estate, Uitkyk Street, Franschhoek ▪ Contemporary fusion ▪ Open for lunch Mon–Sun 12:00–16:00, dinner Fri & Sat 18:30–21:00 ▪ Booking advised ▪ Children welcome ▪ Major credit cards accepted ▪ Corkage R30 ▪ Owners Don & Dane Newton ▪ dnewton@mweb.co.za ▪ www.chamonix-restaurant.co.za ▪ **T (021) 876-2393** ▪ F (021) 876-4950

Innovative menus from chef Dane Newton mix Franco Japanese inspiration (line fish, wasabi mash, tempura prawns and pickled ginger foam) with timeless classics accenting flavour. Admire the view from the terrace, shaded by 200-year old oaks; in winter, relax in the warmth of a crackling log fire.

Dieu Donné Restaurant Dieu Donné Vineyards, Uitkyk Street, Franschhoek ▪ Bistro & classic/modern cuisine ▪ Open for lunch & dinner Mon–Sat 10:00–22:00; Sun 11:00–16:00 – lunch only ▪ Closed Mondays & Sun eve during winter ▪ Booking advised ▪ Children welcome for lunch ▪ Major credit cards accepted ▪ Corkage R25 ▪ Air-conditioned ▪ Underfloor heating ▪ Fireplaces ▪ Owners Robert & Tanya Maingard ▪ info@dieudonnerestaurant.com ▪ www.dieudonnevineyards.com ▪ **T (021) 876-3384** ▪ F (021) 876-2935

For the best seats in a natural amphitheatre overlooking Franschhoek's spectacular panorama, book at this just-completed restaurant. Construction involved scalping a hill; erecting an arched venue for restaurant and micro-brewery; repacking earth and planting fynbos. Two levels: lively outdoor terrace with smarter underground, cellar-styled restaurant above. Seasonal cuisine includes quality seafood and specialities like Cape venison pie and harissa ostrich fillet. With wine from surrounding vineyards. (See also A-Z section.)

Grande Provence – The Restaurant Grande Provence Wine Estate, Main Road, Franschhoek ▪ Modern European cuisine with a South African touch ▪ Open daily for lunch 12:00–14:30 & dinner 19:00–21:30 ▪ Closed Sun nights in winter only ▪ Booking advised ▪ Children welcome lunchtime ▪ Major credit cards accepted ▪ No BYO ▪ restaurant@grandeprovence.co.za ▪ www.grandeprovence.co.za ▪ **T (021) 876-8600** ▪ F (021) 876-8601

Contrasts rule. The 300 year-old estate reflects its Huguenot heritage, the elegantly understated Jonkershuis is perfect for private dining. The Restaurant provides a chic industrial framework to assured and globally-inspired local fare from *Sunday Times* Chef of the Year 2007 Peter Tempelhof, complementing the estate's award-winning wines. Indulge in the menu degustation – and don't miss the bitter-sweet Belgian chocolate fondant with peanut butter ice-cream, honey comb and peanut glass. *Dine* 2007 Top 100 Restaurants. (See also Stay-over & A-Z sections.)

Haute Cabrière Cellar Restaurant Pass Road, Franschhoek ▪ International cuisine ▪ Oct-Apr: lunch & dinner daily; May-Sep: lunch daily, dinner Fri & Sat ▪ Booking advised ▪ Children welcome ▪ Major credit cards accepted ▪ No BYO ▪ Owners Matthew & Nicky Gordon, Penny Gordon ▪ hautecab@iafrica.com ▪ www.hautecabriere.com ▪ **T (021) 876-3688** ▪ F (021) 876-3691

Marry food and wine atop a working wine cellar. No starters or main courses. Full or half portions or platters to share, with wines integral to the menu, by the glass or bottle. Chef/patron Matthew Gordon masterminds mouthwatering specialties like fresh mussels 'Pierre Jourdan' with white wine cream and garlic, and roast Karoo lamb loin with lamb shank ravioli, creamed spinach and Italian tomato sauce. Great Wine Capitals of the World – Best Winery Restaurant 2006. (See also A-Z section for Cabrière.)

La Petite Ferme Restaurant La Petite Ferme, Pass Road, Franschhoek ▪ Contemporary country cuisine ▪ Lunch daily from 12:00–16:00 ▪ Booking advised ▪ Children welcome ▪ Major credit cards accepted ▪ Corkage R25 ▪ Owners Mark & Josephine Dendy Young ▪ restaurant@lapetiteferme.co.za ▪ www.lapetiteferme.co.za ▪ **T (021) 876-3016** ▪ F (021) 876-3624

One of the oldest restaurants in SA's gourmet capital boasts a breathtaking valley view matched by fresh, contemporary country cuisine. You'll find all-time best-sellers - regulars would riot were home-smoked rainbow trout and slow-roasted leg of lamb dropped from the menu - but break out with warthog bresaola or innovative vegetarian options. Pair your meal with boutique wines from the farm, by the bottle or glass. Regular Top 100 choice for the past decade. (See also Stay-over & A-Z sections.)

Le Manoir de Brendel R45 Main Road to Franschhoek ▪ Cosmopolitan cuisine ▪ Open daily 07:00–21:00 ▪ Booking advised ▪ Children welcome ▪ Major credit cards accepted ▪ No BYO ▪ Owner Christian Brendel ▪ lemanoir@brendel.co.za ▪ www.le-manoir-de-brendel.com ▪ **T (021) 876-4525** ▪ F (021) 876-4524

Spoil yourself and your family. Lunch in a tranquil, secluded garden, framed by vineyards and mountains, with seating for ten indoors. Light options like sandwiches, salads and specials (favourite is beer-batter hake and shoestring potatoes), or three-course menus for heartier appetites, with wine suggestions for the set lunch. Enjoy leisurely walks through the vineyards, or visit the spa and gym. Also wedding and conference facilities. (See also Stay-over & A-Z sections.)

Le Quartier Français – 'iCi' 16 Huguenot Street, Franschhoek ▪ Contemporary cuisine ▪ Open Mon-Sun 12:00–22:00 ▪ Booking advised ▪ Children welcome ▪ Major credit cards accepted ▪ No BYO ▪ Owner Susan Huxter ▪ restaurant@lqf.co.za ▪ www.lequartier.co.za ▪ **T (021) 876-2151** ▪ F (021) 876-3105

Consistently good. Fun, funky décor is a backdrop to contemporary food cooked in a wood-burning oven from the finest seasonal produce. Pander to your palate with dishes where each ingredient is distinct and the flavour combinations perfectly judged. An excellent winelist to complement the food, and friendly, informed service. Dine Top 100 Restaurants 2007. (See also Bread & Wine and Le Quartier Français 'The Tasting Room'.)

Le Quartier Français 'The Tasting Room' 16 Huguenot Street, Franschhoek ▪ Contemporary cuisine ▪ Open Mon-Sun 19:00 for dinner only ▪ Booking advised ▪ Children 12+ welcome ▪ Major credit cards accepted ▪ No BYO ▪ Owner Susan Huxter ▪ restaurant@lqf.co.za ▪ www.lequartier.co.za ▪ **T (021) 876-2151** ▪ F (021) 876-3105

A cutting-edge experience. This is innovative cuisine that enchants the palate. Choose four or six courses off an à la carte menu or indulge in an eight-course gourmand version with or without wines. (With enhances the experience). For the fourth time and third consecutive year, named one of the World's 50 Best Restaurants, at the S.Pellegrino World's Best Restaurants Awards - the only South African restaurant to make the top 50 finest culinary hotspots. Also Top 10 Special Occasions and Top 100 Restaurants by Dine 2007; Diners Club Int. Award of Excellence 2006. (See also Bread & Wine and Le Quartier Français – iCi.)

Monneaux Restaurant at the Franschhoek Country House Main Road, Franschhoek ▪ Contemporary cuisine ▪ Open 7 days a week for breakfast, lunch & dinner ▪ Booking advised ▪ Children welcome ▪ Major credit cards accepted ▪ Corkage R30 ▪ info@fch.co.za ▪ www.fch.co.za ▪ **T (021) 876-3386** ▪ F (021) 876-2744

Lunch à la carte on the Tuscan-style fountain terrace; dine in the elegantly understated dining room or enclosed veranda. Cuisine is innovative modern French - from exotic teriyaki quail and macadamia nougat salad with garden leaves, dressed in truffle oil to classic favourites like lamb rack. The winelist highlights local wines, also to be enjoyed by the glass in the cosy wine bar or underground cellar. (See also Stay-over section.)

Mont Rochelle & Mange Tout Restaurants Mont Rochelle Hotel & Mountain Vineyards, Dassenberg Road, Franschhoek ▪ Mont Rochelle - al fresco Mediterranean; Mange Tout - fine dining ▪ Open daily for breakfast, lunch & dinner ▪ Booking advised ▪ Children welcome ▪ Major credit cards accepted ▪ No BYO ▪ Owners Erwin Schnitzler & Miko Rwayitare ▪ res@montrochelle.co.za ▪ www.montrochelle.co.za ▪ **T (021) 876-2770** ▪ F (021) 876-3788

Go gourmet. Mange Tout restaurant offers delectable dining in an elegant, airy ambience or on a shaded terrace, both with wrap-round views of Franschhoek valley. Succumb to orgasmic delights like *foie gras* terrine with dark chocolate, crispy pork belly with Marsala and truffle, or appetizing vegetarian options. For casual Med-style al fresco meals matched to wine, visit Mont Rochelle eaterie at the wine tasting centre. (See also Stay-over & A-Z sections).

Reuben's Restaurant & Bar 19 Huguenot Road, Franschhoek ▪ Global cuisine ▪ Open daily for breakfast, lunch & dinner ▪ Closed Christmas & New Year's days ▪ Booking advised ▪ Children welcome ▪ Major credit cards accepted ▪ Corkage R30 ▪ Owners Reuben Riffel, Marc Kent & Tim Rands ▪ reubens@mweb.co.za ▪ www.reubens.co.za ▪ **T (021) 876-3772** ▪ F (021) 876-4464

Multiple awards haven't turned his head. Chef Reuben Riffel remains modest, his inviting food simply prepared and flavour-rich. Relish tantalizing combos like prawn tempura, ginger relish, orange and avocado salad; or mustard-glazed ostrich fillet with soft polenta, roast pumpkin, tomato *smoor*, creamed spinach, ceps and jus. The extensive winelist offers a wide by-the-glass selection; décor is modern classic, with an alfresco courtyard and smoking bar. *Johnnie Walker Eat Out Awards* Restaurant and Chef of the Year 2004/05; *Johnnie Walker Eat Out Awards* Top Ten in the country 2005/06/07.

The French Connection Bistro 48 Huguenot Street, Franschhoek ▪ French bistro - relaxed atmosphere ▪ Open daily for lunch 12:00-15:30 & dinner 18:30-22:00 ▪ Closed Christmas eve ▪ Booking advised ▪ Children welcome ▪ Major credit cards accepted ▪ No BYO ▪ Owners Matthew Gordon & Trevor Kirsten ▪ french@worldonline.co.za ▪ **T (021) 876-4056** ▪ F (021) 876-4036

Experience that true '*La Provence*' feeling: fresh ingredients and simple, deliciously tasty bistro fare. Watch the activity in the glass-fronted, typical French countryside kitchen or relax on the terraced veranda with local wine. Signature dishes from chef-patron Matthew Gordon (also chef/patron at Haute Cabrière) are all-time classics like *moules frites*, slow roasted crispy duck with raspberry vinegar jus, or well-matured steaks with mop-your-plate homemade sauces. (*Dine* Top 100; British Airways Winelands Restaurants).

Gansbaai

Red Indigo at Grootbos Grootbos Private Nature Reserve, on the R43, between Stanford & Gansbaai (two-hour drive from Cape Town) ▪ Old-school cooking with a modern twist ▪ Open daily for lunch 12:00-14:00 & dinner 19:00-21:00 ▪ Booking advised ▪ Horse-riding ▪ Guided forest walks ▪ Conference facilities ▪ Visa & MasterCard accepted ▪ Corkage R50 ▪ Owners Michael & Tertius Lutzeyer ▪ redindigo@grootbos.co.za ▪ www.grootbos.com ▪ **T (028) 384-8000** ▪ F (028) 384-8042

The name derives from spectacular sunsets and a plant species; the menu (natch) highlights seafood, and the well-stocked wine cellar doubles as a private dining room. Stay over at this peace-inducing five-star coastal fynbos reserve, catch the sunset over Walker Bay, then relax in the hands of chef Duane Lewis and his young team. Simple dishes are refreshingly contemporary: speciality is tempura craytail with wasabi *aioli*. (See Stay-over section.)

Hermanus

B's Steakhouse No 5 Hemel & Aarde Village, National Road (R43), Sandbaai, Hermanus ▪ SA Steakhouse ▪ Open Tue-Sun 18:30-late ▪ Closed Mon (except school holidays) ▪ Booking advised ▪ Children 12+ welcome ▪ Major credit cards accepted ▪ Corkage R20 ▪ Owners Bruce & Christine Henderson ▪ bssteakhouse@absamail.co.za ▪ **T (028) 316-3625** ▪ F (028) 316-2698

Life's too short to eat bad food! That's the motto at B's, a family-run restaurant with a friendly, casual ambience and a caring emphasis on good food, wine and service. Only the best cuts of well-aged meat and fish so fresh it's almost flapping. Steakhouse of the year 2005 (Southern + Western Cape); Diner's Club Winelist Awards - five platinum & one merit award over the past years.

La Vierge Restaurant and Champagne Veranda La Vierge Winery, Hemel en Aarde Valley Road (R320), Hemel en Aarde Valley, Hermanus ▪ French country cuisine ▪ Open daily for lunch & dinner - breakfast weekends only ▪ Booking advised ▪ Children welcome ▪ Major credit cards accepted ▪ Corkage R40 ▪ Owners Sjaak Angenent & Francois Barnard ▪ restaurant@lavierge.co.za ▪ www.lavierge.co.za ▪ **T** (028) 313-2007 ▪ F (028) 313-2300

The new owners promise 'an exquisite experience that combines beauty, culinary indulgence and unsurpassable views', plus a tempting deli. The vineyard panorama extends to the sea and the French-style menu complements the relaxed Provençal ambience. Culinary delights include parfait of chicken liver and *foie gras* with toasted olive bread; and brine-cured beef fillet in red wine jus, with *pomme purée*, wild mushrooms and glazed shallots. (See also A-Z section.)

Seafood at The Marine The Marine Hotel, cnr Marine Drive & Main Road, Hermanus ▪ Seafood ▪ Open daily for lunch 12:00-14:30 & dinner 19:00-21:30 ▪ Booking advised ▪ Children 12+ welcome ▪ Major credit cards accepted ▪ Corkage R50 ▪ Owner Liz McGrath ▪ reservations@collectionmcgrath.com ▪ www.collectionmcgrath.com ▪ **T** (028) 313-1000 ▪ F (028) 313-0160

Though the only sea view is on your plate, the mood's relaxed, service friendly and the fish firmly fresh. All-time favourites from the hectic open kitchen are rich man's fish & chips, seafood bunny chow and Marine seafood soup; menus list regional wines by the glass for easy pairing. The same kitchen team prepares the light seafood served at the convenient Seafood Express One Plate Café. (See also Stay-over section.)

Schulphoek Seafront Guesthouse Restaurant 44 Marine Drive (entrance at 181 Piet Retief Crescent), Sandbaai, Hermanus ▪ Global cuisine ▪ **Restaurant is limited to stay-over guests** ▪ Open 7 days a week ▪ Closed month of June ▪ Booking advised ▪ Children welcome ▪ Major credit cards accepted (excl Amex) ▪ No BYO ▪ Owners Wehrner & Janet Gutstadt ▪ Interactive hosts Mannes & Petro van Zyl ▪ schulphoek@hermanus.co. za ▪ www.schulphoek.co.za ▪ **T** (028) 316-2626 ▪ F (028) 316-2627

Stay over at this 5-star guest house guesthouse overlooking Schulphoek bay (the dining room has uninterrupted sea views) and delight in a four-course *menu du jour*. Chef's specialities centre round local seafood, fresh linefish and venison, enhanced by freshly picked herbs and vegetables. The Diners Club Platinum and Gold Wine award-winning winelist is a wine-lover's dream — the cellar boasts over 7000 bottles of regional wine. (See also Stay-over section.)

The Pavilion The Marine Hotel, cnr Marine Drive & Main Road, Hermanus ▪ South African cuisine ▪ Open daily for breakfast 07:00-10:30 & Tue-Sat 19:00-21:30 for dinner ▪ Closed May to end-Aug ▪ Booking advised ▪ Children 12+ welcome ▪ Major credit cards accepted ▪ Corkage R50 ▪ Owner Liz McGrath ▪ reservations@collectionmcgrath.com ▪ www.collectionmcgrath.com ▪ **T** (028) 313-1000 ▪ F (028) 313-0160

Relaxed and informal, but with understated elegance befitting one of the finest dining experiences in Hermanus. Take your time over the menu and winelist. Dishes with tantalising hints of the Med and the East highlight the creativity of the talented culinary team and encourage adventurous wine pairing. Tempting signature dishes include smoked paprika prawns; mouth-melting slow roast duck and featherlight soufflés from the pastry kitchen. (See also Stay-over section.)

Kuils River

Manor House Restaurant see under Stellenbosch

The Guinea Fowl Restaurant Saxenburg Wine Farm, Polkadraai Road (M12), Kuils River ▪ Continental cuisine ▪ Lunch Wed-Mon, dinner Wed-Sat ▪ Closed Tue, Jun-Aug ▪ Booking advised ▪ Children welcome ▪ Major credit cards accepted ▪ Corkage R25 ▪

Owners Adrian & Birgit Bührer ▪ restaurant@saxenburg.com ▪ www.saxenburg.co.za ▪ **T (021) 906-5232** ▪ F (021) 906-0489

Guinea fowl is a signature dish and fresh fish a speciality at this relaxed country venue run by experienced restaurateur Leo Romer. The birds also decorate the farm's wine labels: choose a bottle for perfect food and wine pairing. Eating options from garden lapa for snacks and light meals, to view-rich terrace and intimate dinners indoors. Awarded a Chaine des Rotisseurs Blazon for culinary excellence. (See also A-Z section.)

Paarl & Environs

Backsberg Restaurant see under Franschhoek

Bistro Allegro Grande Roche Hotel, Plantasie Street, Paarl ▪ Global, casual dining experience ▪ Open daily from 11:00-close ▪ Closed mid-May to 31 Jul inclusive ▪ Booking advised ▪ Children welcome ▪ Major credit cards accepted ▪ No BYO ▪ General Manager Garnet Basson ▪ reserve@granderoche.co.za ▪ www.granderoche.com ▪ **T (021) 863-5100** ▪ F (021) 863-2220

Casual dining with class: expect the care that characterises the Grande Roche chefs. Both savoury and sweet palates are spoiled for choice with tempting salads, seafood (try prawn risotto with saffron sauce, topped with pan-fried cob); pasta, sinful desserts, cakes, homemade ice-creams and cheese platters at competitive prices. Diners Club Platinum award-winning winelist offers first and second labels, half bottles or wine by the glass. (See also Stay-over section.)

Bosman's Restaurant Grande Roche Hotel, Plantasie Street, Paarl ▪ Global cuisine ▪ Breakfast 7:00-10:30, lunch 12:00-13:45 & dinner 19:00-21:00 ▪ Closed mid-May to 31 Jul inclusive ▪ Booking advised ▪ Children welcome (4+ for dinner) ▪ Major credit cards accepted ▪ No BYO ▪ General Manager Garnet Basson ▪ reserve@granderoche.co.za ▪ www.granderoche.com ▪ **T (021) 863-5100** ▪ F (021) 863-2220

Epicurean excellence befitting the first and only hotel-restaurant on the African Continent to achieve Relais Gourmand status. Gracious manor house ambience; sumptuous breakfast buffets; informal terrace lunches overlooking vineyards; array of dinner menus promising taste treats like kingklip on ostrich neck ragoût with Chardonnay foam, and skewer of tandoori-spiced Karoo lamb in Cape Malay broth. Informed sommelier and awesome winelist, Diners Club Award of Excellence 2006. (See Stay-over entry for the five-star, multiple award-winning Grande Roche estate hotel.)

Joostenberg Bistro see under Stellenbosch

Marc's Mediterranean Cuisine & Garden 129 Main Road, Paarl ▪ Mediterranean cuisine with French classics ▪ Open daily for lunch & dinner ▪ Closed Sun night, 3 weeks in July for yearly holiday ▪ Booking advised ▪ Children welcome ▪ Major credit cards accepted ▪ Corkage R30 ▪ Owner Marc Friederich ▪ info@marcsrestaurant.co.za ▪ www.marcsrestaurant.co.za ▪ **T (021) 863-3980** ▪ F (021) 863-3990

Experience the ultimate winelands tasting adventure: 30 top SA wine estates served by the glass. Owner Marc Friederich, experienced restaurateur and award-winning sommelier, dispenses Mediterranean-style hospitality through food and wine. Whether indoors or on the lavender-scented terrace, feast on flavourful delights: generous Lebanese mezze platters; signature paella; pan-seared tuna; luscious dark chocolate mousse. Light lunch offerings include chicken gyros; smoked salmon and crème fraiche wraps. Top 10 in its category, Rossouw's guide 2005-2006-2007. Diners Club International Winelist of the Year 2005; Award of Excellence 2006.

Noop/Kikka 217 Main Road, Paarl ▪ Contemporary/continental cuisine ▪ Noop - Mon-Fri 12:00-15:00 & 17:00-23:00 - booking essential; Kikka (which doubles as a florist) - Mon-Fri 07:30-18:00, Sat 07:30-15:00 - booking advised ▪ Children welcome ▪ Major credit cards accepted ▪ Corkage R25 ▪ Owners Karike & Abe Conradie ▪ kikka@telkomsa.net ▪ **T (021) 872-0685** ▪ F (021) 872-1843

Take an old building, add experienced chef Abe Conradie and the result is two distinct eating spaces. Informal Kikka offers an inviting deli, homebaked cakes and dive-in deli (head for the chicken pie). Uncluttered Noop (through an interleading doorway) introduces some 17 wines by the glass, including lesser-known labels. Specialities on seasonal menus range from kidneys in port reduction, beef fillet, to mouthwatering, wafer-thin pizzas.

On the Terrace@Lindhorst Wines Lindhorst Wines, R45, Southern Paarl ■ Country cuisine ■ Open Thu–Tue, book for evening functions ■ Closed Wed ■ Booking advised ■ Children welcome ■ Major credit cards accepted ■ BYO not encouraged – corkage R20 ■ Owners Mark & Belinda Lindhorst ■ info@lindhorstwines.com ■ www.lindhorstwines.com ■ **T (021) 863-4647** ■ F (021) 863-3694

Hearty, home-style helpings to enjoy overlooking a vista of vines, or indoors, warmed by a fire in winter. This BEE project is powered by local women whose friendliness permeates the premises. Crusty pies, savoury pancakes, Jackie's homemade lasagne, soups, country fresh salads and week-end specials to pair with award-winning Lindhorst wines – and a sure-to-appeal basket for kids with a gift to entertain them over lunch. (See also Stay-over & A-Z sections.)

Seasons at Diemersfontein Wine and Country Estate see under Wellington

The Goatshed Fairview Farm, Suid-Agter Paarl Road, Suider Paarl ■ Cape country farm fare, with Mediterranean influence ■ Open daily from 09:00–17:00 (kitchen closes 16:30) ■ Closed Good Friday, 25 Dec & 1 Jan ■ Booking advised ■ Children welcome ■ Major credit cards accepted ■ No BYO ■ goatshed@fairview.co.za ■ www.fairview.co.za ■ **T (021) 863-3609** ■ F (021) 863-2591

Fairview's welcoming farm eatery in the original wine cellar offers an a la carte menu as well as gourmet cheese platters, meat platters, home-made preserves and seasonal specials - plus moreish breads, baked daily on the premises. Over 40 wines available and excellent coffees (enjoy the aroma). Relax in the informal interior or on the terrace, watched by celebrity goats in the Fairview goat tower. (See also A-Z section.)

Zen Restaurant Glen Carlou, Simondium Road, Klapmuts ■ Contemporary and regional cuisine ■ Open Tue–Fri 11:00–15:00, Sat 11:00–14:00 & Sun 11:00–14:00 (Nov–Mar) ■ Closed Mon & Sun (Apr–Oct) ■ Booking advised ■ Children welcome ■ Major credit cards accepted ■ No BYO ■ Owner The Hess Group ■ zen@glencarlou.co.za ■ www.glencarlou.co.za ■ **T (021) 875-5528** ■ F (021) 875-5314

Designed to fit the new winery's minimalist style, the Zen restaurant occupies the same building as the tasting room, and every dish is paired with a glass of Glen Carlou wine. Fresh, unpretentious food mixes Eastern and Cape influences, with cheese platters showcasing local cheeseries. Best-sellers include prawn and avo salad; beef teriyaki with crushed garlic potatoes and spiced apricot chutney; and traditional Malva pudding. (See also A-Z section.)

Plettenberg Bay
Sand at The Plettenberg The Plettenberg Hotel, 40 Church Street, Plettenberg Bay ■ Global cuisine ■ Open daily 06:30–22:00 ■ Booking advised ■ Children 12+ welcome ■ Major credit cards accepted ■ Corkage R40 ■ Owner Liz McGrath ■ reservations@collectionmcgrath.com ■ www.collectionmcgrath.com ■ **T (044) 533-2030** ■ F (044) 533-2074

Ocean and mountain views are enhanced by contemporary SA cuisine, platinum award-winning wine list and stylish cocktail bar; décor suggests that sea and beach have swept through the light, fresh space. Specialities are local or exotic: butter-tender Karoo lamb; sea-fresh linefish; prawns as brochette with calamari and chorizo stuffing; or crisp fritters with smoked bacon lardons. Romantic dinners for two in the well-stocked wine cellar. (See also Stay-over section.)

Rawsonville
Opstal Restaurant Opstal Estate, Slanghoek Road, Rawsonville ■ Cape country cuisine ■ Open Tue–Sun 10:00–15:00 ■ Closed Christian holidays ■ Booking advised ■ Children welcome ■ Wedding & conference facilities for up to 120 delegates ■ Major credit cards

accepted ▪ Corkage R25 ▪ Owner Stanley Louw ▪ wine@opstal.co.za ▪ www.opstal.co.za ▪ **T (023) 344-3001** ▪ F (023) 344-3002

Enjoy warm hospitality and Cape country cuisine, matched to light-hearted wines in a scenic valley. While the appetizing Opstal menu is seasonal, personal attention extends year-round. Feast on favourites like springbok carpaccio on crisp garlic pita; creamy chicken pie; ostrich kebabs enhanced with apricots and figs; homemade chocolate brownies with mixed berry compote. Only an hour from Cape Town, the estate is also a popular venue for functions. (See also A-Z section.)

Robertson

Fraai Uitzicht 1798 Klaas Voogds East, on Route 62 between Robertson & Montagu ▪ Sophisticated country cuisine ▪ Open Wed-Sun from 08:30 ▪ Closed Mon & Tue, Jun-Aug, 24 & 31 Dec & 1 Jan ▪ Booking advised ▪ Children 12+ welcome ▪ Major credit cards accepted ▪ No BYO ▪ Owner Karl Papesch ▪ info@fraaiuitzicht.com ▪ www.fraaiuitzicht. com ▪ **T (023) 626-6156** ▪ F (023) 626-5265

Enjoy 'the real vineyard experience': indulge in a seven-course fine wine & dine menu in this friendly restaurant on a historic wine and guest farm. Ambience is relaxed and rustic, the hosts attentive and the cuisine country fresh, prepared from just-picked produce from the herb and vegetable garden. The well-chosen winelist highlights a selection of the best labels from the 'valley of wine and roses'. (See also Stay-over & A-Z sections.)

Rosendal Winery & Wellness Retreat Klaasvoogds West, Robertson ▪ French-inspired food with fresh African ingredients ▪ Open daily (Sep-May) for breakfast 08:00-10:00, lunch 12:00-15:00 & dinner 19:00-22:00; Jun-Aug Fri-Sun only ▪ Booking advised ▪ Children welcome ▪ Major credit cards accepted ▪ No BYO ▪ info@ rosendalwinery.com ▪ www.rosendalwinery.com ▪ **T (023) 626-1570** ▪ F (023) 626-1571

The kitchen team is Belgian; the dishes fuse French-inspired food with fresh African ingredients. Tasty light lunches; dinners with temptations like blackened beef fillet and Belgian-style chips; litchi and greenpepper-sauced ostrich; Moroccan sole; indulgent 'hot mud' chocolate pudding. Served with the area's award-winning wines in an ambience that's rustic by day, elegant at night. The bar adjacent to the cellar is available to restaurant guests. (See also Stay-over & A-Z sections.)

Somerset West & Environs

96 Winery Road Restaurant Zandberg Farm, Winery Road, off the R44 between Somerset West & Stellenbosch ▪ Country cuisine with global influences ▪ Lunch daily, dinner Mon-Sat ▪ Closed Sun eve ▪ Booking advised ▪ Children welcome ▪ Major credit cards accepted ▪ Corkage R30 ▪ Owners Ken & Allan Forrester, Natasha Wray & Martin Meinert ▪ wineryrd@mweb.co.za ▪ www.96wineryroad.co.za ▪ **T (021) 842-2020** ▪ F (021) 842-2050

Warm, relaxing venue – unofficial HQ for local and international wine luminaries – celebrating over a decade of fresh, uncomplicated and generous food. Menus change frequently according to the whim and creativity of chef Natasha Wray (back in the kitchen) and Mother Nature. Well-hung beef is a speciality and Hollandse pepper fillet and duck and cherry pie on-going best sellers). Rossouw's Guide, Top Ten, in the R100-R150 category. Diner's Club Wine List Award of Excellence 2006. Wine Spectator 'Grand Award' 2006 (the first such award in SA). Wine Magazine Top 100 since 1996.

The Avontuur Estate Restaurant Avontuur Estate, Stellenbosch Road (R44), Somerset West ▪ Contemporary rustic/modern country cuisine ▪ Open Mon-Fri 09:00-17:00, Sat-Sun 09:00-16:00 ▪ Sunset dinners from Dec-Feb, every Wednesday evening. Dine under the stars from 18:00-21:00 ▪ Closed Easter Fri, Dec 25 & Jan 1 ▪ Booking advised ▪ Children welcome ▪ Major credit cards accepted ▪ No BYO ▪ Patron/Chefs Zunia Boucher-Myers & Melanie Paltoglou ▪ openhand@polka.co.za ▪ www. avontuurestate.co.za ▪ **T (021) 855-4296** ▪ F (021) 855-4600

Champagne breakfasts and languorous lunches, where daily specials include fresh quiches and organic salads; succulent specialities include roast duckling with piquant orange and Van der Hum sauce; and delectable desserts are enjoyed with the estate's 10 year-old pot-stilled brandy. Linger in the restaurant, in the wine tasting area or patio garden with views of vineyards, horses and Table Mountain. Also ideal for corporate functions. Gold star listed by the Tourism Grading Council. (See also A-Z section.)

Vergelegen Vergelegen Wines, Lourensford Road, Somerset West ▪ **Lady Phillips Restaurant** (a la carte/country cuisine) open daily for lunch 12:00-14:30 & teas 10:00-11:45 & 14:30-16:00; **Rose Terrace** (al fresco style - light meals) daily 10:00-16:00 (Nov-Apr); **Camphor Forest Picnic** (luxury/elegant picnics) baskets available 12:00-13:30 (Nov-Apr) ▪ Closed Easter Fri, May 1 & Dec 25 ▪ Booking advised for Lady Phillips & Camphor Forest Picnic ▪ Children welcome ▪ All wheelchair-friendly ▪ Major credit cards accepted ▪ No BYO ▪ Owner Anglo American ▪ ladyphillips@vergelegen.co.za ▪ www.vergelegen.co.za ▪ **T/F (021) 847-1346**

Three lunching experiences, very different in style but with one thing in common: menus, developed to complement Vergelegen's award-winning wines, change seasonally to make the most of fresh produce. **Lady Phillips Restaurant:** In summer, lunch on a patio sheltered by Liquid Amber trees and overlooking manicured lawns; in winter expand your culinary horizons indoors in front of the fire. **Rose Terrace:** Lunch lightly al fresco overlooking the acclaimed Rose Garden. **Camphor Forest Picnic:** Elegant picnics in the deep shadow of a centuries old camphor forest while the children amuse themselves with a treasure hunt.

Stanford

Red Indigo   see under Gansbaai

Stellenbosch & Environs

@ Jakarta Rijsttafel Restaurant   La Provence Road, Stellenbosch (behind Polkadraai farm stall on the M12 Stellenbosch-Kuils River) ▪ Asian - authentic Indonesian food & some Dutch snacks ▪ Open daily for breakfast, lunch & dinner Mon-Sat till late (if no bookings received by 19:00 the restaurant closes) ▪ Closed Sun dinner, New Year's day ▪ Booking essential - owners do have their spontaneous sabbatical short breaks; seasonal closure ▪ Children welcome ▪ Major credit cards accepted ▪ Corkage R15 ▪ Owner Duncan Fransz ▪ sunhillf@iafrica.com ▪ www.jakarta.co.za ▪ **T (021) 881-3243** ▪ F (021) 881-3299

Eccentric, rustic restaurant, with warm service from the owner-patron. Speciality is authentic Rijsttafel, with local wines at pocket-friendly prices. Dine amid antiques and art - your chair will carry a price tag as everything is for sale, except the staff. Outdoor seating makes the most of the roses, sun and view. Courtesy transport (book in advance to/from questhouses/hotels in Stellenbosch) in London taxi or Rolls Royce. (See also Stay-over section for Sunhill Farm self-contained Cottages.)

96 Winery Road Restaurant   see under Somerset West

Blaauwklippen Barouche Restaurant   Blaauwklippen Estate, just outside Stellenbosch on the R44 between Stellenbosch & Somerset West, opposite Techno Park ▪ Cape farm-style cuisine ▪ Open daily from 09:00-17:00 ▪ Closed New Year's day ▪ Booking advised ▪ Children welcome ▪ Horse-drawn carriage rides through the vineyards ▪ Wine centre presenting the history of wine and the herbs and spices represented in wine ▪ Major credit cards accepted ▪ No BYO ▪ Owner Farmers Markt Landhandel GmbH ▪ hospitality@blaauwklippen.com ▪ www.blaauwklippen.com ▪ **T (021) 880-0133** ▪ F (021) 880-1246

Family friendly restaurant, where parents can relax over lunch on the terrace while keeping an eye on offspring on the lawn or jungle gym. Chef Stefan Schmidt and his team use fresh seasonal ingredients in dishes from classic to traditional, influenced by Cape Malay spices and own grown herbs. Dishes are paired with suggested Blaauwklippen wines. (See also A-Z section.)

De Oewer   Aan de Wagen Road (next to De Volkskombuis), Stellenbosch ▪ Global contemporary cuisine ▪ Lunch 7 days a week 12:00-15:00, dinner Mon-Sat 18:30-22:00 &

Sun (Nov-Mar) ▪ Closed Good Friday, Jun-Aug ▪ Booking advised ▪ Children welcome ▪ Major credit cards accepted ▪ Corkage R25 ▪ Owners Dawid & Christelle Kriel ▪ mail@ volkskombuis.co.za ▪ www.deoewer.co.za ▪ **T** (021) **886-5431** ▪ F (021) 883-3413

With a delightfully relaxed setting on the banks of the Eerste River under venerable oaks, this friendly restaurant is well-known for alfresco-style lunches and dinners. An appetising array of Mediterranean dishes and extensive winelist will ensure your enjoyment of the occasion. Ideal for functions.

De Volkskombuis Aan de Wagen Road, Stellenbosch ▪ SA cuisine ▪ Lunch 7 days a week 12:00-15:00, dinner Mon-Sat 18:30-22:00 & Sun (Nov-Mar) ▪ Closed Good Friday ▪ Booking advised ▪ Children welcome ▪ Major credit cards accepted ▪ Corkage R25 ▪ Owners Dawid & Christelle Kriel ▪ mail@volkskombuis.co.za ▪ www.volkskombuis.co.za ▪ **T** (021) **887-2121** ▪ F (021) 883-3413

A specialist in traditional fare for over a quarter-century, serving favourites like baked Karoo lamb rib, honey-roast duck, oxtail and a 'Cape country sampler'. Dawid and Christelle Kriel took over the family business in 2001. Their passion for food, wine and people, and personal touch, have enhanced the restaurant's reputation for meals in good company, seven days a week.

Fishmonger Stellenbosch NPK Building, cnr Ryneveld & Plein Streets, Stellenbosch ▪ Mediterranean - seafood ▪ Mon-Sat 12:00-22:00, Sun & public holidays 12:00-21:00 ▪ Closed Christmas, New Year & Good Friday ▪ Booking advised ▪ Children welcome ▪ Major credit cards accepted ▪ Corkage R15 (if on winelist or more than 1 bottle per 2 pax) ▪ Owners André Viljoen, Craig Seaman & Nico van Staaden ▪ fishmonger@adept.co.za ▪ www. eatingout.co.za ▪ **T** (021) **887-7835** ▪ F (021) 887-7834

A bustling Mediterranean-style alfresco taverna in the heart of the winelands, where patrons enjoy the best and freshest linefish and seafood (sushi is an added attraction), with service to match. The winelist showcases local producers and changes seasonally. Good food, good service and good wine are the watchwords here.

Flavours Restaurant Devon Valley Hotel, Devon Valley Road, Stellenbosch ▪ Contemporary Cape cuisine ▪ Open daily for breakfast 07:00-11:00, lunch & dinner 11:00-22:00 ▪ Booking advised ▪ Children welcome ▪ Wheelchair-friendly ▪ Major credit cards accepted ▪ Corkage R20 ▪ Owner LGI Hotels & Vineyards ▪ info@devonvalleyhotel.com ▪ www. devonvalleyhotel.com ▪ **T** (021) **865-2012** ▪ F (021) 865-2610

Authentic, contemporary Cape cuisine, with an award-winning winelist to complement a pleasurable, relaxed dining experience in a vineyard setting. Focus is on bold flavours, classic, uncomplicated dishes and fresh, clean tastes, with venison as a year-round signature dish. Leisurely light summer lunches on the terrace (admire the view) and cosy winter fireside dinners. Book ahead for local favourites: Sunday lunch and themed month-end dinner dances. (See also Stay-over section & A-Z for SylvanVale.)

Guardian Peak Guardian Peak, Annandale Road, Stellenbosch ▪ Fusion - dishes are paired with Guardian Peak wines ▪ Open Tue-Sat 09:00-17:00 (kitchen closes at 15:00), Tastings Mon-Fri 09:00-17:00, Sat 09:00-15:00 (May-Sep) & 09:00-16:00 (Oct-Apr) ▪ Closed Sun-Mon, Easter Fri, Dec 25 & Jan 1 ▪ Booking advised ▪ Children welcome ▪ Major credit cards accepted ▪ No BYO ▪ Owners Ernie Els & Jean Engelbrecht ▪ info@ guardianpeak.com ▪ www.guardianpeak.com ▪ **T** (021) **881-3899** ▪ F (021) 881-3388

Don't only taste the wines: enjoy them with food. Ernie Els and Jean Engelbrecht's view-rich venture at the foot of the Helderberg pairs Guardian Peak's award winning-wines with dishes created by chef Corli Els. Seared tuna loin macerated in ginger and soy dressing, surrounded by truffle foam, marries merlot; shiraz sings with springbok medallions in blackberry sauce and mushroom ravioli revels in Frontier cab blend. (See also A-Z section.)

Joostenberg Bistro Klein Joostenberg Farm, R304, Muldersvlei ▪ French bistro/country ▪ Open Tue-Sun for breakfast 08:00-11:00 & lunch 12:00-15:00 ▪ Closed Mon ▪ Booking advised ▪ Children welcome ▪ Major credit cards accepted ▪ Corkage R15 ▪ Owners Philip Myburgh, Christophe Dehosse & Susan Dehosse ▪ bistro@joostenberg.co.za ▪ **T** (021) **884-4208** ▪ F (021) 884-4135

Friendly family-run bistro offering traditional French cooking – with fresh bread and filled omelettes to start your day. Joostenberg wines make excellent partners to specialties like charcuterie platter, salad Niçoise, pork cheek casserole and classic crème caramel. Enquire about book-ahead wine and food matching lunches, available to parties over four. Ambience is relaxed, with a cosy fire in winter, and shady stoep in summer. Families welcomed. (See also A-Z section.)

Mana Restaurant & Guest Cottages JC le Roux Farm, Devon Valley Road, Stellenbosch ▪ Contemporary classic cuisine ▪ Open for lunch & dinner Tue-Sat 12:00-14:00 & 19:00-21:00 – check opening times during winter ▪ Closed Sun-Mon ▪ Booking advised ▪ Children welcome ▪ Major credit cards accepted ▪ No BYO ▪ Owners Jonathan & Heather Taylor ▪ dine@mana.co.za ▪ www.mana.co.za ▪ **T (021) 865-2662** ▪ F 086-671-9360

Owner operated and consistently delicious, with well-informed service. Al fresco terrace with stunning vineyard and mountain views; elegant interior. Chef/patron Jonathan Taylor's irresistible offerings include tempura tiger prawns, sesame vegetable and pickled ginger salad with wasabi vinaigrette; refreshing pannacotta of vanilla and pinot noir grappa with summer berries. Well-chosen winelist showcases award-winning wines from the area. Top 10 in *Roussow's Restaurant Guide* 2007. (See also A-Z section.)

Manor House Restaurant Zevenwacht Wine Farm, Langverwacht Road, Kuils River ▪ Global contemporary cuisine ▪ Open 365 days per year for breakfast 07:00-10:00 (Mon-Fri) & 08:00-11:00 (Sat-Sun), lunch 12:00--15:00 & dinner 18:00-22:00 ▪ Booking advised ▪ Children welcome ▪ Major credit cards accepted ▪ No BYO ▪ Owner Manie Wolmarans ▪ restaurant@zevenwacht.co.za ▪ www.zevenwacht.co.za ▪ **T (021) 903-5123** ▪ F (021) 903-5257

The tranquil setting is idyllic: an elegant Cape Dutch Manor House overlooking a lake rich in bird life. Ambience is relaxed and cuisine freshly seasonal – dishes like chicken and prawn curry, stews of the day, from traditional *waterblommetjie* to braised lamb or seafood, and as dessert signature apple & mint brûlée. Picnic baskets are available to enjoy in the farm gardens. (See also Stay-over & A-Z sections.)

Mon Plaisir Restaurant Bottelary Road (M23), Stellenbosch ▪ French cuisine - Plats du jour & A la carte ▪ Open daily for lunch & dinner ▪ Booking advised ▪ Children welcome ▪ Major credit cards accepted ▪ No BYO ▪ Owners Celine & David ▪ cmonplaisir@gmail.com ▪ www.onsgenot.com/monplaisir ▪ **T (021) 865-2456**

Classic French cuisine, fresh products matching Bottelary Road wines, French-owned local wine estates and French wines. Tradition rules: delight in a litany of dishes like foie gras, soufflés, terrines, duck specialities, rib of beef, kidneys, sweetbreads, homemade French-style sauces, pastries and sorbets. Central open fireplace, cosy lounges, terrace and children's playground. (See also Stay-over section for Ons Genot Country Lodge.)

Morgenhof Restaurant Klapmuts Road, Stellenbosch ▪ A la carte, country cuisine ▪ Open daily for lunch 12:00-15:00 (Nov-Apr) & 12:00-14:30 (May-Oct) ▪ Closed Good Friday, Christmas & New Year's days ▪ Booking advised ▪ Children welcome ▪ Major credit cards accepted ▪ No BYO ▪ Owner Anne Cointreau ▪ carolyn@morgenhof.com ▪ www.morgenhof.com ▪ **T (021) 889-2024** ▪ F (021) 889-5266

Complement Morgenhof's award-winning wines with light lunches or hearty meals. Eat al fresco in the garden during summer, shaded by a centuries-old old oak. (Signature dish is sesame chicken salad, the chicken strips marinated in light soya, deep-fried and sprinkled with sesame seeds.) In winter, relish comfort food in the glassed-in and log fire warmed Gazebo, or soak up winter sun under a canopy of vines. (See also A-Z section.)

Olivello Restaurant Marianne Wine Estate, Valley Road, off R44, between Klapmuts & Stellenbosch ▪ Cape Mediterranean ▪ Seasonal opening times, generally closed Mon & Tue ▪ Booking advised ▪ Children welcome ▪ German, Italian & French spoken ▪ Visa & MasterCard accepted ▪ Corkage R35 ▪ Owners Lynne Aberdeen & Laurille Krug ▪ restaurant@olivello.co.za ▪ www.olivello.co.za ▪ **T (021) 875-5443** ▪ F (021) 875-5483

Ex Café Paradiso partners Laurille and Lynne put their passion to work in picturesque surroundings, ensuring that friendly service, delicious food and a lake setting provide a feast for the senses. Sunday speciality is a Mediterranean Table, presented buffet-style in the kitchen. Relax, play boules, row the boat or just laze on the lawns. Ideal for weddings, birthdays or corporate events. (See also Stay-over & A–Z sections.)

Rust en Vrede Rust en Vrede Wine Estate, Annandale Road, Stellenbosch ▪ Fine dining ▪ Open for dinner Tue-Sat 18:00–23:00 ▪ Closed Sun, Mon, Easter Fri, Dec 25 & Jan 1 ▪ Booking advised ▪ Major credit cards accepted ▪ No BYO ▪ Owner Jean Engelbrecht ▪ info@rustenvrede.com ▪ www.rustenvrede.com ▪ **T (021) 881-3881** ▪ F (021) 881-3000

Eagerly awaited new restaurant that promises fine dining in an original barrel cellar dating back to 1783. Rust en Vrede owner Jean Engelbrecht and gourmet chef David Higgs have paired up in a stylish, intimate venue offering a variety of contemporary but classic set menus to complement the international wine list, with fresh produce from the farm gardens. (See also A–Z section.)

Terroir Restaurant Kleine Zalze Wine Estate, Techno Park turn-off, Strand Road (R44), Stellenbosch ▪ Provençal with a Cape twist ▪ Open for lunch Mon-Sun, dinner Mon-Sat ▪ Closed Sun eve ▪ Booking advised ▪ Children welcome ▪ Major credit cards accepted ▪ Corkage R40 ▪ Owner Kobus Basson ▪ Executive chef Michael Broughton ▪ terroir@ kleinezalze.co.za ▪ www.kleinezalze.co.za ▪ **T (021) 880-8167** ▪ **F (021) 880-0862**

Provençal-inspired, with impeccably judged sauces. Chef Michael Broughton (now solo) matches the unpretentious ambience with a constantly evolving chalkboard menu of deceptively simple dishes conveying his 'less is more' philosophy. Specialities include braised pork belly with smoked mash, savoy cabbage and truffle purée, and confit duck pancake with fresh fig jam and classic vinaigrette. Pair your meal with international award-winning wines from the estate. *Eat Out Johnnie Walker* Restaurant of the Year 2006, *Eat Out* Service Excellence Award 2006, *Eat Out* Top 10 2005 and 2006, *Dine* Top 10 2005 and 2006. Best of Wine Capitals of the World South African Wine Tourism Restaurant of the Year 2006. (See also Stay-over & A–Z sections.)

The Duck Pond Welmoed Winery, R310, Baden-Powell Drive (Spier Road), Stellenbosch ▪ Traditional South African cuisine ▪ Open daily for lunch from 12:00-15:00 ▪ Closed Tue (May-Sep) ▪ Booking advised ▪ Children welcome ▪ Major credit cards accepted ▪ Corkage R12 ▪ Owners Ronel & Charlene van der Walt ▪ info@duckpond.co.za ▪ www.duckpond.co.za ▪ **T/F (021) 881-3310**

Craving comfort food like roast duck, slow-roasted lamb shank, chicken and mushroom pie? You'll find it – and other traditional dishes – in hearty helpings at Welmoed Winery, where the restaurant in the Wine Tasting centre overlooks a large duck pond. The relaxed setting (and friendly ducks) make this an ideal venue for families. Seats 50 inside and 70 on wooden benches on the lawn. (See also A–Z section.)

Wellington

Seasons at Diemersfontein Wine and Country Estate Jan van Riebeeck Drive (R301), Wellington ▪ Country cuisine ▪ Open daily 8:00-late (if no bookings received by 19:00 the restaurant closes) ▪ Booking advised ▪ Children welcome ▪ Major credit cards accepted ▪ Corkage R20 ▪ Owners David & Sue Sonnenberg ▪ restaurant@ diemersfontein.co.za ▪ www.diemersfontein.co.za ▪ **T (021) 864-5060** ▪ F (021) 864-2095

Overlooking pastures and farm dam, this welcoming restaurant offers à la carte country cuisine, lightened by a sophisticated touch. The appropriately seasonal menu, devised with Diemersfontein wine in mind, highlights fresh, locally-sourced ingredients. Seasons' handcrafted produce – including must-try chocolate, salami, and preserves is also available. 'Side attractions' for visitors wanting a snack, and gourmet picnics, complete with rug and basket, also available. (See also Stay-over & A–Z sections.)

Worcester

Opstal Restaurant see under Rawsonville

Stay-overs in the Winelands and Cape Town

Featured below are some guest lodges, hotels, country inns, B&Bs and self-catering cottages in the winelands, many of them on wine farms (look for the ⌂ symbol beside the individual entries in the A-Z section of this guide). These are paid entries. The venues supplied information on their cuisine, menus and attractions, which was then edited for consistency of style. Unless stated to the contrary, all speak English and Afrikaans, have parking and gardens/terraces. Rates are for standard double rooms unless otherwise specified – for example per person (pp) or breakfast included (B&B). Tourism Grading Council of South Africa (TGCSA) ratings where provided. Should you wish to know about wheelchair access, please discuss with the relevant venue.

Index of stay-overs

Listed alphabetically, with region.

Villa Exner – Exclusive
   Country Manor . . . . Elgin Valley
Whale Cottage Camps
   Bay . . . . Cape Town
Whale Cottage
   Franschhoek . . . . Franschhoek
Whale Cottage Hermanus . Hermanus

Zevenwacht Country Inn . Stellenbosch
Zorgvliet Vineyard Lodge
   & Spa. . . . . Stellenbosch

Bonnievale

Jan Harmsgat Country House   see under Robertson

Calitzdorp

Calitzdorp Country House   Calitz Street, Calitzdorp ■ TGCSA 5-star guest house ■ 5 Bedrooms ■ Single from R800 B&B, double from R1200 per room B&B ■ Visa & MasterCard accepted ■ Restaurant ■ Pool ■ TV ■ Air-conditioning ■ Ceiling fans ■ Owners Lyn & Allan Fabig ■ calchouse@mweb.co.za ■ www.cchouse.co.za ■ **T (044) 213-3760** ■ F (044) 213-3933

   In a spectacular setting, with views across a fertile valley of vineyards and orchards to the majestic Swartberg mountains, 5-star Calitzdorp Country House lies at the heart of the Klein Karoo's world-class tourist attractions. Furnished with antiques, Persian rugs and original art, the house captures the style of a gentleman's country residence - down to the well-stocked wine cellar. Escape with that special someone.

The Retreat at Groenfontein   Groenfontein Farm, District Calitzdorp (20km from Calitzdorp, off Route 62) ■ TGCSA 3 & 4-star guest house ■ Luxury & standard rooms ■ 9 Bedrooms ■ R570–R750 pp sharing **DB&B**, single & winter rates on request ■ Visa & MasterCard accepted ■ Restaurant (problem diets catered for - advise when booking) ■ Pool ■ Children welcome ■ French, German, Italian & Swedish spoken ■ Owners Grant & Marie Burton ■ info@groenfontein.com ■ www.groenfontein.com ■ **T/F (044) 213-3880**

   A consistent award-winner (AA Accommodation Award 03, 04 & 05, Hall of Fame 2006 & 2007), this three and four-star graded Victorian farmhouse offers both standard and luxury rooms. The inviting lounge and dining room overlook sweeping lawns and the majestic Swartberg, and you'll be pampered with hearty breakfasts and tasty dinners. Enjoy leisurely walks, challenging trails, or simply relax at the pool and let the silence soak into your soul.

Cape Town

Andros Boutique Hotel   cnr Newlands & Phyllis Roads, Claremont, Cape Town ■ TGCSA 5-star hotel ■ 10 Bedrooms ■ May-Sep: single R1 100 B&B, double R1 650 per room B&B; Oct - Apr: single R1 400 B&B, double R2 100 per room B&B ■ Major credit cards accepted ■ Dine at the Andros restaurant ■ Children 12+ welcome ■ Facilities for conferences, exclusive corporate and private functions & elegant weddings ■ Pool ■ TV ■ Air-conditioning ■ Gym ■ Sauna ■ Beauty clinic ■ Dutch & German spoken ■ Owners The Barrow Family ■ info@andros.co.za ■ www.andros.co.za ■ **T (021) 797-9777** ■ F (021) 797-0300

   History and elegance combine in this gracious Sir Herbert Baker designed gabled homestead, lovingly restored and updated. Enjoy gourmet breakfasts on the sun-bathed terrace overlooking park-like gardens and pool; delicious dinners on the candle-lit patio or in the intimate restaurant 'Dine'. With quick, easy access to Cape Town's historic core, the Waterfront and airport, this leafy retreat is ideal for discerning visitors and business travelers. (See also Eat-out section.)

Brooklands House   3 Surbiton Road, Rosebank, Cape Town ■ 4 Bedrooms ■ Low season: single R550 B&B, double R450 pp sharing B&B; High season: single R850 B&B, double R700 pp sharing B&B ■ Major credit cards accepted (excl Diners Club) ■ Conference facilities ■ Pool ■ TV ■ Ceiling fans ■ Owners Philip & Sandra Engelen ■ maxengelen@mweb.co.za ■ **T/F (021) 689-3594** ■ Opening in Dec 07 after renovations

   Charming turn-of-the-century Victorian villa, within walking distance of over 10 restaurants and near Newlands rugby and cricket grounds. Breakfasts are served in the sunroom overlooking the lush garden; dinners (by prior arrangement) by firelight in the cosy red dining room. Sit by the drawing room fire in winter, read a book, chat to new friends - or your hosts, enthusiasts who love talking about wine!

Cape Grace West Quay Road, V&A Waterfront, Cape Town ▪ TGCSA & SATOUR 5-star luxury hotel ▪ 122 bedrooms ▪ Single from R3 925-R4 845 B&B, double from R4 075-R4 995 per room B&B ▪ Major credit cards accepted ▪ onewaterfront Restaurant ▪ Bascule Whisky Bar and Wine Cellar ▪ Café Bascule ▪ Pool ▪ Satellite TV ▪ Air-conditioning ▪ Spa ▪ German, French, Swedish, Xhosa, Spanish, Italian, Czech, Danish, Russian, Norwegian, Serbo-Croatian, Slovak, Portuguese, Greek, Maltese spoken ▪ Owner Meikles Africa Limited ▪ info@capegrace.com ▪ www.capegrace.com ▪ **T (021) 410-7100** ▪ F (021) 419-7622

Grace personified. Overlooking mountains and yachts in Cape Town's Waterfront, this charming 'sanctuary', adds warmth to traditional sophistication, exudes welcome and is a stickler for the detail that ensures guest comfort. (With an award-winning restaurant, bar and café, this extends to the inner man). The hotel's landmark first decade - studded with international accolades for exemplary service — is proof of their commitment to exceed expectations. Latest awards: Top Hotel in Cape Town in *Travel & Leisure's* 2007 annual round up of the World's 500 Best Hotels, Resorts, Lodges, Inns and Safari Camps; Top 10, *Travel & Leisure* reader's poll: 'World's Best Service' in Africa & Middle East 2007. (See also Eat-out section.)

Dunkley House 3B Gordon Street, Gardens, Cape Town ▪ TGCSA 4-star guest house ▪ 11 Bedrooms ▪ From R750-R1 350 per room B&B ▪ Major credit cards accepted (excl Amex) ▪ TV ▪ 3 plunge pools ▪ Air-conditioning ▪ German & French spoken ▪ Owner Sharon Scudamore ▪ reservations@dunkleyhouse.com ▪ www.dunkleyhouse.com ▪ **T (021) 462-7650** ▪ Mobile 083-775-2620 a/h ▪ F (021) 462-7649

Retreat to a tucked-away oasis of luxury, with friendly service and welcoming atmosphere. Enjoy sumptuous breakfasts from a full-time chef, sip sundowners by the courtyard pool and chill out under the shade of banana palms. Set in a turn-of-the-century Dutch-colonial house, surrounded by a private, tropical garden, Dunkley House offers spacious en-suite rooms with all creature comforts (including flat screen TV, ipod compatible radios & beautiful percale linen).

Steenberg Hotel see under Constantia

The Table Bay Hotel Quay 6, V&A Waterfront, Cape Town ▪ TGCSA 5-star hotel ▪ 329 Bedrooms ▪ Rates on request ▪ Major credit cards accepted ▪ Two Restaurants: Atlantic & The Conservatory and Union Bar ▪ Conference facilities ▪ Pool ▪ TV ▪ Air-conditioning ▪ Camelot Health Spa ▪ French, Russian, German, Mandarin, Chinese & Spanish spoken ▪ Owner Sun International ▪ tbhres@sunint.co.za ▪ www.suninternational.co.za ▪ **T (021) 406-5000** ▪ F (021) 406-5686

Ultimate luxury in a Leading Hotel of the World. Spacious reception area with gleaming marble and bowls of orchids, sink-into-comfort en-suite rooms with views of Table Mountain or Robben Island. Two restaurants, gourmet and more casual, to tempt your palate. Business Centre for workaholics; Camelot Health Spa to help shed stress. Direct access to V&A Waterfront activities, from shops, restaurants and movies to boat cruises.

Whale Cottage Camps Bay 57 Camps Bay Drive, Camps Bay ▪ TGCSA 4-star guest house ▪ 10 Bedrooms ▪ Winter R250-R300 pp B&B, summer R550-R590 pp B&B ▪ Major credit cards accepted ▪ Pool ▪ TV ▪ Air-conditioning ▪ German spoken ▪ Owner Chris von Ulmenstein ▪ campsbay@whalecottage.com ▪ www.whalecottage.com ▪ **T (021) 438-3840** ▪ F (021) 876-3107

Welcome to a whale of a stay at Whale Cottage Camps Bay, a beach villa with magnificent views over the Atlantic ocean. Just 500 meters from Camps Bay beach and 25 restaurants (a safe walk) and a 10 minute drive from Table Mountain cableway. Secure parking, sparkling pool and free wireless internet. Wir sprechen Deutsch. Proudly South African.

Clanwilliam

Sanddrif Holiday Resort Dwarsrivier Farm, off the N7, Cederberg ■ 15 Self-catering cottages ■ R420 per cottage for up to 4 people ■ Visa & MasterCard accepted ■ Camping facilities ■ Farm shop ■ Mountain pool ■ Mountain bike trails ■ Hiking trails ■ Observatory ■ Rock climbing ■ Owner Nieuwoudt family ■ sanddrif@cederbergwine.com ■ www. cederbergwine.com ■ **T (027) 482-2825** ■ F (027) 482-1188

Need a break? Sanddrif, on the banks of the Dwars River below Wolfberg, offers camping facilities (with a safe playground), cosy self-catering cottages with spectacular mountain views. Friendly staff at the well-stocked farm shop will supply information and permits needed to explore the area. The vast Cederberg Conservancy, rich in fynbos and wildlife, is a must for adventurous and less energetic nature lovers. (See also A-Z section for Cederberg Private Cellars.)

Citrusdal

Sanddrif Holiday Resort see under Clanwilliam

Constantia

Constantia Uitsig Hotel and Spa Constantia Uitsig, Spaanschemat River Road, Constantia ■ SATOUR 5-star country hotel ■ 16 Bedrooms ■ Single from R1 100–R1 900 B&B, double from R1 500–R2 850 per room B&B ■ Major credit cards accepted ■ Three Restaurants: Constantia Uitsig Restaurant, La Colombe & The River Café ■ Pool ■ Spa ■ TV ■ Air-conditioning ■ Ceiling fans ■ Underfloor heating ■ Wi-fi access ■ Mini bar & coffee making facilities ■ reservations@uitsig.co.za ■ www.constantia-uitsig.com ■ **T (021) 794-6500** ■ F (021) 794-7605

Charmingly unpretentious, this 5-star hotel is set among the vineyards of a private wine estate on the Constantia Wine Route, a mere 20 minutes from the Waterfront. Sixteen garden rooms with sweeping views of the Constantia Valley; a new luxurious spa; and a choice of three world-renowned restaurants on the property, of which La Colombe was voted 28th Best Restaurant in the World in 2006. (See also Eat-out & A-Z sections.)

Hampshire House Guest Lodge 10 Willow Road, Constantia ■ TGCSA 4-star guest house ■ 5 Bedrooms ■ Single from R395–R695 B&B, double from R295–R415 pp sharing B&B ■ Visa & MasterCard accepted ■ Pool ■ TV ■ Air-conditioning ■ Ceiling fans ■ Owners Ricky & Carole Chapman ■ stay@hampshirehouse.co.za ■ www.hampshirehouse.co.za ■ **T (021) 794-6288** ■ F (021) 794-2934

The ideal base for exploring the Cape Peninsula. Set in the Constantia wine valley, this welcoming 4-star guesthouse (runner up - highly commended - in the AA Accommodation Awards 'Guest House of the Year' 2006) offers easy motorway access to Table Mountain, the Waterfront, winelands, beaches and local restaurants. Five individually decorated en-suite bedrooms. English and continental buffet breakfasts; swimming pool and secure off-street parking.

Steenberg Hotel Steenberg Estate, Tokai ■ TGCSA 5-star ■ From R1 825–R2 750 per room B&B ■ Major credit cards accepted ■ Catharina's Restaurant ■ Conference facilities ■ Superb spa ■ Two pools ■ Satellite TV ■ Air-conditioning ■ Championship golf course ■ German & French spoken ■ Owner Graham Beck ■ info@steenberghotel.com ■ www. steenberghotel.com ■ **T (021) 713-2222** ■ F (021) 713-2251

Luxuriate in a national monument established in 1682, sensitively restored and converted into a 5-star hotel - now with three new spacious, butler-serviced suites reflecting Cape history. Past elegance blends with contemporary comforts, including chic pool bar and spa. Sheltered by Steenberg mountains and set in vineyards, with award-winning winery, top-rated restaurant, and 18-hole championship golf course, the hotel is an ideal base for exploring the Cape. AA Accommodation Awards - Gold - Superieur. South Africa's Leading Wine Estate - World Travel Awards 2007. (See also Eat-out & A-Z sections.)

The Cellars-Hohenort Hotel 93 Brommersvlei Road, Constantia ■ SATOUR 5-star Relais & Chateaux Boutique Hotel ■ 53 Bedrooms ■ Low season: single R1 350 B&B,

double R1 750 per room B&B; high season: single R1 950 B&B, double R3 300 per room B&B ▪ Major credit cards accepted ▪ Children 12+ welcome ▪ The Cape Malay Restaurant, The Greenhouse Restaurant & The Martini ▪ Conference facilities ▪ 3 Pools (one heated) ▪ Tennis court ▪ Gary Player designed putting & chipping golf green ▪ Gym ▪ Carchele Beauty Spa ▪ The Collection Boutique ▪ D & D Hair Salon ▪ TV ▪ Air-conditioning ▪ French, Italian, German, Xhosa & Zulu spoken ▪ Owner Liz McGrath ▪ reservations@collectionmcgrath.com ▪ www.collectionmcgrath.com ▪ **T (021) 794-2137** ▪ F (021) 794-2149

This tranquil 5-star haven in the heart of Constantia marries two traditions: the magnificent restoration of the 18th century Klaasenbosch wine cellars and the splendid Hohenort manor house. Combining elegance with charm, the hotel's luxury rooms and suites have breathtaking views across nine acres of world-renowned gardens and vineyard. Also inviting restaurants, swimming pools, gym, tennis court and golf green, hair salon and beauty spa. Member of the International Relais & Chateaux Association. (See also Eat-out section.)

Whale Cottage Camps Bay see under Cape Town

Darling

Darling Lodge 22 Pastorie Street, Darling ▪ TGCSA 4-star B&B ▪ 6 Bedrooms ▪ Double R700 B&B per room - single on request ▪ Visa & MasterCard accepted ▪ Wedding/private function/conference facilities ▪ Pool ▪ TV ▪ Ceiling fans ▪ French & German spoken ▪ Owner Legner Family ▪ info@darlinglodge.co.za ▪ www.darlinglodge.co.za ▪ **T (022) 492-3062** ▪ F (022) 492-3665

Stylish, beautifully restored Victorian home in the gentle Darling valley offers a harmonious blend of old and new in an environment of vineyards, pastures, wheat fields and spectacular wild flower displays. Enjoy the area's award-winning wines and olives in a gorgeous garden with inviting pool. Dinner by arrangement only. An hour from Cape Town and minutes from the Atlantic Ocean. Winelands, beaches, golf, whale watching, art galleries, 'Evita se Perron' nearby.

Trinity Lodge 19 Long Street, Darling ▪ TGCSA 4-star guest house ▪ 6 Bedrooms ▪ Single R400 B&B, double R300 pp B&B ▪ Major credit cards accepted (excl Amex) ▪ Restaurant ▪ Conference facilities ▪ Pool ▪ TV ▪ Owners Shaun & Debbie Mc Laughlin ▪ mclaughlin@worldonline.co.za ▪ www.trinitylodge.co.za ▪ **T (022) 492-3430** ▪ F (022) 492-2693

Think lavender and Provencal charm in the quiet of Darling village. Rooms, opening onto a charming garden, have separate entrances ensuring privacy, with percale linen and ball-and-claw baths setting the tone. The friendly restaurant specialises in fresh country fare (don't miss the tasty home bakes) while the winelist will introduce you to the excellent wines from the area. Trinity also hosts popular wine evenings. (See also Eat-out section for Hilda's Kitchen - the Restaurant at Groote Post.)

Elgin Valley

Glen Stuart Cottages Ross Gower Wines, 114 The Valley Road, Elgin ▪ 6 Cottages with WI-FI: 14 bedrooms ▪ R800 per cottage, 'Top Cottage' sleeps 4 @ R200 pp, 'Lower Cottage' sleeps 6 @ R134 pp ▪ Self-catering - picnic lunches by arrangement ▪ Visa & MasterCard accepted ▪ Wine tastings & sales ▪ Cellar tours by appointment ▪ Walking/hiking/mountain-biking ▪ German & French spoken ▪ Owner Gower family ▪ glenstuartcottages@worldonline.co.za ▪ **T/F (021) 844-0197**

Enjoy magnificent views of vineyards and neighbouring Kogelberg Biosphere from a family-owned wine farm. Four stylishly renovated, individually decorated cottages each with two en-suite double bedrooms and large lounge/diningroom with fireplace; also two three-bedroomed cottages. Well-equipped kitchenettes and Weber braais encourage self catering, though all meals (including picnics) are available by prior arrangement. On Elgin Wine Route, centrally situated between Somerset West, Franschhoek and Hermanus. (See also A-Z section.)

Villa Exner - Exclusive Country Manor 11 Essenhout Avenue, Klipkop, Grabouw/Elgin Valley ▪ TGCSA 5-star boutique hotel ▪ 6 Bedrooms ▪ May-Sep: single from

R650 B&B, double from R450 pp sharing B&B; Oct–Apr: single from R910 B&B, double from R650 pp sharing B&B ▪ Major credit cards accepted ▪ Restaurant ▪ Conferences ▪ Weddings ▪ Pool ▪ TV ▪ Air-conditioning ▪ German, French & Russian spoken ▪ Owner Sascha Sulliman-Exner ▪ info@villaexner.com ▪ www.villaexner.com ▪ **T (021) 859-3596** ▪ F (021) 882-9198

Relax and rejuvenate at this tranquil haven and registered birder-friendly venue, less than an hour's drive from Cape Town. The main house, rich in modern pieces and personally chosen art, is set in smooth lawns and lush private gardens with mountain views. The Green Mountain Eco-Route (the world's first biodiversity wine route) and the Cape's floral kingdom, the protected Kogelberg Biosphere, are on the doorstep.

Franschhoek & Environs

Akkerdal Guest House   Akkerdal Estate, R45, La Motte ▪ 2 Bedrooms ▪ R1 200 per room ▪ Self-catering ▪ Major credit cards accepted ▪ TV ▪ Air-conditioning ▪ Owner Pieter Hanekom ▪ wine@akkerdal.co.za ▪ www.akkerdal.co.za ▪ **T (021) 876-3481** ▪ F (021) 876-3189

Unwind in the picturesque Franschhoek valley, where a friendly artisan winery (less than 10 km from the Cape's food & wine capital) offers accommodation overlooking vineyards and mountains. Two double bedrooms, shared bathroom, fully fitted kitchen and covered braai make this an ideal venue for family or friends. Owner Pieter Hanekom, who recommends sundowners beside the Berg River, suggests visiting the website to sample the enticing environment. (See also A–Z section.)

Burgundy Bourgogne Manor House & Cottages   Burgundy Bourgogne Farm, Excelsior Road, Franschhoek ▪ TGCSA 4-star self-catering ▪ 8 Bedrooms ▪ R630–R750 pp sharing (1–2 people), R500–R630 pp sharing (3–4 people) ▪ Visa & MasterCard accepted ▪ Pool ▪ TV ▪ Air-conditioning ▪ Ceiling fans ▪ Owner Trevor Kirsten ▪ burgundybourgogne@saol.com ▪ www.burgundybourgogne.co.za ▪ **T (021) 876-4623** ▪ F (021) 876-3817

Recapture the style and atmosphere of life on a 17th-century Huguenot wine farm. Set amidst olive orchards, vines and centuries-old oaks, Burgundy Bourgogne Farm offers luxury self-catering accommodation in the historic manor house and fully equipped cottages.

Franschhoek Country House & Villas   Main Road, Franschhoek ▪ TGCSA 4 & 5-star country house ▪ 26 Bedrooms ▪ Standard de luxe rooms from R685–R795 pp sharing B&B; Luxury rooms & garden cottages from R895–R1 075 pp sharing B&B; Villa suites from R1 595–R2 150 pp sharing B&B ▪ Major credit cards accepted ▪ Monneaux Restaurant ▪ Conference facilities ▪ Beauty Salon ▪ 2 Pools ▪ TV ▪ Air-conditioning ▪ info@fch.co.za ▪ www.fch.co.za ▪ **T (021) 876-3386** ▪ F (021) 876-2744

Space combined with luxury: all 14 rooms and 12 villa suites (each 100m^2) provide the features and facilities expected of a first-class hotel. Laze at the pools (one heated), admire the mountain vistas, visit the area's boutique wine farms, or explore the charming village founded by the French Huguenots. Conference facilities for up to 45 delegates available in the fully-equipped, elegant club room. Finalist in the Top Billing Lifestyle Awards. (See also Eat-out section.)

Grande Provence – The Owner's Cottage   Grande Provence Wine Estate, Main Road, Franschhoek ▪ TGCSA 5-star villa ▪ 5 Bedrooms ▪ Rates on request ▪ Major credit cards accepted ▪ Restaurant ▪ Conference facilities ▪ Spa pool ▪ TV ▪ Air-conditioning ▪ Ceiling fans ▪ Art Gallery ▪ ownerscottage@grandeprovence.co.za ▪ www.grandeprovence.co.za ▪ **T (021) 876-8600** ▪ F (021) 876-8601

This heritage wine estate blends past and present, offering a rewarding range of experiences: 5-star, exclusive-use villa (max 10 guests); award-winning winery; chic 'industrial-style' restaurant headed by *Sunday Times* Chef of the Year 2007; elegant Jonkershuis for private functions; and The Art Gallery showcasing contemporary SA art. The super-deluxe Owner's Cottage (with private pool and Jacuzzi overlooking vineyards) made Conde Nast Hotlist for the 60 best new hotels worldwide. (See also Eat-out & A–Z sections.)

La Fontaine Guest House   21 Dirkie Uys Street, Franschhoek ▪ TGCSA 4-star guest house ▪ 12 Bedrooms ▪ Single from R650–R750 B&B, double from R425–R525 pp sharing

B&B ▪ Major credit cards accepted ▪ Children by arrangement ▪ Pool ▪ TV ▪ Air-conditioning ▪ Ceiling fans ▪ Secure off-street parking ▪ Wheelchair-friendly ▪ Owner Linquenda Guest House cc ▪ lafontaine@wam.co.za ▪ www.lafontainefranschhoek.co.za ▪ **T/F (021) 876-2112**

Experience country hospitality in this gracious home in the heart of Franschhoek, within walking distance of restaurants, galleries and shops. Spectacular mountain views from 12 spacious en-suite double rooms (including three garden rooms with fireplace, TV, fridge, separate entrance and patio, and one family suite in tranquil garden). Generous buffet breakfasts served indoors or under vine-covered pergola. AA Quality Assured program 'Superior' rating.

La Maison Bleue Self-catering Guest Accommodation 30 Uitkyk Street, Franschhoek ▪ R1 800 per night for the house – minimum 3 nights ▪ Pool ▪ TV ▪ Fans ▪ German & Dutch spoken ▪ Owners Richard & Rebekah Kelley ▪ Contact Rosemary Beetge ▪ rosemary_beetge@absamail.co.za ▪ www.rlmproperty.co.za ▪ **T/F (021) 876-3849; 083-456-9371**

SA home of sometime Platter Guide contributor and Master of Wine Richard Kelley, La Maison Bleue is located in a quiet area on the edge of Franschhoek village. The house has an extensive living area with three bedrooms (two doubles, one twin), well-equipped kitchen and garden with mountain views, terrace, pool and *petanque piste*. Long- or short-term lets.

La Petite Ferme La Petite Ferme, Pass Road, Franschhoek ▪ TGCSA 5 & 4-star B&B ▪ 5 Vineyard Suites: single from R1 150-R1 350 B&B, double from R650-R750 pp sharing B&B; 4 Lakeside Lodges: single from R800-R900 B&B, double from R450-R550 pp sharing B&B ▪ Major credit cards accepted ▪ Restaurant ▪ Plunge pool per suite (no pools at Lakeside Lodges) ▪ TV ▪ Air-conditioning ▪ Ceiling fans ▪ Fly fishing ▪ Hiking ▪ Wine tasting ▪ Dutch spoken ▪ Owners Mark & Josephine Dendy Young ▪ info@lapetiteferme.co.za ▪ www.lapetiteferme.co.za ▪ **T (021) 876-3016** ▪ F (021) 876-3624

Soak up peace and privacy on a boutique wine farm, now offering more accommodation – with characteristic attention to comfort. Free-standing, individually furnished 5-star Vineyard suites below the restaurant, each with patio and plunge pool, have been augmented by four 4-star rated 2 bedroom/2 bathroom lakeside lodges on the wall of a trout lake across the road. All have spectacular views of the Franschhoek valley. (See also Eat-out & A-Z sections.)

La Petite Providence La Providence Farm, Middagkrans Road, Franschhoek ▪ TGCSA 5-star Country House & AA Travel Superior Accommodation ▪ Two double-bedroomed cottage ▪ Open from 1 Oct - 30 Apr ▪ Rates from R750-R1 250 per person sharing B&B ▪ Visa, MasterCard & Diners Club cards accepted ▪ Pool ▪ Tennis court ▪ TV ▪ Air-conditioning ▪ Ceiling fans ▪ Spanish spoken ▪ Owner Andy Higgins ▪ info@laprovidence.co.za ▪ www.laprovidence.co.za ▪ **T (021) 876-4790** ▪ F (021) 876-4898

Delightfully different accommodation in an elegant gabled guest cottage on a working wine estate in mountain-rimmed Franschhoek village. Two luxurious double bedrooms, one with indulgent leather 'sleigh' bed; both with double doors opening onto the swimming pool. Vast beamed lounge/dining area with array of original artworks; fully-fitted kitchen should you care to self-cater. Stunning mountain views and bird-rich pond on the doorstep. 5-star TGCSA graded and AA 'Superior Accommodation'. (See also A-Z section.)

La Providence Mews Flat La Providence Farm, Middagkrans Road, Franschhoek ▪ One double-bedroomed flat ▪ Open from 1 Oct - 30 Apr ▪ R750 per person sharing – self-catering ▪ Visa, MasterCard & Diners Club cards accepted ▪ Full kitchen ▪ Tennis court ▪ TV ▪ Air-conditioning ▪ Spanish spoken ▪ Owner Andy Higgins ▪ info@laprovidence.co.za ▪ www.laprovidence.co.za ▪ **T (021) 876-4790** ▪ F (021) 876-4898

Attached to the main farmstead and only a short distance from La Petite Providence, the Mews Flat (separate entrance) provides highly original accommodation for two. Antique and original furniture blends East and Africa against a backdrop of artwork, and focal point of the vast room is a carved four-poster 'extra king sized' bed. Features of the art-hung, en-suite bathroom are a freestanding bath and huge walk-in shower. (See also A-Z section.)

Le Manoir de Brendel Spa, Wine & Guest Estate R45 Main Road to Franschhoek ▪ TGCSA 5-star guest house ▪ 10 Suites ▪ Rates on request ▪ Major credit cards accepted ▪ Restaurant ▪ Conference facilities ▪ Chapel ▪ Spa ▪ Gym ▪ Pool ▪ Tennis court ▪ TV ▪ Air-conditioning ▪ Ceiling fans ▪ Owner Christian Brendel ▪ lemanoir@brendel.co.za ▪ www.le-manoir-de-brendel.com ▪ T (021) 876-4525 ▪ F (021) 876-4524

Secluded, view-rich accommodation at the entrance to Franschhoek valley. Unwind amid vines and mountains, sample estate wines in the 'leather bar' and leisurely meals at al fresco tables in the tranquil garden or guest-orientated restaurant. Pamper yourself at the spa or work out at the gym, enjoy tennis and walking trails through the vineyards. The chapel and conference facility are ideal for weddings and functions. (See also Eat-out & A-Z sections.)

Lindhorst Wines Vineyard Cottage   see under Paarl

Mont Rochelle Hotel & Mountain Vineyards Dassenberg Road, Franschhoek ▪ TGCSA 5-star boutique hotel ▪ 22 Bedrooms ▪ Low season: from R1 650 per room B&B; High season: from R2 800 per room B&B ▪ Major credit cards accepted ▪ Two restaurants: Mont Rochelle Restaurant & Mange Tout ▪ Boardroom ▪ Pool ▪ TV ▪ Air-conditioning ▪ Wellness centre ▪ Gym ▪ Horse riding ▪ Hiking ▪ German, French, Xhosa & Zulu spoken ▪ Owners Erwin Schnitzler & Miko Rwayitare ▪ res@montrochelle.co.za ▪ www.montrochelle.co.za ▪ **T (021) 876-2770** ▪ F (021) 876-3788

Previously La Couronne Hotel, Mont Rochelle Hotel and Mountain Vineyards offers ultimate pampering, surrounded by vines on a 33 ha farm with spectacular views of Franschhoek. Enjoy the streamlined luxury of 5-star accommodation, where subtly toned décor induces relaxation. Add the pleasures of fine and al fresco dining, chilling at the pool, a wellness centre, gym and wine tasting facility. Plus hikes and horse riding. (See also Eat-out & A-Z sections.)

Whale Cottage Franschhoek 11 Akademie Street, Franschhoek ▪ TGCSA 4-star guest house ▪ 6 Bedrooms ▪ Winter R250-R300 pp B&B, summer R450-R490 pp B&B ▪ Major credit cards accepted ▪ Pool ▪ TV ▪ Air-conditioning ▪ German spoken ▪ Owner Chris von Ulmenstein ▪ winelands@whalecottage.com ▪ www.whalecottage.com ▪ **T (021) 876-3929** ▪ F (021) 876-3107

Welcome to a whale of a stay at Whale Cottage Franschhoek, a country house with a delightful garden and babbling brook, in the heart of South Africa's gourmet capital. Top restaurants Reubens and Le Quartier Français are 200 meters away. Beautiful mountain views. Sparkling swimming pool. Secure parking. Free wireless internet. Luxury honeymoon suite. Wir sprechen Deutsch. Proudly South African.

Gansbaai

Grootbos Private Nature Reserve On the R43, between Stanford & Gansbaai ▪ TGCSA 5-star lodge ▪ 27 Bedrooms ▪ Single from R2 850-R3 750 full board, double from R1 950-R2 750 pp full board ▪ Visa & MasterCard accepted ▪ Red Indigo Restaurant ▪ Conference facilities ▪ Pool ▪ TV ▪ Air-conditioning ▪ Beauty Salon ▪ Library ▪ Gallery ▪ Close to secluded swimming areas and archaeological caves ▪ German spoken ▪ Owners Michael & Tertius Lutzeyer ▪ info@grootbos.co.za ▪ http://www.grootbos.com ▪ **T (028) 384-8000** ▪ F (028) 384-8042

Set in 1700 hectares of coastal fynbos and forest, this shed-care haven blends hospitality with five-star accommodation, gourmet cuisine and fine wines. A two-hour drive from Cape Town, Grootbos offers guests conservationist-led botanical tours and 4x4 drives, horse riding and boat tours to view the marine big five. Or simply unwind in the space and privacy of richly textured, sink-into-luxury suites with spectacular ocean views. (See also Eat-out section.)

Grabouw

Villa Exner - Exclusive Country Manor   see under Elgin Valley

Hermanus

Schulphoek Seafront Guesthouse   44 Marine Drive (entrance at 181 Piet Retief Crescent), Sandbaai, Hermanus ▪ TGCSA 5-star guesthouse ▪ 7 Suites – superior, luxury & standard ▪ Low season: from R432–R914 pp sharing B&B; High season: from R581–R1 348 pp sharing B&B (includes a 4-course meal on first night); single supplement + 50% to pp rate ▪ Major credit cards accepted (excl Amex) ▪ Restaurant ▪ Body therapy (by appointment) ▪ Heated pool ▪ TV ▪ Air-conditioning ▪ Ceiling fans ▪ Owners Wehrner & Janet Gutstadt ▪ Interactive hosts Mannes & Petro van Zyl ▪ schulphoek@hermanus.co.za ▪ www.schulphoek.co.za ▪ **T (028) 316-2626** ▪ F (028) 316-2627

Five-star guesthouse overlooking an unspoiled, quiet bay, 5 km from Hermanus centre. Luxurious, spacious suites have spectacular sea or garden views. Delectable evening four-course menu du jour, specialising in seafood and venison; choice of over 7000 bottles of local wine. (Diners Club International Platinum and Gold Winelist Awards). Book for body therapy; enjoy the salt pool, golf, walking, birding, fishing, whale watching and great white sighting. (See also Eat-out section.)

The Marine Hotel   Cnr Marine Drive & Main Road, Hermanus ▪ SATOUR 5-star Relais & Chateaux Boutique Hotel ▪ 43 Bedrooms ▪ Low season: single R1 350 B&B, double R1 750 per room B&B; high season: single R1 950 B&B, double R3 300 per room B&B ▪ Major credit cards accepted ▪ Children 12+ welcome ▪ Seafood at The Marine & The Pavilion restaurants ▪ Conference facilities ▪ Heated salt water pool & tidal pool ▪ Carchele Spa ▪ The Collection Boutique ▪ TV ▪ Air-conditioning ▪ Internet lounge ▪ German spoken ▪ Owner Liz McGrath ▪ reservations@collectionmcgrath.com ▪ www.collectionmcgrath.com ▪ **T (028) 313-1000** ▪ F (028) 313-0160

Commanding a spectacular position, the 5-star Marine is set atop seafront cliffs, its bedroom windows providing panoramic ocean views and the world's best land-based whale-watching. Rooms and suites exude understated luxury and the chic Sun Lounge and Bar encourages relaxation. Heated salt water and tidal pool; spa; choice of restaurants: the elegant Pavilion, buzzing Seafood at The Marine and convenient Seafood Express One Plate Café. A Relais & Chateaux boutique hotel. (See also Eat-out section.)

Whale Cottage Hermanus   38 Westcliff Drive, Hermanus ▪ TGCSA 4-star guest house ▪ 6 Bedrooms ▪ Winter R250–R300 pp B&B, summer R450–R500 pp B&B ▪ Major credit cards accepted ▪ Pool ▪ TV ▪ Air-conditioning ▪ German spoken ▪ Owner Chris von Ulmenstein ▪ hermanus@whalecottage.com ▪ www.whalecottage.com ▪ **T (028) 313-0929** ▪ F (021) 876-3107

You'll have a whale of a stay at Whale Cottage Hermanus, a marine-themed beach house with magnificent views over Walker Bay, and of whales B & B (breaching and blowing). Hermanus is the whale capital of South Africa, and offers the best land-based whale watching in the world. Just a 1km walk to village centre and craft market. Sparkling pool. Secure parking. Free wireless internet. Wir sprechen Deutsch. Proudly South African.

Kuils River

Zevenwacht Country Inn   see under Stellenbosch

Montagu

Les Hauts de Montagu Guest Lodge   On Route 62 between Montagu & Barrydale, 3 km after Montagu, second gate on your right ▪ TGCSA 4-star lodge ▪ 6 Bedrooms ▪ Low season: single R650 B&B, double R425 pp sharing B&B; High season: single R750 B&B, double R585 pp sharing B&B ▪ Visa & MasterCard accepted ▪ Restaurant: dinner Tue-Sat ▪ Pool ▪ Ceiling fans ▪ Hiking trails ▪ Small wedding chapel ▪ French spoken ▪ Owners Eric & Myriam Brillant ▪ info@leshautsdemontagu.co.za ▪ www.leshautsdemontagu.co.za ▪ **T (023) 614-2514** ▪ F (023) 614-3517

Tranquility meets romance on a fynbos-rich 600ha farm on the slopes of the Langeberg. Luxuriate in spacious en-suite rooms in thatched cottages, each with fireplace, Victorian bathtub and heated bathroom floor. Sweeping views from veranda (or outside shower) of mountains and olive orchards; French-style cuisine in the converted barn (set four- or five-course dinner Tues-Sat). Plenty to explore, from hiking trails to scenic Route 62.

Oudtshoorn

Rosenhof Country House 264 Baron van Reede Street, Oudtshoorn ▪ TGCSA 5-star country house ▪ 12 Bedrooms & 2 Suites ▪ Low season: single R1 100 B&B, double R1 650 per room B&B; High season: single R1 480 B&B, double R2 250 per room B&B ▪ Major credit cards accepted ▪ Restaurant ▪ Pool ▪ TV ▪ Air-conditioning ▪ Gym ▪ Jacuzzi ▪ Beauty clinic ▪ Art gallery ▪ Owners NJ Barrow & FR Barrow ▪ rosenhof@xsinet.co.za ▪ www. rosenhof.co.za ▪ **T (044) 272-2232** ▪ F (044) 272-3021

Beautiful rose gardens, which gave Rosenhof its name, lead to stylish bedrooms and two totally private suites, each with lounge and swimming pool. Traditional country cuisine is served in the award-winning restaurant, with wine from the extensive private cellar. Revitalise at Rosenhof's wellness centre with gym, jacuzzi, sauna and beauty clinic. Then explore: attractions include the Cango caves, ostrich show farm and wild life centre.

Paarl & Environs

Diemersfontein Wine and Country Estate Guest House see under Wellington

Grande Roche Hotel Plantasie Street, Paarl ▪ TGCSA 5-star hotel, SATOUR 5-star silver, Relais Gourmand ▪ 34 Bedrooms ▪ Terrace Suite from R2 800 low season to R3 900 high season per room B&B; Duplex Suite from R2 400 low season to R3 500 high season per room B&B ▪ Major credit cards accepted ▪ Bosman's Restaurant & Bistro Allegro ▪ Conference facilities ▪ TV ▪ Air-conditioning ▪ 2 Pools (1 heated) ▪ Sauna ▪ Fitness centre ▪ 2 Tennis courts (floodlit) ▪ German, Swedish & Dutch spoken ▪ General Manager Garnet Basson ▪ reserve@granderoche.co.za ▪ www.granderoche.com ▪ **T (021) 863-5100** F (021) 863-2220

Overlooking vineyards and rugged mountains, this multiple award-winning, all-suite estate hotel is the ideal 5-star base from which to explore the Cape. Member of the Relais Chateaux Association, Grande Roche is a byword for 'incredible attention to detail, impeccable grounds, excellent food and superb levels of luxury'. Relax at the swimming pools, go biking, play tennis, visit the fitness centre or the hotel's private masseur. (See also Eat-out section for Bosman's Restaurant - the first and only hotel-restaurant on the African continent to achieve Relais Gourmand status - & Bistro Allegro.)

Landskroon Self-catering Cottage Landskroon Wines, Suid-Agter-Paarl Road, Suider-Paarl ▪ From R400–R500 per cottage – ideal for 2 adults + 2 children ▪ Major credit cards accepted ▪ Picnic lunches on request Oct-Apr ▪ TV ▪ Bass fishing ▪ Owners Paul & Hugo de Villiers Family Trusts ▪ landskroon@mweb.co.za ▪ www.landskroonwines.com ▪ **T (021) 863-1039** ▪ F (021) 863-2810

Idyllic retreat on a wine farm on the southern slopes of Paarl mountain, with views over vineyards to distant Table Mountain. Geared for a family, the one-bedroomed cottage has double sleeper couch in the living room. Fully equipped for self-catering: match your meals to the farm's own wine. And bring your fishing rod - the dam teems with bass. Serviced daily, carport, TV and security. (See also A-Z section.)

Lindhorst Wines Vineyard Cottage Lindhorst Wines, R45, Southern Paarl ▪ 2-bedroomed Cottage ▪ R700 per cottage, plus R100 pp over 2 persons - self catering ▪ Major credit cards accepted ▪ Restaurant - breakfast & lunch ▪ Conference facilities ▪ TV ▪ Ceiling fans ▪ Fireplace ▪ Owners Mark & Belinda Lindhorst ▪ info@lindhorstwines.com ▪ www.lindhorstwines.com ▪ **T (021) 863-0990** ▪ F (021) 863-3694

Revel in wrap-round views of dams and wines from a self-catering luxury cottage on the edge of the merlot vineyards on a working wine and fruit farm. The spacious double-volume living areas, two bedrooms and two bathrooms sleep four comfortably. Alternatively, this is an ideal cosy romantic getaway and springboard to explore the winelands. Well equipped for meals/braais at home and close to fine restaurants. (See also Eat-out & A-Z sections.)

Marianne Wine Estate Guest Apartments see under Stellenbosch

Oak Tree Lodge 32 Main Street, Paarl ▪ TGCSA 3-star guest house ▪ 18 Bedrooms ▪ Single from R420–R440 B&B, double from R295–R325 pp sharing B&B for standard rooms & from R390 pp sharing B&B for garden rooms ▪ Major credit cards accepted ▪ Conference facilities ▪ Pool ▪ TV ▪ Air-conditioning ▪ German spoken ▪ Owners Yvette & Gerd Baudewig ▪ info@oaktreelodge.co.za ▪ www.oaktreelodge.co.za ▪ **T (021) 863-2631** ▪ F (021) 863-2607

Ideal for visitors: accommodation that bridges town and country, offers a full SA breakfast, and is a convenient base for exploring the winelands. Centrally located in the historic town of Paarl, Oak Tree Lodge borders on vineyards at the back, yet is within walking distance of restaurants, wine tasting venues and shops. The large garden, now with rooms beside the pool, overlooks vineyard-clad Paarl mountain.

Sonop Guesthouse Sonop Wine Farm, Windmeul, Voor-Paardeberg, Paarl ▪ TGCSA 3-star ▪ 4 Bedrooms ▪ From R220–R275 pp B&B ▪ Visa & MasterCard accepted ▪ Conference facilities ▪ Pool ▪ TV ▪ Fans ▪ sonop@african-terroir.co.za ▪ www.african-terroir.co.za ▪ **T (021) 869-8534** ▪ F 086-510-4551

Experience farm life in the comfort of a 3-star guesthouse on an organic wine farm with spectacular views of Paarl valley. You'll bask in personal attention and warm hospitality. Just a 45 minute drive from Cape Town, cuddled at the foot of the Paardeberg Mountains, Sonop makes an deal base for exploring the winelands. Enjoy a continental or full English breakfast before setting out. (See also A–Z section for African Terroir.)

Plettenberg Bay

The Plettenberg 40 Church Street, Plettenberg Bay ▪ SATOUR 5-star Relais & Chateaux Boutique Hotel ▪ 38 Bedrooms ▪ Low season: single R1 350 B&B, double R1 750 per room B&B; high season: single R1 950 B&B, double R3 300 per room B&B ▪ Major credit cards accepted ▪ Children 12+ welcome ▪ Sand at The Plettenberg restaurant ▪ Sand Bar ▪ Conference facilities ▪ 2 Pools (one heated) ▪ Carchele Spa ▪ The Collection Boutique ▪ TV ▪ Air-conditioning ▪ Boat based whale & dolphin watching ▪ Golf ▪ Kayaking ▪ Deep sea and rock fishing ▪ Close proximity to 4 beaches ▪ German spoken ▪ Owner Liz McGrath ▪ reservations@collectionmcgrath.com ▪ www.collectionmcgrath.com ▪ **T (044) 533-2030** ▪ F (044) 533-2074

Five-star luxury overlooking sea, mountains and golden sand, with dolphin and whale sighting from hotel terraces. Stylish contemporary décor; chic cocktail bar; sea vistas from the relaxed restaurant, Sand, with modern South African menus; dinners à deux in the well-stocked wine cellar. Spa and two swimming pools, one heated. The adjoining **Beach House** & **Lookout Villa** offer self-contained privacy, sundecks and private swimming pools, large sitting room and dining room with service kitchen. Five-star Relais & Chateaux boutique hotel. (See also Eat-out section.)

Robertson

Ballinderry, The Robertson Guest House 8 Le Roux Street, Robertson ▪ TGCSA 4-star guest house ▪ 6 Bedrooms ▪ Single on request, double from R290–R525 pp sharing B&B low season to R330–R560 pp sharing B&B high season ▪ Major credit cards accepted ▪ Restaurant – dinner served to guests only ▪ Pool ▪ TV ▪ Air-conditioning in some units ▪ Ceiling fans ▪ Dutch, French & German spoken ▪ Owners Luc & Hilde Uyttenhove ▪ info@ballinderryguesthouse.com ▪ www.ballinderryguesthouse.com ▪ **T (023) 626-5365** ▪ F (023) 626-6305

Luxury accommodation in a charming contemporary thatched villa (with 5 double rooms and one deluxe honeymoon suite), set in a large and tranquil tropical garden in the heart of Robertson. Hands-on Belgian owners Luc and Hilde provide personal service and champagne breakfasts: Hilde's fine cooking fuses French, Italian and South African cuisines. Near the region's best-known wineries, with a golf course only five minutes away. AA Superior, Portfolio accredited 'Luxury' accommodation.

Excelsior Manor Guest House Excelsior Estate, Robertson ▪ 9 Bedrooms ▪ Rates on request ▪ Major credit cards accepted ▪ Conference facilities ▪ Pool ▪ TV ▪ Air-conditioning ▪

Owners De Wet Family ▪ guesthouse@excelsior.co.za ▪ www.excelsior.co.za ▪ **T (023) 615-2050/-1980** ▪ F (023) 615-2019

Experience an 'ostrich feather palace' on a working wine farm. During the 1880-1914 ostrich feather boom, affluent SA ostrich farmers erected opulent houses. One such mansion, built by the present owners' grandparents, is now a guesthouse. Of historical value, no changes are allowed to the exterior, but renovations have transformed the interior into comfortable accommodation. Mountain and Breede River valley views, wine-tasting venues nearby. (See also A-Z section.)

Fraai Uitzicht 1798   Klaas Voogds East, on Route 62 between Robertson & Montagu ▪ TGCSA 4-star guest house ▪ 8 Bedrooms ▪ Single from R690 B&B, double from R450 pp sharing B&B ▪ Major credit cards accepted ▪ Restaurant ▪ Pool ▪ TV (in cottages) ▪ Game drives in Private Nature Reserve ▪ Special Klaas Voogds package including game drive and maze walk ▪ Performances by the Makukhanye Choir on certain Wednesdays ▪ German & Xhosa spoken ▪ Owner Karl Papesch ▪ info@fraaiuitzicht.com ▪ www.fraaiuitzicht.com ▪ **T (023) 626-6156** ▪ F (023) 626-5265

Shed stress in the peace of a historic wine and guest farm in the majestic Langeberg hills, at the heart of the Robertson valley. Set amid vineyards and orchards, stylishly appointed guest cottages and suites blend luxurious comfort with spectacular views; attentive hosts ensure fine dining in the award-winning restaurant; vineyard walks and game drives beckon. Ideal for a relaxing, comfortable and culinary few days. AA Travel Superior Guest House. (See also Eat-out & A-Z sections.)

Jan Harmsgat Country House   On the R60, between Ashton (20 km) and Swellendam (25 km) ▪ TGCSA 4-star guest house ▪ 7 Bedrooms ▪ Low season: single R630 B&B, double R525 pp sharing B&B – High season: single R990 B&B, double R825 pp sharing B&B ▪ Major credit cards accepted ▪ Restaurant ▪ Pool ▪ Air-conditioning ▪ Ceiling fans ▪ German spoken ▪ Owners Brin & Judi Rebstein ▪ brinreb@iafrica.com ▪ www.jhghouse.com ▪ **T (023) 616-3407** ▪ F (023) 616-3201

Delight in true Cape hospitality at a genuine country house (four-star graded) set among pecan nut, almond and fruit orchards on a farm famous for cheeses and preserves. Accommodation adds luxury to tradition, cuisine is delectable and the wine collection superb. Two hours from Cape Town between Swellendam and Ashton on the Robertson wine route. Multiple awards for outstanding service in growing local communities in tourism. Awarded Fair Trade in Tourism Trademark 2005.

Pat Busch Private Nature Reserve   Klaas Voogds West, Robertson ▪ 7 Cottages, 3 Farmhouses ▪ Rates vary between R140 pp (standard) & R300 pp (exclusive suite) ▪ Self-catering ▪ Visa & MasterCard accepted ▪ Conference facilities ▪ Indoor fireplaces ▪ German spoken ▪ Owner Busch family ▪ patbusch@intekom.co.za ▪ www.patbusch.co.za ▪ **T (023) 626-2033** ▪ F (023) 626-1277

This country escape in the Langeberg foothills combines nature with comfort, offering exclusive access to some 2000 ha of private nature reserve with hiking trails, swimming and bass fishing. Exclusive self-catering cottages have spa baths, indoor fireplaces, outdoor showers and sweeping vineyard views. A small rustic hall accommodates gatherings, conferences and retreats. On the Robertson Wine Valley route and an ideal base for wine tasting excursions. (See also A-Z section for Rusticus Vintage Cellar.)

Rosendal Winery & Wellness Retreat   Klaasvoogds West, Robertson ▪ TGCSA 4-star Guesthouse ▪ 8 Bedrooms ▪ Low season: single from R610-R760 B&B, double from R800-R900 per room B&B; High season: single from R690-845 B&B, double from R900-R1 100 per room B&B ▪ Visa & MasterCard accepted ▪ Rosendal Restaurant and Wine Bar ▪ Conference facilities ▪ Spa & Wellness Centre with qualified therapists ▪ Pool ▪ Ceiling fans ▪ French & Norwegian spoken ▪ Owners Geir Tellefsen & Sissel Anderssen ▪ info@rosendalwinery.com ▪ www.rosendalwinery.com ▪ **T (023) 626-1570** ▪ F (023) 626-1571

Shed care at a serene haven offering personal service, wine bar and French-inspired restaurant - plus grape-based treatments at the in-house spa and wellness centre. A choice of eight en-suite rooms, elegantly furnished with colonial pieces, in the original farmhouse or new manor house, each overlooking vineyards, pond or beautiful garden. A relaxing getaway and ideal base for Breede River day excursions and wine tastings. (See also Eat-out & A-Z sections.)

Tierhoek Cottages Tierhoek Farm, Noree Valley, Robertson ▪ Single R230, double R460 per room - breakfast R45 pp ▪ No credit card facilities ▪ Pool ▪ TV (in 2 cottages) ▪ Ceiling fans ▪ Owners Bruce & Alison Gilson ▪ gilson@barvallei.co.za ▪ www. tierhoekcottages.co.za ▪ **T/F (023) 626-1191**

Take time out on a certified organic fruit and vine farm. Pepper Tree, Lucky Bean, Quince and Tierhoek House are private, self-catering cottages, elegantly furnished, well equipped, with open fireplaces, private verandas and braai areas. Use of own private pools. Enjoy spectacular scenery with walks in the mountains and an abundance of birds and wildlife. Breakfast and dinner 'baskets' on request.

Van Loveren Farm Cottage Situated in the heart of the Boland, between Robertson & Bonnievale on one of Van Loveren's working wine farms and only 2.5 km from the cellar ▪ 3-Bedroomed Cottage ▪ Rates: 2 persons R600, 4 persons R700, 5 persons R750 & 6 persons R800 for the whole cottage – self-catering ▪ No credit card facilities ▪ Pool ▪ DSTV ▪ Ceiling fans ▪ Owners Stefanie Retief & Francine Conradie ▪ doef@myisp.co.za ▪ www. vanloverenfarmcottage.co.za ▪ **T 082-332-8692** ▪ F (023) 615-1227

Sit on the stoep and drink in the tranquility, unending vistas - and well-priced wines. The three-bedroomed old farm cottage has fully equipped kitchen and enclosed braai with grid and wood. Swimming pool and beautiful garden with large lawn, ideal for children. For the energetic, 13km mountain bike trail and Fish Eagle walking trail. Bedding and towels provided; bring swimming towels and own smartcard for DSTV. (See also A-Z section for Van Loveren Private Cellar.)

Route 62
Les Hauts de Montagu Guest Lodge see under Montagu

Stanford
Grootbos Private Nature Reserve see under Gansbaai

Somerset West & Environs
Fynbos Cottage Miravel Estate, Faure Waterworks Road, Somerset West ▪ 2-Bedroomed Cottage ▪ R500 per night for cottage - self-catering ▪ No credit card facilities ▪ Pool ▪ DSTV ▪ Ceiling fans ▪ Wine tasting ▪ Dutch & French spoken ▪ Owners Maarten & Janine van Beuningen ▪ miravel@adept.co.za ▪ www.miravel.co.za ▪ **T (082) 418-5802**

Self-cater in comfort on a wine estate with breathtaking mountain views. An ideal base for exploring the winelands and Overberg region, this delightful cottage is fully equipped with all amenities. Sleeps four (one double bedroom, one twin); is secure, with private parking. Easy access to shops, to Stellenbosch and Somerset West; 10 minutes from the beach and 20 from Cape Town International airport. (See also A-Z section.)

Ridgemor Ridgemor Farm, R102 Kuilsrivier Road, Firgrove, Somerset West ▪ 6 Bedrooms ▪ Rates on request ▪ Major credit cards accepted ▪ Heated pool ▪ Spa ▪ TV with DSTV ▪ Air-conditioning ▪ Underfloor heating ▪ Wine tasting ▪ Quad drives ▪ Golf driving range ▪ Family-friendly ▪ Picnic/BBQ facilities ▪ Dutch, French & Polish spoken ▪ Owner Veronique Barge ▪ viola@ridgemorwines.com ▪ www.ridgemorwines.com ▪ **T (021) 842-2255** ▪ F (021) 842-3393

Pamper yourself in luxury surrounded by vines. Small, centrally-located Ridgemor boasts every elegant comfort - including heated pool with water bar and mezzanine with home cinema. Enjoy delicious breakfasts, the cosy pub and revitalizing spa. Taste award-winning farm wines; braai at the dam, admiring the view and spectacular sunset. Go Quad biking; try the golf driving range. Or tear yourself away to explore the winelands. (See also A-Z section.)

Stellenbosch & Environs

Alluvia Boutique Winery & Accommodation Glen Arum Road, Helshoogte Pass, Banhoek Valley, Stellenbosch ▪ TGCSA 4-star guest house, 5-star self-catering; AA Superior ▪ 5 Bedrooms + 2 Self-catering apartments ▪ Low season: single from R800–R1 000 B&B, double from R680–R1 100 pp sharing B&B; High season: single from R1 000–R1 450 B&B, double from R850–R1 300 pp sharing B&B ▪ Major credit cards accepted ▪ Restaurant ▪ Pool ▪ Spa ▪ DSTV & DVD ▪ Wireless internet connection ▪ Air-conditioning/ceiling fans ▪ Gas fireplaces ▪ Mountain bikes ▪ Fly-fishing ▪ PGA golf green & golf carts ▪ Scenic flights & heli pad ▪ Wine tasting Mon-Fri 11:00–17:00, Sat & Sun 10:00–17:00 except Good Friday & Christmas day ▪ Cellar tours by appointment ▪ Owners Delarey & Sandie Brugman ▪ info@alluvia.co.za ▪ www.alluvia.co.za ▪ **T (021) 885-1661** ▪ F (021) 885-2064

A carefree 'vineyard lifestyle' is captured in this luxury rural retreat on an active wine estate in the Stellenbosch mountains. Five ultra-premium private suites, each with spectacular views over the estate and valley below, ensure that the rest of the world goes by unnoticed. PGA Golf green, golf carts to roam the estate and picnics at the dam. Custodians of the 'Give me a chance trustfund'. (See also A-Z section.)

Caledon Villa Guest House 7 Neethling Street, Stellenbosch ▪ TGCSA 4-star ▪ National monument ▪ 15 Bedrooms ▪ From R375 pp sharing (in season), R300 pp sharing (out of season) ▪ 15 rooms — suite, luxury, honeymoon, standard or family ▪ Major credit cards accepted ▪ Large pool ▪ Secure off-street parking ▪ Library ▪ Children by appointment ▪ German spoken ▪ Owners Johan & Ode Krige ▪ info@caledonvilla.co.za ▪ www.caledonvilla.co.za ▪ **T/ F (021) 883-8912**

Discover the winelands from this splendid Art Nouveau-style Edwardian guesthouse in the historic core of Stellenbosch. Owners Johan and Ode share their passion for the arts and love of wine, grown from the Krige family's 300-year involvement in wine farming and their historical links with well-known wine estates. Within walking distance of restaurants, shops and sports facilities, with easy access to golf courses and wineries.

Clouds Estate The Villa Clouds Vineyards, Helshoogte Road, Stellenbosch ▪ SATOUR 4-star & AA Superior Guesthouse ▪ 5 Bedrooms ▪ Double from R800–R1 200 per room B&B (out of season) to R1 500–R2 200 per room B&B (in season), single less 40% ▪ Clouds Village: 4 Cottages - self-catering ▪ Major credit cards accepted ▪ Dinners/functions by arrangement ▪ Piazza: wedding venue for 70-100 guests, chapel seat up to 150 persons, conferences up to 70 persons ▪ Pool ▪ TV ▪ Air-conditioning ▪ Ceiling fans ▪ Walks, cycling, horse-riding & easily accessible to many golf courses ▪ Owners Bernard & Petro Immelman ▪ info@cloudsestate.co.za ▪ www.cloudsestate.co.za ▪ **T (021) 885-1819** ▪ F 086-634-1568

Experience informal luxury with your head in the clouds and one of the Cape's most photographed views at your feet. Clouds Villa, on a boutique wine farm at the top of Helshoogte pass, offers five en-suite bedrooms, all with balconies overlooking vineyard-rich, mountain-rimmed Banhoek valley. Furniture, carefully chosen to complement the villa's Mediterranean style and flow, envelops guests in comfort from the moment they arrive. (See also A-Z section.)

Devon Valley Hotel Devon Valley Road, Stellenbosch ▪ TGCSA 4-star ▪ 38 Bedrooms ▪ From R465–R745 pp sharing ▪ Major credit cards accepted ▪ Flavours Restaurant ▪ Pool ▪ TV & DSTV ▪ Air-conditioning ▪ German spoken ▪ Owner LGI Hotels & Vineyards ▪ info@devonvalleyhotel.com ▪ www.devonvalleyhotel.com ▪ **T (021) 865-2012** ▪ F (021) 865-2610

This much-loved, now rejuvenated Stellenbosch landmark (which recently celebrated its 60th birthday), offers spectacular views, stylish rooms, contemporary Cape cuisine, an award-winning winelist and a definitive collection of single malt whiskies. Enjoy garden and vineyard walks, two swimming pools, or relax on the terrace and savour award-winning SylvanVale wines from surrounding vineyards. Winner of The Great Wine Capitals Best of Wine Tourism Award for accommodation; also the Great Wine Capitals - Best of Wine Tourism Award for accommodation for two consecutive years. (See also Eat-out section & A-Z for SylvanVale.)

Kleine Zalze Lodge Kleine Zalze Wine Estate, Strand Road (R44), Stellenbosch ▪ TGCSA 4-star country house hotel ▪ 41 Bedrooms ▪ From R860-R1 180 per room and from R1 615-R2 695 per suite ▪ Major credit cards accepted ▪ Conference facilities ▪ Pool ▪ TV ▪ Air-conditioning ▪ Sauna ▪ Golf ▪ Owner Kobus Basson ▪ accommodation@kleinezalze.co. za ▪ www.kleinezalze.co.za ▪ **T (021) 880-0740** ▪ F (021) 880-2215

Panoramic vineyard and mountain views, award-winning wines, fine dining and luxurious accommodation (bedrooms and suites) on a working wine estate, 3 km from Stellenbosch. Self-cater, or book at the estate's Terroir Restaurant, Eat Out Johnnie Walker Restaurant of the Year 2006. Golf at De Zalze Golf Course, mountain biking, vineyard walks, 17-metre pool and wine tastings. Conference and banqueting venue adjacent to the wine cellar. (See also Eat-out & A-Z sections.)

L'Avenir Country Lodge L'Avenir Estate, Klapmuts Road (R44), between Stellenbosch & Paarl, Stellenbosch ▪ TGCSA 4-star guest house ▪ 11 Guest suites ▪ Low season: single R440-R720 B&B, double R550-R900 per room B&B; High season: single R880-R1 440 B&B, double R1 100-R1 800 per room B&B ▪ Major credit cards accepted ▪ Conference facilities for up to 300 delegates from Dec 2007 ▪ Pool ▪ Flatscreen cable TV ▪ WI-FI facilities ▪ Air-conditioning ▪ Ceiling fans ▪ Wine tastings ▪ Vineyard walks ▪ Owner Michel Laroche ▪ countrylodge@lavenir.co.za ▪ www.lavenir.co.za ▪ **T (021) 889-5001** ▪ F (021) 889-7313

Colonial charm at the foothills of the Simonsberg. Surrounded by 100 ha of vineyards, this newly renovated lodge combines luxury and award-winning wines with warm hospitality. Eleven guest suites; the two icon rooms with splash pool and outdoor shower. Picnics, bird-watching and olives from the farm. Near golf courses, 20 minutes' drive from Franschhoek and Paarl and five from the historic town of Stellenbosch. (See also A-Z section.)

Marianne Wine Estate Guest Apartments Marianne Wine Estate, Valley Road, off R44, between Klapmuts & Stellenbosch ▪ TGCSA 4-star B&B ▪ 5 Bedrooms ▪ Single from R350-R580 B&B, double from R295-R395 pp B&B ▪ Visa & MasterCard accepted ▪ Olivello Restaurant - Wed-Sun for lunch ▪ Pool ▪ TV ▪ German & French spoken ▪ Owner Christian Dauriac ▪ info@mariannewinefarm.co.za ▪ www.mariannewinefarm.co.za ▪ **T (021) 875-5040** ▪ F (021) 875-5036

Relax on the foothills of the Simonsberg in spacious, comfortable apartments (with kitchenettes), uniquely African in style and surrounded by citrus orchards and vineyards. Enjoy scenic walks, taste the estate wines, laze - or braai - at the swimming pool, where barbecue facilities are provided. Children welcome. Centrally located between Stellenbosch, Paarl & Franschhoek. (See also Eat-out & A-Z sections.)

Natte Valleij Farm Natte Valleij, Klapmuts Road (R44), between Stellenbosch and Paarl ▪ TGCSA 3-star B&B & self-catering ▪ 2 Cottages - both private with patio and bbq - Vineyard cottage (sleeps 6) & Cellar cottage (sleeps 2 adults + 2 children) ▪ R280 pp B&B, self-catering from R160 pp ▪ Owners Charles & Charlene Milner ▪ milner@intekom.co.za ▪ www.nattevalleij.co.za ▪ **T (021) 875-5171**

This historic farm in the prime wine making 'Muldersvlei bowl' area, with a magnificent Cape Dutch homestead, was the original land grant of the area. Ideal for families or a group of friends. Relaxing rural ambience; secluded pool set in the large garden. Wonderful walking through vineyards or neighbouring game reserve where one can see wildebeest, gemsbok, zebra, springbok, bontebok and eland. (See also A-Z section.)

Oak Village B&B 7 Hamman Street, Stellenbosch ▪ TGCSA 3-star B&B ▪ 9 Bedrooms ▪ Single R350-R420 B&B, double R550-R650 per room B&B ▪ Visa & MasterCard accepted ▪ Conference facilities ▪ TV ▪ Air-conditioning ▪ Owners Dawid & Christelle Kriel ▪ oakvillage@volkskombuis.co.za ▪ www.oakvillage.co.za ▪ **T/F (021) 887-7889**

Hospitable B&B in the historical heart of Stellenbosch, ideally located for exploring the winelands. Hosts Dawid & Christelle Kriel will make you feel at home, sharing their passion for food and wine. Individually decorated rooms with en-suite bathrooms and tea/coffee making facilities, relaxing sundeck and terrace for braais. Award-winning restaurants, coffee shops and museums all within walking distance and easy motor access to major tourist routes. (See also Eat-out section for De Volkskombuis & De Oewer.)

Ons Genot Country Lodge Bottelary Road (M23), Stellenbosch ▪ TGCSA 4-star guest house ▪ 9 Bedrooms ▪ Single from R440–R620 B&B, double from R350–R490 pp sharing B&B ▪ Major credit cards accepted ▪ Mon Plaisir Restaurant ▪ Conference facilities ▪ Tennis court ▪ Pool ▪ TV ▪ Air-conditioning ▪ Ceiling fans ▪ Dutch, French & German spoken ▪ Owners Eric & Marleen Bovijn ▪ info@onsgenot.com ▪ www.onsgenot.com ▪ **T** (021) 865-**2233** ▪ F (021) 865-2250

'Where guests become friends' sums up the ambience of this welcoming 4-star country retreat on the outskirts of Stellenbosch. Tours are suggested to match individual interests and classic 'bistrot' fare at Mon Plaisir restaurant adds a soupçon of French flair. Luxury air-conditioned en-suite rooms with private terraces, attractive garden, TV, mini-bar, bathroom with bath and shower, jacuzzi in the honeymoon suite. Conference room accommodates 20. (See also Eat-out section for Mon Plaisir Restaurant.)

Sunhill Farm Self-contained Cottages La Provence Road, Stellenbosch (behind Polkadraai farm stall on the M12 Stellenbosch-Kuils River) ▪ 2 Cottages ▪ From R250–R300 per cottage ▪ Major credit cards accepted ▪ @ Jakarta Rijsttafel Restaurant ▪ Small conference facilities (booking essential) ▪ Pool ▪ TV ▪ Dutch spoken ▪ Owners Duncan & Veronica Fransz ▪ sunhillf@iafrica.com ▪ www.jakarta.co.za ▪ **T** (021) 881-**3243** ▪ F (021) 881-3299

Modestly billed as 'probably Stellenbosch's most unpretentious self-contained cottages, but very cosy and romantic', these two comfortable cottages sleep two, and are fully equipped for self-catering. Outside braai facilities and wide verandas make the most of the spreading vineyard view. Fishing and pottery classes available. (See also Eat-out section).

The Wild Mushroom Guest House 15 Ryneveld Street, Stellenbosch ▪ TGCSA 4-star guest house ▪ 5 Suites ▪ Low season: single R550 B&B, double R750 B&B; High season: single R980 B&B, double R1180 B&B ▪ Visa & MasterCard accepted ▪ TV ▪ Air-conditioning ▪ Owner Wynand Nel ▪ info@wildmushroom.co.za ▪ www.wildmushroom.co.za ▪ **T** (021) **886-9880** ▪ F (021) 886-6398

Explore Stellenbosch from an engaging guest house in the town's historical core. Should you wish to learn more about the local lifestyle, culture and wine, discuss this with your host. Decor celebrates wild mushrooms, and suites - from bachelor to two-bedroom - all have private entrances. Full gourmet breakfasts served on the penthouse terrace and continental in the privacy of your room. Secure basement parking available.

Zevenwacht Country Inn Zevenwacht Wine Farm, Langverwacht Road, Kuils River ▪ 13 Suites; 7 three-bedroom cottages & 1 chalet ▪ TGCSA 4-star country house ▪ Low season: single from R395 B&B, double from R270 pp sharing B&B; High season: single from R560 B&B, double from R385 pp sharing B&B ▪ Major credit cards accepted ▪ Manor House Restaurant ▪ Conference facilities ▪ Pool ▪ TV ▪ Air-conditioning ▪ Sauna ▪ Floodlit tennis court ▪ German, Dutch & Xhosa spoken ▪ Owner Harold Johnson ▪ info@zevenwacht.co.za ▪ www.zevenwacht.co.za ▪ **T** (021) 903-**5123** ▪ F (021) 906-1570

Multi-faceted Zevenwacht wine farm offers accommodation ranging from luxury suites in the Country Inn to vineyard cottages and a self-catering chalet. Spectacular views of Table Bay and False Bay. Restaurant in the historic manor house open daily for breakfast, lunch & dinner; garden picnics also available. Facilities for weddings, launches and conferences; cheesery, wine tasting centre, gift shop, chef school, and African Day Spa. Highly Recommended Fine Country Estates; winner International Award Wine Capitals Global Network Best of Wine Tourism 2007. (See also Eat-out & A-Z sections.)

Zorgvliet Vineyard Lodge & Spa Zorgvliet Wine Estate, Helshoogte Pass, Banhoek Valley, Stellenbosch ▪ TGCSA 4 & 5-star guest house ▪ 18 Bedrooms ▪ Single from R995–R1 415 B&B, double from R1 680–R2 200 per room B&B ▪ Visa, MasterCard & Diners

Club cards accepted ■ Herenhuis 1692 Restaurant ■ Conference facilities ■ Pool ■ TV ■ Air-conditioning in 12 rooms ■ Ceiling fans in 6 rooms ■ Owner JS van der Merwe ■ info@ zorgvliet.com ■ www.zorgvliet.com ■ **T (021) 885-1561** ■ F (021) 885-1583

Relax in 5-Star luxury in the beautiful Banhoek valley just outside Stellenbosch, where exclusive lodges in the vineyards of a working wine estate command superb views of mountains and vines. Attractions include a private swimming pool, on-site spa, historic Herenhuis 1992 restaurant, and scheduled barbeques high in the mountains. Spoil yourself. Walk in the vineyards, taste wine and book for a cellar tour. AA Superior accommodation. (See also A-Z section.)

Wellington

Bovlei Valley Retreat Bovlei Road, Wellington ■ TGCSA 4-star guest house - 5 bedrooms + 5-star self-catering cottage - 2 bedrooms ■ Low season: single R500 B&B, double R350 pp sharing B&B; High season: single R650 B&B, double from R475-R700 pp sharing B&B ■ Major credit cards accepted (excl Diners Club) ■ Conference facilities - small ■ Pool ■ TV ■ Air-conditioning ■ Owners Abbi & Lee Wallis ■ info@bvr.co.za ■ www.bvr.co.za ■ **T/F (021) 864-1504**

Peace and tranquility beckon at this luxurious and romantic wine, fruit & lavender estate at the foot of the historic Bains Kloof pass. Magnificent mountain scenery, relaxing comforts and attentive service, complemented by delicious home-cooked breakfasts and gourmet dinners with estate wines. Chill out at the swimming pool, walk through fields of lavender, hike in the mountains and taste wine at local boutique cellars. (See also A-Z section for Dunstone Winery.)

Diemersfontein Wine and Country Estate Guest House Jan van Riebeeck Drive (R301), Wellington ■ 18 Bedrooms ■ From R395 pp sharing B&B ■ Major credit cards accepted ■ Seasons at Diemersfontein restaurant ■ Conference facilities ■ Pool ■ TV in lounges ■ Air-conditioning (some rooms) ■ Ceiling fans ■ Owners David & Sue Sonnenberg ■ hospitality@diemersfontein.co.za ■ www.diemersfontein.co.za ■ **T (021) 864-5050** ■ F (021) 864-2095

Gorgeous gardens provide a colourful backdrop to beautifully appointed garden rooms and vineyard cottages offering 18 double rooms, 16 en suite. (Centrally situated Tulani Cottage boasts lounge, TV room, honesty bar and veranda.) Swimming, horse riding, walks, hikes, and gourmet picnics in summer. Winter weekend packages allow guests to shed city stress and enjoy log fires, great wine and food in breathtaking surroundings. (See also Eat-out section & A-Z sections.)

Disabled Access in SA Wineries

In early 2001, this guide commissioned the first comprehensive audit of estates and farms in the winelands of the Western and Northern Cape, aimed at verifying that venues which are open to the public at set times, and aim to be disabled friendly, in fact are accessible – not only for wheelchairs but for all types of disability.

The initial audit project was carried out in stages, and the results incorporated into successive editions as they become available. Practical difficulties intervened but last year, after a brief hiatus, we were able to restart the initiative in conjunction with disability consultants Andrew Stodel and Guy Davies, and in the region of 100 properties were visited and reviewed.

This edition Guy Davies and his Disability Solutions team carried out the work, covering both new and recently upgraded venues. The results of their evaluations are incorporated into the relevant producer entries in the A-Z section of this book, as well as in the look-up tables which accompany the maps, in the form of the universally recognisable 'wheelchair' icon.

As before, wineries open only by appointment were excluded, as it is felt that in these cases visitors can ascertain their individual requirements when making an appointment.

Of the 30-something venues visited in the current round, La Vierge in the Hemel-en-Aarde Valley was rated the winery with the most accessible facilities — only a minor tweak was needed for a perfect rating.

Guy and his researchers were impressed, as previously, with proprietors' eagerness to attend to the needs of disabled visitors. Owners' best intentions are sometimes negated, however, by design features which are thought to be attractive or to add value but in reality are 'unfriendly', such as gravel surfaces for parking areas and pathways strewn with woodchips. To ensure facilities are truly accessible, Guy's oft-repeated advice is to enlist the help of a recognised disability expert. Accessibility, he believes, is often surprisingly easy and inexpensive to achieve, and it usually benefits many people who are not viewed as 'disabled'.

We would like to extend our appreciation and thanks to Guy, and invite readers who have comments or suggestions to contact him either through the guide's offices or directly on telephone 021·872·1101, mobile 083·289·1199 or email guy@disabilitysolutions.co.za.

In closing, it is important to emphasise that wineries which are not flagged as accessible in the A-Z or the map tables do not necessarily have deficient or non-existent disabled facilities; it might merely mean that we are not yet in a position to comment on them. Our intention remains to not only continue but if possible expand the present coverage of disabled facilities, and we welcome any suggestions on how to achieve this goal.

winelands
MAPS

The maps in this section show locales where wine is available for tasting/sale either at set times or by appointment. The larger-scale map below shows the areas covered by the maps, and the table starting on the next page lists some details for prospective visitors.

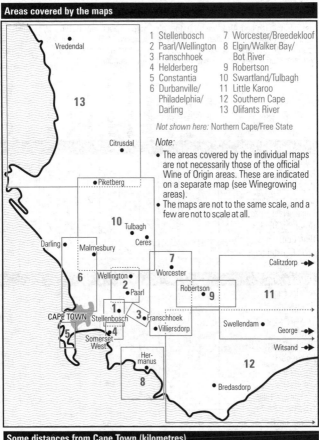

Areas covered by the maps

1 Stellenbosch
2 Paarl/Wellington
3 Franschhoek
4 Helderberg
5 Constantia
6 Durbanville/Philadelphia/Darling
7 Worcester/Breedekloof
8 Elgin/Walker Bay/Bot River
9 Robertson
10 Swartland/Tulbagh
11 Little Karoo
12 Southern Cape
13 Olifants River

Not shown here: Northern Cape/Free State

Note:
• The areas covered by the individual maps are not necessarily those of the official Wine of Origin areas. These are indicated on a separate map (see Winegrowing areas).
• The maps are not to the same scale, and a few are not to scale at all.

Some distances from Cape Town (kilometres)

Calitzdorp	370	Paarl	60	Tulbagh	120
Franschhoek	75	Robertson	160	Vredendal	300
Hermanus	120	Stellenbosch	45	Worcester	110

Key for maps

═══ Main access roads   R62 R60 Road numbers
─── Roads   🔶● Towns
⋯⋯ Gravel roads

Details of Locales Shown on Maps

The tables below are intended to facilitate winery visits by providing summary information about all the winetasting venues which are open to the public, either at set times or by appointment, and appear on our winelands maps. Venues are listed by region, and details provided include a map grid-reference, if applicable; whether the particular venue is open only by appointment (T); open on Saturdays and/or Sundays (✓ = at set times; T = by appointment); open on public holidays (✗ = closed all public holidays; otherwise assume open all or some holidays); and whether meals/refreshments are available (BYO = bring your own picnic). Other details include availability of accommodation, cellar tours and facilities for children. Venues which are friendly to individuals with reduced mobility, as audited by our disability consultants, are highlighted. Other languages spoken (besides English and Afrikaans) are now also noted (Czech = Cz, Dutch = Nl, Flemish = Vl, French = Fr, German = De, Italian = It, Japanese = Ja, Polish = Po, Portuguese = Pt, Russian = Ru, Spanish = Sp, Swedish = Sv, Xhosa = Xh). For more information, particularly items marked with an asterisk, see the A-Z and Eat-out/Stay-over sections.

	Grid reference	Open by appt. only	Open Saturdays	Open Sundays	Open pub. holidays	Meals/refreshments	Accommodation	Cellar tours	Disabled friendly	Child friendly	Languages spoken
Constantia											
Ambeloui		T						T			
Buitenverwachting			✓		✗	✓*		T	✓		
Cape Point Vyds		T						T			
Constantia Uitsig			✓	✓		✓	✓				
Eagles Nest Farm		T						T			
Groot Constantia			✓*	✓*		✓		✓*	✓		
High Constantia			✓	✓				✓			
Klein Constantia			✓		✗					✓	Fr/Sv
Steenberg			✓			✓	✓	T	✓		
Durbanville											
Altydgedacht			✓					T			
Bloemendal			✓	✓		✓			✓		
Capaia		T						T			De
Cloof			✓			✓*			✓		
Darling Cellars			✓			BYO		T	✓		
De Grendel			✓					✓			
De Vallei		T									
Diemersdal			✓			BYO		T			
Durbanville Hills			✓	✓		✓		✓	✓	✓	
Franki's		T				T*	*				
Groote Post			✓	✓		✓/BYO			✓		
Havana Hills		T						T			
Hillcrest			✓	✓		✓		T			
Meerendal			✓	✓		✓			✓		
Nitida			✓	✓		✓		T	✓		
Ormonde			✓			T/BYO			✓	✓	
Elgin/Walker Bay											
Barry Gould Family		T					✓	T			
Barton Farm			✓			BYO	✓				
Beaumont			✓	T		T*	✓	✓	✓		

	Grid reference	Open by appt. only	Open Saturdays	Open Sundays	Open pub. holidays	Meals/refreshments	Accommodation	Cellar tours	Disabled friendly	Child friendly	Languages spoken
Benguela Cove		T						T			
Boschrivier		T									
Bouchard Finlayson			✓		✗				✓		
Creation		T*									
Dispore Kamma		T						T			
Ecology		T*									
Elgin Vintners			✓		✗	T					
Feiteiras		T*						T*			Pt
Goedvertrouw		T				T	T			✓	
Hamilton Russell			✓			T*		T			
Hemelzicht			✓		✗						
Hermanuspietersfontein			✓								Fr
Iona			T	T		BYO	✓	✓*			
Keisseskraal			✓	T		BYO					De
La Vierge			✓	✓*		✓			✓		Fr/Xh/
Luddite		T									Nl
Mount Babylon		T				T				✓	
Newton Johnson			✓		✗	✓			✓		
Oak Valley			T	T							
Paul Cluver			✓			BYO	✓		✓		
Raka			✓*			BYO					
Ross Gower			T	T	T	T	✓	T			Fr/De
South Hill		T				BYO	✓	T			
Southern Right			✓					T			
Spookfontein											
Springfontein		T				BYO	✓	T		✓	
Stanford Hills		T					✓	T			
Sumaridge			✓	✓		✓		✓			
Whalehaven			✓	✓*		BYO		T			
Wildekrans			✓*	✓*		T*				✓	
Wine Village			✓	✓							
Franschhoek											
Akkerdal			T		✗		✓				
Allée Bleue			✓	✓		✓		T	✓		
Blueberry Hill							✓				
Bo La Motte					✗	✓	✓			✓	
Boekenhoutskloof											
Boschendal			✓*	✓*		✓		✓*	✓		
Cabrière			✓			✓			✓		W/Fr/De
Cape Chamonix			✓	✓		✓	✓	T	✓	✓	
Colmant			✓	T							
Dieu Donné			✓	✓		✓*		T			
Eikehof		T						T			
Franschhoek Vyds			✓	✓		✓*					
GlenWood			✓*	✓*				✓			

	Grid reference	Open by appt. only	Open Saturdays	Open Sundays	Open pub. holidays	Meals/refreshments	Accommodation	Cellar tours	Disabled friendly	Child friendly	Languages spoken
Graham Beck			✓					T			
Grande Provence			✓	✓		✓	✓		✓		
Haut Espoir		T						T			
Klein Dassenberg		T					✓				
Klein Genot			✓	✓			✓				
La Bourgogne Farm		T					✓	T			Fr
La Bri			✓	✓*							
La Chataigne		T					✓				Sv
La Chaumiere		T						T			
La Couronne			✓		✗			T		✓	
La Motte			✓			✓*			✓		
La Petite Ferme			✓	✓		✓	✓				
La Vigne			✓					✓			
Landau du Val		T									
Le Manoir de Brendel			✓	✓		✓	✓				
L'Ormarins		T*									
Lynx			T	T			✓				De/Sp
Môreson			✓	✓		✓		T	✓		
Mont Rochelle			✓	✓		✓*	✓	✓			
My Wyn		T*									
Plaisir De Merle			✓*					✓*			De*
Rickety Bridge			✓			BYO	✓	T	✓		
Solms-Delta			✓	✓		✓		✓			
Stony Brook			✓*	✓*							
Von Ortloff		T						T			
Helderberg											
Aeternitas		T									
Assegai Selection		T					✓				
Avontuur			✓	✓		✓		T	✓		
Conspirare		T									
Cordoba		T*			✗			T			
Croydon		T						T			
Dellrust			✓		✗	✓		✓*	✓	✓	
Eikendal			✓	✓		✓*	✓	✓	✓	✓	
Elberti		T									
Flagstone			✓	T				T			
Grangehurst			✓*	✓*			✓				
Heron Ridge		T									
Ingwe											
JP Bredell			✓					T			
Ken Forrester			✓	✓		✓			✓		
L'Auberge du Paysan						✓			✓		
Longridge			✓			T*				✓	
Lourensford			✓	✓				✓			
Lushof			T		✗			T			

	Grid reference	Open by appt. only	Open Saturdays	Open Sundays	Open pub. holidays	Meals/refreshments	Accommodation	Cellar tours	Disabled friendly	Child friendly	Languages spoken
Lyngrove		T					✓				
Miravel		T					✓				N/Fr
Moordenaarskop		T									
Morgenster			✓	✓				T			
Mount Rozier			T		✗	T				✓	De*
Onderkloof		T				T		T			
Post House			T*						✓		
Ridgemor Farm							T				N/Fr/Po
Romond		T									
Ses'Fikile											
Somerbosch			✓	✓		✓		T	✓	✓	
Stonewall			T*								
The Cheviot			T*								
The Co. of Wine People			✓						✓	✓	
The Winery of Good Hope		T									
Vergelegen			✓	✓		✓		✓*	✓		
Waterkloof		T						T			
Waterstone		T					✓				
Wedderwill		T*				BYO		T*	✓		De
Yonder Hill					✗			✓	✓		
Klein Karoo											
Axe Hill		T									
Barrydale Cellar			✓			BYO		T			
Bergwater			✓			BYO	✓				
Boplaas Family			✓					T			
Calitzdorp Cellar			✓			BYO		T			
De Krans			✓			✓/BYO*		T	✓		
Domein Doornkraal			✓*					T			
Excelsior Vlakteplaas											
Grundheim			✓								
Herold			T	T	T	BYO					
Joubert-Tradauw			✓			✓	T	T		✓	
Kango			✓			T/BYO		T		✓	
Ladismith Cellar					✗*	BYO		T			
Mons Ruber			✓				✓				
Montagu Wine Cellar			✓		✗	BYO		T*	✓		
Peter Bayly		T						T			
Rietrivier			✓		✗	✓/BYO		T		✓	
SoetKaroo			✓					T			De
The Goose		T									
TTT Cellar			✓*	✓*		BYO	T	✓*			Xh
Uitvlucht			✓	✓*		✓			✓		
Virgin Earth		T									
Withoek							✓	T			
Northern Cape											

	Grid reference	Open by appt. only	Open Saturdays	Open Sundays	Open pub. holidays	Meals/refreshments	Accommodation	Cellar tours	Disabled friendly	Child friendly	Languages spoken
Douglas					✗	BYO		T			
Goudveld			T					T			
Hartswater Wine Cellar								T			
Landzicht GWK			✓		✗	T/BYO		T		✓	
Oranjerivier Wine Cellars			✓		✗			✓*	✓		
Rostrevor Farm		T									
Olifants River											
Bellpost		T						T			
Cape Rock		T						T			
Cederberg			✓			BYO	T	✓			
Citrusdal Cellars			✓		✗*	BYO	T	T	✓		
Johan van Zyl		T*									
Keukenhof		T*								✓	
Klawer Co-op			✓		✗*	BYO			✓		
Lutzville Cape Diamond			✓			✓		T	✓		
Namaqua			✓		✗	T/BYO		✓*	✓		
Sir Lambert			✓			BYO	✓			✓	
Smit Family		T*									
Stellar								T			
Stoumann's			✓								
Teubes Family		T*			✗		T				
Vleiland			✓			BYO		✓			
Paarl											
African Terroir	C1					T/BYO	✓				Fr/De
Anthony Smook	B2	T									
Anura	C7		✓	✓		✓		T			
Armajaro	C1	T						T			
Arum Lily	E2	T				BYO		T			
Ashanti	F5					✓					
Avondale	F6		✓					T	✓		
Avondvrede	C8	T				T		T			
Ayama	B2	T									
Backsberg	D8		✓	✓		✓		✓*	✓	✓	
Bergheim	E6	T						T			
Bernheim	E3		✓					T	✓		
Black Pearl	D5	T*									
Blyde	E6							T			
Boland Kelder	E4		✓					T			
Bosman Family	G1	T									
Bovlei	G2		✓						✓		
Coleraine	D6		✓		T			T			Fr
Crows Nest	D3		✓	✓		✓		✓		✓	
Détendu	C1	T						T			
David Frost	D1		✓								
De Villiers	E6	T									

	Grid reference	Open by appt. only	Open Saturdays	Open Sundays	Open pub. holidays	Meals/refreshments	Accommodation	Cellar tours	Disabled friendly	Child friendly	Languages spoken
De Zoete Inval	E6	I						I	✓		
Diemersfontein	F2		✓	✓		✓	✓	I			
Domaine Brahms	C3		I		I			I			
Doolhof	H1		✓	✓*		I	✓				
Drakensig	D8		✓*								
Dunstone	H1		✓	✓		✓*	✓	✓			
Eshkol Kosher	F2	I		I		I		I			
Fairview	D6		✓	✓		✓			✓		
Freedom Hill	F7		✓						✓		
Gallop Hill	D4	I				✓					
Glen Carlou	D7		✓*	✓*	I	✓		I	✓		
Groenendal Farm	G1	I						I			Sv
Groot Parys	E5	I						I			
Hawksmoor	A7	I					✓				Fr/De/Ja
Hildenbrand	G2					✓*	✓				De
Horse Mountain	C1	I				BYO					
I Love Wine	E6		✓			✓			✓		
Jacaranda	F1		✓			BYO	✓	✓			
Jacques Smit	F2		✓					✓		✓	
Joostenberg	A8		✓	✓		✓		I	✓		
Juno	E5		✓		X*						
Klein Parys	E5		✓			✓	✓	I			
Kleine Draken	D6				X	BYO		I	✓		
KWV	E6		✓	✓		✓		I	✓		De
Laborie	E6		✓*	✓*	X*	✓		I	✓		
Landskroon	D6		✓			T/BYO*	✓			✓	
Le Fût	F5	I									
Leidersburg	B7	I						I			
Lindhorst	D7		✓	✓		✓*	✓	I	✓	✓	
Linton Park	G1	I				I		I			
Longbarn	F2	I						I			
Main Street	E6	I						I			
Marianne	C8		✓				✓	I			
Maske	G2	I									
Mellasat	G5	I									
Mischa	F1	I			X	I		I			
Mont Destin	C8	I						I			De
Mont du Toit	G2	I									
Mooi Bly	F4	I					✓				
Mount Vernon	C7		✓*	✓*		BYO		I			
Nabygelegen	H1		✓			BYO		I			
Napier	G2		✓	I			✓	I	✓		
Nederburg	F5		✓*	✓*		I		I	✓		Fr/De
Nelson	D3		✓	I		I		✓*	✓	✓	
New Beginnings	D3							I			

	Grid reference	Open by appt. only	Open Saturdays	Open Sundays	Open pub. holidays	Meals/refreshments	Accommodation	Cellar tours	Disabled friendly	Child friendly	Languages spoken
Niel Joubert	D8	T						T			
Noble Hill	D8		✓	✓*		T*		T	✓	✓	
Olsen	G5	T				T					
Oude Denneboom	C2	T						T			
Oude Wellington	G2	T				✓	✓			✓	
Perdeberg	B3		✓					T			
Retief	E4		T	T	✗						
Rhebokskloof	D3		✓	✓		✓		T	✓	✓	
Ridder's Creek	F2	T									
Ridgeback	D3		✓	✓		✓	✓	T			
Rose Garden	C3	T				T/BYO		T			
Ruitersvlei	D6		✓	✓				T	✓	✓	
Rupert & Rothschild	D8	T							✓		
Scali	C1	T					✓	T			
Schalk Burger	F1		✓	T		T/BYO		✓	✓	✓	
Seidelberg	D6		✓	✓		✓	✓			✓	
Simonsvlei	D7		✓	✓		✓		T	✓	✓	
The Chase	G6	T									Sp
The Mason's	E6	T									
Under Oaks	D3		✓			✓*				✓	
Upland	G3	T					✓	T			
Val de Vie	F7		✓	✓		✓		T			
Veenwouden	E3	T			✗			T			
Vendôme	E6		✓		✗			T	✓		
Vrede en Lust	D8		✓	✓		✓	✓	T*	✓	✓	
Vunani	E2				✗	✓		✓			
Wamakersvallei	E2		✓		✗*	BYO		T	✓		
Welgegund	G2	T					✓				
Welgeleë	D7		✓	✓		T					
Welgemeend	C7		✓					T	✓		
Wellington Co-op	E2								✓		
Welvanpas	H1		✓								
William Everson	E6	T				BYO		T			
Windmeul Co-op	D3		✓		✗			T	✓		
Wines of Cape Town	D7		✓	✓		✓					
Ziggurat	D8		✓*	T			✓	T			
Robertson											
Angora		T			✗						
Arabella			✓					T			
Arendsig		T						T			
Ashton Winery			✓		✗	BYO		T			
Bon Cap			✓*	✓*		✓	T	T	✓	✓	
Bon Courage			✓			✓			✓	✓	
Bonnievale Wine Cellar			✓						✓		
Buitehof			✓			BYO					

	Grid reference	Open by appt. only	Open Saturdays	Open Sundays	Open pub. holidays	Meals/refreshments	Accommodation	Cellar tours	Disabled friendly	Child friendly	Languages spoken
BurCon			✓	T		✓	✓			✓	
Bushmanspad			✓	✓		BYO	✓	✓		✓	
Cilandia		T						T			
Clairvaux			✓			BYO		T	✓		
Cloverfield			✓								
De Wetshof			✓					T			
DuVon		T					✓				
Fraai Uitzicht 1798			✓	✓		✓	✓	T			
Goedverwacht			✓			BYO		T			
Graham Beck			✓	✓*				T	✓		
Janéza		T				T*					
Jonkheer		T									
Karusa		T									
Kingsriver		T*						T			
Koningsrivier		T						T			
Kranskop			✓					✓		✓	
Langverwacht					✗			T	✓		
Le Grand Chasseur			✓			✓	T	T			
Lord's		T				BYO		T			
Major's Hill			✓					T		✓	
McGregor Wines			✓						✓		
Mooiuitsig							✓	T			
Quando		T									
Rietvallei			✓			✓/BYO				✓	
Robertson Winery			✓	✓		BYO		T			
Roodezandt			✓					T	✓		
Rooiberg			✓			✓/BYO		T	✓	✓	
Rosendal			✓			✓	✓				
Rusticus			✓			BYO	✓	T			De
Springfield			✓			BYO					
Tanagra			✓	✓		BYO				✓	
Van Loveren			✓			✓*	✓	T	✓		
Van Zylshof			✓					T			
Viljoensdrift			✓*	✓*		✓		T			
Vruchtbaar		T				BYO	✓				
Wandsbeck								T	✓		
Wedgewood			✓	✓							
Wederom		T				T	✓	T		✓	
Weltevrede			✓			✓*	✓	T			
Wolvendrift			✓			BYO		T	✓		
Wonderfontein			✓			BYO					
Zandvliet			✓			BYO			✓		
Southern Cape											
Andy Mitchell		T									
Black Oystercatcher		T									

	Grid reference	Open by appt. only	Open Saturdays	Open Sundays	Open pub. holidays	Meals/refreshments	Accommodation	Cellar tours	Disabled friendly	Child friendly	Languages spoken
Jean Daneel		T						T			De
Lismore		T				BYO	✓			✓	Fr/Sp
Oewerzicht			T	T			✓				
Strandveld						BYO	✓	T			
Zoetendal			✓			T		✓			
Stellenbosch											
Akkerdraai	E8		✓								
Alluvia	H5		✓	✓			✓	T		✓	
Alto	E8		✓								
Amani	B6		✓		✗			T	✓		
Anatu	E5	T						T			
Annandale	E8		✓					T	✓		
Asara	D6		✓*			✓	✓	T	✓		De
Audacia	E7		✓					T	✓		
Beau Joubert	B6	T					✓				
Bein	B6	T						T			Fr/De
Bellevue	C3		✓								
Bergkelder	E5		✓					✓	✓		
Beyerskloof	E3		✓			✓			✓		
Bilton	E8		✓			✓*			✓		
Blaauwklippen	E6		✓	✓		✓		T	✓		
Blue Creek	E7	T						T			
Bonfoi	C5		✓		✗	BYO			✓		
Boschheim	E5	T									
Boschkloof	C6	T*						T			
Bottelary Hills	D3										
Bottelary Winery	D3					✓		T		✓	
Camberley	H5		✓	T	T		✓	T			
Cape Hutton	E7	T						T			
Clos Malverne	D4		✓			BYO		T			
Clouds	G5	T				T	✓				
Clovelly	D3	T						T			
Dalla Cia	E5					✓					It
De Meye	E1		✓								
De Toren	B6	T									
De Trafford	G8		✓					✓			
Delaire	G5	T*				✓			✓		
Delheim	F2		✓	✓		✓		✓	✓		
Devon Hill	D4		T		✗			T	✓		
Devon Rocks	D3	T					T	T			De/Sv
Devonvale	D3	T				✓					Fr
DeWaal	C5		✓*								
Dormershire	B5		✓					✓			
Dornier	F7		✓	✓		✓			✓		
Eaglevlei	E1		✓	✓		✓		✓		✓	

	Grid reference	Open by appt. only	Open Saturdays	Open Sundays	Open pub. holidays	Meals/refreshments	Accommodation	Cellar tours	Disabled friendly	Child friendly	Languages spoken
Ernie Els	F8		✓*			✓			✓		
Ernst & Co	D1		✓								De
Fort Simon	C4		✓		✗	✓		T	✓		
Gilga	D5	T						T			
Glenelly	F4	T*									
Goede Hoop	C3					T/BYO*		T			
Graceland	E7				✗		✓				
Groenland	B3		✓	✓		T		T			
Hartenberg	D3		✓	✓*		✓		✓*			
Haskell	E8		✓*		✗	✓		✓			
Hazendal	B3		✓	✓		✓		✓			De/Ru
Hidden Valley	F8		✓	✓		✓		✓			
Hoopenburg	E1							T			Fr
Jacobsdal	B6	T									
JC le Roux	D4		✓*	✓*				✓*	✓		
Jordan	C5		✓	✓		BYO		T	✓		
Kaapzicht	B4		✓			BYO	✓	T			De
Kanonkop	F2		✓			T/BYO*			✓		De
Kanu	C6		✓*		✗						
KapVino	D3	T						*			
Kholisa	C6	T									
Klawervlei	D1	T							✓		
Klein DasBosch	F7	T									
Klein Gustrouw	G6	T						T			
Kleine Zalze	E6		✓	✓		✓	✓	T	✓	✓	
Kleinood	F7	T						T			
Knorhoek	F3		✓	✓		✓*		✓	✓		
Koelenhof	D1		✓			BYO		✓	✓		
Koopmanskloof	C3				✗	BYO	✓	✓			
Laibach	F2		✓*					T			
Lanzerac	G5		✓	✓		✓	✓	✓*	✓		
L'Avenir	E3		✓			✓	✓	T			
Le Bonheur	F1		✓								
Le Riche	G6		T				✓				
Lievland	F1		✓	✓		✓		✓	✓		
Louiesenhof	E4		✓	✓*		✓*	✓		✓	✓	
Louisvale	D4	T*						T	✓		
Malanot	E8	T									
Marklew Family	F1	T						T			
Meerlust	B8		✓		✗						
Meinert	D4	T									
Middelvlei	E5		✓					✓	✓		
Mitre's Edge	F1		T	T	T			✓*			
MolenVliet	H4	T					✓				
Monterosso	E4		✓					T			It

	Grid reference	Open by appt. only	Open Saturdays	Open Sundays	Open pub. holidays	Meals/refreshments	Accommodation	Cellar tours	Disabled friendly	Child friendly	Languages spoken
Mooiplaas	B4		✓			BYO					
Morgenhof	F3		✓*	✓*		✓			✓		
Morton	G4	T									
Mostertsdrift	E4	T				T		T			
Mulderbosch	E3	T									
Muratie	F2		✓	✓		T	✓	T			
Mvemve Raats	B6	T						T			
Natte Valleij	F1	T					✓	T			
Neethlingshof	D5		✓	✓		✓		T	✓	✓	
Neil Ellis	G6		✓								
Nietvoorbij	F4	T			✗						
Overgaauw	D5		✓					T	✓		
Peter Falke	E8	T*			✗						
Quoin Rock	F3		✓	✓		✓		T			
Raats Family	B6	T						T			
Remhoogte	E3						✓	T			
Reyneke	B6	T					✓				
Rozendal	G5	T				✓	✓	T			
Rust en Vrede	E8		✓*			✓					
Rustenberg	G4		✓						✓		
Saxenburg	A6		✓*	✓*		✓					
Simonsig	E2		✓*			✓/BYO*		✓*	✓	✓	
Skilpadvlei	C6		✓	✓		✓	✓			✓	
Slaley	E2							T			
Spier	C7		✓	✓		✓			✓	✓	De
Stark-Condé	H6		✓								
Stellekaya	E5		✓		✗	T			✓		
Stellenbosch Hills	D6		✓						✓		
Stellendrift	D6										
Stellenrust	E7		✓		✗*	✓/BYO					
Stellenrust	C3		✓		✗*						
Stellenzicht	E7		✓	✓							
Sterhuis	C4	T						T	✓	✓	
Stonehill	D4	T									
Stoney Croft	D3	T									
Sylvanvale	D4		✓	✓		✓	✓	T	✓	✓	
The Co. of Wine People	C7		✓	✓		✓			✓	✓	
The Foundry	B8	T						T			
The High Road	E5	T									
Thelema	G4		✓		✗	BYO		T	✓		
Tokara	G4		✓	✓		✓			✓		
Uitkyk	F2		✓	✓		✓*			✓		
Uva Mira	F8		✓						✓		
Vergenoegd	B8		✓			✓*		T	✓		
Vilafonté	E5	T				✓		T			

	Grid reference	Open by appt. only	Open Saturdays	Open Sundays	Open pub. holidays	Meals/refreshments	Accommodation	Cellar tours	Disabled friendly	Child friendly	Languages spoken
Villiera	D1		✓			BYO*			✓		
Vredenheim	D6		✓			✓	✓		✓		
Vriesenhof	F7		✓*			T		T			
Vuurberg	M4	T						T			
Warwick	F1		✓	✓		T/BYO		T			
Waterford	F7		✓						✓		
Webersburg	E8		✓		✗		✓				
Wedgeview	C6	T					✓			✓	
Welgevallen	F5				✗			✓			
Westbridge	E1		✓*				✓				
Withington	D1	T			✗						
Zevenwacht	B5		✓	✓		✓	✓	✓	✓	✓	
Zorgvliet	H4		✓*	✓*		✓	✓	T		✓	
Swartland											
Abbottshill		T				BYO		T			
Allesverloren			✓		T	✓		T		✓	
Annex Kloof		T				T/BYO	✓				
Babylon's Peak		T					✓	T			
Het Vlock Casteel			✓			BYO		T		✓	
Hofstraat		T						T			
Kloovenburg			✓			BYO		T			
Lammershoek			T	T	T	T/BYO*		T			De
Mac's Hill		T			✗	BYO				✓	
Meerhof			✓			T/BYO		T			
Nieuwedrift			✓	T		✓	✓			✓	
Org de Rac Domain			✓					✓			
Pulpit Rock			✓			BYO		T			
Riebeek Cellars			✓	✓		BYO		T			
Sadie Family		T									
Schonenberg		T				BYO					
Sequillo		T						T			
Swartland			✓			BYO		✓		✓	
The Observatory		T									
Wedgewood											
Wedgewood			✓	✓		✓/BYO	✓				
Winkelshoek			✓						✓		
Tulbagh											
Bianco			✓					✓			
Blue Crane			T					T			
Buck's Ridge		T					✓	T			
Constantia		T						T			
Drostdy-Hof			✓						✓		
Linde		T						T			
Manley			✓	✓			✓	T			
Montpellier			✓			✓/BYO	✓			✓	

	Grid reference	Open by appt. only	Open Saturdays	Open Sundays	Open pub. holidays	Meals/refreshments	Accommodation	Cellar tours	Disabled friendly	Child friendly	Languages spoken
Oude Compagnies Post		T									
Paddagang			✓	✓		✓	✓				
Rijk's			✓			✓/BYO	✓	✓	✓		
Saronsberg			✓			BYO		T			Cz
Schalkenbosch		T				T	T	T			
Theuniskraal			✓			BYO			✓		
Tulbagh Mountain Vyds		T						T			
Tulbagh Co-op			✓			T/BYO		T	✓		
Twee Jonge Gezellen			✓					✓			
Waverley Hills			✓			✓		T	✓	✓	
Worcester											
Aan de Doorns					✗			✓*	✓		
Alvi's Drift		T				T/BYO*		T			
Aufwaerts											
Badsberg			✓		✗	BYO		T*		✓	
Bergsig			✓			✓		T			
Botha			✓			BYO		T		✓	
Brandvlei Cellar					✗			T			
Conradie Family			✓	✓		✓	✓				De
Daschbosch			✓			T/BYO*	T		✓	✓	
De Doorns Winery			✓								
De Wet Co-op			✓		✗	BYO			✓		
Die Huis van Anjé		T				BYO		T			
Du Preez			✓		✗	BYO		T	✓	✓	
Du Toitskloof			✓	✓		BYO		T	✓		De
Eagle's Cliff			✓	✓		✓	T				
Goudini Wines			✓			✓					
Groot Eiland							T	T	✓		
Hex River Crossing		T									
Jason's Hill			✓	T		✓				✓	
Lateganskop								T	✓		
Lorraine		T				BYO		T			
Mountain Oaks			✓		✗	T*	✓	✓			
Mountain Ridge			✓			BYO		T			
Nuy			✓			✓*			✓		
Opstal			✓			✓		T			
Overhex					✗	BYO		T	✓		
Rico Suter		T					✓				
Riverstone			✓				✓		✓		
Slanghoek			✓					T*	✓		
Stettyn			✓		✗	BYO			✓		
Tanzanite		T*			✗						
Villiersdorp Cellar			✓	✓*		✓			✓		
Worcester Winelands			✓			✓	✓				

Constantia/Cape Point

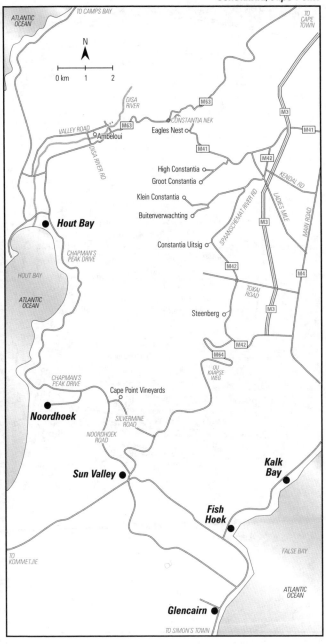

N

0 km 1 2

ATLANTIC
OCEAN

TO CAMPS BAY

TO CAPE TOWN

DISA RIVER

VALLEY ROAD

M63

CONSTANTIA NEK

M3

M41

Ambeloui

Eagles Nest

M63

DISA RIVER RD

M41

High Constantia

Groot Constantia

M42

KENDAL RD

LADIES MILE

Klein Constantia

Buitenverwachting

SPAANSCHEMAT RIVER RD

M3

Hout Bay

Constantia Uitsig

MAIN ROAD

CHAPMAN'S PEAK DRIVE

M42

M4

HOUT BAY

TOKAI ROAD

ATLANTIC OCEAN

Steenberg

M3

M42

M64

OU KAAPSE WEG

CHAPMAN'S PEAK DRIVE

Cape Point Vineyards

Noordhoek

SILVERMINE ROAD

NOORDHOEK ROAD

Kalk Bay

Sun Valley

Fish Hoek

TO KOMMETJIE

FALSE BAY

ATLANTIC OCEAN

Glencairn

TO SIMON'S TOWN

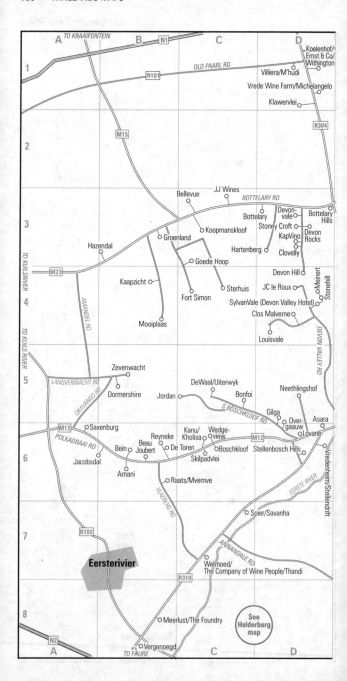

Stellenbosch

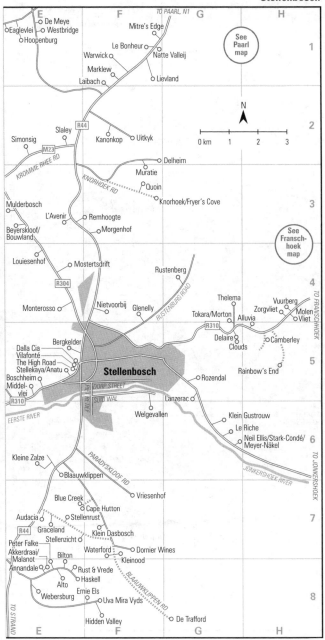

TO PAARL, N1

See Paarl map

E
F
G
H

De Meye
Westbridge
Mitre's Edge
Eaglevlei
Hoopenburg
Le Bonheur
Natte Valleij
Warwick
Marklew
Lievland
Laibach

1

N

Slaley
R44
Kanonkop
Uitkyk

0 km   1   2   3

Simonsig
M23
KROMME RHEE RD

2

Delheim
Muratie
KNORHOEK RD
Quoin
Knorhoek/Fryer's Cove

Mulderbosch
L'Avenir
Remhoogte
Beyerskloof/
Bouwland
Morgenhof

See Franschhoek map

3

Louiesenhof
Mostertsdrift
R304
Rustenberg

RUSTENBERG ROAD

4

Monterosso
Nietvoorbij
Glenelly
Thelema
Vuurberg
Zorgvliet
Molen Vliet
Tokara/Morton
Alluvia
R310
Delaire
Camberley
Clouds

TO FRANSCHHOEK

Dalla Cia
Bergkelder
Vilafonté
The High Road
Stellekaya/Anatu
Stellenbosch
Rainbow's End

5

Boschheim
Middel-
vlei
R310
Rozendal

EERSTE RIVER
DORP STREET
SUID WAL
Lanzerac
Welgevallen

PIET RETIEF

Klein Gustrouw
Le Riche
Neil Ellis/Stark-Condé/
Meyer-Näkel

6

Kleine Zalze
PARADYSKLOOF RD
Blaauwklippen
JONKERSHOEK RIVER

TO JONKERSHOEK

Blue Creek
Vriesenhof
Cape Hutton
Audacia
Stellenrust
R44
Graceland
Klein Dasbosch
Stellenzicht
Waterford
Dornier Wines
Peter Falke
Akkerdraai/
Malanot
Bilton
Kleinood
Annandale
Rust & Vrede
Alto
Haskell
Webersburg
Ernie Els
Uva Mira Vyds
De Trafford
Hidden Valley

BLAAUWKLIPPEN RD

7

8

TO STRAND

TO SITRAND

E
F
G
H

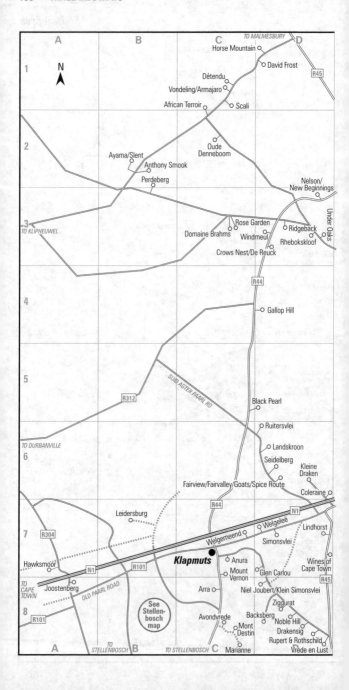

N

TO MALMESBURY

Horse Mountain

David Frost

R45

Détendu

Vondeling/Armajaro

African Terroir

Scali

Oude
Denneboom

Nelson/
New Beginnings

Ayama/Slent

Anthony Smook

Perdeberg

Under Oaks

TO KLIPHEUWEL

Rose Garden

Ridgeback

Domaine Brahms

Windmeul

Rhebokskloof

Crows Nest/De Reuck

R44

Gallop Hill

SUID AGTER PAARL RD

R312

Black Pearl

Ruitersvlei

TO DURBANVILLE

Landskroon

Seidelberg

Kleine
Draken

Fairview/Fairvalley/Goats/Spice Route

Coleraine

Leidersburg

R44

N1

Welgelee

Welgemeend

Lindhorst

R304

Welgemeend

Simonsvlei

Hawksmoor

N1

R101

Klapmuts

Anura

Wines of
Cape Town

TO
CAPE
TOWN

Joostenberg

OLD PAARL ROAD

Mount
Vernon

Glen Carlou

R45

Arra

Niel Joubert/Klein Simonsvlei

R101

See
Stellen-
bosch
map

Avondvrede

Ziggurat

Backsberg

Noble Hill

Mont
Destin

Drakensig

Rupert & Rothschild

TO
STELLENBOSCH

TO STELLENBOSCH

Marianne

Vrede en Lust

Paarl & Wellington

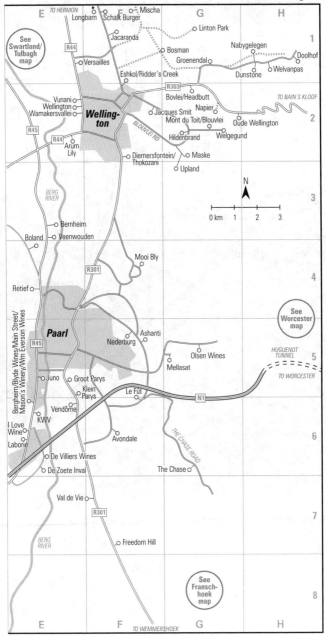

TO HERMON

E — Longbarn — Schalk Burger — Mischa

G

H

Linton Park

Jacaranda

Nabygelegen

Doolhof

1

R44 — Versailles — Bosman — Groenendal — Welvanpas

Dunstone

Eshkol/Ridder's Creek

R303 — Bovlei/Headbutt

TO BAIN'S KLOOF

Vunani — Wellington — Wamakersvallei

Welling-ton

Jacques Smit — Napier

Mont du Toit/Blouvlei

Oude Wellington

2

R45

R44 — Arum Lily

Hildenbrand — Welgegund

BLOUVLEI RD

Diemersfontein/Thokozani — Maske

Upland

N

BERG RIVER

0 km 1 2 3

3

Bernheim — Veenwouden

Boland

Mooi Bly

4

R301

Retief

See Worcester map

Paarl

Ashanti

Nederburg

HUGUENOT TUNNEL

Olsen Wines

5

Bergheim/Blyde Wines/Main Street/ Mason's Winery/Wm Everson Wines

R45

Mellasat

TO WORCESTER

Juno — Groot Parys

N1

Klein Parys

Le Fût

Vendôme

THE CHASE ROAD

I Love Wine

KWV

Avondale

6

Laborie

De Villiers Wines

De Zoete Inval

The Chase

Val de Vie

7

R301

BERG RIVER

Freedom Hill

See Fransch-hoek map

8

E

F

G

H

TO WEMMERSHOEK

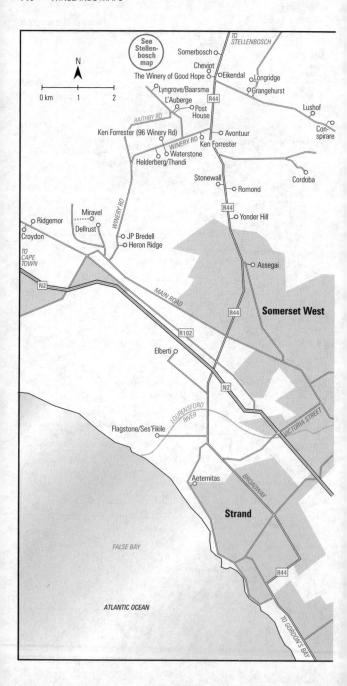

Helderberg

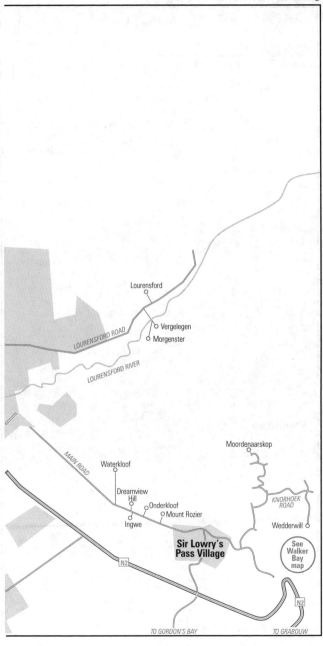

Lourensford

Vergelegen
Morgenster

LOURENSFORD ROAD

LOURENSFORD RIVER

Moordenaarskop

MAIN ROAD

Waterkloof

Dreamview
Hill
Onderkloof
Mount Rozier
Ingwe

KNORHOEK
ROAD

Wedderwill

**Sir Lowry's
Pass Village**

See
Walker
Bay
map

N2

N2

TO GORDON'S BAY

TO GRABOUW

Durbanville/Philadelphia/Darling

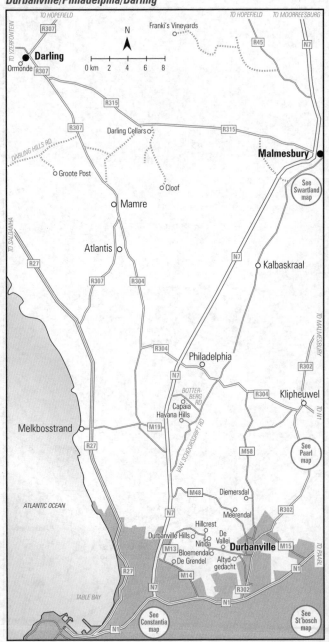

Franschhoek

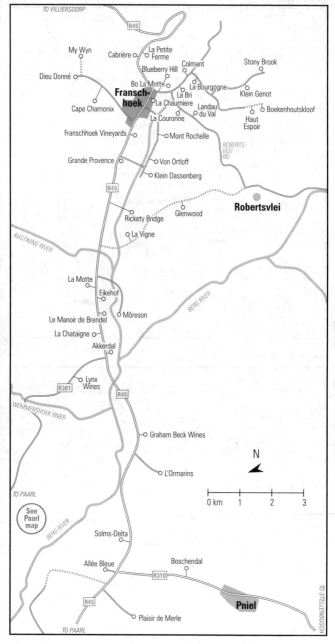

Franschhoek

TO VILLIERSDORP

R45

My Wyn
Cabrière
La Petite Ferme
Blueberry Hill
Colmant
Stony Brook
Dieu Donné
Bo La Motte
La Bri
La Bourgogne
Klein Genot
Cape Chamonix
La Chaumiere
Landau du Val
Boekenhoutskloof
La Couronne
Haut Espoir
Franschhoek Vineyards
Mont Rochelle
ROBERTS-VLEI RD
Grande Provence
Von Ortloff
Klein Dassenberg
R45
Robertsvlei
KASTAIING RIVER
Rickety Bridge
Glenwood
La Vigne
La Motte
Eikehof
BERG RIVER
Môreson
Le Manoir de Brendel
La Chataigne
Akkerdal
R301
Lynx Wines
R45
WEMMERSHOEK RIVER
Graham Beck Wines
L'Ormarins
N
0 km   1   2   3
TO PAARL
See Paarl map
BERG RIVER
Solms-Delta
Allée Bleue
Boschendal
R310
Pniel
R45
Plaisir de Merle
TO PAARL
TO STELLENBOSCH

Elgin/Walker Bay

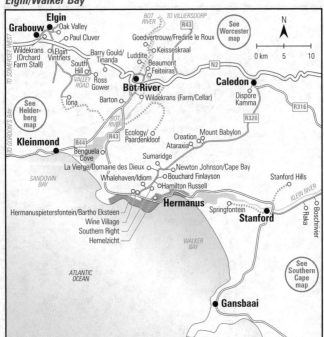

Southern Cape

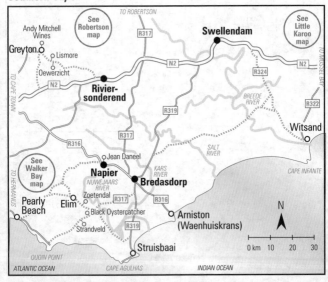

Worcester, Breedekloof & Villiersdorp

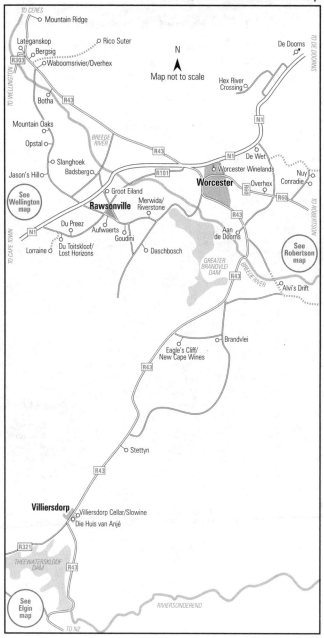

TO CERES

Mountain Ridge

Lateganskop
Bergsig
Rico Suter

R303

Waboomsrivier/Overhex

De Doorns

TO DE DOORNS

TO WELLINGTON

N
Map not to scale

Hex River
Crossing

Botha

R43

N1

Mountain Oaks

BREEDE
RIVER

R43

Opstal

N1

De Wet

Worcester Winelands

Nuy
Conradie

Slanghoek
Badsberg

R101

Overhex

Jason's Hill

Groot Eiland

Worcester

R60

R60

TO ROBERTSON

See
Wellington
map

Rawsonville

Merwida/
Riverstone

R43

TO CAPE TOWN

N1

Du Preez

Aufwaerts

Goudini

Aan
de Doorns

See
Robertson
map

Lorraine

Du Toitskloof/
Lost Horizons

Daschbosch

GREATER
BRANDVLEI
DAM

R43

BREEDE RIVER

Alvi's Drift

Brandvlei

Eagle's Cliff/
New Cape Wines

R43

Stettyn

R43

Villiersdorp

Villiersdorp Cellar/Slowine

Die Huis van Anjé

R321

THEEWATERSKLOOF
DAM

R43

See
Elgin
map

RIVIERSONDEREND

TO N2

Swartland

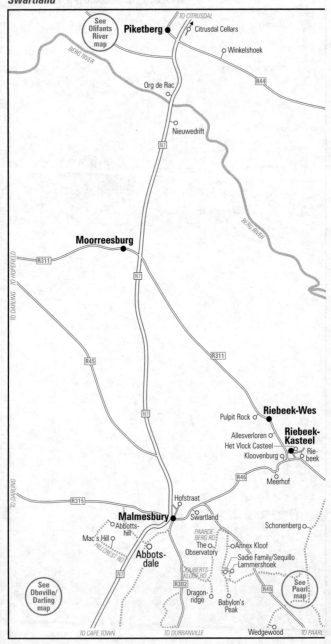

Tulbagh

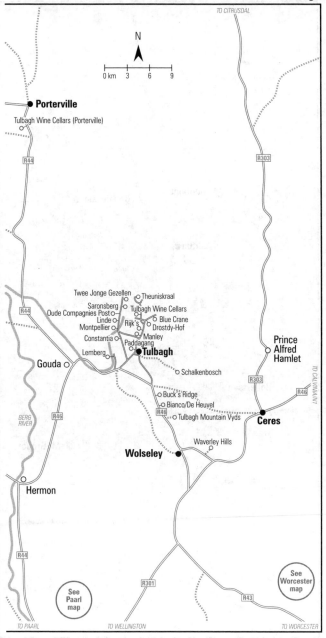

TO CITRUSDAL

N

0 km   3   6   9

● **Porterville**

Tulbagh Wine Cellars (Porterville)

R44

R303

Twee Jonge Gezellen

Theuniskraal

Saronsberg

Tulbagh Wine Cellars

Oude Compagnies Post

Linde

Blue Crane

Montpellier

Rijk's

Drostdy-Hof

Manley

Constantia

Paddagang

R44

Lemberg

● **Tulbagh**

Prince
Alfred
Hamlet

Gouda ○

Schalkenbosch

TO CALVINIA

R303

R46

Buck's Ridge

Bianco/De Heuvel

R46

Tulbagh Mountain Vyds

● **Ceres**

BERG
RIVER

R46

Waverley Hills

Wolseley ●

Hermon ○

R44

See
Paarl
map

R301

R43

See
Worcester
map

TO PAARL

TO WELLINGTON

TO WORCESTER

Robertson

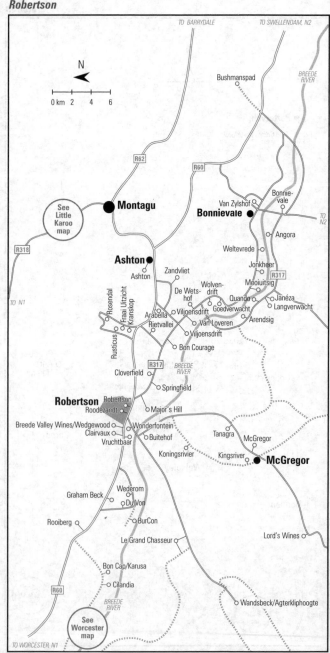

N

0 km 2 4 6

TO BARRYDALE

TO SWELLENDAM, N2

BREEDE RIVER

Bushmanspad

R62

R60

Montagu

See Little Karoo map

Van Zylshof

Bonnie-vale

Bonnievale

Angora

R318

TO N1

Weltevrede

Jonkheer

Mooiuitsig

R317

Ashton

Ashton

Zandvliet

De Wets-hof

Wolven-drift

Quando

Janéza

Langverwacht

Rosendal

Fraai Uitzicht

Kranskop

Arabella

Viljoensdrift

Goedverwacht

Arendsig

Rietvallei

Van Loveren

Rusticus

Viljoensdrift

Bon Courage

Cloverfield

R317

BREEDE RIVER

Springfield

Robertson

Robertson

Roodezandt

Major's Hill

Breede Valley Wines/Wedgewood

Wonderfontein

Tanagra

McGregor

Clairvaux

Buitehof

Kingsriver

McGregor

Vruchtbaar

Koningsrivier

TO N2

Wederom

Graham Beck

Du Von

Rooiberg

BurCon

Le Grand Chasseur

Lord's Wines

Bon Cap/Karusa

Cilandia

R60

BREEDE RIVER

Wandsbeck/Agterkliphoogte

See Worcester map

TO WORCESTER N1

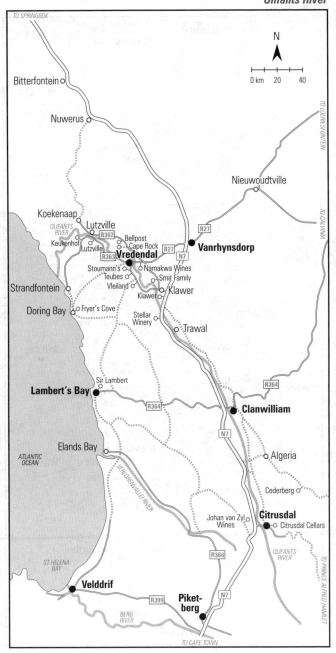

Klein Karoo

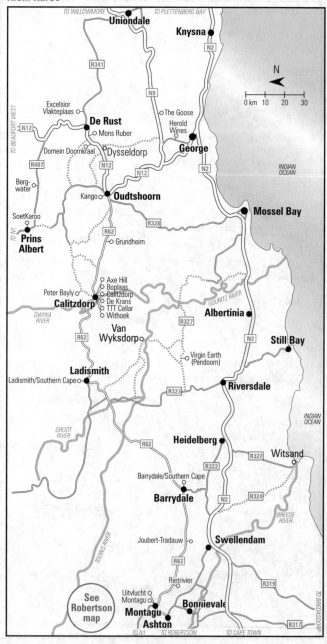

Northern Cape, Free State, North West

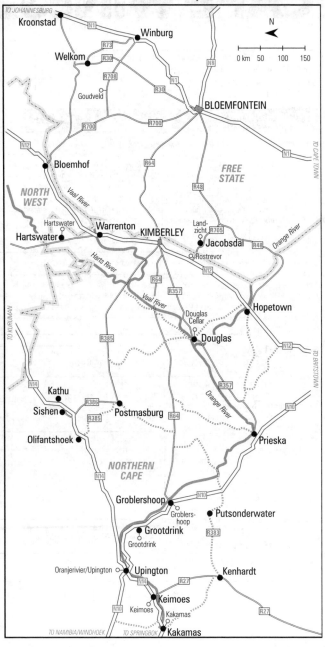

Ratings & descriptions illustrative; see 'How to use this Guide' for further assumptions & abbreviations

Producer's name (only officially recognised 'units for the production of estate wine' identified as 'estate')
See Maps section for location

Boschendal Wines
T 021-870 4200 · F 021-874 1531

Franschhoek ▪ Est 1685 ▪ 1stB 1976 ▪ Tasting & sales daily May-Oct 9-4.30 Nov-Apr 10-6.30 ▪ Fee R15 for 5 wines ▪ Closed Easter Fri, May 1, Jun 16 & Dec 25 ▪ Tours (vyd & cellar in minibus) 10.30, 11.30 & 3 by appt ▪ Restaurants & picnics ▪ Tour groups ▪ Gifts ▪ Conservation area ▪ Museum visits 9.30-5 ▪ Owner DGB ▪ Cellarmaster JC Bekker (1996) ▪ Winemakers Lizelle Gerber (whites, 2006) & James Farquharson (reds, 2004), with Lionel Leibbrandt (1999) ▪ Viticulturist Spekkies van Breda (1995) ▪ 200 ha (cabs s/f, merlot, shiraz, chard, sauvignon) ▪ 3 600 tons 250 000 cs 40% red 44% white 14% rosé 2% sparkling ▪ ISO 9001 & 14001 certified ▪ Pvt Bag X03 Groot Drakenstein 7680 ▪ taphuis@dgb.co.za ▪ www.boschendalwines.com

With DGB's acquisition of the renowned brand, winery, cellar, production facilities and sales centre smoothly completed, CE Tim Hutchinson promises a boosted marketing drive. Jacques Roux, ex-Graham Beck, has come in as marketing director and will work closely with UK agent Paragon to make an impression on the £7 to £10 category of the British market. Five tiers of wine have emerged in a reshuffling exercise, including the premium 1685, the Reserve Collection and the new flagship Cecil John Reserve, each with a Sauvignon and a Shiraz in its ranks, the favourites respectively of cellarmaster JC Bekker (who celebrated 10 years on the historic spread last year) and red-wine maker James Farquharson. Also getting a boost are the farm's conservation areas, with R20m set aside for an alien eradication programme.

★★★★★ **Grand Reserve** Classically crafted & ageworthy blend, mainly cab f, from selected casks. **01** grandly serious, as pvs, but a little easier-going. IWSC gold in 2005. **02** not released. **03** (★★★★) needs time. Green walnuts, summer heath tones from 70% cab f (with equal cab, malbec, shiraz); serious oaking explains peppery nuances, firm structure. Still tightly buttoned mid-2006, shd show better in yr/2. 21 mths Fr, half new.

★★★★ **Cabernet Sauvignon** Elegantly styled red. Brooding, dark, with cassis peeping through, but **03** still evolving; tannins, though ripe, mask true potential. Give another yr, cellar 8+ more. Fr oak 18 mths, half new.

★★★★★ **Shiraz** Deeply coloured **02** offered dried herb, red-fruited aromas, big structure, needing time to harmonise. *Wine* ★★★★. Philosophy of allowing fruit full expression, amply demonstrated in earlier maturing **03** (★★★★): opulent wild berries, smoothly rounded, fleshy palate, accommodating 15.5% alc. Expertly judged oak: 20 mths 300ℓ Fr, qtr new. Drink within 5 yrs.

Sauvignon Blanc ★★★★ Ripe-yet-green **05** has a figgy base, seamed with leafy, fynbos notes, racy acidity. Gd food partner. SAA. EW

Bouchard Finlayson
T 021-312 3515 · F 021-312 2317

Walker Bay ▪ Est 1989 ▪ 1stB 1991 ▪ Tasting & sales Mon-Fri 9-5 Sat 9.30-12.30 ▪ Fee R20 for groups of 8+ ▪ Closed pub hols ▪ Owner Bouchard Finlayson (Pty) Ltd ▪ Winemaker/viticulturist Peter Finlayson ▪ 17 ha (pinot, nebbiolo, sangiovese, chard, sauvignon) ▪ 180 tons 12 000 cs 20% red 80% white ▪ PO Box 303 Hermanus 7200 ▪ info@bouchardfinlayson.co.za ▪ www.bouchardfinlayson.co.za

SYMBOLS

🍾	Bottles own wine on property	📷	Other tourist attractions/amenities on the property
🍷	Open for tasting (no fee unless noted)	🎋	Bring your own (BYO) picnic
☕	Restaurant/refreshments	🏃	Child friendly
🏠	Accommodation	♿	Wheelchair friendly

Tastings, sales & cellar tour times (closed Sundays but open public holidays unless noted)

Other attractions or activities available on the property

Name of owner, name of winemaker, viticulturist & consultant(s); year/month of appointment in brackets

Compliance, where applicable, with internationally recognised quality assurance & food safety standards, eg ISO (International Standards Organisation), HACCP (Hazard Analysis & Critical Control Point) and BRC (British Retail Consortium)

Hectares under vine (not necessarily in production); main varieties planted

Production, in tons and/or 12-bottle cases (cs) and red:white ratio

Brief introduction/news update

Postal & email address, website

Selected recent awards; see also Top Performers section

Wine name, vintage, colour & style

Listings of wines available during the currency of the book

Grape variety/ies & fruit-source; assume own vineyard unless stated; bottlings certified as 'estate wine' flagged as 'EW'; bottlings made by registered 'units for the production of estate wine' but not certified as estate-made, are noted as 'NE'

T = Telephone number
F = Fax number

Date established and/or Date of first bottling

Wine of Origin (WO) geographical unit, region, district or ward where winery or main vinification facility is situated; assume all wines described/rated bear this WO certification, unless noted

OUR TRACK RECORD-BASED RATING SYSTEM

All wines rated 4 stars or more are set in red type.

General rating ★★★★★ **Grand Reserve** Classic

For 4-star or better wines, we give the track record over two or more vintages

Vintage-specific rating 03 (★★★★) needs time.

Any differences from the general rating noted in brackets beside the particular vintage

★★★★★	Superlative. A Cape classic
★★★★★	Outstanding
★★★★	Excellent
★★★★	Very good/promising
★★★	Characterful, appealing
★★★	Good everyday drinking
★★	Pleasant drinking
★★	Casual quaffing
★	Plain and simple
★	Very ordinary
No star	Somewhat less than ordinary

Aan de Doorns Co-operative Winery

T 023-347-2301 • F 023-347-4629

Worcester • Est 1954 • Tasting & sales Mon-Fri 8-5 • Closed pub hols • Tours during harvest by appt • Owner 58 members • Cellarmaster Johan Morkel (Nov 1993) • Winemaker Gert van Deventer (Sept 1997) & Ryno Booysen (Jan 2007) • 1 370ha (pinotage, chard, chenin, colombard) • 23 223/10 300cs own label • PO Box 235 Worcester 6849 • info@aandedoorns.co.za

This Worcester cellar, named after the stretch of thorn trees on the banks of the nearby Doorn River, recently welcomed new assistant winemaker Ryno Booysen to the fold. 2007 saw tonnage up by about 3000 to supply their growing export market.

Pinotage ☺ ★★★ With leather & floral nuances, **06** has soft enough tannins for solo drinking. **Doornroodt** ☺ ★★★ Ruby cab, merlot equal blend **05** has dusty, grassy/hay aromas, light body. **Blanc de Noir** ☺ ★★★ **07** from muscadel; intense rosepetal fragrance, fresh & light (12% alc), some savoury notes. **Chenin Blanc** ☺ 🗐 ★★★ Tropical, passionfruit vibrancy on **07**, nice fresh acidity, light body. **Muscat d'Alexandrie** ☺ ★★★ Ripe & rich, with honey & nuts, **06**'s sugar well balanced by acidity. **Red Muscadel** ☺ ★★★ Warming fireside drinker; **07** Turkish Delight & choc, gd structure & balance.

Colombar Semi-Sweet ★★ Petally **07**, amiable, lively quaffer. Moderate 12% alc. **Sauvignon Blanc** ★★ **07** grass & grapefruit notes, green apple hint, prominent acidity. **Colombar-Chardonnay** ★★ Last ed **06** was zesty, fruity; with pleasantly understated oak. **Sparkling** ★★ Demi-sec bubbly. Last ed had coral glints, fragrant berry aroma. **Cape Ruby** ★★ Last tasted **05** from tinta, touriga, had smoky, fruitcake tones, sweet finish. Discontinued: **Semillon**. *— CvZ*

Abbottshill

T 022-485-7080 • F 022-485-7080

Malmesbury (see Swartland map) • Est/1stB 2004 • Visits by appt • BYO picnic • Owner CA Bain & SP Graham • Winemaker CA Bain • Viticulturist Klaas Coetzee (Swartland Winery) • 10ha (cab, mourvèdre, shiraz) • 30t/350cs 100% red • PO Box 433 Malmesbury 7299 • cameron@empa.co.za

They've come some way from the early days of making chenin in a bathtub, says winemaker and co-owner Cameron Bain. Though still calling themselves garagistes, they're nicely set up in a converted dairy, and marketing their sylvan setting and facilities as the perfect venue for a corporate team-building exercise.

Shiraz ★★ Herbal peppery notes, **06** concentrated flavours a touch rustic. **Shiraz-Cabernet Sauvignon** ★★ Unshowy **06** shows house's stern tannins, austere fruit profile. *— MF*

ACJ Fine Wines
T 021-919-6731 • F 021-919-6731

Durbanville • Est/1stB 2004 • Closed to public • Owner Billy Martin • ±9 200cs own label • Brand for customer: Cattle Baron Group • 33% red 66% white • PO Box 3546 Tyger Valley 7536 • cwacj@telkomsa.net

Negociant Billy Martin's current emphasis is on supplying Cattle Baron's housewines and keeping up with the steakhouse chain's exponential growth. Martin also oversees distribution, marketing and sales for a number of top wine farms, and on a smaller scale, continues with his own brand, Bryde.

Adler
T 011-579-1980 • F 011-579-1981

Est/1stB 2004 • Closed to public • Owner/winemaker Oliver Meckler & Hans J Mamsell • 1 100cs 55% red 45% white • PO Box 104 Linbro Park 2065 • adler@olimeck.co.za • www.olimeck.co.za/adler

Geisenheim-trained Oliver Meckler and wine partner Hans Mamsell make their wines at Mischa Estate in Wellington using fruit they select from the estate's well-tended vineyards.

★★★★ **Modus M** Perfumed bdx blend cab s/merlot/petit v/cab f (42/42/12/4) in **06**. Bouquet broadened by floral & plummy notes; rich & ripe-fruited; attractive warm-region character.

Sauvignon Blanc ★★★ Creamy herbal notes on **07**, lovely peach & pear on fleshy mid-palate. Appealing, but tad less electrifying than **06** (★★★★). **Viognier** ★★ Easy & approachable **07**, peach wafts, ultra-soft styling as pvs but less dimension. — *JP*

■ **Admiralty House** see Cape Bay

Adoro Wines
F 021 880 1585

Stellenbosch • 1stB 2004 • Closed to public • Owner Aspen Freight • Winemaker Ian Naudé (May 2005) • Viticulturist Lucas de Kock (Aug 2005) • 40% red 60% white • PO Box 982, Stellenbosch, 7599 • ian@adoro.co.za • www.adorowines.co.za

Skilled blender Ian Naudé whole-heartedly agrees with UK critic Jancis Robinson's assessment that white wine is SA's forté. Keeping a finger on the pulse of international trends, Ian N tailors his wines by enlisting Lukas de Kock's extensive knowledge of diverse vineyard sites to achieve the style he's after. The resulting blends, he hopes, will always be more than the sum of their parts, combining the complexity and restraint of the Old World with the fruit-driven structure of the New.

★★★★ **Red** Attractive, judiciously oaked blend ex ±9 different vyds, as is Sauv; **04** was a quartet (with grenache), **05** a trio of merlot (62%), shiraz (22%), mourvèdre; fragrant scrub & cherry nuances join white pepper & red berries; fine tannins add grip, length. Approachable now, build for 5+ yrs.

★★★★ **Five Regions Sauvignon Blanc** 🖺 New name reflects the goal of a multi-region mix, yielding 'truly SA sauv'. **07** equally at home in Old World as New: minerality, blackcurrant character of Loire; green tones of New Zealand & cool-climate SA. Shows the intensity, gravitas, possible without big alc - this just tips 11.5%. For food or keeping.

★★★★☆ **Naudé White Blend** 🖺 Classy packaging for **06**, making stellar debut last ed: rich & poised with authoritative weight, length. Mainly Fr oak fermented/aged chenin, semillon (54/37) with dash Elim sauv. Vibrant tropical, thatch, fynbos scents, honeyed/waxy hints. Shd improve with few yrs cellaring. Balanced 13% alc. — *CvZ*

Aeternitas Wines 🍷 NEW
T 021-853-7312

Stellenbosch (see Helderberg map) • Est 2005 • 1stB 2006 • Tasting by appt • Owner Johan & Michelle Grimbeek • Winemaker Johan Grimbeek • Viticulturist Various • 1t/75cs • 21 Livingstone Street, Strand 7140 • aeternitaswines@telkomsa.net

Johan Grimbeek's double-garage cellar in suburban Strand now houses his dream: a handmade shiraz. His quest for individuality in wine began as a student in Bloemfontein when old-style cabs and shirazes called and he responded. Reading, listening and vinifying in France and locally have now culminated in Aeternitas. 'Scary in a sense, but immensely satisfying.'

Syrah ★★★★ Ambitious **05** made with minimal cellar intervention, incl natural yeast ferment. Liqueur-like flavours of cassis & spice but missing some concentration, depth. 16 mths Fr oak, 33% new. — *JPf*

■ **A Few Good Men** see Riebeek Cellars

■ *Affinity* see African Terroir

■ *African Breeze* see DuVon Wines

■ *African Collection* see Rooiberg Winery

■ *African Dawn* see Rooiberg Winery

■ *African Gold* see Old Bridge Wines

■ *African Horizon* see Origin Wine

African Pride Wines
T 021-794-0323 ▪ **F** 021-794-0344

Constantia ▪ Est/1stB 2002 ▪ Closed to public ▪ Owner Afrifresh Holdings ▪ Winemaker Mike Graham (May 2002) ▪ 60% red 40% white ▪ PO Box 518 Constantia 7848 ▪ info@ africanpridewines.co.za ▪ www.africanpridewines.co.za

A firm foothold in America and Western Europe means new MD Harry Loebenstein (ex-Distell) is testing the water in what he terms 'alternative' markets like Russia, the Middle East and West Africa. 'This should enable us to leave our "Footprint" for others to follow,' puns Carno du Toit, adding that this popular brand's packaging has had a revamp.

Lady Anne Barnard range

Cabernet Sauvignon ★★★★ New vintage unready. **02** was elegant & understated, hints wet heath & leafy footpath, tannins supple but structured to age few yrs. 18 mths Fr oak. **Shiraz** ★★★★ Pvsly tasted **02** (listed as 'Syrah') creamy mulberry aroma; lively, juicy palate featuring ripe Hldrberg fruit, well expressed. 16 mths oak, new/2nd fill. Discontinued: **Sauvignon Blanc**.

Footprint Impression range

Petit Verdot-Shiraz ★★★★ With white pepper & prosciutto notes on a bed of dark fruit, **05** had nicely judged oaking last ed plus appetite appeal. Dry finish perfect for food. **Viognier** ★★★★ Gd example of the variety when tasted last yr. **05** appealing peach (fruit & kernel) styling, some floral notes; rounded, almost fleshy mouthfeel, long finish.

Footprint range

Cabernet Sauvignon ★★★ Minty, cranberry-toned **05** provides easy drinking with just a touch of seriousness. **Shiraz** ★★★ Ribena & touch of menthol. Well-made if slightly jammy **06** has hint pepper & dry tannins in sync with juicy fruit. **Merlot-Pinotage** ★★★ Full flavoured & characterful in gutsy mode. **06** ripe, tad rustic, daubed with red fruits. **Chardonnay** ★★★ Pear & baked apple basted **07**. Fullish texture with lick caramel, will suit creamy foods. **Sauvignon Blanc** ★★ Combo pineapple, cinnamon & sweet melon on **07**, clean-cut & well-behaved. **Chenin Blanc-Semillon** ★★★ 50/50 blend in **07**; shy, some citrus in waxy texture. Weightier but simpler than **06**.

Cape MacLear range

Shiraz-Merlot-Pinotage NEW ★★ Smoky, pepper-dosed **06**. Mouthcoating but friendly tannin, attractively lean. **Chenin Blanc-Semillon** NEW ★★ **06** fruit-salad flavours with pines & dash of lime; quite developed mid-2007. Discontinued: **Shiraz-Cabernet Sauvignon, Chenin Blanc-Chardonnay**. —*RP*

African Roots Wine Brands 🍾 NEW
T 021-982-2200 ▪ **F** 021-982-7428

Closed to public ▪ Owner African Roots Wine Brands ▪ Winemaker Andries Blake ▪ PO Box 4560 Tygervalley 7536 ▪ vivian@africanrootswines.com ▪ www.africanrootswines.com

Armed with attractive indigenous branding, a new supplier, and wines named for each of her seven siblings, Vivian Kleynhans (also chair of the SA Vintners Alliance) has broken into the burgeoning US market. Her Seven Sisters line is now listed with Wholefoods and appears on store shelves in 27 American states.

Seven Sisters range

Cabernet Sauvignon Carol ★★★ Combo dark berried fruit & leafy, herbacious touch on **06**. Ripe & dense, with stylish tannins; accessible & food friendly. **Merlot June** ★★★ Ripe, dark, plummy fruit laced with choc, reined in by firm tannins. Warm, chunky farewell makes for full-bodied (14.5 alc) **06** food-pairer.

Pinotage-Shiraz Dawn ☺ ★★★ Pinotage's plummy fruit dominates **06**, with shiraz pepperiness adding a spicy dry appeal to the juicy medium-bodied palate. **Sweet Rosé Twena** ☺ ★★ Cerise **07** with bright red cherry appeal. Semi-sweet, with sherbety acidic lift in tail. Perfect for the sweeter toothed. **Bukettraube Odelia** ☺ ★★★ Soft & gently floral **07**, honeyed, with clean balancing acidity to freshen semi-sweet flavours. Try with fusion food. **Chenin Blanc Yolanda** ☺ ★★★ Balanced, fresh & juicy **07** in cheerful summer style, with enough structure to complement a meal. **Sauvignon Blanc Vivian** ☺ ★★★ Fresh tropical & grassy notes mingle on crisp & refreshing **07**. Lightish 12.5% alc in highly quaffable & food-amenable style. — MW

■ **African Sky** *see Drostdy-Hof Wines*

African Terroir

T 021-869-8103 • F 021-869-8104

Paarl • Est 1991 • 1stB 1991 • Visits Mon-Fri 9-5 (phone ahead) • Fee R15 refunded on purchase of 2+ btls • Closed Dec 25/26 & Jan 1 • Picnic baskets, platters & beverages by appt; or BYO • Sonop Guest house (see Stay-over section) • Tour groups • Conferencing • Owner Jacques Germanier • Winemaker Head winemaker Mathieu Labaki (Jan 2003) • Winemakers Johnnie Loubser (both Nov 2005) • Operations manager Heiko Huber • Viticulturist Francois Brink (Dec 2002) • 75ha (own vyds: cab, shiraz) • 400t • BRC, HACCP & ISO 9001:2000 accredited • Ranges for customers: Indaba, Mooiberge, Unity & Affinity • PO Box 2029 Windmeul 7630 • office@african-terroir.co.za • www.african-terroir.co.za

This Swiss-owned, offshore-focused winery merged its Cilmor operation outside Worcester with its Sonop farm (one of the first to be certified organic and accredited by Fairtrade); released one of SA's first organic viogniers; and at press time was approaching export volumes of almost 8 million litres. A successful import is head winemaker Mathieu Labaki: he arrived from France five years ago as a cellarhand, fell in love with the Cape and now speaks 'lekker Afrikaans'.

Azania range
Cabernet Sauvignon ★★★ Well-structured fireside wine. **06** robust, typical cab notes backed by spiciness & hint of old leather. **Merlot** ★★ Mint & mocha preface, hint dark choc enriches **06** palate. **Pinotage** ★★★ Subtly spicy **06**, palate-inviting ripe berry fruitiness. **Shiraz** ★★★ Appealing **06**, spicy, savoury wafts & chubby, palate-rounding ripe blackberry. **Chardonnay** ★★★ More serious but still companionable **07**, floral touches to tropical fruit salad. **Sauvignon Blanc** ★★ Tad more serious **07**: ripe melon welcomes appley crispness. This range listed intermittently in the guide.

Big Five range

Shiraz ☺ ★★★ Appealing spice & jam character on **06**; warm plummy fruit spiked with cinnamon & clove.

Cabernet Sauvignon ★★ **06** ripe, plummy & undemanding, with Aussie-style eucalyptus. **Pinotage** ★★ Promising earthy opener to **06**, but rather bland follow-through. **Chardonnay** ★ **07** easy-going poolside quaffer. **Sauvignon Blanc** ★ **07** light weight tipple with shy, grassy notes.

Elixir range
Sauvignon Blanc Noble Late Harvest ★★★★ Sticky toffee pudding in a bottle - with intriguing aromas of toasted coconut & dried apricot. **04** complex, deliciously unusual & more charming than pvs **00** (★★★★). Incl dash semillon.

Milton Grove range
Discontinued: **Shiraz**, **Chardonnay**.

Out of Africa range

> **Pinotage** ☺ ★★★ Juicy-ripe **06** sipper with variety's hallmark strawberry nuance. **Shiraz** ☺ ★★★ Spicy fillip adds dimension, interest, to lightweight fruity **06** quaffer.

Cabernet Sauvignon ★★ Shows cab's gentle side: **06** easy blackberry tastes, touch of toast holds interest. **Merlot** ★ **06** roughish, dry, rather tannic red. **Chardonnay** ★★ Aromatic styling for **07**: spicy vanilla, honeysuckle & gentle fruit. **Sauvignon Blanc** ★ Usual lightweight profile, **07** clean grapefruit aroma & flavour. Discontinued: **Rosé**.

Sonop Organic range

Cabernet Sauvignon ★★ Slightly stalky stewed fruit character on **07**. **Merlot** ★ Astringent, stalky **07** invites rich food. **Pinotage** ★★ Delicate, unshowy **07** with unusual hints of dried mango & pear. **Shiraz** ★★ Spicy, earthy nose introduces ripe plum jam flavours on **07**. **Chardonnay** ★★ **07** biscuity notes & some green melon; tad one-dimensional. **Sauvignon Blanc** ★★ Clean grassy preamble to very dry, light & crisp **07** food wine. **Viognier** NEW ★★★ Complex conversation starter, **07** with pear, musk rose & dried peach hints.

Tribal range

Merlot NEW ★ **06** mineral & austere with bitter choc notes. **Pinotage** NEW ★ **06** unfleshy entry-level food wine. **Dry Red** ★★ Appealing fruity quaffer, with berry flavours. **NV. Rosé** ★★ Follows pvs as poolside refresher. **07** from cab. **Dry White** ★ Grassy & astringent three-way blend, best well-chilled. **NV. Sauvignon Blanc-Colombard** ★★ Balanced **07** blend: guava hints complemented by green apple flavours. **Sparkling White Off-Dry** ★★★ **NV**. Last tasted, light sweetish hanepoot with brisk bubbles & soft citrus tone. **Sparkling Semi-Sweet** ★★ **NV**. Appreciably sweet, last ed lifted by lemon sherbet character,

Tribal Spear range

> **Cabernet Sauvignon** ☺ ★★★ **06** ripe blackberry nose with firm tannin underlying berry flavours. **Merlot** ☺ ★★★ Dusty flintiness on **06**, nicely offsetting ripe black cherry flavours. **Pinotage** ☺ ★★★ **06** comforting spice & plum pudding backed by firm tannin. **Shiraz** ☺ ★★★ **06** spicy intro to stewed plum flavours, finishing dry.

Chardonnay ★★ **07** seasonal compote of winter melon, florals & summer fruits. **Chenin Blanc** ★★ Variety's signature warm hay on **07**, delicate green apple crispness.

Winds of Change range

Fairtrade Organic Pinotage-Shiraz NEW ⚘ ★★★ Shiraz to the fore in **06**, followed by appealing appletart warmth. Comfortable wine. **Fairtrade Organic Chardonnay** NEW ⚘ ★★ **07** uncomplicated, with biscuit notes, banana & pineapple flavours. **Fairtrade Organic Sauvignon Blanc** NEW ⚘ ★★★ Classic grassiness & some summer fruit ripeness. **07** uncomplicatedly appealing. Discontinued: **Fairtrade Organic Shiraz, Pinotage-Cabernet Sauvignon, Pinotage-Shiraz, Fairtrade Chardonnay, Sauvignon Blanc**. Fruit for all ranges sourced widely, so various WOs.— *DB*

■ **African Treasure** *see* Vin-X-Port South Africa
■ ***African Wine Adventure*** *see* Mooiuitsig Wine Cellars

African Wines & Spirits
T 021-506-2600 • **F** 021-510-4560

Cape Town • Est 1999 • Closed to public • Owner Edward Snell & Co • Directors DV Hooper & CC Weeden •40% red 60% white • PO Box 318 Paarden Eiland • chrisw@esnell.co.za

This wholesaling and marketing company is owned by Edward Snell & Co, and has the Craighall range made to spec by The Company of Wine People in Stellenbosch. Other brands in the stable include Cinzano sparkling, bottled in Italy and imported.

■ **Afrikaanse Plesier** *see* Oaklands Wine Exporters

■ *Agostinelli*   *see Fairview*
■ *Agterkliphoogte*   *see Wandsbeck Wines*

Agterplaas Wines
T 021-886-5446 • F 021-886-5446

*Stellenbosch • Est/1stB 2003 • Visits by appt • Owner/winemaker James Basson • 5t/250cs •
PO Box 863 Stellenbosch 7599 • agterplaas@adept.co.za*

Lack of space at Somerbosch cellars, home to Agterplaas for the past three years, meant it
became necessary to look at alternatives. Winemaking was put on hold and the time spent on
designing a cellar and acquiring equipment and tanks. Operations will resume from the home
base this year.

'Bordeaux Blend' ★★☆ Cinnamon-infused jammy fruit on **05**, from cab, merlot, petit v &
malbec, with soft tannins, but moderate finish a bit hot from 15% alc. 14 mths oak, some
new. *— JPf*

■ *Agulhas Wines*   *see Strandveld Vineyards*

Akkerdal Estate
T 021-876-3481 • F 021-876-3189

*Franschhoek • Est 2000 • 1stB 2001 • Tasting & sales by appt Mon-Fri 8-5 Sat 9-1 • Sales also
at La Cotte Inn Wine Sales (see Wine shops section) • Closed pub hols • Self-catering guest
house (see Stay-over section) • Owner/winemaker Pieter Hanekom • Viticulturist Pieter
Hanekom, advised by Eben Archer & Dawid Saayman • 18ha (12 vars r/w) • ±3 000cs own
label 95% red 5% white • ISO certification in progress • PO Box 36 La Motte 7691 • wine@
akkerdal.co.za • www.akkerdal.co.za*

Pieter Hanekom has his finger on the winegrowing pulse, from the establishment of a wide
and varied range of varieties to the final boutique bottling. Regular testing and fine tuning,
from natural nourishment to trellising, have paid wine award-winning dividends. Never com-
placent, he's off on an educational trip to Bordeaux and the Rhône.

★★★★   **Merlot** Pieter H understandably pleased with **05**, opulent yet elegant vintage, polished tannins, hints spice & menthol to lush mulberry tone. 18 mths Fr oak. Gd
prospects.

★★★★   **Syrah** Sweeter, rounder, more accessible **05**, as gd though not as punchy as **03**.
Fynbos & fennel edge, malty, toasty finish. 18 mths Fr oak. No **04**: made in only exceptional vintages.

Passion Red ★★★★ **04** last tasted; peppery shiraz-led blend spiced up by malbec & pinotage.
Red meat friendly. 14 mths combo Fr/Am/Hung oak. **Wild Boar** ★★★★ Suitably 'wild' red (blend
incl roobernet, tempranillo). **05** sturdier but more fruitily delicious, accessible, than **04** (★★★★).
18 mths Fr oak. Swiss gold. **Kallie's Dream** ★★★ Smooth, buttery, food-friendly white from
viognier, sauv, chard & semillon; **NV**; not retasted. **Passion White** ★★★ Softer & leaner **05**, less
complex than pvs; dry yet creamy sauv, sem, chard & viognier, unoaked. *— RP*

Akkerdraai
T 021-881-3861/083-264-1463 • F 021-881-3861

*Stellenbosch • Est 1956 • 1stB 2007 • Tasting Mon-Fri 9-5 Sat 9-12:30 • Closed Easter Fri-
Mon, Dec 25 & Jan 1 • Fee R10, refundable on purchase • Walking/hiking trails • Owner Salie
de Swardt • Winemaker Marius Malan (consultant), with Salie de Swardt (both Jan 2004) •
Viticulturist Marius Malan (Jan 2004, consultant) • 1.75ha (cab) • 5t/500cs 100% red •
sdswardt@mweb.co.za*

Wine has been a hobby of Salie de Swardt's for many years, so when he retired as head of
one of SA's biggest media companies, his next move was obvious. He'd bought a property in
Stellenbosch's 'Golden Triangle' ten years ago, replanted the vineyard, built a boutique cellar
and in 2007, with Malanot owner/winemaker Marius Malan, made the farm's first Cab. Too
young for review this ed, it will be released later this year.

■ **Alexanderfontein** *see Ormonde Private Cellar*

Alkmaar [NEW]
T 021-873-0191 ▪ F 021-873-0191

Wellington ▪ Est 2001 ▪ 1stB 2005 ▪ Closed to public ▪ Owner Bouwer & Janet Nell ▪ Winemaker Matthew Copeland ▪ Vineyard Manager Dawid Futhwa ▪ 5.6ha (cab, merlot, mourvèdre, petit v, shiraz, chard, viognier) ▪ 7t/275cs 100% red ▪ PO Box 1273 Blouvlei Road Wellington 7654 ▪ janet@alkmaarfarm.co.za

'A welcome surprise,' was winemaker Matthew Copeland's response to the gold medal reception at the Swiss Awards for their maiden vintage. Owner Bouwer Nell is equally modest about this 'best kept secret' in Wellington's Blouvlei area, averring that the support from his neighbours, Schalk Burger & Sons, has made it all possible.

★★★★ **The Old School Master** Bright berry fruit & fine leafy tannins on **05** make for creditable debut of this cab/merlot blend (60/40), 18 mths in Fr oak, 25% new.— *CvZ*

Allée Bleue
T 021-874-1021 ▪ F 021-874-1850

Franschhoek ▪ Est 1690 ▪ 1stB 2001 ▪ Tasting & sales daily 9-5 ▪ Café Allée Bleue daily 9-5 ▪ Deli, banqueting area, corporate winetasting venue & other attractions ▪ Tours by appt ▪ Tour groups ▪ Owner DAUPHIN Entwicklungs-und Beteiligungs GMH (Germany) ▪ Winemaker Gerda Willers (Dec 2001) ▪ Viticulturist Douw Willemse & Rob Meihuizen (2001, consultant) ▪ 13ha (cab, merlot, pinotage, shiraz, sauv) ▪ 80% red 18% white 2% rosé ▪ PO Box 100 Groot Drakenstein 7680 ▪ info@alleebleue.com ▪ www.alleebleue.com

Eucalyptus trees provide the 'Blue Avenue' leading to this lovely visitor-friendly German-owned wine, fruit and herb-growing property. Vinified off-site since the critically acclaimed 2001 maiden vintage, the wines are now made in a new top-of-the-line on-site cellar, widely experienced Gerda Willers still at the winemaking controls.

★★★★ **Isabeau** Fine wooded semillon/chard blend, 60:40 in 2006. Citrus peel & buttered toast, verging on savoury, with enough vibrant freshness to hold your attention, give drinking pleasure. Mainly Fr, 9 mnths, third new. Friendly 13% alc.

Pinotage ★★★ Rippling muscles on **06**; chewy tannins, opulent dark fruit, 15% alc. Uncompromisingly pinotage, could tame with some ageing. Yr oak, half new. **Shiraz** ★★★ Meaty dark fruit & spice, **06** already drinking smoothly, but given firm backing by yr oak, half new, to age few yrs. **Cabernet Sauvignon-Merlot** ★★★★ Harmonious 70:30 blend in **06**; deep plum, tobacco, mint choc layers, finely judged tannins. Built to age 3+ yrs but already fine food match. Yr Fr, half new. **L'Amour Toujours** ★★★★ Range flagship. Cab's lead in **06** (merlot, dabs shiraz, grenache noir) dictates cassis styling, gd structure & length. 15% alc not intrusive; 60% new Fr oak. **Starlette Rouge** ★★★ Changing mix 4 varieties, always approachable. **06** has mocha choc, spice fragrance, juicy-fruited palate. Lightly oaked, bold 15% alc. **Rosé** ★★★ From shiraz, **06** more Provençal than red. Savoury touch from seasoned oaking. Dry, light textured, great food partner. **Chenin Blanc** [NEW] ★★★★ Portion new-oak matured, **07** sample promises well; rich melon & peach, long piquant finish, wood adding biscuit tones. **Sauvignon Blanc** ★★★★ Lemongrass minerality given boost by touch sugar, but **07**'s balancing acidity creates appealing tangy dry effect, sweet/sour finish. Delicious solo or with food. **Starlette Blanc** ★★★ Mainly sauv, some chenin, grenache bl, **07**'s perky fruit salad flavours refreshed by racy acidity. Dry, perfect food fare. All above WO W Cape unless noted.— *CR*

Allesverloren Estate
T 022-461-2320 ▪ F 022-461-2444

Swartland ▪ Est 1704 ▪ Tasting & sales Mon-Fri 8.30-5 Sat 8.30-2; phone ahead on pub hols ▪ Tours by appt ▪ Steakhouse-style meals, function venue, play area for children & other amenities ▪ Owner/winemaker/viticulturist Danie Malan (Nov 1987) ▪ 187ha (cab, shiraz & various port varieties) ▪ 50 000cs 100% red ▪ PO Box 23 Riebeek West 7306 ▪ info@allesverloren.co.za ▪ www.allesverloren.co.za

Major developments at this, the oldest winery in the Swartland and seat of the Malan family for five generations, include a large (up to 250 guests), tastefully appointed conference and function venue, augmenting a variety of child-friendly amenities such as the Pleasant Pheasant Restaurant, al fresco picnics and a tasting area where visitors can sample the estate's first Vintage Reserve Port. Otherwise, deadpans Danie Malan, 'it's been a good year'.

★★★★ **Shiraz** Excellent flavours in medium-full bodied **06**: big black pepper nose; palate ripe with strawberries, cherries & raspberries. Well-structured & -oaked, mainly 2nd & 3rd fill barrels with some new Am. 13.41% alc lighter than **05** (★★★★).

★★★★☆ **Port** Spice, rich dark fruit, caramel & nutty nuances. **04** (★★★★) spirity when tasted mid-2007; needs time to integrate to classic styling of last-tasted **02**. Aged 49 mths, 97.5g/l sugar; (less sweet than **02**'s 120 g/l).

★★★★☆ **Vintage Port** NEW **04** made in a style that would please fans of classic Portuguese ports. Exciting malty, nutty aromas & flavours enhanced with choc, coffee & prunes. Dry, no-nonsense finish.

Cabernet Sauvignon ★★★★ Leafy nose on **05**, backed by ripe black fruit & well-rounded tannins with gd grip. More elegant than **04** (★★★★), with well-managed oak (30% new, 18 mths). **Tinta Barocca** ★★★ **06** chunky, with raspberry/cherry notes & charred wood nuances. Continues combo barrel/tank fermentation, with micro-oxygenation. **Touriga Nacional** ★★★☆ Spicy, mulberry pie notes to light (13.14% alc), easy-drinking & fruity **06**. Lovely outdoor wine. — JN

Alluvia Boutique Winery & Guesthouse
T 021-885-1661 • F 021-885-2064

Stellenbosch • Est 2002 • 1stB 2005 • Tastings Mon-Fri 11-5 Sat & Sun 10-5 • Closed Easter Fri & Dec 25 • Sales office open daily • Tours by appt • Luxury guest suites (see Stay-over section) • Facilities for children • Gifts • Conferences • Walks • Mountain bike trails • Owner Brugman Family • Cellarmaster Delarey Brugman • Production team Delarey Brugman (convenor), Kevin Watt & Chris Kalp • Viticulturist Kevin Watt • 8ha (cabs s&f) • 18t/1 100cs 88% red 12% white • PO Box 6365 Uniedal 7612 • info@alluvia.co.za • www.alluvia.co.za

Naming their wine range 'Ilka' reflects the Brugmans' pride in their twin daughters, Ilse and Karla. They're also proud of the achievements of 10 local children they've 'adopted' through their Give Me A Chance trust fund. 'We did this to make a difference, not for any empowerment scorecard,' says Delarey B.

Ilka range

★★★★ **Sauvignon Blanc** Complex **07** zings with capsicum & white asparagus, tingles with bright acidity, finishes slatey-dry. Combo alc (14%) & fruit intensity give vg palate weight & mouthfeel - could be even better in yr.

Cabernet Sauvignon ★★★★ Step-up for classy, claret-style **05**, with sophisticated smoke, cassis & forest notes, polished tannins & endless length. Super now & for gd few yrs. More complete, ageworthy, than restrained **04** (★★★★). — CvZ

■ **Alphen Hill** *see* Wines of Cape Town

Alter Ego Wines
T 014-577-4762 • F 023-230-0774

Rustenburg • Est 2001 • 1stB 2002 • Visits by appt • Owner Vin de Parr cc • Winemaker/viticulturist John Parr (Sep 2001) • 35t/2 000cs 50% red 40% white 10% port • Postnet Suite #75, Private Bag X7, Parkview, 2122 • playberg@icon.co.za • www.alteregowine.com

John Parr has taken a breather from winemaking to make the films he's been scriptwriting, but he has some bottles of his wine left 'for those who truly appreciate it'. Included are Boonducks Red (cab), Ethan Asher (cab/merlot), Semillon and Elroy's Pawt (sweet fortified from cab & merlot). He'll be back, he hints, with a new and rather different winemaking project in the near future.

Alto Estate

T 021-881-3884 • **F** 021-881-3894

Stellenbosch • Est 1906 • 1stB 1918 • Tasting & sales Mon-Fri 9-5 Sat & pub hols 10-4 • Fee R10 (R20 incl glass) • Owner Lusan Premium Wines • Winemaker Schalk van der Westhuizen (Jul 2000) • Viticulturist Eben Archer • 93ha • 25 000cs 100% red • PO Box 104 Stellenbosch 7599 • altoestate@telkomsa.net • www.alto.co.za

Good news is that winemaker Schalk van der Westhuizen's cellar is being enlarged: space has been so tight that he's had to store wine on neighbouring Stellenzicht and 'two cooks in one kitchen is never a good thing'. A new tasting area is also on the cards, with a breathtaking view across False Bay towards Table Mountain.

★★★★ **Cabernet Sauvignon** Stylistically one of SA's slow-maturing wines. **05** follows savoury, meat extract track record, dark fruit concentration. Despite current accessibility, great rewards lie ahead.

★★★★ **Shiraz 05** in similar mould to pvs, savoury, spicy tones, no shortage of fruit. Heart is more in Rhône than SA but appeal is universal: it's the quality that attracts. Combo Am/Fr wood, 18 mths, some new.

★★★★ **Alto Rouge** 'Estate' outside SA. One of Cape's oldest, best-loved labels. Bdx varieties & shiraz. In **05** cab f dominates, adding edgy green walnut piquancy to usual layered fruit. Well-oaked structure. Class & interest remain, fans will too. — *CR*

Altydgedacht Estate

T 021-976-1295 • **F** 021-976-8521/4318

Durbanville • Est 1698 • 1stB 1981 • Tasting & sales Mon-Fri 9-5 Sat 9-3 • Closed Easter Fri, Dec 25 & Jan 1 • Tours by appt • Pampoenkraal boma-style function venue T 021·913·4962/3 • Conferencing • Conservation area • Owner Parker family • Cellarmaster Oliver Parker • Winemaker Etienne Louw (Jan 2006), advised by Mark Carmichael-Green • Viticulturist John Parker, with Adanté Roux (2002) • 170ha (12 varieties, r/w) • 1 500t/±5 000cs own label 55% red 45% white • Export label: Tygerberg • PO Box 213 Durbanville 7551 • altydgedacht@ mweb.co.za • www.altydgedacht.co.za

'2007 produced the sauvignon of the millennium,' enthuses Etienne Louw, and to better reflect it, he made his first Reserve. Next year he hopes to fulfil an ambition by making a chardonnay bubbly, perhaps with a touch of pinot which, despite having access to a home-farm viticultural cornucopia (dozen varieties, 170ha), he reckons he'll have to pinch. Durbanville farmers beware!

Cabernet Franc Rosé NEW ☺ 🗐 ★★★ Delicious tangy-fruity **07**, redcurrant pastille in sweet/sour tussle, long finish. Pink charmer perfect for summer picnics.

Cabernet Sauvignon ★★★ Dark mulberry on **04**, hints tobacco; firmer tannins as expected from cab, but soft enough for the impatient, some earthiness on finish. 10 mths oak, 70% new. **Barbera** ★★★ SA pioneer of this Italian variety. **04** with forest floor & dried herb intro, soft tannins & ultra-soft acidity, makes interesting alternative to usual reds. 14 mths Fr oak, 40% new **Merlot** ★★★★ **05** distinguished by soft tannins, plush fruit, cassis & dark choc fruit; approachable, as expected of variety. 10 mths Fr oak, 70% new. **Pinotage** ★★★★ Latest **05** meaty & savoury, velvet tannins allow for drinking now, further ageing, too. Well behaved - a treat! 11 mths mainly Fr oak, 20% new. **Shiraz** ★★★★ Last ed **04** beckoned with lovely display of ripe red fruits, smoky touch; well-judged wood (only Fr, 50% new), elegant meaty flavours. **Chardonnay** ★★★★ Always stylish; **06** poised ripe lemon aromas/flavours with fine acid balance from cool vyds, shows elegance. 50/50 oak/tank fermented, 5 mths all new Fr casks. **Chenin Blanc** ★★★★ Vines now 35 yrs old; latest **07** ripe apple tart flavours backed by chenin's steely acidity for excitement & balance. 15% oak fermented, balance tank. **Gewürztraminer** ★★★★ One of handful in SA; **07** particularly good; lovely early morning rose scents, just off-dry, muscat intensity balanced by lively acidity. **Sauvignon Blanc** 🗐 ★★★★ Picked in batches to capture spectrum of varietal flavours; vg spread of shrill capsicum, dusty green fig through to fat greengage, flavours to match. **07** tangy, juicy & quite individual. NE.

Sauvignon Blanc Reserve NEW ▤ ★★★★ **07** less showy than regular, more finesse & restraint, pleasing ripeness & poise, marginally drier. Some will prefer. From high-lying vyd on already cool farm. NE. **Chatelaine** ✓ ★★★ Dainty & pretty, **07** in established style: off-dry, light-hearted gewürz & riesling blend (59/41). *—IvH*

Alvi's Drift Private Cellar

T 023-340-4117 • F 023-340-4557

*Worcester ▪ Est 1928 ▪ 1stB 2002 ▪ Tasting, sales & tours by appt ▪ Canoe trips, game drives, visits to dairy/cheesery, BYO picnics, walks, eco-friendly 4×4 excursions by arrangement ▪ Owner Bertie, Alvi & Johan van der Merwe ▪ Winemaker Alvi van der Merwe ▪ Viticulturist Pierre Snyman (consultant) ▪ 350ha (17 varieties w/r) ▪ 5800t ▪ PO Box 827 Worcester 6850 ▪ alvi@intekom.co.za ▪ www.alvi*sdrift.co.za*

The wines and cheeses (now available at Melissa's) co-marketed under the Alvi's Drift banner are rapidly gaining recognition. For a match made in heaven, visit the farm and try the Red Muscat de Frontignan with their Mature Cheddar, Shiraz with Port Cheddar or Chenin with Havarti, suggests former GP and driving force behind the brand, Alvi van der Merwe.

Premium Selection
★★★★ **Chardonnay 06** (★★★★) less showy than **05**, more slender, finer. Gd marriage tropical fruit & oak (yr Fr barrel fermented/aged), silky drinkability.
Cabernet Sauvignon NEW ★★★ **06** attractively perfumed, sweet berry intro, well supported by firm ripe tannins. Drink now or age 2-3 yrs. **Cape Fusion** ★★★★ Warm, aromatic blend shiraz, pinotage, cab (33/40/27); last ed **05** was firm, ripe tannins providing grip & structure. Deserved yr/2 to develop. VDG. **Chardonnay-Viognier** NEW **06** blend 90/10 blend, yr small Fr oak, not ready for tasting.

Alvi's Drift range
★★★★☆ **Muscat de Frontignan White** ✓ Fortified dessert (as is Red version below); seductive barley sugar, crystallised fruit richness on **06**, mouthcoating, never-ending yet not cloying. Gorgeous. 14 mths Fr barriques.
Pinotage NEW ★★★ Mulberry tones in 06 (yr Fr/Am oak) don't offset chunky tannins. Early stage, will show better in ±yr's time. **Shiraz** NEW ★★★ **06** still tightly structured, needs ±yr to meld. Dark choc, coffee grounds, savoury character, firm oak backbone (yr Fr/Am). **Chenin Blanc Barrel Fermented** ★★★ Last-tasted **05** well structured, with broad flavours, acids & fruit tannin, oak adding interest/mouthfeel. **Chenin Blanc Unwooded** ★★★ **06** sold out, **07** unready. **Sauvignon Blanc 07** not tasted. **Muscat de Frontignan Red** NEW ✓ ★★★★ Expected raisin perfume, flavours, essence of fruit; light textured despite 177g/l sugar; chillable for summer sundowners, what a pleasure! *— CR*

■ **Amandalia** *see Rooiberg Winery*

Amani Vineyards

T 021-881-3930 • F 021-881-3931

Stellenbosch ▪ Est/1stB 1997 ▪ Tasting & sales Mon-Fri 9-4 Sat 10-4 ▪ Closed pub hols ▪ Tours by appt ▪ Owner Jim Atkinson ▪ Winemaker Carmen Stevens, with Dirk Tredoux (both 2005) ▪ Viticulturist Kevin Watt (consultant) ▪ 32ha (cabs s/f, merlot, mourvèdre, shiraz, chard, sauv, viognier) ▪ 20 500cs 53% red 47% white ▪ PO Box 12422 Die Boord 7613 ▪ wine@amani.co.za ▪ www.amani.co.za

Amani, traditionally known for its Merlot and Chardonnay, now boasts Shiraz as its biggest volume in production; the first vintage will be released in new packaging. 'We sort every batch of grapes by hand,' says winemaker Carmen Stevens, 'and we love to experiment - it keeps us on top of our game.'

Atkinson Ridge range
★★★★ **Sauvignon Blanc** More nettles & minerality in **07**, both desirable attributes. Despite lacking zing of **06** (pvs ed rated provisionally), lovely mouthfeel still offers enough greenpepper freshness to impress, do justice to food.

Chardonnay ★★★★ Powerful citrus zest, savoury & nutty aromas/flavours on punchier, showier **06**. Generous oaking easily handled by fruit. Bold yet tangy, drinkable, ultra-long finish. Fhoek fruit. Pvs **04** was savoury & steely (★★★★).

Amani range

★★★★ **Merlot 05**, barrel sample last ed, now shows ripe dark berries, plums, violet nuances, creamy smooth texture, long finish. Incl 14% shiraz. Ageing credentials 4+ yrs. 14 mths Fr, 30% new, as for all reds.

★★★★ **Chardonnay Reserve** Classy **04**, subtle citrus & white peach, noticeable mineral seam, expertly oaked, integrated fruit. Likely to develop further. **05** not tasted.

Forest Myers Shiraz ★★★★ Tribute to GM Rusty Myers's late son. Touches cab, viognier. **05** previewed last ed, retasted: wild berry piquancy, ultra-smooth body, fully integrated oak.

Cabernet Franc-Merlot ★★★★ **05** now bottled. Creative blend (18% shiraz) gives complex array fragrances, flavours: fynbos, hedgerow fruit, smoke & choc. Already drinking well; gd potential. **I Am 1** ★★★★ Merlot-led red with other bdx grapes plus shiraz. **05** revisited (pvsly sample), gorgeous perfume, choc, dark fruit, whiffs spice; evolved tannins offer drinkability. **Chardonnay** ★★★ Integrated oak gives biscuity overlay to **06** peach, tropical tones. Gd drinkability, if touch restrained; could develop in bottle. WO W Cape. **Sauvignon Blanc** ★★★★ Grapefruit & crunchy apple freshness on **07**, nettly vein adding interest, complexity. Tiny portion barrelled: here, fruit's the thing. — *CR*

■ **Ama Ulibo** *see Goedverwacht Estate*

Ambeloui Wine Cellar

T 082-441-6039 • F 021-790-7386

Hout Bay (see Constantia map) • Est 1995 • 1stB 1998 • Visits by appt • Owner Nick & Ann Christodoulou • Winemaker/viticulturist Nick Christodoulou, with Alexis Christodoulou • 0.6ha (pinot, chard) • 600cs 100% MCC • PO Box 26800 Hout Bay 7872 • wine@ambeloui.co.za • www.ambeloui.co.za

It's babes and bubbly in the nursery at this boutique MCC producer in Hout Bay. Matthew is the name of the new grandson and the newest vintage being nursed with love and attention for the loyal clientele, who queue for wine on release day, the first Saturday in November.

★★★★ **MCC** Fine, really 'brut' cap classique. **04** (★★★★★), subtitled 'Alex', gorgeous baked apple/toast complexity lifted by brilliant sparkle, mineral acidity from chard (60%, with 40% pinot). 10% barrelled, 3 yrs on lees. Weightier **03** ('Nicholas'), showed pinot predominance. **05** ('Ashley') unready for tasting.

★★★★ **Rosanne Rosé** Delicate, classy brut MCC. Latest is beguiling blush-coloured **NV**, 2 yrs on lees. Lovely creamy vitality, rounded dryness, showcasing dainty raspberry & apple flavours. 75/25 chard/pinot.

Both WO Coastal. — *AL*

■ **Amira** *see Avondale*

Anatu Wines

T 082 378 1008

Stellenbosch • Est/1stB 2002 • Visits by appt • Owner André & Freda Hamersma, Wickus & Anina Guelpa • Winemaker Anina Guelpa • 340cs 70% red 30% white • PO Box 5792 Cresta 2118 • sales@anatu.co.za • www.anatu.co.za

Harvest time at this expanding family winery witnessed sisters Anina and Freda juggling babysitting (the youngest just three weeks old) and winemaking responsibilities with respective husbands. Sauvignon grapes from Darling were deemed to be 'stunning' and grenache from Swartland dryland vineyards may one day see its own label.

★★★★ **Shiraz** Robust, fruit-lashed number from Dbnville; **04** ripeness (15.5% alc), sweet raisiny lushness shored up by spicy tannins. Loads of personality, interest noted last ed. 50% barrel fermented.

The most intelligent liquor store.

Change the way you look at liquor stores.

For info on your nearest TOPS liquor store ,
phone our Share Call number 0860 313141

Nicholas Pentz (front) of family-owned Groote Post, and **Peter Duckitt**, viticulturist at Cloof, back-dropped by the Darling Hills. The cohesive Darling winegrowers have embraced conservation, protecting the Swartland renosterveld and Atlantis sand fynbos on their farms and ensuring the famed spring flowers will bloom for decades to come. The Pentzes have dedicated a sizeable portion of their land to the Cape West Coast Biosphere Reserve. BWI champions Cloof are conserving endangered vegetation here and at their neighbouring property, Burghers Post, where they've established a 750ha game camp.

WINE FREIGHT SPECIALISTS AND FINE WINE MERCHANTS

When it comes to the professional export and shipping of wines, our proud reputation spans more than 20 years. We will ship anything upwards of three bottles right to your door - anywhere in the world.

POLKADRAAI ROAD (M12) STELLENBOSCH 7600 SOUTH AFRICA
TEL +27 21 881 3477   FAX +27 21 881 3476
EMAIL wine@capegrape.co.za OR freight@capegrape.co.za

CAPE GRAPE & WINE COMPANY

SPECIALIST WINE FREIGHT SERVICES

FINE WINE MERCHANTS

www.capegrape.co.za   TEL: +27 21 881 3477

Winemaker **Francois van Zyl** (left) and MD/viticulturist **Michael Malherbe** in Laibach's vineyards in the Simonsberg foothills, increasingly converted to organic farming. Techniques employed include planting cover crops like yarrow and fennel, a convenient nesting place for wasps which naturally predate on mealy bug. Cover crops also help restore soil structure, improve water infiltration, and replenish organic matter and nutrients. This practice, combined with discontinuing the use of insecticides, has seen the soil recover significantly and earthworm numbers multiply as a result.

Things that taste good, taste even better in glass. Glass is 100% pure and natural which means there's no better place for your favourite wine than in one of our Consol Glass bottles.

Consol

IT'S GOOD. IT'S IN GLASS.

Frans Smit is cellarmaster at Spier Wines. Certified by WIETA and a BWI member, Spier is committed to improving the land by restoring endangered species and introducing biodynamic farming methods. It has engaged in a zero waste policy by introducing on-site waste recycling programmes and water conservation initiatives, significantly reducing environmental impacts. Innovations outside of wine include producing bio-diesel as an alternative energy source, and making environmentally sound adobe bricks for use in all new building projects.

The largest selection of South African wine in the WORLD!
If it's in Platter, it's in our cybercellar [or it's sold out]
cybercellar.com
www.cybercellar.com

Spot the chameleon? If not, zoom in just below **Gary Jordan**'s chin. He and wife **Kathy**, long protectors of the Cape Dwarf Chameleon (Bradypodion pumilum), initiated the Jordan Chameleon Research Bursary last year, motivated by research carried out by scientists from the SA National Biodiversity Institute (SANBI). Their study indicated that chameleons are not found in Jordan's vineyards but in shrubs and trees around them, allaying industry fears that they may be harmed by automated harvesters, viticultural practices or tools.

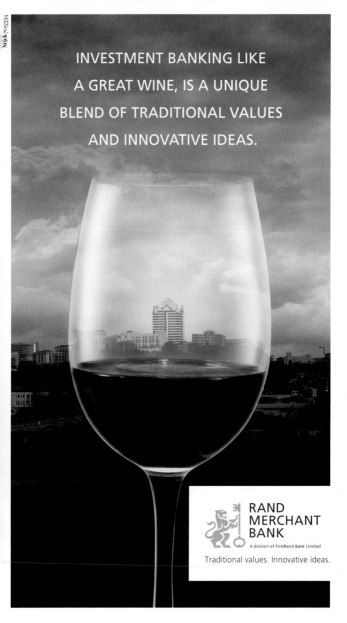

INVESTMENT BANKING LIKE
A GREAT WINE, IS A UNIQUE
BLEND OF TRADITIONAL VALUES
AND INNOVATIVE IDEAS.

RAND
MERCHANT
BANK
A division of FirstRand Bank Limited

Traditional values. Innovative ideas.

Rand Merchant Bank's long and happy association with the South African wine industry
is no coincidence. The wine-makers' individuality and flair for combining time-honoured
techniques with cutting-edge thinking is very much at the heart of our founding philosophy
of 'Traditional values. Innovative ideas'. www.rmb.co.za

Thinking that can change your world

An Authorised Financial Services Provider

Winemaker **Bertus Albertyn** (left) with viticulturist and 'bio-logic' exponent **Johnathan Grieve**, whose family owns BWI-accredited **Avondale** as well as a leading health products business. Their novel approach combines organic certification and a variety of nature-harnessing practices, ranging from teams of ducks which pick snails off vines, to wasps and beetles that deal swiftly with mealy bug. They now have a thriving ecosystem of buck, rabbits, eagles, hawks and owls – tall poles have been strategically placed for predator birds to naturally control the rodent population.

Stockist of a wide variety of Quality
South African & Imported Wines
including Nederburg Auction Wines

For the __BEST__ Prices in Town

The __KING__ of Liquor!

Sauvignon Blanc ★★★ Lightish, aperitif-style **06** last yr offered zip & zing without jarring acidity. Clean gooseberry/greenpepper tang. — *CT*

■ **Ancient Africa** *see Baarsma Wine Group*

■ *Andreas see Groenendal Farm*

■ *Andrew Bain see Cape Vineyards*

Andy Mitchell Wines
T 028-254-9045, 083-558-5085 · F 021-510-1266

Greyton (see Southern Cape map) · Est/1stB 2003 · Visits by appt · Owner Andy & Vikki Mitchell · Winemaker Andy & Vikki Mitchell, advised by Marais de Villiers (vini) & Terroir Wines (viti) · Viticulturist Benny Diederichs · 320cs 60% red 40% rosé · PO Box 543 Paarden Eiland 7420 · andy@za.northsails.com · www.andymitchellwines.com

Andy Mitchell is celebrating both his graduation as a Cape Wine Master and rescuing his rosé from a stuck fermentation. All's well in the end, he says, the wine is dry as intended, and the extra time on the lees added dimension. A top-rank chenin and a bubbly are next in his sights.

Breakfast Rock Syrah ★★★ Oaky notes to warm, jammy & slightly volatile **05**. Firm but juicy tannins, sweet/sour finish. Sbosch grapes, as for next wine. **Nerina Shiraz Rosé** 📖 ★★★ Dry party wine with slight petillance & vibrant colour. **07** baked apple wafts through to palate. — *MM*

■ **Angels Tears** *see Grande Provence*

Angora
T 021-881-3475 · F 021-881-3248

Robertson · Est/1stB 2002 · Tasting & sales by appt · Closed pub hols · Owner Gerrit Joubert · Winemaker Gerrit Joubert & sons, with Danie Slabber · Viticulturist Danie Slabber · 16ha (cab, port varieties, ruby cab, shiraz, chenin, muscadel) · 300t/900cs own label 100% red · PO Box 343 Bonnievale 6730 · chris.joubert@gilga.com · www.gilga.com

Most of the grapes grown by the Joubert family are delivered to nearby Bonnievale Cellar, but each harvest Gerrit J and son Chris (ex-Overgaauw, now solo and consulting to dad, amongst others) divert enough to their Angora label for at least two wines. Volumes were too low for a Rosé last year, so the 07s are a Chenin and a Shiraz.

Shiraz ★★★★ **05** continues upward trend set by **04** (★★★★); cardamom, fenugreek & fennel mingle with lily perfume, firm tannins mould around juicy, refreshing fruit core. 18 mths oak, 30% new. **Shiraz Rosé** ★★★ **06** last ed was off-dry with simple strawberry aromas, sweet raspberry flavours, tangy acidity. **Chenin Blanc** ★★★ Step up for lightly oaked **07**; though shy on nose, explodes with guava/melon flavours & vibrant acidity; smidgen sugar prolongs finish, fleshes out palate. All above WO Bonnievale. — *CvZ*

Annandale Distillers & Vintners
T 021-881-3560/1 · F 021-881-3562

Stellenbosch · Est/1stB 1996 · Tasting & sales Mon-Sat 9-5 · Fee R15 refundable on purchase · Closed Christian hols · Tours by appt · Collection of antique wine objects · Owner/ winemaker/viticulturist Hempies du Toit · 45ha (cabs s/f, merlot, shiraz) · 5 000cs own label · 100% red · Annandale Farm, Annandale Road, Stellenbosch 7600 · info@annandale.co.za · www.annandale.co.za

Time moves slowly at this idiosyncratic, Old-World cellar, and Hempies du Toit is paying it homage with a five-year barrel-matured shiraz. It celebrates five generations of winemakers: 'I was born into wine, not bought into it,' says amiable Hempies, who admits that he loves to see his wines grow up, but not leave home.

★★★★ **Cabernet Sauvignon 01** 'masculine' cab, with classic cedar & blackcurrant profile, solid dry finish; 15.5% alc no drawback, neither is no-holds-barred oaking in 3 yrs new Nevers. As below, not retasted.

★★★★ **Shiraz** Beautifully packaged maiden **01** last time noted as quintessentially Cape: warm, spicily intense but neither over-rich nor too showy. 30 mths 2nd fill barrels, all Fr. New vintage mentioned in intro not ready.

Cavalier ★★★★ Balanced & classy blend merlot, cab s & f, shiraz (40/25/25/10), 36 mths oak, all Fr; **01** was last reviewed. **CVP** ★★★★ 'Cape Vintage Port'; 100% shiraz, fortified with matured brandy, contributing to rich spiciness of **03**; sweet fruitcake flavours; ready to drink or keep a few more yrs. 76g/l RS, 20% alc. — IM

Annex Kloof Wines

T 022-487-3870 · F 022-487-3870

Swartland · Est 2005 · 1stB 2006 · Tasting by appt · Cheese platters by appt · BYO picnic · Self-catering cottages · Conference facilities · Walking/hiking/4x4 & mountain biking trails · Conservation area · Fishing · Owner Hugo, Toeloe, Thys & Tobie Basson & Martin Burger · Winemaker/viticulturist Hugo Basson · Cab, malbec, merlot, pinotage, shiraz, chard, chenin, sauvignon, viognier · 2 500 cs 60% red 40% white · PO Box 772 Malmesbury 7299 · hugo@annexkloofwines.co.za

'Wine is a story in a bottle that begins in the vineyard,' philosophises Hugo Basson, whose own story has many important characters – from the all-too-often unsung farm workers to his two brothers, who each have a farm providing different fruit character, and most of all his dad: 'He hasn't taught me technical things so much as perseverance – that you don't just give up but rather learn from your mistakes.' Selling off all but the best grapes, enlisting Wynand Hamman (Fryer's Cove) as adviser, offering visitor-friendly amenities in the exciting but as-yet-undeveloped Paardeberg… Doesn't sound like they're making too many errors! The wines, a red and white blend not ready for review this edition.

AntHill Wines

T 082-895-9008 · F 021-851-5914

Somerset West · Est/1stB 2000 · Tasting by appt · Owner Mark Howell & Hylton Schwenk · Winemaker Mark Howell · 300cs · 19 Immelman Rd, Somerset West 7130 · anthill@absamail.co.za

Mark Howell is unflinching in his low opinion of vintage 2007: 'It was s***t!' But he and fellow garagiste Hylton Schwenk are still having fun, garnering experience for day-job retirement time. They're hinting at providing their own private tasting room, this year or next, instead of borrowing space here and there.

★★★★ **Ietermagô Chardonnay** An elegant & classy 'Armadillo'. **04** (★★★★) pvs ed showed rich melon, clementine & shortbread tones. Shade lighter (12.5% alc), less opulent than maiden **03** but still v gd. No **05** as yet.

Entre Nous Cabernet Sauvignon NEW ★★★★ Luscious cassis, macerated plums, drink-me juicy accessibility. **05** new-barrel treatment, fully integrated. Sbosch/Hlderbrg fruit. Only 70 cs. **The Persian Shiraz** ★★★★ Southern-rhône-style **04**, with dash viognier, pvs ed layered & elegant with well-managed oak (16 mths, mainly Fr, 50% new). — CR

Anthony de Jager Wines

T 021-863-2450 · F 021-863-2591

Paarl · Est/1stB 2001 · Closed to public · Owner/winemaker Anthony de Jager · 175cs 100% red · PO Box 583 Suider-Paarl 7624 · homtini@absamail.co.za

'Not much happening with the couple of barrels of Homtini,' says self-effacing Fairview winemaker Anthony de Jager about his own small-scale production of fine shiraz. On a personal note, the mountain bike enthusiast rode the 900km Cape Epic race.

★★★★★ **Homtini Shiraz** Since debut **00** (★★★★★) satisfyingly merges shiraz & dash viognier. Last tasted **05** carefully minimised burly 15% alc, maintained balanced medium-term drinking. Co-fermented/14 mths oak, 15% new. Old Paarl Mntn vines. — AL

Anthony Smook Wines
T 083-376-9924 / 021-869-8655 • F 021-869-8655

Voor Paardeberg (see Paarl map) • Est/1stB 2000 • Tasting & tours by appt only; tasting/sales also at I Love Wine (see entry) • Owner/cellarmaster Anthony Smook • Winemaker Francois Louw • Viticulturist Johan Wiese (2001, consultant) • 30ha (cab, viognier, pinotage, shiraz, chard) • 36t/2 500cs 75% red 25% white • PO Box 7038 Northern Paarl 7623 • info@ smookwines.co.za, zelda@smookwines.co.za • www.smookwines.co.za

Entrepreneurial winemaker Anthony Smook has relocated 'down the road' to a renovated 18th-century cellar on quaintly named property Staart van Paardeberg ('Tail of Horse Mountain'), officially part of Voor Paardeberg wine ward. New endeavours include planting shiraz amid fynbos on other Paarl farm, Elandsjacht, and making wine and olive oil on his newly acquired Italian spread.

★★★★ Shiraz Reserve Rich, tightly knit woodspice & sappy fruit in seamless harmony in **05**. Svelte tannin & layers of flavour in powerful yet elegantly balanced style.

Pinotage ★★★ Usual elegant 'burgundian' style. **05** balanced, soft & appealing; bright, rich red fruit & touch earthiness. **Shiraz ★★★★** Elegant spice & vibrant red fruit in **05**, enhanced by judicious oaking. Juicy, balanced tannins. Eminently drinkable. **Cabernet Sauvignon-Merlot ★★★ 04** not ready. **03** last ed was savoury, steely, well- & elegantly fruited. **Chardonnay ★★★** Ripe lime & pear shine through **06**. Approachable; integrated oaking & refreshing acid balance. Discontinued: **Chardonnay Reserve**. — *MW*

Anura Vineyards
T 021-875-5360 • F 021-875-5657

Paarl • Est 1990 • 1stB 2001 • Tasting & sales daily 9.30-5 • Closed Easter Fri/Mon, Dec 25/26 & Jan 1 • Fee R20 (cheese & wine) • Lilly Pad Restaurant • Tours by appt • Farm produce sold • Owner Tymen & Jenny Bouma • Winemaker Tymen Bouma & Carla Pauw, with Johnnie Calitz (Jan 2007) • Viticulturist Hannes Kloppers (Oct 1997) • 118ha (cab, malbec, merlot, mourvèdre, pinotage, sangiovese, shiraz, chard, sauv) • 45 000cs own label 80% red 20% white • PO Box 244 Klapmuts 7625 • info@anura.co.za • www.anura.co.za

'Lifestyle' rings a bell for Tymen Bouma (co-owner with wife Jenny): 'It's an essential part of getting people to visit us.' Hence his delight that plans are advanced for a 50-bed hotel and spa at Anura, completely integrated with the red-wine cellar. It's a model he's seen in France and he's sure it'll satisfy a local demand.

Reserve range

★★★★ Cabernet Sauvignon Last ed complex **04** showed rich & juicy palate with cassis & cedar from serious oaking (23 mths older barrels). Long, dry, scented black fruit on finish; 15% alc in balance. **05** not ready.

★★★★ Merlot 05 as sybaritic as pvs. Ripe, fruity, Christmas pud aromas gain coffee/ mocha flavours on richly textured palate. Sustained finish with elegant tannins; develops in glass. 18 mths mixed-age barrels.

Syrah-Mourvèdre ★★★★ Elegance & fruit combine in **05**'s Old-World-meets-New approach. Long, dry tannic finish (20 mths, shiraz 35% new Fr, mourvèdre 3,4 fill).

Limited Release range

Pinot Noir NEW **★★★★** Maiden **06** in dense, full style. Ripe black fruit & rich black berries; chunky tannins with dry finish; 15% alc. **Petit Verdot ★★★** Meaty nose with hints tomato leaf on well-made, warm & tannic-tailed **06**. 18 mths 30% new Fr oak. **Syrah ★★★★** Opulent dark fruit in showy, New-World **04**. Last ed concentrated & juicy — like biting into a dark ripe plum. Supple tannins with 20 mths oak maturation (40% new) providing support. **Viognier** NEW **★☆ 06** newcomer very shy; hot & simple with sweet finish. **Cap Classique Brut** NEW **06** not ready for tasting.

Anura range

Malbec ★★★☆ Pleasant spice & cherries on now-bottled **05**. Ripe, round with soft tannins & creamy finish. 18 mths seasoned barrels. **Merlot ★★★★** Pvsly tasted **04** was lean & edgy, with sour plum/herbaceous nuances & taut tannins; needed food. **Pinotage ★★★** Dash mourvèdre in austere, minerally **05**. Soft, complex oaking regime (staves & 3rd/4th fill brls) results in fine, dry tannic finish. **Sangiovese Limited Edition** ★★★☆ Serious & well-made, characterful **05** (now bottled). Savoury, biscuity, strawberry aromas; gd, fine tannins & long finish. **Legato** NEW Bdx-style **05** blend merlot/cab (53/47) not ready. **Chardonnay** ★★★ Refreshing lime nuances to **06**; well-managed subtle oaking supports fruit. Pleasant drinking wine, solo or with food. **Chenin Blanc** ★★★ Broad-shouldered **06** mingles perfumed citrus with pleasant oak/vanilla hints; hot, oaky finish. Fr oak, 11 mths. **Sauvignon Blanc** ★★★ Greenpepper & waxy hints to **06**, shows some age but still fresh, long nutty finish. Discontinued: **Syrah**, '**Bordeaux Blend**', **Syrah-Mourvèdre**.

Frog Hill range
Pinotage NEW ★★★ **06** incl dash mourvèdre; farmyard character, ripe plums in modest debut; obvious tannic finish. Stave ferment/ageing plus 6 mths older barrels. **Rana** ★★★ **06** reduces pvs 4-way blend to cab/merlot (70/30). Fruity choc/toffee notes & black plums; full & dry, tannic finish. **Rosé** ★★★ Last-tasted **05** combined tart cranberry flavours from cab with dash merlot in light, refreshing al fresco option. Discontinued: **Chenin Blanc**. *— MM*

Anwilka
T 021-842-3225 • F 021-842-3983

Stellenbosch • Est 1997 • 1stB 2005 • Closed to public; sales from Klein Constantia • Owner Bruno Prats, Hubert de Boüard & Lowell Jooste • Winemaker Trizanne Pansegrouw (2005), with Hubert de Boüard & Bruno Prats • Viticulturist Piet Neethling, advised by Johan Wiese (May 1998/Dec 1997) • 40ha (cab, merlot, shiraz) • 250t total; ±100t own label; 100% red • PO Box 5298 Helderberg 7135 • lowell@anwilka.com • www.anwilka.com
'Just got back from Oz, a fantastic trip! Learnt so much!' reads a message from winemaker Trizanne Pansegrouw to Klein Constantia's Lowell Jooste, local proprietor of this premium red-wine producer. (Bruno Prats, formerly of Bordeaux second growth Cos d'Estournel, and Hubert de Boüard de Laforest of St-Emilion premier grand cru L'Angélus are co-owners and advisers). Some 90% goes to the Bordeaux trade, selling on to 'very similar customers as the top Bordeaux châteaux', says Lowell J. Quality dictates quantity, so a second label (and a new cellar) are on the cards.
★★★★★ **Anwilka** Released young to catch Bordeaux 'en primeur' previews. **06** initially less settled than maiden **05**, but layered sweet fruit, intensity & persistence all suggest potentially more complex & long-lived wine. 66/29 cab/shiraz, elegantly perfumed by dash merlot (5%); Fr oak, 50% new, 10 mths.*—AL*

▮ **Apiesklip** *see Baarsma Wine Group*
▮ **Aprilskloof** *see Lammershoek Winery*

Arabella

T 023-615-2256 • F 023-615-2257

Robertson • Est 2005 • 1stB 2006 • Tasting & sales Mon-Fri 9-5 Sat 9-2 • Tours by appt • Owner Stephen & Jamie de Wet • Winemaker/viticulturist Stephen de Wet • 176ha (cab, sauv) • 1 250t/±20 000cs 50% red 50% white • HACCP certification in progress • PO Box 155 Ashton 6715 • info@arabellawines.com • www.arabellawines.com
In only 2 years the De Wet family have a new cellar, new plantings of shiraz and nouvelle, and are breeding the next lineage of thoroughbred Arabian horses. Perseverance is useful not only in successfully completing projects - both father (Stephen) and son Jamie are in the national top line-up of endurance horse riders.
Cabernet Sauvignon ★★★ Cassis, cedar & herbaceous whiffs, **06** has classic styling, lively drinkability but enough backbone for 2/3yrs ageing. **Merlot** ★★★ Plum/prune fruit & sweet spice in tasty **06**, enough tannin structure for hearty stews. 1/2 yrs ageing potential. **Shiraz** ★★★ Molten plums, smoky nuances, ultra-smooth texture, **06** is a charmer, has 'drink me' written all over it. **Pink Panacea** NEW ★★ A crowd pleaser, **06** has tropical fruit, light touch of sweetness. **Chenin Blanc** ★★★ **06** last ed was lightly textured, aromatic & floral. **Sauvignon Blanc** ★★★ Blend early- & later-picked fruit improves **07**'s leafy, gooseberry styling.

Bone-dry, appetisingly fresh, seafood-friendly. **Viognier** ★★ Pvsly reviewed **06** offered fresh melon & fruit salad, undemanding drinkability. — *CR*

▪ **Ardens Andreu** *see* Groenendal Farm

Arendsig Hand-Crafted Wines
T 023-616-2835 ▪ F 023-616-2090

Robertson ▪ Est/1stB 2004 ▪ Visits by appt ▪ Vineyard tour & tasting with winemaker by appt ▪ Owner/winemaker/viticulturist Lourens van der Westhuizen ▪ 12ha (cab, shiraz, chard, sauv, viognier) ▪ 12t/2000cs ▪ PO Box 170 Robertson 6705 ▪ info@arendsig.co.za ▪ www.arendsig.co.za

Although he's invested in a cellar mattress for harvest time, catching Lourens van der Westhuizen napping could prove a challenge. Determined to produce individual wines, he's involved from vineyard to bottling and has now entered the creative department: the catchy labels for his Sauvignon and Viognier are his design.

Shiraz ★★★★ Showstopper! **06** liquorice, choc, cinnamon mingle with ultra-ripe, dense fruit. Exceptionally concentrated micro-cuvée; big structure sure to have many followers. 80% new oak, mainly Fr. **05** (★★★★) was more Rhône than New World. **Chardonnay** ★★★★ Sumptuous vanilla & pineapple character, with almond, citrus notes. Rich Burgundian profile (partly from Fr oak maturation, 20% new) though purists might decry sweet exit (4g/l RS). **05** (★★★★) was appealing & tangy. **Sauvignon Blanc** NEW ★★★ Maiden **07**, from single vyd, is super-racy, lemon-fruited & pungent; carefully made: could develop interestingly. **Viognier** NEW Barrel-fermented **07** not tasted. — *RP*

Arlington Beverage Group
T (021) 794-6697

Stellenbosch ▪ Est 1996 ▪ 1stB 1997 ▪ Closed to public ▪ Owner Richard Addison ▪ ±200 000 cs 45% red 55% white ▪ PO Box 1376 Stellenbosch 7599 ▪ richard@arlingtonbeverage.com ▪ www.arlingtonbeverage.com

Arlington markets and sells SA wines to countries such as the UK, Ireland and Argentina. With local partners, it has built a number of successful on-trade brands including Broken Rock, Landsdowne, Millbrook and Rocheburg. Arlington also represents a number of leading Cape properties in the international markets, including Riebeek and Ridgeback.

▪ **Armajaro** *see* Vondeling
▪ *Arniston Bay* *see* The Company of Wine People

Arra Vineyards
T 021-875-5363 ▪ F 021-875-5866

Paarl ▪ Est 1998 ▪ 1stB 2001 ▪ Tasting by appt ▪ Owner Coventry & Novak Families ▪ Winemaker Ronell Wiid (2004), with Etienne Southey & Alpheus Ntoa (2006) ▪ Viticulturist Paul Wallace (May 2001, consultant) ▪ 43ha (cab, merlot, mourvèdre, pinotage, ruby cab, shiraz, viognier) ▪ 140t/10 000cs own label 90% red 5% white 5% rose ▪ PO Box 298 Klapmuts 7625 ▪ info@ arrawines.com ▪ www.arrawines.com

Arra Vineyards, previously Royle Family Vineyards, belong to the Novak and Coventry families, who picked up the wine bug on a visit here ten years ago. While aiming to continue producing elegant, hand-crafted wines, they're ringing the changes, including opening the farm doors to visitors (by appointment). Other innovations include a music stage, to be unveiled in the near future.

Cabernet Sauvignon ★★★★ Released after **04**, now at perfect readiness, **03** impresses with cassis & blackberry concentration; finely judged oak structure (18 mths Fr). **Shiraz** ★★★ Dominated by oak last yr, needing time; **04** gd leathery flavours, dry tannins. 15 mths mainly Fr oak. **03** (★★★★) was elegant, showed promise. **Viognier** ★★★★ Previewed pvs ed, debut **06** showing beautifully; peach & floral perfume rendered food-friendly by biscuity shading. Lively drinkability remains intact. — *CR*

■ **Arumdale** *see* Thelema Mountain Vineyards

Arum Lily Wines 🍷 🌳 [NEW]
T 083-230-5618 ▪ F 021-933-2161, 022-772-2163

Wellington (see Paarl map) ▪ Est/1stB 2006 ▪ Visits by appt ▪ Closed Dec 25 ▪ BYO picnic ▪ Owner Chris Pretorius Family Trust ▪ Winemaker Hein Hesebeck (2007) ▪ Viticulturist Nico Uys (2007, consultant) ▪ 32ha (cab, pinotage, shiraz, chard, chenin) ▪ 260t/5 600cs own label 60% red 20% white 20% rosé ▪ PO Box 1098 Wellington 7654 ▪ cjpretorius@gogga_connect.co.za

Arum Lily Wines is the latest project of Chris Pretorius, whose family's business interests include property development and a number of Spar stores. The family bought the 69ha farm some time ago, but its first vintage, produced by seasoned winemaker Hein Hesebeck and viticulturist Nico Uys, only went on sale at the end of last year.

Dry Red ★★ Concentrated black fruit, herbal aromas, puckering dry tannins. **NV. Shiraz Rosé Off-Dry** ★★★ Ribena & red fruit prelude to **07**, firm fleshy flavours but dilute finish. **Chardonnay** ★★ Lime-citrus notes on **07**, dense flavours still unsettled mid-2007. **Chenin Blanc Wooded** ★★★ Pear-drop & vanilla overlay to concentrated grapefruit flavours, **07** balanced, harmonious & lingering. **Chenin Blanc Unwooded** ★★ **07** melon & apricot notes on uncomplicated dry white. **Dry White** ★ **06** doubtless better in youth. **Cabernet Sauvignon Rosé Natural Sweet** ★★ Herbaceous **07** v sweet & syrupy, needs more freshness. *— MF*

Asara Estate 🍷 ☕ 🏛 📷 ♿
T 021-888-8000 ▪ F 021-888-8001

Stellenbosch ▪ Est 1691 ▪ 1stB 1970 ▪ Tasting & sales Mon-Fri 9-5 Sat 10-5 (Oct-Apr), 10-2 (May-Sep) ▪ Fee R15 ▪ Closed Easter Fri, Dec 25/26 & Jan 1 ▪ Tours by appt ▪ Amenities/attractions: see intro ▪ Owner Markus & Christiane Rahmann ▪ Winemaker Jan van Rooyen (Oct 1999) ▪ Viticulturist Pieter Rossouw (1995) ▪ 120ha (cab, merlot, shiraz, chard, sauv) ▪ ±500t/ 25 000cs 60% red 40% white ▪ PO Box 882 Stellenbosch 7599 ▪ info@AsaraWine.com ▪ www.AsaraWine.com

This handsome estate, named after a trio of ancient gods, is about to become an even more attractive destination. A luxury hotel will open early this year and feature a high-end restaurant, tapas bar, cigar and whisky lounge, as well as extensive conference and wedding facilities. Add to this their already comprehensive range of wines and you realise that thinking big is part of the Asara way.

★★★★☆ **Cabernet Sauvignon** Quite expressive fruit & appealing fine, soft tannin on **02** (★★★★), which lacks concentration of **00** (no **01** made), but similar fruit profile. Cherries, cassis & coffee on palate with lingering minerality. Gd oaking (2 yrs, 30% new).

★★★★ **Merlot** Concentrated & elegant **02** does well in difficult vintage: fresh & inviting plummy fruit with gd underlying minerality & spicy, well-managed oak (18 mths).

★★★★ **Avalon** Fascinating amarone-inspired 'meditation wine' from vine-dried pinotage - hedonistic, high-toned, savoury & intense, with tannic grip. Richly firm maiden **04**; ±16.5% alc, dry finish. Last tasted was sample **05**.

★★★★ **Shiraz** Vibrant **03** (★★★★★), not retasted, allured with lily, black pepper & red berry scents, deliciously tangy fruity tannins; greater depth & concentration than **01**, **02**. Mixed Fr/Am, older/new oak. NE.

★★★★ **Bell Tower Collection Estate Wine** Classic Bdx blend cabs s & f, petit v, splash malbec & merlot. Forward from **99** to **03**, classy restrained nose with choc, black fruit, vanilla; complicated by soya & graphite on palate, rounded with obvious 4.6g/l sugar. 2 yrs oak, 40% new.

★★★★ **Cape Fusion** 'Cape blend' of pinotage, merlot, shiraz, cab. Interesting aromas of fresh red fruit, Oriental spice on **02** (★★★). Elegant palate with substantial tannins, but without delicious decadent richness of **01**.

★★★★ **Chardonnay Reserve** Restrained, judiciously oaked **04** not retasted; citrus, vanilla, nutmeg notes; focused acidity & well knit tannins. Fermented/±yr mix new & older Fr oak.

★★★★★ **Noble Late Harvest** Luscious dessert from barrel-fermented chenin. Last tasted was lightly intense **03**, with 11.5% alc, fine acidity, following unctuous **02** (★★★★).
Ebony 🔲 ★★★★ Elegant, well structured **01** blend cab/merlot, aromas/flavours of blackcurrant, humidor & wet earth; more depth & complexity than pvs. **Rosé** ★★★ **07** v dry summery blend shiraz, gamay, pinotage, with lovely floral/red fruit tones, hint of spice. **Chardonnay Unwooded** ★★★ **07** appealing, well balanced, typical of variety but unexceptional. **Sauvignon Blanc** ★★★ Juicy **07** shows typical aroma/flavour of gooseberry & grenadilla. **Ivory** 🔲 ★★★ Early tired-looking blend of 71% sauv & chard, but fresher-tasting, with gd palate weight. **Pineau** NEW ★★★★ **04** fortified pinotage juice; ideal sweet aperitif with lots of fruit, balancing acidity & evident spirit (21% alc). 2 yrs oak, 70% new. **Spirit of Chenin** ★★★★ White-port-style fortified from chenin, made intermittently. Last tried was **04**, with nicely integrated spirit. 108g/l RS, 20% alc, 14 mths Fr oak. *— JPf*

Ashanti
T 021-862-0789 · F 021-862-2864

Paarl ▪ Est 1997 ▪ 1stB 1998 ▪ Tasting & tours by appt ▪ Restaurant at Ashanti lunches Tue-Fri 11-4 year-round; in season also Sat dinner/sundowners 6.30pm-9pm & Sun lunches; booking advised ▪ Owner Ashanti Estates ▪ Winemaker Kosie Moller ▪ Viticulturist Anton Laas ▪ 96ha ▪ 70 000 cs ▪ PO Box 934 Huguenot 7645 ▪ info@ashantiwines.com ▪ www.ashantiwines.com

'Exciting, innovative new wines to be launched soon,' promises well-known Klein Parys owner/winemaker Kosie Möller, now also in charge of operations at this Tuscan-style Paarl property after forging a partnership with the new owners. Noted for its lakeside setting and mountain views, the restaurant is headed up by Christine Veldsman, previously of Le Quartier Francais.

★★★★ **Chiwara** The flagship. **04** (★★) cab, merlot, cab f (72/21/7) in lightweight successor to last-tasted **02**. Shy, dusty, jammy ripe fruit; soft tannins & sweetish finish.
Cabernet Sauvignon ★★★ Sociable **06** combines warm, jammy nose & blackcurrant character with ripe tannins & juicy mouthfeel. Enjoy solo or with food. **Malbec 04** & **05** sold out. **06** not ready. **Merlot** ★★★ **05** sold out; **06** untasted. **Petit Verdot** NEW 🔲 ★★ Savoury, with touch spiciness on **06**, raspberry glimpse from 12% shiraz. **Pinotage** ★★ Ripe banana, rosepetal fragrances & flavours on **06** supplant pvs vintage's firmness; would benefit from more acid. **Shiraz** ★★ Reclusive **06**, hints black pepper & berries, cinnamon note, sweet oak tannins from 20% new wood. **Chardonnay** NEW ★★ **06** light, with lime & mineral whiffs, nutty vanilla tail. **Chenin Blanc** NEW **07** unready.

Concept wines
Discontinued: **Joseph's Hat**, **Sunset Hat**, **Nicole's Hat**, **French Kiss**. *— MM*

Ashbourne
T 028-312-3595 · F 028-312-1797

Hemel-en-Aarde Valley ▪ Est 1996 ▪ 1stB 2001 ▪ Closed to public ▪ Owner Anthony Hamilton Russell ▪ Winemaker Hannes Storm ▪ Viticulturist Johan Montgomery ▪ ±13ha (pinotage, sauv) ▪ 8t/600cs 70% red 30 white ▪ PO Box 158 Hermanus 7200 ▪ hrv@hermanus.co.za

Anthony Hamilton Russell continues his quest to develop wines with a uniquely South African fingerprint on this property bordering Hamilton Russell Vineyards, his Hemel-en-Aarde estate. 2008 will see the first crop from experimental vines for blending trials; these include bushvines planted in virgin soils. Indigenous innovations involve clearing alien plants to pasture a herd closely related to original Khoi cattle, for making 'real Cape cheese'; and the planting of native Cape olives to investigate their oil potential.

★★★★★ **Ashbourne** First of these elegant, bdx-styled pinotages since maiden **01** was excellent, raspberry-fruited **04**, last ed showing fresh charm, with mineral undertone & serious subtle structure. This, below, WO W Bay.
★★★★ **Sandstone** Tasted last yr, **06**'s aroma, flavour dominated by sauv (60%), needed decanting to bring out contributions of chard (30%) & barrel fermented semillon; yr/2 wanted to augment simplicity. *— TJ*

Ashton Winery
T 023-615-1135/7 • F 023-615-1284

*Ashton (see Robertson map) ▪ Est 1962 ▪ 1stB ca 1970 ▪ Tasting & sales Mon-Fri 8-5 Sat 9-12.
30 ▪ Closed pub hols ▪ Tours by appt ▪ BYO picnic ▪ Owner 68 members ▪ Winemaker Philip
Louw (Aug 2000) & Jozua Joubert (Dec 2006), with Surina Conradie (Jan 2007) ▪ Viticulturist
Willem Botha (consultant) ▪ 1 200ha (cab, ruby cab, shiraz, chard) ▪ 18 000t (6 000cs own
label) 35% red 65% white ▪ Range for customer: Berryfields ▪ PO Box 40 Ashton 6715 ▪ info@
ashtoncellar.co.za ▪ www.ashtonkelder.co.za*

What with a very successful Klein Karoo arts festival, visiting agents from Europe, a brand-new website with a focus on wine-and-food pairing, it's been busy, says Philip Louw, now GM. Stellenbosch graduate Surina Conradie joined the cellar as quality controller/assistant winemaker, and Stephen Anthony as concentrate production manager (they also produce grape juice concentrate for the wine, canning and beverage industries).

Reserve range
Shiraz ✓ ★★★★ Steps up the quality ladder with lovely lily/red fruit bouquet, peppery note, fine tannins all part of polished **05**'s appeal. **Chardonnay** ★★★ 40% new-oak adds pleasant vanilla cloak to **06**'s lemony profile; 13,8% alc slightly warming.

Ashton Winery range

Cabernet Sauvignon ☺ ★★★ Forthcoming cassis aromas on **04**, beguiling freshness despite extreme ripeness. Friendly 13,7% alc. **Satyn Rooi** ☺ ★★★ Reliable unoaked 50/50 ruby cab & pinotage mix, perennial favourite at bargain price. **06** smooth as name suggests. **Colombar-Chardonnay** ☺ ★★★ Charming guava/orange wafts on **07**; zesty acidity ensures lively mouthful.

Pinot Noir Limited Release ★★★ Pvs without 'Limited Release' moniker. **04** authentic varietal notes of cherry & forest floor, soft lemony acidity. **Shiraz** ★★★ Uncomplicated fruity **05**, easy, soft, touch of resin on finish. **Cabernet Sauvignon-Merlot** ★★ Tasted last ed, approachable **04** showed restrained red fruits, soft tannins. **Rosé** ★★ Nicely balanced, so **07** tastes juicy rather than sweet; appealing red berry tone. **Chardonnay Unwooded** ★★ Work-in-progress **07** shows fair vinosity but little varietal character. **Chenin Blanc** ★★ **07** raises the bar with attractive floral/thatchy bouquet, rounded flavours. **Colombar** ★★ Sample **07** guava hints, easy alc (11.6%) & racy freshness. **Sauvignon Blanc Winemaker's Choice** ★★ **07** green aromas & flavours, bracing acidity (6.1g/l) balanced by solid fruit core. **Pascali** NEW ★★ Frothy brut-style party-starter with sauv's grassy, zippy acidity. **NV Bonica** NEW ★★ Onion-skin-hued bubbly with grapey aromas, slightly sweet lift. **NV. Special Late Harvest** ★★ **07** sweetly pleasant, grapey & effortless. **Red Muscadel Jerepigo** ★★ **06** raisined, tea-leaf-scented fortified dessert, vast sweetness (216g/l RS) refreshed by 17% alc. **White Muscadel** ★★★★ No new vintage. Last ed jasmine-scented **02** brimmed with silky peach & honey flavours. **White Muskadel Jerepiko** NEW ★★★ **03** fortified sweetie with sun-kissed grape & honey notes, lovely persistence. **Port** ★★ Unpretentious winter warmer, raspberry & treacle lifted by low but active alc (17.5%). **NV. Pétillant Blanc** ★★ Lightly perlant crowd-pleaser, now **NV**. Fresh, sweetish, with moderate 13% alc. Discontinued: **Late Harvest**.

Berryfields range NEW
Cabernet Sauvignon-Merlot ★★ Approachable **06** slips down easily, courtesy fresh ripe fruit & soft tannins. **Rosé** ★★ Pretty pink sipper; **07** light (11.7% alc), with delicate raspberry tones. **Chenin Blanc** ★★ Soft dry, slender quaffer; **07** delicate floral/thatch glimpses. **Colombar-Chardonnay** ★★ Ultra-shy **07** zings with zippy citrus acidity. — *CvZ*

Assegai Selection
T 021-855-2249 • F 021-855-4924

*Stellenbosch (see Helderberg map) ▪ Est 1999 ▪ Tasting & sales by appt ▪ Assegai Guest Lodge
▪ Owner Woodlands Import Export ▪ 18 000cs 60% red 40% white ▪ 10 Harewood Ave,
Somerset West, 7130 ▪ rbuchner@worldonline.co.za*

Raimund Buchner launched four new Assegai wines last year – with four more under the Patrys label (none tasted this edition) – and is now shipping 800 000 bottles mainly to Germany. With a long-term goal of 4 million, Buchner appears unfazed by the 'wine glut'. 'It's about who you know, he says, and being very, very competitively priced.'

■ **Astonvale** *see Zandvliet Estate*

Ataraxia Mountain Vineyards
T 028-212-2007 • F 028-212-1921

Est 2004 • 1stB 2005 • Tasting by appt • Reception facilities • Owner Kevin Grant Wines (Pty) Ltd • Winemaker Kevin Grant • Viticulturist Andrew Teubes • 25ha planned • 10 000cs 40% red 60% white • PO Box 603 Hermanus 7200 • info@ataraxiawines.co.za

It took little more than two years for success to challenge Kevin Grant's careful business plan. While he remains unshaken is his belief in pinot and chardonnay as the 'vins de terroir' of Walker Bay, and envisages planting an additional 5ha a year until 2011, and still selects grapes from the best cool-climate vines to augment his own, the (enviable) reality is that the reception given Ataraxia in Holland, Scandinavia, the UK and the US means that chardonnay production this year will be at levels projected for 2010. However, 'we'll remain relatively boutiquey,' promises KG, 'and we won't jump onto new fashion bandwagons.'

★★★★ **Serenity** 'Ataraxia' pvs ed. Spicy red blend from selected vyds, undisclosed areas/ varieties. **06** work in progress shows brilliant blackcurrant, cherry, raspberry aromas; fine tannins, elegant fruit; still youthful but already seamless. 38% new wood, Fr, yr.

★★★★★ **Chardonnay** New-generation Cape benchmark, from ungrafted vines; **06** bright mineral notes, penetrating lime aromas; creamily intense, slightly tropical favours; oak (10 mths, Fr) evident but integrating. Worthy successor to sumptuous **05**, now filling out.

★★★★ **Sauvignon Blanc** Similar capsicum/flint fragrance to **06**, but outstanding **07** (★★★★★) adds riper green fig complexity; concentrated & leesy but zesty, with v fine texture. Still tight & edgy but showing ample development potential. — *MF*

■ **Atkinson Ridge** *see Amani Vineyards*

■ *At the Limiet* *see Nabygelegen Private Cellar*

■ *Auberge du Paysan* *see L'Auberge du Paysan*

Audacia Wines
T 021-881-3052 • F 021-881-3137

Stellenbosch • Est 1930 • Tasting & sales Mon-Fri 8-5 Sat 10-3 • Fee R10 refundable on purchase • Closed Christian hols & Jan 1st • Tours by appt • Owner Strydom & Harris families • Winemaker Elsa Carstens (Apr 1999), with Louis van Zyl • Viticulturist Elsa Carstens, with Willem Booysen • 20ha (five bdx reds, roobernet, shiraz) • 154t/12 000cs 100% red • PO Box 12679 Die Boord 7613 • info@audacia.co.za • www.audacia.co.za

2007 saw the first release of wine, the Merlot 04, made from grapes grown only on Audacia. Another milestone for the owners and long-time winemaker Elsa Carstens was their debut on the annual Nederburg Auction, with their 01 Shiraz. The original Audacia hand-press featured on the label symbolises personal involvement in every aspect of winemaking.

Merlot ★★★★ **04** cassis & cherries, cedar tones & succulent drinkability, capturing all charm variety can give. Delicious. Yr Fr oak. **Shiraz** ★★★ Bright-fruited, well spiced **03** meets tasty shiraz drinking requirements, smooth yet lively. Oak as above. **Coeur de Rouge** ★★★★ Mainly cab, dab malbec in **02**, softly generous, all flesh & perfume. Lavish berry fruit, meaty spice tones, for early drinking. Yr 2nd fill Fr oak. — *CR*

Aufwaerts Co-operative
T 023-349-1202 • F 023-349-1202

Rawsonville (see Worcester map) • Visits by appt • PO Box 15 Rawsonville 6845 • aufwaerts@breede.co.za

This well-established winery, owned by the De Villiers family, markets a portion of its bulk production under an own-label, and invites visitors to pop in anytime for a tasting of the Dry Red and Dry White, and new Semi-Sweet White and Full-Sweet Hanepoot. ('Best to phone ahead though,' says Hennie de V, 'as we bottle very small batches at a time.') Also available is the Twee Eeue 5-year-old potstill brandy.

Autumn Harvest Crackling

Long-established perlé white by Distell.

NV ☺ 🍶 ★★ Latest wallet-pleaser more off-dry than semi-sweet, lifted by slight prickle & zesty acidity. **NV**. — *MW*

Avondale

T 021-863-1976 • F 021-863-1534

Paarl • Est 1997 • 1stB 1999 • Tasting & sales Mon-Sat & pub hols 10–4 • Fee R20, refunded on purchase • Tours by appt • Conferencing • Owner Grieve Family through The Avondale Trust • Winemaker Bertus Albertyn, with Corné Marais • Viticulturist /GM Johnathan Grieve (2000) • 100ha (cab s/f, grenache, malbec, merlot, mourvèdre, shiraz, chard, chenin, muscat de F, roussanne, semillon, viognier) • 290t/20 000cs 74% red 20% white 6% fortified • PO Box 602 Suider-Paarl 7624 • wine@avondalewine.co.za • www.avondalewine.co.za

'Approved by Mother Nature' is the new tagline for wines from Avondale, where the Grieve family prefers to talk about their farm's 'bio-logic' future more than its Cape Dutch history. It's neither fashion trend nor marketing ploy, 'but the only way to produce honest, authentic wines in a sustainable way', says man-in-charge Johnathan Grieve, whose grandfather founded Vital Health Foods. The seriousness of their commitment to organic farming has been delightfully leavened by a racy, sophisticated advertising campaign illustrating their au naturel approach.

Les Pleurs range

★★★★☆ **Syrah** Magisterial **05**, discreetly luxurious, the stuff of boardrooms & five star dining. Deep-pile velvet texture, supple understated fruit, so well groomed & suave, disguises insistent power. Tannins unobtrusive. 14 mths Fr oak 40% new.

Viognier NEW ★★★★ **07** has a certain gravitas, combines elegance with power, not over-rich. White peach & violets, beautifully proportioned, oak infusion coming along well. Whole-bunch pressed, natural yeast; still in barrel, rating provisional.

Avondale Reserve range

★★★★ **The Owl House Cabernet Sauvignon** Dark mulberry berries, some leafy notes to handsome charmer **03**. Tannins have yielded, slight come-back on finish. Will delight cab lovers. 14 mths Fr oak, 25% new.

★★★★ **Camissa Syrah** Leather, smoke, meat on **05** - the braai special! Savoury, dry, muscular, still taut but plenty waiting for chance to perform. Cold soak, fermentation completed in oak, all used Fr.

★★★★ **Graham** Cuvée named for Grieve family's Scottish clan. Lesser vintage **04** (★★★★), shows delicacy, perhaps somewhat diffident. Carefully judged, less dense style, led by cab. 19 mths used oak. **03** was classy & multi-layered.

★★★★ **MCC Brut** NEW Satisfying blanc de blancs sparkling. Lemon & apricot freshness; firm, steely palate, fine mousse. Gd length to dry finish. **NV** from 100% chard, portion oaked. 2 yrs on lees.

Pinotage NEW ★★★ Previously tasted ex-barrel; **06** upfront crushed raspberry/red cherry flavours; mouthwatering & cheerful; light oaking. **The Weir Chardonnay** ★★★☆ **06** peaches & custard notes to firm-fleshed & toned body. Showy, with underlying seriousness. Nudges next rung. Whole bunch pressed, fermented/oaked 9 mths Fr. **Chardonnay** ★★★☆ Now bottled, **05** buttered toast, lime marmalade, some gd rich flavours, oak supportive rather than intrusive, still fresh. Earns another half star.

The Green Duck Range NEW

★★★★ **Green Ducks The Duke** Cab f-led red with splash shiraz. Understated **05** class instantly apparent: mulberry, some plum & hint tobacco, impressive example of reined-in power. 19 mths Fr oak, 15% new.

★★★★ **Green Ducks The Duchess** Undisclosed white blend, wild yeast fermented. Dense & richly flavoured **06**, loads of white peach, tangy greengage flavours. Fat & round, weighty, though only 13.5% alc, with long finish. Fr oak, 20% new.

Organic range NEW

Jonty's Ducks ▣ ✿ ★★★ Shiraz, with plums & prunes on **06**, well judged, as are all these wines, nice ripeness with contrasting dry tannins. 9 mths used oak.

Avondale Premium range

> **Rosé** ☺ ▤ ★★☆ Pretty floral & talcum powder aromas, after which juicy dryness unexpected.

Cabernet Franc NEW ★★★ Shy-ish **06**, some modest leafiness to cassis flavours, has the cellar's signature down-played tannins. This is the 'feminine' cab, with charm, too. **Merlot** NEW ▤ ★★★ Blackcurrant pastille, seems less ripe & more elegant than the 14.5% alc suggests, unobtrusive tannins. US market only. **Pinotage** ▤ ★★★ SA spin on 'nouveau' carbonic maceration style. **06**, now bottled, still delightful crushed berries, soft, easy drinking. **Syrah** ▤ ★★★ **05** plump & friendly, well rounded with soft, v approachable tannins, slight sweetness on finish. Export brand. **Julia** ★★★★ More stuffing, concentration in **03** than other reds. Mature, generously endowed, smooth dry tannins. Blend mainly cabs s&f, shiraz. **Cabernet Sauvignon Rosé** ▤ ★★★ **07** fresh cab cedar notes, tangy, dab sugar goes unnoticed. US market only. **Chardonnay Unwooded** ▤ ★★★ **07** delicate peachy invite, firm-fleshed, brisk acidity & clean finish. With 9% semillon. **Chenin Blanc** ▤ ★★★ Shy, thrilling acidity, delicately fruity **07**. **Sauvignon Blanc** ▤ ★★★ Subtle varietal character in **07**, some grass, green figs, bouncy & dry.

Fortified Sweet range

★★★★ **Muscat Rouge** Fortified red muscat de F. Billowing muscat aromas on pvsly tasted **04** conjure up incense, exotic spices. Intensely sweet & raisiny (192g/l sugar), slight tannic grip adding textural contrast, subtle grip. Alc 18%. Small portion oaked. 375ml, like white version.

★★★★ **Muscat Blanc** These in modern, less sweet mode. Muscadel Awards 'platinum' plaudit for gorgeous **05**. Latest **06** (★★★★) less impressive, like plain Jane sister: sugar down to 170g/l & alc to 15.5%. Pleasant nightcap.

Amira range

Red NEW **07** unready. **Rosé** NEW ▤ ★★ Tuti-frutti **07**, gentle quaffer. Pinotage-based with sauv & chenin. **White** NEW ▤ ★★ Fresh-faced & lively **07** (sample), sauv plumped up with semillon (58/42). Discontinued: **Cabernet Franc**, **Syrah**, **Cape Red**. *— IvH*

Avondvrede
T 083-658-0595 • F 021-875-5609

Paarl • Est 1995 • 1stB 1999 • Tasting, sales, cellar tours & light lunches by appt • Tour groups • Function room • Owner John & Christine Enthoven • Winemaker John Enthoven • 3ha (cabs s/f, merlot) • 20t/500cs 100% red • PO Box 152 Klapmuts 7625

John and Christine Enthoven have downscaled, both in their vineyard, where they've taken out a hectare of merlot, retaining 1.5ha and the same area of cab; and in their cellar, where they made only 1 500 bottles of Koningshof 07, a varietal cab to be released mid-year.

Avontuur Estate
T 021-855-3450 • F 021-855-4600

Stellenbosch (see Helderberg map) • Est 1850 • 1stB 1990 • Tasting & sales Mon-Fri 8.30-5 Sat & Sun 8.30-4 • Fee R20 for 5 tastings, incl glass • Closed Easter Fri, Dec 25 & Jan 1 • Tours by appt ▪ The Avontuur Restaurant (see Eat-out section) ▪ Winemaker Adél van der Merwe (2006) ▪ Viticulturist Pippa Mickleburgh (Sep 1999) ▪ 50ha (cab s/f, merlot, pinot, pinotage, shiraz, chard, sauv) ▪ 20 000cs own label 70% red 30% white ▪ Export brand: Klein Avontuur ▪ PO Box 1128 Somerset West 7129 ▪ info@avontuurestate.co.za ▪ www.avontuurestate.co.za

Owner Tony Taberer passed away in April 2007, leaving big shoes to be filled on the estate. Winemaker Adél van der Merwe went through her first harvest here, and made her mark with new stainless-steel tanks and a new crusher system that allows efficient harvesting in bins instead of crates. There are also about 20 more hectares of sauvignon on conducive sites that promises future quality. The Avontuur farmworkers' community soccer team is playing in the Stellenbosch league, and foreman Hennie Bunding visited Australia as a beneficiary of the Patrick Grubb Scholarship.

Avontuur Estate range

★★★★ **Pinotage** Pinot noir-like **02**, attractive floral note to leather, spice & buchu nose, following to fine, classy palate. Tannins bit dry but enough strawberry padding. 18 mths seasoned oak.

★★★★ **Baccarat** Elegant bdx blend cabs s/f & merlot; **04** deep cab-dominated bouquet with leafy hint; concentrated, poised cassis flavours cradled by new Fr oak (18 mths). Gd maturation potential. No **03**, **02**.

★★★★★ **Luna de Miel** Emphatic barrel-fermented chard. **06** not ready; pvsly tasted **04** exotic & pungent with asparagus suggestion, tangy grapefruit flavour; touch sugar (5.8g/l) & viscous alc (14.5%) sweeten the tail. 8 mths Fr oak.

Cabernet Sauvignon ★★★ Herbaceous **03** easy-going, with enough black-fruit flesh to cover fine soft tannins. Classy early drinking. **Minelli** ★★★ Light-toned **05** still in rustic mode, but step-up from overly tannic **04**. Sweet raspberry notes; soft & attractive for early drinking. **Vintner's Pinotage** ★★★ Gluggable mulberry-hued & raspberry-toned **03**, fruit well-meshed with yr older wood. **Shiraz** ★★★★ Tasted last ed, **04** showed smoky red fruits well-knit with approachable tannins, white pepper hint adding interest. **Cabernet Sauvignon-Merlot** ★★★ Cedar & cassis from cab dabbed with 20% merlot. **04** fruity & quaffable but has enough substance for the steak-house. **Vintner's Red** ★★★ **04** fruity wallet-pleaser. Healthy dash merlot adds flesh, weight, to usual cabs f/s (50/25) duet. Dusty finish from oak freshened by acidity. No retasted, as for V's Pinotage & Blend. **Vintner's Blend** ★★★ **06** sunset-pink, medium-bodied easy-drinker from chard & pinot (60/40), briefly oaked. **Sauvignon Blanc** ★★★ Pungent **07** alive with greenpepper & tropical fruits, lightweight & firm, v easy & pleasant to drink. **Brut Cap Classique** In abeyance. Discontinued: **Cabernet Franc**, **Merlot**. — *RP*

Axe Hill 🍷
T 021-780-1051 • F 021-780-1178

Calitzdorp (see Klein Karoo map) ▪ Est 1993 ▪ 1stB 1997 ▪ Open by appt; when closed, sales from Queens Bottle Store, Voortrekker Road (R62), Calitzdorp ▪ Owner Axe Hill Trust ▪ Winemaker Miles Mossop ▪ Vineyard Manager Boets Nel ▪ 1.3 ha (touriga, tinta, souzão) ▪ 6-9 tons 1 600 cs 100% port ▪ PO Box 43942 Scarborough 7975 ▪ lyn@axehill.co.za, info@axehill.co.za ▪ www.axehill.co.za

The 05 Vintage Port is special: the last made by port aficionado Tony Mossop before his death. His legacy lives on in talented winemaking son Miles (of Tokara), with the Axe Hill focus now solely on port once more. Lyn M deals with the business side and Boets Nel of De Krans the viticulture.

★★★★★ **Cape Vintage Port** A stylish, consistently stellar Cape port. **05**, Tony M's last, celebrates his legacy: an explosion of fruit pud & nuts tightly wound in oak now, a beauty for ageing. **04** (★★★★★) tense, less overt. Traditionally vinified touriga/tinta blend from low-yielding vyds, yr seasoned casks. 20% alc, 88g/l RS.

★★★★ **Dry White Port** Fortified linctus coaxed from chenin 'solera-style': 450litres/yr added to reserves from which new bottlings drawn (thus **NV**). Crisp freshness braces oxidative girth, 20% alc stiffens. 40g/l sugar. A tingling icy aperitif.

Discontinued: **Touriga Nacional**. — *DS*

Ayama Wines
T 021-869-8313 • F 021-869-8313

Voor Paardeberg (see Paarl map) ▪ Est 2004 ▪ 1stB 2005 ▪ Tasting by appt only ▪ Owner Slent Farms (Pty) Ltd (6 partners) ▪ Winemaker Kobus de Kock & Pieter Carstens (Perdeberg Co-op) ▪ Viticulturist Morné Kruger (2004) ▪ 41ha (cab, merlot, shiraz, chenin) ▪ 416t/20 000cs 60% red 40% white ▪ PO Box 2180 Windmeul 7630 ▪ info@slentfarms.com ▪ www.slentfarms.com

Ayama is an isiXhosa word which loosely translates as 'aslant', describing the location of the home-farm, Slent, on the lower slopes of Perdeberg. The enthusiastic Dalpiaz family, their investor friends back in Italy and the local staff, fronted by viticulturist Morné Kruger, are as proud of their consumer-friendly wines as of the farm's conservation status: 16 Red Data List plant species are found here, plus abundant birds and animals.

Cabernet Sauvignon ★★★ Well-structured **05** not revisited;, ruby ripe clarity, palate pleasing tannin/fruit integration. **Merlot** ★★★ Last-tasted **05**, rounded & substantial, dry but lively with ripe plummy fruit. Try with game. **Pinotage** NEW ★★★ Hedgerow, sweet spice in full-ripe **05** with food-friendly dry tannin underpinning. **Shiraz** ★★★ **06** not tasted. Last ed **05** straightforward yet pleasing choc & red berries, balanced freshness & grip. **Shiraz-Pinotage** NEW 🔲 ★★★ Smoky shiraz dark fruit lifted by lively pinotage freshness. Lightly oaked. WO W Cape. **Chardonnay** NEW ★★ Tinned peach & biscuit on **06**, soft, uncomplicated structure. **Chenin Blanc** ★★★ **06** better than pvs: appealing floral & peach styling underpinned by tangy freshness. **Sauvignon Blanc** NEW ★★★ Leafy green thread permeates **06** peardrop tones, but overall character friendly & easy drinking. Mainly Paarl WOs. — *CR*

■ **Azania** *see African Terroir*

Baarsma Wine Group
T 021-880-1221 • F 021-880-0851

Stellenbosch ▪ Closed to public ▪ Owner Baarsma Wine Group B.V. ▪ MD Chris Rabie (since Jul 2001) ▪ Cellarmaster Hannes Louw (since Jan 2005) ▪ PO Box 7275 Stellenbosch 7599 ▪ info@baarsma.co.za ▪ www.baarsma.co.za

Baarsma SA, headquartered in Stellenbosch, is a major export marketer of SA wines, shipping more than 1m cases a year to the major international wine markets, notably Europe. Ranges owned or exported include Ancient Africa, Apiesklip, Blydskap, Boschveld, Cape Reality, Drie Berge, Goede Moed, Goedgenoegen, Jacobus de Wet, Lazy Bay, Lyngrove (see entry), Meerland, Podium, Rotsvast, The Mask, Veelplesier, Volmaak, Voorspoed, Vreughvol and Wild Tales. Baarsma also represents a number of top SA brands in Europe.

■ **Babbling Brook** *see Makro*

Babylon's Peak Private Cellar
T 022-487-1614 • F 022-487-1614

Swartland ▪ Est/1stB 2003 ▪ Visits by appt ▪ Self-catering guest cottage ▪ Walks ▪ Conservation area ▪ Owner/winemaker/viticulturist Stephan Basson ▪ 200 ha (cab, carignan, merlot, pinotage, ruby cab, shiraz, chard, chenin, sauv) ▪ 80t/1 200cs own label (70% red 30% white) + ±40 000litres bulk wine ▪ PO Box 161 Malmesbury 7299 ▪ info@babylonspeak.co.za

Four years' experience in the vineyards and cellar have moved husband and wife team, Stephan & Inalize Basson, from trying to please every taste to concentrating on wines that perform best on their soils, and deliver consistent quality. To simplify matters further, the Basson brand has been incorporated into the Babylon's Peak label.

Cabernet Sauvignon ★★★ At press time, still selling stock of modern, fresh-faced **05**, previewed pvs ed. **Syrah** ★★★★ Continuing cellar's trademark savoury styling, improved **06** has dark fruit, dried herbs, smoky nuances; a delicious mouthfeel, sleekly harmonious, packed with flavour. Pvs **04** (★★★★) nudged next notch; Fr/Am 18 mths. **Babylon** ★★★ Near equal blend pinotage, cab & merlot in showy **05**, ultra-ripe plummy fruit, voluptuous curves. 18 mths Fr/Am, fully integrated, adds vanilla spicing. **Basson Family Wines 19 Nineteen** ★★★ Pvsly 'Stephan's Blend'. Riper vintage, big-boned & gregarious, **05** shows prunes & black fruit, liberally spiced from toasty oak (Yr, Fr/Am). **Basson Family Wines Chenin Blanc** 🗎 ★★★ Peardrop flavours & variety's trademark freshening acidity give **07** lively appeal. **Viognier** ★★★★ Fragrant yet sophisticated, **07** more Old World thanks to 1st/2nd fill barrel fermentation. Lavender, biscotti styling, lovely juicy palate. Nudges next level. Discontinued: **Chardonnay**. — *CR*

■ **Babylons Toren** *see* Backsberg Estate Cellars
■ ***Babylon's Vineyards*** *see* Mount Babylon

Backsberg Estate Cellars
T 021-875-5141 · **F** 021-875-5144

Paarl ▪ Est 1916 ▪ 1stB 1970 ▪ Tasting & sales Mon-Fri 8-5 Sat 9.30-4.30 Sun 10.30-4.30 ▪ Fee R10 refunded on purchase ▪ Closed Easter Fri, Dec 25 ▪ Self-guided tours during tasting hours ▪ Backsberg Restaurant Tue-Sun (see Eat-out section); cheese platters at tasting room ▪ Play area for children ▪ Maze ▪ Gifts ▪ Conferences & weddings by appt ▪ Owner Backsberg Estate Cellars ▪ Winemaker Alicia Rechner (since Dec 2001) ▪ Viticulturist Clive Trent (Jul 1992) ▪ 130ha (cab, merlot, shiraz, chard) ▪ 1 000t/±90 000cs 65% red 30% white 5% rosé ▪ PO Box 537 Suider-Paarl 7624 ▪ info@backsberg.co.za ▪ www.backsberg.co.za

'I want my kids to grow grapes at Backsberg, not avocado pears!' says Michael Back, referring to predictions that global warming could result in the Western Cape becoming a summer rainfall area. Hence his decision to sequestrate Backsberg's carbon emissions, becoming the first carbon-neutral wine farm in SA. He has also allocated 10% of the property to plant trees as a renewable energy source. Meanwhile, the Freedom Road project is complete, with almost all who work at Backsberg now living in their own houses. 'From corporate social responsibility to caring for the environment, we'll do everything we can as long as it doesn't compromise our wine quality – that's non-negotiable.'

Babylons Toren range

★★★★ **Red** Last-tasted **03** got 33% shiraz injection plus powerful shot new oak (3 yrs!). Ripe mint-plum fruit held its own, needing yr/2 to grow into massive structure of tannin & alc (15%), should carry the wine decade+.

★★★★ **Chardonnay** 🗎 Last available, bold & characterful **03** had plentiful lime/greengage fruit, toasted hazelnut; appealing combo leesy breadth, racy-dry freshness. Fermented/yr oak, 100% new.

★★★★ **Viognier** 🗎 Back on track, strikingly individual **07** (sample) impresses with sweet floral & toasted brioche tones, tangy citrus freshness. Now bone-dry, deserves solo enjoyment to appreciate styling. Oaked 6 mnths, 70% new. More convincing than sweet **05** (★★★★).

Black Label range

★★★★ **Klein Babylonstoren** With supple grace & alluring fruit purity, **04** showcases its near-equal cab/merlot partnership: cassis & violets on a bed of integrated, well-judged oak. Will easily go a 6+ yr distance. 24 mnths wood, half new.

★★★★ **Elbar** ✓ Pvsly 'Elba'. Idiosyncratic medley 5 red grapes & viognier, led by malbec, mourvèdre & sangiovese, **06** captures old world underbrush, venison, crushed pepper tones. Robust tannins beg cellaring, will reveal more over time.

Pumphouse Shiraz ★★★ With touch merlot, malbec, **05** retains earthy, tarry notes of pvs, has forceful structure allowing future development. **Bella Rosa** ★★★ Last-tasted **06** ('Elba Bella Rosa') comprised juice bled from varieties headed for Elba red (mourvèdre mainly). Dry, fruity & light but charming. **John Martin Reserve Sauvignon Blanc** 🗎 ★★★★ Partly barrel-fermented, blend own & Dbnvlle fruit. Fruit still hero in **07**, lovely intensity, step up in quality on **05** (★★★★): fynbos, gooseberries & mouthwatering, zinging freshness. **Elbar White Blend** NEW 🗎 Not ready.

Premium range

★★★★ **Special Late Harvest** NEW ✓ Proudly sweet with noticeable botrytis, **07**'s grapefruit marmalade flavours underpinned by bright seam of acidity, giving sweet/sour effect, delicious appetite appeal. A beauty. Semillon, chenin 80/20.

> **Chenin Blanc** ☺ ★★★ **07** surpasses pvs in quality, fresher styling: lime & pear, mouth-awakening acidity balancing touch sugar.

Cabernet Sauvignon ★★★ Hard to ignore, sample **05**'s prominent mint & cassis aromas, flavours nicely delivered in medium-proportioned, accessible form. **Merlot** ★★★ Dark choc & mixed berries show in **06**, clothing the dry but amenable tannins. Flavourful, for earlier drinking. Yr oak. **Pinotage** ★★★ Unwooded **06** successfully combines dark fruit & liquorice with an easily accessible palate. Satisfying, tasty. **Dry Red** ★★★ Latest (**07**) all-sorts unoaked blend; **NV**; plums, smoky notes accompany mid-weight structure, food-friendly dry grape tannins. **Rosé** ★★★ Cerise-hued & sweet, latest is fruit basket of flavours, light textured enough (12% alc) for easy summertime quaffing. **NV. Chardonnay** ★★★ Last ed showy **05** had textbook citrus peel & buttered toast character; rounded mouthfeel from 50% Fr oak fermentation. **Sauvignon Blanc** ★★★ Leafy, asparagus perfume & flavours in **07**, retaining fresh-fruity drinkability.

Kosher range

Merlot NEW Not ready. **Pinotage** ★★ Last available **04** was fruit salad melange with banana hint. **Chardonnay** ★★ Last **04** had whiffs lawn cuttings, compost, was drier than pvs. Oaked. Made under supervision of Cape Town Beth Din.

Niche range

Pinneau ★★★ Tasting room favourite: unfermented semillon fortified with own potstill brandy. Pvs ed **04** had fruity/toffee flavours with medicinal finish. **Port** ★★★★ Last-tasted **04** from cab f, fortified with 3 yr old house-brandy. Choc-sloshed burnt toffee character; pungent flavours & grip.

Organic range

Merlot NEW Not ready. **Chardonnay** ★★★★ Last tasted was characterful **03**; medium bodied, balanced creamy/crisp contrast, roundly dry. *— CR*

Badsberg Wine Cellar
T 023-344-3021 • F 023-344-3023

Breedekloof (see Worcester map) ▪ Est 1951 ▪ Tasting & sales Mon-Fri 8-5 Sat 10-1 ▪ Closed Easter Fri-Mon & pub hols ▪ Tours by appt during Dec ▪ BYO picnic ▪ Tour groups ▪ Play area for children ▪ Conservation area ▪ Owner 26 members ▪ Cellarmaster Willie Burger (Oct 1998) ▪ Winemaker Henri Swiegers and De Wet Hugo (Dec 2002/Dec 2006) ▪ Viticulturist De Wet Hugo (Dec 2006) ▪ 1 000ha ▪ 20 000t 20% red 74% white 2% rosé 4% fortified ▪ PO Box 72 Rawsonville 6845 ▪ enquiries@badsberg.co.za ▪ www.badsberg.co.za

Situated in the scenic Rawsonville area, this 26-member co-op is confidently focused on growth, with more vineyards being planted with petit verdot, cab franc and nouvelle. At current expansion rates, they're looking at an intake of 25 000 tons a year by 2010.

Merlot ★★★ **06** amiable version, gentle cassis, dry tannins, undemanding but pleasing. **Rosé** ★★ Pleasant semi-sweet, soft strawberry notes in **07**, delicate brush of tannin. **Chardonnay Sur Lie** ★★★★ Last tasted was v pleasant **05**, SAYWS champ, generous lemon/lime fruit, touch buttered toast, discreet oaking (5 mths, Fr/Hung). **Chenin Blanc** ★★ Last was delicate, sappy **06**, floral aromas & soft acidity. **Sauvignon Blanc** ★★ Ripe melon, greengage; smooth & bouncy, dash sugar adds some plumpness in **07**. **Vin Doux Sparkling** ★★ **06** from muscat d'A, wafting fresh honeysuckle, really sweet. **Special Late Harvest** ★★★ From hanepoot & chenin; pvsly tasted **06** light, attractively balanced, with a genteel sweetness. **Noble Late Harvest** ★★★★ Usually chenin & hanepoot; **04** unctuously sweet & gentle, last ed noted as needing drinking. **Hanepoot Jerepigo** ★★★★ Another outstanding **05** fortified from this cellar; abundantly sweet but fresh, excellent fruit concentration in an elegant frame. **03** (★★★) oozed hanepoot character. **Red Muscadel** ★★★★ Fortified dessert **04** tasted out of vintage sequence; hint malt in aroma with incense & Turkish Delight; gorgeous sweetness, could do with touch more balancing acidity. Mucadel Awards 'platinum'. **05** (★★★★) was unreservedly gorgeous. **Red Jerepigo** ★★★★ **02** pvsly showed a lavender bouquet & sweetness livened by alc (15.6%) for agreeably warming fruity finish. **Port** ★★ Last was **01** unclassic mix shiraz, cab f, ruby cab; Fr oaked; plain but pleasant. Wrcstr & Breedeklf WOs. — *IvH*

Bain's Way *see* Wamakersvallei Winery

Bakenskop *see* Jonkheer

Balance *see* Overhex Wines International

Barefoot Wine Company *see* Catherine Marshall Wines

Barrel Select *see* Graham Beck Wines

Barrydale Cellar

T 028-572-1012 • F 028-572-1541

Klein Karoo ▪ Est 1941 ▪ 1stB 1976 ▪ Tasting & sales Mon-Fri 8-5 Sat & pub hols 9-3 ▪ Closed Easter Fri-Mon, Dec 25 & Jan 1 ▪ Book ahead for tours ▪ BYO picnic ▪ Heritage garden ▪ Owner 25 members ▪ Winemaker Riaan Marais, with Ferdie Smit (Jan 1999/May 1985) ▪ Viticulturist Willem Botha (2000, consultant) ▪ 152ha (cab, merlot, ruby cab, shiraz, chard, colombard, sauv) ▪ 2 000t ▪ Range for customer: Decent Red ▪ PO Box 59 Barrydale 6750 ▪ sales@scv.co.za ▪ www.scv.co.za

Legendary Overberg trader and namesake Joseph Barry would surely approve of parent company Southern Cape Vineyards' decision to reassert the identity of Barrydale Cellars and its well-established label, Tradouw. Joining the portfolio is a new label, Merchant's Mark, a reference to Barry's seal - a replica of which also appears on the potstill brandies of this cellar, SA's largest independent producer.

Sauvignon Blanc ☺ ★★★ Charming & zesty **07** brims with capsicum & blackcurrant, balanced & light on its feet (12% alc).

Decent Red ★★★ New bottling untasted. Pvs was ripe-fruited unoaked blend ruby cab, merlot, pinotage. **NV**, as for White. **Decent White** ★★★ Pvs was cheerful everyday tipple with tropical notes, zippy acidity, satisfying mouthfeel. From chenin, chard, gewürz.

Merchant's Mark range NEW

Merlot ★★★ **04** decently dry, with taut tannins bracing plum/meat flavours; some new oak. **Shiraz** ★★ Reticent **05** has high-toned red fruit & soft spices. Firm tannins provide structure, feature dominantly on finish. Yr Hung oak. — *CvZ*

Barry Gould Family Wines

T 028-284-9827 • F 028-284-9624

Elgin (see Elgin/Walker Bay map) ▪ Est 2003 ▪ 1stB 2004 ▪ Visits by appt ▪ B&B/self-catering accommodation ▪ Owner Barry Gould ▪ Winemaker Barry Gould, with Niels Verburg & Gould family ▪ 160cs 70% red 30% white ▪ PO Box 7 Elgin 7180 ▪ gould.arc@wildekrans.co.za

'Winemaking is great when things go well,' says Barry Gould. 'It's like an 18-year-old in a Golf GTi - impressive on a straight road, but beware the curves, because when things go wrong, it needs some serious experience to correct the skid.' After his first stuck fermentation last year, he says: 'I think I'll pull through. But I did ding the car.'

A Simple Red ★★★ Dual Elgin/Overberg WO for **05**, interesting combo dried tobacco leaf & warm toffee, perceptibly fresh. **Chenin Blanc** ★★★ Light, uncomplex **06**, now bottled, honey & golden delicious apples with slight nutty hint. — *MM*

Bartho Eksteen Family Wines *see* Hermanuspietersfontein Vineyards

Bartinney Cellars

T 021-885-1013 • F 021-885-2852

Stellenbosch • Est 1920 • 1stB 1999 • Sales Mon-Fri 9-5 • Tours by appt only • Self-catering guesthouse • Owner Michael Jordaan • Winemaker/viticulturist Carl Potgieter • 19ha (cab, chard, sauv) • 62t/4 500cs 51% white 49% red • PostNet Suite #231, Private Bag X5061, Stellenbosch 7599 • info@bartinney.co.za

Bartinney is back in the Jordaan family's hands – the current generation is the fourth to farm the property on the Helshoogte heights outside Stellenbosch – and extensive cellar renovations are planned for the 2008 harvest. Some 20ha are being converted from pine and bluegum forest to fynbos as part of an eco-responsible approach, which also includes adherence to IPW guidelines.

Barton Farm

T 028-284-9283 • F 028-284-9776

Walker Bay (see Elgin/Walker Bay map) • Est 2001 • 1stB 2003 • Tasting & sales Mon-Fri 9-5 Sat 9-1 • Four self-catering villas • Owner Peter Neill & Charles Lousada • Winemaker Danie Truter & Niels Verburg (Onderkloof/Luddite) • Viticulturist Noeil Vorster (Oct 2005) • 28ha (cab, malbec, merlot, mourvèdre, shiraz, chenin, sauv, semillon) • 2 430cs • PO Box 100 Bot River 7185 • peterjneill@aol.com • www.bartonfarm.co.za

Niels Verburg made Barton's first Sauvignon from recently planted vines, and is following the unwooded style for the Chenin. Red and white bottling takes place at the new cellar from this year. 'Part of the farm is being designated as a nature reserve and there are some idyllic spots for picnics,' says owner Peter Neill.

★★★★ **Shiraz-Cabernet Sauvignon** Sample **06** (★★★★), like **05**, lighter, less grippy than cab-driven **04**; very fruity oak-kissed raspberry features in soft, accessible package. WO W Cape, incl Elgin shiraz & W Bay cab.

Chenin Blanc ★★★★ Sumptuous white pear flesh in round, leesy texture; **07** full & inviting, offering interest without weight. Bone-dry, 13% alc. **Sauvignon Blanc** NEW ★★★ Free-run juice cold-fermented to preserve flavours; **07** gently tropical aromas, subtly racy finish. *– DS*

■ **Basson Wines** *see Babylon's Peak Private Cellar*

■ **Bat's Rock** *see Lutzville Cape Diamond Vineyards*

■ **Bay View** *see Longridge Winery*

■ **BC Wines** *see Brandvlei Cellar*

■ **Beacon Trail** *see Overhex Wines International*

■ **Beaufort** *see Ultra Liquors*

Beau Joubert Vineyards & Winery

T 021-881-3103 • F 021-881-3377

Stellenbosch • 1stB 2000 • Visits by appt • Self-catering guest houses • Conference facility for max 100 • Functions & weddings for max 150 • Owner Joubert family & US investors led by Andrew Hilliard • Winemaker Christian Kuun • Viticulturist Lukas Joubert • 80ha (cab, merlot, chard, sauv) • 600t/20 000cs own label 50/50 red/white • Other export brands: Oak Lane & Veelverjaaght • PO Box 1114 Stellenbosch 7599 • info@beaujoubert.com • www.beaujoubert.com

Elsenburg-trained Christian Kuun has taken over winemaking duties, equipped with plenty of hands-on experience (including California & Germany), and is ready to take the wines to the next level. With an 'incredible amount of time' spent in the vineyards bearing fruit, they have better prospects than ever in global markets, says MD Andrew Hilliard.

Beau Joubert range
Cabernet Sauvignon ★★★ **04** pine needle-perfumed, with vanilla hint. Tannic edge daunts, but time may soften. Yr 2nd/3rd fill oak. **Merlot** ★★★ Choc-mint-rich **04**, succulent & full ripe-plum flavours, with herbaceous edge. Oaking as for Cab. **Chardonnay** ★★☆ Ripe **07** redolent

of marzipan & pineapple; rich & full, but sample still needed to meld mid-2007. 3 mths oak, 25% new. **Sauvignon Blanc** ★★★ Flavoursome **07** (sample), ripe tropical fruit leaps from glass, greenpepper & smoky hint, roundish finish.

Oak Lane range NEW

> **Merlot-Cabernet Sauvignon** ☺ ★★★ 50/50 blend in **05**; soft tannins, bright & chewy fruit, hint leather & spice. Seasoned oak.

Pinot Noir Rosé ★★★ Attractively rustic **06**, perky, with creamy texture best enjoyed soon.
Chenin Blanc-Sauvignon Blanc ★★★ Previewed **07** fleshy, chenin giving breadth & weight, gd firmness with mineral notes. — RP

Beaumont Wines
T 028-284-9194 · F 028-284-9733

🍴🍷☕🏛📷♿

Walker Bay (see Elgin/Walker Bay map) · Est 1750 · 1stB 1994 · Visits Mon-Fri 9.30–4.30 Sat 10-3 Sun by appt · Fee R20 for groups of 10+ · Closed Easter Sat/Sun, Dec 25 & Jan 1 · Meals for small groups by appt · 2 self-catering guest houses · Art/jewellery exhibits · Conservation area · Owner Raoul & Jayne Beaumont · Winemaker Sebastian Beaumont (Aug 2003), Marelise Jansen van Rensburg · Viticulturist Andrew Teubes (consultant) · 34ha (13 varieties, r/w) · 200t/12 000cs 55% red 45% white · PO Box 3 Bot River 7185 · info@beaumont.co.za · www.beaumont.co.za

Chenin rules here. In fact, in the face of current convention, they've stopped making sauvignon to better focus on chenin - 'probably the first winery in the country to do so', surmises winemaker Sebastian Beaumont, now backed by assistant winemaker Marelise Jansen van Rensburg and viticulturist Neil de Beer. 'We have great old vines and excellent quality chenin, which gives us a strong point of difference.' They're in the process of restoring the watermill, which dates back to 1800, and their first stone-ground flour using the original equipment is available in limited quantities at the winery. A BWI member, on the Green Mountain Eco-Route, they're conserving 350ha of mountain fynbos and clearing their Bot River frontage.

Beaumont range

★★★★ **Mourvèdre 05** fresher, better balanced than brutish **04**, though still clocks 15% alc. Distinctive pristine leather notes, hint of decadent gaminess. Quite ruggedly firm & dry but fruit/structure are synched; promising. Oak, 30% new, 2 yrs.

★★★★ **Pinotage** Latest **06** (sample) promises usual juicy mouthful, raspberries, redcurrants & spicy Am oak. Exceptionally fine, dry tannins. Carries 14% alc with balanced ease. Oak matured, Fr/Am, 14 mths. No '**05**.

★★★★ **Shiraz** Cooler-climate influence suggested in previewed **05**'s fresh white spice fragrance, tangy flavours. Refined, with classic N Rhône delicacy, despite solid 14.5% alc. Should be one of best to date. 2 yrs oak, 45% new.

★★★★ **Chenin Blanc** ✓ Elegant, natural feel to these, from 25-30+ yr vyds. **07** exceptionally concentrated, full of fruity vitality; pure floral, honey fragrance; untiring medium body. 2-3 yrs will benefit youthful exuberance. 3% oaked.

★★★★ **Hope Marguerite Chenin Blanc** Chenin in seductive guise. Oak & sugar (7g/l) enhancements to ripe pear & honeycomb succulence, natural ferment complexity. **06** surprisingly unheavy, deliciously long.

★★★★ **Goutte d'Or** Irresistible combination of honeyed semillon, dusty botrytis & sauv's freshening element. 65/35 mix in **06**; still to fill out, fully express flavour spectrum, silky succulence. Small oak, 10 mths. Higher general rating for this & gorgeous **05**.

Ariane ★★★★ Bdx quintet in cab-led **05**. Back on form after ultra-ripe **04** (★★★★); fragrantly fresh blackberry & oak tones beautifully melded in well-tailored but unsevere frame. Lovely potential. 2 yrs Fr oak. Sample tasted, rating provisional. **Shiraz Rosé** ★★★ Shimmering ruby lights, basketful fresh summer red berries delight both eye & palate in **07**. Slightly drier than **06** (4.4g/l RS) for compatibility with wide range dishes. **Jackals River Unwooded Chardonnay** ★★★ Mouthwatering summer sipper. **07** the usual forthcoming lime/citrus zest fragrance matched by stimulating fruity acids, cleansing finish. **Cape Vintage** ★★★ Hearty tinta/pinotage duo, for really cold nights. **04** lots of earthy ripeness, warming alc glow (20.5%) but not over-sweet. 2 yrs oak. Discontinued: **Chardonnay**, **Sauvignon Blanc**.

Raoul's range

> **Willow Tree White** NEW ☺ ★★★ Quaffability & interest in **07**, 80/20 chenin/chard blend. Satisfying citrus/nut concentration captured in crisp, medium bodied mouthful. EW.

Old Basket Press Red ★★★ Intended as full-bodied quaffer, unoaked for distinctive fruit. **06**, tinta plus bdx quartet, admirably fulfils goal with spicy, earthy warmth, comfortable padding. —*AL*

Bein Wine
T 021-881-3025 • F 088-021-881-3025

Stellenbosch • Est/1stB 2002 • Open by appt only • Owner/winemaker/viticulturist Luca & Ingrid Bein • 2.2ha (merlot) • 1 000cs 100% red • PO Box 3408 Matieland 7602 • lib@beinwine.com • www.beinwine.com

Forsaking Swiss veterinary science for Cape winemaking, the Beins continue to fine-tune their 80 rows of merlot. Leading the way towards an ever more eco-friendly approach, two donkeys, Gloria and Poppy, wander the vineyard, occasionally needing a reprimand for sampling a tender shoot or two.

★★★★ **Merlot** Serene, unshowy yet increasingly compelling. Youthful **06** as beguilingly scented as superb **05** (★★★★★), though richer, bigger, with denser texture & tannins; well able to handle increased new wood (66% vs 40%). Yr oak.

Little Merlot ★★★ **06** realises accessibility, fruity charm of young vines; satisfying but not simple. Spiced/seasoned with 14% bought-in cab f, yr older oak. **Pink Merlot** ★★★ Pretty pink bled from best grapes. **07** spirited dry flavours; guaranteed affable partner with or without food. —*AL*

Belbon Hills
T 021-557-7143 • F 021-557-1351

Worcester • Est/1stB 1999 • Closed to public • Owner Directors Mirella Corsetti Kruger & Pedro Estrada Belli • 30ha (cab, pinotage, ruby cab, shiraz, chenin, colombard, sauv) • 260t/10 000cs own label 60% red 40% white • PO Box 457 Bloubergstrand • info@belbonhills.com

Having entered the Italian market with a hand-picked portfolio ('we want the locals to associate SA with only top quality'), Italians Mirella Corsetti Kruger and Pedro Estrada Belli are actively marketing in neighbouring African countries and as far as Nigeria, reaping the benefit of increasing wine awareness as consumption moves beyond the mining and oil fraternities into the popular arena.

Cabernet Sauvignon ★★ Tasted last ed, **04** balanced, easy-sipper courtesy plentiful berries, comfortable tannins. **ASCS Cabernet Sauvignon** NEW ★★★★ Marketed in Italy, most profit diverted to local charities & upliftment projects. Maiden **04** stylish, lip-smacking; dark berries & dry finish combine for satisfying drinkability. **Shiraz** ★★ Ultra-ripe & warming last ed, **04** was uncomplicated everyday tipple. Wood-staved. **White** ★★ Granny Smith apple tang, hint of sweet spice on fresh **07**, from chenin. **Passito** ★★★ Fortified dessert from hanepoot; Step up for latest bottling (**NV**), like sipping liquid sunshine: rich, unctuous glacé pineapple flavours. **Sauvignon Blanc** ★★★ **07** sample has attractive fig notes, sweet/sour acidity, lingering finish. —*IvH*

Belfield
T 021-848-9840 • F 021-848-9840

Elgin • Est 2000 • 1stB 2005 • Closed to public • Owner Mike & Mel Kreft • Winemaker Mike Kreft, with Lawrence Lebenya & Kreft family, advised by Mark Carmichael-Green (2004) • Viticulturist Paul Wallace (2002, consultant) • 2.5ha (cabs s/f, merlot, shiraz) • ±16t total 75cs own label 100% red • PO Box 191 Elgin 7180 • phkreft@mweb.co.za • www.belfield.co.za

Proteas are close to the hearts of the Kreft family (they grow them on their Porterville Mountain farm), so no surprise to see the 'Magnifica' celebrated on the label of the new Cab Reserve, unreleased at press time along with a Cab-Merlot blend. The wines are handcrafted by the Krefts at the nearby Valley Green cellar with the help of right hand man Lawrence Lebenya.

Belfield range NEW

★★★★☆ **Cabernet Sauvignon 05** stellar debut from 'Julia' vyd, named for favourite aunt. Subdued, but unfolds to reveal cassis, wet earth & cool 'tomato leaf' aromas. Cool, too, on palate, with fine savoury tannins. Should improve over 5+ yrs. 100% Fr oak. — *CvZ*

Bellevue Estate
T 021-865-2055 · F 021-865-2899

Stellenbosch · Est 1701 · 1stB 1999 · Tasting Mon-Fri 10-4 Sat & non-religious pub hols 10-3 · Owner Dirkie Morkel · Winemaker Wilhelm Kritzinger (Feb 2002) · Viticulturist Dirkie Morkel (1979) · 193ha (14 varieties, incl 5 bdx varieties, pinotage, shiraz, sauv) · 13 000cs own label 97% red 3% white · PO Box 33 Koelenhof 7605 · info@bellevue.co.za · www.bellevue.co.za

Fourth-generation vinegrower Dirkie Morkel sold grapes until 1998, when winning awards for others prompted his own-label release. Exports are buoyant, and the new Sizanani range (isiXhosa for 'to help one another') is produced in partnership with the labour force, delivering quality at affordable prices - Bellevue's keen pricing policy due to Dirkie M's reluctance to sell a wine for more than he would be willing to pay for it himself.

Morkel range

★★★★ **Pinotage** Pure-fruited **05** has plummy, savoury bouquet & entry, banana-toned tail. Focussed & lithe, mouthcoating juicy fruit & lengthy farewell.

★★★★☆ **PK Morkel Pinotage** Site of SA's first commercial pinotage; now a vyd selection. **05** not ready, **04** last ed was accessible, with up-front fruit, velvet texture, ripe tannins.

★★★★ **Tumara** Classically inclined bdx blend. Sample **05** opulent, deep & balanced. Hint mint adds complexity to luscious cassis aromas/flavours; long, velvet finish. Structured for cellaring ±5 yrs. Cab 70%, smidgens cab f, merlot, malbec, petit v.

Malbec ★★★ **05** less complex than pvs, still a gd drink; eucalyptus & cured meat naunces, spicy, smoky tannins, pleasantly dry finish. **Petit Verdot** ★★★☆ Thick & chunky sample **05** has blueberry jam & black olive tones; chalky tannins add refinement to otherwise rustic fruit. 22 mths Fr oak. **Rozanne** ★★★ Oak-dominated, fruit-shy **05** tasted last ed. Mainly merlot (60%), with shiraz, pinotage. **Shiraz** ★★★ **05** sample in leathery guise, red berry note; oak dominates palate giving charry complexion, dry finish. **Atticus** ★★★ Classy **04** sample smooth, sweet fruited; only detractor a somewhat dilute mid-palate. Blend cab, pinotage & petit v. NE. **Sauvignon Blanc** 🍷 ★★★☆ Gunflint & tinned peas do the business on sample **07**. Piercing acidity balanced by gooseberry concentration, lengthy bone-dry finish. Discontinued: **Limited Release Malbec, Pinot Noir**.

Sizanani range NEW

Pinotage ✓ 🍷 ★★★ Attractive gamey **06**, flavoursome package, soft, juicy; slips down easily. NE. **Red Blend** ★★★ Choc-laden **03** equal portions merlot & pinotage with dash shiraz. Forest floor notes, fleshy centre, chewy tannins. NE. **Chenin Blanc** 🍷 ★★★ **06** shows ripe apple notes in crisp, light-tripping style. NE. All these for early drinking. — *RP*

Bellingham
T 021-870-4200 · F 021-876-1531

Wellington · Est 1693 · 1stB 1947 · Closed to public · Owner DGB · Winemaker Niël Groenewald, with Mario Damon (Jul 2004, Jan 2002) · Viticulturist Stephan Joubert (2006) · 5 000t/350 000cs 50% red 49% white 1% rosé · HACCP, ISO 9001:2000 & WIETA certified · Private Bag X03 Groot Drakenstein 7680 · bellingham@dgb.co.za · www.bellinghamwines.com

The well-established brand has relaunched with a new range called Fusion which experiments with dashes of other varieties - pinotage with a splash of petit verdot, for instance. Another new introduction is a line of handcrafted blends, the Legends Collection. 'It's true: it is all about the grapes,' says winemaker Niël Groenewald, 'but a lot of the magic happens in the cellar. It's when playing around during vinification and at bottling time that the fun and creativity really start.'

The Maverick range

★★★★ **Syrah 05** lots of bitter choc, spice (fruit & oak) aromatic appeal. Echoed in clean, fluid mouthfeel with supple tannin support. Surprisingly elegant, fresh for 15% alc. Gd now, probably better around 2011.

★★★★ **SMV** Classy blend syrah, mourvèdre & dash viognier. **05** creamy, concentrated with chewy ripe tannins, balanced oak support for perfumed red fruits.

★★★★ **Chenin Blanc** Limpid gold hue immediate attraction to this multi-award winner. Barrel ferment, soupçon sugar, freshness & chenin's floral/honeysuckle delicacy offset each other in charming **06**.

★★★★ **Sauvignon Blanc 06** sample promises similar sleek refinement, rating as **05**. Oaking seamlessly applied to highlight cool sauv fruit, taut savoury acid. Combines freshness & breadth.

★★★★ **Viognier** Welcomingly fresh, unblowsy version of this too-frequently overdone variety. **06** subtle ripe peach woven into succulent yet lively texture. Balanced oaking adds note of attractive savoury decadence.

The Legends Collection

★★★★ **Fair Maiden** NEW New-wave white blend led by chenin, chard, viognier, with splashes grenache bl, roussanne & verdelho. Previewed **06** rich yet refined; lovely mineral vinosity within firm structure. Provisional rating.

St George NEW 'Cape Blend' featuring merlot, cab f & pinotage. **05** ex-cask shows concentrated sweet fruit, fine freshening backbone, telltale insistent grip. Too unformed to rate.

Dragon's Lair NEW ★★★★ Bright-fruited shiraz blend; small amounts mourvèdre & viognier (10/2%). Full bodied with balanced freshness; **05** ex-barrel, rating tentative.

Fusion range

Cabernet Sauvignon with a splash of Cab Franc NEW ★★★ Tasty cab spiced with cab f; **05** ripe, crunchy fruit underscored by light texture, nip of tannin. **Merlot with a dash of Malbec** NEW ★★★ Succulent red plum merlot twins perfectly with mineral malbec in **05**. Brisk, juicy tannins, clean, savoury tail enhance quaffability. **Pinotage with a dash of Petit Verdot** NEW ★★★ Clever pairing; petit v adding perfume & lively, light touch to carefully oaked pinotage. **05** gd now, further yr/2. **Shiraz with a splash of Viognier** NEW ★★ Simple, rustic **05**; meagre flesh revealing alc glow in tail. **Chardonnay with a splash of Viognier** NEW ★★ Heavy, rather lifeless **06** with cloying finish. **Sauvignon Blanc with a dash of Semillon** NEW ★★★ **07** wild, cool-climate green pea, lemongrass nose & flavours; balancing richer mouthfeel, sweet/sour conclusion slight detraction.

The Blends range

Cabernet Sauvignon-Merlot ▨ ★★ Previewed **05** with reticent sweet strawberry tones in lean, tannic frame. **04** not tasted. **Shiraz-Cabernet Sauvignon** NEW ★★★ Bowlful spice, juicy sweet blackberries crammed into lively yet youthfully accessible frame. **07** uncomplicated & tasty. **Pinotage Rosé** NEW ★★★ **07** with soupçon more red winey bite, liveliness than its pink partners. Happy in both sundowner & food partner roles. **Rosé** ★★ Sunset pink **07**; medium bodied with smooth strawberries & cream quaffability. **Rosé Sec** NEW ★★ Strawberry pink lights on **07** matched by abundant juicy flavours, fruity farewell. **Chardonnay-Semillon** ★★★ Last tasted **04** was unwooded 50/50 mix. No new vintage available. **Sauvignon Blanc-Chardonnay** ▨ ★★★ Bright-fruited **07** (sample) in usual easy-drinking form. Medium-bodied, lively with gd tropical persistence. **Chenin Blanc-Viognier** NEW ★★★ **07** happy marriage chenin fruit, rounded viognier weight; hint of latter's alc glow slight detraction. Characterful but not too blowsy.

Bellingham range

Premier Grand Cru The original PGC, introduced 1951, undergoing branding change at press time. Not tasted. **Johannisberger** Now a standalone brand, Legacy; see entry.

Spitz range

Discontinued: **Cabernet Franc**, **Merlot**, **Pinotage**, **Chardonnay**. *— AL*

Bellpost
T 027-213-2562, 082-619-2428 • F 027-213-2562

Olifants River • Est/1stB 2005 • Visits by appt • Owner Lollies Thiart • Winemaker Koos Thiart (2005) • Viticulturist Nico Thiart (2005) • 2ha (merlot, shiraz, ruby cab, chard) • 15t/975cs 80% red 20% white • PO Box 39 Vredendal 8160 • bellpost@starmail.co.za

Formerly at Saxenburg and with experience in France, Koos Thiart works at local giant Spruitdrift Cellars and now brings his skills and ideas to the family farm on the west coast. Saying 'you don't need the latest technology to make world-class wines', he aims to help raise the bar for the region.

> **Ruby Cabernet** ☺ ★★★ One of the nicest we've tasted. **06** robust fruit sleeked & groomed by yr oak, 28% new. Like sewing diamonds on blue jeans. It works! **Chardonnay** ☺ ★★★ Maiden **07** peach and lime packed, juicy and vibrant, lovely example of unoaked style

Merlot ★★★★ **06** meaty, savoury with dark choc appeal, soft dry tannins for further ageing, hide hefty 14.9% alc successfully. Yr Fr/Hung oak. **Shiraz** ★★★★ **06** charming black cherry & cassis, smooth, almost formless, then brush of dry tannin on finish. Seems soft & gentle, but watch the brawny 15.4% alc. Oak as above. *— IvH*

Benguela Cove
T 021-794-0751 • F 021-794-0737

Walker Bay (see Elgin/Walker Bay map) • Est 2004 • 1stB 2007 • Visits by appt • Owner Chris Drummond & Mike Nixon • Winemaker Johan Joubert (2007 harvest) • Viticulturist Schalk du Toit (2002) • 65ha projected (cabs s/f, merlot, mourvèdre, petit v, pinot, shiraz, chard, sauv, semillon, viognier) • PO Box 112 Onrusriver 7201 • dutoitsr@lando.co.za • www.benguelacove.co.za

Co-owner Mike Nixon summited Mount Everest last May, but that was easy compared to overcoming initial scepticism about establishing a vineyard on this cool but windy ocean-facing site near Hermanus, with its brackish, clay rich soils. 'We created our own specialised techniques,' reveals Schalk du Toit, 'and we now have industry people visiting and phoning for advice!' Equally welcome are visits from a pair of Fish Eagles and over 100 Blue Cranes.

Benguela Cove range NEW

★★★★ **Sauvignon Blanc** Freshly mown grass, greengage nuances & persistent blackcurrant leaf finish are part of maiden **07**'s appeal; suggestion sweetness (3.3g/l RS) beguiling counterpoint to grapefruity acidity. *— CvZ*

Bergheim
T 082-770-8001 • F 021-862-7852

Paarl • Est/1stB 2000 • Visits by appt; tasting/sales also at I Love Wine (see entry) • Owner E & H Jordaan • Winemaker Edwin Jordaan • 500cs 80% red 20% white • PO Box 6020 Main Street Paarl 7622 • bergheim@micron.co.za

'All that's changed, except for making a little less wine, is that I've added a bit more soul,' says medical doctor Edwin Jordaan (aka 'Jorrie'). He's getting to grips with the pinotage he sources from a particular vineyard, and his love for semillon has found expression in a maiden commercial release.

Pinotage ☺ ★★★ Juicy **05** bursts with strawberry & mulberry, succulent tannins. One of more attractive - if rustic - available. 15 mths old oak. **Shiraz** ☺ ★★★ Rounded **05** slips down easily thanks to succulent fruit, smidgen sugar, friendly tannin grip. Portion new oak, 15 mths. **Semillon** [NEW] ☺ 🗎 ★★★ Sedate but appealing **06**, poised, with waxy notes, stonefruit flavours. Partly oak-fermented, 8 mths on lees. — *CvZ*

Bergkelder Wine Centre
T 021-809-8582 • F 021-887-9081

Stellenbosch • All day tasting & sales Mon-Fri 8-5 Sat 9-2 • Tour fee R20 • Open non-religious pub hols • Tours Mon-Fri 10, 11& 3; Sat 10, 11 & 12; incl AV presentation; bookings: info@bergkelder. co.za • Tel 021-809-8582. Special group tours, private tastings by appt • Owner Distell • Cellarmaster Andrea Freeborough • Winemaker Pieter Badenhorst (whites) & Justin Corrans (reds), with Schalk van der Merwe & Jaco van der Walt • Viticulturist Bennie Liebenberg • 17 000t 45% red 55% white • PO Box 184 Stellenbosch 7599 • info@bergkelder.co.za • www.bergkelder.co.za

Literally 'Mountain Cellar', after the maturation facilities deep within Stellenbosch's Papegaaiberg, the Bergkelder winery is responsible for production of the Fleur du Cap range, listed separately. Also on the premises are a visitor centre, where FdC and other ranges in the Distell portfolio are available for tasting and sale, and the Vinoteque Wine Bank. The latter, now in its 24th year, markets fine wines with the option of having purchases stored in perfect cellar conditions at surprisingly low cost. T 021-809-8281; info@vinoteque.co.za; www.vinoteque.co.za.

Bergsig Estate
T 023-355-1603 • F 023-355-1658

Breede River Valley (see Worcester map) • Est 1843 • 1stB 1977 • Tasting & sales Mon-Fri 8-5 Sat & pub hols 9-5 • Tasting fee for groups • Closed Easter Fri & Dec 25 • Tours by appt • Bistro for light meals • Conference/function facilities • Owner Lategan family • Winemaker De Wet Lategan, with Chris du Toit (Jan 1989/Jul 2003) • 253ha (cab, pinotage, shiraz, chard, chenin, sauv) • 3 200t/50 000cs own label • 35% red 60% white 4% rosé 1% port • Exported as Lategan & White River • PO Box 15 Breede River 6858 • wine@bergsig.co.za • www.bergsig.co.za

As it celebrates the 250th anniversary of the arrival in SA of its pioneering ancestor, the Lategan family steps into the future: it has sold a bundle of assets - some 140ha of its Romansrivier farm, 15% of the Bergsig marketing company and 10% of shares in the cellar - to a 60% worker-owned joint venture. Comments director Louis L: 'It's our social responsibility and our contribution to land reform.' He notes that the Bergsig Chardonnay '04 bottle now sports five award seals, just five of the many it's won.

★★★★ **Pinotage** Elegant **04**, back on form after unheralded blip in **03** (★★★), bright red berry fruit & well-integrated Am oak.

★★★★ **Chardonnay 06** (★★★★) shade less fleshy & charming than weighty, buttery **05**. Vanilla aromas from all-new Fr & Am oak precede apple & citrus flavours with crunchy acidity.

★★★★ **Cape Ruby** ✓ Unoaked **NV** fermented in kuipe; from tinta, more serious than average ruby style. Tobacco, leather, spice aromas, with fine grape tannins supporting rich, dark plum fruit, long, savoury finish. 19.5% alc, 90g/l RS.

★★★★ **Cape Vintage** Traditionally vinified, from tinta, fortified with brandy spirit, 36 mths older oak; **00**, pvsly tasted, succulent, smooth & harmonious; should mature fruitfully.

★★★★ **Late Bottled Vintage 99** from tinta, oak matured 40 mths (20% alc. 98g/l RS). Richly succulent & complex: dark cherry & plum with spicy clove, cinnamon & black pepper. Firm tannins on warm, savoury & flavoursome finish. **97**, **98** also still available.

Shiraz Rosé ☺ ★★★ Soft, balanced, cherry-toned **07**, 10g/l sugar adds charm but finishes clean & dry. Moderate 12.9% alc. **Gewürztraminer** ☺ ★★★ Fresh, aromatic litchi & Turkish Delight on **07**. Light (12% alc) but characterful, exotic flavours & dry, spicy finish.

Cabernet Sauvignon ★★★ 04 mid-2005 showed attractive red-berry intro & stern, gripping tannins, which may since have settled. **Ruby Cabernet-Merlot** ★★★ Hint charry oak on 05 with lean, elegant cherry fruit flavours, chewy tannins. Honest, uncomplicated drinking. **Chenin Blanc** ★★ 07 undemanding, lightly fruited & straightforward. **White River Chenin Blanc** ★★ Undemanding, tropical, pleasant quaffer in 06. **Weisser Riesling** ★★★ Last tasted was 03, with few yrs cellaring potential. **Sauvignon Blanc** ★★ Overt pineapple tropicality on simple light (12% alc) quaffer. **Sauvignon Blanc Brut** ★★ Brisk, dry & simple carbonated sparkler; ideal for Buck's Fizz. NE. **Special Late Harvest** ★★★ 07 from lightly botrytised chenin; pineapple glacé & sweet melon aromas, raisin flavours & delicate, clean finish. **Noble Late Harvest** Made in conducive yrs, currently sold out. NE. **Bouquet Light** 📖 Await new release. Mainly WO Breedeklf.

Lategan Family Reserve range

Shiraz ★★★★ Youthful, balanced 06 shows savoury spicy oak & soft mulberry, some meatiness, for early, pleasant drinking. **Touriga Nacional** Sold out. **Merlot-Petit Verdot** Out of stock. Range exclusively for export customer Direct Wines. Mainly WO Breedeklf. — IM

Bergwater Vineyards

T 023-541-1703 • F 021-541-1081

Prince Albert (see Klein Karoo map) • Est 1999 • 1stB 2002 • Tasting & sales Mon-Fri 9-4 Sat 10-2 • BYO picnic • Farm accommodation • Owner Heimie & Stephan Schoeman & a Dutch investment group • Winemaker Mariska Schreuder (Jan 2003) • Viticulturist VinPro advisers (1999) • 70ha (cab, merlot, shiraz, sauv) • 90% red 10% white • PO Box 40 Prince Albert 6930 • wine@bergwater.co.za • www.bergwater.com

The curious tasters visiting this Great Karoo winery 'leave with renewed vigour', say the Bergwater team, who declare themselves 'rather chuffed' with the 2007 harvest, citing excellent grape balance in all respects. Another highlight was winemaker Mariska Schreuder making it to the finals of the Woman Winemaker of the Year.

Reserve range

Cabernet Sauvignon ★★★ 14.5% alc well hidden by fulsome fruit on 05, though tannins still rather brusque, need time. Special oak treatment for all Reserves: 17 mths Fr barrels. Sample tasted, as for most in this range. **Merlot** NEW ★★★ Debut 05 has lashings plum fruit, creamy mouthfeel & playful tannic twist. Slips down easily, so watch the 14.5% alc. **Shiraz** ★★ 04 flew with KLM; 05 lively quaffer with indistinct varietal character, coconut/vanilla sweetness from wooding. **Royal Reserve** ★★★ Merlot leads 05 blend, souped up by cab & shiraz (60/30/10). Signature ripeness cut by racy acidity, sturdy tannins. Finishes dry, with bitter tickle. 10% Am oak. **Rosé** ★★★ Juicy pink tipple with alc punch (14%), mainly unwooded pinotage, dash shiraz. Strawberries & cream on gently sweet 05. Discontinued: **Sauvignon Blanc**. These, below, mainly WO Prince Albert Vlly.

Bergwater Vineyards range

Rendezvous Red NEW ☺ ★★★ Well-priced blend merlot (70%) & shiraz. Maiden 06 very drinkable, dry, with fair tannic grip from staves (70% Fr & Am).

Cabernet Sauvignon ★★★ This, standard Merlot, Shiraz bottlings & Reserve Rosé tasted last ed. Oak-chipped 05 sweet fruit entry, rather quick, chunky farewell. Wine Best Value award. **Merlot** ★★★ 05's oodles fruit & broad tannins mask beefy 14.5% alc, finish slightly bitter. **Shiraz** ★★ Gamey 05 unyielding, 'unsweetened' even by sojourn on Am oak. **Chardonnay** NEW 📖 ★★ 07 reticent chard aromas/flavours, sweetish underpin (11g/l RS) lifted by zesty acidity. Fermented with Am oak chips. **Sauvignon Blanc** NEW 📖 ★★ Fresh & friendly sipper with succulent Granny Smith apple aromas/flavours. — CvZ

Bernheim Wines
T 021-869-8384 • F 021-869-8365

Paarl • Est/1stB 2004 • Tasting & sales Mon-Fri 8.30-5 Sat 9-12 • Fee R5 refunded with purchase • Closed Christian holidays • Tours by appt • Owner Pieter & Anneke Taljaard, Hermann Helmbold, Jacques Kruger/Pacas Winery (Pty) Ltd • Winemaker Jacques Kruger (Feb 2004) • Viticulturist Gawie Kriel (Mar 2004, consultant) • 11ha (cabs s/f, merlot, pinotage, shiraz) • 6 000cs 100% red • PO Box 7274 Noorder-Paarl 7623 • bernheim@iafrica.com • www.bernheimwines.com

A three-year search for additional quality vineyard land culminated in the acquisition of hilltop Kersfontein farm in the Voor Paardeberg ward. This jump-started further cellar upgrades to 150-ton capacity and delighted veteran winemaker Jacques Kruger with the addition of 'some lovely' cab franc and petit verdot to celebrate 2007 as their first red-only vintage.

JH Pacas & Co range

Cabernet Sauvignon ★★★☆ No follow-up on harmonious & supple **03** from Sbosch fruit.
Shiraz ★★★☆ Last was showy New-World style **04**, billowing cardamom & sweet spice from new oak (17 mths, Fr/Am).

Bernheim range

Pinotage Rosé NEW ☺ 🍸 ★★★ **07** friendly & just off-dry; crushed berry character. Gd summertime companion.

Pinotage ★★★ Last-reviewed **05** was pleasant & drinkable, wholesome tannins made for gd food wine. **Merlot-Cabernet Sauvignon** ★★ As yet no follow-up to **04**, 61/39 blend, eucalyptus-fragrant, but still taut last yr. — *IvH*

■ **Berrio** *see* Flagstone Winery
■ **Berryfields** *see* Ashton Winery

Beyerskloof
T 021-865-2135 • F 021-865-2683

Stellenbosch • Est 1988 • 1stB 1989 • Tasting & sales Mon-Fri 8.30-4.30 Sat 10-4.30 • Closed Easter Fri/Sun/Mon, Dec 25/26 & Jan 1 • Farm produce • Red Leaf Restaurant Mon-Fri 9-4 Sat 10-3 • Groups by appointment • Conference facilities • Owner Beyers Truter & Simon Halliday • Winemaker Beyers Truter, with Anri Truter (Jan 2004) • Viticulturist Johan Pienaar (2000, consultant) • 70ha (cab, merlot, pinotage) • 550t/130 000cs + 225 000litres for customers • 98% red 2% rosé • PO Box 107 Koelenhof 7605 • wine@beyerskloof.co.za • www.beyerskloof.co.za

'Beyerskloof may be synonymous with pinotage, but it's about much more than that,' asserts brand manager Francois Naudé. 'Our premium blends attract serious attention, too, and there's more to come.' Winemaker Beyers Truter, confident of son Anri's assistance, has begun what he calls 'creative blending' with his favourite grape. In the pipeline: a light, refreshing easy-drinker inspired by vinho verde; a bi-continental melange featuring touriga nacional from Portugal's Quinta Nova, and third variation on the Cape Blend theme, this time involving pinotage's 'parents', cinsaut and pinot noir. The new restaurant is cooking (Pinotage Burgers the hot favourite) and, on a more serious note, The Faith Fund, initiated by Beyers T to tackle foetal alcohol syndrome, has raised over R4 million.

★★★★★ **Pinotage Reserve 05** back on track after oak-dominated & somewhat sombre **04** (★★★★). Powerful yet not forceful, fruit in confident balance with acid & oak; rounded, richly textured & persistent. 14 mths Fr oak, half new.

★★★★☆ **Field Blend** New name (pvsly 'Beyerskloof') alludes to the 5ha cab & merlot planted 80/20, harvested en-bloc & vinified traditionally. Keenly focused **03** (★★★★★) understated yet complex cassis & choc-mint beautifully wrapped in silken tannins. Alc more moderate & balanced (13.5% vs macho **02**'s 15%). Superb now but, like **02**, built for a decade.

★★★★☆ **Synergy Reserve** Cape blend, make-up varying each yr, ±18 mths 100% new Fr oak. Pinotage the headline in **05** with cab & merlot (30/20). Perfumed; almost decadent fruit & bold tannin. Cab-led **04** also very classy. No **03**.

Pinotage ✓ ★★★★ Extraordinary quality, consistency & value. **06** lightly wooded & full flavoured; black fruit bouquet, ripe berry palate & tangy acidity. 6 mths Fr oak, none new. **Synergy** ★★★★ 'Cape blend' from cab, pinotage, merlot &, in **05**, also dollop petit v (43/33/19/5). No bells & whistles - just bright fruit, deft oaking & satisfying choc-mint finish. ± 15 mths Fr oak, 30% new. **Brut Pinotage Rosé** ★★★ Sunset-hued sparkler, frothy & ebullient **06** earthy & sweet fruited but vibrant & dry. Drink well-chilled. Charmat process. **Pinotage Rosé** ★★★☆ V pretty **07** ideal for al fresco entertaining, esp lunchtime friendly 12% alc. Sweet fruited yet dry with mouthwatering acidity. **Lagare Cape Vintage** ★★★★ Lacks depth & concentration of SA's fortified first team but **06** has confident spiritous grip, interesting Turkish Delight aromas & bitter cherry farewell. Equal blend tinta, touriga &, of course, pinotage. — *CvZ*

■ **Big Ears** *see Groupe LFE South Africa*
■ **Big Five** *see African Terroir*
■ **Big Six** *see Old Bridge Wines*

Bilton Wines
T 021-881-3714 • *F* 021-881-3721

Stellenbosch • 1stB 1998 • Tasting & sales Mon-Fri 9.30-4.30 Sat 10-3 • Fee R20 • Wine & Chocolate tastings (R30) • Refreshments & summer picnics • Function venue • Owner Mark Bilton • Winemaker Rudi de Wet (Nov 2005), advised by Giorgio Dalla Cia • Viticulturist Ruan du Plessis (Dec 2004) • 52ha (cab, merlot, mourvèdre, petit v, pinotage, shiraz, chenin, sauv, semillon, viognier) • 100t own label 80% red 20% white • PO Box 60 Lynedoch 7603 • sales@biltonwines.com • www.biltonwines.com

Sir Percy, Bilton's flagship bordeaux blend, and the new Boules Court launched, winemaker and avid pétanque player Rudi de Wet travelled to St-Emilion for a month's skills-honing. Matthew Bilton, eldest son of owner Mark, strengthens the team as new blocks of pinot and sauvignon are added to the mix.

★★★★ **Cabernet Sauvignon** Built on sleekly powerful lines, **04**'s rich cassis, plum fruit reined in by fine, beautifully judged tannins: a class act. 18 mths mainly Fr oak. **03**, with 10% petit v, Wine (★★★★). This, Merlot, from registered single vyd.

★★★★ **Merlot** Succulent & sophisticated. **04** (★★★★★) lesson in grape's local potential: deeply fruit-rich, raspberries, fresh prunes, layered with dried herbs & smoke; beguiling complexity. Deft wooding provides backbone for 4+ yrs ageing. Oak as for Cab. **03**, with 10% cab, similarly multi-layered, firm but harmonious tannins.

★★★★ **Shiraz** Modern, showy, voluptuous, lashings creamy vanilla-oak. Intensity continues into **04**'s fruit, raspberries, cherries, with prosciutto hovering in background. Svelte structure, harmonious tannins mean it's accessible already, but min 4 yrs ahead. Oak as for Cab.

★★★★ **Sir Percy** Statement bdx blend honours owner's grandfather, knighted for charitable work. Another Giorgio hand in **04** whose classic 60/30/10 proportions (cab, merlot, petit v) have New World concentration: cassis, mature beef, savoury oak. Tight structure, built to last gd few yrs. 18 mths combo new/used oak, mainly Fr.

★★★★☆ **Matt Black** Named jointly after wine-loving 17th-century pirate & combo Bilton family names. Shiraz, merlot, petit v blend (53/31/16) bearing fingerprint of vini guru Giorgio Dalla Cia. Impressive **04** supple, juicy, vibrates with health, but 18 mths Fr/Am oaking confirms seriousness & ageing potential. Note: no reds retasted this ed.

White NEW ☺ 🍴 ★★★ Blend sauv, semillon, chenin. **07** has real flavour, nice concentration, firm flesh with flint & mineral notes, lively acidity & bone-dry finish.

Discontinued: **Sauvignon Blanc**. — *IvH*

■ **Birdfield** *see Klawer Co-operative Cellars*

Blaauwklippen Agricultural Estate
T 021-880-0133 • F 021-880-0136

Stellenbosch • Est 1682 • 1stB 1974 • Tasting & sales Mon-Fri 9-5 Sat 10-5 Sun 10-4 • Fee: R25 formal tasting (incl tour); R25 informal (incl tasting glass); R35 informal (incl red wine glass) • Closed Dec 25 & Jan 1 • Tours by appt 10-3 • Blaauwklippen Barouche Restaurant (see Eat-out section) & many other amenities • Owner Farmers Markt Landhandel GmbH • Winemaker Rolf Zeitvogel with Albert Basson • Viticulturist Kowie Kotze (1987) • 100ha (cabs s/f, malbec, merlot, petit v, shiraz, zinfandel, viognier) • 480t/35 000cs own label • 98% red 2% white • PO Box 54 Stellenbosch 7599 • mail@blaauwklippen.com • www.blaauwklippen.com

Last year this landmark farm celebrated is 325th anniversary with, among others, the inauguration of an annual Farm Festival & Market to give the farmworkers and the rest of the Stellenbosch community a place to sell home-grown produce and hand-made crafts. A commemorative 10-Year Vintage Reserve Port was released, along with a trio of new zinfandel wines 'reflecting the unique tradition here at Blaauwklippen' (none reviewed this edition). The Blaauwklippen Blending Competition remains a firm favourite; 2008 is its 25th consecutive year.

Blaauwklippen Vineyard Selection (BVS)
★★★★ **Cabernet Sauvignon** Complex nose on **05**, notes tobacco leaf, blackberries & spice. Rich, jammy, v silky tannins, alc (13.5%) slightly up from pvs but in keeping with Old-World styling. Only seasoned wood. No **04**.
Merlot ★★★ **05** dry dusty tones of coffee, choc & distant plums, retained on palate. Soft, chewy tannins. **Shiraz** ★★★★ Ripe, jammy fruit on **06**, some cassis & hint spice persisting on palate. Quite rich & intense; silky tannins. **Zinfandel** ★★★ Ripe, jammy aromas on **05**, hint of kelp, mellow tannins. For early enjoyment. **Cabriolet** ★★★☆ **05** reinstates cab f (50%) in mix with cab, dashes malbec & merlot. Rich plum spiciness, hint of forest floor. Just misses heights scaled by concentrated **03** (★★★★). No **04**.

Blaauwklippen Cultivar range
Cabernet Sauvignon ★★★ Dry, quite intense, with tobacco leaf, spice & friendly tannins on **05**. **Merlot** ★★★ Minty **05**'s light mid-palate needs food supplement: try with waterblommetjie bredie or potjiekos. **Shiraz** ★★★ Whiffs spice & toffee on **04**, soft dry-prune flavours, refreshing acids are food-friendly. Can keep yr/2. Coastal vyds. **Barouche Blend** ★★★ **05** cab-led with shiraz, merlot & dash mourvèdre. Easy drinking, companionable tannins. **Sauvignon Blanc** ★★★★ **07** (sample) rich tropical fruit with pleasing follow-through; clean & well-balanced. S/West, W/Coast vyds.

Landau range
Red Landau ★★☆ Pvs seven-variety blend down to cab, shiraz & zin in **04**. Juicy, easy & forthcoming, with soft tannins. Coastal WO. Under screwcap, as are all in range. **Rosé** ★★ Blueberry hints to light, easy-drinking **07**; now 50/**05** cab/shiraz. **White** ★★ Pvs chenin/viognier blend gains sauv in **07**, uncomplicated braai wine from S/West fruit. **Semi-Sweet Landau** ★★ **06** adds gewürz to blend (incl Dbnville fruit). Muscat & litchi flavours; needs firmer acids. *— MM*

■ **Black Label** *see Backsberg Estate Cellars*

Black Oystercatcher
T 082-779-5439 • F 028-482-1938

Elim (see Southern Cape map) • Est 1998 • 1stB 2003 • Tasting by appt • Owner/winemaker/viticulturist Dirk Human • 14.5ha (cab, merlot, shiraz, sauv, semillon) • ±90t; 48% red 52% white • PO Box 199 Bredasdorp 7280 • dirk@blackoystercatcher.co.za

Lest fans of the Semillon are disappointed about its discontinuation, Dirk Human insists that it's going to better use in White Pearl, his bordeaux-style blend. 'I personally think it's a more complex wine, so we're going to stick to it.' He remains determined to protect the wetlands on and around the family farm Moddervlei, along with the plants, animals and birds that make this remote area so special. 'But it's the wine that makes people want to come out here,' he insists.

★★★★ **Sauvignon Blanc 07** (tank sample) follows in steps of impressive **06**, with more power & presence. Complex bouquet brimming with cut grass, capsicum & almond, all in sync with zesty gooseberry flavours.

★★★★ **White Pearl** NEW Thrilling maiden **06**, barrel fermented/aged older Fr oak (7 mths). Pungent aromas of thatch, dust & lemon from 60% semillon, capsicum nuance from sauv, spiced with whiff fresh ginger. Satisfying now, has structure to grow in bottle.

Shiraz ★★★★ Scented nose of white pepper, tomato leaf & lily part of **05**'s charm, these cool-climate hallmarks contrasting attractively with ripe 15% alc, strident savoury & salty palate. Distinctive & worth watching. 14 mths Fr/Am oak, ±20% new. **Cabernet Sauvignon-Merlot** ★★★☆ **05** supple, with vibrant cassis fruit & cardamom notes. Unknit mid-2006, noted as needing short time to meld. Discontinued: **Blanc Fumé, Semillon.** —*CvZ*

Black Pearl Vineyards

T 021-863-2900, 083-297-9796 • F 0866-178-507

Paarl • Est 1998 • 1stB 2001 • Tasting, sales & tours just about anytime but please phone ahead (note: no credit cards) • Closed Dec 25 • Walks • Conservation area • Owner Lance Nash • Winemaker/viticulturist Mary-Lou Nash • 8ha (cab, shiraz) • ±1 800cs 100% red • PO Box 609 Suider-Paarl 7624 • info@blackpearlvineyards.com • www.blackpearlvineyards.com

'Consume and conserve' is the Nash family's mantra. They've just been honoured with a Cape Action Plan for People & the Environment (CAPE) award apropos of Stewardship in a Priority Biodiversity Site in the Cape Floristic Region. They've also dedicated the shiraz under their new Nash Family Vineyards label to biodiversity, and maintain a 'contract conservation area' (184ha of pristine Swartland shale renosterveld) with Cape Nature.

★★★★ **Shiraz** Less juicy, more tannic than pvs; **05** (★★★★) has black berry & coffee perfume, flavours, a dry finish. Contrast with **04**, an explosion of dark fruit & spicy black pepper.

★★★★ **Shiraz-Cabernet Sauvignon** Delicious New-World-style **05** shows complex black pepper, smoked meat & cigarbox notes, ripe berry undertones, pliable tannins.

Cabernet Sauvignon 🗎 ★★★★ Step-up **06** has lovely concentration, ripe dark berries & cassis, attractively spiced, well balanced tannins & a juicy finish. **05** untasted; **04** (★★★★) hearty food partner. **Nash Family Vineyards Shiraz** NEW ★★★★ **04** combo Old/New World style: leather, filigree of spice, underlying dark berries & soft tannins; an elegant food wine. 50% new oak. —*MM*

■ **Black Rock** *see The Winery of Good Hope*

BLANKbottle

T 0861 106 106 • F 0865-030-974

Somerset West • Est 2005 • Tasting by appt • Owner/winemaker Pieter Walser • 2 890cs 90% red 10% white • Postnet Suite 160 Pvt Bag X15 Somerset West 7129 • thebestwines@blankbottle.co.za • www.blankbottle.co.za

'I can't tell what my next wine will be like until I've formed an alliance with a winemaker and cellar,' says internet-savvy entrepreneur Pieter Walser, whose latest creation is 'Mystery', so-named because its label gives no clues as to cultivar, vintage or area of origin. 'It's up to the consumer to guess what it is!'

Isa 42 ★★★ Last tasted **03** ex-Smnsberg was minty berry style from merlot, dry tannic finish. **Mystery** NEW ★★☆ Fresh & fruity red; **06** quirky twists: portion fermented with oak essence, another underwent 'extreme-thermo-ferment'; aged 2nd/3rd fill oak, 30% on sauv/riesling lees! **Phortion Shiraz** NEW ★★ **04** dominated by caramel, malt & wood flavours; sprawling but short. Fr/Am oak, 100% new. **Sorga Cabernet Sauvignon-Shiraz** NEW ★★★ **06** brims with shiraz red fruit, cab's tangy acidity, firm tannins in long farewell. Sbosch vyds. **Luca Merlot-Cabernet Sauvignon-Shiraz** NEW ★★★ **05** merlot-led blend (cab s/f 15/10). Appealing winter warmer (14.7% alc) with berry/herby notes, meaty hints. **Walser/Malan Alliance** NEW ★★★☆ **06** barrel sample shows smart if sweet oak, generous Smnsberg fruit

(70/30 cab/shiraz) & herbal high notes mid-2007. By Walser & Slaley's Marius Malan. **Graphé Shiraz-Viognier** NEW ★★★ Full-throttle fun in **05**; dash (2%) viognier adds verve, perfume. Older-oak biscuity tones, 15% alc extends a warm farewell. Paarl fruit. Striking minimalist packaging a feature throughout.— *CvZ*

Bloemendal Estate
T 021-976-2682 • F 021-976-2682

Durbanville ▪ Est 1902 ▪ 1stB 1987 ▪ Tasting & sales Mon-Fri 9-5 Sat 9-4 Sun 11-3 ▪ Fee R15 pp for groups ▪ Closed Dec 25 ▪ Deli/oyster bar, weddings, evening functions & full conference facilities etc ▪ Owner Bloemendal Trust ▪ Winemaker Jackie Coetzee ▪ Viticulturist Johan Pienaar (consultant) ▪ 140ha (cab, merlot, shiraz, sauv) ▪ 5 000cs own label 73% red 25% white 2% rosé ▪ PO Box 466 Durbanville 7551 ▪ bloemendal@isoft.co.za

Laid-back Jackie Coetzee becomes animated when talking about his 07 Sauvignon. 'Better than the 05' (which won the inaugural Terroir Wine Award), it was released only towards the end of last year. 'I hold my Sauvignon back longer than most, allowing it to marry in the bottle. ' This year he releases his first Malbec. With a lot less hair, he adds!

★★★★ **Cabernet Sauvignon** Pinnacle of estate's reds, recent vintages much improved, prompting higher general rating. Refined tannins wind around **02**'s plush fruit, capsicum & cassis nuances; opulent with delicate silky finish. Yr Fr oak.

★★★★ **Shiraz** Last ed, **03** (★★★★) was savoury & austere, less rich than burly **02**, whose tannins were approachable on release. Yr Am oak.

★★★★ **Sauvignon Blanc Suider Terras** Named for mature s-facing vyd, 30 yr old bushvines benefiting from bracing sea breezes. Pungent **06** has capsicum, fig & fresh-cut grass aromas, gooseberry flavours; mineral, slightly coarse farewell compared to **05**'s assertive but elegant palate.

★★★★ **Semillon 05** (★★★), tasted last ed ex-barrel, now confirmed in bottle: ripe yet lean, oak adding chunky finish to rather tired lime cordial fruit. Livelier **04** was large (14.6% alc) but friendly.

Merlot ★★★★ **03** charms with poised plum, bacon & tar notes; gentle, slightly salty finish giving an Old-World feel. **Blosend Rooi** ★★ 'Blushing Red', barrel-fermented dry rosé; **04**, tasted last ed, blended shiraz (70%) & merlot, had less fleshy fruit than pvs. **Brut** ★★ MCC from chard, ±9 mths lees; new bottling not ready. Pvs **NV** was light textured & focused, with attractive citrus tones & busy bubbles. **Natural Sweet** ★★★ Back after several yrs in abeyance. **04** sorbet & melon with floral twist; gently sweet entry followed by dry finish, for attractive if uncomplicated sipping. — *RP*

■ **Blouberg** *see Graça*

Blouvlei Wines
T 021-873-7745 • F 021-864-2737

Wellington ▪ Est/1stB 2003 ▪ Visits Mon-Fri 8-5 Sat by appt ▪ Fee R7/tasting ▪ Closed pub hols ▪ Meals by appt ▪ Guesthouse ▪ Owner BEE company ▪ Winemaker Pieter-Niel Rossouw, with Jerome van Wyk ▪ 8 000cs 100% red ▪ PO Box 817 Wellington 7654 ▪ blouvlei@cknet.co.za

It's all systems go for Mont du Toit's workers' trust, marketing its own wines mostly on-consumption and overseas (though local retail sales are up to 40%). Director Abelia Lawrence, combining motherhood with global marketing trips and a 'wine-related' MBA (the joint Cape Town/Adelaide University course), hopes to see Blouvlei in UK chain Marks & Spencer soon.

White ☺ 🍷 ★★ Gentle tropical & stonefruits on crisp, easy-drinking **07**. W Cape WO.

Red 🍷 ★★ Cabs s & f plus merlot mesh to provide ripe-berried friendliness in soft, approachable **05**. **Klassique** 🍷 ★★★ **05** less serious, more rustic than pvs. From cab, merlot & shiraz; jammy dark fruit & liquorice, chunky tannins, spiritous farewell. **Silver Lining Rosé** NEW 🍷 ★ Maiden **07** crimson hued, savoury, dry; bitter cherry flavours & tannic goodbye. All WO Coastal.— *MW*

Blueberry Hill

T 021-876-3362 · F 021-876-2114

Franschhoek · Est/1stB 1998 · Visits by appt · 2 self-catering cottages · Owner Blueberry Hill Trust (Brian & Lindy Heyman) · Winemaker Nigel McNaught (1998, adviser) · Viticulturist Paul Wallace (2000, adviser) · 0.6ha · 350-400cs 100% red · PO Box 580 Franschhoek 7690 · bhwine@iafrica.com · www.blueberryhillcottages.co.za

South Africa does produce merlot of high quality, asserts co-owner Brian Heyman. And the success of their 04 (best of 26 in a Wine of the Month Club tasting) evidences his claim to have found the right site for this fastidious grape. Crop thinning and careful canopy management are further keys to quality, he adds.

Blueberry Hill

Merlot ★★★ Caramel note on **05**, toffee richness with some minerality; vintage's big alc (15. 3%) evident, as is oak (24 mths 90% Fr), tannins bit sticky. Needs time. — *MM*

Blue Cove Wines

T 082-492-3213 · F 021-671-9031

Robertson · Est/1stB 2006 · Tasting by appt · Owner Blue Cove Holdings Ltd (UK) · Winemaker/viticulturist Stephen de Wet (Jan 2006) · 176ha owned plus grower partnerships (cab, merlot, shiraz, chenin, nouvelle, sauv, viognier) · 1 250t/72 000cs 42% red 6% rosé 52% white · HACCP accreditation in progress · PO Box 155 Ashton 6715 · murray@netconnect.co. za · www.bluecovewines.com

Soaring sales of the Blue Cove brand (72 000 cases in only 2 years, 85% exported) have the partners (two UK-based and three SA) looking to expand into the US and other markets while ensuring locals also enjoy the wines, particularly by the glass in wine bars and restaurants.

Cabernet Sauvignon ★★★ **06** classic profile; plums, grass nuance, pencil shavings. Firm but ripe tannins; will soften given 2/3 yrs. **Merlot** ★★★ Harmonious oaking of **06** allows plummy fruit full rein for satisfying drinkability. Best now. **Shiraz** ★★★ Meaty flavours & velvety texture of **06** ensure wide appeal; not for ageing. Lightly oaked. **Rosé** ★★★ Cerise-hued party-goer **06**; bright berries, easy drinking, off-dry. **Chenin Blanc** ★★★★ **06** tasted last ed was ripe & fleshy Golden Delicious apple combined with tangy acidity. **Sauvignon Blanc** ★★★★ **07** shows more concentration than **06**. Intriguing lemon tones whet appetite, crisp tangy finish fulfills the promise. **Viognier** ★★★ **06** tasted pvs ed was highly aromatic & perfumed with notes of jasmine & muscat; gd acid. — *CR*

Blue Crane Vineyards

T 023-230-0823 · F 023-230-0825

Tulbagh · Est 2001 · 1stB 2004 · Visitors welcome but phone ahead · Owner Henk & Anita Jordaan · Winemaker/viticulturist Henk Jordaan, advised by viticulturist Andrew Teubes & suppliers · 6ha (cab, merlot, shiraz, sauv) · 2 000cs 75% red 25% white · PO Box 306 Tulbagh 6820 · henk@bluecrane.co.za · www.bluecrane.co.za

'If only you had photos in Platter - this is the most beautiful place,' says former corporate executive Henk Jordaan of his and wife Anita's farm in Tulbagh's mountain-ringed valley, increasingly the domain of excellent reds, including their own new handcrafted Blue Crane flagships. Next is a Jagger's Peak dry Pinotage Rosé, and 'big things' in the planning for 2008.

Blue Crane Vineyards range NEW

★★★★ **Cabernet Sauvignon 04** array berries, cedar, dried herbs assault senses. Surehanded winemaking here: 2 yrs barrel treatment give fine-grained tannins, structure for gd few yrs further ageing, yet already drinking superbly.

Full Flight ★★★★ Ripe strawberries on **05**, hint savoury spice, accessible structure, harmoniously oaked. Drink now & over 2/3 yrs. Merlot, cab, shiraz 50/35/15.

Jagger's Peak range

Cabernet Sauvignon ★★★★ Choc-minty **04** last time full & ripe but well formed. **05** unready. **Merlot** ★★★ Generous **05** pvs ed showed ultra-ripe cassis & plums; tasty drinkability from refreshing acidity. **06** not ready for tasting. **Shiraz** ★★★ Smoky, dark-fruited & satisfying **06**.

Yr Fr/Am oaking adds nuance, tannins ripe, already accessible. **Chenin Blanc ★★★ 06** not made. Pvsly reviewed **05** distinctive, with hints resin & fynbos. **Sauvignon Blanc ★★★** Gooseberry & greengage, intriguing savoury vein throughout flavourful, different **07**. Tangy dry finish. — *CR*

Blue Creek Wines

T 021-887-6938, 021-880-0522 • F 021-886-5462

Stellenbosch • Est 1995 • 1stB 1996 • Visits by appt • Owner/winemaker Piet Smal • Viticulturist Johan Smith (1996, consultant) • 7.5ha (cab, merlot, pinotage) • 1 000cs own label 100% red • 26 Piet Retief Str Stellenbosch 7600 • blue_creek@email.com

Holidaying in Europe whilst working in England introduced Piet Smal to the idea of making your own wine from a relatively small parcel of vines. Back in South Africa, he convinced his grape-growing father and, for a name, turned to the nearby Blaauwklippen River. And thus, Blue Creek wines.

★★★★ **Cabernet Sauvignon** ✓ **05** athletic rather than opulent, as **04** (★★★★★) was. Fruit in confident balance with oak & alc (14.5%, up on pvs 13.5%). Wooding (14 mths Fr, 30% new) imparts platform for gd few yrs maturation. Ex-own yds in Sbosch's 'Golden Triangle'. — *CvZ*

▮ **Blue Grove Hill** *see Capaia Wines*

▮ **Blue White** *see Old Vines Cellars*

Blyde Wines

T 083-270-5706 • F 021-871-1619

Paarl • Est/1stB 2000 • Tasting & sales at I Love Wine (see entry) • Tours by appt • Owner/winemaker Lieb Loots • 400 cs 90% red 10% white • PO Box 3231 Paarl 7620 • lieb@blyde.com • www.blyde.com

Garagiste Lieb Loots has downscaled his wine business to a hobby. 'That way,' he says, 'I can stop operating at a loss and still make good wine at affordable prices that I can sell to real wine lovers.'

Bona Dea ★★★★ Impressive **04** relies more on shiraz (80%) than pvs vintages; merlot & cab (12/8) in support. Red fruit melange nicely spiced up with toasty oak; 14.6% alc well hidden, tannins still bit raw on finish. — *CvZ*

Bodega

T 021-987-6647 • F 021-987-5828

Paarl • Closed to public • Owner/winemaker Adriaan Stander • Vineyard Manager Willem Carelse • P O Box 2472 Dubanville 7551 • rednats@eccsystems.co.za

Adriaan Stander purchased this Paarl property at auction in 2005, and is taking time and care to ensure the wines which materialise will carry the Bodega name with pride. An 07 cab, merlot and pinotage had been vinified and were works-in-progress at press time, and hence not rated this edition. Stander was in discussion with prospective consultants to help style the wines to spec, his preference being full-bodied blends.

Boekenhoutskloof

T 021-876-3320 • F 021-876-3793

Franschhoek • Tasting & sales Mon-Fri 9-5 • Owner Boekenhoutskloof Investments (Pty) Ltd • Winemaker Marc Kent & Rudiger Gretschel, with Heinrich Tait & Heinrich Hugo • Viticulturist Pieter Siebrits • PO Box 433 Franschhoek 7690 • boeken@mweb.co.za • www.boekenhoutskloof.co.za

Marc Kent and wife Brigitte celebrated the birth of twins on Freedom Day. What spare time he has is now spent working with Walker Bay fruit for the first time, and devoting more energy and thought to sweet wines. Cement 'eggs' have been installed for small-batch white wine fermenting, and the decision to open to the public Monday to Friday in the ultra-chic tasting room has been a huge success. This is one of six SA wineries financially supporting an initiative to bring opera to schoolchildren – a premium-priced wine will carry a motif from William Kentridge's designs for Mozart's Magic Flute.

★★★★☆ **Cabernet Sauvignon** Classically styled & ageworthy, **05** a stunner: cedar scented, intense blackcurrant fruits pleated in beautifully woven structural support; elegance defined. Superb **04** (★★★★★) echoed claret-like minerality & sophistication. 27 mths all new Fr oak complementary. Single hillside Fhoek vyd.

★★★★★ **Reserve Syrah** NEW **05** altogether different beast alongside 'regular' bottling; deeper, denser, even more finely textured, a masterpiece. So thick one could stand a spoon in it, yet with finesse, delicacy. Best barrel selection, 27 mths seasoned Fr oak.

★★★★★ **Syrah** Admirable consistency, traditional styling & exhilarating fruit expression. **05** (★★★★☆) has heady pimento spice layered with dense, tense palate, breathtaking finale. Splendid **04** both sensuous & sophisticated. Old Wllngtn vyd yielding 1500cs. Native yeast ferment, 27 mths Fr oak, none new. Regular 90+ pts WS.

★★★★☆ **The Chocolate Block** Hedonistic; smouldering dark choc sheen, viscous texture to bold, ripe, polished **06** (★★★★). Shiraz-led compendium with grenache, cinsaut, cab & viognier (55/17/15/9/4). 15 mths Fr oak, mix new/used. WO Coastal. Sleek, shiny, but tad less serious than warm & sensuous **05**.

★★★★☆ **Semillon** Refined charm, with personality. **05** (★★★★) quiet at review mid-2007, nicely balanced citrus fruits, candle wax breadth & fine Fr oak (yr all new), but not (yet) as riveting as richly vinous **04**. Needs few yrs. Fhoek vyds, 40-100+ yrs old.

★★★★☆ **Noble Late Harvest** Semillon **04** harbinger of glorious development that awaits CWG sibling. Tangerine glints herald sumptuous, viscous, vanilla scented fruit; fresh finish cuts lushness of caramel/custard core. 9.5% alc. 29 mths new Fr casks. 375ml, 100cs.

★★★★ **CWG Auction Reserve Noble Late Harvest** NEW Pale **06** deceptive: proffers overt botrytis & a light body mid-2007, but penetrating fruit intensity & fine length of flavour suggest many semillon treasures to unfold over time. Autumn-harvested fruit lavished new Fr oak 13 mths, 12% alc, 140g/l RS. 45 cs, 375ml. EW.

The Wolftrap ☺ ★★☆ Unpretentious red with clean spicy flavours in **06**. Shiraz, mourvèdre & viognier, Fr oaked. WO W Cape.

Porcupine Ridge range

★★★★ **Syrah** 06 (★★★★) spicy purple fruit compote interest, ends hot & hard, showing 14.65% alc. **05** riper, but balanced despite chewy concentration. 1/3 each used Fr cask, oak stave & tank portions. Chiefly Mbury, Wllngtn vyds.

Cabernet Sauvignon ★★★ 06 aromatic red berries tucked into spicy Fr oak; splashes cab f & malbec add sappy tension to big alc impact. Mainly Mbury fruit. **Merlot** ★★★ 06 mulberry tones to tart, mint-bordered red plum core; rough Fr oak (stave/old cask) stands apart. WO Coastal. **Sauvignon Blanc** ★★★ Clear varietal notes to unaggressive 07; refreshing 12.5% alc in lunchtime style. WO W Cape. — DS

Bo La Motte 🍷 ⌂ 🏃 NEW
T 021-876-3067 • F 021-876-3498

Franschhoek ▪ Cellar est 2001 ▪ 1stB 2003 ▪ Visits Mon-Fri 10-5 ▪ Fee R15p/p refunded on purchase of wine ▪ Closed all pub hols ▪ Facilities for children ▪ Guest accommodation ▪ Owner Maarten de Graaf & Jennie Troth ▪ Winemaker Anelle le Roux (Dec 2006) ▪ Viticulturist Pietie le Roux ▪ 10ha (cab, grenache, merlot, mourvèdre, shiraz, chenin, semillon, viognier) ▪ 45t/ ±200cs 60% red 40% white ▪ PO Box 521 Franschhoek 7690 ▪ reservations@bolamotte.com ▪ www.bolamotte.com

Winemaking started as a hobby after Maarten de Graaf and Jennie Troth converted this property back to its Huguenot wine farm roots. 'But with the arrival of three little boys, we just ran out of time!' Their cellar is small but well-equipped, and their target is to become fully organic.

Cabernet Sauvignon ★★ Herbal **04** has peppery tealeaf & gamey notes, dry & austere tannins. 30% new Fr oak, 14 mths.

Middagkrans range

Shiraz ★★★ Bold tutti-frutti flavours dominate **07**, lush velvet texture, long, sweet-fruited finish. **Cabernet Sauvignon-Shiraz** ★★★ Equal blend **05**, pepper, cassis & tobacco aromas, nutmeg hints promise complexity not yet evident on grippy palate; give time to develop. 20% new Fr oak, rest 2nd fill Am/Fr. — MF

◼ **Boland Cellar** *see Boland Kelder*

Boland Kelder

T 021-862-6190 • F 021-862-5379

Paarl • Est 1947 • 1stB 1948 • Tasting & sales Mon-Fri 8-5 Sat 9-2 • Closed Easter Fri/Sun, Dec 25/26 & Jan 1 • Tours by appt • Underground cellar for functions & gatherings (max 45 people) • Events programme during Dec/Jan; phone for details • Tour groups • Owner 96 producing shareholders • Cellarmaster Altus le Roux (Sep 1984) • Winemaker Naudé Bruwer & Bernard Smuts (Dec 1996/Nov 1999), with JG Auret & Chris Crawford (Dec 2002/July 2005) • Viticulturist Jurie Germishuys (Jul 1998) • 2 400ha (cab, merlot, pinotage, shiraz, chard, chenin, sauv) • ±21 500t 56% red 44% white • Export brands: Boland Cellar, Lindenhof & Montestell • PO Box 7007 Northern Paarl 7623 • info@bolandkelder.co.za • www.bolandkelder.co.za

The winery's tally of golds, at time of writing, was 99, latest awards being from the Mondial de Bruxelles for the Shiraz **05** and the Mondiales des Vins Canada for the Shiraz Reserve **02**. No doubt this year the score will be a century! Visitors to Boland get more than award-winning wines (or a tour, if one's been booked): they can buy cheese and olives grown in the area and enjoy them with a picnic under the trees, or in the cool of the underground cellar.

Single Vineyard Selection NEW

★★★★ **Shiraz** Elegantly packaged **05** determined to impress, & does: fynbos, pepper, leather & red berries mingle on nose & palate, generous fruit core, well-hidden alc (14.9%) & refreshing acidity make for big, satisfying mouthful. Distinct sweet impression from 100% new Am oak (18 mths); approachable, plenty potential for development.

No 1 Reserve range

★★★★ **Cabernet Sauvignon** Classy **04** spicy, savoury nuances mingle with big ripe blackberry & dark cherry flavours, underpinned by confident tannins from 24 mths all-new oak (60/40 Fr/Am). Potential to improve gd few yrs.

★★★★ **Shiraz** Impossible-to-ignore charmer: **05** boldly spicy, smoky & savoury, dark fruit flavours wonderfully fluid & flamboyant, as are the tannins. Natural fermentation, 18 mths oak, Am/Fr/Hung (70/20/10), unfiltered.

Chardonnay ★★★★ Delicious oak fermented/aged version. **05** vanilla biscuit note, creamy mouthfeel from 18 mths lees ageing; nuts & toffee finish, crisp lemon tang throughout. All-new oak, Fr. **Sauvignon Blanc** ★★★★ All-new Fr barrique fermentation/ageing for these; wood better wielded in **06** than pvs, provides gd platform for ripe pineapple/tropical fruit; brisk, dry.

Winemakers Selection

Merlot ★★★★ **05** raises the bar with a warm, inviting coffee-tinged bouquet, dark choc & black plum palate; more than sufficient juicy fruit to mesh with 100% new oak, 70/30 Fr/Am. A wine to savour… & age a few yrs. **04** (★★★★) was shrouded in oak when tasted mid-2006. **Pinotage** ★★★★ Extra care taken in the cellar shows in improved **05**. Earthy aromas, succulent plummy fruit, tantalising spices; complex & mouthfilling. 60/40 Am/Fr oak, all new. **Nouvelle** ★★★ BK's was first varietal bottling of semillon-crouchen cross. **06** winter melon aromas & flavours, crisp acidity, perfect for grilled fish.

Boland Kelder range

★★★★ **White Muscadel** Elegant fortified dessert, **07** filled with honeyed sunshine & florals; tantalising sweetness checked by crisp lemon acidity.

Sixty 40 [NEW] ☺ ★★★ Name alludes to blend proportions of chenin & sauv in debut **07**, latter contributing herbal notes & brisk acidity, former tropical fruit salad flavours.

Cabernet Sauvignon ★★★ **06** layered with blackberries, spice & dark cherries; extra complexity from Am/Fr oak, 60% new. Lovely red meat partner. **Merlot** ★★★ Inviting mocha nose, plum fruit on an unobtrusive oak base; **06** finish is dry & satisfying. Like most in range, for drinking not keeping. **Pinotage** ★ Banana-tinged fruit not up to task of cushioning hefty oak tannins in **06** (Am/Fr 60/40, 40% new). **Shiraz** ★★★ **06** a pleasant dinner companion; dry finish, understated oak detail (12 mths, 44% new) & inviting smoky red fruit. **Cabernet Sauvignon-Shiraz** ★★★★ Always unwooded. Smooth & friendly **06** a step up; led by pure, ripe fruit, subtle smoke, well-managed grape tannins. **Rosé Off-dry** [NEW] ★★★ **07** pretty pink maiden from cab & shiraz (60/40); charming berry fruit, appealing fruit/acid balance. **Chardonnay** ★★ Accessible partially oaked version. **07** light textured & biscuity, cleansing lemon acidity & persistent finish. **Chenin Blanc** ★★★ Green fig & slight note of guava on **07**, crisp lemon-fresh finish. **Sauvignon Blanc** ★★★ Easy-drinking **07** has typical grass aromas, riper apple & pear flavours. **Red Muscadel** ★★★ Slightly dusty tealeaf nose on warm-hearted **07**, honeyed notes lifted by satisfying dry finish. **Port** ★★ **06** from shiraz, as pvs. V dry & dusty, awkwardly tannic. 14 mths older oak.

Bon Vino range

Dry Red ☺ ★★★ Smiling-faced quaffer; spicy, inviting, approachable; well-made, too.

Rosé Sweet [NEW] ★★ Gently sweet (30g/l RS) newcomer from cab & shiraz; touch herbal. **Dry White** ★★ Styled for easy-drinking pleasure; uncomplicated grassy wafts, refreshing acidity. Chenin, with 30% sauv, 20% riesling. **Semi-Sweet** ★★ As name implies, unpretentious grapey sipper; mainly chenin with crisp acidity from 30% sauv. All **NV**, in 500ml bottles & 2/5litre packs, bargain priced.— *CvZ,DB*

Bon Cap Organic Winery

T 023-626-1628 • **F** 023-626-1895

Robertson • Est 2001 • 1stB 2002 • Tasting & sales Mon-Fri 8-5 at winery; Sat, Sun & pub hols 10-4 at Bon Rouge Bistro • Fee R15 for groups of 10+ • Tours only by appt • Bistro/function/ conference centre serving meals Mon-Sun 8-5; evenings by appt • Guest house (self-catering & B&B by appt), weddings & conferences T 023-626-2073 • Farm produce • Facilities for children • Tour groups • Walks • Owner Roelf & Michelle du Preez/SHZ Winecellar (Pty) Ltd • Winemaker Jacques Conradie (2004) • Viticulturist Roelf du Preez • 45ha (cab, pinotage, shiraz) • 500t/21 000cs • 80% red 20% white • PO Box 356 Robertson 6705 • info@boncap.co. za • www.boncaporganic.co.za

This is SA's largest privately owned and internationally registered organic wine producer. Despite their success, with exports to 13 countries and stylish wine launches accomplished, this seventh-generation family still have their feet planted firmly on their sustainable soil. Growth from 5 000 cases in 2001 to the current 21 000 is attributable to Roelf du Preez's dedication in the vineyard, fine wine-making by Jacques Conradie, and Michelle du P's marketing and hospitality skills (the latter boosting a new wedding facility and guest house).

Bon Cap range

★★★★ **Cape Blend** [NEW] Bright, juicy blend pinotage, cab & petit v (42/33/25). **05** complex berry compote balanced by judicious oak (14 mths all-new Fr/Am); ripe savoury tannins persist to finish.
Cabernet Sauvignon ★★★★ Vivid blackcurrant & medicinal aromas on **06**, with well-extracted, compact fruit, balanced acidity & spicy, grippy tannins. 14 mths Fr/Am oak, 10% new. **Pinotage** ★★★★ Forthright smoky bacon notes overlie ripe, rich plum fruit in **06**, ensuring savoury finish. 14 mths Fr/Am oak. **Syrah** ★★★★ Exotic dark fruit & spiciness in **05**. Touch less concentration than **04**, with dry, spicy oak finish. 30% new/older Fr/Am oak, 16 mths.

Chardonnay ★★★★ Pale gold **06**, previewed last ed, more oak & lees character than fruit; soft citrus & oatmeal flavours with firm mineral finish. **Viognier** ★★★★ Abundant apricot, exotically spicy aromas. Bold wood flavours impart slightly phenolic finish perfectly suited to food.

The Ruins range

> **Pinotage** ☺ ★★★ **06** half-staved (Am), giving vanilla & juicy mulberry sweetness on entry; soft, pleasingly plummy finish. **Syrah-Cabernet Sauvignon** ☺ 🍷 ★★★ 60/40 blend of staved shiraz, unoaked cab; **06** balanced smoky, spicy blackberry flavours for easy & early drinking.

Rosé ★★★ **07** from free-run pinotage juice; sweet cherry aromas & sour plum flavours. 12.5% alc & screwcap ideal for picnics. **Sauvignon Blanc** ★★★ Stylishly packaged, zingy **06** from Tradouw vyds sold out. Next is 08. **Chardonnay-Viognier** ★★★ 75/25 unwooded blend in **07**. Peach, apricot aromas, broad, rich flavours & firm, brisk finish. **Sparkling Vin Sec** ★★ Claimed SA's first organic sparkling; frothy, spicy & fruity, ideal for off-dry cheer. — *IM*

Bon Courage Estate

T 023-626-4178 • **F** 023-626-3581

Robertson ▪ *Est 1927* ▪ *1stB 1983* ▪ *Tasting & sales Mon-Fri 8-5 Sat 9-3* ▪ *Restaurant Mon-Fri 9-4.30 Sat 9-3* ▪ *Closed Easter Fri & Dec 25* ▪ *Play area for children* ▪ *Owner/viticulturist André Bruwer* ▪ *Winemaker Jacques Bruwer* ▪ *150 ha* ▪ *Export brand: Three Rivers* ▪ *PO Box 589 Robertson 6705* ▪ *wine@boncourage.co.za* ▪ *www.boncourage.co.za*

The boom in the méthode cap classique market – 'We've had to up production by at least 30%,' observes Jacques Bruwer – has spurred more expansion here: a new, fully automated MCC cellar with a 300 000-plus bottle capacity will be used from this year's vintage. The Bruwers are enthusiastic participants in the Robertson Wine Valley's marketing initiatives: 'As an area, we must stand together and bring people in, not to just one big venue but on to private farms as well.'

★★★★ **Cabernet Sauvignon Inkará** Latest **05** softer, more fleshy version, similarly flavoured to pvs: mocha, dried prune, less cedar though. So seductively flavoured & well clad, vg structure goes unnoticed. 18-24 mths new Fr oak.

★★★★ **Shiraz Inkará 05** (★★★★★) ultra-ripe & -soft, also ultra-luxurious velvet tone & texture. So rich, almost like sipping liqueur, watch the 15% alc, tells tales about that ripe fruit. 18-24 mths Fr oak, all new. **04** was richly flavoured & complex as an Oriental rug.

★★★★★ **Cap Classique Jacques Bruére Brut Reserve Blanc de Blancs 04** (★★★★) younger than pvs **02** (no **03**) when reviewed, yet to develop complexity. Spiced peach aromas/flavours, soft acidity creates impression of slight sweetness, lovely. 10% oaked. On 2nd lees 36-60 mths, hand-riddled, 9 mths on cork before release for this, version below.

★★★★ **Cap Classique Jacques Bruére Brut Reserve** Pleasing toastiness & yeasty notes on **03**; supple & stylish. Pinot, chard in 60/40 blend. Made as Bl de Bl above.

★★★★ **Noble Late Harvest** Sumptuously sweet riesling dessert, with rapier fruit acid to balance. Following **02**, standout **04** (★★★★★) pvsly noted for its ethereal aromas/flavours, peaches & cream texture, racy finish. Next is **05**.

★★★★ **White Muscadel** Long history of excellence; wafting exotic tropical aromas in **06** (★★★★★), tangy sweet-sour tussle on palate - teasing & pleasing. Intricately wrought, one of few to show true complexity & excitement alloyed to sweetness. **05** was voluptuous & slow-moving.

Cabernet Sauvignon ★★★ Warm prune flavours on **05**, plumping sweetness reinforces impression of ripeness, though marginally more tannic than cellarmates. 12-15 mths Fr oak, 30% new. **Bruére Gold Reserve** In abeyance. **Pinotage** ★★★★ Latest **06** more serious; attractive oaking to black plum fruit, cellar's signature soft tannins allow drinking now. 18 mths Fr/Am oak, 30% new. NE. **Shiraz** ★★★ Baked prunes & leather on **05**, ripe tannins in estate's smooth, boneless style. 12-15 mths Fr oak, 30% new. **Chardonnay Prestige**

Cuvée ★★★☆ Barrel-matured version, 8 mths on lees in new to 3rd fill Fr oak. **06** subtle wood support to delicate peach, not showy or overdone, just gd drinking. **05** (★★★★) quieter, more reticent flavours. **Sauvignon Blanc** ★★★ Lipsmacking **07** more focused, gd varietal expression. Delicate greenpeppers, gooseberries, zippy acidity. **Blush Vin Doux** ★★ Uncomplicated sweet bubbly from red muscadel. Billowing muscat - fresh as a daisy. **NV**. NE. **Gewürztraminer Special Late Harvest** ★★★★ Last tasted was petally **06**, usual lilting sweet-sour music for the palate; 66g/l sugar, mere 12% alc. **Red Muscadel** ★★★★ Heartwarming **04** (sample, tasted last ed) combines elegance & pristine muscat flavours with sweet raisin character. **Vintage Port** ★★★ **05** proper vintage style: beefy/savoury rather than sweetly rich, distinctly dry, tannins have yet to yield, suggest waiting another few yrs. Discontinued: **Weisser Riesling Natural Sweet**.

Cabernet Sauvignon-Shiraz ☺ ★★☆ **05** v approachable, warm & welcoming flavours. 60/40 blend. **Chardonnay** ☺ 🍷 ★★☆ Unoaked **07**'s delicate peach flavours, appealing fleshy style & soft acidity make for casual summer drinking. Enjoy soon. **André's Fame** ☺ 🍷 ★★☆ Pvsly plain 'Colombard'. **07** curiously quiet, some rather distant ripe guavas, soft easy quaffer. Might pep up, given time. **Riesling** ☺ ★★☆ From Cape riesling, perennial favourite; amiable, soft & a welcome 11.5% alc together translate into perfect lunchtime companion. **Colombard-Chardonnay** ☺ 🍷 ★★☆ Recalls days when colombards were really dry! **07** terrific guava zestiness & freshness, slender middle filled out with curvy chard (30%).

Like Father Like Son range NEW

Merlot-Cabernet Sauvignon ☺ ★★☆ Generous ripeness not overdone, **06** beautifully balanced & approachable. 1litre bottle (as is white rangemate), great value! **Chenin Blanc-Colombard** ☺ ★★☆ Crisp dry & juicy, **07** loads fresh guava aromas/flavours. Another bargain.

Shiraz Rosé ★★ **07** (sample) charming orange-tinted rosé from shiraz. Semi-sweet & lightish at 12.5% alc. — *IvH*

Bonfoi Estate
T 021-881-3774 • F 021-881-3807

Stellenbosch ▪ Est 1699 ▪ 1stB 1974 ▪ Tasting & sales Mon-Fri 9-5 Sat 10-2.30 ▪ Fee R10, refunded with purchase ▪ Closed pub hols ▪ BYO picnic ▪ Walks ▪ Conservation area ▪ Owner/winemaker/viticulturist Johannes van der Westhuizen ▪ 101ha (cabs s/f, merlot, pinot, pinot meunier, pinotage, shiraz, chard, chenin, sauv, semillon) ▪ 700t/3 000cs own label 60% red 40% white ▪ PO Box 9 Vlottenburg 7604 ▪ bonfoi@mweb.co.za ▪ www.bonfoiwines.co.za

Johannes van der Westhuizen now bottles his wines on-site, and has planted pinot for the first time. The challenge, he says, is remaining adaptable enough to jump at new niche opportunities while holding on to existing markets by producing good-value wines.

- ★★★★ **Cabernet Sauvignon 04** back on form; interesting contrast to Ouverture, has the sharper focus, firmer (but surprisingly approachable) tannins of cab without the soft padding. Delicious. 18 mths Fr oak, 80% new.

- ★★★★ **Shiraz 04** another terrific vintage, sensitively handled; last ed we noted usual smoked beef aroma, here with peppery tang, fine dry tannins. Tasty & not too full bodied. For now & over 3-5 yrs.

- ★★★★ **Ouverture 04** maintains style & class of pvs; richly clad in deep-pile mulberry, disciplined by firm tannins & 18 mths Fr oak, 80% new. This vintage omits shiraz (as in **02**), now cab/merlot 80/20. No **03**.

Merlot ★★★ Attractive dark cassis/mulberry flavours, some mulberry leaf tones adding freshness on pvsly tasted **03**. Yr oak. **Chardonnay** ★★★★ **05** fuller & better balanced than pvs; some leesy richness to generous tangerine palate; integrated oaking (fermented/6 mths aged). **06** unready. NE. **Sauvignon Blanc** ★★★★ No successor to **06** sample, which offered usual balanced bounce, juicy curvaceousness. — *IvH*

■ **Bonne Esperance** *see KWV Limited*

Bonnievale Wine Cellar

T 023-616-2795 • F 023-616-2332

Robertson • Tasting & sales Mon-Fri 8-5 Sat & pub hols 10-1 • Closed Easter Fri-Mon, Dec 25/26 & Jan 1 • Owner 135 members • Winemaker Gerhard Swart, Esmarie Smuts, Simon Basson & Jolene Calitz-Le Roux • Viticulturist Willem Botha (consultant) • 1 771ha (15 varieties r/w) • 23 500t/60 000cs 25% red 75% white • PO Box 206 Bonnievale 6730 • office@bonnievalecellar.co.za • www.bonnievalecellar.co.za

The first year of operation, after members of the Merwespont, Nordale and Bonnievale wineries pooled their grapes towards the three Bonnievale ranges, went smoothly, says Henk Wentzel. Newcomers include a cab/shiraz blend, a semi-sweet - and a winemaker, newly-wed Jolene Calitz-le Roux, ex-Franschhoek Vineyards.

Vertex Reserve range
Cabernet Sauvignon ★★★★ Carefully made **04** on review showed ripe fruit & tannins with wild berries & hint of cedar from 50% new oak. **Shiraz** ★★★ Style change in **04**; trimmer oak, less alc, still plenty fruit, structure & interest noted pvsly. **Chardonnay** ★★★★ Last **05** was especially well-wooded, showing creamy lime-zest fruit & mineral texture.

Bonnievale range
Shiraz ★★★ Warmer vintage **05** has strawberry & plum perfume; nicely spiced; friendly & approachable. **Cabernet Sauvignon-Merlot** ★★★ Pvs ed showed upfront fruity exuberance; **04** 70/30 blend well-oaked. Enjoy soon. **Kelkierooi** ★★★ Lightish & quaffable unwooded **NV**; mix varieties. Warm ripe fruit, softly rounded body. **Chardonnay** ★★★ Pre-bottled **07** has appealing peach tones, light oaking, for drinking soon. **Sauvignon Blanc** ★★★ Sample **07** shows crunchy fresh pear & apple character, amicable 12.5% alc. **Kelkiewit** No new bottling tasted of this light & crisp summertime white. **NV**. **Sauvignon Blanc Brut** ★☆ Crisp, refreshing carbonated sparkling; **06** last time had fruit salad flavours. **Cape Vintage** ★★ **03**, last tasted was a winter warmer with charry notes. Discontinued: **Pik 'n Wyntjie**.

CCC range

Red ☺ ★★★ Cab, cab f & cinsaut in **06**, showing array red berries, juicy, approachable structure. Perfect braai wine.

White ★☆ **07** bone-dry, squeaky clean, refreshing mix chenin, colombard & chard. — CR

■ **Bon Vino** *see Boland Kelder*

Boplaas Family Vineyards

T 044-213-3326 • F 044-213-3750

Calitzdorp (see Klein Karoo map) • Est 1880 • 1stB 1982 • Tasting & sales Mon-Fri 8-5 Sat 9-3 • Fee R20 p/p for tour groups • Closed Easter Fri/Sun & Dec 25 • Tours by appt • Gifts • Ring of Rocks, Guinea Fowl Walking Trail • Owner/cellarmaster Carel Nel • Winemaker Morne Landman (Sept 2006) & Margaux Nel (Jan 2007) • Viticulturist Johannes Mellet (Vinpro) • 70 ha (cab, merlot, pinotage, shiraz, touriga, chard, sauv) • 35 000cs 50% red 45% white 5% blanc de noir • PO Box 156 Calitzdorp 6660 • boplaas@mweb.co.za • www.boplaas.co.za

Port-making doyen Carel Nel sees carbon footprinting as the next big issue for environmentalists and winegowers. He's proud of the fact that his winery has a negative footprint, thanks to the family's acquisition over the past decade of 2 200ha of pristine 'spekbos', which research shows absorbs 400kg of carbon dioxide a day. In addition, the Nels plan deliveries and maintain machinery to use fuel efficiently, and advocate the abolition of domestic animals like ostriches which damage the veld. A source of pride for Carel N is daughter Margaux's MSc - the subject for her thesis was touriga nacional; this year, she joins her father in the cellar.

Family Reserve range

★★★★ Pinotage Last was complex & supple yet slightly spiritous **02** (★★★☆). Creamy, banana-toned **01** should be reaching its peak.

★★★★ Shiraz 06 continues on higher quality trail blazed by **05**. Lively fruit still checked by firm ripe fruit tannins & oak (9 mths new Fr). Black pepper & tobacco wafts mingle with cool fruit tones from Bo-Langkloof vyds. Should reward gd few yrs cellaring.

★★★★ Ring of Rocks Pvsly 'Kuip & Clay', now named for circle of stones the Nels have placed on the farm to mark sun's journey through the sky. Youngberries & spice in tight tussle with firm tannins on **05** (★★★☆). Cab, merlot & touriga powerfully styled, now chunky/unknit; will need several yrs to open to full potential. **03** was commanding but not as overpowering as latest.

★★★★ Sauvignon Blanc ✓ Darling fruit's dusty minerality on **07** (sample) complements profusion herby green tones, asparagus, fig leaf & passionfruit flavours. Balancing zesty acidity & long slatey farewell; brimming with confidence.

Cabernet Sauvignon ★★★★ Generous cassis & dark choc on powerful (15%), well-toned, muscular **06**. Dry cedary tannin, slick fruity farewell. Bo-Langkloof grapes, yr oaked, 50% new. Notch up on less juicy, more tannic **05** (★★★★). **Shiraz-Cabernet Sauvignon ★★★★** Much improved **06** crosses the Old World/New World divide with rich cassis, spice & liquorice supported by supple tannins & integrated oaking (yr Fr, 50% new). Structure to gain complexity with bottle-age. **05** (★★★★) was perfumed & red-fruit-toned.

Boplaas range

★★★★★ Red Muscadel Vintner's Reserve Latest vintage a **75**. Tasted mid-2004 was complex, indulgent, with dried fruit finish, spirit addition integrated smoothly with fruit, tannins.

★★★★★ Cape Tawny Vintner's Reserve Port 80 last ed was poised & sedate after 15 yrs seasoning in old oak; nutty, with hints maraschino cherries, it was a pure delight. 100% tinta, 17.5% alc, 102g/l sugar.

★★★★★ Vintage Reserve Port Concentrated & viscous **05** from 60% tinta, touriga. Dense dark fruit, cassis & choc nuances, peppery grip from firm yet ripe tannin, integrated spirit (19%). Delicious now but should only be broached 5+ yrs hence, when it will have gained additional complexity. Wine (★★★★).

★★★★☆ CWG Auction Vintage Reserve Port Selection of best barrels, tiny quantities. **05** has similar density, powerful structure to **05** Vintage Reserve but richer, slightly sweeter. Orange peel hints to opulent fruit core, balanced, creamy, with persistent peppery farewell.

★★★★★ Cape Tawny Port ✓ Unctuous amber **NV** elixir from tinta b, wood matured 12 yrs. Complex, with nutty, caramel & choc/orange tones. Sleek, balancing candied peel tang & spirit (18.8%). Peter Schulz Trophy, Wine (★★★★), Best Tawny at TWS. Just keeps getting better.

★★★★ Cape Vintage Port Shy nose on tinta-led **05** followed by spicy fruit intensity; prunes & dark choc mesh with 18.4% alc, peppery finish. Sublime elegance & concentration. Wine (★★★★★), Peter Schulz Excellence Award.

★★★★ Cape Ruby Port Best-selling **NV** ruby, always in drier Douro style (±89g/l sugar, 18.5% alc). Souzão now solid partner in blend with tinta (60%), touriga (25%). Version tasted last ed's velvety fruit, integrated oak/alc made it super-sippable.

Cabernet Sauvignon ★★★ 06 takes step up with juicy cassis, pleasant minerality balanced by firm, ripe tannin. Food-friendly. **Merlot ★★★** Restrained, red-fruited **06** brushed by oak spice. Medium bodied, uncomplex BBQ red. **Tinta Barocca ★★★** Tightly knit, dry tannins rein in core of dark fruit on **06**; 'lovely with food,' says the team. **Touriga Nacional ★★★ 06** more understated than pvs; dark fruit centre currently muted but spicy finish very obvious & moreish. **Late Harvest ★★★** Light 11% alc ideal for lunchtime sipping. **06** last ed equal blend hanepoot/colombard had dried mango & muscat tones. **Ruby Light NEW ★★★** No new vintage of sweetie made for 'those who like port's flavours but not its alcs'. Last ed, maiden **NV** was plummy, slightly scrubby; 12.5% alc. **Hanepoot ★★★** Aromatic lemon syrup flavours, lively sherbet tang on **07** fortified dessert. 16% alc but light-footed - this tipple can dance!

Drink soon, over ice or ice-cream. **Muscadel Reserve ★★★★** Fans of this sweet fortified will bemoan the fact that no **05** was made. Last-tasted **04** had scintillating orange peel/lemon zest entry, syrupy finish (200g/l RS). **Red Dessert ★★★** Last ed, latest **NV** was 50/50 tinta/muscadel mix fortified to 16% alc; ambrosial choc-raisin, berry-toned sipper. **Late Bottled Vintage Option Port ★★★★** Last-tasted **93** spicily opulent, deliciously harmonious & balanced. Tinta, touriga, 4½ yrs Portuguese oak. 18.5% alc. **Cape White Port ★★★** From chardonnay, latest **NV** picks up the pace; nutty, sherry-like oxidative nuances balanced by zesty acidity, creamy mid-palate. Spirit well integrated. Yr older oak.

Pinotage ☺ ★★★ Variety's signature plums & spice on lively **06**. Balanced, fresh & quaffable. **Shiraz ☺ ★★★** 06's smooth tannin, bright fruit, medium body deliver early accessibility. By contrast, Tinta & Touriga below will gain complexity & integration from 2-3 yrs aging. **Dry Red ☺ ★★★** Unwooded **NV** blend shiraz, pinotage, cab & merlot invariably slips down easily. Enjoy young. **Blanc de Noir ☺ ★★** 07 unassuming, gently off-dry aperitif with refreshing savoury farewell. **Rosé ☺ ★★** 07 combo pinotage & shiraz bursts with red-fruit joviality & gluggability, courtesy zesty acidity. **Chardonnay Unwooded ☺ ★★** Yellow peach aromas/flavours, piercing citrus finish to party-starter **07**. Quaff this summer. **Sauvignon Blanc ☺ ★★★** 07 flavoursome tropical & herbaceous mix, slender 11.8% alc ideal for summer tippling. **Classic Dry White ☺ 🍽 ★★** 07 blends chard & sauv for a plumpish, placid & gently aromatic quaffer. **Pinot Noir Sparkling ☺ ★★★** 07 refreshing anytime bubbly with gentle savoury red-fruited flavours, dusty cinnamon finish. Nod from Wine's Good Value guide. **Sweet Sparkling ☺ ★★** Pinotage & muscat melange gives scented appeal, sweetish touch to tail. **NV. Muscadel ☺ ★★★** 07 raises the bar, enters the mouth like liquid raisins, exits lemon-fresh thanks to tangy acidity. Over crushed ice, makes a delightful aperitif. — MW

Borg Family Wines `[NEW]`
T 021-863-2492

Coastal ▪ Est 2004 ▪ 1stB 2005 ▪ Visits by appt ▪ Home-cooked gourmet dinners by appt ▪ Owner Jeremy & Emma Borg ▪ Winemaker Jeremy Borg (Dec 2004) ▪ 18t/350cs 95% red 5% white ▪ PO Box 1483 Suider Paarl 7624 ▪ info@borgfamilywines.com ▪ www.borgfamilywines.com

After years of working in cellars in the US, UK and locally, the dreams of Jeremy Borg and professional photographer wife Emma became reality in 2004, but not without some challenges. Balancing winemaking here and retaining overseas jobs was tricky. In 2006 they returned for good and found a cellar in Simondium which they're still kitting out. The 07 Viognier was made in bins filled with frozen bottles of water replenished daily from their freezer. Plans are to extend and upgrade the facilities for the next vintage.

Pinotage ★★★★ 07 still in oak (50% new) mid-2007, so rating provisional. Soft, round tannins & chocolatey dark fruit; extra spice from 10% shiraz. Swtland grapes. **Shiraz ★★★** 06 from Sbosch, with 10% cab; peppery, Asian spice-loaded fruit now dominated by oak (40% new, half Am), giving coconutty, drying finish. **Painted Wolf ★★★** 07 sample of blended shiraz, pinotage, merlot, t amarela, viognier; ex-barrel shows mulberries, bitter choc. Gd concentration, some creaminess. Tentative rating. **Viognier ★★★★** Sample 07 (from the one sold-oak barrel made!) has floral, apricot tones wih gd mineral expression. Unirrigated Mlmsbry vyd. Rating provisional. — JPf

---

Boschendal Wines
T 021-870-4200 ▪ F 021-874-1531

Franschhoek ▪ Est 1685 ▪ 1stB 1976 ▪ Tasting & sales daily May-Oct 9-4.30 Nov-Apr 10-6.30 ▪ Fee R15 for 5 wines ▪ Closed Easter Fri, May 1, Jun 16 & Dec 25 ▪ Tours (vyd & cellar in minibus) 10.30, 11.30 & 3 by appt ▪ Restaurants & picnics ▪ Tour groups ▪ Gifts ▪ Conservation area ▪ Museum visits 9.30-5 ▪ Owner DGB ▪ Cellarmaster JC Bekker (Oct 1996) ▪ Winemaker Lizelle Gerber (whites, 2006) & James Farquharson (reds, 2004), with Lionel Leibbrandt (1999) ▪ Viticulturist Stephan Joubert (since 2006) ▪ 200ha (cabs s/f, merlot, shiraz, chard, sauv) ▪ 3

600t/250 000cs 40% red 44% white 14% rosé 2% sparkling ▪ *ISO 9001 & 14001 certified* ▪ *Pvt Bag X03 Groot Drakenstein 7680* ▪ *cellardoor@dgb.co.za* ▪ *www.boschendalwines.com*

Boschendal, with roots in the 17th century, got the contemporary nod from Russian President Vladimir Putin, who was treated to a private tasting and lunch accompanied by the flagship 1685 range. This estate, once part-owned by Cecil John Rhodes, celebrates the empire-builder in its handcrafted Cecil John range, which has shiraz and sauvignon as its focus varieties. Recently acquired by DGB, Boschendal is undergoing a rejuvenation under chief winemaker JC Bekker, Lizelle Gerber (ex-Bellingham) and James Farquharson; viticulturist Stephan Joubert; and marketing manager Wynand van Schalkwyk. Future developments include a return of the popular Boschendal Brut as well as a new Rosé Cap Classique. The property is famous for its exquisite grounds – the perfect place for one of their gourmet picnics, traditional buffet meals or country-style teas.

Cecil John Reserve range

★★★★ **Shiraz** Named for Boschendal founder. Surpassing maiden **03**, **04** (★★★★) is gorgeous; interleaved with ceps, creamy dark plums, prosciutto, a basket of spices. Silky texture but 27 mths oaking promises good future.

★★★★ **Sauvignon Blanc** Last ed saw first release; previewed **06** captured capsicum, grapefruit, leafy minerality from cool growing conditions; tastebuds were alive with steely acidity, seeking food.

Reserve Collection

★★★★ **Cabernet Sauvignon** Elegantly styled red. Last ed **03** was brooding, dark, with cassis peeping through, but tannins, though ripe, masked true potential. Needed another yr, cellar 8+ more.

★★★★★ **Shiraz** Opulent dark fruit, liquorice & campfire smoke, **04** is a hedonist's delight. Accessible, curvaceous, heaps of flavour & just enough tannin structure to remain serious. 19 mths mainly seasoned oak. **03** (★★★★) was opulent, rounded & fleshy but earlier maturing.

★★★★★ **Grand Reserve** Bdx varieties led by cab f, some shiraz. Impressive **04** is powerhouse of cassis & spice, hint of mint, already seduces with interwoven fine tannins, ultra-long finish. Has 6+ yr future. Fr/Am 20 mnths, third new. **03** (★★★★) was still tightly buttoned on review mid-2006, needed time.

Sauvignon Blanc ★★★★ Unshowy, refined **06** has intriguing layers of fynbos, nettle & lemongrass, satisfyingly smooth, tangy texture. Perfect oyster, shellfish match.

1685 range

★★★★ **Brut** Vintaged MCC from pinot, chard. Last-tasted **99** disgorged Jan 2003 (date on label). Biscuit/brioche bouquet presaged almost decadently rich but well-balanced palate offering strawberry & ripe apple notes.

Shiraz ★★★☆ Admirable restraint in warm vintage, **05** has smoked beef, dried herb & black pepper styling, lithe tannins promising 3/4 yr future. Gd food wine. 50% Faure fruit. **Shiraz-Cabernet Sauvignon** ★★★★ Well-suited partnership in just off-dry **05**, with dark fruit, smoky aromatics from shiraz, firm foundation ex-cab, all nicely integrated & tasty. **Chardonnay** ★★★★ Appealing savoury biscuit slant to **06**'s citrus character, designed with food in mind, reinforced by lovely zesty acidity. **Sauvignon Blanc Grand Vin Blanc** ★★★★ 'Grand Cuvée' internationally. Bursting with freshness, **07**'s quivering lime & gooseberry tones, racy acidity stimulate the tastebuds, cry out for food. Dab semillon. Nudges next level. **Chardonnay-Pinot Noir** ★★★★ Fruit remains main focus in **07**, fresh peach, strawberry, with portion older barrel fermentation/lees contact adding texture, savoury nuances. 70/30 blend.

Boschendal Favourites

Lanoy ★★★★ Tasty big-volume oaked blend, named for 17th century part owner. Bdx in **95**, minty red berries, robust but drinking smoothly. Yr seasoned barrels. **Blanc de Noir** ★★★ Pale cerise colour from red all-sorts, **07** shows gd fruit purity, light texture (12% alc) & quaffability for which it's famous. Just off-dry. **Chenin Blanc** ★★★★ From 27 yr old bushvines, giving fruit concentration. Intriguing earthy note in **07**, with melon, peach, usual satisfyingly full body, gd length. **Blanc de Blanc** ★★★ Easy drinking 80/20 chenin/chard blend, **07** is simpler than pvs, a fruit basket of summer flavours, friendly appeal. **Le Bouquet** ★★★ Aromatic off-dry blend. With muscat, sauv, chenin, **07** continues in same mould: tropical fruit, floral notes, nicely flavourful experience.

The Pavillion range

> **Blanc** ☺ ★★★ All-sorts blend **07** has exhuberant peach flavours, plenty crisp appetite appeal.

Shiraz-Cabernet Sauvignon ★★★ Offering best of both partners, **06** shows shiraz dark fruit, cab structure. Seasoned oak; could age few yrs. **Rosé** ★★★ Light-hearted red-mix quaffer. Last ed **06** had cranberry/fruitgum tones, rounded mouthfeel from touch sugar. Discontinued: **Rouge**, **The Grand Pavillion**. — *CR*

Boschheim

T 021-808-3175 · F 021-886-4731

Stellenbosch · 1stB 2003 · Visits by appt · Owner/winemaker Andy Roediger · 900cs 90% red · PO Box 3202 Matieland 7602 · ahar@sun.ac.za

A year of graduations for polymer scientist Andy Roediger: from wine student to qualified Cape Wine Master; from garagiste-style facilities to a full-fledged winery currently producing some 13 000 bottles; and from red-only producer to 'really chuffed' maker of a viognier and a verdelho, both still in barrel, along with a new red blend from a vineyard near Anwilka.

Cabernet Sauvignon ★★★★ Already approachable **05** nudges next class. Ripe & generous, warm baked plum fruit, tannins to match. **Ella Marie** NEW ★★★ Attractive, accessible & stylish blend cab, shiraz, merlot (71/20/9). **06** well-judged black cherry & choc flavours, unobtrusive structure. **Elemental** ★★★★ Last tasted **05** shiraz, laced with splash viognier, pervasively spicy, hints bramble & liquorice. — *IvH*

Boschkloof

T 021-881-3293 (office); 021-881-3268 (cellar) · F 021-881-3032

Stellenbosch · Est/1stB 1996 · Tasting & sales by appt only Mon-Fri 8-6 (sales 8-5) Sat 8-1 · Tours by appt · Owner Reenen Furter & Jacques Borman · Winemaker Jacques Borman · Viticulturist Reenen Furter · 19ha (cabs s&f, merlot, shiraz, chard) · jborman@adept.co.za · www.boschkloof.co.za

It has taken Jacques Borman eleven years to release a flagship wine - hence 'Conclusion'. His holy grail (reflected on the label) is a special wine made in limited quantities with as little human interference as possible. The potential of Rhône varieties in the Cape is inevitably drawing his attention. Meanwhile his youngest son keeps him on his toes with wine-related calls from Elsenburg.

★★★★   **Syrah** Considerable power within svelte frame. **05** (★★★★★) demurely scented, intensely spiced & superbly structured. Breathtaking balance & echoing length - delicious. Like generous **04**, 14.7% alc. 50:50 native/Rhône yeasts, 15 mths in cask, mainly Fr.

★★★★   **Cabernet Sauvignon-Merlot** Stylish 2:1 blend. **05** (★★★★) tight, dark & smoky, very firm finish. **04** showed choc-vanilla sheen to plum fruits with coffee interest. 17 mths Fr oak.

★★★★   **Conclusion 04** previewed pvs ed not released, now bottled blend (56/20/14/10 cab s, merlot, shiraz, cab f) re-tuned to proprietors' satisfaction. Densely coloured & fruited, the beauty's in the balance; a classicists delight (despite 15% alc). All new oak 2 yrs.

★★★★   **Five Acres Shiraz-Viognier** Tad more boisterous than Syrah. **04** burly, ripe black fruit buffed by fragrant blending partner; imposing 15.7% alc tethers jostling tannins. Own shiraz, Darling viognier, natural ferment in oak. Not revisited this ed.

Cabernet Sauvignon ★★★★ Won't win shows but delights with restraint. **04** svelte, textured; blackcurrant fruit woven into tannic trellis. 19 mths Fr oak. No **03**. **Merlot** ★★★★ **04**

stamped with cellar's class; plush nutty fruit in lilting balance with muscle-toned structure. 19 mths used wood. No **03**. **Chardonnay ★★★★** Unflashy, rich & complex. **07** more fruity than pvs, still with gravitas. 4 mths seasoned Fr oak. — *DS*

Boschrivier
T 023-347-3313/2 • **F** 023-342-2215

Kleinrivier (see Elgin/Walker Bay map) • Est 1997 • 1stB 2002 • Tasting by appt (T 028-341-0630, 072-208-6572 - Louise van der Merwe) • Owner Theo de Villiers • Winemaker Mike Dobrovic (Mulderbosch) • Viticulturist Johan van der Merwe • 14ha (cab, shiraz) • 367cs 100% red • 70 Fairbairn Str, Worcester, 6850 • drnjtdevilliers@mweb.co.za • www.boschrivier.co.za

If it's true that vines are like children, then paediatrician Theo de Villiers has had good training for this shiraz-only label (with cab planned for sometime in the future). Meanwhile, the old farmhouse on the property is being renovated to offer public tastings in 2008.

Shiraz ★★★★ Taking a step up, **04** shows salty liquorice, prosciutto & macerated dark plum styling with silky smooth lines; designed for drinking pleasure. All-new Fr oak fully integrated. **03** (★★★★) was ultra-ripe, warm & chunky. — *CR*

■ **Boschveld** *see Baarsma Wine Group*

Bosman Family Vineyards
T 021-873-3170 • **F** 021-873-2517

Wellington (see Paarl map) • Est 1699 • 1stB 2004 • Visits by appt • Owner Jannie Bosman • Cellarmaster Petrus Bosman • Winemaker Corlea Fourie • Viticulturist Pierre Carstens & Heinie Nel • 250ha (cab, chenin) • 120t/8 500cs own label 85% red 15% white • PO Box 9 Wellington 7654 • info@bosmanwines.com • www.bosmanwines.com

A 50-year-old dream became reality last year when the restored and modernised cellar on the Bosman property, Lelienfontein, crushed the first harvest from family vineyards. Inspired by a grandfather's winemaking tales, and supported by the growth of Lelienfontein Vinegrowers - one of the largest vine nurseries in SA - Petrus Bosman Jnr is focusing on a limited number of high-end wines. The flagship Cab is joined by an unusual 07 blend of shiraz, mourvèdre, primitivo (zinfandel) and viognier, named Adama after the forebear of many of the workers on the farm, and by a pair of **07** Chenins, one from 50-year-old bushvines and branded Optenhorst. All but the Cab were too young at press time to rate realistically.

Cabernet Sauvignon ★★★ **05** classic cassis & leafy nuances with firm tannic grip. Riper style, needs (& will benefit from) time to knit. — *MW*

■ **Bosman's Hill** *see Saxenburg*

Botha Wine Cellar
T 023-355-1740/789 • **F** 023-355-1615

Breedekloof (see Worcester map) • Est 1949 • 1stB 1974 • Tasting & sales Mon-Fri 8-5 Sat 10-1 • Closed Easter Fri/Sun, Dec 25 & Jan 1 • Tours by appt • BYO picnic • Facilities for children • Tour groups • Conservation area • Owner 71 members • Cellarmaster Gerrit van Zyl (Nov 2006) • Winemaker Johan Linde & Michiel Visser (Nov 1996/1999), with Pierre Hugo & Cobus Brink • Viticulturist Hennie Visser • 1 880ha • 30 000t 35% red 65% white • PO Box 30 Botha 6857 • admin@bothakelder.co.za

There's fresh energy here, generated by new manager Gerrit van Zyl and a reshuffled team. On the drawing board are new wine labels and a trimming of the range. Dassie Smith has retired but fans will be pleased to note that Dassie's Rood will live on in new livery, partnered by a Dassie's White.

Dassie's Reserve range
Cabernet Sauvignon ★★★ Gd fresh bouquet plum & caramel on **03**, crisp dark fruit, charming cherry finish. **Merlot ★** Old leather & baked fruit on **04**, lifted by firm tannins, inkling of fruit on finish. **Pinotage ★** Volatile & oxidative tones on **03** completely mask varietal

character. **Shiraz** ★★★ Shy **04**, firm, restrained red berry fruit & prominent tannins. **Sauvignon Blanc** ★★ Upfront sauv lime & herbaceousness on **07**, simple light palate, slightly high acid.

Botha range

> **Late Bottled Vintage Port** ☺ ★★★ Toasty caramel, coffee & plum on **04**; sweet ripe entry, full & quite sumptuous, nice brandy-spirit finish. Great fireplace aid.

Merlot ★★ Plummy **06** with herbaceous note, smoky/charry slightly green flavours. **Pinotage** ★★ Dry banana & earthy touch on **06**, youthful & vibrant flavours. **Dassie's Rood** 🗎 ★★ Winery's top seller; fresh & fruity **06** hits the spot for everyday drinking. **Dassie's Blanc** 🗎 ★★ Pvsly 'Blanc de Blanc'. **07** pungent tropical tones, gd flavours, decent weight. **Red Jerepigo** ★★ Interesting **04**, red berry & intriguing chilli-tomato relish note; balanced; ideal with the cheese platter. **Hanepoot Jerepigo** ★★★ Honeyed **04**, slightly herbal, simple but satisfying. — *CvZ, JP*

Bottelary Hills Wines
T 021-903-6286 ▪ F 021-906-1553

Stellenbosch ▪ Est/1stB 2003 ▪ Tasting & sales at Bottelary Wine Centre, T 021-865-2955 Mon-Sat 9-7 Sun 9-5 (closed Dec 25) & cellars mentioned below ▪ Owner Bottelary Hills Wines (Pty) Ltd ▪ 70% red 30% white ▪ PO Box 42 Koelenhof 7605 ▪ goede@adept.co.za ▪ www.bottelaryhills.co.za

This is a joint-venture brand for six family farms, Bellevue, Goede Hoop, Groenland, Kaapzicht, Sterhuis and Mooiplaas, which provide selected wines for blending and venues for tasting (sales also at Bottelary Hills Wine Centre at Koelenhof). In a new BEE deal, a third of the profits will go to farmworkers.

Bottelary Hills range
Shiraz 03 available but not tasted. **Cabernet Sauvignon-Pinotage 01** not reviewed.

M23 range
Cabernet Sauvignon-Merlot 02 untasted. **Rhapsody** 🗎 ★ Dry, leathery **06**, all-sorts red blend. **Sauvignon Blanc** 🗎 ★★★★ Capsicum, gooseberry & ripe fig hit all the right notes; **07** tangy, lovely concentration, long finish; really good. **Limerick** 🗎 ★★ 50/50 blend sauv, chenin; **07** straightforward & dry. — *IvH*

Bottelary Winery
T 021-865-2781 ▪ F 021-865-2780

Stellenbosch ▪ Tasting & sales Mon-Fri 8-5.30 Sat 9-1 ▪ Closed Easter Fri & Sat, Dec 25 & Jan 1 ▪ Tours by appt ▪ Light meals during office hours ▪ Private functions after-hours/weekends by appt ▪ Facilities for children ▪ Winemaker Ewald Kellerman & Pieter Carstens (both 2004), with Carla Myburgh (Dec 2005) ▪ Viticulturist Callie Coetzee (2007) ▪ ±3 000t from contract vyds ▪ 100 000cs 48% red 48% white 4% rosé ▪ Also exported as Rocco Bay ▪ PO Box 214 Paarl 7620 ▪ info@bottelary.com

One of the oldest cellars in the Bottelary area, this winery's new labels indicate that it's keeping pace with the times. Visitors can take advantage of personalised wine tastings, and light meals around a cosy fireplace in winter or under umbrellas on the verandah in summer. The venue is also available for small functions.

Reserve range
Cabernet Sauvignon ★★★★ No newer versions tasted of any in this range. Last **03** was modern yet elegant, combining fruit-richness with restraint & seriousness. **Merlot** ★★★★ Supple tannins underpinned **02**, imparting backbone to ripe fruit & platform for development. **Pinotage** ★★★★ **02** polished performance; delicious black cherry fruit, elegant dry tannins. **Shiraz** ★★★ **02** ripe red fruit firmly supported by savoury tannins, twist liquorice in tail. Gd potential.

Bottelary range

Cabernet Sauvignon 🗔 ★★★ **06** attractive mulberry ripeness, rounded & fleshy, no cab austerity, ripe tannins. Pdberg vyds for this, most below. **Merlot** NEW 🗔 ★★★ **06** delicate black cherry note, softish tannins & gd dry finish. **Pinotage** NEW 🗔 ★★ Understated raspberry & redcurrant on **06**, with variety's unsubtle tannins. **Shiraz** 🗔 ★★ Not patch on pvs; little varietal character & powerful tannins on **06**. **Cabernet Sauvignon-Merlot** 🗔 ★★ pleasing dryness, merlot portion lends softer tannins for accessible quaffing. **Cinsaut-Shiraz** ★★★ No newer vintage available; **03** was jovial & lively 70/30 blend. **Classic Red** NEW 🗔 ★★ Not quite dry red **06**; cab, shiraz, cinsaut blend; plummy with soft tannins. **Chenin Blanc Dry** 🗔 ★★★ **06** last ed was light & fruit-driven with ripe guava flavours. **Semi Sweet** NEW 🗔 ★★ **06** delightful tropical-tinged & balanced sweetie from chenin. **Sauvignon Blanc** ★★★ Untasted. **Tropical White** NEW 🗔 ★★ Pears & apples on light-bodied blend, **06** with firm acidity. **Smooth Red** NEW 🗔 ★★ Lightish feel & flavour, semi-sweet (17.8g/l sugar), **06** grapes as for Classic Red. Screwcaps for most in this range. **Hanepoot** ★★★ No follow-up for grapey **05**, with ripe & balanced sweetness.

Rocco Bay range

Pinotage Not tasted. **Soft Smooth Red** ★★ Pvs **NV** a crowd-pleaser; sweet & undemanding, with wild berry flavours. **Rosé** No new vintage tasted. — IvH

Bouchard Finlayson

T 028-312-3515 • F 028-312-2317

Walker Bay (see Elgin/Walker Bay map) ▪ Est 1989 ▪ 1stB 1991 ▪ Tasting & sales Mon-Fri 9-5 Sat 9.30-12.30 ▪ Fee R20 for groups of 8+ ▪ Closed pub hols ▪ Owner Bouchard Finlayson (Pty) Ltd ▪ Winemaker/viticulturist Peter Finlayson ▪ 17ha (pinot, nebbiolo, sangiovese, chard, sauv) ▪ 180t/12 000cs 20% red 80% white ▪ PO Box 303 Hermanus 7200 ▪ info@ bouchardfinlayson.co.za ▪ www.bouchardfinlayson.co.za

Peter Finlayson is more enamoured than ever with his beloved pinot noir. 'I have maintained that pinot is like opera. When it is great it is pure seduction, almost hedonistic. Most of all, like opera, there is no middle road' Finlayson's fascination and experience with this grape's delicate ways has made Bouchard Finlayson an A-list producer, and one of the keys that's unlocked the Hemel-en-Aarde Valley's great potential - not only for pinot. Internationally, fans of his wines may well include opera buffs, but sports heroes like them too - witness his invitation to hold a tasting at American Football coaching legend Don Shula's Steakhouse at Miami's Alexander Hotel.

★★★★☆ **Galpin Peak Pinot Noir** Burgundy-inspired leading Cape pinot, **05** with complex notes choc/mocha-dusted black fruit & forest floor. Broad & powerful, with concentrated flavours, vibrating spice & minerals in lengthy finish. Expert use of oak (30% new, 10 mths).

★★★★★ **Tête de Cuvée Galpin Peak Pinot Noir** Cellarmaster's (stellar!) barrel selection in best yrs only (pvs was **03**). **05**, our Wine of the Year this ed, precise aromas of sour cherries & blood orange underlined by spicy oak. Immense, concentrated & penetrating flavours are powerful without excessive weight. Silky finish made complex with mineral note. Needs & deserves time in bottle to fully integrate 75% new Fr oak.

★★★★ **Hannibal** Red berries & floral tones on well-balanced **05** combo sangiovese, pinot, nebbiolo, barbera, shiraz. Delicately built, with vibrant acidity, silky tannins, ending with cool mineral undertone. 16 mths Fr oak, 30% new.

★★★★ **Kaaimansgat Chardonnay** 'Crocodile's Lair' the cool Vllrsdorp source of fruit, fermented/8 mths Fr oak (30% new). **06** has vibrant limy, floral notes & mineral backbone, but needs time to integrate butterscotch & hazelnut flavours. Classic: nothing overpowers; a great food partner.

★★★★ **Kaaimansgat Chardonnay Limited Edition** Same source as above, but different handling for **04** (not retasted). Only half 8 mths in oak, giving clear peach/pear flesh, with nutty breadth from time in bottle.

★★★★ **Missionvale Chardonnay** Flagship white from home grapes. **06** (★★★★★) has ripe pear character, complicated by fig, toast. Mineral palate, superbly balanced &

integrated oak (25% new Fr, 7 mths); nothing flashy or obvious: a gran signor of a wine, with (even) more elegance & graceful power than complex, persistent **05**.

★★★★ **Sans Barrique Chardonnay** Unoaked version, with 5 mths lees ageing. After quieter **05** (★★★☆), burgundy-like organic funkiness on **06**, with green pear & wet stone aromas. Mid-2007 bit closed on palate, but lime notes & refreshing acidity augur well. WO Ovrberg.

Sauvignon Blanc ★★★☆ Sample **07** has cool-climate crispness, notes of grapefruit & granadilla; lithe body with vibrant mineral finish. **Blanc de Mer** ★★★☆ Riesling leads **07** blend with peachy tangerine, plus aromatic viognier, sauv zestiness, chenin depth: great drinking fun. WO W Cape. — *JPf*

Bouwland �
T 021-865-2226 • F 021-865-2227

Stellenbosch • Est 1996 • 1stB 1997 • Tasting & sales at Beyerskloof • Owner Bouwland Deelnemings Trust & Beyerskloof • Winemaker Beyers Truter, with Anri Truter (1997/2004) • Viticulturist Johan Pienaar (2003, consultant) • 40ha (cab, merlot, pinotage) • 360 tons 30 000cs 100% red • PO Box 62 Koelenhof 7605 • bouwland@adept.co.za

Currently using Koelenhof's wine cellar, Bouwland has plans for a tasting room, bottling plant and warehouse on its own premises, and is also planning to increase its product range to include a Chenin and a Shiraz blend. Ebullient winemaker Beyers 'Mr Pinotage' Truter helps keep Bouwland's products front and centre both nationally and abroad.

Cabernet Sauvignon-Merlot ★★★☆ Gently firm tannins, light oak supporting gd fruit make **04** an engaging, well made blend which should win friends with its honest decency. **Cabernet Sauvignon-Merlot Reserve** ★★★☆ Richer, fuller version of above **04**, more focused berry fruit; touch more structure & wood. Both lovely when reviewed last ed but should keep gd few yrs. **Chenin Blanc** In abeyance. — *TJ*

■ **Bovlei Valley Retreat** *see Dunstone Winery*

Bovlei Winery
T 021-873-1567, 021-864-1283 • F 021-864-1483

Wellington (see Paarl map) • Est 1907 • Tasting & sales Mon-Fri 8.30-5 Sat 8.30-12.30 Non-religious pub hols 9-4.30 • Olive & grape seed products • Owner 38 members • Cellarmaster Jacques Theron • Production manager Frank Meaker • Viticulturist Dawie le Roux (consultant) • 920ha • 8000t/7m liters 52% red 48% white • PO Box 82, Wellington, 7654 • merlene@ bovlei.co.za • www.bovlei.co.za

The second-oldest co-op in SA celebrated 100 years of winemaking in late 2007 with the release of their Centennial wines. The winery, in the foothills of the Hawequa Mountains, is a deservedly popular destination, with a range of fun- and food-related activities: try, for example, the annual harvest festival and the 45km quad bike trail.

The Centennial range
★★★★ **Shiraz-Mourvèdre** Scrubby **06**, 60/40 blend, meets std set by pvs but is more sedate, with 'lower' 14% alc (vs 15%). Exceptionally persistent, allowing pepper, lily, dark plum notes to mingle with gentle oak nuances. Worth cellaring.
Cabernet Sauvignon ★★★☆ Tasted last ed, **05** was pliable & succulent but boisterous, with choc-lavender hints, needing bottle-ageing to settle. **Merlot** ★★★☆ Long espresso-tinged finish on complex, plummy **05**, tasted pvsly. **Zinfandel-Pinotage** ★★★☆ Vibrant newcomer with charming strawberry/mulberry fruit & vanilla edges from 15% new oak. Nicknamed 'ZinPin'.

Bovlei range
Merlot ★★★ **06** more 'red wine' than 'merlot', still gd everyday tipple; fresh, whisper of tannin, hint alc on finish. **Pinotage** ★★ Firm, modest **06**. Some varietal character on nose but more tannin than fruit on taste. **Grand Rouge** ★★★ No new wine since **04**; was 10% shiraz plus equal portions merlot & cabs/f. Easy-going, smooth. **Chardonnay** ★☆ **06** plays hide &

seek; white asparagus & mango nuances waft in & out, to zippy finish. **Sauvignon Blanc** ★★ Sample **07** light in body & flavour, zinging freshness, faint ocean spray scent. **Beaukett** ★★ Lightish, gently sweet party-starter (12% alc, 12g/l RS). **NV** blend chenin, colombard & muscat. **Port** ★★ New bottling of ruby-style fortified ups alc from 15.3% on pvs to 17%; remains undemanding with plump fruit & soft tannins. **NV**. Discontinued: **Pinotage Rosé, Bukettraube.**

Cabernet Sauvignon ☺ ★★★ **06** gd restaurant option, well fruited with long oaky goodbye. **Shiraz** ☺ ★★★ Step up for **06** with solid red berry core, firm tannins, lengthy & balanced farewell. Spiced up with 8% mourvèdre. **Chenin Blanc** ☺ ★★★ Change from fruity **06** to steely **07**; light flavour, vibrant acidity make for early quaffing with food. — *CvZ*

■ **Bowe Joubert**   *see Beau Joubert Vineyards & Winery*
■ **Bradgate**   *see Jordan Winery*
■ **Brahms**   *see Domaine Brahms Wineries*

Bramon Wines

T 044-534-8007 • F 044-534-8007

Plettenberg Bay • Est 2000 • 1stB 2004 • Visits Tue-Sun 11-sunset • Fee R25 (full glass) • Closed Dec 25 • Light lunches • Gifts • Cheeses • Owner Private company • Winemaker Pieter Ferreira, with Irene Waller (Graham Beck Wines) • Vineyard Manager Peter Thorpe • 5ha (sauv) • 100% white • PO Box 1606 Plettenberg Bay 6600 • peter@bramonwines.co.za • www.bramonwines.co.za

Plans are being drawn up for a cellar at this Plettenberg Bay sparkling wine boutique, which has elephants for neighbours (it adjoins a sanctuary). Their lunches are proving very popular, leading to restaurant extensions, and a wellness centre is planned, 'except that here we will not starve you!'

Cap Classique ★★ Brut-style MCC from sauv; short-lived mousse on flinty **06**; refreshing steeliness & wet pebble character. — *MM*

■ **Brampton**   *see Rustenberg Wines*

Brandvlei Cellar

T 023-340-4215 • F 023-340-4332

Worcester • Est 1955 • 1stB 1956 • Tasting & sales Mon-Thu 7.30-5.30 Fri 7.30-4.30 • Closed pub hols • Tours & group tastings by appt • Owner 32 members • Winemaker Jean le Roux, with Jandré Human & Tertius Jonck • Viticulturist Danie Conradie (2004) • 1 400ha (13 varieties r/w) • 10 000cs own label 20% red 75% white 5% jerepiko • PO Box 595 Worcester 6849 • brandvlei@breede.co.za • www.brandvlei.co.za

Hard at work behind the scenes at this Best Value Cellar (according to Wine magazine's latest Best Value tastings – their Ruby Cab-Merlot scoring a perfect 10), viticulturist Danie Conradie is excited about plans to expand the BC range to include a rosé after a successful trial run in 2007. 'We're also upgrading the tasting room to ensure a convivial experience, and planning a revamp of the front-labels.'

BC range

Cabernet Sauvignon ★★ Last ed, light-textured **NV** showed sturdy tannins, some berry fruit, touch earthiness. **Ruby Cabernet-Merlot** ★ **06** sweet upfront fruit but gritty dry finish. **Chardonnay** ★★ Bruised apples with soft, creamy finish, **07** pleasant drinking. Unwooded. **Chenin Blanc** ★★★ Step-up **07** has bright green apple notes; punchy, crisp & lively. **Bacchanté** ★★ **07** off-dry chenin quaffer with tropical fruit & waxy texture. **Sauvignon Blanc** ★★★ Picked young for freshness, **07** intense gooseberries & steely finish, ups the ante on pvs. **Hanepoot Jerepiko** ★★ Straightforward sweet & grapey, **07** hot, spicy finish. — *RP*

■ **Bredell's** *see* JP Bredell Wines

■ *Brederode* *see* Groupe LFE South Africa

■ *Breede Valley Wines* *see* Wedgewood Wines

Brenthurst Winery

T 021-863-1154/1375 · F 021-424-5666

Paarl · Est 1993 · 1stB 1994 · Open to public only by special appt · Owner José Jordaan · Winemaker José Jordaan with advisers · Viticulturist Johan Wiese (1991, consultant) · 5ha (cabs s/f, merlot, petit v) · 50-70t · PO Box 6091 Paarl 7622

Advocate José Jordaan was introduced to winemaking by two good friends, viticultural consultant Johan Wiese and winemaker Charles Hopkins (De Grendel). 'It started as a hobby but you've got to work a lot harder in the wine industry these days!' But he still enjoys making his bordeaux-style blend (not tasted this edition), mostly for export to Holland and Germany.

■ *Britz Vineyards* *see* Under Oaks

■ *Broad Reach* *see* Devonvale Golf & Wine Estate

■ *Broken Rock* *see* Arlington Beverage Group

■ *Broken Stone* *see* Slaley Estate

■ *Bryde* *see* ACJ Fine Wines

Buck's Ridge Wines & Olives

T 023-230-1160 · F 023-230-4444

Tulbagh · Est 2005 · Visits by appt · Self-catering cottages & camping site · Olives & olive products · Walks, mountain biking & other attractions · Owner Brendon & Sue McHugh · Winemaker/viticulturist Brendon McHugh, with Marius Slabber · 6ha (cab, mourvèdre, petit v, shiraz, viognier) · ±2 555cs 80% red 20% white · PO Box 222 Tulbagh 6820 · info@bucksridge.co.za · www.bucksridge.co.za

Brendon McHugh distance-learnt his winemaking before fleeing the corporate world for these shores. He first vinified bought-in grapes in 2005, selling to his guest-cottage clients and exporting to his old European stomping grounds; his own vines are coming on-stream with a chenin release imminent and rhône-style blends in the pipeline.

Cabernet Sauvignon ★★★ These reds both **05**, tasted last ed. Cedar, tobacco aromas, plus lurking black fruit. Modest oaking (14 mths older Fr), modest fruit on palate, finishing dryly tannic. **Shiraz ★★★★** Forward fruit, nice ripe tannins. 15.3% alc obtrusive, but gratifying toasty, smoky, tasty persistence. Wooded like Cab. WO Coastal. **Chenin Blanc ✓ ★★★★ 06** has touch viognier, but chenin's honey, thatch, herbs reign quietly. Creamy texture from older oak ferment, maturation. Understated & pleasing. — *TJ*

Buitehof

T 023-626-4044 · F 023-626-2918

Robertson · Est 2002 · 1stB 2003 · Tasting Sat 9-2 · BYO picnic · Owner Johannes & Gideon van Zyl · Winemaker Gideon van Zyl (Jan 2002) · Viticulturist Briaan Stipp (consultant) · 100ha (cab, merlot, shiraz, chenin, colombard, sauv) · 500cs 70% red 30% white · PO Box 248 Robertson 6705 · buitehof@breede.co.za

Gideon van Zyl was inspired to make wine on a student exchange visit, where he worked on a farm – in Ohio of all places – and saw what could be achieved with little equipment and lots of enthusiasm. Since delivering his maiden vintage in 2003, equipment has improved, but enthusiasm remains the mainstay.

Cabernet Sauvignon ★★★ Italianate sour cherry note on **06**, walnut whiff; 40% new oak smartly used for subtle spicing & vanilla sweetness, lets fruit shine; slips down easily. **Sauvignon Blanc NEW ★★★** Flint & hints freshly mown grass, full flavour & moderate alc do the business on promising **07** maiden. — *CvZ*

Buitenverwachting

T 021-794-5190 • F 021-794-1351

Constantia • Est 1796 • 1stB 1985 • Tasting & sales Mon-Fri 9-5 Sat 9-1 • Closed pub hols • Tours by appt • Buitenverwachting Restaurant Mon-Sat • T 021·794·3522 (see Eat-out section). Summer only: Café Petite for light lunches (tel as above) & picnic baskets by appt (T 083-257-6083) • Teddy Bear Fair May 1; Valentine's Day Picnic • Conferences • Owner Richard & Sieglinde (Christine) Mueller, Lars Maack • Winemaker Hermann Kirschbaum & Brad Paton (Dec 1992/Dec 2004) • Vineyard Manager Peter Reynolds (Jun 1997), advised by Johan Pienaar • 120ha (cabs s/f, merlot, pinot, chard, sauv, riesling) • 1 300t/90 000cs 18% red 80% white 1% rosé 1% sparkling • PO Box 281 Constantia 7848 • info@buitenverwachting.com • www.buitenverwachting.com

Last year saw the final leg of a four-year plan to upgrade the cellar; from this year, the buildings on this historic Constantia estate are in line for what MD and co-owner Lars Maack calls 'cosmetic developments'. A succession plan has cellarmaster Hermann Kirschbaum (now celebrating his 15th year here) alternating with Brad Paton as chief honcho on reds or whites. Lars M quips: 'That way, we always have one relaxed winemaker to chat to our many visitors.' More seriously, he believes the practice encourages a healthy competitiveness. In the vineyards, an experimental block, as always, tries out organic viticulture - this year only organically approved sprays are being used - and extends what's successful across the farm.

★★★★ Cabernet Sauvignon Classic-styled **03** with enough fruit, serious oaking & gd structure for long ageing. Savoury fruit, with Asian spice, hint Kirsch, toasty oak; gd balance between power & finesse.

★★★★ Merlot Typically unshowy, elegant **02**, followed by **04** (★★★☆) with plummy, tobacco-scented fruit but slight green edge, & wanting more concentration to offset fresh acidity. Seriously oaked. No **03**.

★★★★☆ Christine One of Cape's finest classically minded bdx blends (cabs s/f, merlot & drop malbec), but **03** concedes to riper style, as 14.5% alc shows. Rich, deep cassis & cherry fruit, spicy cedar & minerals. Great balance, with fine-grain tannin. Yrs to go. All-new new Fr oak.

★★★★ Chardonnay New-World styling, but some classic touches. Flavoursome, medium-bodied **06** featuring lime, ripe pear, with oak prominent mid-2007 (50% new; but 15% unwooded) & moderate 13% alc; finishes with vibrant acidity. Needs time to fully integrate.

★★★★☆ Husseys Vlei Chardonnay 05 (not retasted) a vyd-based selection - more subtle, refined. Quietly forceful & will become more gorgeously so with few yrs. Gd balance. 90% new oak.

★★★★ Husseys Vlei Sauvignon Blanc Following crisp & silky **05**, tank sample **06**, from granitic soil, brings forceful greenpepper aromas. Richer, more powerful than above, but not as refined & subtle yet, with obvious lime & herbal flavours.

★★★★ Sauvignon Blanc Long tasted only as sample. Delicate **07** offers range of aromas from herbaceousness & asparagus to granadilla & peach. Typical Constantia white & yellow fruit on palate, with sense of chalky minerality on fresh finish. Should age interestingly.

★★★★ Semillon Last tasted was flavourful, crisp **03**. Not enough for bottling **04** or **05**.

★★★★ Brut MCC NV bubbly from 85/15 chard/pinot; full & round, with spice, ripe apple, nutty brioche notes; rich & creamy, ending with interesting sweet-sour play.

Meifort ★★★★ Rocket fuel for everyday drinking. Appealing blackcurrant, cedar on **03**; elegant, open-knit, refreshing, with beautiful fruit & gd depth. **Blanc de Noir ★★★** Delightfully pink & dry **07** bled off top reds; full-flavoured straw/raspberry character. **Gewürztraminer ★★★★ 05** (tasted last ed) varietal rosepetal character, pleasant fresh balance, almost dry. Lightly oaked. **Rhine Riesling ★★★★** Tank sample **07** attractively aromatic, with green apple & peach; balanced but a bit rustic in youth, with vibrant acidity. Maturation might bring higher rating. **Buiten Blanc ★★★☆** Reliable, winning sauv-based blend. **07** has sexy fruit notes in crisp but not aggressive structure. Thirst-quenching & moreish. WO Coastal. **Natural Sweet ★★★☆** Like last **02**, **05** is from riesling. Sample offers notes of dried apricot, pineapple, honey

& nuts, with refreshing acidity on tight palate making for lovely sipping, but finishes quickly. **Rhine Riesling Noble Late Harvest** In abeyance. **Noblesse** This NLH returns after long absence, with rich, opulent **06**: lots of overripe peach & apricot, with honey & spices, finishing with oak spice & nuttiness. Sample tasted; needs time, should rate ★★★★ or more. — *JPf*

■ **BunduStar** *see Vin-X-Port South Africa*

BurCon Wines
T 023-626-2012 ▪ F 023-626-2012   🍷 ☕ ♨ 📷 🎿 NEW

Robertson ▪ 1stB 2004 ▪ Tasting Mon-Fri 9-4 Sat 10-2 Sun by appt only ▪ Many amenities/ attractions incl restaurant, conference facilities, farm produce, facilities for children & tour groups, walking/hiking & mountain biking trails. See intro for more ▪ Owner Frans & Amanda Conradie, Renée Burger ▪ Winemaker Christie Steytler (Feb 2004, Roodezandt) ▪ 25ha (pinotage, shiraz, muscadel) ▪ 16t/1 250cs ▪ PO Box 86 Robertson 6705 ▪ info@ nerinaguestfarm.com ▪ www.nerinaguestfarm.com

Amanda Conradie of Nerina Guest Farm describes herself and her family – husband Frans, daughter Renée, son-in-law and two grandchildren – as ordinary Afrikaans-speaking farmers. 'We decided to make our own wines not to win medals or impress anyone, but for the pure enjoyment of it.' The farm also has a restaurant, B&B and bush camp, and offers horse-riding.

Oompie se Oeps ★★ **04** herbaceous Old World style pinotage (75%), shiraz; easy-drinking & rustic. **Meskien Christine** ★★★ Lush & delicious fortified muscadel. **05** ripe, spirity nose with raisin & honey; full-sweet flavours of sunny ripe fig & sultana. — *JP*

■ **Bushbuck Ridge** *see Long Mountain Wine Company*

■ **Bush Camp** *see Landskroon Wines*

■ **Bushman's Creek** *see Wines of Cape Town*

Bushmanspad
T 023-616-2961 ▪ F 023-616-2961   🍴 🍷 🚜 ♨ 📷 🎿

Robertson ▪ Est 2000 ▪ 1stB 2006 ▪ Visits (from Oct 2007) Mon-Fri 8-5 Sat/Sun 9-3 ▪ Closed Easter Sun, Dec 25 & Jan 1 ▪ Luxury B&B/self-catering cottages ▪ BYO picnic ▪ Gifts ▪ Walks ▪ 4×4 trail ▪ Mountain biking ▪ Facilities for children ▪ Tour groups ▪ Owner Menno Schaafsma ▪ Winemaker Pieter Ferreira & Irene Waller (Graham Beck, Mar 2006) ▪ Viticulturist Marco Ventrella (Graham Beck, Dec 2005) ▪ 51.5 ha (cabs s/f, malbec, merlot, mourvèdre, shiraz, sauv) ▪ 190t/1 500cs own label ▪ Export brand: Bushmanspad Red Gold ▪ PO Box 227 Bonnievale 6730 ▪ info@bushmanspad.co.za ▪ www.bushmanspad.co.za

The traditional Bushman path over the mighty Langeberg Mountains for trade traversed this farm. In similar spirit, current owner Menno Schaafsma is traveling widely to develop markets for the maiden-release reds, starting in Holland with intentions to explore China.

Red Gold range NEW

Cabernet Sauvignon ★★★ This, following, all ±14.5% alc, barrel fermented/15 mths new Fr oak. Nicely handled wood, firm tannins & refreshing cab acidity star in **06**. Hints cassis, forest floor; length & balance. **Merlot** ★★★ **06** savoury whiffs, meaty cranberry flavours. Fresh entry, slightly dilute, lifted by persistent grippy palate. **Shiraz** ★★★ Expressive **06** shiraz 'furniture polish', leather, lilies & red fruit. Broad & appealing, warming finish. Of the trio, this most needs time for tannins to knit with fruit. — *CvZ*

Buthelezi Wines
T 021-422-5206 ▪ F 021-422-5238

Cape Town ▪ Est/1stB 2002 ▪ Closed to public ▪ Owner/winemaker Khulekani Laurence Buthelezi ▪ 800 cs 100% red ▪ PO Box 12481 Mill Street Cape Town 8010 ▪ buthelezi@winery. co.za

The focus for this label, by Burgundy-trained Signal Hill winemaker Laurence Buthelezi, for his own account, is the export market, mainly France and the US, though limited quantities may be found in select restaurants and wine bars locally.

Tutuka Syrah ★★★ Introverted last yr, **05** hinted at complexity to come: prosciutto & blackberries, freshly ground spices, ripe yet firm tannins should now be softening. 2nd fill Fr oak, 18 mths. WO W Cape. — *CT*

■ **BWC Wines** *see* Catherine Marshall Wines

Cabrière
T 021-876-8500 • F 021-876-8501

Franschhoek • Est 1982 • 1stB 1984 • Tasting Mon-Fri 9-5 Sat & pub hols 10-4 • Fee R20p/p for 3 wines • Formal tasting/tour Mon-Fri 11 & 3 Fee R30 p/p • Private tasting/tour (pre-booked) Fee R35 p/p • Achim vA's tasting/tour Sat 11 Fee R30 p/p • Closed Good Fri, Dec 25 & Jan 1 • Haute Cabrière Cellar Restaurant (see Eat-out section) • Tour groups • Conferencing for groups of max 60 • Owner Clos Cabrière Ltd • Winemaker Achim von Arnim (1984), with Takuan von Arnim (2005) • Viticulturist Sakkie Lourens (May 2002) • 30ha (pinot, chard) • 500 000litres 40% red 60% white • PO Box 245 Franschhoek 7690 • cabriere@iafrica.com • www. cabriere.co.za

When we talk to Achim Von Arnim, he's been up till 2.30am, painting a self-portrait. He's a published poet too, but Franschhoek's most flamboyant character remains down to earth, scoffing at the cult of 'pedestal wines'. For him, wine should have the entertainment value of good art - not only in its creation but in the palette of flavours. 'Certain food can make a wine dance. Like when I dance with my bookkeeper Mabel. You wouldn't think we could, but when we do, it's magic!' Experience the AVA magic first-hand at the award-winning Haute Cabrière Cellar Restaurant, with its 'en suite' winetasting venue.

Haute Cabrière range

★★★★ **Pinot Noir** Tasted last ed, **04** was one of Von Arnim's finest. From densely planted vyds, it had bright cherry, generous fruit, flawless tannin/acid integration.
Arnim Sauvignon Rouge ★★★ Rosé-style summer refresher from cab & sauv bl. **NV**. Latest deeper hues, balanced & soft, gd with food or solo. WO W Cape. **Chardonnay-Pinot Noir** ★★★ **07** clean floral nuances, rosepetals, & big shoulders but lacks usual joie de vivre.

Pierre Jourdan range

★★★★ **Blanc de Blancs** 100% chardonnay, portion of base-wine briefly wooded. Latest lacks honeyed bottle-age overlay, so shows tad less complexity; does have usual lilting lime/citrus character, yeasty touch & long crisp finish.

★★★★ **Cuvée Reserve** Brut-style MCC from chard, pinot (60/40); **NV**, as are all in range. Latest has caramel & cassis notes, biscuit richness (from 60 mths on lees) not in pace with racy freshness; misses completeness, integration of pvs bottlings.

★★★★ **Cuvée Belle Rose** MCC from 100% pinot. Latest blushes palely but comes to life on nose with delightful rosepetal & fruitgum perfume. Crisp, refreshing - a real mood-lifting celebration wine.
Tranquille ★★ This, Ratafia below, the non-MCC sparklers in range. Softly dry pinot & chard blend, 60/40, pleasant, delicate, shows some gd bottle-age. **Brut** ✓ ★★★★ Their top-selling MCC; latest shows classy elegance & style; fresh, appealing green apple & grapefruit tones, gd creamy mousse & decidedly moreish finish. 60/40 chard/pinot. **Brut Sauvage** ★★★★ 'Savagely' dry cap classique from 60/40 pinot/chard, bare 1g/l sugar. Effusive lime & citrus perfume, yeasty undertone reflecting some maturity, though less definition & freshness than usual. **Ratafia** ★★★★ Other non-sparkling in line-up. Sweet jerepiko-style aperitif from chard, stiffened with estate's (chard) potsill brandy. Rich biscuit & caramel notes, warming glow from 20% alc. Some above incl W Cape fruit. — *CvZ,MM*

Calitzdorp Cellar
T 044-213-3301 · F 044-213-3328

Calitzdorp (see Klein Karoo map) · Est 1928 · 1stB 1977 · Tasting & sales Mon-Fri 8-1; 2-5 Sat 8-12 · Closed Easter Fri & Dec 25 · Tours by appt · Tour groups · BYO picnic · Farm produce · Owner 60 members · Winemaker Alwyn Burger (Nov 1990) · Viticulturist Johannes Mellet (consultant) · 160ha (13 varieties, r/w) · 3 000cs 60% red 30% white 10% fortified · PO Box 193 Calitzdorp 6660 · calitzwynk@telkomsa.net

This hillside cellar with wonderful views across the Gamka Valley offers visitors more than award winning wines (Veritas and Swiss medals among the latest harvest). A veld garden of named indigenous Karoo plants, a BYO picnic, and all the fun of the ever-popular, energetic 'grape stomp' at harvest time.

Cabernet Sauvignon ★★★ 05 attractive, with variety's slightly firmer tannins well cushioned by ripe mulberry & black choc fruit. Not retasted, as for all reds, BdN & Ruby Port. **Merlot ★★** Softer-styled **05**, honest cassis flavours & dry, food-friendly tannins. **Shiraz ★★★ 05** sound everyday quaffer with smoky aromas, ripe fruity flavours & nice dry finish. These reds 10-14 mths Fr/Am oak. **Touriga Nacional ★★★** Well made **05**, rounded soft red fruit, slight earthy note, drinkable & satisfying. **Blanc de Noir ★** Orange-tinted **05** from shiraz pleasant & sweet, needs drinking. **Chardonnay ★★** Canned peach flavours on **06**, tiring - drink up. **Sauvignon Blanc ★ 07** not tasted. **06** was sweetish, soft & pleasant. **Vonkelwyn ★★** Sparkling from chenin, on sweeter side of demi-sec, exotic tropical aromas/flavours. **NV. Hanepoot ★★★ 06** more golden in colour than Golden Jerepigo; at 260g/l sugar, hugely sweet & syrupy. **White Muscadel ★★★★** Shy on nose but **07** palate really expressive: rich, unctuous & sweet. These in modern mode with lower alcs (15.5%). **Golden Jerepigo ★★★★** Equal portions hanepoot & white muscadel in **NV** fortified dessert. Loads of sugar balanced by clean acidity. Terrific! **Vintage Port ★★★★** 'Cape Vintage' pvs ed. 75/25 touriga/tinta; **06** classically drier & more aloholic; some gd leathery, meaty fruit, still in the grip of tannin, though, so best cellared few yrs. **Ruby Port ★★★** 'Cape Ruby' pvs ed. Equal tinta & touriga in delicious **NV** bottling; last ed was richer, fuller than classic ruby style, well wooded/fortified (yr seasoned Fr) for spice, grip. — IvH

Camberley Wines
T 021-885-1176 · F 021-885-1176

Stellenbosch · Est 1990 · 1stB 1996 · Tasting & sales Mon-Sat & pub hols 9-5 Sun preferably by appt · Fee R10 · Closed Dec 25 & Jan 1 · Tours by appt · B&B guest cottage · Owner John & Gaël Nel · Winemaker John Nel · 7ha (cabs s/f, merlot, petit v, touriga, shiraz) · ±35t/2 500cs 100% red · PO Box 6120 Uniedal 7612 · john@camberley.co.za · www.camberley.co.za

Exports have doubled over the past year, and now account for over 75% of sales. 'We've just been lucky,' says John Nel, describing his Reserve Cab - equally modestly - as a mistake. 'We suddenly discovered four barrels in the cellar and didn't have a clue what they were! When I realised it was some 04 which had spent 28 months in barrel, I thought it would be finished. Then I tasted it - and now I just hope I can make a few more mistakes like that!'

★★★★ **Cabernet Sauvignon Reserve** NEW Mint & mocha-choc in bold New-World-styled maiden **04**, with pleasant chalky finish. Dense fruit core, seriously crafted structure (20% new oak, Fr/Am) & balanced 15% alc suggest wine will hold/improve many yrs.

★★★★ **Pinotage 06** muscular, with brooding fruit & chewy tannins; ripe prune & liquorice juiciness checked by dry oak tannin from higher new-oak content (75% vs pvs 50%). 16% alc back to heady **04** levels, **05** only marginally lower at 15.4%; all easily buffered by signature fruit concentration.

★★★★★ **Shiraz** Last ed **04** appeared set for long, gentle development; was succulent, full-ripe, richness & oak (14 mths Fr/Am 70/30, all new) taming 15.5% alc.

★★★★★ **Philosophers' Stone** Cab-led bdx blend seldom failing to impress with opulence, structure. **05** concentrated fruit compote with liquorice & tobacco highlights, dry tannins, 15.5% afterglow.

★★★★☆ **Ten** NEW Celebrating 10 yrs of Camberley wines, a blend of cabs s/f & merlot. Complex, rich cassis/mint tones, smooth texture, chalky tannins ex-24 mths mainly Fr oak, 20% new. 15.5% alc tad evident mid-2007.

★★★★ **Cabernet Sauvignon-Merlot 04** offers that elusive quality in fine wines; immediate access yet ageing ability courtesy seamless integration between plum/cassis fruit, judicious oak (14 mths Fr, half new). 72/28 blend. Not revisited.

★★★★ **Charisma** Cab joins usual trio of shiraz, merlot & cab f in succulent **04**. Bold cassis/ mint attack, yet elegantly styled & gd for 3-7 yrs cellaring. 20 mths Fr oak, 15% new. **Sparkling Shiraz** NEW ★★★☆ Rare-in-SA MCC sparkler debuts with fine mousse, exuberant savoury black cherry flavours & dusty finish. **04** base-wine oak matured for extra verve & texture; 23.6g/l sugar barely noticeable. Sure to find fans among those seeking an out-of-the-ordinary bubbly. **Elixir Fortified Red** NEW ★★★ **05** port-style dessert from shiraz, fortified to 20%; offers molten cassis & liquorice flavours, sweet & spicy finish. Cockle warming. Discontinued: **Merlot, Cabernet Franc-Merlot**. — *MW*

Cameradi Wines
T 021-873-1225 • F 021-873-4910

Wellington ▪ Est 1999 ▪ 1stB 2000 ▪ Closed to public ▪ Owner Stelvest cc (Pieter Laubscher, Niel Smith, Nic Swingler, Hendrik du Preez & Casper Lategan) ▪ Winemaker Casper Lategan (Jan 1999) ▪ 8t/600cs 100% red ▪ 48 Bain Str, Wellington, 7655 ▪ latsement@telkomsa.net

Garagiste brand Cameradi, started by former university pals, remains focused on hand crafting small quantities of reds. Frontman Casper Lategan believes their philosophy of producing individualistic wines, full bodied in style, is the reason people from the Seychelles to Amsterdam now enjoy their symbol of camaraderie.

★★★★ **Cabernet Sauvignon-Shiraz** Beefy **04** from Sbosch fruit upped ante for this winery last ed. Full-bodied with a confident tannin handshake; balanced, vibrant, clean finish. 50% new oak, mainly Fr. — *CvZ*

Capaia Wines

T 021-972-1081 • F 021-972-1894

Philadelphia (see Durbanville map) ▪ Est 1997 ▪ 1stB 2003 ▪ Visits by appt ▪ Owner Alexander & Ingrid von Essen ▪ Winemaker Stephan von Neipperg & Manfred Tement (consultants), with Werner Geldenhuys (2007) ▪ Viticulturist Mattie Bothma ▪ 60ha (cabs s/f, merlot, petit v, shiraz, sauvignon) ▪ 175t/±9 500cs 85% red 15% white ▪ PO Box 25 Philadelphia 7304 ▪ info@capaia.co.za ▪ www.capaia.co.za

This modern winery, which employs the second largest array of French oak fermentation barrels in the world, has appointed a new winemaker. Werner Geldenhuys, previously of La Motte, enjoys the experienced counsel of leading European wine men Stephan von Neipperg (reds) and Manfred Tement (whites). In the last year volumes were 40% up as younger vines came on-line (full production is expected next year) but hungry guinea fowl put paid to the anticipated first crop of shiraz.

Capaia Wines range

★★★★☆ **Capaia** Dark, handsome & suave. Cab-led (55%), sappy vinosity from 15% petit v; but **06** tight, brooding, like a pacing cougar in youth. As promising as inky **05** (55% merlot); cool minerality; super-fine tannins. 14 mths new Fr oak.

Blue Grove Hill range

Blue Grove Hill ★★★☆ Recent more seriously styled; **06** choc sheen to bright berries & smoky tail. From merlot & cab. 8 mths 2nd fill Fr oak. **Sauvignon Blanc** ★★★★ Waxy gloss to tropical **07**; portion new oak 2 mths, less minerality than **06**. All NE. — *DS*

■ **Cape 1652** *see Origin Wine*
■ ***Cape Aurora*** *see False Bay Vineyards*

Cape Bay

Nautical-themed range of easy-drinkers by Newton Johnson. Ready on release, and well priced.

Admiralty House range

Cabernet Sauvignon-Shiraz ★★★★ Elegant & spicy **04**, lavender & pepper notes, choc-mocha flavours; integrated; added interest from ±yr Fr oak. **Sauvignon Blanc** ★★★ Restrained 'European' feel to mineral **05**, mainly Wrcstr fruit given extra zing by 35% ex-cooler Hemel-&-Aarde Vlly & Firgrove. Export only range, to be discontinued after current stocks sell out; not retasted.

Cape Bay range

Pinotage ★★★ Lovely carmine coat for **06**, mulberry, strawberry & hint banana; softly fruity middle & friendly tannic hug. Not retasted, as for other reds. **Cabernet Sauvignon-Merlot** ★★★ Sample **06** incl dashes petit v & shiraz. Rather nice, dark fruits & tealeaf; balanced; slips down cheerfully. **Mellow Red** ★★★ Berried quick-quaffing quartet of grapes. **06** dusty nose, refreshing acidity; ideal with steak or solo, even slightly chilled. **Chenin Blanc** ★★ **07** crisp, medium bodied (13%), easy summer quaffer. **Sauvignon Blanc** ★★★ Tangy, crisp tropical-toned tipple. Drink **07** fresh & young. 12.6% alc. Discontinued: **Chardonnay, Bouquet Blanc**. — *MW*

■ **Cape Cab** *see* Groupe LFE South Africa

Cape Chamonix Wine Farm
T 021-876-2494 • **F** 021-876-3237

Franschhoek ▪ Est 1991 ▪ 1stB 1992 ▪ Tasting & sales daily 9.30-4 ▪ Fee R15 ▪ Chamonix Restaurant (see Eat-out section) ▪ Fully equipped self-catering cottages ▪ Facilities for children ▪ Tours by appt ▪ Gifts ▪ Tour groups by appt ▪ Farm-distilled schnapps & spring water ▪ Owner Chris & Sonja Hellinger ▪ Winemaker Gottfried Mocke (Sep 2001) with Werner Muller ▪ Viticulturist Rodney Kitching, with Gottfried Mocke ▪ 50ha (cabs s/f, merlot, pinot, pinotage, chard, chenin, sauv) ▪ 200t/17 000cs 60% red 36% white 4% MCC ▪ PO Box 28 Franschhoek 7690 ▪ marketing@chamonix.co.za ▪ www.chamonix.co.za

It was an extremely successful year for Cape Chamonix, including the Chardonnay Reserve earning Gottfried Mocke the 2006 Diners Club Winemaker of the Year (the standard bottling came a close second). He's the youngest-ever winner and, for this avowed admirer of Burgundy, winning the award with one of his favourite varieties is the cherry on top – it was this farm's chardonnay and pinot vines that initially drew him here. Mocke attributes Chamonix's accumulating successes to a combination of his growing familiarity with the vineyards, hard work with the vines, and experimentation in the cellar, all of which helps individual, characterful wines to emerge.

★★★★☆ **Pinot Noir** Clean, fresh, pure fruit on **06**, with perfume & earthy note on red berries. Tannins more harmonious than pvs, in lithe muscular balance. Natural ferment in open wooden vats; then 14 mths oak, 80% new. Quite oaky in youth; needs few yrs to show at best.

★★★★ **Troika** Serious, slightly austere but well-fruited & not over-modest blend cabs s/f plus merlot. Solid fruit copes well with 2 yrs new oak, gives decent length. Will benefit from time in bottle.

★★★★ **Chardonnay** Serious 2nd label, but fruitier, for earlier drinking than Rsv. Delighful orange, floral notes on **05**, gd balance fruit with integrated oak (these fermented, 11 mths new Fr). Intense, lingering **06** similar, but more stress on mineral core.

★★★★☆ **Chardonnay Reserve** Serious, elegant flagship, increasingly applauded: Museum Trophy for **97** at 2007 TWS; **05** Diners Club winner. Tasted mid-2007, refined, steely **05** still oakier than current **06** which highlights minerality & pure fruit, built on uncompromisingly elegant lines. Fine wine, subtle balance with lowish 13.1& alc. Natural ferment/14 mths new oak. Deserves few yrs at very least.

★★★★★ **Sauvignon Blanc Reserve** In house style, **06** unshowy & elegant. Fermented/11 mths oak, 30% new - but this well absorbed in vibrant, fresh fruit, typically with passionfruit, earth, citrus. Satisfying, lingering, lime-green finish. Has track record for ageing gd few yrs.

★★★★ **MCC Blanc de Blancs** Chard bubbly, 11 mths big older oak, 3 yrs on fine lees. **03** (not retasted) usual undemonstrative elegance; subtle yeast, apple-pie character; dry, green-apple finish.

★★★★ **MCC Reserve** Occasional special release, degorged after 5 yrs lees-ageing. Last was richly refined **00**; next up **01** in magnum.

> **Rouge** ☺ ★★★ Generous, scented aromas on **05**; light-fruited, firmly structured & food-friendly blend cab, merlot, pinotage, malbec; modestly oaked.

Cabernet Sauvignon ★★★☆ Serious, flavourful **05** shows more oak (2 yrs, 90% new) than **04**; with cedar, tobaco over juicy fruit; herbal (tarragon?) notes; savoury dry tannin. **Pinotage** ★★★ Last-tasted **04** with usual gd varietal character, light & bright flavours, firm tannic grip. **Rosé** ★★★ **06** (last ed) mix red/white grapes; fresh, fruity, not-quite-dry easy-drinker. **Sauvignon Blanc** ★★★★ Long since tasted except as sample - usually generously flavoured, with ripe tropicality, crisp. **Blanc** ✓ ★★★★ Generous, fruity **06** blends chard, sauv & a litle chenin. Fresh, green-tinged citrus fruit, well-rounded approachability. — TJ

■ **Cape Circle** *see* Vin-X-Port South Africa

Cape Classics
T 021-847-2400 • F 021-847-2414

Somerset West ▪ Est 1991 ▪ 1stB 1995 ▪ Tasting by appt only ▪ Owner André Shearer ▪ Winemaker Bruwer Raats (consultant) ▪ 70 000cs own label 45% red 55% white ▪ Lourensford Estate, Lourensford Road, Somerset West 7130 ▪ info@capeclassics.com ▪ www.capeclassics.com; www.indaba.co.za

Cape Classics' Indaba range is one of the most successful SA brands in the US, supported by partners like the Darden Restaurant group, the world's largest. Winemaker Mzokhona Mvemve, the original Indaba Scholarship recipient and part of the Cape Classics' team for almost a decade, is now pursuing his own-label development; and Bruwer Raats of Raats Family Wines is consulting for the Indaba range. Cape Classics completed a shareholder buyout during 2007, and one of its new partners, Mark Schwartz (ex-chairman of Goldman Sachs Asia), brings a wealth of corporate experience to the board.

Indaba range
Merlot ★★★ No **06**. Last ed, **05** was a friendly solo glassful with ripe & juicy blueberries, subtle vanilla overlay (3 mths Fr/Am oak) & silky tannins. **Pinotage** ★★★ Toasted spice & dusty red fruit dominate **06**. Lacking gruff tannins, could be a red-wine match for light curries or spicy food. **Shiraz** ★★★★ No **06**. Last we enjoyed **05**'s abundant roast beef, cracked pepper & spicy red fruit. Ripe vintage well managed (13.5 alc). **Chardonnay** ★★★ **06**'s ripe pear & buttered toast, zesty acid bite & mineral finish suggest solo sipping or pairing with creamy dishes. **Chenin Blanc** ★★★ Granny Smith apple & tropical fruit in **06** everyday tipple. **Sauvignon Blanc** ★★★ Fresh guava & other tropical notes in ripe, easy-drinking **07**. Friendly 13.5% alc. All bottled under screwcap for quick refreshment. — MW

Cape Coastal Vintners
T 021-860-8840 • F 021-872-9262

Paarl ▪ Est/1stB 2004 ▪ PO Box 6141 Paarl 7620 ▪ stan-h@mweb.co.za ▪ www.matuba.co.za

Ownership of this company and its brands, including Matuba, Kleinbosch and Jabulani, was changing hands at press time, and no wines were available for tasting.

■ **Cape Cobra** *see* Klein Dauphine
■ **Cape Concert** *see* Daschbosch Wine Cellar

■ *Cape Diamond* see Lutzville Cape Diamond Vineyards

■ *Cape4* see Groupe LFE South Africa

Cape Grace Wines
T 021-855-5639 • F 021-855-5639

Stellenbosch ▪ Est/1stB 2004 ▪ Closed to public ▪ Owner Thierry's Wine Services & Afrifresh ▪ Winemaker Carno du Toit ▪ 200 000cs for export only, incl Waitrose, Asda, Sainsbury's, Tesco, Somerfield & Thresher ▪ 40% red 40% white 20% rosé ▪ PO Box 1376 Stellenbosch 7599 ▪ info@itjustdid.com ▪ www.capegracewine.co.za

This partnership between UK wine importer Thierry's and Vineyard 41 (the wine division of Afrifresh) has strengthened and developed 'a real family atmosphere', reports Lucy Warner, Thierry's SA-based portfolio manager. New are a Shiraz and Chenin, two blends, a Pinotage-Merlot and Semillon-Chenin, while the popular Pinotage Rosé is now partnered by a Pink Pinotage Fizz due to hit UK shelves just in time for Christmas. No wines in either the Cape Grace or Diversity ranges were ready for tasting.

■ *Cape Haven* see Pulpit Rock Winery

■ *Cape Heights* see False Bay Vineyards

Cape Hutton
T 021-880-0527 • F 021-880-0666

Stellenbosch ▪ Est 2003 ▪ 1stB 2004 ▪ Visits by appt ▪ Owner/viticulturist Gerrit & Lesley Wyma ▪ Winemaker Piet Smal (Cab) & Wynand Hamman (Sauvignon) ▪ 4 ha (cab, merlot) ▪ 19t/1 000cs 93% red 7% rosé ▪ PO Box 2200 Somerset West 7130 ▪ lesley@capehutton.com ▪ www.capehutton.com

Small is beautiful, believe Gerrit and Lesley Wyma, who now bottle their West Coast Sauvignon (courtesy of Fryer's Cove's Wynand Hamman), Rosé and Cabernet in 375ml screwcapped bottles - much to the delight of guest lodges. A tiny potstill in their maturation cellar may soon produce a grappa from their miniature - that word again! - hanepoot vineyard.

Cape Hutton range
Cabernet Sauvignon ★★★★ 05 step up in quality; classic cedar tones, austere tea-like tannins; cassis fruit very ripe, hint raisin, but refreshing acidity makes for gd food wine. 14 mths Fr oak, 35% new. **Merlot** NEW Not tasted **Merlot Rosé** NEW **07** unrated barrel sample should make interesting addition to line-up. Brimming with sugared plums & vanilla aromas, sweet-sour flavours. **Sauvignon Blanc** NEW **★★★** Maiden **07** bottled shortly before review; sweetish impression, warming afterglow (courtesy 14% alc) follows appealing fresh-cut grass & dusty notes. — *CvZ*

Cape Legends
T 021-809-8330 • F 021-882-9575

Stellenbosch ▪ Closed to public ▪ Owner Distell ▪ PO Box 184 Stellenbosch 7599 ▪ ekrige@capelegends.co.za ▪ www.capelegends.co.za

Stand-alone marketing and sales organisation within the Distell group representing a portfolio of well-regarded brands including Alto, Allesverloren, Flat Roof Manor, Hill & Dale, Ixia, Jacobsdal, Le Bonheur, Lomond, Neethlingshof, Plaisir de Merle, Stellenzicht, Theuniskraal, Tukulu and Uitkyk, all listed separately.

■ *Capell's Court* see Linton Park Wines

■ *Cape Maclear* see African Pride Wines

■ *Cape Maidens* see Juno Wine Company

■ *Cape Mist* see Thorntree Wines

Capenheimer

SA's original perlé wine, launched 1962.

> **Capenheimer** ☺ 🍷 ★★ Light summer quaff from chenin & colombard. Ripe pear balanced by fresh acidity & slight spritz. **NV.** *— MW*

■ **Cape Original** see Origin Wine

Cape Point Vineyards

T 021-785-7660 · F 021-785-7662

Cape Point (see Constantia map) • Est 1996 • 1stB 2000 • Visits by appt • Owner Sybrand van der Spuy • Winemaker Duncan Savage (Dec 2002), with Jean du Plessis (May 2007) • Viticulturist Duncan Savage (Dec 2002), advised by Kevin Watt • 31ha (cab, shiraz, chard, sauv, semillon) • 140t/7 000cs own label; 1000cs for Woolworths • 20% red 80% white • PO Box 100 Noordhoek 7985 • info@cape-point.com • www.capepointvineyards.co.za

No doubt about it, winemaker Duncan Savage is enjoying himself. Lots of reasons - working in vineyards which surprise and delight with their sea views; sauvignon with special promise in the cellar; better than ever sales; a launch into the US on the back of three 90+ point ratings in Wine Spectator magazine ('Not that we think we're going to conquer America, but still…'); and the challenge of getting vines to trellis in the teeth of the wind on seven newly planted hectares at the top of the Noordhoek farm. A small disappointment in 2007 did nothing to dampen his enthusiasm: production was 20 to 30% down but then there's not enough CPV wine to meet demand anyway.

★★★★☆ **Sauvignon Blanc** Formula 1 sauvignon: sleek, racy, filled with sophisticated complexities. **06**, TWS trophy winner, heady, cool scents; richly flavoured with plenty tangy drive. Staying power enhanced by 5% barrel-fermented portion, 10% splash semillon.

★★★★ **Stonehaven Sauvignon Blanc** 'Junior' sibling never shy to show off. **07** exhilarating citrus & gooseberry freshness, resounding dryness, all in refined package with admirably moderate 13% alc.

★★★★☆ **Semillon** Intricately composed, fine dry white. **06** (★★★★★) exciting potential in concentrated, ripe, tangerine-led citrus aromas; full-throttle silky richness, flavour concentration beg 2-3 yrs development. Partially barrel fermented, incl 4% sauv. Fr oak, 30% new. **05**, **03** Trophy winners TWS 2007.

★★★★★ **Isliedh** One of few exceptional cool-climate bdx-style whites in Cape. **06** echoes splendid **05**, though bigger, more powerful; similar potential. Semillon (22%) supplies rich aroma, structure; the triumph in all 3 CPV whites is in the resonating length. Barrel fermented, 70% new, 10 mths.

Scarborough Red ★★★★ **05** cab/shiraz blend tad deeper, more structured than maiden **04**, still friendly, velvety & rich; dark berries & spice, supple grip. Yr Fr oak, 8% new. **Chardonnay** ★★★☆ Last **04** showed richness in tandem with citrus freshness, spicy oak. No **05**, **06**; **07** untasted. **Semillon Noble Late Harvest** None since **01**; waiting for sufficient botrytis. *— AL*

■ **Cape Promise** see WaverleyTBS/uniWines
■ *Cape Reality* see Baarsma Wine Group

Cape Rock Wines

T 027-213-2567 · F 027-213-5567

Olifants River • Est 2001 • 1stB 2002 • Visits by appt • Permanent art exhibit • Owner Willie Brand • Winemaker WP Brand & Gavin Brand (Jan 2002/Feb 2005) • Viticulturist Jeff Joubert & WP Brand • 30ha (cab, merlot, pinotage, roobernet, ruby cab, shiraz, chard, chenin, sauvignon) • 605t/150cs own label 100% red • PO Box 261 Vredendal 8160 • caperockwines@gmail.com • www.caperockwines.co.za

Most of the floodplains on the Brands' farm on the Olifants River banks are undisturbed, leaving abundant wildlife and scarce bird species protected and thriving. Winemaking on the property involves the entire family – from picking to labelling and wrapping bottles – and everything is done by hand.

Red Shoe NEW ★★★ From shiraz; **06** ripe dark-berry fruit, caramel & vanilla from wood, dry chunky tannins. Attractive now, but perhaps better in 2/3 yrs. Natural ferment, 9 mths oak, 30% Am. **Shiraz-Viognier** ★★★ Plum-pudding & coconut aromas on pvsly tasted **05**, big 15. 3% alc well tucked away in opulent fruit. 7% viognier adds floral note & a bit of polish. WO W Cape. – *MM*

■ **Cape Sauv** *see* Groupe LFE South Africa
■ *Cape Table* *see* Riebeek Cellars
■ *Cape View* *see* Kaapzicht Estate

Cape Vineyards
T 023-349-1585/1466 • F 023-349-1592

Rawsonville • Est 1994 • 1stB 1996 • Closed to public • Owner 4 shareholders • 47 300cs + 2m litres bulk • 70% red 30% white • Ranges for customers: Pearl Springs (UK/Japan); Andrew Bain Reserve, Jantara, Wildfire (all UK) • PO Box 106 Rawsonville 6845 • hanno@cape-vineyards.com • www.cape-vineyards.com

This four-member (Merwida, Slanghoek, Bainskloof and Opstal Estate), Rawsonville-based alliance came together in 1994 for synergies in a highly competitive industry, and to help establish brands for international clients. It exports both bulk and bottled wine, and has its own portfolio of bottled wines for SA consumption.

Andrew Bain Reserve range
Pinotage ★★★ **05** a sleeping giant; incl 15% shiraz, dense savoury/spicy fruit & powerful tannins. Should hold gd few yrs. 30% 1st fill oak. **Chardonnay** ★★ **05**, with 15% chenin; understated oak, unheavy styling makes for food compatibility. Slnghoek fruit for these.

Andrew Bain range
Cabernet Sauvignon-Merlot ★★★ **05** generous & warming (14.5% alc); 60% cab & equal dollops merlot/malbec provide flavoursome mouthful coffee, choc & red fruit. **Chardonnay** ★★★ Tropical **05** weighty, with zesty lift; appealing.

Jantara range
Pinotage ★★★ Splash malbec adds extra colour & fruit-richness to **05**, dry tannins make it a food wine. Fr/Am oak, 2 mths. **Shiraz** ★★★ **05** gets density & flavour boost from 15% malbec; pvsly noted as v dry, needing rustic food. **Chardonnay** ★★ **05** restrained & shy; fruit aromas & flavours gently buoyed by 6 wks combo Fr/Am oak. **Chenin Blanc** ★★★ **05** attractive nectarine & lime tones balanced by light vanilla (oak as for Chard). Sensible 13% alc. **Sauvignon Blanc** ★★☆ **03** had unusual peach whiff; bright, zesty finish, when last reviewed.

Rawson's range
Ruby Cabernet-Merlot ★★★ Unoaked blend. **05** ready to drink, merlot/malbec (20/10) add structure to ruby cab's sweet fruit & accessibility.

Wildfire range
Malbec ★★ Vibrant fruit runs riot on **05**, spicy aromas & tannic bite add interest. Best young. **Chardonnay** ★★ **06** friendly poolside quaffer; lightish pine & peach notes, not-so-light 14% alc. W Cape/Breede Rvr Vlly WOs for all above. – *CT*

■ **Cape Wine Cellars** *see* Cape Coastal Vintners
■ *Cap Vino* *see* Winkelshoek Wine Cellar
■ *Cardouw* *see* Citrusdal Cellars
■ *Caresse Marine* *see* Wildekrans Estate

Carl Everson *see* Opstal Estate
Carpe Diem *see* Diemersfontein Wines
Casa do Mar *see* Ruitersvlei Wines
Cathedral Cellar *see* KWV Limited

Catherine Marshall Wines

T 083 258 1307 • F 021-788-8390

Est/1stB 1997 ▪ Tasting by appt ▪ Owner Jeff Jolly, Cathy Marshall, Greg Mitchell & Peter Oxenham ▪ Winemaker Cathy Marshall (1997) ▪ 40t/2 500cs + 300cs for Woolworths ▪ 75% red 25% white ▪ PO Box 13404 Mowbray 7705 ▪ cathy@cmwines.co.za ▪ www.cmwines.co.za

Ten years on from a fun-driven grape-treading party, the Barefoot Wine Company (BWC) has acquired even more gravitas and matured into Catherine Marshall Wines, a move the team feels emphasises the commitment to consistency and quality, and which has dramatically upped sales. Cathy M values the flexibility to vinify good grapes from carefully selected sites. She's excited about sourcing pinot from ultra-cool, high-altitude Langkloof (where pinot-loving baboons tightrope-walk telephone lines to get at the vines), and a new Elgin home for the brand is being renovated.

★★★★ **Pinot Noir** Consistent star blips in **06** (★★★☆) as Darling/Elgin fruit struggles to carry charry Fr oak. Raspberry & black cherry aromas with signature Darling oystershell character show elegance, while flavours need time to meld. **05**, ex-Elgin/Sbosch vyds, was beguiling & quite dainty.

★★★★ **Syrah** Enticing pure red fruit & smoke on bright, youthful **05**, elegant & expressive rhône style. Fine weave of fruit & oak on mineral palate, with light peppery finish. WO Paarl.

★★★★ **Syrah-Mourvèdre** NEW Magenta-rimmed, youthful **05** with 14% mourvèdre; entices with sweet, dark fruit & sour cherry flavours still masked by firm tannins. Moderate 12.5% alc, poised acidity & savouriness make ideal refreshing food wine. Coastal vyds.

Sauvignon Blanc ▤ ★★★☆ Plenty verve in sample **07** from Dbnville fruit, ample fig & citrus balanced by steely acidity, finishing firm & flinty. **Myriad** ★★★ Foot-pressed, part-fermented, brandy-fortified blend pinot & merlot. Last tasted was **02**; **03** sold out; **04** in barrel. Discontinued: **Wholeberry Cabernet Sauvignon**. *— IM*

Cattle Baron *see* ACJ Fine Wines
CCC Wines *see* Bonnievale Wine Cellar
Cecil John *see* Boschendal Wines

Cederberg Private Cellars

T 027-482-2827 • F 027-482-1188

Cederberg (see Olifants River map) ▪ Est/1stB 1977 ▪ Visits Mon-Sat 8-12.30; 2-5 Pub hols 9-12; 4-6 ▪ Fee R10 ▪ Closed Easter Fri/Sun/Mon & Dec 16/25 ▪ BYO picnic ▪ Sanddrif Holiday Resort - fully equipped self-catering cottages (see Stay-over section) ▪ Walks/hikes ▪ Mountain biking ▪ Owner Nieuwoudt family ▪ Winemaker David Nieuwoudt, with Jan Taylor & Mark Jentzel (1997/2005) ▪ Viticulturist Ernst Nieuwoudt ▪ 56ha (cab, shiraz, chenin, sauv) ▪ 18 000cs 60% red 40% white ▪ PO Box 84 Clanwilliam 8135 ▪ info@cederbergwine.com ▪ www.cederbergwine.com

The Nieuwoudt family and team may seem like kings of their castle in their elevated Cederberg cellar, with local wine sales up 45% and international acclaim. Their success, however, grows out of dedicated involvement: from vineyards and cellar, to hospitality and marketing, with a sound environmental ethic (they're part of the Greater Cederberg Biodiversity Project and Cape Leopard Trust). Winning a Decanter World Wine Awards trophy for the V Generations Cab is a source of pride… but the arrival of sixth-generation Emma, daughter to David and Cisca, on the day their third MCC was bottled, is cause for even greater celebration.

V Generations range

★★★★☆ **Cabernet Sauvignon** In homage to the family's guardianship of this snowline wilderness area; grapes ex-30+ yr old vyd enjoys handcrafting, all new Fr oak indulgence (18 mths). **05** impressively ordered blackcurrant fruits within dense tannic trellis; grippy, more assertive than softer **04** (★★★★), which open structure suggests earlier accessibility. 100 cs.

★★★★ **Chenin Blanc** Selection of 3 best barrels off 33 yr old vyd. **06** carries the gravitas conferred well; biscuit patina over creamy oak, lovely zesty tropical tones to underlying fruit. 11 mths Fr cask, third new. 100 cs.

Cederberg Private Cellars range

★★★★ **Cabernet Sauvignon** Well-established quality styling: pure fruit, ample ripe tannins. **06** melange cassis, mint & fragrant oak, tight but full enough to cellar few yrs. Yr Fr oak, 60% new.

★★★★★ **CWG Auction Reserve Teen die Hoog Shiraz** Best fruit of best vyd afforded best new Fr oak; only best barrels for 75cs parcel. 'Old style' whisper critics: 'Multi-dimensional!' is David N's retort. **05** thrills: highly concentrated red fruits coiled in wafts of spice, beautifully toned muscular frame promising many fruitful yrs cellaring.

★★★★ **Shiraz** Authoritative yet unflamboyant, & much fêted. **06** plummy, choc-pud & sweet vanilla frame; a generous alternative to the sometimes lean spicy style. 80/20 Fr/Am oak, 70% new.

★★★★ **Sauvignon Blanc** Racy **07** fuller, more fig flesh to still-minerally frame than explosive **06**, which bristled with cut grass & rapier-like flintiness. Pleasing 13% alc.

★★★★ **CWG Auction Reserve Elim Semillon** NEW Maiden **07** still a coiled spring when reviewed just after bottling; very fresh, focused grassy fruits jostle with riverstone flint, almost too big for the bottle; needs time. Free-run juice, 25% new Fr oak, 4 mths on lees.

Cederberger ★★★★ Frequent WOM selection; merlot & pinotage, with shiraz (50/30/20). **06** chunky, ripe plum & bright berry flavours lifted by spicy unintimidating tail. 14 mths old oak. **Bukettraube** ★★★ Enchanting **07**, cumin, honey & melon complexity to sweet grapiness (24. 5g/l sugar). **Chenin Blanc** ★★★★ More demure than white cellarmates, but no less interesting; flavourful **07** has brisk pink grapefruit seam in balanced weight, invigorating finish. —DS

Cellar Cask

Budget range by Distell 'for people who value simplicity'. SA's first bag-in-box (1979); now also in 750ml glass.

Select Johannisberger Rosé ★★ Salmon hue, sweetly floral flavour but more balancing acidity than white version. **Select Johannisberger White** ★ Blowsy fruit salad-toned tipple from mainly chenin & colombard. **Select Johannisberger Red** ★★ Similar berry-rich bouquet & flavour as pvs but softer; gently sweet finish. All **NV**, all ±11.5% alc, semi-sweet, widely sourced.—MW

▪ **Cellar Door** *see* Villiera Wines

▪ **Cellar Hand** *see* Flagstone Winery

▪ **Cellarmaster's Release** *see* Stellenzicht Vineyards

▪ **Cellar Selection** *see* Kleine Zalze Wines

Cellar-Vie Wines
T 073-386-2618 • F 011-975-4482

Est/1stB 2004 • Closed to public • Owner Hendri Nagel & Adam Simcock • Viticulturist Teddy Hall & Bob Cartwright (Rudera/Leeuwin Estate) • 320cs 50% red 50% white • PO Box 10136 Edleen 1625 • sales@cellar-vie-wines.co.za, hermitage@iburst.co.za

Cellar-Vie partners Hendri Nagel and Adam Simcock buy in grapes and juice from various regions for vinification by selected high-profile winemakers. The virtual winery's latest offering is an 06 chardonnay, made by Australian winemaker Bob Cartwright of Leeuwin Estate and Weltevrede Estate's Philip Jonker, chardonnay aficionados and exponents both.

★★★★ **Chardonnay** NEW **06** delicious debut. Confident & poised; alc & well-integrated oak (13.9%, 100% new Fr) cradle lemon-lime fruit rather than smother it. EW.

Commitment Reserve ★★★★ Last-tasted **04**, by Rudera's Teddy Hall, modern but serious bdx blend cab/merlot (53/47); generous padding, fresh, moderate 13.5% alc. — *CvZ*

■ **Chameleon** *see* Jordan Winery
■ *Chamonix* *see* Cape Chamonix Wine Farm

Chateau Libertas

SA's 'iconic' affordable red blend, made uninterrupted since 1932. By Distell.

Chateau Libertas ★★ **05** cab-dominated, merlot, shiraz & malbec more evident on nose than chunky, tannic palate; touch gruff, needs food. — *MW*

■ **Cherry Hill** *see* Liquor World

Christo Wiese Portfolio
T 021-847-2200 • F 021-847-0910/1669

Stellenbosch • Owner Christo Wiese • Contact Anton du Toit • PO Box 16 Somerset West 7129 • cwp@lourensford.co.za

This is the umbrella for big-businessman Christo Wiese's extensive wine interests, which include Stellenbosch farms Lanzerac and Lourensford, and branded ranges Five Heirs and Eden Crest (the latter pair listed under Lourensford).

Cilandia
T 023-626-5209 • F 023-626-5209

Robertson • Est 2002 • 1stB 2003 • Visits by appt • Owner AA Cilliers Jnr & AA Cilliers • Winemaker Albie Cilliers • Viticulturist Abraham Cilliers • 60ha (cab, cinsaut, pinotage, roobernet, shiraz, chard, chenin) • 700t/1 200cs own label 100% red • PO Box 504 Robertson 6705 • wine@cilandia.co.za

Despite his belief that the main growth markets for SA wines are overseas, AA 'Albie' Cilliers is not interested in pursuing opportunities on foreign shores. In fact, the aim of this down-to-earth winemaker is to downscale; producing less wine, better quality, with a reduced carbon footprint. No new vintages tasted of the Cab, Pinotage or Shiraz.

■ **Cilliers Cellars** *see* Stellendrift
■ *Cinzano* *see* African Wines & Spirits
■ *Circumstance* *see* Waterkloof
■ *Cirrus* *see* Ernie Els Wines

Citrusdal Cellars

T 022-921-2233 • F 022-921-3937

Citrusdal (see Olifants River map) • Est 1957 • 1stB 1958 • Tasting & sales Mon-Fri 8-5 Sat 9-12.30 (sales also at retail outlet in Citrusdal village Mon-Fri 9-7 Sat 8-5) • Closed all pub hols except Easter Sat • Tours by appt • BYO picnic • Citrusdal Cellars Guest House • Tour groups • Owner 78 members • Winemaker Ian Nieuwoudt, with Jaco Brand & Andries de Klerk (2005) • Viticulturist VinPro advisers • 1 200ha (grenache, pinotage, chenin) • 6 000t/90 000cs own label + 20 000cs for clients • 30% red 60% white 5% rosé 5% dessert • Export brands: Cardouw, Ivory Creek & Danckaert • HACCP certified • PO Box 41 Citrusdal 7340 • citrusdalcellars@yebo.co.za • www.citrusdalcellars.co.za

New major stakeholder Charles Back (of Fairview fame) is exuberant about his latest venture: 'the terroir, the old grenache vines in Piekenierskloof, astonishing sales in Russia... it's looking good!' The Goue Vallei brand may be joined by others in the future, but the current focus is on creating a holistic viticultural, winemaking and marketing package, says Back. The social aspect is not being forgotten: one of SA's first wineries to commit to ethical trading, Citrusdal is on its way to becoming 100% certified and UK listings already include Thresher, Marks & Spencer, and Sainsbury's. WIETA accreditation is their next goal. No wines tasted this edition.

Clairvaux Private Cellar
T 023-626-3842 ▪ F 023-626-1925

Robertson ▪ Est 2000 ▪ 1stB 2001 ▪ Tasting & sales Mon-Fri 8-5 Sat 9-12.30 Pub hols 9-3 ▪ Closed Easter Fri-Mon, Dec 25/26 & Jan 1 ▪ Tours by appt ▪ BYO picnic ▪ Owner Wouter de Wet Snr & Jnr ▪ Winemaker Pieter van Aarde (Jan 2004) ▪ Viticulturist Briaan Stipp (consultant) ▪ 180ha (cab, malbec, merlot, pinotage, petit v, shiraz, chard, colombard, muscadel, sauv) ▪ 3 100t ▪ PO Box 179 Robertson 6705 ▪ appelsdrift@lando.co.za ▪ www.clairvauxcellar.co.za

It was all systems go at Clairvaux last harvest, with a 'fast and furious' crush, a new dry white under screwcap, and a new baby (Pieter and Ria van Aarde's second). And their witty brand names remained hits: who could resist Madonna's Kisses?

Cabernet Sauvignon ★★ **04** last ed offered ripe & succulent berry fruit, silky tannins, gd persistence. **Shiraz** ★★ Meaty, savoury, with touch of spice, **06** invites braaied boerewors. **Sandberg Purple** ★★★ Fullish in body & flavour, **07** meaty red with some rustic charm. Equal cab & merlot. **Rosé** ★ Last we tasted overtly sweet, somewhat simple **05**, from white muscadel. **Chardonnay** ★★ **05** on review was amiable & plump, well flavoured & supportively oaked. **Sauvignon Blanc** ★★ Pleasing **07**, has some charm & modest varietal character. **Appelsdrift White Blend** NEW 🔖 ★★ Innocuous dry white, **07** equal blend sauv, chard, chenin. **Soleil** ★★ Sweet but refreshing **05**, mainly white muscadel & colombard, straightforwardly pleasant. **Madonna's Kisses Golden Muscadel** ★★★ Super-sweet, appealing raisiny fruit, though **06** could benefit from a tad more freshness. **Port** ★ Old-style fireside fortifier from ruby cab; **03** showed treacle-like sweetness last yr. Discontinued: **Chardonnay-Colombar.** *— IvH*

Cloof
T 022-492-2839 ▪ F 022-492-3261

Darling (see Durbanville map) ▪ Est 1997 ▪ 1stB 1998 ▪ Tasting & sales Mon-Fri 10-5 Sat 10-2 ▪ Closed Easter Fri/Sun, Dec 25/26, Jan 1 ▪ Tasting room lunches Mon-Sat; occasional Sun gourmet BBQ events - pre-bookings only ▪ Owner Cloof Wine Estate (Pty) Ltd ▪ Winemaker Christopher van Dieren (Jan 2002) ▪ Viticulturist Peter Duckitt (2005) ▪ 166ha (cabs s/f, cinsaut, merlot, pinotage, shiraz, chard, chenin) ▪ 600t/90 000cs 88% red 5% white 7% rosé ▪ PO Box 269 Darling 7345 ▪ info@cloof.co.za ▪ www.cloof.co.za

For their conservation efforts and environmentally sensitive vineyard and cellar management, Cloof and neighbouring property Burghers Post - Cloof's prime source of bought-in grapes - now hold Biodiversity Champions status. To consolidate the achievement, a conservation officer has joined the team. Dark Side, Darling Daisy and The Very Sexy Shiraz continue the practice of naming wines after the characteristics they display. Purchase of the last-named gets the buyer an option on a bottle (from only 400 cases) of the 2006 Crucible Shiraz. The register of Crucible Futures is being held by a private asset management company, enabling a secondary market in the trading of the futures.

Cloof range

★★★★☆ **Crucible Shiraz** Individal, powerful, but less harmonious than pvs, **06** (★★★★) impresses with black pepper, dark fruit, prosciutto layers. Trademark high acidity more intrusive this time, helps offset bold 15.6% alc. All new Fr, 15 mths. No **05**. **04** a showstopper, with enormous concentration of flavour.

★★★★ **Merlot-Cabernet Franc** Last available **04** (★★★), choc & sweet tobacco jostled with racy acidity & firm, almost austere tannin, mid-2006 needing food & time to tame. Concours Mondial 2006 judges felt differently, awarded gold. **03**, wearing pvs tag, flew with SAA, impressed Wine judges (★★★★).

★★★★ **Lynchpin** NEW Named for important cab f role in merlot-led blend. Brambly touches on **05**'s smoked meat, plummy depths; curvaceous drinkability masks serious structure, sheathed power needing time. 13 mths oak, 75% new.

★★★★ **Cellar Blend** Tinta, pinotage & shiraz blend in **05** (★★★), last available. Subtlety & finesse outgunned by vintage's extreme ripeness; warm, hollow palate with notes of dark spice & liquorice. Shade less alluring than sweetly rustic **04**. Yr Fr oak, 20-30% new.

★★★★ **Inkspot** NEW 🍷 Light oaking for full expression of low-yielding bushvines (pinotage, some shiraz, cinsaut): **05** molten black plums, whiffs scrub, salty liquorice. Silky palate completes seduction. Not for long ageing, just enjoy.

Pinotage ★★★ Ultra-ripe **05** is big in every way, dense dark fruit, chewy tannins, generous 15.5% alc, plenty of smoky spice. **The Very Sexy Shiraz** 🍷 ★★★★ Unfinished sample **06** focuses on ripeness (15.2% alc), sacrificing nuance: robustly fruity, big dollop spicy tannin needing time's smoothing hand. Unashamedly bold, gutsy. Fr oak, half new. No **05**. **Ubuntu** ★★★ Name alludes to 'the African principle of humanity'; sales proceeds to worthy education initiatives; last **05** (sample) cab-led blend with shiraz & merlot, bold & powerful (15.5% alc) but gd with robust fare. **The Dark Side** NEW 🍷 ★★★★ Cab, shiraz (89/11), aptly named for wine's richness. **05**'s showy ripe black plums infused with mocha choc, prosciutto flavours reward with plump, juicy drinkability. Partially oaked. **'Darling Daisy'** NEW ★★★ Name provisional at tasting **07** chenin/sauv sample; lush melon fruit, perky appetite appeal from taut acid structure. Occasional release. **Chenin Blanc Natural Sweet** NEW 🍷 ★★★★ Barley sugar & preserved tropical fruit richness pervades **06**, chenin's trademark acidity adding fillip of freshness to 58g/l sweetness. For cheese, dessert or solo, enjoy well chilled. New oak 5 mths. In 375ml.

Bush Vines range

CPS ★★★ Blend cab, pinotage, shiraz. **04** gruff & brooding mid-2006 but gd earthy, spicy wild berry character; deserved time to show its latent charms.

Dusty Road range

Cabernet Sauvignon 🍷 ★★★ Last-tasted **05**, ripe cassis with whiff spice (from dash shiraz) imparting sweet impression to chunky wine. Touch hot & hollow, from vintage. **Pinotage** 🍷 ★★★ Last ed, **05** (sample) unwooded & softer than pvs, with ripe squishy fruit & friendly 12.4% alc. **Cabernet Sauvignon-Shiraz** ★★★ Made intermittently for particular customers. Last was smoky & austere **03**. **Rosé** 🍷 ★★ **06**, last available, equal parts cinsaut & shiraz infused dry crisp quaffer with spicy, savoury nuances. Short & brisk. **Chardonnay Unwooded** 🍷 ★★ Soft, understated, light & brisk **06**, last reviewed, had limy acidity & short sherbet finish. **Chenin Blanc** 🍷 ★★ Tasted last ed, **06** lighter styled with shy winter melon aromas & very brisk palate. — CR

■ **Clos Cabrière** see Cabrière

Clos Malverne
T 021-865-2022 • F 021-865-2518

Stellenbosch • Est/1stB 1988 • Tasting & sales Mon-Fri 10–4.30 Sat 10-1 • Fee R15 • Closed Christian hols & Jan 1 • Tours by appt • Free picnic facilities • Owner Seymour & Sophia Pritchard • Winemaker/viticulturist I.P. Smit (Nov 1997) • 25ha (cab, merlot, pinotage, shiraz, sauv) • 350t/24 000cs 80% red 20% white • PO Box 187 Stellenbosch 7599 • info@ closmalverne.co.za • www.closmalverne.co.za; www.capeblend.co.za

'We were happy to let the business trundle along,' muses Seymour Pritchard, co-owner with wife Sophia, 'but now that Zaine's involved we've been given a new shot of energy.' Zaine is Seymour P's nephew, and he's credited with a 40% increase in sales, still largely export oriented. He is, says his uncle, 'the new face of Clos Malverne'. Not that Seymour is retiring; far from it. He's become fascinated by sauvignon, now accounting for a surprising (for a red wine producer) quarter of wine sold.

★★★★ **Pinotage Reserve** Seriously styled **04** entices with complex damson & red berry aromas. Compact, succulent fruit underpinned by firm tannins, balanced, spicy-dry finish. Yr Fr/Am oak.

★★★★ **Cabernet Sauvignon-Merlot Limited Release 01** once-off 60/40 blend which won Jan Smuts Trophy at SAYWS 2001 released early 2006. Decanter gold, Calyon Top 10; pvsly noted as beautifully proportioned, with deep-pile velvety richness.

★★★★★ **Auret Cape Blend 05** (★★★★) version cellar's flagship cab, pinotage, merlot blend (65/25/15) not as sleek or luxurious as pvsly rated **03**. Unyielding tannins overwhelm ripe mulberry fruit, & persist to sweet-sour warm (14.5% alc) finish.

★★★★★ **Auret Cape Blend Limited Release** Once-off **01** still available; features SAYWS winning cab (60%) & merlot, plus cellar's best pinotage (25%). Mid-2004 showed compact flavours & understated power.

Cabernet Sauvignon ★★★★ Forthcoming cassis, violets, cedar charms in perfumed, step-up **04**; plush, juicy blackcurrant fruit in balance with ripe, integrated tannin & savoury finish. For medium term. Yr Fr oak. **03** (★★★☆) was classically styled but foursquare. **Pinotage** ★★★ **04**, reviewed mid-2005, showed savoury spiciness to ripe fruit, dry tannins accentuated slightly bitter finish. 4 mths Fr/Am oak. **Cabernet Sauvignon-Merlot** ★★★ Herbal, brambly 80/20 blend in **05**, stalky tannins masking blackberry fruit flavours. 4 mths Fr/Am oak. **Cabernet Sauvignon-Shiraz** ★★★ Usual 75/25 blend & 4 mths Fr/Am oak in **05**. Spicy pepper & blackcurrant aromas, dry tannins grasping sinewy fruit. **Sauvignon Blanc** ★★★★ **07** overt tropical fruit aromas & more herbaceous fig & gooseberry flavours. Fresh, minerally finish. Enjoy now. Discontinued: **Shiraz**. All reds basket-pressed, fermented in traditional open-topped kuipe. — *IM*

Clouds Vineyards
T 021-885-1819 • F 021-885-2829

Stellenbosch ▪ Est 2002 ▪ 1stB 2003 ▪ Visits by appt ▪ Lunches/dinners for small groups by appt ▪ Luxury self-catering & B&B suites (see Stay-over section) ▪ Weddings & functions ▪ Owner Bernard & Petro Immelman ▪ Winemaker Gyles Webb & Rudi Schultz (Thelema) ▪ Viticulturist Matthew Castle ▪ 2.5 ha (sauvignon) ▪ 750 cs 100% white ▪ PO Box 540 Stellenbosch 7599 ▪ info@cloudsvineyards.co.za ▪ www.cloudsestate.co.za

For owner Bernard Immelman, the 'cherub' on top of Clouds, their idyllic wedding and accommodation venue situated on the scenic Helshoogte pass, is their single-vineyard Sauvignon. Gyles Webb of Thelema makes the wine, a portion of which is marketed under the Clouds label. Contemplated plans include a small winery, vinoteque and restaurant.

Sauvignon Blanc ★★★★ **07** picks up the pace on **06** (★★★☆): juicy blackcurrant nuances to tropical flavours; poised, silky mouthfeel, long farewell. — *CvZ*

Clovelly Wines
T 021-865-2511 • F 021-865-2511

Stellenbosch ▪ Est/1stB 2000 ▪ Visits by appt ▪ Guesthouse with B&B/self-catering option (082-853-7190) ▪ Owner Mineke Toerien-Fourie, Jacques Fourie & Deon Toerien ▪ Winemaker Jacques Fourie ▪ 3ha (cab) ▪ 6t/2 600cs 70% red 30% white ▪ Postnet Suite 215, Private Bag X5061, Stellenbosch 7599 ▪ info@clovellywines.com ▪ www.clovellywines.com

Careful juggling of winemaking responsibilities at the family-owned winery with his expanding role as consultant allows Jacques Fourie just enough time to assist in international marketing activities. Gaining 89 points for the Cab from UK Wine & Spirits magazine made the balancing act all the more worthwhile.

Cabernet Sauvignon ★★★ **03** last ed was few yrs off peak; very ripe dark-choc & cherry notes balanced by tangy acids & savoury tannins. 14 mths oak, some new. **Patina Shiraz** ★★★★ **05**, (unacknowledged) sample pvs ed, still dense, broody, packed with blackcurrant, hint smoked bacon. 100% new Fr oak integrating nicely. Classy & opulent in savoury mould. **Triangle** ★★★ Now NV; slightly dusty & robust, summer berries augmented by meaty hint, lean & food-friendly. **Chardonnay** ★★★ Chardonnay only made in equal years, thus no **05**.

Flavour-packed **06**, baked pear & lemon zest • still slightly gawky acidity. 40% new oak adds creamy/toasty touch. — *RP*

Cloverfield Private Cellar
T 023-626-4118/3 • F 023-626-3203

Robertson • Est ca 1945 • 1stB 2002 • Tasting & sales Mon-Fri 9-5 Sat 10-2 • Closed Easter Fri-Sun, Dec 25 & Jan 1 • Facilities see intro • Owner/viticulturist Pieter Marais • Cellarmaster Cobus Marais • Winemaker Cobus Marais (Jan 2002) • 100ha (10 varieties r/w) • ±1 000t/±2 000cs own label 40% red 60% white • PO Box 429 Robertson 6705 • info@cloverfield.co.za • www.cloverfield.co.za

The Irish patrimony of materfamilias Liz is the inspiration behind the Marais family's four-leaf clover motif. With a new conference and wedding venue now completed, your ventures, both commercial and matrimonial, can share in the associated good luck. Production of wine continues in the upgraded wine cellar.

Winemaker Selection

★★★★ **Chardonnay Wooded** Usually elegantly voluptuous, rich but with pert lime acidity to ward off cloy. Work-in-progress **07** showing all hallmarks of MIWA-applauded **05** & pvs, too unformed, sweet-oak-dominated to rate.

Shiraz ★★★ No successor in sight for **04**, warm & creamy, touched with spice.

Clover Selection

Shamrock Red [NEW] ☺ ★★★ Cranberries, ham & black pepper abound in friendly-tannined maiden **06**. Mainly shiraz, unwooded. WO W Cape. **Sauvignon Blanc** ☺ ★★★ Typically early-harvested for zesty acidity, green-spectrum flavours, moderate alc. **07** doesn't disappoint; fresh, delicately dry.

Chardonnay Unwooded ★★★ Enticing lime & banana, refreshing acidity on **07**; pvs brawny alc down to manageable 14%, but not as flavoursome as last-tasted **05**. **Chenin Blanc** ✓ ★★★★ Bold, vibrant & long **07** brims with dried peaches, pears, orange pith. First tasted since equally characterful **04**. — *CvZ*

■ **Cocoa Hill** *see Dornier Wines*
■ **Cogmans Kloof** *see Zandvliet Estate*
■ **Cogmans River** *see Zandvliet Estate*

Cold Duck (5th Avenue)

Carbonated sparkler by Distell. Signatures are its gentle sweetness, low alc (8%) & pineapple scents from Ferdinand de Lesseps grapes (50%, with pinotage, chenin).

5th Avenue Cold Duck ★★ Latest **NV** has strawberry & candyfloss extras, exuberant bubbles. — *MW*

Coleraine Wines
T 021-863-2073 • F 086-617-8723

Paarl • Est 1998 • 1stB 1999 • Tasting & sales Mon-Fri 10-3 Sat 10-1 • Fee R10 • Closed Easter Fri-Mon, Dec 25/26 & Jan 1; phone ahead on other pub hols • Tours by appt • Walks • Owner C & HK Kerr • Winemaker Reinhard Odendaal • Viticulturist Clive Kerr & Reinhard Odendaal • 30ha (cab, cinsaut, merlot, mourvèdre, petit v, ruby cab, shiraz, chard, sauv, viognier) • 4-5 000cs own label • PO Box 579 Suider-Paarl 7624 • info@coleraine.co.za • www.coleraine.co.za

Owner Clive Kerr has handed winemaking duties over to ex-Beyerskloof Reinhard Odendaal, as well as curtailing all use of herbicides and pesticides towards a holistic, more eco-attuned approach. Odendaal predicts further improvements to the range, but also a sore back from stoppering all 2 000 bottles of the maiden Viognier by hand.

Culraithin range

★★★★ **Merlot** Last tasted was plump-fruited TWS trophy winner **03**, which showed butcher-shop richness with elegance & finesse.

★★★★ **Syrah 04** pvs ed was amply fruited, but with lingering elegance & refined minty, spiced berry character. No **03**. Exceptional **02** (★★★★★) won Paarl Vintners Challenge. **Cabernet Sauvignon** ★★★★ Heady fruit, oak & fynbos aromas on **04**, sample pvs ed; rich, sappy fruit well controlled by tight yet elegant tannins. Ready to enjoy; will evolve. **Coleraine Fire Engine Red** ★★★ New **05** blend, 50/50 merlot/shiraz; appealing fruit richness, charry oak notes, gd grip; drinks easily. Seasoned oak. **Chardonnay** NEW ★★★ Vanilla & orange blossom on ripe-style **07**; previewed, has soft entry, gd oak & fruit integration. Still youthfully taut mid-2007; may rate higher once bottled. **Chenin Blanc** NEW Introverted **07** barrel sample difficult to rate; oxidative style, promising broad palate. Only 100cs. **Viognier** ★★★★ Attractive spicy white peach notes on now-bottled **06**. Litchi & hint honey; fresh, ripe flavours; medium bodied & balanced. — *JP*

Colmant Cap Classique & Champagne

T 021-876-4348 • F 021-876-3732

Franschhoek • Est/1stB 2005 • Visits Fri 10-6 & Sat 10-1 or by appt (T 072·368·4942) • Fee R15 for glass of champagne • Owner Jean-Philippe & Isabelle Colmant • Winemaker Jean-Philippe Colmant, with Nicolas Follet (2006/2007) • Viticulturist Paul Wallace (consultant) • 2.8ha (chard) • 18t/3 400cs 100% MCC • PO Box 602 Franschhoek 7690 • jp@colmant.co.za • www.colmant.co.za

Belgians Jean-Philippe and Isabelle Colmant source chardonnay and pinot from six different areas for their handcrafted cap classique, the maiden Brut Tradition and Rosé due in September this year (and unready for review), the Blanc de Blancs to follow. In the meantime, they offer champagne tastings. Say they: 'We pride ourselves on being the right place for the discerning bubbly lover.'

■ **Compagnies Wijn** *see* Oude Compagnies Post

■ **Condé** *see* Stark-Condé Wines

■ **Confluence** *see* Douglas Wine Cellar

Conradie Family Vineyards

T 023-342-7025/1258 • F 023-347-1356

Worcester • Est/1stB 2004 • Visits Mon-Sat 9-5 Sun 10-3; sales also after-hours by appt • Closed Good Fri, Ascension Day, Dec 25 & Jan 1 • Fully licensed restaurant, guest house & other amenities • Owner Conradie family • Cellarmaster/viticulturist CP Conradie • Winemaker CP Conradie (2004), with Elsabé Conradie (Jan 2007) • 91ha (cabs s/f, merlot, pinotage, red muscadel, chard, chenin, colombard, crouchen, sauv) • 1 500t/5 300cs own label • Other export brand: Saw Edge Peak • 45% red 45% white 10% rosé • PO Box 5298 Worcester 6851 • wine@conradievineyards.co.za • www.conradie-vineyards.co.za

Fifth-generation winegrowers CP and Elsabé Conradie are rekindling interest in this private family cellar after an absence of 40 years. 'We now use only the very best 5% for our premium wines,' reveal the young brother-and-sister team, proud of their 'very hands-on' approach and promising a friendly welcome.

Cabernet Sauvignon ★★★ Sweet vanilla & coconut from 15 mths new Fr/Am oak; **06** powerful tannins need few yrs to meld with cranberry fruit. SAYWS champ. **Pinotage** ★★★★ **06** leap in quality from **05** (★★★). Quintessential strawberries & cream plus lightest hint rubber, subtle oakspice. Juicy, coconut-dusted; long & intense. 15 mths new oak, 50/50 Fr/Am. Awards incl Winemaker's Choice 'diamond'. **Chardonnay** ✓ ★★★★ **06** judiciously oaked to showcase zesty lemon & lime notes; delicious now, potential for yr/2 ageing. 33% barrel fermented, rest tank. **Chenin Blanc** ★★ After lees-enriched **06**, slightly sweet-centred **07** simpler, less convincing. **Sauvignon Blanc** ★★ **07** shy, some kiwi & greengage, racy acidity despite 5.3g/l sugar. **Werdoux Semi-Sweet** ★★ Gently sweet (20g/l RS) **07** from colombard, enlivened by sweet-sour acidity. **Sweet Rosaline Perlé Rosé** 🖺 ★★ Petillant pink party girl. Sauv bl & cab with red muscadel upping sweetness. Carbonated, **NV. Merlot** **NEW** ★★ 05 serious intent, but fruit currently too slender for grippy tannins. Give time. Mostly WO Nuy. — *CvZ*

Conspirare

T 021-855-0722 ▪ F 021-855-0706

Stellenbosch (see Helderberg map) ▪ Est/1stB 2002 ▪ Tasting by appt ▪ Owner HB Dowling/ LRD Trust ▪ Winemaker Henry Dowling ▪ Viticulturist Francois de Villiers ▪ 24ha (cab s/f, merlot, shiraz, chenin) ▪ 250t/425cs own label 100% red ▪ PO Box 1210 Stellenbosch 7599 ▪ dowls@ mweb.co.za

All quiet on the eastern front, reports Henry Dowling, winemaker and owner (with wife Lesley Rae), although he has been planting on the home farm, the aptly named Angel's View on the Helderberg. This year, he assures us, he'll be making wine again, for the first time since 2003.

★★★★ **Conspirare** Quietly powerful & intense 03 added 14% shiraz to pvs cabs s/f, merlot blend, with no reduction of appeal. Still available, not retasted. — *TJ*

Constantia Glen

T 021-794-7865 ▪ F 021-794-9705

Constantia ▪ Est 2000 ▪ 1stB 2005 ▪ Closed to public ▪ Owner Tumado Investments ▪ Winemaker Karl Lambour (Nov 2006) ▪ Viticulturist Andrew Teubes ▪ 29ha (cabs s/f, malbec, merlot, petit v, sauv) ▪ 120t 80% red 20% white ▪ PO Box 780 Constantia 7848 ▪ wine@ constantiaglen.com ▪ www.constantiaglen.com

Karl Lambour took up the baton to conduct the 2007 harvest in the new state-of-the-art cellar. The score here will always be for two works, a Sauvignon (the applauded 2006 won IWC gold and 90 Wine Spectator points) and, from 2009, a red bordeaux-style blend – with consultant Dominique Hebrard, of Cheval Blanc repute, to advise on fine tuning.

★★★★☆ **Sauvignon Blanc 06** (not retasted) another cool-climate classic, but green character not exaggerated or pungent: some greenpepper, citrus, flint. Flavour will develop with deserved yr/2 in bottle; beautifully balanced, taut-silk structure can cope with that & more. — *TJ*

Constantia Uitsig

T 021-794-1810 ▪ F 021-794-1812

Constantia ▪ Est 1988 ▪ 1stB 1993 ▪ Tasting & sales Mon-Fri 9-5 Sat & Sun 10-5 ▪ Closed Easter Fri, Dec 25/26, Jan 1 ▪ Constantia Uitsig & La Colombe restaurants (see Eat-Out section); The River Café for light meals 8-5 ▪ Constantia Uitsig Hotel & Spa (see Stay-over section) ▪ Owner David & Marlene McCay 50% & a consortium headed by Tokyo Sexwale 50% ▪ Viticulturist André Rousseau & John Loubser (Mar 1998/2001, consultants) ▪ 32ha (cab, merlot, chard, sauv, semillon) ▪ ±200t/±12 000cs 30% red 70% white ▪ PO Box 402 Constantia 7848 ▪ wine@uitsig.co.za ▪ www.uitsig.co.za

A firm favourite with locals and visitors for their internationally regarded wine and restaurants, the McCays and team have worked on subtle changes 'while guarding the essence'. Encouraging results from natural mealy bug control have led to insecticide-free weed-control programs, part of a collaborative Constantia Valley winegrowers bio-diversity initiative. A new arrival is their first bubbly (missed our deadline, unfortunately); their red is getting more time in the bottle before release. A brand new spa opened last year, complete with wine therapy. Extensive restaurant refurbishments too, as well as a new chef at the celebrated La Colombe.

★★★★ **Constantia Red** Half merlot, with cab & dash cab f; 04 melds sassy woodspice with velvety red-berry fruit & finely tuned tannins. 03 had tad Am oak; showy, lushly ripe, woodier than pvs. Now 15 mths Fr cask (down from 19), 70% new.

★★★★ **Chardonnay Unwooded** 🖻 Convincing, appealing example in increasingly popular genre. Preview 07 usual untrammelled varietal aromas & flavours, broad mouthfilling viscosity focused by cool acidity in flourishing finish. Gentler 13.5% alc.

★★★★ **Sauvignon Blanc** 🗎 Focused & full flavoured, splendidly combines green fruit & tropicality. Sample **07** in stony form, grassy tension to flowing length; skin & lees contact abets richness. 14% alc firmer than **06** (13%). Better yr+ in bottle.

★★★★☆ **Semillon Reserve** 🗎 Serious & rather grand, now even more focused with less oak (7 mths, seasoned). Lanolin aromas mingle with wood vanilla, measured mouthful briefly upset by pushy 14.5% alc. Like toasty **05**, needing yr/2 to harmonise.

★★★★☆ **Constantia White** 🗎 Breathtaking intensity of flavour without weight, a touch of beeswax breadth adding gravitas to flinty core. Dry **06** (60:40) reverts to more equal blend sem/sauv (as for serious **04**) after brief flirtation with earlier style of 70:30 proportions in not-quite-dry **05** (★★★★). 7 mths used oak.

Discontinued: **Chardonnay Reserve**. — *DS*

Constantia Wines
T 023-230-0656 • F 023-230-1574

Tulbagh • Est 1965 • 1stB 2000 • Visits by appt • Owner Lucas J van Tonder • 35ha (cab, merlot, pinot, chenin, riesling, sauv) • 3-5 000cs own label 15% red 80% white 5% blanc de noir • PO Box 79 Tulbagh 6820 • montpellierwine@tiscali.co.za • www.montpellier.co.za

Seasoned Anton Krynauw, former colleague of legendary Günter Brözel, returned from retirement in 2002 to help Johannesburg advocate Lucas van Tonder manage his Tulbagh wine ventures… and stayed. The winemaker is now running two cellars: replanted 18th-century Montpellier and neighbouring Constantia, with its own independent spread of red and white vineyards.

Constantia de Tulbagh range

Merlot ★ Tasted out of vintage order, **05** shows green stalky character. **Pinot Noir** ★ Tasted last ed, **06** light coloured/styled, suggestion of pinot fragrance. **Red** NEW ★★ Porty, full-bodied, tannic & touch oxidised **05**. **Chenin Blanc** ★★ Honeyed notes on dry, light-bodied **06**. **Selene** NEW Semi-sweet blend mainly chenin, riesling & soupçon gewürz. This, next wine, unrated. **Jesse's View** NEW Light-bodied dry white from chenin, sauv. **NV**. **Cap Classique** ★ Sunny-ripe character to latest **NV**, fizzy mousse, slightly oxidative, dry. — *IvH*

Cordoba Winery
T 021-855-3744 • F 021-855-1690

Stellenbosch (see Helderberg map) • Est 1982 • 1stB 1994 • Tasting only by appt Mon-Fri 8.30-5 • Sales Mon-Fri 8.30-5 • Closed pub hols • Tours by appt • Owner Jannie Jooste • Winemaker/viticulturist Christopher Keet (Oct 1993) • 31ha (cabs s/f, merlot, shiraz, chard) • 100t/7 000cs 90% red 10% white • PO Box 5609 Helderberg 7135 • mail@cordobawines.co.za • www.cordobawines.co.za

'We remain focused in our objective of "perfecting viticulture" to create great wines, as opposed to "making" great wine,' says grower-vintner Christopher Keet. For him, this means farming in harmony with nature. 'Alien clearing, reducing fungicidal sprays, virtually eliminating insecticides and pesticides, preventing erosion, and protecting our wildlife are all in a day's work at Cordoba.' As is attention to detail in tending to these mountain vineyards, with severe crop reduction and canopy management appearing to be paying off even in the young vineyards: 'They keep surprising us with the quality of grapes they are producing.'

★★★★ **Merlot** One of Cape's more serious. **02** was more severe (though savoury & well structured on review pvs ed) than standout **01** (★★★★★); signature coffee/dark choc notes over cherry & minty-leafy element. 17 mths Fr oak, 20% new.

★★★★☆ **Crescendo** Classically-oriented cab f-based blend: beguiling early charm to **03** (15% each cab & merlot), but lovely berries, sappy minerality & savoury tannins suggest long stayer. 18 mths gd new Fr oak. Not reviewed for this ed.

Cabernet Sauvignon-Merlot ★★★ Cab noses ahead in 51:49 blend (hence name change from pvs ed), adds leafy austerity to **03**. 16 mths 20% new oak unyielding mid-2007. **Chardonnay** ★★★★☆ Developed patina, crème brûlée roundness & buttery oak (fermented/9 mths, 33% new) offset by mineral character, limy tail & gentle 12.5% alc. Enjoy now. — *DS*

■ **Cowlin Wines** *see* Noble Hill Wines

■ *Craftsman* *see* Val de Vie Winelands Lifestyle Estate

Craighall

Popular range of budget-priced easy-drinkers, by African Wines & Spirits.
Cabernet Sauvignon-Merlot ★★★ Perennially tasty & unassuming. **05** 60/40 mix, last ed had distinct claret feel, blending elegance & carefree quaffability. **Sauvignon Blanc** ★★ Pre-bottling sample **07** dry & racy; attractive Granny Smith apple notes. **Chardonnay-Sauvignon Blanc** ★★ **07**, ex-tank, friendly dry party-goer with acid nip in tail. 60/40 mix. Discontinued: **Rosé**. — *CvZ*

Creation Wines

T 082-858-6562 (JC); 072-673-1880 (CM) • F 028-313-1512

*Walker Bay (see Elgin/Walker Bay map) • Est 2002 • 1stB 2007 • Tasting by appt Mon-Sat •
Owner JC & Carolyn Martin, Heidi Kellerhals Kaser & Christoph Kaser • Winemaker JC Martin
& Christoph Kaser with Kevin Baatjies (Jan 2007) • Viticulturist JC Martin & Christoph Kaser,
advised by Johan Pienaar • 22ha (cab, grenache, merlot, petit v, pinot, shiraz, chard, sauv,
semillon, viognier) • 70t/5 000cs 65% red 35% white • PO Box 1772 Hermanus 7200 • info@
creationwines.com, cmartin1@telkomsa.net • www.creationwines.com*

A new cellar, featuring equipment imported from Germany, Switzerland and France, was completed in time for the vintage last year on this property owned by winemakers Christoph Kaser, JC Martin and their partners (Carolyn M a member of the respected Finlayson winemaking family). They plan to hit full production on the 22ha Hemel-en-Aarde Valley farm this year with what they describe as a fabulous Côtes-du-Rhône-style blend as well as a Viognier and Chardonnay, aged in barrel.

Merlot-Cabernet Sauvignon-Petit Verdot ★★★ Nutty blackcurrant & mulberry aromas on **06**, some sweet fruit lurking behind youthful, puckering tannins. **Sauvignon Blanc** ★★★ Elegant & restrained **07**, lime-citrus aromas, some flinty/mineral notes & a hint of capsicum; racy & bright but not austere. — *MF*

Crios Bríde

T 021-883-9568 • F 086-694-0728

*Est/1stB 2007 • Closed to public • Owner Yorke-Smith Family & Martin Bates • Winemaker
Carla Pauw (Jan 2007) • 80t/4 000cs 7% red 13% white 80% MCC • PO Box 2290 Dennesig
Stellenbosch 7601 • criosbride@gmail.com*

Brighid – goddess of nature – wears a Crios Bríde (a girdle of straw crosses) during her spring festival – and is the inspiration behind the name of Neil Yorke-Smith and London-based financier Martin Bates' vinous venture, with its emphasis on cap classique. The MCC is remaining on its lees, until deemed ready by winemaker Carla Pauw.

Sauvignon Blanc ★★★ Ripe & grassy **07**, mown hay, oyster & iodine notes, soft & amply textured. Limited release from Darling fruit. — *MF*

Crossroads Wines

T 021-461-3629 • F 021-465-0581

*Cape Town • Est/1stB 2005 • Closed to public • 5 000cs • 4 Church Square Building, 5th Floor -
Suite 514, Cape Town • simphiwe@crossroadsmail.co.za*

Ahead of the Soccer World Cup, this BEE company kicks off with a '2010' red blend, to be repeated annually until 2010, together with a final representative 4-wine pack. New wine Bayete joins the team with China and the US as export goals, while Soweto White also stars locally at Wandis tavern.

Crows Nest

T 021-869-8712 • F 021-869-8714

*Paarl • Est/1stB 2003 • Tasting & sales daily 8-5 • Tours Mon-Sat 9-5 • Farm/country-style
lunches 12-3; also picnics in summer by appt • Farm produce • Facilities for children • Tour*

groups ▪ *Owner Marcel & Deidre de Reuck ▪ Winemaker Marcel de Reuck ▪ Viticulturist Viti consultant Paul Wallace (Aug 2003) ▪ 11ha (cab, mourvèdre, shiraz, tinta amarella, chard, viognier) ▪ 48t/4 000 cs 85% red 15% white ▪ PO Box 2571 Paarl 7620 ▪ info@dereuckwines. co.za*

Many winemakers rate marketing as the worst part of the job, and Marcel de Reuck is no exception. 'But it's leather to the pavement,' he shrugs, looking for growth in the US, Eastern Europe and China, while adding value back home with new varieties (mourvèdre and tinta amarela), horse-drawn carriages, and an ever-spreading lawn to accommodate picnics.

Marcel de Reuck range

★★★★ **Cabernet Sauvignon** Combines power, extraction & elegance; **04** dense tannins, opulent blackcurrant flavours. Very youthful still last yr, deserved time to show potential. Yr Fr oak, 20% new. Paarl, Dbnvlle fruit.

Syrah ★★★☆ **04** juicy, rich, attractive spicy barrel character (20% new oak), but pvsly noted as yard short of seriousness, complexity of **03** (★★★★), MIWA DG. **Cabernet Sauvignon-Merlot** ★★★ Sinewy, even austere **04**, powerful tannins & herbaceous green walnut fruit noted last ed. Oak as for Syrah. WO Coastal. **Chardonnay 04** sold out; **05** unready. **Sauvignon Blanc** ★★★ Lees-matured 14 mths before release, hence attractive bottle-age nuance on last tasted **05**; fig & nettle flavours, clean acid bite. **06** not ready. Note: Crows Nest range in abeyance. — *CT*

Croydon Vineyard Residential Estate

T 021-843-3610 ▪ F 021-843-3609

Stellenbosch (see Helderberg map) ▪ Est 2005 ▪ Visits by appt (see intro) ▪ Owner Croydon Vineyard Estate Homeowners Association ▪ Cellarmaster Beyers Truter ▪ Winemaker Corius Visser (2005), advised by Beyers Truter ▪ Viticulturist Corius Visser ▪ 7ha (cabs s/f, malbec, merlot, pinotage, shiraz) ▪ 56t/±5 000cs ▪ 100% red ▪ Croydon Wine Company, Unit 1, Croydon Vineyard Estate, Croydon, Somerset West 7130 ▪ winemaker@croydon-estate.co.za ▪ www. croydon-estate.co.za

Residents of this 'signature development' near Faure hold an equal share in the winery and vineyards, so they're able to rub shoulders with one of SA's most celebrated winemakers, Beyers Truter - preferably after studying their personal copy of Truter's Introduction to Winemaking. Non-residents can taste and buy the wines, and tour the cellar by appointment.

Covenant ★★★★ Similar blend to sibling but enjoys 100% new-oak (Fr) fillip; **05** intricate, classy lead pencil fragrance; firm but integrated tannin backbone. Notch up from persistent & spicy **04** (★★★★). **Title Deed** ✓ ★★★★ Attractive & finely tuned blend cab (47%), roughly equal pinotage & merlot, 7% petit v; **05** ups the ante with suave tannins meshed with plush black fruit; 13.9% alc not obvious. 30% new Fr oak. **04** (★★★☆) not quite as rich, flavoursome. — *CvZ*

■ **Cru Wines** *see* Wines of Cape Town

Culemborg

This big-volume range of easy-drinkers is made by DGB.

Cabernet Sauvignon ★★★ Dusty blackberry nose on **05**, soft tannins underpin luscious berry flavours. **Cinsaut** ★ **06** continues undemanding style of pvs. Tasted as sample, as were most of these; ratings provisional. **Merlot** ★★☆ Steely **05**, mocha hints & well-managed tannins. No rush to consume. **Pinotage** ★★★ Earthy black cherries on **05**, usual sweet plum jam finish. **Shiraz** NEW ★★★ A charmer. **05** inviting spicy bouquet; warm, savoury dark berry fruit. **Cape Red** ★★ Ruby cab & cinsaut in **06**, fresh & uncomplicated fruit-driven quaffer. **Blanc de Noir** ▤ ★★ Crisp, almost dry picnic/poolside splasher. **07** from pinotage. **Rosé** ★★ **07** a crisp, fruity lunchtime pink with pinotage's strawberry hints. **Chardonnay** ★★ Perfumed limy **07**, citrus & green melon flavours, easy drinking. **Chenin Blanc** ★★ Fresh outdoor aromas on **07**, clean undemanding tastes. **Sauvignon Blanc** ★★ Sauv's typical grassy notes on **07**, green apple zing. **Cape White** ★★ Crisp, dry everyday white, **07** with leafy notes. — *DB*

■ **Culraithin** *see* Coleraine Wines

Dalla Cia Wine & Spirit Company
T 021-888-4120 • **F** 021-887-2621

Stellenbosch • Est 2004 • Tasting, sales & traditional Italian meals at Pane E Vino Food & Wine Bar • Owner/winemaker Giorgio Dalla Cia • 9 000cs • 7A Lower Dorp Street, Bosman's Crossing, Stellenbosch • info@dallacia.com • www.dallacia.com

After more than 25 years at Meerlust, the Dalla Cias have moved into a new, larger home in Stellenbosch's Bosman's Crossing. Like an Italian family of old, all lend a hand in the various enterprises. Son George helps Giorgio make the family grappa (and small quantities of brandy for other brands) while daughter-in-law Elena serves gourmet Italian food at the adjacent trattoria, Pane E Vino, which also houses winetasting and sales.

★★★★☆ **Giorgio** Always impressive bdx blend. Reflecting vintage, **05** ripe, rich; plums, mocha, meat extract, all assimilating 80% new oak. Italian-style dry tannins food friendly but still unfolding, future pleasures in store. No **04**.

Special Selection NEW ★★★★ For Wine Society & by glass ex-Pane E Vino. **03** bdx blend, cab dominant, explains firm structure, lead pencils styling. Quality in place, just needs time. 70% new oak. **Chardonnay** ★★★★ True individual; unwooded. Expressive **07** shows floral, fennel notes of **06**, this time citrus veined. Vibrant appetite appeal no surprise: food is major family focus. **Sauvignon Blanc** ★★★★ Vibrating with tension, freshness, **07** surpasses **06** (★★★★), showing cool fruit class: nettles, 'oyster shell' minerality, elegant sustained finish. — *CR*

■ **Danckaert** *see* Citrusdal Cellars
■ *Danie de Wet* *see* De Wetshof Estate

Darling Cellars
T 022-492-2276 • **F** 022-492-2647

Darling (see Durbanville map) • Est/1stB 1996 • Tasting & sales Mon-Thu 8-5 Fri 8-4 Sat 10-2 • Closed Easter Fri/Sun, Dec 25 & Jan 1 • BYO picnic • Tours by appt • Owner ±20 shareholders • Cellarmaster Abé Beukes (Dec 1997) • Winemaker Johan Nesenberend (reds, Dec 1996) & Albé Truter (whites, Dec 2003) • Viticulturist Gawie Kriel (Sep 2001, consultant) • 1 300ha (cab, merlot, pinotage, shiraz, cinsaut, chard, chenin, sauv) • 6-7 000t/300 000cs • 65% red 33% white 2% rosé • BRC, IFS & ISO 9001:2000 certified • PO Box 114 Darling 7345 • info@darlingcellars.co.za • www.darlingcellars.co.za

Their tenth anniversary year was a great one, beams Abé Beukes. A new importer in Scandinavia sees exports looking healthier than ever; locally wines are flying out as fast as they can be produced (the downside is pressure to release them earlier than Abé B would like). He also has a few things in mind - like a light-and-fruity summer-style grenache with lower alcohol, for chilled lunchtime enjoyment. And several new red blends come on-stream, including a rhône-style wine utilising 'very nice' plantings, a classic blend of the Bordeaux five, and a shiraz-grenache. But he's not just seeing reds - the sauvignon's 'going great guns!'

Onyx range

★★★★ **Cabernet Sauvignon** Step-up **04** (★★★★☆) svelte, balanced & accessible, yet structured to reward cellaring 5+ yrs. Abundant cassis, silky/cedary tannins, dry elegant finish; oak (12 mths, 60% new) harmonises with dense fruit core. **03** tad sleeker, with supportive dry tannins.

★★★★ **Pinotage** Less oak on **04** (Fr/Am/Hung combo, 50% new vs 100% pvsly) complements earthy, dark berried fruit; contributes to full mouthfeel. More elegant, pinot-like than extroverted, fruitier **03**; neither unbalanced by 14.6%+ alcs.

★★★★ **Shiraz** **04**'s ripe, dense fruit in confident balance with 14.5% alc, acid & oak; firmly structured (18 mths, 50% new oak), built for cellaring 3-7 yrs. Shares leather/game characteristics with **03**, **02**.

★★★★☆ **Kroon** ▤ Cellar's flagship of co-fermented shiraz, pinotage, grenache & cinsaut usually layered & richly textured, but stumbles in **04** (★★★★). Leaner, more austere, unyielding than **03** & pvs; 14.9% alc stands out, fights against tight fruit core. May develop greater charm over time. No grenache; oak 13 mths 100% new.

★★★★☆ **Noble Late Harvest** None tasted since **03**, from chenin, which benefited from variety's piercing acidity, cutting through a rather daunting 240g/l RS. 5-9 mths Fr barrels. An occasional label, as is Barrel Selection, literally the two best **02** casks, 14 mths older oak, drier (120g/l).

Sauvignon Blanc ★★★★ **07**'s focussed minerality & wafts white asparagus raise the bar on **06** (★★★★). Seriously styled, with zesty acidity & long chalky farewell, to accompany food. Groenekloof WO unless noted.

DC range

★★★★   **Black Granite Shiraz** Flagship of this fruit driven varietal range; **06** opulent & liquorice toned, broad tannins support brooding fruit, 14.5% alc. Deserves 3-5 yrs to show best.

Terra Hutton Cabernet Sauvignon ★★★★ **06** notch up on pvs courtesy elegant cassis, choc-mocha flavours, juicy core, fine grained tannins. Accessible, friendly, even with 14.5% alc; some potential to develop. Pvs **04** (★★★★) was leafier & more restrained. **Six Tonner Merlot** ★★★ Fleshy, dark-fruited **06** has hints choc, chunky/toasty mid-palate. Robust 14.5% alc needs hearty fare. **Old Block Pinotage** ★★★★ Intense red plum fruit & spice, bright acidity & firm, ripe tannins do the business in full-bodied **06**. **Unwooded Chardonnay** 🔖 ★★★ Pvsly 'Quercus Gold' despite being decidedly 'quercus-free'. **07**'s fleshy pear & apple palate pierced by lime acidity; moderate 12% alc ideal for solo or lunchtime imbibing. **Chenin Blanc** ★★★ **06** sample last ed was soft & rounded, with big-tasting 14% alc, toasty notes ex-light wooding. **07** unready. **Bush Vine Sauvignon Blanc** 🔖 ★★★ **07** quieter, more subdued than friendly predecessor. Dusty, mineral, with some leesy breadth & grapefruit pith farewell. These all WO Darling.

Flamingo Bay range

Chenin Blanc-Sauvignon Blanc ☺ 🔖 ★★ Clean & zesty **07**, leaner-styled al fresco partner with moderate 12.8% alc.

Cinsaut-Cabernet Sauvignon 🔖 ★★★ **06** foursquare & amiable summer barbeque companion. Warm youngberry fruit & toasty finish. **Pinotage Rosé** 🔖 ★★ Sunset-tinged **07** has strawberry tones. Tangy & slender styling (12.5% alc). Coastal WOs for these.

Zantsi Natural Sweet range

Rosé ★★ Sweet-&-sour scented, red-berry toned pink, with svelte build. **White** ★★ Tangy passionfruit flavours from 100% buket. Still finds favour in France as aperitif, say winemakers. These **NV** & just over 10% alc. — *MW*

Daschbosch Wine Cellar
T 023-349-1110 • F 023-349-1980

Breedekloof (see Worcester map) ▪ Est 1956 ▪ 1stB 1965 ▪ Tasting & sales Mon-Fri 8-5 Sat & pub hols 10-2 ▪ Closed Christian holidays ▪ BYO picnic ▪ Children welcome ▪ 'Fear Factor' wine tasting, cheese platters & accommodation by prior arrangement ▪ Conference facilities for max 50 ▪ Tour groups ▪ Walks ▪ Owner 30 shareholders ▪ Winemaker Johan Lotz (Jun 2004), with Wilhelm le Roux (Sep 2002) ▪ Viticulturist Johan Möller (Okc 2006) ▪ 890ha (15 varieties, r/w) ▪ 17 500t/3 500cs own label 50% red 40% white 10% fortified ▪ Ranges for customers: Sibeko & Cape Concert , Cape Promise, Lambertsbay, Oliver & Gregg (UK) & Waverley (TBS), Victoria Peak ▪ BRC & HACCP accredited ▪ PO Box 174 Rawsonville 6845 ▪ cellar@daschbosch.co.za ▪ www.daschbosch.co.za

Daschbosch and nearby Groot Eiland are long-time collaborators, exporting in a successful joint venture to the UK since 1997. Combined export volumes now top 28 million litres, prompting the partners to formalise their relationship in a new company, uniWines Marketing, setting the stage for further growth.

Chardonnay ☺ ★★★ Lively medium-weight **07** sample showing ripe dried peach & lime. Fresh, balanced & eminently quaffable. **Sauvignon Blanc** ☺ 🗎 ★★★ Pleasant, refreshing summer white. Riper than pvs, **07** retains zesty lemon acidity.

Pinotage Reserve ★★ **07** ripe banana & spice. Youthful sample still sweet, hunky & unknit. **Shiraz** ★★ **07** preview all smoke & spice. Ripe, bold & brawny New World babe! **Cabernet Sauvignon-Cabernet Franc** ★★★ Well-rounded **02** pvs ed showed muted but ripe mint & plum tones. **Chenin Blanc** 🗎 ★★ **07** undemanding, drink-young style. Passionfruit, ripe apple & crisp farewell. **Sparkling Demi-Sec NV** carbonated bubbly from hanepoot. Untasted. **Nectar de Provision Red** ★★ Pvsly tasted spiritous, unctuous **NV** sample from fortified merlot juice, partly barrelled. **Nectar de Provision White** ★★★★ First local version of Cognac's classic aperitif, Pineau des Charentes. **NV** from colombard, pvs ed burst with orange, choc-mint & vanilla; silky, decadent but not cloying. Discontinued: **Rosé**. — *MW*

■ **Dassie's Reserve** *see Botha Wine Cellar*

David Frost Estate
T 021-869-8339 • F 021-869-8732

Voor Paardeberg (see Paarl map) ▪ Est 1994 ▪ 1stB 1997 ▪ Tasting & sales Mon-Fri 10-4 Sat 10-2 ▪ Owner David Frost ▪ Winemaker Ettienne Malan ▪ Vineyard Manager Wynand Pienaar ▪ ±24ha (five bdx reds, shiraz) ▪ 100% red ▪ PO Box 7358 Noorder-Paarl 7623 ▪ davidfrost@ global.co.za ▪ www.frostwine.com

David Frost says he played a lot of golf in 2007. Doable if you're a pro; you qualified for The Open at Carnoustie (where son Shawn, an aspirant pro, caddied); and you can rely on international consultant Michel Rolland, former Rust en Vrede winemaker Etienne Malan and farm manager Wynand Pienaar to oversee matters vinous.

★★★★ **Cabernet Sauvignon 02** (★★★) tasted mid-2006 showed powdery tannins & big (15%) alc fighting for dominance over ripe blackcurrant flavours. Cellaring suggested to give fruit the upper hand. 18 mths 42% new Fr oak. **01** had velvet tannins, tapered slowly to persistent finish.

★★★★ **Par Excellence** Youthful **03**, cab-dominated blend 5 bdx varieties, plenty extract, abundant ripe blackberry, mulberry fruit with cedar and cinnamon. Ripe palate, firm integrated tannin & acidity. Warm finish from 14.5% alc. 26 mths Fr oak.

Merlot ★★★ Savoury & high-toned **02** tasted last ed packs big fruit & alc (15.4%). **Shiraz** ★★★★ Ex-barrel last ed, **04** growing into large frame with berry compote & aniseed flavours, tannin-coated finish partly from 18 mths Fr oak. No **05**. Discontinued: **Cabernet Sauvignon Reserve, Merlot Reserve, Cabernet Sauvignon-Merlot**. — *IM*

■ **Dawning** *see Elberti Wines*
■ *DC Wines* *see Darling Cellars*
■ *Decent Red/White* *see Barrydale Cellar*

De Doorns Winery
T 023-356-2835 • F 023-356-2101

Worcester ▪ Est 1968 ▪ Tasting & sales Mon-Fri 8-5 Sat 8-12 ▪ Winemaker /manager Danie Koen, with Ferdi Coetzee ▪ PO Box 129 De Doorns 6875 ▪ ddwk@hexvallei.co.za

A tweak to the tasting facility - to make it more accessible - and a change to the range, in that it now boasts a sauvignon, which has the members of the co-op enthusing. 'Everybody wants it; these trends…' tut-tuts manager/winemaker Danie Koen. Off the list is the hanepoot (those trends again!).

Sauvignon Blanc NEW 🗎 ★★ **07** attractive grass & green apple aromas; herbal notes on finish. **Demi-sec Sparkling** ★ Uncomplicated semi-sweet fizz, **07** with soft, creamy citrus aromas. **Late Harvest** 🗎 ★ Honey-sweet **07** with floral aroma & hint of rose. **Red Muscadel** ★★★ Maraschino cherry, tealeaf & raisins on **07**; gd structure & well-balanced sweetness.

Available but not tasted: Cabernet Sauvignon, Roodehof Dry Red, Rosé, Chardonnay, Chenin Blanc, Colombar. — *JP*

De Grendel Wines
T 021-558-6280 • F 021-558-7083

Durbanville • Est 1720 • 1stB 2004 • Visits Mon-Fri 9-5 Sat 10-4 • Closed Easter Fri, Dec 25 & Jan 1 • Farm produce • Walks • Conservation area • Owner David Graaff • Cellarmaster Charles Hopkins (Oct 2005) • Winemaker Elzette du Preez (Jan 2006) • Viticulturist Leon Dippenaar (consultant) • 104ha (cabs s/f, malbec, merlot, mourvèdre, petit v, pinot, shiraz, chard, sauv, semillon, viognier) • 17 000cs 40% red 60% white • PO Box 15282 Panorama 7506 • info@ degrendel.co.za • www.degrendel.co.za

Cellarmaster Charles Hopkins is climbing steadily towards maximum output of 35 000 cases; production reached 20 000 in 2007. 'I would have found it a tough task to beat the quality of the 06 Sauvignon,' he confides, 'but it happened. We didn't rush into picking after the February heatwave, just nursed the vines with plenty of irrigation.' On the sales front, Righard Theron focuses on experiential marketing, as in a successful co-operative venture with the fashion house Habits: 'Husbands waiting patiently in the store are offered a glass of wine and when their ladies have spent a certain amount they're presented with a bottle.'

★★★★ **Sauvignon Blanc** 🖥 Tropical notes, white peach & dust on nose & palate of very satisfying, beautifully dry **07**. 4 different blocks, 5 different clones ensure complexity.

★★★★☆ **Koetshuis Sauvignon Blanc** NEW Arresting New Zealand-influenced maiden. 'Best I've had the privilege of working with,' enthuses Charles H. Asparagus & green pea overlain with 'Dbnville dust' & khaki bush; fleshy white peach & passionfruit flavours; poised, complex, with thrilling nervy acidity. 250cs only ex-cellar door.

★★★★ **Winifred** Careful winemaking makes for another gem. **07** has chard's richness, semillon's freshness, all the spice & joi de vivre viognier can muster. Partially barrel fermented (chard/viognier), harmonious. A lovely food wine worth cellaring.

Merlot ★★★★ Confident & polished **06** with scented bouquet, savoury tannins & tangy tail; slightly warming alc (14.8%) also evident on step-up **05** (★★★★). This & other **06** reds first vintage vinified in new cellar. **Op Die Berg Pinot Noir** NEW ★★★★ First commercial pinot from Dbnville. **06** sample still intensely oaky mid-2007 (9 mths Fr, 40% new); cherries & wet earth tickled by spiritous lift (14.5% alc). **Shiraz** ★★★★ Touches mourvèdre & viognier add perfumes & floral notes to previewed **06**'s lifted white pepper profile; juicy fruit core wrapped in fine tannin. Yr oak, 70% Fr, rest Am. Sweetness, not heat, imparted by 15% alc, also feature of muscular **05** (★★★★). **Rosé** NEW ✓ 🖥 ★★★☆ Crisp, dry newcomer perfect for al fresco occasions. **07** well flavoured, brimming with red berries & spicy biltong. Near-equal mix cab & pinotage with 15% cab f. — *CvZ*

■ De Groene Heuwel *see Linton Park Wines*

De Heuvel Estate
T 023-231-0350 • F 023-231-0938

Tulbagh • Est/1stB 1997 • Tasting & sales Mon-Fri 8.30-5 Sat 9-2 • Fee R10 p/p for groups • Closed Easter Fri/Sun, Dec 25 & Jan 1 • Tours Mon-Fri 9-4.30 • Olive oil/olive products • Owner Gaëtan Bovit • Winemaker/viticulturist Marinus Potgieter (2005) • 16 ha (cab, nebbiolo, pinotage, shiraz) • 70 tons 6 000 cs 70% red 30% white • PO Box 103 Tulbagh 6820 • bianco@lando.co.za • www.bianco.co.za

Enthusiastic Gaëtan Bovit's initial infatuation with the beautiful historic farm De Heuvel (previously listed as Bianco Fine Wines) has blossomed into a love affair. The 1806 cellar has been revamped, and, in the first of a series of developments aimed at attracting 'a more lifestyle-orientated crowd', a wine bar is being opened where visitors can enjoy boutique brands by the glass (including the new De Heuvel Muscadel and Port).

■ Dekker's Valley *see Mellasat*

De Krans

T 044-213-3314/64 • F 044-213-3562

Calitzdorp (see Klein Karoo map) • Est 1964 • 1stB 1977 • Tasting & sales Mon-Fri 8-5 Sat 9-3 • Tasting fee for groups R10 pp • Closed Easter Fri/Sun, Dec 25 • Tours by appt • Vintners platters 12-2 Wed & Sat during Feb (also pick your own hanepoot grapes) • BYO picnic • Olive oil for sale • Tour groups • Self-guided vineyard walks year round • Owner/winemaker Boets & Stroebel Nel (1982, 1988) • Viticulturist Willem Botha (2001, consultant) • 45ha (cab, pinotage, tempranillo & port varieties, chard, chenin & muscats) • 500t/20-25 000cs 50% red 10% white 3% rosé 37% fortifieds • PO Box 28 Calitzdorp 6660 • dekrans@mweb.co.za • www.dekrans.co.za

'An 1870 Madeira I had in Portugal in 1996, which still tasted youthful after 126 years.' This is co-owner/winemaker Boets Nel's most memorable wine, and his continuing love affair with fortified wines shows in De Krans's Cape Tawny and Cape Ruby ports, both of which have had great reviews. Their flagship red, Red Stone Reserve, is 'getting better all the time'. 'We believe in producing wines and ports that express the Calitzdorp terroir best,' says Boets. De Krans is the first Klein Karoo member of the Biodiversity & Wine Initiative. Also new is their white and rosé wines in screwcap bottles.

★★★★ **Red Stone Reserve** Flagship red from touriga plus 30% cab, named for ruddy cliffs viewed from the cellar. **06** not ready. Tasted last ed, **05** tightly wound & showy (yr Fr oak) in same mould as focused, fruit-rich **04**; both needing few yrs to meld.

★★★★ **Muscat Reserve** ✓ May have changed its name from 'White Muscadel Reserve' but there's no change in quality. **06** sunshine in a bottle, fortified to 15.5% (156g/l sugar); attractive spicy pineapple notes linger.

★★★★ **White Muscadel Jerepigo** ✓ Varietal character preserved by picking before too many grapes raisin. Melon, papino & raisin on viscous but not syrupy **07**, alc (15.5%) well integrated.

★★★★★ **Vintage Reserve Port** A Cape classic from tinta b, touriga, souzão & tinta r (50/35/10/5), fortified with unmatured spirit to 20% alc, matured 20 mths in large oak to preserve fruit. Powerful yet elegant, seductive with a sweet (90g/l) nudge.

★★★★ **Cape Vintage Port** ✓ Doing the family business for yrs; from tinta b, touriga, souzão (55/35/10 in **05**); 18 mths in large, old oak, 19% alc. Teasing rhubarb nuance to **05**'s fruit & nut, beautifully spiced mouthful; even more delicious than choc/Christmas cake-toned **04** (★★★★).

★★★★☆ **Cape Tawny Port** ✓ Tinta b & touriga (80/20, no tinta r in current **NV** bottling), average age 8 yrs. Now less sweet (102g/l), touch more spiritous (19.5% alc). Gloriously nutty with tealeaf, fudge & coffee notes. JCWCA Best Port.

★★★★ **Cape Ruby Port** ✓ Solid blend tinta, touriga, souzão (50/40/10). Latest **NV** bottling rich, dense fruitcake, sweetness (95g/l RS) lifted by bracing 19% alc. Yr old 500litre brls. Wine Best Value 2007; Peter Schulz 2007 Best Ruby. Also available in screwcapped 250ml.

Cabernet Sauvignon ☺ ★★★ No **05**. **06** pre-bottling sample: cassis fruit overwhelmed by tannic grip; needs time to settle. 5 mths older oak. **Rosé** ☺ 🍷 ★★★ Sunset-hued, decently dry **07**, now 100% cab, picked early for freshness. **Chardonnay** ☺ 🍷 ★★★ Tasted ex-tank, **07** already well formed with pleasing lime-lemon acidity & flavours, pithy tail. **Chenin Blanc** ☺ 🍷 ★★★ Pre-bottling sample **07**'s tropical whiffs, sourball twists make attractive early drinking. **White Port** ☺ ★★★ NV from chenin; drier (65g/l) than reds versions, 14 mths old 500litre brls adding oxidative complexity to nutty, creamy nose & palate.

Merlot NEW ✓ ★★★★ Plummy, well-fleshed maiden **06** v pleasant & easy-going thanks to empathetic wooding (5 mths older oak). EW. **Pinotage** ✓ ★★★★ No **05**. **06** ex-tank, proudly pinotage with strawberry & tar hints, juicy mouthful & pleasant bitter lift, couched in gentle choc oak (5 mths older brls). **Tempranillo** ✓ ★★★★ SA's only stand-alone bottling. **06** full flavoured, with sour cherry & green herb notes, luscious fruit core, judicious oak accents. Light on its feet despite 14% alc. **Tinta Barocca** ✓ ★★★★ Authoritative tannic grip matches exuberant mulberry fruit, high-toned spices & pleasant leafiness on briefly oaked **06** (4 mths old wood). **Touriga Nacional ★★★★** This & stablemates Tinta B, Tempranillo, among Cape pioneers of unfortified reds from stalwart port varieties. Tasted last ed, **05** packed with berries & hefty tannins. 6 mths older oak. **Relishing Red ★★★** No new bottling; last-tasted **NV** was juicy, gluggable (13.5%), from 50% pinotage, dash ruby cab & merlot. **Merlot-Pinotage ★★★** No **05**, **06** unready. Pvsly tasted **04** was comfortable & dry, with slightly bitter finish. **Golden Harvest ★★★** Early-drinking Natural Sweet from 50/50 hanepoot & gewürz. Last ed was gently sweet rose-lime combo. **NV**. — *CvZ*

Delaire Winery

T 021-885-1756 ▪ F 021-885-1270

Stellenbosch ▪ Est 1982 ▪ 1stB 1986 ▪ No tastings till end Mar 2008 due to renovations; sales from office ▪ See also intro ▪ Owner Laurence Graff ▪ Winemaker To be advised ▪ Viticulturist Benjamin Booysen (Oct 2002) ▪ ±20ha (cabs s/f, merlot, petit v, shiraz, chard, sauv) ▪ 170t/12 500cs 60% red 40% white ▪ PO Box 3058 Stellenbosch 7602 ▪ info@delaire.co.za ▪ www.delairewinery.co.za

In spring of 2008 Laurence Graff launches his latest creation, a new restaurant and cellar with spectacular views from the top of the Helshoogte Pass, polished as carefully as his exquisite gems. Plans include a 5-star boutique hotel, aiming to make Delaire 'the most fabulous wine farm in the Cape'.

★★★★☆ **Botmaskop** Austere & mineral **04** & pvs were Lilliputian parcels 100% cab, best vintages only; named for peak above farm. Unready **05** & future will be blends.

★★★★ **Driven by Cab** Pvs variously listed as 'Delaire' & 'Cab-Merlot'. Excellent **04** last time showed seductive & complex fruit but still too-tight tannins, which might have softened by now; cab, merlot, cab f (51/33/16). 14 mths barriques Fr oak, 40% new.

★★★★ **Chardonnay Barrel Fermented 06** less austere & without dominating toasty charriness of **05** (★★★★). Rich butterscotch & toast with hint of lime; full, well-structured & -balanced, elegant finish. Great food partner.

★★★★ **Sauvignon Blanc 07** (sample) back up to speed; gushing spice, flint & capsicum; full, serious & refreshing; excellent food wine. **06** (★★★★) elegant, but not quite as much authority as pvs.

Blush ☺ **★★★** Some complexity to previewed **07** bone-dry rosé (five-way r/w blend). Ideal al fresco melange of rosepetals, strawberry, spice; crisp & refreshing.

Discontinued: **Chardonnay Unwooded**. — *MM*

▪ De Leuwen Jagt *see Seidelberg Estate*

Delheim

T 021-888-4600 ▪ F 021-888-4601

Stellenbosch ▪ 1stB 1961 ▪ Tasting & sales daily 9-5 ▪ Fee R20 (tasting) R25 (tour & tasting) ▪ Tours Mon-Sat 10.30 & 2.30 Sun 10.30 ▪ Closed Easter Fri/Sun, Dec 25 & Jan 1 ▪ Delheim Garden Restaurant for country/traditional meals daily 9.30-4.30 ▪ Tour groups ▪ Gifts ▪ Farm produce ▪ Owner Sperling Family ▪ Cellarmaster/viticulturist Victor Sperling (Aug 1993) ▪ Winemaker Brenda van Niekerk, with Marius Prins (Oct 2002/July) ▪ 148ha (15 varieties, r/w) ▪ 850t/60 000cs 70% red 28% white 2% rosé ▪ Wines for client: Woolworths ▪ PO Box 210 Stellenbosch 7599 ▪ delheim@delheim.com ▪ www.delheim.com

The infectious energy and enthusiasm of Pappa 'Spatz' Sperling is continued by son Victor - the viticulturist - and daughter Nora. Commercial know-how and social responsibility are given equal importance in sustaining life on the farm. Delheim also walks the biodiversity talk; from installing a water-recycling plant in its cellar to serving both snails and mushrooms that have been harvested on the farm in its Garden Restaurant. Rising like a phoenix from the ashes of another fire on their Klapmutskop conservancy, a new initiative - overseen by Nora - will extend the conservancy to some important Simonsberg wineries.

Vera Cruz Estate range

★★★★☆ **Shiraz** Last available **04** darkly handsome, muscular, well groomed. Firm, meaty dark fruit, with formidable tannin, suggesting wait yr/2, will easily last 8-10 yrs. 16 mths Fr/ Am oak.

Delheim range

★★★★ **Cabernet Sauvignon** Tightly knit **05** (★★★☆) needs another yr to show full potential. Fruit in thrall of tannins, ripe but firm; suggestions of savoury spice, brambleberries, promise that wait will be rewarded. 15 mths, mainly Fr. **04** confirmed recent new seriousness.

★★★★ **Shiraz** Deep concentrated berries in **05**, without losing trademark svelte structure. Polished & stylish, with seamless oak integration, already delivering accessibility, but wine has gd 4+ yr future.

★★★★ **Grand Reserve** Remains successful 20+ yrs on; mostly cab; serious, 10+ yr future but so well-crafted, accessible on release. Lovely scents, flavours in improved **04** (★★★★★), hedgerow fruit, fennel, roasted spice, usual lithe tannins. Dab merlot, as for youthfully introverted **03**.

★★★★ **Chardonnay Sur Lie** Well-flavoured **05** mooted higher general rating, confimed with **06**; yellow peaches & blanched almonds, yet savoury/citrus underpin, finish. Not showy but many layers inviting quiet contemplation. 11 mnths Fr barriques.

★★★★ **Natural Sweet** NEW From almost equal riesling & chenin, **06** is the nearest thing to liquidised honey & pineapple you'll ever taste. Piquantly sweet, delicious, try it with dessert or cheese.

★★★★ **Edelspatz Noble Late Harvest** From riesling single vyd. Unbottled **07** (★★★★★) should be NLH template, it's so good: botrytis-infused, pineapple-flavoured richness, lifted by arresting acidity, giving an irresistable, tangy appetite appeal. Friendly 11% alc. **06** was a cornucopia of scented fruits dusted with botrytis.

Sauvignon Blanc-Chenin Blanc Heerenwijn ☺ 🍷 ★★★ Equal blend in fruit-driven **07**, touch colombard. Crunchy-fresh appley fruit salad, sauv minerality on finish; gd food partner.

Merlot ★★★★ **05** is all curves, succulent berries, smooth-textured charm. Oaking (15 mths Fr, mainly seasoned), gives underlying structure but wine so delicious, there'll be none to age. **Pinotage** ★★★ Textbook rhubarb & hedgerow fruit in **06**, with integrated oak, enough juicy ripeness to perk up any occasion. Enjoy at its youthful best. **Cabernet Sauvignon-Shiraz Dry Red** ★★★ Still unfinished but already showing well, **06** sample more fruit-driven than pvs, cab predominance lending berry & herbaceous tone, firm tannin structure. Could age 3/4 yrs. **Pinotage Rosé** 🍷 ★★☆ Cerise-hued **07**'s almost dry fruitiness is light textured enough (12.5% alc) to be perfect summertime fun. Dash muscat de f. **Chardonnay** ★★★ Partially oaked **07** sample already satisfies with ripe melon, peach flavours, softly curvaceous body, expected fresh-dry finish. **Gewürztraminer** 🍷 ★★★★ Heaps of flavour; textbook litchi & rosepetal in **07**, all wrapped in a rounded, softly sweet package, with just enough freshness for definition, without distraction. **Sauvignon Blanc** ★★★★ More intensity, cool fruit charac- ter in **07**, green figs, lemongrass, with racy acidity giving the tastebuds a wake-up call. **Spatzendreck Late Harvest** ★★★ Chenin/pinot bl blend, touch riesling, **06** shows full-ripe honeydew melon flavours, nicely rounded appetising sweetness, perfect for long summer evenings. Discontinued: **Rhine Riesling**. — *CR*

Dellrust Wines 🍴 🍷 ☕ 📷 🎿 ♿
T 021-842-2752/2457 • F 021-842-2456

Stellenbosch (see Helderberg map) • Est/1stB 1998 • Tasting & sales Mon-Fri 8-5 Sat 10-2 • Closed pub hols • Tours on request • Restaurant Tue-Sat 9.30-3.30 Sun 12-4 • Play area for children • Quadrides.com Tue-Sun; bookings 084-874-8730 • Owner/winemaker/viticulturist Albert Bredell • 97ha (11 varieties, r/w) • 600t/6 000cs own label 75% red 25% white • PO Box 5666, Helderberg, 7135 • winesales@dellrust.co.za • www.dellrust.co.za

It's difficult not to have fun at Dellrust. You can explore the farm on quad bikes, play paintball in the vineyard, or harvest and crush your own grapes. Be sure to bring al fresco accoutrements in November as they're official hosts of the annual Helderberg Picnic Festival.

★★★★ **Three Vines** Flagship, harmonious blend merlot, pinotage, shiraz; selected blocks vinified & blended pre-maturation in small Fr oak, ±14 mths. Still-current **03**, 40/30/30 ratio; last ed plummy with lead pencil hint.

Merlot ★★★ Cherry-toned ripe red fruit on **04**, meatiness, brisk acidity, grip & structure, savoury finish. 18 mths new Fr oak. **Rosé** ★★ Cherry pink off-dry **07** (sample) from shiraz & tinta, sweet/spicy finish. **Sauvignon Blanc** ✓ 🗎 ★★★★ Pungently herbaceous **07** picked at various stages of ripeness; abundant greenpepper aromas, grapefruit flavours; zingy & crisp; forceful finish. **Jerepigo** 🗎 ★★ Last tasted **06** sweet, light-textured, shy on fruit & freshness. No new vintage. **Cape Late Bottled Vintage** ★★ Last ed we noted **02** beginning to dry out. Discontinued: **Pinotage, Tinta Barocca-Cinsaut, Steen & Groen.**

Vinehills range NEW

Red ★★ **06** uncomplicated blend ruby cab/tinta, firm acidity harnesses ripe fruit. **White** ★ **07** blend sem, chard, sauv for immediate drinking. Both screwcapped. — *IM*

De Meye Wines

T 021-884-4131 • F 021-884-4154

Stellenbosch • Est/1stB 1998 • Tasting & sales Mon-Fri 9-5 Sat 9-2 • Closed Easter Fri, Dec 25/26 & Jan 1 • Home-grown lavender & lavender essential oil • Owner Jan Myburgh Family Trust • Winemaker Marcus Milner, with Aby Bodlani (Sep 1999/Sep 2000) • Viticulturist Johan Pienaar • 60ha (cab, shiraz, chenin, chard, merlot, cab franc) • 14 000cs 80% red 20% white • PO Box 20 Elsenburg 7607 • info@demeye.co.za • www.demeye.co.za

You can bottle and label your own wine in De Meye's new tasting room. Actually, you pay a deposit and fill a magnum with De Meye wine yourself. Your returned bottle is sterilised and reused, all part of a farm-wide recycling ethos. In the same vein, the Myburghs are replacing invasive alien plants with local varieties, an effort linked to the recently established indigenous plant nursery on the property. Plans are underway to bio-filter winery wastewater for irrigation, using locally made purifying plants.

De Meye range

★★★★ **Shiraz** Last tasted was **03**. Sweet fruit, decent structure, well-integrated oak in approachable understated style.

★★★★ **Trutina** Warm, expressive cab/shiraz blend, 80/20 in **03**, not re-tasted. Concentrated but not heavy; savoury acid, fine tannins ensure gd potential. 2 yrs Fr oak, 35% new. Unfiltered.

★★★★ **Chardonnay** Carefully oaked, attractive **05** last ed offered usual spice, nuts, orange zest plus honeyed element.

Cabernet Sauvignon ★★★ Ripe vintage reflected in **04** (sample); sturdy but gentle extraction, judicious oaking highlight tasty blackberry, cassis breadth. **Shiraz Rosé** ★★★ **07** unoaked (pvs were barrel matured). Gentle structure with complementary spice, savoury flavours. Equally happy as aperitif, food partner. **Chardonnay Unwooded** ★★★ Previewed **07** happy balance between texture & freshness. As pvs, fairly intense lime pith flavour, medium body, dry finish. **Chenin Blanc** ★★★ Bounteous floral/honey attractions in **07**, lively & satisfying. Milner's praiseworthy moderate alc, pleasing dryness.

Little River range

Cabernet Sauvignon ☺ ★★★ Freshness, moderate alc, purity of varietal character promise satisfying drinking in pre-bottling **05**. **Shiraz** ☺ ★★★ Preview **05** reveals elegant & generous choc, red fruits & spice; pleasing chewy concentration, fruity length within usual rounded frame. **Cabernet Sauvignon-Shiraz** ☺ ★★★ 'Blend' pvs ed. Happily forged ripe spice & cassis flavours in **05**'s 70/30 partnership. Smoothed in older Fr oak for immediate enjoyment. — *AL*

De Morgenzon
T 021-881-3030 • **F** 021-881-3773

Stellenbosch ▪ Closed to public ▪ Owner Wendy & Hylton Appelbaum ▪ Manager Anton Ferreira ▪ Winemaker Teddy Hall (2005, consultant) ▪ Viticulturist Kevin Watt (Sep 2003, consultant) ▪ PO Box 1388 Stellenbosch 7599 ▪ info@demorgenzon.co.za

Now three-quarters of the way through their replanting programme, Wendy & Hylton Appelbaum see their Stellenboschkloof farm as 'nearly 100ha of gardens which include 60ha of vines'. Committed to a bio-diverse future, they are experimenting with wildflowers as a spring cover crop to enhance both the soils and local ecosystem. 'It also unquestionably improves the appearance of our vineyards,' says Hylton A, who has now moved onto the spectacularly situated property with his family.

★★★★★ **Chenin Blanc 06** (★★★★) as seamless, if not as show-stopping as stellar **05**. Myriad aromas/flavours from orange blossom to Brazil nut to sea spray. Tad less sweet (4.7g/l vs 6.8g/l), not quite as vivacious, distinctive, as pvs but should age well. Fermented/8 mths Fr oak, 30% new.

Rosé NEW ★★★★ **07** crackerjack first vintage. Lovely freshness, suppleness; dry impression despite touch sugar thanks to lively natural acid. From shiraz. Rosé for grown-ups. — *CvZ*

■ **Den Dulk & Siddle** *see De Toren Private Cellar*
■ **Denneboom** *see Oude Denneboom*
■ **De Sonnenberg** *see Premium Cape Wines*
■ **Destiny** *see Mont Destin*

Détendu Wines
T 021-863-3282 • **F** 021-863-2480

Paarl ▪ Est 1995 ▪ 1stB 2001 ▪ Visits by appt ▪ Owner Western Investments Company ▪ Winemaker Francois Louw (Jan 2003) ▪ Viticulturist Johan Wiese (2002, consultant) ▪ 33ha (cab, merlot, pinotage, shiraz, chard, chenin, colombard) ▪ 300t/1 500cs own label 90% red 10% white ▪ PO Box 2917 Paarl 7620 ▪ info@detendu.co.za

Co-owner Garry Roberts loves cooking. 'I think having a developed palate for tastes and flavours complements my appreciation of wine,' he says. Part of the new Voor Paardeberg Visitors' Centre, Détendu reserves the best fruit for its own label and sells the balance to other producers.

Pinotage ★★★ Youthful purple-rimmed **05**, lean red fruit & feisty acidity. 15 mths 3rd fill Am oak. **Shiraz** ★★★ Sweet-sour rhubarb & plum flavours on **05**; v fresh & zippy. Older (mostly Fr) oak 21 mths. **Shiraz Reserve** ★★★ Mostly new (Fr) wood for this riper & more serious version; **05** better balanced, fruit nicely focused by firm acidity. 21 mths oaked. **Cabernet Sauvignon-Merlot** ★★★ Last-tasted **03** showed a savoury character, pliable tannins, black-fruit concentration. Coastal fruit, all others Voor Pdberg WOs. **Chardonnay** ★★★ Crisp, fresh, green-apple flavours on **06**. Oak (third new) more perceptible on nose; gd lively acidity. — *IM*

De Toren Private Cellar
T 021-881-3119 • **F** 021-881-3335

Stellenbosch ▪ Est 1996 ▪ 1stB 1999 ▪ Visits by appt ▪ Fee R180, waived on purchase ▪ Owner Edenhall Trust ▪ Winemaker Albie Koch (Aug 1998) ▪ Viticulturist Ernest Manuel (Mar 2003), advised by Johan Pienaar ▪ 20ha (cabs s/f, malbec, merlot, petit v) ▪ 7 000cs 100% red ▪ PO Box 48 Vlottenburg 7604 ▪ info@de-toren.com ▪ www.de-toren.com

Patience paid off last harvest, resulting in grapes displaying near-perfect analyses, reports winemaker Albie Koch, demonstrating the attention which goes into these polished and consistent performers. De Toren 'Z' 04 is following in the charmed footsteps of sibling Fusion V, which influential US critic Steve Tanzer also awarded 90 points on debut. Experts aren't the only ones who rate the wines highly: though De T has probably the smallest signpost in Stellenbosch, owner Emil den Dulk says visitors turn in to stock up in such numbers that a case-per-family limit has had to be regretfully imposed.

★★★★☆ **Fusion V** Glossy top-ranker acclaimed both sides of the Atlantic; 57% cab leads bdx 'Big 5'. Explosion of **05** flavour: luscious berries in firm tannin basket, long ripe finish. 50% new Fr oak, 10% Am.

★★★★ **Z** Different to flagship: merlot dominates, fleshy, earlier accessibility. **05** smoked meats mingle with blueberries in easy structure, ends tad sweet. With cabs s & f, malbec, dash petit v; yr oak, 35% new.

Discontinued: **DDS Shiraz**. — DS

De Trafford Wines
T 021-880-1611 · F 021-880-1611

Stellenbosch · Est/1stB 1992 · Tasting, sales & tours Fri & Sat 10-1 · Owner David & Rita Trafford · Winemaker David Trafford · 5 ha (cabs s/f, merlot, pinot, shiraz) · 80 tons 3 500 cs 75% red 25% white (5ha Mont Fleur, 10ha bought in) · PO Box 495 Stellenbosch 7599 · info@detrafford.co.za · www.detrafford.co.za

'The morning I walked into our cellar and smelled the exotic, heady aromas of our first (98) shiraz that had just started fermenting, I realised that we had something special,' says David Trafford. 'I'm convinced there's something magical about that vineyard.' An exciting new shiraz vineyard has now been planted, on a steep, rocky, clay-soil site. But it's not only the shiraz that's shining: 'The **05** vintage was beyond expectations,' says David T of the merlot, cab, shiraz and roobernet. 'The reds developed beautifully in the barrel and we kept them all a little longer before bottling' – which they did just before the 'difficult but promising' 2007 harvest. A personal highlight for David and wife Rita was an eight-day trek to the Himalayas in Nepal.

★★★★☆ **Cabernet Sauvignon** Regal Cape cab from parsimonious 1kg fruit/vine. **05** sublime: tobacco whiffs & cassis sewn into dense, tense structure; fantastic grip rides 15% alc. 14% merlot, 23 mths Fr oak, 5% Am, 40% new.

★★★★ **Merlot** Watermark elegance: polished plum fruits shaped by careful wooding (35% new Fr, 20 mths) & splash cab f. **05** earthy nuts & spice, easier than super **04** (incl petit v), which had deep violet scents, nutty black fruits, lithe tail.

★★★★ **Pinot Noir** Only 2 barrels, finely tuned & always in demand. **04** showed black cherry gloss to earthy aromas & breathtaking concentration when last sampled. 18 mths Fr cask, 15% alc. Mix burgundian (80%) & older BK5 clones.

★★★★ **Blueprint Shiraz** Younger Keermont vyd fruit accorded cellar's gentle natural treatment. Scented, fruitier & a little lighter than stablemates. **05** fennel/berry fruit; like **04**, accessible in youth, probably best at 5-6 yrs. 23 mths 25% new oak, mix Fr/Am.

★★★★ **Heap of Stones Shiraz** One-off **04** made by assistant winemaker Hendry Hess & Keermont grower Alex Starey from Pru Crawley's vyd of same name. More herbaceous than siblings, tightly structured for food. Fr oak, 25% new. Only 42cs. Not retasted.

★★★★☆ **Shiraz** Singular display of handcraft, heads cellar's three renditions of the grape. **05** (★★★★★) magical: like **04**, big boned yet finely drawn; ethereal spice & pastille fruits woven into fine tannins. 2 yrs 50% new Fr oak. 154cs.

★★★★☆ **Elevation 393** Name alludes to home vyd's height above sea level. Best cab, merlot & shiraz; 2 yrs all new Fr oak. **05** folds berries with woodspice into aristocratic tannins. Dangerously accessible, but try to keep 10 yrs. 14.5% alc.

★★★★ **Chenin Blanc** New-wave chenin ex-venerable Hldrberg vyds, full & complex but stitched with elegance: polished **06** luscious yet brisk, fruit with flair. Serial 90+ pts WS. Naturally fermented/8 mths 2:1 Fr/Am oak, 18% new; unfiltered.

★★★★☆ **Straw Wine** Passion taken to the edge with this elixir from 'air-dried' chenin. Bottled **05** bigger than sample (pvs ed) suggested: heady marmalade in luscious mouthful. 180g/l sugar, 6% alc. Mostly new oak, 50% Fr/Am, 17 mths. 375ml. — DS

De Vallei Boutique Winery
T 082-413-3564 · F 086-664-0881

Durbanville · Est/1stB 2006 · Visits Mon-Fri 9-5 by appt · Owner JJ De Villiers Trust · Cellarmaster/winemaker Nikie de Villiers (2006) · Viticulturist Nikie & Koos de Villiers · 104ha (cab, merlot, shiraz, chard, sauv) ▪ *9t/±130cs 60% red 40% white* ▪ *PO Box 488 Durbanville 7551* ▪ *boutiquewine@gmail.com*

For many years, this 150ha family farm delivered top-quality grapes to Durbanville Hills, until vinegrower Koos de Villiers' son Nikie decided to make wine himself instead. Nikie vinified his first (2006) vintage in the farm's cool-room but since restored the historic cellar and crushed the 2007 there.

Syrah ★★★ Clove & pepper notes on **06**, off low-yielding vines. Pleasing redcurrant fruit slightly out of kilter with tart acidity. Yr Fr oak, 25% new. **Sauvignon Blanc** ★★★ Cool-grown **06**, shy greengage & fig aromas, some minerality, but needing more fruit concentration to balance & enliven. — *IM*

De Villiers Wines
T 021-863-4441 • **F 086-6538-988**

Paarl ▪ *Tasting & sales by appt* ▪ *Owner De Villiers Family Trust* ▪ *Cellarmaster Villiers de Villiers* ▪ *50 000cs 60% red 40% white* ▪ *PO Box 659 Southern Paarl 7624* ▪ *vadev@mweb.co.za* ▪ *www.devwines.co.za*

A new acquisition for De Villiers Wines is their marketing head office in Paarl's Main Street, directly opposite KWV. Tastings here will include a range of personally selected international wines, including a malbec from Argentina, a Côtes-du-Rhône and a riesling from Alsace.

De Villiers Heritage Wines

Cape Riesling ☺ ★★★ **07** pleasing typicity, succulent green notes, firm acidity, dry.

Cabernet Sauvignon ★★★ **05** fruitily quaffable was last tasted. Rounded & well-fattened with wild berries. **Merlot** NEW ★★★ **03** attractive mineral quality to cassis fruit; approachably soft tannins but no pushover. **Pinotage** ★★★ Baked plum aromas make way for dry prune flavours. **05** nice brush of oak, though tannins still gruff mid-2007. **Shiraz** ★★★ Whiff of vanilla oak to dry, leathery & typical **04**. **Rosé** ★★ Dry **04** from pinotage was last tasted. **Chardonnay** ★★★ **06** last ed lightish, with perky acidity & good flavour layering. **07** unready. **Chenin Blanc** ★★ **07** pleasing balance & character, quick finish. **Sauvignon Blanc** ★★ Gentle floral notes on previewed **07**, unlingering flavours. **Blanc de Blanc** ★★ Light, soft **07**, with easy 10.7% alc. Mainly W Cape WOs. — *IvH*

■ **Devon Air** *see* Terroir Wines of SA

Devon Hill Winery
T 021-865-2453 • **F 021-865-2444**

Stellenbosch ▪ *Est 1996* ▪ *1stB 1997* ▪ *Tasting & sales Mon-Fri 10-4 Sat by appt* ▪ *Fee R10* ▪ *Closed pub hols* ▪ *Tours by appt* ▪ *Walks* ▪ *Winemaker Erhard Roux (May 2004)* ▪ *Viticulturist Johan Carinus (May 2002)* ▪ *46ha (cabs s/f, merlot, pinotage, shiraz, sauv)* ▪ *±300t 80% red 20% white* ▪ *PO Box 541 Stellenbosch 7599* ▪ *info@devonhill.co.za* ▪ *www.devonhill.co.za*

Winemaker Erhard le Roux still has high hopes for this Swiss-owned hilltop winery's pinotage. Competition success and buyer interest inspired him to nurture some of the 05 vintage 'like a baby' into a gentle giant. His obvious compassion stretched to rescuing some 300 khoi from a cracked guesthouse dam, temporarily housing them in two concrete wine tanks.

★★★★ **Bluebird** Elegant, full-flavoured 'Cape blend', varieties/proportions vary with the vintage. Last was beautifully balanced **02**, merlot (50%), pinotage & cab with luxurious, well-modulated berry character.

Cabernet Sauvignon ★★★★ Attractive ripe mulberry, touches tobacco & spice on **05**, pleasing roundness & generosity, tannins under control, add dryness to finish. **Merlot** ★★★★ Distinct mintiness on **03** (retasted mid-2007), tannins have evolved revealing classy mulberry, fine-grained oak for dry finish. Manageable 14% alc. **Pinotage** ★★★★ Latest **05** bursting with black plum fruit, fat & fleshy, much more modern. Oak a sideshow rather than star attraction (new 300-litre casks). 'Ripe' the key word: 15.2% alc. No **04**. **Shiraz** ★★★★ **05** a standout, nudges next rung. Deep velvet texture, ripe tannins, discreet oaking make for hedonistic mouthful. Drink at home: 15% alc. No **04**. **Four Stars** ★★★★ Last-tasted **02** light textured blend pinotage, merlot, shiraz, cab. Easy-drinking pleasure with touch of seriousness. Yr oak, none new. **Sauvignon Blanc** ✓ ★★★★ Ultra-pale does not equate to lacking flavour: **07** crammed with gooseberry & fig, smooth acidity, finishes with a dry flourish. Discontinued: **Shiraz Reserve**. — *IvH*

Devon Rocks

T 021-865-2536 • **F** 021-865-2621

Stellenbosch • *Est 1998* • *1stB 2003* • *Visits by appt* • *B&B accommodation* • *Owner Jürgen & Brita Heinrich* • *Winemaker Simon Smith (Louisvale)* • *Viticulturist Gawie du Bois & Paul Wallace (consultants)* • *3.5ha (pinotage, shiraz)* • *775cs 100% red* • *PO Box 12483 Die Board 7613* • *info@devonrocks.co.za* • *www.devonrocks.co.za*

When it comes to building a brand, says Jürgen Heinrich, 'it's slowly, slowly'. He and wife Brita now have a small export market in Germany and Holland, several Cape Town restaurants and hotels list their pinotage, and they're happy to be involved in an informal co-operative marketing effort taking shape in the Devonvale and Bottelary areas.

Pinotage ★★ Foursquare **06**, pear-drop, boiled fruit & blackberry aromas, savoury flavours. Yr 1st fill Fr oak. — *MF*

Devonvale Golf & Wine Estate

T 021-865-2080 • **F** 021-865-2601

Stellenbosch • *Est/1stB 2004* • *Tasting by appt* • *Fee R10 / R25 (incl glass)* • *Sales Mon-Sat 10-6* • *Closed Easter Fri-Mon, Dec 25 & Jan 1* • *Breakfasts, lunches & dinners* • *Gifts* • *Conferences* • *Tour groups* • *Golf* • *Owner Devonmust (Pty) Ltd* • *Winemaker Wilhelm Kritzinger (Bellevue, Feb 2004)* • *Viticulturist Ruben Nienaber* • *5.5ha (cab, shiraz)* • *40t/3 000cs 100% red* • *PO Box 77 Koelenhof 7605* • *proshop@devonvale.co.za* • *www.devonvale.co.za*

This 'lifestyle estate' inaugurated a new cold-room for barrel maturation, opened their tasting room to the public, held their first wine show, and broadened the range with a shiraz (untasted). The tradition of getting everybody involved in the harvest continued, with members, homeowners, friends and families getting together for a day of grape picking.

Broad Reach range
Provoyeur Cabernet Sauvignon ★★ Oak-staved **05** has dense black fruits & savoury tones.
Provoyeur Cabernet Sauvignon-Shiraz ★ **05** choc-rich dry red with earthy notes. — *RP*

■ Devon View *see Devon Hill Winery*

DeWaal Wines

T 021-881-3711 • **F** 021-881-3776

Stellenbosch • *Est 1682* • *1stB 1972* • *Tasting & sales Mon-Fri 9-4.30 (Oct-Apr) Mon-Fri 10-12. 30; 2-4.30 (May-Sep) Sat 9-4.30 (Aug-May only)* • *Fee R10* • *Closed Easter Fri/Sun, Dec 25/ 26 & Jan 1* • *Owner De Waal brothers* • *MD Pieter de Waal* • *Winemaker/viticulturist Chris de Waal & Daniël de Waal (whites/reds, Jan 1976/1989)* • *120ha (pinotage, shiraz, sauv)* • *800t/ 20 000cs 50% red 50% white* • *PO Box 15 Vlottenburg 7604* • *info@uiterwyk.co.za* • *www. dewaal.co.za*

The 9th generation De Waals, Chris, Daniël and Pieter, continue to reap the rewards of their family's pioneering work with pinotage and, more recently, viognier. Their pinotages are regulars on the Absa Top 10 awards and the viognier's food-friendly personality has devotees as far flung as Hong Kong, Spain and Canada. SA's only gold medal for merlot at the 2007 Concours Mondial, a Wine magazine Best Value citation for the DeWaal Pinotage, and additions to the fruit-driven Young Vines wines bear testimony to their continuing success.

DeWaal range
★★★★ **Merlot** Slow developer, **04** (★★★★) last ed still tightly knit; savoury spice, violets, dark-toned fruit, all vying for attention, firm tannins needed another yr. Fr oak, half new. By contrast, **03** was early harmonious. EW.

★★★★ CT de Waal Pinotage From 40 yr old vines, less oaked than TotH version, but **05** still 24 mths Fr wood, 60% new. Quality shows in bewitching complexity, smooth liquo-rice-toned palate. Still an infant, as was **04** (★★★★) on release; watch both develop over 6+ yrs. EW.

★★★★☆ Top of the Hill Pinotage One of the more serious expressions of this grape, from 50+ yr old bushvines. Reined-in opulence, savoury nuances, rich mix crushed herbs & spices, accompany dark fruit. Multi-layered, individual. Expert oaking, 27 mths, all new Fr, gives backbone, 6+ yrs ageing potential. EW.

★★★★☆ Shiraz Beautifully crafted wine; last tasted **04** enticed with smoky depths, scrub & blackberry-veined opulence, promised 5+ yr future. Fr oak 35% new, rest 2nd fill. No **03**; **06** is next.

★★★★☆ Cape Blend Serious-minded, soberly elegant pinotage blend. Last was **03**, with merlot dominant at 50% (pinotage/shiraz 30/20), 50% new Fr oak; should develop & keep gd few yrs. Next is **05**. EW.

Young Vines Merlot NEW 🍷 ★★★ Unbottled **04** offers robust enjoyment, spiced ripe plums, chewy but ripe tannins. EW. **Pinotage** ★★★★ From 35+ yr old vyds. Lightest of the pinotage trio, **04** last ed showed varietal-true rhubarb & dried banana, juicy palate appeal. Accessible, thanks to balanced oaking, but few more yrs ahead. 18 mths Fr wood, third new. **Young Vines Red** ★★★ Last ed **04** showed perky plummy fruit, gentle oak support, youthful charm. Merlot 60%, balance equal shiraz, pinotage. **Sauvignon Blanc** ★★★★ **07** sample appeals with sleek minerality, leafy asparagus tones. Brisk acidity ensures perfect food fare. **Young Vines Sauvignon Blanc** NEW 🍷 ★★ **07** sample shows pear-drop freshness, tasty quaffability. EW. **Viognier** ★★★ Stil reticent mid-year, **07** preview has floral/peach kernel typicity, bone-dry finish. **Young Vines White** ★★ Uncomplicated quaffer; **06** last yr was crisply dry, with pear-drop character. Sauv, chenin, colombard; modest 12.5% alc.

Uiterwyk range
Discontinued: **Merlot**, **Shiraz**. — CR

De Wet Co-op Winery   🍷🎋📷♿
T 023-341-2710 • F 023-341-2762

Worcester • Est 1946 • Tasting & sales Mon-Fri 8-5 Sat 9-12 • Fee R1/wine • Closed pub hols • BYO picnic • Conferencing • Owner 60 members • Winemaker Piet le Roux (1995) & Hugo Conradie (2003) • Viticulturist Newald Marais (Jan 2003, consultant) • ±1 000ha (chard, chenin) • 19 000t 20% red 80% white • PO Box 16 De Wet 6853 • piet@dewetcellar.co.za • www. worcesterwinelands.co.za

No new 'children', reports a relieved Piet le Roux of his and the De Wet team's role in giving birth to FirstCape, the hugely successful export joint-venture snapping at Kumala's heels as top SA brand in the UK. Nowadays they're focusing on De Wet's increased red-wine contribution to FirstCape, helped by new cellar addition Tertius Jonck.

Sauvignon Blanc ☺ ★★★ Melon, greenpepper & gooseberry melange in **07**. Bone-dry & steely, with lowish 11.5% alc. **Hanepoot** ☺ ★★★ Misreported discontinued last ed. **05** litchi heaven, hint of clove; syrupy & simple but finishes delightfully clean. **Petillant Fronté** ☺ 🍷 ★★★ New bottling of popular light-bodied (8% alc), perlé-style white has litchi & rosepetal aromas, softly sweet flavours. **NV**.

Cabernet Sauvignon NEW ★★★ Ground coffee aromas on **06**, fruit quite lush but marred by vegetal touch. **Pinotage** ★★★ **06** not ready to be tasted. Last ed **05** was friendly, bright & breezy. **Shiraz** ★★ **06** as pvsly, somewhat raisin-like fruit but rescued by nice chalky tannins. **Dry Red** ★★★ Blend varies from yr to yr; last tasted **06** equal shiraz, cab & merlot, lightly oaked. 5litre party-ready packs. **Chardonnay** ★ **07** not ready. Last tasted **02** was better in youth. **Chenin Blanc** ★★ Sample **07**, has some wet wool & citrus notes, but fruit's a touch dull. **Bouquet Blanc** ★★★ Unpretentious **06** last ed had a white-fruit bouquet, pithy acidity balancing 9.8g/l sugar. **Special Late Harvest** ★★ Last-tasted **06** was light, off-dry, with muscat & potpourri scents. **Red Muscadel** NEW ★★★★ Alluring & elegant **05**; musky, unctuous (223g/l RS) & packed with ripe flavours, lengthy mixed-berry conclusion. **White Muscadel** Critically acclaimed **03** sold out. No newer vintage. **Port** ★★★★ Last-tasted **03**, savoury rather than fruitcake flavours, dry (85 g/l) with well-woven 17.3% alc. Future releases will be **NV**. — *RP*

De Wetshof Estate
T 023-615-1853 ▪ F 023-615-1915

Robertson ▪ Est 1949 ▪ 1stB 1972 ▪ Tasting & sales Mon-Fri 8.30-5 Sat 9.30-1 ▪ Closed Easter Fri/Mon, Dec 25/26 & Jan 1 ▪ Tours by appt ▪ Owner Danie de Wet ▪ Winemaker Danie de Wet (1973), with Mervyn Williams (2001) ▪ Viticulturist George Thom (1996), advised by Phil Freese & Francois Viljoen (both 1997) ▪ 180ha (cab, merlot, pinot, chard, sauv, semillon, riesling) ▪ 10% red 90% white ▪ ISO 9001, BRC & HACCP certified ▪ PO Box 31 Robertson 6705 ▪ info@dewetshof.com ▪ www.dewetshof.com

It took some time to get his sons into the family business, says industry heavyweight Danie de Wet wryly, but now he has Johann assisting veteran Bennie Stipp with the marketing, and Peter in the cellar. Does he have more free time? 'I wish!' More philosophically, he notes that the era of Wine As A Commodity has yielded to an age of Produce To Plan, whether the plan is for easy-drinkers in big volumes or intellect-pleasers at the top end of the market. For the latter, production must be site-specific, he believes.

De Wetshof range

★★★★ **Bateleur Chardonnay** Last-tasted **05** showing style & finesse, with toasty oak, grilled hazelnut, ripe stonefruit - all restrained, with fruit tautened by racy acidity. New Fr oak fermented/yr. Next is **06**.

★★★★ **Rhine Riesling** Floral, orange blossom aromas & green apple flavours on steely **07**. Pithy grapefruit finish & bone-dry despite 5g/l RS.

★★★★★ **Edeloes** Botrytised riesling last tasted **00** vintage. Charming **05** (★★★★★) returns with complex honey & dried apricot aromas, pleasingly sweet entry & long, mouthwatering citrus zest finish. Delicate 9% alc & poised acidity balancing 157g/l RS. Pvs **00** was honeyed, with lovely balance between opulent sweetness & acid.

Chardonnay D'Honneur ★★★★ Bigger, more generous style. **05** previewed mid-2006 on form with ripe peachiness, deft oaking & signature clean acidity. **Finesse Chardonnay** ★★★★ Most lightly oaked chard in range. **06** last ed round, stylish, showing citrus & stonefruit with subtle oaking. **Bon Vallon Chardonnay** ★★★ SA's first unwooded chard; **07** citrus & yeasty lees aromas & fresh apple flavours make easy lunchtime drinking. **Sauvignon Blanc** ★★★ Subdued gooseberry & capsicum aromas; **07** fig flavours & hints of flintiness with crisp acidity throughout. Discontinued: **Blanc Fumé**.

Danie de Wet range

★★★★ **Limestone Hill Chardonnay** 🞑 Abundant orange blossom & lees character in **07**. Charming lemon & lime fruit balancing crisp acidity & minerally finish. On-form **06** showed terrific concentration of fruit in lengthy finish. NE.

★★★★ **Cape Muscadel** Last tasted was **00**. **06** spicy, grapey muscat aromas; sweet raisined fruit on entry lifted by zesty acidity. (15% alc, 185g/l RS). NE.

Cabernet Sauvignon Naissance ★★★★ Enticing blackcurrant-scented **05**, approachably soft & juicy blackberry fruit & spiciness. Smoothly textured & friendly. **Nature in Concert Pinot Noir** ★★★★ Brambly fruit & tobacco aeomas abundant in **06**; easy, light, toasty plum entry with fruit, alc. & acid in perfect balance. **Chardonnay Sur Lie** 🞑 ★★★ **07** delicate & stylish sipper. Floral aromas & stone fruit flavours dominated by fresh acidity. Light, lemony finish. NE. **Sauvignon Blanc** ★★★ Shy, herbaceous **07** made in soft, dry, easy-drinking style for early enjoyment. NE. Discontinued: **Merlot, Dukesfield Cape Blend, Blanc De Wet**. — *IM*

■ **Deza Collection** *see* Oaklands Wine Exporters

De Zoete Inval Estate

T 021-863-1535 • F 021-863-2158

Paarl • Est 1878 • 1stB 1976 • Tasting & sales at I Love Wine (see entry); farm tastings & tours by appt • Owner DZI Agricultural Investments CC (John Robert & Eulalia Frater) • Cellarmaster John Robert Frater • Winemaker/viticulturist John Robert Frater (1999) • 20ha (cab, petit v, port varieties, shiraz, chard, sauv) • 100t/5 000cs own label 50% red 50% white • PO Box 591 Suider-Paarl 7624 • info@dezoeteinval.co.za • www.dezoeteinval.co.za

An exciting air of rejuvenation reigns at the Fraters' place: there are new vineyards cultivated as organically as possible (shiraz, cab and especially chardonnay are well suited to the Berg River Valley terroir, they say); there's a cellar being revamped, and the 'friendliest, craziest new tasting room' should be ready in time for summer visitors.

Cabernet Sauvignon ★★ **03** pvs ed was light, with tart cranberry flavour, dusty dry conclusion. 20 mths oaked. **Pinotage** NEW Not tasted. **Cabernet Sauvignon-Shiraz** ★★★ Rustically appealing **NV**. Pvs bottling had almost porty prunes & plums, savoury touch, chunky 15+% alc. **Yvette Dry Red** ★★ Light, slightly dusty **NV** from cab, yr Fr oaked. No newer 1 000ml bottling tasted. **Shiraz Rosé** ★ **05** was light in tone & taste, with slight salty tang. **Chardonnay** ★★★ Last was **03**, which revealed some complexity; dry, attractively austere. **Vintage Brut** ★★★ **03** was maiden MCC from chard. Fine bubbles, arresting acidity, bone-dry yet balanced. Not revisited. **Vin Sec Sparkling** ★★ From chenin; last yr **06** was delicate, effervescent, with decidedly sweet crème caramel note. **Cape Vintage** ★★ Port-style fortified; Pvs **01** showed mature tawny tint; dusty dried-fruit nose, soft, silky & attractively dry. Next is **03**. Discontinued: **Blanc de Blanc**, **Late Harvest**.

Eskdale range
Discontinued: **Merlot**, **Pinotage**, **Shiraz**. *— MM*

DGB

T 021-864-5300 • F 021-864-1287

Wellington • Est 1942 • Closed to public • Owner DGB management, Brait Capital Partners & Kangra • Winemaker/viticulturist See Bellingham & Boschendal • PO Box 246 Wellington 7654 • exports@dgb.co.za • www.dgb.co.za

Well established merchant house with a strong portfolio of premium and own-brand table wines, ports and sherries. See separate listings for Bellingham, Boschendal, Culemborg, Douglas Green, Legacy, Millstream, Oude Kaap, Tall Horse, Text and The Saints.

Die Huis van Anjé

T 028-840-2115 • F 028-840-2115

Villiersdorp (see Worcester map) • Est/1stB 2006 • Visits by appt • Fee R10 p/p • BYO picnic • Owner Petrus Roux Trust • Winemaker Petrus Roux • 1 Upington Str, Villiersdorp 6848 • huisvananje@lando.co.za

Youth is a permanent state of mind for Annetjie Roux (aka Anjé) and husband Petrus, who began making wine in their retirement. Their sauvignon and chardonnay come from vineyards in the famous Kaaimansgat Valley, which is cold enough to witness winter snow. New additions include a semi-sweet rosé 'for the ladies'.

Swartstomp Merlot NEW ★★★ Sample **07**, lightly-staved Vllrsdorp fruit; needs time to settle. Savoury & smoky rather than fruity; plenty of grip in youthful state. **Kroonland Chardonnay** ★★★ **07** fresh citrus aromas, imperceptible oak from staves. Light, crisp apple flavours with fine acidity throughout. **Sauvignon Blanc** ✓ ★★★★ **07** herbaceous grass & capsicum aromas from high-altitude vyds, deceptively light feel despite 14.5% alc; crisp, mineral finish.

Pastorie range
Pastorie Rosé NEW ▤ ★★ **07** strawberry pink blend of chenin & merlot, gulpable semi-sweet (15g/l), chill well. **Pastorie Chenin** ▤ ★★ **07** semi-sweet from ripe Wrcstr fruit, charming, light, easy-drinking style. *— IM*

■ **Die Krans** *see De Krans*

Diemersdal Estate
T 021-976-3361 ▪ F 021-976-1810

Durbanville ▪ Est 1698 ▪ 1stB 1979 ▪ Tasting & sales Mon-Fri 9-5 Sat 9-3 ▪ Closed Easter Fri/ Sun, Dec 25 & Jan 1 ▪ Tours by appt ▪ BYO picnic ▪ Walks ▪ Owner Tienie Louw ▪ Winemaker Thys Louw & Mari van der Merwe ▪ Viticulturist Div van Niekerk (1980) ▪ 172ha (cab, merlot, pinotage, shiraz, chard, sauv, petit v, malbec) ▪ 1 750t 70% red 30% white ▪ PO Box 27 Durbanville 7551 ▪ wines@diemersdal.co.za ▪ www.diemersdal.co.za

The new team at Diemersdal, led by sixth-generation Thys Louw, will continue to focus on sauvignon as a variety where the cool Durbanville climate gives a proven competitive advantage. Value entry-level wines should groom future fans, and while SA remains core, significant export markets are multiplying.

MM Louw range

★★★★☆ **Red Blend** NEW Bdx blend, selection 6 barrels, only 150cs. Distinctive fynbos, green walnuts terroir note accompany red fruit; supple tannins promise long evolution. Beautifully crafted, epitomises elegance, refinement.

★★★★☆ **Sauvignon Blanc** NEW Grape selection & special yeast ferment for this 200-case wine. Ultra-sophisticated: bone-dry & with cellar's trademark nettly, fynbos character, **06** exits with a sleek, intense minerality ideal for all seafood.

Diemersdal Estate range

★★★★ **Chardonnay Reserve** Careful cellar attention for max flavour concentration. **06** again shows individual styling, preserved clementines, roasted nuts & a wonderful savoury vein keeping it food-friendly rather than showy. Could age few yrs.

★★★★ **Sauvignon Blanc 8 Rows** Selected 8 rows within single vyd, even better in **07** (★★★★★), the essence of fresh: cut grass, spring meadow plus an edgy fynbos wildness on the palate. Unfiltered. Complex, individual & truly fine. **06** delighted fans of an edgier, 'sauvage' style.

★★★★ **Sauvignon Blanc Single Vineyard** Topping impressive debut **06** last yr, **07** (★★★★★) has similar rivetting intensity but greener styling, Old-World leafy minerality on finish. Classic, designed for fine dining. On lees 5 mths, bottled unfiltered.

Matys ☺ 🍴 ★★★ Pronounced Mah-tace, honest, well-made quaffer. Half pinotage in **06**, rest equal shiraz, merlot; gently oaked plummy fruit, nicely dry finish. NE. **Blanc de Blanc** ☺ 🍴 ★★★ Mainly sauv in **07**, some chenin; irresistible crunchy asparagus salad flavours, bursting with vitality. NE.

Cabernet Sauvignon ★★★☆ Showing all attributes of warm vintage, & then some, **05**'s plush black plums allowed centre stage, reflected in creamy palate. Expert oaking provides good support. Cab at its generous best. **Merlot** ★★★★ **05** not just a pretty face: creamy berries & spice, proving compatibility of terroir, given firm oak foundation for further enjoyment over time. **Pinotage** ★★★☆ Reflecting warmer vintage, **05** has ripe dark fruit, leavened by well-judged oak treatment (16 mnths Fr, half new) adding backbone, definition. Trademark drinkability remains intact. **Shiraz** ★★★★ Modern, accessible style. As affable as pvs, **05** combines hedgerow berries, cedar spicing & smoothly integrated tannins. 16 mths Fr barriques, 60% new. Could keep few yrs. NE. **Private Collection** ★★★★ Bdx blend, make-up varies. Plenty fruit in improved **05**, cab-led cassis to support 24 mths barreling, all new. Busy evolving, whiffs cocoa-rich choc, dried herbs, promising further depths over next 4/5 yrs. **Chardonnay Single Vineyard** ★★★★ Only half-oaked for better fruit expression, showing tinned peaches in **07**. Such gentle curves, attractive freshness, almost best enjoyed solo without food distraction. **Sauvignon Blanc** ★★★★ Distinctive house style appears in more concentrated **07**, nettles, fynbos, with invigorating acidity holding freshness intact. Delicious solo or with food. Friendly 13% alc. **Noble Late Harvest** ★★★ Bunch pressed, barrel fermented/matured dessert from sauv. To date only **03**, still available; mid-2005 billowed ripe peach fruit & fresh baked bread; racy acidity, nutty flavours & long, elegant finish. NE. Discontinued: **Blanc de Noir**. — *CR*

Diemersfontein Wines
T 021-864-5050 • F 086 516 1560

Wellington (see Paarl map) • Est/1stB 2001 • Tasting & sales daily 10-5 • Fee R15 • Closed Dec 25 • Tours by appt • Restaurant & guest house (see Eat-out & Stay-over sections) • Conferencing • Walks • Mountain biking • Owner David & Susan Sonnenberg • Winemaker/ viticulturist Francois Roode & Brett Rightford (Sep 2003/Nov 2005) • 55ha (cab, merlot, mourvèdre, petit v, pinotage, shiraz, viognier) • 600t/80 000cs • 95% red 5% white • HACCP & ISO 9001 accredited • PO Box 41 Wellington 7654 • wine@diemersfontein.co.za • www. diemersfontein.co.za

The Wellington pinotage specialist is beginning to see homes spring up among the vines as its residential estate development takes off. Also growing are areas under pinotage, chenin and shiraz, and their 'protégé school', Wellington Preparatory, is progressing nicely. Recently accreditation by WIETA was celebrated, but the biggest festivity is the annual (and growing) Pinotage-on-Tap Party, which launches the new vintage on the farm and in Gauteng.

Carpe Diem range

★★★★ **Cabernet Sauvignon** Last ed we tasted **05** sample, exuberant cassis, livening touch mint, oak as 'wood shaving' presence; was busy integrating fine-grained tannins. 15 mths new Fr.

★★★★★ **Pinotage** Not a shy bone in its body, **05** parades opulent black plums, prunes & heaps of vanilla, spicing. Remarkably accessible, curvaceous & silk-textured, despite 15 mths new Fr/Am oak. Delicious.

★★★★ **Shiraz** Last ed ex-barrel, **05** yr later shows more pronounced dark choc, ripe plummy tones, now with mocha overlay. Tannins fully integrated, a warm-hearted, effusive wine. Cellaring potential 4+ yrs.

★★★★ **Chenin Blanc** NEW As expected in this range, an impressive rendition: unbottled **07** is bold, showy, with melon & peach concentration, savoury shading from oak treatment, a delicious tangy finish. Has few yrs ageing prospects.

Malbec ★★★★ Maiden **05**, previewed last ed, more accessible tannins yr later, same individual wet heath, hedgerow fruit styling. With 10% cab f. One of few bottlings of this variety, gd typicity. **Merlot** ★★★★ Last-tasted **03** showed house style, delivered herbal warmth to tightly arrayed palate. ±18 mths oak **Viognier** ★★★★ Stylish & individual, more Old World than New. Same graceful lines as pvs in **06**, same lavender & violet perfume. Dry, with balanced acidity, it's good enough to enjoy on its own.

Diemersfontein range

★★★★ **Pinotage** Despite reduced complexity, concentration, **05** (★★★★) still confidently struts the classic shiraz road: campfire smoke, dark fruit, plenty of black pepper flavours. **04** signalled return to form after blip in **03** (★★★).

★★★★ **Shiraz** Despite reduced complexity, concentration, **05** (★★★★) still confidently struts the classic shiraz road: campfire smoke, dark fruit, plenty of black pepper flavours. **04** signalled return to form after blip in **03** (★★★).

★★★★ **Heaven's Eye 04**, reviewed last yr, saw blend change to mainly cab, with petit v, shiraz, roobernet; oodles of sweet spice accompanied by enough tannins for 10+ yrs. 10 mths mainly Fr oak.

★★★★ **Summer's Lease** Blend changed to 65/35 shiraz, mourvèdre, dab viognier in **04**, bringing out rhône-like dark fruits, salty liquorice, nuances of scrub. Last yr noted as already delicious, needing more time to show true potential, as all these. Mix Fr/Am oak, 10 mths.

Cabernet Sauvignon ★★★ Cedar-infused cassis in **06**, with firm tannin underpin from yr mainly Fr barrels. Accessible & robust, perfect for hearty casseroles. **Merlot** ★★★ **06** has appealing berry fruit & savoury tannins, promising cellaring longevity but dry, noticeable at this early stage. **Maiden's Prayer** ★★ Last was **04**, unoaked merlot, cab, shiraz, pinotage blend, for early drinking. — *CR*

■ **Die Rivierkloof** *see* Viljoensdrift Wines

■ *Die Tweede Droom* *see* Groot Parys

Dieu Donné Vineyards
T 021-876-2493 • **F** 021-876-2102

Franschhoek • Est 1984 • 1stB 1986 • Tasting & sales Mon-Fri 9-4 Sat/Sun 10.30-4 • Fee R10 • Closed Dec 25/26 & Jan 1 • Restaurant (see Eat-out section) • Cheese platters • Picnic lunches in summer (booking essential) • Tours by appt • Tour groups • Owner Robert Maingard • Winemaker Stephan du Toit (May 1996) • Viticulturist Hennie du Toit (Apr 1988) • 40ha (cab, merlot, pinotage, shiraz, chard, sauv) • ±280t/16 500cs 60% red 35% white 3% rosé 2% MCC • PO Box 94 Franschhoek 7690 • info@dieudonnevineyards.com • www.dieudonnevineyards. com

Will winemaker and Cape Wine Master Stephan du Toit be able to bridge the gap and make beer as well as wine? That's the question now that a micro-brewery forms part of the new restaurant with its splendid views over the valley, not to mention a variety of picnic menus and platters designed to complement the liquid produce.

Cabernet Sauvignon ★★★★ Always low-fruited with food-cordial taut tannins. Classic **03** has cassis core, tobacco hints, savoury tail. 16 mths Fr oak, third new. **Merlot** ★★★ Confident **03** raises bar on pvs, lithe tannins moulding attractively around solid plum centre. 18 mths Fr oak, 30% new. **Pinotage** ★★☆ Alc (14.7%) detracts from **04**'s charming strawberry & banana fruit, teasing acetone farewell. Yr oak, some new. **Shiraz** ★★★★ **04** resist the inviting pepper & salami aromas for now: fruit, taut tannins & alc (15.5%) need time to mesh. Yr oak, some new. **Cabernet Sauvignon-Shiraz** ★★★ Last ed **03** maiden was smooth & accessible, with New World fruitiness, light oak touch. **Rosé** ▤ ★★ Formula changes to chard (80%) & cab for **06**, party-ready, gently sweet (20g/l RS). **Chardonnay Wooded** ★★★ Lemon-cream palate, vibrant acidity flatter pronounced oakspice & spiritous note (14.3% alc) on **05**. Yr Fr oak. **Chardonnay Unwooded** ★★★ Shy, gently-flavoured **06** blossoms in glass; relatively light bodied (12.4% alc) with lingering lemony tail. **Sauvignon Blanc** ★★☆ **07** unready. Grassy **06** last ed was pleasant but short, for early drinking. **Maingard Brut MCC** ★★★★ Pvsly tasted **02** delicate, with fine mousse, brioche whiff; honeyed, creamy finish from 30 mths on lees. Next is **05**. **Noble Late Harvest** ★★★★ Fr oak matured **05** last time noted as subtly oaked, botrytis nuances entwined with pineapple & marzipan. Successor is **07**. — *CvZ*

■ *Die Vlakte* *see* Cloverfield Private Cellar

■ *Discover* *see* Spier Wines

Dispore Kamma Boutique Winery
T 028-214-1057 (a/h), 083-448-1670, 028-2121096 (o/h) • **F** 028-214-1077

Caledon (see Elgin/Walker Bay map) • Est/1stB 2002 • Visits by appt • Owner Philip Mostert & Hannes Coetzee • Winemaker Philip Mostert, with Hannes Coetzee (Jan/Jun 2002) • Viticulturist Willie de Waal (consultant) • ±150-200cs 100% red; 50cs white from bought-in wine • PO Box 272 Caledon 7230 • disporekamma@overnet.co.za

This winery can now add (™) behind its name (derived from the Khoi word for Caledon, physician Philip Mostert's hometown). The after-hours winemaker is proud of his Syrah's consistent performance over the years but it's the 07 which currently has him enthused: 'It's back to the same recipe as **02/03**, and all the grapes are from Willie de Waal of Scali in the excellent Voor Paardeberg ward.'

Cabernet Sauvignon Dark berried appeal in **06**, but sample too cloaked with barrel character (mostly older wood) to rate conclusively. **Merlot** ★★ Off organically grown Ovrberg vines, pvsly tasted **05** ripe-style country red with obvious oak & alc, big dry tannins. **Syrah** Enviable MIWA record for this handcrafted red, incl best garagiste producer. Spicy **06**, barrel sample dominated by vanilla oak, warming alc, unfair to rate. **Sauvignon Blanc** NEW ★★ Quaffable **07** with crisp grassy notes for summer refreshment. — *MW*

Distell
T 021-809-7000

Stellenbosch • PO Box 184 Stellenbosch 7599 • www.distell.co.za

Operating from two corporate-owned wineries in Stellenbosch (Bergkelder and Adam Tas), Distell vinifies some of SA's most successful and enduring wine brands. They are: 5th Avenue Cold Duck, Autumn Harvest Crackling, Capenheimer, Cellar Cask, Chateau Libertas, Drostdy-Hof, Flat Roof Manor, Fleur du Cap, Graça, Grand Mousseux, Grünberger, Hill & Dale, Ixia, Kellerprinz, Kupferberger Auslese, Libertas, Monis, Obikwa, Oom Tas, Oracle, Overmeer, Pongrácz, Sedgwick's, Ship Sherry, Table Mountain, Tassenberg, Taverna, Two Oceans, Virginia and Zonnebloem. Distell also owns the House of JC le Roux, a dedicated sparkling-wine cellar in Devon Valley. Then there are the stand-alone 'estate' labels: Nederburg, Plaisir de Merle and Lomond. Distell is also the co-owner, together with Lusan Holdings, of a handful of top Stellenbosch properties (Alto, Le Bonheur, Neethlingshof, Stellenzicht, Uitkyk), and, with seven local growers, of Durbanville Hills. Distell also has agreements with a few independently owned cellars (Allesverloren, Jacobsdal, Theuniskraal) for which it provides a range of services. Finally, there's the black empowerment venture on Papkuilsfontein farm near Darling, source of Tukulu wines. See Bergkelder for details about the Vinoteque Wine Bank; Cape Legends; and separate entries for the above brands and properties.

■ **Diversity** *see* Cape Grace Wines
■ **Dixon's Peak** *see* Waverley Hills Organic Wines
■ **Dolphin Bay** *see* Wines of Cape Town

Domaine Brahms Wineries

T 021-863-8555 • F 021-869-8590

Paarl • Est 1998 • 1stB 1999 • Tasting & sales Mon-Fri 9.30-5 Sat & pub hols by appt (closed Easter Fri-Mon, Jun 16, Sep 24, Dec 25/26 & Jan 1) • Fee R5/wine • Tours anytime by appt • Chapel & wedding/function venue • Owner Johan & Gesie van Deventer • Winemaker/viticulturist Gesie van Deventer (Lategan) (1998) • 15ha (cab, merlot, pinotage, shiraz) • 100% red • PO Box 2136 Windmeul 7630 • brahms@iafrica.com

While still involved in upliftment and mentoring (of women in particular), Gesie van Deventer is progressively quitting public life to concentrate on winemaking. She is dismayed that buoyant demand takes her wines away at such a young age, but consoled by the happiness the new wedding chapel brings to the farm.

★★★★ **Pinotage** Rich, robust blackberry fruit, medicinal spiciness from 14 mths Fr oak (15% new) which checks sweetness with savoury tannins. **05** ready for early enjoyment with food.

★★★★ **Shiraz** Brooding **03**, dark fruit & violet aromas; opulent flavours show some meatiness, firm acidity & drying tannins paring richness & finishing warm from 15% alc. 18 mths Fr oak, 15% new.

Cabernet Sauvignon ★★★★ Ripe **02**, tasted pvsly, expressive dark plum aromas with rich fruit, supple tannins & textured finish. Yr Fr oak, 20% new. **03** unready. **Quartet** ★★★★ Pvsly tasted **03** stylish blend merlot, pinotage, cab, shiraz (50/30/10/10), with well proportioned wood, cassis & spicy meatiness. **Judex Provisional Judgement** ★★★ Earthy blend **02** from pinotage, merlot, ruby cab, shiraz, with attractive berry, herb & oak tones. Not revisited. **Chenin Blanc** ★★★★ Bright, golden **05** with wood, tangerine & sweet almond aromas, harmonious & integrated, fruit adequately supporting 60% new Fr oak (yr). Ex-35 yr old bushvines. MIWA gold. *— IM*

Domaine des Dieux

T 028-313-0130 / 083-536-5916 • F 028-312-1388

Walker Bay • Est 2002 • 1stB 2006 • Tasting by appt at La Vierge Winery • Owner Domaine des Dieux (Pty) Ltd • Winemaker Marc van Halderen • Viticulturist Augustus Dale, advised by Andrew Teubes • 16ha rising to 20ha (pinot, shiraz, chard, sauv) • 2500cs 25% white 75% MCC • PO Box 1580 Hermanus 7200 • gparnell@tiscali.co.za

In its first vintage (2006), the poetically named 'Home of the Gods' pioneered an MCC in the Hemel-en-Aarde Valley. It's set for release later this year. Two other cap classiques, a Blanc and Rosé, are maturing sur latte. Plans include a Pinot, Chardonnay, an underground maturation cellar and a tasting facility. Meanwhile visitors are welcomed at nearby La Vierge, where the maiden Sauvignon below was vinified.

★★★★ **Sauvignon Blanc** Zesty citrus & green fig aromas, restrained mineral & flint flavours belie bracing aperitif-style finish on **07** (sample), persistent limy/peppery finish. — *MF*

■ Domaine Finlayson *see Edgebaston*

Domaine Newman
T 021-855-5528

Stellenbosch · Est/1stB 2006 · Closed to public · Owner Chris Newman · Winemaker Chris Newman with Edouard Labeye & Guillaume Nell · Viticulturist Edouard Labeye & Guillaume Nell · 2t/115cs 100% red · c/o The Winery of Good Hope, Postnet Suite 124, Private Bag X15, Somerset West 7129 · thewineryofgoodhope@thewineryofgoodhope.co.za

'It's all about watching, learning and tasting,' declares Chris Newman, second-generation owner of Domaine Newman in Burgundy, about his view on making wine. In the French 'off-season', he's in SA making a Syrah, a project he started in 2006 with The Winery of Good Hope's Alex Dale. 'I've always liked the best-of-both-worlds feel of SA wine,' Newman says.

★★★★ **Syrah** With all the black pepper, smoky & dark wild fruit styling of the Rhône, this beauty seduces you with its trim muscle tone, savoury dry tannins. A good 5+ yr future. 14 mnths Fr, 40% new. Unfiltered. — *CR*

■ Dombeya *see Haskell Vineyards*

Domein Doornkraal
T 044-251-6715/2556 · F 044-251-6715

Klein Karoo · Est 1890 · 1stB 1973 · Tasting & sales Mon-Fri 9-5 Sat 8-1 (Sep-May) & Sat 9-1 (Jun-Aug) · Pub & school hols 8-5; school hols (summer) 8-6 · Closed Easter Fri/Sun, Dec 25/ 26 & Jan 1 · Tours by appt · Seasonal farm produce · Tour groups · Gifts · Owner Swepie & Piet le Roux · Winemaker Swepie & Piet le Roux, with Schantelle Swiegelaar (2005) · Viticulturist Piet le Roux · 22ha · 2 000cs own label 50% white 50% red · PO Box 14 De Rust 6650 · doornkraal@xsinet.co.za · www.doornkraal.co.za

The Le Roux vision of organic farming with integrated and sustainable practices means coaxing 'Mother Earth into becoming her voluptuous self again'. The past cold winter, with its snow and rain, benefited grapes and wine, as well as the tourist-friendly gift and coffee shop at their tasting venue.

Domein Doornkraal range

★★★★ **Pinta** Luscious jerepiko-style dessert from pinotage, tinta; lately dash touriga too (necessitating name change?); harmonious with fresh dry finish. 30/50/20 mix; alc now set at 17%. **NV**. Note: no new vintages/bottlings tasted for this, any below.

★★★★ **Ten Year Old Tawny Port** Among handful of SA vintaged tawnies; old-fashioned but delicious. last tasted **92** VDG was beautifully balanced; from pinotage, tinta.

Cabernet Sauvignon ★★★ 02 ripe cassis aromas; focused & quite rich; quick finish but pleasant enough. **Merlot ★★** Quirky, sweet & simple **03**, fermented with native yeasts **Kannaland (Red) ★★★ 05** cab, merlot mix, unwooded; undemanding, lightish berry flavours finishing slightly sweet. **Kannaland (White) ★★ 05** chardonnay/semillon mix; semi-dry boiled-sweet flavours, lively, for early enjoyment. **Tickled Pink ★★** Light, sweet, festively foamy blanc de noir sparkler; sold with shocking pink ostrich feather. **Kuierwyn Natural Sweet** Available but not tasted. **Muscadel Jerepigo ★★★** Comfortable & warming fortified dessert; rich raisiny flavours with hint of pipe-tobacco. 18% alc. Discontinued: **Kuierwyn Dry, Ruby Port, White Port**.

Military' range
Majoor ★★★ Idiosyncratic white jerepiko from chenin. Great Martini mixer, avers Piet le R. **NV**, like all in range. **Kaptein** Not assessed. **Luitenant** Still AWOL. —*DH*

Dominion Wine Company
T 021-883-8879 • F 021-883-8782

Stellenbosch • Est/1stB 2002 • Closed to public • Owner 63 Capital, Wine of the Month Club, Merwida Vineyard • Winemaker Lelanie Germishuys (2004) • 120 000cs own label 40% red 60% white • Export brands: Longwood, Harvest Moon & Dominion • Postnet Suite 280, Private Bag X29, Somerset West 7135 • info@dominionwineco.co.za • www.dominionwineco.co.za
Seventy-five percent black owned, 'virtual winery' Dominion's philosophy is 'innovation is the key to survival'. Winemaker and blender Lelanie Germishuys says, 'I consult with a few selected wineries and work closely with them to produce quality wines in a style that our consumers require.'

Dominion Wine Company range
Kingsview Pinotage ★★ Still-listed lusty **03**. Red-berry pungency, big tannins, warming 14. 3% alc. **Big Red** ★★ **NV** cab/merlot sold only in magnum (1.5litre); last ed showed strong tannins & slightly stewed fruit. **Sauvignon Blanc** ★★ Early-drinking **06** (sample) pvs ed noted as vinified for light-bodied freshness & verve. **Sauvignon Blanc Brut** ★★★ Mouthfilling fizz with gd sugar/acid balance & some sauv character. **NV**. All ranges sourced widely, so various WOs. Discontinued: **Milestone Chardonnay Limited Release, Rolling Hills Chardonnay**.

Harvest Moon range
Discontinued: **Shiraz, Chardonnay, Sauvignon Blanc**.

Longwood range
Cabernet Sauvignon-Shiraz NEW ★★★ Old-style **05**, v tight & dry but gd lingering finish. **Chenin Blanc-Colombard** ★★ Zingy **07** (sample), light-bodied dry summer cooler. Discontinued: **Pinotage-Shiraz, Sauvignon Blanc**.

Sugar Bush Ridge range
Cabernet Sauvignon-Merlot ★★★ Pvsly tasted **05**, approachable, deliciously harmonious & flavourful combo. **Sauvignon Blanc** ★★ **07** not tasted. —*IvH*

■ **Donatus** *see Dornier Wines*

Doolhof Estate

T 021-873-6911 • F 021-864-2321

Wellington (see Paarl map) • Est 1995 • 1stB 2001 • Visits Mon-Fri 8.30-4 Sat/Sun Sep-May 10-4, Jun-Aug Sat only 10-2 • Fee R20 • Closed Easter Fri, Dec 25 & Jan 1 • Picnics by appt • Guest cottage • Walks • Mountain biking • Owner Dennis Kerrison • Winemaker Therese de Beer (Aug 2004) • Viticulturist Hendrik Laubscher (Aug 1996) • ±36ha (cabs s/f, malbec, merlot, petit v, pinotage, shiraz, chard, sauv) • 220t • PO Box 157 Wellington 7654 • wine@doolhof.com • www.doolhof.com
Good news from the Kerrisons' Wellington estate, some close to home: creating footpaths to make a labyrinth (the word translates as 'Doolhof') and winemaker Therese de Beer (née Swart) celebrating her nuptials. Other updates from further afield: a slew of awards for their wines and prestigious new listings, including the Ritz-Carlton Singapore, the UK's Du Vin luxury hotel chain and Harrods of London.

Signatures of Doolhof range
★★★★ **Chardonnay Wooded** Well-judged oaking in **06**, fermented/matured Fr oak; 50% new, giving roasted nut overlay to peach, citrus flavours. Harmonious, showy & delicious.
Cabernet Sauvignon ★★★ Sample **05** pvs ed; distinctive 'roasted corn' element remains, warm-textured pruney fruit, integrated tannins. 70% new Fr oak. **Merlot** ★★★ Smoked meat notes have emerged in **05**, previewed pvs ed; accompanying cassis flavours & smoothly

rounded body. Yr Fr wood, 50% new. **Pinotage** ★★★★ Ex-barrel last ed, **05** since settled into dark-fruited, smooth-textured delight. Touch rhubarb adds typicity. Yr Fr oak, 70% new. Michelangelo gold, Terroir Awards best pinotage. **Shiraz** NEW ★★★ **05** affable ripe plum & spice flavours, well supported by integrated tannins, juicy drinkability. **Chardonnay Unoaked** ★★★ Gentle but characterful **07**, tropical & peach tones, friendly, fresh approachability. **Sauvignon Blanc** ★★★★ Cut grass, vibrant leafy perfume; **07** quietens down enough for elegant (12.5% alc) & tasty food pairing. Regional Terroir Award.

Doolhof Estate range

Pinotage Plus NEW ★★★ Toasty oak & hedgerow fruit intro, **06** pure creamy mocha flavours; nothing shy about this one! **Renaissance Cabernet Sauvignon-Merlot** In abeyance. **Cape Boar** ★★★★ No follow-up reviewed for **04**, equal shiraz, merlot with ripe plum pudding fruit & assertive tannins. **Cape Roan** ★★★★ **05** unready. Explosively fruity **03** was last tasted, blend of shiraz, cab, merlot (70/20/10); massive alc (15%) not unbalanced. **The Dukes Blend** Not tasted. Discontinued: **Maiden's Prayer**. — *CR*

Dormershire
T 021-903-1784 • F 021-945-1174

Stellenbosch • Est 1996 • 1stB 2001 • Visits Mon-Fri 10-5 Sat 10-4 • Owner SPF Family Trust • Winemaker Michelle Loots, advised by Kowie du Toit • Viticulturist Johan Pienaar (consultant) • 7ha (cab, shiraz, sauv) • 60t/4 000cs 75% red 15% white 10% rosé • PO Box 491 Bellville 7535 • wine@dormershire.co.za

For new winemaker Michelle Loots, who aims to build on good vineyard management, the old adage 'quality starts in the vineyard' rings ever true. The reduced yields of the 2007 harvest lead her to expect a classic vintage, and a cab-shiraz blend will join the range.

Rosé ☺ 🍽 ★★★ Charming summer quaffer, soft acidity, nice & dry in **06**. Lightly oaked.

Cabernet Sauvignon ★★★★ Classically constructed, stylish **04**, liberal cassis fruit, fragrant pencil-shaving oak; mid-2006 needed more time to show true worth. 15 mths Fr oak, 20% new. Not revisited, as for other reds. **Shiraz** ★★★ **04** similar uninhibited ripe fruitiness as pvs, plus aromatic enticements incl smoked bacon, though tannins drier, bit more herbaceous. Oak as above. **Stoep Shiraz** ★★★★ Higher rating for this version courtesy riper tannins/fruit, more generosity & concentration. **04** similar attractive flavours. Wood as above. **Sauvignon Blanc** 🍽 ★★★ Bottled **06** misses effusiveness of last ed's sample; diffident herbal, grassy tones, but still pleasant. — *IvH*

Dornier Wines
T 021-880-0557 • F 021-880-1499

Stellenbosch • 1stB 2002 • Tasting & sales daily 10-5 • Fee R20 • Closed Good Fri, Dec 25 & Jan 1 • Bodega Restaurant daily 10-5 (May 1-Sep 30 closed Mon & Tue) • Tour groups • Owner Delfinarte Foundation • Winemaker JC Steyn (2005) • Viticulturist Bob Hobson (2005) • 60ha (cabs s/f, malbec, merlot, petit v, pinotage, shiraz, chenin, sauvignon, semillon) • 300t 80% red 13% white 7% rosé • PO Box 7518 Stellenbosch 7599 • info@dornier.co.za • www. dornier.co.za

From the outside, this winery is an architectural gem; on the inside the team has been fine-tuning their knowledge with the help of French consultant Florent Dumeau, as well as looking after their natural habitat as part of the Biodiversity & Wine Initiative: witness plans to reintroduce indigenous fish to the farm's waterways. A new tasting centre has opened, along with the new Bodega Restaurant helmed by internationally trained Tullishe le Roux, in the charmingly restored barn.

Dornier range

★★★★ **Dornier Donatus** Classy bdx-red. No **05** produced; last ed **04** (★★★★★) was alluringly spiced, taut; typical claret tealeaf finish courtesy 71/29 cab f/merlot mix. **03**, with touch cab, classically structured. New Fr oak, 18 mths.

★★★★ **Donatus White** Confident barrel-fermented/aged chenin (81%) & semillon, the latter's weight lovely counterpoint to chenin briskness. **07**'s nutty oak mingles with thatch/lemon notes; will reward 2yrs+ aging. 8 mths Fr oak, 43% new.

Cabernet Sauvignon NEW ★★★☆ Straight arrow yet vivacious **05** has high-toned cassis fruit, refreshing lemony acidity & friendly tannins from 18mths 2nd fill Fr oak. **Merlot** ★★★★ Well formed **05** needs a few yrs for strident tannins to meld with plush fruit, live up to alluring bouquet spice, smoke. Fruity **04** had fine tannins, minerals; **03** was rich, if slightly astringent. 18 mths Fr oak, 30% new. **Pinotage** ★★★★ Smart & confident **06** (no **05**) lifts the bar on oak-driven **04**. Has all of the fruit, none of the bitterness of the variety; finishes long & succulent. 12 mths Fr oak, 30% new.

Cocoa Hill range

Cocoa Hill ★★★☆ Polished, gently oaked blend. Merlot plays leading role in **06** (55% vs **07**'s 23%) with cab s & f, shiraz as supporting cast (21/6/18). Balanced, more-ish red/black fruit mélange. **Rosé** NEW ▤ ★★★ **07** maiden - mainly cab f (83%) with dash merlot - perfect for al fresco dining. Decently dry, brimming with red berry flavour, party-starting 13% alc. **Chenin Blanc** ▤ ★★★ No oak on **07** versus 30% for **06**. Water-white with thatch notes, Granny Smith Apple flavours, long zesty farewell. *— CvZ*

Douglas Green
T 021-864-5300 • F 021-864-1287

Wellington • Est/1stB 1938 • Closed to public • Owner DGB • Cellarmaster Blending cellar: Gerhard Carstens, with Liezl Carstens (2003) • Oenologist Jaco Potgieter (2000) • Vini advisor John Worontschak • Viticulturist Stephan Joubert (2006) • 23 000t/1 600 000cs 50% red 50% white • ISO 9001 2000 & HACCP certified • PO Box 246, Wellington, 7654 • douglasgreen@ dgb.co.za • www.douglasgreenwines.com

Sourcing grapes from throughout the Cape winelands and keeping the flexibility to change styles - these are the elements that make Douglas Green tick, according to oenologist Jaco Potgieter. Updated packaging will also give this trusty old label a new lease of life - 'We're focusing on a younger, female target market,' explains brand manager Liné Marais.

Reserve Selection NEW

Merlot ★★★ **05** step-up on standard bottling; appealingly ripe damson fruit with harmonious fruit, oak & acid balance. **Shiraz** ★★★ Meaty **05** with serious leather & spice tones, red fruit sweetness checked by savoury acidity. **Chardonnay** ★★★★ Pop-style **05**, vanilla & butterscotch aromas, rich peachy flavours & creamy texture balanced by crunchy acidity. 50% new oak fermented/matured. This range international only.

Vineyard Creations NEW

Cabernet Sauvignon ★★★ **05** brightly fruited & focused, with hint oak from 3 mths Am staves, refreshing savoury finish. **Merlot** ★★☆ Stalky & vegetal **05**, simple sour plum flavours & spiky acidity. **Pinotage** ★★★ Well-made, meaty **05**, succulent red fruit flavours & juicy freshness; some structure & texture from oak staving. **Shiraz** ★★★ Commercially styled **05** with spicy, smoky aromas; sweet blackberry flavours tempered by warm savouriness. **Chardonnay** ▤ ★★★ Melon & peach **07** offers hint butterscotch from stave ferment & richness from lees contact, zingy acidity. **Chenin Blanc** ▤ ★★☆ Pineapple tropicality on **07** balanced by crisp apple flavours & tangy, flavoursome finish. **Sauvignon Blanc** ▤ ★★★ Preview **07** lightly herbaceous, passionfruit flavours & fresh acidity with low 12% alc. Ideal for seafood lunch. Replaces the Single Varietals range.

Diversity range NEW

Cabernet Sauvignon-Merlot ☺ ▤ ★★★ Juicy, characterful 50/50 blend, **05** balanced & savoury for fresh, uncomplicated, everyday drinking.

Cabernet Sauvignon-Shiraz ▤ ★★★ Ripe 60/40 blend; **05** mulberry aromas restrained by balanced acidity & savoury, spicy finish. **Cinsaut-Pinotage** ★★ Preview **06** simple, juicily fruited quaffer. **Shiraz -Viognier** ▤ ★★★ Spicy redcurrant **05**, with aromatic viognier lift to sweet red berry flavours & warm (14.5% alc) finish. **Cinsaut-Ruby Cabernet Sauvignon** ★★ Light **06** sample, 50/50 blend, simply fruity for easy, early drinking. **Pinotage Rosé** ★★★ Salmon-pink **07**, bright & breezy picnic wine, friendly fruitgum notes. **Chardonnay-Colombard** 🔲 ★★★ Preview **07** for early drinking. Intense melon flavours, Fr oak chip fermented. **Chenin Blanc-Colombard** 🔲 ★★ Fresh tropicality in preview **07**, light, balanced 60/40 blend. **Sauvignon Blanc-Semillon** 🔲 ★★ **07** (sample) herbaceous, grassy 60/40 'dry white', pleasant drinking. **Sauvignon Blanc-Chardonnay** 🔲 ★★★ Preview **07** grassy sauv character (70%), fresh acidity & light 12.5% alc. **Chardonnay-Viognier** ★★★ Apricot & peach aromas from splash viognier in **07**, sweet fruit flavours & fresh acidity, appealing breadth. Replaces 'Faces of Africa' range; sold internationally, some locally; all WO W Cape.

Douglas Green Signature Brands

St Augustine ★★★ Favourite SA red since the 1940s. **05** easy charmer; soft, juicy commercial appeal & warmly spicy sweet red fruit. **The Beachhouse** NEW 🔲 ★★ **07** aptly named summery, easy-drinking sauv/semillon blend; 12% alc. **Cape Ruby Port** ★★★★ Spicy **NV** in lighter style, from tinta & souzão; welcoming nutty sweetness & fruitcake richness. — *IM*

Douglas Wine Cellar

T 053-298-8314 • F 053-298-1845

Northern Cape ▪ Est 1968 ▪ 1stB 1977 ▪ Tasting & sales Mon-Fri 8-5 ▪ Fee R5 ▪ Closed pub hols ▪ Tours by appt ▪ BYO picnic ▪ Gifts ▪ Owner 45 shareholders ▪ Winemaker Willie Stofberg ▪ Viticulturist Pou Le Roux ▪ 360ha (cab, merlot, ruby cab, shiraz, chard, chenin, colombard, gewürz) ▪ 6 000s own label 19% red 43% white 8% rosé 30% dessert ▪ PO Box 47 Douglas 8730 ▪ wynkelder@gwk.co.za ▪ www.confluencewines.co.za

After earning his stripes at De Wetshof and Deetlefs, Willie Stofberg is now determined to put the Northern Cape on the quality-wine map. 'Yes, it's hot here, but you wouldn't believe how many amazing terroirs we have.' You'll find him working on a few special projects in his 'small cellar within the big cellar'.

Barney Barnato range NEW

Shiraz ★★★ Dusting warm spice on **05** pruney fruit, dry, some savoury notes; shows subtle side of the variety. 6 mths oak. **Cabernet Sauvignon-Merlot** ★★★★ Cool cedary notes & dark choc mesh on **03** equal blend. Gd sappy fruit sourced in Sbosch, approachable tannins, though grippy on finish. 6 mths oak. **Chardonnay 05** sold out before we could taste. **Sauvignon Blanc** ★★★ **06** asparagus & canned peas, attractive varietal character in riper style. Take cue from label: serve with food.

Confluence range

Classic Red ★★ Light, savoury 50/50 cab s/ruby cab mix, **06** ideal for chilling. **Pinotage Rosé** Not tasted. **Chenin Blanc** NEW ★★ Maiden **07** has fruit pastille flavours, is light-bodied & crisp. **Classic White** ★★ **06** easy-drinking 60/40 chenin/colombard blend; light 11.5% alc. **Johannisberger White** ★★ Bland, semi-sweet **NV** blend (70/30 chenin/colombard). 10% alc. **Johannisberger Red** ★★ Tutti-frutti cab s/ruby cab blend (80/20); soft tannins, semi-sweet. **NV**. **Red Muscadel** ★★ No new vintage. **04** was raisined & treacle-rich, with well-integrated alc. Discontinued: **Shiraz-Cabernet Sauvignon, Red Jerepigo**.

Provin range

2/5litre casks untasted: Dry Red, Grand Cru, Stein, Special Harvest & Late Harvest. — *IvH*

■ **Down to Earth** *see Villiera Wines*

Dragonridge Winery

T 022-487-1153 • F 022-487-1153 (telephone first)

Swartland ▪ Est 1997 ▪ 1stB 2004 ▪ Visits by appt ▪ Tasting fee R30 against orders of 6 btls ▪ Meals/refreshments for groups by arrangement ▪ BYO picnic ▪ Guesthouse B&B ▪ Aged wine vinegar, olive oil, honey ▪ Conferences/workshops ▪ Walks/hikes ▪ Conservation area ▪ Mountain biking ▪ Birding tours by arrangement ▪ Owner Fynbos Estate (3 partners) ▪ Winemaker Johan Simons, with Peter Narun (2004/2005) ▪ Viticulturist Johan Simons (1997) ▪ 30ha (cab, mourvèdre, pinotage, sangiovese, shiraz, chard, chenin, viognier) • *200t (10t/500cs own label) 60% red 40% white* • *P O Box 526 Malmesbury 7299* • *info@dragonridge.co.za, info@ fynbosestate.co.za* • *www.fynbosestate.co.za*

'I feel like an Italian peasant who describes his wine as "wine from grapes",' laughs Johan Simons. Not because he doesn't know what's in the wine, but because he believes in minimal intervention. 'We try to get it right in the vineyards.' His focus is rhône-style wines, but sangiovese is also planted 'because I like Super Tuscans but cannot afford them.'

Sangiovese ★★★ Unusual **06**, packed with ripely plush sweet maraschino cherry aromas/ flavours untrammelled by modest oaking. Fresh despite 15.7% alc; sharp & dry-tannined. **Jack's Red** Not tasted. **Galaxy ★★★★** Chenin-based **06**, viognier (23%) adding subtle peach to fynbos, chard (31%) augmenting breadth; characterful, with freshness, flavour, power; though restrained & lightly wooded. — *TJ*

Drakensig Wines

T 021-874-3881 • **F 021-874-3882**

Paarl • *Est 1999* • *1stB 2000* • *Tasting & sales Mon-Fri 9-5 Sat 9-1; low season by appt* • *Closed Easter Sun, Dec 25/26 & Jan 1* • *Farm-grown olive oil for sale* • *Conference facilities for groups of 5-10* • *Owner/viticulturist Marais Viljoen* • *Winemaker Marais Viljoen, advised by Chris Joubert* • *13ha (cab, pinotage, shiraz)* • *4 000cs 80% red 20% white* • *HACCP implementation in progress* • *PO Box 22 Simondium 7670* • *drakensig@mweb.co.za*

'Olives are the flavour of the month,' is Marais Viljoen's understatement of the year, given that olive production here is up by 100%. The multi-tasking owner now has help in the cellar from experienced winemaking consultant Chris Joubert, originally with Overgaauw. They pronounce themselves happy with the last vintage: 'Maturity of the vines is showing in the grapes.'

Marais Viljoen range

★★★★ **Shiraz** Leader of this pack. Spicy wild-berry intro to **04**, off Darling vyds (as all in range); full, robustly extracted, with strong, tight tannins promising gd few yrs development. 14 mths 50/50 Am/Fr oak.

Cabernet Sauvignon ★★ Returned to guide with **04**, showing some chalky-dry tannins tending towards austerity. **Merlot ★★★** **05** lashings sweet-ripe plummy fruit, low acid, ±15% alc, last ed made a big, rich, winter warmer. **Pinotage ★★** Big & unsubtle **01** last time.

Drakensig range

Cabernet Sauvignon No new vintage. **Merlot** Sold out. **Pinotage** No wine reviewed. **Shiraz** No new vintage. **Chardonnay** NEW Unwooded **07** not ready for tasting. **Sauvignon Blanc ★★★** **06** better, more expressive than pvs; appealing **07** unready. — *CT*

Drostdy-Hof Wines

T 023-230-0203; 012-809-8177 • **F 023-230-0211**

Tulbagh • *Est 1804* • *Tasting & wine sales at De Oude Drostdy Mon-Fri 10-5 Sat 10-2* • *Owner Distell* • *PO Box 213 Tulbagh 6820* • *www.drostdywines.co.za*

De Oude Drostdy, Tulbagh's old magistracy, built in 1804 and now a national monument, is the spiritual home of Drostdy-Hof wines. The range, intended to be fruity and accessible early, is now distributed globally.

Pinotage ☺ **★★** **06** reverts to mulberried amiability, with quaffable rounded tannins & bright acidity. **Chardonnay-Sémillon** ☺ **★★★** Comfortable quaffing or food-styled partner. **06** plump, waxy ripe pear on nose & palate, zesty lime acidity.

Cabernet Sauvignon ★★ **05** contrasting ripe cassis fruit & austere tannins ex-barrels/ staves. Invites food. **Merlot ★★** Earthy, tight, lean & dry **06**; lacks plummy spiciness of pvs. **Shiraz ★★★** Approachable & balanced, medium-bodied **06**; more understated, stylish than burly pvs. Spicy hint from gd oaking. **Cape Red ★★** **06** brawny pinotage-led blend with berry hints; lean & tannic despite dollop sugar. **Claret Select ★★** Last-tasted version was cheery, light, pleasantly dry. **NV**. 750ml, 2 & 5litre cask. **Rosé** ★★ Brisk, tart, cherry-toned 5-way melange. **07** light in alc (11.7%). **Chardonnay** ★★ Ripe pear with tangy lime & pithy twist on **06**, crisp finish. **Extra Light** ★ Super-light, extra-dry low-alc (9.5%) chenin for slimmers/ salad fans. **NV**. 750ml, 2 & 5litre. **Steen/Chenin Blanc** ★★ **07** delicately crisp & fruity, fresh flinty edge. Made for seafood. **Sauvignon Blanc** ★★ Lemongrass & passionfruit nuances enhance delicate, light & crisp **07**. **Chardonnay-Viognier** ★★★ Frisky, edgy summer sipper. **06** gentle viognier aromas overtaken by citrus zestiness. Combo staves/barrels. 2litre cask. **Premier Grand Cru** ★★ Summer slimmer's tipple. Low alc (11.7%), dry, fresh-apple crisp. 750ml, 2 & 5litre. **NV**. **Stein Select** ★★ Gently fruited, balanced white blend; **NV**; semi-sweet, vaguely tropical, with honeyed tail. 750ml, 2 & 5litre. **Late Harvest** ★★ Honeyed **NV** from chenin; sweet, textured, but tad soft & blowsy. 750ml, 2 & 5litre. **Adelpracht** ★★★ SLH from chenin, botrytis touched in **06**. Delicately sweet with refreshing lime twist. Gd with spicy cuisine or curries. **Natural Sweet Red** NEW ★ Soft, scented, accessible three-way blend. **NV**. **Natural Sweet Rosé** NEW ★★ Innocuous sweet charmer, soft, alluring deep rose hue. **NV**. **Natural Sweet White** NEW ★★ Low-alc sweetie. Delicate, perfumed, with crisp, refreshing acidity. **NV**.

African Sky
Cabernet Sauvignon, **Merlot**, **Shiraz**, **Cirrus** (mainly pinotage, with cab, merlot, cab & shiraz), **Crux** (chiefly cab, splash ruby cab), **Cape Red**, **Cumulus** (chenin), **Chenin Blanc**, **Cape White** (chenin), **Sauvignon**, **Celeste** (sauvignon, semillon). — *MW*

■ **Dry Creek** *see* Du Preez Estate
■ *Due South* *see* Wines of Cape Town

Dunstone Winery  NEW
T 021-873-6770 • **F** 021-873-6770

Wellington (see Paarl map) ▪ *Est/1stB 2006* ▪ *Visits Mon-Sat 10-6 Sun 10-4* ▪ *Fee R10p/p* ▪ *Closed Easter Sun, Dec 25 & 26, Jan 1* ▪ *Lunch from 12; teas 4-6; private dinner parties by arrangement* ▪ *Bovlei Valley Retreat - luxury guest house & self catering cottage (see Stay-over section)* ▪ *Owner Abbi & Lee Wallis* ▪ *Winemaker Corlea Fourie (Jan 2006)* ▪ *2.7ha (mer-lot, shiraz)* ▪ *4t/350cs 80% red 20% rosé* ▪ *PO Box 901 Wellington 7654* ▪ *wine@dunstone.co.za* ▪ *www.dunstone.co.za*

A passion for wine became a full-scale wine business for Lee and Abbi Wallis, who moved to SA from the UK in 2002, eventually settling on a smallholding in Wellington. Lee is Professor of Emergency Medicine at the University of Cape Town; Abbi takes care of the guesthouse; and in the cellar, finished in 2006, is winemaker Corlea Fourie who also takes care of the 2.7ha in production.

Shiraz ★★★ White pepper & black cherry on **06**, allspice aromas, delicate, lace-like textures, hot chunky finish. **Shiraz Rosé** 〓 ★★★ Raspberry-toned **07**, nutmeg whiffs, spicy palate, some vinosity & length. — *MF*

■ **Du Pleina** *see* Vrede Wine Farm
■ *Du Plessis Reserve* *see* Havana Hills

Du Preez Estate
T 023-349-1995 • **F** 023-349-1923

Goudini (see Worcester map) ▪ *Est 1995* ▪ *1stB 1998* ▪ *Tasting & sales Mon-Fri 8-12.30; 1.30-5 Sat 10-1* ▪ *Closed pub hols* ▪ *Tours by appt* ▪ *BYO picnic* ▪ *Facilities for children* ▪ *Tour groups* ▪ *Owner Du Preez family* ▪ *Winemaker Hennie du Preez Jnr (1995)* ▪ *Viticulturist Jean du Preez (Dec 1996)* ▪ *300ha (cab, merlot, petit v, chard, chenin, sauv)* ▪ *56% red 40% white 2% rosé 2% sparkling* ▪ *Other export brands: Hendrik Lodewyk, Dry Creek, Route 101* ▪ *PO Box 12 Rawsonville 6845* ▪ *info@dupreezestate.co.za* ▪ *www.dupreezestate.co.za*

'Watching my dad make wine made me want to do it too,' says Hennie du Preez, whose two children are now growing up on the same farm he did. Polla's Red, the estate's flagship, was named after Hennie's grandmother. 'It was made sort of by coincidence and turned out to be an award winner.'

Du Preez Estate range

★★★★ **Hendrik Lodewyk Petit Verdot** Blueberry & cedar spice joined by mocha choc on rich mouthfilling **04**, but austere tannins & bright acidity need time to meld, settle. Seriously wooded (30 mths small oak), as for last-tasted **01**.

★★★★ **Hanepoot** Dried peach, jasmine, barley sugar & tropical fruit abound on ripe, succulent **05**. Full-sweet, but sufficient bright acidity to balance. Great winter warmer or on crushed ice.

Merlot ★★★☆ Ripe, dark fruited **04** with mocha choc & hint of eucalyptus; last ed offered creamy, persistent, balanced flavours with smoke & spice from integrated wooding (9-18 mths). **Shiraz** Not tasted. **Polla's Red** ★★★★ Character/flavourful vintage blend. Last we reviewed **02**, four-way mix pinotage, cab, petit v & shiraz; spicy welcome, ripe plummy flavours, rich texture with supple tannin, well fused oak (6-12 mths). **Chardonnay** ★★☆ **07** ripe pear & lemoncurd flavours in rounder style than pvs, hint of acidity overwhelmed by warm alc finish. **Sauvignon Blanc** ★★ Dusty nettle intro to plump but dilute **07**, brush of tropical fruit & mineral, warm finish despite low 11.6% alc. **Hendrik Lodewyk Cap Classic** NEW ✓ ★★★★ Bright, lively sparkler in MCC style. Clean citrus & apple appeal with zesty fresh acidity & some creaminess ex-39 mths on the lees. Still youthful, potential to age but delicious now. Discontinued: **Merlot Reserve**.

Rockfield range

Cabernet Sauvignon ★★★ Ripe cassis & fruit pastille combine with bright acidity on clean, juicy **04**. Medium bodied & unoaked, for early drinking. **Merlot** ★★ Leaner, fresh style (13% alc), **04** unwooded with sweet/sour cranberry & rhubarb notes. **Shiraz** ★★ Spicy wild-berry & fynbos scrub introduce lighter, sappy **04**; mild tannins & tangy touch make gd barbeque red. **Red Stone Blend** ★★★★ Spicy, red berried **02** was last tasted. **Dry Creek Red** ★★☆ Shiraz, merlot & petit v mix in **07** sample, sweet-sour plum, savoury hints, still unknit mid-2007, rating tentative. **Chenin Blanc** ★★★ Friendly ripe-apple aromas & zesty acidity enliven rounded **07**, finishes touch warm. **Sauvignon Blanc** ★★ Tart, lemony dry white with hint of mineral. **07** has low alc (11.4%) yet is plump & warming. **Dry Creek White** ★★ Neutral, 3-way, low alc (11.3%) blend **07**, fresh, crisp acid lift for casual summer quaffing. **Dry Creek Bouquet Blanc** ★★☆ Last we tasted **04** delicate & still fresh off-dry easy-drinker from chenin & colombard. *— MW*

Durbanville Hills   🍷🍴☕🎿♿

T 021-558-1300 · F 021-558-8169

Durbanville · Est 1998 · 1stB 1999 · Tasting & sales Mon-Fri 9-4.30 Sat & pub hols 9.30-2.30 Sun 11-3; fee R10 · Tours Mon-Fri 11 & 3; Sat/Sun by appt; fee R20 · Closed Easter Fri/Sun, Dec 25/26 & Jan 1 · @ The Hills Restaurant (see Eat-out section) · Facilities for children · Tour groups · Owner Distell, 8 farmers & workers' trust · Cellarmaster Martin Moore with winemakers Louw Engelbrecht & Günther Kellerman (Nov 1998/Jun 2005/Nov 2003) · Viticulturist Johan Pienaar (consultant) · 770ha (cab, merlot, pinotage, shiraz, chard, sauv) · 6 000t/ 140 000cs own label 50% red 50% white · ISO 9000,14000 & BRC certified · PO Box 3276 Durbanville 7551 · info@durbanvillehills.co.za · www.durbanvillehills.co.za

There are local fans and awards aplenty for the Durbanville wines (witness another Veritas Merlot hat trick). Canadians joined the devotees after Martin Moore was invited to cook up a real South African barbeque storm on their national TV channel, pairing his wines with kebabs, sosaties, sousboontjies and potbrood! Doubts about the monkeys in monkeygland sauce took some dealing with - but what of the renosterveld vegetation alluded to on the Rhinofields label and the creatures in the Luipaardsberg? Talking of the stylish new labels: to help Canadians and locals alike remember the wine they enjoyed, they feature peel-off, memory-prompting stickers.

Durbanville Hills range

★★★★ Luipaardsberg Merlot Reserve Ex-single vyd on Klein Roosboom farm. Intense blackberry & mint flavours in **03**, savoury whiffs, exotic spices. Structurally elegant, with lurking seriousness: 2 yrs new Fr, 4+ yrs ageing potential. VDG. No **02**.

★★★★☆ Caapmans Cabernet Sauvignon-Merlot Veritable choco box (mint & dark), **03** has such well-tailored tannins, layers of interest, you'll be tempted to drink it all up. Resist; 2 yrs new Fr oaking laid down structure for rewarding future. VG. No **02**.

★★★★☆ Biesjes Craal Sauvignon Blanc Only cool vintages, ex-steep, mature south-facing vyd. Always individual: greenpepper & lime zest in **07**, less acidity this time but no compromise on intensity of flavours, elegant appeal. Only 11.9% alc. Could age few yrs.

Rhinofields Reserve range

★★★★ Merlot Distinctive, individual **05** has much to offer: dark cherries, whiffs mint choc, liberal dusting oakspice. Elegant, balanced, with sheathed power, gd 3/4 yrs cellaring future. **02-04** sold out before we could taste.

★★★★☆ Chardonnay Carefully blended from 3 vyds, unwooded portion, rest new oak, yr lees. Less intensity than pvs, **06** (**★★★★**) still delivers drinking pleasure: peach/apricot, toasted brioche layers, lemony vein of acidity. Ex-barrel last ed, on-song **05** was a powerhouse of toast, yellow cling peach & citrus peel.

★★★★☆ Inner Valley Sauvignon Blanc This & next designed to show terroir diversity. From trellised vines, one vyd, **07** (**★★★★**) gentler than **06**, same green styling: leafy, asparagus, core of minerality, ideal for seafood. Gd ageing potential, 2/3 yrs.

★★★★ Outer Valley Sauvignon Blanc Bushvines from one vyd, riper style than sibling. Gooseberries & lemongrass in **07** (**★★★☆**), friendly rather than steely palate, gd minerality. Would benefit from yr/2 ageing, to allow further flavour evolution. Full, ripe **06** was delicious solo or with food.

★★★★ Sauvignon Blanc Combo 5 vyds for full-spectrum flavours. Unfolding in glass, **07** proves benefits of this strategy; cut grass, fennel, with gooseberry underpin, appealing drinkability.

The Hill Range

★★★★ Bastion Confident, classy 60/40 blend cab/shiraz. Allowing appealing plum & smoky spice aromatics of shiraz to dominate in **05**, cab takes care of elegant structure, supple tannins. Satisfyingly dry, food-friendly. **Cabernet Sauvignon ★★★★** Like reds below, for earlier drinking. Varietal-true as always, **05**'s cassis core given extra fillip by herbaceous nuances, oak spicing. Elegant, lively, harmonious. **Merlot ★★★** More mocha-choc than red fruit in **05**, hardly grounds for complaint! Sleek structure & enough lifting acidity to please most palates. **Pinotage ★★★** Black plums & liquorice perfume, flavours in **06** but balance hasn't strayed from variety's trademark lively drinkability. **Shiraz ★★★★** Rhône elements in **05**, dried brush, campfire smoke, with plum core & harmonious tannins adding to tasty appeal. Nicely made; has few yrs ageing potential. **Chardonnay ★★★** Largely unwooded for earlier drinking, accessible but not simple. **06** peach flavours, creamy texture from long lees contact. **Sauvignon Blanc ★★★★** Entry-level, high-volume version, yet **07** more to show than usual: green fig, gooseberry styling, lipsmacking freshness; v satisfying. — CR

■ Dusty Road see Cloof

Du Toitskloof Winery 🍷 🌳 ♿
T 023-349-1601 • F 023-349-1581

Rawsonville (see Worcester map) ▪ Est 1962 ▪ 1stB 1970 ▪ Tasting & sales — Winery: Mon-Fri 8-5 Sat 9-12.30; wine shop: Mon-Fri 9-5 Sat 10-5 Sun 11-16h00 ▪ Closed Easter Fri/Mon, Dec 16/25/26, Jan 1 ▪ BYO picnic ▪ Tours by appt ▪ Formal tasting for groups max 20 ▪ Owner 20 Members ▪ Winemaker Philip Jordaan & Shawn Thomson (May 1983/Oct 1999), with Derrick Cupido & Christo Basson (1993/Jan 2002) ▪ Viticulturist Viti consultant Leon Dippenaar

(2005) • *750ha* • *13 500t 30% red 70% white* • *PO Box 55 Rawsonville 6845* • *info@ dutoitskloof.co.za* • *www.dutoitskloof.com*

Winner of innumerable good-value awards, Du Toitskloof is focusing its substantial capacity and resources on exports. In the past year, it's opened new markets for bottled wines in Europe, Brazil, Russia and China. It's also expanding in Central Africa. Locally it's tweaking the flagship Du Toitskloof line-up, and taking Hemisphere and all but one of the Quantum wines off the domestic market (exports of these brands continue, however). Lost Horizons, acquired in 2006, is being re-launched. Set for roll-out at press time were a Nebbiolo, Chardonnay-Viognier and Nouvelle.

Du Toitskloof Winery range

★★★★ **Hanepoot Jerepigo** ✓ Back in style with brassy hued **06**; choc-orange flavours in unctuously sweet delight - neither cloying nor heavy.

★★★★ **Red Muscadel** ✓ No simpering sweetie: a fortified dessert of substance & complexity. **06** full aromatic intensity, fine texture to raisiny fruit-pud flavours, even a hint of dryness amid massive 256g/l sugar, courtesy of a kiss of tannin.

Merlot ☺ ★★★ Extra juicy from 50% carbonic maceration. **06** charming mocha aromas, succulent mulberry flavours, stylish 10 mths good oak. **Pinotage** ☺ ★★★ Initially trenchant **06** mellows in the glass, drinks more easily, so give bit of time to settle. 10 mths wood. **Bukettraube** ☺ ★★★ Real character in full-flavoured **07**; gorgeous rose & incense bouquet, usual balanced sweetness. **Chardonnay** ☺ ★★★ Earthy & foursquare; **07** big on fruit, flavour & - for this cellar - burly 14% alc. **Chenin Blanc** ☺ 🍷 ★★★ **07** tropical & honeyed, easy-going pleasure with now standard low 12% alc. **Sauvignon Blanc** ☺ 🍷 ★★★ 'Our "flagship"', says Team DTW. Appealing, light but flavourful **07**, tropical tones lanced by nettle features, not quite dry. **Sparkling Brut** ☺ ★★★ Light, fresh & brisk, grapey white muscadel here with sauv, chard. **NV. Cape Ruby** ☺ ★★★ Modern styling with tinta, souzão, touriga; **05** light & undemanding, brilliantly priced.

Cabernet Sauvignon ✓ ★★★★ Bright cassis sparks carnival of brambly fruit on lush tannin roundabout. **04** yummy now, will develop 3-5 yrs. **Shiraz** ✓ ★★★★ Rich spicy nose leads to harmonious smoky/savoury flavours; **05** medium bodied, balanced elegant tones. **Cabernet Sauvignon-Shiraz** 🍷 ★★ Austere, rather lean frame, despite 6g/l sugar & 14% alc. **NV. Pinotage-Merlot-Ruby Cabernet** 🍷 ★★ Feisty young pinotage leads charge in semi-dry braai buddy. **NV** 500ml. **Rosé** 🍷 ★★ Light cherries in soft, sweet mouthful. **NV. Rosé** [NEW] ★★ **07** vibrant copper, off-dry texture better balanced with delicate fruit. **Cape Riesling** ★★ **07** hay notes fleshed out in sweet tail, but technically dry. **Blanc de Blanc** 🍷 ★★ Softly dry chenin, sauv blend, now only **NV**, 500ml bottle. **Special Late Harvest** ★★★ Light bodied, zesty freshness of **07** sample keeps sweet muscat from cloying. For an Asian table. Discontinued: **Blanc de Noir, Late Vintage, Noble Late Harvest**.

Lost Horizons range

Cabernet Sauvignon ★★ Unwooded **03** easy everyday red, bolstered by 6g/l sugar. **Merlot** ★ **04** unripe, with 'green stick' tone. **Pinotage** ★★ Lightly wooded **05**, bacon/banana aromas, tangy dry finish. **Cabernet Sauvignon-Merlot** ★★ 60/40 blend in **03**, trattoria-friendly as always. **Classic Red** ★★ Cheerful **05** mix pinotage, ruby cab, merlot; spicy, undemanding. **Chardonnay** ★★ **05** uncomplicated sweet-ripe peach/mango flavours. Discontinued: **Classic White, Sauvignon Blanc**. Entire range being redesigned, no listings retasted.

Quantum range

Classic Ruby Red ★★ Sole survivor of range rationalisation; **05** pinotage, ruby cab & merlot in gulpable, juicy cahoots. Not retasted. —*DS*

DuVon Wines

T 023-626-5981 • *F 023-626-5981*

Robertson • *Est/1stB 2003* • *Visits by appt* • *Little France luxury country house (T 023-626-4174; F 023-626-3359; ida@intekom.co.za)* • *Owner Du Toit & Von Klopmann families* •

Winemaker Armand du Toit (2003) ▪ Viticulturist Armand du Toit (Jan 2003) ▪ 29ha (cab, ruby cab, chenin, colombard, sauvignon) ▪ 450t/10 000litres ▪ PO Box 348 Robertson 6705 ▪ duvon@vodamail.co.za

DuVon is one of the new micro cellars boosting Robertson Valley's growing popularity as a wine tourism and lifestyle destination. Like many others, the Du Toit and Von Klopmann families grow grapes for the bigger brands but conclude it's more profitable - and fun! - selling their own-brand wines, and welcoming guests to their luxurious Little France country house.

Cabernet Sauvignon ★★★ Blend of two vintage for this maiden (so **NV**), showing bottle-age character in garnet rim, savoury aromas; comfortable tannins, soft fruit to enjoy soon.
Sauvignon Blanc ★★★ Pre-bottling sample of **07** already shows complexity: cat's pee & sweaty whiffs mingle with fynbos, dust & capsicum; gd sustained flavours. — *CvZ*

■ **D'Vine** *see* Swartland Winery

■ *Dwyka Hills* *see* Eagle's Cliff Wines/New Cape Wines

■ *Eagle Crest* *see* Swartland Winery

Eagle's Cliff Wines/New Cape Wines
T 023-340-4112 ▪ F 023-340-4132

Worcester ▪ Est/1stB 2000 ▪ Visits Mon-Fri 8-4.30 Sat, Sun & pub hols 10-3 ▪ Closed Easter Fri, Dec 25 & Jan 1 ▪ Eagle's Cliff Restaurant Wed-Sun (breakfast & lunch); Sun buffet lunch; booking essential; functions, small weddings etc ▪ Arendskloof Self-catering Cottage; Karin Groenewald karin@ncw.co.za; T 082-886-9839 ▪ Owner/winemaker/viticulturist Christiaan Groenewald ▪ 80ha ▪ 40% red 60% white ▪ PO Box 898 Worcester 6849 ▪ christiaan@ncw.co.za ▪ www.newcapewines.co.za

'We like to keep busy,' laughs Christiaan Groenewald, his and better half Karin's guest house and restaurant now rolling out the welcoming carpet. In the cellar, Christiaan G's standouts are the Sauvignon and Nouvelle - the latter a locally developed cross of crouchen blanc and semillon. 'In time, this could become an unbelievable wine and something of a signature for us,' he enthuses.

Eagle's Cliff Reserve range

Cabernet Sauvignon ★★★ **05** cassic cab: touch cedar & blackcurrant, nice dry tannins, balanced, lingering dry finish. **Shiraz** ★★★ Plummy, smooth **03**, retasted last ed, showed potential for few yrs cellaring. **Chardonnay** ★★★ Last ed found oak still strong on bold **05**, but beginning to meld with peachy aromas & flavours. **Sauvignon Blanc** 🗋 ★★★★ Last tasted **06** cool-fruited, restrained & mineral, more Old World than New. **Viognier** 🗋 ★★★★ Revisited last ed, **05** offered mellowing fruit & subtle, savoury nuances from gentle wooding.

Eagle's Cliff range

Pinotage 🗋 ★★★ **05** last ed was a fleshy easy-drinker, with brambleberry & banana flavours. **Merlot-Cabernet Sauvignon** 🗋 ★★ **06** mid-weight, serene dark berries, dry tannic grip on finish. No **04**, **05**. **Shiraz-Pinotage** ★★★ Last tasted **02** was plummy, plump & silky. **Shiraz Rosé** 🗋 ★★ Fruit pastille aromas, off-dry, easy quaffing **07**. **Chardonnay** ★★ Last time **06** was a softly rounded summer sipper. **Chenin Blanc** 🗋 ★★ Apricot fruit somewhat marred by touch burnt match, **07** insubstantial. **Nouvelle** NEW 🗋 ★★ **07** dry white with very little varietal character. **Sauvignon Blanc** 🗋 ★★ Freshly floral, light & easy **07**. **Viognier** 🗋 ★★★ Last ed **06** floral & aromatic, blending character with delicacy. Wine Best Value pick. Various WOs.

Dwyka Hills

Shiraz 🗋 ★★ **06** light & soft-fruited, with dry tannins. **Sauvignon Blanc** NEW 🗋 ★ **06** sinewy dry white, bracingly fresh. Both WO W Cape. — *IvH*

Eagles Nest Farm

T 021-794-4095 • F 021-794-7113

Constantia ▪ Est 2001 ▪ 1stB 2005 ▪ Visits by appt ▪ Winemaker Martin Meinert (July 2004), with Steve Roche ▪ Viticulturist Steve Roche (Oct 2001) ▪ 12ha (merlot, shiraz, viognier) ▪ 36t 95% red 5% white ▪ PO Box 535 Constantia 7848 ▪ info@eaglesnestwines.com ▪ www. eaglesnestwines.com

Carved out of the Constantiaberg, the new eyrie cellar is in close harmony with its surroundings. Construction was hampered last winter by heavy rains (they experienced two of the wettest months on record). Undeterred, director Peter Stewart announced that the production facility, with its on-site laboratory, would be ready for this year's crush 'come hell or high water'. The 2007 wines, meanwhile, were vinified at two nearby wineries by Martin Meinert (Meinert Wines) with resident viticulturist/winemaker Steve Roche. The maiden Merlot was released as the guide went to press and not ready for tasting.

Shiraz NEW ▤ ★★★☆ Most promising debut from soaring Constia vyds. 05 honest, expressive dark spice, savoury fruit, gentle grip, freshness & moderate alc. 18 mths used oak.
Viognier ▤ ★★★★ 06 introduced by refined apricot/honeysuckle perfume, whisper clean oak (used Fr, fermented/matured 6 mths). Agreeably fresh, fruity succulence prolonged by 4g/l sugar. — AL

Eaglevlei

T 021-884-4713 • F 021-884-4716

Stellenbosch ▪ Est/1stB 1997 ▪ Visits daily 10-5 ▪ The Vineyard Kitchen Restaurant Tue-Sun 10-6 ▪ Functions & weddings ▪ Facilities for children ▪ Owner Tony Hindhaugh ▪ Winemaker Maria le Roux ▪ Viticulturist Henri Fisk, advised by Johan Pienaar ▪ PO Box 969 Stellenbosch 7599 ▪ tony@eaglevlei.com, enquiries@eaglevlei.com ▪ www.eaglevlei.com

The subject of an international TV programme, The Grape Escape, Tony Hindhaugh has created a must-visit wineland venue with floor-to-ceiling glass-walled tasting room, restaurant run by adventurous chef Herbie van Schalkwyk, art gallery, and arts foundation, opening up the creative world to neighbouring children. Other youngster-friendly facilities include probably the largest jungle gym in the province.

Eaglevlei Special No 7 range NEW

Pinotage ★★★★ Red/black berries, earthy note & smoky oak (50% new, some Am); sweet fruit dominated in youth by strong, drying tannins. Screwcapped, as are all below. **Shiraz** ★★★★ Appealing, forthcoming, ripe nose, with spice, leather, dark fruit. Rich, powerful, savoury palate shows heavy oak (25% new Am, rest new/older Fr), & fruit soon falls away. **Blend** ★★★★ 06 (like all reds in range; all from Sbosch grapes) dry, serious-minded blend cab (46%), merlot, shiraz, some pinotage. Oak (mostly Fr, half new) now obscuring lurking dark fruit. On the lean side; gd food companion.

Eaglevlei Reserve range

Cabernet Sauvignon ★★★★ 06 ripe, spicy, gd plummy fruit; savoury satisfaction. Firmly built: robust tannins need few yrs maturing. **Merlot** NEW ★★★ 06 choc, berry aromas, but a little angular & sharp, with 14.5% alc too big for the fruit. Lightly oaked. Sample tasted, rating tentative, as for Shiraz & Sauv. **Shiraz** NEW ★★★ Previewed 06 slightly richer than std version, with fresh red berry fruit, but a slightly forbidding austerity of structure in yth. **Beccy's Blush Pinotage Rosé** ★★★ Swiggable 12% alc & crisp acid are selling points of lightly soft, lightly flavoured, off-dry 07 from pinotage. Ex-Sbosch, like reds in this range. **Sauvignon Blanc** NEW ★★★☆ 07 ex-tank mixes greenpepper, grass, passionfruit. Fresh & elegant, ending with green plum.

Eaglevlei range

Merlot ★★★ Pleasant spice, fruitcake notes on 06; moderate tannic/acid grip softened by some ingratiating sugar. All WO W Cape except where noted. **Shiraz** ★★★ Softly flavourful 06 - some will find 6g/l RS too sweet, but decent backbone supports the fat. Herbaceous finish. **Sauvignon Blanc** ★★★ 07 gd varietal character, some plumping sugar but still a crisp, green bite to it. Useful modest 12% alc. Discontinued: **Cabernet Sauvignon**, **Pinotage**, **Chardonnay**, **Chenin Blanc**. — TJ

Ecology [NEW]
T 082-578-1030; 028-284-9824 • F 028-284-9419

*Walker Bay (see Elgin/Walker Bay map) • Est 2003 • 1stB 2007 • Tasting & tours by appt •
Sales Mon, Wed & Fri 9-12 • Winemaker Niels Verburg (Dec 2006, Luddite) • Viticulturist Kevin
Watt (Dec 2006, consultant) • 23.6ha (cab, shiraz, sauv) • 16t 25% red 75% white • PO Box
381 Bot River 7185 • info@ecologywines.com • www.ecologywines.com*

On much of the 'nature conservation farm' Paardenkloof no farming activities occur at all.
Where they do, it's predator-friendly sheep farming, indigenous Nguni cattle, and 23 hectares of fynbos-bounded vineyards from which the aptly named wine, Ecology, is made. 'We
have an embarrassing wealth of biodiversity and this is reflected in our wine,' says owner
Valli Moosa.

■ **Eden Crest** *see Lourensford*

■ **Edenhof** *see Schalkenbosch Wines*

■ **Eden's Vineyard** *see Women in Wine*

Edgebaston
T 021-880-1633 • F 021-880-1633

*Stellenbosch • Est/1stB 2004 • Closed to public • Owner Woodlands & Finlayson Family trusts
• Winemaker Walter Finlayson with David Finlayson (Jan 2004) • Viticulturist David Finlayson,
with Riaan Coetzee (Jan 2004/Jan 2006) • 24ha (cab, merlot, mourvèdre, shiraz, sauv) • 70t/
±3 000 cs 80% red 20% white • PO Box 2033 Dennesig 7601 • lizelf@lantic.net*

'There's no big rush to take over the world; the focus is purely on quality,' says one of the
Cape's finest young winemakers, David Finlayson, of his family's private-vineyard venture in
the Simonsberg foothills. Cab and shiraz are the current suit, with a blend of shiraz,
mourvèdre and tannat, as well as classic whites to follow. David's father, the very experienced Walter F, oversees; daughter Daniella (7) 'assists' in the cellar.

★★★★★ **CWG Auction Reserve 'GS' Cabernet Sauvignon** [NEW] After legendary
winemaker George Spies, who inspired the father-son team's desire to match his
fabled 66 & 68 vintages. **05** should meet GS's approval: perfumed, multi-dimensional,
seamless; in a word, regal. Structured for cellaring. 100% new Fr oak, 18 mths.

★★★★ **Shiraz 05**'s lifted red fruit, lilies usher in lively, spicy, berried mouthful; suave tannins
give appealing dry finish, build for 5+ yrs. 16 mths oak, 40% new, 30% each older Fr/
Am.

★★★★★ **Chardonnay** [NEW] 100% barrel-fermented version from distinguished shale-on-clay
vyd in Sbosch: 'We grabbed this fruit with both hands.' **06** handcrafted, complex; lime
top notes to creamy oak, invigorating acidity, taut mineral core & persistent chalky finish; 14.6% alc tad evident. 60% new oak, partial malo. — *CvZ*

■ **1855** *see Hermanuspietersfontein Vineyards*

Eikehof Wines ♀
T 021-876-2469 • F 021-876-2469

*Franschhoek • Visits by appt • Owner/winemaker/viticulturist Francois Malherbe • 43ha (cab,
merlot, shiraz, chard) • 70t/4 000cs 60% red 40% white • PO Box 222 Franschhoek 7690 •
eikehof@mweb.co.za • www.eikehof.co.za*

Eikehof has scaled back a little in recent years and continues to 'read the market carefully'
says Francois Malherbe. Plans are afoot for a small function venue on the property.

Cabernet Sauvignon ★★★ Softer, less chunky styling continues with **04**. Earthy, distinctive
ripe blackberry flavours, pleasantly firm tannin. **Merlot** ★★★ Last ed **04** was herbaceous &
restrained, with elegant fruit. **Shiraz** ★★★ Last-tasted **04** soft, fruity & well-spiced. **Chardonnay** ★★★★ Briefly oaked **06** sample not retasted. Pvsly noted as rounded, silky, with liberal citrus flavours. **Bush Vine Semillon** In abeyance. — *DB*

Eikendal Vineyards

T 021-855-1422 • F 021-855-1027

Stellenbosch (see Helderberg map) • Est 1981 • 1stB 1984 • Tasting & sales daily 9.30-4.30 • Fee R10 (5 wines) • Tours Mon-Fri 10 & 2.30 • Closed Easter Fri, Dec 25 & Jan 1 • Harald's@ Eikendal for lunch/dinner; T 021-855-5033 for opening times • Eikendal Lodge Guest House/ B&B; lodge@eikendal.co.za, T 021-855-3617, F 021-855-3862 • Facilities for children • Tour groups • Small conferences • Walks • Owner Substantia AG • Winemaker Henry Kotze (Sep 2004), with Nico Grobler (June 2007) • Viticulturist Johan Pienaar (Sep 2001, consultant) • ±65ha (cabs s/f, merlot, shiraz, chard, chenin, sauv, semillon) • ±350t/±20 000cs 65% red 35% white • PO Box 2261 Stellenbosch 7601 • info@eikendal.co.za • www.eikendal.com

Eikendal has celebrated the traditional end-of-harvest festival in March every year for over a decade, and this 'Weintaufe' is mutating into a full-scale wine festival. The name means 'wine baptism', and traditionally involves new wines being named, blessed, and having a godfather appointed. Other European touches at this Swiss-owned property include the popular cheese fondue at Harald's restaurant, now served year round. Cellar alterations are under way to facilitate smaller batch handling in time for the 2008 harvest, which Henry Kotzé and new assistant Nico Grobler expect to bring forth more of the potential that the acorn on the label symbolises.

Black Label range

★★★★ **Classique** Cabs s & f blend (83/17); **04** delicious, minty notes to plump cassis supported by supple structure, fresh & tasty. Gd now, warrants yr/2 for further integration.

★★★★ **Chardonnay** More showy **06** rich & broad, plushly upholstered fruits kept in check by brisk acid. Pvs 9 mths half new Fr oaking regimen changed to mix ages/Am & European origin.

★★★★ **Semillon** Gorgeous **06** anchors re-rating started by **05**, fresh grapefruit features beautifully countered by viscous toffee character. Fermented/6 mths new oak. Potential to develop.

Shiraz ★★★ **04**, revisited, porty nose & v ripe fruit amongst dry tannins. Big 15% alc dominant. 20 mths oak. **Noble Late Harvest** ★★★★ Bold preserved-peel character, yet **06** still delicate. 100% new oak 6 mths. From chenin. 119g/l sugar, 12% alc.

Premium range

★★★★ **Cabernet Franc** Spicy fragrance & fennel/pepper fruit of now-bottled **04** (★★★★) offset by sappy austerity, hard tannins detract. 16 mths Fr oak, 30% new. Delicious **03** Wine (★★★★).

★★★★ **Merlot** Earthy grip to meaty mulberry fruit of **05**. In style of pleasing red fruit/choc-mint **04**, sufficiently serious, rich & round, dryly refined. Nicely weighted, easily carries 18 mths oak (100% new 9 mths, then 3rd fill).

Cabernet Sauvignon ★★★★ Oak dominance of **03** abets big dry tannins; but gd red berry fruit makes for gratifying (if slightly severe) effect. 20 mths cask, half new. Not retasted. No **04**. **Janina Chardonnay** 🖩 ★★★ **06** back after hiatus (no **05**) with limy fruit given oatmeal gloss by 4 mths lees contact. Trifle tart. **Chenin Blanc** 🖩 ★★★★ Pvs ed noted impressive **06** in trendy new, showy styling with very ripe honeyed fruit & spicy oak (50% new, cask fermented), subtly off-dry. Warm farewell from 14.5% alc. **Sauvignon Blanc** 🖩 ★★★★ Penetrating grassiness, bracing freshness lift **07** & switch on the salivary glands. Now bone-dry (tropical **06** had 4.5g/l sugar), what an aperitif! Mainly Lutzvlle fruit, 10% semillon ex-Sbosch.

Wicked Wines

Rosé ☺ 🖩 ★★★ New bottling of **06**, mainly merlot; off-dry, for imminent enjoyment.
Blanc ☺ 🖩 ★★★ Sauv & chard co-operate happily to offer generous flavours in now vintage-dated **06**, sweet finish pierced by racy tail. W Cape WO.

Rouge 🖩 ★★ **05** vegetal, with tough dry tannins. 80/20 merlot, shiraz. **Sparkling Brut** ★★★ Now vintage dated, from sauv & chard, dash chenin. **06** rather neutral, sour twist in tail. WO

W Cape. **Sparkling Brut Rosé** NEW ★★★ 'Pink & bright', 'berries or cherries', 'fruity & light', 'fun & sun' flirts the back label. Enough said. — *DS*

■ **Elandsberg** *see Viljoensdrift Wines*

Elberti Wines
T 021-851-4760 ▪ F 021-851-4761

Stellenbosch (see Helderberg map) ▪ Est 2005 ▪ Tasting & sales by appt ▪ Owner Steyn family ▪ Winemaker Pieter Steyn ▪ 8 000cs own label 75% red 25% white ▪ PO Box 2401 Somerset West 7129 ▪ info@elbertiwines.com ▪ www.elbertiwines.com

This odyssey-themed winery has travelled another year, and paused to release the first wine in the Sojourn range, a light-style red which will show itself convincingly after some cellaring, believes Eppie Steyn. Elberti entered the screwcap arena with its Sauvignon, and winemaker Pieter S's unusual Syrah-Malbec hit the market on a high note.

Sojourn range NEW
Cape Blend Red ★★★ Maiden **05** combines 58% pinotage with cab & merlot; fascinating wet biltong/new leather aromas, pleasant tannic counterpoint to ripe fruit. Coastal WO.

Dawning range
Cabernet Sauvignon ★★★ **03** nutty black fruit notes, slightly green & tannic finish when tasted last ed. **Merlot** ★★★ **03** last yr showed lots of ripe fruit aromas, promising greater richness than lean, slightly austere palate delivered. **Syrah-Malbec** ★★ Wooded 15% malbec joins majority unoaked shiraz on **05**, marked mid-2006 by smoky tones & persistent sappy tannins. **Sauvignon Blanc** 🗒 ★★★ **07** ups ante with gd vinosity; nettly khaki bush notes, slender yet juicy body, appealing grapefruit tang. — *CvZ*

Eldorado Wines
T 021-869-8830 ▪ F 021-869-8830

Paarl ▪ Est 1999 ▪ 1stB 2001 ▪ Closed to public ▪ Owner Proteus Trust ▪ Winemaker/viticulturist Shannon Booth (1999) ▪ 1 ha ▪ 4 tons 300 cs 100% red ▪ PO Box 2042 Windmeul 7630 ▪ tmurray@iafrica.com ▪ www.eldorado.co.za

Fans of this boutique winery will be pleased to hear that though there was no 04 bottling of the cab-merlot blend, the (untasted) **05** should be on the shelf when the guide appears. And there's more to look forward to: a Syrah is due to make its debut this year.

■ **Elements** *see Hartswater Wine Cellar*

Elgin Heights NEW

Elgin ▪ Closed to public ▪ Owner Ryk Joubert ▪ 60 ha (cab, merlot, shiraz, chard, sauv, viognier) ▪ mwddj@mweb.co.za

Wine farmers in Stellenbosch since 1913, the Jouberts say it was a natural transition to extend their grape and wine activities to Elgin. However, they grew deciduous fruit here until DD Joubert finished his viticulture studies and established vineyards in 1999. Now launching his first wine, vinified at Rustenberg, he says: 'Winemaking is the completion of the circle for a grape grower.'

★★★★ **Sauvignon Blanc 07** combines aromatic & complex layers of asparagus, greenpepper, passionfruit & ripe lemon; some herbal notes & excellent weight. — *JP*

Elgin Vintners
T 021-848-9587 ▪ F 021-848-9587

Elgin (see Elgin/Walker Bay map) ▪ Est 2003 ▪ 1stB 2004 ▪ Tasting & sales Mon-Fri 9-5 Sat 10-3 ▪ Closed pub hols ▪ Light meals by arrangement ▪ Owner Derek Corder, Max Hahn, Alastair Moodie, James Rawbone-Viljoen, Rob Semple & Paul Wallace ▪ Winemaker see intro ▪ Viticulturist Paul Wallace ▪ 75.5ha (cab, malbec, merlot, shiraz, pinot, chard, sauv, viognier) ▪ 3 950cs ▪ PO Box 121 Elgin 7180 ▪ elginvintner@mweb.co.za ▪ www.elginvintners.co.za

This partnership of six farmers employs specialist winemakers for specific wines and styles. Known for its sauvignons, Elgin's reds look set to be surprising. 'Although the vineyards are young, we're finding very elegant wines coming through,' says business manager Nicky Wallace of the reds, which have already scooped some awards. Elgin Vintners has also made progress in the export market, with the UK, Singapore, Brazil, Germany and the Netherlands on their list.

★★★★ Agama NEW New Fr barrel selection, cab/merlot blend, **05** can't be hurried. Complex array hedgerow fruit, fennel, dried herbs; sleekly muscular, fine-grained tannins evident in dry finish. Could age 5+ yrs. Decanter gold.

Cabernet Sauvignon ★★★★ Still restrained but promising well, **05** shows dark plum, prosciutto, white pepper dusting; an elegant wine, nicely constructed. Fr barriques 11 mths. Ex-2 vyds. **Merlot ★★★★** Untasted pvs ed, maiden **05** captures red fruit charm & graceful lines variety delivers at best; sheathed power promises few yrs further development. Ex-2 vyds. **Easy Red** 🍷 **★★★** Last-available **05** had attractive clean cherry fruit, unobtrusive oak, demure 12% alc. **Pinot Noir ★★★★** Riper than earlier submissions (14.5% alc) but **06** has lost no class: dark fruit, barnyard hints, sinewy construct & savoury finish thanks to yr oaking, third new. From one vyd. **Shiraz** 🍷 **★★★★** Last tasted **05**, 50/50 blend wines independently crafted by Niels Verburg & Clive Torr from young vyds. Lightly weighted, more spice than pepper, elegant exit. **Sauvignon Blanc** 🍷 **★★★★** Admirable cool-climate intensity, **07**'s asparagus & greenpepper tones not too aggressive to interfere with appetite appeal, zesty drinkability. From 4 vyds. — *CR*

■ **Elixir** *see African Terroir*
■ ***Engelbrecht-Els Vineyards*** *see Ernie Els Wines*
■ ***Enon*** *see Zandvliet Estate*
■ ***Enoteca Bottega*** *see Idiom*

Epicurean Wines
T 011-880-5730 · F 011-880-5731

Est 2001 · 1stB 2003 · Closed to public · Owner Global Pact Trading 125 (Pty) Ltd · Cellarmaster Schalk-Willem Joubert · Winemaker Mbhazima Shilowa, Mutle Mogase, Ron Gault & Moss Ngoasheng with Schalk-Willem Joubert (Nov 2002, chief consultant) · 250cs 100% red · PO Box 280 Parklands 2196 · mutle@mogase.co.za

This is the child of a consortium of high-profile businessmen, politicians and friends who've had the privilege of tasting the world's finest: messieurs Shilowa, Mogase, Ngoasheng and Gault aim to craft an icon that doesn't pander to market whims but respects the less transitory ideals of fine wine.

Epicurean range NEW

★★★★ Epicurean Authoritative cab/merlot blend crafted at Rupert & Rothschild from barrels selected by the four partners. Maiden **03** not tasted; **04** classically styled, generous black fruits, fine tannins, cranberry acidity in faultless harmony. 2.8g/l RS, oak vanilla, substantial alc (14.5%) leave sweetish impression. Deserves 5+ yrs cellaring. — *CvZ*

Ernie Els Wines
T 021-881-3588 · F 021-881-3688

Stellenbosch · Est 1999 · 1stB 2000 · Tasting & sales Mon-Fri 9-5 Sat: May-Sep 9-3 Oct-Apr 9-4 · Closed Easter Fri, Dec 16/25 & Jan 1 · Guardian Peak Restaurant (see Eat-out section) · Gifts · Owner Ernie Els & Jean Engelbrecht · Winemaker Louis Strydom (2000) & Mark van Buuren, Guardian Peak (2007) · Viticulturist Hardie Van Den Heever · 72ha (cab, merlot) · 45 000cs 100% red · PO Box 7595 Stellenbosch 7599 · info@ernieelswines.com · www.ernieelswines.com

Pro golfer Ernie Els' easy-flowing game continues to draw standing ovations - as do his wines. Rooted in prime red-wine country, the winery he owns with Jean Engelbrecht remains focused on high-end blended reds, which E & E consider 'consistently the top performing category for SA wines internationally'. (To sample the white bottlings, call at their Guardian Peak Restaurant, stylish and exclusive outlet for portions of the portfolio.) Els spends much of his time in the US, which suits their marketing strategy to a T. 'We believe the US has the greatest potential for growth, but it requires a constant presence to create and maintain market share.'

Ernie Els Wines range

★★★★☆ **Engelbrecht-Els Proprietor's Blend** Cab/shiraz-headed merger (59/21), sprinklings cab f, p verdot, merlot, malbec; whole greater than sum of parts in splendid **05**. Triumph of structure & minerality over ripe fruit; lively, good grip & delicious savoury length. Fr oak, 17 mths.

★★★★ **Cirrus Syrah** SA/US joint venture, aiming for best of both worlds. Mission accomplished in generous yet refined **05**; beautifully balanced, drier than pvs; fresher, more savoury edge to rich texture. Lifted, livened by dash viognier. W Cape vyds.

★★★★☆ **Ernie Els 05** master-crafted to limit excesses of ripe cab yr (59% with 25% merlot, 6% cab f, 5% each p verdot & malbec). Realises tightrope balance through gentle extraction, elegant mineral core. Class shows in fine cab/clean oak scents (from 100% new Fr wood), great length.

Guardian Peak range

★★★★ **Lapa Cabernet Sauvignon** 'Cabernet Sauvignon' last ed. GP team's take on California-style cab: **05** big, sumptuous, generously oaked (100% new Fr) - as compared with classic **04**. Even at 15% alc, achieves freshness, balance. Packaging suitably super-heavyweight.

★★★★ **Frontier** ✓ Bright-fruited, creamy cab-led blend, **05** with shiraz/merlot (42/13) still available, not re-tasted. Modern, plenty of interest, ageworthy. Yr used oak. Sbosch, Elgin vyds.

★★★★ **SMG** After slight dip in 04 (★★★☆), **05** back on form: shiraz-led (63%) blend with 29% mourvèdre, peppery grenache builds character. Already smooth, but plenty to give. Fr/Am oak, all new.

Merlot ★★★★ **06** in usual satisfying mould: pure, unshowy fruit, comfortably rich & fresh, clean dark choc tail. Immediately accessible, few yrs potential. Sbosch/Elgin fruit, stave/barrel aged. **Shiraz** ★★★★ Quality with approachability hallmark of range. **05**, now bottled, pure-fruited, supple & rounded; freshness lightens 14% alc. Combo stave/barrels. WO W Cape. *— AL*

Ernst & Co Wines

T 021-865-2895 • F 021-865-2894

Stellenbosch • Est/1stB 2004 • Tasting & sales at Koelenhof Winery Mon-Thu 9-5, Fri 9-4.30, Sat & pub hols 9-1• Closed Easter Fri, Ascension Day (Jun 6), Dec 25/26 & Jan 1 • Owner Ernst & Gwenda Gouws • Winemaker Ernst Gouws & Ezanne Gouws • 12ha (chenin, sauv) • 10 000cs 50% red 50% white + 10 000cs under export brands Imbizo, Four Gates & Timbili • PO Box 7450 Stellenbosch 7599 • info@ggwines.co.za • www.ernstco.co.za

'Wine is what we do - a way of life,' says Ezanne Gouws, winemaker daughter of husband-and-wife team Ernst and Gwenda, whom she describes as the soul and drive behind this dedicated family affair. Well established locally and overseas, they modestly attribute their success to 'a sound marketing strategy, constant hard work, total dedication and lots of grace from our Lord'. But Ernst and Gwenda are understandably less modest about their daughter's first solo Shiraz 07, still awaiting release: 'An absolute stunner!'

Ernst & Co Wines range

Cabernet Sauvignon ★★★ **03** last ed was fruity, layered with cedar/herbaceous notes, fresh balanced palate. Few yrs potential. Yr new Fr oak. **Merlot** ★★★ Forthcoming red berries, plums, nicely rounded body to soft, appealing **05**. 18 mths Fr oak, fully integrated, supporting fruit. **Shiraz** ★★★★ Accessible, New-Worldish **04**, tasted last ed, shd hold another few yrs. **Chardonnay** ★★★★ **06** toned down to 13% alc, allowing more citrus character, fresher finish. Well-integrated oaking provides nutty tones. Eminently drinkable. **Chenin Blanc** ★★★☆ Melon & apple flavours, nicely rounded. **07** appetising summer drinking. **Sauvignon Blanc** ★★★★ Good fruit purity, leafy/green pepper, finish of minerality. **07** slender but attractive, friendly 11.5% alc.

Imbizo range

Cabernet Sauvignon [NEW] ★★ **05** unwooded, red berries & scrub, grape tannins providing definition. **Chenin Blanc-Sauvignon Blanc** ★★★ Food-friendly, crisply dry 60/40 blend. **07** gooseberry tones give satisfying drinkability. — *CR*

■ **Escape** *see* Kanu Wines

Eshkol Kosher Winery
T 021-864-3356 • F 021-873-0871

Wellington (see Paarl map) • Est/1stB 2003 • Tasting & sales only by appt Mon-Thu 10-5 Fri 10-12 Sun by appt • Fee R15 • Closed Jewish holidays • Tours by appt • Cheese platters by appt; also (non-kosher) meals at Onverwacht Restaurant • Small tour groups • Owner ERIE Trading • Winemaker Shalom Epstein & Ryan Wyness (2003/2007) • Viticulturist Ryan Wyness (2007) • 15 ha (merlot, pinotage, ruby cab, shiraz, chenin) • 10 000 cs 90% red 10% white • PO Box 151 Wellington 7654 • eshkol@ezinet.co.za • www.eshkol.co.za

Ryan Wyness, ex Freedom Hill, joined Shalom Epstein for last year's vintage, and both are delighted with an addition to the range - ruby cab Sweet Liati Port (named for Shalom's daughter). Tastings are now by appointment in the barrel cellar, but the plan is to convert into a tasting room an old building overlooking the valley. Note: no new vintages tasted.

King Solomon range

Cellar Masters Choice Red ★★★ **04** roughly equal four-way blend with dusty dried-currant fruit, sweet-stalky finish. **Shiraz Rosé** ★★ Raspberry whiffs on semi-sweet **05**, juicy, balanced by touch dry tannin. **Chardonnay** ★★ **05** tasty dry white, 100% Am oak surprisingly subtle; grapefruit hints, citrus-salad flavours. **Premier Chenin Blanc** ★★★ Ex-30 yr old vyd on Rose Garden farm, Paarl; **06** pleasing citrus flavours & dry straw hint. **Cellar Masters Choice White** ★★ Chard, chenin blend (53/47), **04** high-toned, with fresh acidity. **Kiddush** ★★ V soft & sweet sacramental wine from cinsaut, shiraz, ruby cab.

Eshkol range

Cabernet Sauvignon ★★ Hot-country 'baked' quality on **04**, plum jam flavours with slight stalky edge. **Cabernet Sauvignon Reserve** ★★★ **04** ripe-fruit style with raisined nuance; comfortable, not too full-bodied. **Merlot** ★★★ Restrained but appealing **03**, leafy cassis hint; light, harmonious, accessible dry flavours. **Merlot Reserve** ★★ **04** off own vyds; jammy plum whiffs with volatile touch, tart flavours, unsustained dry finish. **Pinotage** ★★ **04** lightish country-style red with choc-prune fruit, tangy dry savoury flavour. Unwooded. **Walker Bay Pinotage** ★★★ Pinot-like delicacy on **04**; red berry flavour, juicy & dry. **Shiraz** ★★★ Medium-bodied **04** expressive leather & spice, tangy tannins & sweet-sour farewell. **Classic Dry Red** ★★★ Light but succulent cab, merlot, shiraz convivium; **03** classy cedar whiff & berry ripeness, balanced leafy tannins. — *CT*

■ **Eskdale** *see* De Zoete Inval Estate
■ **Eventide** *see* Mischa Estate
■ **Evolution** *see* Origin Wine

Excelsior Estate
T 023-615-1980 • F 023-615-2019

Robertson • Est 1859 • 1stB 1997 • Closed to public • Guest House (see Stay-over section) • Owner Freddie & Peter de Wet • Winemaker Johan Stemmet (Nov 2003) • 200ha • 175 000cs own label 67% red 33% white • BRC certified • PO Box 17 Ashton 6715 • info@excelsior.co.za • www.excelsior.co.za

This family-owned Robertson spread remains closed for public tastings, but visitors to their new guest house, resplendent in a renovated 'ostrich palace', not only relive the grandeur of the ostrich boom but can also enjoy private showings of their wines, 80% of which are exported, mainly to the US, where they are among the top three Cape brands.

Cabernet Sauvignon ★★ Hot-country ripeness & contrasting racy freshness on **06**, gawky tannins & hot alc finish. Sample tasted, rating tentative. Export version will be screwcapped.

Cabernet Sauvignon Reserve ★★★ No **05**. Last ed **04** was massively ripe, with black fruit & tarry notes from 22 mths oaking. **Merlot** ★★★ Shy mocha & welcoming, friendly red fruit, **06** dry & dusty farewell from oak staving. **Paddock Shiraz** ★★★ Exuberant ripe mulberry appeal, palate harnessed by grainy wood tannins. **06** needs time to settle, then drink early. **Purebred Red** ★★★ Ripe & somewhat rustic **05** tasted pvs ed; high tannins implore food. **Chardonnay** ★★ Rounded, ripe & peachy, just enough acid to balance. Enjoy wood-brushed **07** soonest. **Sauvignon Blanc** ★★★ Combo ripe tropical fruit & refreshing acidity makes **07** plump, pleasant summer quaffer (12.5% alc). Discontinued: **Merlot Rosé**, **Paddock Viognier**. — *MW*

Excelsior Vlakteplaas

T 082-821-3556 • **F** 044-241-2240

Klein Karoo • Est 1934 • 1stB 1998 • Tasting & sales Mon-Fri 9-5 • Closed Easter Fri-Mon, Ascension Day, Dec 16/25/26 & Jan 1 • Owner Jurie & Danie Schoeman • Winemaker Danie Schoeman (1981) • 41ha (merlot, pinotage, ruby cab, chenin, muscadel r/w) • 490t/1 000cs own label 50% red 50% white • Export brand: His Master's Choice • PO Box 112 De Rust 6650 • jjschoeman@telkomsa.net

Muscadel has entered a promising new period with a focus on quality and image, and renewed interest shown by young winemakers. Representing the fifth generation on this Klein Karoo farm, Danie Schoeman reports that they've bottled the first Red and White Muscadel under their top-end His Master's Choice label, and anticipate good feedback. And ample rains made a refreshing change from the dry seasons of late.

Red Muscadel ★★ **04** at review time showed mature caramel & thatch aromas, soft raisiny sweetness. New vintage unready. **White Muscadel** ★★ Multi-awarded **04** still availble at press time; pvsly noted as best enjoyed soon; ultra-smooth, syrupy. — *IvH*

■ **Excelsious Wines** see Stoumann's Wines
■ **Faces of Africa** see Douglas Green
■ **Fairbridge** see Paarl Wine Company
■ **Fairhills** see Origin Wine

Fairseat Cellars
T 021-797-1951

Cape Town • Closed to public • Owner Dick Davidson • PO Box 53058 Kenilworth 7745 • fairseat@mweb.co.za

Negociant and Cape Wine Master Dick Davidson sources wines locally for export to Europe, chiefly buyers' own brands (BOBs) for the German market.

Fairvalley Farmworkers Association

T 021-863-2450 • **F** 021-863-2591

Paarl • Est 1997 • 1stB 1998 • Tasting & sales at Fairview • Owner Fairvalley Association • Winemaker Awie Adolph (Feb 1997) • ±50 000litres for own label 50/50 red/white • PO Box 6219 Paarl 7620 • marlene@fairview.co.za

This long-established empowerment venture, involving Fairview farmworkers and their families, continues to grow in the US and UK, and enquiries are being received from potential buyers in a variety of Continental markets.

Pinotage 🍷 ★★ **05** packed with dark fruit, palate roundly ripe. Bold 14.9% alc. **Chenin Blanc** 🍷 ★★ **06** appley fruit salad, easy, fresh-dry quaffability. **Sauvignon Blanc** 🍷 ★★ Intriguing lime peel fragrance on **06**, amenable, softly fruity body. — *CR*

Fairview

T 021-863-2450 • **F** 021-863-2591

Paarl • Est 1693 • 1stB 1974 • Tasting & sales Mon-Fri 8.30-5 Sat 9-4 Sun 9.30-4 • Fee R15 • Closed Easter Fri, Dec 25, Jan 1 • The Goatshed for meals/refreshments daily 9-5 (see Eat-out section) • Groups by appt • Also tasting & sales of Fairview cheese • Owner Charles Back • Winemaker Charles Back & Anthony de Jager (Dec 1996), with Erlank Erasmus (Jan 2001) • Viticulturist Johan Botha, advised by Andrew Teubes • 300ha (cab, barbera, malbec, merlot, mourvèdre, nebbiolo, pinotage, shiraz, sauv, viognier) • 1 700t 80% red 15% white 5% rosé • ISO 9001:2001 & HACCP certified • PO Box 583 Suider-Paarl 7624 • info@fairview.co.za • www.fairview.co.za

'Every day there's something new,' smiles Charles Back, who has grown this family concern into a global wine and cheese success story. (In a stroke of marketing genius, he's turned the farm's resident goat herd into an integral part of the branding.) Restless, creative, determined to push the envelope and with a bloodhound's nose for future trends, he's full of surprises. This year is no exception and wine lovers can rest assured of their share of innovations. In the pipeline is a low-alcohol 'little white', Bianchino; new grenache blanc, roussanne and petite syrah vines are looking promising; and Fairview's fortified red now features the Portuguese variety tinta amarella. The cheese tasting facility has been revamped, and a new wine sampling venue allows for sit-down, tutored tastings.

Red Seal range

★★★★ **Pegleg Carignan** Features some of the oldest carignan in SA. Last reviewed **04** showed high toned sweet nose of ripe fruit & oak, typical firm acid of the variety.

★★★★☆ **Primo Pinotage** Massively flavourful & aromatic; off bushvines on eponymous Agter-Paarl farm. **04** when last tasted was a serious wine with positive savoury elements, firm tannins needing to settle.

★★★★☆ **Solitude Shiraz** Ex-dryland Pdberg vyd, standout **04** (★★★★★) revealed loads of fruit & spice while showing restraint; gd potential noted last ed. Oak fermented, further 16 mths Fr barrels. Earlier accessible **03** widely hailed: 91 pts WS, Concours Mondial & Santé Classic golds.

★★★★☆ **The Beacon Shiraz** From low-vigour Koelenhof vyd. Ultra-ripe **04** (★★★★) last ed was noted as having lost some mid-palate definition & class in going bolder (15.1% alc). Fermented/matured Fr oak, 40% new. Gold IWSC. **03** elegantly styled, with pure fruit expression.

★★★★ **Jakkalsfontein Shiraz** Mature bushvine vyd on western Pdberg slopes. Reviewed pvsly, **03** serious, sturdy but showing its origin. Juicy fruit, great structure & vibrant acidity, so holds its 15% alc well; will benefit with keeping. 91 pts WS.

★★★★ **Caldera** Selected Swtland shiraz, mourvèdre, 53 yr old grenache bushvines. Step up, **05** (★★★★★) combines opulent hedgerow fruit, garrigue & tar notes with velvet tannins, reflecting masterly cellar handling. Characterful, scrumptious, as was elegant **04**.

★★★★ **Oom Pagel Semillon** One of more serious Cape examples. Sample pvs ed, **06** combo own & Darling fruit, half barrel fermented, given fresher styling, citrus, beeswax typicity. Main attraction is tangy kumquat flavours, sweet/sour freshness.

Fairview range

★★★★ **Stellenbosch Cabernet Sauvignon** From 2 Firgrove vyds giving authentic maritime influenced fruit. Last was **04**, likeable extrovert; perfectly ripe plums, blackcurrants, well partnered by 14 mths Fr oaking, partial barrel ferment. Already drinking well, but a gd future.

★★★★ **Shiraz** 🗒 The winery's signature since 1974. Dustinctive Rhône tones to **05**, dark fruit, tar & campfire smoke wrapped in a svelte, silky package. Well-judged oaking, 14 mths, portion new.

★★★★ **Cyril Back Vintage** NEW Barrel-select flagship from shiraz, **05** shows molten black plums, glimpses dried herbs, smoked meat. Impressive harmony despite hefty 15.5% alc; seamless & polished. New Fr 16 mnths. Only 200cs.

★★★★ **Sauvignon Blanc** 🗒 Unirrigated bushvines incl Darling. Again showing ripe yet intense character so delicious to drink; **07** is crisply dry, grapefruit & mineral-flavoured delight.

★★★★ **Viognier** Lauded example of the fashionable Rhône variety. **06** last ed showed class variety can deliver in good hands: wafting jasmine, peach pip perfume partnering savoury oak notes. Majority fermented/4 mths seasoned barrels. Despite 14.9% alc, elegant, poised.

★★★★ **La Beryl Rouge** Unique local 'straw red'; shiraz & merlot in **05**. Unusual perfume: prosciutto, roast vegetables, cheese straws; deeply rich sweet-savoury flavours. Remarkably drinkable, lifted by oak-toned finish, vein of acidity.

★★★★☆ **La Beryl Blanc** Straw wine. Equal chenin, semillon in **06**: liquidised apricots & kumquats, mouthcoating richness, 195g/l sugar, but tangy, uncloying, thanks to racy acidity. Friendly 11.7% alc another reason to enjoy this beauty.

Stellenbosch Merlot ★★★ **04** tasted pvsly; from Firgrove, as with Cab. Good, bright varietal fruit; taut palate that would benefit from some ageing. **Mourvèdre** ★★★ No follow up to sturdy & tarry **04**, expresses variety's typical monolithic girth, flattered by oak (9 mths older Am). Dryland Swtland grapes. **Pinotage** 🍷 ★★★★ Full-ripe style in **06**, dark fruit, meaty/liquorice richness, but drinkability never sacrificed; fleshy & smooth texture, supple tannins. **Pinotage-Viognier** 🍷 ★★★★ Shows varieties' compatibility. **05** retains red-fruit vibrancy of pinotage, given aromatic lift by 4% viognier. 14 mths mainly Am oak, third new. **Rosé** 🍷 ★★★ From four varieties, cerise-hued **07** delivers fresh berry-toned appetite appeal; ideal summer lunch fare. **Chardonnay** 🍷 ★★★★ **06** weightier, more impressive than **03** (★★★), parades citrus peel, dried peach & nutty oak characteristics, curvaceous body adding to seduction. Brisk acidity ensures food compatibility. **Viognier Special Late Harvest** ★★★☆ Arresting floral & pineapple perfume in **07** & palate doesn't disappoint either: racy acidity counters 25g/l sugar, giving off-dry effect, long aromatic tail. **Sweet Red** 🍷 ★★★ Fortified changing blend; in **06** shiraz 65%, rest tinta amarela. Sweet, full-bodied brandied fruitcake winter warmer. Added flavour from 8 mths oaking. Discontinued: **Formosa Peak Cabernet Sauvignon-Shiraz**. WO Coastal unless noted.

Agostinelli range

Barbera ★★★☆ Herbal whiffs in piquant sour cherry compote, **05** last ed sparkled with youthful vibrancy, sinuous appeal. 10 mths used Fr wood. **Sangiovese** ★★★★ Streamlined & designed to please, **06** is all sleekly integrated sweet spice, cherries, seasoned oak. Well crafted, with good varietal expression; perfect solo or with food. Discontinued: **Agostinelli**. WO Coastal unless noted. — *CR*

False Bay Vineyards
T 021-873-2418/2639 • F 021-873-7580

Est/1stB 2000 ▪ Closed to public ▪ Owner Paul Boutinot ▪ MD Jean du Toit ▪ Winemaker Werner Engelbrecht (2004) ▪ Viticulturist Werner Engelbrecht ▪ 470 000cs 45% red 40% white 15% rosé ▪ Export brands: Cape Aurora, Cape Heights, False Bay/Vals Baai, Hoop Huis, Paarl Heights, Post Stones ▪ PO Box 1286 Wellington 7654 ▪ ceo@boutinotsa.co.za; admin@boutinotsa.co.za

This brand forms part of the UK Boutinot portfolio, whose SA assets include Somerset West farm Waterkloof (see entry). Founder and owner Paul Boutinot and False Bay winemaker Werner Engelbrecht both believe that, in the pursuit of more elegant wines, a less interventionist way is good practice regardless of price or volume – and worth the few stuck fermentations that might result from relying on wild yeast fermentations.

Pinotage NEW ★★★ Attractive first appearance in **06**; only partly wooded, so variety's vivacious strawberry fruit & naturally fiesty tannins shine through. **Shiraz** ★★★ Debuts in guide with **06**; Old-World game & lily styling, gripping tannins inviting food, only older oak (8 mths). **Chardonnay** ★★★☆ Wooded **07** ups quality. Lime/lemon delicacy, vibrant orange-zest acidity, satisfying mouthfeel ex-3 mths lees-ageing. 14% alc well hidden. **Chenin Blanc** ★★★ Maiden **06**, tasted pvs ed, showed fine, varied character, weight & persistence. Should gain complexity over few yrs. **Sauvignon Blanc** ★★★ **07** lifts the bar. Appealing dusty/peppery notes mingle with green cool-climate flavours; balanced, persistent, tingling acidity. All Coastal WOs; all screwcapped. — *CvZ*

■ **Family Reserve** see Kleine Zalze Wines
■ **Fantail** see Morgenhof Estate

Fat Bastard

Tongue-in-jowl international label created by European wine-partners Thierry Boudinaud and Guy Anderson. Now made in serious quantities (500 000+ cartons) and distributed in Europe, America and the Far East. The SA versions, featuring a cartoon hippo on the front-label, are from Robertson Winery.

Shiraz ★★★★ Dark spicy fruit & hint leather on **07**, juicy, lively flavours & supple structure. Versatile braai red - rung below the elegant & classy standout we reviewed in **04** (★★★★). **Chardonnay** ★★★ Plump but gutsy **07**, ripe pear flavours balanced by zesty acidity. Drink within 2 yrs. **Sauvignon Blanc** ★★★ **07** less ripe than pvs, leaner, with piercing lemon acidity & grapefruit-pith finish. Best with food. 13% alc. — *MW*

■ **Fat Ladies** *see* Spier Wines

Feiteiras Vineyards

T 082-453-1597 · F 028-284-9525

Walker Bay (see Elgin/Walker Bay map) ▪ Est 2003 ▪ 1stB 2004 ▪ Visits by appt Mon-Fri 9-5 Sat/Sun 9-12 ▪ Closed Easter Fri/Sun, Dec 25 & Jan 1 ▪ Owner De Andrade family ▪ Winemaker Jose de Andrade (Mar 2003) ▪ Viticulturist Manuel de Andrade (Mar 2003) ▪ 4. 5ha (cab, merlot, mourvèdre, petit v, shiraz, verdelho) ▪ 1 200cs ▪ 80% red 10% white 10% fortified ▪ PO Box 234 Bot River 7185 ▪ feiteiraswine@icon.co.za ▪ www.feiteiraswine.co.za

Last harvest the De Andrades were particularly proud... of their neighbours' wines! Says Jose de A: 'They bought the grapes our tiny cellar couldn't handle, and were so impressed they immediately booked more for this year.' After launching a dry Verdelho, a variety from their native Madeira, they wonder: 'Why don't more people try it here?' Meanwhile, there's some interesting packaging on the cards for their port: individual oak casks with a brass tap and wooden bung, sealed with wax.

Troca Tintas ★★★ Name means 'changeable', which blend is: **06** cab/merlot (pvs merlot/ tinta); unfussy; juicy tannins, low acid enhance readiness. Oak-rounded. **Verdelho** NEW ▤ ★★★★ **07** most promising debut. Distinctive, amply spiced tropical fruit medley; tangy, green freshness hints at vinho verde; bone-dry, satisfying length. EW. **Vinho Fino Tinto** ★★★★ Warming fruit-driven dessert from mourvèdre, 10% cab, 18% alc. **06** smooth, luscious, not over-sweet. Chocolate ideal partner. 4.5/9litre oak vats. **Vinho Fino Branco** ★★★★ Verdelho in characterful fortified guise. **06** intriguing nuts & spice plus oxidative complexity. Concentrated, persistent though sweetish. 4.5/9litre oak vats. All WO Ovrbrg. — *AL*

■ **Finlayson Family Vineyards** *see* Edgebaston
■ **Fiona** *see* Flagstone Winery

FirstCape Vineyards

T 023-349-6720, 021-555-1442 · F 023-349-6727, 021-555-0852

Paarl ▪ Est 2002 ▪ Closed to public ▪ Owner De Wet, Aan de Doorns, Stettyn & Badsberg co-op wineries, Goudini Wines, Newton Johnson family & BrandPhoenix ▪ Winemaker David Smit & Newald Marais ▪ PO Box 88 Rawsonville 6845; Suite 22 Private Bag X4 Century City 7446 ▪ charmaine@firstcape.com ▪ www.firstcape.com

Sustained growth and reliability remain the theme at this export success story, SA's second-biggest bottled brand in the UK, twice as big as last year. Here they've grown their supermarket footprint, while moving into convenience stores and restaurants; elsewhere, they've moved into Scandinavia and Ireland. The recent launch of their 'little black box', a 3-litre pack, outstripped expectation. There's now a home base outside Simondium, where they can do their own blending and bottling, 'for even greater control and consistency' says partner Bevan Newton Johnson.

First Selection range

Shiraz ★★★ Lively, savoury **05**, pleasing roundness from touches Am oak & sugar (3g/l). **Shiraz-Cabernet Sauvignon** ★★★ Decent length, tannic grip at end of juicy red- & black-berried

05. Shiraz Rosé ★★ Uncomplicated quaffing style; **07** soft red ruit, some savoury tones & gentle sweetness. **Chardonnay** ★★★ **06** delicately citrus; hint spice/fatness from small portion Fr staves/barrels. Tasted pvs ed, as were all except Shiraz Rosé. **Chardonnay-Viognier** ★★★ Tropical **06**, with dollop sauv, deft oaking (combo Fr staves/Am barrels) adds spice & breadth; slight alc glow (13.6%).

Limited Release range

Cabernet Sauvignon ★★★ **05** solid example, with variety's austere tannin, fresh acidity, lush cassis fruit. **Merlot** ★★★ Jammy, malty tones on **06**, lifted by spice nuance & slightly stalky finish. **Shiraz** ★★★ Tasted last ed, **05** was easy to drink though sweet-sour, with firm tannins. **Pinotage Rosé** ★★ **06** earthy, sweet entry checked by pleasantly drying fruit tannins when tasted last ed. **Chenin Blanc** ★★★ Pvs ultra-low sugar slightly up in **07**, still dry, satisfying, should complement most salad/fish dishes. **Pinot Grigio** NEW ★★★ Tasty debut, **07** musky, nutty, peachy; racy acidity softened by hint sugar. Close your eyes & you could be in Italy. **Sauvignon Blanc** ★★★ Drink-soon **06**, untasted last ed, still nicely balanced, with gooseberry & quince tones, relatively light 11.8% alc. **Sauvignon Blanc-Semillon** ★★★ **07** slender (11.7% alc) but well-formed, refreshing; a lovely food wine.

Café Selection NEW

Rosé ★★ Pretty pink **07** from shiraz & pinotage, fresh & undestated; low 10% alc for sipping away the hours. **Chenin Blanc** ★★ **07** water-white with 'sea spray' hint, bracing acidity, fuller than 9.8% alc suggests. Screwcap (here & throughout the ranges) makes the café waiter's task a little easier.

FirstCape range

Pinotage ★★★ **05** bursts with creamy strawberry aroma & flavour, wags a long, juicy tail. **Cabernet Sauvignon-Merlot** ★★★ Drink-some-more **06** wonderfully fruity, uncomplicated by oak, screwcapped for easy access. **Shiraz-Pinotage** ★★★ Shiraz-led (55%) **06** a really gd drink thanks to sappy tannins & exuberant fruit; pinotage adds hint of bitterness though. **Shiraz Rosé** NEW ★★ **07** alluring sweetie (16g/l RS) with dusty berry & biltong nose. **Chenin Blanc** NEW ★★★ Lovely bruised apple compote, 'brusque' chenin acidity make **06** a satisfying sipper. **Chardonnay-Semillon** ★★★ 50/50 blend **06** tasted last ed, ligtish but flavoursome, with fresh finish. **Colombard-Chardonnay** ★★ Pre-bottling sample **07** fun & fresh with forthright guava, bubble-gum & banana aromas. 60/40 blend. All ranges WO W Cape, for current consumption. — *CvZ*

▪ **First Selection** *see FirstCape Vineyards*

▪ **First Sighting** *see Strandveld Vineyards*

▪ **Fish Hoek** *see Flagstone Winery*

▪ **Five Generations** *see Cederberg Private Cellars*

▪ **Five Heirs** *see Lourensford*

▪ **Five's Reserve** *see Van Loveren Private Cellar*

Flagstone Winery
T 021-852-5052 ▪ **F** 021-852-5085

Somerset West (see Helderberg map) ▪ *Est 1998* ▪ *1stB 1999* ▪ *Tasting & sales Mon-Fri 10-5 Sat 10-3 Sun by appt ('phone to avoid disappointment')* ▪ *Fee R20 redeemable with any purchase* ▪ *Tours by appt* ▪ *Owner Jack family* ▪ *Winemaker Bruce Jack, Wilhelm Coetzee & Gerald Cakijana* ▪ *Viticulturist Bruce Jack* ▪ *90ha under management* ▪ *400-600t/40-70 000cs (varying % reds/whites)* ▪ *PO Box 3636 Somerset West 7129* ▪ *admin@flagstonewinery.co.za* ▪ *www.flagstonewines.co.za*

The Mary le Bow 04 made news on two fronts last year: it took gold at the Sélections Mondiales in Canada, and is one of two Flagstone wines to hold the top price spots in UK retail chain Tesco. 'Ample proof,' declares winemaker Bruce Jack, 'that Ashton, bizarrely unheralded as a red-wine growing area, can underpin world-beating wine quality.' Talking Tesco, the Fish Hoek range is now listed there: Bruce J intends to grow it into the biggest SA brand in the world and is using a new UK sales office as HQ for his campaign. The Fish Hoek, Cellar Hand and A Few Good Men ranges, as well as new ventures like Barbarossa, now fall under The Springtree Wine Company, a collaboration between Flagstone and Riebeek Cellars. Last of the newsmakers are the La Báscula range, bringing the taste of Spain to SA palates, and a vintaged cider, from Elgin fruit.

Cape Winemakers Guild Reserves

★★★★☆ **Love Handles** 🗒 Name from Bruce's physique (!!), this **04** shiraz pvs ed showed prosciutto, coffee beans, New World plush dark fruit underpinned by spice. Impossibly smooth; cellaring could reveal more layers. 2 yrs new Am oak. Mainly Swtberg fruit. For 2006 Auction.

★★★★ **CWG Chenin Blanc** Preserved citruspeel, almond biscotti-styled **07** takes chenin to a more sophisticated level; still tightly held, savoury rather than fruity, with requisite seam of acidity, will reward cellaring for next 5+ yrs. 100% new Am oak. With dab sauvignon.

★★★★☆ **Months of Sundays** For 2005 Auction, now replaced with Weather Girl.

★★★★☆ **Weather Girl** NEW 🗒 Elim-sourced near-equal sauvignon, semillon, unadulterated by oak, **06** glories in the terroir. Admirable complexity, fennel, spring-fresh leafy salad, lime zest, finishing with food-versatile minerality. A beauty.

Fiona range

★★★★ **Pinot Noir** 🗒 No **04**, **05**. Latest **06**, with cab, pinot meunier & all Am oak, has found a different voice to **03**: red berries, svelte lines & wonderfully perfumed; violets, organic & wild scrub notes of pinot at its best. A beauty.

★★★★ **Sauvignon Blanc Reserve** 🗒 From Elim fruit, **06** has altogether riper flavour & textures than pvs; gooseberry, lime & greengage, without sacrificing freshness. Remains delicious & involving.

Foundation range

★★★★ **Music Room Cabernet Sauvignon** 🗒 Expert handling gives cab dominant **05** perfume of fully ripe grapes, none of the excess. Cassis & cherries, spiced by Am oak, complex strands of barnyard, smoke-cured meat. 15% alc smoothly assimilated.

★★★★ **Writer's Block Pinotage** 🗒 Ever popular with pundits. **04** last ed had spicy plum richness in medium-tannined tail. Third whole-berry crush, 14 mths barrelled, 30% new Am.

★★★★ **Dark Horse Shiraz** 🗒 Aptly named, last tasted **04** had sheathed power, touch of the untamed in hedgerow fruit, scrub, moorland. Glossy texture, sleekly approachable tannins, with yrs of pleasure ahead. Barrel selection. Deep & brooding **03** houseful of awards incl VDG, SAA, Wine ★★★★.

★★★★ **Dragon Tree** 🗒 Cape individuality in flagship blend. **05** mainly cab, with pinotage & 5 others, gaining structurally as result. Wild berries, underbrush & cedar; althletic, muscular, built to last but no impediment to current enjoyment.

★★★★ **Two Roads** 🗒 Cellar's 'icon white'. Last available **05** sauvignon, chard, with 4 others, mostly Am barrel ferment/matured. Result assaulted the senses: preserved peach/pineapple, citrus peel, yet underlying green fig, coming together in tangy sweet-sour way. Admirably creative, complex.

Semaphore ☺ 🗒 ★★★ Almost-dry rosé from mainly pinotage. Sample last ed, **06** now shows piquant red berries, hint of fresh banana, appealing freshness.

Longitude 🗒 ★★★☆ Consistent value, usually blend 7 varieties, cab, shiraz led. Smoky, dark-fruited **06** retains the curvaceous lines, smooth texture its many fans have come to expect. **"Reserve Rosé"** NEW Not ready. EW. **Heywood House Barrel Fermented Sauvignon Blanc** 🗒 ★★★★ Sophisticated handling of often fractious sauvignon/wood marriage. Last tasted **04**'s warm custard breadth of spiced oak softened sauvignon spikes. **Free Run Sauvignon Blanc** 🗒 ★★★★ Elim fruit in last available **06**, beefed up leafy/fynbos tones; racy acidity was balanced by soupçon body-plumping sugar. With 15% semillon. **Noon Gun** 🗒

★★★ Chardonnay, sauvignon, riesling based miscellany of 6 varieties, **07** is a peach-perfumed & floral delight, characterful & refreshingly dry. **The Field Day** 🔲 ★★★☆ Pinot blanc (84%), sprinkle of 5 others in last available **05**; unpretentious, with layers of floral, fruity notes to admire while enjoying the shapely, refreshingly tangy drinking experience. **The Last Word Port** 🔲 ★★★★ From Tulbagh shiraz, **05** has distinctive espresso notes accompanying the fruitcake richness; a hedonist's delight, silky & sweetly delicious. Discontinued: **BK5 Pinot Noir**.

Joint Ventures

★★★★ **Berrio Cabernet Sauvignon** 🔲 Last ed, **04** had intriguing blueberry/wild fruit character, hints wintergreen, mocha choc; a refined elegance. Dabs cab f, petit v, merlot. Gd 4-6 yr future.

★★★★ **Bowwood** Cab/merlot blend in technicolour, last tasted **04**'s cassis/black plums were given vanilla-rich 14 mths Am oak treatment; lush, velvety mouthful. Only 126 cs made. Partnership with Johnsens in Pdberg.

★★★★ **Mary Le Bow** Cooperation with Fraters of Rbtsn. Fruitcake richness at first glance in last tasted **04** blend, but intriguing nuances: mint choc, smoky cigarbox, roasted veggies, showing how clever it was adding shiraz to a bdx blend. Big (14.9% alc) & impressive.

★★★★ **Berrio Sauvignon Blanc** 🔲 Refined & sophisticated, last available **06** showed nettles, grapefruit & a deep seam of minerality. Ideally suited to food, but gd enough solo.

Strata Series
Discontinued: **Cape Blend**, **The Wallflower**. — *CR*

Flamingo Bay *see Darling Cellars*

Flat Roof Manor

'Laid-back, unpretentious and quirky' screwcapped range made by Estelle Lourens of Uitkyk (where the wines may be tasted). The name an allusion to the flat-roofed neoclassical manor house on the property.

Merlot ★★ **06** appealing plum & vanilla notes, but light on fruit with overly tight oak grip. **Shiraz-Mourvèdre** ★★★ **06** ±60/40 blend. Spicy vanilla oak (9 mths Fr/ Am) dominates red fruit; youthful, lighter (13.5% alc) than pvs. **Cabernet Sauvignon-Sangiovese** ★★★ **06** intriguing tar & roses from 30% sangiovese component; savoury & lean-fruited flavours, matured in combo Fr & Am oak, adding tannic grip. **Pinot Grigio** ★★★ **07** focused, spicy forthright flavours for easy enjoyment. 12.5% alc lunchtime white; will work well with food. **Semillon** ✓ ★★★★ Lemony **06** with 15% sauv, gains breadth from 5 mths lees & barrelled component; pithy, firm finish, will stand up to curries. — *IM*

Fleur du Cap
T 021-809-7000 • F 021-883-9651

Stellenbosch • 1stB 1968 • Tasting & sales at Bergkelder Wine Centre (see entry) • Owner Distell • Cellarmaster Andrea Freeborough • Winemaker Pieter Badenhorst (white wines) & Justin Corrans (red wines), with Schalk van der Merwe & Jaco van der Walt • Viticulturist Bennie Liebenberg • 2 100t/180 000cs 55% red 45% white • fleurducap@distell.co.za • www.fleurducap.co.za

The awards keep coming, with the Unfiltered Viognier Limited Release 06 one of only three SA wines to win a trophy at the 2007 International Wine Challenge. The policy of 'handpicked in the vineyard and handcrafted in the cellar' dates back to the 80s, when Bergkelder cellarmaster Dr Julius Laszlo was a key protagonist in bringing noble grape varieties to SA and in introducing small oak barrels for red-wine maturation. The red-wine team has therefore launched a limited-release blend in his honour, while Kobus Gerber (now Distell group winemaker) has handed over the white-wine reins to Pieter Badenhorst (ex-Nederburg).

Unfiltered Collection

★★★★ **Cabernet Sauvignon 05** substantial, demanding mouthful. Modern classic in its cassis, mint decoration to very fresh, firm frame, concentrated fruit core. Just absorbs 14.9% alc punch. Smartly oaked: new Fr, 16 mths. Bottlry single-vyd.

★★★★ **Chardonnay** Hints of lime, buttered toast & spice in elegantly poised **06**. Carries oak (new Fr/Am 80/20, 9 mths) & alc (14.2%) with ease. Vigorous acid (no malo) firms, lengthens & ensures gd potential.

★★★★ **Sauvignon Blanc** Serious sophisticate ex-cool Cape Agulhas/Koekenaap vyds. Previewed **07** deep, long, dusty greenpepper, lemongrass flavour; substantial but lithe, bone-dry.

★★★★ **Sauvignon Blanc Limited Release** Extrovert Kiwi styling, bursting with passionfruit, gooseberry, green pea drama. Sample **07** huge juicy concentration, still restless acid needs time to calm. Koekenaap, Groenekloof fruit.

★★★★ **Semillon 06** (★★★★) pleasant honey, tangerine aromas, more transient flavours; lowish acid, contrasting alc grip in tail. Fr/Am oak fermented/7 mths, 50% new. Limey **05** was shapely, even statuesque.

★★★★ **Viognier Limited Release** White peach, sunny honeysuckle fragrance make explosive return in **06** - missing in **05** (★★★★). Concentrated, succulent but not too sweet (4.2 g/l RS), with firming mineral core; enjoy before beefy 15% alc asserts itself.

★★★★ **Viognier-Chardonnay-Sauvignon Blanc-Semillon 06** attractive equal blend buffed by careful oaking (9 mths, some new). Refined pot pourri scents; full, creamy & structured but surprisingly fresh; lovely finish.

Merlot ★★★★ **05** powerful, sternly built with still edgy grip, though 18 mths new Fr oak well absorbed. Pleasing mint/red-plum tones, incipient silkiness should emerge after yr/2. S West/Bottlry fruit. **04** (★★★★) was v dry & firm.

Fleur du Cap range

★★★★★ **Laszlo** [NEW] Handsomely packaged, merlot-based bdx blend honouring Julius L, Bergkelder cellarmaster 1975-1992. **04** mint-edged cedary intensity, plush yet graceful, fresh; properly tight for beneficial further few yrs development. 18 mths in Dr L's trademark small Fr oak.

★★★★ **Chenin Blanc** Previewed **07** promises charm, complexity. Faint winter melon, apple blossom concentration from selected older vyds, spiced by subtle oak. Vigorous, firm, mouthwateringly long. Am/Fr barrels, some new; 25% unoaked.

★★★★ **Noble Late Harvest** Thrilling riesling dessert; **06** (★★★★★) subtle botrytis & honeycomb touches to variety's spice & muscat; racy acid/sweetness tussle sumptuous fruit, finishing tingly-clean. Low 9.9% alc a bonus. 207g/l RS, 9.3g/l TA; unwooded. Sbosch vyds. Zesty **05** featured dollops chard, gewürz.

Cabernet Sauvignon ★★★★ **05** bright, crunchy fruit; balanced, integrated tannin grip supplies approachability plus few yrs ageing potential. Yr mainly Fr oak, 30% new. **Merlot** ★★★★ Since maiden 90, among most expressive, interesting reds in range. **05** alive with fresh plum flavours & spice; velvety concentration balanced by mineral lift; gd now & for few yrs. Mainly Fr oak, 5% new, 14 mths. **04** (★★★) shade less exciting. **Pinotage** ★★★ **05** mouthful smooth, crushed mulberries followed by 15% alc kick in tail. **Shiraz** ★★★ Rich smells of warm stony soil, black fruits, cured meat on robust **05**. Austere, grippy palate less enticing. Fr/Am oak 14 mths, 30% new. **Chardonnay** ★★★ Everyman's (& woman's) chard. **06** harmonious, smooth; clean citrus, tropical flesh; unobtrusive brush spicy oak (6 mths, mainly Fr). Gd for few yrs. **Sauvignon Blanc** ★★★★ Quality of vintage evident in **07** (ex-tank, provisional rating): expressive, expansive flavours hinged on invigorating steely core. **Natural Light** ★★ Refreshing **07**; pick-me-up green apple acid, fruitily balanced 9g/l sugar matches low ±9% alc. —AL

▪ **Foot of Africa** *see* Kleine Zalze Wines

▪ **Footprint** *see* African Pride Wines

▪ **Forge Mill** *see* Franschhoek Vineyards

For My Friends
T 083-658-8691 ,083-379-3941

Darling • Est/1stB 2002 • Tasting by appt • Owner/winemaker Abé Beukes & Johan Nesenberend • 200 cs 100% red • PO Box 114 Darling 7345 • winemaker@darlingcellars.co.za

The ever-widening circle of friends who share a love for this private-label Shiraz have bought up the 02 vintage. The **03** – which Abé Beukes and Johan Nesenberend, cellarmaster and red-wine maker at Darling Cellars respectively, are very happy with – was launched, and the **05** bottled for future release (no **04** was made).

For My Friends range
Shiraz ★★★★ **03**, last a preview (so provisionally rated), more elegant than maiden **02** (★★★☆), lingering, harmonious, though also big boned. 18 mths Fr oak, 60% new. — *CvZ*

■ **Forresters** *see Ken Forrester Wines*

■ **Fortress Hill** *see Fort Simon Estate*

Fort Simon Estate

T 021-906-0304 • F 021-903-8034

Stellenbosch • Est/1stB 1998 • Tasting & sales Mon-Fri 9.30-5 Sat 10-2 • Fee R2/wine • Closed pub hols • Tours by appt • Venue for after-hours receptions & conferences (max 40 guests) by appt • Gourmet cheese platters • Owner Renier & Petrus Uys • Winemaker Marinus Bredell & Stander Maass • Viticulturist Renier Uys • 126ha (cabs s/f, malbec, merlot, petit v, pinotage, shiraz, chard, chenin, sauv, viognier) • 800t/30 000cs own label 50% red 50% white • PO Box 43 Sanlamhof 7532 • fortsimon@telkomsa.net • www.fortsimon.co.za

'Try it – it's making the news,' advises winemaker Marinus Bredell, talking about his NLH 06, a pioneering product from viognier, named Top Dessert Wine at the 2007 Terroir Awards. Now assisting Marinus B in the cellar is newcomer Stander Maass, whose CV includes a stint in New Zealand.

Fort Simon Estate range
★★★★ **Chardonnay** Prominent citrus & lime; 50% new oak deftly judged to reinforce fruit & structure on **06**; well-balanced acidity invigorates.

★★★★ **Sauvignon Blanc** No follow up as yet for concentrated & complex **05** (★★★★☆), which achieved perfect ripeness at moderate 12.3% alc. **04** was more showy & intense.

Anna Simon Merlot-Pinotage ★★★ None tasted since **01**; savoury, ground coffee aromas & flavours, touch pinotage sweetness on finish. **Cabernet Sauvignon** ★★★★ Rich, meaty **04**, with hints of spice, still-juvenile tannins & clever use of oak (18 mths, no new barrels). Preview assessed, rating tentative. **Merlot** ★★★★ Well-made **04** intense & rich with toffee, choc & raspberry; ripe, fairly soft tannins; 2 yrs Fr/Am oaking well absorbed. **Pinotage** ★★★★ Refreshing, clean rosepetal note on **04**, pleasing soft tannins; elegant, well structured, but probably not for keeping. **Shiraz** ★★★ **03**, pvs ed, warm & ripe (14% alc); savoury edge with hints fynbos & leather. **Barrel Select** NEW ★★★ Bdx-style blend merlot & malbec (88/12); **03** shy, lightish, with austere minerality & v soft tannins. For drinking now. Fr oak, 18 mths. 375ml. **Rosé** ★★★ **06**, tasted pvsly, mainly pinotage with merlot. Juicy & easy, with dry finish. **Chenin Blanc Barrel Fermented** Discontinued. NE. **Chenin Blanc** ★★★★ Refreshing, ripe **06**, tropical & quince nuances to be enjoyed within the next yr. **Viognier Noble Late Harvest** NEW ★★★★ Unusual & interesting **06**, floral, biscuity & rich (142g/l RS); dried apricot & almond notes - volatile touch too. Unwooded. 375ml. Discontinued: **Sauvignon Blanc Barrel Fermented**, **Restelle**.

Fortress Hill range
Merlot ★★★ Light-toned **04** hints of spice, nuances of blackberry & mint, friendly tannins. Third Fr oaked, 24 mths. **Pinotage** Sold out. **Shiraz** NEW ★★ **02** pleasant bottle-age tone, hints red berries & spice, but needs drinking soon. **Merlot-Pinotage** ★★★ Last tasted **01** was lightly oaked & easy; smooth tannins for early drinking. **Chardonnay** Out of stock.

. **Chenin Blanc** ★★★ **06** rich, ripe-fruit flavours, hint papaya, appealing & friendly. Gd solo or with food. 30% Am oaked. **Sauvignon Blanc** No new vintage tasted. —*MM*

■ **Foundation Series** *see Flagstone Winery*
■ **Founders** *see Bellingham*
■ **Fountain Head** *see Jason's Hill Private Cellar*
■ **Four Clover** *see Cloverfield Private Cellar*
■ **Four Cousins** *see Van Loveren Private Cellar*
■ **Four Gates** *see Ernst & Co Wines*

Four Paws Wines [NEW]
T 021-874-1033 • F 021-874-2110

Paarl • Est/1stB 2005 • Closed to public • Owner Rob Meihuizen, Gerda Willers & Anne Jakubiec • Winemaker Gerda Willers (2006) • Viticulturist Gerda Willers (consultant) • 15t/1 100cs 75% red 25% white • PO Box 69 Simondium 7670 • anne@southerntrade.co.za

'Put three wine buffs around a table and before long they are making the stuff,' say Rob Meihuizen, Anne Jakubiec and Gerda Willers, winemaking consultant to a number of farms. Since the start, grapes have come mainly from the mountainous Piekenierskloof region, and most of the finished product goes to the UK.

Four Paws

★★★★ **Pablo** ✓ Bargain-priced cab-dominated bdx blend with dab grenache noir, **06** shows dark hedgerow fruit, smoked beef, dried herbs, sinuous lines. Complex, intriguing, remarkably accessible but lurking power promises 4+ yr future.

Pinotage ★★★ **06** abounds with rich, smoky dark fruit, given firm foundation by yr oaking, third new. Already accessible, could cellar few yrs. **Chardonnay** ★★★ Savoury, honeyed peach perfume, flavour reflects **06**'s ripeness, yr oaking. Backing acidity adds spark, refreshing drinkability. **Sauvignon Blanc** ★★★ Pear drop & gooseberry ripeness in **07**, with mouthfilling succulent freshness. Good food wine. —*CR*

Fraai Uitzicht 1798
T 023-626-6156 • F 023-626-5265

Klaasvoogds (see Robertson map) • Sales at reception/restaurant during opening hours (see Eat-out section) • Closed Jun-Aug & Jan 1 • Tours strictly by appt • For amenities & activities, see Stay-over section • Owner Karl Papesch • Winemaker/viticulturist Karl Papesch, advised by local experts • 10ha (cab, merlot, shiraz) • 500cs 100% red • PO Box 97 Robertson 6705 • info@fraaiuitzicht.com • www.fraaiuitzicht.com

It seems more guesthouse than winery: ask for Merlot and you get shown either the en-suite cottage or one of the bottles of wine, made in the oldest and smallest wine cellar in the Breede River Valley. But for Karl Papesch, who fell in love with the farm during the 2001 crush, making wine is a dream come true. He consults many of the winemakers who are regulars at his restaurant, and the results, he believes, are indeed 'fraai'.

Merlot ★★★ 40% new oak perhaps a touch too generous for **05**'s shy, tight fruit; mid-2007 vanilla tone & woody mouthfeel; might just need time to attain harmony. —*MM*

Franki's Vineyards [NEW]
T 022-482-2837, 082-888-3702 • F 086-660-3677

Swartland (see Durbanville map) • Est2004/1stB 2007 • Tasting by appt only • Light meals by appt • Conference facilities • Walks • Classic- & race-car museum, guesthouse & restaurant opening end 2008 • Owner Franco Afrique Technologies (Pty) Ltd • Winemaker Erica Joubert with Nicolaas Hanekom (both Jan 2004), advised by Francesca Cordier • Viticulturist Han Yao (consultant) • 20ha (grenache, mourvèdre, viognier) • 15t/670 cs own label 65% red, 25% white, 10% rosé (2007 rosé only) • PO Box 972 Malmesbury 7299 • erica.joubert@cropspec.co.za

Franki's Vineyards are set on combining the old with the new to the best possible effect. Modern technologies, including innovative vinicultural practices, and elements from the Old-

World, such as a specially tailored 'goblet' vine-training system, are harnessed to produce this high-aiming newcomer's wines (none ready for tasting, unfortunately). Noteworthy are a rooibos tea plantation and, from late this year, an extensive collection of classic and competition automobiles.

■ **Franschhoek Cellar** *see Franschhoek Vineyards*

Franschhoek Vineyards
T 021-876-2086 • **F** 021-876-3440

Franschhoek • Est 1945 • 1stB ca 1975 • Tasting & sales Mon-Fri 9.30-5 Sat 10-4 Sun 11-3 • Fee R15 • Closed Easter Fri & Dec 25 • La Cotte Restaurant (booking advised) • Owner 35 shareholders • Winemaker Richard Duckitt (Dec 2005) • 2 000t/43 000cs own label 45% red 55% white • Ranges for customers: Franschhoek Cellar Gold- & Silver; The Stonewalker; export labels: Anvil Road, Ancient Earth, Forge Mill, Keate's Drift & Millberg • PO Box 52 Franschhoek 7690 • info@franschhoek-vineyards.com • www.franschhoek-vineyards.co.za, www.franschhoekcellar.co.za

Success at the 2007 Swiss and Terroir awards for their top-tier Semillon, Merlot and Petit Verdot was the best sort of 'welcome gift' for the incoming new management team, who took over the helm of a ship buoyed by the past few years' concerted fine tuning. Revitalisation continues with an upgrade of the visitor centre at the gateway to Franschhoek Village, and new labels waiting to be unveiled as the guide went to press.

Franschhoek Cellar Reserve range
Cabernet Sauvignon ★★★★ No new vintage for this, Merlot; respective notes from pvs ed. **04** set the tone for range with ripe-fruited lushness controlled by rich but chewy tannins; 14% alc finished warm. **Cabernet Franc** NEW ★★★★ Promising debut **04** has sweet-sour tang in tail, sweet-ripe lift to leafy red-fruit flavours. Subtle oak note from 3rd fill Fr wood. **Merlot** ★★★★ **04** very ripe & sweet with touch of wildness about the nose; chunky but balanced. **Petit Verdot** ★★★★ Step up for powerful **05**, still needing few yrs to show best. Sugared prune nose followed by full, fruity palate, shaped by taut tannins, brisk acidity. 2007 Terroir Awards 'best on show'. 18 mths 20% new Fr oak. **Shiraz** ★★★ Improved **05** still ripe & ultra-powerful but not hot or port-like as pvs; gd fruit weight, acidity & roundness, lashings coconut/banana from 21 mths Am oak. **Semillon** ★★★ Barrel fermented/aged version; attractive **06** a treat for the sweeter-toothed: ±5g/l sugar combines with 14% alc & vanilla overlay to give an unctuous profile, vibrant acidity notwithstanding. 60/40 Fr/Am wood, yr. **Semillon-Chenin Blanc** NEW ★★★ Maiden **06** blend (55/45) not shy & retiring, but has charm. Unoaked to showcase expressive lemon-waxy character, grape tannin nudge on finish. **Chardonnay-Pinot Noir MCC** NEW ★★★★ **00** makes sparkling debut; 5 yrs on lees adding weight & texture to enticing honey-soaked brioche, apple tones. Invigorating mousse, lively acidity complete the package. 51% chard.

Franschhoek Vineyards range
La Cotte Port ★★ Returns to guide with **00**, bucks trend with only 50g/l RS (vs usual 85+) but walks the alc talk with 19%. Gentle tealeaf, gentle Christmas cake tones. — *CvZ*

■ **Fredericksburg** *see Rupert & Rothschild Vignerons*

Fredine le Roux Wines
T 028-284-9765 • **F** 028-284-9765

Caledon • Est/1stB 2004 • Tastings/sales at Goedvertrouw • Owner Josias and Fredine le Roux • Winemaker Fredine le Roux • 240cs 60% red 40% white • PO Box 338 Caledon 7230 • josiasfredin@mweb.co.za

The demands of a young family have placed Fredine le Roux's winemaking career on a temporary hold, but no doubt she'll be back next year with her 06 wines, currently awaiting final polishing prior to release.

Cabernet Sauvignon ★★★★ Big-boned **04**, on review oozed ultra-ripe but gorgeous cassis & plum fruit, toasty oak & pipesmoke notes added complexity. 18 mths Fr oak. **Grenache-Cabernet Sauvignon** Sells out before we can taste. **Chenin Blanc** ★★★ **04** marked by sinewy elegance when tasted in youth; kiwi & passionfruit on nose, fairly prominent oak but enough vivacious lemon fruit to carry it. — *MM*

Freedom Hill Wines
T 021-867-0085 ▪ F 021-867-0576

Paarl ▪ Est 1997 ▪ 1stB 2000 ▪ Tasting & sales Mon-Thu 9-5 Fri 9-4 Sat 10-3 ▪ Owner Francois Klomp ▪ Winemaker Kowie du Toit advised by Francois Naudé (Jan 2007) ▪ Viticulturist Chris Immelman (June 2006) ▪ ±19ha (cab, merlot, pinotage, shiraz) ▪ 140t/6 000cs 90% red 10% white ▪ PO Box 6353 Uniedal 7612 ▪ info@freedomhill.co.za ▪ www.freedomhill.co.za

Owner Francois Klomp has enlisted namesake Francois Naudé, former L'Avenir winemaker, to massage his wines into even finer fettle. The seasoned consultant fine-tunes the trimmed range in rented cellar space, relying on new viticulturist Chris Immelman for invaluable 'donkey work'. Shiraz and cab still shine, heralding the duo's re-introduction in a blend.

★★★★ **Shiraz** More modest version in **05** (★★★); seems slimmed down; still the meaty/beefy character we appreciated in last-tasted **03**, though, & some elegance.

★★★★ **Shiraz-Cabernet Sauvignon 05** (★★★) more elegant but seems to have lost some fruit en route. Pleasing, with approachable tannins & subtle oak. Last-tasted **01** had generous New-World ripeness, fairly extracted but harmonious.

Pinotage ★★★★ Introverted **05**; last ed muted cappuccino & earth tones but a gd structure with fleshy fruit, lively acidity, generous tannins. **Cape Blend** ★★★ New blend of **05**, still cab, pinotage, shiraz, but somewhat diffident, more approachable than last yr's version. **Sauvignon Blanc** ★★★ Light & refreshing **07** (sample), undemanding sauv character. Discontinued: **Cabernet Sauvignon, Merlot, Shibula Merlot, Merlot-Cabernet Sauvignon, Blanc de Noir.** — *IvH*

■ **Friends** *see Lutzville Cape Diamond Vineyards*
■ **Frisky Zebras** *see United Nations of Wine*
■ **Frog Hill** *see Anura Vineyards*
■ **Frost Vineyards** *see David Frost Estate*

Fryer's Cove Vineyards
T 027-213-2312 ▪ F 027-213-2212

Bamboes Bay ▪ Est 1999 ▪ 1stB 2002 ▪ Tasting/sales at Knorhoek (see entry) ▪ Owner Jan Ponk Trust, JH Laubscher Family Trust & Wynand Hamman ▪ Winemaker Wynand Hamman (Apr 1999) ▪ Viticulturist Jan van Zyl (Apr 1999) ▪ 6ha (cab, merlot, pinot, sauvignon) ▪ 35t/2 500cs 66% red 34% white ▪ PO Box 93 Vredendal 8160 ▪ tharowynand@telkomsa.net

There are plenty of reasons – and seasons, like spring for the flowers - to visit these partners-in-wine up the West Coast. There's a tasting in the wooden cabin and dinner in the lapa (by arrangement) in Strandfontein for starters. Then there's Jan 'Ponk' van Zyl's bush camp near Vredendal, where you can savour a glass of pinot while watching buck drink at the waterhole, followed by a braai. 'It's a challenge working with pinot but I'll find my feet,' says winemaker Wynand Hamman. If the Sauvignon and Richard Fryer blend are the yardsticks, they're already on terra firma.

★★★★ **Richard Fryer** Near-equal blend cab, merlot. Sample **05** following **04**'s lead: deep opulent fruit, intriguing asphalt nuances, cocoa. Sleekly muscular, refined, 24 mths oaking perfectly judged, promises gd furture.

★★★★★ **Sauvignon Blanc** 🔖 Confirming variety's perfect fit with terroir, **07** explodes with flavour: greengage & lime, just-picked gooseberries, long tangy intensity. A beauty.

Pinot Noir ★★★★ Unbottled **06**'s beguiling raspberry tones & svelte fresh-fruity palate promise well, only second crop. Oak fully integrated, 14 mnths mainly seasoned barriques. — *CR*

Furstenburg Wines
T 082-552-7063 ▪ F 021-465-2428

Stellenbosch ▪ Est 2004 ▪ 1stB 2005 ▪ Closed to public ▪ Owner Victor van Aswegen & Anton van Aswegen family trusts ▪ Viticulturist Vini consultant Jeff Wedgwood (Oct 2004) ▪ 1 600 cs 67% red 33% white ▪ PO Box 212 Stellenbosch 7599 ▪ victor@furstenburg.com ▪ www. furstenburg.com

With no premises, Victor van Aswegen describes Furstenburg as a 'virtual winery', with only two labels, a Cab and a Chardonnay (neither tasted this edition). He has no immediate plans to bottle more, partly because he's involved with a project 'on a somewhat more ambitious scale': putting together a group of BEE companies in the wine industry supply chain.

Galleon Wines
T 021-976-1786, 028-272-9511 ▪ F 021-976-8129

Betty's Bay ▪ Est 2003 ▪ 1stB 2004 ▪ Visits by appt ▪ Owner BK Investments/Andries Brink ▪ Winemaker Andries Brink, advised by Bertus Fourie (2004) ▪ 600cs 100% red ▪ PO Box 62 Durbanville 7551 ▪ cvjsa@cvjsa.co.za

Retired cardiologist Andries Brink says winemaking has brought him many new friends: 'Wine people are nice people.' In fact, they've taught this Betty's Bay garagiste so much that it's his turn: "An auditor friend became so interested that I trained him in the art of winemaking and he is now vinifying his own wine too.'

> **Chardonnay** NEW ☺ ★★★ Fat, peachy **06** refreshed by zesty acidity. Medium bodied, balanced; long, fruity farewell. Lightly wooded.

Cabernet Sauvignon ★★★★ Pvsly-tasted **05** classically styled; gd but reined-in varietal aromas of lead pencil, blackcurrant. Tight tannins, slightly herbal finish. **Cabernet Sauvignon Reserve** NEW ★★★★ **05** accessible cassis & liquorice flavours, hint dark choc; tannins tamed by ripeness; softer, friendlier than expected of a Rsv. 20 mths new oak. **Shiraz** NEW ★★★ Juicy & quaffable **06**, smooth & balanced, with spicy red-fruited appeal; warm & friendly farewell. Barrelled 15 mths. – *MW*

Gallop Hill
T 021-869-8956 ▪ F 021-869-8133

Paarl ▪ Est 2001 ▪ 1stB 2002 ▪ Visits by appt; contact Dijonne at 076-169-4547 ▪ Many attractions & amenities incl polo arena ▪ Owner Dijonne du Preez & Jim Deane ▪ Winemaker/viticulturist Louw Schabort (consultant) ▪ 20ha (cab, shiraz) ▪ ±50t/2 500cs 100% red ▪ PO Box 2125 Windmeul 7630 ▪ info@gallophill.co.za ▪ www.gallophill.co.za

The name alone has made their Polo Cap Classique the bubbly of choice at international polo events. 'It sold out an hour after we launched it,' marvels Dijonne du Preez. After hosting several 'huge' polo events at Gallop Hill last year, he says: 'Our customers arrive on Friday and leave on Sunday. They play polo, they drink, and they pre-order our wine 2-3 years in advance.' Note: neither the new MCC sparkling nor newer vintages of previously listed The First Chukka red blend or Sauvignon Blanc tasted this edition.

■ **Gecko Ridge** *see Long Mountain Wine Company*

Gentis Family Vineyards

Walker Bay ▪ Est 1992 ▪ 1stB 1993 ▪ Closed to public ▪ Owner FV Gentis Trust ▪ Winemaker Emile Gentis (1992), Frans Gentis (1989) & Victor Gentis (1992) ▪ 60% red 30% white 10% port ▪ PO Box 14 Vlottenburg 7604 ▪ emilegentis@yahoo.com

After selling their Stellenboschkloof wine farm De Morgenzon, the father-and-sons team of Frans, Victor and Emile Gentis settled at Fisherhaven on the Bot River Lagoon. Victor, through his Ciatti wine brokerage, sources grapes from top blocks, and Emile (Long Mountain winemaker) vinifies the family's L'Emigré, Nutwood Grove and Azure ranges.

Nutwood Grove Cabernet Sauvignon ★★★ This, Port, return to guide after extended hiatus with mature **00**. Evasive fruit, some forest floor aromas, soft cobwebby tannins. Needs drinking. **L'Emigré Shiraz** ★★★ Black fruit, raspberry & pepper notes, full & harmonious flavours with oak still evident on attractive previewed **06**. **L'Emigré Port** NEW ★★ Faded aromas of hazelnut & dark fruit, spicy flavours, but **98** rather tired now. *— MF*

■ **GG Wines** *see Ernst & Co Wines*

Gilga Wines
T 021-887-1861 • F 021-887-1861, 011-646-8754

Stellenbosch • Est/1stB 1998 • Visits by appt • Winemaker/viticulturist Chris Joubert • 2.5ha (shiraz) • 700cs 100% red • PO Box 26 Vlottenburg 7604 • Chris.Joubert@gilga.com • www.gilga.com

No longer at Overgaauw, Chris Joubert is able to concentrate his considerable talent on the own-label, Gilga. Besides building a cellar, he is pleased with the progress of his 7000 shiraz vines, now trellised and due for a maiden harvest next year; cab vines to follow. Having positioned Gilga as a top-end producer, he delayed the release of the 05, citing the need for oak to balance what he describes as a highly concentrated vintage.

★★★★☆ **Syrah** Last ed, youthful **04** showed densely fruited, compact style; tight but supple tannins, weighty, persistent finish. Balance, concentration & ample oaking (18 mths) for grand evolution in bottle.

★★★★ **Amurabi** Serious **05** with gravitas, blending shiraz with 17% cab & dash grenache; aromas of exotic flowers & blue/blackberry liqueur interwoven with spicy oak (60% new), which needs more time to integrate, now finishing rather tannic. *— JPf*

Glen Carlou
T 021-875-5528/96 • F 021-875-5314

Paarl • Est 1984 • 1stB 1988 • Tasting & sales Nov-Mar: Mon-Fri 8.30-4.45 Sat & Sun 10-3; Apr-Oct: Mon-Fri 8.30-4.45 Sat 10-3 • Fee R15 p/p, refundable on any purchase of R100 or more p/p • Closed Easter Fri/Sat/Sun, Dec 25/26 & Jan 1; phone ahead on other pub hols • Cellar tours by appt • Zen Restaurant Tue-Fri 11-3 Sat 11-2 (see Eat-out section) • Gifts • Conferences • Fine art gallery (book ahead for guided tour) • Owner The Hess Group (Switzerland) • Cellarmaster David Finlayson • Winemaker Arco Laarman & Gielie Beukes (2000/2006) • Viticulturist Marius Cloete (2000) • 75ha (cab, pinot, shiraz, chard) • 8-900t/65 000cs 60% red 40% white • PO Box 23 Klapmuts 7625 • welcome@glencarlou.co.za • www.glencarlou.co.za

The Hess Group, Swiss owners of this top-notch Paarl winery, have altered and renovated its various facilities so that they're of a piece, allowing visitors an holistic experience. Pairing the wine-tasting and buying – wines from Hess farms in Argentina, Australia and California are available alongside the local range – is something for foodies: the new restaurant, Zen (in harmony with the style of the garden), offers lunch with a local flavour five days a week in high season. Signature dish from chef Neil Smit is a retro favourite: a prawn and avo salad with lemon mayo. Nothing retro, however, about works from the Hess Art Collection which are on exhibition in the Glen Carlou gallery, with a new African artist featured at the start of each year.

★★★★★ **Gravel Quarry Cabernet Sauvignon** Powerful yet streamlined red named for old quarry found by pvs owner Walter Finlayson when he bought the farm in the '80s. **05** layered with dense dark fruit, violets & cedar. 18 mths new Fr oak well integrated, supportive. Built for a decade, as was concentrated **04**.

★★★★ **Pinot Noir 06** (★★★★) not as impressive as **05**. Slender, with earthy red berry notes & bright acidity, lacks complexity & concentration. Dry, no-nonsense tannins demand time to harmonise. 10 mths Fr oak, some new.

★★★★★ **Syrah 06** (★★★★) a shade off the mark. Same touches mourvèdre & viognier but chunkier, more austere, tannins masking dark fruit, liquorice & sweetly spiced opulence. Allow more time to harmonise. **05** was deep & brooding, in similar style to **04**, our 2006 Wine of the Year.

★★★★ Grand Classique Classically styled red from five bdx varieties, cab-led since **03**. Inviting cedar, cassis/cinnamon & polished leather in understated **04**. Fruit & refined tannins mask 14.5% alc, contribute to vg development potential. 24 mths Fr oak, 40% new.

★★★★☆ Quartz Stone Chardonnay 06 complex & focussed, 11 mths new Fr oak adding toasted nut nuance to lithe streamlined form (13.5 alc). Abundant lime & quince marmelade, marzipan & peach flavours threaded with trademark tangy acidity.

★★★★ Chardonnay 06's (**★★★★**) 14.2% alc too bold for latent citrus fruit, overall glassful perhaps not as complex as pvs. Possibly only needs time to show same form as **05** & pvs. 10 mths mainly new Fr oak.

Cabernet Sauvignon NEW **★★★★** With 13.8% alc, subtle fruit, dry yet chalky finish, **06** most classically styled of all the reds. Restrained core of cassis, dark choc & cedar ex-14 mths oak (Fr/Am 60/40), sappy, fine tannins; combines elegance with ageability. **Zinfandel ★★★★** Step up from last-tasted **01** (**★★★☆**) to sumptuous **05**, brimming with brambles, sweet tobacco & cloves; tempered by ripe yet firm tannin & spicy oak (16 mths, Am/Fr, Am new). Accessible now with hearty fare. **Tortoise Hill Red** 🍷 **★★★★** Friendly cab-led blend; juicy, balanced & supple. **05** a great fireside drink. 14 mths Fr/Am oak. **Tortoise Hill White** 🍷 **★★★** **07** tangy, al fresco-styled blend from sauv (79%) plus dashes viognier & chard. Discontinued: **Chardonnay Reserve**. — *MW*

Glenelly Estate 🍷 NEW
T 021-809-6440 • F 021-809-6448

Stellenbosch • Est/1stB 2003 • Visits from May/Jun 2008; phone for details • Owner May-Eliane de Lencquesaing • Winemaker Stéphane de Saint Salvy (Jul 2006) • Viticulturist Heinrich Louw (2003) • 47ha (cab, merlot, petit v, shiraz, chard) • ±100t/7500cs (2007 vintage) 100% red • PO Box 1079 Stellenbosch 7599 • info@glenelly.co.za

Bringing a wealth of knowledge and cachet to the Cape is May-Eliane de Lencquesaing, grande dame of the Bordeaux wine industry and former owner of classed growth Pichon Longueville Comtesse de Lalande. Since acquiring Glenelly in 2003, she's restored the manor house, planted 47ha of new vines (another 7 planned) and built a 600-ton gravity cellar, due for completion early this year. One of their strengths, reports winemaker Stéphane de Saint Salvy (also from Bordeaux), was to have distribution in place before establishing the winery. Their red blend is available locally and exported to several countries via commercial agreements with Pichon Longueville.

★★★★ Glenelly Hill Cab leads **03** maiden with dollops merlot, shiraz (28/24), dash pinotage; grapes ex Smnsberg, Agulhas. Restrained fruit plays second fiddle to savoury/mineral notes, notable tannins; yet mid-palate is well fleshed. 14.5% alc a tad warming. One to watch. — *CvZ*

■ **Glenhurst** *see Quoin Rock Winery*

Glenview Wines
T 021-438-1080 • F 021-438-3167

Cape Town • Est/1stB 1998 • Closed to public • Owner Robin Marks • Winemaker Reino Kruger & Neil Hawkins (white, red; both consultants) • 7 000cs 50% red 50% white • PO Box 32234 Camps Bay 8040 • bayexport@kingsley.co.za • www.glenview.co.za

Glenview's Chenin, a restaurateur's favourite, so impressed a recent French visitor to Cape Town that he later emailed Robin Marks to ask for more. 'I'm so proud of its quality,' says Robin M, who's discontinued the Shiraz to concentrate on it and the Merlot.

Merlot ★★★ 05 (sample) definite notch up; choc plum & herbs; slightly wild character with gd mouthfeel; Sbosch vyds. Interesting. **Chenin Blanc ★★★** Charming **07**, quite rich & juicy with mineral & touch pineapple; fruit from Paarl. Discontinued: **Shiraz**. — *JP*

GlenWood
T 021-876-2044 · **F** 021-876-3338

Franschhoek · Est/1stB 2000 · Tasting & sales Mon-Fri 11-4; Sat/Sun (Sep-Apr only) 11-3; pub hols (except Christian holy days) 11-3; fee R20 · Tours daily 11; fee R30 · Owner Alastair G Wood · Winemaker/viticulturist DP Burger (May 1992) · 23ha (merlot, shiraz, chard, sauv, semillon) · ±150t/6 000cs own label 30% red 70% white · PO Box 204 Franschhoek 7690 · info@glenwoodvineyards.co.za · www.glenwoodvineyards.co.za

GlenWood's credo of 'simple, natural, quality' pervades everything that happens on the farm and in the winery, assures DP Burger. Vine plantings are now complete, and a quarter of the property is dedicated to fynbos. Semillon, which has deep roots in Franschhoek, is being reintroduced this year and looks set to follow in the successful trail of the chardonnays.

★★★★ Chardonnay Vignerons Selection Bold, big **06** follows showy trend set by **05** (★★★★★) & pvs. Toasted nut with oak & hints of lime; strong impression of sweetness from 14% alc. 11 mths new Fr oak. Gd food wine.

Merlot ★★★ Dry tobacco leaf aromas, with toffee nuances on **06**. Impression of sweetness, though tannins dry throughout, warm 14.5% alc. 30% new oak, 10 mths. **Shiraz ★★★★** Tasted last ed, fleshy **05** offered combo dark fruit, roasted spice & fully integrated oak. **Syrah Vignerons Selection NEW ★★★** No machines used: foot crushed, hand bottled. **05** stewed fruit & boiled sweets, cassis flavours well integrated with wood, tight tannins will soften in 2/3 yrs. All-new Fr oak. **Unwooded Chardonnay ★★★** Floral & sherbet nuances to light, friendly picnic-style **07**. **Sauvignon Blanc ★★★** Green apple intro to uncomplicated **07** (sample), firmly structured, clean, refreshing. *— MM*

■ **Goats do Roam** *see The Goats do Roam Wine Company*

Goede Hoop Estate
T 021-903-6286 · **F** 021-906-1553

Stellenbosch · Est 1928 · 1stB 1974 · Tasting & sales Mon-Thu 10-4 Fri 10-3 · Open pub hols · Tours, meals & refreshments by appt · BYO picnic · Conferencing for max 20 · Owner Pieter Bestbier · Winemaker Carel Hugo (Dec 2002) · Viticulturist Johan de Beer (Apr 2000) · 80ha (cab, carignan, malbec, merlot, pinotage, shiraz, chard, chenin, sauv) · 11 000cs + 90-100 000litres bulk 91% red 9% white · PO Box 25 Kuils River 7579 · goede@adept.co.za · www.goedehoop.co.za

'We're improving our white wines quite dramatically,' says Pieter Bestbier, citing several recent accolades including a nomination for WOM's Wine of the Year. Another source of satisfaction is that all the reds currently on the market are older than five years. Some shiraz was picked last season at higher-than-usual sugar, so they hauled Bestbier Snr (and his trusty notes) out of retirement and made a barrel of port.

★★★★ Cabernet Sauvignon 00 nose more open than pvs but gd maturation prospects, thanks to fine structure & balanced tannin. 2nd/3rd fill Fr, 18 mths. This, following wines, not retasted.

★★★★ Merlot-Cabernet Sauvignon Aka 'Vintage Rouge'. Charming & delicious **01**, juicy, ripe & accessible with plenty to give. 19 mths 2nd/3rd fill barrels.

Pinotage ★★★★ 02 less full-figured than pvs, vegetal touch with savoury undertone. 8 mths oak, 2nd/3rd fill. **Shiraz ★★★★** Stylish **02**, aromatic combo black fruit & white pepper, savoury spicing; quite chewy/youthful, might have softened since review. **Domaine ★★★ 02** lightish unwooded cab/carignan blend (53/47). Redcurrants & cherries, accessible weave, savoury & peppery fruit. **Chardonnay ★★★★** Subtle wood presence in **05** gives appealing nutty citrus effect; rounded bonhomie thanks to grain sugar. 8 mths Fr wood, 20% unoaked. **Sauvignon Blanc ★★★★** Exciting combo of minerality & juiciness on **06**, pungent capsicum/green fig whiffs, zesty nettle flavour. *— IvH*

■ **Goede Moed** *see Baarsma Wine Group*
■ *Goedgenoegen* *see Baarsma Wine Group*

Goedvertrouw Estate

T 028-284-9769 • **F** 028-284-9769

Bot River (see Elgin/Walker Bay map) ▪ Est 1990 ▪ 1stB 1991 ▪ Visits by appt ▪ Home-cooked meals & accommodation by appt ▪ Play area for children ▪ Farm produce ▪ Small conferences ▪ Conservation area ▪ Small art gallery ▪ Owner/winemaker/viticulturist Elreda Pillmann ▪ 8ha (cab, pinot, chard, sauv) ▪ 70% red 30% white ▪ PO Box 37 Bot River 7185 ▪ goedvertrouwestate@telkomsa.net

Elreda Pillmann must be one of the few winemakers who never touches the stuff, but she remains determined to prove her late husband right: that with minimum intervention and organic principles you can make a truly honest wine that will stand SA proud. She hopes her Pinot will one day be that wine.

Cabernet Sauvignon ★★★ Native yeast fermented (as are stablemates); **06** similar to pvs but purer fruit, interesting baked bread aroma, riper tannins; still needs yr/2 to marry. **Pinot Noir ★★** Elegant **04**, now bottled, fragrant mineral bouquet, hints game & damp earth, attractively restrained 12.7% alc. Yr older oak. **Pardoemps ★★★** Onomatopoeic name a favourite of the late Arthur Pillmann's for once-off **03** blend pinot, pinotage, cab (50/25/25). Like all Gvtrw wines, artisanal, sometimes quirky, with a loyal following. **Chardonnay ★★★** None since **01**. **Sauvignon Blanc ★★★** Low-ish alcs on **05** (11.4%) & **06** (12.5%); former more 'dry white' than sauv, latter more zesty, blackcurrant & fig. Individual, for early drinking. *— CvZ*

Goedverwacht Estate

T 023-616-3430 • **F** 023-616-2073

Robertson ▪ 1stB 1994 ▪ Tasting & sales Mon-Fri 8.30-4.30 Sat 10-2 ▪ Closed Easter Fri/Sun, Dec 25 & Jan 1 ▪ Tours by appt ▪ Snacks served with wine tasting; also BYO picnic ▪ Owner Jan du Toit & Sons (Pty) Ltd ▪ Winemaker Henry Conradie ▪ Viticulturist Jan du Toit, advised by Francois Viljoen ▪ 110 ha (cab, merlot, shiraz, chard, colombard, sauvignon) ▪ 1 500 tons 40 000 cs own label 43% red 50% white 7% rosé ▪ Exported as Soek die Geluk & Ama Ulibo ▪ PO Box 128 Bonnievale 6730 ▪ goedverwachtestate@lando.co.za ▪ www.goedverwacht.co.za

After completing his second harvest here, winemaker Henry Conradie is happy with the results in the winery, and with the effect that the new entrance (which 'could put Sun City to shame') had on the municipality. Bulldozers came to break it down, but the whole farm sat on the wall until the authorities relented. The allegedly troublesome entrance has already lured many more visitors down to the cellar, where one of the most intimate and hospitable experiences is promised.

★★★★ Triangle Friendly **05** (**★★★**), blend cabs s/f & merlot (down to 4% from pvs 49%), gently rounded, dark berry & plum, ultra-soft tannins. Misses seriousness, structure of refined **04**. 14 mths mainly Fr oak.

★★★★ Maxim Chardonnay `NEW` Pricey addition to range, stylishly presented. **06** generously proportioned; sweet peach, well oaked; musters some elegance too. Fermented/aged 7 mths new Fr oak.

> **Shiraz Rosé** ☺ 🗐 **★★★ 07** delicious strawberry-tinged quaffer. Red-wine aroma & weight with white-wine freshness, just off-dry. **Crane White Colombar** ☺ 🗐 **★★☆** Juicy, limy **07**, with mouthwatering fruit acid.

Maxim Cabernet Sauvignon ★★★★ 05 not ready. **04** last ed was suave & stylish, with structure to suggest ageing for gd few yrs. **03** (**★★★**) VDG. **Crane Red Merlot ★★** Soft **06** boneless style, some gentle plum & winegum flavours. **Acre of Stone Shiraz ★★★☆ 06** not ready; last-tasted **05** intriguing black choc, bramble & liquorice bouquet, well-judged oak & silky flavours. **Great Expectations Chardonnay ★★★** Fat **07**, juicy & peachy; subtle oak influence (staves 3 mths), slight sweetness on finish. NE. **The Good Earth Sauvignon Blanc** 🗐 **★★☆** Bouncy **07**, more 'dry white' than sauv, but gd fresh acidity. **Suiderkruis Vonkel ★★** Lively carbonated sparkler. **06** just off-dry, tangy greengage flavours. *— IvH*

■ **Goeie Tye** *see* Rooiberg Winery

■ *Gôiya* see Namaqua Wines

Golden Kaan [NEW]

Est/1stB 2002 ▪ Tasting Mon-Sun 9-4.30 Sales 9-5 Tours 10, 10.30 & 2.30 (Eng), 10/15 (German) ▪ KWV Emporium ▪ marketing@goldenkaan.com ▪ www.goldenkaan.com

This brand, KWV's 50/50 joint venture with German wine company Racke, boasts market leadership in Germany and representation in Europe, Russia and the US. The three-tiered range is now also available locally.

Golden Kaan range

Cabernet Sauvignon ★★★ 04 was ripe & cassis-infused; ready to drink after 9 mths seasoned Fr oak. This, merlot & shiraz tasted mid-2006. **Merlot** ★★★ Medium-weight 04 lightly oaked, cassis & raspberry rich. **Pinotage** ★★★ Sweet fruit/gentle oak dance well together on soft, very gulpable 05. **Shiraz** ★★★ 04 forthcoming with luscious red berries, spice. 9 mths Fr oak. **Pinotage Rosé** ★★★ Ultimate picnic enjoyment delivered by 07's subtle savoury aroma, dense blueberry/strawberry palate. Dry & refreshing. **Chardonnay** ✓ ★★★☆ 06 raises the bar, is rich & beguiling with oodles pear/citrus, gentle oaking. Classiest in the range. **Sauvignon Blanc** ★★★ 07 light bodied; round & attractive tropical quaffer.

Golden Kaan Reserve range

★★★★ **Winemaker's Reserve Cabernet Sauvignon** 03 tasted pvs ed; had cassis/raspberry depth, cigar box nuances ex serious oaking (26 mths new Fr). Structured for 3-7 yrs cellaring.

Reserve Selection Cabernet Sauvignon ★★★☆ Intensely toned, pure fruited 04 seamless & deep, attractively smoky; Yr Fr oak ensuring ageability. **Reserve Selection Shiraz** ★★★☆ 04's herby edge contrasts with its bacon savouriness; has grip yet is accessible. **Winemaker's Reserve Chardonnay** ★★★★ 100% new oak ensures 06 (★★★★) is ultra rich, more satisfying than pvs 03 (★★★★). Pear, almond, marzipan bouquet follow through to palate, marry with zesty lemon acidity, buttery notes for added complexity. Should improve 3-5 yrs aging. **Reserve Selection Sauvignon Blanc** ★★★☆ Flinty, grassy-toned 07 very rewarding, classy; touch sugar helps crisp acidity to integrate, adds breadth & depth. *— RP*

■ **Golden Triangle** see Stellenzicht Vineyards
■ **Gordon's Bay** see Zidela Wines

Goudini Wines

T 023-349-1090 ▪ F 023-349-1988

Rawsonville (see Worcester map) ▪ Est 1948 ▪ Tasting & sales Mon-Fri 8-5 Sat 9.30-12.30 ▪ Closed Easter Fri-Mon, Dec 25/26, Jan 1 ▪ Coffee shop ▪ Conferences ▪ Gifts ▪ Owner 40 members ▪ Cellarmaster Hennie Hugo (Dec 1984) ▪ Senior winemaker Dominique Waso (Oct 2001), with Ruaan Terblanche & Samuel Viljoen (Nov 2001/Sep 2004) ▪ Viticulturist Hendrik Myburgh (Nov 2001, consultant) ▪ 1 040ha (merlot, ruby cab, shiraz, chard, chenin, semillon) ▪ 20 000t/33 000cs own label 45% red 45% white 10% rosé ▪ PO Box 132 Rawsonville 6845 ▪ winesales@goudiniwine.co.za ▪ www.goudiniwine.co.za

The plan's coming together: 'A couple of years of putting new technology like thermoflash into the cellar is giving us softer, fruitier reds,' says cellarmaster Hennie Hugo. He refers with equal satisfaction to a three-year project to trellis for better fruit exposure and more effective leaf function.

Reserve range

Ruby Cabernet ★★★☆ Last ed 04 was a generous varietal expression of sweet ripe plum with well massaged tannins/oak, some new. Showed typical stalk & thatch varietal character, too. Discontinued: **Chardonnay Barrel Fermented**.

Goudini range

> **Blanc de Noir** ☺ ★★ **07** pretty salmon-pink party wine, brimming with strawberry fruit, clean, dry finish. **Brut Sparkling** ☺ ★★★ **NV** bubbly from sauv. Latest crisp & fresh, appealing dry finish offset by creamy mousse.

Pinotage ★★★★ Last ed **05** had plums, choc-banana wiffs, agile tannins; demonstrated all the style which earned it Concours Mondial gold. Yr oak, some new, 10% Am. **Shiraz** ✓ ★★★★ Smoky, cigarbox aromas on briefly staved (6 mths) **05**, followed by rich, plummy fruit, balanced tannins; a fine food accompaniment. **Ruby Cabernet-Merlot** ★★★ Tasted last ed, **05** offered thatch & lavender tinged with choc-toffee, healthy tannins added interest. **Unwooded Chardonnay** ★★★ **06** brimmed with tropical fruit last ed. Bold 14.4% alc was well tucked in. **Chenin Blanc** ★★ **07** understated poolside quaffer with friendly wafts of pear & apple. **Sauvignon Blanc** ★★★ **07** shy, grassy nose followed by crisp green apple flavours; uncomplex & unchallenging. **Natural Sweet** ★★★ Pvsly tasted **06**, from chenin, was engaging, had bright fruit, zippy acidity, charming honeyed tones. **Ruby Cabernet-Merlot Semi-Sweet** ★★★ Oak staves add a extra dimension to 60/40 blend; warm, spicy nose & a splash of sugar ensure **06** slips down easily. **Hanepoot** ★★★★ Muscat & honeysuckle flavours did the business for luxuriously scented, fortified **05** last ed. **Port** ★★★★ **04** tempts with rich layers prunes & pipe tobacco, dry & dusty farewell. A contemplative fireside warmer.

Umfiki range

> **Merlot** ☺ ★★★ Thumbs up for friendly dry red; dark mocha-choc wafts, soft & ripe cherry flavours. **Sauvignon Blanc** ☺ ★★★ Soft, leafy scents introduce crisp summer fruit-salad flavours; a happy tipple.

Cabernet Sauvignon ★★★ Smooth, berry toned easy-drinker at a wallet-pleasing price. Tasted mid-2006. **Dry White** ★★ Latest fresh & cheerful, deftly controlled acidity, crisp pineapple flavour. Discontinued: **Pinotage-Cinsaut, Clairette Blanche-Colombar.** All **NV**. – *DB*

■ **Goudriaan** *see Groupe LFE South Africa*

Goudveld Winery
T 057-352-8650 • F 057-352-8650

Free State (see Northern Cape map) • Tasting & sales Mon-Fri 8-6 Sat by appt • Tours on request • Owner See intro • Winemaker/viticulturist Merkil Alers (1985), advised by Ian Sieg • 15ha • 120t/1 000cs own label • PO Box 1091 Welkom 9460 • isieg@vodamail.co.za

With some three decades of experience in summer-rainfall areas, consultant Ian Sieg has a vested interest in weather patterns. 'Soon it'll be a summer rainfall area in the Western Cape – and we'll switch to winter,' is his dry prediction. Developments at Goudveld, including a change of ownership, have been delayed. In the meantime, Sieg continues teaching Viticulture & Oenology at the Central University of Technology.

■ **Goue Vallei** *see Citrusdal Cellars*

■ **Gouverneurs** *see Groot Constantia Estate*

Graça

Vinho verde-inspired, lightly spritzy sippers, the original white version still SA's top-selling cork-closed wine. By Distell; exported as Blouberg.

Graça ★★★ Zesty crowd-pleaser with lively petillance. Mainly sauv & sem; low 11.8% alc. Great with seafood & al fresco-style fare. **Rosé** ★★ Crisp, cheerful quaffer, now featuring semillon in 4-way blend. Low in alc (10.7%) with fresh raspberry appeal. Both **NV**; WO W Cape. – *MW*

Graceland Vineyards
T 021-881-3121/021-881-3394 • F 021-881-3341

Stellenbosch ▪ Est 1997 ▪ 1stB 1998 ▪ Tasting & sales Mon-Fri 9-5 ▪ Fee R30 ▪ Closed pub hols ▪ Two-bedroom B&B + self-catering vyd cottage ▪ Owner Paul & Susan McNaughton ▪ Winemaker/viticulturist Susan McNaughton (2001) ▪ 10ha (cab, merlot, shiraz) ▪ 60 t/4 300cs 100% red ▪ PO Box 7066 Stellenbosch 7599 ▪ graceland@iafrica.com ▪ www.gracelandvineyards.com

This boutique cellar's husband and winemaking wife team make only red wines, and they're happy to report that growth is steady, with their wines now listed in 35 leading restaurants in 10 countries. As they concentrate on improving their wines, Paul McNaughton gears up for a year of 'living with reduced yields'.

★★★★ **Cabernet Sauvignon** Traditional fermentation in open kuipe with punch downs, full malo in wood (Fr, 30% new, 20 mths). **05** shows sappy cassis in chewy, well textured mouthful; 13.9% alc nicely integrated.

★★★★ **Three Graces** Best barrels of cab, merlot & shiraz selected at 20 mths for flagship, then blended & further matured 3 mths in new oak. **05** (40/30/30 blend) restrained, judiciously fruited cab backbone & extra-fine tannins give super structure for longevity. 14.5% alc. No **04**.

Merlot ★★★★ Meaty **05** lanced by hot 15% alc mouthfeel, not as elegant as SAA-selected **04** (★★★★), which boasted bright plum notes & silky tannins. Latest 20 mths Fr casks, 30% new. **Shiraz** ★★★★ Nutty aromas of **05** lead to lovely plum fruit hung on gravelly tannic lattice, carries evident 14.5% alc well. 16 mths Fr wood, 30% new. **Amazing Grace** NEW ★★★☆ Quirky dessert wine in fetching package: shiraz juice run off at crush, native yeast ferment before fortification & 16 mths oak, 30% new. **05** golden, oxidative & sweet. 15% alc. Just 25cs x 500ml. *— DS*

Graham Beck Wines
T 023-626-1214, 021-874-1258 • F 023-626-5164, 021-874-1712

Franschhoek/Robertson (see Franschhoek map) ▪ Est 1983 ▪ 1stB 1991 ▪ ISO 14001 certified ▪ Robertson Estate: Tasting & sales Mon-Fri 9-5 Sat & 1st Sun of mth 10-3 ▪ Closed Easter Fri/Sun, Dec 25/26 & Jan 1 ▪ Tours by appt ▪ Franschhoek Estate: Tasting & sales Mon-Fri 9-5 Sat 10-4 ▪ Closed Easter Fri/Sun, Dec 25/26 & Jan 1 ▪ Tours by appt ▪ Owner Graham Beck ▪ Cellarmaster Pieter Ferreira (Aug 1990) ▪ Winemaker Robertson Estate: Irene Waller (Dec 2004); Franschhoek Estate: Erika Obermeyer (Jan 2005) ▪ Viticulturist Marco Ventrella (Sep 2004) ▪ Robertson Estate: 173ha (cab, merlot, pinot, sangiovese, shiraz, chard, viognier) ▪ 1 500t ▪ 45% red 20% white 35% MCC ▪ Franschhoek Estate: 162ha (cabs s/f, merlot, petit v, pinotage, shiraz, sauv, viognier) ▪ 1 200 tons ▪ PO Box 724 Robertson 6705, PO Box 134 Franschhoek 7690 ▪ market@grahambeckwines.co.za ▪ www.grahambeckwines.com

No avenue for increasing the quality of grapes and wines, high-tech or low, goes unexplored in the Graham Beck operation. Satellite information improves vineyard blocks, while winery personnel gain international experience abroad. The winery can now take more whole-bunch grapes, and the bottling line will soon accommodate screwcaps. The not strictly vinous dimensions of the operation show the same dedication to quality. GBW is setting a benchmark in wine industry community upliftment, spearheading the establishment of a skills centre in Robertson. In the conservation sphere, where their efforts have already earned them Biodiversity Champion status, they are likewise acting as a collective catalyst for efforts in the area. Man-made beauty also gets a look-in with the new designer Franschhoek tasting and visitor centre.

Ultra Premium range

★★★★ **Coffeestone Cabernet Sauvignon** From Sbosch vyd, imposing, powerful **04** (14.7% alc) shows blackcurrant, herb aromas. Spice & tobacco reflect mostly new oak, as does big dry tannin jostling with juicy fruit & bright acidity - still v youthful.

★★★★ **The Old Road Pinotage** From old Fhoek vines. **03** still youthful; evolving varietal notes earth, strawberry, with acetone element. Elegant entry, dry but well-placed tannins supporting juicy fruit; tiny bitter hint adds to interest of long fruit-sweet finish. Yr new Fr/Am oak. EW.

★★★★ **The Joshua** Ultra-ripe, powerful 03 followed by somewhat toned-down 04 (★★★☆); disconcerting dank note on nose, but then well-knit & savoury with smooth tannin, modest flavour. 5% viognier well integrated, as is Fr/Am oak mix (35% new).

★★★★☆ **The Ridge Syrah** Icon wine named for its Rbtsn vyd. Full flavour of 03 (not retasted) held in place by elegant structure. 14 mths 60/40 new Am/Fr oak assists ageing potential. EW.

★★★★ **The Andrew** Bold, serious-minded 05 (no 04 made), cab-led with 4 other Bdx varieties; dominated in youth by lavish expensive oak (70% new) adding to spiciness & big tannins, but fruit likely to cope with this & 14.5% alc. Best hold few yrs first.

★★★★☆ **The William** Successful, harmonious blend cab (65%) & pinotage, 05 more light-footed than 14.6 alc implies, with lots of fresh, sweetly juicy fruit controlled by big, rather dry tannins. Young, needs gd few yrs. No 04 made.

★★★★ **Lonehill Chardonnay** Last tasted 05, from Rbtsn mountain vyd, had hazelnut, lime; lightly toasty oak on creamy, full-flavoured palate. Fermented/10 mths Fr oak, 80% new.

★★★★ **Pheasants' Run Sauvignon Blanc** Only samples tasted for many yrs: 07 looks promising as ever, with grassy pungency & passionfruit edge; powerful, bracing & dry, richly textured. From Dbnville, Darling fruit. These all WO Coastal, except where noted.

★★★★ **Rhona Muscadel** Like 02 (with mature terpene hint), 03 (★★★★) version of this elegant fortified muscat de F all grapey, flower-scented sweet charm - which no less delightful for its ultimate simplicity. Fresh, with lightish 16.2% alc. 500ml. Rbtsn. EW.

Super Premium range

★★★★ **Shiraz** 03 had dollops other varieties, last-tasted 04 (★★★☆) all ultra-ripe shiraz: big, fruity & chunky; acidic rather than fresh. 13 mths mostly Am oak.

★★★★ **Viognier** Deliciously vibrant 05, 06 sold out before we cld taste; now a promising 07 (ex-tank) with typical but restrained perfumed apricot aromas; powerful but fresh, partial wooding giving creaminess to texture. WO Robtsn. EW.

Cabernet Sauvignon ★★★★ Firm & serious, drily tannic 05 has pleasant lightish fruit coping well with power of 14.5% alc. 15 mths oak, 30% new. 04 not tasted. Various origins in range. This WO Sbosch. **Merlot** ★★★ Substantial juicy fruit on 05, but ungraceful dry tannic thrust & strong herbal edge. 14 mths oak, 30% new. WO Coastal. **Pinotage** ★★★ Provisional rating - ex-tank, 06 has ripe acetone aromas/flavours; sweet fruit but drily tough. WO Coastal. **Pinotage Rosé** NEW ▤ ★★☆ Pinotage gives earthy-raspberry character to crisp, dry 07. WO Rbtsn. **Chardonnay** ★★★★ Attractive nut, smoke & orange notes on easy-going but fresh, firm & creamy 06; well integrated supportive oak. From Rbtsn. **Sauvignon Blanc** ★★★★ Satisfyingly mixing tropical & greenpepper elements, 07 also fresh, well-textured (3 mths on lees adds some richness) & bone-dry. WO Coastal.

Premium range

Pinno Pinotage ★★★ Sample 05 promised to be particularly charming of unwooded & fruit-focused ptage, with gentle grip. **Cabernet Sauvignon-Merlot** NEW ★★★ These reds all tasted for last ed. Slightly lean, lightly wooded respectable 03 blend, with subdued fruitcake notes. EW. **Shiraz-Cabernet Sauvignon** ★★★ UK only. Pepper & soft plummy fruit in accessible 04; supportive tannins. **Railroad Red** ★★★★ Smoky, spicy, agreeable 05 blended 60/40 shiraz/cab. Juicy fruit well supported by gd tannin, lightly oaked. **Waterside Chardonnay** ★★★ Forward boiled-sweet charm on light-flavoured, boldy structured 07. **Chardonnay-Viognier** ★★★★ Last yr, vibrantly fresh 06 had 16% viognier adding fragrance, chard in charge of balanced structure. Discontinued: **Pinno Rosé**, **Pinno Chardonnay**.

Méthode Cap Classique range

★★★★ **Brut** Latest NV from equal own chard & Sbsch pinot lively, sophisticated & delicious as ever, with Marmite note on the nose & fresh apples everywhere, finishing green-apple crisp & dry.

★★★★☆ **Brut Blanc de Blancs** Amongst most respected & awarded bubbly labels. A little new oak (50% fermented in wood) adds to **03**'s richness, complexity, as does ±4 yrs on lees. Notes of brioche, spicy citrus, strawberry & apple. Deeply refreshing; satisfying afterglow. EW.

★★★★ **Brut Rosé** Exquisite pinky gold rather than rose-coloured, unique in SA in pinot (80%) being crushed with chard as grapes. Subtle, scented raspberry, with flair & finesse, long dry finish. — *TJ*

Grande Provence

T 021-876-8600 • **F** 021-876-8601

Franschhoek • Est 1694 • Tasting & sales daily 10-6 • Fee R20 • Tours Mon-Fri 11 & 3 • 'The Restaurant' & 'The Owners Cottage' (see Stay-over & Eat-out sections) • Fine art exhibit in 'The Gallery' • Winemaker/viticulturist Jaco Marais (Oct 2003), advised by Kevin Watt (2001) • 22ha (cab, merlot, petit v, shiraz, chard, sauv) • 250t/25 000cs own labels 35% red 55% white 10% rosé • PO Box 102 Franschhoek 7690 • enquiries@grandeprovence.co.za • www. grandeprovence.co.za

A beautiful showcase of a winery in a superb setting, Grande Provence also features a luxury hotel and restaurant, the former frequented in the last year by the likes of Prince Edward and Jude Law. The restaurant has a new chef, Peter Tempelhoff, straight from Automat in London, and their art gallery showcases some of SA's best contemporary artists (recent exhibits included Christo Coetzee and sculptor Angus Taylor). On the wine side, they were recently to present their flagship red blend, named Angelus, as the guide went to press.

Grande Provence Premier range

★★★★ **Cabernet Sauvignon 05** not ready for tasting; last ed, **04** was seamless, well constructed & elegantly fleshed with a pronounced minty tone. 15 mths new Fr barrels.

★★★★ **Shiraz** No **05**, **06** unready. **04**'s savoury & aromatic styling mid-2006 won us over, as did its sweet-fruited finish, lavish vanilla spice. 15 mths 85/15 Fr/Am oak.

Chardonnay ★★★★ Focused, well-made **05** epitomises chard expression: bruised apple, some nutty notes, well-integrated oak (Yr Fr, 60% new). Rich & complex. Takes step up from **04** (★★★☆). **Sauvignon Blanc** Previewed **07** (★★★) tart, limy with clean, zesty palate wakeup call. Shade off the rousing, athletic **06** (★★★★) version, from cool Elim vyds.

Angels Tears Collection

Pink ☺ ★★☆ **NV** off-dry quaffer showing blackcurrants, fruit pastilles. Weighty yet vibrantly alive.

Red ★★ Smoky & red fruits in a lean style; cab, merlot & smidgen shiraz savoury. **NV**. **Sauvignon Blanc** ★★★ Last ed, **06** was supple, with leafy freshness, hint of gooseberry, smooth lemony finish. **White** ★★ 50/50 chenin/muscat d'A; crisp, textured, with hanepoot adding grapey fullness, 14.5g/l RS a sweet lift in its tail. **NV**. All in this range WO W Cape. — *RP*

Grand Mousseux

Anytime, anywhere non-vintage carbonated bubbly by Distell.
Vin Doux ★★ Fresh, floral, frothy summer sparkler for the sweeter tooth. — *MW*

Grangehurst Winery

T 021-855-3625 • **F** 021-855-2143

Stellenbosch (see Helderberg map) • 1stB 1992 • Tasting & sales Mon-Fri 9-4 Sat, Sun & pub hols 'please phone' 10-4 • Self-catering guest cottage • Owner Grangehurst Winery (Pty) Ltd • Winemaker Jeremy Walker, with Gladys Brown (1992/2002) • Viticulturist Viti consultant Thys Greeff • ±14ha (cab, merlot, mourvèdre, petit v, pinotage, shiraz) • 80t/5 000cs 90% red 10% rosé • PO Box 206 Stellenbosch 7599 • winery@grangehurst.co.za • www.grangehurst.co.za

The light, quaffing Rosé that Jeremy Walker initially produced for home consumption is now available under the Grangehurst label, to be enjoyed as an aperitif before moving on to its

fine cultivars deserve nurturing

With variable settings for red or white wine, electronic temperature control and UV Protection, the Samsung Wine Chiller is the contemporary solution to the classic art of wine.

www.samsung.co.za

Michael Back, proprietor of **Backsberg**, leaves his 'carbon neutral' footprints on the upper reaches of the Simonsberg farm. The first wine producer in South Africa – and one of only three in the world – to gain carbon neutral status, Back believes each generation is the custodian of the land for a limited time only. His farsightedness has already seen several plant species saved from extinction: 10% of the farm has been set aside to preserve the endangered fynbos biome. Sequestration solutions include a greening programme at nearby Klapmuts Village.

Turn new money into old money.

Viticulturist son **Victor Sperling** (left), **Inge Kotze**, project co-ordinator of the BWI, patriarch '**Spatz**' **Sperling**, marketer daughter **Nora Thiel** and a posse of farm dogs take a stroll on a part of the Delheim property left for the fynbos to re-establish itself after a fire razed the pine plantation. The nature-loving Sperlings have been committed to protecting the environment for decades – they're BWI members and farm sustainably within IPW guidelines.

Chris Baker

Farm Specialist

ell: 083 407 5024| Email: chrisbaker@remaxoaktree.co.za

Want to live in the Winelands?

If you can afford to do it...
You can't afford not to do it!

osition Position Position   P.O.A

/ww.remaxoaktree.co.za

We keep good company.

Wine Cellar is passionate about identifying, acquiring and
cellaring South African wines with investment potential. For more
information on our current and back vintages of South Africa's

The rugged terrain around Calitzdorp encompasses three biomes –
fynbos, thicket and succulent Karoo (a biodiversity hotspot with 92
Red List species) – and houses more plant species than are found in
the whole of Europe. Boplaas Family Vineyards channel part of their
export earnings into protecting endangered plant species on 2 200ha
of pristine veld, acquired by owner and Cape Wine Master **Carel Nel**,
here surveying the land from a vantage point on the Kleinberg. Boplaas'
protected area falls within the sprawling Rooiberg Conservancy, of
which Nel is chairman.

Eco-friend **Mossie Basson** spreads the conservation message to staff at **Graham Beck**'s Robertson farm, where vast tracts of land have been set aside for a conservancy, including a significant portion of endangered Breede sand fynbos. (The reserve covers the eastern slopes of the Rooiberg in the background, to give you some perspective of the scale.) Stocked with game and with the condition of the veld restored, this ongoing project is managed by Basson, the resident gamekeeper.

DELI
T 021 8844 303

BUTCHERY
T 021 8844 206

BISTRO,
RECEPTIONS
& CONFERENCES
T 021 8844 208

J.

Joostenberg

KLEIN JOOSTENBERG FARM
R304, Muldersvlei , Western Cape, South Africa
Deli: 021 8844303; Butchery: 021 8844206;
Bistro, Receptions & Conference: 021 8844208
Website: www.joostenberg.com

THE ULTRA
winebox

Why buy 12 bottles of the same wine, when you could choose any 12 wines (or more) and still pay the case lot price per bottle?

ANY MIXED CASE OF WINE AT CASE LOT PRICES

EXCLUSIVE

It's the best way to buy wine.
Drink wine? Think Ultra.
Toll free: 0800 00 44 14.

GO Advertising 52187

companion reds. Mantra of the latter is 'traditional, unhurried', so it's no surprise that the wines released last year were of the 01 vintage. They're now reaching the US, where Jeremy W's new agent received a fillip from a 92-pt Robert Parker rating for the Nikela **00**. New importers in Sweden, Belgium and Ireland are spreading the G-word, as are Vins du Monde in France. Informal weekend tastings are on the cards at the cellar, but in the interim visitors are invited to 'phone/take a chance and see if the family's in'.

★★★★☆ **Cabernet Sauvignon Reserve** Pvs mostly under CWG Auction label; **02** (★★★★) rich for lesser vintage, well structured. **03** less austere, but forceful, even richer: big 14.8% alc balanced by mouthfilling fruit. 3 prime Sbosch vyds, 25 mths Fr oak. To mature decade+. No newer vintages reviewed for this, wines below.

★★★★ **Pinotage** Serious version, with some cab - 11% in **01**. Gd varietal aromas lead to powerful, sweetly fruity flavours & big dry tannins. Impressive & rather tough when reviewed, should since have softened somewhat. Like others, fermented in open tanks, then to basket press.

★★★★☆ **Cabernet Sauvignon-Merlot** Authoritative & satisfying, sombrely rich fruit balanced with grippy tannins, savoury acid. Big, still-young **01** (72% cab), offering dusty, spicy blackcurrant, fits fine pattern. 14.2% alc. 2 yrs oak (mostly Fr) well integrated. Shd grow over a decade.

★★★★ **CWG Auction Reserve Cape Blend** Characterful, serious & long lived melding pinotage, cab & shiraz; **03** (★★★★★) near-equal mix, pinotage just ahead. Delicious & sweet fruited, supported by ripe tannins. Similarly flavourful **01**, elegant structure rhymes with slightly bigger cab portion (49%).

★★★★☆ **Nikela** Richly austere in youth, ageworthy **01** has intense, winning aromas & flavours, bdx-like & meaty on nose, some sweet jam on palate. Always ±50% cab, with merlot, pinotage - latter 31%. 22 mths oak, mostly Fr. Some will discern bitter note on finish.

★★★★ **Shiraz-Cabernet Sauvignon Reserve 03** brighter, sweeter, lighter-seeming, though more forthright tannins than pure Cab - 55% shiraz - generous, with sweet, spicy red fruit. Again, more than simply a stayer: shd develop. 28 mths mainly Fr oak.

Cabernet Sauvignon ★★★★ Restrained, austerely balanced **01**, dryly tannic but fruit lurks, perhaps to fully emerge in few yrs. 24 mths oak, mostly Fr. **Cape Rosé** ★★ Half pinotage, with merlot & shiraz; light berry & boiled sweet character on **05**. Lowish alc, dry. — *TJ*

■ **Griekwaland West Co-op** *see* Douglas Wine Cellar

■ *Groblershoop* *see* Oranjerivier Wine Cellars

■ *Groenekloof* *see* Neil Ellis Wines

Groenendal Farm
T 021-873-2286 · F 021-873-2268

Wellington (see Paarl map) ▪ *Est/1stB 2003* ▪ *Tasting & sales by appt Mon-Fri 9-5* ▪ *Fee R10* ▪ *Closed pub hols* ▪ *Tours by appt* ▪ *Owner Jan & Anita Bokdal* ▪ *Cellarmaster/winemaker Ettienne Malan* ▪ *4.6ha (mourvèdre, shiraz)* ▪ *30 t/1 900cs 100% red* ▪ *Export brands: Andreas & Ardens Andreu* ▪ *PO Box 892 Wellington 7650* ▪ *andreas@ezinet.co.za* ▪ *www.andreas.co.za*

The milestone 2007 crush was the first time their shiraz was made from 100% own grapes; it was also their first olive harvest. Ettienne Malan, ex-Rust en Vrede, is now making the wine, and a tasting room is coming in early 2008.

Andreas Shiraz ★★★★ Raspberry, nutmeg/black pepper notes, sweet fruited, raisiny, fine tannins, almond allspice finish **05**, MIWA DG. **Ardens Andreu** ★★ Coffee, mocha aromas on **04**, herbal farmyard whiffs, robust tannins. — *MF*

Groenland
T 021-903-8203 · F 021-903-0250

Stellenbosch ▪ *Est 1932* ▪ *1stB 1997* ▪ *Tasting & sales Mon-Fri 10-4 Sat & pub hols 10-1* ▪ *Fee for large groups* ▪ *Closed Easter Fri/Sun, Dec 25, Jan 1* ▪ *Meals for 20-60 by appt* ▪ *Tours by appt* ▪ *Conference & reception facilities* ▪ *Owner Kosie Steenkamp* ▪ *Winemaker Kosie*

Steenkamp, with Piet Steenkamp (1975/2001) · *Viticulturist Kosie & Piet Steenkamp* · *152ha (cab, merlot, pinotage, shiraz, chard, chenin, sauv)* · *1 200t/6 250cs own label + 75 000 blts* · *93% red 7% white* · *PO Box 4 Kuils River 7579* · *steenkamp@groenland.co.za* · *www. groenland.co.za*

More accolades for 'owner-etc' Kosie Steenkamp's Reserve range, with the Antoinette Marié named by Swissair judges as top Cape Blend Without Pinotage and by the Juliet Cullinan panel as Best Red Blend. A touch of white now offsets the farm's reds - last year marked the launch of the Steenkamps' maiden sauvignon.

Reserve range

★★★★ **Antoinette Marié** Equal cab, shiraz, merlot. Yr later, **04** drinking beautifully, worth higher rating: cassis-rich tones, shiraz showing in savoury finish, smooth-textured palate. Delicious.

Cabernet Sauvignon ★★★★ Retasting shows same brooding, dark-toned fruit, harmoniously balanced oaking, all Fr barrels. Designed for pleasurable enjoyment now & next few yrs.

Shiraz ★★★★ **04** retasted, more Rhône than New World: meaty, wild fruit, but main appeal is lively drinkability, appealing lift to the flavours. Am barrels. Yr new oak all these.

Groenland range

Cabernet Sauvignon ★★★ **05**'s cigarbox, brambleberry character more savoury than fruity, nicely so, with enough vitality to ensure appetite appeal, popularity. **Shiraz** ★★★★ Better than pvs, **05** pleases all senses: spice-toned plummy fruit, smoothly rounded texture, flavours that last. **Antoinette Marié** ★★★ Range focus on drinkability admirably achieved. Shiraz, cab blend, touch merlot in **05**, plenty spice, ripe fruit, with trademark fresh, amenable finish. All yr oaking, 40% new. **Sauvignon Blanc** NEW ★★★★ Garden-fresh greenpepper & lime fragrance, flavours & zinging acidity of **07** wets appetite, switches you into food mode. Admirable debut. **Port** ★★★ 'Cape Port' pvs ed. Lighter, drier (43g/l RS) than usual ports, **01** has brandied fruitcake aromas & flavours & flavours. From shiraz. 500ml. — *CR*

Groot Constantia Estate
T 021-794-5128 · F 021-794-1999

Constantia · Est 1685 · 1stB 1688 · Tasting & sales daily 9-6 (Oct-Apr) 9-5 (May-Sep) · Fee R22, R27 (tasting & tour) · Closed Easter Fri, Dec 25 & Jan 1 · Tours on hour (large groups plse book ahead), every hour 10-4; also 'theme' tours/tastings · Simon's at Groot Constantia Restaurant (T 021·794·1143); Jonkershuis Restaurant · Tour groups · Gift shop · Conferencing · Walks · Museum · Managed by Groot Constantia ('Section 21' company) · Winemaker Boela Gerber (Jan 2001), with Michelle Rhodes · Viticulturist Callie Bröcker, advised by Johan Pienaar (1996) · ±90ha (12 varieties,r/w) 458t/400 000 bottles 75% red 25% white. · Private Bag X1 Constantia 7848 · enquiries@grootconstantia.co.za · www.grootconstantia.co.za

Things are moving at this historic estate. Boela Gerber keeps expanding his red-wine capacity, enabling him to experiment more (he's particularly keen on varying length of skin contact during the fermentation process). He's also planting more pinotage - a variety he thinks has a great future in the Constantia Valley - and is experimenting with barrel-ageing small quantities of sauvignon and semillon-sauvignon. According to CE Jean Naudé, the results are 'amazing'. But then Naudé rates 2007 as a potentially spectacular year for Constantia whites, particularly sauvignon. Given two restaurants, the manor house and the gorgeous setting, there's even more reason to call here.

Gouverneurs range

★★★★ **Reserve** Flagship blend, **04** cab led (54% with merlot, cab f & malbec). Sensuous; mocha & spicy dark fruit flavours held by firm tannins, detailed pvs ed. Accessible, but will improve over next 5+ yrs. Swiss gold **03** as elegant.

★★★★ **Chardonnay** Huge whack of oak on **05** needing time to integrate (10 mths 60% new small Fr). Pvs ed noted weighty limpid gold, with ripe marmalade flavours beneath showy wood. Resolute textured tail. Sante Classic, JCWCA gold/'first'.

Discontinued: **Merlot**.

Groot Constantia range

★★★★ **Sauvignon Blanc** Pvs ed noted **06** as exuberantly herbaceous with trademark green fig, fresh & vibrant, some fruit depth to pleasing minerality.

★★★★ **Grand Constance** Flies flag for famous GC sweet muscats of yesteryear. Ochre **05** delineated by its delicacy; naartjie twist to sweet seduction. First **03** satin texture with spice/litchi wafts. Old oak fermented muscat de F, 18 mths. No **04**.

Cabernet Sauvignon ★★★★ 05, in mould of **04**, generously oaked & more leanly structured, herbal, than pvs; delicate raspberry fruits battle through hearty tannins. 14 mths 40% new Fr oak. **Merlot ★★★★** Ethereal violet scents tone nicely weighted restraint of **05. 04** smoky, plummy spiciness in structured ripe tannins. Small Fr cask, 40% new 15 mths. **Pinotage ★★★★** More serious since **04, 05** as attractively styled with sweet plum fruit couched in oak, yr 40% new Fr. IWC gold, Wine (**★★★★**). **Shiraz ★★★★ 05** earthy mulberry fruits touched with spice, as classically constructed as unshowy **03** (**★★★★**), exudes style. Yr 40% new Fr barrels. **Constantia Rood ★★★** Six variety ensemble led by merlot & cab. Now more serious; **05** good fruit & grip. 15 mths old Fr oak. **Blanc de Noir ★★★** All cab **07** onion-skin pink, simple red berry fruits, ends sweeter than 4.2g/l suggests. **Semillon-Sauvignon Blanc ★★★★** Bracing, grassy herbaceous **06**, with 60% dusty semillon, makes statement on entry but fades on finish; fine mineral acid backbone throughout. Not retasted this ed. SAA; VG; Sante Classic gold. **Cap Classique ★★★★** Last noted was a **NV (00)**; untasted successor due by Christmas 2007. **Muscat ★★★** Barrel fermented/aged red & white muscadel in simple, sweet (101g/l sugar) grapey style. **NV. Cape Ruby Port ★★★** Chunky **04**, sweet plum pudding notes shot with bracing spirit. Third each pinotage, touriga, shiraz blend. Discontinued: **Chardonnay**. — DS

■ **Grootdrink** *see Oranjerivier Wine Cellars*

Groot Eiland Winery

T 023-349-1140 • **F** 023-349-1801

Breedekloof (see Worcester map) ▪ Est 1962 ▪ 1stB 1980 ▪ Tasting & sales Mon-Fri 8-5 ▪ Tours by appt ▪ La Bri guest house (T 023-349-1547) ▪ Gifts ▪ Owner 30 members ▪ Winemaker Albertus Louw, with Lindi Kotzé & Christo Smit ▪ Viticulturist Johan Möller (2003, consultant) ▪ 1 000ha (cab, merlot, pinotage, shiraz, chard, chenin, colombard, sauv) ▪ 50 000cs own label 30% red 50% white 20% rosé ▪ PO Box 93 Rawsonville 6845 ▪ grooteiland@lando.co.za ▪ www.grooteiland.co.za

Groot Eiland and neighbouring Daschbosch have joined marketing forces under the banner of uniWines, which will now be handling both wineries' selling, locally and abroad. 'We want to give our buyers a one-stop opportunity to buy consistently good quality wines,' says winemaker Albertus Louw.

Limited Releases NEW

Merlot-Ruby Cabernet ★★★ Starbucks special with cappuccino notes & fruit muffin richness on **06. Shiraz-Pinotage ★★★ 06** invites with cedarwood fragrance & ripe fruit flavours, manicured tannins.

Groot Eiland Winery range

Cabernet Sauvignon ★★★ Earthy scents precede **06**, juicy berry fruit & twist of pepper, gd firm tannins. **Merlot ★★** Understatedly styled **06**, light colour belying gd, lingering dark choc flavours. **Pinotage ★★** Robust & spicy **06**, some floral notes, touch cherry, strong tannic finish. **Shiraz ★★★** Big & ripe **06**, spicy cherry fruit & extended conclusion. **Rosé Semi-Sweet ★★ 07** from shiraz; easy-drinking, uncomplicated semi-sweet patio wine. **Chardonnay ★★** Savoury intro to **07**, followed by green apple crispness. **Chenin Blanc ★★** Frisky **07**, brisk, clean pineapple scents & flavours. **Sauvignon Blanc ★★★** Lively **07** layered with everything you'd expect from variety: melon, greenpepper, grass & gooseberry. **Honigtraube ★★** Last ed **04** was supple, easy, with uncloying sweetness. No **05/6; 07** not ready. **Sparkling Brut** NEW **★★** Big, explosively fizzy **05**, redolent of vanilla biscuit, clean dry exit. **Hanepoot**

Jerepigo ★★★★ Beautifully balanced **06**, bottled sunshine slathered with honey; delightful all-year-round pudding wine.

Meander range

Merlot-Shiraz ★★ Replaces pvs 'Fruity Red'. Quaffable **06**, dusty notes to ripe plum flavours. **Chenin Blanc-Colombar** ★☆ 'Crisp Dry' pvs ed. **07** summertime blend, guava-scented, clean & yes, crisp.

Nuwehoop range NEW

Merlot ★ Undemanding braai slosher with earthy tone on **06**. **Blanc de Noir** ★★ **06** delicate pale salmon hue, dry, with lick of honey. **Chenin Blanc** ★★ Fresh fruit salad aromas & some pineapple notes on **07** relaxed fruity quaffer. **Colombar Semi-Sweet** ★☆ Dried grass notes on **06**, undemanding poolside sipper. —*DB*

Groote Post Vineyards
T 022-492-2825 • **F** 022-492-2693

Darling (see Durbanville map) ▪ 1stB 1999 ▪ Tasting & sales Mon-Fri 9-5 Sat/Sun 9-2.30 Pub hols 9-5 ▪ Closed Easter Mon, Dec 25 & Jan 1 ▪ Fee R10 for groups of 10+ ▪ Hilda's Kitchen (see Eat-out section) or BYO picnic ▪ Tour groups (40 people) ▪ Conferencing ▪ Walks ▪ Game drives (T 022-492-2825) ▪ Conservation area & bird hide ▪ Owner Peter & Nicholas Pentz ▪ Winemaker Lukas Wentzel (Nov 2000) ▪ Viticulturist Jannie de Clerk, advised by Johan Pienaar (1999) ▪ 117ha (cabs s/f, merlot, pinot, shiraz, chard, chenin, sauv) ▪ 600t/28 000cs 35% red 65% white ▪ PO Box 103 Darling 7345 ▪ wine@grootepost.co.za ▪ www.grootepost.com

Sparkling wine and festivity have figured large at Groote Post of late, with more weddings than ever before being celebrated in the restaurant and a maiden MCC tabled for release as the guide went to press. 'We grafted over some vines to semillon and riesling,' says co-owner Nicholas Pentz, 'and we'll see the first of these being produced this year.' Future plans include game drives through a camp holding 10 different antelope species, including eland and bontebok.

★★★★ **Wooded Chardonnay** Bottled **06** (★★★★★) exceeds expectations of sample tasted last ed. Complex with toasted nuts, lime marmalade & honey, tangy acidity. 8 mths Fr oak (50% new) enhances sumptuous mid-palate, increases concentration, lengthens aftertaste & ensures ageability. **05** sold out before we could taste. **04** was showy & sumptuous.

★★★★ **Sauvignon Blanc Reserve** Intensely aromatic **07** (★★★★☆) ups the ante with greater fruit concentration, less RS than pvs. Dusty cat's pee, fig & asparagus aromas flow through to focused, sleek & steely palate; medium body, slender 13% alc. Debut **05** showed a powerful style which demanded food.

Merlot ★★★★ Step up **05** has plush red fruit, bright acidity. Balanced with well hidden 14.5% alc, svelte, dry tannins from 15 mths Fr oak (20% new). Accessible, but with structure to improve. **04** (★★★★) was ripe but brooding; needed time to evolve. **Pinot Noir** ★★★★ Now bottled, **06**'s gutsy, ripe New-World style still evident. Pleasant core of earthy rhubarb fruit, supple tannins & liquorice finish. All new oak, Fr, 10 mths. **Shiraz** ★★★★ Bottled **04** shows confident New-World styling. Sumptuously ripe & spicy with black pepper & scrub nuances; supple tannins & supportive oak (15 mths 40% new), 14.5% afterglow. Notch up from Youthfully taut **03** (★★★★). **The Old Man's Blend Red** ★★★ Merlot-led bdx **06** blend in smooth-tannined, accessible style, mingling warm fruit compote with spicy sweet tobacco. **Unwooded Chardonnay** ★★★☆ Vivacious **07** brims with zesty citrus & ripe pear, touch clean minerality. Balanced & food-friendly. **Chenin Blanc** ✓ ★★★★ Ripe apple & almond flavours on **07**, waxy breadth & clean-cut, slatey acidity. Poised, unshowy but focused. **Sauvignon Blanc** ★★★★ Vivacious **07** rung above pvs. Dusty, herbaceous & minerally aromas follow through to mouthfilling palate. Bursting with summer freshness. **06** (★★★★) was refreshing & balanced, without edges. **The Old Man's Blend White** ★★★ **07** not ready. Last-tasted **06** (70/30 sauv/chenin) was lively, combined grassy aromas with ripe chenin fruit, finished with twist fresh grapefruit. —*MW*

Groot Parys
T 021-872-7140 • F 021-872-7140

Paarl ▪ Est 1699 ▪ 1stB 2003 ▪ Visits by appt ▪ Owner Eric Verhaak & Peter & Mariëtte Ras ▪ Winemaker Naudé Bruwer (consultant) ▪ Viticulturist Gawie Kriel (consultant) ▪ 45ha (ruby cab, chard, chenin, colombard) ▪ 550t/±1 500 cs ▪ PO Box 82 Huguenot 7645 ▪ grootparys@ wam.co.za ▪ www.grootparys.co.za

The original 1699 deed of this land fulfilled one farmer's dream. Its 2002 acquisition by Eric Verhaak, Peter and Mariëtte Ras fulfilled a second, hence the 'Tweede Droom' alluded to on the labels. The owners have an organic approach, not only with regard to the vines but also the property's flowers and livestock.

Die Tweede Droom range

★★★★ **Chardonnay Wooded** Attractive vanilla & apple pie character on **06** (★★★), rich fruit hiding 15.3% alc. Shows potential; wooding tad more enthusiastic than on impressive & well-crafted **05**.

★★★★ **Chenin Blanc Wooded Wild Yeasts** NEW Intriguing & characterful maiden. Citrus, almond with melon layers, **06** full yet elegant mouthfeel, long dry finish. Natural yeasts, unsulphured, unfined. Has few yrs ahead.

Chardonnay Unwooded ★★★★ Last tasted was **04**, with more intensity, character than most. **Chenin Blanc Wooded** ★★★ Serious but dusty nose, savoury **06**'s barrel fermentation adds richness, but lacks juicy fruit focus. **Chenin Blanc Unwooded** ★★★ Sprightly aperitif-style **07** (sample), tropical fruit & textured mouthfeel. Unfiltered. *– RP*

Groupe LFE South Africa
T 021-850-0160/1 • F 021-851-3578 NEW

Somerset West ▪ Est/1stB 2006 ▪ Closed to public ▪ Owner Groupe LFE BV Netherlands ▪ ±200 000cs 50% red 30% white 20% rosé ▪ Other export brands: Brederode, Cape Cab, Cape Sauv, Goudriaan, Schoonenberg, Wonderboom ▪ PO Box 88 Somerset Mall 7137 ▪ info@groupelfe. co.za ▪ http://winesofsouthafrica.blogspot.com

Part of a Netherlands-based concern, Groupe LFE South Africa is nonetheless proudly South African. 'We buy only from Black Economic Empowerment companies and promote "bottled in SA",' says MD Rob Coppoolse.

Cape 4 range

Cabernet Sauvignon ★★★★ Restrained herbaceous notes on **06**, cassis fruit currently tempered by austere dusty tannin. Solid structure; few yrs potential. **Merlot** ★★★ Rounded, warm & ripe **06**, with dry, chalky tannin. Medium bodied (13% alc) & long, fruit-filled farewell. **Shiraz** ★★★★ **06** black pepper & dense fruit, mouthfilling & full-bodied (14.5%), firm but ripe tannins. **Chardonnay** ★★★★ Ripe melon & pear on plump, rounded **07**. Full, creamy/nutty texture ex-lees ageing, balanced by limy acidity. **Sauvignon Blanc** ★★★ **07** ripe, tropical & herbaceous tones; lively balancing acidity; clean, fresh finish. As all above, below, WO W Cape.

Cape Cab & Cape Sauv

Cape Cab ★★ Robust **06** full-blown & chunky winter warmer, with charry tannins. **Cape Sauv** 🗌 ★★★ Soft **07** ripe & quaffable tropical sauv, with refreshing crisp acidity. Clean & carefree summer tipple (12.9% alc).

De Vloot range

Brederode Merlot ★★★ Red fruit & herbaceous leafy tinge to **06**; some tight, bright acidity & tannin still masking fruit. **Goudriaan Shiraz** ★★★ Bold, ripe & spicy, with dark fruit & liquorice on **06**. Still chewy & unknit - will be tamed by hearty food. **Schoonenberg Chardonnay** ★★ Blowsy pear flavours on plump **06** (14.5 alc); citrusy acid finish.

Elephantasy range

> **Long Nose** ☺ ★★ Light, floral **06** mix chenin & colombard in crisp & carefree quaffing style.

Big Ears ★★★ Braai-mate-style **06** blend cab, shiraz & cinsaut. Soft, dark, berry jam flavours & dry raspy tannins, 13 % alc. All in range under screwcap; labels feature sketch of appropriate part of elephant anatomy. **Short Tail** ★★ **07** cheery, simple cherry-fruited summer quaffer with tart, tangy (but not short) tail.

Inkathi range

Merlot-Cinsaut-Pinotage ★★ Smoky, red-fruited pinotage character leads **06** blend in juicy, easy drinking style. **Pinotage Rosé** ★★ Undemanding **07** gentle, strawberry toned just-dry blusher. Screwtopped, as all Inkathi range. **Chenin Blanc-Chardonnay-Sauvignon Blanc** ★★★ Crisp, fruity **07** combines chenin, chard & sauv in easy drinking blend, medium bodied (13.5% alc), mouthfilling & food-friendly. — *MW*

Grundheim Wines

T 044-272-6927 • F 044-272-6927

Klein Karoo • Est/1stB 1995 • Tasting & sales Mon-Fri 8-5 Sat 9-1 • Fee R10 for groups of 10+ • Closed Easter Sun, Dec 25 & Jan 1 • Owner Danie Grundling • Winemaker Dys Grundling (1997) • 25 ha (cinsaut, tinta, touriga, ruby cab, r/w muscadel, colombard, hanepoot, palomino) • 360t/10 000litres for own labels 100% fortified • PO Box 400 Oudtshoorn 6620 • grundheim@absamail.co.za

Stalwarts of the Klein Karoo Wine Route and its fortified wine tradition, the father-and-son Grundling team continue to make a full range, while bringing their skills to bear on their potstill brandy, already a medal winner.

Classic Red New bottling (**NV**) not ready. **Chenin Blanc** Unready for tasting. **Late Harvest** Untasted. **Red Muscat** ★★★ Subtitled 'Muscat de Frontignan'. Well-aged **95** last ed had lovely tawny hues, aromas of Karoo bush & raisins, soft caramel texture. **White Muscadel** ★★ **07** unready. Plump **06** last ed had flavours & textures of liquid raisins, very soft acidity imparted little structure or refreshment. **Red Jerepigo** ★★★★ Delicious winter-warming **NV** from ruby cab, touriga & tinta, permeated with ripe, luscious blackcurrants & raisins. Yr in barrel. **Golden Jerepigo** ★★★ **04** a tad tired, syrupy, last ed. **Cape Ruby Port** ★★★ Eccentric style: darker & richer than true Ruby, with notes of ground coffee & raisins; chunky & sweet, warming. **NV**. **Cape Vintage 99** is newest bottled vintage, untasted. — *IvH*

Grünberger

Frankish 'bocksbeutel' bottles a nod to German oenologist Alfred Baumgartner, who originally developed this brand for the Bergkelder, now part of Distell. All are off-dry or semi-sweet, and quaffably light.

Spritziger 🗎 ★★ **06** vivacious, spritzy poolside chenin. **Stein** ★★ **06** innocuous off-dry but still crisp quaffer, with restrained thatch & apple nuances. **Rosenlese** ★ **07** coral-hued Natural Sweet, now with chenin addition to sauv/ruby cab blend. **Freudenlese** ★ **07** perfumed Natural Sweet. Soft, generous if somewhat blowsy charmer. All WO W Cape. — *MW*

■ **Guardian Peak** *see Ernie Els Wines*
■ **Guinea Fowl** *see Saxenburg*

Gusto Wines

T 082-807-4447 • F 021-790-8000

Stellenbosch • Est 2001 • 1stB 2002 • Tasting by appt • Owner PG Slabbert & Nicolette Waterford • Winemaker Nicolette Waterford • Viticulturist PG Slabbert • 500 cs 30% red 70% white • PO Box 6045 Uniedal 7612 • wine@base4.co.za

'2007 was by far my most difficult harvest,' reports Nicolette Waterford. 'Not because of anything relevant to the harvesting process, but because of the little man now ruling the roost - Walter

Marck Edward Waterford.' Working from home is set to become a doddle, however, when her own 'garden vineyard' in Llandudno on the Atlantic seaboard comes on-line, possibly next year.

Destino ★★★★ Last was unshowy **01**, firm merlot/cab blend. **Sauvignon Blanc** ★★★ **06**'s sweet-fruited notes yield attractive if not cultivar-typical easy-drinker. Both wines ex-Sbosch vyds; no successors ready. — *MF*

🟦 **Hagelsberg** *see Middelvlei Estate*

🟦 **Hakuna Matata** *see Remhoogte Estate*

Hamilton Russell Vineyards

T 028-312-3595 • F 028-312-1797

Hemel-en-Aarde Valley (see Elgin/Walker Bay map) • Est 1975 • 1stB 1981 • Tasting & sales Mon-Fri 9-5 Sat 9-1 • Also tasting/sales of estate olive oil • Closed Easter Fri/Sun, Dec 25/26 & Jan 1 • Tours by appt • BYO picnic by appt • Conservation area • Owner Anthony Hamilton Russell • Winemaker Hannes Storm (2004) • Viticulturist Johan Montgomery (2005) • 52ha (pinot, chard) • 180t/13 500cs 40% red 60% white • PO Box 158 Hermanus 7200 • hrv@hermanus.co.za • www.hamiltonrussellvineyards.com

It's been year of consolidation at this blue-blooded Hemel-en-Aarde estate, with proprietor Anthony Hamilton Russell making fewer international marketing trips. 'We've been told to return when we have more wine!' It's probably no coincidence that 2007 saw solid growth in local wine markets, though international acclaim – and demand – continues. The development of the two farms that abut HRV is now fine-tuned: the larger (to the west) dedicated to Southern Right, the eastern property to Ashbourne. HRV's focus on 'expression of origin' is unwavering, and not only in the wines. Wife Olive HR has been testing recipes for an upcoming cookbook on last year's nearly 1800 lunch guests, including dishes featuring indigenous renosterveld herbs.

★★★★★ **Pinot Noir** Pure, perfumed red berry fruit in harmony with oaking (regime as for Chard, as is use of inoculated native yeast), around mineral core. **06** shaped more by fine acidity than the subtle tannins. Serious & delicately powerful, with long future. Both EW.

★★★★★ **Chardonnay** After superbly elegant **05** (★★★★★), **06** has bright fruit in ascendent, focused by big fresh, savoury acid. Gd balance with youthfully obvious toasty oak (fermented/8 mths, third new); harmony will grow with few yrs. Silkily rich – never heavy; authoritative – never ponderous. — *TJ*

Handcrafted Wines

T 0861-235-527 • F 086-688-9482

Sandton • 1stB 2006 • Tasting & sales Mon-Fri 9-5 Sat & Sun 9-5 • Closed religious holidays • Tours by appointment • Owner Handcrafted Wines • Winemaker Oliver Meckler • 20 000 cs own label 100 % red • Export brand: Ikapa • PO Box 781960 Sandton 2146 • info@handcraftedwines.co.za • www.handcraftedwines.co.za

'There are 1000-plus winemakers in the Cape but only one in Gauteng,' laughs Oliver Meckler of Adler Wines who, in a partnership (named Handcrafted Wines) with Sunninghill wine and food destination Cellar d'Or, tailors wine for airlines under the Ikapa label. Meckler's other major role at Cellar d'Or is educational, offering Gauteng wine lovers 'a very hands-on' winemaking experience, from destemming grapes right through to designing their own label.

Hartenberg Estate

T 021-865-2541 • F 021-865-2153

Stellenbosch • 1stB 1978 • Tasting & sales Mon-Fri 9-5 (Nov 1 till Easter 9-5.30); Sat 9-3; Sun Dec 1 till Jan 31 (tasting & lunches) 10-4 • Closed all other Sundays, Easter Fri, Dec 25 & Jan 1 • Nominal tasting fee for groups, refunded with purchase • Vintners lunches (al fresco, weather permitting) Mon-Sat 12-2 (picnic platters in summer; soup & vetkoek in winter); booking advisable • Seasonal cellar tours by appt • Excellent birding trails (obtain permission from tasting room) • Owner Hartenberg Holdings • Cellarmaster Carl Schultz (Nov 1993) •

Winemaker Jaco van der Merwe with Patrick Ngamane (Jan 2001/May 2002)) • Viticulturist Alberto Antonini • 95ha (cab, merlot, pinotage, shiraz, chard, riesling, sauv) • 600t/35 000cs 80% red 20% white • PO Box 12756 Die Boord 7613 • info@hartenbergestate.com • www.hartenbergestate.com

Unless you are blinded by the silverware after a 'very successful year award-wise' for Hartenberg, you might enjoy a sighting of lynx, porcupine or the rare Burchell's Coucal along a new 2.5km wetland hiking/birdwatching trail. 'We have successfully completed the clearing of alien vegetation from 65ha of indigenous wetland,' reports MD Paddy Bomford, 'and we're continuing to re-establish fynbos, with indigenous plants and trees being planted along the drive up the farm.' Where the planting of vineyard poles and recycling of glass and plastic used to be outsourced, this is now offered to Hartenberg staff. Meanwhile, Howard Booysen, the first protégé in the Cape Winemaker's Guild's empowerment initiative, is working under Carl Schultz, and Samuel Paulse has been appointed as assistant vineyard manager.

★★★★ **Cabernet Sauvignon 05** textbook cellar-worthy cab: for starters there's cassis, forest floor, ink & gentle oaky notes; then smooth, taut tannins & dense fruit core. So plush you won't even notice the 14.9% alc. 16 mths Fr oak, 50% new.

★★★★ **Merlot 05** maintains step-up in quality made by classy **04**. Luxurious bouquet of sugared plums, hints iodine lead to composed palate. With deep-veined tannins/succulent fruit, built for the long haul. 17 mths Fr oak, 55% new.

★★★★★ **CWG Auction Reserve Gravel Hill Shiraz** Made for CWG since 1995, from single vyd ferrous stone on clay. **04** shows quiet reserve, elegance (thanks partially to modest 12.5% alc). Lilies mingle with cranberries, velvet tannins linger. 17 mths Fr oak, 100% new. EW.

★★★★★ **Shiraz** Highly regarded version, typically with rich fruit, smoky notes, fleshy accessibility. **05** in same vein: nose a tapestry spice/lilies/red currants; tannins assured. 14.9% alc peeps out on finish. 50% new Fr oak, 15 mths. EW.

★★★★ **The Stork** Honours Ken Mackenzie ('Stork' for height & thin legs!). From clay, style contrasts with athletic Gravel Hill. **05** not ready, **04** was irresistible, but with structure for ±10yrs ageability. All new Fr oak, 18 mths.

★★★★★ **The Mackenzie** Cab-led with dollop merlot/dash malbec honouring family regenerating the estate. **05** (★★★★★) a marvellous exercise in restraint, 100% new Fr oak moulds around concert of black berries, tobacco & leafy glens. Beautifully crafted as was **04**.

★★★★ **Chardonnay** Powerful, barrel-fermented version. **06** as showy, nutty as **05**, **04** but with more tangy citrus refreshment. 5 vyds, 5 clones (mix Burgundian, California Davis); full batonnage, partial MLF. 11 mths Fr oak, 60% new. EW.

★★★★ **The Eleanor Chardonnay 06** not ready; **05** was refined, poised, with perfectly judged oak framing citrus & peach dash. Fermented/10 mths new Fr barriques; named after Eleanor Finlayson, property's former doyenne.

Pinotage ★★★★ Opulent fruit, refreshing acidity hide whopping 15.3% alc on assertive **05**. Oak well integrated, too (17 mths Fr, 50% new). EW. **Cabernet Sauvignon-Shiraz** ★★★★ Juicy melangé red/black fruits in confident balance with tight tannins. Not as refreshing as pvs. 12 mths Fr oak, 10% new. **Chatillon** ★★★★ Charming sipper with enticing pear drop aromas, steely acidity & rounded palate from 3 mths sur lie, 14% alc. 100% chenin. **Weisser Riesling** ★★★★ 30% botrytis adds apricot/pineapple nuances, weight & texture to gloriously jasmine scented, slightly off-dry **07**. Rich, with signature acidity ensuring balance & length. **Sauvignon Blanc** ★★★★ **07** not ready for tasting. Last ed, **06** was delicious solo or with food; had zesty freshness. **L'Estreux** No new bottling. Occasional label. Discontinued: **Bin 9**, **Bin 3**. — *CvZ*

Hartswater Wine Cellar
T 053-474-0700 • **F** 053-474-0975

Northern Cape • Tasting & sales Mon-Fri 8.30-1, 2-5 • Sales also from outlet in Hartswater town; orders delivered to liquor stores in Northern Cape (350km radius), Free State & North West • Tours by appt • Owner Senwes • Winemaker Deon Truter • 5 000t • PO Box 2335 Hartswater 8570 • deon@wynkelder.co.za

Biggest news here is a new winemaker, Deon Truter, who says he keeps moving further from the sea: after 22 years in Franschhoek, he spent four at Oranjerivier Wine Cellars and now finds himself mere hours from the Botswana border. 'It's dry up here,' he notes. 'Any chance the guys in the Cape could send us some rain?'

Elements range

Cabernet Sauvignon NEW ★★ New Fr oak staves, 4 mths, for **07**, sour cherries & earth, tangy dried fruit tail. **Earth** ★★★ NV tasted pvs ed had herby edge with soft red fruits. **Thunder** ★★ No new bottling of **NV**, pvs showing rich & juicy fruit; 11% alc. **Wind** ★★ Fruity, soft, off-dry colombard; **07** with pineapple & pear flavours. **Rain** ★★ **07** shy, delicate pear note; palate fleshed out with attractive sweetness. **Fire** ★★ Sweet ruby cab, with lowish 10.5% alc. Dry guava & cherry fruit tones, **07** tad syrupy. Most screwcapped.

Hinterland range

Cabernet Sauvignon Not tasted. **Chardonnay** Not ready. **Chenin Blanc** No new bottling. **Doux Sparkling** Untasted. **Red Jerepigo** No newer bottling ready. **Port** New version not ready. Discontinued: **Ruby Cabernet**, **Late Harvest**, **Special Late Harvest**.

Overvaal range

Red Jerepico NEW 🍷 ★ From ruby cab; fruity, full-sweet & honeyed **07**. **White Jerepico** NEW 🍷 ★★★ Lovely **07** layered notes of ripe apple, lemon & honey; vanilla custard flavours & sweet finish. Discontinued: **Grand Cru**. — JP

■ **Harvest Moon** *see* Dominion Wine Company

Haskell Vineyards
T 021-881-3895 • **F** 021-881-3986

Stellenbosch • Est 2002 • 1stB 2003 • Tasting, sales & tours Mon-Fri 9-5 Sat (Sep-Apr only) 10-3 • Closed pub hols • Vineyard Kitchen for breakfasts & light lunches Mon-Sat 9-4.30 • Walks • Owner Preston Haskell • Winemaker Rianie Strydom (Jan 2005) • Vineyard Manager Wikus Pretorius (Dec 2005) • 15 ha (cab, merlot, shiraz, chard) • ±65 tons ±6 000 cs 80% red 20% white • 'Foundation brand': Dombeya • PO Box 12766 Die Boord 7613 • info@ haskellvineyards.com • www.haskellvineyards.com

Last year was a watershed: winemaking GM Rianie Strydom produced the first of the Samara range (a cab-based blend) and added the Boulder Road Shiraz to the Dombeya label. The Haskell wines are still in barrels in the cellar, awaiting launch, perhaps in 2009. Everyone on the farm was involved in production, wearing their Ts and coming in for a day's work in the cellar, with their families. 'Yes, we are having fun,' agrees Rianie S, adding that she and her team had the time to try all sorts of processes, from basket pressing to wild fermentation.

Dombeya range

★★★★ **Chardonnay** Cements higher general rating with classically styled **06**, bright lime & grapefruit aromas; sweet almost spicy citrus notes; beautiful concentration of pear-drop & melon flavours; edgy, restrained, persistent. 14 mths oaked.
Boulder Road Shiraz NEW ★★★★ Rianie S aiming for younger consumers with **05**, raspberry & white pepper aromas, bramble, bayleaf notes; **05** not fully formed yet on the palate, grippy, tad insubstantial, but still integrating. **Samara** NEW ★★★★ Elegant & restrained bdx blend cab, merlot, cab f (54/40/6). Unshowy but concentrated **05**, classic tobacco, blackcurrant & tealeaf notes, densely textured, tannins evident but not intrusive. Discontinued: **Shiraz**, **Amalgam**, **Sauvignon Blanc**. — MF

Haut Espoir
T 021-876-4000 • **F** 021-876-4038

Franschhoek • Est 1999 • 1stB 2004 • Tastings & tours by appt; sales Mon-Fri 9-4 (phone ahead) • Owner Armstrong family • Winemaker/viticulturist Nikey van Zyl (Oct 2003) • 12ha (cab, merlot, petit v, shiraz) • 80t/4 000cs 70% red 30% white • PO Box 681 Franschhoek 7690 • wine@hautespoir.co.za • www.hautespoir.co.za

Winemaker Nikey van Zyl had a relatively relaxed harvest: the varieties behaved themselves and didn't rush him too much, reports Rob Armstrong. To counteract the effects of what Rob A describes as 'significantly drier rainy seasons, with uncharacteristically hot winter spells', a sweet-pea species is being tested as an indigenous cover crop. This year sees the first wines made from grapes grown on Haut Espoir. And another homegrown special: Rob and Erica are expecting their first child, a son.

★★★★ Chardonnay Reserve Last ed delicious **05** was well integrated & lively, had potential to improve. Barrique fermented with native yeasts; 13 mths on lees. **04** (★★★) woodier but well-liked by Veritas, MIWA judges.

Cabernet Sauvignon Reserve NEW **★★★★** Opulent, cassis-rich **04** preview shows some development; chalky tannins & alluring deep texture perfect match for rare fillet. 14 mths new Fr/Hung oak. **Syrah ★★** Tightly-wound yet sweet-fruited **05**, herbal, earthy notes, touch astringency. 9 mths 2nd fill Fr oak. **Shiraz Reserve ★★** Leather & candied fruit contrast on **04** (sample) will appeal to some; tannins show a serious side. 14 mths 2nd fill Fr oak. **Shiraz Rosé ★★★ 06** sexy dinner party companion. Cinnamon & cured ham layered with dense red fruit. **Sauvignon Blanc ★★★** Stylish, classic **06** a step-up; tangy, cool-fruited, with minerals & stonefruit giving a long finish. 9 mths lees contact. **Semillon ★★★** Last available **05** had gentle leafy aromas, pure waxy fruit, slender body (12% alc). Small portion oaked. **Viognier ★★★★** Perfumed & off-dry, with extra depth from partial malo, lees contact, **06** is finely fruited, with lively peach & candy notes. Should develop. Nudges next level. 50% oaked, Fr. — *RP*

Havana Hills

T 021-972-1110 • F 021-972-1105

Philadelphia (see Durbanville map) ▪ Est 1999 ▪ 1stB 2000 ▪ Visits by appt ▪ Owner Kobus du Plessis ▪ Winemaker Nico Vermeulen & Paul Engelbrecht (Jun 1999/Jan 2006) with Joseph Gertse (Jan 2000) ▪ Viticulturist Rudi Benn (2001) ▪ 65 ha (barbera, cabs s/f, merlot, mourvèdre, petit v, pinot, sangiovese, shiraz, nouvelle, sauvignon, viognier) ▪ 400t/35 000cs 80% red 20% white ▪ Export brands: Lime Road 1481 & Virgin Earth (see entry) ▪ Postnet Suite 57, Pvt Bag X18, Milnerton 7435 ▪ sales@havanahills.co.za

A trio of winemakers runs this cellar on the slopes of Olifantskop: consultant Nico Vermeulen, Paul Engelbrecht, settled in after his second vintage, and young Joseph Gertse, who has a bent for blending. He's bound to be pleased with wider scope promised by new blocks of barbera, sangiovese, petit verdot and nouvelle, all tended by Rudi Benn, who's not averse to namedropping - when it comes to the vines, that is: each one has its own moniker!

Kobus

★★★★★ Kobus Flagship made only in exceptional vintages. **05** blends 67% cab with dollop merlot, petit v & smidgen cab f. Myriad black & red berry aromas/flavours tantalise on nose, seamless tannins cosset sweet fruit on palate; majestic with considerable depth, ageability. Only 300 cases.

Du Plessis range

★★★★ Reserve Shiraz Nuanced, refined **04** lauded with VDG; **05** (★★★★) lighter toned, more floral with conservative leather & white pepper; velvety structure/mouthfeel puckered by acid streak.

★★★★★ Du Plessis Médoc-style blend using all but malbec from bdx's usual 5 varieties. **05**, which like others in range, will only be released after several mths bottle maturation, has choc/truffle tones, beguiling fruit depth & restrained power. Needs ±3 yrs to blossom fully.

Reserve Cabernet Sauvignon ★★★★ Amarillo cherry & trademark fynbos edge on reticent **05**. Focussed tannins add class, structure. Shuld open, gain complexity with cellaring. This & Merlot following back in stable. **Reserve Merlot ★★★★** Ground coffee & grassy hints hide floral bouquet in **05**. Big & ripe with sweet-sour finish.

Havana Hills range

Merlot ★★★ Back to range after pvsly noted as discontinued. **05** mushroom/herb notes to baked plum mouthful; fleshiness curtailed by fine tannin, hint sour fruit acidity. **Shiraz ★★★★**

Cracked black pepper standout aromas/flavours on **05**. This, plus leathery, dry tannins reining in sweet fruit makes it star of range. Yr Fr oak, 30% new; same for other reds. **Lime Road** ★★★☆ Almost equal proportions cab/shiraz/merlot on smoky, earthy **05**. Full-bodied with leafy edge. Good now, should improve 2-3 yrs. **Italian Job** ★★★ Rustic **04** last ed was 'cross cultural' blend sangiovese, nebbiolo, barbera, pinotage, shiraz & even touriga! EW. **Chardonnay** ★★★★ Tasted pvs ed; **05**'s toasty, mature aromas balanced by fruity freshness; some lingering sweetness. **Sauvignon Blanc** ★★★★ Slender yet fruitful **07** laced with asparagus, edged with greenpepper, touch sugar softens piercing acidity. — *RP*

Hawksmoor at Matjieskuil ♀ 🏠 [NEW]
T 021-884-4587 ▪ F 021-884-4465

Paarl ▪ Est 1692 ▪ 1stB 2005 ▪ Tasting by appt daily 10-4; sales by appt Mon-Sat ▪ Fee R20 refunded with purchase of wine ▪ Closed Easter Fri-Sun, Dec 25/31 & Jan 1 ▪ Hawksmoor House luxury guest lodge ▪ Owner Mark Borrie & Simon Olding ▪ Viticulturist Paul Wallace (2004) ▪ ±23ha (cab f, mourvèdre, pinotage, shiraz, chenin) ▪ ±160t/500cs own label 65% red 35% white ▪ PO Box 9 Elsenburg 7607 ▪ wines@hawksmoor.co.za ▪ www.hawksmoor.co.za

From making wine from elderberries, gooseberries (and even carrots!) during his English south coast youth, Mark Borrie has graduated to grapes. He and partner Simon Olding, enthusiastically assisted by German Pointers Cosmo and Max, now farm at historic Hawksmoor at Matjieskuil, run Hawksmoor House guesthouse, sell English antiques, handcraft Shiraz and Pinotage at their other farm, Die Laaitjie, in Robertson, and generally live life according to the maxim: 'Be prepared to be adventurous, but always heed good advice'.

Pinotage 🗄 ★★ Meaty, slightly varnishy aromas on **06**, herbal hints, concentrated, tannic **Chenin Blanc** 🗄 ★★ Zesty, light & bracingly fresh **07**.

Limited Releases
Pinotage 🗄 Six barrels of **06** made; not tasted. **Shiraz** 🗄 ★★★ Super-ripe, opulent raspberry notes, massive (16.3%) alc, **06** intense sweet almond finish. — *MF*

Hazendal
T 021-903-5112 ▪ F 021-903-0057

Stellenbosch ▪ Est 1699 ▪ 1stB ca 1950 ▪ Tasting & sales daily 9-4.30 (closed Mon in winter) ▪ Fee R10 for 5 wines ▪ Tours Mon-Fri 11 & 3 ▪ Closed Easter Fri, Dec 25 & Jan 1 ▪ Hermitage Restaurant ▪ Museum of Russian art & culture ▪ Gifts ▪ Conferencing ▪ Owner Mark Voloshin & partners ▪ Winemaker Ronell Wiid (Jan 1998, consultant) ▪ Viticulturist Schalk du Toit (2000, consultant) ▪ 52ha (cab, merlot, pinot, shiraz, chenin, sauv) ▪ 350t/25 000cs own label 40% red 60% white ▪ PO Box 336 Stellenbosch 7599 ▪ info@hazendal.co.za ▪ www.hazendal.co.za; www.myspace.com/hazendal

'I was worried, trying to balance grapes and pickers,' says winemaker Ronell Wiid of 2007's heat-beset harvest, 'and then the huge, lovely flavours of the whites dispelled my nervousness.' Since 1994, the property has been carefully restored by the owners, Russian-born Germans Mark Voloshin and his business partner and friend Leo Schumacher. The family members now take care of the management, international marketing, and restaurant and function areas. A goal is to establish the brand in the major European and Eastern markets.

★★★★ **Shiraz 04**, featured last ed, due for release this year. Dark-fruited, hints liquorice & smoked salami, well-judged tannins supple, but ensure firm skeleton for ageing.

★★★★ **Shiraz-Cabernet Sauvignon 03** last ed was everything needed for a gd drinking experience: creamy, fully ripened berries, deepening woodsmoke notes; balanced structure. Drink now, but the real pleasure is 4-5 yrs off. 54/46 blend, yr Fr barrels, 40% new.

★★★★ **Chenin Blanc Wooded** From miserly 30+ yr old bushvines. **06** unshowy, but lots of class: pervasive tropical/citrus intensity, elegant structure. Potential to age few yrs.

★★★★☆ **The Last Straw** Aptly, amusingly named meal-ending straw wine. Last tasted **05** (★★★★☆) mouthcoating, resonating apricot & quince flavours, rich & irresistible. Notch up the scale from **04**. Fermented/9-10 mths Fr oak.

Bushvine Chenin Blanc ☺ ★★★ **06** off old vines. Deep tropical, citrus concentration, tangy 'drink-me' appeal. 'My most favourite Bushvine since I arrived at Hazendal,' says winemaker.

Merlot ★★★★ **05** seductive nose & palate: full-ripe plums, black cherries, curvaceous body; enough tannin structure to take seriously, but main focus is enjoyment. **Pinotage** ★★★★ Limited quantities for UK market. No **05** produced. **04** captured the variety perfectly with rhubarb pie richness, touch green fynbos. **Reserve Red** ★★★ **05** own grapes, merlot/cab (52/48) blend. Plum, smoky spice, firm structure. Built to last few yrs, yet drinkable now. **Blanc de Noir** ★★★ **06** (now bottled) pinot derived, fruity/savoury, easy-drinking, perfect al fresco fare, esp with ham, cheeses. **Chardonnay** ★★★ Last we noted **04** as gd summer white with modest alc & ripe tropical fruit core. Fermented/aged Fr barrels, 20% new. **Konynwijn** ★★☆ No **06**. Last ed **05** was appealing semi-sweet chenin quaffer with glacé pineapple flavours. **Sauvignon Blanc** ★★★★ Previewed **07** already shows classic fruit purity, gooseberries, lime. Palate is clarion call for food: vibrant, juicy, flavourful, delicious. Potential (★★★★). **White Nights Brut Cap Classique** ★★★★ New vintage not ready. **01** from pinot, tasted last ed; 4 yrs on lees, rich & creamy; enjoy soon to catch at peak. Discontinued: **Marvol Pinotage**. *— CR*

Headbutt Wines

T 021-873-1567 • **F** 021-864-1483

Wellington ▪ Est/1stB 2003 ▪ Tasting & sales at Bovlei Winery ▪ Owner Jan du Preez & Marius Erasmus ▪ Winemaker Frank Meaker (Bovlei), with Jan du Preez ▪ Viticulturist Dawie le Roux (consultant) ▪ 120t/10 000cs 60% red 30% white 10% sparkling ▪ BRC accreditation in progress ▪ PO Box 7210 Stellenbosch 7599 ▪ headbutt@leidersburgwines.co.za ▪ www. leidersburgwines.co.za

Big celebrations as the guide went to press for this collaboration between Leidersburg's Jan du Preez and wine industry administrator/financial strategist Marius Erasmus, as two years of negotiations paid off in a substantial listing with major US group Wholefoods. Local tasting and sales are at Bovlei, where the wallet-friendly wines continue to be made.

Vinters Reserve Merlot-Pinotage-Cinsaut ★★ Spicy melange sour cherries & raspberries on **06**, generous jammy/raisin flavours reined in by robust tannins. For hearty casseroles. **Chardonnay** ★★ Unoaked **07** has little varietal definition but is fresh & quaffable, with fleeting lemon scents. **Sparkling Brut** ★★★ Carbonated **NV** bubbly from chenin & chard (70/30). Pvs bottling was frothy & fun, with peaches & cream flavours. Discontinued: **Vinters Reserve Pinotage, Cabernet Sauvignon-Merlot, Sauvignon Blanc-Steen**. *— CvZ*

■ **Hegewisch Wines** *see* Solms-Delta
■ **Helderberg Winery** *see* The Company of Wine People
■ **Helgerson Wines** *see* La Bri
■ **Helshoogte Vineyards** *see* Vuurberg

Hemelzicht

T 028-313-2215 (cellar); 028-313-3512 (a/h) • **F** 028-313-2215

Upper Hemel-en-Aarde Valley (see Elgin/Walker Bay map) ▪ Est 1998 ▪ 1stB 2003 ▪ Tasting & sales Mon-Fri 8.30-5 Sat 8.30-1 at 19 Long Street Hermanus ▪ Closed pub hols ▪ Owner Louis Saaiman ▪ Winemaker Hannes Storm (2003) ▪ 16ha (cab, malbec, shiraz, chard, sauv) ▪ 800cs 100% white ▪ PO Box 469 Onrusrivier 7201

Louis Saaiman's wine and flower business in the Hemel-en-Aarde Valley is blooming. Two-thirds of his BWI-registered Hemelzicht property is being restored to fynbos, and the balance is or will be given to vines (currently 16ha under vineyard). Saaiman channels the best fruit into his own labels, available mainly through local restaurants and guesthouses (untasted this edition); the balance is sold off.

■ **Hemisphere** *see* Du Toitskloof Winery

■ **Hendrik Lodewyk** *see* Du Preez Estate

■ **Hercules Paragon** *see* Simonsvlei International

Hermanuspietersfontein Vineyards
T 028-316-1875 • **F** 028-316-1293

Walker Bay (see Elgin/Walker Bay map) ▪ Est/1stB 2005 ▪ Tasting & sales Mon-Fri 9-5 Sat 9-1
▪ Closed Easter Sun/Mon, Dec 25/26 & Jan 1 ▪ Farmers' Market Sat 9-1 & other attractions ▪
Owner Johan & Mariette Pretorius, Bartho Eksteen ▪ Winemaker Bartho Eksteen, with Kim
McFarlane ▪ Vineyard Manager Derick Steyn ▪ 250t/12 000cs 68% red 32% white ▪ Suite 47
Private Bag X15 Hermanus 7200 ▪ kelder@hpf1855.co.za ▪ www.hpf1855.co.za

'My wife greets me with a handshake, and the kids call me oom,' jokes Bartho Eksteen when asked how much of his time is devoted to winemaking. Last year things eased somewhat, thanks to a fully operational cellar (bar pangs of guilt when leaving at 9pm rather than 2am) and the results have already borne fruit. Besides extending the 'family' to include Die Arnoldus and Die Martha, there's Kleinboet, Swartskaap and Bloos (in typical maverick fashion Bartho E uses only Afrikaans on his labels), he's also taking an unorthodox view on his sauvignons, deferring bottling of the new harvest so the late-ripening grapes have more time to develop on their fine lees.

★★★★ **Die Arnoldus** NEW Well-structured **05** blend from cab (50%), merlot, malbec, petit v, cab f. Refined & savoury with masses of sweet fruit supported by soft, lithe tannins in valiant struggle with 14.5% alc & influence of 2 yrs Fr oak (half new): time should bring resolution.

★★★★ **Die Martha** NEW **05** has shiraz aromas dominant: pepper, fynbos herbs, herbaceous hint. Cab (28%), merlot (18%) add to complexity. Characterful, delightful & approachable, its fresh liveliness belying 15% alc. Firm ripe tannins; woody in youth (20 mths; half new). W Bay/Dbnville grapes.

★★★★★ **Die Bartho** 目 **07** looks set to match excellent **06** in concentration & harmony, its superiority manifest in fine, ripe silkiness as much as in subtlety of its asparagus-tinged blend of passionfruit & grass. From Langkloof; has a little nouvelle. These sauvs all tasted ex-tank, but finished wines. The range mostly WO W Cape.

★★★★ **Sauvignon Blanc No 3** 目 Like **06**, **07** stresses rich ripeness & tropicality, here with notably lovely passionfruit, but with bracing freshness & taut green grip. Like No 7, includes wooded semillon element, adding subtly to texture, richness.

★★★★ **Sauvignon Blanc No 7** 目 **07** (★★★★☆) adds some nouvelle grapes to enhance grass, greenpepper notes - effect here is of ripe, succulent greenness. Poised & elegant, long-lingering, promise of gd development over few yrs; rating provisional. **06** was steely & flinty rather than fruity.

Swartskaap ★★★★ The **05** (★★★☆) (red) 'Black Sheep' showed heavily woody in youth; **06** (sample, rating provisional), also from cab f, much less so, though 16 mths oak, half new. Leafy fragrance, plus Marmite note; chewy, firm, ripe & confident. **Kleinboet** NEW ★★★☆ Arnoldus's friendly, easier-going brother. **05** same varieties, different mix; fruit-driven, softer & very ripe, showing less oak (but 20 mths, half new). **Bloos** NEW ★★☆ **07** lightly, softly fruity rosé from 5 Bdx varieties; dry, with a gd little bite.

1855 range
'Red' ★★☆ **06** in ripe, fruity & easygoing (but not dumbed down) mode of **05**; also from 5 Bdx varieties. Like White, tasted pre-bottling. **'White'** ★★★ Softer & lighter version of grand sauvs; fresh, juicy & pleasantly dry. These WO W Cape. — *TJ*

Herold Wines
T 072-833-8223 • **F** 0866-204-248

Outeniqua (see Klein Karoo map) ▪ Est 1999 ▪ 1stB 2003 ▪ Tasting & sales weekdays; other
times by appt ▪ Fee R15 refundable on purchase ▪ BYO picnic ▪ Walks ▪ Conservation area ▪
Owner Mark Chandler ▪ Winemaker Mark Chandler & Vivien Harpur ▪ Viticulturist Vivien

Harpur (1999) • *6 ha (pinot, sauv)* • *30t/1 200cs 80% red 20% white* • *PO Box 10 Herold 6615* • *harpie@xsinet.co.za*

Herold Wines' vines endured their coldest, wettest, windiest season to deliver over 30 tons, most to their own cellar. The new 'underground' bottle cellar (a converted fodder trench) and its stock of 12 000 bottles survived the August floods. Their new official brown tourist signs – a wine farm in the Garden Route! - brought curious travellers to the don't-trip-over-the-pipes tasting room in the fermentation cellar. 'Many fulfilled long-held winemaking aspirations,' says winemaker Vivien Harpur, 'punching the reds and manhandling buckets of overflowing yeast into the whites.'

★★★★ **Sauvignon Blanc** ✓ 🗐 **07** a treat for fans of nervy, athletic sauvs. Thrilling, intense & lean. Contrast with **06**, similar quality but plump, concentrated.

Merlot NEW ★★★★ **06** makes creditable debut with ying-yang of savoury bacon & sugared plums. 15% cab adds backbone of approachable tannins for early enjoyment. **The Black Sheep Pinot Noir** ★★★ Pvs prosaically 'Pinot Noir'. **05** valiant attempt to replicate burgundy-styled **04**; unfortunately gruff oak overwhelms younger vintage's delicate fruit. **Shiraz** ★★★ With lush fruit & moderate oak (14 mths Fr), **06** makes pleasant winter fireside companion. Like Red Man below, carries dual Bo-Langkloof & Outeniqua WO. **Red Man Blend Shiraz-Cabernet Sauvignon** ★★★ New name for blend of two compatible red grapes. Shiraz (73%) leads charry **06** with red fruit, pepper aromas/flavours. **Gertrude** NEW ★★★ Now for something completely different: fortified dessert from pinot. Maiden **06** has enchanting tealeaf & lifted cherry notes; only slightly sweet & spirituous (53.4g/l RS, 16.5% alc). 14 mths old Fr oak. 375ml. Discontinued: **Rosé**. — *CvZ*

Heron Ridge
T 021-842-2501 • F 021-842-2501

Stellenbosch (see Helderberg map) • *Est 1997* • *1stB 2001* • *Visits by appt* • *Fee R10 p/p for groups* • *Closed pub hols* • *Owner Orpen family* • *Winemaker Pippa Orpen* • *Viticulturist Paul Wallace (Mar 1999, consultant)* • *4ha (cab, shiraz)* • *30t/1 800-2 000cs 100% red* • *PO Box 5181 Helderberg 7135* • *orps@xsinet.co.za* • *www.heronridge.co.za*

The sad passing of winemaking father, Pete, sees daughter Pippa Orpen ably continuing the good work in vineyard and cellar. Passionate about her new career (graphics and photography were her first love), she gladly ploughs, sows and prunes before becoming creative in the winery. The Pete Orpen Flight carries her label design.

★★★★ **Shiraz 05** (★★★★) style maintained, finely textured black cherry & dark choc backed by elegant tannins, adding texture & subtle grip, but a lesser vintage. **04**, tasted as sample, showed sumptuous ripeness & lovely concentration.

★★★★ **Pete Orpen Flight** Refined & classy 76/24 shiraz/cab blend; **05** sumptuous fruit held in check by cab's tannins & gd oak (mainly Fr, 15% new). — *IvH*

Het Vlock Casteel
T 022-448-1433 • F 022-448-1610

Swartland • *Est 2005* • *1stB 2006* • *Tasting & sales Mon-Fri 9-5 Sat 9-2* • *Fee for groups R10* • *Closed Christian holidays* • *Tours by appt during tasting hours* • *Export grape farm: tours & grape picking during season by appt (Jan-Apr)* • *Olive oil tasting* • *BYO picnic* • *Farm-grown olive products, fruit, jams, chutneys, chilli sauces, dessert toppings, preserves for tasting/sale (range of 65 products)* • *Child friendly* • *Owner Johan Louw Vlok* • *Winemaker Alicia Hamman (consultant)* • *Viticulturist Johan Louw Vlok & Hanno van Schalkwyk (consultant)* • *100ha (cab, merlot, pinotage, shiraz, chard)* • *1 300t/7 000cs own label 100% red* • *PO Box 8 Riebeek-Kasteel 7307* • *jlvlok@iafrica.com* • *www.hetvlockcasteel.co.za*

When Attie Vlok put down roots in the Kasteelberg Valley in 1958 to establish an export fruit business, he could hardly have predicted his domain's tourist potential. Today the lures include son Johan Louw Vlok's wines, created with 'biodynamic equilibrium methods', farm-grown olives and oils, and wife Ansie's vast range of preserves. The singular castle-like cellar, alluded to in the brand name, looks set to become a tourist attraction in its own right.

Merlot ★★★ Savoury, meaty & with dark fruit, maiden **05**'s ripeness gives mouthfilling drinkability despite new-oak treatment (85/15 Fr/Am). **Shiraz** ★★★ Heaps of spice in fully ripe **05**; warm-hearted, gutsy. All-new Fr oak (yr) readily assimilated. — *CR*

Hex River Crossing Private Cellar

T 083-455-5194 • F 023-347-4734

Worcester • Est/1stB 2004 • Visits only by appt • R15 per tasting • Owner De Villiers Graaff, AJ Reyneke & Leon Dippenaar • Winemaker/viticulturist Leon Dippenaar (2004) • 2ha (mourvèdre, shiraz, viognier) • 15t/500cs 90% red 10% white • Export brand: The Auction Crossing • PO Box 5 Hex River 6855 • leon@vinpro.co.za

This small, traditional cellar is now grooming the third vintage of their rhône-style wines, with a view to inaugurating yearly auctions where the wines will be knocked down while festivities proceed alongside. Meanwhile winemaker/shareholder Leon Dippenaar eagerly waits for their junior vines to mature.

The Auction Crossing range
★★★★ **Viognier** Classic peach & flower aromas on previewed **07**; rich but vibrantly fresh palate belies big 15% alc, with integrated wood influence, lingering finish. Wllngtn fruit. Drier than pvsly tasted off-dry **05** (**06** sold out).

Syrah-Viognier ★★★★ Viognier's apricot quality a little too obvious in **05**'s easy-going delciousness. Oaky too, but plenty of fruit & ripe, firm tannins. Widely sourced grapes. — *TJ*

■ **Hidden Agenda** *see* Hidden Valley Wines

Hidden Valley Wines

T 021-880-2646 • F 021-880-2645

Stellenbosch • Est/1stB 1995 • Visits Mon-Fri 9-4.30 Sat/Sun & pub hols 9.30-3.30 • Closed Good Fri, Dec 25 & Jan 1 • Restaurant Tue-Sat 12-7, dinner Thu-Fri 7-10 & Sun 12-5 lunch only, closed Mon & mnth of July • Amenities: see intro • Owner David Hidden & Hidden Family Trust • Winemaker Chris Kelly (2005), with Corina du Toit (Oct 2005) • Viticulturist Johan 'Grobbie' Grobbelaar (Feb 1999) • 44ha (barbera, cabs s/f, malbec, merlot, mourvèdre, petit v, pinotage, shiraz, tannat, sauv, semillon) • 220t/15 000cs 75% red 25% white • PO Box 12577 Die Boord 7613 • info@hiddenvalleywines.com • www.hiddenvalleywines.com

Dave Hidden has made the move from Johannesburg to his hi-tech, 220-ton gravity-flow winery high up on the slopes of the Helderberg. Here, Hidden Valley's 'lifestyle' cellar and new restaurant offer visitors a food and wine experience; and there is also the option to picnic. Olives and olive oil are an additional passion that's emerging on the farm. Dave H aims to return the valley to its pristine natural state, and to this end employs and mentors Nomzame Ngame and her team of 20 to clear all alien vegetation. Frequent trips to his Elim vineyards at the southern tip of Africa keep him in touch with his Lands End Range.

★★★★ **Pinotage** From 30+ yr Devon Vlly vyd. Sample **05**, provisional (★★★★★), full-bodied yet refined with warming spice & meaty tones; rich layers encased in/lengthened by comfortable savoury tannins. Incl splashes cab & viognier. Fr/Am oaked, none new.
★★★★ **Sauvignon Blanc** 📖 **07** worthy inaugurator of new Hlderbrg cellar. Whistle clean, polished, with expressive passionfruit & tropical tones, invigorating & prolonged juicy flavours. 3% barrel fermented.

Cabernet Sauvignon ★★★★ **01** last available, ex-Firgrove/Hldrberg vyds. Next **05** not ready for tasting. **Shiraz** ★★★★ **05** satisfying & balanced without being overly complex. Quietly warming spice scents; light texture, gentle grip yielding to savoury length. Restrained oaking, none new.

Hidden Agenda range
Shiraz ★★★ Ripe **05**, incl splashes cab & pinotage, plentiful fruit, easy tannins. Not reassessed. **06** unready. **Shiraz-Viognier** NEW 📖 Preview **06** 85/13 blend with 2% cab, delicately scented; sturdier palate with apricot tones revealing viognier's presence. Fr/Am oak, 25% new. Too unformed to rate. **Chenin Blanc** 📖 ★★★★ Variation on chenin, viognier, sauv

theme: **07** (ex-tank) the more voluptuous, with honeyed breadth, succulence & hints dried apricot. 30% of chenin new-oak fermented. **Chenin Blanc-Viognier** 🔲 ★★★★ Suave chenin, viognier, sauv combo; 75/21/4 composition in **07** (★★★★) Preview characterful though easy-drinking, with complementary gentle spice/apricot aromas. Portion new-oak fermented. 'White' pvs ed.

Land's End range

★★★★ **Sauvignon Blanc** 🔲 Unbottled **07** has cool, refreshing profile; greater gooseberry/minerals intensity than **06**, expanded by dash barrel-fermented wine (2%) & 8% semillon. Refined, v long; gd potential.

Syrah NEW ★★★☆ Maiden **06** with eager, pure white spice & red berry character. Dense, soft texture in harmony with 14.3% alc. Carefully oaked, yr, used Fr. —*AL*

High Constantia
T 021-794-7171 • F 021-794-7999

Constantia • Est 1693 • 1stB 2000 • Tasting, sales & tours 8-5 • Fee R25 • Closed Dec 25 & Jan 1 • Owner David van Niekerk • Winemaker David van Niekerk & Roger Arendse • 14.5ha (cabs s/f, malbec, merlot, pinot, chard, sauv) • 40t/5 500cs own label • 64% red 1% white 5% rosé 30% MCC • Range for customer: High Constantia (UK) • Puck's Glen, Groot Constantia Rd, Constantia 7800 • david@highconstantia.co.za • www.highconstantia.co.za

Driven by the competitive wine world's pressure to market, David van Niekerk has been tramping the highways and byways of Europe and the Far East, sample case in hand. But it's paying off: 'Whatever that guy's doing in SA, tell him not to stop!', to quote the chief taster for Sweden's Systembolaget. Johannesburg claims a good proportion of his time too - not quite saturated yet, and 'there's always a market for good wine', as Van Niekerk says. Closer to home, development of the Wynberg Zonnestraal vineyards continues apace, and demand means increasing production of the much sought-after Clos André cap classique.

★★★★ **Cabernet Franc** Leafy fragrance, dusty spice & earthy notes make for unusual, characterful **03**. Sweet fruit on smoothly tannic palate; dusty finish elegantly dry with moderate 13% alc. 32 mths new oak. Note: no wines tasted this ed; notes from pvs guide.

★★★★☆ **Sebastiaan** Splendid cab s/f blend (63/32), with a dab malbec. Handsome **03** darkfruited & lightly fragrant, with gravitas to absorb spicy oak (mix new/2nd fill Fr, 2+ yrs). Understated muscular elegance & authoritative composure.

★★★★ **Sauvignon Blanc** Last tasted was **05**, showing cool-country characters: gooseberry & grapefruit edged with passionfruit, not too green. Richness tempered by steely acidity, balanced by adequate 12.5% alc.

★★★★ **Clos André MCC** Refined, & about as dry as you can go. **04** (76% chard, rest pinot) mineral character, just hinting at yeast; lightly rich & austerely elegant. **05** nearer 50:50 blend, fuller, more brioche-like but as delicate.

Cabernet Sauvignon ★★★ Herbal notes of **04** signal cool origin, some varietal cassis; big dry tannins overwhelm fruit on shortish finish, 19 mths new oak apparent. **Malbec 04** sold out; no newer vintage tasted. **Merlot** NEW Not tasted. **Rosé** ★★★★ **05** more than just 'fun wine': big (14.5% alc), pure-fruited & as vinous as it is berried, with dry finishing grip. Mostly cab f, some MCC press-wine, other bits & bobs. **Viognier** NEW Not tasted. —*DS*

■ **High Gables** *see* Klein Constantia Estate

Hildenbrand Wine & Olive Estate
T 021-873-4115 • F 0866-700-147

Wellington (see Paarl map) • Est 1998 • 1stB 1999 • Tasting & sales by appt • Tasting fee R15 for wine & R10 for olives & olive oil • Hildenbrand's Table only open for guests & functions at Klein Rhebokskloof Country & Guest House • Farm-grown olives & olive oil • Owner Reni Hildenbrand • Winemaker/viticulturist Reni Hildenbrand, with Ruani Visser • 18ha (cab, malbec, shiraz, chard, chenin, semillon) • 5 000cs own label 40% red 60% white • P.O box 270 Wellington 7654 • info@wine-estate-hildenbrand.co.za • www.wine-estate-hildenbrand.co.za

Perennially upbeat, the female team at this small, traditional wine and olive oil house is excited about burgeoning international relationships (Thailand the latest to succumb, after Sweden), as well as making more headway in Johannesburg recently. A first for the 2007 harvest was a cab rosé; future plans include 'a couple more trophies and to keep on selling out as we are doing now'.

★★★★ Shiraz Classic Hildenbrand styling: perfumed, hints bluegum & dark choc, flick spice; **06** well balanced, focused tannins & savoury biscuit conclusion.

Cabernet Sauvignon Barrique ★★★★ Lovely ripe blueberry notes & velvety spices on **06** (sample); tannins should lose their slight astringency over few yrs. **Cabernet Sauvignon Unwooded ★★★** Spicy hint to ripe blueberry perfume of **06**; pleasantly dry, fresh & convivial. **Inspiration** NEW **★** From cab; **07** light, almost rosé colour & texture; leathery, mushroomy styling; short lean finish. **Malbec ★★★★** Usually sells out before we get to taste, but... **06** intro is New-World-style blackberry voluptuousness yet palate is dry, food inviting. **Shiraz Autumn Leaf ★★★** Gleaming ruby lights on **07**, gushing red plum & peach, pleasant off-dry rosé-style quaffer. **Chardonnay Barrique ★★★★** Well-balanced, rich yet uncloying **05**, orange-peel & honey, hint vanilla, coconut aftertaste marries well with Thai curries. **Chardonnay Unwooded ★★** Light, easy drinking, with citrus & marmalade flavours. **Chenin Blanc ★★★ 06** combo early, later picked grapes, wooded & unoaked; tad less enthralling than last but attractively floral, ripe melon notes, hint oakspice. **Semillon ★★★** Heat-impacted **06**, spicy oak accompanying the citrus/nut-infused mouthfull. **Sleepless Nights Semillon Noble Late Harvest ★★★** Maiden **06**, now bottled, dried apricot & joyful juiciness, but fewer fireworks than promised. — *MM*

■ **Hilko Hegewisch** *see Solms-Delta*

Hill & Dale

Easy-drinking wines vinified from fruit off selected Stellenbosch vineyards by Guy Webber at Stellenzicht (see entry for tasting/sales information).

Merlot ★★ Dusty, mint-seamed stewed fruit on **06**, slight bitterness to soft core. **Pinotage ★★★** Typical banana & blackberry plus smidgen choc on **06**. Fleshy, yet austere finish similar to **04**. **Cabernet Sauvignon-Shiraz ★★★** Smoky & savoury **05**, bold frame of tannins hold ripe black fruits, vanilla edge from Fr/Am oak. **Merlot Rosé ★★★** Strawberry-infused, bone-dry picnic partner. **07** tad richer than pvs, long, pleasing finish. **Chardonnay ★★★** Fr/Am oak adds toasty note; attractive peach & apricot lingers. Food-friendly **06** touch purer & fresher than shy **05**. **Sauvignon Blanc ★★★** Sprightly **07** offers pungent greenpepper & gooseberry flavours, balanced acidity & quick finish. — *RP*

Hillcrest Estate
T 021-975-2346 • F 021-975-2195

Durbanville • Est/1stB 2002 • Tasting & sales daily 9-5 • Closed Easter Fri, Dec 25 & Jan 1 • Restaurant for breakfast & lunches during tasting hours • Tours by appt • Owner PD Inglis, R Haw & G du Toit • Winemaker Graeme Read (Jan 2003) • Viticulturist G du Toit • 25ha (cab, merlot, shiraz, chard, sauv) • 60t/±3 000cs 45% red 55% white • Private Bag X3 Durbanville 7551 • cellardoor@hillcrestfarm.co.za

'We have focused on improving the quality of Hillcrest Merlot to elevate it to signature status along with our Sauvignon,' says Graeme Read, who's employed vertical shoot positioning, green harvesting and precision irrigation, among others, to accentuate the grape's 'characteristic abundance of fruit on the nose and palate'. All the care and attention bore abundant fruit at last year's Trophy Wine Show, when the 05 vintage scooped the category trophy. 2007 also saw the first crops of cab franc, malbec and petit verdot, earmarked for a 'pure' bordeaux red.

★★★★ Cabernet Sauvignon-Merlot In 60/40 proportion for **06**, which manages to balance cassis, red berry concentration, harmonious oaking & refined structural elegance, with aplomb. Oaked 10 mths, third new.

★★★★ **Sauvignon Blanc** Gets it right every time: more fynbos & lemongrass in **06**, same expected minerality, racy acidity as predecessors. Designed for food & sharing with friends. As all these, 3+ yrs ageing potential.

★★★★☆ **Chardonnay Noble Late Harvest** Last available **05**, astonishing perfumes of honeyed dried peaches & preserved melon, but palate was the real surprise: tangy, zesty citrus. Third used barrels. 105g/l sugar, 11.5% alc. NE.

Cabernet Sauvignon NEW ★★★★ Structurally sound, from all-new barrique oak treatment, showing fruit ripeness of vintage, **05** also has attractive fennel, dried herb, black pepper nuances. Accessible, with 3/4 yr cellaring potential. **Merlot** ★★★★ Last available **05** showed greater concentration than **04** (★★★★); trademark red berries, candied violets, oakspice & backbone from Fr barrels, 80% new. Ageing potential 5+ yrs. Incl touch cab. NE. **Robbenzicht** NEW ★★★ For earlier drinking, merlot-led **06** has satisfying ripe plum flavours, lively juiciness. With 20% cab. **Chardonnay Wooded** ★★★★ Only 40% oak fermented, allowing full expression of peach & citrus tones, zesty drinkability. **06** excellent food partner. **Chardonnay Unwooded** ★★★ Characterful **06**'s tropical flavours given buttery richness, body plumping by 6 mths lees ageing. **Sauvignon Blanc Reserve** ★★★★ Last available **05**, coolly austere whiffs nettle & grapefruit, tad lean. NE. — *CR*

■ **Hinterland** *see Hartswater Wine Cellar*

Hippo Creek

By Vintage International Brands. Originally exclusive to the PicardiRebel chain, now more widely available following its success in the export arena.

Cabernet Sauvignon ★★★ **02** vanilla & red berries, ripe rounded tannins (only 2nd fill oak) make for easy early drinking. **Merlot** ★★ Drink-soon **03** juicy but uncomplex, some smoky/savoury nuances. ±Yr Fr oak oak, 20% new. **Pinotage** ★★ Unwooded, swiggable **04** earthy & plummy with rugged tannins — good with hearty/braai food. **Shiraz** ★★ **03** fruity with dusty note from combo new/old Fr oak. Showing maturity, time to pull the last corks. **Chardonnay** ★★★ **02** pvsly noted as low-keyed but attractive. **Sauvignon Blanc** ★★ Light **05** (sample) lacks varietal character, somewhat dilute.

River Horse range NEW
Red & White in this range, both **NV**, not ready for tasting. — *DH*

■ **Hirondel** *see Thor Wines*
■ **His Master's Choice** *see Excelsior Vlakteplaas*

Hofstraat Winery
T 022-487-3202 • F 022-487-3015

Swartland • Est/1stB 2002 • Visits by appt • Owner/winemaker Wim Smit, Loch Nel & Jack de Clercq • 3.5t/310cs 100% red • PO Box 1172 Malmesbury 7299 • wimsmit@wcaccess.co.za

The Hofstraat trio's Shiraz was judged best garagiste wine at the 2006 Michelangelo Awards. Another reason their informal tasting room is likely to keep attracting foreign buyers looking for exclusive, rare wines not found on the internet - one client left with 70 cases last year! Their first Port will debut at the end of the year.

Renosterbos range
Cabernet Sauvignon ★★★★ Provisionally rated **04**, flavoursome fresh cassis teamed up with noticeable but gd oak. **Barbera** ★★★ **05** big, smoky & sweet, with strong dry tannins, 15.3% alc. **Merlot** ★★★★ **04** focused red plum, choc freshness; light textured with some fruity succulence. **Shiraz** ★★★ **05** pleasant, smoky fireside drink — 15.5% alc guaranteed to banish any winter chill. No newer releases of this, any above, ready for review. — *DH*

■ **Homtini** *see Anthony de Jager Wines*

Hoopenburg Wines
T 021-884-4221/2/3 • **F** 021-884-4904

Stellenbosch • Est 1992 • 1stB 1994 • Tasting & sales Oct-Apr only Mon-Fri 9.30-4.30 Sat & pub hols 9.30-2 • 'Buy 11 get one free' • Closed Easter Fri-Mon & Dec 25/26 • Tours by appt (see also intro) • Owner Gregor Schmitz • Winemaker/viticulturist Neil Hawkins (Jan 2005) • 34ha (cab, merlot, pinot, shiraz, chard) • 150t/10 000cs 75% red 25% white • PO Box 1233 Stellenbosch 7599 • info@hoopenburg.com • www.hoopenburgwines.co.za

Winemaker Neil Hawkins is thrilled with the IWC 2007 gold for his Chardonnay under Hoopenburg's new top-end Integer label. 'The only SA chardonnay to get gold,' he marvels. He's equally excited about new visitor facilities: tastings in the barrel room and on a wooden deck overlooking the harvest action.

★★★★ **Cabernet Sauvignon** Unlike big, bold **02**, which needed time to mesh, **03** more Old World; evocative leathery hints to polished fruit, fresh acidity & long, fine tannins. 18 mths, 30% new Fr oak. Cellar, & uncork earlier-ready **02** (★★★★).

★★★★ **Integer Chardonnay** NEW Replaces South Barrel. **05** barrel selection, fermented/ aged Fr oak, 60% new. Well-handled wood cradles lemon/lime fruit, adds creaminess. Buttery richness & 14.5% alc cut by zesty citrus acidity.

Merlot ★★★★ Plush plum fruit & herbal hints in confident balance with well-handled oak on **04**. 18 mths Fr oak; 30% new. Balance & poise lifts the bar on **03** (★★★★). **Pinot Noir** ★★★ **04** was light-textured last ed, hints cherry, raspberry & charry oak. **Shiraz** ★★★ When last tasted **03** was somewhat rustic with noticeably drying tannins. May now have melded with fruit. **Chardonnay** ★★★ New vintage not ready. **05** was elegant, with subtle varietal character, fine acidity & judicious oaking. **Sauvignon Blanc** ★★★★ **06** change from unwooded New Zealand-styled **05** (★★★★) to Loire- & barrel-influenced. Restrained & refined grassy sauv character enhanced by nutty oak; 10% semillon adds weight, roundness. MIWA gold. Discontinued: **South Barrel Chamber Chardonnay**. — *CvZ*

■ Hoop Huis *see False Bay Vineyards*

Horse Mountain Wines
T 021-869-8328, 082-444-4568 • **F** 021-869-8329

Voor Paardeberg (see Paarl map) • Est 1997 • 1stB 2001 • Visits by appt Mon-Fri 9-5 Sat 9-1 • BYO picnic • Owner Far Horizons Wine Estate (Pty) Ltd • Winemaker Charles Stassen (Jan 2002) • Viticulturist Paul Wallace (Jan 2000, consultant) • 45ha (cabs s/f, merlot, pinotage, shiraz) • 400t/20 000cs own labels + 80 000litres for clients • 70% red 20% white 10% rosé • PO Box 2143 Windmeul 7630 • wine@horsemountainwines.com • www. horsemountainwines.com

'Continuity of quality prevails,' remarks Craig Lardner of Horse Mountain's repeated success at last year's IWC and Decanter tastings. At home, Lardner was instrumental in setting up the WO Voor Paardeberg Visitors' Centre, and he is still running The Quagga Project - come and view these animals at your next tasting.

Horse Mountain Wines range

★★★★ **Pinotage** 🖿 Intro wild berry & rhubarb typicity, unfolding to mocha flavours, long savoury finish. **05** individual, harmonious & delicious.

★★★★★ **Shiraz** 🖿 Layered cocoa & savoury spice, but **05** palate is long way off showing full potential. Still tight, fine-grained tannins promise rewarding development over 4+ yrs. New oak, yr, mainly Fr.

★★★★☆ **Michele** 🖿 Deeply serious, complex, classy. **05** layers dark fruit, fennel, campfire smoke. Firm but ripe tannins provide dry finish, longevity. Will age beautifully 5+ yrs. 14 mths Fr oak.

Quagga Ridge range

Cabernet Sauvignon-Merlot 🖿 ★★★ Pvsly listed as 'Red'. **05** fruit-driven & juicy, extra fillip from Fr staves. Cab & merlot 55:45. **Pinotage-Merlot Rosé** 🖿 ★★ Name change from

'Rosé' for **07**, boiled sweets fruitiness, off-dry quaffer. **Sauvignon Blanc-Semillon** 📖 ★★
Pvsly 'White'; **07** 80/20 sauv/sem, dictating gooseberry flavours, crisp acidity. — *CR*

■ **Houmoed** *see* Teubes Family Wines
■ **Hugo's Hill** *see* Landskroon Wines

Huguenot Wine Farmers

T 021-864-1293 • F 021-873-2075

*Wellington • Closed to public • Owner Kosie Botha • Cellarmaster Bill Matthee (1984) • Trade
enquiries Gert Brynard • PO Box 275 Wellington 7654 • jcb@mynet.co.za*

Privately owned wholesaling company which blends, markets and distributes a wide range of
wines, liqueurs and spirits.

■ **Hunting Family** *see* Slaley Estate
■ **Husseys Vlei** *see* Buitenverwachting
■ **Icon** *see* Ken Forrester Wines

Idiom

T 028-316-1633 • F 028-316-1640

*Sir Lowry's Pass • Est 1999/1stB 2003 • Tasting & sales: see Whalehaven • Vineyard tours by
appt (Da Capo Vineyards, Sir Lowry's Pass) • Owner Alberto/Valerie Bottega & family •
Winemaker Reino Thiart (2007) • Vineyard Manager Tim Clark • 32ha (barbera, cabs s/f, merlot, shiraz, mourvèdre, nebbiolo, pinotage, sangiovese, zinfandel, viognier) • 90% red 10%
white • PO Box 3802 Somerset West 7129 • wine@idiom.co.za • www.idiom.co.za*

Wind and baboons ensure low yields from the Bottega family's 8-year-old vines on their Da
Capo Vineyards farm, on the slopes of the Hottentots Holland Mountains near Sir Lowry's
Pass – they get a mere 1-3 tons for barbera and nebbiolo. The quality of the latter reportedly
gave a visiting Italian sommelier goosebumps: 'As good as Italian,' he averred.

Idiom range

★★★★ **Nebbiolo** NEW Premium-priced new addition from extremely low-yield Sbosch vyds.
04 fennel, menthol, cassis & vanilla affirmed on palate. New-World sweet fruit coupled with beefy (big & savoury) tannins. Only 25 cs.

★★★★ **Cabernet Sauvignon-Merlot-Cabernet Franc** No successor sighted for elegantly
configured (57/28/15) **04**; maraschino cherry flavours & firm, classy tannins. Poised,
shrugs off substantial alc, sweetness. Good prospects. Yr Fr oaked, 60% new.

Sangiovese ★★★★ **04** last ed realised potential implied in maiden 03; well crafted, so 15%
alc barely noticeable; juicy berry fruit, lithe tannin, tangy tail. Yr Fr/Am, some new. **Zinfandel**
★★★★ Mammoth **06** explodes with Ribena & Turkish Delight flavour; sweet, cinnamon laced &
somewhat alcoholic though already quite soft, yielding. **Cabernet Sauvignon-Pinotage-
Merlot** NEW ★★★☆ Flashy, forward & round for younger enjoyment. Maiden **05** cherry-toned,
40% pinotage giving sweet tannins & some appealing rusticity. **Shiraz-Mourvèdre-
Viognier** ★★★★ Viognier now identified in wine's name, having anonymously spiced up pvs
04 (★★★★). Follow-up **05** arresting combo cured meat, tar & Chinese spice. Nice density,
poise & focus; should develop attractive savoury patina with time. 100% Fr oak absorbed in
stride. **Wooded Viognier** ★★★☆ **04** offered stonefruit aromas last ed, 'sweet' butterscotch
& barley sugar flavours. Oak overwhelming on release but sufficient fruit to carry few yrs.
Sbosch WOs for all.

Enoteca Bottega range NEW

Super Rosso ★★★ **04** more Old World than stablemate; herbaceous, stalky texture, dry tannin yet a sweet fruit core. Cellaring may bring harmony. **Rosso** ★★☆ Merlot-shiraz duo
labelled 'Vino da Tavola'. **04** showing v little Italian character: soft, sweet & juicy. — *RP*

■ **Ikapa** *see* Handcrafted Wines
■ **Ilka** *see* Alluvia Boutique Winery & Guesthouse

I Love Wine
T 021-863-2375 • F 021-863-3120

Paarl • Open Mon-Sat 9-5; pub hols 10-3 • Closed Good Fri, Dec 25 & Jan 1 • 40A Main Rd Paarl 7646 • info@ilovewine.co.za • www.ilovewine.co.za

Paarl boutique-wine and fully licensed coffee shop, doubling as tasting venue for Anthony Smook Wines, Bergheim, Blyde Wines, De Zoete Inval, Southern Sky and The Mason's Winery, all listed separately.

◼ **Imagine**   *see Southern Sky Wines*

◼ **Imbizo**   *see Ernst & Co Wines*

◼ **Imbongi Wines**   *see Crossroads Wines*

◼ **Imvelo**   *see Premium Cape Wines*

◼ **Indaba**   *see Cape Classics*

◼ **Indalo**   *see Swartland Winery*

◼ **Infiniti**   *see The Company of Wine People*

◼ **Inglewood**   *see Neil Ellis Wines*

Ingwe
T 083-280-0137(FB)/ 083-327-3887 (PJG) • 021-8581063 • F 021-858-1063/021-852-7346

Stellenbosch (see Helderberg map) • Est 1998 • 1stB 1999 • Visits Mon-Fri 10-4 • Owner Alain Mouiex • Winemaker PJ Geyer (Sep 2001) • Viticulturist Francois Baard (Sep 1999) • 28ha (own/leased; cabs s/f, malbec, merlot, shiraz, tempranillo, chard, sauv) • 11-18 000cs 95% red 5% white • PO Box 583 Somerset West 7129 • sales@ingwewines.co.za

Viti man Francois Baard, with 20 years' experience behind him, gives 2007 the title of Hottest Year Ever. 'We're definitely noticing climate change.' For the first time, winemaker PJ Geyer last year produced a pinotage, a sauvignon, a rosé and a shiraz, all by request: 'We now have a BEE partner, Sheila Hlanjwa of Lathithá Wines, and that's what she wanted.' In the pipeline are organic wines, preferred by Bordeaux owner Alain Mouiex's European customers.

★★★★   **Ingwe** Refined & classic merlot-led red ('Leopard' in isiXhosa). Has 48% cab partnering standout **03** (★★★★★), sampled mid-2005. Classy **02** also displayed refined minerality & mid-palate fruit density; 60% new Fr oak compared to **03**'s 40%.

★★★★   **Amehlo White** Sophisticated & harmonious bdx-style blend sauv & sem. Textured, aromatic **06** (★★★★★) continues upward trend. Probably gd for another few yrs (not retasted, as for rest of range). Impressively taut, minerally **05** raised the bar.

Amehlo ★★★★★ 'Leopard's Eye' another take on the bdx style; mainly cab (46%) with merlot, malbec, shiraz (25/15/10), dash petit v in **03**, leap up from austere & leafy **02** (★★★★). 14-18 mths Fr oak. — *CvZ*

◼ **Initial Series**   *see Jean Daneel Wines*

◼ **Inkathi**   *see Groupe LFE South Africa*

Iona Vineyards

T 028-284-9678 • F 028-284-9078

Elgin (see Elgin/Walker Bay map) • Est 1997 • 1stB 2001 • Tasting, sales & tours Mon-Fri 8-5 Sat/Sun by appt only • Closed Easter Fri/Sat/Sun, Dec 25 & Jan 1 • BYO picnic • Self-catering guest house • Walks • Mountain biking • Owner Andrew & Rozanne Gunn, Workers Trust • Winemaker Niels Verburg (consultant), with Thapelo Hlasa (both Feb 2004) • Viticulturist Joseph Sebulawa, advised by Kevin Watt (Nov 2001) • 35ha (cab, merlot, petit v, shiraz, mourvèdre, chard, sauv, semillon, viognier) • 10 000cs 25% red 75% white • PO Box 527 Grabouw 7160 • gunn@iona.co.za • www.iona.co.za

Quality and not quantity remains the focus here. 'Instead of planting more vines we are very selectively grafting over excesses of one variety to varieties which have exceeded our expectations,' says Andrew Gunn. Thanks to empowerment by way of on-the-job training and equity participation, assistant winemaker Thapelo Hlasa, formerly in charge of irrigation, has also exceeded expectations: 'The best right hand I've ever had,' says consultant Niels Verburg. They made their first Noble Late Harvest last year. 'Something to look forward to if we manage to put a restraining order on Andrew from tasting it every five minutes!'

★★★★ **Chardonnay** NEW Sensational debut for low-cropped 2.5ha beauty. Wonderfully balanced citrus fruits, oak (60% in Fr, 20% new) & leesy complexity within mineral core; stony ring to farewell flourish. 13.5% alc. 300cs.

★★★★★ **Sauvignon Blanc** Classically styled upland example: mineral rather than tropical. **07** (just post-bottling) more pithy than pvs, figgy flesh to fresh natural acid seams. Style consistent with nettly **06**, fine fruit texture on cleanly dry palate. 13% alc.

Shiraz ★★★★ Piercing spice aromas focus cool, mineral core of **05**; N Rhône fruit intensity without blowsiness. Accessible but will go 4+ yrs. Yr Fr oak, 13.5% alc. Only 120cs. **Merlot-Cabernet Sauvignon** ★★★★ **04** showed bright mulberry fruit when tasted pvs ed. Savoury, herbal hints, tannins lending grip. Yr Fr oak, 25% new; 13.2% alc. — DS

▮ **Isabelo** see WaverleyTBS/uniWines

▮ **Isis** see Schalkenbosch Wines

▮ **Ivory Creek** see Citrusdal Cellars

▮ **Ivy Du Toit** see Jason's Hill Private Cellar

▮ **Ixia** see Theuniskraal Estate

▮ **Jabulani** see Cape Coastal Vintners

Jacaranda Estate

T 021-864-1235

Wellington (see Paarl map) • Est 1993 • 1stB 1994 • Tasting, sales & tours Mon-Sat 10-5 • Closed Easter Fri & Dec 25 • Self-catering/B&B cottage • BYO picnic • Farm-grown/made cheeses, jams & olives • Owner Jan & Trish Tromp • Winemaker/viticulturist Jan Tromp • 2.8ha (cab, merlot, chenin) • 25t/300cs own label • 75% red 25% white • PO Box 121 Wellington 7654 • jacaranda@iafrica.com • www.jacarandawineestate.co.za

Jan Tromp planted 3 000 tinta barocca vines last year. 'I like drinking unfortified tinta b myself,' he explains, 'otherwise I might turn it into port.' JT and wife Trish continue to make small quantities of cheese from Nutmeg, their new Jersey cow, and the olives, they assure, are as good as ever.

Cabernet Sauvignon ★★ **01** individual & rustically charming; no **02/03**; follow-up unready, as for rest of range. **Merlot** ★★★ **03** soft & light textured with pleasing tannin structure & smart wooding (Fr staves). **Debutante** ★★★ Idiosyncratic **03** cab/merlot blend with scents of farmyard & wild scrub, firm dry finish. **Chenin Blanc** ★★ Pear-toned **03** soft, fruity-dry, uncomplicated by wood **Jerepigo** ★★★ Individual & attractive **05** brimful of baked apples & sultana, very sweet & just a touch cloying. — IvH

▮ **Jackals River** see Beaumont Wines

Jack & Knox Winecraft

Somerset West • Est/1stB 2001 • Tasting & sales at Flagstone (see entry) • Owner Graham Knox & Bruce Jack • Winemaker See under Flagstone

Vinous chameleon Graham Knox (Siyabonga, Stormhoek) here collaborates with Bruce Jack of Flagstone Winery, uncovering exciting and unusual vineyards, capturing their essence, nurturing the young and nursing the old back to life. And bottling under descriptive names like Frostline, from a sky-high Swartberg vineyard, and Green on Green, ex the lower foothills of Wellington's Groenberg ('Green Mountain'). Great critical acclaim, great fun.

★★★★ **Green on Green Semillon** From Wllngtn vyd. Last tasted **04** beautifully elegant (13% alc); candlewax notes, ripe quince flesh, limy seam. Native yeasts; Am/Fr oak, 30% new.

The Outsider Shiraz ★★★★ Lovely fruit purity in last-available **04** (★★★★). Complex layers violets, café au lait, dark plums, coupled with svelte body. 14-16 mths mainly Am. Pvs was brooding blockbuster **02** (★★★☆). **Coincidence Chardonnay** NEW ★★★★ Buttered toast & citrus peel perfume on **05**, with a savoury flavour from gd oak & long lees ageing. Combo Fr/Am 10 mnths. Nudges next level. **Frostline Chardonnay** ★★★★ **04** pvs ed had crème brûlée, roast hazelnut girth & white pear aromas; smooth, less robust (13% alc) than pvs. Barrel fermented 4 mths Am/Fr oak, 60% new. **Frostline Riesling** ★★★★ Variety's aromatic pepper/lime delicacy given steely glint in last-tasted **05**, broad fruit richness finishes tinglingly bone-dry. — *CR*

■ **Jackson's of Stanford** *see Stanford Hills Winery*

Jacobsdal Estate
T 021-905-1360 • F 021-905-1360

Stellenbosch ▪ Est 1916 ▪ 1stB 1974 ▪ Tasting & sales at Bergkelder (see entry) or by appt ▪ Owner Dumas Ondernemings (Pty) Ltd ▪ Winemaker/viticulturist Cornelis Dumas, with Hannes Dumas ▪ 100ha (cab, pinotage, chenin, sauvignon) ▪ 600t/9-13 000cs own label 100% red ▪ PO Box 11 Kuils River 7579 ▪ dumas@iafrica.com ▪ www.jacobsdal.co.za

'The secret to our success is traditional winemaking,' says third-generation winemaker Cornelis Dumas, who is gradually handing over to son Hannes. They believe what makes their wine unique is that they rely solely on natural wild yeasts present in the vineyards to complete the fermentation in the cellar.

★★★★ **Pinotage** Perfumes not out of place at a grand ball! Pinot-like feel to silky plum fruit; soft & attractive. **04** lighter in body but just as charming as **03**.

Cabernet Sauvignon ★★★☆ **04** similarly softer-toned as **03**, still attractively lean, classic, with well-knit tannins. Warming ripe-fruit profile ideal with winter stews. Welcome lowish alc (12.3%). — *RP*

■ **Jacobus de Wet** *see Baarsma Wine Group*

■ *Jacoline Haasbroek Wines* *see My Wyn*

Jacques Smit Wines
T 021-873-1265 • F 021-873-2143

Wellington (see Paarl map) ▪ Est/1stB 2003 ▪ Tasting, sales & tours Mon-Fri 9-5 Sat 8-1 ▪ Closed Easter Fri/Sun/Mon, Ascension Day, Dec 25/26 & Jan 1 ▪ Facilities for children ▪ Owner Jacques & Marina Smit ▪ Winemaker Jacques Smit ▪ Viticulturist Jacques Smit ▪ 32ha (cab, shiraz, chenin, crouchen) ▪ 300t total/6t/±5 000 btls own label 100% red ▪ PO Box 137 Wellington 7654 ▪ info@vines2wine.com ▪ www.vines2wine.com

Flying the family flag at their first wine shows, the vine- and wine-growing Smits basked in positive comment about their (as yet untasted) Rooibernet Port and long lees-matured Chenin - crowd-pleasers both. The Wellington nursery owners report an uptick in demand for traditional varieties like riesling and crouchen blanc, hanepoot and muscadel, all high on the graftings list for new vineyards.

Cabernet Sauvignon ★★★★ **03**, tasted out of vintage sequence (as is Shiraz), super-ripe, pure-fruited & silky; well-balanced despite 15% alc. Notch up on slightly stalky **04** (★★★). **Shiraz** ★★★★ Thick & rich **05**, dense fruit hides massive alc (16%) on surprisingly lively palate. Contrast with **04** (★★★), showing rhône-like savouriness & elegance. **Chenin Blanc** NEW ★★☆ Fresh, appealing **06**, apple & dash melon, lees-ageing gives rounded drinkability. — *RP*

■ **Jagger's Peak** *see Blue Crane Vineyards*

Janéza Private Cellar

T 023-616-3547 • **F** 023-616-3547

Robertson • Est 2000 • 1stB 2001 • Visits by appt • Fee for tour groups R5 • Platters by appt Mon-Fri • Owner Jan & Eza Wentzel • Winemaker Jan Wentzel • Viticulturist Willem Botha (consultant) • 18ha (cab, merlot, petit v, shiraz, chard, sauv) • 3 000cs own label 60% red 40% white • PO Box 306 Bonnievale 6730 • jan.eza@lando.co.za • www.janeza.co.za

'I make it, so she has to sell it,' jokes Jan Wentzel of his better half, Eza, both great believers in the personal touch. Hence their regular participation in wine and cheese festivals, and the individual attention given to visitors to their farm. The newer Merlot and Cab brands are doing well but top seller remains the Tresuva.

Cabernet Sauvignon ★★★ Hazelnut-toned **05** last ed noted as needing ±yr to soften & fruit to emerge. **Merlot** ★★★ Pleasing tannin structure & smart wooding (staves) supported soft, light-textured **03** last ed. **Tresuva** ★★★ Pvsly tasted **03** bdx blend with shiraz, vinified traditionally; medium bodied, slightly raisined fruit. **Chardonnay** ★ Uncomplicated, unwooded **07** has delicate citrus & lime flavours. **Sauvignon Blanc** ★★ Crisply light (11% alc) & uncomplicated **07**, with tropical fragrance, flavour. — *MM*

■ **Jantara** *see Cape Vineyards*
■ **Jardin** *see Jordan Winery*

Jason's Hill Private Cellar

T 023-344-3256 • **F** 023-344-3146

Slanghoek (see Worcester map) • Est/1stB 2001 • Tasting & sales Mon-Fri 9-5 Sat 10-3 Sun by appt • Fee R10 • Closed Easter Fri, Dec 25 & Jan 1 • Bistro @ Jason's Tue-Sat 9-5 (also available for functions) • Facilities for children • Farm produce • Conferencing for max 50 • Owner Sakkie du Toit • Winemaker Ivy du Toit-Oates (Jan 2001) • Viticulturist Sakkie du Toit & Alister Oates (2004) • 100ha (13 varieties r/w) • 600t 50% red 45% white 5% rosé • Brand for customer: Wolvenbosch Family Vineyards (UK) & Fountain Head (Denmark) • PO Box 14 Rawsonville 6845 • info@jasonshill.co.za • www.jasonshill.com

Winemaker Ivy du Toit-Oates took time off last year for a very special harvest: the birth of her first baby, Ivy-Ann. At the cellar, there are now more activities for children, including a menagerie of birds and monkeys. On the wine side, says Ivy, 'We're looking to export more, particularly to Denmark and Holland.'

Limited Release Pinotage 02 not tasted. No successor in sight. **Limited Edition Sauvignon Blanc-Semillon-Chardonnay** ★★★ SA Woman Winemaker of Yr award for last tasted **03**, equal blend with prominent sweet-oak vanilla, gd balancing acid. Various WOs for all ranges.

Jason's Hill Private Cellar range

Chenin Blanc ☺ ★★★ Ripe Golden Delicious apple on generous **07**. Fat, juicy & food-friendly. **Sauvignon Blanc** ☺ ★★★ Tropical, refreshing summer quaffer; **07** hints asparagus & crisp, balancing acidity.

Cabernet Sauvignon ★★ **05** dense, ripe fruit with porty nuances, somewhat unbalanced. **Pinotage** ★★★ Tart red mulberry notes in **05**, strong tannins call for food. **Shiraz** ★★★ Sweet-oak-dominated **06**, firm dry tannin, subdued red fruit needs time to assert itself. **Rosé** ★★ Touch cranberry & rosepetal to rounded, easy-drinking, off-dry **07**. **Chardonnay** ★★ Soft **06** offers honeyed butterscotch & ripe pear for early drinking. **Jasonté Sparkling** ★ Off-dry pinotage based fizz, **06** with savoury, bitter-cherry twist. **Noble Late Harvest** ★★★★ Last tasted was **03**, 50/50 chenin/muscat d'A; golden, luscious but not over-heavy.

Jason's Creek Classic range

Red ☺ ★★★ Cab f & merlot in sappy, smoky red fruited combo. **06** medium bodied & bright, friendly tannins, v quaffable. **White** ☺ ★★★ Aromatic, peachy, crisp & nutty sav, chenin, viognier. **07** pleasant summer aperitif. — *MW*

JC le Roux
T 021-865-2590 • F 021-865-2586

Stellenbosch • 1stB 1983 • Tasting & sales Mon-Fri 8.30-4.30 Sat 10-4 (Nov-Apr) 10-3 (May-Oct) Sun 10-3 (Nov-Apr only) • Fee R20 • Tour & AV show Mon-Fri 10, 11.30, 3 Sat 10, 12 Sun (Nov-Apr only) 11, 12 • Closed Easter Fri/Sun, Dec 25 & Jan 1 • Tour groups • Gifts • Owner Distell • Winemaker Elunda Basson (2007) with Hentie Germishuys (Oct 2002) • Viticulturist Bennie Liebenberg (both Jan 2000) • 27ha own vyds • 20% red 80% white • ISO 9200 certified • PO Box 184 Stellenbosch 7599 • ebasson@distell.co.za • www.jcleroux.co.za

Elunda Basson was until recently red-wine maker for Nederburg and helped place that household name back on the local and international pop charts. She has now assumed the mantle of bubblemeister at this, the country's largest dedicated sparkling-wine house, after winemaker Wilhelm Pienaar was offered the unmissable opportunity to do an MBA at the prestigious Montpellier Oenology School in France.

Méthode Cap Classique range

★★★★☆ **Pinot Noir 98** was elegant, creamy, delicious. **99** (★★★☆) less impressive, lacking mousse, but good minerally palate with some length. Matured in bottle for 6.5 years before disgorging.

★★★★ **Scintilla** Creamy fine-pearled mousse on chard-dominated **00** (75%, with pinot; released after already-tasted **01**). Reflects 5 yrs on its lees with gd depth & complexity, underlain by refreshing mineral tones, lengthy finish.

★★★★ **Pinot Noir Rosé** Another version released only after time in bottle. **97** was delightfully fresh; **98** (★★★★) also with fresh, pleasant raspberry/strawberry flavours, after slightly rustic fruity bouquet; gd weight & refreshing minerally finish.

La Vallée ★★★ Now **NV**, semi-sweet version mostly from pinot; bland to sniff, but distinct nutmeg on palate, & a gently sweet finish. Discontinued: **Chardonnay**. Both ranges Coastal or W Cape origin.

Sparkling range

Sauvignon Blanc ★★☆ Just a touch of sweetness on uncomplicated **07**, which bubblingly offers green apple & grenadilla notes. **Le Domaine** ★★ Floral, lemon zest aromas, cloying sweetness (80g/l RS) & mere 7.5% alc (like Chanson). From sauvignon/muscat de F. **La Chanson** ★★★ Big-volume, ruby-hued sparkler. Sweet & overtly fruity, for uncomplicated celebrating. Discontinued: **JC Blue**. These all carbonated; **NV** unless noted. — *JPf*

Jean Daneel Wines
T 028-423-3724 • F 028-423-3789

Napier (see Southern Cape map) • Est/1stB 1997 • Visits by appt • Owner Jean & René Daneel • Cellarmaster/viticulturist Jean Daneel • Winemaker Jean-Pierre Daneel • 3.25ha • 57t/4 000cs 30% red 70% white • PO Box 200 Napier 7270 • jdwines@worldonline.co.za

Winemaking in Napier means a good deal of DIY, smiles Jean Daneel. He and his family have been busy, developing their own town vineyard, as well as finishing the restoration of an old house and a barn on the main road for the now-open restaurant and deli, operated by wife Renée, where Mediterranean flavours, cheese and fresh produce are the mainstays. Son Jean-Pierre, who helps with management, is now married, and younger son Marchand is training as a chef, much to his parents' delight.

Signature Series

★★★★ **Cabernet Sauvignon-Merlot** Last tasted were elegant **01** (★★★★★) & generously ripe **02**, well structured & gd for difficult yr, but focus diffused. Next will be **05**.

★★★★☆ **Chenin Blanc** Always sophisticated, suave; **06** in more restrained mode than pvs (more like **04**), with fine acid thread binding incipient complex, gorgeous flavours (give it time!), with 13 mths oak, 20% new still apparent. Silky texture, long finish.

★★★★☆ **Directors Signature Chenin Blanc** NEW Brilliant greenish gold of **06** tells of quality - but, mid-2007, young wine's rich fruit restrained, almost austere under the oaking (17 mths new), which needs yrs to (hopefully) integrate. Subtly forceful & v supple, almost slithery. Like std version, WO Coastal. EW.

★★★★ **Chardonnay Brut** Last tasted **01**, MCC from Fhoek chard, had biscuit notes, delicious suppleness, great lift & focus.

Syrah NEW This & maiden versions of Directors Signature Red & Signature Red, also 05s, still in barrel at press time; to be released later this yr.

JD Initial Series

Red ★★★ Savoury **05** shows herbal red-fruit notes; firmly, perhaps sternly built; herbaceous finish. Integrated oak, 20% new. 70/30 merlot/cab. No **04** made. WO Fhoek, like next. **White** ★★★ **06** blends chenin with semillon, chard, sauv, for well-textured, mildly attractive wine with a rather sharp bite. **Port** ★★★ Last was **00** from Barrydale cab; raisiny & oxidative, dense & soft. 3 yrs oak. — TJ

■ **JH Pacas & Co** see Bernheim Wines
■ **JJ Handmade Wines** see Stellenrust
■ **Johan de Wet Wines** see Lorraine Private Cellar

Johan van Zyl Wines
T 022-921-3328 • F 022-921-2740

Piekenierskloof (see Olifants River map) • Est/1stB 2002 • Visits by appt 10-5 • Owner Johan van Zyl • Winemaker Gerda Willers • Viticulturist Johan Viljoen • 50ha (cab, cinsaut, grenache (r/w), pinotage, tempranillo, chard, viognier) • 250t/500cs own label • PO Box 251 Citrusdal 7340 • hannalise@heidedal.co.za

Buoyed by the response to his 'still-developing' Grenache 05, Johan van Zyl has now planted grenache blanc. He increasingly sees grenache as his flagship, 'somewhat unique to my area, and the ideal wine to share with friends who share my passion for it.'

Grenache ★★★ Bright ripe red fruit on **05**, hint spice, pleasing harmony between fruit, alc & acid. **Pinotage** ★★ **04** slightly wild aromas & Am oak 'sweetening', warming 15% alc. **Chardonnay** ★★★ Lovely full-ripe **05**, touch of pear, integrated oak, though lowish acidity. **Chardonnay Unwooded** NEW ★★★ Soupçon sugar on **06** gives extra plumpness to sunripe tropical fruit flavours. — JN

■ **John B** see Rietvallei Estate

Jonkheer
T 023-616-2137/8/9 • F 023-616-3146

Robertson • Est 1912 • 1stB 1956 • Visits by appt only • Owner Nicholas Jonker & sons • Cellarmaster Erhard Roothman (1970) • Winemaker Dirk Jonker (1992) • Viticulturist Andries Jonker & Nicholas Jonker (1985/1942) • 185ha (cab, chard, muscat d f) • 2500t/17 000cs own label + 150 000cs for customers 30% red 70% white • PO Box 13 Bonnievale 6730 • info@ jonkheer.co.za • www.jonkheer.co.za

'Look north-west and north-east. Not north,' is Dirk Jonker's advice to SA winemakers wishing to expand their international horizons. Heeding his own counsel, he launched his Pinotage in China and scored an instant hit – good news not only for Jonker but also for other pinotage producers looking to crack the Far East market. Still thinking out of the marketing box, Dirk J invited a group of top-rated Mauritian sommeliers to Jonkheer for a memorable masterclass in winemaking.

Jonkheer range

★★★★ **Chardonnay Family Reserve** Serious & classically styled. **04** (sample) held nothing back, with crème brûlée intensity & palate-lengthening sugar; **05** (★★★) on review showed similar opulence without a containing structure, giving an ultra-soft character which some would prefer. Single vyd, new Fr oak fermented/±18 mths, native yeasts.

★★★★ **Dead Frogge Chardonnay** Vastly less frivolous than name implies. **05** (★★★★) bold & vibrant as pvs, a ringing freshness to the yellow peach fruit, wood well integrated; only quibble is the sweetish finish, which **04** (sample) avoided though it had more residual sugar. 75% fermented new/2nd fill oak, natural yeasts.

★★★★ **Muscatheer Family Reserve Muscat de Frontignan** Last was massively sweet **04**, which billowed caramelised peel, dried fruit, toasted nuts. IWSC gold, Muscadel Assoc platinum. 500ml.

Dead Frogge Merlot Sold out. **Pinotage** ★★★ Characterful **05** was last reviewed; ex-single vyd block; thick & chunky with high-toned edginess. Portion barrel fermented/aged new Fr oak. **Cabernet Sauvignon-Merlot** ★★★★ **03** evolved beautifully; last time had curves in the right places to please most palates. Yr oaked. **Chardonnay** Not tasted. **Buccanheer Touriga Nacional** ★★★★ Ruby style port; **02** Christmas cake, tea leaves & marzipan; lighter than expected body doesn't detract from enjoyment. 18 mths 2nd fill oak, 500ml. Not retasted. Discontinued: **Cabernet Sauvignon Family Reserve**.

Bakenskop range

★★★★ **Red Muscadel** ✓ Previewed **07** already delicious; distinctive tealeaf aromas, raisin sweetness nicely balanced by acidity & hint of tannin. Beautifully elegant & poised. Deserves hordes of fans.

★★★★ **White Muscadel** ✓ Fortified dessert, beloved of competition judges. Fresh-as-a-daisy **07** (★★★★★), entrancing veldflower & incense bouquet, uncomplicated sweetness, but not all are like this! From healthy, tiny berries, cold soaked. **04** was also gorgeous & luscious.

Chardonnay ☺ ★★★ **07** gentle peach note, soft acidity, lovely varietal character. Exceptional value. **Chenin Blanc** ☺ ★★★ Melon with sprinkling spice, clean acidity not overdone. **07** refreshing, perfect for hot summer's day in gd company.

Cabernet Sauvignon Not tasted. **Merlot** ★★★ **04** a real charmer last ed: sappy red berry fruit, silky mouthfeel helped by 4.7g/ℓ sugar. **Pinotage** ★★★ **04** textbook ripe-style pinotage, last time with forceful tannins which should have relaxed by now. **Roothman Cape Red** ★★★ Fruit the hero of this **NV** blend; last bottling offered bright fresh-picked mulberries & blackcurrants, backed up by creamy palate. **Blanc de Noir** ★★ Last was simple & honest off-dry **05**, with redcurrant/cherry character from its red muscadel source. **Sauvignon Blanc** Not tasted. **Natural Sweet Rosé** Not tasted. **Es la Vida Perlé** [NEW] **07** not ready for tasting. Discontinued: **Muscat Perlé**. — IvH

Joostenberg Wines 🍴 🍷 ☕ ♿
T 021-884-4932 · F 021-884-4135

Paarl ▪ Est 1999 ▪ Tasting & sales daily 10-5 at Klein Joostenberg Deli & Bistro ▪ Tours by appt ▪ Bistro hours Tue-Sun 8-5 (see Eat-out section) ▪ Owner Myburgh Winery (Pty) Ltd ▪ Cellarmaster/viticulturist Tyrrel Myburgh ▪ Winemaker Gareth Hardres-Williams ▪ 31ha (cab, merlot, mourvèdre, shiraz, touriga, chenin, viognier) ▪ 200t/8 000cs own label 35% red 50% white 15% dessert ▪ PO Box 82 Elsenburg 7607 ▪ joostenberg@mweb.co.za ▪ www.joostenberg.co. za

Gareth Hardres-Williams completed his first full vintage here, overseeing the creation of a cabernet rosé and shepherding the new Little J range into the Joostenberg fold. In the vineyards, the team have grafted more viognier onto old cabernet vines and are looking at other Mediterranean varieties suited to their climate, such as mourvèdre and grenache. The winery continues to move towards more eco-friendly practices like biodegradable packaging and organic viticulture, while composting is being explored as an alternative to chemical fertiliser.

★★★★ **Bakermat** Farm's flagship off their best vyds. Last ed noted **04** more robust & showy than pvs, but still seriously styled, with firm tannins. Blend cab, merlot, shiraz (50/41/ 9), 2 yrs Fr oak, 25% new.

★★★★ **Shiraz-Viognier** 🗌 Always fresh & elegant with beguiling fruit purity, vibrancy & balance. **06** dense hues, white pepper sewn into cool, mineral core. 6% viognier lifts fresh, dry finish. 14.5% alc. 10 mths Fr oak.

★★★★ **Fairhead** 🗌 **06** now 2:1 chenin/viognier blend barreled 6 mths; latter's dried apricot dominance kept in check, so tangy succulence & seamless balance are the lasting impressions. Step-up **05** included dash oaked chard. 14% alc. Wild yeasts, seasoned wood.

★★★★★ **Chenin Blanc Noble Late Harvest** Wow! **06** shimmers golden; redolent of full, luscious marmalade, with great viscosity in echoing length. More showy than **05**, but as sophisticated: fine acidity counters unctuous depth of flavour. Swiss gold; drier than pvs (114g/l sugar), & strong (14.5% alc). Barreled 6 mths.

Little J Rosé NEW ☺ 🗌 ★★★ Vibrant salmon hues suggest not just candy-floss: **07** brims with cherry/berry fruit, fresh tangy tail. Good enough grip for the eponymous Bistro's food. Cab, agreeable 12.5% alc, dry. EW.

Shiraz-Merlot 🗌 ★★★★ **05** (previewed as Merlot-Shiraz pvs ed) now resplendent in purple robes with just-dominant (51%) shiraz leading moniker; racy spice aromas lifting red berry flesh. Fresh & refreshing. **Chenin Blanc-Viognier** ✓ 🗌 ★★★★ Bang for your buck: quince fruits, apple pie warmth, a bit of grip & a tinge of oak wrapped up in appealing **07**. Like **06** (★★★★), fuller, more textured than pvs. 5% viognier. Discontinued: **Walker Bay**. — *DS*

Jordan Winery 🍾 ⏵ 🎋 ♿
T 021-881-3441 • F 021-881-3426

Stellenbosch • Est 1982 • 1stB 1993 • Tasting & sales Mon-Fri 10-4.30 Sat & Sun 9.30-2.30 • Fee R15 refundable with purchase • Group tastings for up to 15 by appt • Closed Easter Fri-Mon, Dec 25 & Jan 1 • Tours by appt only (no pub hols) • BYO picnic • Owner Jordan family • Winemaker Gary & Kathy Jordan with Sjaak Nelson (2002) • Viticulturist Ted & Gary Jordan (1982) • 105 ha (cabs s/f, merlot, shiraz, chard, chenin, sauvignon, riesling) • 900 tons 65 000 cs 55/45 red/white • PO Box 12592 Die Boord 7613 • info@jordanwines.com • www.jordanwines.com

Gary Jordan's online harvest diary, started in 2006, had readers asking for more: it now has an interactive question and answer slot and regularly updated video clips. Last year's vintage was memorable for the release of a maiden Rosé, shiraz-based, under the Chameleon label. 'We visited France in 2006 to taste and research our ideal rosé style,' explains Kathy J, 'and selected particular vineyards to ensure an elegant wine with a slightly lower alcohol.' The label honours the Cape Dwarf chameleons which, as SA National Biodiversity Institute researchers last year ascertained, live in the shrubs and trees around the vineyards. They're further commemorated by the Jordans' newly-established research bursary which donates a percentage of sales of the Chameleon range towards the tuition and research costs of a PhD candidate studying the endangered animal.

Jordan Winery range

★★★★ **Cabernet Sauvignon** Leading modern style, watermarked with restraint. Concentration, complexity evident in **05**, in herbaceous genre. Tight yet ripe tannins of macho **04** need yr/2 to unfurl classic flavours. 20 mths new/used Fr oak.

★★★★ **Merlot** Stylish & understated, as usual. Lithe yet confident **05** offers butcher's door aromas, measured mulberry fruit & judicious oak; a satisfying whole. **04** contrasts ripe fruit & freshness, eminently drinkable. 17 mths Fr oak.

★★★★★ **Cobblers Hill** Flagship Bdx blend celebrates family heritage in shoes. Best barrel selection cab, merlot & cab f (46/33/21) lavished 2 yrs Fr oak. **04** sensational; complex spicy allure to tightly wound mouthful, striking elegance. Will reward - demands - up to 10 yrs evolution. Majestic cab austerity on **03** (55/30/15) upped ante from pvs. Swiss gold.

★★★★★ **Sophia CWG Auction Reserve** Named for mother of Faith, Hope & Charity, representing the three best barrels selected from above wine for this impressive show bottling. Dominant cab on **04** gives austere, tannic feel to underlying sweet fruited richness & freshening acidity. 46/33/21 cab, merlot, cab f, 26 mths new Fr barriques. Not revisited this ed.

★★★★ **Chardonnay** Perennial hit with both judges & consumers. **06** bold & beautiful; ripe grapefruit/lime napped in leesy hazelnut richness. **05** had steely tension. **04** Winemakers' Choice, VDG. Fr oak sur lie 9 mths, fresh 13% tank element.

★★★★☆ **CWG Auction Reserve Chardonnay** Stringent all-new-barrel selection ex Nine Yards vyd. **05**, star of 2006 auction (not retasted this ed), distinguished & refined, gorgeous buttery sheen, assertive - needs time to round out. Native yeasts, 14 mths Fr oak.

★★★★☆ **Nine Yards Chardonnay Reserve** A New World classic: outspoken yet sophisticated. **06** masterful; mineral edge to delicious quince fruits, myriad flavours ghost super length. 14% alc. **05** balanced freshness with rich textures. Barrel selection of farm's best vyd; fermented/yr new Fr oak, portion native yeast for complexity. **03** (★★★★★); Wine (★★★★); VDG; JCWCA gold.

★★★★ **Blanc Fumé** Riper, more complex than unwooded sibling; finely tuned melange creamy oak sparring with spiky fruit in **06**. **05** reliable as ever, elegant vanilla enhancing fig/citrus features. 13% alc. 40% tank portion freshens.

★★★★ **Sauvignon Blanc** Full blast of grass, hay & riverstone minerality announce **07**, bracing & intense but not quite best-yet **06** (★★★★★). Latter more dramatic than pvs, fantastic purity of fruit; ripe, concentrated but agile.

★★★★ **Mellifera Noble Late Harvest** Riesling's propensity for botrytised dessert style paraded in scintillating **06**, reviewed pvs ed. Spicy/limey aromas herald lush fruit; sweetness pepped up by racy acid. Touch bigger than best-to-date **05** (★★★★★). No **07**.

Syrah ★★★☆ Aromatic guile to refined wood spice folded with dark berry fruits in **05**. Full enough but not too heavy. **04** also richly textured with balanced freshness. Harmoniously Am/Fr oaked, 16 mths. **Chardonnay Unoaked** ★★★★ Good fruit retention & enough secondary interest without blowse in next **07**; well harmonised structure, substantial nutty concentration with focusing freshness. On lees 4 mths. **06** sold out before tasting. **Chenin Blanc** ★★★★ Beautiful balance tropical fruit, creamy oak vanilla & fresh acidity of **06** testimony to cellar's wood management skills. **05** rich, honey notes in supple texture. 55% in used Fr oak 8 mths, rest ex tank. **04** TWS trophy. **Rhine Riesling** ★★★ **06** developed, lightly spicy & slightly sweet. Best aside Asian/poultry/fish dishes.

Bradgate range

Syrah ✓ ★★★★ **05** redolent of pears-in-redwine, lovely clove warmth to easy but interesting mouthful. Reliable fallback on winelists. Fr/Am oak finish. **Cabernet Sauvignon-Merlot** ★★★ Modern, bright-fruited, easygoing ensemble cab s & merlot (splash cab f). **05** leather scents, showing 'warm' 14% alc. Mix new/used Fr oak 10-15 mths. **Chenin Blanc-Sauvignon Blanc** ★★★ **06** bottle-aged, honeyed flavours held by perky acid. 81/19 mix. These easy drinkers developed for world markets but also available locally.

Chameleon range

Cabernet Sauvignon-Merlot ★★★☆ Approachable, yet flavoursome with ageing potential. **05** gravelly ring to bright cassis/plum fruits, structured Fr oak (14 mths). Like **04**, small shiraz component (11%) adds to fruit. **Rosé** NEW ★★★ Summer fruits explode through the salmon sheen, spicy edge to clean, refreshingly dry send-off. 13% alc. EW. **Sauvignon Blanc-Chardonnay** ★★★ Successful marriage of difficult partners: flashy, tense sauvignon tempered by leesy chard adding fruit weight to **07**. — DS

Joubert-Tradauw Private Cellar

T 028-572-1619 • F 028-572-1315

Tradouw (see Klein Karoo map) ▪ Est/1stB 1999 ▪ Tasting & sales Mon-Fri 9-5 Sat 10-2 ▪ Breakfasts, teas & 'Karoo tapas'/al fresco lunches Mon-Sat ▪ Tours by appt ▪ Lentelus B&B (T 028-572-1636, www.lentelus.co.za) ▪ Facilities for children & many other attractions ▪ Owner Joubert Family Trust ▪ Winemaker/viticulturist Meyer Joubert (1995) ▪ 30ha (cab, merlot, shi-

raz, chard) ▪ *2 500cs own label 70% red 30% white* ▪ *PO Box 15 Barrydale 6750* ▪ *info@ joubert-tradauw.co.za* ▪ *www.joubert-tradauw.co.za*

Visit this family-friendly farm in the Tradouw Valley and experience real country conviviality, including delicious food by Beate Joubert (try the 'Karoo tapas' or a generous Mediterranean-style platter), handcrafted wines by husband Meyer, lovely views, a new art gallery, upmarket farm stays and more.

Syrah ★★★★ Notes of black pepper, flint & wild spicy fruit on **06**, complexity underpinned by refreshing acidity, rounded by 45% new oak. Long cool natural fermentation no doubt played part in v interesting wine, which should be gd with food. **05** (★★★★) was well-crafted given warm vintage. **R62** ★★★★ Bdx-style blend, 60/40 merlot/cab in **06** (sample); well structured; appealing aromas of lead pencil & red fruit; promises complexity, but mid-2007 oak dominant (50% new), rather tannic. **Unplugged 62** NEW ★★★ Red-fruited **05** merlot-shiraz blend juicy & unpretentious. Appropriately for 2nd label, lightly oaked. **Chardonnay** ★★★★ From mature vyd, elegant **06** shows an Old-World persona in New-World dress: rich, earthy minerality interwoven with ripe apple & melon; smooth, soft finish. Fermented/14 mths 40% new oak. Toasty **05** (★★★★) was more ebulliently New World. — *JPf*

Journey's End Vineyards
T 082-612-7607; 021-852-6564 • F 021-852-4374

Sir Lowry's Pass ▪ *Est 1996* ▪ *1stB 2001* ▪ *Closed to public* ▪ *Owner Roger Gabb (Gabb family)* ▪ *Winemaker Leon Esterhuizen, advised by Ben Jordaan (Jan 2005, Jan 2004)* ▪ *Viticulturist Paul Fourie (Jan 1998)* ▪ *25ha (cab sauvignon & franc, merlot, shiraz , chard)* ▪ *95 tons/37 500cs 90% red 10% white* ▪ *Export brands: Journey's End, Chairman's Reserve, Kendal Lodge Estate* ▪ *PO BOX 3040 Somerset West 7129* ▪ *leone@journeysend.co.za, paulf@ journeysend.co.za*

Previously the flagship of the Kumala/Constellation SA portfolio, Journey's End Vineyards go solo this year. The Gabb family and winemaker Leon Esterhuizen, who honed his skills post-Elsenburg in Spain and the US, have their sights set on on-site vinification and maturation, and the establishment of a tasting room, by 2009.

Chairman's Reserve range NEW
Cabernet Sauvignon Not tasted. **Shiraz** Not ready. **Chardonnay** Unready; due for release this yr.

Journey's End range
★★★★ **Merlot** NEW Restrained greengage/mulberry aromas & some herbal notes; savoury, with powdery tannins, elegant & persistent.

★★★★★ **Chardonnay** Sumptuously fruited **05**, concentrated tropical, lime & pear-drop notes, textured, with sweet-sour finish.

Cabernet Sauvignon ★★★ Pepper/pimento, sweet almond & vanilla notes on **05**, restrained tannins, shy fruited; spicy finish. Barrel selection, limited release. **Shiraz** ★★★ Leathery, gamey aromas on **05**, forest floor notes, ample dry tannins; muscular style.

Kendal Lodge Estate range NEW
Cabernet Sauvignon Not ready. **Shiraz** Untasted. — *MF*

JP Bredell Wines

T 021-842-2478 • F 021-842-3124

Stellenbosch (see Helderberg map) ▪ *1stB 1991* ▪ *Tasting & sales Mon-Fri 9-5 Sat 10-2* ▪ *Tours by appt* ▪ *Owner Helderzicht Trust* ▪ *Winemaker Anton Bredell* ▪ *95ha (cab, merlot, pinotage, shiraz, souzão, tinta, tourigas f/n)* ▪ *15 000cs own label 80% red 20% port* ▪ *PO Box 5266 Helderberg 7135* ▪ *info@bredellwines.co.za* ▪ *www.bredellwines.co.za*

This year sees the re-launch of value-driven Vineyard Collection range under the brand name Helderzicht. 'Over the years we've established ourselves as a premium red wine and port producer. We're now ready to show this quality and style in wines that taste R50, look R50 and cost R25,' says MD, Donald Keys. Other new releases are a 10yr old tawny port and the 2003 vintage port in a 375ml packaging. A focus on conservation sees their CWG wines carry this theme, and winemaker Anton Bredell a regular visitor to their expansive Karoo game farm, Aasvoelsvallei, where he's refining its eco tourism potential.

★★★★ **Cabernet Sauvignon 03** last ed was huge yet refined; dense colour & masses cassis fruit; followed unbridled mould of pvs. **04** unready for tasting.

★★★★ **Bredell's CWG Auction Shiraz** Emphatic & individual **01** was last, with extra-fine tannins & tantalisingly 'different' finish. Yr mix Fr/Am wood, 25% new. Not retasted; 2nd lot offered at 2006 Auction.

★★★★ **De Rigueur** None since **03**, Sbosch bushvine cab/merlot (60/40), Calyon Top 5. Succulent bramble & woodsmoke flavours; plump fruit just contained by ripe tannins. Yr Fr oak.

★★★★★ **Bredell's Cape Vintage** Pvsly listed as 'Cape Vintage Reserve'. Long-admired benchmark Cape port. Long-lived too: refined **03** has substance, build for 15-20 yrs though delectably lush now; its cornucopia candied citrus, leather & spice warmingly memorable enticements. Multi-gonged fusion tinta, touchings & souzão. 20% alc. 86g/l RS. No **02**.

★★★★ **Late Bottled Vintage** Rich & silky 'fireside port'. None since **02**, which seduced with plush fruitcake features, promising velvety finish. Tinta, souzão, tourigas; 3 yr old oak; 19% alc; ±90g/l sugar.

★★★★★ **Bredell's CWG Auction Reserve Port** Last was **03**, which needed to slumber for ±decade, in vintage style. Traditional Portuguese varieties, 2 yrs large old Fr oak; 87g/l RS.

Merlot ★★★★ Last was big, plummy **01**. **02** sold in bulk. **03** is next. **Shiraz** ★★★★ **03**, revved up with whiffs oak, berry & spice, still available, not retasted.

Vineyard Collection

> **Helderzicht Shiraz** NEW ☺ ★★★ Modern, crowd-pleaser style. **04** rounded, friendly mouthful, abounding with spice, oak vanilla scents & flavours. Soundly dry finish.
> **Helderzicht Red** ☺ 🍷 ★★★ Honest country-style red; cinsaut-dominated **NV** (with tinta, cab, pinotage, shiraz), pleasant winey flavours, rounded dry conclusion.

Helderzicht Chenin Blanc ★★★ **07** modest floral/pear ripeness; sweet kick in tail from 14% alc. —AL

JP le Hanie Wines [NEW]
T 021-887-1277 • F 021-887-1288

Stellenbosch ▪ Est 2007 ▪ 1stB 2008 ▪ Closed to public ▪ Owner Johan & Anne-Mari le Hanie ▪ Winemaker Johan le Hanie ▪ 500cs 100% red ▪ PO Box 12695 Die Boord 7613 ▪ johan@email4life.co.za

After a dozen years as a winemaker, Johan le Hanie and his wife, Anne-Mari, are going solo. Their first wine will become available this year. They have plans for a barrel-fermented Pinot Noir-Chardonnay, and are looking to establish their own cellar on a Boland farm within the next two years.

Sixteen Barrels Cabernet Sauvignon-Merlot ★★★ **06** slightly vegetal cab-dominated blend. Austere & inscrutable at present though inky black fruits could fill out given time. **Mea Culpa Cabernet Sauvignon-Merlot** ★★★★ Attractive meaty exterior, soft & juicy fruit core. **03** eminently drinkable now with enough structure for another yr/2. —RP

▌ Juhantha *see Stellar Winery*

Julien Schaal
T +33-9-53-9-3775 • F +33-3-90-29-8127

Walker Bay ▪ Est 2004 ▪ Closed to public ▪ Owner/winemaker Julien Schaal ▪ 28 tons 2 000 cs 85% red 15% white ▪ PO Box 832 Stellenbosh 7599 ▪ julien@vins-schaal.com ▪ www.vins-schaal.com

'Making wine in SA is still like a dream,' says Julien Schaal, a young winemaker from Alsace, of his local wine venture. The new Hemel-en-Aarde cellar built by his 'awesome' partners, the Newton Johnsons, has, he believes, made all the difference to his wines. New among them is Les 5 Pierres (The 5 Stones), a shiraz/cab blend.

★★★★ **Les Cinq Pierres** NEW Maiden **06** tank sample rather gawky mid-**07** but gives distinct impression will ease into cohesive whole. Already balanced & long, opulent lily/red currant aromas & flavours from Elgin syrah; 10% Hemel-en-Aarde cab giving tangy acidity, firm backbone. 30% new Fr oak.

★★★★ **Chardonnay** Fr oak ferment/aged **06** for fans of 'in your face' chardonnay. Lashings of vanilla/butter, sun-ripe tangerines enlivened by tart lime acidity. Less overtly sweet than pvs (2.1g/l vs 4.7g/l). WO O'berg.

Syrah ★★★★ Tailored tannins balanced by bright fruit, brisk acidity help **06** take step up. Adding allure to Elgin fruit are garrigue/lily top notes & persistent creamy finish, 14.5% alc well disguised. Oak as for Les Cinq Pierres. **Merlot-Petit Verdot** ★★★★ **06** intensely flavoured with black plum fruit, almost palate-cleaving acidity. Built for cellaring with moderate 13.3% alc (vs 14.5% of pvs), integrated tannins. 40% new Fr oak. WO W Cape. — *CvZ*

Juno Wine Company   ♟
T 021-872-0697 • F 021-872-1863

Paarl • Est/1stB 2004 • Tasting & sales at 191 Main Str, Paarl, Mon-Fri 8-5 Sat 10-1 • Closed most pub hols • Winemaker/viticulturist Newald Marais (Nov 2004, consultant) • ±60 000cs 40% red 40% white 20% rosé • PO Box 68 Main Road Paarl 7622 • info@junowines.com • www.junowines.com

'It seems that our two artists, 'wine' [Newald Marais, oenologist] and 'fine' [Tertia du Toit, label designer], have created a product that appeals to almost everyone,' says marketing director Oliver Kirsten of the newly released Pinotage Rosé. A variety of breads and deli goods are now also available from Juno's Paarl headquarters.

Cape Maidens range

Chardonnay ☺ ★★☆ Like pvs, **06** is fruity & dry, pear-toned & very quaffable.

Shiraz ★★☆ Tasted last ed, **05** was easy-drinking, its intense black fruit seasoned with pepper. **Cabernet Sauvignon-Merlot** ★★ **05** not revisited; last ed was aproachable & unchallenging with fresh, zesty finish. **Rosé** NEW ★★ Maiden **07** perky salmon pink, subtly pleasant berry/cherry nuances. **Sauvignon Blanc** ★★ Tasted pvsly, **06** lightish (11.5% alc) & dry, understated tropical tones. — *IvH*

■ **Kaapdal** *see Robertson Wide River Export Company*
■ **Kaap Hollands** *see Origin Wine*

Kaapzicht Estate   ♟♟♈ 🅰 📷
T 021-906-1620 • F 021-906-1622

Stellenbosch • Est 1946 • 1stB 1984 • Tasting & sales Mon-Fri 9-4.30 Sat & pub hols 9-12 • Fee R10 • Closed Easter Fri-Sun, Dec 25 & Jan 1 • Tours by appt • BYO picnic • Self-catering chalet & separate 'Wingerd Kraal' braai area for ±70 people; conference/entertainment venue (T 082·737·8329 - Mandy Steytler) • Conservation area • Owner Steytdal Farm (Pty) Ltd/Steytler Family Trust • Cellarmaster Danie Steytler • Winemaker Danie Steytler, with Charl Coetzee (Jan 1979/2003) • Viticulturist George Steytler, Charl Coetzee & Schalk du Toit (Jan 1984; Mar/Jun 2003) • 146ha (cab, merlot, pinotage, shiraz, chenin, sauv) • 1 100t/40 000cs own label 65% red 35% white • PO Box 35 Koelenhof 7605 • kaapzicht@mweb.co.za, sales@ kaapzicht-wines.com; exports@kaapzicht-wines.com • www.kaapzicht.co.za

The Steytlers have bought an extra 16ha, atop the highest hill on their farm, formerly a part of Eikenhof. Generally east facing, its wind-cooled slopes are destined in the main for sauvignon; west-facing sites will contribute to Danie S's goal: a full bordeaux blend. On the export front, Yngvild S is flying north, west and east five times a year, and recently engaged a new importer in Indonesia; plans, she discloses, are to bottle more under the Kaapzicht label and to sell less unbottled wine.

Steytler range

★★★★☆ **Pinotage** Leader of pinotage pack, regularly glitters with awards. **04** similar to regular bottling but fresher, thanks to plush new Fr oak (2 yrs) & livelier spice. Finely tailored individual from single old vyd.

★★★★★ **Vision** Multi-awarded flagship, melds classic duo, cab & merlot, with pinotage; regular 50/10/40 mix in **04** (★★★★). Expresses vintage ripeness, redoubtable structure, big alc (15%); all in check now but will need careful monitoring if cellaring. Tad less convincing than triumphant **03** & pvs. All new Fr oak, 2 yrs.

Kaapzicht range

★★★★ **Cabernet Sauvignon** Classic style with New World breadth. Last **02** showed signature ripe blackcurrant, dark choc fruit, authoritative oaking. **03** destined for CWG auction; **04** unready for tasting.

★★★★☆ **CWG Cabernet Sauvignon** 🖿 Ripeness always feature of this Bottelary Hills farm's reds. **03** tipping into Marmitey/porty tones of over-ripeness; fresher palate but 15% alc glow lingering memory. 100% new Fr oak 2 yrs.

★★★★ **Pinotage** Smart junior member of cellar's pinotage family. **04** chewily rich, full bodied; very ripe fruit contrasted/balanced by fresh acid, bone-dry finish. Fr oak, 40% new, 22 mths.

★★★★ **Shiraz** Sturdily-framed **05**, just pre-bottling, needs time to settle & reveal usual arresting perfumed spice, floral elegance. Core freshness & polished oak (35% new Fr) alleviate effects of 14.5% alc.

★★★★☆ **CWG Auction Reserve Blend** Selection Danie S's favourite barrels of Vision. Latest **05** imposing, powerful, its more robust features smoothed by new-oak vanilla, rich sweet mulberry fruit. New Fr oak, 2 yrs.

Chenin Blanc ☺ 🖿 ★★★ Heady concentration of apple blossom & floral fragrance on **07**. Perky freshness offset by 4.5g/l sugar. **Sauvignon Blanc** ☺ 🖿 ★★★ **07** packed with invigorating ripe fruity acids; medium body, tangily moreish. **Combination** ☺ 🖿 ★★★ Combines chenin's fragrance, sauvignon's bounce in **07** equal partnership. Delicious warm weather sipping. **Natural Sweet** ☺ 🖿 ★★★ **07** salutes bushvine vyd's diamond anniversary. Steamlined, dainty 11% alc with elegant tropical succulence, lingering sweetness.

Merlot ★★★★ **03** from excellent vintage. Deep minerally, meaty bouquet showing some development; tighter, fresher palate, velvety richness checked by dry tannin. Buffed by all new Fr oak, 22 mths. More satisfying than solid **02** (★★★★). **Bin-3** ★★★ Fruity blend, incl splash sweetening pinotage. **05** promising ripe, plummy nose, less generous in mouth, disappointingly short tail. **Estate Red** ✓ ★★★★ Fulsome, savoury mouthful; rich cab melded with supple shiraz; 66/33 in **05**. Comfortable & comforting. **Classic Red** 🖿 ★★★ **04** still available, not re-tasted. Classier than allsorts red with cinsaut would suggest. **Chardonnay** 🖿 ★★ Fr-oaked **06** tiring; mere wisps pickled lemon/lime, sweet flesh. Drink up. **Hanepoot Jerepigo** ★★★ **06** sunny gold colour; intense minty/grapey sweetness, but very clean, unheavy. —AL

🟥 **Kakamas** see Oranjerivier Wine Cellars

🟥 **Kalkveld** see Zandvliet Estate

Kango Winery

T 044-272-6065 • **F** 044-279 1038

Klein Karoo • Est 1976 • 1stB 1977 • Tasting & sales Mon-Thu 8-5 Fri 9-4.30 Sat 9-1 • Tours by appt • Cheese platters, picnic baskets by appt, or BYO • Conferences & other amenities (see intro) • Owner 36 members • Winemaker Flip Smith • Viticulturist Johannes Mellet (consul-

tant) ▪ 295ha (cab, merlot, pinotage, shiraz, chard, chenin, colombard, hanepoot, muscadel r/w, sauv) ▪ 3 000t 18% red 82% white ▪ PO Box 46 Oudtshoorn 6620 ▪ wynhuis@kangowines.com ▪ www.kangowines.com

Champion co-op cellar for the Klein Karoo, Kango Winery's other 2007 honours included a gold at the Swiss Wine Awards. Not resting on its laurels, the winery produced a regional first: a Noble Late Harvest. Also new is the petting zoo, a great drawcard for kids. And for adults, there's the winetasting facility which also offers platters of food from the area.

Swartberg Reserve range

Pinotage ★ Raisined, intense bouquet of **05** did not follow through to palate. Tasted last ed, as were others in range. **Shiraz ★★★ 05** had pleasing varietal smoke & thatch, salty meat hint, firm, hearty finish. **Chardonnay ★** Straw aromas on last-available **05**, light & dry. Grapes from elevated vyds in Meiringspoort area, among highest in S Hemisphere.

Kango range

Cabernet Sauvignon-Merlot-Shiraz ☺ **★★★ 06** elegant, fine-tannined blend; dollops lush fruit in a compact style, excellent drinking. Swiss gold.

Cabernet Sauvignon ★★★ Last ed black-berried **05** had meat extract & nutmeg whiffs, sustained friendly dry farewell. **Merlot ★** Eucalyptus touch to **06** robust pizza partner. **Pinotage ★★** Unceremonious braai slosher. Last ed **05** dusty, dry tail, savoury green-banana whiffs. **Ruby Cabernet ★★** Wine 'Best Value' pick for unpretentious **05**, last yr juicy wild-berry fruit, any edges smoothed. **Shiraz ★★** Last-tasted **05** restrained savoury intro, fairly robust tannins gd with heartier foods. **Chardonnay ★** Honey-laced appley **06** quaffer. **Chenin Blanc ★** Last-available **05** was soft, lightish & foursquare, dry. **Sauvignon Blanc ★★ 06** resembles pvs uncomplicated dry white with overt melon tones. **Morio Muscat Sparkling ★★★** Lemon sherbet follows through to a sweet yet fresh, spicy mouthfeel. Interesting Thai food match. **Semi-Sweet ★** Kiwifruit & lime in an ordinary sweet style. This, range below, WO W Cape unless noted.

Rijckshof range

- **★★★★** **Hanepoot** Alluring golden glints; deep spice & nutty fruit; super integration of alc, sugar; intense & warming - a great fireside companion.
- **★★★★** **Red Muscadel** Strawberry perfume leads to a tangy rhubarb & red berry palate; deep flavoured & warming, with a clean classy finish.

White Muscadel ★★★★ Melon & cinnamon lead to syrupy mouthfeel, but clean, fresh acidity provides gd balance. Best young, over ice. **Red Jerepigo ★★★** Tealeaves & molasses, malt-like, with a savoury character hiding primary fruit. **Gold Jerepigo ★★** Sultanas & spice in a shy style. **Ruby Port ★★** Faded fruit in a simple ruby style. **Vintage Port** In abeyance. All above fortified desserts **NV**. – RP

Kanonkop Estate

T 021-884-4656 ▪ F 021-884-4719

Stellenbosch ▪ Est 1910 ▪ 1stB 1973 ▪ Tasting & sales Mon-Fri 9-5 Sat 9-2.30 Pub hols 10-4 ▪ Fee R10 ▪ Closed Easter Fri, Dec 25 & Jan 1 ▪ Cheese platters in summer; traditional snoek barbecue only by appt (min 15 people); or BYO picnic ▪ Owner Johann & Paul Krige ▪ Winemaker Abrie Beeslaar (2002), advised by Beyers Truter ▪ Viticulturist Koos du Toit ▪ 100ha (cabs s/f, merlot, pinotage) ▪ 600t/±50 000cs 100% red ▪ PO Box 19 Elsenburg 7607 ▪ wine@kanonkop.co.za ▪ www.kanonkop.co.za

'Why not chilled Kadette with Sunday brunch?' muses irrepressible Johann Krige. His straightforward approach to wine encourages everyone to eschew hype and stuffiness and just enjoy it. A refreshing perspective for an estate with a consistent track record of success locally and overseas; with 115ha of terroir-matched vineyards aged an average 25 years; and with markets in over 50 countries (latest include Korea, Mexico and Brazil). And how many other producers can (and generously do, from time to time) offer tastings of 15 consecutive vintages of their top wines? Including the Cab, a wine dear to Johann K's heart – the 2003 perhaps the best in 20 years, he thinks.

★★★★★ **Paul Sauer** A classic since 1981. **04** has 70% cab, with equal cab f, merlot. Winning aromas cedar, spice, subtle berry, leading to oaky palate a touch lighter, less fruit-substantial than usual, but promising useful development. Vinified traditionally, like all these, in open fermenters. 2 yrs new Fr oak.

★★★★★ **Pinotage** Customary pure-fruited aromas/flavours on **05**, well supported by oak (80% new Fr, 16 mths), with big but very ripe, soft tannins on long, full-fruited palate. Manages 14.5% alc well. Rather delicious as well as serious.

★★★★ **Cabernet Sauvignon** After sternly elegant **01** & lighter **02** (★★★★), a splendid **03** (★★★★★), richly elegant, fresh, firmly structured; fruit intensity harmonising with oak (half new), leading to long, satisfyingly savoury finish. Should develop well over 5-10 yrs. WO Smnsberg-Sbosch (as all are, bar Kadette which WO Sbosch/NE).

Kadette ★★★★ Not trivial, but enjoyably approachable, with softly chunky tannins. **05**'s usual sophisticated rusticity stresses pinotage (43%) over cabs & merlot. — *TJ*

Kanu Wines

T 021-881-8140 • **F** 021-881-3514

Stellenbosch ▪ Est/1stB 1998 ▪ Tasting & sales Oct-Mar: Mon-Fri 10-5 Sat 9-1; Apr-Sep Mon-Fri 10-4.30 Sat closed ▪ Fee R3/wine ▪ Closed pub hols ▪ Gifts ▪ Cheese Bar for farm-style products ▪ Functions venue ▪ Permanent art exhibition ▪ Owner Hydro Holdings ▪ Cellarmaster Richard Kershaw ▪ Winemaker Johan Grimbeek (Jan 2002) ▪ Viticulturist Werner de Villiers (Nov 2004) ▪ 39ha (cabs s/f, merlot, petit v, roobernet, shiraz, nouvelle, viognier) ▪ 860t/38 000cs own label 40% red 60% white ▪ PO Box 548 Stellenbosch 7599 ▪ info@kanu.co.za ▪ www. kanu.co.za

Kanu's Noble Late Harvest is named Kia-Ora, a Maori greeting which literally means 'be well/ healthy'. This reflects a keen awareness that consumers are demanding healthier, lower alcohol wines, a challenge that winemaker Richard Kershaw is addressing by using more natural winemaking techniques, including wild yeast fermentation.

Limited Release range
★★★★ **Chenin Blanc Wooded 04** (★★★★) tasted pvs ed not quite in league of **03** (★★★★) more seriously oaked version. Tropical/floral scents with forceful structure.

★★★★★ **Kia-Ora Noble Late Harvest** No follow up yet on textured and luscious **04**. Botrytised dessert from chenin with excellent sweetness/acid balance. 14 mths Fr oak (60% new).

Shiraz ★★★★ Deeply coloured with spicy pepper aromas & roasted herbs. **04** (★★★★) rich red & blackberry fruit; more seamlessly integrated than **03** (★★★★). Well judged Fr oak 25 mths. Delicious finish. Discontinued: **Merlot**.

Reserve range
Sauvignon Blanc ★★★★ Also no follow up on food friendly **05**. Well assembled green fig and long mineral finish.

Kanu range
★★★★ **Keystone 04** tobacco & blackcurrant signals seriously-styled earthy Bdx blend (78% Cab); ripe concentrated fruit somewhat masked currently by firm oak tannins from 25 mths Fr oak maturation.

★★★★ **Chardonnay 05** not ready for tasting. **04** (★★★★) tasted perhaps at awkward stage; 10 mths oak (mainly Fr) gives extra dimension, but still unintegrated. **03** (★★★★) was deep & sophisticated.

Rockwood ☺ ★★★ Preview **06** just bottled; loads of juicy, spicy ripe fruit from shiraz, cab & merlot. Delightful. Gd everyday drinking - won't disappoint. **Chenin Blanc** ☺ ✓ ★★★★ Fresh, mouthwatering **06**, abundant green apple fruit focuses broad and complex flavours; firm, rich, solid finish. K'hof grapes.

Sauvignon Blanc ★★★ **06** overt capsicum/fig aromas, with less-induced breadth, though surpringly light on flavour with minerally finish.

Escape range
Sourced & made on request. None tasted this ed. — *IM*

KapVino Estate
T 021-865-2821 • F 021-865-2821

Stellenbosch • Est 2000 • 1stB 2005 • Tasting by appt only • 2 self-catering cottages • Owner Allemann Properties CC • Winemaker Urs Allemann (2005) advised by local experts • Viticulturist Urs Alleman (2000) advised by local experts • 2.5ha (shiraz) • 5t/300cs 100% red • PO Box 108 Stellenbosch 7599 • info@kapvino.com • www.kapvino.com

After 25 years in the electronics business, Emilia and Urs Allemann left Joburg's bright lights to grow shiraz in quiet Devon Valley. Most of the production is bought up but last year saw their first 'baby' in bottle. Plans are to increase volumes gradually whilst developing a local and overseas market following.

Shiraz ★★★ A pleasant lighter-styled version, **05** with smoky black-fruit aromas & smooth peppery flavours, 8 mths Fr oak a supportive background presence. — *MF*

Karmosyn *see* Terroir Wines of SA

Karusa Vineyards
T 023-626-1628 • F 023-626-1895

Robertson • Est/1stB 2004 • Tasting by appt • Owner Karusa Partnership • Cellarmaster Jacques Conradie • Vineyard Manager Theo Landmann • PO Box 529 Robertson 6705 • jacques@karusavineyards.co.za • www.karusavineyards.co.za

Convinced of the potential of high-altitude sites in the Klein Karoo, Jacques Conradie has planted exotics mourvèdre, grenache and petit syrah at 600m in the Swartberg foothills. The first fruit is expected in 2010; meanwhile he continues as winemaker for Bon Cap in Robertson, where he also vinifies his own Karusa label.

★★★★ **The Fifth Element** Co-fermented **06** blend shiraz/viognier (5%), youthful magenta rim & pure, bright redcurrant fruit structured by firm tannins. Well-measured acidity ensuring clean finish. Unfiltered/fined. Montagu fruit, as for **05** (★★★★) equally characterful albeit shade lighter. — *IM*

Karuwa *see* Vrede Wine Farm

Katbakkies Wine
T 021-424-6883 • F 021-426-1967

Est/1stB 1999 • Tasting & sales by appt • Owner Andries van der Walt • Winemaker Teddy Hall & Andries van der Walt • 550cs 57% red 43% white • PO Box 21675 Kloof Street 8008 • Avdwalt@inds-ct.co.za

Planning an environmentally friendly cellar, with the smallest possible energy footprint, on a plot he's bought in Devon Valley, Andries van der Walt is thinking positively: 'My first vintage there will be in 2008. Then I'll be a fully-fledged independent.' Last year was another first: he produced a maiden petit verdot, a single barrel that's 'a wild child'.

★★★★☆ **Cabernet Sauvignon 04** (★★★★) less opulent, more tightly knit than **03** debut. Firm oak & fruit tannins restrain red berry core, bright acidity gives length to cherry/cedar farewell. All elements in place for fruitful bottle-development. 22 mths new Fr oak.
★★★★ **Chenin Blanc** Nutty oak nuances (11 mths, 2nd & 3rd fill) complement tightly focussed lime & apple flavours on **06**. tingles with sweet-sour tension, 14% alc well hidden. Cellar few yrs to elicit full potential.
Syrah ★★★★ **05** more in line with lighter-styled **04** than concentrated **03**. Lean & savoury, refreshing sweet & sour plum acidity, lively tannins. Moderate 12.5% alc a big plus. 11 mths oaked. **Syrah Reserve** NEW ★★★★ Promising **04** debut's 18 mths in older oak sees fruit evolve into dense, opulently spiced mouthful. Complex, appealing, with firm chalky tannic

structure, leather whiffs. 15% alc bold but balanced. **Viognier ★★★★ 06** plump but beautifully proportioned, brimming with perfumed white peach, apricot kernel, almond flavours, clean-cut lime acidity; all enhanced by yr older oak. Notch up on intricately perfumed **05** (★★★★). All above WO Sbosch. — *MW*

Kautzenburg
T 021-842-3903 • F 021-842-3903

Stellenbosch ▪ Est 2000 ▪ 1stB 2002 ▪ Closed to public ▪ Owner Peter & Nina Ruch ▪ Winemaker Jeremy Walker (2002, Grangehurst) ▪ Viticulturist Peter Ruch, advised by De Waal Koch ▪ 5ha (pinotage) ▪ ±25t total 10t/±300cs own label 100% red ▪ PO Box 91 Somerset West 7129

This small Helderberg vineyard slopes due west, a favourable aspect, and throughout the pruning process the fragrance of khaki bush is in the air. 'This makes for a distinctive herbaceous aroma and taste in our Pinotage,' say Peter and Nina Ruch. Their wine is made by Jeremy Walker of Grangehurst.

★★★★ **Pinotage** From low-yielding bushvines. Riper vintage **05** (★★★★), preview packed with prunes & liquorice, contrasting with peppery oak & dry tannins. Needs melding; could rate better over time. **06** was layered, with finer tannins. — *CR*

▪ **Kaya** *see Overhex Wines International*

▪ **KC** *see Klein Constantia Estate*

▪ **Keates Drift** *see Franschhoek Vineyards*

▪ **Keimoes** *see Oranjerivier Wine Cellars*

Keisseskraal Vineyards

T 028-284-9219 • F 028-284-9219

Bot River (see Elgin/Walker Bay map) ▪ Est 2004 ▪ 1stB 2005 ▪ Tasting & sales Mon-Sat 10-4 Sun by appt ▪ Closed Christian holidays ▪ BYO picnic (if tasting) ▪ Farm produce ▪ Walks ▪ Owner Johann & Ulrike Mendelsöhn ▪ Winemaker Johann Mendelsöhn, advised by Bartho Eksteen (Jan 2005) ▪ Viticulturist Johann Mendelsöhn ▪ 4ha (cab, malbec, merlot, petit v, shiraz, viognier) ▪ 250cs 100% red ▪ PO Box 85 Botrivier 7185 ▪ ultramontani@telkomsa.net

Architect/winemaker Johann Mendelsöhn has partially signed off plans to transform the original farm cottage into a tasting room and barrel maturation area. The bushvines have been trellised ('to save my back'), and biodynamic farming is bringing delicious results: 'Yellow milk and even yellower butter and eggs!'

Galantskloof Syrah ★★★★ 06's fruit better balanced than pvs, pushes higher rating; same slightly rustic, sweetly spicy deliciousness, with prominent oak vanilla (yr new). Very natural: biodynamically farmed vyds, native yeasts. — *TJ*

▪ **Keizer's Creek** *see Roodezandt Wines & Vineyards*

Kellerprinz

High-volume semi-sweet white swigger in 2 & 5-litre bottles, by Distell.

Late Harvest 🗎 ★ From chenin/colombard. Latest **NV** is a light (11% alc), honeyed apple-toned sweetie. W Cape vyds. — *MW*

▪ **Kendal Lodge Estate** *see Journey's End Vineyards*

Ken Forrester Wines

T 021-855-2374 • F 021-855-2373

Stellenbosch (see Helderberg map) ▪ Est/1stB 1994 ▪ Tasting & sales on home farm, cnr R44 & Winery Rd: Mon-Fri 9-5 Sat 10.30-1.30; closed Easter & Dec 25; Sun & after hours at 96 Winery Road Restaurant (see Eat-out section) ▪ Owner Ken & Teresa Forrester ▪ Viticulturist Jannie Fourie (Jan 2005) ▪ Vini consultant Martin Meinert (1995) ▪ 33ha (cab f, grenache, merlot, mourvèdre, shiraz, chenin, sauv) ▪ *200t/65 000cs own label + 500 000litres for clients* ▪ *35% red 65% white* ▪ *HACCP, SEDEX certified; WIETA pending* ▪ *PO Box 1253 Stellenbosch 7599* ▪ *info@kenforresterwines.com* ▪ *www.kenforresterwines.com*

It's the eponymous winemaker's 15th year in the industry, and his best reward ever is last year's Decanter Trophy for the Forrester Meinert Chenin '04, as the best white single-variety wine over £10 from SA. It proves two things for the chenin champ: his faith in the variety's future as this country's leading white is well-placed, and he was right to believe his first employer, hotel tycoon Sol Kerzner, when he indicated that nothing was impossible. Hence the likelihood of best-in-the-world chenin, given more sun than the Loire valley, 40-year-old vines, a deep bowl of vineyards collecting cool sea air, and clever winemaking from Martin Meinert. Less cause for celebration is the SA industry's blindness to the serious damage that's wrought by leafroll virus: 'It's as virulent as AIDS,' warns Ken F.

Icon range

★★★★★ **Gypsy** More 'dark & brooding' than 'flamboyant' in **04** (★★★★). Shiraz/grenache combo delivers dense, scrub-tinged fruit & spice, tight chalky tannins, savoury farewell, but needs few yrs for more harmonious richness. Youthfully accessible & expressive **03** raised the bar & provided surprises at every turn.

★★★★☆ **The FMC Chenin Blanc** Ken F describes this as 'full throttle chenin', showcasing the best SA can offer; we agree. **05** (★★★★★) enhanced by yr Fr oak (50% new) & beautifully proportioned: vivacious acidity lifts 9.7g/l sugar & mouthfilling 14.5% alc. Rich, layered with dried apricot, lime marmelade & honey. Will gain additional complexity with cellaring. Some under screwcap. Powerful & gorgeous **04** was also among their best.

★★★★★ **'T' Noble Late Harvest Chenin Blanc** Stellar botrytised dessert from old bushvine chenin, up to five pickings each vintage; **06** not ready. **05** sumptuous, yet with racy acidity to balance quince-infused sweetness. Silky & long, as were tantilising **03** (★★★★★) & **01**; no **04**, **02**. 18 mths new Fr oak.

Ken Forrester range

★★★★ **Chenin Blanc** 🍷 Alluring **06**, portion botrytis lending honeyed notes, ripe apple flavours reined in by piercing lime acidity, judicious oak ensuring early drinkability but also structure for several yrs ageing. Fermented/9 mths Fr oak, 20% new; vines manicured for low yields.

Merlot 🍷 ★★★☆ **05** takes step up with more seriously styled ripe berry & choc, supported by smooth, firm tannin. Firm favourite with the punters, says Ken F. Yr Fr oak. **Shiraz-Grenache** ★★★★ Robust **04** fires on all cylinders with 14.5 alc, spicy red fruit, savoury black olive farewell, food-friendly tannins. **Sauvignon Blanc** 🍷 ★★★★ Step-up **07** fresh, vivacious; dusty minerality mixing it up with fig & tropical flavours.

Petit range

Pinotage 🍷 ★★★ Cheerfully styled for al fresco fare; **06** juicy, accessible, brimming with mulberry & cherry. **Chenin Blanc** 🍷 ★★★☆ **07** tropical & apple toned; tangy acidity delivering flavour & length.

Winery Road range [NEW]

Pinotage ★★★★ **06** sample given a potential score. Mulberry & liquorice exuberance tamed by integrated oak & dry, supple tannins. Food styled. **Shiraz-Grenache** ★★★★ **03** succulent & accessible blend; bursts with smoky cranberries, finishes with pleasantly dry tannins. 9 mths old oak. **Chenin Blanc** ★★★ Restrained & steely **06** has waxy, almond flavours, whiffs buttery oak from fermentation/lees ageing in mostly older oak. **Sauvignon Blanc** ★★★ Moderate 12.5% alc on **06** should find favour with lunchtime sippers. Dust & herbs, balanced acidity also do the business. On-consumption range for the UK market. — *MW*

■ **Keteka** *see Dominion Wine Company*

Keukenhof Wines
T 027-217-2623 • F 027-217-2623

Olifants River • 1stB 2003 • Visits by appt Mon-Sat 8-5 • Fee R10 p/p • Closed Good Fri-Mon, Ascension Day & Dec 25 • Play area for children • Owner Smuts family • Winemaker Riaan Smuts, with Nadine Smuts (both Jan 2003) • Viticulturist Riaan Smuts (Jan 2003) • 65ha (cab, merlot, chard, chenin, colombard, sauv) • 1 200t/250cs own label • PO Box 49 Lutzville 8165 • tazu@kingsley.co.za

Winemaking is very much a hobby for Riaan and Nadine Smuts, and what with their commitments (Riaan harvests 1 500 tons for the local co-op, Nadine's a teacher), they didn't get round to making wine last year. 'Besides, we still had plenty of 06 to see to our own needs!'

Cabernet Sauvignon ★★ Sweet blackcurrant & fine herbal hints on **04**, some greenish tannin & alc evident. **Merlot ★★** Chalky mulberry intro to **04**, succulent, though fruit battled nearly 15% alc last ed (neither wine revisited). — *MF*

■ **Keurfontein** *see Viljoensdrift Wines*

■ ***Kevin Arnold*** *see Waterford Estate*

Kholisa Wines
T 021-881-3331 • F 021-881-3331

Stellenbosch • Est 2005 • 1stB 2004 • Tasting by appt • Owner Kholisa Wines cc • Winemaker Richard Kershaw (Jul 2007, consultant) • Viticulturist Werner de Villiers (Jul 2007, consultant) • ±10 000litres • PO Box 1514 Brackenfell 7560 • kholisawines@telkomsa.net • www. kholisawines.co.za

The word 'kholisa', 'to satisfy' in isiXhosa, prompted five rugby- and wine-loving South Africans to consider the wine needs of their own circles, and, working backwards from the concept and the label, joined up with winemaker Richard Kershaw and the rest of the team at Kanu to start this promising new wine venture.

Brilliant Red ★★ Herbaceous blackcurrant notes on **04**, greengage/plum flavours & food-inviting tannins. **Chardonnay ★★★** **05** still lively & flavourful, with butterscotch & succulent melon notes, delicate citrus flavours & crisp finish. — *MF*

■ **King Solomon** *see Eshkol Kosher Winery*

Kingsriver Estate
T 023-625-1108

Robertson • Est 2004 • 1stB 2005 • Visits Sun 10-4, otherwise by appt • Owner De Clercq family • Winemaker Ruud de Clercq (2005), advised by Kobus van der Merwe • Viticulturist Anton Laas • 26ha (ruby cab, shiraz, chard, chenin, colombard) • 250t total 900cs own label 100% red • PO Box 203 McGregor 6708 • kingsriver@breede.co.za • www.kingsriver-estate.com

Owner and winemaker Ruud de Clercq has developed his wine philosophy over the three harvests since the farm's inception: 'I extract as many healthy elements as possible from the skin; I try to achieve high quality from low yields; and I ferment a large part of my grapes with natural yeast.' The line-up, untasted this edition, includes Mzansi 05, a cab-ruby cab blend, a Ruby Cab and a Shiraz, both **06**.

Klawer Co-operative Cellars
T 027-216-1530 • F 027-216-1561

Olifants River • Est 1956 • Tasting & sales Mon-Fri 8-5 Sat 9-1 • Fee R5 • Closed pub hols except during wildflower season • BYO picnic • Conferences • Owner 120 members • Cellarmaster Hermias Hugo • Winemaker Hermias Hugo, Roelof van Schalkwyk & Dewald Huisamen • Viticulturist Gert Engelbrecht • 2 095ha ±40 000t 14% red 85% white 1% rosé • PO Box 8 Klawer 8145 • klawerwyn@kingsley.co.za • www.birdfieldwines.co.za

There's been movement aplenty at this modern facility: Hermias Hugo was made production manager, the winemaking team of Dewald Huisamen and Roelof van Schalkwyk was joined by Christo Beukes, and Gert Engelbrecht now oversees the Klawer Valley vineyards, where careful canopy management is key.

Birdfield range

Cabernet Sauvignon Reserve NEW ★★☆ 06 dark berry flavours well underpinned by oak, dry, firm tannins. Yr wooded. **Merlot** ★★★ 06 soft oak & dark chocolate; could benefit from yr's cellaring. **Pinotage** ★ Earthy 06 shows variety's bold tannins. **Shiraz** ★★★ Spice & violets intro to 06, juicy Rhône-style flavours cut short by pushy tannins. **Shiraz-Merlot** ★★★ Shiraz spice & merlot mocha on 06, succulent plum flavours carry through to finish. **Blanc de Noir** 🍷 ★★ 07 sweet but balanced charmer with spicy hints & delicate blush from shiraz. **Chardonnay** 🍷 ★★ 07 undemanding & food-friendly, some vanilla biscuit aromas. **Chenin Blanc** 🍷 ★ Dusty grass & bracing acidity on 07. **Sauvignon Blanc** 🍷 ★ Grassy-toned 07, lean dry style. **Michelle Sparkling** ★★ Light NV froth with Barbie-pink label reflecting wine hue & reading 'For ladies only'. **Hanepoot** ★★★ 07 easy, friendly, honey-rich fortified in warming West Coast style. **Red Muscadel** ★★★ Treacle-sweet 06, fruitcake flavours offset by lively alc (16.5%). **White Muscadel** ★★☆ Last tasted 05 soft & rounded melon flavours, lifted by unobtrusive 17% alc. **Travino Matador** ★★ Dusty nose & sweet warmth create welcoming 06 charmer. Discontinued: **Late Harvest**, **Special Late Harvest**.

Klawer range NEW

Dry Red ★★ Meaty, mocha notes precede crisp tangy berries on NV newcomer. **Rosé** ★ Pale pink, strawberry-sweet NV from pinotage. **Grand Cru** ★ Undemanding, everyday dry white quaffer. NV. **Late Harvest** ★★ Guavas & pineapple zing in sweet beguiler from chenin. **African Ruby Vermouth Rooibos Infused** ★★★ Intriguing & different rooibos-infused red muscadel in friendly, pretty, pale red NV. This range mainly screwcapped. — RP

Klawervlei Estate

Stellenbosch • Est 1994 • 1stB 1995 • Tasting & tours by appt • Owner Strobe Props • PO Box 2081 Cape Town 8000 • skeate@mweb.co.za

This year, we'll see the first wines from the new, improved (and non-organic) Klawervlei: at time of going to print the vineyards had been spruced up, buildings had been cleaned and repaired, distribution channels had been established and decisions were being made about what new varieties were required.

■ **Klein Avontuur** see Avontuur Estate
■ *Klein Begin* see New Beginnings Wines
■ *Kleinbosch* see Cape Coastal Vintners

Klein Constantia Estate
T 021-794-5188 • F 021-794-2464

Constantia • Est 1823 • 1stB 1986 • Tasting & sales Mon-Fri 9-5 Sat 9-1 • Fee R20 for groups • Closed pub hols • Owner Duggie & Lowell Jooste • Winemaker Adam Mason, with Sebastiaan Cloete (Jul 2003/Jul 2006) • Viticulturist Floricius Beukes (Jan 2006) • 82ha (cabs s/f, merlot, pinot, shiraz, malbec, petit v, chard, muscat de F, riesling, sauv, semillon) • 500t/40 000cs 25% red 75% white • Export brands: High Gables, Rowans Ridge • PO Box 375 Constantia 7848 • info@kleinconstantia.com • www.kleinconstantia.com

Klein Constantia has undergone restructuring over the past few years and is now raring to go with its once-again full range of wines. After a hiatus of three vintages, the Marlbrook red was relaunched and quickly snapped up an award. Michel Roux Jr of London's gastronomic icon, Le Gavroche, visited during harvest for the local release of the award-winning title, Vin de Constance with Michel Roux Jr. The estate celebrated by hosting 10 top chefs to prepare dishes from the book. The harvest lunch for 80 people prepared by Peter Goffe-Wood on an enormous braai, finishing with a sorbet of freshly harvested chardonnay, is set to become a tradition. And, after relocating the marauding water mongoose, the swans have returned to the pond in the Charolais paddock.

Marlbrook Range

★★★★ **Marlbrook** Relaunched with **05** (pvs was **01** (★★★☆), noted last ed as crafted from carefully selected vyd sections; showed savoury if austere promise, needed time to develop from oaky, dark fruited mouthful. 15 mths oak, third new.

★★★★☆ **Mme Marlbrook** Consort for flagship red; **06** continues style set by serious, rich **05**. Spicy, pungent semillon (60%) adds weight to floral, lighter-toned sauv. 2-3 yrs should see latter's racy acidity soften & former's waxy fullness bloom.

Klein Constantia Estate range

★★★★ **Rhine Riesling** 🟰 Sample **07** already gorgeous, like strolling through a spring meadow; luscious & mouthwatering pineapple chunks laced with cinnamon but finishes crisply dry. Cellar few yrs for extra depth, complexity.

★★★★☆ **Perdeblokke Sauvignon Blanc** 🟰 Selection from higher-altitude vyd named for the ploughing Percherons that helped till it. **07** expressive tinned pea & stonefruit, marvellous intensity, stern backbone, composure & length. Showing class before bottling. Only 280cs made.

★★★★ **Sauvignon Blanc** Gunflint puff on classy **07**, tropical fruit & Oriental spice, full & rich partly thanks to 12% semillon, persistent chalky mineral adieu. Like subtly forceful **06**, deserves time to open fully. Not just for drinking - merits contemplation too.

★★★★☆ **Vin de Constance** Luscious unfortified dessert with international reputation spanning 2 centuries, typically from unbotrytised yet lusciously ripe muscat d F. **02** more slender than pvs (13% alc vs 14.8%) but follows generous sun-blessed style, with tightrope balance. Marmalade, Asian spice hints, unctuous but uncloying.

★★★★☆ **Rhine Riesling Natural Sweet** NEW A once-off (though consumers might have other ideas). Botrytised riesling 18 mths seasoned barriques. Sample **06** rather sexy: citrus & more unusual cherry hints, delightful floral depths. Sultry sweetness (250g/l RS) nipped by firm acidity.

★★★★ **Sauvignon Blanc Noble Late Harvest 05** pvs ed was a rich, focused, botrytised pleasure, fermented/matured in older oak. Honey-lemon freshness deliver tangy balance, modest 86g/l sugar a welcome return from woody **02** (★★★).

Cabernet Sauvignon ★★★★ Previewed **06** first since austere **01** (★★★★). More fruit-filled style though cassis-soaked palate still encased by burly tannins; dense & punchy with potential to raise the bar to (★★★★). **Pinot Noir** ★★★★ Appealing medley of ripe fruit (from warmer vintage) & orange choc-truffle on **06**. Firmly structured, elegantly poised but finishes somewhat abruptly. 50% new-oak obvious mid-2007, should mesh given 2-3 yrs. **Shiraz** ★★★★ **04**, tasted pvsly, ripe, almost lush, subtly oaked for firm, gd structure. **Chardonnay** ★★★★ Charming **06** a macadamia nut, straw & mineral melange; lime flavours & acidity fuse with creamy oak, finish pleasantly lean. As with all in range, will replay cellaring few yrs. **Semillon** ★★★★ None tasted since **05**, immensely drinkable, 14% sauv adding verve to lemongrass, fennel & lanolin glassful.

KC range

Shiraz ★★★☆ No follow-up to **04**, showing darker fruit, more power than estate version. Savoury tannins ex-18 mths oak. **Cabernet Sauvignon-Merlot** 🟰 ★★★☆ **04** tasty berry mix given structure & length by chunky tannins. 86/14 blend. **Rosé** NEW ★★★☆ Vivid pink **07** delightful newcomer. Sumptuous raspberry cheesecake & candyfloss notes without compromising driness; amiable, with sufficient gravitas for the dinner table. **Sauvignon Blanc** NEW 🟰 ★★★☆ Elim & Elgin fruit combo for **07** maiden; lean but alluring passionfruit & citrus tones. Range includes grapes from Anwilka farm in Hldrberg, so NE. — *RP*

■ **Kleindal** *see Robertson Wide River Export Company*

Klein DasBosch
T 021-880-0128, 083-272-4575 ▪ F 021-880-0999

Stellenbosch ▪ Open by appt ▪ Owner James Wellwood Basson ▪ Marketing Director Nikki Herbst ▪ Viticulturist Viti/vini consultant Jan Coetzee (1997) ▪ 5.5ha ▪ 35t/16 000cs own label

89% red 11% white ▪ *PO Box 12320 Stellenbosch 7613* ▪ *wine@kleindasbosch.co.za* ▪ *www. kleindasbosch.co.za*

Range made at Vriesenhof Vineyards by rugby-and-wine legend Jan Coetzee for his neighbour James 'Whitey' Basson, CEO of retailing empire Shoprite/Checkers. Current releases include an 05 Merlot and 06 Chardonnay. Mostly exported, though some do appear on selected local restaurant lists and wine shops. The wines can now be tasted by appointment.

Klein Dassenberg
T 021-876-2107 ▪ F 021-876-2737

Franschhoek ▪ Est 1997 ▪ 1stB 2002 ▪ Tasting by appt ▪ 4 self-catering guest houses ▪ Owner Francois & Sally Marais ▪ Winemaker Nigel McNaught (2002) ▪ Viticulturist Pietie le Roux (adviser, 1997) ▪ 5ha (cab, shiraz, sauv) ▪ 22t/400cs 50% red 50% white ▪ PO Box 553 Franschhoek 7690 ▪ marais@kleindassenberg.co.za ▪ www.kleindassenberg.co.za

After a career at BBC Television, Francois Marais and wife Sally returned to fulfil their wine farming dream. Their renovated property now boasts self-catering cottages with great views and a recently completed maturation cellar for their wine, made by neighbour Nigel McNaught of Stony Brook.

Shiraz ★★ Charry **04**, mocha notes, herbal peppery whiffs, rustic tannins, sweet finish. **Sauvignon Blanc** 🗒 ★★★ Delicate grassy notes on **06**, citrus, green fig whiffs, fine-textured & crisp. — *MF*

Klein Dauphine `NEW`
T 021-876-2244 ▪ F 021-876-2398

Franschhoek ▪ Est 2001 ▪ 1stB 2003 ▪ Closed to public ▪ Owner John & Liz Atkins ▪ Winemaker Justin Hoy (consultant) ▪ 1ha (cab, merlot) ▪ 4t/300cs 100% red ▪ PO Box 151 Franschhoek 7690 ▪ liz@kleindauphine.co.za ▪ www.kleindauphine.co.za

Owners of a tiny vineyard, John and Liz Atkins decided on an own label (mainly for export to the UK) with winemaker Justin Hoy advising. When it comes to the vineyards, 'the biggest challenge is knowing what we are doing - it is a very steep learning curve but our friends and neighbours are extremely supportive.'

Cape Cobra range
Merlot ★★★ Coconut, almond & plum aromas on **05**, sumptuous soft tannins, rich, savoury, olivaceous, ample fruit layering Fr/Am oak. — *MF*

Kleine Draken
T 021-863-2368 ▪ F 021-863-1884

Paarl ▪ Est 1983 ▪ 1stB 1988 ▪ Tasting & sales Mon-Fri 8-12.30; 1.30-5 ▪ Closed pub hols & Jewish holy days ▪ Tours strictly by appt ▪ BYO picnic ▪ Owner Cape Gate (Pty) Ltd ▪ Winemaker Mabusa Nyaniso (Jul 1999) ▪ Viticulturist Frank Pietersen (1984) ▪ 9ha (cabs s/f, malbec, merlot, chard, riesling, sauv) ▪ 90t/10 000cs own label 50% red 50% white ▪ Brand for customer: Tempel Wines ▪ ISO 9000 certification in progress ▪ PO Box 2674 Paarl 7620 ▪ zandwijk@capegate.co.za ▪ www.kosherwines.co.za

Kleine Draken's kosher wines are made with juice pasteurised prior to fermentation, and every step of the process, from crushing to bottling and labelling, is done under the supervision of the Cape Beth Din. As export demand for Kleine Draken's wines increases, more and more grapes are sourced from suitable vineyards.

Cabernet Sauvignon ★★★ **02** cassis & black berries, clever oaking (6 mths old/new Fr) for gd dry mouthfeel. Not retasted, as for all these. **Pinotage** ★★ **04** distinct varietal plum & mulberry, big tannin, bitter touch. Yr seasoned Fr oak. **Shiraz** ★ **05** attractive red berry & smoked beef bouquet, astringency noted last time might since have softened. **Dry Red** ★★★ Bdx-style blend **04**, lightish (11.9% alc) & elegant red-berry character, friendly tannins. Older Fr wood. **Chardonnay** ★★ Appealingly restrained **05**, white peach notes brushed with vanilla oak. **Sauvignon Blanc** ★★ **05** subdued, barely vinous, but nicely fresh. **Bouquet Blanc** New **NV** bottling unready. **Kiddush** ★★ Natural Sweet sacramental wine from cinsaut. **NV**. — *CvZ*

■ **Kleine Hazen** *see* Hazendal

■ *Kleine Parys* *see* Klein Parys Vineyards

Kleine Zalze Wines
T 021-880-0717 · **F** 021-880-0716

Stellenbosch · Est 1695 · 1stB 1997 · Tasting & sales Mon-Sat 9-6 Sun 11-6 · Closed Easter Fri, Dec 25 & Jan 1 · Fee R15 · Tours by appt · 'Terroir' Restaurant (see Eat-out section) · Four-star luxury Kleine Zalze Lodge (see Stay-over section) · Play area for children · Tour groups · Conferences & functions · Owner Kobus Basson & Rolf Schulz · Winemaker Johan Joubert, with Bertho van der Westhuizen (Nov 2002/Dec 2004) · Viticulturist Henning Retief, advised by Schalk du Toit (May 2006/2000) · 60ha (cab, merlot, shiraz) · ±2 000t/80 000cs 50% red 50% white · PO Box 12837 Die Boord 7613 · quality@kleinezalze.co.za · www.kleinezalze. com

Kobus and Mariette Basson took a major leap of faith in buying a run-down Stellenbosch farm a decade ago. Their subsequent emotional and financial commitment to a ten-year plan (assisted by a dedicated staff who are, says Kobus 'the building blocks of the Kleine Zalze wall') has created a multi-faceted, popular tourist destination. The cornerstone being the quality and good value of their wine, linked to the equally lauded Terroir restaurant, golf course and hotel. The next decade's business goals include growth and fine tuning, assisted by some top new appointments, including Johan Bestbier (ex-KWV) and Thelma du Plooy (ex-WOSA).

Family Reserve range
★★★★ **Cabernet Sauvignon** Dark choc & cedar on **05**; dense, concentrated mulberry with the variety's distinctive tougher tannins but more than enough fruit to balance. Cold soak, 18 mths Fr oak. Impressive awards list incl Decanter & IWC golds.

★★★★★ **Shiraz 05** gorgeous black cherry, toffee, classy oak intro to velvety mouthful. Poised & stylish, layers of ripe fruit padding, fine tannins for contrast, lengthy finish. Has a certain presence. Cold soak, 16 mths Fr oak. MIWA gold.

★★★★ **Sauvignon Blanc 06** (★★★★) not quite in same league, quiet but main action on palate. Ripe, expansive; good acid tang, green pea & asparagus ripeness; lingering but less freshness mid-2007. VDG. On-form **05** was rather stately & ageworthy.

Vineyard Selection
★★★★ **Cabernet Sauvignon Barrel Matured** After elegant **01**, last-tasted **03** (★★★★) big & bold, showing nice cedarwood touch to gd, ripe fruit. Well managed oak in balance with sweet fruit & soft, dry tannins. Winemakers Choice 'diamond'.

★★★★ **Chardonnay Barrel Fermented** Full breakfast special in **06** (★★★★) - marmalade, buttered toast, then palate comes as surprise - less generous with taut lemon fruit, brisk acidity, unobtrusive oak (fermented/4 mths Fr oak, 20% new). Contrast with **05**, which was creamy & rich.

★★★★ **Chenin Blanc Barrel Fermented** Just off-dry **06**, aroma of bruised apple, sprinkling warm spice, supportive oak does not dominate expansive creamy palate. Success lies in excellent fruit/acid balance, lovely long finish. 7 mths oak, 30% malo.

Pinotage Barrel Matured ★★★★ More power than charm on **03**, pvsly marked by severe tannins, dusty cedar notes from 18 mths new Fr oak — but dark fruit lay in wait. **Shiraz Barrel Matured** ★★★★ **05** smoked beef aromas; firm muscular wine, tannins still taut, very savoury, dry finish with grippy tannins. Needs time. 16 mths used Fr oak.

Cellar Selection
Cabernet Sauvignon ★★★ Strangely quiet but appealing cab mulberry, cedar signature on **05**. Smooth, rounded profile, dry tannins but approachable. Honest, some charm, too. **Merlot** ✓ ★★★★ Blueberry & choc on **05**; smooth, succulent, black-hearted core, integrated oak. Tangy acid balanced by touch sweetness. Yr used Fr oak. Mundus Vini gold. **Pinotage** ★★★ Perhaps more 'dry red' than pinotage, **05**'s varietal exuberance curbed; firm-ish tannins to dry baked character, rustic appeal. 50% oaked. **Shiraz-Mourvèdre-Viognier** NEW ★★★★ Fragrant **06**, shows what viognier can do for blend. Curvaceous black cherry flavours, softly rounded with smooth caressing tannins. Hedonist's delight. 16 mths used Fr oak. Export

only. **Sauvignon Blanc** ★★★★ Arresting green fig, dusty capsicum on previewed **07**, with Old World raciness. Dry & flinty, crisp acidity, mouthwatering finish. Loads typicity, style.

Gamay Noir ☺ ★★★ Fresh from the press **07**, nouveau-style softness, though no carbonic maceration. Juicy, gd red wine flavours, ready to enjoy. **Gamay Noir Rosé** NEW ☺ ✓ ★★★ Fruity & dry, attractive style, some engaging blackberry flavours mop up acidity. **07** perfect picnic wine. **Chardonnay** ☺ ★★★ Lovely freshness, zippy flavours of lemon & lime in **07**, unoaked. From bought-in fruit. **Chenin Blanc Bush Vines** ☺ ★★★ Muchgonged **07** (sample) plump & juicy as a slice of melon, lovely welcoming glassful, tastes sweeter than 3.6g/l sugar would suggest.

Foot of Africa range
Cabernet Sauvignon ★★★ Tart sweet/sour tension in **05**, baked prune flavours, grippy tannins. Swedish market only. **Shiraz-Viognier** ★★★ Boldly fruity **06**; plump, sweet prune flavours & soft tannins. **Chardonnay** NEW ★★★ Big & fleshy in **07**; juicy peach & lime flavours, unfettered by oak. Exclusive to Sweden. **Chenin Blanc** ★★★ **07** rounded & bouncy, ripe melon sprinkled with spice. — *IvH*

Klein Genot Country & Wine Estate
T 021-876-2738 • F 021-876-4624

Franschhoek ▪ 1stB 2005 ▪ Tasting Mon-Fri 10-4 Sat & Sun 11-3 ▪ Fee R20 ▪ Luxury B&B guesthouse ▪ Owner Angie Diamond ▪ Winemaker Mark Carmichael-Green (Aug 2004) ▪ Viticulturist Paul Wallace (Aug 2004) ▪ 16ha (cab s/f, merlot, shiraz) ▪ 28t 100% red ▪ PO Box 620 Franschhoek 7690 ▪ info@kleingenot.com ▪ www.kleingenot.com

General manager Johan Bothma says it was a lifelong ambition to make wine for ordinary folk - not only those staying at this luxurious Franschhoek guesthouse. Great believers in organic farming, they say the biggest influence on their wines is Mother Nature: 'We believe in getting the basics correct in the vineyard.' They're currently building a cellar where the motto will be 'keep it simple'.

★★★★ **Black Swan** This, following maidens, confirm the Diamonds & winemaker MC-G are on track with quest for small quantities of high-quality modern wines. **05** a 50/50 blend cabs/f. Structured for cellaring; forceful oak tannins (yr Fr) swamp youthful fruit, yet tannin-acid combo work together for persistent.Yr new Fr oak. One to watch.

Cabernet Sauvignon ★★★★ Impressive **05** combines typical Old World tones of cassis/cedar/fennel with New World fruit purity & verve. Taut tannins rein in riotous, fleshy fruit. 12 mths Fr oak, 20% new. Should develop complexity, greater harmony with ±5 yrs cellaring. **Merlot** ★★★ Only 10% of **05** was aged in barrel, remainder kept in tank to retain overt fruit characters. Early drinking in style, mulberry/plum aromas/flavours. With raisin nuances, only one of these 4 to hint at how warm the vintage was. **Shiraz** ★★★★ Rhône-like **05** has peppery red fruit, St Joseph lily scent appeal; balanced & juicy, super now or within 2yrs. Like merlot, partially oaked for almost immediate gratification. All above 14% alc, from 4 yr old vyds, so expect improvement as vines mature/viticultural practices fine-tuned. — *CvZ*

Klein Gustrouw Estate
T 021-887-8039 • F 021-887-8039

Stellenbosch ▪ Est 1817 ▪ 1stB 1993 ▪ Tasting, sales & tours by appt '24x7' but phone ahead (closed Dec 25/26) ▪ Conservation area ▪ Owner Klein Gustrouw (Pty) Ltd ▪ Winemaker Chris McDonald ▪ Viticulturist Wynand Pienaar ▪ 16ha (cab, merlot) ▪ 21t/1 600cs 100% red ▪ 17 Koloniesland, Noordwal Oos, Stellenbosch 7600 ▪ suzanne.slabbert@gmail.com

The McDonalds and the lovelorn Scottish deerhound of past editions are on the move from Klein Gustrouw. No 2007 vintage was made, so the new owners will have to make what's left last. But with 2006 in barrel and 2005 not yet released, that's a problem for the future.

★★★★★ **Cabernet Sauvignon-Merlot** Usual pleasing perfumed aromas on already approachable **05**, with interesting 'wild' notes. Has friendly, restrained charm, with gentle tannins & integrated smoky oak (12-17 mths, third new) on warm, broad palate. Attractive herbaceous note to finish. — *TJ*

Kleinood
T 021-880-2527 ▪ F 021-880-2884

Stellenbosch ▪ Est 2000 ▪ 1stB 2002 ▪ Visits by appt ▪ Owner Gerard de Villiers ▪ Winemaker Gunter Schultz (2007) ▪ Viticulturist Aidan Morton (Dec 2000, consultant) ▪ 9.6ha (mourvèdre, shiraz, viognier) ▪ 6300cs own label ±99% red ±1% white ▪ PO Box 12584 Die Boord 7613 ▪ winemaker@kleinood.co.za ▪ www.kleinood.com

Gerard de Villiers was naturally delighted when the 04 Tamboerskloof Syrah sold out sooner than expected. 'We had to limit sales to try and stretch the wine and keep everyone happy.' The team was sad to lose winemaker Willem Grobbelaar, off to farm in the Free State, but Gunter Schultz (ex-Delaire) is his welcome replacement.

Tamboerskloof range

★★★★ **Viognier** NEW Attractive **06** maiden has more delicacy, poise than most SA examples. Peach, floral & nut nuances stay the distance from nose to lingering farewell.
Syrah ★★★★ **05** solid zesty fruit centre, white pepper flick on meaty mouthful, tailored tannins, hint of 14% alc in tail. Delightful now, perhaps better in 2-3 yrs. *— CvZ*

Klein Optenhorst
T 021-864-3155 ▪ F 021-864-1744

Wellington ▪ Est/1stB 2001 ▪ Closed to public ▪ ±150cs 100% red ▪ See Siyabonga for details ▪ PO Box 1209 Wellington 7654 ▪ graham@stormhoek.co.za

The limited-release red below is grown by hand - and by hoof, the latter belonging to the charmingly named Percheron, Poppie, who draws the plough that clears away winter growth between the rows of this thumbnail-sized vineyard in Wellington. The process aids rapid absorption of moisture into the comparatively shallow soils and creates a 'water bank' for the drier months, explain marketer Graham Knox and grower Naas Ferreira.

★★★★ **Pinot Noir** Individual SA take on classic grape. **05** (★★★★) released ahead of **04**, as former more open; last ed noted as softly textured, ending touch sweet. 11 mths Fr casks - just six of them. *— DS*

Klein Parys Vineyards
T 021-872-9848 ▪ F 021-872-8527

Paarl ▪ Est 1692 ▪ 1stB 2003 ▪ Tasting & sales Mon-Fri 10-6 Sat 10-4 ▪ Closed Easter Fri/Sun, Dec 16/25/26 & Jan 1 ▪ Tours by appt ▪ Restaurant, cheese platters, olives, olive oil & other farm-style produce ▪ Self-catering accommodation ▪ Tour groups ▪ Gifts ▪ Art, clothing & other exhibitions ▪ Owner/winemaker/viticulturist Kosie Möller ▪ 56ha (cab, chard, chenin, nouvelle, semillon, viognier) ▪ 700t/80 000cs 50% red 50% white ▪ Export brands: Kleine Parys & Miller's Mile ▪ PO Box 1362 Suider-Paarl 7624 ▪ parys@kparys.co.za ▪ www.kleinparysvineyards.co.za

'Life is about balancing the downside with truly great things, such as great wine, great company and great challenges,' says owner-winemaker Kosie Möller. And on family-owned Klein Parys, one of Paarl's oldest wine estates, he's put this philosophy into action. The estate's amenities include well-known restaurant La Masseria.

Kleine Parys range

Cuvée Brut ☺ ★★★ Pineapple crispness in an explosion of bubbles make quite a sophisticated but fun celebration wine. **NV**.

Cabernet Sauvignon ★★★ Warm toasty oak over very ripe dark cherries & berries, **06**'s clean dry tannins make up a satin mouthfeel & lingering crisp finish. **Pinotage** ★★ Earthy, Marmite notes with hint acetone & almost over-ripe fruit on **06**. **Sangiovese** 🗎 ★★★★ **05**, tasted last ed, a hit in Sweden, says Kosie M. Tightly bound spicy melange (incl hints anise & salt); needed yr/2 or decanting it opened then. Yr 2nd fill barrels. **Shiraz** ★★★★ Typical smoky, spicy sun-ripe berries in harmony with clean, silky tannins & gentle acidity. **06** sustained dry finish. **Classic Red** ★★★ Inviting plum pudding prelude to **06**. Ripe, rich, juicy dark fruit add up to a comfortable welcome-home drink. **Beatrix Selection** ★★★★ Meaty/spicy blend shiraz (60%), cab, pinotage; pvsly tasted **02** fruitcake flavours, rich & ripe. Contrived & obvious in the nicest way. New oak 18 mths, 40% Am. **Pinotage Blanc de Noir** ★★★ **07** not tasted. **06** was palest shell-pink, softly dry, with delicate honeysuckle tones. **Chardonnay** ★★★ Buttery caramel biscuit aromas partnered by toffee flavours & hint rosewater. **07** mouthfilling, lingering nuttiness. **Chenin Blanc** ★★★ Green leaves on **07** nose give way to some nice peachy fruit, balanced by suggestion of gentle oak-vanilla. **Sauvignon Blanc** 🍴 ★★★ Pineapples, fruit salad & greenpeppers combine in **07** crisp, multi-layered food wine.

Miller's Mile range

> **Pinotage** ☺ ★★★ Dusty ripe & spicy **06**, charming dried banana layers & well-managed tannins followed by long juicy finish. **Shiraz** ☺ ★★★ Suggestion of old leather-bound books in **06** warm-hearted fireside wine. Tannins could make for some longevity.

Cabernet Sauvignon ★★★ Walnut & mulberries opening to **06**. Bold tannins almost dominate fruit mid-2007, will probably soften. **Pinotage-Shiraz** ★★ **06** continues shy & dry style of pvs, with hint of ripe plum added. **Chardonnay** ★★ Quiet hints of lemon & pear. **07** easy-drinking food wine. **Chenin Blanc** ★★ Light & leafy **07**, undemanding with appealing ripe-fruit character. — *DB*

▪ **Klein Simonsvlei** see Niel Joubert Estate
▪ *Klein Tulbagh* see Tulbagh Wine Cellars
▪ *Klompzicht* see Freedom Hill Wines
▪ *Kloofzicht* see Alter Ego Wines

Kloovenburg Vineyards

T 022-448-1635 ▪ **F** 022-448-1035

Swartland ▪ Est 1704 ▪ 1stB 1998 ▪ Tasting & sales Mon-Fri 9-4.30 Sat 9-2 ▪ Fee for groups R10 ▪ Closed Christian holidays ▪ Tours during tasting hours by appt ▪ BYO picnic ▪ Farm-grown olive products for tasting/sale ▪ Walks ▪ Conservation area ▪ Owner/winemaker Pieter du Toit ▪ Viticulturist Kobus van Graan (Jun 2000, consultant) ▪ 130ha (cab, merlot, shiraz, chard, sauv) ▪ 6 000cs own label 70% red 30% white ▪ PO Box 2 Riebeek-Kasteel 7307 ▪ info@kloovenburg.com ▪ www.kloovenburg.com

In 2005 a baby antelope was found in the cellar, and 2007 is, apparently, the year of the pig! A hungry herd polished off the entire sauvignon harvest, leaving Kloovenburg to buy in grapes for the vintage. All things olive (including a new chutney and an olive-and-fig jam) and half of the White From Red Shiraz stock flew out the cellar during the annual Olive Festival, which was merry enough to make humans – and even a few animals – go wild.

★★★★☆ **Shiraz** Northern rhône-style red lacks some of the sophistication & harmony of pvs in big **05** (★★★★) vintage. Very ripe & fleshy, yet silky, with black olive notes, fynbos hints, & fine tannins. Alc (15%) still a little disjointed. **04** (ex-barrel) was elegant & seamless.

★★★★ **Chardonnay** New-World-style **07** leesy, apple toned & citrus infused. Big, creamily soft with sweet finish & well-hidden 15% alc.

Cabernet Sauvignon ★★★☆ Leafy whiffs on classy **05**. Though a tad stalky, succulent & well-balanced, with firm acid contrasting savoury red fruit. Elegantly styled **04** (★★★★) was a standout. **Merlot** ★★★ Shy **06** tank sample; sappiness of fruit toned down by wood tannins. Gd balance, but finish shortened by tannic dryness. **Eight Feet** ★★★★ No new vintage. Last ed, serious **05** cab/merlot blend showed tight tannins restraining fruit the Du Toit boys helped stomp. Only ex-cellar. **White from Red Shiraz** ★★ **07** coral-pink charmer in blanc de noir style, lightish & dry. **Sauvignon Blanc** ★★★ Last-tasted **06** showed typical (for this wine) cat's pee character & appealing lemongrass lift. Friendly 12% alc. — *JN*

Knorhoek Wines
T 021-865-2114 ▪ F 021-865-2627

Stellenbosch ▪ Est 1827 ▪ 1stB 1997 ▪ Tasting & sales daily 9-5 ▪ Fee R10 ▪ Closed Easter Fri & Sun, Dec 25 & Jan 1 ▪ Restaurant/lapa Sep-May 12-4 ▪ Guest house (B&B) with conference, function, entertainment area ▪ Facilities for children ▪ Tour groups ▪ Walks ▪ Conservation area ▪ Owner Hansie & James van Niekerk ▪ Cellarmaster Hansie van Niekerk ▪ Winemaker Arno Albertyn (2005) ▪ Viticulturist James van Niekerk ▪ 105ha (cabs s/f, merlot, pinotage, shiraz, chenin, sauv) ▪ 900t/6 000cs own label 70% red 30% white ▪ Export label: Two Cubs (9 000cs) ▪ PO Box 2 Koelenhof 7605 ▪ office@knorhoek.co.za ▪ www.knorhoek.co.za

A cool summer with phenolic ripeness at lower sugars resulted in an excellent harvest at this family-friendly farm, the reds showing good colour and the whites benefiting from additional tank capacity, allowing for separate vinifications. The Two Cubs easy-drinkers are a roaring success, says Arno Albertyn, and the new versions have been tweaked for extra quaffability. The Lapa Restaurant has been upgraded, the guesthouse redecorated and two new self-catering cottages opened.

★★★★ Cabernet Sauvignon 05 not ready. Last-tasted **03** impressed 2007 Terroir judges with concentrated fruit, finely handled tannins. **Pinotage ★★★** Savoury mushroom & earth aromas gain coconut touch mid-palate; **05** elegant tannin, added complexity from dollops cab f, merlot. **Shiraz ★★★** Pvsly 'Syrah'. Shy nose to **04**, white pepper & berry nuances; some earthy, mushroomy character; gripping tannic finish. 15% alc. **Pantére ★★★★** 'Reserve' pvs ed. **04** not ready; **03** was tightly wound four-way blend mainly cab (65%), shiraz, merlot, pinotage. **Chenin Blanc ✓ ★★★★** Hints of green apple & watermelon on **07**, following through to clean, sweetish palate. **Sauvignon Blanc ★★★★** Flinty, greenpepper & green fig typicity on **07**; mild tastes with refreshing acidity, long, clean finish.

Two Cubs range

White Blend ☺ **★★★** Friendly **07** mixes sauv, chenin & dollop semillon into delicious quaffability. Opulent appley flavours, hints ripe pineapple & honey.

Red Blend ✓ 目 ★★★★ 'Cape Blend' pvs ed. **06** complex, upfront nose mingling mint, choc & spices; rich blackberry flavour, juicy tannins, long toffee/coffee finish. 6 mths Fr oak. **Rosé ★★★** No new wine. Pretty, light, maiden **06** intended for early drinking. WO Coastal for the Cubs, rest Smnsberg-Sbosch. – MM

■ **Koelenbosch** *see* Koelenhof Winery

Koelenhof Winery
T 021-865-2020/1 ▪ F 021-865-2796

Stellenbosch ▪ Est 1941 ▪ 1stB 1974 ▪ Tasting & sales Mon-Thu 9-5 Fri 9-4.30 Sat & pub hols 9-1 ▪ Closed Easter Fri, Ascension Day, Dec 25/26 & Jan 1 ▪ BYO picnic (excellent deli nearby) ▪ Play area for children ▪ Function venue ▪ Owner 75 shareholders ▪ Winemaker Wilhelm de Vries & Martin Stevens (Jan 2001/Oct 2003) ▪ Viticulturist Herman du Preez (Jan 2002) ▪ 14 000 tons 6 000 cs own label ±9m litres bulk 60% red 38% white 1% rosé 1% sparkling/grape juice ▪ HACCP certification in progress ▪ PO Box 1 Koelenhof 7605 ▪ koelwyn@mweb.co.za ▪ www.koelenhof.co.za

Last year third-generation Andrew de Vries took the helm, in a family succession uncommon in grower-owned cellar. Koelenhof vinifies some 14000 tons, gleaned from a wide area (Malmesbury to Somerset West), but bottles only a fraction under its own label, including their first Sangiovese, released after the guide went to press.

Koelenbosch range

> **Merlot** ☺ ★★★ **04** old-Cape dried-fruit characters plumped up with plum/choc/vanilla notes; tannins more approachable. **Shiraz** ☺ ★★★★ Most complex of reds: myriad red fruits jostle with charry oak, lilies, new leather. 15% alc well masked; strident tannin backbone suggests may drink better few mths hence. **Cape Blend** ☺ ★★★ Step up for decently dry, quaffable **04**. Equal merlot/pinotage mix with 20% cab. Better integrated than range-mates. **Chenin Blanc Wooded** ☺ ★★★ Trend to subtler oaking continues with **06** (now 8 mths, older Fr). Exotic spices, white peach & brisk acidity part of charm.

Cabernet Sauvignon ★★ 24 mths Fr oak, 60% new, for all reds in this range. Too long for lean **04**, appealing black fruit not sufficient to counter gruff tannins. **Pinotage** ★★ Refreshing acidity, pleasant dry grip & strawberry-rubber nuances for step-up **04**. **Chardonnay Wooded** NEW ▤ ★★ Ambitious acid:sugar ratio (7.2g/l:1.9g/l RS) results in bracing maiden **06**; barely there lemon & vanilla flavours, despite 6 mths Fr oak aging. **Sauvignon Blanc** ▤ ★★ Shy **07** relies on bracing acidity for presence, but light on its feet (12% alc).

Koelenhof range

> **Pinotage Rosé** ☺ ★★★ **07** seems to follow in footsteps of VG **06** with appealing sugar-dusted strawberry tones, leafy hints, gently sweet lift. **Koelnektar** ☺ ★★★ Quintessential semi-sweet gewürz. **07** sample delightful rose petal & litchee nuances, lively acidity should please, as always, its many fans. **Hanepoot** ☺ ▤ ★★★ Tasted pvs ed, **06** warmed the cockles (and the heart) with 17% clean spirity filip, lovely pure grapey wafts.

Koelenberg NEW Dry red **07** not ready for tasting. **Pinotage Rosé Vin-sec** ★★ **06** tasted pvs ed was undemanding; dried-fruit bouquet, sweetish flavours without any grip. **Koelenhoffer** ★★ Off-dry sauv; lightish (12% alc), fresh but that's it. Also available in 1000ml. **Sauvignon Blanc Vin-sec** ★★ Frothy semi-sweet carbonated **07** bubbly. Latest is balanced, sea spray fresh. **White Jeripigo** ▤ ★★ Despite 17% alc fortification, 176g/l unctuous **06** needs more zip, either from alc or acidity. **Pino Porto** ★★ LBV-style (**NV**) port usually from pinotage with 2 yrs seasoned small oak, low fortification (16.4%). **03** was cheek-rougeingly spiritous, latest not ready for tasting. Discontinued: **Shiraz**, **Chardonnay Wooded**. *– CvZ*

Koelfontein

T 023-313-3130 ▪ F 023-313-4898

Ceres ▪ Est 1832 ▪ 1stB 2002 ▪ Visits by appt ▪ BYO picnic ▪ Farm produce, walks & other amenities ▪ Owner Handri Conradie ▪ Winemaker Dewaldt Heyns (consultant) ▪ 10ha (cab, merlot, shiraz, chard) ▪ 50t/2 000cs own label + 18 000litres for customers ▪ 70% red 30% white ▪ PO Box 702 Ceres 6835 ▪ wine@koelfontein.com

Sales of flagships Shiraz and Chardonnay gained such momentum last year that some fans were left empty-handed. The consolation: vineyard expansion of these is planned, with the possible addition of sauvignon and pinot to make the most of the varying mesoclimates on this high-altitude (750m) Ceres property.

★★★★ Chardonnay ✓ More refined oaking (now 80% new Fr, 11 mths), greater integration & balance cements re-rating from **04**. **06** has a classy sheen, gravelly citrus fruit spine & 'warm' (14% alc), satisfying finish. **05** not tasted.

Merlot ★★★★ Jolly opulence in a glass: rich meaty exuberance bursting with cherry & plums, oak & 14.5% alc lead the taste tango of **04**. Yr Fr cask, half new. No **03**. **Shiraz** ★★★★ Smoke & coffee, bustling 15% alc & fruit-rich red berry flavours on **05**, gear up on smouldering **04** (★★★★); tighter, more restrained in youth, needs food. Flashy all-new oak, 20 mths. *– DS*

■ **Kogmans Kloof** *see Zandvliet Estate*
■ **Koningshof** *see Avondvrede*

Koningsrivier Wines
T 023-625-1748 • **F** 023-625-1748

Robertson ▪ Est/1stB 2002 ▪ Visits by appt ▪ Owner SW Colyn ▪ Cellarmaster/winemaker Niël Colyn ▪ Viticulturist Briaan Stipp (consultant) ▪ 9ha (cab) ▪ 435cs 100% red ▪ PO Box 144 Robertson 6705 ▪ koningsrivier@barvallei.co.za

Niël Colyn describes his winemaking style as producing 'heavy, full wines – not easy drinkers but thoroughly drinkable'. This year he adds a wooded viognier to his portfolio; next is a chardonnay. But what he'd really like to try is sauvignon, his preferred tipple. True to form, he plans a wooded version.

Cabernet Sauvignon ★★★ **03** a cab at full throttle! Liquorice & port-like notes unrestrained by chewy oak tannins (100% new), 15.4% alc. For hearty fare. **Shiraz** ★★★★ Ripe, dense **04**'s bronco fruit corralled by sweet vanilla oak (25/75 Fr/Am, all new) & 16% alc frame. **Merlot-Cabernet Sauvignon** ★★★★ Merlot-led bear hug - 14.7% alc is bold but balanced by cassis, prune & savoury notes. Perfect winter warmer. **NV.** *— MW*

Koopmanskloof Vineyards

T 021-865-2355 • **F** 021-865-2421

Stellenbosch ▪ Est 1801 ▪ 1stB 1970 ▪ Tasting & cellar tours Mon-Fri 9-4 ▪ Sales 8-5 ▪ Fee R20 to taste 5 wines ▪ Closed pub hols ▪ Tour groups ▪ Olives ▪ BYO picnic ▪ Walking/hiking trails ▪ Private nature reserve ▪ Self-catering accommodation in mountain lodge for up to 16 people ▪ Owner Stevie Smit ▪ Winemaker Louwtjie Vlok (1992) with Anriënka Vlok (Oct 2006) ▪ Viticulturist Louwtjie Vlok (1992) & PD Koegelenberg (2000, consultant) ▪ 520ha (cab, merlot, pinotage, shiraz, chenin, sauv) ▪ 3 500t/50 000cs 40% red 40% white 20% rosé ▪ ISO 9001/2000 ▪ PO Box 19 Koelenhof 7605 ▪ kmkwingerde@adept.co.za ▪ www.koopmanskloof.co.za

This Stellenbosch farm has a winemaking history dating back to 1777, and owner Stevie Smit represents the third generation of his family there. Tradition extends to conservation, with 98ha set aside for fynbos, nature trails to walk and a mountain chalet to overnight in.

Koopmanskloof range NEW
Cabernet Sauvignon-Shiraz ★★★ Elegant black fruit aromas, **05** somewhat austere tannins but gd concentration of fruit to balance, slightly chunky finish. **Dry Red** ★★★ Almond, vanilla & black berry notes; velvet tannins; supple, subtle, harmonious; **05** mainly cab lifted by carignan. **Semi-Sweet Rosé** ★★★ Coppery salmon-pink **06**, black cherry & pineapple whiffs, luscious & sweet but ends crisply. **Chenin Blanc** ★★★★ Apricot/melon aromas, classic lime & pear-drop flavours, **07** sample austere mid-2007 but ample fruit presages gd development. **Sauvignon Blanc** ★★★ Khaki bush & mown-hay, **07** lean, tangy, green & fruit-shy. *— MF*

■ **Kosher** *see* Backsberg, Eshkol, Kleine Draken, Tempel

■ **Kosie Möller** *see* Klein Parys Vineyards

Kranskop Estate

T 023-626-3200 • **F** 023-626-3200

Robertson ▪ Est/1stB 2001 ▪ Tasting & Sales Mon-Fri 10-4.30 Sat 10-2 ▪ Closed Easter Sun, Dec 25 & Jan 1 ▪ Tours during tasting hours ▪ Tour groups ▪ Facilities for children ▪ Walks ▪ Owner/winemaker/viticulturist Nakkie Smit ▪ 43ha (cab, merlot, shiraz) ▪ 500t/2 500cs own label 100% red ▪ PO Box 18 Klaasvoogds 6707 ▪ kranskop@barvallei.co.za ▪ www.kranskopwines.co.za

An ancient and distinctive rock formation, Kranskop is the backdrop to this family winery where hand-picking, basket-pressing and barrel-ageing are the order of the day. The traditional approach is complemented by an unhurried tasting outside on the deck, personally conducted by owner-winemaker Nakkie Smit.

Cabernet Sauvignon ★★★ Classy, mint-lined **06** (preview), firmly structured with fine tannins, sweet cassis. This, following, barrel-aged up to yr. **Merlot** ★★★ Sturdy structure of **06** sample matched by dense mulberry fruit & hint menthol. **Shiraz** ★★★ Soft, lush & strawberry fruited, with dusty notes on **06** (ex-barrel). Shares stablemates' chunky tannin backbone, which should soften with ±yr's ageing. Like all these, WO Klaasvoogds. Discontinued: **Chardonnay**. — RP

■ **Krone** see Twee Jonge Gezellen Estate/The House of Krone
■ ***Kuikenvlei*** see Terroir Wines of SA

Kumala/Constellation South Africa

T 021-882-8177 · F 021-882-8176

Stellenbosch · Est 1981 · 1stB 1996 · Closed to public · Winemaker Ben Jordaan (Jul 2002) · PO Box 769 Stellenbosch 7599 · ben.jordaan@cbrands.co.za · www.kumala.com

Now part of the largest wine company in the world, the US Constellation Brands group, Kumala flies the SA flag around the globe. In the UK, where the 'Kumala phenomenon' began, it is still the leading SA brand and well supported by a £5-million campaign which includes radio, press, event sponsorship and extensive PR. The local arm is focusing on wine development with its winemakers and growers. Recently, former colleague Rhyan Wardman returned to help James Reid and the rest of the Stellenbosch team in their mission: to own the SA category on a global level.

Kumala Reserve range

Cabernet Sauvignon ★★★ Mulberry leaf & berry on mid-weight **06**, soft dry tannins. **Merlot** ★★★ **05** a delight. Handsome, dark & juicy, fulfilling merlot's promise of soft body & tannins. **Shiraz** ★★★ Earthy, dry & grainy tannined **05** has shed **04**'s plump allure & suppleness. **Chardonnay** ★★★★ Balanced, tangy & lively **07** (sample) serves up buttered toast & orange marmalade, with ripe, sunny fruit & brisk acidity. **Sauvignon Blanc** ★★★ Previewed **07** has a tropical spring in its step, offering passionfruit, lime & smooth acidity. W Cape WOs for all ranges.

Kumala Limited Release range NEW

Cabernet Sauvignon ★★★ Maiden **06**, previewed, honest & appealing. Ripe mulberry; sweetness of ripe fruit, ripe tannins to match. Nice example. **Merlot** ★★★ Black cherry & liquorice on **06**; impressive concentration; typically softer merlot tannins. **Shiraz** ★★★ Attractive warm prune fruit dusted with cinnamon spice, soft ripe tannins in warm-hearted, amiable **06** (sample). **Chenin Blanc** ★★★★ Cinnamon baked apples, lees, subtle oak/fruit interplay on **07**. Chenin's clean acidity balances fruit; lingering finish. Barrel sample nudges next rung. **Sauvignon Blanc** ★★★ Dbnville's dusty, capsicum signature apparent on **07**. Racy acidity, bone-dry, but neither shrill nor aggressive.

Kumala range

Cabernet Sauvignon-Shiraz ★★★ Cab is senior partner in new 50/50 (sample) blend, offering fresh cedary notes & ripe tannins. **Merlot-Ruby Cabernet** ★★★ Sweet-tempered **07** plump, with ultra-soft tannins, & slight sweetness on finish too. **Ruby Cabernet-Merlot** ★★★ No new wine; **06** sold out. Last tasted **05** was soft, smooth & quaffable. **Intulo Red** ★★★ **07** gutsy, vibrantly fruited red quaffer from robust pinotage/ruby cab. **Merlot-Pinotage** ★★ Some charry oak on chunky **07**. **Pinotage-Cabernet Sauvignon** ★★★ Pinotage dominates **07**; edgy berries, soft tannins, loads fruit. **Pinotage-Cinsaut** ★★ 50/50 mix in **07**, dry & austere despite dab sugar, though tannins are soft. **Pinotage-Shiraz** ★★ **07** blend yet to marry mid-2007, seems to be pulling apart. **Shiraz-Mourvèdre** NEW ★★ **06** trendy blend, earthy, bit foursquare. Note big 15% alc. **Rosé** ★★ Boiled sweets, candyfloss; the whole confectionery shop in **07**, just off-dry. **Chardonnay** ★★ Ripe citrus-tinged style, **07** laudably modest oaking. **Chardonnay-Semillon** ★★ Equal blend in **07**, with dried peach & v soft acidity. **Chenin Blanc-Chardonnay** ★★★ **07** chenin's acid balances chard's fleshy, peachy tones. Successful marriage. **Intulo White** NEW ★★ Modestly fruity, appley **07** blend, 50/50 chenin/colombard. **Sauvignon Blanc-Colombard** ★★ **07** fresh & lively; zippy acid; not as light as pvs. **Sauvignon Blanc-Semillon** ★★★ Herbal notes & capsicum on balanced **07** blend. **Chenin Blanc-Viognier** NEW ★★★ Maiden **07** melange of peach kernel & marzipan; spicy, tangy, mouthwatering & quite stylish. **Colombard-Chardonnay** ★★★ Fruit pastille & juicy peach combine in **07** appealing, everyday blend. Most in range tasted as samples; ratings tentative.

Kumala Organic range
Pinotage-Shiraz ★★★ No new wine. **05**, **06** sold out. Pinotage dominated **04**'s ripe, plummy 60/40 blend. **Colombard-Chardonnay** NEW ★★ No new wine. **06** sold out. **05** Gentle, dry with usual modest oak influence.

Kumala USA range NEW
Cabernet Sauvignon ★★★ Pleasant baked black fruit backed by ripe, dry tannins; **06** grippy on finish. **Merlot** ★★ Soft, easy **06** entices with sweet choc aromas & baked plums. **Shiraz** ★★★★ Whiffs smoked beef, mocha, berries & spice interplay on complex **06**; ripe fruit balanced by just-right tannins; gd dry finish. **Chardonnay** ★★★ Tropical-toned, v soft acidity enhances **07**'s slight sweetness. **Sauvignon Blanc** ★★★ Tropical **07** mixes passion- & kiwifruit salad with tangy acidity & fun sweet-sour notes. All in range tasted as samples, ratings provisional.

Winemakers Selection
Discontinued: **Shiraz-Cabernet Sauvignon**. — *IvH*

■ **Kumkani** *see* The Company of Wine People

Kupferberger Auslese

Crowd pleasing, medium-bodied white blend by Distell.
Kupferberger Auslese ★★ Current lowish alc (12%) version is mainly chenin, with sauv & riesling. Refreshing & tangy despite semi-sweet 27g/ℓ sugar. **NV**. — *MW*

■ **KwaZulu-Natal** *see* The Stables

KWV Limited
T 021-807-3900 • F 021-863-2000

Paarl • Est 1918 • KWV Wine Emporium daily tastings 9-4.30; fee R15 • Sales 9-5 • Tours Eng: 10, 10.30 & 14.15; Ger: 10.15 • Tour groups • Gifts (T 021-807-3007/8) • Winemaker KWV SA: chief winemaker Sterik de Wet • Senior winemakers Bertus Fourie & Thys Loubser, with Nomonde Kubheka (reds) & Johan Joubert (whites) • Viticulturist Senior viticulturist Cobus van Graan • ±13 000t • PO Box 528 Paarl 7624 • customer@kwv.co.za • www.kwv-international.com

Continuing developments at KWV show this industry giant's determination to be market-oriented. Their re-branding strategy, begun in 2006, continued last year with the introduction of a new look for the KWV Reserve range and the Laborie, Robert's Rock and Pearly Bay brands – the last three now also screwcapped. 2007 saw the launch of a new range of easy-drinking single-varietal wines – named 'Ubuntu', meaning 'To Share'; dual-varietal wines became a feature of the new KWV Lifestyle and entry-level Pearly Bay lines. There were some changes in the winemaker department, too, with two new appointments, Johann Fourie and Belinda van Eyssen, following Tania Joubert's move to the marketing team. Bertus Fourie, now senior winemaker, is focusing all his attention on creating innovative wines, in line with company ethos.

Cathedral Cellar range
★★★★☆ **Cabernet Sauvignon** Well-crafted, ageworthy cab. **04** shows array cassis, cured meats, liquorice; 26 mths new oak unobtrusive, provides beguiling vanilla/spice-perfumed overlay for graceful fruit. Like pvs, should repay cellaring.
★★★★ **Merlot 04** fine fruit laced with mint, enhanced by supportive oaking, stylish but austere tannins. Impenetrable mid-2007, will soften & evolve given time.
★★★★ **Pinotage** Typically a generous mouthful of lush fruit, abundant but friendly tannins. **04** more reined in, showing refinement of variety's Burgundian parent. Spicy, menthol notes; new oak yet to integrate mid-2007.
★★★★☆ **Shiraz** Bridges the Old/New World divide with elegance & panache. **04** has pvsly tasted **02**'s savoury tones & brambly fruit, well-dusted with black pepper (not white this time!); measured opulence, carefully crafted tannins suggest well worth keeping few yrs.

★★★★☆ **Triptych** Classy, iron fist in velvet glove-style blend cab, merlot & shiraz. **04** (★★★★) ultra-fine tannins, touch eucalyptus, expansive breadth; 26 mths new oak for longevity. Excellent, but misses exceptional depth & precision of **01**.

★★★★ **Chardonnay** Widely & frequently lauded. **06** won't disappoint: in footsteps of showy **05** with generous oaking, lush aromas of pineapple dusted with almonds & vanilla. Smidgen sugar, silky texture for immediate gratification.

Sauvignon Blanc ★★★★ Nettle & asparagus notes allude to cool-climate origin of **06**. Compact, steely & polished; attractive lingering finish. Step up on brawny (15.5% alc) **05** (★★★☆). This range WO W Cape unless noted.

Roodeberg range [NEW]

Roodeberg ★★★☆ Enduring brand, make-up morphed over yrs into current cab, merlot, shiraz configuration. **04** refined, spicy, & rather saturated with oak mid-2007 yet big, juicy fruit core to match, so should flesh out given some bottle age. WO W Cape.

KWV Reserve range

★★★★ **Cabernet Sauvignon** Clasically styled **04** still touch brooding & tight, cedary oak combining well with cassis basting. Elegant body & tannin suggest gd ageing potential. 14.5% alc well covered.

★★★★ **Merlot** Choc-coated plum flavours & sour cherry acidity on **05** (★★★★); sturdy tannins & herbaceous note recall pvsly tasted **03**, though latter more seductive in youth. W Cape vyds.

★★★★ **Shiraz** Higher general rating cemented by **04**, broad, savoury & appealing. Cherry, cured meat, liquorice & mint complexity; moderate 13.5% alc. 16 mths Am oak pleasantly obvious in sweet vanilla tones.

★★★★ **Chardonnay** ✓ Hedonistic **06**, cinnamon-spiced apple pie aroma, lime & crème brûlée favours, toasty hazelnut oaking. What can dinner guests say except 'yum!' Ex-single vyd.

★★★★ **Sauvignon Blanc 06** same mould as **05**: rich tropical fruits hung on grassy backbone. Balanced, suggestion sugar (3g/l) taking edge off piercing acidity.

This range WO Sbosch unless noted.

KWV Vintage Reserve range

★★★★ **Red Muscadel** Pvs eds reported 75's expressive tealeaf & brandy-soaked raisin complexity, long sweet/savoury finish, richness & sophistication. From selected Rbtson vyds, large-oak 8 yrs, 17.3% alc, 150g/l RS. Muscadel Awards laureate.

Cape Vintage Late Bottled [NEW] ★★★★ **00** from tinta & souzão, matured in older Fr oak. Round, soft & medium bodied with nuts, dried figs & brandy cream delights.

KWV Classic range

Cabernet Sauvignon ★★★☆ **06** big & full with cinnamon, capsicum highlights. Tannins serious enough for few yrs cellaring. **Merlot** ★★★ Tasty **06** brims with plums, herbs, dusty spices ex large seasoned oak; take 2 bottles, 1 won't be enough. **Pinotage** ★★★☆ **03** juicy, with vibrant raspberry & brambleberry fruit, fine tannins. Tasted last ed, as was next wine. **Shiraz** ★★★ Medium-bodied **03** pepper-infused early-drinker, dry tannins perfect for food. **Cape Blush** ★★ Blanc de noir-style al fresco companion; **06** a gentle passionfruit & strawberry cocktail. **Chardonnay** ★★ Touch oak on pinapple- & butterscotch-laden **06**, needs touch more sugar to cushion puckering acidity. **Steen** ★★☆ 'Old Cape' name for bone-dry chenin. Last ed, **06** was grassy & refreshingly dry. **Chenin Blanc** ★★☆ Textbook tropical crowd-pleaser, **07** ripeness adds texture, off-dry slick in tail. **Cape Riesling** ★★ Guava-toned **07** a little terse, perky & uncomplex for youthful quaffing. **Sauvignon Blanc** ★★★ Zesty **07** delivers the goods with fig & cut grass tones; light yet flavoursome, balanced finish. **Mousseux Blanc Cuvée Brut** ★★ NV crowd-pleaser finishing dry & slender (11.5% alc). **Mousseux Blanc Demi-Sec** ★★ NV sparkler from chenin has attractive Granny Apple hints, treacle-sweet finish. **Late Vintage** ★★★ Pvs ed, **05** made comeback with grapey notes, charming balance between 23g/l sugar & brisk acidity. This range WO W Cape.

KWV Fortified range

★★★★ **Red Muscadel** Eminently sippable, with honeyed raisins, candied citrus peel, freshening acidity, enlivening 17.6% spirit. 8 yrs large oak. **NV** not retasted.

★★★★ **White Muscadel NV** unfettered by oak, a glorious expression of the richness, layered complexity of fully ripe muscadel. Toffee, savoury whiffs; beautifully balanced 17.5% alc. WO Breede Rvr Vlly.

★★★★ **Millennium Port 99** from cinsaut & tinta, pvsly noted as ageing gracefully courtesy perfect balance between 19.5% alc, 110g/l sugar, substantial grape-tannin structure. Unwooded.

Ruby Port ★★★ Tinta/souzão star in soft, easy-drinking **NV**. Ripe cherries, spice from 2-3 yrs large oak. **Tawny Port** ★★★★ Long maturation (5-8 yrs) in old cask renders tinta/souzão into sun-packed compote raisin, hazelnut, dried peach. Latest **NV** drier than pvs (100g/l vs 120g/l RS). All WO W Cape unless noted.

KWV Lifestyle range NEW

Cabernet Sauvignon ★★ Ribena scented **07**, soft & vinous, for early enjoyment. **Merlot** ★★ Herbaceous **05** shows some depth & grip; finishes lean but long. **Pinotage** Not tasted. **Shiraz** ★★★ **05** sweet-fruited centre, savoury farewell. **Pinotage Rosé** ★★ Party starter **07**, banana & cream intro, gently sweet flavours. **Chardonnay** ★★ **06** honeyed, uncomplicated quaffer. **Chêne** ★★ From chenin, partly oaked. Understated bouquet & palate on **07**, some latent minerality, soft finish. **Steen** 'Old Cape' name for chenin. **07** not tasted. **Chenin Blanc** ★★★ Riper-styled **07** with tropical & red apple notes, slightly sweet farewell. **Sauvignon Blanc** ★★ **07** has loads of green aromas but is tad dilute on palate. **Sparkling Brut** Not tasted. **Sparkling Demi-Sec** ★★ Musky **NV** bubbly with citrus notes, medium-sweet finish. Fun wine; drink soon after purchase. **Sparkling Doux** ★★ Carbonated any-occasion celebrator. Honey-sweet palate infused with Granny Smith apple. **NV. Late Harvest** ★★ From chenin, **06** filled with grapey ripeness, tangy sweet-sour finish. **Red Muscadel** Not tasted. **White Muscadel** Not tasted. **Cape Ruby** Not ready. **Cape Tawny** Untasted.

Val du Chêne range

Merlot NEW ★★★ Maiden **03** ground-coffee aromas, choc flavours, approachable tannins for easy drinking (watch out for big alc, though). **Chenin Blanc** ★★★ Oak-brushed chenin; **04** last ed sassy but well rounded, brimful lemon zest & melon; mineral slant adds complexity. Wine (★★★★), 2007 Chenin Challenge winner.

Ubuntu range NEW

Shiraz ★★ Maiden **05** peppery, jammy quaffer with firm finish; 5g/l sugar adding extra gluggability. **Sauvignon Blanc** ★ **05** debuts this ed; simple melon-toned sipper starting to tire.

Robert's Rock range

Cabernet Sauvignon-Merlot ★★★ Cassis-licked **06**, firmly generous, 2 mths oak adding texture. Braai friendly. **Merlot-Cinsaut** ★★★ None tasted since **02**. **Pinotage-Pinot Noir** ★★★ Perfumed 60/40 blend, **06** soft & sumptuous banana/plum duet. 12 mths in oak. **Shiraz-Cabernet Sauvignon** ★★★ **06** extremely ripe & forward; dense, smoky & appealing. 60/40 combo. **Shiraz-Malbec** ★★★★ **05** flavoursome, wacky salami/fruit gum combo, leaner than siblings but more interesting. **Cinsaut-Ruby Cabernet** ★★★ Lively sweet red fruits leap from glass in **06**, chewy, juicy & uncomplicated. **Chenin Blanc-Cinsaut** No tasted. **Chardonnay** ★★★ Last tasted was easy & uncomplicated **04**. **Chardonnay-Semillon** ★★★ Pear & melon-laced **06** also has mellow citrus flavours, creamy mouthfeel, friendly 12.5% alc. **Chenin Blanc-Chardonnay** ★★ **07** plain yet pleasing, off-dry, creamy. **Chenin Blanc-Colombar** NEW Not tasted. All WO W Cape.

Pearly Bay range

Cabernet Sauvignon-Shiraz NEW ★★★ **06** most serious in range: bright blueberry fruit, mixed spice in chewy tannin shell. **Pinotage-Pinot Noir** NEW ★★★ 60/40 blend, **06** floral notes & sweet red fruit, yr oak well integrated. **Cape Red** ★★★ We last tasted an unoaked **NV**, lightly perfumed, with generous fruit. **Celebration Rosé** NEW Not tasted. **Cape Rosé**

NEW Unready. **Chenin Blanc-Chardonnay** **NEW** ★★★ Debut **06** melange Granny Smith apples, minerals & fresh citrus fruit; dab sugar (5g/l) adds richness. **Chenin Blanc-Colombar** **NEW** ★★ Crisp apple & macadamia nuts on attractive, light & flavoursome **06**. Tasty newcomer.

Bonne Esperance range

Dry Red ★★ This, below, **NV**, in 1litre screwcap, sold internationally. Unwooded, moderate 12.5% alc, variable blend, usually drop pinotage. Last ed was softly friendly with baked plum flavours. **Dry White** ★★ Tasty grape flavours & easy-going 12.1% alc. — *RP*

■ **La Beryl** *see* Fairview
■ *La Bonne Vigne* *see* Wonderfontein

Laborie Cellar

T 021-807-3390/3196 • F 021-863-1955

Paarl ▪ Est 1691 ▪ Tasting & sales daily 9-5 (Nov-Apr) Mon-Sat 9-5 (May-Oct) ▪ Fee R10 for 5 wines; tour & tasting R20 ▪ Closed all Christian pub hols ▪ Tours for groups 10+ by appt ▪ Laborie Restaurant open daily 10-5 (T 021-807-3095) ▪ Owner KWV International ▪ Winemaker/viticulturist Dave Boyes ▪ 39ha (cab, merlot, pinot, pinotage, shiraz, chard, sauv, viognier) ▪ 550t/40 000cs ▪ PO Box 528 Suider-Paarl 7624 ▪ wolhuter@kwv.co.za ▪ www.kwv-international.com

'Heritage with vision' sums up the approach at KWV's prestige Paarl property, where young Dave Boyes respects the three centuries of winemaking that preceded his arrival but isn't letting them stop him from looking into alternative styles and approaches. Committed to eco-friendly vineyard practices, his experiments last year included a pinot and a botrytised dessert.

★★★★ **Jean Taillefert** A bold New World shiraz flagship typically loaded with berries & choc-moccha; made intermittently. Last tasted **03** densely structured, with staying power for 5 yrs+.

★★★★ **Blanc de Blanc Brut** MCC from chard, ± 3 yrs lees aging in bottle. Brioche flavoured **03** has fine mousse, reveals focussed lemon fruit, touch minerality; finishes with zesty acidity, nutty nuances.

★★★★ **Pineau de Laborie** Standalone dessert from (mostly) unfermented pinotage fortified with Laborie pinotage potstill brandy. The variety's trademark plums/strawberries are very evident on exuberent **03**; 17.5% alc is integrated, imparts clean, dry edge. 18 mths old Fr barriques add spice, not tannin.

Cabernet Sauvignon ★★★ **05** perenially soft & ripe with red berries, hint liquorice, smooth & friendly tannins; 13.5% alc slightly warming on farewell. Yr Fr oak, 30% new. **Merlot** ★★★ **05** (★★★) more food wine than solo sipper given its rather reticent aromas/flavours, leaner & more herbaceous tones than pvsly featured **03**. **Pinotage** ★★★ Chunky & bold **05** (★★★) finishes with a warming glow ex 14% alc. Oak (30% new) lends dry, spicy edge to rich plummy fruit. **Shiraz** ★★★ **04** has trademark rustic styling; leather & drying tannins take centre stage, fruit plays a supportive role. **Merlot-Cabernet Sauvignon** ★★★★ **04** a stylish, accessible food partner; medium bodied, juicy, supple tannin balancing bright acidity. **Chardonnay** ★★★ **06**'s butter richness (ex 30% oak ferm) tempered by tangy lime acidity; balanced, should complement fine seafood, poultry dishes. **Sauvignon Blanc** ★★★ Cleansing acidity, grapefruit pith texture & dry, mineral farewell part of **06**'s charm. **Viognier** **NEW** ★★★ Maiden **06** delicate & aromatic on the nose, poised on the palate; tangy dried apricot & almond nuances add extra interest, charm. EW. Discontinued: **Blanc de Noir**. — *MW*

La Bourgogne Farm

T 021-876-2115 • F 021-876-2567

Franschhoek ▪ Est 1694 ▪ 1stB 2005 ▪ Visits by appt ▪ Self-catering cottages ▪ Owner La Bourgogne Farm (Pty) Ltd ▪ Winemaker Justin Hoy ▪ Viticulturist Pietie le Roux (2006, consultant) ▪ 2.5ha (mainly semillon) ▪ 25t 100% white ▪ PO Box 96 Franschhoek 7690 ▪ george@cpsa.co.za ▪ www.labourgogne.co.za

George Mayer is delighted with the reception his maiden semillon has had; next up is his first straw wine, a blend of semillon and hanepoot. Top of mind for the owner/winemaker is the need to keep alcohol levels around 13 percent. Planting is going ahead, but own vinification facilities are still a dream.

★★★★ **Progeny Semillon** Excellent, finely textured maiden **05** was last tasted. Sweet waxy, lanolin aromas, slightly creamy with crisp, food-friendly greengage finish. Modest 13% alc a bonus. Fermented/±8 mths oak. **06** held back for further maturation.

Progeny White Honey NEW Not ready. — *MF*

La Bri
T 021-876-2593 • **F** 021-876-3197

Franschhoek • Tasting & sales Mon-Fri 9.30-5 Sat & pub hols 10-4, Sun (in season only) 11-3 • Fee R12pp, redeemable with any purchase • Closed Easter Sun, Dec 25 & Jan 1 • Owner Robin Hamilton • Cellarmaster/winemaker Jocelyn Wilson • Viticulturist Claude Uren • 18ha (cabs s/f, merlot, petit v, shiraz, chard, viognier) • 4 000cs own label 85% red 15% white • Ranges for customers: Makro (SA) • PO Box 180 Franschhoek 7690 • info@labri.co.za • www.labri.co.za

In less than a year, recently graduated winemaker/manager Jocelyn Wilson has overseen a complete make-over of this established brand, including a range streamlining, boutique cellar, website and - later this year - a new tasting room, with lovely valley views and plans to open daily.

La Bri range

Affinity ★★★★ No new vintage. Flagship cab-driven bdx blend with merlot & dollops petit v, cab f. Last ed, succulent & approachable **04** showed structure for 5+ yrs ageing.

Limited Release range

★★★★ **Shiraz-Viognier** Ying-yang of spice & floral notes well integrated on **05** thanks to co-fermentation of red & white (10%) grapes. Abundant red fruit to tame lofty 15.6% alc, big tannins. Yr older Fr/Am oak.

Cabernet Sauvignon ★★★★ Textbook tobacco leaf & spice, fruity core to supple, early-drinking **03** noted last ed. **04** sold to Makro. **Merlot** ★★★ 100% new oak for athletic **04**. Solid fruit core hides 14.6% alc, matches robust tannins built for long haul. **Chardonnay** ★★★★ Citrus freshness to rich, weighty (±15% alc) **05**. Fermented/yr 100% new Fr oak. Not retasted. — *CvZ*

■ La Cave *see Wamakersvallei Winery*

La Chataigne

T 021-876-3291 • **F** 021-876-3220

Franschhoek • Est 1972 • 1stB 2003 • Visits by appt • 3 guest cottages • Owner Parkfelt family • Winemaker Gerda Willers (2002, consultant) • Viticulturist Pietie Le Roux (1996, consultant) • 15ha (merlot, shiraz, pinotage, chenin, sauv, semillon) • 150t/1 000cs own label 25% red 45% white 30% rosé • PO Box 7 La Motte 7691 • info@lachat.co.za • www.lachat.co.za

'Our first year of providing accommodation, cookery courses and wine tastings has been very rewarding,' says Richard Parkfelt. All La Chataigne's wines (which, he says, they have great fun making and sell reluctantly) now have individually hand-written labels. And the family's focus on their Swedish heritage has helped to grow that market.

Marron ★★★★ Amiable combo merlot, pinotage & cab. Step-up **05** red berry, cherry character, hint bay leaf; smooth, elegant tannins make for a charming food wine. 8 mths 2nd/3rd fill Fr oak. **Rosé** ★★ Last available **04** a slightly sweet picnic companion from merlot, refreshing addition two blancs (chenin, sauv, 25% each). Next is 08. **Sauvignon Blanc** ✓ ★★★★ Showing increased intensity, concentration, **06** has tropical, gooseberry aromas, touch of spice, well-balanced firm structure; a wonderful food wine. Another rung up from much improved **05** (★★★). **Semillon** NEW Not ready for tasting. **Kastanje** ★★★ Sweetly friendly chenin-led blend with 15% dollop sauv in **06**. Herbaceous & almond notes, soft flavours. — *MM*

La Chaumiere Estate

T 021-876-2135

Franschhoek • Est 2001 • 1stB 2003 • Tasting & tours by appt (sales only from local outlets) • Owner Ian & Margaret Slack • Winemaker Johan Haasbroek & Ian Slack • Viticulturist Johan Haasbroek • 3.6ha (shiraz, chard) • 12t/600cs • PO Box 601 Franschhoek 7690 • slacki@telkomsa.net

'We're trialling cap classique from the chardonnay harvest this year,' says Ian 'Slacki' Slack, who notes that it will be three years before the results can be tasted – 'but we intend it to be good!' Johan Haasbroek, formerly of La Bri, has joined La Chaumiere as estate manager and winemaking consultant.

La Chaumiere

Slacki's Shiraz ★★★★ Attractive **04** last ed was for early drinking with its spiciness & exuberant tannins lifted by refreshing acidity, light texture. 18 mths oak. EW.

La Chimere

Shiraz NEW ★★★★ Rhône-like lilies dominate the maiden **05** bouquet, red berries & spicy oak the long & balanced flavours. 24 mths old Fr oak. EW. **Chardonnay** ★★★ **04** on review offered lovely butterscotch & lees aromas, refreshing citrus acidity. Fr oak, third new. EW. *— CvZ*

■ **La Chimere** *see La Chaumiere Estate*
■ **La Cotte** *see Franschhoek Vineyards*

La Couronne

T 021-876-3939 • F 021-876-4168

Franschhoek • Est/1stB 1999 • Tasting & sales Mon-Fri 10-4 Sat 9-1 • Fee R15 • Tours by appt (R10 p/p) • Closed pub hols • Weddings & conferences • Facilities for children • Tour groups • Owner The Austrian Trust • Winemaker Anneke du Plessis (2007) • Viticulturist Dirk Husselmann • 21ha (cabs s/f, malbec, merlot, petit v, shiraz, chard, sauvignon) • 60-90t/±13 000cs 60% red 40% white • PO Box 459 Franschhoek 7690 • ninette@lacouronne.co.za • www.lacouronne.co.za

This farm is named after the warship which transported 277 French Huguenots to the Cape in 1685. It boasts an extraordinary garden (perfect setting for picnics and wedding receptions) which inspired an illustrated children's book about Franschhoek and the Cape. Anneke du Plessis (ex-Mont Rochelle) recently took the winemaking helm.

La Couronne range

★★★★ **Cabernet Sauvignon** 15.5% alc stands out on well-crafted, if very ripe, **05** (★★★★). Hint raisin, but oak & tannins well handled (yr, 33% new). No **04**. **03** classically styled with finessed tannins.
Merlot ★★★★ Full-flavoured **05**, packed with scrub & mulberry notes; slightly warm (15.5% alc) but fresh & appealing. Yr Fr oak, 35% new. **Pinotage** NEW **05** not ready for tasting. **Shiraz** ★★★ Big, forthright **05** has 16% alc kick, tight tannins & dash sugar for accessibility. Varietal character, not obvious mid-2007, may evolve. **Ménage à Trois** ★★★★ **04** unpretentious but satisfying bdx-style red, mainly cab & cab f/merlot (22/21). Classic black fruit & green herbs; fine, well-knit tannins. Yr Fr oak. **Chardonnay Wooded** ★★★★ Appealing toasty oak, lemon & lime on poised **06**; almost back to std set by elegant **04**. 8 mths Fr oak, 40% new. **Chardonnay Unwooded** 🍾 ★★★ Oatmeal & minerals on **06**; light bodied & textured but lacking joie de vivre. Both ranges widely sourced, so various WOs.

277 range

Exodus Dry Red ★★★ Pvsly bdx blend, now incl shiraz. Well-handled staves give added dimension to fresh, supple fruit. **NV. Sauvignon Blanc** 🍾 ★★ **07** picked tad riper for more body (now 13.6% alc); vinous & shy. Discontinued: **Etienne Chenin Blanc**, **Cevennes Blanc**. *— CvZ*

Ladismith Cellar
T 028-551-1042 • F 028-551-1930

Klein Karoo • Est 1941 • 1stB 1988 • Tasting & sales Mon-Fri 8-5 • Closed all pub hols except Easter Sat • BYO picnic • Tours by appt • Conferencing • Owner 75 members • Winemaker Emile Schoch (2005) • Viticulturist Johannes Mellet (Aug 2006, consultant) • 600ha (ruby cab, chard) • 8 000t/4 200cs own label + 3.2m litres bulk • PO Box 56 Ladismith 6655 • info@ scv.co.za • www.scv.co.za

Previously listed under umbrella company Southern Cape Vineyards, Ladismith Cellar and sibling Barrydale Cellar have regained their own identities, packaging and product ranges. Ladismith's varietal wines and blends now appear under the Ladismith Cellar Towerkop label (thus linking the brand with the eponymous town, experiencing new-found fashionability as a tourist destination). The cellar also continues producing Amalienstein White Muscadel and Towersoet, its popular traditional sweet wines.

Towerkop range

Chardonnay-Sauvignon Blanc ☺ ★★☆ **07** cheery quaffer from equal portions chard, sauv. Well-defined varietal character, long & balanced finish; just needs extra intensity to lift the bar. **Amalienstein Muscadel** ☺ ★★★ Lovely fortified sweetie; **06** nicely balanced thanks to deft fortification; overt grapey notes, nutty undertones.

Pinotage ★★★ We last reviewed Regional Young Wine Show winner **03**. **Ruby Cabernet** ★★ Lively & juicy, quaffable **05** (modest 12.2% alc helps), mulberry & thatch tones last yr, long fruity finish. **Shiraz** ★★ Interesting bread/baked fruit notes on briefly oaked (6 mths) **07**; soft fruit core, slightly astringent aftertaste. For early drinking. **Rosé** ★ Semi-sweet **NV** from pinotage, chard, last ed noted as needing drinking soon. **Chardonnay** NEW **06** not ready for review. **Chenin Blanc** NEW **06** not tasted. **Viognier** NEW Review sample of **06** not received. **Stein** ★★ Last we tasted an **NV**; supple, lightish summer tipple, dry for this style. **Towersoet** ★★★ Fortified hanepoot, literally 'Magic Sweet', which it is. When last tasted **03** had enchanting muscat & Oriental market smells & fresh acidity. Discontinued: **Blanc de Blanc**. — *CvZ*

■ **Lady Anne Barnard** *see African Pride Wines*

Lady Auret Wines
T 082-773-7059, 082-377-2661

Paarl • Est/1stB 2002 • Tasting by appt • Owner Corius & Gina Swart • Winemaker Corius Swart (Jan 2002) • 2 200 btls 100% red • 14 Auret Str Paarl 7646 • ladyauret@polka.co.za

Shiraz, the first Lady of this House (located at 14 Auret Street, Paarl), has played her starring role and now Corius Swart's new leading lady, a wooded Chenin-Viognier **07**, makes her debut. Fashionably late for our deadline, she will be released in the course of the year.

Laibach Vineyards
T 021-884-4511 • F 021-884-4848

Stellenbosch • Est 1994 • 1stB 1997 • Tasting & sales Mon-Fri 10-5 Sat 10-1 (Nov-Apr only) Pub hols 10-1 • Closed Easter Fri/Sun, Dec 25 & Jan 1 • Fee R10 refunded on purchase • Tours by appt • Owner Laibach family • Cellarmaster Francois van Zyl & Stefan Dorst • Winemaker Francois van Zyl (Jan 2000) • Viticulturist/MD Michael Malherbe (Jun 1994) • 42ha (cabs s/f, malbec, merlot, petit v, pinotage, chard, viognier) • 300t/24 000cs own label • 600cs for Woolworths • 70% red 30% white • PO Box 7109 Stellenbosch 7599 • info@laibachwines.com • www.laibachwines.com

MD/viticulturist Michael Malherbe will be implementing ideas gleaned on a visit to California's leading organic farms, as the team pursues their goal of having two-thirds of the farm certified organic by 2010. Organic flagship The Ladybird showed judges her true spots, taking gold at last year's Swiss Awards. Not to be outshone, the Merlot is becoming a front-runner in its category with repeated 4-star ratings in Wine magazine. The death of founder Friedrich Laibach sees the farm in the hands of daughter Petra and her husband.

★★★★ **The Widows Block 05** reviewed last yr being held back for further maturation. From oldest cab vyd on farm. Beautifully proportioned/toned, with pure fruit & burnished tannins. 100% new Fr oak, 16 mths. SAYWS champion. EW.

★★★★ **Merlot** FvZ's goal to emulate classic Pomerol. **06** (★★★★★), incl malbec & cab f, probably best to date. Gorgeous spice, bitter choc perfume; silky, with fine, youthfully insistent tannins. Full delights still 6-8 yrs off. Fr oak, 40% new.

★★★★ **Pinotage** Consistent award-winner from old dryland bushvines. **06** modern but refined, classy. Full body tempered by lively sweet-spicy concentration, finely-tuned tannins. Still tight; give 2-3 yrs before opening; can mature longer. Fr oak, 40% new.

★★★★ **Friedrich Laibach** Farm's flagship, a bdx blend, made only in best yrs. Last **03** cab, merlot, cab f, petit v quartet (64/16/13/7) sumptuous mocha, mulberry features. Skilfully tailored; 100% new Fr oak, 16 mths. No **04**; **05** untasted, released mid-2008.

★★★★ **White Ladybird** NEW Interesting new-wave white blend. **06** seamless home-grown organic chard & bought-in viognier (25%), chenin (13%). Silky & substantial; some oxidation adding complexity to attractive savoury length. Wild ferment/8 mths Fr oak, none new. Unfiltered/fined.

Cabernet Sauvignon ★★★★ **05** extremely ripe, soft-centred & a little hollow. Careful extraction & judicious oaking allow for agreeable drinking in short/medium-term. 14% alc. 5% new Fr oak. **The Ladybird** ★★★★ Step-up **06** similar organically-grown merlot, cabs s/f blend as **05** (★★★★). The younger wine richer, more dimension; balanced by hallmark 'minerally' tannins. Promising. Fr oak, some new. **Chenin Blanc** ★★★ **06** last ed was an attractive quaffer with easy-going richness. Pdberg/Bottlry Hills vyds. **07** not ready for tasting. **Sauvignon Blanc** ✓ ★★★★ Invitingly moreish **07** purer, more intense than **06** (★★★★). Cool gooseberry & mineral attractions; rich yet agile, invigorating, with sustained finish. WO Sbosch. **Natural Sweet** In abeyance. Discontinued: **The Dogleg, Chardonnay**. —AL

La Kavayan

T 021-881-3289, 021-881-3246 • F 021-881-3095 & 021-881-3211

Stellenbosch • Est 1999 • 1stB 2001 • Closed to public • Owner Gabriël Kriel & Theo Beukes • Winemaker PG Slabbert (2001, consultant) • Viticulturist Gabriël Kriel • 4ha (cab, shiraz) • 1 000cs 100% red • PO Box 321 Stellenbosch 7599 • minpro@adept.co.za

Bodraai's name change to La Kavayan ('Jan's Cellar', after previous owner Prof Jan Sadie) reflects the place where the vines are cultivated under the watchful eyes of close friends Theo Beukes and Gabriel Kriel. Emphasis is placed on limited release and exclusive distribution.

La Kavayan range

Cabernet Sauvignon ★★★ Intriguing almond/walnut & not unappealing volatile notes on ready-to-drink **04**; balanced, as was pvs, firmly friendly tannins, juicy cassis fruit. **Cabernet Sauvignon-Shiraz** ★★★★ Undemanding fireside sipper **04**, well-upholstered with red & black fruit, some leather & farmyard, mild tannins for current enjoyment. —CvZ

■ **Lambertsbay** *see Daschbosch Wine Cellar*

Lammershoek Winery

T 022-482-2835 • F 022-487-2702

Swartland • Est/1stB 1999 • Visits Mon-Fri 9-5; Sat/Sun & pub hols by appt • Tours Mon-Fri 9-5 by appt • Special house platter (R65 p/p) Mon-Fri 9-5 by appt; or BYO picnic • Walks • Conservation area • Mountain biking • Owner Paul & Anna Kretzel, Stephan family • Winemaker Albert Ahrens (Jun 2002) • Viticulturist Albert Ahrens & Anna Kretzel • 130ha (12 varieties, r/w) • 200t/10 000cs own label 75% red 25% white • PO Box 597 Malmesbury 7299 • info@lammershoek.co.za • www.lammershoek.co.za

'We're delighted that Carla Kretzel, daughter of owners Paul and Anna, has joined us in marketing,' says winemaker Albert Ahrens. The winery is applying an old European method of trellising which allows for the vines to grow in natural bush form, but has the benefit of each vine being tied to its own pole to keep the bunches out of the heat. 'The change of viticultural practices over the past five years to improve quality is starting to show very nicely in the wines,' says Albert A.

Lammershoek Winery range

★★★★ Syrah 05, with dollop mourvèdre, remarkably delicate & elegant given 14.5% alc. Herbal fynbos notes plus sweet red fruit - & evident oak (16 mths Fr/Am; 80% new) which also dries out finish. Savoury & smart, with room to grow over few yrs.

★★★★ Roulette Fruit-filled but seriously vinous **05** blends 70% shiraz with carignan, grenache, mourvèdre, viognier. Shows dark cherry, mulberry notes along with Swrtlnd scrubby herbs; lively palate well structured - 14.5% alc in balance; sensitively restrained yr oak (20% new) supporting.

★★★★ Zinfandel-Syrah Delicious, savoury **03** last tasted (next will be **06**). Individual & unusually refined given zin's boisterousness.

★★★★ Chenin Blanc Barrique After showy, oaky-sweet **05** (**★★★☆**), **06**, with straw & honey-tinged notes, more modest & lovely; just off-dry with big 14.5% alc, but gd balancing freshness for lingering charm. Clever blending of different parcels, pickings; mostly older barrels.

★★★★ Roulette Blanc Powerful, rich & tasty **06** chenin-led blend (with 24% chard, 10% viognier, touches of clairette, hárslevelü) much along lines of pvs, but more refined, less oak-driven (mixed older, new), with floral, peach & earth notes. Not quite dry, which is a pity here.

Pinotage Barrique ★★★ Attractive aromas on well rounded **03**, with big dry tannins tussling with sweet red fruit flavours. 16 mths oak, 20% new. **Tinta Barocca Barrique ★★★☆** Last was balanced, supple **02**. **Cape Vintage Zinfandel ★★★** Last was sweet, scarcely gripping **02**. **Straw Wine ★★★☆** Last 375ml **NV** from sun-dried hárslevelü not retasted. Fresh & lingering; sweet, but dryish, grippy effect, with 12.5% alc.. **Pinodoux ★★★** Fortified, lightly oaked pinotage; last was smooth, rich **03**. Discontinued: **Viognier Barrique**.

Aprilskloof range

Tinta Barocca NEW ★★★ Sweetly ripe fruit on **05**, with choc, cola notes; a little new oak adds to awkward tannic dryness. **Red-Red Wine ★★★** Pinotage-based allsorts red, lightly wooded, giving lots of fresh red fruit in firm structure. **Rosé ★★** Last **NV** blend tasted few yrs back; label's future uncertain. **Sauvignon Blanc ★★★** Bone-dry, well textured **07** has fresh, savoury greenness. Decent, straightforward stuff. — *TJ*

La Motte

T 021-876-3119 • F 021-876-3446

Franschhoek • Est 1984 • Tasting & sales Mon-Fri 9-4.30 Sat 10-3 • Fee R15 • Closed Christian hols • Seasonal Food & Wine Experiences • Monthly classical concerts • Owner Hanneli Koegelenberg • Winemaker Edmund Terblanche (Dec 2001), with Michael Langenhoven (Dec 2006) • Viticulturist Pietie le Roux (May 1986) • 108ha (cabs s/f, merlot, shiraz, chard, sauv) • 900t/32 000cs own label 53% red 47% white • ISO 14001 certified • EurepGap & WIETA accredited • PO Box 685 Franschhoek 7690 • cellar@la-motte.co.za • www.la-motte.com

Already a member of the Biodiversity & Wine Initiative and home to SA's largest private collection of indigenous orchids, eco-conscious La Motte has been turning land not suitable for vines over to flower cultivation and the production of organic essential oils. The Franschhoek farm is converting to organic, while Bot River grapes supply the organic sauvignon in the medal-winning Pierneef range, named after the famous SA landscape artist whose works grace the labels. Upliftment initiatives include new housing and facilities for the estate workers, and a new assistant winemaker Michael Langenhoven, with wide sauvignon experience, has been appointed.

Pierneef Collection

★★★★☆ Shiraz-Viognier In powerfully perfumed **05**, floral notes vie with hedgerow fruit, savoury spice - pepper, cloves. There's tensile strength, but silk-clothed. 15 mnths Fr, half new. Int Wine Challenge gold; Concours Mondiale gold.

★★★★☆ **Sauvignon Blanc (Organically Grown)** ⚘ Walker Bay fruit, stylistically cooler than sibling. Specially cellar-handled, bone-dry **07** has remarkable complexity: asparagus, lime, fennel, plus a pervading palate minerality that speaks of fine seafood dining.

Classic Collection

★★★★☆ **Shiraz** Going for class rather than overt appeal, **05** is a new world take on the Rhône: smoky whiffs, blueberries, white pepper, presented in a lithe, beautifully tailored package. Already drinkable, will reward 4+ yrs cellaring.

★★★★ **Millennium** Mainly merlot in **04**, rest bdx varieties. Boosts perfume, plush dark berries, choc nuances, sweet spice; then an enthralling smooth, structured elegance. 18 mnths Fr barriques, half new. Concours Mondiale gold.

Cabernet Sauvignon ★★★★ In warm vintage, **05** has no shortage of plump ripe fruit, handled with finesse through 16 mth Fr barrique treatment. With enough nuances to hold your interest, cedar, dark choc, this is made for enjoyment. **Chardonnay** ★★★★ Much to admire in **06**: roasted almond & citrus peel perfume, flavours, sleekly curvaceous body & an appealing freshness from third unoaked portion that keeps it food-friendly. Incl dab semillon. **Sauvignon Blanc** ✓ ★★★★ Lovely fresh-fruity tones to improved **07**; gooseberry core with leafy, green fig overlay, coming together in a zesty, palate-awakening finale. Hard to resist, espec at the price. — CR

Landau du Val
T 082-410-1130 • F 021-876-3369

Franschhoek • Tasting by appt • Sales at La Cotte Wine Sales, Franschhoek • Owner Basil & Jane Landau • Winemaker Anina Guelpa (Anatu Wines); Jean Daneel (2004 vintage) • Viticulturist Jaco Schwenke • landau@mweb.co.za

Basil and Jane Landau and new winemaker Anina Guelpa were understandably delighted with their form at last year's Trophy Show, where Anina's G's first Semillon for this label garnered a bronze medal. The team is quick to acknowledge the gnarly, unirrigated bushvines which supply the fruit: amongst the most venerable in SA, they're 103 years old but clearly still capable of producing winning wines.

★★★★ **Semillon Private Selection** Fr oak-fermented/aged 5-6 mths. **06** (★★★★) awarded by Trophy Show but to us shade off **04** & pvs; waxy semillon character in place, gd fruit & follow-through, but less lip-smacking grip than pvs. — MM

■ **Landsdowne** *see Arlington Beverage Group*
■ **Land's End** *see Hidden Valley Wines*

Landskroon Wines
T 021-863-1039 • F 021-863-2810

Paarl • Est 1874 • 1stB 1974 • Tasting & sales Mon-Fri 8.30-5 Sat 9-1 • Fee R3 p/p for groups • Closed Easter Fri, Dec 25 & Jan 1 • Tours by appt • Picnics in summer by appt or BYO • Self-catering cottage (see Stay-over section) • Play area for children • Tour groups • Gifts • Walks by appt • Permanent display of Stone Age artefacts • Owner Paul & Hugo de Villiers Family Trusts • Winemaker Paul de Villiers (Jan 1980) • Viticulturist Hugo de Villiers Jnr (1995) • 270ha (14 varieties r/w) • 1 100t 81% red 14% white 5% port • PO Box 519 Suider-Paarl 7624 • huguette@landskroonwines.com • www.landskroonwines.com

Recent plantings of shiraz, cab and merlot are set to uphold Landskroon's reputation for good-value big reds and port. The past year included the successful launch of the Hugo's Hill and Bush Camp labels in the US, while the Landskroon range now travels to several new Far Eastern destinations.

Paul de Villiers range

★★★★ **Cabernet Sauvignon** Long-lived flagship from select vyds, treated to all-new Fr oak. Mid-2005, **03** was youthful with generous cassis core wrapped in taut tannin; in similar vein to **02**. Not retasted.

Shiraz ★★★★ Showier than version below, courtesy 18 mths new Am oak. Despite **05**'s powerhouse of flavours, smoky plums & vanilla spice, the palate lacks concentration of pvs. Still attractive, smooth-textured, eminently drinkable. Could age 3/4 yrs. **Reserve ★★★★** Mainly shiraz, merlot, touch touriga, cab, which **05** showcases delightfully. With graceful lines, savoury notes & fruit vying for attention, it's an engaging experience. mainly new Am/Fr oak.

Landskroon Wines range

★★★★ **Cabernet Sauvignon** Recent releases approachable sooner rather than styled for extended cellaring, still v satisfying. **05** sold out before we could taste, **06**'s rich fruit-cake perfume misleads: the palate is streamlined, welcoming, harmonious. Drink now or age few yrs.

★★★★ **Port** Approachable medley tinta b/r, touriga, souzão. **03** follows cellar styling of fruit-cake richness delivered in a smooth-textured form; appetising & ready to be enjoyed.

Cinsaut ☺ **★★☆** From older bushvines. Savoury tone in **06**'s warm ripe fruit; generous, flavourful, unwooded braai/outdoor red. **Blanc de Noir Pinotage Off-Dry** ☺ **★★☆** Successful house style: **07** has bright fruit, curvy lines & enough lively acidity for pleasurable drinking.

Merlot ★★★ Exuberantly fruity (cherries, red berries) **05** steps up with finely judged oaking (some new) adding structure & definition. **Pinotage ★★★** Showing typicity & gd fruit purity, **06**'s plum & rhubarb flavours firmly supported by oak, heralding 3/4 yr future. **Shiraz ★★★ 05** sticks to full-ripe house style: dark plums, vanilla spice, curvaceous body harmoniously oaked. Yr seasoned Am. **Tinta Barocca** NEW **★★★** Lightly oaked maiden **06** shows expected charm: wild berry fruit nicely coupled with juicy quaffability. **Cinsaut-Shiraz ★★★** Equal blend plus dabs cab, touriga, give **06** wild-berry nuance, but main focus is warm-hearted drinkability. Lightly oaked. **Cabernet Franc-Merlot ✓ ★★★★ 05** tasted last ed, needed time for slightly astringent tannins to marry with herbaceous fruit; should be ready now or soon. Dash cab added to 49/37 blend. **Chardonnay ★★** Unwooded **07** softly rounded, with appealing tropical tones, slips easily down. **Chenin Blanc Dry ★★** Friendly, appley fruit salad flavours in **07**; refreshing dry quaffer with well hidden 14% alc. **Chenin Blanc Off-Dry ★★☆** Melon & peach nuances in **07**, touch sugar (8g/l) plumps out body, gives extra drinkability. **Sauvignon Blanc ★★★ 07** ripe fruity version, gentle pear-drop tones. **Morio Muscat Jerepico ★★★★** Lively fortified dessert; **06**, tasted pvs ed, delicious lightly chilled, its sugar richness (196g/l) lifted by zingy acidity & alc (17.5%). — *CR*

Landzicht GWK Wines

T 053-591-0164 • **F** 053-591-0145

Jacobsdal (see Northern Cape map) • Est 1976 • 1stB ca 1980 • Tasting & sales Mon-Fri 8-1; 2-5 Sat 8-11 • Tasting fee on application • Closed pub hols • Tours by appt • Meals/refreshments by appt, or BYO picnic • Farm produce sold • Play area for children • Tourgroups • Conferences • Owner GWK Ltd • Winemaker Chrisna Botha • Viticulturist Pou le Roux • 300ha (cab, merlot, pinotage, shiraz, chard, chenin, colombard, muscadels r/w) • ±2 200t/40 000cs own label 20% red 40% white 20% rosé 20% fortified • PO Box 94 Jacobsdal 8710 • landzicht@kby.gwk.co.za • www.landzicht.co.za

Three maidens stepped out of this Jacobsdal cellar last year: two wines in the Reserve range - a barrel-matured Cab, followed by a Chardonnay - and finally a Port. It was second year in the driving seat for winemaker Chrisna Botha, whose only concern (almost trifling, given the challenging climate) was the dryness of the summer.

Cabernet Sauvignon ★ Stalky, raisiny **06**, v pushy tannins. **Cabernet Sauvignon Reserve** NEW **★★★** Fresh vanilla & cassis, dark choc & black cherries on **05**; could repay few yrs keeping. Fr barrels 18 mths. **Merlot ★** Mint & red cherry notes in undemanding **05**. **Pinotage ★** Earthy & robust **05**, tannins tend to overwhelm fruit. **Shiraz ★★** Burnt sugar nose on **05**, ripe plum flavours. **Chardonnay Reserve** NEW **★★** Buttered popcorn, subtle lime & honey nuances on barrelled **05**, low-alc easy-drinker. **Chenin Blanc ★★** Easy-drinking **06** last ed, softly rounded, off-dry summery tipple. **Vin Doux ★** Sweet, grapey party bubbly from colombard. **NV**. **Rosenblümchen ★★** Natural Sweet-style **NV** from colombard & cab. Honey on nose, fresh, unchallenging. **Blümchen ★★** Continues tradition as low-alc lunchtime sweetie. **NV. Sweet Hanepoot** ✓ **★★★★** Clean muscat scent, rich malt & honey flavours. **07** quite complex & yummy. **Red Muscadel ★★★** Typical brick/pinky red muscadel colour, **06** honey bouquet, well-controlled acid. **White Muscadel ★★★** Bright golden colour **05**, honey & lavender, pleasing balance. Veritas gold achiever. **Red Jerepigo ★★** Blend pinotage & ruby cab. **06** unusual savoury touch, warm molasses palate. **Ruby Port** [NEW] **★★★** 60/40 blend ruby cab & touriga. **05** dusty & nutty, pleasingly dry finish (100g/l RS). Discontinued: **Gewürztraminer, Blanc de Blanc**. — DB

■ **Langeberg Wineries** *see* Wonderfontein
■ *Langkloof Vineyards* *see* The Goose Wines

Langverwacht Cellar
T 023-616-2815 • F 023-616-3059

Robertson • Est 1954 • Tasting & sales Mon-Fri 8-12.30; 1.30-5 • Closed pub hols • Tours by appt • Owner 30 members • Winemaker Johan Gerber, with Theunis Botha (Dec 1986, Dec 2005) • Viticulturist Willem Botha (2005, consultant) • ±600ha (shiraz, chenin, chard, colombard, sauv) • ±9 800t/±9 000cs own label 60% red 31% white 9% rosé • PO Box 87 Bonnievale 6730 • langverwacht@lando.co.za

'Bumper' isn't enough to describe Johan Gerber's 2007 harvest (the previous year's yield was dented by heavy hail). 'Bigger, better, exceptional!' exults the winemaker, adding that the new tasting room has attracted many visitors, especially during Robertson's Wacky Wine Weekend, boosting cellar door sales.

> **Cabernet Sauvignon** ☺ **★★★** Burst of cassis, cedar & eucalyptus on **04**, supporting ultra-ripe blackberry flavours. Al fresco wine with touch of sophistication. **Chardonnay** ☺ **★★★** Peaches & kiwifruit with clean acid balance in **06**; pleasant, unusual interpretation of this variety.

Ruby Cabernet ★★ 05 no-worries braai quaffer, with unwooded scents of new thatch & red berries. **Shiraz ★★★** When last tasted, **04** was warm, ripe, with friendly tannins & slightly sweet finish. **Chenin Blanc ★★** Easy & undemanding **07**, green (melon & pepper) tastes, hint clean apple. **Colombar ★★★ 06** (sample) last ed showed juicy guava fruit in light, zesty, dry frame. **Sauvignon Blanc** [NEW] **★★** Pungently grassy **07** (sample), greenpepper flavours & crisp acidity. A seafood wine. **Colombar-Chardonnay 07** unready. — DB

Lanzerac Wines
T 021-886-5641 • F 021-887-6998

Stellenbosch • Est 1991 • 1stB 1995 • Tasting & sales Mon-Thu 8.30-5; Fri & pub hols 9-4; Sat 10-2; Sun 11-3 • Fee R15 (incl tasting glass) • Tours Mon-Fri & pub hols 11 & 3 • Closed Easter Fri, Dec 25 & Jan 1 • Five-star Lanzerac Hotel for stay-overs; also Governor's Hall Restaurant & Craven Lounge (T 021-887-1132) • Tour groups • Gifts • Conferences (T 021-887-1132) • Walks • Owner Christo Wiese • Winemaker Wynand Lategan (Nov 2004) • Viticulturist •50ha (cabs s/f, malbec, merlot, petit v, pinotage, shiraz, chard, sauv) •500t/30 000cs 80% red 20% white • ISO 14000 & HACCP certification in progress • PO Box 6233 Uniedal 7612 • winesales@lanzerac.co.za • www.lanzeracwines.co.za

Good news for those who remember the legendary Lanzerac cheese lunches at this historic estate is that they're back, along with wine and food pairings, and, in a dedicated tasting room, the opportunity to savour earlier vintages of their pioneering pinotage. Special attention has been paid to this variety, and experiments with open canopies, bushvines and micro-vinification are leading to the imminent unveiling of a limited-release Reserve. Work on refining the house style continues and, given that the merlot and chardonnay typically sell out before the next harvest, the efforts are bearing fruit.

Cabernet Sauvignon ★★★★ Classic bxd style **01** exhibiting cigarbox, cassis aromas; taut tannins from skins & third new oak draw in spicy, peppery & austere mid-palate, still obscuring fruit to lean, dry finish. **Merlot ★★★★** Classic style accomplished in **05**, step up from **03**

(★★★). Juicy, plummy fruit with aromatic hints of cedar, mint & chocolate checked by firm tannins from yr in third new Fr oak. Mineral core persists to finish. **Pinotage** ★★★ Pioneer pinotage label (59 vintage was Cape's first) shows ripe red fruit & funkiness in **03**, with spicy meatiness & dry tannins. **Pinotage Reserve** NEW Untasted. **Shiraz** ★★★★ Judiciously oaked, stylish **03** tasted mid-**04** still available; deep black fruit, whiffs smoke, savoury spice. **Classic** ★★★★ Generously styled & balanced **03** merlot dominated blend all 5 bdx varieties, with graphite & cherry tobacco aromas and approachable ripe cassis & mulberry flavours structured by half new Fr oak. Spicy, savoury finish. **Rosé** ★★★ Marketed again after long absence with **06** (not tasted) in original curvaceous bottle. Portion cab f plays part in appealing strawberry aromas. Simple, with dry finish despite 7g/l sugar. **Chardonnay** ★★★★ Limpid, weighty gold **06** fermented (some natural yeasts) & matured (7 mths) third new Fr oak to offer creamy texture & lees complexity to bright lemoncream & marmalade fruit, finishing with fine grapefruit pithiness. **Sauvignon Blanc** ★★★★ Sample **07** expressive capsicum and passionfruit aromas/flavours. Lively mouthfeel from splash sem; sweet-sour finish. — *IM*

La Petite Ferme

T 021-876-3016 • F 021-876-3624

Franschhoek • Est/1stB 1996 • Wines below available in the restaurant or from the cellar 12-4 daily • French country-style lunches daily; luxury guest suites (see Eat-out/Stay-over sections) • Gifts • Owner Dendy Young family • Winemaker Mark Dendy Young (Jan 1996) • Viticulturist John Dendy Young • 8ha (merlot, shiraz, chard, nouvelle, sauv, viognier) • 6 000cs 40% red 60% white • PO Box 55 Franschhoek 7690 • info@lapetiteferme.co.za

'We're still plagued by baboons,' sighs Mark Dendy Young. But that's not why there isn't a single fruit tree left here. 'There's so much demand that we've planted more chardonnay and sauvignon, and also a bit of viognier and nouvelle.' When possible, he still takes visitors on a personalised cellar tour: 'People seem to enjoy getting juice on their shoes or taking photos of me standing on a tank!'

★★★★ **Barrel Fermented Chardonnay 06** even more delicious than buttery **05** (★★★★). Elegant lemon curd & pineapple invitation; stylish entry, warm, toasty lemon fruit; broad, with super balance.

Cabernet Sauvignon ★★★★ Rich, modern & fruit-driven **05**, brooding basket fruit showing lovely flavour, complexity; satisfying fleshy aftertaste. **Merlot** ★★★ Plummy **05**, entice charry preamble to zingy tart fruit & slightly dominant but food-accommodating tannin. **Bush Vine Pinotage** ★★★ No follow-up vintage made to well-padded, creamy & structured-to-cellar **04**, still available. **Shiraz** ★★★★ Tobacco, spice & red berries/cherries combine appealingly in **06**, ex-single vyd. Full, juicy, elegant despite cheek-ruddying 15.5% alc. Yr Am oak. **Maison Rouge** ★★★ Upfront youngberry with choc & coffee undertones, youthful vibrance & freshness ensure **07**'s easy drinking appeal. **Maison Rosé** NEW ★★★ **07** lovely pale salmon colour; light, delicate, but enough dry grip to complement canapés & lighter-style foods. **Chardonnay Unwooded** Misreported discontinued pvs ed; lives on as 'Baboon Rock', regrettably unready for review. **Blanc Fumé** ★★★ **07** pear-toned & herbaceous with suggestion vanilla; creamy, balanced & gentle. We say every yr: great with their smoked rainbow trout. **Sauvignon Blanc** ★★ **06** broad tropical welcome, gd light-bodied flavours for summer pleasure. **Maison Blanc** 🔖 ★★ Tropical fruit & fresh lime on light **07** summer charmer. Discontinued: **Semillon**. — *JP*

La Providence

T 021-876-4790 • F 021-876-4898

Franschhoek • Est 2001 • 1stB 2002 • Luxury self-catering guest cottage (see Stay-over section) • Owner Andy Higgins • Viticulturist Nigel McNaught (consultant) • 2.2ha (cab) • 10t/ 6500litres 100% red • PO Box 363 Franschhoek 7690 • info@laprovidence.co.za • www. laprovidence.co.za

Encouraged by the reception of his Cab, owner Andy Higgins is turning his attention to export. China, Japan and Russia are his target countries, and Andy is encouraging their citizens to visit his boutique wine farm themselves, and avail themselves of the luxury of the five-star guest cottage.

Cabernet Sauvignon ★★☆ Comprehensively oaked **02** when last tasted showed caramel overtones to cab's blackcurrant, ultra-ripe flavours & well concealed 14.4% alc. — MF

■ **La Siesta** *see* Signal Hill
■ *Lategan Family* *see* Bergsig Estate

Lateganskop Winery
T 023-355-1719 • **F 023-355-1719**

Worcester • *Est 1969* • *1stB 2004* • *Tastings & sales Mon-Fri 8-12.30; 1.30-5* • *Tours by appt* • *Owner 5 members* • *Winemaker Vlam Fourie, with J Manewick (Aug/Dec 1990)* • *238ha (cab, cinsaut, merlot, pinotage, ruby cab, chenin, colombard, hanepoot, riesling, sauv, semillon, viognier)* • *650cs + 2.2m litres bulk* • *50% red 50% white* • *PO Box 44 Breërivier 6858* • *lateganskop@mweb.co.za*

Vlam Fourie is as ebullient as ever. Besides looking forward to his first chardonnay harvest (earmarked for Twin Peaks), he's thinking of producing a range of cask wines, 'with a clear "best before" date - so a man knows he's got to get on and empty the thing!'

Lion's Drift range
Cabernet Sauvignon ★ Meat & spice hints on compact, food-styled **03**, with volatile touch.
Ruby Cabernet Sold out.

Twin Peaks range
Pinotage-Cinsaut ★★ **05** appealing bouquet of dark fruit, liquorice & caramel; dry, firm favours. Regional YWS class winner. **Sauvignon Blanc** ★★ Ripe, fruity **07** (sample), pineapple & guava tones, undemanding whistle-wetter. **Hanepoot Jerepigo** ★★ Billows raisined sultana; full-sweet, warming hanepoot flavours. **NV**. — JP

L'Auberge du Paysan
T 021-529-3980 • **F 021-842-2008**

Stellenbosch (see Helderberg map) • *Est 1995* • *1stB 1998* • *Tasting & sales during restaurant hours* • *Closed Easter Fri-Mon, Dec 26, Jan 1* • *Art gallery* • *Owner Michael Kovensky* • *Winemaker Tjuks Roos, with Ricardo Adams* • *Viticulturist Tjuks Roos* • *3.8ha (merlot, pinotage)* • *14t/±1 250cs 100% red* • *PO Box 315 Somerset West 7129* • *kovensky@aroma. co.za*

Former chef/patron Frederick Thermann has retired to Canada but it's silver service as usual at this French-toned winelands auberge, where guests are currently enjoying the 01 vintage; **02** to **05** are still maturing in bottle. Fruit from the young merlot vines will be blended with the pinotage in future.

Pinotage ★★★★ Unpretentious but vg **05** (pvsly unrated) lifts bar: subtle oak, lively fruit, 'wild' nuance adding interest. 18 mths old Fr oak. **04** (★★★★) was elegant & amenable but touch less serious. — CvZ

L'Avenir Estate
T 021-889-5001 • **F 021-889-5258**

Stellenbosch • *Est/1stB 1992* • *Tasting & sales Mon-Fri 9-5 Sat 10-4* • *Fee R15* • *Closed Easter Fri, Dec 25 & Jan 1* • *Tours by appt* • *Picnic hampers available* • *Luxury B&B guest house (see Stay-over section)* • *Tour groups* • *Farm-grown olives & olive products* • *Owner Michel Laroche* • *Cellarmaster Tinus Els* • *Winemaker Abraham de Klerk (June 2007), with Samantha Pugh (Nov 2006)* • *Viticulturist Johan Pienaar (consultant)* • *71.9ha (7 varieties r/w)* • *500-550t/32 500cs 60% red 31% white 9% rosé* • *PO Box 7267 Stellenbosch 7599* • *info@lavenir.co.za* • *www.lavenir.co.za*

Another step in his expansion out of Chablis via the south of France and Chile, famed producer Michel Laroche (partnered with AXA Insurance) bought L'Avenir in 2005, another signal Franco-South African development to place alongside other investments in this area. In with him came new CEO/winemaker Tinus Els to build upon the estate's pinotage and chenin reputation; he's now assisted by winemaker Abraham de Klerk. Laroche also acquired neighbouring Sentinel, and those who don't particularly care for that property's Hollywood-style castle will no doubt be gladdened to hear it's undergoing a thorough facelift and will house the new tasting and functions venue.

★★★★ **Cabernet Sauvignon** None since perfectly proportioned **03**; was opulently fruited & firm tannined. 18 mths Fr oak, 33% new, rest 2nd fill. Last tasted mid-2005, as was Cape Vintage below.

★★★★☆ **Grand Vin Pinotage** Regal hue to **05**; noble bouquet & elegant palate, too. Choc top notes to raspberry fruit, savory tannins, lingering aloe-toned aftertaste. Should gain complexity, mellow with ±5-10yrs cellaring. 12 mths 100% new Fr oak.

★★★★ **Pinotage** Quintessential pinotage doing business for L'Avenir for yrs. Confident **06** has wet earth & mineral notes to bright mixed berry fruit, fine athletic tannins for ±5yrs aging. 14 mths Fr oak; 33% each new/2nd/3rd fill.

★★★★☆ **Stellenbosch Classic** Bdx-style blend (cab 60/merlot 20/cab f 20); pvsly with dash pinotage. **05** regal; sweet but reserved dark fruits enlived by deft touches vanilla, linear tannins. Harmonious & long. 14 mths used Fr oak.

★★★★ **Chenin Blanc** 🖹 One of first success stories in the Cape chenin renaissance. **06** had pleasant thatch & floral notes, long, tangy farewell; 5% oaked portion adds mid-palate weight. No new vintage to taste mid-**07**.

★★★★ **Cape Vintage** Portugese-led in style (beefy 19% alc, low 85g/l sugar) if not by variety. **03** from cab, as was preceding and delicious **99**. EW.

Merlot ★★★★ **05** first since **01**; opulent plum & cranberry bouquet belies austere palate, gruff fruit tannins hiding soft fruit. Not for the long haul. 3rd fill Fr oak, 11 mths. **Chardonnay** 🖹 ★★★★ Despite a string of Chardonnay-du-Monde medals for pvs oak-led vintages, **06** changed focus; took steely, minimally oaked (15% Fr barrel ferment) Chablis path. Tasted last ed, was charming; also took home gold. **Sauvignon Blanc** 🖹 ★★★★ Thrilling blackcurrent/greengage nuances to zesty, flavoursome **07** mouthful; brief 6 wks lees contact adding breadth & weight. **Discontinued: L'Ami Simon, Rosé Maison Dry, Rosé Maison, Vin d'Erstelle, Vin de Meurveur.**

By L'Avenir

Pinotage NEW 🖹 ★★★ Following 3 all new, all for export. Bright & cheerful **07** aiming to make new friends which appealing strawberry & cream aromas/flavours. **Rosé de Pinotage** NEW 🖹 ★★★ Watermelon hued wallet-pleaser combines tangy acidity with hint 4.6g/l sugar lift. **Chenin Blanc** NEW 🖹 ★★★ Supple, decently dry sipper set to do SA proud; modest 12.5% alc a perfect match for international al fresco dining scene. — *CvZ*

■ **Lavida** *see Overhex Wines International*

La Vierge Wines
T 028-313-0130 ▪ F 028-312-1388

Walker Bay (see Elgin/Walker Bay map) ▪ Est 1997 ▪ 1stB 2006 ▪ Visits Mon-Sat 9-5 Sun during season ▪ Closed Easter Sun/Mon, Dec 25/26 & Jan 1 ▪ La Vierge Restaurant & Champagne Verandah (see Eat-out section) ▪ Tour groups by appt ▪ Permanent art exhibition ▪ Owner La Vierge Wines (Pty) Ltd & Viking Pony Properties 355 (Pty) Ltd ▪ Winemaker Marc van Halderen, with Petrus Bothma (Jun 2005, Jan 2007) ▪ Viticulturist Andrew Teubes (Jul 2005, consultant) ▪ 46ha (pinot, sangiovese, shiraz, chard, riesling, sauv, semillon) ▪ 180t 30% red 50% white 20% MCC ▪ PO Box 1580 Hermanus 7200 ▪ info@lavierge.co.za ▪ www.lavierge. co.za

'The building slog is over,' says winemaker Marc van Halderen, referring to two years' extensive renovations at this promising Hemel-en-Aarde Valley winery. In the vineyards the focus remains on pinot, chardonnay and sauvignon - this under the watchful eye of viticulturist, Augustus Dale, with 13 years' Burgundian experience. This year sees the launch of the Temptation range with a sauvignon, a syrah-blend and a rosé, best enjoyed at the Champagne Verandah & Restaurant.

★★★★ **Temptation Sauvignon Blanc** NEW ▤ Elegant **07** green fig, gooseberry notes, nettley yet quite tropical, bracing lime/grapefruit freshness, intense, persistent. Staggered harvest, three separate W Bay blocks, long lees contact, 13.6% alc

★★★★ **Sauvignon Blanc** Green-fruited & herbaceous **07**, lemongrass, gunflint whiffs, mineral notes, dry, lean, persistent.

'Shiraz Blend' NEW ★★★ Light, leathery fruit, **06** ground white pepper notes, infused with choc/moccha aromas from malo in barrel and 14 months Fr oak ageing. **Temptation Rosé** NEW ★★ Salmon-pink **07**, copper-edged, red fruit & parmesan whiffs, tangy. — *MF*

La Vigne Estate
T 021-876-3357 • F 021-876-3357

Franschhoek • Est/1stB 2005 • Visits Mon-Sat 11-4 • Fee R15 pp • Closed Easter Sat/Sun, 25 Dec & 1 Jan • Owner Robert Joergensen • Winemaker Oswald 'Ossie' Sauermann with Gerda Willers (2006/2005) • Viticulturist Oswald 'Ossie' Sauermann (2006) • 4.3ha (cab, shiraz, semillon) • 19.9t/1 370cs 82.5% red 17.5% white • PO Box 69 Simondium 7690 • wine@ lavigne.co.za • www.lavigne.co.za

Norwegians Vanja and Robert Joergensen (they bought what was TenFiftySix Winery three years ago) believe that playing classical music in the maturation cellar not only gives 'a nice working atmosphere' but improves the end product. The proof is in the drinking: the first 'musical release', a red blend named Edvard Grieg Edition, was due to be launched as the guide went to bed.

Owner's Selection Red ★★★ Bdx trio, cab, merlot, p verdot in light-textured, vigorous **05**. Some pretty violet notes peep from behind prevailing Fr oak vanilla. Wine (★★★★). **Private Selection Red** ★★★ Merlot-led **05** with 18% cab. Very ripe, plummy aromas; more austere, thinner palate, despite 14.5% alc. 30% new Fr oak. **Owner's Selection White** ★★★★ Fresh-honey semillon, lemon-crisp chard make compatible mix in personable **05** blend (80/20). Vanilla hints from gd Fr oaking, 40% new. EW. **Winemaker's Selection White** ★★★ Unoaked sem/chard blend (68/32). **05** inviting honey, waxy notes; just dry. EW. — *AL*

■ **La Vinette** *see Olsen Wines*

Lazanou Organic Vineyards
T 083-265-6341 • F 086-670-9213

Wellington • Est/1stB 2006 • Closed to public • Owner Jo Lazarus & Candice Stephanou • Winemaker Corlea Fourie (Jan 2006) • Viticulturist Johan Wiese (consultant) • 5.5ha (mourvèdre, shiraz, chard, chenin, viognier) • 18t/1025cs 60% white 40% red • PO Box 834 Wellington 7654 • wine@lazanou.co.za • www.lazanouwines.co.za

Ducks to gobble the snails and sheep to mow the weeds – and both to complement the wines. That's Lazanou's pest-control policy since 2006, when all their vineyards were declared organic by international certification company SGS. Last year they harvested their first chardonnay and shiraz, and this year will be the turn of their first mourvèdre.

Syrah NEW **07** unready for review. **Chardonnay** NEW ★★★ Deceptively pale **07**, lemon & lime-tinged flavours, poised, elegant, with gd length. **Wooded Chenin Blanc** ★★★★ Early sample **06** not revisited; last ed was lovely, complex & succulent, with lively acidity. 10 mths new Fr oak. **Chenin Blanc** ★★★ Feisty **07**, from old vines; assertive ripe peach flavours, densely packed. Really tasty. — *IvH*

■ **Lazy Bay** *see Baarsma Wine Group*
■ **Leatherwood** *see Prospect1870*

Le Bonheur Estate
T 021-875-5478 • F 021-875-5624

Stellenbosch • Tasting & sales Mon-Fri 9-5 Sat 10-4 • Fee R10 • Special tastings on request • Functions & conferences by appt • Owner Lusan Holdings • Winemaker Sakkie Kotzé (1993) • Viticulturist Eben Archer • 435t/±31 000cs • PO Box 104 Stellenbosch 7599 • info@lebonheur. co.za • www.lebonheur.co.za

Winemaker Sakkie Kotze revels in the yearly excitement of winemaking, from pruning to the finished product. A challenge, he says, is our ever-changing weather: 'Global warming is a worry.' A new red-wine maturation cellar is being built, and, in the vineyards, there are new blocks of shiraz and cab franc.

★★★★ **Prima** Enduring Cape red is particularly gd in **05** (★★★★★), wafts of creamy dark fruits, fruity abundance on palate. Well-managed oaking (40% brl fermented in Fr oak, remainder in stainless steel), lovely soft tannins. Wine with finesse, should keep min 5 yrs. **03** was gorgeous, velvety & persistent.

Cabernet Sauvignon ★★★★ Well-flavoured perennial. **04** redolent of classic cassis, blackberries & spiciness. Medium/full bodied & well structured with grippy ripe tannins, should keep 5+ yrs. One for the table. **Chardonnay** ★★★ **07** tank sample follows delicate tone of pvsly reviewed **05**. Crisp citrus notes, delicious lemon & ripe peach. Augurs well for an elegant wine. **Sauvignon Blanc** ★★★ Invariably pale-hued yet full-flavoured. **07** Powerful green fig & asparagus; softer acid than many, attractive lingering aftertaste. — *JN*

■ **Leef op Hoop** *see Le Riche Wines*
■ **Leeurivier** *see Terroir Wines of SA*

Le Fût
T 021-863-0322 • F 086-675-5114

Paarl • Est/1stB 2005 • Tasting by appt • Owner Trevor & Joan Ernstzen • Winemaker Trevor Ernstzen (2005) • Viticulturist Joan Ernstzen (2005) • 14ha (shiraz, chenin) • 200-350cs 95% red 5% white • PO Box 156 Paarl 7622 • wine@lefut.co.za • www.lefut.co.za

Once the vinous bug had bitten, the only cure for the Ernstzens was to buy and restore a Paarl farm, build a new cellar and make wine for themselves. Joan E tends the vineyards and equally enthusiastic Trevor makes the wine from their well-aged chenin and shiraz vines.

Shiraz ★★★ Concentrated fruit compote flavours on **05**, hints of prune & maraschino. 6 mths oak, 2nd fill. — *MF*

Legacy

New name and stylish packaging for one of SA's longest-established brands (1957), Johannisberger, previously in the Bellingham range. By DGB.

Legacy range
Johannisberger ★★ Delicate, light-bodied (12% alc) with 'sea spray' aroma, sweetish (18g/ l RS) fruity flavours. Chenin & trio of white grapes. **NV**. W Cape. — *CvZ*

Le Grand Chasseur Estate
T 023-626-1048/5781 • F 023-626-5781/1048

Robertson • Est 1881 • 1stB 1999 • Tasting & sales Mon-Fri 8.30-5 Sat 9-3.30 • Closed Easter Fri/Sun/Mon, Dec 25/26 & Jan 1 • Tours by appt • Deli & gifts • Guest accommodation by appt • Owner Albertus de Wet • Winemaker Albertus de Wet, with Wickus Erasmus (Jan 2001) • Viticulturist Francois Viljoen (Jan 1998, consultant) • 275ha (cab, merlot, pinotage, ruby cab, shiraz, chard, chenin, colombard, sauv) • 3 100t/8 000cs own label 37% red 60% white 3% rosé • PO Box 439 Robertson 6705 • cellar@lgc.co.za, sales@lgc.co.za • www.lgc.co.za

Wickus Erasmus reports an uneventful but excellent 2007 harvest, from which has emerged a new white muscadel, and a promising shiraz and pinotage earmarked for extended barrel maturation. The majestic African Fish Eagles which give the estate its name still patrol the Breede River close by.

Sparkling ☺ ★★★ Raspberry fruited jazzy pinotage sparkler in sweet style. **NV**.

Cabernet Sauvignon ★★★ Last-tasted **03** more straightforward than pvs, lacked fruit stuffing. **Pinotage** ★★ Lean & simple **06** with smoky edge. Yr oak. **Shiraz** ★★ **04** not ready;

jammy & soft **03** needed drinking last yr. **Chardonnay** ★★★ Well made, attractive **07**; oak fermented, supple & pure with pear notes. **Sauvignon Blanc** ★★ **07** early harvested, clean & tropical with grassy notes. **Sauvignon Blanc-Chardonnay** ★★★ Will be culled after rounded, green-toned **05** sells out. **Cap Classique** ★★★ NV from chard, last ed showed mouthfilling mousse, mushroom hint on bone-dry finish. **White Muscadel** [NEW] ★★★ Thick & creamy **07**, super-ripe caramel centre & rich, sweet finish. **Grand Port** [NEW] 🍷 ★★★ Ultra-ripe first vintage from ruby cab. Burnt toffee & black cherry flavours, touch raw, give some time. **NV**. Discontinued: **LGC Red**, **Rosé**. — RP

Leidersburg Vineyards
T 021-886-6251 • **F** 021-886-6251

Paarl • Est 1996 • 1stB 1997 • Visits by appt • Owner Jan du Preez & Brian Craddock • Winemaker Jan du Preez, with Jacques du Preez • Viticulturist Jacques du Preez • 6ha/2 000cs 100% red • PO Box 7210 Stellenbosch 7599 • leidersburgwines@telkomsa.net • www. leidersburgwines.co.za

Father-and-son team Jan and Jacques du Preez are concentrating their export efforts in Florida, US, where they sell about 60% of their Cab, Sauvignon, Muscadel and Cape Ruby (none tasted this edition). 'Our other important market is the Netherlands, which is doing very well for us,' says Jan dP. Locally, they sell only in the Gauteng area.

Le Manoir de Brendel
T 021-876-4525 • **F** 021-876-4524

Franschhoek • Est/1stB 2003 • Tasting & sales Mon-Sat 11-4 Sun 11-3 • Fee R25 • Lunches daily 12-3 (see Eat-out section) • Luxury accommodation & other facilities (see Stay-over section) • Owner Christian Brendel • 26 ha (cab, merlot, shiraz, chardonnay, chenin, sauv, semillon) • PO Box 117 La Motte 7691 • lemanoir@brendel.co.za • www.le-manoir-de-brendel.com

Unwind at this five-star establishment in scenic Franschhoek where winetasting can be done at leisure over lunch in the garden or indoors. A wedding chapel and conference facilities are available, as well as a spa and sporting activities aplenty for those who refuse to rest. See the Eat-out and Stay-over sections for details.

Cabernet Sauvignon ★★ Elegant herbaceous overtones & hints of black fruit, **04** light, unwooded, sweet-sour finish. **Merlot** ★★ Lightly-fruited **05**, unknit last ed but should have melded by now. **Shiraz** ★★★ Tad less ebullient, but **04** still pleasant, rounded, with clove-like flavours. **Sauvignon Blanc** ★ **06** again very light, with understated varietal character. No new vintage of this, above, tasted this ed. Discontinued: **Pinotage**. — JN

Lemberg Estate
T 023-230-0659 • **F** 023-230-0661

Tulbagh • 4 ha (pinot, pinotage, sauv) • PO Box 317 Tulbagh 6820

Klaus Schindler has sold this boutique winery to focus on his personalised game hunting tours (see Schindler's Africa), and no update was received from the new owner/s.

▮▮ L'Emigré *see Gentis Family Vineyards*

Leopard Frog Vineyards
T 011-884-3304 • **F** 011-883-0426

Stellenbosch • 1stB 2003 • Closed to public • Owner Brookwood Capital Corporation • Winemaker David John Bate • 1 000cs 100% red • 8 Royal Ascot Lane, Sandown, Sandton 2196 • firstfrog@leopard-frog.com • www.leopard-frog.com

Winemaker David Bate completed his MSc at the Bordeaux International Wine Institute; by the time he and his family returned home, 'My four-month-old daughter had spent most of her life in France – and her French was as good as her English!' Expanding into the Middle East is his latest project – 'Hot wines for a hot climate,' says Bate. See also United Nations of Wine.

Tantra ★★★★ Serious bdx-inspired blend cabs f/s & petit v; **04** pvsly noted as well extracted & wooded (18 mths Fr oak, some new); satisfying, gd maturation prospects. **Kiss & Tell**

Reserve ★★★ Attractively taut **04** last ed deserved time to show best; malbec plus equal mix merlot & shiraz, dollop mourvèdre. — *CT*

Leopard's Leap Wines
T 021-876-8002 • **F** 021-876-4156

Franschhoek ▪ Est 2000 ▪ Closed to public ▪ Owner Leopard's Leap Wines (Pty) Ltd ▪ Winemaker Eugene van Zyl (Nov 2002) ▪ 310 000cs 60% red 40% white ▪ ISO 1400 certified ▪ PO Box 685 Franschhoek 7690 ▪ Hs.marketing@leopardsleap.co.za ▪ www.leopards-leap.com

Owned by Hein Koegelenberg and Hanneli Rupert Koegelenberg, this affordable range is vinified by Eugene van Zyl. Launched in 2000, the wines are available locally, throughout Europe, North America and Asia. A contribution is made to the Cape Leopard Trust with every purchase.

Leopard's Leap Wines range

Cabernet Sauvignon ★★★ Meat extract, dark fruit styling; **05** firm but accessible tannins, could age few yrs. **Shiraz** ★★★ Fruity, juicy, nicely curvaceous **05**, v easy drinking. **Cabernet Sauvignon-Merlot** ★★★ **05** not ready. Previewed last ed, undemanding **04** brimmed with berry fruit. Drink young. **Pinotage-Shiraz** ★★★ Meaty, dark-fruited **05**, compatible & tasty 52/48 blend, pinotage adding lively freshness to palate. Lightly oaked. **Sangiovese-Pinotage-Cabernet Sauvignon** ★★★★ Spicy, wild shiraz-like aromas in attractive **03** (last ed); sweet-fruited suppleness boosted by touch sugar. Equal blend. New vintage unready. **Chardonnay** ★★★ Honeyed, tropical character from lees contact, light oak. **06** softly rounded, tasty, fresh. **Chenin Blanc** ★★★ Crunchy apple & peardrop fruitiness on **07**, tangy dry finish. **Sauvignon Blanc** ★★★ Leafy gooseberry perfume/flavours on tangy, lively **07**. Appetising solo or with food. **Semillon-Chardonnay** ★★★ Last tasted unoaked **04** attractively light & supple equal blend. **Chenin Blanc-Viognier** ★★★ Last tasted **04** loaded with citrus & tropical fruit, plumped by ±4g/l sugar.

The Lookout range

> **Cabernet Sauvignon-Shiraz-Cinsaut** ☺ ★★ Pvs ed 'Cape Mountain Red'. **06** delightfully fruity, light-textured, easy summertime red. **Rosé** ☺ ★★★ Fruit pastille-toned, characterful & appetising **07** dry charmer from pinotage & chenin (85/15). **Chenin Blanc-Chardonnay-Colombar** ☺ ★★★ 'Cape Mountain White' pvs ed. **07** appealing crisp quaffer with pear drop nuance, bargain priced. Equal blend.

Chenin Blanc Semi Sweet Pvsly under LL range. **07** untasted. Both ranges mostly W Cape WOs. — *CR*

■ **Le Pavillon** *see Boschendal Wines*
■ *Le Pommier* *see Zorgvliet Wines*

Le Riche Wines
T 021-887-0789 • **F** 021-887-0789

Stellenbosch ▪ Est 1996 ▪ 1stB 1997 ▪ Tasting & sales Mon-Fri 10-12.30 2-4.30 Sat & pub hols by appt ▪ Self-contained B&B (T 021·887·8958) ▪ Owner Etienne le Riche ▪ Winemaker Etienne le Riche, with Mark Daniels (1998) ▪ 5 000cs ▪ PO Box 6295 Stellenbosch 7612 ▪ wine@leriche.co.za ▪ www.leriche.co.za

A collection of Mouton Rothschild labels from 1945 onwards is a clear hint that traditionalist Etienne le Riche's first love is cab. At his cellar in Jonkershoek you'll also see open fermenters, and bottling and labelling is still done by hand. His family hide out now that they are around more: son Christo put in a harvest at Stag's Leap and daughter Yvonne gained some London wine merchant experience, while wife Marcelle and long-time assistant Mark Daniels remain indispensable. Etienne went fishing in Angola between business trips and winemaking in France's Bergerac - of this venture, the 03 vintage is available ex-cellar.

★★★★☆ **Cabernet Sauvignon Reserve** Cape classic; gentle yet persuasive, reflecting Etienne le R's signature light touch. Last tasted **03** Best Red Trophy SAA 2006; ripe, dry & showing unusual completeness for varietal cab. 45% new Fr oak, 10% Jnkrshoek Vlly vyds.

★★★★☆ **CWG Auction Reserve Cabernet Sauvignon** Grander, more opulent than Reserve above, still with usual balance & refinement. **04** dark berried, choc intensity, plush texture, augmented by 100% new Fr oak, presently restrained by insistent tannins. Livelier than 14% alc suggests.

★★★★☆ **Cabernet Sauvignon 03** shines in gorgeous vintage. Deep, mint-edged cassis, cedar oak enhancement suggest full riches still dormant within structured, clean lines. Further 4-5 yrs shd confirm it as one of most satisfying unblended examples. 2 yrs Fr oak, 30% new. Lightish **02 (★★★★)** reflected difficult yr.

★★★★ **Cabernet Sauvignon-Merlot-Shiraz** 'Blend' pvs ed. Seamless partnership (even incl splash pinotage), with appealing lightness of touch in hot **04** vintage. Ripe vinosity lifted by bright, juicy acid, fine-grained tannins, all harmonised in used Fr oak.

★★★★ **Chardonnay** Celebrates Le R's 'ten years of independence' **06** realises promise suggested in last ed's preview. Citrus freshness, minerals & creaminess knit in understated yet persuasive style. 100% new Fr oak deftly handled.

Leef op Hoop Merlot ★★★ Accessibly styled **04** still available. Mouthfilling, meaty, rounded by yr in older oak. *— AL*

■ **Les Pleurs** *see* Avondale

Libertas

Distell range named for venerable Stellenbosch farm on which current Adam Tas vinification facility is situated.

Cabernet Sauvignon ★★★ Rich blackcurrant nose & palate on **06**; ripe (6.5g/l RS), yet with astringent tannins, long liquorice finish. **Merlot** ★★★ **06** muted bouquet; more flavour on palate: sweet/sour red plum & cherry, tannins tad stalky. **Pinotage** ★★★ Big, bouncy **06** billows with pinotage's ripe red-fruit character, spicy toastiness ex-oak. Perfect braai companion. **Chardonnay** ★★★ **05** last yr showed peach & tangerine aromas, lemon/lime flavours, good grip & brisk acidity. **Chenin Blanc** ★★★ Dusty muted tones with crisp Granny Smith flavours & acidity. **07** plumper than pvs, trimmed by clean, tart zestiness. **Sauvignon Blanc** ★★★ Pleasing varietal figs & nettles on **07**: plus ripe tropical flourish & hint sugar, offset by bright acidity. Drink young. All WO W Cape. *— MW*

Lievland Estate

T 021-875-5226 • F 021-875-5213

Stellenbosch • Est 1982 • Open daily all year except Dec 25 • Tastings noon to sunset • Fee R20, free with purchase • Wine sales 10-6 • Winter soups & hotpot; summer picnic baskets • Owner Susan Colley • Winemaker Kowie du Toit (Jan 2004) • 50ha (cabs s/f, merlot, mourvèdre, petit v, roobernet, shiraz, riesling, viognier) • 250t/15 000cs 50/50 red/white • lievland@icon.co.za • www.lievland.co.za

Edward Colley, son of owner Susan C, and his wife Johanna have taken over the running of this historic Simonsberg estate, and are imbuing the property with new energy and vision. Efforts are being concentrated on the finest hectares, winemaker Kowie du Toit encouraged by good award recognition to develop the estate's shiraz potential. The popular sauvignon, in abeyance since 2005, is back in the line-up.

Shiraz ★★★★ When last tasted, **03** showed renewed vigour & form, plus fruit & structure to improve over few yrs. **Lievlander** ★★★ Braai accessory from shiraz & cab; aromas coffee & tobacco leaf on **04**; black berry fruit & ripe tannins. EW. **Sauvignon Blanc** ★★★ **07** limy, hints honey, Golden Delicious apple; long refreshing finish. Discontinued: **Chardonnay**, **Weisser Riesling**, **Natural Sweet**. *— MM*

■ **Lifestyle** *see* Simonsvlei International

L'illa
T 028-312-3862 • F 028-312-3867

Robertson • Est/1stB 2005 • Tasting & sales by appt • Owner/winemaker Nadia Cilliers & Gordon Newton Johnson • Viticulturist AA Cilliers • 1 ton/600 btls (375ml) 100% white • PO Box 225 Hermanus 7200 • gordon@newtonjohnson.com

Catalan for 'island', L'illa (pronounced leeya) is an allusion to both the Wine of Origin area Eilandia and the Cilliers family farm where the grapes are grown. Though the gnarled vines yield very little, volume has doubled over the last year: instead of only one barrel, wine-partners Nadia C and Gordon Newton Johnson (of Newton Johnson Wines) have managed to squeeze out two!

Noble Late Harvest ★★★★ Ripe glacé pineapple, quince & botrytis on **06** dessert. Unctuous & velvety, marmalade & crème caramel tones, moderate 12.8% alc. Rich, not cloying, but dash more acidity would add welcome verve. — MW

■ **Lime Road** *see Havana Hills*

■ **Lindenhof** *see Boland Kelder*

Linde Vineyards

T 023-230-0742 • F 023-230-2838

Tulbagh • Est 1998 • 1stB 2001 • Visits by appt • Walks • Owner Olof Gregor & Sylvia Linde • Winemaker Sylvia Linde • Viticulturist Jean Kotzè • 14ha (cab, merlot, shiraz, chard) • 130t 100% red & 15 tons 100% white • PO Box 146 Tulbagh 6820 • diggershome@mweb.co.za

American owners Olof Gregor and Sylvia Linde plan to continue supplying most of their fruit to KWV and producing own-label wines only on a small scale. In conjunction with farm manager Jean Kotze, they also run by-appointment Wine Boot Camps, introducing small groups to the basics of winemaking.

Digger's Home range

Shiraz ☺ ★★★ **05** liquid velvet, liquorice & dark fruit, not a rough edge in sight. Drink soon. Will make many friends.

Cabernet Sauvignon ★★★ **05** smoky, meaty, liberally sprinkled with dried herbs. Showing some maturity, but still satisfyingly drinkable. **Merlot** NEW ★★★ Easy-drinking **05** with a meaty, plum ripeness & wide appeal. **Chardonnay** NEW ★★★ Lemon peel with savoury overlay, full-bodied individual style; **06** compatible with antipasta & al fresco spreads. **Sauvignon Blanc** NEW ★★★ **06** very ripe style. Melons, stewed apples with expected full body; drink solo rather than with food. — CR

Lindhorst Wines

T 021-863-0990 • F 021-863-3694

Paarl • Est 1996 • 1stB 2002 • Tasting daily 10-5 • Fee R20 (incl tasting & snacks, redeemable against purchase of 6 btls) • Cellar tours by appt • Closed Easter Sun, Dec 25 & Jan 1 • Lunches Wed-Sun year round (see Eat-out section) • Functions by arrangement • Self-catering Vineyard Cottage (see Stay-over section) • Facilities for children • Gifts • Farm produce • Owner Mark & Belinda Lindhorst • Winemaker Ernie Wilken with Cathy Marshall (consultant) • Viticulturist Ernie Wilken with Kevin Watt (Jan 2001, consultant) • 18ha (cab, merlot, pinotage, shiraz) • 75t/4000 85% red • PO Box 1398 Suider-Paarl 7624 • info@lindhorstwines.com • www.lindhorstwines.com

Max's Tribute, the red created by Mark Lindhorst in honour of his late father, had more than just a tribute last year at the Swiss Awards. 'The day before the results were announced, we were told we'd better be there with a case for the crowd to taste,' remembers Mark L. 'The next day - a gold!'

Cabernet Sauvignon ★★★★ Last ed **04** richly fruited, balanced & accessible, with potential for few yrs development. **Merlot** ★★★★ **05** herbaceous nuance to berry styling; palate shows well-judged oaking, fully integrated despite 22 mths barrique treatment. Built to last 3+ yrs. **Pinotage** ★★★☆ Leap in quality in **06**. Impressive fruit breadth, opulence throughout, variety's lively freshness confirming appeal. Oak combo Am/Fr/Hung in support role. **Shiraz** ★★★★ Last ed noted **04**'s youth & potential. Intro of spicy white pepper; palate rich with New World fruit, reined in by 22 mths oaking. **03** (★★★★) was an elegant food wine. **Max's Tribute** ★★★★ Touch merlot with cab dictates character of **05**: dark choc, black plums & cedar, white pepper spicing. Fr barriques 22 mths. **Statement** ★★★★☆ Deep, rich, spice-layered mocha-choc & red fruit. **05** shiraz (60%(, cab & merlot. Built for few yrs but already rewardingly accessible. **Sauvignon Blanc** ★★★ Dbnvlle fruit reveals area's distinctive fynbos & lime intensity; **07** racy acidity calls for food. Could handle few yrs ageing. *— CR*

Lindiwe Wines
T 021-949-6013/4 • F 021-949-6036

Paarl • 1stB 2003 • Closed to public • Winemaker Chris Jansen (Oct 2003) • Viticulturist Chris Albertyn & Cobus van Graan • 20 000cs 50% red 50% white • ISO 9001 certified • Suite 170, Postnet, X3036, Paarl 7620 • info@lindiwewines.com • www.lindiwe.com

Owned by Reinvest, a black empowerment company, Lindiwe ('The One We Have Been Waiting For') has achieved enviable market penetration. With the exception of the Chazaa sparkling, supplied by Namaqua Wines, CEO Nosey Pieterse says all bottlings are now sourced from African Terroir. With volumes ever rising, the wait is over…

Cabernet Sauvignon ★★★ Seasoned oak gives creamy texture, sweet vanilla tones to generously berried **03**, an easy-drinker with hint of mint. Not retasted, as for all these. **Merlot** Sold out. **Pinotage** Sold out. **Shiraz** ★★ **03** charry wood whiffs, soft ripe fruit, amenable tannins & alc for pleasant drinking. 8-12 mths older oak. **Chardonnay** ★★ Butter & cream notes on partly barrel fermented/matured **04**, gains extra smoothness, body, from touch sugar. **Chenin Blanc** ★★ **05** shy hay aromas, mellowing mid-2006 but still lively apple flavours, gd solo or with food. **Sauvignon Blanc** ★★ Easy-going **05**, lightish, unaggressive, with just a hint of nettle. **Chazaa** ★★ Frothy semi-sweet sparkling from chenin, with happy gingerbeer flavour. Carbonated, **NV**. All WO W Cape. *— CvZ*

Linton Park Wines

T 021-873-1625 • F 021-873-0851

Wellington (see Paarl map) • Est 1995 • 1stB 1998 • Tasting & sales Mon-Fri 8-5 by appt • Tours by appt Mon-Fri 9-4; also guided cellar/vineyard tours by appt (incl barrel tasting) • Light lunches/picnics for small groups by appt Mon-Fri 9-4 • Owner Linton Park plc • Cellarmaster Hennie Huskisson • Winemaker Hennie Huskisson, with Danie Stevens (Jan 2001/Oct 1999) • Viticulturist Vlok Hanekom • 67ha (cab, merlot, shiraz, chard, sauv) • ±500t/20 000cs 50% red 50% white • Export brand: De Groene Heuwel • PO Box 1234 Wellington 7654 • sales@lintonparkwines.co.za • www.lintonparkwines.co.za

Vlok Hanekom, the new farm manager, has 'a presence that can be noticed when you enter the gate,' says winemaker Hennie Huskisson. Another newcomer is ,Alana Lochner (ex-La Motte), who joined as marketing manager and now works out of a new office complex symbolising the renewed energy and enthusiasm.

Reserve range

★★★★ **Cabernet Sauvignon** Signature ripe-fruited styling shown in **01**, yet still fairly easy to drink when last tasted, with spicy oak bit more evident. Same block ('Bush Vine') as version below, more extensively barrelled (yr new Fr, further yr 4th fill).

★★★★ **Merlot 03** impressively concentrated & deep-flavoured, hints mint & dark choc to attractive wild berry tone; ripe, but tight tannins needed time when tasted. Selection of best barrels, oaked as per Rsv Cab. 15% alc. WO Paarl.

★★★★ **Shiraz** Same 'Summer Hill' vyd as std version, different wooding: yr Am, followed by extra yr Fr. **01** brazenly New World but not a fruit bomb: had some seriousness, structure for maturation.

Linton Park range

★★★★ **Shiraz** From same Summerhill vyd as Rsv, **02** softer & lighter. Sweet brambly fruit, hints of flowers & fynbos. Yr Am oak, third new, 2nd & 3rd fill.

Cabernet Sauvignon ★★★★ Extrovert **02** burst with bright bramble aromas & plump, juicy fruit. Hint cigarbox from yr new Fr oak. Not retasted, as for other reds & Port. **Merlot** ★★★ Light-hued **02** characterised by red plum jam aromas & simple jammy fruit. **Chardonnay** ★★★★ Less expansive & opulent than pvs. Vanilla & citrus aromas on fruit salady **05**, backed by apples & pears, with slight green melon tones. For early drinking. Yr oak, third new. **Reserve Port** ★ Limited-release fortified dessert, 3 yrs oaked. Latest **NV** from cab very ripe & sweet, distinct alc glow.

Capell's Court range

Cabernet Sauvignon ★★★ **06** (sample) wide-girthed, as pvs, sweet & earthy. These unwooded unless mentioned; reds not retasted. **Merlot** ★★★ Seductive **05** coupled Peppermint Crisp character with ripe fruit succulence. **Shiraz** ★★ Herbaceous **06** showed pleasing fleshiness & fruity succulence. **Chardonnay** ★★★ Revisited **06** light, easy-drinking, refreshing pear & apple flavours with slight vanilla-like undertone. **Sauvignon Blanc** ★★★ Easy-drinking outdoor wine. **07** grassy gooseberry notes with hint passionfruit, good, lively & not overdone acid. — *JN*

■ **Lion's Drift** *see* Lateganskop Winery

■ *Lion's Gate* *see* Origin Wine

■ *Liquor Boys* *see* Oranjerivier Wine Cellars

Liquor World
T 011-490-2300 • F 011-689-2560

Enquiries Keith Simms • ksimms@metcash.co.za

Cherry Hill wines are selected and marketed exclusively by the Metcash Africa group through its Liquor World outlets nationwide.

Cherry Hill range

Merlot ★★★ **04** light but harmonious & persistent fruit with evident tannin. **Pinotage** ★★ **03** gamey & vegetal notes, light tannins & gd length make for easy drinking. **Cabernet Sauvignon-Merlot** ★★★ Herbal notes to light cherry & plum on **04**, grainy mid-weight body. All WO Coastal; none retasted. — *MF*

Lismore Estate Vineyards  NEW
T 028-254-9848

Greyton (see Southern Cape map) • Est 2003 • 1stB 2006 • Visits by appt • BYO picnic • Walks, hikes, mountain bike trails • Self-catering accommodation in original farm house (ca 1896) - sleeps 6 • Children welcome • Owner Jake Easton & Samantha O'Keefe • Winemaker Jake Easton & Samantha O'Keefe (Nov 2003) • Viticulturist Jake Easton with Andrew Teubes (consultant) • 12ha (cab f, shiraz, chard, sauv, viognier) • 750cs 75% red 25% white • PO Box 76 Greyton 7233 • wine@lismore.co.za • www.lismore.co.za

What brings two young Hollywood executives to an old dairy in the foothills of the Sonderend Mountains? 'An opportunity to make world-class wine in small quantities using traditional methods,' they say. 'And to set an example to our children: have a passion for life and create something that you love which you can share.'

Chardonnay ★★★ Serious oaking imparts toasty butterscotch overlay to **06**, adds textural element to lively citrus flavours. Bunch-pressed, fermented/11 mths Burgundian barriques. — *MF*

■ **Little River** *see* De Meye Wines

■ *Live-A-Little* *see* Stellar Winery

■ *Livingstone* *see* Withington

■ *Living World* *see* Oranjerivier Wine Cellars

Lomond
T 021-8098330 • F 021-8098864

Cape Agulhas ▪ Est 1999 ▪ 1stB 2005 ▪ Closed to public ▪ Winemaker Kobus Gerber (white) & Justin Corrans (red) ▪ Viticulturist Wayne Gabb & Johan Wiid ▪ 105 ha (merlot, shiraz, sauvignon, nouvelle, semillon, viognier) ▪ 750 tons ▪ ISO 9002 certified ▪ PO Box 1269 Gansbaai 7220 ▪ wayne@biogrow.co.za ▪ www.lomond.co.za

A BWI Champion, over 660 indigenous plant species and three entirely new species of fynbos have been identified here – hence all single-vineyard wines take fynbos names. An 80-km hiking trail is planned for 2008, and for spectator-sport fans, Lomond's wines were served at Wimbledon 2007.

★★★★ Sauvignon Blanc 🔲 Blending seems to add complexity: **06** developed with finesse, with nettles, dry-grass supported by earthy minerality over savoury, fresh core telling of cool-climate origins. Previewed **07** with tropical fruit & lemongrass in pleasing balance, a little sugar bringing out flavour.

Merlot ★★★ Attractive choc, spice aromas/flavours; fresh, but a little lean & simple. 16 mths new Fr oak. **Syrah ★★★** Lightly fruited, with ripe berry flourishes to dominant oak tones (16 mths new Fr), but ungenerous edge to finish. **Conebush Syrah** `NEW` **★★★★** Ripening cool-climate shiraz means big alc (14.5%); lavish new Fr oak now rather obscuring the delicate fruit, adding dry tannin (as in next). But one to watch as vyds mature. EW. **Pincushion Sauvignon Blanc** 🔲 **★★★★** A year on, the **06** single vyd wines starting to merge their distinctiveness, but a rich, dry austerity with mineral element appeals. Sample **07** again with fig, gooesberry to start; flint & grass emerging against firm acid structure. **Sugarbush Sauvignon Blanc** 🔲 **★★★★** Acid of young **07** (tank sample) better balanced than **06**, with lemongrass succulently triumphing over passionfruit. Nice green finish a little short. *— TJ*

Longbarn Winery
T 021-873-6396 • F 021-873-7059

Wellington (see Paarl map) ▪ Est 2006 ▪ Visits by appt ▪ Owner David & Sue Power ▪ Winemaker David Power, advised by Marais de Villiers ▪ 7ha (cab, pinot, sauv) ▪ 10t/110cs 100% white ▪ PO Box 1295 Wellington 7654 ▪ david@longbarn.co.za ▪ www.longbarn.co.za

In 2003, retired paediatrician David Power planted Turkish figs and Indian pomegranates on his Wellington property, but kept some of the existing grapes, which he vinifies himself. Along with the sauvignon, he made 600 litres of pinot last year. 'Small scale, hard work,' he smiles.

Sauvignon Blanc ★★ Previewed **07** similar to pvs: grassy & riper gooseberry notes, laudably moderate 12.6% alc & rather bracing, food-inviting acidity. *— JN*

Long Beach

Mediterranean-inspired range by Robertson Winery for Vinimark, pitched at SA's 'ever-burgeoning café society'. Attractively presented with twist-off caps.

Chardonnay ★★★★ Particularly flavoursome **06**, last ed was packed with citrus fruit; layer of toasty oak for lively drinking pleasure. **Sauvignon Blanc ★★★** Top sauv vintage lends zinging freshness to last-tasted **06**; crisply round, with greenpepper & green grass flavours, modest 12.5% alc. *— DH*

■ **Longmarket** *see* Woolworths

Long Mountain Wine Company
T 021-880-8800 • F 021-880-8860

Stellenbosch ▪ Est/1stB 1994 ▪ Closed to ptublic ▪ Owner Pernod-Ricard SA ▪ Cellarmaster/ winemaker/viticulturist Emile Gentis (Oct 2006) ▪ 50% red 49% white 1% MCC ▪ PO Box 1324, Stellenbosch, 7599 ▪ jaco.boonzaaier@pernod-ricard-southafrica.com, emile.gentis@pernod-ricard-southafrica.com ▪ www.longmountain.co.za

This brand in the Pernod-Ricard stable has shown enviable growth in the past two years, says production manager Jaco Boonzaaier, and double-digit increases in key markets like Russia and the US bode well for the future. Incoming winemaker Emile Gentis (ex-Meerhof) brings fresh vitality, working with new vinegrowing partners in Elgin and the Riebeek Valley as well as long-time suppliers in Breedekloof and Robertson. Also making their debut are the Long Mountain Premium Reserves.

Long Mountain Premium Reserve range NEW

Mourvèdre ★★★☆ **07** (sample) earthy, toasty notes from Am oak ferment/ageing, well-weighted flavours of cranberry & mulberry; tasty (try with venison pie), & gd potential. **Pinotage** ★★★★ 'Our flagship & the way we want to go with our Reserves' says winemaker. Big, bold but friendly **07**, inviting freshly roasted coffee aromas, flavours of dark choc & plump ripe plum. Moreish. **Chenin Blanc** ★★★ **07** (sample) still tad oaky but showing gd tropical fruit. Complex & characterful yet elegant. Will please widely.

Bushbuck Ridge range

Cabernet Sauvignon ★★ **04** pvs ed was fairly robust with leafy tones matching wild berry fruit. **Shiraz** ★★★ New-Fr-oaked **05** warm, toasty aromas with ripe plum pudding fruit; rich & mouthfilling. **Chardonnay** ★★ Tasted pvs ed, **05** textbook citrus with touch mineral & buttery lees. **Sauvignon Blanc** ★★ Grassy greenpepper & crisp acidity make **07** (sample) a good seafood wine.

Long Mountain range

Cabernet Sauvignon ★★★ **04** last ed had distinctive cassis moderated by firm, balanced tannins. Structure to age. **Pinotage** ★★★ Soft, approachable, ripe-berried **06**, comfortable & companionable style for immediate enjoyment. **Ruby Cabernet** ★★★ Basket of perfectly ripe fruit, delicately balanced & tasty; **06** incl dash pinotage. **Shiraz** NEW Not ready. **Merlot-Shiraz** ★★★ Herbal **06**, ripe minty notes & red berry flavours; crisp dry finish. Serve with oxtail casserole. **Shiraz-Cabernet Sauvignon** ★★★★ No follow up yet for **04**, generous red berries & v accessible. **Chardonnay** ★★ **07** pleasantly fresh, with splash of lemon/lime crispness. **Chenin Blanc** ★★★ Pineapple & geranium scents; delightful **07** with dry, clean finish. **Sauvignon Blanc** ★★ **07** grassy, greenpepper & tropical tones; comfortable food style. **Semillon-Chardonnay** ★★★ **07** (sample) vanilla biscuit & guava notes. Blend 70/28, dash sauv adds fruit salad crispness. **Chardonnay-Pinot Noir Cap Classique** ★★★ Just-brut style sparkling with bright lime & lemon crispness & persistent, bouncy mousse. Happy, celebration wine. **NV**.

Gecko Ridge range

Cabernet Sauvignon ★★★ **04** multi-layers of cedar, blackberry, cherry & cranberry; clean, crisp flavours. Nice! Gd for few yrs too. **Chardonnay** ★★★ **05** few notches up; ripe pineapple & citrus. Inviting, toasty biscuit tones from long lees contact & 25% new oak. Riebeek Vlly fruit. — DB

■ **Long Nose** see Groupe LFE South Africa

Longridge Winery
T 021-855-2004 • **F** 021-855-4083

Stellenbosch (see Helderberg map) ▪ Est 1994 ▪ Mon-Fri 8.30-5 Sat & pub hols 8.30-2 ▪ Closed Easter Fri & Sun, Dec 25 & Jan 1 ▪ Picnics & cheese platters by appt ▪ Childrens' playground ▪ Owner Aldo van der Laan ▪ Cellarmaster/winemaker Clinton le Sueur ▪ Viticulturist Johann Schloms ▪ 40ha (incl new cab f, petit v, chard, chenin, verdelho, viognier) ▪ 13 000cs 75% red 25% white ▪ ISO 9001 certified ▪ PO Box 2023 Dennesig 7601 ▪ info@longridge.co.za ▪ www.longridge.co.za

Previously under the Winecorp banner and now owned by Hollander Aldo van der Laan, this well-equipped winery on the Helderberg flanks is now manned by Clinton le Sueur (ex-Mulderbosch). 'It's great to have lots of space, tanks and barrels,' he enthuses. 'The ranges will remain the same with the future addition of a white blend, a shiraz and a red blend featuring a whole bunch of varieties, from cabernet franc to verdelho.' Now they're intent on reviving that 'small farm with a family feeling' atmosphere.

★★★★ **Cabernet Sauvignon** Cab's characteristic herbaceous 'green stick' nuance mingles with dark berried fruit in **05**. Dense & robust, tight structure sheathed in powerful tannins. Needs time to tame. 14.8% alc. 15 mths oak.

★★★★ **Merlot** Dark fruit & mint nuances hint at **05**'s latent core of dense fruit, currently held in taut tannic embrace. Powerful, full-bodied with potential; needs time to integrate fully.

★★★★ **Pinotage** Much awarded rendition of the variety, though **05**'s soft, savoury & plummy fruit overwhelmed by austere spicy wood tannin mid-2007. Layers of lurking fruit, interleaved by enticing cinnamon spice, need time to show full potential. Big, bold style (14.9% alc), as pvs.

★★★★ **Chardonnay** Explosion of orange marmalade & clove (ex-oaking, yr Burg barrels) in bold **06** (★★★☆). Some fat, buttery appeal, but wood overwhelms subtler flavours. **05** broader, more open than pvs, in process lost some definition compared with stellar pvs.

★★★★ **Sauvignon Blanc** Fresh minerality & hints of granadilla & figleaf on delicious **07** (sample), enlivened by bright, clean acidity. Pleasing richness, oak (portion 4 mths new) subtly integrated. Shows verve & character.

★★★★ **Brut** MCC sparkling with inviting brioche & apple aromas & fine mousse. Rich, leesy & complex with nutty toasted nuances, clean finish. Developed & approachable but will hold few yrs yet. **NV**.

Rosé NEW ★★★ Sappy, savoury & juicy **07** from merlot, pinotage & cab f. Red-berried spicy appeal with refreshing acidity & dry finish.

Bay View range
Discontinued: **Cabernet Sauvignon**, **Merlot**, **Pinotage**, **Shiraz**, **Chenin Blanc**, **Sauvignon Blanc**. – *MW*

■ **Longwood** *see* Dominion Wine Company

Loopspruit Winery
T 013-930-7025 • F 013-935-8020

Mpumalanga ▪ Tastings, sales & tours by appt ▪ Restaurant lapa or picnic baskets available ▪ Conferences ▪ Owner Mpumalanga Agricultural Development Corporation ▪ Winemaker Matthew Sibanyoni, advised by Ian Sieg ▪ Viticulturist Ian Sieg (adviser) ▪ ±19ha (cabs s/f, ruby cab, shiraz, chard, chenin, colombard, hanepoot, raisin blanc) ▪ ±150t/±10 000 cs ▪ PO Box 855 Bronkhorstpruit 1020 ▪ manie@madc.co.za ▪ www.madc.co.za

SA's northernmost winery is doing exceptionally well, says consultant Ian Sieg, thanks to CEO Manie Grobler and winemaker Matthew Sidanyoni. The lab has been upgraded; the revamped thatched-roof cellar and tasting room offer a welcome respite from the heat; and picnic baskets (on request) and barbecue sites ensure an unhurried visit. 'And don't miss the mampoer,' Sieg urges. Note: no wines ready for review this edition.

■ **Lord Neethling** *see* Neethlingshof Estate

Lord's Wines
T 023-625-1265 • F 023-625-1265

McGregor (see Robertson map) ▪ Est/1stB 2006 ▪ Visits by appt (T 082-378-3987) ▪ BYO picnic ▪ Walks ▪ Conservation area ▪ 4×4 trail by appt ▪ Tour groups ▪ Owner 12 shareholders ▪ Winemaker Newald Marais ▪ Viticulturist Briaan Stipp (consultant) ▪ 12ha (pinot, shiraz, chard, sauv) ▪ 27t/1 400cs 50% red 50% white ▪ PO Box 165 McGregor 6708 ▪ groottoren@telkomsa.net

A great start in 2006/7 for this organic boutique winery high in the mountains above McGregor, selling all 9 000 bottles of its maiden sauvignon within just four months. Expansion and development continue, including new cellar equipment, a new shiraz (not ready for tasting), and an additional 4ha of pinot noir. Marketing possibilities include branding as a 'pinot farm', and tying up with icon namesake Lord's Cricket Ground.

Sauvignon Blanc ★★★ Delicate, nuanced **07** has flinty green fig hints; well-rounded flavours with firm pithy grip, super with seafood. **Sauvignon Blanc Organic** ⚘ ★★★ **07** shows subdued grass & green fig aromas & pleasant vinosity, but flavours are somewhat insubstantial. — *CvZ*

L'Ormarins Private Cellar
T 021-874-9000; 021-874-9020 • F 021-874-9100

Franschhoek • Est 1714 • 1stB 1982 • Tastings Mon-Fri 9-4.30 Sat 10-3 • Booking essential, Franschhoek Motor Museum visits Tue-Sun 9-4.30 • Closed Easter Fri/Sun, Dec 25 & Jan 1 • Owner Johann Rupert • Winemaker Terra Del Capo cellar: Winemaker Neil Patterson with Christo Hamerse • L'Ormarins cellar: Thierry Haberer with Dawie Botha • Viticulturist Rosa Kruger • ISO 14001 certified • PO Box 435 Franschhoek Valley 7690 • tasting@lormarins.co.za • www.lormarins.com; www.terradelcapo.com

This fine, historic farm, owned by international businessman Johann Rupert, has opened its doors to the public after three years of renovations and a brand restructure. New wines, from vineyards on the property and hand-picked sites in the Western Cape, will be released this year. A white blend, a Sauvignon and a Chardonnay, along with the Italian-inspired range, Terra del Capo, are made in the white-wine cellar. From the red-wine cellar, a range of single-varietal bordeaux-style wines will emerge this year. Meanwhile, car enthusiasts have discovered the resident Franschhoek Motor Museum, showcasing dozens of rare and exotic cars, from a 1928 Rolls-Royce Phantom to a 2003 Porsche Carrera GT.

Terra del Capo range
Sangiovese ★★★ Softish, dry **04**, wood dimming usual varietal focus, freshness. 12.3% alc. 15 mths Fr oak, 30% new. Reviewed last ed, still available. **Pinot Grigio** ★★★ Easy-drinking **07** with quiet winter melon & green apple interest. Lightish body, balanced freshness, just-dry. — *AL*

■ **Lorna Hughes** *see* Stonehill

Lorraine Private Cellar
T 023-349-1224 • F 023-349-1224

Goudini (see Worcester map) • Est 1875 • 1stB 2002 • Visits by appt • Tasting fee R15 (incl glass) • BYO picnic • Conservation area • Owner Lorraine Trust (Johan & Lori Ann de Wet) • Winemaker Johan de Wet • Viticulturist Leon Dippenaar (2003, consultant) • 150ha (cab f, merlot, petit v, pinotage, ruby cab, shiraz, chard, chenin, sauv, viognier, nouvelle) • 2 000t total; 50t/±4 200cs own label • 50% red 50% white • PO Box 2 Rawsonville 6845 • info@lorraine.co.za • www.lorraine.co.za, www.lorraine-wines.com

Accredited by the Biodiversity & Wine Initiative for his Du Toitskloof mountainside farm, approved by Fairtrade, and a member of the Proudly South African campaign, Johan de Wet has impressive social and environmental credentials. Naming his Pinotage Rosé 'Love of my Life' after wife Lori Ann shows his heart is in the right place, too.

★★★★ **Chardonnay** NEW ✓ Gorgeous whiff vanilla oak, dried peach & marmalade, expansive creamy flavours. Lighter wooding (5 mths Fr) abets greater harmony, balance, yet **06** makes a (delicious) statement. Big step up from **03** (★★★) crowd pleaser. No **04/05**.

> **Love Of My Life Pinotage Rosé** NEW ☺ 🍽 ★★★ Charmingly named & styled **07**, ex-pinotage, slight candyfloss sweetness; well made, lots of creamy concentration.

Shiraz ★★★ Last-tasted **03** was modern, with fragrant aromas framed by oak, dense mouthfeel. **Cape Harmony** ★★★ **04** serious-minded 'Cape Blend' (30% pinotage). Last ed noted as still needing time to develop. 2 yrs Fr/Am oak. **Sauvignon Blanc** ★★★ Welcoming tropical flavours, no shrill acidity here; notch-up **07** gd solo sundowner. — *IvH*

■ **Lost Horizons** *see Du Toitskloof Winery*

Louiesenhof Wines
T 021-865-2632 ▪ **F** 021-865-2613

Stellenbosch ▪ Est/1stB 1992 ▪ Tasting & sales daily 9-5 (summer) Mon-Sat 10-3 (winter) ▪ Fee R10 ▪ Closed Christian holidays ▪ Accommodation: see intro ▪ Light picnic meals in summer ▪ Play area for children ▪ Function facilities ▪ Farm produce ▪ Walks ▪ Conservation area ▪ Owner WS Smit Watergang Trust ▪ Winemaker Jos le Roux ▪ Viticulturist Gawie Kriel (2000, consultant) ▪ 130ha (cab, merlot, pinotage, tinta, chard, chenin, sauv) ▪ 1 000t/2 000cs own label 70% red 28% white 2% rosé ▪ PO Box 2013 Stellenbosch 7601 ▪ lhofwine@iafrica.com ▪ www.louiesenhof.co.za

A trendy dry rosé and less-aged pinot grigio have joined the line-up which includes, besides wine, a handsomely packaged Marbonne brandy. Hospitality has also been upgraded and now features a luxurious accommodation suite (sleeps 4) complete with Jacuzzi and massage options.

Pinotage ★★★ Unwooded **04**, rich plum & black berry notes, soft ripe tannins, dry finish. As all in range, not retasted. **Tinta Barocca** ★★★ **02** Mediterranean-style food-friendly red, briefly oaked. **Cabernet Sauvignon-Cabernet Franc** ★★★★ Well-crafted, harmonious equal blend; **05** attractively full & rounded, leafy wild berry flavours. Fr oak, 2nd fill, yr. **Pinotage Rosé Secco** Unready for tasting. **Chardonnay Unwooded** ★★★ **04** pear & green melon, mineral & restrained, gd foil for seafood. **Pinot Grigio** Not reviewed. **Sauvignon Blanc** ★★★ Water-white **05** liberal tropical aromas, brisk dusty finish. **Sweet Red** ★★ Individual fortified dessert from cellar known for characterful bottlings. **NV. Perroquet Cape Tawny** ★★★★ Rustic glow-inducer from tinta, pvsly noted as fairly developed, with savoury touches. **NV**; 19% alc. Discontinued: **Pinotage Blanc de Noir**. — *CT*

Louisvale Wines
T 021-865-2422 ▪ **F** 021-865-2633

Stellenbosch ▪ Est/1stB 1989 ▪ Tasting & sales by appt only Mon-Fri 9.30-4.30 ▪ Fee R10 ▪ Closed Easter Fri-Mon, Dec 25/26 & Jan 1 ▪ Tours by appt ▪ Owner Michael A Johnston, Hendrik Kotzé & Martin Delaney ▪ Winemaker/viticulturist Simon Smith (Jul 1997) ▪ 13 ha (chard) ▪ 200t/15 000cs 20% red 80% white ▪ PO Box 542 Stellenbosch 7599 ▪ winery@louisvale.com ▪ www.louisvale.com

The decision at Louisvale to specialise exclusively in chardonnay has been cemented with the sale of neighbouring property Nooitgedacht, previously their source of red grapes. Intent on constantly increasing quality across the board, a vine replacement programme has begun and the ever-popular Unwooded Chardonnay is now under screwcap.

★★★★ **Chardonnay 06** pronounced oak & bags of citrus; buttery entry broadens into delicious tangerine. Well-made, will appeal to fans of big, woody chards. No **05**.
Dominique ★★★ Still available **02** was somewhat austere, in line with lesser vintage & higher proportion cab f. Not for keeping. No **03**. **Chavant Chardonnay** ★★★★ **06** continues signature elegance & finesse. Attractive vanilla & hint quince, lively acid backed by ripe stonefruit, yummy peaches-&-cream farewell. Could cellar few yrs. WO W Cape. Improves on juicy & curvaceous **05** (★★★★). **Chardonnay Unwooded** 🗒 ★★★ Citrus, green peaches & waft pears enhance crisp **07** (sample). Lively, medium-bodied, with flavourful finish. — *JN*

Lourensford
T 021-847-2300 ▪ **F** 021-847-0896

Stellenbosch (see Helderberg map) ▪ Est 1999 ▪ 1stB 2003 ▪ Tasting & sales Mon-Fri 8.30-5 Sat 10-2 Sun 11-3 Pub hols 9-4 ▪ Fee R15 ▪ Closed Easter Fri, Dec 25 & Jan 1 ▪ Tours Mon-Fri 11 & 3 ▪ Conferencing ▪ Fly-fishing ▪ Annual SAA Cape Town Flower Show ▪ Polo ▪ Cheesery ▪ Owner Christo Wiese ▪ Cellarmaster Philip Costandius ▪ Oenologist Hannes Nel ▪ Winemaker Adéle Louw ▪ Viticulturist Piet Uys & Ronel Bester ▪ 362ha (cab, merlot, pinotage, shiraz, sauv, viognier) ▪ 1 300t/80 000cs 67% red 33% white ▪ BRC certification completed. ▪ PO Box 16 Somerset West 7129 ▪ winetastings@lourensford.co.za ▪ www.lourensford.com

Oenologist Hannes Nel has diversified into making honey liqueur – preservative- and additive-free, and unfiltered. There's also a new arts venue on the property, operated by the Bell-Roberts Gallery. 'And we are looking at growing olives,' reveals cellarmaster Philip Costandius. But all this doesn't mean focus is shifting from the vineyards. On the contrary, a leafroll virus laboratory has been established on the farm to monitor and manage infection. 'We have also started a programme to remove alien invasive plants on a large scale, which ties in with our recent accreditation by the BWI.

Lourensford range

★★★★ **Seventeen Hundred** Named for date property established. Worthy flagship cab s, shiraz 75/25 blend in **05**. Black cherry, hint tobacco, classy feel & flavours with supportive oak for fine-grained dry finish. 10 mths Fr oak, 85% new.

★★★★ **Viognier** Newest **07** keeps flag flying, but too young to rate realistically. Rich (but elegant) dried peaches 'n cream with splash lime for freshness. 30% used Fr oak.

★★★★ **Semillon Noble Late Harvest** Distinctive, original, hedonistic. Previewed last ed, **05** reached to new heights with silky opulence, never-ending sweet-savoury flavours. Potential (★★★★★). **04** showed lavender scent, citrus freshness on long, silky finish. Partially oaked. 500ml.

Cabernet Sauvignon ★★★★ **03** pvsly noted as one to watch: dark fruit, smoked beef & fynbos nuances; finely honed tannins. Yr Fr oak. **Sauvignon Blanc** 🍷 ★★★ Assertive **07**, some grass, nettles; swingeing acidity upsets balance, drinkability. Addition 2% semillon helps, but demands fried fish, forget the lemon.

Eden Crest range

Merlot ☺ ★★★ Easy-drinking **06**, hints coffee & dried plum, dry tannins. **Shiraz** ☺ ★★★ Touch smoked beef in **06**, easy tannins, sweet finish (6g/l sugar).

Cabernet Sauvignon-Merlot NEW ★★★ Gd everyday red. Whiff vanilla on **06**, pleasing berry fruits, soft tannins, sweetish finish. **Chardonnay** Light oaking & soupçon semillon in **06** last ed added interest to a crisp, melon/citrus-toned summer quaffer. **Sauvignon Blanc** ★★ **07** hints of grass, greenpeppers, fullish bodied at 14% alc. **Sauvignon Blanc-Chardonnay-Chenin Blanc** In abeyance. Discontinued: **Merlot-Shiraz**, **Cape Blend**.

Five Heirs range

Chardonnay ☺ 🍷 ★★★ Latest **06** hints oak & peach; more lively, fresh flavours with citrus tang. Portion oaked.

Cabernet Sauvignon ★★★★ Last-tasted **04** had fruit as main focus, firm vein of oak tannin ensured food compatibility, few yrs ageing potential. **Merlot** 🍷 ★★★ **06** meaty, savoury; soft approachable tannins, finish seems dry despite dab sugar. **Shiraz** 🍷 ★★★★ Attractive smoke & vanilla in **06**, lovely pure fruit reined in by gd oak (only 10% new), discernibly dry. An absolute treat. **Shiraz-Mourvèdre** ★★★★ **06** initially oaky, gives way to savoury, beefy flavours with mourvèdre's gravelly tannins, muscular feel. 10 mths oak. **Shiraz-Viognier** NEW ★★★★ **06** the 'feminine' version of the shiraz blends: fragrant & delicate, smooth silky body, elegant. 100% new oak. **Sauvignon Blanc** ★★★★ Loads gooseberries, greenpeppers on **07**, follows through in flavour, racy acidity for extra excitement. Good typicity. **Viognier** NEW ★★★ Gentle peach, evening flowers intro in **06**; gd assertive flavours, firm acidity, more like dried peaches. Portion oaked 7 mths. **Chardonnay-Viognier** 🍷 ★★★ **06** more weight, less bouquet & freshness than solo Chard above, flavours resonate in lower key, some will prefer. Discontinued: **Cabernet Franc**, **Pinotage**, **Rosé**, **Chenin Blanc**. — IvH

■ **Louwshoek** see Daschbosch Wine Cellar

Lovane Boutique Wine Estate  NEW

T 021-881-3358 • F 021-881-3546

Stellenbosch • Est 2003 • 1stB 2006 • Tasting Mon-Fri 10-5 Sat 9:30-4 • Closed Easter Fri-Mon, Freedom Day (Apr 27), Pentecost (May 11), Dec 25 & Jan 1 • Fee R10, refundable on purchase • Tours by appt only • Conferencing for 16 delegates • Functions venue for 80 guests • Restaurant for breakfast & lunch from Sep 2008 • B&B guesthouse (no children under 12) • Owner Philip, Gail & Francois Gous • Winemaker/viticulturist Philip & Gail Gous • 2.5ha (cab s/f, petit v) • 12t/140cs 90% red 10% rosé • PO Box 91 Vlottenburg 7604 • info@lovane.co.za • www.lovane.co.za

Lovane (Xhosa for 'Chameleon') was established on virgin land and is truly family owned and run – the Gous kids helped with the planting of the vines as well as all the other hard work. Lovane's visitor facilities – a small functions venue and upmarket conference facility, plus a guesthouse – cater particularly for businesspeople, while plans are on the drawing board for a restaurant.

Blanc de Noir ★★ Salmon-hued 06, apricot edged, softly sweet. *– MF*

■ Luca & Ingrid Bein *see* Bein Wine

Luddite Wines

T 028-284-9308 • F 028-284-9045

Bot River (see Elgin/Walker Bay map) • Est 2000 • Tastings by appt • Owner Niels Verburg & Hillie Meyer • Winemaker Niels Verburg • Viticulturist Penny Verburg • 5.5ha (shiraz, mourvèdre, cab) • 2 500cs 100% red • Export brands: Niels Verburg & Mudge Point • Ranges for customers: Barton, Elgin Vintners & Iona • PO Box 656 Bot River 7185 • luddite@telkomsa.net

A tasting room and office complete, a cellar in the foundation stages, up to 60% of their own fruit... 'Now first prize will be 100% our own and natural yeasts all the way,' says Niels Verburg, longing to stay put after an overload of travel. Meanwhile Penny V's as happy as the proverbial, what with pigs producing litters, olive trees flourishing (extra-virgin oil next up), and fruit trees and a vegetable garden starting to supply the household. 'We're well on our way to being self-sufficient – oh, and the vineyards are happy too.'

★★★★ **CWG Auction Reserve Shiraz Dos Años** Selected for two consecutive Auctions; pvs ed noted peppery, black fruited notes; has developed rich, silky mocha fullness. Real oomph. Yr all new Fr barrels then yr seasoned casks.

★★★★★ **Shiraz** Pure-fruited & elegant, unshowy yet intense. Pvs ed noted 04 silkier, more concentrated than 03, but same seamless style. Yr oak, 80/20 Fr/Am, 25% new. Successfully draws on vyds from Mbury, via Sbosch to Bot R.

★★★★ **CWG Auction Reserve 'Two for Listening' Shiraz-Cabernet Sauvignon** NEW Named for Master Verburg's inability to listen in class - his mark out of 5! 05 super compendium nutty notes, lovely concentration of cassis fruit & plush opulence; beguilingly open in youth. 80/20 blend, half new Fr oak.

Mudge Point Sauvignon Blanc NEW ▤ ★★★★ Done no justice by funky label or tropical aromas, a beautifully flinty, mineral, clean-fruited mouthful makes 06 a delight. *– DS*

Lusan Premium Wines

T 021-883-8988 • F 021-883-8941

Stellenbosch • Closed to public • info@neethlingshof.co.za

Umbrella organisation for Alto, Flat Roof Manor, Hill & Dale, Le Bonheur, Neethlingshof, Stellenzicht and Uitkyk. Wines from these farms, totalling some 800 ha of prime Stellenbosch vineyards, marketed by Cape Legends. See individual entries.

Lushof Estate

T 021-855-3134 • F 0866-189-154

Stellenbosch (see Helderberg map) • Est 1997 • 1stB 2000 • Tasting & sales Mon-Fri 10-4 Sat by appt • Closed pub hols • Tours by appt • Owner Steyn Trust • Winemaker/viticulturist Petré

Morkel (Dec 2005) ▪ 12.5ha (cab, merlot, shiraz, chard, sauv) ▪ 70t/3 500cs 75% red 25% white ▪ PO Box 899 Stellenbosch 7599 ▪ info@lushof.co.za ▪ www.lushof.co.za

Hennie Steyn sadly having passed away suddenly at the end of 2006, the Steyn farm now in the hands of the Steyn Family Trust. The estate is finally at full production, and winemaker Petré Morkel cannot wait to release the new vintages.

★★★★ **Sauvignon Blanc** Tropical, passionfruit nuances coming through on pleasant & refreshing **07** (★★★★), crisp, clean cut-grass finish. Misses persistence & zest achieved by **06** & pvs.

Cabernet Sauvignon ★★★ Forthcoming coffee, toffee, dry tobacco leaf aromas on **04**; savoury flavours with hints forest floor & barnyard; brief warm exit. **Merlot** ★★★ New vintage not ready. Strong tannins & beefy 15% alc noted last ed on leafy **04**. **Shiraz** ★★★ Sweet porty aromas on last-tasted **04**, chunky, savoury flavours & big spicy tannins. **Signet Red** ★★★★ When last reviewed, fruity **04**'s earthy, well-oaked & balanced structure augured well for further cellaring. Mainly cab, smidgens shiraz & merlot. **Chardonnay** ★★ Canned pineapple note on oak-brushed **07**; quickish, somewhat blowsy tropical fruit flavours. — *MM*

Lutzville Cape Diamond Vineyards

T 027-217-1516 ▪ F 027-217-1435

Lutzville Valley (see Olifants River map) ▪ Est 1961 ▪ 1stB 1980 ▪ Tasting & sales Mon-Fri 8-5 Sat & non-Christian hols 10-14 ▪ Tours by appt ▪ 'Lutzville Cape Diamond' coffee shop ▪ Function/conference venue ▪ Tour groups ▪ Gifts ▪ Farm-style produce ▪ Owner 109 shareholders ▪ Winemaker Gideon Theron, Albie Rust & Piet Sebenje ▪ Viticulturist MG van der Westhuizen ▪ 2 100ha (cab, merlot, pinotage, ruby cab, shiraz, chard, chenin, colombard, sauv) ▪ 47 500t/ 40 000cs own label 10% red 87% white 1% rosé 2% fortified/sparkling ▪ PO Box 50 Lutzville 8165 ▪ info@lutzvillevineyards.com ▪ www.lutzvillevineyards.com

Winemaker Gideon Theron and his team have a handle on which are the better-performing vineyards in the cooler sites, so they're now able to better select fruit for the styles they're intending to make. Theron is also introduced wooding for all the reds – which previously were mostly unoaked – and started maturing selected reds in barrel. 'The change of style and adjustment in winemaking techniques are producing wines with far more fruity flavours, better balanced on the palate,' says Gideon T. 'As always, there is room for improvement, but we do try to leave absolutely nothing to chance.'

Cape Diamond range

Cabernet Sauvignon ☺ ★★★ Cassis & pipe tobacco notes on **06**, blackberry kick & well-managed tannins. **Merlot** ☺ ★★★ **06** dark choc & black cherries, ripe & spicy food wine. **Pinotage** ☺ ★★★ **06** vanilla biscuit & spice give way to choc & ripe plums. **Shiraz** ☺ ★★★ Step up **06**; dark choc & black cherries on firm tannic foundation. Gd partner to meat dishes. Could go yr/2. This, all red stablemates, pvsly unwooded, now lightly oaked. **Rosé** ☺ ★★★ **06** strawberry jam scents introduce a crisp summer patio charmer. **Chenin Blanc** ☺ ★★★ Notch up; leafy scents & crisp pineapple, balanced touch of sweet fruitiness in off-dry (9g/l RS) **07**, sampled ex-tank.

Chardonnay ★★ **07** (sample) clean citrus flavours on unoaked seafood partner. **Sauvignon Blanc** ★★ Quiet & unassuming **07**, preview shows gentle greenpepper notes. **Muscadel** ★★★ **07** fortified dessert continues honeysuckle fragrance of pvs, adds jasmine note; balanced; alc nicely judged. Discontinued: **Ruby Cabernet**.

Bat's Rock range

Ruby Cabernet ★★ **06** mint & eucalyptus tones, somewhat austere. **Rosé** ★★ **06** from pinotage, colombard; rich, mid-weight & dry character that belies its 20g/l RS. **Chenin Blanc** ★★ Wafts of dry grass & tropical fruit on uncomplicated **07** sample. Discontinued: **Bouquet Blanc**.

Diamond River range NEW

> **Merlot** ☺ ★★★ Coffee & mocha notes; **05** light touch of sweetness makes for approachable sharing wine. **Shiraz** ☺ ★★★ Smoky wafts & dark cherries; **05** gd combo, with friendly fruity sweetness typical of the range. **Chardonnay** ☺ ★★★ Shy wood adds complexity to cheerful **06**, well-balanced & off-dry (8.5g/l RS). **Sauvignon Blanc** ☺ ★★★ Earthy, herbal **06**; ripe & juicy, off-dry (8.6g/l RS) charmer.

Cabernet Sauvignon ★★ **05** spicy cedarwood with plum pudding ripeness & firm tannins. Screwcapped, as are all these.

Diamond Collection NEW

Cabernet Sauvignon ✓ ★★★★ Seriously styled **06** (sample) rich, warm, spicy; big blackberry body (15.5% alc) & clean oak notes from barrel fermentation/14 mths ageing. **Shiraz** ★★★ Sample **06** smoky cedar notes & firm tannins. Serious intent (14 mths barrelled) but needs time to develop. **Chardonnay Wooded** ★★★ Charmingly approachable **06**, toasty, nutty notes lifted by lick of sweetness, lingering flavours. **Sauvignon Blanc** ★★★ **06** understated & accessible; confirms sauv character with a clean grassy aroma.

Friends range
Discontinued: **Ruby Sunset**, **Misty Morning**, **Sunny Day**. —*DB*

Lyngrove
T 021-880-1221 · F 021-880-0851

Stellenbosch (see Helderberg map) · 1stB 2000 · Tasting & sales by appt (T 021-842-2116) · Five-star Lyngrove Country House · Owner Baarsma's Holdings B.V. · Winemaker Hannes Louw, with Danielle du Toit (Jun 2006) · Vineyard Manager John Fullard · 76ha (cab, merlot, shiraz, petit v, pinot, pinotage, chard, chenin, sauv) · 50 000cs 80% red 20% white · PO Box 7275 Stellenbosch 7599 · info@baarsma.co.za · www.lyngrove.co.za; www.baarsma.co.za
Part of the 1m-cases-a-year Baarsma Wine Group, this winery shares its name and Helderberg locale with Lyngrove Country House, a luxury stay-over and conference venue.

Platinum range
★★★★ **Pinotage** Touches eucalyptus & cedar, coconut flavours in balance with rich dark fruit on **05**. 18 mths oak, 35% new, 10% Am.
Shiraz ✓ ★★★★ Smoky & leathery **04**, fruity & generous but more elegant than **03** (★★★★); alc down a fraction (14%) & 15 mths in 35% new oak add welcome dimension. **Cabernet Sauvignon-Merlot** ✓ ★★★★ Appealing home-baked aroma on previewed **04**, deep, rich black cherries & firm supporting tannins notch up on **03** (★★★★). Ingredients in place for long life. 60/40 blend, Fr oak. **Chardonnay** ★★★★ Lemon/citrus elegance, inviting caramel character throughout **06**. Subtle (Fr) oak & just enough sweetness to add excitement.

Reserve range
Shiraz-Pinotage ★★★★ Redolent of old leather-bound books; **05** v ripe fruit & lovely clean dry finish. **Chardonnay** ★★★★ Gentle use of wood underscores delicious citrus & melon flavours on **06**. Combo 85% tank, 15% Fr older oak. Discontinued: **Cabernet Sauvignon-Merlot**.

Lyngrove Collection

> **Shiraz** ☺ ★★★ Relaxed **05** with attractive leafy nose & juicy mulberry flavour.

Cabernet Sauvignon ▤ ★★★ Mint & herbs on preview of unwooded **05**, dark choc & lengthy finish. **Merlot** ★★ Light hued **03**, eucalyptus whiffs preceded greenish, fairly tart sour plum palate last ed. **Pinotage** ★★★ Last-tasted **05**, sweetly ripe, soft & ingratiating; redberry/banana flavours & hint vanilla from 9 mths oak (equal Fr/Am). **Chardonnay** ★★★ Pvsly reviewed **05** wooded, but subtly; easy, light; enjoy young. **Sauvignon Blanc** ▤ ★★★ Shy grassy nuances to understated, easy-quaffing **07** (sample). —*DB*

Lynx Wines
T 021-867-0406 ▪ F 021-867-0397

Franschhoek ▪ Est/1stB 2002 ▪ Tasting & sales Mon-Fri 10-5, otherwise by appt ▪ Self-catering cottages ▪ Owner Vista Hermosa (Pty) Ltd ▪ Winemaker Dieter Sellmeyer (2002) ▪ Viticulturist Kevin Watt (Apr 2002, consultant) ▪ 11ha (cabs s/f, grenache, merlot, mourvèdre, petit v, shiraz, viognier) ▪ 2 000cs 85% red 15% rosé/blanc de noir ▪ PO Box 566 Franschhoek 7690 ▪ winemaker@lynxwines.co.za ▪ www.lynxwines.co.za

A fan of traditional concrete fermenters, Dieter Sellmeyer broke down in 2007 and installed a stainless steel tank for his first white, a viognier. Then, stuck without enough viognier for solo vinification, he co-fermented it with shiraz - in good old concrete! Outdoors, 200 CDs were strung from the vines as a quirky but eminently successful form of bird deterrence.

Premium Range

★★★★ **Cabernet Sauvignon** Back to form, berry-toned **06** seduces with svelte structure, fruit concentration, lively finish; pure drinking pleasure, oak (yr, 42% new) fully integrated. Swiss gold winner **05** (★★★★) warmed by lusty 15% alc.

★★★★ **Xanache** Supple, sweet-fruited bdx-style red led by cab in **06**. Fully ripe, cedar toned, warmly generous, rounded & accessible but with backbone for few yrs further development.

Merlot NEW ★★★★ Barrel selection for maiden **06** showing charm & verve; red berries & cedar, yr oaking (3rd new) in support. Drink now or age few yrs. **Shiraz** ★★★★ Wild berries & smoked meat, salty liquorice takes drinkability to the nth degree in **06**. Succulent, generous, delicious. 12 mths Fr oak, 35% new. **05** (★★★★), Swiss gold, super-ripe & showy. Both ranges EW.

Classic Range

Vino Tinto 🗒 ★★★★ Bdx varieties plus shiraz for berry compote styling in **06**; lifted by fynbos note. Appealing, lively & juicy. **Blanc de Noir** 🗒 ★★★ Merlot-based **07** fulfills all the requirements: pretty fresh berry perfume, light tone, dry finish for summertime quaffing. **Rosado** NEW 🗒 ★★★ Equal cab, shiraz debut **07** is hard to ignore: cerise-hued dry rosé, powerfully fruity, with vibrant freshness, long finish. — CR

🟦 **M23** see Bottelary Hills Wines

🟦 **Maankloof** see Mountain River Wines

Mac's Hill Winery
T 022-485-7035 ▪ F 022-485-7035

Swartland ▪ Est 2004 ▪ 1stB 2005 ▪ Tasting by appt ▪ Closed pub hols ▪ BYO picnic ▪ Facilities for children ▪ Olive & lavender oils ▪ Owner Rick & Colleen McCrindle ▪ Winemaker/viticulturist Rick McCrindle ▪ 32ha (cab, cinsaut, shiraz, zinfandel, chenin, viognier) ▪ 165t/250cs 100% red ▪ PO Box 630 Malmesbury 7299 ▪ mccrindle@intekom.co.za

'We used to park our bakkie in our cellar until a few years ago, when the "garage" was converted to what is now the "cellar"', says Rick McCrindle, who heads up the enterprises on this 50-hectare Swartland farm that also produce olive and lavender oils. They've come some way since starting out crushing grapes with their feet. Progress has seen them move to small-scale Italian winemaking machinery.

Mac's Hill Winery range

Barrel Cinsaut ★★ Pale cerise **06**, unpretentious easy-drinker with light raspberry fruit & a touch of savoury. Older wood. **Cabernet Sauvignon-Zinfandel** ★★★ Pleasing varietal combo of blackcurrant & wild berry on **05** country red; farmyard note, robust spicy tannins, chunky finish. **Rick's Red** ★★ Mainly shiraz, dollops cab, cinsaut on **05**; gamey black fruit, leathery notes, rustic & food-friendly. 1st/2nd fill Fr oak. — MF

Maiden Wine Cellars

T 021-856-3052 • **F** 021-856-5085

Gordon's Bay • *Est 1995* • *1stB 1999* • *Tasting/tours by appt; also tailor-made wine tours (max 6 people)* • *Owner Danie Hattingh* • *1 000cs 100% red* • *PO Box 185, Gordon's Bay, 7151* • *mwines@mweb.co.za* • *www.maidenwines.com*

'It's getting beyond my imagination,' says MD Danie Hattingh, delighted that 890 cases of his 900-case production were shipped off to a single buyer in Malaysia. The balance was distributed locally as gifts, leaving him with only seven bottles of his Private Reserve 05 red for personal consumption: 'I'll just have to double the volume next year.'

Main Street Winery
T 021-872-3006 • **F** 021-872-3006

Paarl • *Est/1stB 1999* • *Tasting & tours by appt* • *Owner/winemaker Marais de Villiers* • *700cs 50% red 50% white* • *PO Box 2709 Paarl 7620* • *mainstreet@mweb.co.za*

What a marvellous service Marais de Villiers provides, gearing up fledgling winemakers then giving continuing support. The business is taking this one-man-Elsenburg far - last year even to the Natal Midlands to launch a maverick new winemaker.

Main Street range `NEW`
Main Street ★★ Oak dominates fruit on **03** bdx-style combo caf, petit v & merlot, will need time to integrate.

Stoep range
Merlot ★★★★ Provisionally rated sample **03** (★★★★) showed big improvement: deep, densely layered mulberry/choc fruit; ripe dry tannins & already integrated oak. **Shiraz** ★★★★ Also tentatively rated as a preview last ed, **03** (★★★★) upped the wattage with well-extracted savoury fruit, excellent varietal spice & classically dry finish. **Chenin Blanc** ★★★☆ **06** serious little chenin with appealing Golden Delicious apple & pear, extra touch vanilla & well-balanced, zingy acid. **Sauvignon Blanc** ★★★☆ Crisp & flavourful **06**; medium-weight; gooseberry & passionfruit; lively, refreshing acid in balance with fruit. Discontinued: **Pinotage**, **Dry Red**, **Chardonnay**. *— JN*

Major's Hill Estate

T 023-626-6093 • **F** 023-626-6096

Robertson • *1stB 2002* • *Tasting & sales Mon-Fri 9.30-1; 2-5 Sat 10-4* • *Closed Good Fri, Dec 25/26* • *Tours by appt* • *Facilities for children* • *Owner Dewald, Johan & Anton Louw* • *Winemaker Alkie van der Merwe, with Nico Renoster (both Jan 2003)* • *Viticulturist Dewald Louw* • *52ha (cab, merlot, pinotage, shiraz, chard, sauv)* • *15 000cs own label + 15 000cs for customers + 100 000litres bulk* • *60% red 40% white* • *PO Box 561 Robertson 6705* • *info@ majorshill.co.za* • *www.majorshill.co.za*

The history of the vine on this farm dates back to Major Kosie Marais (at rest on his favourite hill, hence the name) who built one of the first cellars in Robertson and brought the enduring Klipdrift brandy to life. No 'major' news at present, says co-owner Dewald Louw, but there are plans to upgrade the visitor facilities once planning permission is obtained. The range, not tasted for this edition, includes a Merlot, Cabernet Sauvignon, Shiraz and Pinotage (all 05), Chardonnay and Sauvignon Blanc (**07**), and Pinotage Port **03**.

Makro
T 011-797-0503 • **F** 011-797-0366

See Selected wine shops section for contact details • *Enquiries Carolyn Barton* • *cbarton@ makro.co.za* • *www.makro.co.za*

This national chain, now 13 stores strong, continues to offer a crowd-pleasing mix of retail and wholesale offerings (with case discounts on all buys), as well as limited editions and auction wines. In-house, monthly panel tastings update the range and review existing listings; customer care extends to a wine education course and e-mail and sms/text communication.

Private Reserve range

★★★★ Boplaas Cape Vintage Port Private Bin Ex-30 yr old touriga (50%), plus tinta (35%), introducing splash souzão in **01**. Last ed, maple-syrup toned still seriously delicious, great then & for many years. Follow-up **05** (also in 1.5-litre magnum) untasted.

Leef op Hoop Merlot ★★★★ By Etienne le Riche (Le Riche Wines). Classically restrained **03** still in stock. **Vriesenhof Vineyards Pinot Noir** See Vriesenhof. **Landskroon Merlot-Cabernet Franc ★★ 05** shade less appealing than last-tasted **03** (**★★★★**). Restrained , v fresh & slightly hollow. **Truter's Reserve ★★★** From Beyerskloof's Beyers T. **04** usual blend cab/merlot, last ed noted as more dimension, flavour; ripe fruit core should emerge given time. **Villiera Merlot-Cabernet Sauvignon** NEW **★★★ 05** minty, dusty notes with hints of boiled beans; red berry flavours with dry, tannic farewell. Consume soon. Yr Fr oak. **Morgenhof Cabernet Sauvignon-Merlot** NEW **★★★ 02** barnyard, earthy, blackberry hints following on to palate; firm tannic structure. 18 mths oak, 40% new. **Villiera Cape Blend Merlot-Pinotage ★★★★** Last-tasted attractive **02** firmer, punchier than usual, with 14.6% alc. Yr Fr oak, some new. **Diemersfontein Shiraz-Mourvèdre ★★★** Savoury notes on **04**, new blend from this vintage shows farmyard hints, liquorice touch, needs drinking. Fr/Am oak, 10 mths. **Porcupine Ridge Collection Syrah-Cabernet Sauvignon ★★★★** Pvsly tasted **02** v ripe, creamy bramble palate with spicy tannins, touch portiness in finish invites early enjoyment. **Morgenhof Estate Private Bin 44 Chardonnay ★★★** Barrel sample **07** brims with lemongrass, honey & oak flavours; tangy, lively acids. 20% new oak, some wild yeasts. **Steenberg Sauvignon Blanc** NEW **★★★★ 07** nuances honey & lime with hints of flintiness; racy acidity; pleasant finish. Incl smidgens colombard, muscat, semillon. **Misty Mountain ★★ 07** pleasant, juicy, lemongrass-scented off-dry quaffer by Bon Courage. **The Field Day** See under Flagstone. Discontinued: **La Bri Cabernet Sauvignon Reserve, De Toren Diversity Shiraz, Yellowwood Ridge Merlot-Cabernet Sauvignon, Flagstone Strata Series Cape Blend, Overgaauw Touriga Nacional-Cabernet Sauvignon.**

Babbling Brook range
Currently unavailable.

Mont d'Or range

Brut ★★ Both **NV** carbonated sparklings in range are by Van Loveren. Uncomplicated, hints spice & tropical fruit, short-lived mousse. **Vin Doux ★★★** Crowd-pleasing, full-sweet **NV**, interesting bouquet honey & lime, cinnamon & rosepetal. Discontinued: **Vin Sec.**

Thomas Kipling range
Currently unavailable. — *CR*

■ **Malan de Versailles** *see* Versailles

Malan Family Vintners

Pair of easy-drinking non-vintage blends by the Malan brothers of Simonsig.

Cape Rouge ★★★ Raises Cape flag high with ripe, succulent shiraz flavours; easy appeal bolstered by additions fragrant cab f & petit v, & dollop sugar. **Malan Cape Blanc ★★★** Playful mix of sauv & semillon (66/31), fresh & brisk despite smidgen sugar (7g/l). — *CvZ*

Malanot Wines
T 082-784-1297

Stellenbosch ▪ Est 2007 ▪ 1stB 2008 ▪ Tasting by appt ▪ Fee R20, refunded on purchase ▪ Owner Marius & Salicia Malan ▪ Winemaker/viticulturist Marius Malan (2007) ▪ 20t/3 000cs 70% red 10% white 20% MCC ▪ PO Box 22 Lynedoch 7603 ▪ malanot@vodamail.co.za ▪ www.malanot.co.za

'I'm spreading my wings a bit,' declares Marius Malan about this new venture he and his wife, Salicia, have started. While he's still making wine for Slaley, he's looking forward to the first bottling of Malanot Wines, which happens this year. The wines, Cab, Merlot, Syrah, red blend and Semillon, are to be sold here and exported to the UK and US.

Manley Private Cellar
T 023-230-0582 ▪ F 023-230-0057

Tulbagh ▪ Est/1stB 2002 ▪ Tasting & sales daily 10-4 Sat/Sun 10-12 ▪ Fee R5/wine ▪ Cellar tours by appt ▪ Closed Good Fri & Dec 25 ▪ Luxury B&B ▪ Gifts ▪ Walks ▪ Owner/winemaker/viti-culturist David Manley Jordan ▪ 8ha (cabs s/f, merlot, mourvèdre, pinotage, shiraz) ▪ Target: 5 000cs ▪ PO Box 318 Tulbagh 6820 ▪ info@manleywines.co.za ▪ www.manleywines.co.za

David Manley Jordan, who describes his transition from conventional farming to vinegrowing and winemaking as 'very easy and comfortable', is happy and excited about the 2007 harvest. This one-man show might stretch to an assistant winemaker in the future; for now, though, David MJ plans to continue to produce his red-only range solo.

★★★★ **Shiraz 05**, revisited, confirms promise of last yr's sample in opulent brooding fruit, glimpses coffee, spice & dried fennel, admirably balanced & ripe tannins. For those with willpower, gd few yrs ahead.

Cabernet Sauvignon ★★★★ No new vintage tasted, but last ed we enthused about **05** barrel sample's expert winemaking & fulsome fruit. **Merlot** ★★★★ Last-tasted **05** was still in development but showing deliciously ripe fruit, elegance, polished tannins & balancing acidity. **Pinotage** ★★★★ Full-blown New-World style continues with **06**; voluptuous, creamy nose; juicy red berry fruit; lovely dry palate courtesy refined tannins. 16 mths oak, combo Fr/Am, 60% new. Notch up on **05** (★★★★), with intriguing salty liquorice overlay. Discontinued: **Sauvignon Blanc**. *— JP*

▪ **Manor House** *see Nederburg Wines*

MAN Vintners
T 021-886-7532 ▪ F 021-887-4340

Paarl ▪ Est/1stB 2001 ▪ Tasting & sales by appt ▪ Owner MAN Vintners (Pty) Ltd ▪ Winemaker Tyrrel Myburgh ▪ 100 000cs 70% red 30% white ▪ PO Box 389 Stellenbosch 7599 ▪ info@manvintners.co.za ▪ www.manvintners.co.za

Grapes sourced from WIETA-accredited growers, predominantly in the Perdeberg area, reflect the social and environmental responsibility of the partners in this low-key but swiftly expanding venture: Charles Back of Fairview, José Conde of Stark-Condé, Tyrrel Myburgh of Joostenberg and Perdeberg Winery. Production of their modern, fruity wines now tops 100 000 cases and includes exports to 12 countries plus local distribution.

MAN Vintners range

Pinotage ☺ ★★★ **06** pronounced oak vanilla aromas, lifted by honeysuckle from dash viognier & spice from dollop shiraz. Morello cherry & damson structured by tannins, savoury finish. 10 mths Am oak.

Cabernet Sauvignon ✓ ★★★★ Approachable **06** with modestly serious intentions. Splashes shiraz & merlot add juicy plumpness to blackcurrant & spice, balanced by supple tannins. 20% small Am oak. **Shiraz** ✓ ★★★★ Youthful **06** distinctively shiraz - red fruit, black pepper mingle with vanilla from 10 mths Am oak. Grippy, ripe tannins add seriousness to spicy, vibrant fruit; drinking well now. **Chardonnay** ★★★ **06** winter melon, honeysuckle well-fused with buttery aromas, rich stonefruit flavours balanced by crisp acidity. Light oak & lees contact add complexity. Finishes slightly warm (14% alc). **Chenin Blanc** ✓ ★★★★ Abundant pineapple tropicality with hints of marzipan on **07**. Concentrated baked apple flavours from old bushvines & lees contact, tingly green-apple finish. **Sauvignon Blanc** ★★★★ Herbaceous zing & tropical note in engaging **07**, blend of cool Dbnville & Pdberg fruit. Rich, concentrated, but checked by enticingly crisp acidity. Moderate 12.5% alc. All screwcapped.

Sénga range
Discontinued: **Shiraz**, **Merlot-Cabernet Sauvignon**. *— IM*

▪ **Marais Viljoen** *see Drakensig Wines*

■ *Marcel de Reuck* see Crows Nest

Marianne Estate

T 021-875-5040/5672 ▪ F 021-875-5036

Paarl ▪ Est/1stB 2004 ▪ Tasting & sales Mon-Fri 9-4.30 Sat 9-1 ▪ Fee R10 ▪ Closed Easter Fri, Dec 25 & Jan 1 ▪ Tours by appt ▪ Four-star B&B guest apartments (see Stay-over section) ▪ Olivello Restaurant (see Eat-out section) ▪ Owner Dauriac family ▪ Winemaker Laure Ininger, with Stephan du Toit ▪ Viticulturist André van den Berg (Jan 2004) ▪ 17ha (cab, merlot, pinotage, shiraz, sauv) ▪ 86t 90% red 10% white ▪ PO Box 7300 Stellenbosch 7599 ▪ info@ mariannewinefarm.co.za ▪ www.mariannewinefarm.co.za

A year on, and the Dauriacs are cross-pollinating: 30kg of grapes to a lug as on their farms in Bordeaux, a day's wait in the cold room, sorting by bunches then by berries. French staff too: marketing man Franck Malassigne arrived on the estate at the beginning of last year, and winemaker Laure Ininger is another newcomer. Like farm manager André van den Berg and assistant winemaker Stefan du Toit (ex-L'Avenir), they spend part of the year in Paarl and part in Bordeaux.

Cabernet Sauvignon ★★★ **05** sweet black berries, vanilla fragrance; reasonable concentration, robust dry tannins. Oak fermented. Like all these reds, massive alc (15.5%). **Merlot** ★★★ MIWA gold winning **05**, nearly porty mulberry & plum notes lifted by new oak (20%). **Pinotage** ★★★ **05** echoes old-style **04**. Agreeable red fruit juiciness diminished by rustic tannins & glowing alc. Used oak, 18 mths. **Shiraz** ★★★★ Forceful Aussie-style **05**, gd supple texture, moderate grip but spicy concentration truncated by whopping 16% alc. 100% new Fr oak, 18 mths. **Desirade** ★★★★ Merlot-led blend (81%) with cab, better balanced, able to handle substantial alc. Silky, fleshy sweet plum filling & fine grip. Oak fermented, 20% new. **Floreal** ★★★ **05** merlot, cab, shiraz trio. Very ripe, dense & extracted. 16% alc. Oak fermented. **Sauvignon Blanc** ★★★ **06** atypically quiet aromas/flavours; weighty, powerful, just balanced by some mineral notes. WO Coastal. All but Sauvignon NE.—*AL*

■ *Marimba* see Wines of Cape Town

Marklew Family Wines

T 021-884-4412 ▪ F 021-884-4412

Stellenbosch ▪ 1stB 2003 ▪ Visits by appt ▪ Tour groups (max 20) ▪ Pvt/business functions for small groups ▪ Walks ▪ Mountain biking ▪ Conservation area ▪ Owner Marklew family (Edward Dudley, Edward William, Lyn & Haidee) ▪ Winemaker Duan Brits, with Haidee Marklew Higgs (both Jan 2003) ▪ Viticulturist Billy Marklew & Duan Brits (Jun 2001/Jan 2003), advised by Cobus van Graan ▪ 45ha (cabs/f, merlot, pinotage, shiraz, chard, sauvignon) ▪ ±300t/2 700cs own label 70% red 30% white ▪ PO Box 17 Elsenburg 7607 ▪ wine@marklew.co.za ▪ www. marklew.co.za

Personable siblings Billy and Haidee Marklew made a good start to the world of international wine competitions last year, winning a gold medal at their very first attempt. With only a small percentage of the farm's production under own label, 'we make as much wine as we can afford to put into the best barrels,' says Haidee. Both Marklews celebrated personal milestones in the last year – she married local celebrity chef David Higgs and he tied the knot with Georgia Percy.

★★★★ **Capensis Reserve** Cab-led blend with splash pinotage. This, other **05** reds, unready for tasting; to be released later this yr. **04** (★★★★) showed assertive tannins softened by sweet cassis/mint flavours & generous new oak (18 mths).
Cabernet Sauvignon ★★★★ Last-tasted **04** had bit more heft than **03** (★★★★), though both showed the understated power typical of Simonsberg vyds. Yr Fr/Am oak, 40% new. **Merlot** ★★★★ **04** last ed was well structured, powerful yet elegant, with fresh plum & dark choc flavours. Third new barrels, Fr/Am. **Chardonnay** ★★★☆ **06** modern & bright but not too showy. Well-judged Fr oak (15% new) gives hazelnut hint, allows ripe, creamy lime flavours to come to the fore. All above WO Smnsberg-Sbosch.—*AL*

■ **Martins Red** *see Major's Hill Estate*

Maske Wines
T 021-873-3407 ▪ F 021-873-3408

Wellington (see Paarl map) ▪ Est 1987 ▪ 1stB 2000 ▪ Tasting & sales by appt ▪ Owner Erich Maske ▪ Winemaker Hein Hesebeck (2004, consultant) ▪ Viticulturist Erich Maske, advised by Hein Hesebeck ▪ 5ha (cab, merlot, chenin) ▪ 10-15t/500cs ▪ PO Box 206 Wellington 7654 ▪ maske@iafrica.com

'The Maskes are still feeling their way into the industry,' laughs Janine M. But she hopes to take things to new heights as soon as she has finished her D.Litt in Afrikaans & Netherlands. A special wine made from their 53-year-old chenin vineyard is still on the cards; this year's bottling is an easy-drinking trial run.

Merlot ★★★ Dry & firm, but gd spicy, plummy fruit; **05** just needs bit of time to fill out. 18 mths 1st-fill Rum oak. **Chenin Blanc** NEW ★ Individually styled **07**, nutty, earthy notes, honeyed doughy flavours. —*JP*

■ **Mason's Hill** *see The Mason's Winery*
■ **Matuba** *see Cape Coastal Vintners*

Matzikama Organic Cellar
T 082-801-3737

Olifants River ▪ Est 1999 ▪ 1stB 2001 ▪ Closed to public ▪ Owner/winemaker/viticulturist Klaas Coetzee ▪ 4ha (shiraz) ▪ 180cs 100% red ▪ PO Box 440 Vredendal 8160 ▪ info@matzikamawyn.co.za ▪ www.matzikamawyn.co.za

Newly appointed Swartland Winery viticulturist, Klaas Coetzee, still finds time to produce limited quantities of organic wine; but last year he wasn't satisfied with the quality of the shiraz, so the 07 barrels (all two of them) instead are filled with cab.

McGregor Wines
T 023-625-1741/1109 ▪ F 023-625-1829

McGregor (see Robertson map) ▪ Est 1948 ▪ 1stB 1978 ▪ Tasting & sales Mon-Fri 8-5 Sat 10-3 ▪ Closed Easter Fri, Ascension Day, Dec 25 & Jan 1 ▪ Owner 42 members ▪ Winemaker André Scriven (Dec 2005) ▪ Viticulturist Jaco Lategan ▪ 780ha ▪ 11 000t 25% red 75% white ▪ PO Box 519 McGregor 6708 ▪ marketing@mcgregorwinery.co.za, mcg@intekom.co.za ▪ www.mcgregorwinery.co.za

Awards aplenty have been coming McGregor's way, from numerous Best Value medals to National Terroir and Young Wine Show class winners, endorsing a solid reputation as a producer of affordable quality wine. New manager Adam Hobson and his team are now looking north and east, taking their message to Russia, Japan and China. '

Winemaker's Reserve range
Cabernet Sauvignon ★★★ **04** lighter but more serious than **03**. Combo mint/cassis laden fruit & gd dry tannins show potential. 14 mths oak. **Chardonnay** In abeyance. Discontinued: **Sauvignon Blanc**.

McGregor range

Pinotage ☺ ★★★ **06** (sample) perfumed, cherry-packed, savoury mouthful with well-integrated soft, spicy tannins (6-8 mths oak). **Colombard** ☺ ★★★ Light-bodied **07**, guavaroll & apples as foretaste of fresh, mouthwatering finish.

Ruby Cabernet ★★★ Soft & appealing **06**, preview shows juicy quaffer with grassy finish. **After Five Ruby Cabernet NV** not tasted. **Shiraz** ★★★ Sample **05** lean & savoury with sweet plum core. 5 mths oak, could use yr/2 to settle. **Cabernet Sauvignon-Merlot** ★★ Previewed **06** touch hard but serious, gd backbone. Allow time to settle. **Chardonnay** ★★★ **07** (ex-tank) flavoursome creamy mouthful uncluttered by oak. **Chenin Blanc** ★★ Dry & easy **07**, Granny Smith apple-toned glugger. Sample reviewed. **After Five Chenin Blanc NV** not tasted. **Sauvignon Blanc** ★★ Early-drinking **07**, citrus & candy flavours with dry but juicy finish. **Colombar-Chardonnay** ★★ **07** (sample) more peaches & cream breadth than cheerful, undemanding **06**. **Red Muscadel** ★★★ Elegant treacle & strawberry-laced **07** sipper. Turkish Delight & Asian spice add complexity. **White Muscadel** ★★★ Ripe litchis & sultana lining a juicy palate. **07** lighter than pvs but nicer. **Cape Ruby** ★★★ Port-style fortified from ruby cab. **06** (sample) lovely herbaceous tones, fleshy christmas cake core, fine tannins. Discontinued: **Merlot**, **Late Harvest Bouquet**. — *RP*

MC Square
T *083-303-5467* ▪ **F** *021-852-7740*

Somerset West ▪ Est/1stB 1996 ▪ Closed to public ▪ Winemaker/viticulturist Jean-Luc Sweerts ▪ 300 cs 100% white ▪ PO Box 436 Somerset West 7129 ▪ mcsquare@iafrica.com

Jean-Luc Sweerts has been consulting for the last year in KwaZulu-Natal fine-tuning a project in that province's emerging wine areas started nearly 10 years ago. His MC Red Square and a Cap Classique are both waiting for release, but when is another story. 'Maturation is the key to the development of finesse, so time will decide.'

★★★★ **Cuvée Chardonnay** Subtitle - 'Méthode Classique' - sets tone for last-tasted **01** & pvs; full, rich, citrus-fruited with attractive toasty hints. Yr Fr oak, 20% new. — *CR*

■ **Meander** see Groot Eiland Winery

Meerendal Estate
T *021-975-1655* ▪ **F** *021-975-1657*

Durbanville ▪ Est 1702 ▪ 1stB 1969 ▪ Tasting & sales daily 8-5 ▪ Fee R10 per person, refunded on purchase of 6 btls ▪ Closed Easter Fri & Dec 25 ▪ Restaurant, bistro, deli & function venue (see Eat-out section) ▪ Owner HN Coertze, AF Swanepoel ▪ Cellarmaster Liza Goodwin (Apr 2006) ▪ Viticulturist Kevin Watt (Jul 2005, consultant) ▪ 100ha (cab, merlot, pinotage, shiraz, chard, chenin, sauv) ▪ 650t/25 000cs 80% red 20% white ▪ Private Bag X1702 Durbanville 7551 ▪ info@meerendal.co.za ▪ www.meerendal.co.za

Links were woven last year to Meerendal's historic past. Liza Goodwin stepped into cellarmaster Karl Lambour's boots, thus becoming the sole current female winemaker in the Durbanville Valley but not the first: Maria Stans, wife of Meerendal's founding farmer, managed a 60 000-vine spread, as well as the cellar, after her husband died in 1712. And 2007 saw the launch, 305 years to the day after the granting of land to the first owner, of three flagship wines, among them the Heritage Block Pinotage 05, from 50-year-old bushvines.

Prestige range NEW
★★★★☆ **Heritage Block Pinotage** Concentrated spicy fruit on **05** from 60 yr old, low-yielding bushvines (Cape's oldest registered pinotage). Seriously styled, should integrate oak (all new) & develop complexity over next decade.
Bin159 Shiraz ★★★★ Blockbuster **05** (15% alc), ripe black fruit & earthy mint undertones but sweetish all-new oak overwhelms rather hot finish. **Bin 242 Sauvignon Blanc** ★★★☆ Replaces 'Reserve'. Interesting **06** has heaps of tropical flavours & touch of oak. Extended lees contact gives smooth softness. NE.

Meerendal range
★★★★ **Chenin Blanc** NEW **06** half fermented in tank, half in 2nd fill oak, giving room for pure fruit expresion in flavours of orange blossom, tropical fruit, green tea. Full bodied, gd concentration, but finishes slightly hot.
Cabernet Sauvignon ★★★★ Last tasted **04** with lavish blackberry flavours, vigorous dry tannins. Some new oak. **Merlot** NEW ★★★★ Focused raspberry/plum on **05** (★★★★) has better expression of freshness than bemedalled blockbuster **04**. Tobacco-infused, restrained & elegant palate with flesh to absorb 40% new oak. **Pinotage** ★★★★ Lightly oaked **04** (not retasted) generous & fresh, with balanced tannic grip. **Shiraz** ★★ **04** porty, overripe aromas; simple sweetish palate. **Cabernet Sauvignon-Merlot** In abeyance. **Chardonnay** NEW ★★★★ Baked apple & some complicating brown spice on **06**; opulent fruit copes with 14.5%

alc. Half fermented in new oak. **Sauvignon Blanc** NEW ★★★ Sample **07** with green fig/tropical flavours - powerful but a bit rustic. **Natural Sweet** NEW ★★★★ Jump from **02** (★★★) gewurz to **06** (TWS gold) from chenin. Delicate honey, with dried pineapple, apricot flavours complicated by clove on finish. 170g/l RS beautifully balanced by big, cleansing acid, low 10% alc. Fermented in older oak. Discontinued: **Sauvignon Blanc Single Vineyard Reserve**. —JPf

Meerhof Winery

T 022-487-2524 ▪ F 0866-838-132

Swartland ▪ Est/1stB 2000 ▪ Tasting & sales Mon-Fri 8.30-4.30 Sat & pub hols 10-2 ▪ Closed Easter Fri-Mon, Dec 25, 31 & Jan 1 ▪ Sunday lunch by appt (T 022-482-2088); also BYO picnic ▪ Functions for up to 50 by appt ▪ Tours by appt ▪ Owner C Kotze, Kotze Steyn Family Trust & private investors ▪ Winemaker Rudi Wium 2006 ▪ Vineyard Manager Gert Borcherds & Gert Kotze ▪ ±65ha (cab, merlot, pinotage, shiraz, chard, chenin) ▪ ±200t 90% red 10% white ▪ PO Box 1229 Malmesbury 7299 ▪ meerhof@wcaccess.co.za ▪ www.meerhof.co.za

New winemaker Rudi Wium is brimming with fresh ideas and passionate about this growing Swartland cellar. Previously they bottled all their wine but now select only the very best. Rudi W says: 'Through new labels and packaging, we've created a feeling of boutique-style wines. And the 2007 vintage was a cracker!'

Meerhof Private Cellar range

★★★★ **Winemaker's Reserve Shiraz-Cabernet Sauvignon-Merlot** NEW **06** more elegant, less robust than stablemates, dry tannins not overdone. Way to go! 50/25/25 configuration, blended after ageing in new/used brls.

Cabernet Sauvignon ★★★ Rich, ripe **06** in cellar's distinctive chunky style, marred by hint of VA. 100% new Fr oak. Sample tasted, rating provisional, as for all new wines above, below. **Merlot** ★★★ From low-yielding dryland bushvines. **06** ripe mulberry, chunky fruit, ripe tannins, supportive older oak. **Pinotage** ★★☆ Returns to line-up with **07** after extended absence. 'Banged with wood to give mocha & dark choc flavours,' says winemaker. Nothing more to add! **Shiraz** ★★★★ Coffeebean, toast & smoked beef on **06**; full bodied & quite rich, ripe tannins; needs yr/2 to show best. Combo new/used Fr oak. **Winemaker's Reserve Syrah** ★★ No new wine. Last-tasted **03** was light & well-fruited, for early enjoyment. **Rosé** Not tasted. **Chardonnay** ★★ **07** lightly oaked, lightish body & feel. **Weisser Riesling** ★★☆ Last we tasted a sample of **05**, showing delicate flowers & spice, controlled sweetness. **06** sold out & no follow-up for review.

Rolling Hills range

Dry Red ★★ **NV**, in macho, meaty style, older oak aged. —IvH

■ **Meerland** *see Baarsma Wine Group*

Meerlust Estate

T 021-843-3587 ▪ F 021-843-3274

Stellenbosch ▪ Est 1693 ▪ 1stB 1975 ▪ Tasting & sales Mon-Fri 9-5 (9-4 May-Sep) Sat 10-2 ▪ Fee R20 ▪ Closed pub hols ▪ Owner Hannes Myburgh ▪ Cellarmaster Chris Williams (Jan 2004) ▪ Viticulturist Roelie Joubert, advised by Paul Wallace (both 2001) ▪ 110ha (cabs s/f, merlot, pinot, chard, petit v) ▪ 600t/±50 000cs 90% red 10% white ▪ PO Box 7121 Stellenbosch 7599 ▪ info@meerlust.co.za ▪ www.meerlust.co.za

'Climate change? Bring it on!' says Chris Williams. 'It's getting colder and wetter on the farm - making us optimistic about coaxing more finesse and balance from our long-ripening vines.' But, he adds, Meerlust is always working on sustainability - and a breeding pair of Fish Eagles approves, having taken up residence. 'We've also been joined by a pair of swans, the male of which is so aggressive the guard dogs have handed farm security over to the interloper!' Then there's Skip, the sheep dog with a taste for cab grapes, who will surely approve of Meerlust's first Cab release since 1993. Magnums of the 04, sporting William Kentridge's depiction of The Magic Flute, are dedicated to the memory of opera singer Deon van der Walt, a close friend of proprietor Hannes Myburgh.

★★★★☆ **Rubicon** One of SA's most famous & revered bdx-style reds. **03** captures vintage's charm & approachability; cab-led (69%) with merlot & cab f (19/12); also has legs to age. Fr oak, 80% new, 20 mths. Not re-assessed; **04** unready.

★★★★ **Red** Second label for Rubicon, when vintage doesn't permit flagship quality. Delicious & wallet-cordial, at less than half the price. To date 85, 90 & **02**.

★★★★☆ **Cabernet Sauvignon** Estate's original label in 75, now occasional release. **04**, first since **93**, a most impressive resurrection. Classic, tight, delicious crunchy cab fruit anchored by vibrant, ripe tannins, bone-dry. Polished in classy Fr oak, 80% new, 17 mths. Unheavy 14% alc.

★★★★ **Merlot 04** Chris W's debut red, TWS gold. Tighter, less youthfully accessible than some pvs, also more noticeable oak, but with lithe elegance, balance to age. Spiced with 10% cab; 60% new Fr oak.

★★★★ **Pinot Noir 03** gentler, more expressive than pvs. Dainty yet convincing pinot tones; full yet supple; tender tannins. 100% new Fr oak. No **02**.

★★★★ **Chardonnay** Since **04**, extra freshness & complexity from natural ferment portion. **06** still vigorous, tight; lime blossom & earthy mineral perfumes, rich, peachy flavours; classy development possibilities. Fr oak, 60% new. — *AL*

Meinert Wines
T 021-865-2363 • F 021-865-2414

Stellenbosch ▪ Est 1987 ▪ 1stB 1997 ▪ Tasting & sales by appt (see also Eat-out section) ▪ Owner/winemaker Martin Meinert ▪ Vineyard Manager Henk Marconi ▪ 13.5ha (cabs s/f, merlot, petit v, pinotage) ▪ 90t/6 500cs 100% red ▪ PO Box 7221 Stellenbosch 7599 ▪ info@ meinertwines.com ▪ www.meinert.co.za

Assistant winemaker Allison Adams left last year, leaving Martin Meinert working solo in the cellar and homebound, which suits him rather well. Hardly surprising: Martin has tied the knot with - of all ironies - someone who doesn't really like red wine (yet?). He's promised to make a sauvignon for his bride, but is taking his time, carefully sourcing grapes (the home-farm being strictly red wine territory) and experimenting in the cellar. 'It would be so embarrassing if I made something really awful in honour of the woman I love!' No doubt sauvignon lovers everywhere will rejoice in his betrothal promise.

★★★★☆ **Synchronicity** Sexy, modern blend; deeply fruited; simmers with tension as spiced vanilla berries held captive by fine-grained tannins (until at least 2010). **04** barrel-selected cab & merlot (60:30) plus perfect proportion pinotage for harmony. 2 yrs new Fr oak. As all in range, not retasted.

★★★★ **Devon Crest** Bdx red bears name of home-farm with confidence. **04** (★★★★☆) masterly display of power & elegance; a beauty. **03** restored form after lighter but still excellent **02**. Cool s-facing vyds 10-15 yrs old. 81/19 cab/merlot blend (pvs 69/31), 18 mths new Fr oak.

★★★★ **Merlot** Urbane table companion, laden with panache. **04** minty edge to sleek black & red berry fruit, plush, upholstered frame; understatement without austerity. Dash pinotage, cab. 18 mths used Fr oak. — *DS*

Mellasat
T 021-862-4525 • F 021-862-4525

Paarl ▪ Est 1996 ▪ 1stB 1999 ▪ Visits by appt, but encouraged ▪ Owner Stephen Richardson ▪ Winemaker Stephen Richardson, with Poena Malherbe ▪ Viticulturist Poena Malherbe ▪ 8ha (cab, pinotage, shiraz, tempranillo, chenin, chard) ▪ 50t/2 500cs 85% red 15% white ▪ PO Box 7169 Paarl 7623 ▪ mellasat@mweb.co.za ▪ www.mellasat.com

A 'surreal' experience tasting fine Bordeaux with his grandfather when he was 16 pushed Stephen Richardson towards a career in wine. 'We're continuing to build awareness of our flagship blend,' he says of the Mellasat M, 'a process starting in the vineyard and followed through in the cellar.'

Mellasat range

Shiraz ★★★☆ None ready for tasting. Last ed work-in-progress **02** showed improved tannin management. **Mellasat 'M'** ★★☆ Flagship blend shiraz (64%), pinotage & cab; **03** was oak-dominated when tasted mid-2006 but, avers SR, has now reached full potential. **04** not ready. **'White Pinotage'** NEW ★★★★ Blanc de noir-style **07** intriguing melange of floral, coconut, pineapple, white choc & vanilla spice. Juicy, with soft acidity; 85% new Am oak. **Tuin Wyn** ★★ From chenin grapes air-dried on racks under the oaks, barrel-fermented/aged 30 mths. Revisited **03** (sample last ed) honeyed, prominent coconut notes ex-100% Am oak, balanced sweet finish. Discontinued: **Cabernet Sauvignon**, **Pinotage**.

Dekker's Valley range

Revelation ☺ 🍷 ★★★ **05** combines shiraz, pinotage & cab (41/32/27) in fruity, characterful easy drinker. 22 mths 3rd & 4th fill Fr/Am oak.

Chenin Blanc 🍷 ★★ **07** upfront fruity nose, youthful easy drinking. — *JP*

🔲 **Merwespont Winery** *see Bonnievale Wine Cellar*
🔲 **Merwida** *see Riverstone Vineyards*

Metzer Wines

T 084-340-8278 • F 021-422-5238

Cape Town • Est/1stB 2004 • Tasting by appt • Owner/winemaker Wade Metzer • 5t/300cs 100% red • 3 Village Close, 17 Drama Str, Somerset West 7130 • metzerwines@gmail.com

Wade Metzer is a passionate advocate of pedestrianisation - particularly when trying to unload grapes at Cape Town's inner-city Signal Hill winery for his own-label wines. The latest vintage is from Swartland grapes which, he says, give lie to the belief that great wines only come from cooler or marginal areas.

★★★★ **The Kitchen Sink Syrah** Evocative & individual **05** last ed was burly but also amazingly fine, gentle; no ungainly hint of 15% alc. Hldrberg/Firgrove fruit natural yeasts, unfined/filtered. Older Fr oak, 15 mths. No **06**.

★★★★ **Syrah** NEW Swtland fruit imparts flavour richness to **06**; Metzer's hands-off approach (native ferment, unfined/-filtered) & sensitivity used oak (only Fr, 15 mths) give delicate & refined feel, despite ripe 14.5% alc. Gd few yrs potential.— *AL*

M'hudi Wines

T 021-865-2002/3 • F 021-865-2314

Est/1stB 2003 • Visits as for Villiera (see entry) • Owner Rangaka family • Cellarmaster Jeff Grier • Winemaker Jeff Grier & Anton Smal, with Tseliso Rangaka (all 2004) • Viticulturist Simon Grier (2004) • 3 000cs 33% red 67% white • PO Box 66 Koelenhof 7605 • wine@villiera.com • www.villiera.com

The name of this family winery means 'harvester' in Setswana, and the Rangakas are hard at the appropriate work, with the assistance of the team from neighbouring Villiera. Son Tseliso R is fast learning the skills of vine and barrel, having ditched the advertising world in Johannesburg for this more earthy endeavour. Lebogang, his sister, has now joined the wine marketing fray in Gauteng.

Merlot NEW ★★★ From Elim, **05** shows red berries, dusting of white pepper from fine-grained tannins; harmony & tasty drinkability fully achieved. **Pinotage** ★★★ Extrovert **05** abounds with dark plums, vanilla spicing, without sacrificing palate appeal: juicy, smoothly rounded, gregarious. **Chenin Blanc** ★★★★ Pvsly tasted as sample, **05** since evolved into luscious, waxy, tropical, golden-hued beauty. Drinking well, should hold for yr/2. **Sauvignon Blanc** ★★★ Elgin/Sbsch fruit in **07**, hence leafy, mineral tones. Light textured, perfect summertime fare. — *CR*

🔲 **Mia Bella** *see African Roots Wine Brands*
🔲 **Mia Cara Wines** *see African Roots Wine Brands*

■ *Michelangelo Wine Company* see Vrede Wine Farm

Micu Narunsky Wines
T 021-713-3163

Cape Town ▪ Est 2005 ▪ 1stB 2006 ▪ Closed to public ▪ Owner/winemaker Micu Narunsky ▪ ±120cs 80% red 15% white 5% rosé ▪ PO Box 30994 Tokai 7966 ▪ nmicu@hotmail.com

Jazz pianist Micu Narunsky's predilection for Portuguese varieties has led to a new red blend, Iemanjá, named after an ancient African sea goddess whose influence was transplanted, in the cruel diaspora of slavery, to various American countries including Brazil. 'Brazil and South Africa were both discovered by Portuguese, and this name links Africa, Portugal and my passion for Brazilian music and culture.' Also novel is a dry, barrel-fermented muscat de Frontignan, from old vines in Paarl.

Tinta Barocca NEW ★★ **06** light & fruity, wild shrub & spice notes, appealing tartness. Enjoy chilled. **Touriga Nacional-Tinta Barocca** ★★★ Rare pairing of Portuguese varieties in (unfortified) dry red. **06** lighter than pvs, tart entry follows through to redcurrant finish. **Iemanjá** NEW ★★★★ Brooding dark-fruited blend touriga, tintas b & r plus souzão. **06** gd ripeness, showing some spice; lively palate & refreshing acidity. ±11 mths Fr oak for all the reds. **La Complicité** NEW ★★★ Easy, fruity, light & dry **06**, from white muscat de F, unfortified; approachable, upfront muscat nose, gd purity of fruit & soft entry. *— JP*

■ *Middagkrans* see Bo La Motte

Middelvlei Estate
T 021-883-2565 ▪ F 021-883-9546

Stellenbosch ▪ Est 1919 ▪ 1stB 1973 ▪ Tasting & sales Mon-Sat 10-4.30 ▪ Fee R15 ▪ Closed Easter Fri & Dec 25 ▪ Combo cellar tour/barrel tasting Mon-Fri 11 & 3 ▪ Small conference facility ▪ Walks ▪ Owner Momberg family ▪ Winemaker Tinnie Momberg (Jan 1992) ▪ Viticulturist Ben Momberg (Jan 1992) ▪ 130 ha (cab, merlot, pinotage, shiraz, tinta, chard, sauv) ▪ 1 000t/ 35 000cs own labels 95% red 5% white ▪ Export brand: Hagelsberg ▪ PO Box 66 Stellenbosch 7599 ▪ info@middelvlei.co.za ▪ www.middelvlei.co.za

Refreshingly traditional, Middelvlei's approach remains true to the family identity: Their new premium blend carries the Momberg name and The Red Falcon (also newly launched) refers to the family crest. The restaurant opening suffered delays but a Michelangelo silver and three golds (including one for the Middelvlei Momberg) kept spirits high.

★★★★ **Shiraz** Worth seeking out. **04** tasted last ed had signature earth-after-rain & white pepper notes; polished dark cherry & oak flavours. Yr 2nd fill oak, 80% Fr.

★★★★★ **Momberg** NEW **04** impressive debut for full-flavoured blend pinotage, shiraz, merlot & cab (37/29/17/17). Enticing lily bouquet complements savoury, balanced palate, fine tannins (17 mths oaked, 100% new, 50% Am). Worth keeping ±5 yrs. EW.

Cabernet Sauvignon ★★★★ Intense bacon-seasoned cassis & appealing vanilla notes the hallmarks of quietly satisfying **05**. Yr Fr oak. EW. **Pinotage** ★★★★ **05** gentle & appealing, with fresh cherries, soft oak detail from 24 mths seasoned oak (mostly Fr, sprinkling Am). **Red Falcon** NEW ★★ **05** rather old-fashioned maiden. 60/40 merlot/shiraz, meaty & v ripe fruited, broad & soft, tad short. EW. **Pinotage-Merlot** ★★★★ Plenty of party fun in juicy **06**; slips down easily courtesy light oak touch (yr 2nd fill, 85% Fr). **Chardonnay** ★★★ Tasted pvs ed, **06** paired dried pear & spiced peach with well-judged oak flavours. *— CvZ*

Migliarina Wines
T 072-233-4138

Stellenbosch ▪ Est/1stB 2002 ▪ Closed to public ▪ Owner/winemaker Carsten Migliarina ▪ 500cs 100% red ▪ PO Box 673 Stellenbosch 7599 ▪ carsten@migliarina.co.za ▪ www. migliarina.co.za

With ten years as a sommelier and 12 seasons assisting on various vintages behind him, Carsten Migliarina finally felt qualified to start making his own wine in 2002. Preserving varietal and fruit character is the focus of his winemaking. Most of his output goes overseas, a small proportion into SA hotels and restaurants.

Shiraz ★★★ Well-structured, Old-World-style **05**, nice interplay between power & finesse; finishes with typical gamey/peppery notes. 40% new oak, 16 mths. WO W Cape. — *JPf*

■ Migration-Serengeti   *see Leidersburg Vineyards*

Mike's Kitchen
T 011-463-9269 • F 011-463-9300

Sandton • 298 Main Rd, Bryanston Ext 1, Sandton • fran@oldvines.co.za • www. mikeskitchen.co.za

Exclusive, easy-drinking range for the Gauteng-based restaurant chain, by Old Vines Cellars.

Reserve Red ★★★ Sample **05** combines shiraz & merlot (60/40), needs time for gruff tannins to meld with spicy, very ripe fruit. Staved, with small portion barrel-aged. **Stein Select** ★★★ Last bottling (**NV**) was from chenin, with butterscotch & bready aromas, appealing sweetish finish. **Classic White** ★★★★ Fresh, food-friendly **07**. Sauv dominates in glass (if not on paper - only 30%, plus chenin) with intense capsicum tone throughout. — *CvZ*

Miles Mossop Wines
T 082-413-4335 • F 021-808-5911

Stellenbosch • Est/1stB 2004 • Closed to public • Owner/winemaker Miles Mossop • 12t/ 900cs 67% red 33% white • PO Box 7339 Stellenbosch 7599 • miles@tokara.com

Tokara winemaker Miles Mossop is delighted about demand for his two own-label wines, named after daughter Saskia and son Max. 'I thought Saskia would be more difficult to sell because it's a fairly strange white blend, but it's flying off the shelves.' However, he was in a quandary as this edition went to press: 'My wife is pregnant again, so it looks like I have to make a third wine. The problem is, I can't expand because I'm already at maximum production!'

★★★★   **Max** Expressive, classically styled bdx blend. Pure, violet-perfumed **05**; ripe vinosity, savoury features & admirably fine tannin. Already harmonious but also ageworthy. Cab/merlot (56/24) with freshening 20% petit v. Natural ferment. Sbosch vyds. 20 mths Fr oak, 40% new.

★★★★   **Saskia** Classy new-wave chenin/viognier blend; 67/33 in seamless **06**. As pvs, powerful & sumptuous but lifted by freshening acid. Natural ferment adds further intrigue. Fr oak, 10 mths, 8% new. Sbosch & Pdberg fruit. — *AL*

■ 'Military' Wines   *see Domein Doornkraal*
■ Millberg   *see Franschhoek Vineyards*
■ Millbrook   *see Arlington Beverage Group*
■ Miller's Mile   *see Klein Parys Vineyards*
■ Millstone   *see Stettyn Winery*

Millstream

Range by DGB for export chiefly to the UK, Ireland and the Netherlands.

Pinotage ★★★ Previewed **05** earthy & herbal, bold savoury palate & choc nuance. **Cinsault-Ruby Cabernet** ▤ ★★★ Ripe berries & blossoms in pre-bottling **06**, 50/50 friendly, juicy seductress. **Rosé** ▤ ★★ Jolly quaffer with dusty strawberry nose & clean finish on **07**. **Chardonnay** ★★★ **07** perky summer wine with pretty floral honeyed notes. **Chenin Blanc** ▤ ★★★ Casual **07** with typical chenin tones of sun-warmed hay, some winter melon & pineapple. — *DB*

■ Milton Grove   *see African Terroir*

Minke Wines
T 083-273-4561

Stellenbosch • Closed to public • Owner Henry Davel • PO Box 693 Springs 1560

No grapes last year from Vriesenhof for Minke owner Henry Davel ('There was a miscommunication between me and Jan Coetzee!') so no 'virtual winemaking' for this Gauteng-based doctor. However, he'll be following his pinot recipe again this year, threatening to phone JC every day to ensure those grapes are delivered.

Pinot Noir ★★★★ Characterful & ageworthy **04** last ed opened in glass to classic pinot fragrance (earth/sour cherry), silky mocha, choc ebb & flow. Fine tannins give focus, grip. — *CvZ*

Miravel
T 072-212-4668 • F 021-842-2456

Stellenbosch (see Helderberg map) • Est 2002 • 1stB 2005 • Visits by appt • Self-catering Fynbos Cottage (see Stay-over section) • Owner Maarten van Beuningen • Winemaker Bartho Eksteen (sauv), Albert Bredell (cab) • Viticulturist Paul Wallace (Jun 2004, consultant) • 26ha (cab, merlot, petit v, pinotage, chenin, sauv) • 135t/525cs own label • PO Box 5144 Helderberg 7135 • miravel@adept.co.za • www.miravel.co.za

'Given that we're still starting out, it's an honour to get awards in two prestigious competitions,' says owner Maarten van Beuningen of Miravel's medal-winning Sauvignon and Cab. MvB, who's made the transition from Zimbabwean ostrich farmer to Cape wine grower, is busy rationalising the varieties in his vineyard.

Cabernet Sauvignon NEW **★★★★** Promising debut: **05** minted ripe berries, elegant balance with long-legged tannins, healthy but unintrusive 14.5% alc. 18 mths Fr oak, third new. **Merlot ★★★** Last-tasted **03** showed mulberry, herbal hints; choc flavours & robust tannins from 18 mths oak. **Sauvignon Blanc ★★★★** Freshly-mown lawn, wet gravel & pithy lees contribute to poised **06**'s appeal; only cavil is fairly brief farewell. — *CvZ*

Mischa Estate
T 021-864-1016/19/20 • F 021-864-2312

Wellington (see Paarl map) • Est/1stB 1999 • Tasting, sales & tours (vine nursery in winter & cellar in summer) by appt • Fee R250, waived if 6+ btls purchased • Closed pub hols • Snacks & meals by appt • Walks • Mountain biking • Owner JA & GH Barns • Cellarmaster Andrew Barns (Jan 1999) • Viticulturist Ruiter Smit (Jun 1960) • 40ha (cab, merlot, shiraz, sauv, viognier) • 97t/4,000cs own label 75% red & 25% white • PO Box 163 Wellington 7654 • info@ mischaestate.com • www.mischaestate.com

New at Mischa is the estate's first white blend, Eventide Classic White, an innovation in that it includes the still-rare variety nouvelle. A very small quantity was produced, mainly for sale from the farm. The Eventide Viognier and Sauvignon 06s both scored 90 points with Wine Enthusiast. New markets entered include Thailand, Sweden and Switzerland.

Mischa Estate range
★★★★ **Cabernet Sauvignon** Characteristic blueberry signature of poised Wllngtn cab, admirable elegance & balance to **04**, which carries 33% new oak & 14% alc with ease. Stunning **03** (★★★★★) geared up from pvs.
★★★★ **Shiraz 04** lowers the alc power (to 14%), ups the subtlety without forfeiting generous spicy red fruit or scented pepper attractions. Pvs ed we noted ripe & supple tannin, sleek texture & long chalky finish. Yr Fr oak.
Merlot ★★★★ Refreshing **04** shows racy edge to dark berry fruits, soft tannins in measured length. Minerally, with hints of olive. 33% new casks. 13% alc.

Eventide range
Cabernet Sauvignon ★★★ Very brambly fruit intensity of **05** offset by 'hot' alc finish. **03** (★★★★) a 'lunchtime cab' with more moderate 13.5% alc. Third new casks. **04** flew the coop before review. **Merlot ★★★** Pvs ed detailed sour cherry flavours & racy freshness of light **03**. Just 12.6% alc. Sold out **04** untasted. NE. **Shiraz ★★★★** 'Syrah' last ed. **06** leather & spice notes, red berry fruit within mid-weight, slightly chunky mouthful. Refreshing despite 14% alc. Yr oak, third new. **04, 05** untasted. NE. **Sauvignon Blanc** 📖 **★★★★** Zesty green edge to tropical **07**, touch oily. **06** (★★★★) herbaceous aromas, lemon barley tones; bright acidity

with hints of minerality. NE. **Viognier** 📖 ★★★★ Caresses with ethereal delicacy: lovely orange blossom, dried peach & rosepetal notes to demure **07**, gentle 12% alc. 75% fermented in seasoned oak. NE. *— DS*

■ Misty Point *see Ladismith Cellar*

Mitre's Edge
T 021-875-5960 ▪ F 021-875-5965

Paarl (see Stellenbosch map) ▪ Est 1999 ▪ 1stB 2004 ▪ Visits Mon-Fri 9-5 or by appt; pub hols by appt ▪ Small tasting fee, refunded on purchase ▪ Farm-grown olive oil ▪ Owner Bernard & Lola Nicholls ▪ Winemaker Lola Nicholls (2004), with Bernard Nicholls (Feb 2006) & Alexander Milner (Feb 2007) ▪ Viticulturist Paul Wallace (1999, consultant) & Francois Roux (2007) ▪ 18ha (cabs s/f, malbec, merlot, petit v, shiraz) ▪ 95% red 5% rosé ▪ PO Box 12290 Die Boord 7613 ▪ info@mitres-edge.co.za ▪ www.mitres-edge.co.za

Mitre's Edge, previously owned by Lola Nicholls' father, is named after the cleft profile of Klapmuts Hill rising above the property. The Nicholls replanted the entire farm in 1999, and 2007 saw the first release from the revamped vineyards. In the winery, neighbour Alexander Milner supplements Lola N's six years' experience at round-the-corner Warwick.

Mitre's Edge range [NEW]
Shiraz ★★★ Bright peppery fruit, notes of raspberry & wild scrub on **04**, elegant light tannins, unshowy, with appealing savoury finish.

Fynbos range [NEW]
Shiraz ★★ Sherbet & black cherry whiffs, real fruit-bomb flavours, soft, uncomplicated finish on **04**. **Rosé** ★★ Coppery pink, gamey & grapey aromas, **06** dryish, with bold 15.4% alc. *— MF*

MolenVliet Wine & Guest Estate
T 021-885-1597 ▪ F 021-885-1684

Stellenbosch ▪ 1stB 2005 ▪ Tasting & sales by appt ▪ Luxury B&B/self-caterging accommodation ▪ Conferences, private parties/receptions, corporate functions for up to 30 ▪ Owner Ockie & Susan Oosthuizen ▪ Winemaker Ettiene Malan ▪ Viticulturist Wynand Pienaar ▪ 7.5ha (cab, merlot, shiraz) ▪ 28t/1 500cs 100% red ▪ PO Box 6288 Uniedal 7612 ▪ elize@molenvliet.co.za ▪ www.molenvliet.co.za

Etienne Malan has some big shoes to fill, the first wines here having been made by Miles Mossop, winemaker at neighbouring Tokara. But MolenVliet's location in the Banhoek Valley is precisely why owner Ockie Oosthuizen is confident he'll succeed: 'This area is known for some of the best red wines in SA.'

Proprietors Choice ★★★ Plum & mulberry notes, fresh herbal hints, **05** savoury flavours with slightly leafy tannins. Oak (30%) well managed. *— MF*

Monis Wines
T 021-860-1601 ▪ F 021-872-2790

Paarl ▪ Est 1906 ▪ Closed to public ▪ Owner Distell ▪ Winemaker Dirkie Christowitz (Aug 1979) ▪ 22 000 cs 100% fortifieds ▪ PO Box 266 Paarl 7620 ▪ dchristowitz@distell.co.za ▪ www.distell.co.za

These long-aged muscadels and ports continue to win favour with competition consumers and judges alike, as demonstrated recently when the Vintage Muscadel clinched a gold medal at the 2007 Muscats du Monde international competition in France. Another plume in the well-feathered cap of Dirkie Christowitz, who next year celebrates a remarkable three decades as winemaker at the Cape's original fortified-wine house.

★★★★★ **Vintage Muscadel** Acclaimed **00** continues path trodden by exalted forebears. Amber glints, inviting scents of raisined fruit, toffee, coffee & mulled-wine spices, followed by languid, silky flavours. Shd improve, hold, decade+.

★★★★ **Tawny Port** Competition hero (Veritas, Peter Schultz, TWS et al). Among handful of dated tawnies in SA. Gorgeous 96 sweeter than pvs, also longer in oak (109g/l RS; ±8 yrs, Fr). Paarlberg tinta & cinsaut. Only 1500 cs made. Neither this, Muscadel, revisited. — *MW*

Mons Ruber Estate

T 044-251-6550 • F 044-251-6550

Klein Karoo ▪ Est ca 1850 ▪ Tasting & sales Mon-Fri 9-5 Sat 9-1 ▪ Closed Easter Sun & Dec 25 ▪ Self-catering overnight accommodation ▪ Estate produce for sale ▪ Hiking trail in proclaimed conservation area ▪ Owner Radé & Erhard Meyer ▪ Winemaker Radé Meyer ▪ Viticulturist Johannes Mellet (consultant) ▪ 38 ha (cab, muscadels r/w, chard, chenin, hanepoot, palomino) ▪ ±500t/10 000cs own label 50% red 50% white ▪ PO Box 1585 Oudtshoorn 6620 ▪ monsruber@lantic.net ▪ www.geocities.com/monsr_za

'A treasure that shouldn't be allowed to go to waste,' is how the Meyer brothers view muscadel, which explains their recent decision to replant a vineyard with the variety. They're on the new R62 Brandy Route, providing increased exposure for their estate brandies, created in a wood-fired potstill dating from 1936. About to be bottled at press time was a 7 Year Old, distilled from sultana and, yes, muscadel.

Conari ★★★ 05 easy-drinking unoaked cab with cheery plum & berry notes, friendly 13% alc. As for entire range, not retasted. **Chardonnay ★★** 06 (sample) full of melon & honey aromas/ flavours; modest 12.4% alc. **Vino ★★** NV from chard, last time showed bottle-age honey & peach notes. **Regalis ★★★** Current bottling (**NV, 03**) of fortified white muscadel sweeter, more syrupy than stablemates, with caramel & tealeaf nuances. **Cabernet Sauvignon Jerepigo ★★★** Aka Elegantia. 06 succulent sweetness, mouthcoating prune & tealeaf flavours, irresistible. **Red Muscadel Jerepigo ★★★** In abeyance. **Hanepoot Jerepigo ★★★** 04 ripe & grapey, with harmonious acid & spirit. Also labelled Bonitas. **Sultana Jerepigo ★★** 99 nutty character infused with hints honey & anise, silky & proudly sweet. **White Muscadel Jerepigo ★★★** Flavour-packed fortified dessert with pretty floral notes accompanying citrus peel/sultana richness. 06 sweet & full bodied, & really delicious. **Port ★★★** Gentle tawny-style NV, drier than most Cape ports; from cab. Mature looking russet-ruby, stewed fruit & mocha hints. Discontinued: **Cabernet Sauvignon, Muscadel Liqueur**. — *CR*

Montagu Wine Cellar

T 023-614-1125 • F 023-614-1793

Klein Karoo ▪ Est 1941 ▪ 1stB 1975 ▪ Tasting & sales Mon-Fri 8-5 Sat 9-12 ▪ Closed pub hols ▪ Tours during harvest by appt (call Marguerite van der Merwe) ▪ BYO picnic ▪ Owner 68 members ▪ Winemaker Eben Rademeyer, with Collin Wright (2006/1990) ▪ Viticulturist Johannes Mellet (consultant) ▪ 660ha (11 varieties r/w) ▪ 12 500t/5 500cs own label ▪ 12% red 82% white 6% muscadel ▪ PO Box 29 Montagu 6720 ▪ manager@montaguwines.co.za ▪ www. montaguwines.co.za

Modernising and changing consumer perceptions about this grower-owned winery remain a focus, hence the new website and planned additions to the Reserve range. (A second debut for their Hanepoot, long in abeyance, suggests they're not abandoning their traditional market.) It's a slow but sure shift, says winemaker/marketer Eben Rademeyer, revelling in 'folk who walk in for two bottles today, and tomorrow are back for six'.

Cabernet Sauvignon-Shiraz Reserve ★ Spicy intro to uncomplicated dry red 06. **Merlot-Ruby Cabernet ★** Unwooded 06 offers lean & tangy flavours. **Mont Rouge** Not ready. **Mont Rosé** Not tasted. **Chardonnay** Only bottled in exceptional years. **Chenin Blanc ★** Early-picked 07 light on fruit & in body. **Colombard ★** Off-dry 07 fruity easy-drinker. **Mont Blanc** Not tasted. **Vin Doux Sparking Wine** Sweet grapey bubbly, new (**NV**) bottling not ready. Pvs were lively, with muscat notes. **Late Harvest ★** From colombard; 07 with zippy grassy nose, less lively sweet palate. **Hanepoot ★★** Work-in-progress on first hanepoot release in years. 07 v pale colour belies forthcoming aroma & rich raisin palate, prominent alc. **Red Muscadel ★★★** 'Cellar's flagship & must for any wine lover,' says ER. 06 candyfloss & strawberry with spirity lift; red cherry adds interest on elegant finish. Try lightly chilled. **NV. White Muscadel ★★★** 07 gentle honey & white peach notes, raisined flavours on full, lush palate,; gd spiritous conclusion. — *JP*

Mont Destin

T *021-875-5870* ▪ **F** *021-875-5870*

Paarl ▪ Est/1stB 1998 ▪ Visits by appt ▪ Owner Ernest & Samantha Bürgin ▪ Winemaker Samantha Bürgin, advised by Bruwer Raats (Jan 2003) ▪ Viticulturist Bertus de Clerk since 2006 ▪ 7ha (cab, cinsaut, grenache, mourvèdre, shiraz, viognier) ▪ 15t/1 000cs 80% red 20% white ▪ PO Box 1237 Stellenbosch 7599 ▪ info@montdestin.co.za ▪ www.montdestin.co.za

The TLC lavished on the family, the wines, labels and facilities have borne bountiful fruit. The wines have won awards, and the new afro-chic tasting room now features happy silhouettes of young von Destin, bold springbok hides and a 210-bottle chandelier.

★★★★ **Passioné** Pvsly '1482'. Seamless & stylish blend cab, shiraz, merlot 57/33/10, 50% new oak. **05** seductive black berry/cherry flavours backed by fine, caressing tannins.

The Pink Door Rosé NEW ☺ ★★★ **07** fully kitted out in pink: pink fruit pastille aromas with light berry flavours to match, includes startling pink stopper!

Destiny Shiraz ★★★★ Strikingly packaged, handmade limited release. Gutsy **03** last ed noted as artisanal & personality packed. 20 mths new Fr/Am oak. Relatively plentiful 800 btls. **02** (★★★/) but Wine (★★★★). **The Pink Door Cabernet Sauvignon-Shiraz** NEW ★★★ Attractive **05** a serious addition to range; dark brooding berry & prune aromas matched by firm dusty tannic grip. Future vintages to carry Red Stiletto label. **Chenin Blanc** ★★★ **06** less beguiling than pvs, still ample charms though at 14.5% alc, with pineapple & mineral signature. — *IvH*

▪ Mont d'Or *see Makro*

Mont du Bleu

T *0861-11-11-50* ▪ **F** *021-880-0152*

Stellenbosch ▪ Est 2005 ▪ Closed to public ▪ Owner Chilled 24/7 (Pty) Ltd ▪ Winemaker Wine sourcing Johann Strauss ▪ 500 000litres own label 30% red 70% white ▪ PO Box 12429 Die Boord 7613 ▪ chilled247@yebo.co.za ▪ www.montdubleu.co.za

Johann Strauss and Rian Kerkhoff are doing their bit for chenin. Having launched an innovative wine dispensing system serving Spur outlets, other restaurant franchises and casinos, he reports chenin sales of 170 800 litres or 2340 glasses a day! The system, now able to link electronically to point-of-sale, is moving into Africa as well as the UK and Australia. The range is now also available in bottled form.

Dry Rosé ☺ ★★★ **06** from shiraz, liquidised strawberry flavours, lip-smacking fruitiness, structured for light-hearted quaffing.

Cabernet-Sauvignon-Merlot ★★★ **04** last ed pleasantly plump with loads of prune fruit, low tannins, generous 14.2% alc. 50/40 blend, smidgen cab f. **Rosé Semi Sweet** ★★ **06** from shiraz. Ripe berry fruit intro, fruitgum sweetness, simplicity. **Chenin Blanc** ★★★ Refreshing, lively **07** (preview), dry quaffer with marzipan & boiled sweets nose & flavours. **Colombard Natural Sweet** ★★ Gently sweet, friendly & low-alc (11%) **07**, sherbet & floral notes. W Cape WOs for all. — *CR*

Mont du Toit Kelder

T *021-873-7745* ▪ **F** *021-864-2737*

Wellington (see Paarl map) ▪ Est 1996 ▪ 1stB 1998 ▪ Tasting & sales by appt ▪ Owner Stephan du Toit ▪ Winemaker/viticulturist Pieter-Niel Rossouw (Jan 2000), advised by Bernd Philippi (1997) ▪ 26 ha (alicante bouschet, cabs s/f, merlot, petit v, tintas b & r(a), shiraz & mourvèdre) ▪ ±130t/±10 000cs 100% red ▪ PO Box 704 Wellington 7654 ▪ kelder@montdutoit.co.za ▪ www.montdutoit.co.za

They've completed their tenth harvest, and winemaker Pieter-Niel Rossouw and the team are moving steadily towards a more organic approach, with ducks and specially-bred wasps helping with pest control. Grenache has now been added to their palette to join the young tinta barocca, while the older cab vines continue to satisfy.

★★★★ **Mont du Toit** Blend varies, usually cab, merlot, shiraz, cab f. Plush black velvet texture on last tasted **03**, evidencing cab in big-boned, warm-climate mode; balanced tannic grip, shd unfold with ease. 2 yrs oak (⅙plusmn;30% new) imparted loads of spice. Deserved 4-6 yr wait.

★★★★☆ **Le Sommet** Ambitious blend (composition secret). **03** last ed not fully accessible, less presence than magisterial **02** but still dignified, controlled. Concentrated mulberry fruit, notes of roast beef, oak char; very dry, verging on austere. Shd reward cellaring 5-7 yrs.

Hawequas ★★★ From cab/merlot, occasional shiraz. Last tasted **03**, took on new seriousness. Gd oak (16 mths) showing, with cassis; ripe tannins but a touch bitter on long finish. All these Wllngtn/Kmuts fruit; WO Coastal. **04** sold out before we could taste. **Les Coteaux** NEW ★★★★ Kept back for yr after **05**'s release, slower maturing **04**'s brooding dark-fruited depths sure to reveal further delights over time. Currently accessible but still quiescent. — CR

Monterosso Estate
T 021-889-5021 • F 021-889-5021

Stellenbosch • Est/1stB 2000 • Tasting & sales Mon-Fri 10-4 Sat 10-12 • Closed Easter Fri/Mon, Apr 27, May 1, Jun 16, Dec 25 & Jan 1 • Tours by appt • Owner Socrate, Orneglio & Francesco De Franchi • Cellarmaster/winemaker Orneglio De Franchi (Jan 2000) • Viticulturist Francesco De Franchi • 68ha (cab, merlot, pinotage, sangiovese, shiraz, chard, chenin, sauv, semillon) • 6 600cs own label 60% red 40% white • PO Box 5 Stellenbosch 7599 • monterosso@mweb.co.za • www.monterosso.co.za

I'm doing something right!' beams winemaker Orneglio "Meaty" De Franchi, whose wines are winning awards (including Michelangelo Grand d'Or for the Cab-Merlot) and selling out. 'The Sangiovese is in such demand that it sold three vintages in two years! We need to look at substantially increasing production on all four wines.'

Sangiovese Socrate ☺ ★★★ Bright, cherry-red **05** similar Italianate styling to pvs. Sour cherry acidity & maraschino flavours; 10% new oak needs bit of time to mellow. **Sauvignon Blanc** ☺ 🔲 ★★★ **07** fun-filled wallet-pleaser, as zesty & flavoursome as always. Stock up for summer.

Cabernet Sauvignon-Merlot ✓ ★★★★ Appealing, medium-bodied & rustic **04** shows refreshing acidity & integrated tannins. 16 mths Fr oak, 16 mths bottle-ageing. **Old Bush Vine Chenin Blanc** 🔲 ★★★ Unoaked **07** not quite up to rich, poised **06** (★★★★). Still complex, pear/thatch notes, lovely minerality, but mid-palate tad dilute. — CvZ

▮ Montestell *see Boland Kelder*

Montpellier
T 023-230-0656 • F 023-230-0656

Tulbagh • Est ca 1950 • 1stB ca 1968 • Tasting, sales & tours Mon-Fri 9-12; 2-5 Sat 9-12 • BYO picnic • Restaurant, farm-style guest house, conferences & many other attractions • Facilities for children • Tour groups • Owner Lucas J van Tonder • Winemaker Anton Krynauw (Jan 2003) • Viticulturist Gawie Kriel (Apr 2003, consultant) • 50ha (11 varieties, mainly white) • 300t/10 000cs 30% red 70% white • PO Box 79 Tulbagh 6820 • montpellierwine@tiscali.co.za • www.montpellier.co.za

Winemaker and bio-chemist Anton Krynauw was delighted with the trial run of his Exergy plant (of Austrian origin, locally made to his specs), aligning positive/negative ions in grape mash, resulting in purer juice and the need for less preservative. Viognier and chardonnay joined the juvenile red varieties in the continued replanting of what consultant Gawie Kriel describes as Châteauneuf-du-Pape-like terrain.

Cabernet Sauvignon ★★ **05** hearty & ripe with choc tones, very dry tannins. Sample tasted, as for most of these. **Mourvèdre** NEW ★★ **06** hints of fynbos & liquorice, dry cherry flavours. **Pinot Noir** NEW ★ Pitch black **05**, massive (16% alc), brooding & over-ripe. **Petit Verdot** NEW ★★ Dark-fruited **07**, earthy blackberry fruit, dry tannins. **Shiraz** ★★ Porty & gamey **06**, with sweet finish (10g/l RS). **Blanc de Noir** ★ **06** pale salmon pink, strawberry notes, easy-going food companion from pinot. **Chardonnay** ★ Last ed **05** was off-dry & very ripe (15.5% alc). **Chenin Blanc** ★★ Tropical & guava tones on **06**, uncomplicated poolside quaffer. **Viognier** NEW ★★ **07** promising, complex layers peaches, melon, floral & pepper; finishes tad flabby. **Méthode Cap Classique** ★★★ Perfumed dry sparkling from semillon; boiled sweets & passionfruit notes over honeyed bottle-age. **NV Port** ★★ Uncomplicated & full-sweet **04**, raisins & jam, more correctly named 'sweet fortified pinotage'. — *JN*

■ **Montpellier du Sud** *see Constantia Wines*

Mont Rochelle Hotel & Mountain Vineyards ▪🍷☕⌂📷
T 021-876-3000 ▪ F 021-876-2362

Franschhoek ▪ 1stB 1996 ▪ Tasting & sales daily 10-6 ▪ Fee R15 ▪ Tours 11, 12.30 & 3 ▪ Five-star hotel & restaurant (see Eat-out/Stay-over section) ▪ Cheese platters; picnics & gourmet tastings by appt ▪ Functions & events ▪ Farm produce ▪ Art gallery ▪ Owner Mont Rochelle Mountain Vineyard Ltd ▪ Winemaker Dustin Osborne ▪ Viticulturist Danie Botha (consultant) ▪ 19ha (cab, merlot, shiraz, chard, sauvignon) ▪ 15 000cs own label 50% red 50% white ▪ ISO 14001 certified ▪ PO Box 334 Franschhoek 7690 ▪ info@montrochelle.co.za ▪ www.montrochelle.co.za

New winemaker Dustin Osborne has joined the team in this mountain eyrie; last project on his predecessor's watch was the rationalisation of the Mont Rochelle range, which will eventually comprise three tiers. Palates are pampered here - there are now two restaurants, and gourmet tastings offer food-pairing too.

★★★★ **Syrah 04** (★★★★) moderately oaked showing leathery spice and smoke. Hint of mint, leather & black fruits add complexity. Notch down on hedonistic **03**.

★★★★ **Barrel Fermented Chardonnay 06** experimented with Hungarian oak! Buckets of spice and butter. Full and round from lees and malolactic. Sample not quite complete but showing lots of toasty potential.

Cabernet Sauvignon ★★★☆ Savoury **04** sample; herbaceous & cassis laced. Fine-grained; deep and luscious seamless oak integration. Elegant and honest. **Merlot** ★★☆ No follow up yet on **03**; vintage was stern and unyielding vs plump and velvety pvs. **Merlot-Cabernet Sauvignon** ★★★☆ Also no follow up on debut **03**. Ripe tannins with rich choc-laced fruit. Beefy 15% alc. **Artemis** ★★★☆ **03** tasted pv ed was velvety easy-drinker; minty and juicy with soft tannins. Merlot, cab, pinotage, shiraz (40/30/20/10). **Rosé** 📖 ★★★ **07** sample sleek and sexy strawberry-fruited. Dry crisp and textured, leaning more to savoury-stardom. EW. **Natural Chardonnay** ★★★ Ultra soft pear and naartjies; mouth-filling but simple **07**. **Sauvignon Blanc** ★★★☆ **06** last ed was from Wllngton fruit; fresh and tangy kiwifruit & gooseberry flavours. Excellent concentration with ripe fig fruit. **Sauvignon Blanc Reserve** ★★★★ **07** unready for tasting. **06** was definite notch up from easy drinking **05** (★★★). Excellent concentration with ripe fig fruit. Moderate 13.5% alc. — *RP*

■ **Mooiberge** *see African Terroir*

Mooi Bly Winery 🍷⌂
T 021-868-2808 ▪ F 021-868-2808

Paarl ▪ Est/1stB 2003 ▪ 'Vine to wine tour' by appt ▪ Self-catering cottages ▪ Owner Wouters family ▪ Winemaker/viticulturist Erik Schouteden & Theunis van Zyl ▪ 19ha (cabs s/f, malbec, petit v, tannat, chard, chenin) ▪ 2 300cs own label + 40 000litres bulk ▪ 35% red 65% white ▪ PO Box 801 Huguenot 7645 ▪ info@mooibly.com ▪ www.mooibly.com

Erik Schouteden says he's not superstitious, but it was Friday 13th when he fell from a 4m-high tank. 'I forgot to put my wings on,' he jokes, nursing a broken arm. He's still able - touch wood - to export everything he bottles to Holland and Belgium; Germany and Sweden will hopefully come on-stream this year.

Rosé NEW ☺ ★★★ Gutsy yet friendly quaffer; **07** off-dry, with cranberry & savoury appeal, bright acidity. From shiraz & pinotage. **Chenin Blanc** ☺ ★★☆ Delightful easy-drinking **07**, ripe apple & tropical flavours; fleshier than pvs but lively; solo or with food.

Cabernet Sauvignon ★★★ Bold & chunky **06**, smoky dark berries & firm wood tannin (50% 12 mths oak); youthful, needs time to mellow. **Pinotage** NEW ★★☆ Big, chewy & rustic **07**, ripe mulberry & toasted spice, firm dry tannins. 75% 6 mths oak, 15.2% alc. **Chardonnay** ✓ ★★★★ Rich & fleshy **07**, attractive creaminess enlivened by balancing acidity & citrus tang on exit. — *MW*

Mooiplaas Estate
T 021-903-6273/4 ▪ F 021-903-3474

Stellenbosch ▪ Est 1806 ▪ 1stB 1995 ▪ Tasting & sales Mon-Fri 9-4 Sat & pub hols 10-2 ▪ Closed Easter Fri-Mon, Dec 25/26 & Jan 1 ▪ Fee R10 refundable with purchase ▪ BYO picnic ▪ Conservation area ▪ Owner Mooiplaas Trust ▪ Winemaker Louis Roos (1983) ▪ Viticulturist Tielman Roos (1980) ▪ ±120ha ▪ 750t/8 000cs own label 57% red 43% white ▪ PO Box 104 Koelenhof 7605 ▪ info@mooiplaas.co.za ▪ www.mooiplaas.co.za

The 50-hectare renosterveld conservation area established, the Roos brothers wanted to celebrate their SAA first/premium class listings (Sauvignon and Cab) and a TWS museum class silver (Sauvignon, again), and did so in sparkling style, with a new bubbly. First sampled over December, it 'just about shot Father Christmas's beanie off his head!'

★★★★ **Cabernet Sauvignon 03** displays elegance & completeness of vintage. Beguiling cab fragrance; fine structure gives focus & form to fresh, creamy richness; lovely length. Small but influential spicing from 14% cab f. Fr/Am oak, 35% new, 23 mths.

★★★★ **Pinotage** Unoaked (except for 14% cab stiffening) for approachability. Generous juiciness on ripe **04** (★★★★) dampened by vintage robustness, twist finishing bitterness. NE.

★★★★ **Rosalind** ('Blend' pvs ed.) Most serious, ambitious red in range. **04** cabs f/s & merlot (53/37/10) harmoniously & elegantly fused. Serene rich concentration, integrated textured tannins, savoury persistence; all presage delicious maturity. Fr oak, 68% new.

Merlot ★★★★ Last ed **03** touch severe in youth though ample tobacco, choc-plum notes, dry tannins. Incl 10% cab. 22 mths, 20% new. **Shiraz** ★★★★ **04** quite sturdy with firm, fresh core; robust edges smoothed by gentle spice & red fruits notes, dash sugar. 28 mths oak, 48% new. **Chenin Blanc** ✓ ★★★★ Concentration & densely textured mouthfeel on **06**, from 35 yr old bushvines. Generous, balanced, sophisticated honeyed tropical persistence. Potential for further few yrs. **Sauvignon Blanc** ★★★★ Invigorating gooseberry & capiscum scents on **07**. Good attack, bounce & clean tangy finish, but nothing too aggressive. — *AL*

Mooiuitsig Wine Cellars
T 023-616-2143 ▪ F 023-616-2675

Robertson ▪ Est 1947 ▪ Sales Mon-Thu 8-5 Fri 8-2 ▪ Tours by appt ▪ Stay-overs at De Rust Lodge info@outdoorarena.co.za; T 023-616-2444 ▪ Owner Jonker & Claassen families ▪ Winemaker Nico van der Westhuizen ▪ Viticulturist Casper Matthee ▪ 2 500t ▪ PO Box 15 Bonnievale 6730 ▪ info@mooiuitsig.co.za ▪ www.mooiuitsig.co.za

Founder, now chairman, 'Oom' Boet Jonker, still puts in a good day's wine-blending work at SA's biggest family-run liquor wholesale business, which last year celebrated its 60th anniversary. Almost as many years as own brands: Mooiuitsig includes 64 house labels in its wide range of spirits and wines for sale to the mass market.

African Wine Adventure range

Red ★★ Cheeky zebra-striped cork sets the tone of this sunny, ripe **NV** quaffer. Discontinued: **Chardonnay**.

Mooiuitzicht range

> **Bonwin Ruby Dessert Wine** ☺ ★★★ Ripe raisins in this rich, well-balanced sweetie, evoking liquid toffee pudding.

Vin Doux ★★ Sweet (55g/l RS) party-pleasing bubbly with wide appeal. **NV**, as are all these. **Sweet Hanepoot** ★★ Uncomplicated full-sweet dessert, with suggestion of plump, ripe sultanas. **Nagmaalwyn** ★★ Sacramental wine. Ripe, full-sweet muscat flavours, slightly cloying finish. **Marsala** ★★★ Similar to Bonwin. **Old Tawny Port** ★★ Comfortable old-Cape-style fortified with dusty dried apricot tones. Discontinued: **Overberger**, **Vin Brut**.

Oude Rust range

Sweet Hanepoot ★★★ All these are certified desserts, fortified to ±17.5% alc. **05** last ed combined rich gooseberry preserve aromas & hearty flavours; spirity, yet silky texture. **Red Muscadel** ★★★ **06** tealeaf scents & raspberry/cranberry lushness; well-rounded mouthful. **White Muscadel** ★★★ **06** in early-drinking style; lusciously sweet with floral & apricot tones.

Rusthof range

Oulap Se Rooi ★★ Quirkily packaged red blend, styled for traditional potjiekos partnering. Latest with dusty cinnamon notes. Also as Droë Rooi in more conventional attire. **Droë Rooi** See above. **Rosé** ★ Like pvs, light, uncomplicated pink; slight cherry tone, not overly sweet. **Sauvignon Blanc** ★ **07** light, undemanding dry white (11.5% alc). **Premier Grand Cru** ★★ Light & flinty, with green apple nuances. Chill well for poolside quaffing. **Blanc de Blanc** ★★ Floral & peach tones make for pleasing off-dry lunchtime drink. **Potjie Effe Droog** ★★ Cheap & cheerful white designed for outdoor glugging. 500ml. **Late Harvest** ★★ Relaxed, uncomplicated semi-sweet white. These cork-closed wines **NV** unless mentioned. — *DB*

Moordenaarskop
T 021-858-1202 ▪ F 086-672-6797

Stellenbosch (see Helderberg map) ▪ Est 1999 ▪ 1stB 2002 ▪ Tasting by appt only ▪ Owner/viticulturist Graham Smith ▪ Winemaker Graham Smith, advised by Daniël Truter (Onderkloof) ▪ 0.3ha (cab) ▪ 2.2t/150cs 100% red ▪ PO Box 2889 Somerset West 7129 ▪ mwsmiths@mweb.co.za

'Complete garagiste' Graham Smith's decision to plant a small vineyard in front of his house was made in 1998 over a glass or two of wine. 'The making followed on naturally in 2002, with lots of panic, somewhat eased by good advice from Danie Truter at Onderkloof.' The harvest is always on a Sunday, so friends can be involved – 'We destalk and crush on the driveway.' Fermentation, maturation, and hand bottling and labelling all take place in the garage. **Cabernet Sauvignon Reserve** ★★★ Notch above std version, as expected from small-oak-ageing (Yr, Fr). Restrained & well-integrated dark fruit, persistent. **Cabernet Sauvignon** ★★ Karoobush spice & juicy fruit on **05**, friendly, gregarious yet elegant. — *JP*

Môreson
T 021-876-3055 ▪ F 021-876-2348

Franschhoek ▪ Est 1986 ▪ 1stB 1994 ▪ Tasting & sales daily 11-5 ▪ Fee R10 ▪ Closed Dec 25 ▪ Tours by appt ▪ Bread & Wine Restaurant, Farm Grocer & other amenities (see Eat-out section) ▪ Owner Richard Friedman ▪ Winemaker Hannes Meyer (2006) with Clayton Reabow (since June 2007) ▪ 18ha (chard, chenin, sauv) ▪ 300t/18 000cs 40% red 55% white 1% rosé 4% MCC ▪ Export brands: Pinecrest & MorningSide ▪ ISO 14000 & Eurogap certified ▪ PO Box 114 Franschhoek 7690 ▪ sales@moreson.co.za ▪ www.moreson.co.za

Hannes Meyer has moved into the GM/winemaker's seat, and, assisted by Clayton Reabow in the cellar, is building on steadily rising production and sales, particularly of their MCC sparklers. Feathers in the year's cap include their Magia winning best bordeaux blend and best red overall at the 2007 Trophy Wine Show, and their Bread & Wine Restaurant landing a berth in the SA Top 10, says owner Richard Friedman, whose sister Susan Huxter is the name behind another critically acclaimed Franschhoek establishment, Le Quartier Francais.

Môreson range

★★★★ **Pinotage** Benchmark modern style; **06** engaging mulberry/raspberry scents follow through on to dense yet supple palate. Oaked to frame fruit, round tannins. On form of ABSA Top Ten **03**. Sbosch vyd.

★★★★ **Shiraz** NEW Experimental one-off from Sbosch fruit to 'explore new blending components'. Comfortable & balanced **05**, subtle (seasoned) oak backdrop to characteristic red fruits/spice, supple mouthfeel. Gd prospects.

★★★★ **Magia** Handsome **04** (★★★★☆), classy follow up to TWS Trophy winner **03**. Slightly bigger, more intense but similar evocative spice & cedar. Plush, dense but refined; delicious savoury length. Give yr-2 to settle. Cab, merlot, cab f (48/33/19), 80% new oak, ±18 mths. Coastal vyds.

★★★★ **Premium Chardonnay 05** generous dimensions (14.2% alc) & flavours, yet also elegant; last yr showed lovely white peach fragrance, nutty butterscotch creaminess, more new oak (60%) than pvs but well judged.

Merlot ★★★★ Lively, spicy red plum aromas belie full-bodied, robust structure on **04**. Dry tannins, glow from 14.8% alc. 30% new Fr oak, 18 mths. Sbosch vyd. **Chenin Blanc** ★★★★ Old-vine white that helped establish farm from 1986. Latest **07** still exudes graceful, fragrant charm of original, lovely ripe pear/winter melon flavours. **Sauvignon Blanc** ★★★☆ **07** deemed 'exceptional' vintage by Môreson team. Pure gooseberry & tropical notes; unaggressive build with gd long flavours. Sample tasted, rating tentative. **Blanc de Blanc** ★★★★ Quiet but authentic brut MCC from chard with 10% chenin. 'Champagne' wheaten tones follow through on gently toasty aromas, fine, persistent mousse. Portion oaked for extra dimension. **Cuvée Cape** ★★★☆ Aptly named white MCC sparkling, blends local heroes pinotage & chenin. Vigorously refreshing; Granny Smith apples & ginger biscuit hints, whistle clean tail. **NV.** Discontinued: **Cabernet Sauvignon**, **Cabernet Franc**.

Pinehurst range

Chenin Blanc ☺ 🍷 ★★★ Striking pineapple fragrance on newly screwcapped **07**. Succulent, flavoursome, appealing fruitily dry-ish finish.

Cabernet Sauvignon ★★★ **04** mouthful ripe, tasty brambly fruit; robust but unaggressive. Seasoned oak. Still selling; not re-assessed. **Pinotage** 🍷 ★★★ Lightly oaked **06** first red under screwcap. Ripe stewed plum/choc tones, juicy flavours complemented by vin ordinaire tannins. Fhoek grapes. **Merlot-Cabernet Sauvignon** ★★★★ Last ed we noted attractive plump fruit, comfortable tannins, gd length on **04**. 6 mths older wood. **Rosé Dry** ★★ Pinotage's tart red-fruit flavours tiring on **06**. Drink up. **Chardonnay** ★★ Quiet bruised apple tones on unwooded **07**. Bone-dry, slightly rough finish. **Sauvignon Blanc** ★★★☆ Previewed **07** shows benefits of gd vintage; bowlful passion/grapefruit & other tropical juiciness. Comfortably fresh & not over-assertive. Rating tentative. This range WO Coastal unless noted. — *AL*

Morewag

T 021-875-5626 ▪ F 021-875-5626

Stellenbosch ▪ Est 1996 ▪ 1stB 2002 ▪ Tasting by appt: T 073-420-3300 (Lorna Hughes) ▪ Owner Michael & Ulrike Merkel ▪ Winemaker Rudi Schultz (Thelema, 04 vintage) ▪ PO Box 290 Klapmuts 7625 ▪ morewag@mweb.co.za

New German partner/winemaker Franz-Josef Blomendahl has rented a cellar in Elgin, and the entire harvest (previously predominantly sold to Boschendal and Thelema) is now bottled under own labels. Despite a smaller yield due to hail, 2007 production jumped from 5000 to 75 000 litres - just as well Blomendahl also brings extensive marketing connections to the table.

Pinotage ★★ Organic notes & hint lavender on **04**, drying tannin & savoury flavours. Not your typical fruit bomb! 18 mths Fr/Am oak. — *CvZ*

Morgenhof Estate

T 021-889-5510 ▪ **F** 021-889-5266

Stellenbosch ▪ Est 1692 ▪ 1stB 1984 ▪ Tasting & sales Nov-Apr: Mon-Fri 9-5.30 Sat/Sun 10-5; May-Oct: Mon-Fri 9-4.30 Sat/Sun 10-3 ▪ Fee R10 ▪ Closed Easter Fri, Dec 25 & Jan 1 ▪ Light lunches/coffees & other amenities (see Eat-out section) ▪ Tour groups ▪ Owner Anne Cointreau ▪ Winemaker Jacques Cilliers (Dec 2004) ▪ Viticulturist Pieter Haasbroek (1998) ▪ 72ha (cabs s/f, merlot, pinotage, touriga, chard, chenin, sauv) ▪ 35 000cs 60% red 40% white ▪ PO Box 365 Stellenbosch 7599 ▪ info@morgenhof.com ▪ www.morgenhof.com

No glass ceiling here (but then the owner of the picture-perfect, award-winning estate is Anne Cointreau): last year Lee-Anne Bosman, who started in the tasting room 15 years ago, was appointed COO, and another tasting-room graduate, Helga Truter, took over as marketing manager. In the vineyards, new chenin is being planted, to supplement the tiny yield from blocks of 37-year-old vines. Both the Morgenhof Chenin, 'very popular, especially abroad', and the Chardonnay have been made to pre-orders since 2006, when the Chenin sold out after a month.

Morgenhof Estate range

★★★★ **Merlot** Returns with a flourish; **05** black cherry, choc appeal; some classic restraint to poised palate. Not a tannin out of place - dry, smooth, contrasts with supple berry fruit, lingering dry finish. 18 mths Fr oak. **04** (★★★★) was more savoury, with softish tannins.

★★★★☆ **Première Sélection** Latest **04** right on the money, perhaps more elegance than power. Oak-cloaked mulberry & cassis shows classic restraint, tannins firm, needs time to loosen. Balanced, has presence. Blend cab, merlot, malbec, cab f 65/25/6/4; will easily keep 5-10 yrs.

★★★★ **Chardonnay** Cellar rethink revives label (**05** was to be last). Barrel sample **07** grilled nuts, dried apricot with the tang to match, oak still dominant. Too young to rate realistically. No **06**.

★★★★ **Chenin Blanc** Vyds nearing 40 yrs of age. Bruised apple, peach kernel on classy **07**, firm flesh disciplined by good oak, chenin's fresh acidity. Tangy & crisp, like biting into an apple. Fr oak, 6 mths.

★★★★ **Brut Reserve 04** tasted while still on lees, where it rests 2 yrs. Toasted nuts, crisp & biscuity, fine creamy mousse. Base-wine fermented/7 mths used oak. Chard/pinot(60/40).

Cabernet Sauvignon ★★★★ **04** back on form; stylish mulberry-tinged, cedar & fine oak interplay. Tannins cleverly worked to allow drinking now or long-term cellaring. Fr oak, 18 mths,40% new. **03** (★★★★) appealing, but lacks the new vintage's gravitas. **Sauvignon Blanc** ★★★☆ **07** a real show-off! Whiffs capsicum, green fig to racy palate, crisp acidity, lingering fig, peppers on finish. Bone-dry. Try with any seafood - garlic butter an absolute must. **Noble Late Harvest** ★★★☆ Last was **02**, not over-sweet, with balancing acidity, dry finish. Fermented/6 mths in oak. **Cape Vintage** ★★★★ Latest **03** combines delicacy & power. Subtle & refined, rather than fruitcake intensity; retains drier Portuguese styling of pvs **00** (★★★★), though alc low at 17.5%. 100% touriga. Matured 2 yrs oak, 2 yrs bottle. Discontinued: **Cabernet Sauvignon Reserve**, **Merlot Reserve**, **Natural Sweet**.

Fantail range

Merlot ☺ ★★★ Delightfully fruity & accessible; **05** crushed red & black berries, soft juicy texture with added bonus of subtle oaking (14 mths).

Pinotage ★★★ Loads crushed red cherries in **06**, soft & juicy, very appealing. Barrel aged, 9 mths, seasoned. **Vineyards Red** ★★★ **04** plump & pleasing merlot-led all-sorts red; last ed was approachable & easy with some underlying seriousness; gd dry finish with brush of tannin. Up to 18 mths oak, some new. WO W Cape (others mainly Sbosch). **Rosé** ★★★ **05** sweet plum & red cherry aromas/flavours, very dry, moderate 12.8 % alc. Not retasted. **Vineyards White** ★★★ **07** less freshness, excitement, broader flatter flavours than pvs. Sauv dominated blend. — *IvH*

Morgenster Estate
T 021-852-1738 · F 021-852-0835

Stellenbosch (see Helderberg map) ▪ Est 1993 ▪ 1stB 1998 ▪ Tasting & sales Mon-Fri 10-5 Sat/ Sun & pub hols 10-4 ▪ Fee R12; additional R12 for estate grown olive oil & olive products ▪ Closed Good Fri & Dec 25 ▪ Tours by appt ▪ Owner Giulio Bertrand ▪ Winemaker Marius Lategan, with Cornea Cilliers (Aug 1999, Jan 2004), advised by Pierre Lurton ▪ Vineyard Manager Gerhard Bruwer, advised by Francois Viljoen ▪ 35ha (cabs s/f, merlot, petit v) ▪ 150t 100% red ▪ PO Box 1616 Somerset West 7129 ▪ wine@morgenster.co.za ▪ www.morgenster.co.za

The focus after ten vintages at this rejuvenated wine and olive estate in prime Helderberg terroir remains on world-class bordeaux blends, released under two distinct labels: Morgenster and Lourens River Valley. Both the wines and the olive products (the 'liquid gold' has garnered the highest accolade, 'Mill of the Year', by L'Extravergine) enjoy wide national representation, thanks to a targeted marketing drive and an online purchasing facility. Internationally, new markets include China, Russia, Finland, Singapore and New Zealand. A bonus for collectors is the availability of limited stocks of older vintages going back to 1998.

★★★★☆ **Lourens River Valley 04** claret with a modern, vibrant fruit twist: poised; polished tannins rub against leafy, cassis notes. Best in 3yrs+. 46% merlot, equal portions cab s/f, ±yr in Fr oak. **03** more merlot (68%), less cab s/f than **02**; had mushrooms accents, leafy tannins. Unlikely '2nd' blend if ever there was one.

★★★★☆ **Morgenster** Aristocratic Old-World-style flagship. **04**, like **01**, merlot driven (69%) with cabs f/s (17/14), ±13 mths Fr oak, 93% new. Perfumed, plush, persistent; tapered tannins contributing to fine, noble structure, seemingly endless finish. **03** beguiling, mixed herbs, cassis & eucalyptus with spice.

Discontinued: **The Summer House.** — *CvZ*

■ **Morkel** *see Bellevue Estate*

■ ***MorningSide*** *see Môreson*

Morton Wines
T 021-808-5972 · F 021-808-5971

Stellenbosch ▪ Est 2003 ▪ Tasting & sales by appt ▪ Owner Aidan & Mandy Morton ▪ Winemaker Miles Mossop ▪ Viticulturist Aidan Morton ▪ 10t/700cs 100% red ▪ PO Box 12242 Stellenbosch 7613 ▪ aidan@tokara.com ▪ www.mortonwines.co.za

The 05 Shiraz is the third vintage that Tokara viticulturist Aidan Morton and cellarmaster Miles Mossop have made together, and they believe it's the best to date. The vineyards which produce the grapes are models of modern viticulture, as you'd expect from this youthful but critically acclaimed team, and both parcels are hand picked.

Shiraz ★★★ Comfortable **05**, plenty dark spice, choc & lifted red fruit. Big 15% alc in balance with tannins, savoury richness. Subtle Fr/Am oak, 25% new, 18 mths. — *AL*

Mostertsdrift Noble Wines
T 021-889-5344 · F 02-887-1780; 086-516-1730

Stellenbosch ▪ Est/1stB 2001 ▪ Visits & meals by appt ▪ Owner Anna-Mareè Mostert-Uys & André Mostert ▪ Winemaker Anna-Mareè Mostert-Uys (Jan 2001) ▪ Viticulturist Nico Mostert (Jan 2001) ▪ 7.5 ha (merlot, pinot, cab, chard, hanepoot) ▪ 40 tons 600-800 cs 70% red 30% white ▪ PO Box 2061 Dennesig 7601 ▪ mostertsdrift@telkomsa.net

The Mosterts don't get swept up in the competitive undercurrents one sometimes feels when talking to winemakers. 'As producers we have to stop challenging each other and concentrate on uplifting wine, particularly SA wine. Let's take on the world!' Doing their bit for kin and countrymen, the Mosterts have made a new Rosé, and it's proved a big hit with locals.

Merlot Rosé NEW ☺ 🖺 ★★☆ Startlingly fruity, bouncy, show-off **07**. Heaps of red berries; even a touch of tannin in dry finish.

Cabernet Sauvignon ★★★★ Previewed **05** cassis & cedar from 50% new Hungarian wood, tannins still very firm but appear better managed than on oak-staved **04** (★★★), retasted, showing classic cab tones of dark berry, dry dusty finish. **AnéRouge** ★★ **04** blend changes to cab/merlot (82/18); dried herbs, lean & very dry, some austerity. **Chardonnay** 📖 ★★★ Largely unwooded; **07** (sample) gentle limy fruit & soft acidity; easy summer white. Discontinued: **Chenin Blanc, Blanc de Blanc, Sauvignon Blanc**. *– IvH*

Mountain Oaks Winery

T 023-344-3107 • F 023-344-3688

Slanghoek (see Worcester map) ▪ Est/1stB 2003 ▪ Visits Mon-Fri 10-4 Sat/Sun 10-2 ▪ Closed public hols ▪ Picnics by arrangement ▪ Guest cottage ▪ Organic farm produce ▪ Owner Stevens family ▪ Winemaker Christine Stevens (Jun 2003) ▪ Viticulturist Christine & Mark Stevens ▪ 20ha (cabs s/f, mourvèdre, pinotage, shiraz, chard, chenin, viognier) ▪ 40-50t/2 000cs 30% red 70% white ▪ PO Box 68 Rawsonville 6845 ▪ christine@mountainoaks.co.za

Mountain Oaks' farmers' markets, run in summer, attract hordes of visitors from Cape Town and surrounds, who snap up fresh local produce to enjoy with the winery's certified organic wines. The appreciation at home is echoed abroad, with a growth in export wine sales, particularly to the UK.

★★★★ **Pinotage** Youthful **06** sample with redcurrant & cherry tobacco aromas; lovely, expressive fruit, complemented by spiciness & fine acid. Integrated oak from 16 mths older barrels, but needs time to soften.

★★★★ **Cabernet Franc-Cabernet Sauvignon** NEW Sample **06** still v youthful; vibrant plum aromas, astringent tannins currently masking underlying rich, succulent fruit. Needs time to reveal its ample charms. 18 mths older Fr oak. Rating tentative.

★★★★ **Chardonnay** Repeats stellar performance in **06** with pale gold limpidity & seductive Fr oak, mingling easily with rich, expressive stonefruit & citrus. Leaner, more minerally on palate than particularly opulent **05**.

★★★★ **Chenin Blanc Barrel Reserve** Occasional label. **05** buttoned up when tasted last ed, but with gd length & texture; fruit in confident balance with acid & oak; long, richly textured finish.

Chenin Blanc ★★★★ Unoaked **06** pineapple & boiled sweet aromas, rich & promising: fulfills on concentrated, structured palate with firm acidity balancing robust fruit sweetness. Step up on **05** (★★★★), perfect lunchtime wine. **Le Jardin** ★★★ 65/35 unoaked chenin/chard blend in **06**; sweet aromas from muscat clone chard, with dry, pithy grapefruit finish. *– IM*

Mountain Range
T 021-552-9251 • F 021-555-4280

Cape Town ▪ Closed to public ▪ Owner Belinda Traverso, Paul Finlayson & Paul de Waal ▪ 1 000 cs ▪ 67 Belmont Ave Oranjezicht 8001 ▪ shelley@mountainrange.co.za ▪ www.mountainrange.co.za

Many wineries claim to market 'icon wines'; this merchant house sells its wines in an icon. Its Table Mountain-shaped bottles, filled with wines from a reputable Stellenbosch estate, fly off the shelves — and often fly home with tourists too. The distinctive bottles, available in miniature 50ml size as well, also hold local sherry, brandy and extra-virgin olive oil. The Red and White wines not tasted this edition.

Mountain Ridge Wines

T 023-231-1080/70 • F 023-231-1102

Wolseley (see Worcester map) ▪ Est 1949 ▪ 1stB 1976 ▪ Tasting & sales Mon-Fri 8-5 Sat 10-1 ▪ Closed Easter Fri-Sun, Dec 25/26, Jan 1 ▪ Tours by appt ▪ Tour groups ▪ BYO picnic ▪ Conference facilities ▪ Owner 30 members ▪ Cellarmaster Francois Agenbag ▪ Winemaker Rikus Neethling ▪ Viticulturist Leon Dippenaar ▪ 500ha (cab, chard, chenin, colombard) ▪ 8 000t/5 000cs own label 40% red 60% white ▪ PO Box 108 Wolseley 6830 ▪ sales@mountainridge.co.za ▪ www.mountainridge.co.za

Francois Agenbag has several reasons to be delighted: he won the Diners Club Young Winemaker of the Year in 2006; and since the winery changed its name (it was previously

Romansrivier Cellar), 'everything's been going full steam ahead,' he says. A second winemaker, Rikus Neetling, has been appointed to ensure a fully hands-on approach to the winemaking process.

Sauvignon Blanc ☺ 🍷 ★★★ **07** delicious, friendly & crisp summer quaffer, with lively tropical fruit.

Cabernet Sauvignon Reserve ★★★★ Dense core dark, smoky fruit on rich, balanced **05**. Generous, enhanced by new oak; structure to age few yrs. **Shiraz Reserve** ★★★★ Rich, peppery, savoury appeal on **05**, juicy, supple tannins & complementary oaking (Fr/Am). Medium-bodied. **Dimension** NEW ★★★ **05** juicy melange cab, merlot, shiraz in bold New-World style, with structure. Full-bodied, with savoury twist. **Malbec-Pinotage** ★★ Subdued red fruit on smooth palate. **05** unwooded, undemanding 60/40 blend. **Chenin Blanc-Colombard** 🍷 ★★ Crisp summer tipple with Granny Smith apple tartness. **07** light & dry. **Natural Sweet Rosé** 🍷 ★★ Easy off-dry summer pink with red-berry appeal. **NV**. W Cape & Breedeklf WOs for all above. Discontinued: **Pinotage**, **Chenin Blanc**. — *MW*

Mountain River Wines
T 021-872-3256/7 • F 021-872-3255

Paarl ▪ Est 1993 ▪ 1stB 1998 ▪ Closed to public ▪ Owner De Villiers Brits ▪ Winemaker De Villiers Brits with advisers ▪ 62 000cs 60% red 40% white ▪ 146 Main Road Paarl 7646 ▪ dev@ mountainriverwines.co.za ▪ www.mountainriverwines.co.za

Fifteen years down the line, this export-focused company is very much on track. 'We see quality as the most important factor to differentiate us from the competition,' says owner De Villiers Brits, and to this end consultant Chris Joubert (ex-Overgaauw) has been brought on board for the flagship Mountain River range.

Mountain River range

★★★★ **Pinotage** NEW DVB describes this as 'father' of range (though 'son' & 'daughter' older vintages!). Delicious **06** vanilla oak wafts; savoury, ripe plummy fruit on firm tannic base (18 mths 100% new Fr oak). Will soften & keep beautifully. **Merlot** Sold out. **Cabernet Sauvignon-Merlot** No new release tasted. **Pinotage-Cabernet Sauvignon** ★★★ Dubbed flagship's 'youngest daughter'; **05**, revisited, cedar spices, eucalyptus, ripe cherry & dark choc; firm, well-managed tannins. **Pinotage-Shiraz** NEW ★★★★ Range's 'youngest son' shows more care than pvs. **05** warm, inviting shiraz spice; wood prominent but will probably harmonise with age. **Chardonnay** Sold out. All ranges widely sourced, mainly W Cape WOs.

Altyd Somer range NEW

Cinsaut-Pinotage ★★ **06** maiden release under new label is suitably summery quaffer.

Estuary range

Sauvignon Blanc ★★★★ Tasted last ed, **05** offered cool nettle & ripe gooseberry, delicate acid balance & crisp finish.

Maankloof range

Chenin Blanc NEW ☺ ★★★ Overflows with geranium & pineapple scents; pleasing biscuity notes & ripe melon on **07**.

Cabernet Sauvignon NEW ★★ Spices, pencil shavings, vanilla on undemanding **05** braai wine. **Pinotage** ★★ Fruit-ripe **05** (sample) brims with mango, plump prune & black cherry. **Shiraz 04** sold out; no follow-up sighted. **Chardonnay** ★ Pvsly tasted **04** invited drinking soon. **Sauvignon Blanc** ★★ Clean, green **07**, previewed, redolent of peppers & winter melons; crisp finish.

Rijckbosch range

Pinotage ✓ **★★★★** Warm choc wafts on sample **06**, lovely berry ripeness; convivial wine - share with good friends. **Shiraz ★★★** Mint & spices enliven **04**, some cheeky melon notes mingling with dark cherry ripeness. **Chenin Blanc ★★☆** Herbal notes with guava & fruit salad layers in **07**; nice clean finish. **Viognier** [NEW] **★★★** Big friendly food wine: lovely buttery notes & ripe cape gooseberry flavours on **06**.

Stripes range [NEW]

> **Cabernet Sauvignon-Shiraz** ☺ **★★★** Merry ruby colour to **06**, appealing choc notes, ripe plummy richness. A braai-side winner.

Chenin Blanc-Chardonnay ★★☆ 07 pleasant, undemanding patio wine with herbal & lemongrass hints. Both tasted as samples; ratings tentative.

Zaràfa range

Pinotage 05 sold out. Successor unready. **Shiraz** [NEW] **★★** Previewed **05** spicy old-leather, ripe plums on fruit-driven fireside red. **Sauvignon Blanc ★★** Grassy nose, pineapple crispness & dry finish on easy-drinking **07**. — *DB*

■ **Mountainside** *see Fairseat Cellars*

Mount Babylon
T *021-855-2768* · **F** *021-855-2768*

Hemel-en-Aarde Valley (see Elgin/Walker Bay map) · Est 2002 · 1stB 2007 · Tasting by appt only · Closed Easter Fri-Mon, Apr 27, May 11, Dec 25 & Jan 1 · Cheese platters by prior arrangement · Facilities for children · Owner Johan Holtzhausen · Winemaker Marc van Halderen (Jan 2006, consultant) · Viticulturist Johan Pienaar (Feb 2002, consultant) · ±7ha (malbec, shiraz, viognier) · 22t/370cs own label 40% red 40% rosé 20% other · PO Box 7370 Stellenbosch 7599 · info@babylonsvineyards.co.za · www.babylonsvineyards.co.za

'Walter and Peter Finlayson encouraged me to plant grapes such as shiraz, malbec and viognier. The results show they were correct,' declares Johan Holtzhausen who, with the help of consultant winemaker Marc van Halderen, turned the varietal trio into the farm's flagship blend, named SMV, launched after the guide went to press.

Mount Rozier Estate
T *021-858-1130* · **F** *021-858-1131*

Stellenbosch (see Helderberg map) · Est/1stB 1997 · Visits Mon-Thu 9-5 Fri 9-4 Sat by appt · Closed pub hols · Amenities see intro · Owner Atlantic Wine Agencies, Inc · Winemaker Eikendal winemaking team (2007) · Viticulturist Jaco Mouton · 20ha (cab, merlot, shiraz, sauv, semillon) · ±2 500cs own label 90% red 10% white · PO Box 1241 Somerset West 7129 · wines@mountrozier.co.za · www.mountrozier.co.za

Mont Rozier is worth visiting for its setting alone - a natural amphitheatre in the Schapenberg foothills - but there's more reasons to earmark this as-yet-unexplored winelands corner: there's horse riding with a view, picnics by appointment, a recreation area with child-appeal - and, of course, the wines.

Mount Rozier Estate range

★★★★   **Cabernet Sauvignon** Bold, touch showy **04** international award winner gaining gravitas when retasted last ed. New vintage not available for tasting.

★★★★   **Shiraz** Blockbuster New-World profile continued in last tasted **04**. Ripe fruit, athletic tannin for keeping, 15% alc. No newer vintage reviewed.

Merlot ★★★★ Tasted last ed, oak in **04** still too powerful for fynbos-scented fruit & tannins still dry. New vintage unready. **Pioneer Blend** [NEW] **★★★★** Serious **04** nudges next rung. Merlot, shiraz, cab, shiraz playing pivotal role. Dark plum & cherry, oak well-woven, properly dry. **Sauvignon Blanc ★★★** None reviewed since **05**, then fresh & lively with intense tropical notes.

Rozier Bay range

Merlot-Cabernet Sauvignon NEW 🔲 ★★★ Attractive oak overlay to serene dark berry flavours. **04** well-judged, balanced sprinkling spice on finish. **Chardonnay** NEW ★★★ Fresh lemony tang to slimmed-down **06**. 2nd-fill barrels & some staves. **Sauvignon Blanc** ★★ Last tasted **06** dry, light (12% alc) & modestly flavoured.

Rozier Reef range

Pinotage ★★ **05** showed sweet vanilla veneer, youthful tannic grip when last tasted. **Shiraz** ★★★ Deliciously balanced flavours found in **05** last ed. **Shiraz-Pinotage** ★★ **05** last tasted mid-2006 when fruit & tannin not yet melded. **Chardonnay** ★★★ Pvsly we found **05** food friendly, with tropical notes & smooth acidity. **Chenin Blanc** ★★ No follow-up to **05**, light, with hints green apple & pear. **Sauvignon Blanc** ★★★ Last **06** was light bodied, but touch riper & more flavourful than RBay version. **Chenin Blanc-Chardonnay** ★★★ **06** last ed easy drinker, rounded & fruity with moderate 12.5% alc. — IvH

Mount Vernon Farm

T 021-875-5073 • F 021-875-5073

Paarl • Est/1stB 2003 • Open Mon-Fri 9-4; check noticeboard for weekend times • Cellar tours by appt • Closed Easter Fri/Sun, Dec 25/26 & Jan 1 • BYO picnic • Walks • Mountain biking • Owner David & Debbie Hooper • Winemaker Debbie Hooper, with Anele Mangena • Viticulturist Philip du Toit • 28ha (cab, malbec, merlot, petit v, pinotage, shiraz, chard) • 205t total 7000litres own label • PO Box 348 Klapmuts 7625 • laurna@threepeakswine.co.za

Debbie Hooper is delighted with the good exposure her reds have had, and hopeful her new Chardonnay, made with the assistance of Anele Mangena in between Cape Wine Academy studies, will also strike a responsive chord. The new tasting room is open weekdays and by appointment over weekends.

Three Peaks range

Cabernet Sauvignon ★★★ More grace, charm in **05**, retains fruit generosity, nudges next rung. WO W Cape. **Cantata** ★★★ Earthy, somewhat brusque notes in **05**, honest & workmanlike grenache, mourvèdre, shiraz & pinotage. Smnsberg-Paarl WO. **Rosé** ★★★ **06** (sample) incl 36% chenin infusion (pvs 100% pinotage). Gd summer al fresco wine, with low 12% alc. Not retasted. **Chenin Blanc** ★★★ **06** noted as weightier than pvs (14% alc) last ed, but not inelegant. Engaging fynbos/lemon scents, lengthy farewell with hint of nut. — IvH

■ **Mudge Point** *see Luddite Wines*

Mulderbosch Vineyards

T 021-865-2488 • F 021-865-2351

Stellenbosch • Est 1989 • 1stB 1991 • Sales: Mon-Fri 8-5; tasting by appt only • Closed pub hols • Owner Hydro Holdings • Cellarmaster Mike Dobrovic (1991) • Winemaker Nic van Aarde (Sep 2005) • Vineyard Manager Danie Williams • 23ha (cabs s/f, malbec, merlot, petit v, chard, sauv) • 500t/30 000cs 30% red 70% white • PO Box 548 Stellenbosch 7599 • info@mulderbosch.co.za • www.mulderbosch.co.za

Last crush cellarmaster Mike Dobrovic was in tune with his feminine side and his inner poet waxed lyrical. His 26th harvest yielded the most beautiful chardonnay and cabernet he's ever worked with (11 barrels were kept apart for possible future release under their Centauri label). All the reds, for the first time in years, reached full phenolic ripeness at lower-than-normal sugar. They last picked such perfect sauvignon in 1993. Cinderella-like, the chenin was shy but her charms were coaxed out by ample rains and just the right amount of botrytis. And the sauvignon NLH is so perfumed he's thinking of dabbing it on his cheeks. 'This wine, like me, will only get better with age.'

★★★★ **Faithful Hound** Crafted rather than confected red, a bastion of honest earthiness amongst new wave pretenders. Now full bdx quintet. **04** unflashy, balanced & satisfying. 13% alc. 18 mths Fr oak 50% new.

★★★★ **Beta Centauri** Only in exceptional vintages. Last **02** plush cabs f/s merger with 12% petit v. More modern than 'Hound' cellarmate, would benefit from ageing. Harmonious 18 mths new Fr oak. Not retasted.

★★★★ **Chardonnay** Contrasting with range mate, only partly barrel fermented (60% Fr oak, half new): combines elegance & depth of flavour. Citrus fruit of **05** folded in spicy wood, mature sweet tail.

★★★★ **Chardonnay Barrel Fermented** Busty components - ripe tropical fruit in new oak (80% Fr, 9 mths), full malo & off-dry 6.3g/l sugar - arranged with surprising harmony in **06**. **05** (★★★★) tad disjointed. **04** Wine (★★★★), Tri-Nations class winner.

★★★★ **Chenin Blanc** Subtitled 'Steen-op-Hout', **06** (★★★☆) oak-buffed flutter of grape's floral/honey charm in sweet, simple, finish. 5.2g/l sugar aided by 5% botrytised sauv. 18% oaked, mix age/origin. **05** showed just a whisper of wood.

★★★★☆ **Sauvignon Blanc 07** (★★★★) less compelling than pvs, full of steely promise but showing some middle-age spread. Just-dry. Maybe 12.5% alc too gentle? Yard off minerally **06** with distinctive greengage allure & synchronised weighty fruit.

★★★★ **Sauvignon Blanc Noble Late Harvest** `NEW` Edgy, steely interpretation of the generally luscious NLH genre. **07** pale, but stunning balance to shimmering tangerine fruits, oak-in-relief & refreshing dry tail. 100% Fr cask fermented/6 mths. 500ml. EW.

Shiraz ★★★★ Dark-hued **04** noted pvs ed as expressive but straightforward; enlivened with 12% petit v. Pure-fruited modern **03** (★★★★) lively, supple. **05** unready. **Cabernet Sauvignon Rosé** ★★★★ **07** lovely composite of salmon pink with cheerful cherries in a tangy tail; engaging & food friendly. Cabs s & f. 7g/l sugar doesn't jar. Sold out **06** untasted. — DS

■ **Muldersvlei** *see* Westbridge Vineyards

Mullineux Family Wines `NEW`
T 082-333-6888 · F 082-131-333-6888

Swartland · Est 2007 · Closed to public · Owner Mullineux Family Wines (Pty) Ltd · Winemaker/viticulturist Chris & Andrea Mullineux (Jun 2007) · 30t 85% red 15% white · info@mullineuxwines.com · www.mullineuxwines.com

'We're making the Swartland and its wines our life and home,' say newlywed Chris and Andrea Mullineux, who put Tulbagh Mountain Vineyards on the map, and have now based themselves in Riebeek-Kasteel. 'We've brought together an exciting and diverse group of vineyards which we feel will properly reflect the character of the Swartland, and placing our family name on each bottle will be our guarantee to the consumer of something special.' Their maiden wines were too young for review but, we predict, will be well worth the wait.

Muratie Estate

T 021-865-2330 · F 021-865-2790

Stellenbosch · Est 1685 · 1stB ca 1920 · Tasting & sales daily 9-5 · Fee R15, waived on purchase · Closed Easter Fri & Sun, Dec 25 & Jan 1 · Picnic baskets by appt · Tours by appt · Guest house · Art gallery · Owner Melck Family · Winemaker Francois Conradie (Dec 2005) · Viticulturist Paul Wallace (1998, consultant) · 42ha (cabs s&f, merlot, pinot, shiraz, chard, hanepoot, port varieties) · 210t/8 000cs own label 85% red 15% white · PO Box 133 Koelenhof 7605 · info@muratie.co.za · www.muratie.co.za

There's no want of character at Muratie. Last year a Cape Times reader hailed the atmospheric (and cobwebbed) tasting room as one of the Cape's Seven Wonders; their limited release Ronnie Melck Shiraz (from 30+ year old vines) is dedicated to a larger-than-life personality, the late father of current owner Rijk Melck. Stalwart Shiraz continued to perform (it and the Merlot won their WOM category tastings), while new characters emerged in the form of an as yet untasted cap classique sparkling and a pink from cab franc.

★★★★ **Cabernet Sauvignon 04**'s lighter-textured palate evolves into Old World austerity in **05** (★★★★) - with New World alc (15.5%) evident. Earthy, juicy; young tannins.

★★★★ **Shiraz 05** (★★★★) less generous than welcoming **04**. Hints spice & red berries, but obvious oak (15% new Am) dominates. Ripe 15% alc.

★★★★ **Ronnie Melck Reserve Shiraz** NEW Estate's first single-vyd wine. **05** obvious black pepper & origanum, touch bluegum. Juicy; silky tannins; 15% alc. Worth ageing few yrs. ±16 mths new Fr oak.

★★★★☆ **Ansela van de Caab** Classically built, subtle merlot/cab blend. **05** is gorgeous: ripe blackberry & spice well-intertwined, evolves in glass. Gd structure, balance; harmonious berry fruit & oak (yr Fr, 30% new); tannins integrated, but 14.5% alc noticeable.

★★★★ **Isabella Chardonnay** 🍷 Ripe, rich **07** (sample) well up to std. Golden Delicious character, honeycomb, with intense oak, well structured & integrated. Prevailing richness follows through to finish, where good acidity freshens.

★★★★ **Cape Vintage 05** (★★★☆) continues classic vintage styling of firmly dense **04**; tad disjointed mid-2007, with dried fruit tone, perhaps just needs more time. Field blend of tintas b/r/f, souzão, block planted in 70s. 2+ yrs old oak.

Merlot ★★★ **05**'s barnyard character deviates from established mould. Rich & juicy, tannins still prominent. **Pinot Noir** ★★★★ SA's first pinot planted here over 75 yrs ago. **05** bold & forthcoming. Spice, earth, black stonefruits; chunky, chewy tannins better after 2/3 yrs. Fr oak, Yr, used. **Melck's Red** 🍷 ★★☆ Off younger vines. **05** blend now merlot, shiraz (70/30). Shy, hints of blueberries, noticeable tannins: drink with food. **Cabernet Franc Rosé** NEW 🍷 ★★ **07** pretty, pale pink picnic wine, strawberry toned, light & softly dry. **Amber Forever** ★★★ Fortified muscat d'A, popular for over 75 yrs. Hazelnut & almond on previewed **07**, warming, & not for the faint-hearted! NE. **Cape Ruby** ★★★ Ever-popular **NV**, varieties as above, yr+ oak. Intense colour, woody nose, molasses & cassis, dry finish. This, all above, mainly Smnsberg-Sbosch/Sbosch WOs. *— MM*

Mvemve Raats 🍷

T 021-881-3078 ▪ F 021-881-3078

Stellenbosch ▪ Est/1stB 2004 ▪ Visits by appt ▪ Owner/winemaker/viticulturist Mzokhona Mvemve & Bruwer Raats ▪ 5t/150cs 100% red ▪ PO Box 2068 Dennesig 7601 ▪ braats@ mweb.co.za

Partner Mzokhona Mvemve contemplated mortgaging his house to launch their maiden (04) De Compostella. Unnecessary, as it turned out, as inherent wine quality prompted 13 top SA restaurants and hotels to take 60% and the remainder was exported. Their faith was justified as the wine has since blazed a successful trail locally and internationally, garnering 93pts from US Wine Spectator, the highest rating for a SA bordeaux blend to date.

De Compostella ★★★★ **05** raises the bar, carefully marries each of the main five bdx varieties even while cab f leads. Violets & friar's balsam on nose, opulent fruit reined in by taut tannins. Needs & deserves few yrs to develop & show its undoubted potential. **04** (★★★★) similar but lower keyed. *— MW*

■ My Best Friend *see Zandvliet Estate*

Mystery Wine Corporation
T 083-628-5160 ▪ F 086-50-50-212

Cape Town ▪ 1stB 2002 ▪ Closed to public ▪ Owner Saul Gorin ▪ 4 000cs 40% red 50% white 10% rosé ▪ PO Box 281 Sea Point 8060 ▪ gorin@isoft.co.za ▪ www.mysterywines.co.za

Saul Gorin has the negociant's nose for the market's preference and the consumer's appreciation for an affordable price. These attributes combine in his Mystery label, whose mainstays are a Dry Red and Dry White. Occasionally Saul G comes across an unmissable opportunity, like the 'crisp and refreshing' Sauvignon he discovered last year.

Dry Red ☺ ★★★ Approachable as always; **06** sweet melange berry fruits & caramel ex-oak staves, slight alc glow.

Rosé ★ 'Tickled Pink' pvsly. Strawberry hint to easy **07**, medium-sweet flavours. **Sauvignon Blanc** ★ Lemon & pineapple hints on **07**, uncomplicated, with bracing freshness. **Dry White**

★★★ Bright & breezy summer drinking. Last ed **06** mainly chenin, plumped with chard fatness & sauv granadilla. —*JP*

My Wyn

T 021-876-2518, 083-302-5556 · **F** 8660-80233

Franschhoek · Est/1stB 2001 · Tasting & sales at cellar door Mon-Fri 10-12.30 Oct-Apr, or by appt (T 083-302-5556) · Owner/winemaker Jacoline Haasbroek · 400cs · 50% red 50% white (incl 4 barrels chard for MCC) · PO Box 112 Franschhoek 7690 · tastewine@telkomsa.net

'Every year I try something new.' Last year it was sauvignon, made for the first time in Jacoline Haasbroek's new in-home cellar. The micro-vintner sticks to limited quantities – no more than three barrels – but last year made five casks of viognier, falling for a second harvest on Valentine's Day because the grapes were irresistible.

Cabernet Franc ★★ No **05/06**; tannins in last-tasted, herbaceous **04** needed time. **Petit Verdot** ★★★ Strong, tight tannins in ripe, mulberry-toned **05** last ed invited further bottle-maturation. **Sy Shiraz** ★★★★ Named for JH husband Johan ('Sy' meaning 'His'). Last was **04**, powerful (15% alc) but well extracted & balanced. **My Shiraz** NEW ★★★★ **04** spirituous top notes to intense scrub & raspberry; ripe palate further bolstered by bold tannins. 15% alc; 2 yrs oak, 2nd fill. **Viognier 06** sold out & **07** unready. Discontinued: **Cabernet Sauvignon**. —*CvZ*

Mzoli's Wines
NEW

T 021-638-1355

Cape Town · Owner Mzoli Ngcawuzele · Shop 15 NY 115 Gugulethu

The immensely popular Mzoli's eatery in Gugulethu, Cape Town works on a choose-'n'-char basis: you pick your meat cut, which is then flame-grilled for your eating pleasure. Mzoli's own-label Chardonnay is intended as a chilled-out match to the fare, while the Merlot isn't too proud to take a block of ice in summer.

Merlot ★★ So pale, you could read the menu through a glass of **05**; red berries & tannin robust enough to withstand the fattiest chop. **Chardonnay** ★★★ **06** slips down easily courtesy moderate 13% alc, dollop sugar. Lacks overt varietal character but pleasantly firm & fleshy. —*CvZ*

Nabygelegen Private Cellar

T 021-873-7534 · **F** 021-873-7534

Wellington (see Paarl map) · Est 1712 · 1stB 2002 · Tasting & sales Mon-Fri 9-5 Sat 9-1 · Closed Easter Fri/Sun, Apr 27, May 1, Dec 25 & Jan 1 · Tours anytime by appt · BYO picnic · Walks · Owner/cellarmaster James McKenzie · Winemaker Charles Stassen (Jan 2003) · Viticulturist Johan Wiese (May 2001, consultant) · 20ha (cab, merlot, petit v, tempranillo, chenin, sauvignon) · 5 000cs 60% red 40% white · PO Box 302 Wellington 7654 · sales@nabygelegen.co.za · www.nabygelegen.co.za

Plans for this property include a four-bedroom boutique guesthouse, a new tasting room and wine bar, and a small commercial bakery that will be run by the wives of the vineyard team. 'The winery is going at full speed and this year's white-wine vintage could be exceptional,' comments owner James McKenzie.

★★★★ **1712** Lauded by Decanter as Top New World Red. Merlot-led (60%) bdx blend, exceptional **05** (★★★★★) baked plums lead to inky, elegant choc-toned core. Serious crumbly tannins from 35% cab give weight, structure. Well poised & already more sumptuous than **04**; long finish shows class. 16 mths Fr oak.

★★★★ **Scaramanga** Funky blend cab, malbec & tempranillo. **05**, tasted pvs ed, suave & sophisticated. Wild, aromatic leather & tight tannin structure. 6 mths Fr oak.

★★★★ **Natural Sweet** New name & packaging for 'At the Limiet'. From rare-in-Cape hárslevelü, **04** (★★★★) interesting savoury bouquet, raisined & honeyed mouthfeel directed by firm acidity; lees contact adds richness though overall effect less convincing than **03**, showing focused fruity persistence.

Chenin Blanc ★★★ Ripe bruised apples contrast caramel texture. **06** soft & round; 11 mths Fr oak, ex-single vineyard. **Sauvignon Blanc** ★★★ Ultra-crisp **07** from early harvest, light alc

(12%) with Granny Smith apple zing. **Chenin Blanc-Sauvignon Blanc** ★★★ **06** same melon & peach flavours as last-tasted **04**, though tad foursquare. — *RP*

Namaqua Wines
T 027-213-1080 • F 027-213-3476

Olifants River • Est 2002 • Tasting & sales Mon-Fri 8-5 Sat 8.30-12 (sales close 30 mins later) • Closed pub hols • Tours at 10 & 3 during harvest • Light meals by appt or BYO picnic • Tour groups (±42 people) • Conferences • Audio-visual presentation • Gifts • Owner 224 members • Winemaker Alwyn Maass, Pieter Verwey, Driaan van der Merwe & Len Knoetze (1997/1999/2000/2002), with Koos Thiart, Johan Weideman & Renier van Greenen (all Jan 2004) • Viticulturist Marina Bruwer & Heine Janse van Rensburg (Jan 2004/Jan 2004) • 4 990ha (cab, merlot, pinotage, ruby cab, shiraz, chard, chenin, colombard, sauv, hanepoot) • 107 000t/8.9m cs 30% red 70% white • PO Box 75 Vredendal 8160 • info@namaquawines.com • www.namaquawines.com

One of the company's two cellars, that in Vredendal, last year installed the biggest tank press seen in SA, able to process up to 200 tons of grapes. WCI is still growing its export market: the Namaqua range of bottled wines has been expanded, pushing more product into retail chains Tesco, Asda and Morrisons. On the local front, Namaqua has launched stylish new three- and five-litre cartons, and a new wine for local palates, the Natural Sweet Rosé, packaged in a striking pink box. 'The ladies will love this one,' predicts marketing director Fanie Augustyn.

Gôiya range
Shiraz-Pinotage ★★ Simple game & smoked meat flavours on **06**, 70/30 mix. **Chardonnay-Sauvignon Blanc** ★★ Semi-dry equal blend; **07** uncomplicated everyday quaffer. Discontinued: **Shiraz**, **Merlot-Cabernet Sauvignon**. Large volumes, for export only.

Namaqua range

Late Harvest ☺ ★★★ Inviting dried peach intro to sweet, juicy tropical fruit flavours. **Natural Sweet Rosé** NEW ☺ ★★★ Sweet charmer with floral nose introducing peaches & Turkish delight.

Dry Red ★★ Dry fynbos tones on bold food-inviting three-way blend. **Rosé** ★ Simple, light, lunchtime pink from chenin & pinotage. **Blanc de Blanc** ★ Undemanding picnic white, even simpler than pvs. **Extra Lite** ★ Straightforward dry white, approved by Weigh-Less. **Johannisberger** ★★★ Big, mouthfilling sweetness, brimming with muscat & honey. **Stein** ★★ Herbal notes to undemanding off-dry sipper. **Johannisberger Red** ★★ Three-grape medley with firm tannins, so tastes off-dry rather than full-sweet. All **NV**, available in 3 & 5litre packs.

B4 range
B4 Spumante ★★ Party all night on this cheerful, low-alc **NV** bubbly, popping with sherbet & guavas.

Spruitdrift range

Cabernet Sauvignon ☺ ★★★ **06** (sample) savoury nose; ripe blackberry flavours on pleasantly firm tannic base. **Pinotage** ☺ ★★★ Easy **05**, earthy, herbal nose, ripe plums & cherries, less astringency than pvs. **Shiraz** ☺ ★★★ Wafts of herbs & earth on **06**, ripe plums on foundation of relaxed tannins.

Merlot ★★ **06** savoury smoked meat character & big dry tannins. Discontinued: **Sauvignon Blanc**, **Grand Cru**, **Johannisberger**, **Brut Sparkling**, **Vin Doux Sparkling**, **Hanepoot Jerepigo**, **Red Muscadel**, **White Muscadel**.

Gôiya D-Lite-Ful range
Discontinued: **Red**, **Rosé**, **White**, **Brut**, **Rosé Sparkling**.

Spencer Bay range
Discontinued: **Merlot**, **Shiraz**. — *DB*

Napier Winery
T 021-873-7829 • F 021-864-2728

Wellington (see Paarl map) • *Est 1993* • *1stB 1994* • *Tasting & sales Mon-Fri 9-5 Sat 10-4 Sun & pub hols by appt* • *Cellar tours by appt* • *Self-catering cottage (sleeps 4)* • *Small conference facility* • *Owner Michael & Catherine Loubser, Leon Bester* • *Winemaker/viticulturist Leon Bester (Apr 2000)* • *34ha (five bdx reds, shiraz, chard, chenin)* • *±5 500cs 30% red 70% white* • *PO Box 638 Wellington 7654* • *sales@napierwinery.co.za* • *www.napierwinery.co.za*

Nadia Pieterse and Jeanette Booysen have brought a woman's touch to the cellar and tasting room respectively. 'We're following the trend in SA to provide opportunities for women,' they say.

Cabernet Sauvignon ★★★ 04 cherries & red berries with some minerality; soft tannins, light & pleasant shorter-term drinking. Yr Fr oak, 30% new. **Red Medallion ★★★★** Bdx-inspired blend cabs s/f & merlot. Minerality & spiciness on blackberry-brushed **03**; nutty tannins on dry finish. Trophy Show-lauded **00** & **01** also still available. 18-20 mths Fr oak. **St Catherine ★★★** Barrel-fermented/aged chardonnay, **03** tasted last ed. Balanced; tropical fruits & walnuts, well-integrated 14% alc. **Greenstone ★★★★** Last-tasted **06** was unwooded chenin, poised & elegant with lunch-time 12% alc. — *MM*

Natte Valleij
T 021-875-5171

Paarl (see Stellenbosch map) • *Est 1715* • *Visits by appt* • *B&B/self-catering accommodation (see Stay-over section)* • *Owner/winemaker Alexander Milner* • *10t (2007) 500cs 100% red* • *PO Box 4 Klapmuts 7625* • *milner@intekom.co.za* • *www.nattevalleij.co.za*

One-man show Alexander Milner not only rode the week-long Giro del Capo cycle race (which took place during harvest), he also supplied the wine, his Swallow Cab, presented to Argus tour winner Robbie Hunter. Natte Valleij production tripled this year: 'It's human nature to want to buy quality well-priced wine by the case, rather than by the bottle,' explains Milner.

Swallow range
Cabernet Sauvignon ★★ Joyous & generously fruited **06**, hints mint &, more unusually, tomato leaf. **Merlot ★★ 06** similar herbaceous tone to Cab, soft, pleasantly chewy texture. Both modestly priced, open-fermented, aged 11 mths in 2nd/3rd fill barrels. — *RP*

Naughton's Flight
T 021-794-3928 • F 021-794-3928

1stB 2003 • *Closed to public* • *Owner Francis Naughton* • *Winemaker Ronell Wiid (consultant)* • *8 000 btls* • *25 Willow Rd Constantia 7806* • *naughts@mweb.co.za*

Francis Naughton is as upbeat as ever about SA and his wine (which all sells out), especially the new food-friendly Viognier. If this is the wine that 'moved' an Irish lady journalist, 'imagine the reaction to the planned Noble Late Harvest', quips the irrepressible Irishman.

★★★★ Shiraz Gentle approach of Ronell W evident in these; **05** (**★★★**) light toned, supple, though missing depth & length of **04**; some varnishy notes, still prominent Am oak (20%). WO Paarl.

Vionier NEW Two vintages to date; **06** is latest, neither tasted by us. — *AL*

Nederburg Wines
T 021-862-3104 • F 021-862-4887

Paarl • *Est 1792* • *1stB ca 1940* • *Tasting & sales Mon-Fri 8.30-5; Sat 10-2 (Apr-Oct); Sat 10-4 & Sun 11-4 (Nov-Mar)* • *Informal tasting fee dependent on wine; tasting & tour: R25* • *Closed Easter Fri, Dec 25 & Jan 1* • *Tours in Afrikaans, English, French & German by appt* • *Picnic lunches by appt Mon-Sun Nov-Mar* • *Corporate & private lunches/dinners by appt* • *'Incredible Journey of Tastes' food & wine matching, by appt* • *Tour groups* • *Gifts* • *Conferences* • *Conservation area* • *Owner Distell* • *Cellarmaster Razvan Macici (Jan 2001)* • *Red-wine maker Wim*

Truter (Jun 2007) ▪ *White-wine maker Tariro Masayiti (Aug 2005), with Pieter Badenhorst (Mar 2001)* ▪ *Viticulturist Hannes van Rensburg & Drikus Heyns* ▪ *18 000t/1.1m cs* ▪ *Private Bag X3006 Paarl 7620* ▪ *nedwines@distell.co.za* ▪ *www.nederburg.co.za*

Legendary winemaker Günter Brözel's Nederburg Edelkeur 69, his pioneering Noble Late Harvest wine, received the first of a string of accolades at the Concours Mondial in Budapest in 1972. When his successor, Razvan Macici, saw that the biennial Botyritis Wine & Sweet Competition was being held in Budapest last year, he decided there could be no more fitting tribute than to enter GB's Edelkeur 77. In the tradition of all romantic gestures, his had a fitting consequence – the Edelkeur, the oldest table wine in the line-up and the only contender from outside Europe, was awarded Top Ten status. Razvan M now has a new red winemaker: assistant Wim Truter has taken over from Elunda Basson. Promoted to co-star (in a recent Nederburg TV campaign) is Razvan's shadow, his Jack Russell, Vladimir.

Private Bin range for Nederburg Auction

The famous Nederburg Auction, now in its 35th yr, is SA's biggest. It's open to any producer whose wine passes the selection process (Nederburg also subject to the screening). The Nederburg wines listed here are made in small quantities, usually from special vyd blocks, offered in lots of ±500 cs. Originally labelled under a meaningless Bin number, prefaced by a letter (R=dry red, D dry white, S dessert, C Cap Classique), they now also carry the variety/blend.

★★★★ **Cabernet Sauvignon Private Bin R163** Striking **04** from Darling grapes. Compact, concentrated dark-berried allure, tannin still taut. Shd easily last 10 yrs. Notes from last ed for all these auction reds; new vintages not ready.

★★★★ **Merlot Private Bin R181** Fruit-forward & rounded **04**, with ripe cassis, ripe meatiness, oak adding fragrant cinnamon. Juicy, dense fruit, plus fine tannins, long finish. This & Pinotage less dry than others in range at ±4.1g/litre RS.

★★★★ **Pinotage Private Bin R172 04** has nuances of wild brambleberry, tangy morello cherry & touch of tar. Suave & stylish, with gd varietal character, but will benefit from 5-7 yrs. Darling/Dbnville fruit.

★★★★ **Shiraz Private Bin 121** Savoury, compact, dense **04** last yr took time to open in glass & reveal subtle black cherry, choc, smoke; elegantly styled with taut tannins needing at least 3-6 yrs. Darling/Philadelphia grapes.

★★★★ **Cabernet Sauvignon-Merlot Private Bin R109** Classic aromas/flavours cassis, lead pencil, choc truffle on **03**. Cab leads in 58/42 blend, supporting merlot's gentler attractions. Midweight, elegant; more approachable than R163. These auction reds have 10% juice bled off after crushing to concentrate wine; mix open fermenters, steel tanks; 18 mths in small Fr oak.

★★★★ **Cabernet Sauvignon-Shiraz Private Bin R103** After taut **03**, very fine **04** (★★★★★) with concentrated black-berried fruit & notes of toast & tar. Firmly structured, still youthful, needing few yrs to unravel. 60/40 blend, converse below.

★★★★ **Chardonnay Private Bin D270** Generous, forthcoming **06**, whose citrus-tinged, sweetly soft fruity richness is cut by firm acidity (not quite integrated in youth); sympathetic oak (yr); stony undertone, forceful limy finish. **05** (★★★★★) boldy impresive. Dbnvlle, Sbosch grapes.

★★★★ **Sauvignon Blanc Private Bin D215** As usual, exuberant **07** contrasting with D234 version: this riper & fleshier, with showy tropical fruit, savoury rich acidity giving lip-smacking succulence, gd length.

★★★★ **Sauvignon Blanc Private Bin D234** The more restrained version, but **07**'s capsicum, grass & nettles no less intense for being unaggressive, even delicate; balance no less succulent. A little flint adds further interest.

★★★★ **Viognier Private Bin D212** NEW Variety's potential excessiveness here well disciplined, shows as delicate peach on **07**'s nose & well-balanced, structured palate. Lingering flavours. Lovely sipping, but restraint & fresh, dry firmness make gd food partner.

★★★★ **Edelkeur** The botrytised chenin that gave rise to SA's NLH industry. **06**'s glowing mid-gold offers apricot, honey, citrus zest & jasmine amongst its complexities: but its (adequate) acidity not quite thrilling, its charm not intense or long-lingering.

★★★★ **Eminence NLH** Achieves fragrant freshness - redolent of jasmine tea, apricot & tangerine - rather than powerful finesse; but softly firm, well balanced, delightful. From muscat de F. WO Paarl, like Edelkeur.

Malbec Private Bin R101 ★★★☆ Black plum, smoked beef, mocha aromas in **04**; berries jostling toasty oak on dry palate, with youthful austerity on finish.

Private Bin range

★★★★☆ **Cabernet Sauvignon** Big, serious **05** confirms **04**'s success. Shows lots of cedary oak but depth of fruit flavour & intensity to match. Warm, ripely powerful but refined, paying deference to traditional styling, with tannic structure demanding ±5 yrs for max pleasure.

★★★★ **Sauvignon Blanc** Appealing, convincing varietal character, **07** initially more grass & fig than passionfruit notes, but subtle rather than over-pungent, with breadth & depth on offer. EW.

These more readily available than Auction versions.

Manor House range

★★★★ **Collection Cabernet Sauvignon** [NEW] Forceful but elegant (& slightly conservative) **05**, opening with fine cedar, tobacco & cassis, then revealing well balanced tannins, acid & oak plus gd silky texture; finishing on herbaceous note. A few yrs will benefit.

★★★★ **Shiraz** Last was shapely & accessible **04** (**05** sold out). **06** (★★★☆) with spicy red fruit, coffee, leather, built on smooth clean lines, with light grip, but v dependant on sweet oak for effect.

★★★★ **Sauvignon Blanc** After thrillingly balanced **06**, **07** (★★★☆) perhaps more ordinary, though gd varietal character, succesfully mixing ripeness with freshly crisp green bite.

Cabernet Sauvignon ★★★☆ Tasted last ed, reserved **04** was tightly woven, classically oriented. Yr oak, most new.

Classic range

★★★★ **Edelrood** ✓ A little too much easy sweetness on **05** puts high rating in doubt, but cab's structure asserts quality, merlot asserts prettiness; there's lovely fruit, gd structure, appropriate oaking - so we are seduced. Approachable, but shd keep.

★★★★ **Noble Late Harvest** Lovely honey & tangerine notes on rich, powerfully sweet yet delicate **07**; a subtle balance with satisfactory acid bite, but trifle short-finishing - pity, given the pleasure involved.

Rosé ☺ ★★☆ Light-red **07** replete with red berry scents, the sweet softness deftly balanced by a pleasing freshness. **Stein** ☺ ★★☆ Loads of soft, mellow ripe fruitiness on semi-sweet **07**, with bracing of fresh acidity to enhance quaffability. **Premier Grand Cru** ☺ ★★★ This style can be bleak - but not this crisply dry **07**, full of lip-smacking green-tinged fruit.

Cabernet Sauvignon ★★★☆ **05** sold out, untasted by us. Unshowy (not trivial) **06** has spicy, fruity nose & decent, firm palate for gd everyday drinking. **Merlot** ★★★★ Smoothly soft red-berried plumpness of **05** neatly complemented by a touch of firm tannin, herbaceous lift & hint of spicy oak. EW. **Pinotage** ★★★ Outgoing & so eager to please, fruity **05** just fails to offer enough to cope with its dry tannins, before retreating crestfallen. **Shiraz** ★★★ Gd varietal notes on v satisfactory **06** (incl lilies, smoke), all in appropriate, undemanding, lightish balance. **Baronne** ★★★★ Suave but with firm tannic control over its smooth fruitiness, **05** expertly blends cab, shiraz. Easy but not at all trivial. Moderately, expertly oaked - as are all reds in range. **Chardonnay** ★★★ Last yr **06** ripe & soft, slightly sweet on finish. 30% fermented/6 mths new oak. **Paarl Riesling** ★★ Masquerader actually made from crouchen; **07** lightly fruity & dry; dully respectable. **Rhine Riesling** ✓ ★★★★ Distinctive nutmeg & pineapple notes on fresh but off-dry **07**; a satisfying & even elegant mouthful with lingering charm.

Sauvignon Blanc ★★★☆ Well-balanced **07**, deploying both grassy & riper tropical notes: a gd mouthful of juicy green fruit. **Sauvignon Blanc-Chardonnay** ★★★ Tasted last ed, **06** had real interest: ripe & juicy but dry. Chard portion oaked. **Special Late Harvest** ✓ ★★★☆ Always fragrant, flowery sweet stuff from aromatic varieties. Delightfully light-feeling & fresh **07** happily maintains tradition.

Lifestyle range

> **Lyric** ☺ ★★★ Light fruity-floral aromas/flavours on off-dry **07**, giving undemanding pleasant drinking.

Duet ★★★ From **06** 'Shiraz-Pinotage' (as the int. version calls it); a chunky & robust just-dry 60/40 blend (not retasted). Like next, a light oak influence (3 mths staves, with micro-oxygenation). **Shiraz-Viognier** ★★★ Like next, mostly for int. sales; locally from tasting room only. **06** (tasted last ed) for easy, early drinking: succeeds admirably, with soft berry fruit & leather hint; modestly tannined, a little sugar. **Chardonnay-Viognier** ★★★ Minority viognier dominates peachily in youth, with chard adding some gravitas. **07** dry, with a nice tannic touch. **Prelude 07** another unexceptional and unexceptional dry, crisp, well-made quaffer. **Cuvée Brut** ★★★ As ever, reliable carbonated **NV** threaded with fragrant citrus & not all that dry; but it's really the happy bubbles that matter. — *TJ*

Neethlingshof Estate

T 021-883-8988 • F 021-883-8941

Stellenbosch ▪ Tasting & sales Mon-Fri 9-5 (open till 7pm Dec 1-Jan 31); Sat/Sun & pub hols 10-4 ▪ Fee R30 (R35 incl cellar tour) ▪ Closed Easter Fri & Dec 25 ▪ Tours by appt ▪ Lord Neethling Restaurant, Palm Terrace ▪ Play area for children ▪ Tour groups ▪ Conferences ▪ Owner Lusan Premium Wines ▪ Winemaker DeWet Viljoen, with Lauren Snyman ▪ Viticulturist Eben Archer ▪ 210ha ▪ 50 000cs 60% red 40% white ▪ PO Box 104 Stellenbosch 7599 ▪ info@ neethlingshof.co.za ▪ www.neethlingshof.co.za

'Neethlingshof is like a big puzzle, every piece slowly but surely falling into place…' reflects DeWet Viljoen. An extensive uprooting and replanting programme, initiated by Eben Archer, over the halfway mark and due for completion in 2011, is already reaping dividends. In the cellar, this 'small team with big plans' has been striving to establish a specific style for their wines. Sauvignon sales have soared and they're hoping for similar growth for the red wines of the 04 vintage, DWV's first here.

Lord Neethling range

★★★★ **Cabernet Sauvignon** None since **00** (★★★), still selling. Last noted as very dry with pronounced acidity. 16 mths Fr oak. Similar to taut **98**, which needed time. NE.

★★★★ **Cabernet Franc 03** generous floral bouquet, serious structure, fine tannins. 14 mths Fr oak. Not-retasted, still available. NE.

★★★★ **Pinotage** Last ed **03** showed promising richness, plush tannins embracing fine concentrated cherry/tobacco fruit. Youthful exuberance allows for both current drinking & few yrs aging. NE.

★★★★☆ **Laurentius** The flagship, quietly composed in **02** (★★★★), rounded & ready. Harmonious & satisfying cab, cab f, merlot, shiraz fusion, showing gentle savoury development. Yr oak, Fr/Am 90/10, 70% new, same as for refined & balanced **01**. NE.

★★★★☆ **Weisser Riesling Noble Late Harvest** Striking botrytis-enriched dessert. Last ed we noted typical honey & apricot scents on **05**, sweet marmalade flavours, 137 g/l RS lengthened by acid lift. Classic low 9.5% alc. NE.

Shiraz NEW Not tasted. Discontinued: **Chardonnay**.

Neethlingshof range

★★★★ **Cabernet Sauvignon** Last ed we noted **03** as serious, textbook cab; spice & dark berries restrained by supple tannins, fine acid spine. Fr/Am oak, 16 mths, almost half new. NE.

★★★★ **Cape Blend** None since youthfully tight **01**; mainly unwooded mix cabs s/f, pinotage (40/28/22). NE.

★★★★ **Gewürztraminer** Regular charmer - why aren't there more? Scented yet refined spice & Turkish Delight tones on **07**; rich but not heavy; flavours intensified & lengthened by perfectly matched 6.3 g/l sugar/acid. NE.

★★★★ **Special Reserve Sauvignon Blanc** NEW **07** sleeker, cooler feel than std label. Agile, with good weight; plentiful lemongrass & mineral juiciness extended by clean savoury acid.

Merlot ★★★ **04** more rustic than pvs; pleasant fruit marred by aggressive dry tannins, bitter twist in tail. No **03**. NE. **Pinotage** ★★ **03** last yr was ripe but unknit, needing more time. 43% new Fr/Am oak. NE. **Shiraz** ★★★ **03** ultra-ripe, somewhat cloying creamy texture, warming 15.3% alc. NE. **Cabernet Sauvignon-Merlot** ★★★ Rather sombre **06**; quiet dark fruits, soft-centred but grainy tannin contrast. **04/05** sold out before we could taste. NE. **Blanc de Noir** ★★★ Well-balanced, characterful **06**, redcurrant flavours, sweet entry (7 g/l RS). Not retasted. **Chardonnay Wooded** ★★★★ Oaking on **06** was evident though restrained last yr (50% left unwooded). Citrus, nutty oatmeal combo, sweet-fruit tail. Not re-tasted. **Chardonnay Unwooded** ★★★★ Uncluttered peach, pineapple flavours, citrus finish in food-friendly **06**. Not re-assessed. NE. **Sauvignon Blanc** ★★★ **07** big, rich mouthful of tropical fruit & lemongrass. Lacks zing; alc glow in tail. NE. — *AL*

Neil Ellis Meyer-Näkel
T 021-887-0649 • **F** 021-887-0647

Stellenbosch ▪ Est/1stB 1998 ▪ Tasting & sales at Neil Ellis Wines ▪ Owner Neil Ellis Meyer-Näkel (Pty) Ltd ▪ Winemaker Neil Ellis & Werner Näkel ▪ Viticulturist Pieter Smit ▪ 10ha ▪ 3 500cs 100% red ▪ Box 917 Stellenbosch 7599 ▪ info@neilellis.com

A joint venture between Werner Näkel, known as the 'king of red wine' in his native Germany, and one of our own winemaking aristocrats, Neil Ellis. Last year they harvested the Stellenbosch farm's first grapes; now it's all about fine-tuning, says Neil E. 'Once we're really satisfied with the quality, we'll consider a tiny on-site winery.'

Z ★★★★ **05** from merlot; forceful cedar & cassis ensemble, touch herbaceous freshness on palate with spirited tannin finish. Needs yr/2 to settle & fill out. **Zwalu** ★★★★ **06** cab, merlot, cab f blend; ex-barrel shows sweet-fruited ripeness, gd creamy concentration & length in medium body. No **05**. — *AL*

Neil Ellis Wines

T 021-887-0649 • **F** 021-887-0647

Stellenbosch ▪ 1stB 1984 ▪ Tasting & sales Mon-Fri 9.30-4.30 Sat & pub hols 10-2 ▪ Fee R15 p/p, waived on purchase ▪ Closed Easter Fri, Dec 25/26 & Jan 1 ▪ Owner Neil Ellis Wines (Pty) Ltd ▪ Winemaker Neil Ellis, with Warren Ellis & Reginald Holder ▪ 40 000 cs ▪ 50% red 50% white ▪ PO Box 917 Stellenbosch 7599 ▪ info@neilellis.com ▪ www.neilellis.com

Plans to streamline the range are somewhat hamstrung by commercial factors, says Neil Ellis. 'Markets temper egotistical attitudes to winemaking.' Instead, he's considering adding to the portfolio. 'Before I'm dead and buried I'm going to find the perfect site for riesling. It's a variety that's not taken seriously enough here - unsurprisingly, given that most local bottlings bear no resemblance to the German versions. But it's such a beautiful wine when it's good.' Ellis is looking beyond his Stellenbosch home base, perhaps to cooler Elgin where he's just replanted chardonnay, and his pioneering work with red varieties in this predominantly white-wine area continues to bear fruit.

Vineyard Selection

★★★★☆ **Cabernet Sauvignon** More classically styled than Premium version, which helps account for **05**'s relative tautness, austerity. But concentration of sumptuous ripe fruit, classy 100% new Fr oaking & plentiful tannin should permit similar gd 5+ yrs maturation as more youthfully expressive & splendid **04** (★★★★★).

★★★★☆ **Syrah 05** (★★★★) usual mix of black spice & smoked meat, generous charry oak. Tighter structure & fresher acidity than **04** & some pvs will require some time to relax & allow full expression of delicate sweet fruit. 100% new Fr oak, 18 mths.

★★★★☆ **Sauvignon Blanc** 🔲 Texture & vinosity accented over forward fruit in this food-friendly style. **06** (★★★★) attractive balance of freshness & richness from 70% barrel-fermented portion, extended lees maturation; concludes with clean varietal flourish. **04** similar if tad more sophisticated. No **05**.

Premium range

★★★★ **Cabernet Sauvignon** Pvsly listed with 'Stellenbosch' prefix, as were some below. **05** substantially built, without losing unshowy modernity of pvs. Youthfully vigorous, with Fr oak polish, bright cab fruits & sturdy though balanced tannin frame. Needs yr/2 to unwind. Small barrels, 18 mths.

★★★★ **Pinotage** Modern & delicious. **06** introduced by velvety purple sheen; juicy, sweet-fruited with moreish mulberry tang, supported by pleasantly firm tannins for immediate enjoyment. Fr oak, 15 mths. No **05**.

★★★★ **Shiraz** Elegant **04** ex-7 yr old Grnekloof vyd. Supple, well-textured drinking until ±2010. Unobtrusive oak, Fr, 15 mths. Not re-assessed this ed. **05** unready for tasting.

★★★★ **Cabernet Sauvignon-Merlot** Characteristic **05** power noticeable but not out of tune with wine's hallmark soft black fruits & choc. Neil E's usual tempered approach evident in freshening whisper-clean Fr oak, controlled tannins.

★★★★ **Aenigma** Occasional, experimental label. First & only **03** was a burgundy-like chard, barrel fermented with native yeasts, matured 10 mths.

★★★★ **Elgin Chardonnay** 🔲 Cool, citrus-toned **06** reflects its highland origin. Lightness of touch, taut minerally acid belie creamy undercurrents, dainty but satisfying hazelnut/oatmeal flavours. Barrel fermented, seasoned 10 mths.

★★★★ **Stellenbosch Chardonnay** 🔲 Ellis trademark elegance beautifully realised in **06**. Laced with quiet yet pure nuts & tropical tones, subtle oak; liveliness anchored by creamy undertones, limy fresh conclusion. Plenty in store. Fr oak fermented/aged 8 mths.

★★★★☆ **Groenekloof Sauvignon Blanc** 🔲 Unusually vivid gooseberry/capsicum concentration on **07**, with the std minerally attractions. Skims across palate with determined verve to mouthwatering, fruitily dry conclusion. —AL

Nelson Estate 🍴🍷☕📷🎿♿
T 021-869-8453 • **F** 021-869-8424

Paarl ▪ Est/1stB 1993 ▪ Tasting & sales Mon-Fri 9-5 Sat 9-2 Sun by appt ▪ Wine & vineyard tour R20 p/p ▪ Closed Easter Fri/Sun, Dec 25 & Jan 1 ▪ Tours Mon-Sat 10; Sun by appt ▪ Meals/ refreshments by appt ▪ Facilities for children ▪ Tour groups ▪ Gifts ▪ Walks ▪ Conference/function/lapa venue ▪ Conservation area ▪ Owner Alan Nelson ▪ Winemaker Jean van Rooyen & Lisha Nelson (2003, 2007) ▪ Viticulturist Daniel Nelson (Apr 2005) ▪ 60ha (cab, merlot, pinotage, shiraz, chard, sauv) ▪ 340t/20 000cs own label 65% red 30% white 5% rosé ▪ PO Box 2009 Windmeul 7630 ▪ info@nelsonscreek.co.za ▪ www.nelsonscreek.co.za

Indefatigable owner Alan Nelson regards the Pearl's Gate 'mini-region' as the undiscovered winelands gem. Something he's actively changing, abetted by three wedding and conference venues, making his family estate perfect for crowd-pulling events like the Horse & Wine Festival, The Pearl's Gate Barrel Tasting Festival, monthly farmers' markets and regular sunset concerts. Daughter Lisha joined as winemaker at the end of 2007 after completing her Masters degree in Oenology at Stellenbosch University.

★★★★ **Pinotage** Not for the faint-hearted. Opaque, extracted **03** (★★★★), smoked meat & high-toned aromas of ultra-ripe fruit, cut through on palate by firm acidity & held by gripping oak tannins. High alc gives porty impression on finish. **02** similarly showy, settled down after yr in bottle.

★★★★ **Cabernet Sauvignon-Merlot** Stylish **02**, 81/19 blend, 18 mths Fr oak, 80% new. Classic cassis & cigarbox tones, firm tannins, deftly applied wood.

★★★★ **Chardonnay** Native yeasts; fermented/aged new Fr barrels, 10 mths. **05** (★★★★) tad lighter than pvs; honeyed lemon-butter tone checked by racy acidity. Regional winner 2007 Terroir Awards. **04** was forceful, creamy & concentrated.

Shiraz ★★★☆ **02** full-flavoured/bodied (14.8% alc) but not overpowering; well layered with peppery red fruit, warm toast & coffee tones. All except Pinotage tasted pvsly.

Nelson's Creek range

Cabernet Sauvignon ★★★ **02**, with dash merlot, dry, savoury, slightly earthy flavours, firm tannins. 8 mths new Fr staves. **Merlot** ★★★ Graphite & cassis announce **03**, clean ripe fruit, big dry tannins from yr Fr oak. **Pinotage** ★★★ Wooded **03**, different to silky pvs; savoury & rustic, 15% alc showing in hot finish. **Shiraz** ★★★★ Suave, supple **02**, appetising dark choc/black cherry flavours; fine pervasive smokiness. From single 'Stony Hill' vyd; older Am oak. VDG & regional winner 2006 Terroir Awards. **Albenet** ★★ Blend changes into merlot-led unwooded quintet in **03** (sample); earthy mulberry flavours & somewhat rustic dry tannins. **Cabernet Sauvignon-Merlot Rosé** ★★★ **07** bled from Estate range cab & merlot to produce richly fruity but dry rosé, some structure, flavoursome finish. Only this, next three wines, retasted this ed. **Chardonnay** ★★★ Lightly staved **06** in restrained citrus style for early, easy drinking, with food. No **05**. **Sauvignon Blanc** ★★★ **07** fresh mix herbaceousness & tropical pineapple, pleasant fruitiness balanced by zingy acidity. **Triple Creek** ★★★ **06** chard, sem, chenin blend too unformed to rate last ed, now maturity shows in gold tinge & nutty aromas, citrus finish; drink soon. **Marguerite** ★★ Litchi-scented **06** blend chenin & muscat d'A finishes crisply despite generous dollop sugar. — *IM*

New Beginnings Wines
T 021-869-8453 • F 021-869-8424

Paarl • Tasting & sales Mon-Fri 9-5 • Fee R20 for groups • Vineyard tours by appointment • Owner Klein Begin Farming Association • Winemaker Sollie Hendriks, with Jean van Rooyen (Nelson Estate) since 2003 • 13 000cs 40% red 60% white • PO Box 2009 Windmeul 7630 • victor@nelsonscreek.co.za

SA's first black wine producers made no wine last year. Instead, they restructured their venture, says spokesperson Victor Titus. Remaining stock of Pinotage and Cab is still flying via export channels, and their first shiraz and chardonnay vines are in the ground, heralding the first white wine from own grapes (chardonnay previously sourced from mentor Nelson Estate).

■ **New Cape Wines** *see Eagle's Cliff Wines/New Cape Wines*

Newton Johnson Wines
T 028-312-3862 • F 028-312-3867

Hemel-en-Aarde Valley (see Elgin/Walker Bay map) • Est 1996 • 1stB 1997 • Tasting & sales Mon-Fri 9-4 Sat 10-2 • Closed pub hols • Heaven Restaurant • Owner Dave & Felicity Johnson • Cellarmaster Gordon Newton Johnson (Jan 2001) • Winemaker Nadia Cilliers (Aug 2006) • Viticulturist Christopher Cloete (Jul 2005) • 11ha (pinot, shiraz, chard, sauv) • 120t/7 000cs 44% red 48% white 8% rosé • PO Box 225 Hermanus 7200 • wine@newtonjohnson.com • www.newtonjohnson.com

Following a 'great' first year in the new winery, the Newton Johnsons have completed their new tasting room, offering panoramic views of the Hemel-en-Aarde Valley; and Heaven restaurant has increased in size after a 'sensational' first season. In the vineyards there are new high-density plantings of shiraz, mourvèdre and pinot, with some alternative training methods, and there are plans to plant more pinot, sauvignon and chardonnay in cooler sites on a new 100ha property. While pinot is still the primary focus (the limited quantities sell out quickly), the Syrah-Mourvèdre blend has overtaken the Sauvignon as the best-selling wine.

★★★★ **Cabernet Sauvignon** Features dollop shiraz; **03** still available; pvsly we admired its restrained smoky bouquet, black cherry flavours & persistent cool finish.

★★★★ **Pinot Noir** Historically a softer pinot, **06** touch more dense, notch up on lightish **05** (★★★★); has earthy, cranberry appeal, focused sweet & sour berry fruit & lively acidity.

Supple tannins in balance with 14.4% alc & oak (9 mths Fr oak, 41% new). 'Our most ageworthy yet,' says the team.

★★★★ **Syrah-Mourvèdre** Bold & modern rhône-style blend off W Bay, Dbnvlle vyds. **06** not ready; retasted **05** has developed softer, less tarry note, tannins more supple & integrated; still lots of life, 14.8% alc in sync with fruit, wood.

★★★★ **Chardonnay** Highlights virtues - tight mineral core, preserved by partial malo - of reputed Vllrsdorp-area single vyd 'Kaaimansgat' ('Crocodile's Lair'). **06** poised, creamy but crisp citrus flavours cradled in toasty oak (10 mths Fr, 33% new), gd few yrs ageing potential.

★★★★ **Sauvignon Blanc** 🖺 Usually from H-en-A Vlly, Elgin fruit (65/28) plus 7% fermented/aged semillon ex-Bot Rvr. **07** combines asparagus & earthy minerality of pvs with greater creamy breadth, less fruit/acid tension. Modest 13.5% alc, serious dinner companion.

★★★★ **Pour Mes Amis** Occasional label; last was harmonious **05**, mainly sauv (75%), splash semillon ex-W Bay for extra flesh. 3 mths new Fr barriques.

Felicité ★★★ Sophisticated, food-friendly dry rosé. **07** first with oaked component; shiraz & sauv (73/37), dash semillon. Savoury & raspberry flavours in tangy, plumper style. — *MW*

■ **New World** *see* The Winery of Good Hope

■ **Nicholas L Jonker** *see* Jonkheer

Nick & Forti's Wines
T 012-460-4367 • F 012-460-5173

Est/1stB 2004 • Closed to public • Owner Fortunato Mazzone & Saronsberg • Winemaker Dewaldt Heyns (2004) • 200cs 100% red • Box 25032 Monument Park Pretoria 0105 • ritrovo@mweb.co.za

Collaboration between Nick van Huyssteen of Saronsberg and Forti Mazzone, chef and co-owner of acclaimed Ritrovo Ristorante in Pretoria, celebrating 'life, friendship and superb wine'.

Shiraz ★★★★ Juicy, early-drinking **04**, friendly tannins & lovely roundness from dollops malbec, petit v & cab. Yr Fr, 40% new. **Epicentre** ★★★★ TWS gold winner **04** food-friendly bdx blend with fine tannins. Cab, merlot, petit v, malbec; Coastal grapes; yr Fr oak, some new. No successor or this or Shiraz. — *CvZ*

Nico van der Merwe Wines
T 021-903-9507 • F 021-903-9507

Stellenbosch • Est/1stB 1999 • Closed to public • Owner Nico & Petra van der Merwe • Winemaker Nico van der Merwe • 45t/3 500cs 85% red 15% white • PO Box 12200 Stellenbosch 7613 • wilhelmshof@xsinet.co.za

What's in a name? Globalisation has taken the sting out of Van der Merwe jokes, reports Nico vdM, and his Robert Alexander - the name evoking both a maternal grandfather and a brother - strikes a note with customers the world over. 'Mas' is southern French for 'farmhouse', and Nico and wife Petra vdM still hope someday to build one on their Bot River family farm, where increasing vineyard development on all sides bodes well.

★★★★★ **Mas Nicolas** Invariably a shiraz/cab blend. **03** last ed joined classy ranks with black cherry fruit, deeply veined tannins, liquorice & dried herb notes. Already supple, but deserved more time. 14 mths combo new, 2nd fill, all Fr. Same vyds since first **99**: Kuils Rvr shiraz, Smnsberg cab.

Robert Alexander range

Merlot ★★★ Slender frame but **05**'s creamy fruit, ripe tannins make welcome addition to repertoire. Few yrs ageing potential. **Shiraz** ★★★★ No rough edges in **06**, just textured drinkability, wonderful fruit purity & savoury infusion of yr seasoned oak, Fr/Am. Enough structure to cellar further 2/3 yrs. Sbosch WO.

Nicolas van der Merwe range

Merlot-Shiraz-Cabernet Sauvignon ★★★★ Fruit ex-Mas N vyd. Last tasted **04**, accessible, but built to last few yrs. Appealing choc-mint & cassis, reflecting bdx varieties' two-thirds pre-eminence. Yr equal Fr/Am oak, some new. **Sauvignon Blanc-Semillon** ★★★★ Equal blend **06**'s clear focus on appetite appeal gives pear-rich fruit salad styling, enough leafy freshness for tasty food accompaniment. WO W Cape for all unless noted. — *CR*

Nico Vermeulen Wines
T 021-863-2048 · F 021-863-2048

Paarl · Est/1stB 2003 · Closed to public · Owner/viticulturist Nico Vermeulen · Winemaker Nico Vermeulen, with Judy & Izelle Vermeulen · 1 000cs · 3 Pieter Hugo Str Courtrai Suider-Paarl 7646 · nicovermeulen@webmail.co.za

Winemaker Nico Vermeulen (consultant to Havana Hills) is very positive about his own venture, showcasing his two most favoured cultivars, sauvignon and shiraz. 'For the first time I'm doing what I really love most!'

★★★★★ **The Right Red** NEW Shiraz makes impressive debut. Cracked pepper & red berries highlighted by game, smoke & floral notes, pure fruit encased by fine tannins; **06** poised, with depth & structure for lengthy ageing.

The Right Two Reds ★★★ **05** almost equal blend merlot/cab combines herby scents with forest floor nuances, sleek mouthful courtesy refreshing acid, friendly tannins. **The Right White** NEW 🍷 ★★★ Sauv from Dbnville. **07** sprightly, eminently drinkable despite leanish centre; cool tinned pea & sunnier gooseberry combo working together tastily. **The Right Two Whites** 🍷 ★★★★ Glossy textured maiden **07** blends 85% sauvignon with semillon, both ex Dbnville. Round & accessible, sweet fruited & lengthy. — *RP*

Niel Joubert Estate

T 021-875-5936 · F 021-875-5936

Paarl · Est 1898 · 1stB 1996 · Visits by appt · Walks · Owner Joubert family · Winemaker Ernst Leicht (May 2000) · Viticulturist Daan Joubert · 305ha (cab, merlot, pinotage, shiraz, chard, chenin, sauv, viognier) · 2 000t/40 000cs own label 40% red 60% white · PO Box 17 Klapmuts 7625 · wine@nieljoubert.co.za · www.nieljoubert.co.za

'Simply South African' is a slogan the Jouberts fancy for their wines: 'They're as at home on SA tables as is Mrs Ball's Chutney,' claims Niel Snr. He reports that growth in the local market last year was gratifying, with restaurants accounting for well over 50% of sales.

Shiraz Rosé ☺ ★★★ Breaks mould of inconsequential quaffing rosés. Whiff red cherries on **06**, red-wine flavours, touch tannin, properly dry, too.

Cabernet Sauvignon ★★★ **05** tasted pvs ed from Paarl sourced fruit; well made, with cab's signature grippy tannins & cedar notes from yr-oaked portion. (Assume NE unless noted). EW. **Merlot** ★★★ Blackcurrant jam on nose, but more classically flavoured **05**. Dark choc & good berry fruit, tannins still youthful. **Pinotage** ★★★ 05 really dry, with firm tannins, continues in Italianate style, ideal for pastas/pizzas. **Shiraz** ★★★ **05** sample shows attractive black cherry, mulberry, with firmish tannins; needs another yr to unfurl, could be a star. **Christine-Marie** ★★★★ 03 tasted last ed was stylishly constructed; ripe mulberry with cool mint complex flavours. **Chardonnay** ★★ Wooding more assertive in sample **07**, creamy weight with some citrus, fresh peach. Definite notch up. EW. **Chenin Blanc** ★★★ **07** fresh melon & spice with racy acidity, better than everyday. EW. **Sauvignon Blanc** ★★ **07** fresh & fruity, appealing dry white. W Cape fruit. **Viognier** ★★ Amiable off-dry styling, plump & big boned, good freshening acidity in sample **07**. **Viognier Reserve** NEW Attractive toasty oak on barrel unrated sample **07**, still in formative stage but well built & imposing. Overshadowed by oak, but watch this one. **Blanc de Blanc** NEW ★★★ Big whiff (Hung) oak in **07**; viognier's distinctive white peach intro, exciting & racy despite big build; could rate higher when bottled. Blend chenin, nouvelle, viognier. EW. — *IvH*

■ **Niels Verburg** *see Luddite Wines*

Nietvoorbij Wine Cellar

T 021-809-3084/3091 ▪ F 021-809-3202, 086-520-4521

Stellenbosch ▪ Est 1963 ▪ 1stB 1992 ▪ Tasting & sales Mon-Fri 9-4; phone ahead on Sat ▪ Fee R1/wine ▪ Closed pub hols ▪ Conferences ▪ Owner Agricultural Research Council ▪ Winemaker Neil Strydom (2005) ▪ Viticulturist Guillaume Kotzè (Apr 2002) ▪ 32ha (cab, malbec, merlot, pinotage, shiraz, sauv) ▪ 150t/6 000cs own label 74% red 24% white 1% port ▪ Private Bag X5026 Stellenbosch 7599 ▪ cellar@arc.agric.za ▪ www.arc.agric.za

Last year Neil Strydom and team experimented with sauvignon at this cellar owned by the Agricultural Research Council, crushing in separate phases and blending the results. But their real passion is pinotage: both the rosé and port are entirely from the variety, and the red blend is pinotage based. In a pragmatic approach to 'global oversupply', they eschew far-flung markets, carving instead a niche in Namibia.

Rosé ☺ 🍷 **★★** Sour cherry with fresh juicy acid to balance sweetness of **07** preview. Low alc (11%).

Merlot ★★★ 04, tasted last ed, had ripe blackberries & plums; vanilla & spice richness rescued by dry tannins. **Pinotage ★★★★** Dark fruit & liquorice notes on **03** pvs ed; gd support from oaking, with firm dry finish. **Sauvignon Blanc** 🍷 **★★★** Pleasant **07** summer drink with variety's dusty fig leaf signature. Sample shows balanced fruit & acid, fresh tart farewell. **Port** 🍷 **★★★** Fruit-filled winter warmer **05** (sample). Pinotage's ripe exuberance restrained by fortification with brandy, adding a drier edge to this vintage. All WO Smnsberg-Sbosch. — *MW*

Nieuwedrift Vineyards

T 022-913-1966 ▪ F 022-913-1966

Swartland ▪ Est 1996 ▪ 1stB 2003 ▪ Visits Mon-Fri 9-1; 2-5 Sat 9-2 Otherwise by appt (phone mobile no. below) ▪ Restaurant open Wed & Fri-Sun ▪ B&B guesthouse ▪ Facilities for children ▪ Tour groups ▪ Conferences & weddings ▪ Walks ▪ Owner Johan Mostert ▪ Winemaker Johan Mostert, advised by Marais de Villiers ▪ Viticulturist Juliana Booysen (consultant) ▪ 31ha (shiraz, chard, chenin, colombard) ▪ ±7t, 35% red 65% white ▪ PO Box 492 Piketberg 7320 ▪ nieuwedrift@telkomsa.net

Demand last year necessitated that the Chenin be bottled early but the upside was that the Shiraz, usually bottled simultaneously, matured in barrel six months longer, reports Johan Mostert, whose wife Karen has commissions for her paintings here and in Namibia. The restaurant, previously open on request only, is opening its doors at regular hours.

Shiraz ★★★ Wood-driven **05**, last ed inadvertently listed as **04**. Step up on pvs; bit fleshier but still fairly light fruited & tannic. **Chenin Blanc ★★** Relaxed, everyday **07**, green leafy nose; easy, grapey dry flavours. — *DB*

Nitida Cellars

T 021-976-1467 ▪ F 021-976-5631

Durbanville ▪ Est 1992 ▪ 1stB 1995 ▪ Tasting & sales Mon-Fri 9-5 Sat 9.30-3 Sun 11-3 ▪ Closed Easter Fri/Sun, Dec 25/26 & Jan 1 ▪ Tours by appt ▪ Team building, facilities for children & conferences; see also intro ▪ Owner Veller family ▪ Winemaker/viticulturist Bernhard Veller with Jacus Marais (1995/1999), advised by Eugene van Zyl & Johan Wiese ▪ 15ha (cab s/f, merlot, pinotage, shiraz, sauv, semillon) ▪ 140t/7 500cs own label 45% red 55% white ▪ PO Box 1423 Durbanville 7551 ▪ nitida@mweb.co.za ▪ www.nitida.co.za

Co-owner and winemaker Bernhard Veller is extremely happy with the development of the new vintages in the cellar. On the food side, Café Nitida serves light lunches and picnic baskets, while the brand-new restaurant, Cassia, is owned and run by the two world-renowned chefs, Dave Grier and Peter Goffe-Wood. Off the menu, but on the cards, are selected adventure sports, to join a variety of existing child-friendly and business-orientated facilities.

★★★★ **Cabernet Sauvignon** Jump from **03** to light-hearted, attractive **06** (**★★★★**), forward ripe fruit & firmly gentle structure, modestly oaked. Ready for early, satisfying drinking.

★★★★ **Calligraphy** Last sampled was unchallenging but not trivial **04**: smooth-tannined, ripe, pleasing, with choc notes to fruitcake flavours. From merlot, cabs f & s; 18 mths Fr oak, 30% new.

★★★★ **Sauvignon Blanc** Reliably winning style, deftly & exuberantly blending light greenness & passionfruit on **07**, with savoury elegance amounting to a steely finesse. Drop semillon as usual.

★★★★☆ **Sauvignon Blanc Club Select** As pvsly, **07** shares essential character, make-up, well-balanced freshness of above, but adds concentration, with a mineral seriousness taking over from some of the more obvious fruitiness, promising interesting development over few yrs.

★★★★ **Semillon 07** has length, fresh acidity & fine silkiness plus full-fruited aromas/flavours (grassy citrus, wool, wax). Ready for delicious early drinking, though shd keep. Successfully integrated 50% portion ex-oak, half new. 5% sauvignon adds to freshness.

★★★★ **Coronata** NEW Well balanced, appealing **05** happily blends sauv with 30% oak-fermented semillon. Citrus, honey, light tropicality all mingle with fresh, delicate, lingering charm. Like Speciosa, mostly grabbed by Club members.

Pinotage ★★★★ **06** same showy, sweet-fruited, toasty oak mode as **05** MIWA DG; soft, densely textured - & tasty, but some will find bitter note. **Shiraz** ★★★★ Name returns after brief spell as 'Syrah', but usual forward, sweet-fruited charm on **05**, with soft but shapely tannins, thick texture. Yr in Fr oak shows attractively. **Speciosa** NEW ★★★★ From 45% merlot, with cabs s & f. Ripe, fragrant aromas with lots of ripe sweet fruit, touched with herbaceousness; gd firm structure, but **06** finishes a little hard & short. **Chardonnay** ★★★☆ Last tasted was oak-dominated **03**. **Sparkling Shiraz** ★★★ **05** sold out; last tasted was **04** MCC in soft ripe style: fresh, dryish, simply fruity, with some tannic grip. Unusual but drinkable. — *TJ*

■ **Noble Cape** *see* Origin Wine

Noble Hill Wines   🍴🍷☕📷✗&

T 021-874-3844 · F 021-874-2948

Paarl ▪ Est 2001 ▪ Tasting & sales Mon-Fri 8-5 Sat-Sun 10-5 ▪ Closed Sun mid-Apr to Nov, Dec 23 & 24 ▪ Picnics/deli meals (Dec-Apr): phone for details ▪ Farm-grown olive oil ▪ Tours by appt ▪ Walks along dam ▪ Facilities for children ▪ Owner Noble Hill Family ▪ Winemaker Kowie du Toit (2006, consultant) ▪ Cellar manager/asst winemaker Rodney Zimba (2003) ▪ Viticulturist Gideon Malherbe & Paul Wallace (consultants) ▪ 17ha (cab, merlot, shiraz, mourvèdre, chard, viognier) ▪ 150t/7 500cs own label ▪ 80% red 20% white ▪ PO Box 111 Simondium 7670 ▪ wines@noblehill.com ▪ www.noblehill.com

New owners of what was Cowlin Wines, are Americans and Europeans who've travelled the world and visited this country over a decade or more. They fell in love with their Paarl wine farm some two years ago and are now 'students of the process, learning and participating at the same time'. Consultants Kowie du Toit and Paul Wallace have joined an otherwise unchanged wine team; physical changes include a new barrel maturation cellar and a private viewing, tasting and dining room.

Noble Hill range

★★★★ **Shiraz** NEW Maiden **05** sets high standard with alluring bouquet of lilies & smoked meats, concentrated mouthful. 15% alc warms finish, but is tamed by powerful tannins, bold fruit & refreshing acidity. 14 mths new/old Fr oak.

★★★★ **Sauvignon Blanc** Thrilling 'wet stone' steeliness to fresh tropical mouthful in **07** (tank sample); racy, poised & v persistent. Perfect for oysters.

Noble Hill ★★★☆ Stylish cab-driven **04**, with merlot & petit v. 14 mths Fr oak, 30% new. Well-rounded last yr, & less beefy than pvs with elegant dry finish. **Viognier** NEW ★★★★ **06** promising debut; stonefruits & hint pepper (courtesy used Fr oak fermentation/ageing) delight on bouquet & broad, almost Rubenesque palate.

Cowlin range

Cabernet Sauvignon ★★★ Ripe & plummy **03** spent yr in Fr oak, 30% new; had dry tannic flick in its tail when last tasted. **Merlot** ★★★★ **04** classically styled with pencil shavings & plum, soft tannins. Oak as for Cab. **Jack's Jug** ★★★ Steakhouse-friendly **05**, near equal mix shiraz/cab, full-flavoured & smoky. 6 mths Fr staves. Discontinued: **Shiraz**, **Poodle's Passion Sauvignon Blanc**, **Chardonnay-Semillon**. — *CvZ*

■ **No Name** *see* Pick 'n Pay

■ **Nordale Winery** *see* Bonnievale Wine Cellar

■ **Nottingham Road** *see* The Stables

■ **No 1 Reserve** *see* Boland Kelder

■ **Nutwood Grove** *see* Gentis Family Vineyards

■ **Nuwehoop** *see* Groot Eiland Winery

Nuy Wine Cellar

T 021-347-0272 • F 023-347-4994

Nuy (see Worcester map) • Est 1963 • 1stB 1967 • Tasting & sales Mon-Fri 8.30-4.30 Sat 8. 30-12.30 • Fee R15 for groups of 10+ • Closed Easter Fri/Sun, Dec 25 & Jan 1 • Braai facilities • Owner 19 members • Winemaker Christo Pienaar, with Juan Slabbert (Sep/Oct 2003) • Viticulturist Newald Marais (Oct 2002, consultant) • 9 500t • 9% red 79% white 12% muscadel • PO Box 5225 Worcester 6849 • wines@nuywinery.co.za • www.nuywinery.co.za

'There was nothing funny about the big 2007 harvest,' sighs Christo Pienaar. 'The grapes just kept coming and coming…' But so did the awards, much to his delight - especially at being joint top achiever at Veritas 2006. 'We're famous for muscadel but we now want to bring people's attention to our other wines.'

★★★★ **Red Muscadel** ✓ Deeply delicious fortified dessert to sip on a rainy day or cellar for some yrs. Exceptional **06** (★★★★★) deceptively delicate pink; spice-edged muscat fruit; admirable balance, intensity & persistence. Powerful **05** also muscat scented & silky, with harmonious 16% alc.

★★★★ **White Muscadel** ✓ Rich, unctuous but uncloying fortified; **07** spicy grape aromas, signature mint & iced tea flavours, delightfully light finish. Drink chilled now, or cellar for future pleasure.

Chenin Blanc ☺ ★★★ Light & easy **07**, fresh lunchtime white with tropical flavours, crisp, balanced acidity. **Colombar Dry** ☺ ★★★ Pale **07**, delightfully fresh & dry; light, zippy acidity, breezy 12% alc. **Sauvignon Blanc** ☺ ★★★ Refreshing & delightful **07**, crisp & fresh, with citrus twist. **Sauvignon Blanc Sparkling Vin Sec** ☺ ★★☆ Energetic mousse to carbonated **07**. Tropical fruit hints, sweetly flavourful finish.

Cabernet Sauvignon ★★☆ **04** effusive ripe aromas followed by unexpected restraint on palate; oak staves add spicy vanilla. **Barrel Selection Cabernet Sauvignon** NEW ★★★ More seriously styled version. **05** smoky oak, blackcurrant fruit, well-judged tannin & acid. For now & few yrs. **Barrel Selection Syrah** ★★★ Spicy, smoky, red-berried **05**, like maiden **04**, result of stringent (Fr/Am) barrel selection. Approachable but best wait another yr. **Rouge de Nuy** ★★ Cab-merlot blend. Staves overwhelm lean fruit on **04**, adding bitter twist. **Rosé** ★★☆ Pale pink **07**, red muscadel & splash hanepoot; soft & semi-sweet for easy, early quaffing. **Chardonnay** ★★★ **06** last ed showed delicious stonefruit with vanilla oak suggestion. **07** unready. **Colombar Semi-Sweet** ★★★ Honeysuckle & summer apples on **07**, soft sweetness & lively acidity; pleasant early drinking. **Chant de Nuit** ★★ Light, pineapple-scented, bone-dry NV featuring Ferdinand de Lesseps table grape. **Noble Late Harvest** ★★★★ Botrytised chenin & hanepoot. **04** last ed offered apricot-toned fruit, slight citrus tang to tail. — *IM*

Oaklands Wine Exporters
T 021-886-9626 ▪ F 021-887-0441

Est 2002 ▪ 1stB 2003 ▪ Closed to public ▪ Owner Danie Zeeman ▪ PO Box 12398 Die Boord 7613 ▪ info@oaklandswines.com ▪ www.deza.co.za

Widely experienced Danie Zeeman sources wines locally for clients in Europe to market under their own brands, and in some cases creates special blends to suit clients' requirements. Deza is his own label, and it flies to America, Switzerland, Singapore and Russia. Note: the wines below all still available. In the Deza range, a Merlot, Shiraz, Pinotage Rosé, Chenin & Merlot Natural Sweet, all 06s, were added since the last ed.

Deza Collection
Reserve Shiraz ★★★☆ **02** modern, ripe but not over-extracted, lots of toasty wood noted last ed (combo Fr/Am barrels, 80/20). Not retasted, as for all below. **Shiraz-Pinotage** ★☆ 60/40 mix, fruit ex-Wllngtn, unoaked; **04** dry leaves/damp earth tone, rustic, sharpish finish. **Chardonnay Reserve** ★★★ Food-friendly **04** (sample), fresh & balanced, weighty, with lime marmalade aromas & flavours. **Sauvignon Blanc 06** not tasted.

Afrikaanse Plesier range
Merlot ★★ Pleasantly nutty **05**, mulberry flavours & firm but friendly tannins, fullish body. **Shiraz Rosé** ★★★ Tasty, dry al fresco quaffer; strawberry-red **06**, slight grip of tannin, pert cherry bite on finish. **Chenin Blanc** ★★★ **06** well-crafted, harmonious easy-drinker with softly persistent apple flavours. All WO W Cape. — DH

◾ **Oak Lane** *see Beau Joubert Vineyards & Winery*
◾ **Oak Ridge** *see Shoprite Checkers*

Oak Valley Wines
T 021-859-4110 ▪ F 021-859-3405

Elgin (see Elgin/Walker Bay map) ▪ Est 1898 ▪ 1stB 2003 ▪ Tasting & sales Mon-Fri 9-5, otherwise by appt ▪ Closed Easter Fri-Mon, Dec 25/26 & Jan 1 ▪ Conservation area ▪ Owner AG Rawbone-Viljoen Trust ▪ Winemaker Pieter Visser ▪ Viticulturist Pieter Visser, advised by Kevin Watt ▪ 40ha (cabs s/f, merlot, petit verdot, pinot, shiraz, chard, sauv, viognier, semillon) ▪ 7 500cs white 3 500cs red ▪ PO Box 30 Elgin 7180 ▪ wines@oak-valley.co.za ▪ www.oakvalley.co.za

Ugly flames swept across Oak Valley's mountain slopes in early spring, destroying a stand of rare Protea Stokoei, the largest known colony of these plants on earth. A third of the Mountain Reserve single-vineyard sauvignon block as well as the edges of the pinot vineyard were scorched, but since this was prior to blossom, fortunately the threat of smoke taint to the grapes was averted. The fire aside, a cool, quality conducive growing season means the 07 wines show good potential, particularly the sauvignon, and winemaker Pieter Visser hopes to make a Mountain Reserve this year.

★★★★ **Pinot Noir** Like **05**, soft red berries & earth on finer, lovelier **06** (★★★★☆). Clean, pure fruit held lightly in fresh & charming, rather than forceful, structure; subtly wooded (50% new), well balanced.

★★★★ **The Oak Valley Blend** Mostly merlot in **04** (9% cab f, dollop cab s), tasted last ed. Big & self-assured, with gd succulent tannic structure. Herbaceous twist pleasantly stresses cool-climate origins, 14.5% alc testifies to ripeness. Decanter regional trophy winner.

★★★★☆ **Chardonnay 06** in usual elegant, restrained & charming style, with aromas of hazelnut & oatmeal. Fresh, incisive - though not over-concentrated; balanced, with fine acidity, moderate 13.5% alc; light oakiness (40% new) should soon integrate.

★★★★☆ **Mountain Reserve Sauvignon Blanc** From high vyd block - so far only maiden **05**, which was thrilling, compelling & immensely drinkably tasted last yr. More powerful than standard version, fuller & richer yet more steely & mineral; concentrated & complete.

★★★★☆ **Sauvignon Blanc** 🗒 **06** not tasted, but **07** in expected delicately restrained mode, though with subtly intense flavours: passionfruit, grass, gooseberry. Finely structured, with flinty minerality on sustained finish. Will grow in interest over yr/two min. — *TJ*

Obikwa

Distell brand named for the indigenous Obikwa people, the front label featuring a stylised ostrich. In fruity, easy-going style for current enjoyment.

Chenin Blanc ☺ ★★★ Al fresco patio companion. **07** bright, fresh & lively melange of ripe apple & zingy acidity. **Sauvignon Blanc** ☺ ★★★ Lively green fig & nettle on **07**, ripe tropical flourish & hint sugar, balanced by bright acidity. Low alc (11.5%).

Cabernet Sauvignon ★★★ Bold & hearty **06** with chunky tannins (more prominent & austere than pvs) & hot finish. **Merlot** ★★★ Leaner, sappier **06** with juicy red fruit & clean, tight tannins. Alc touch lower than pvs but still punchy. **Pinotage** ★★★ **06** same style as pvs: easy drinking, friendly tannins from combo barrels/staves & unoaked portion, sturdy 14.5% alc. **Shiraz** ★★★ Am oak (2-3 mths) adds sweet vanilla spiciness to **06**'s smoky bacon & chunky fruit. Firm tannins & savoury finish. **Chardonnay** ★★★ **06** friendly & accessible, solo or with summer fare. Soft, ripe stone fruit with marmalade twist, zesty acid & subtle oak. All WO W Cape. — *MW*

▮ **October Red** *see* Vrede Wine Farm

▮ **Oddbins** *see* Shoprite Checkers

Oewerzicht Private Cellar   🚹 🍷 ⌂ 📷
T 028-254-9831 • F 028-254-9968

Greyton (see Southern Cape map) • Est/1stB 2002 • Tasting & sales Mon-Fri 8-5 & by appt • Luxury guest cottages & tents • Wedding, conference & function facilities • Mountain biking/ hiking trails • Owner/winemaker/viticulturist Kootjie Viljoen • 3ha (cab) • 1 000cs 100% red • PO Box 18 Greyton 7233 • oewerzicht@telkomsa.net

When not delighting in his newborn twins, Kootjie Viljoen remains a firm cab fan. That said, he's convinced the Greyton climate will suit Rhône varieties too, so last year saw new vines of shiraz (and 'Burgundian' chardonnay); with any luck their coming-of-age will coincide with a new on-site cellar.

Cabernet Sauvignon ★★★★ Quality leap for **03** noted pvsly; showed softer side of variety thanks to gentle vinification & oaking. Ripe & accessible tannins, juicy finish. Yr Fr wood. Modest 13% alc. WO Ovrberg. — *DH*

Old Bridge Wines
T 082-777-1519

Closed to public • Owner Paulinas Dal Farm Holdings (Pty) Ltd • 20 000cs 60% red 40% white • PO Box 557 St Francis Bay 6312 • rickety@iafrica.com

Export-focused producer and negociant sourcing wines for a variety of brands, including private labels for specialised corporate clients. The wines, untasted, include limited-edition African Gold Collection: Cabernet-Merlot, Shiraz, Merlot mainly for US, Europe and Far East; Big Six Collection: boxed sets of Cabernet, Merlot, Shiraz, Pinotage, Sauvignon, Chenin for local game lodges/retreats and for export; and Old Bridge: Cabernet, Merlot, Shiraz, Pinotage, Sauvignon & Chenin.

▮ **Old Brown** *see* Sedgwick's Old Brown Sherry

▮ **Old Chapel** *see* Robertson Winery

Old Vines Cellars
T 021-685-6428 • F 021-685-6446

Cape Town ▪ Est/1stB 1995 ▪ Closed to public ▪ Owner Irina von Holdt & Françoise Botha ▪ Winemaker Irina von Holdt with Jan van Rooyen ▪ 12 500cs own label + 2 500cs for pvt clients ▪ 35% red 65% white ▪ 50 Liesbeek Rd Rosebank 7700 ▪ fran@oldvines.co.za ▪ www.oldvines.co.za

'Fran and I will just have to make sure we wear the pants around here,' laughs Irina von Holdt, Cape Wine Master and taster for this guide, in response to the growing number of men in this 'women's initiative'. The latest male addition is a son born to IvH's daughter and co-owner Fran Botha, and husband/production manager Jurgen. The 'little baron' helps fill the void left by the passing, at 96, of Irina's father, a German nobleman and wine lover. Chenin remains their passion, but the success of their 'modest' Spring Valley Shiraz-Merlot, which won big orders from Wine of the Month Club, shows how seriously they take their reds.

Old Vines Cellars range
★★★★ **Baron von Holdt** Elegant rather than powerful bdx-style blend. **04** mid-2006 had plentiful cassis & sugared plum, reined-in tannins. 2 yrs new/older Fr oak.

★★★★ **Barrel Reserve Chenin Blanc** None since minerally **04**; mid-2005 had creamy bouquet, was drier than **03** (2.3g/l RS), longer in oak (10 mths Fr casks), & received 10% new wood (pvs only older oak).

★★★★ **Chenin Blanc** Made to showcase the v best chenin fruit IvH can find, always released yr after harvest. **06** balanced & restrained with honeyed aromas & bruised apple flavours.

★★★★ **Vintage Brut** Elegant & unusual MCC-style sparkling from chenin, ex-Sbosch bushvines, made with help from Villiera's Jeff Grier. **04** has seemingly endless mineral conclusion, creamy/honey palate & sea-spray-fresh bouquet.

Blue White ★★★☆ 07 sample should prove to be a lovely food wine; bright & firm flavours, sustained & balanced.

Spring Valley range
Shiraz-Merlot ★★★ Food-friendly 60/40 mix, sample **05** needs time for gruff tannins to meld with spicy fruit. Very ripe, but not raisined. Mainly oak-staved, small portion barrelled. **Stein Select ★★★** No new wine tasted; last **NV** was from chenin, butterscotch & bready aromas led to honeyed palate, 14g/l sugar gave soft, sweet lift. **Sauvignon Blanc ★★★ 07** a work-in-progress, mid-2007 subdued yet gd palate weight, zesty acidity. Unknit, should evolve & improve. **Chenin Blanc-Sauvignon Blanc ★★★★** Always fresh, floral & fruity, friendly. Sample **07** more than meets the bill; 30% sauv plays key role with intense capsicum aromas/flavours & aftertaste. — *CvZ*

■ **Old Well House** *see Thorntree Wines*
■ **Oliver & Gregg** *see Daschbosch Wine Cellar*

Olsen Wines
T 021-862-3653 • F 021-862-2589

Paarl ▪ Est/1stB 2002 ▪ Visits by appt ▪ Fee R10 ▪ Home-style light meals for groups of ±10 by appt ▪ Farm-style jams ▪ Owner Greg Olsen ▪ Winemaker Helene van der Westhuizen (2005) ▪ Viticulturist Armand Botha (2000) ▪ 30ha ▪ 500cs 90% red 10% white ▪ Europgap registered ▪ PO Box 9052 Huguenot 7645 ▪ olsenwines@mweb.co.za

Since becoming only the third private citizen to enter space, Greg Olsen has been earth-bound, touring, giving motivational lectures to schools and auctioning wines with labels that made it into orbit. New at the 10-ton cellar are a barrel maturation facility and a Chenin. Not ready for tasting, no doubt it is of 'stellar' quality.

★★★★ **Cabernet Sauvignon** Ripe & well balanced **03**; fine, firm, slightly herbal tannins give structure to sweet finish.

Pinotage ★★★ Easy-drinking **03**, attractive banana & black fruits, surprisingly soft tannins for variety. 9 mths Fr oak. **Vinette Cabernet Sauvignon-Shiraz ★★** Just 'Cab-Shiraz' pvs ed. Herbaceous green-fruit aromas on **05**, intrusive tannins softened by sweet fruit.

South Africa pioneered the internationally ground-breaking Integrated Production of Wine (IPW) programme, aimed at ensuring environmentally sustainable farming and winemaking practices, and addressing a range of environmental concerns. Over 95% of SA's producers now farm according to these guidelines, introduced in 1998. Former manager **Andries Tromp** (right), past president of the OIV's Oenology Commission and a prime mover behind the SA-spearheaded drive to draw up global guidelines for environmentally sustainable grape growing and winemaking, has handed over the green baton to new incumbent **Jacques Rossouw**.

THE PRESERVATION OF PERFECTION

Through our patented co-extrusion technology, we've created a line of wine closures that provide consistent, predictable oxygen management. As a result, off-flavors due to oxidation and reduction or cork taint are a worry of the past. That's why the world's most recognized brands have chosen Nomacorc to protect their wines billions of times over.

NOMACORC®

NOMACORC.COM

NOMACORC IS A REGISTERED TRADEMARK OF NOMACORC LLC ©2007 NOMACORC LLC

MCG INDUSTRIES

93 Carlisle Street, Paardeneiland, Cape Town, 7405, South Africa
Tel (Direct): 021-508 7189 - Tel: 021-508 7100 - Fax: 021-508 7198
E-mail: andreb@mcgind.co.za - Website: www.mcgindustries.com

the Thoroughbred Group

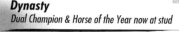

. **Chardonnay** ★★ **05** some marzipan aromas, fleeting flavours, curiously low alc (11.9%) for ripe Paarl fruit. This, above wines, not retasted. — *MF*

Onderkloof Vines & Wines
T 021-858-1538 • F 021-858-1536

Stellenbosch (see Helderberg map) • Est 1998 • 1stB 1999 • Tasting Mon-Fri by appt • Sales & tours by appt • Private functions (lunch/dinner) by appt • Member of Schapenberg-Sir Lowry's Conservancy • Owner Daniël Truter & Beat Musfeld • Winemaker/viticulturist Daniël Truter • 25ha (cab, pinotage, shiraz, chenin, crouchen, muscat d'A, sauv) • 100t/4 000cs own label 30% red 70% white • PO Box 90 Sir Lowry's Pass 7133 • wine@onderkloofwines.co.za • www.onderkloofwines.co.za

Daniël Truter is very excited about WO ward status for the Schapenberg Mountain range, pending final approval of the Wine & Spirit Board. The launch of their first two single-vineyard wines - the 06 Sauvignon and 06 Chardonnay - was a significant milestone for DT and wine partner Beat Musfeld, both great believers in the wind-cooled Schapenberg terroir.

★★★★ **Chardonnay** From single Schapenberg vyd, combo tank/barrel. **06** (★★★★) now finished wine, retains a bone-dry, focused citrus freshness; savoury oak note an attractive counterpoint. Friendly 12.2% alc. **05** sleekly muscular, boldly oaked.

Cabernet Sauvignon ★★ Concentrated, attractive **02** (★★★★) succeeded last ed by pre-bottling sample **03**, showing more freshness & oak (14 mths Fr). **Pinotage** ★★★★ **04**, now bottled, confidently parades mocha-infused dark fruit character, invites sampling of its smoothly accessible, tasty wares. Ex-single vyd. **Shiraz** ★★★ Pvs New World in style, though last-tasted **04** less fruit-rich & open-textured; had dusty sweet-sour flavours, which departed fairly hastily. **Floreal Rouge** ★★★ Interesting & unusual unwooded red, easy drinking. Last available **05** was malbec/merlot mix with brambly flavours, light & refreshing. **Chenin Blanc** ★★★ Well-applied oak chips added dimension, texture to last-tasted, unbottled **06**; had taut mineral flavours & brisk acidity. Unfiltered. **Sauvignon Blanc** ★★★★ Now registered single vyd. Previewed last ed, **06** has benefited from extra yr: intriguing lime pickle, preserved pineapple perfume, with enough elegance & palate minerality to handle seafood. **Floreal Blanc de Blanc** ★★★★ An aptly named charmer, **06**'s chenin, sauv, muscat blend is a floral bouquet, with just enough refreshing sweetness to complete the seduction. — *CR*

■ **Onyx** *see Darling Cellars*

Oom Tas

With 2m-plus cases sold each year, all in returnable glass, this is one of SA's biggest-selling budget-priced brands. By Distell.

Oom Tas ▤ ☆ Tawny-coloured blend chenin, muscat & colombard. Looks sweet but it's dry & lean. 750ml & 2-litre bottles. **NV**. — *MW*

■ **Open Sky** *see Premium Cape Wines*

Opstal Estate
T 023-344-3001 • F 023-344-3002

Slanghoek (see Worcester map) • Est 1950 • 1stB 1978 • Tasting & sales Mon-Fri 9-5 Sat 10-2 • Closed Christian holidays • Tours by appt • Restaurant Wed-Sun 10-3 (see Eat-out section) • Conference/function centre • Owner Stanley Louw • Winemaker Stanley Louw, with Jaco Theron (Jan 1999) • 103ha (13 varieties, r/w) • 1 500t/10 000cs own label 35% red 65% white • PO Box 27 Rawsonville 6845 • wine@opstal.co.za • www.opstal.co.za

There's dedication here: to the Breedekloof district (owner/winemaker Stanley Louw is a tireless tourism marketer), to the Slanghoek Valley and, more specifically, to the food-and-wine experience purveyed by Opstal's restaurant and tasting venues. An unusual offering at the latter is Stanley L's shiraz-viognier blend, a first for the valley when it made its debut in 2006.

Cabernet Sauvignon ★★★ Characterful, lightish **02** not resampled; red berry flavours & plentiful dry tannins. ± Yr Fr oak. **Cabernet Sauvignon-Shiraz** ★★★ **04** shows spicy red fruit, well structured & oak-framed, but rather thin, with slightly bitter tannins. **Syrah-Viognier** NEW 🏷 ★★★ **07** delicate, with spiced strawberries with creamy dry finish; chilled, could be cool at the pool. **Chenin Blanc** ★★★ **06** not tasted, but sample **07** is uncomplicated fruit-laden summer wine, ideal for early enjoyment. **Sauvignon Blanc** 🏷 ★★ Dry, lightly fruity **07** for drinking soon. **Viognier** NEW ★★★ Some juicy fun in **07** tank sample; nice apricot/floral tones & not unappealing bitterness on slightly hot finish. Rating provisional. **Hanepoot** ★★ Fortified dessert **05**, typically warming, appealingly smooth & fragrant, but sweetness cloys. No **04** bottled. — *JPf*

Oracle

Distell export brand, styled for 'easy and versatile enjoyment'.

★★★★ **Sauvignon Blanc** Fig, herb & wet stone aromas on **07**, with some riper stone fruit hints. Nicely rounded & soft. Moderate12.6% alc.

Cabernet Sauvignon ★★★★ Stylish, balanced **06**. Smoky, rich dark berries, juicy mid-palate, savoury tannins & pleasing dry finish. **Pinotage** ★★★★ Juicy, lithe **06**; Dbnville's signature dusty character adds dry elegance to plummy fruit, counters slight sweetness. **Shiraz** ★★★ Rotund **06** with stewed red fruit, smoky leather profile. Dollop sugar cut by acidity & spicy lift from oak chips. **Chardonnay** ★★★ Tangy lime/mango melange with complementary oak spice. **06** harmonious, approachable & food friendly. All WO W Cape. — *MW*

Oranjerivier Wine Cellars
T 054-337-8800 • F 054-332-4408

Lower Orange (see Northern Cape map) ▪ Est 1965 ▪ 1stB 1968 ▪ Tasting Mon-Fri 8-4.30 Sat 9-11.30 ▪ Fee R5 for 1-5 wines; R10 for 5+ wines ▪ Sales Mon-Fri 8-5 Sat 8.30-12 ▪ Closed pub hols ▪ Tours Mon-Fri 9, 11 & 3 Jan-Mar ▪ Owner ±930 shareholders ▪ Cellarmaster Gert Visser ▪ Winemaker Johan Esterhuizen (Upington cellar), Jan Steenkamp (Grootdrink), Johan Dippenaar (Groblershoop), Chris Venter (Keimoes) & Bolla Louw (Kakamas), with (in same cellar order) Jopie Faul/Philani Gumede, Tinus Kotze, Ferdinand Laubscher, Rianco van Rooyen/Riaan Liebenberg & George Kruger/André Smit ▪ Viticulturist Henning Burger, senior viticulturist (2005); Nic Smit (2005) & Stoney Steenkamp (2007) ▪ 3273.45ha (pinotage, ruby cab, chard, chenin, colombard,) ▪ ±150 000t ▪ Export labels: River's Tale, Quiver Tree, Living World & Oranjerivier ▪ Ranges for customers: Liquor Boys & Season's Collection (Liquor City); Country Cellars & Carnival (Spar) ▪ ISO, BRC & HACCP certified ▪ PO Box 544 Upington 8800 ▪ marketing@owk.co.za ▪ www.owk.co.za

This is a socially responsible big-scale wine operation: raising awareness of alcohol abuse, sponsoring a soccer club, providing training for its workers and those on affiliated farms, funding local festivals, donating to schools and becoming actively involved in BEE are among its community-building efforts. But with a protective pricing policy it also extends its support to its 900-odd growers in this huge area (the largest vineyard in the southern hemisphere) following the course of the Orange (Gariep) River. Delighted with their SA Young Wine Show success, GM Herman Cruywagen reports continuing quality improvements in vineyard and cellar, and a marketing strategy with varieties attuned to demand - though, while innovative products are being introduced, their best-seller remains the sweet Nouveau Blanc.

Pinotage ☺ ★★★ Unwooded **06** full of plum/strawberry fruit, brisk mouth-cleansing acidity. **Ruby Cabernet** ☺ ★★★ Unlike pvs, **06** opens its arms with sweet brambly fruit, gently tugging tannins. Unoaked, like Shiraz. **Shiraz** ☺ ★★★ Smoky bacon & vibrant red fruit do the business on **06**. **Chardonnay** ☺ ★★★ Bright, tangerine-toned **06** a super sip, unwooded & refreshing. **Nouveau Blanc** ☺ ★★★ Usually chenin, but **07** ex-colombard. Nice guava & blackcurrant cocktail, uncloying. **Sweet Hanepoot** ☺ ★★★ Easy-sipping nutty & syrupy fortified with muscat spiciness & hint of rose on **06**. **Red Muscadel** ☺ ★★★ 17% alc has firm hold on **06**'s muscat spice & flavour, cuts through the powerful sweetness. **White Muscadel** ☺ ★★★ Balanced **06** fortified dessert has welcome spirity kick, Turkish Delight finish.

Rouge ★☆ **NV** from cab. Smoky & savoury with hint oak ex-staves. **Cabernet Sauvignon** ★☆ Jammy, soft-centred **06** finishes sweetish, though technically dry. **Blanc de Noir** ★☆ **NV** from ruby cab. Juicy, dryish tasting despite dollop sugar. **Rosé** ★ Semi-sweet pink, from colombard & pinotage. **NV**. **Chenin Blanc** ★☆ Sample **07** charms with Granny Smith apple nose & palate. **Light** ★ Fruit-free, austere **NV** from chenin; low 8% alc. **Stein** ★☆ Late Harvest from colombard/chenin; sweetness masks otherwise austere profile. **NV**. **Colombard** ★★☆ Vinous **07** makes quality leap with teasing tangy flavours, long finish. **Grand Cru** ★☆ Chenin/ colombard equal partners in tingling **07**. **Blanc de Blanc** ★☆ Floral quaffer from colombard; **07** has woody note from 3 wks oak chips. **Sparkling Brut** ★☆ **06** frothy carbonated bubbly from colombard; slightly sweet rather than 'brut' as on label. **Sparkling Doux** ★☆ **07** happy sparkler from colombard; lightish & sweetish (11% alc). **Late Harvest** ★ Demure barley sugar aromas on **07**'s colombard/chenin combo. **Special Late Harvest** ★☆ Delicate **04** with hint of fruit; varieties as for Late Harvest. **Red Jerepigo** ★☆ Stalwart from ruby cab; **06** malty &, unusually, a tad short. **White Jerepiko** ★☆ 16% alc barely refreshes ultra-sweet **06** (228g/l RS). **Red Port** ★☆ Traditional-style fortified from ruby cab. **06** short & unknit mid-2007, with spirtous kick. N Cape & Lower Orange WOs for all.

River's Tale range

Classic Red ★☆ **05**'s succulent fruit & gruff tannins mask 14% alc. Oak-staved 6 mths. **Shiraz-Cabernet Sauvignon** ★★★ Tasted last ed, **05** was balanced, easy-going with 80/20 mix providing juicy sour-plum tones. **Chenin Blanc-Chardonnay** ★☆ Fleeting gooseberry aromas & flavours on light, chenin-led **06**; 12% alc. Dual W/N Cape WO. Mostly N Cape & Lower Orange WOs. — *CvZ*

■ **Oranje Straat** see Rooiberg Winery

Org de Rac Domain

T 022-913-2397 • F 022-913-3162

Swartland ▪ Est 2001 ▪ 1stB 2005 ▪ Visits Mon-Fri 9-5 Sat 9-1 ▪ Closed Easter Fri/Sun/Mon, Dec 16/25/26 & Jan 1 ▪ Tour groups ▪ Conferences ▪ Game viewing ▪ Owner Org de Rac Domain (Pty) Ltd ▪ Winemaker Hugo Lambrechts (Nov 2004) ▪ 42.5ha (cab, merlot, shiraz) ▪ 380t/30 000cs 100% red ▪ Accredited by Soil Association; HACCP certification in progress ▪ PO Box 268 Piketberg 7320 ▪ orgderac@mweb.co.za ▪ www.orgderac.com

A Swartland cattle ranch before turning to (red only) vines from 2002, this organic winery's hilltop location is a commending presence when viewed from the N7 route north from Cape Town. Meaning 'Organic on the Shelf', it's the only SA producer certified by the UK's Soil Association, and is on track to receive full HACCP credentials this year. Maturing vines, continuing fine-tuning (of strategies, staff, winemaking) signal a brand going places.

Family Reserve range

Cabernet Sauvignon ★☆ This new range unfinished at press time last year & so not rated. Now bottled, **05** has menthol & cranberry flavours, is somewhat tart. Serious structure needs food. **Merlot** ★★★ Baked fruit, Christmas cake & fynbos notes on maiden **05**. Ripe yet v dry tannins & marked freshness need time or food. **Shiraz** ★★★ **05** shows combo rhône-style black pepper & raisined fruit; seamlessly wooded, with savoury solid tannins. Yr Fr oak for all. Both ranges certified organic, both EW.

Org de Rac range

★★★★ **Merlot** Last ed maiden **05** had abundant berry aromas/flavours, accessible succulent tannins giving potential to improve over few yrs.

Cabernet Sauvignon ★☆ Last-tasted **05** was firm & v dry, unsoftened by berried, slightly earthy fruit. **Shiraz** ★★★★ Last-available **05** was big, bold with well-handled tannins. **Rosé** ★☆ Last ed demure **05** was light on fruit, v dry & savoury. — *MM*

Origin Wine
T 0861-ORIGIN/021-865-8100 • F 021-865-2348

Stellenbosch • Est/1stB 2002 • Closed to public • Owner Bernard Fontannaz • Winemaker Alain Cajeux, Grant Michaels & Quintin van der Westhuizen • 4 million cs • 55% red 40% white 5% rosé • Export brands: Cape Original & ranges below • PO Box 7177 Stellenbosch 7599 • reception@originwine.co.za • www.originwine.co.za and www.fairhills.co.za

The key to growth in a difficult market, CEO Bernard Fontannaz advises, is to be innovative - whether in one's packaging or product line - and competitive, by cutting out agents and distributors. Answering the innovation call is Origin's Fairhills range, carrying the Fairtrade label: 'It has a good footprint in the UK,' Bernard F discloses, 'and is progressing in Denmark and Finland. We can do good business by doing good.' Presenting another point of difference is the Oorsprong Organic range, also showing growth.

African Horizon range
Merlot NEW **★★★ 07** dark choc followed by ripe plummy fruit, bold tannic texture & savoury finish. **Pinotage ★** Touch ruby cab, but **05** last ed chiefly banana character & puckering dryness. **Shiraz ★** Warm spicy character to **07**, slight metallic edge detracts from fruit. **Pinotage-Cinsaut ★★★** Fresh bread aroma & accessible blackberry flavours on firm tannic base in **07**. **Dry Red ★★** Comfortable anytime red, pinotage-led **05** has berry/banana whiffs, low tannins. **Pinotage-Ruby Cabernet-Cinsaut ★** Little fruity cinsaut juiciness last noted on **05**, faint raisin notes, challenging dry tannins. **Pinotage-Shiraz ★★★** Pinotage-led **05** easier, fruitier than pvs; whiffs spice & bacon to fleshy fruit. Not retasted. **Pinotage-Ruby Cabernet** NEW **★★★** Deep ruby colour, dry grass wafts; **07** soft, ripe, juicy fruit & subtle tannins. **Cabernet-Pinotage-Ruby Cabernet ★★** Last tasted **05** showed cassis/vanilla, fruit restrained by dry tannins which might since have softened. **Rosé ★★** Delicately dry pink from pinotage; **05** last ed offered subdued but easy strawberry flavours. **Chardonnay ★★** Retiring **05** insubstantial & unmemorable last yr. **Chenin Blanc ★** Dry grass aromas, soft & understated in **07**, with modest 12.5% alc. **Chardonnay-Viognier ★★★** Plump, peachy **05** (ex Rbtson vyds) last ed pleasant, lightish quaffer with spicy floral nuances. **Chenin Blanc-Colombard ★★** Dusty aromas to **07**, some tropical fruit, clean, dry finish. **Colombard-Chardonnay ★★** Some tropical ripe melon on **07**; crisp green apple farewell. **White ★★** Cheerful **05** light chenin, colombard, muscat mix; pvsly showed delicate fruit salad aroma.

Cape 1652 range
Merlot-Cabernet Sauvignon ★★ 07 ripe berry fruit on firm tannic foundation, lingering dry finish. **Cabernet Sauvignon-Shiraz ★★★ 07** mouthfilling food wine with warm, toasty aroma & ripe, plummy Christmas pud character. **Pinotage-Cabernet Sauvignon ★★** Some berry fruit on **07** bed of firm tannin. Dry finish. **Pinotage-Shiraz ★★** No new vintage. **05** spice & red cherries, fruity & uncomplex. **Rosé ★★** No follow-up tasted for refreshing **06** picnic basket filler, ex pinotage. **Rosé Pinotage** NEW **★★★ 07** floral bouquet, some strawberry juiciness, pleasant, dry finish. Moderate 12.5% alc. **Chenin Blanc-Chardonnay ★★** Crisp **07** dry & undemanding 75/25 blend, modest 12.8% alc.

Cape Organic range NEW
Cabernet Sauvignon ★★★ Inviting berry nose on **07**, some ripe plum flavours. Finishes dry with suggestion of oaky tannin. 14% alc. **Shiraz ★** Dusty straw nose, slightly baked flavours on **07**. 14% alc. **Chenin Blanc ★★** Relaxed summer drinking. **07** pale straw colour, grassy, with crisp green-apple flavours.

Cape Original range
Shiraz-Cabernet Sauvignon NEW **★★** 60/40 juicy joy: **07** sheer plummy fun in a box (3litre).

Evolution range
Merlot ★★ Incl 10% ruby cab. **05** stalky flavours, big dry tannins; 10% oaked. This range not retasted. **Pinotage ★★★** Partly wooded **04** melange of red fruits, gentle tannins for easy drinking. **Shiraz ★★★** Peppery touch to **04**, palate padded by touch sugar (±4g/l); 20% Am oaked. **Merlot-Ruby Cabernet ★★★** Rhubarb tartness to appealing **04**, plum & choc

flavours; firmish tannins. 15% Fr oak. **Rosé** ★★★ From pinotage; **04** plummy red berry character, crisp & refreshing, satisfyingly dry. **Chardonnay** ★★★ Peaches & cream aromas, vanilla whiff, crisp liveliness. Portion of **04** wood-aged. **Colombard** ★★★ Tropical fruit aromas, crunchy, boiled-sweet aftertaste to **04**. **Sauvignon Blanc** ★★★ Gooseberry intro to light-bodied **05**; some flinty hints; lively acidity. **Semillon-Chardonnay** ★★ Light **05** crisp, dry & minerally, for early enjoyment. 10% Fr oaked.

Fairhills range

Cabernet Sauvignon ★★★ Red cherry fruit on friendly, no frills **06** complements underlying flintiness & hint cedarwood on soft departing tannins.13.85% alc. **Merlot** NEW ★★★ Big berry introduction to polished wood aromas & lingering mulberry flavours. **06** gentle, round tannins with flick mocha on finish. **Shiraz** ★★★★ Smoky/herbal notes on robust **07**; black pepper & dark cherries; long tannic finish. Cries out for big, juicy rump steak! **Cabernet Sauvignon-Shiraz** ★★★ Undemanding **07**'s toasty, spicy welcome followed by rollicking, ripe blackberry celebration. Pure pleasure. **Merlot-Shiraz** ★★ Mocha & spice **05**, last ed lively flavours, youthful but balanced tannins. 10% oaked. **Merlot-Pinotage** NEW ★★★ Attractive garnet colour, earthy mocha intro to dark cherry & well-handled tannins. **07** long dry finish. **Pinotage-Cabernet Sauvignon** NEW ★★ Juicy mulberry & vanilla nose, **07** clean berry fruit & pleasing crisp tannic bite. 13% alc, dry finish. **Cinsaut-Shiraz** ★★★ **07**'s earthy, ripe wafts introduce coffee/choc flavours & plump, sun-ripe mulberries. **Rosé** NEW ★★ From pinotage. **07** gentle strawberry aroma, juicy fruit, crisp dry farewell. **Low Alcohol Rosé** NEW ★★ Equal blend pinotage & shiraz; **07** crisp, dry, with pleasant strawberry notes. **Chardonnay** ★★★ Warm butterscotch wafts followed by fresh lime notes. **07**, like pvs, attractively lively & dry. A drink to wow the ABC (Anything But Chard) crowd. **Chenin Blanc Wooded** NEW ★★★ Charming **07** pale gold colour & skilful use of oak to underscore clean, crisp melon & pineapple fruit. **Low Alcohol Chenin Blanc** NEW ★★ **07** leafy, herbal aroma, gentle melon fruit & crisp, dry finish. **Low Alcohol Colombard** NEW ★★ Guava scents & austere acidity on **07**. For dedicated calorie counters. **Sauvignon Blanc** ★★★ Dusty, leafy nose to light-bodied but fullOflavoured **07**, liberal tropical fruit. **Viognier Wooded** NEW ★★★ Spices, herbs & yellow peach, plus clever use of wood (medium-toasted Fr), combine in big, mouthfilling **07**. **Chenin Blanc-Chardonnay** ★★★ **07** inviting biscuity lemon-cream aromas from gentle oaking, delicate apple fruit & clean nutty finish. **Sauvignon Blanc-Colombar** ★★ Light, undemanding **07** shows fresh fruit salad character for easy enjoyment. **Semillon-Chardonnay** ★★★ Vanilla & pineapple wafts precede crisp green apple freshness on appealing, refreshing **07**. **Colombard-Chardonnay** ★★ Hint oak vanilla adds dimension to crisp, firm **07** quaffer. **Colombard-Sauvignon Blanc** ★★ Light, crisp & compact 75/25 blend. **07** fresh, simple everyday white. Approved/certified by the Fairtrade Labelling Organisation (FLO).

Kaap Hollands range

Pinotage-Shiraz ★★ Cheerful **05**, jammy wild-berry flavours, generous but balanced tannins noted last ed. **Chenin Blanc-Chardonnay** ★★ Fruity, easy **05**, 10% Fr oaked, apricot/ orange zest aromas, short finish. Not retasted.

Lion's Gate range

Dry Red ★★ Robust **05** berry flavours/tannins demand full-flavoured food. 10% lightly oaked. Range tasted last yr. **Dry White** ★★ Light bodied, dry **05** quaffer, mainly chenin, with colombard & muscat.

Noble Cape range

Pinotage-Shiraz ★★ Strawberry-toned **05** boasts tannins to partner braais. Portion lightly oaked. None in range retasted. **Chenin Blanc-Chardonnay** ★★ **05** effortless quaffer, light pineapple & dried peach flavours; 5% Fr oaked. **Vonkel Wijn** ★★ Explosion of straw-toned bubbles in hugely festive **05** brut-style sparkler.

Oorsprong Organic range

Cabernet Sauvignon ★★ Herbaceous profile, with leaves & damp earth noted last ed; **05** unfruity flavours/tannins. **Merlot** ★★★ Robust & assertive **07** brims with big mocha/choc notes, ripe black cherry & dark choc, finishing long. **Shiraz** ★★★ Inviting youthful purple hue & hint new leather on softly spicy **05**, not retasted. **Colombard** ★★ Signature guava notes last yr on appealing, crisply dry **06**. **Chenin Blanc-Chardonnay** NEW ★★★ Fresh leafy nose, nicely rounded papaya in tasty **07** mouthfiller.

Pier 42 range

Merlot ★ Sappy, stalky **05**, green tone only partly offset by dash fruity ruby cab. 10% oaked. **Chardonnay** ★★ Restrained, lightly buttery notes on **05**; dry & fresh, fairly soft flavours for comfortable quaffing. None in range retasted. **Sauvignon Blanc** ★ More 'crisp dry white' than varietal hero; some wet wool character & racy acidity on **05**.

Rocktail Bay range

Merlot-Cabernet Sauvignon ★★ No new vintage. Casual tippling **05**, mild cranberry flavours titivated by dollop sugar. **Cabernet Sauvignon-Cabernet Franc-Petit Verdot** NEW ★★ Ruby-hued **06**, 75% cab s, fresh berries, kiss of dark choc. **Rosé** ★★ **06** last ed was similar to Cape 1652 version, though mite drier on analysis (4.5g/l RS). **Pinotage Rosé** NEW ★★ Pretty pink **07**, suggestion of strawberries, light & frisky, finishes dry. **Chardonnay-Sauvignon Blanc** NEW ★★ **07** grassy nose; crisp, lemon/lime layers; fresh, dry finish.

South Point range

Pinotage ★★ Rustic **05** wild strawberry fruit & fairly severe tannins. None in range retasted. **Dry Red** ★★★ Pleasant al fresco **04**, smoothed by smidgen sugar. Mainly pinotage & shiraz, with dash ruby cab. **Chenin Blanc** ★★★ Gentle, fresh-tasting guava flavours, **04** styled for undemanding quaffability. **Sauvignon Blanc** ★★ Lightish **05** green-toned, crisply dry, with asparagus hint.

Stellenbosch Drive range

Cabernet Sauvignon NEW ★★★★ **07** cassis nose & clean vanilla oak; dark cherry fruit in silky mouthfeel & long dry finish. Styled for early drinking. **Merlot** NEW ★★★ Big, robust **07** invites with mocha notes & toasty wood, black cherry & dark choc flavours. Long dry finish. **Shiraz** NEW ★★★ Toasty oak, spice & smoke on **07**. Ripe plummy fruit on a foundation of crisply balanced acid & gentle tannin. **Red Blend** ★★★ Cab-led blend with shiraz & merlot. **06** spice, smoke, blackberry & dark choc combo; crisp & firm tannins. Fr oaked. **Chardonnay** NEW ★★★★ Soft vanilla biscuit scents on gentle, nutty **07**; clean peach & pear flavours, & lingering touch coconut on finish. **Chenin Blanc in Barrels** NEW ★★★ **07** pretty wine with lingering charm & modest 13.8% alc. Gentle blossoms introduce pleasing melon & citrus flavours; Fr oak nicely tucked away. **Sauvignon Blanc** NEW ★★ Herbal, grassy **07**, clean, crisp food wine. **Viognier in Barrels** NEW ★★★★ Pale gold, big-hearted charmer. **07** ripe fig/vanilla nose, satin mouthfeel, peachy fruit & lingering finish. Fermented in Fr oak. **White Blend** ★★★ Complex **07** blends chenin, chard, sauv & drop viognier, adds Fr oak. Herbal/vanilla nose, tropical fruit layers, citrus finish. — DB

Ormonde Private Cellar

T 022-492-3540 · F 022-492-3470

Darling (see Durbanville map) · 1stB 1999 · Tasting & sales Mon-Fri 9-4 Sat & pub hols 9-1 · Closed Easter Fri, Dec 25/26 & Jan 1 · Vineyard tours by appt · Picnic baskets by appt or BYO · Function hall · Facilities for children · Farm produce · Walks · Owner Basson family · Winemaker Michiel du Toit · Viticulturist Theo Basson · ±400ha (cabs s/f, merlot, mourvèdre, petit v, shiraz, chard, chenin, sauv, semillon) · 1 000t/35 000cs own label 40% red 60% white · PO Box 201 Darling 7345 · info@ormonde.co.za · www.ormonde.co.za

'Activity on this farm never stops,' marvels Theo Basson. The new cellar, which 'ran like clockwork' for the 2007 harvest, now awaits Fairtrade accreditation. Meanwhile, the Bassons have a new project: a flower route and nature reserve complete with hiking trails and camping site. But they're especially proud of their Alexanderfontein Cab - one of only nine SA wines to win gold at the Decanter World Wine Awards.

Alexanderfontein range

Sauvignon Blanc ☺ 🏵 ★★★☆ **07** (★★★★) lively & cheerful with similar dusty fig & asparagus scents to **06** & pvs, yet lacks its vivaciousness, lengthy finish.

Cabernet Sauvignon ★★★☆ **05** not retasted, pvs ed was opulent, smooth & creamy with ripe tannic structure. 9 mths Fr, 25% new, micro-oxygenation during ferment. WO Coastal. **Merlot** ★★★ **05** more quaffer than keeper; rich & ripe, overloaded with dark fruit & liquorice flavours. **Chardonnay** ★★★ **07** riper than pvs, also less serious, more amiable with less focus. Pear & apple notes buttered with toasty oak ex-30% wood fermented portion. **Chenin Blanc** ★★★ Warm vintage yields riper (14.3%) more rounded **07**; greengage & pine flavours very quaffable.

Ormonde range
Cabernet Sauvignon-Merlot ★★★★ **05** an opulent dark fruited compote with silky mouthfeel & supple tannins. Balanced & accessible now, yet with few yrs ageability. **Chardonnay** ★★★★ Step up for **06**; toasty oak marrying marmalade & lemongrass flavours; understated minerality ensuring its place at the dinner table. **Sauvignon Blanc** ★★★ **06** dusty aparagus, mineral core deliver a crisp al fresco companion, to enjoy early. — *MW*

Oubenheim Estate
T 083-509-9885 • F 027-213-5624

Olifants River ▪ Est/1stB 2002 ▪ Closed to public ▪ Owner DW Viljoen & Philip Viljoen ▪ Winemaker Philip Viljoen ▪ 800cs 100% red ▪ PO Box 52 Vredendal 8160 ▪ oubenheim@telkomsa.net
Having registered the first 'estate' in the Olifants River region in 2002, Philip Viljoen is concentrating on producing quality reds – 'ideal for the Olifants soil' – specifically merlot, pinotage and shiraz, each harvested from a single vineyard. Last year saw the launch of his new midtier range, Philip's Creek. None tasted for 2008.

Oude Compagnies Post
T 023-230-1578 • F 023-230-0840

Tulbagh ▪ Est 1699 ▪ 1stB 2003 ▪ Tasting only by appt ▪ Owner Jerry Swanepoel Family Trust (Jerry & Henriette Swanepoel) ▪ Winemaker Jerry Swanepoel ▪ Viticulturist Hanno van Schalkwyk (consultant) ▪ 18ha (cab, merlot, pinotage, ruby cab, shiraz, chard, sauv) ▪ 80t/3 000cs 100% red ▪ PO Box 11 Tulbagh 6820 ▪ swanepoel@intekom.co.za
This is a family wine business. 'My three sons do jobs in the cellar to earn extra pocket money, my wife does the marketing and I make the wine,' says Jerry Swanepoel. 'I love what I do!' This year's addition to the historic stone cellar was a dry rosé 'for those hot summer months'.

Compagnies Wijn range
★★★★ **Merlot 06** might be diverted to Caap Ensemble, as **05** was. Last-reviewed **04** was pleasantly approachable.
★★★★ **Caap Ensemble** Cab, merlot & pinotage (40/40/10) with meaty mineral hints, tart cranberry sauce-like flavours, fine tannins. Great food partner. Matches quality of maiden bottling, a sample last ed.
Cabernet Sauvignon ★★★★ Sampled ex-barrel last ed, **05** not retasted. Plenty gd fruit; looked promising beneath wood. **Pinotage** ★★★★ Minerality, hints sweet vanilla, spiciness & blackberry fruit on **06**; blackcurrant extra on palate, ripe yet grippy tannins. Nudges next level. **Shiraz** ★★ **06** lacks juice of pvs. Black pepper & leather hints, dusty oak, dry finish. **Cabernet Sauvignon-Pinotage** ★★★☆ Last was **03**, hollow-centred, but gd fruit & firm structure. **Ruby Blanc** NEW 🏵 ★★ **06** light & breezy rosé from trio of reds with honey & lemon aromas. — *MM*

Oude Denneboom
T 021-869-8073 • F 021-869-8073

Voor Paardeberg (see Paarl map) ▪ 1stB 2003 ▪ Visits by appt ▪ Owner Daniel de Waal ▪ Winemaker/viticulturist Hannes Aucamp ▪ ±41ha (cab, mourvèdre, pinotage, shiraz, nouvelle, viognier) ▪ 400t/150cs 85% red 15% white ▪ PO Box 2087 Windmeul 7630 ▪ hannesaucamp@mweb.co.za

Winemaker Hannes Aucamp's been having a grand time experimenting in the cellar. There are nice new varieties available locally, he says, and he's been playing around with Rhône grapes. The results? A Chenin-Viognier (mentioned last guide), a stand-alone Viognier for 'curiosity' value, and a Shiraz-Mourvèdre-Viognier blend in the making, for good measure.

Oude Denneboom range

Shiraz ★★★★ Apologies, we overlooked **05** last yr, but **06** barrel sample agrees to be very friendly... with lily/violet perfume, bluegum notes; mouthfilling, finishes with gentle tannins but slightly hot. Rating provisional. — *JPf*

Oude Kaap

Range by DGB for export mainly to the Netherlands, Germany and Scandinavia.

Oude Kaap range

Cabernet Sauvignon ★★★ Sociable unwooded **05** (sample) invites with ripe berry & mint aromas, plum pudding flavours. **Pinotage** ★★★ Generous, earthy & plummy **05**, ex-tank, comfortable everyday quaffer. **Cabernet Sauvignon-Merlot** ★★★ Warm & welcoming, previewed **05** redolent of dark choc & black cherries. **Klassiek Rood** ★★ Gd everyday savoury dry red **06**, equal cinsaut & ruby cab. **Cinsaut-Ruby Cabernet** NEW ★★★ Earthy, plummy equal blend, pre-bottling **06** pleasant, undemanding, gd dry finish. **Blanc de Noir** 🗒 ★★ Dusty strawberry nuances on **07**, crisp finish. From pinotage. **Rosé** NEW ★★ Lunchtime sipper from pinotage. **07** subtle flavours, fresh & dry. **Chardonnay** ★★ **07** poolside quaffer with lemon hints & appealing honey overlay. **Chenin Blanc** 🗒 ★★★ Typical chenin nose on brisk **07**, grapey flavours finishing dry. **Elegant Wit** ★★ Light, multi-variety white quaffer, **07** drier than 'Semi-Sweet' label suggests. **Klassiek Wit** 🗒 ★ Slightly bland sauv-led dry white; serve chilled. **NV.** Discontinued: **Ruby Cabernet**. — *DB*

■ **Oude Rust** *see Mooiuitsig Wine Cellars*

Oude Wellington Estate
T 021-873-2262 • F 088021-873-4639

Wellington (see Paarl map) ▪ Visits by appt ▪ Closed Dec 25 ▪ A la carte restaurant ▪ Guest house & self-catering cottages ▪ Tour groups ▪ Facilities for children ▪ Conferencing ▪ Owner/ viticulturist Rolf & Vanessa Schumacher ▪ Winemaker Vanessa Schumacher (Jul 1995) ▪ 13 ha (cab, ruby cab, shiraz, chard, chenin) ▪ 80t/±2 500cs own label 60% red 20% white 20% rosé ▪ PO Box 622 Wellington 7654 ▪ info@kapwein.com ▪ www.kapwein.com, http://estate. kapwein.com

The Schumachers were recently incommunicado for some months, over-landing to Kenya and back. Now in residence at their convivial weingut again, they'll tell you about their adventure while offering a personalised experience of their wine, food, potstill brandy and grappa. 'We love to share our home and experiences with like-minded people.'

Cabernet Sauvignon ★★★ Back after 4 yr absence, **04** has choc, coffee aromas, red berries showing through dry tannins; fresh & pleasant. **Vasecco** NEW 🗒 ★ **05** blanc de noir from ruby cab makes a jolly debut; has dry hay perfume, sweet/sour flavours. **Chardonnay Unwooded** ★★ Showing bottle-age character, **05** also has prominent acids, ideal for food. — *MM*

■ **Out of Africa** *see African Terroir*

Overgaauw Estate
T 021-881-3815 • F 021-881-3436

Stellenbosch ▪ Est 1905 ▪ 1stB 1971 ▪ Tasting & sales Mon-Fri 9-5 Sat & pub hols 10-12.30 ▪ Closed Mar 21, Easter Fri-Mon, Dec 25/26 & Jan 1 ▪ Fee R10 ▪ Tours by appt ▪ Owner Braam van Velden ▪ Winemaker David van Velden Jnr (Nov 2002) ▪ Viticulturist Johan Pienaar (consultant) ▪ 75ha (11 varieties) ▪ 60% red 40% white ▪ PO Box 3, Stellenboschkloof Road, Vlottenburg 7604 ▪ info@overgaauw.co.za ▪ www.overgaauw.co.za

The wisdom of 100 years of Van Velden winemaking at Overgaauw stand David Jnr in good stead as he takes over the reins and puts his youthful stamp on the portfolio. Recognising the modern trend for fruity, accessible and well-priced wines, he's introducing the Shepherd's Cottage range, after the 18th century rustic abode on the estate and starter home to several Van Velden newly-weds. Ready on release, the new wines are perfect, David Jnr believes, for those who do not have time to waste/wait for the longer-maturing Overgaauw bottlings to reach their peak.

★★★★☆ **Cabernet Sauvignon 04** (★★★★) focused red berry flavours & ripe tannins give classic Cape elegance with a slight rustic edge. Less lavish than vintage-boosted **03**, it has flesh & structure for min 3-4 yr maturation. 100% new Fr oak.

★★★★★ **Merlot** First Cape bottling of this variety (82); after lavish **03**, **04** (★★★★) now shows savoury plum & cocoa fruit framed by unobtrusive oak; green edge gives freshness & tobacco hint on rather diluted palate.

★★★★★ **Tria Corda** Aromas of scorched earth on **04**, scents of kirsch & cassis. Medium bodied, with fine ripe tannins binding flavours; interesting aftertaste incl hints smoked wood, raspberry. Cab-based with 34% merlot, touch cab f. 18 mths new Fr oak.

★★★★ **Chardonnay** Finished wine not tasted for few yrs. Sample **07** (★★★★) fruit-driven, with some toast notes & lifted finish, but not as characterful as **06** & pvs. Fermented/8 mths oak, 20% new.

★★★★★ **Cape Vintage** Pioneer of classic styling, use of Portuguese varieties. Exceptional **97** (★★★★★) showed great balance & intensity; latest **98** structured, grippy, richly balanced, still needing time. Mid-2007 tasting of all since **93** (available as 'collector's pack') shows great quality, with **96** lightest & least, **95** & **97** standouts. All very drinkable, most still maturing. Blend touriga with tintas b/f/r, souzão & cornifesto.

Shiraz-Cabernet Sauvignon ★★★★ Shiraz (80%) offers red berry & black pepper on lightly oaked **04**; restrained & food-friendly. **Sylvaner** 🔲 ★★★★ Cape's sole varietal bottling, since 71. **07** at 13.5% alc bigger than pvs (giving warm finish), but same individuality, melon allure, supple spice. **Sauvignon Blanc** 🔲 ★★☆ **07** asparagus, zesty tropical flavours with a little sugar; finish a bit hot.

Shepherd's Cottage range NEW

Cabernet Sauvignon/Merlot 🔲 ★★ **05** unfussily offers well-structured, easy-going drinking. **Pinotage Rosé** 🔲 ★★ Rhubarb flavours, pleasant off-dry finish on **07**. **Chenin Blanc-Semillon-Chardonnay** 🔲 ★★ Uncomplicated, tropical, lively **07** with good palate weight. All tasted as samples. —*JPf*

Overhex Wines International 🍴 🎋 📷 ⚙

T 023-347-6838 ▪ F 023-347-6837

Worcester ▪ Est 2006 ▪ Owner Overhex Private Cellar & Waboomsrivier Co-op ▪ Cellarmaster/ production Kobus Rossouw, with JC Martin ▪ Winemaker Kobus Rossouw, JC Martin, Johan Rossouw, Bennie Wannenburg, Natalie van Rooyen ▪ Viticulturist Pierre Snyman ▪ PO Box 139 Worcester 6849 ▪ karin@overhex.com ▪ www.overhex.com

Overhex Cellar: Tasting & sales Mon-Fri 8-5 ▪ Closed pub hols ▪ Tours by appt ▪ BYO picnic ▪ Farm produce ▪ Winemakers Johan Rossouw, with Natalie van Rooyen, Seugnet Rossouw & Willie Malan ▪ Viticulturist Pierre Snyman ▪ 10 000 tons ▪ HACCP, BRC & ISO 9000 certification in progress ▪ T 023-347-5012 ▪ F 023-347-1057

Waboomsrivier Cellar: Tasting & sales Mon-Fri 8–12.30; 1.30-5 Sat 8-10 ▪ Closed pub hols ▪ Cellar tours by appt ▪ BYO picnic ▪ Winemaker Bennie Wannenburg, with Wim Viljoen & Paul Burger ▪ ±15 500 tons ▪ wabooms@mweb.co.za ▪ T 023-355-1730 ▪ F 023-355-1731

This two-cellar operation went into a joint venture last year with Langguth, one of Germany's biggest producers of branded wines and owner of the well-known Blue Nun label. Their new brand is Kaya, its theme 'South Africa's True Nature', hence the predominance of pinotage and chenin in the four blends in the range.

Soulo range

Cabernet Sauvignon ★★ **05** last ed showed mint, earth & choc, nutty flavours & steak-taming tannins. **Shiraz** ★★☆ Well-textured **05**, pvsly noted as having dry, amenable leathery tannins with spicy touch. **Sauvignon Blanc** ★★ Dusty grass prelude, pleasing pineapple, tangy mouthfeel & clean, lemony finish on **07**. **Red Muscadel** ★★★ **06** rich raisin wafts precede honey-sweet fruit, offset by clean acidity & velvety mouthfeel. R/S 239g/l as pvs. From single vyd block. **White Muscadel** ★★ **04** powerfully sweet & muscatty last ed, with touch lemon. SAYWS reserve champ.

Soulo Five Senses range [NEW]

Cabernet Sauvignon-Petit Verdot 06 unready. **Sauvignon Blanc 07** not ready for review.

Balance range

Merlot-Cabernet Sauvignon ★★★ As the label states, **06**'s vanilla/mocha & ripe, plump fig fruit nicely balanced with easy tannins. Long dry finish. **Pinotage-Shiraz** ★★ Fruit-driven **06**, nicely pitched blend (70/30) for comfortable quaffing, abetted by grain sugar. **Shiraz-Merlot** ★★★ Equal blend **06** combines wafts spicy pencil shaving & ripe, plummy fruit, sitting well on bed of crisp tannins. **Shiraz Rosé** [NEW] ★★★ **07** light, uncomplicated charmer, just off-dry, with suggestion of strawberry, finishes dry. **Muscat d'Alexandrie** ★★ Delicate floral & honey notes on light-bodied **07** (11% alc), drier tasting than 24g/l sugar suggests. **Chenin Blanc-Colombard** ★★ Warm hay & tropical fruit salad in light & undemanding **07**. **Sauvignon Blanc-Semillon** ★★ **07** grassy entry, soft, figgy sweetness from sprinkle sugar (9.5g/l). **Vin Sec** ★★ Bouncy explosion of mouthfilling bubbles in dry-finishing party sparkler. **NV**. **Vin Doux** ★★★ Lively mouthfilling mousse & sun-ripened grapes make for cheerful party fun. **NV**. Discontinued: **Pink, Colombard-Chardonnay**.

Kaya range [NEW]

Pinotage-Shiraz ★★ Interesting combo spices & herbs, plum pudding on **06**; touch sugar smoothes rather than sweetens. **Pinotage-Merlot** ★★ Meaty, savoury whiffs, ripe plums, juicy finish to soft 50/50 mix in **06**. **Pinotage-Cabernet Sauvignon** ★★★ Equal blend **06**, easy-tippler with wafts choc/mocha, sunny-ripe black berries & soft mouthfeel. **Chardonnay-Viognier** ★★ **07** shy, with understated tropical-fruit sweetness & lemony finish. **Chenin Blanc-Chardonnay 07** not tasted.

Lavida range

Cape Red ★★ Bright, red-fruited quaffer; firmish & dry, unpretentious. Pvsly tasted **04** mainly shiraz, briefly oaked. **Cape White** ★★ Early-drinking **05** from chenin, 40% colombard; rounded & pleasantly dry. Neither revisited for current ed. *— DB*

Overmeer Cellars

Since 1996, big-selling no-frills quaffing range mostly in 2 and 5-litre packs, ex-Western Cape vyds by Distell.

Selected Red ★★ Low-alc (11%) unpretentious red-berried quaffer with leanish dry farewell. **Grand Cru** ★★ Pear & apple aromas & flavours, bone-dry & lean. **Stein** ★★ Friendly summertime easy-drinker, gently sweet with brisk finish. **Late Harvest** ★★ Crisp, fruity, appletoned quaffer. Dollop of sweetness adds personality. All **NV**. *— MW*

■ **Overvaal**   *see Hartswater Wine Cellar*
■ **Paardenkloof**   *see Ecology*
■ **Paarl Heights**   *see False Bay Vineyards*

Paarl Wine Company
T 021-862-0616 • **F** 021-862-6400

Paarl • Closed to public • 9 Zuidmeer Str, Huguenot, Paarl 7646 • izak.v@pwcwines.co.za

Wine wholesalers and owners of the Fairbridge range.

Paddagang Wines
T 023-230-0394 • *F 023-230-0433*

Tulbagh • *Est 1987* • *Tasting & sales daily 9-4* • *Fee R5* • *Paddagang Restaurant daily 8.30-4.30* • *Closed Easter Fri, Dec 25 & Jan 1* • *Guest house, gifts & other attractions* • *Owner Paddagang Vignerons* • *Winemaker Elsabé Roux (Dec 2002)* • *Viticulturist Wedré Lourens (Nov 2006)* • *5 300cs 52% red 21% white 27% other* • *PO Box 303 Tulbagh 6820* • *paddagang@mweb.co.za* • *www.tulbagh.net*

This cheerful amphibian-themed range finds its home in an equally convivial setting: the Paddagang Wine House in Tulbagh's historic Church Street (other wines from the area also available for tasting and sale). The revamped labels have been well received, especially the Brulpadda Port, says marketing manager Quintus Basson of Tulbagh Wine Cellars, where the wines are made.

Paddarotti ★★★ Mainly cab (plus dollop shiraz) with variety's food-friendly firm tannins. **NV**, as are all these; none retasted. **Paddajolyt** ★★★ Tangy, lightish, unwooded vin ordinaire from pinotage & ruby cab (50/50). **Paddadundee** ★★ From chard, with fragrant passionfruit hints; creamy-dry finish. **Paddasang** ★★ Lightish sauvignon, apple & pear tones tinged with bottle-age. **Paddapoot** ★★★ Deliciously aromatic, fortified hanepoot, very soft & sweet. **Brulpadda** ★★★ Old-style Cape port from ruby cab & pinotage; soft, sweet & silky. — *DH*

■ *Pangolin* see MAN Vintners

■ *Papillon* see Van Loveren Private Cellar

■ *Papkuilsfontein* see Tukulu

■ *Paradyskloof* see Vriesenhof Vineyards

■ *Patrys* see Assegai Selection

Paul Cluver Estate
T 021-844-0605 • *F 021-844-0150*

Elgin (see Elgin/Walker Bay map) • *Est 1896* • *1stB 1997* • *Tasting & sales Mon-Thu 9-5, Fri 9-4, Sat & pub hols 9-3 (Sep-Apr), 10-2 (May-Aug)* • *Fee R10 for groups of 8-12* • *Closed Easter Fri/Mon, Dec 25 & Jan 1* • *BYO picnic* • *Guest house* • *Summer sunset concerts in amphi-theatre* • *Conservation area* • *Owner Cluver family* • *Winemaker Andries Burger (Nov 1996)* • *Viticulturist Kevin Watt (since Mar 2005)* • *85ha (cab, merlot, pinot, chard, gewürz, riesling, sauv)* • *300t/20 000cs 45% red 55% white* • *PO Box 48 Grabouw 7160* • *info@cluver.com* • *www.cluver.com*

The Lion King came to Elgin this year. Not the full cast, just Mufasa, head of the pride, aka cellarmaster Andries Burger. 'It's because of how I am over harvest time,' he chortles. Losing his assistant to her homeland, France, didn't help, and a stop-start season fixed his mind, but looking back on vintage 2007 the chief's pleased with better ripeness levels in the reds than in 2006, anticipating more concentrated, bigger flavours. Winning fans, particularly in Scandinavia, is the collaborative Slowine brand (and here he doffs his cap to father-in-law Paul Cluver for a well-chosen name). See seperate entry for Slowine.

★★★★ **Pinot Noir** Unlike **04** which had a hedonistic edge to its taut tannin-acid structure, **06** lacks perfumed charm, is more earthy; yet its austere tea leaf tannins are brushed with sweet cherry fruit on exit making it a more kingly, than queenly, version. 9 mths Fr oak, 20% new.

★★★★★ **Chardonnay** Barrel fermented/aged version, now 100% natural ferment. Lemon-lime nuances, thrilling acidic vein to rich, buttery mouthful on **06**; 9 mths on lees, regular battonage adds creaminess. Not everyone's glass of chard, but expertly crafted.

★★★★★ **Gewürztraminer** 🔲 Always a treat, as much for its uniqueness (there are less than 2 dozen gewürz in SA) as its poise. **06** has signature rosepetal & honeysuckle notes, lime acidity; sweeter than pvs (now 10g/l) but still finely balanced.

★★★★ **Sauvignon Blanc** Aromatic & poised **07** maintains standard set by **05**. Well rounded, yet zesty & dry, with wet pebble finish. Sweaty suggestion to cool greenpepper/ruby grapefruit aromas, flavours. Enjoy now, or even better in ± yr's time.

★★★★ **Weisser Riesling 06** flew out the tasting room before we could taste it, sample **07** considered, deliberate. Characteristic peach/perfumed notes highlighted by lime, nut hints; steely core & piercing acidity ideal tipping point for 9g/l hint of sweetness. Will gain complexity with 3 yrs+ bottle aging.

★★★★★ **Weisser Riesling Noble Late Harvest** Doing the family business for yrs - with pinpoint elegance, style. **06** incredibly complex already with dried apricots, honeycomb, rosepetal & cinnamon oak aromas, flavours. Brisk, joyful. Portion matured 3rd fill Fr oak, 8 mths.

Cabernet Sauvignon ★★★★ Precisely structured **04**'s cedary-toned cassis opulence contrasts beautifully with its regal tannin backbone, characteristic dry cab finish. Should improve with few yrs cellaring. Usual 18 mths Fr oak, this yr 50% new. **The Elgin Blend** ★★★★ Tasted last ed, **04** ripe, rather thick, but very appealing even in youth; soft fruit paired with intelligent supportive oaking. Blended home cab & bought-in Elgin merlot with dash shiraz. — *CvZ*

■ **Paul de Villiers** *see Landskroon Wines*

Paul Wallace Wines
T 021-848-9744 • F 021-848-9744

Elgin • Est 2004 • Closed to public • Owner/viticulturist Paul Wallace • Winemaker Paul Wallace with Inus Muller • Malbec, pinot, sauv • PO Box 141 Elgin 7180 • wallovale@mweb. co.za

After 27 years of consulting, Paul just loves having his own farm, says wife Nicky Wallace. Some wildlife is happy too - not the vineyard snout beetles, but the guinea-fowl that devour them, and the Cape Clawless Otter in the natural dams on the 25-hectare farm, nearly a third of which falls within the Groenland Conservancy.

★★★★ **Malbec** Intriguingly different, rather wild aromas on fruit-packed **05** (ex-Paarl), with 50% new oak adding spice to the ripe berries, all underpinned by velvet-soft but pervasie tannins, leading to long dry finish. — *TJ*

Pax Verbatim Vineyards
T 021-855-5244 • F 021-855-5244

Stellenbosch • Est 2004 • Closed to public • Owner/winemaker Richard Hilton • 500cs 50% red 50% white • 21 Topaz Street, Heldervue, Somerset West 7130 • info@paxverbatim.co.za • www.paxverbatim.co.za

'Quantities are still "micro" and quality still the focus," declares winemaker/negociant Richard Hilton. His Syrah enjoys a growing following locally and overseas, and this year a maiden Viognier 'from top-end Stellenbosch grapes' will be released. A trip to Tuscany was inspiring - can a Sangiovese be far off?

Blazing Hill Syrah ★★★★ Svelte tannins embrace dense fruit core in aromatic **05**, rhône-like bouquet with pepper, smoked ham & floral notes. Structured for the long haul, as were pvs. 18 mths Fr oak, 35% new. Rung above unflamboyant **04** (★★★). — *CvZ*

■ **Peacock Ridge** *see Waterkloof*
■ **Pearl Springs** *see Cape Vineyards*
■ **Pearly Bay** *see KWV Limited*
■ **Pecan Stream** *see Waterford Estate*

Pella Wines
T 021-881-3026 • F 021-881-3026

Stellenbosch • Est/1stB 2004 • Closed to public • Owner Ingrid de Waal • Winemaker Ingrid & Daniël de Waal • Viticulturist Daniël de Waal • 100cs • 100% red • PO Box 89 Vlottenburg 7604 • pella@adept.co.za

This may be a venture of garagiste proportions, but inspired couple Ingrid and Daniël de Waal are serious about the quality of their Shiraz, handcrafted from low-yielding 30-year-old vines. So there's nothing from what they consider the lesser 05 vintage, and just nine barrels of the (untasted) **06**, destined for an early summer release. Export agents are being sought 'to establish greater horizons'.

Hoogland Shiraz ★★★★ Striking **04** with peppery, earthy & mineral notes; when reviewed was concentrated & well extracted. 15 mths Fr oak, 20% new. —*MF*

■ **Pendoorn** *see* Virgin Earth

■ **Pendoring** *see* Havana Hills

Perdeberg Winery
T 021-869-8244/8112 ▪ F 021-869-8245

Paarl ▪ Est 1941 ▪ Tasting & sales Mon-Fri 8-5 Sat 9-1 ▪ Closed Easter Fri/Sat, Dec 25 & Jan 1 ▪ Tours by appt during tasting hours ▪ Owner 40 members ▪ Winemaker Kobus de Kock, Ewald Kellerman & Pieter Carstens (1989/1997/2004) ▪ Viticulturist Callie Coetzee (2006) ▪ 3 100ha ▪ 23 000t 60% red 40% white ▪ PO Box 214 Paarl 7620 ▪ info@perdeberg.co.za ▪ www. perdeberg.co.za

Motivated to fulfil the promise of their good-value wines, this BWI-accredited winery recently introduced a 'satisfaction guarantee' to their range, and have also embarked on a country-wide merchandising blitz. Internationally they now have a joint venture brand, named SAAM (see separate entry), with the UK's Bibendum Wine Limited, available locally soon.

Reserve Range
★★★★ **Pinotage** ✓ From old bushvine vyd. **05** better balanced than drily tannic **04** (★★★☆); deliciously savoury, with forward fruit, good varietal character, long finish. Well calculated 14 mths Fr/Am oak.

Shiraz ★★★★ **05** last ed showed spicy-peppery, perfumed aromas; serious structure, yr in Fr/Am oak supporting sweet red fruit, but a touch tart, **Classic Red** NEW ★★★★ Lovely aromas black & red berries on **05**, cedar, tobacco; palate hints at oak & tannic grip satisfies - though 4.5g/litre RS less than 'classic'. Herbaceous note on end. **Chenin Blanc** ✓ ★★★★ Softly rich (just-dry) but fresh & lively **06** (not retasted) oak fermented/aged 5 mths - spicy wood well integrated. 14.5% alc a touch hot on finish. TWS gold. **Sauvignon Blanc** ✓ ★★★★ **07** confirms pattern of grassy, greenpepper liveliness; flavourful, substantial, well textured & dry (Durbanville grapes). **'Elitist Sauvignon Blanc'** NEW **07** sample has more tropicality than straight Rsv version, adding interest; full, lengthy flavours & winning fresh balance. Shd rate at least ★★★★. **Viognier** ★★★ Aromas/flavours more subdued than in **05** (★★★★) on rather oxidative, oaked **06** - pity, as structure crisply rich. **"Icon White"** NEW ★★★★. Ambitious, emphatically wooded **06** blends 45% chenin, with semillon, viognier, sauv. Deepish yellow, from time on lees & oxidative handling. Fruit lurks, somewhat hidden, in thick-creamy texture; finish a little awkward & hard.

Perdeberg range

Merlot NEW ☺ 🍷 ★★★ Savoury, tasty **06**'s light wooding highlights choc, sweet-fruit-cake; just off-dry & very easy-going. **Pinotage** ☺ 🍷 ★★★ Nice aromas, gd varietal char on **06**, but struggle of dry tannins vs sugar & ripe fruitiness means less success than pvs version. **Shiraz** ☺ 🍷 ★★★ A little background tannin sets off **06**'s spicy plumminess - sweetish like most of these reds, but more characterful. **Cabernet Sauvignon-Merlot** ☺ 🍷 ★★★ **06** cab adds some seriousness & firmness, a little sugar takes some away, juicy fruit and light oaking do their bit. **Soft Smooth Red** ☺ 🍷 ★★★ Allsorts red now vintage-dated with **06**; still semi-sweet, with some structure to control its outgoing juiciness. **Chenin Blanc Dry** ☺ 🍷 ★★★ As ever, **07** leaps from the glass with tropical fruit aromas & continues lipsmackingly. **Chenin Blanc Semi-Sweet** ☺ 🍷 ★★★ Latest **06** as usual a freshly balanced, not-too-sweet version. Discontinued **Cinsaut-Shiraz**.

Fresh & Fruity White NEW 🍷 ★★ Not so fruity, but vaguely pleasant, just-dry quaffer. **Cinsaut Liqueur Wine** ★★★ **05** lush fortified dessert last yr a little spirituous & sweet (125g/litre sugar; 18% alc). 375m Discontinued: **Cinsaut**. —*TJ*

■ **Perold** *see* KWV Limited

Peter Andrew Signature Collection [NEW]
T (516) 357-2070 • F (516) 357-8799

Est 2005 • 1stB 2003 • Closed to public • Owner Peter Morales • Winemaker Wilhelm Kritzinger (Bellevue Estate) • Viticulturist Dirkie Morkel (Bellevue Estate) • 200cs • 57 Main Street Imports, 585 Stewart Ave, Suite 544, Garden City NY 11530 USA • info@57mainstreet.com • www.57mainstreet.com

This brand, owned by New York-based Peter Morales, benefits from his considerable experience in the international wine and spirits sphere, which includes importing and marketing wines from some of the Cape's foremost wineries. The collection commences with Ingenium, a 'Collaboration of brilliance' (the literal meaning) with Bellevue owner Dirkie Morkel and winemaker Wilhelm Kritzinger.

Ingenium ★★★★ Menthol-tinged bdx blend, **03** showing some gd development with structure for another few yrs. Soft, floral & refined in classy, lean style (13.2% alc). EW. — *RP*

Peter Bayly
T 044-213-3702 • F 086-513-2727

Calitzdorp (see Klein Karoo map) • Est 2002 • 1stB 2004 • Visits by appt • Conservation area • Owner Peter & Yvonne Bayly • Winemaker Peter Bayly • 1.2ha (tinta, touriga, souzão) • 700cs 100% port • PO Box 187 Calitzdorp 6660 • info@baylys.co.za

A freak accident – the Baylys' solar-powered electric fencing burnt out – allowed a troop of baboons into the vineyard, destroying unripe grapes on their way to raid a walnut tree. Frost had a hand in further reducing the crop to a miserly 20%, 'but what we have is superb', says Peter B cheerfully. He bought in local grapes and made a white port; just released is a Cab, from grapes ex the Langkloof.

Peter Bayly range
★★★★ **Cape Vintage Port** From foot-trodden touriga, tinta, souzão, **05** notable for fresh, fruity, grapey styling; appealing acidity & only lightly gripping tannins make for delicious early drinking. Firm dry finish. Charming 500ml bottle.

Cabernet Sauvignon [NEW] ★★★★ Dark, extracted, ripe, powerful, rich, grippy **06** - & aromatic reminders of port too; also lovely fresh cab cassis. Characterful, delightful; might mature into something starrier. Bo-Langkloof grapes. — *TJ*

Peter Falke Wines   [NEW]
T 021-881-3266 • F 021-881-3256

Stellenbosch • Est/1stB 2003 • Tasting by appt Mon-Fri 9-4 Sat 9-2 • Fee R15 • Closed pub hols • Owner Franz Peter Falke • Winemaker/viticulturist Tertius Naudé (Aug 2005) • 8ha (cab) • 60t/5 000cs 95% red 4% white 1% rosé • PO Box 228 Bellville 7535 • info@peterfalkewines.co.za • www.peterfalkewines.co.za

Previously supplying grapes to top-notch wineries such as Rust en Vrede, Waterford and Neil Ellis, an on-site winery to vinify fruit for an own brand was completed in 2007 (a tasting room is in the planning). Now also buying in grapes, the range has been expanded, the main outlet being Europe, plus some local restaurants.

Signature range
Cabernet Sauvignon ★★★★ Elegant & structured if not electrifying **03**; everything you want from cab (violets, plums, coffee & tobacco) in tailored mouthful. 18 mths Fr oak (70% new).
Sauvignon Blanc ★★★ **06** reticent pear nuances but gd rounded mouthfeel from 7 mths lees enrichment. Best in lively youth with delicate foods.

PF range
Cabernet Sauvignon ★☆ Red berry & earth notes; **03** unwooded, sinewy & lightish, for easy drinking. — *JP*

■ **Petit** *see* Ken Forrester Wines

Philip Jordaan Wines
T 023-349-1601 • F 023-349-1581

Rawsonville ▪ Est/1stB 1998 ▪ Closed to public ▪ Owner/winemaker Philip Jordaan ▪ Viticulturist Leon Dippenaar (consultant) ▪ 1ha ▪ 500cs 100% red ▪ PO Box 55 Rawsonville 6845 ▪ philipjordaan@intekom.co.za

Philip Jordaan, by day cellarmaster at Du Toitskloof, makes a small quantity of fine Cab Franc for his own label. 02 still in stock at press time; no **03**; **04** not ready for tasting.

■ **Philip's Creek** *see* Oubenheim Estate

PicardiRebel
T 021-700-5500 • F 021-700-5515

Cape Town ▪ Est 1994 ▪ PO Box 18130 Wynberg 7800

The wine profile of this national group changes slightly as Colin Frith takes over as GM Wines. The emphasis will be re-establishing the 'wine destination' role of PicardiRebel stores, enabling greater customer interaction with the best of the new releases and rarer wines, together with the popular brands. Frith will continue to seek out exceptional wines both locally and from overseas for the Picardi/Rebel house brands.

Pick 'n Pay
T 021-936-8400 • F 021-934-6355

Enquiries Elsa Gray ▪ Bahrain Drive Extension, Airport Industria, 7490 ▪ egray@pnp.co.za ▪ www.picknpay.co.za

This national chain of supermarkets and hyperstores offers its 'No Name' house-brand wines in 3- and 5-litre casks. All are made by Robertson Winery, and commendably moderate in alcohol.

No Name range

Dry White ☺ ★★☆ Latest version more quaffably fresh & light than pvs, offering balanced floral aromas & flavours.

Dry Red ★★ Selected fruity varieties styled for easy imbibing; soft berry flavours & moderate 13% alc. **NV**, as are all these. **Semi-Sweet Rosé** ★★ Sweet but crisp & lively, with strawberry flavours & a light body. **Dry White Light** ★ Fragrant but ordinary off-dry glassful, with light 10.3% alc. **Stein** ★★ Zesty semi-sweet flavours & gentle tropical notes in a light, easy-drinking package. **Late Harvest** ★★ Friendly sun-ripened semi-sweet, melange of dried fruit & tropical flavours. — *MW*

Pick's Pick
T 011-784-8676/7 • F 011-784-8674

Owner Alan Pick ▪ thebutchershop@mweb.co.za

Successful Gauteng restaurateur Alan Pick is routinely one of the biggest buyers at the CWG Auction. A good reason he can persuade the Cape's finest to bottle for his Butcher Shop & Grill in-house brand and great-value off-sales, which he sees as a joint venture between himself and the winemaker.

★★★★★ **Pinotage Reserve 05** by Beyerskloof, should delight Beyers Truter fans: generous rasp/strawberry tones lifted by subtle tarry hints; composed, persistent, with aloe suggestion on finish.

★★★★ **Late Bottled Vintage** Tasted pvs ed, **02** had all correct qualities for style: ripe & accessible fruit, measured structure, almost stately finish with persistent spiciness. From leading port house JP Bredell.

Cabernet Sauvignon ★★★ **05** ex-Paul Cluver in Elgin had cool-area raciness etched into red fruit, powerfully structured yet subtle, deserved few yrs bottle-ageing. Not retasted. **Merlot** ★★★★ **05** big & forthright but with interesting nutty nuances, attractive plum-choc flavours, soft tannins, long warm finish (14.5% alc). Lifts the bar on leafy & jammy **04** (★★★). Both from

Jordan, as is Sauvignon. **Shiraz** ★★★ Zevenwacht the source of **04**; tasted mid-2006, approachable with soft tannins, meaty/savoury styling appropriate for restaurant's carnivorous clientele. **Cabernet Sauvignon-Shiraz-Merlot** ★★★★ Near-equal cab & shiraz fleshed out by 13% merlot in vintage-boosted **05**. Modern, overt fruit profile kept in check by austere tannins & bright acidity. 11 mths Fr/Am oak, 30% new. **04** (★★★★) similar but tad less exciting. Both ex-Guardian Peak. **Chardonnay** ★★★★ Barrel fermented/aged **06** ideal for creamy (sea)food. Well-judged oak ensures buttery nuance does not overwhelm citrus flavours, mineral/nutty aromas. 9 mths Fr oak. Ex Jordan, as was pvsly tasted **04** (★★★★), which showed a pleasing firmness. **Sauvignon Blanc** ★★★★ **06** full flavoured, with myriad tropical/green notes & asparagus; lightish (13% alc) with pleasing mouthfeel & minerality. Solo or with food. **05** (★★★) few shades lighter than regular Jordan version. **Chenin Blanc-Viognier-Chardonnay** ★★★★ Delightfully aromatic **06** blend (60/33/7) by Rudera's Teddy Hall; last ed we noted body-plumping sugar, balancing crisp acidity. — *CvZ*

■ **Pier 42** *see* Goedverwacht Estate
■ *Pierneef Collection* *see* La Motte
■ *Pierre Jourdan* *see* Cabrière
■ *Pikkewyn* *see* Groupe LFE South Africa
■ *Pinecrest/Pinehurst* *see* Môreson

Plaisir De Merle

T 021-874-1071 • **F** 021-874-1689

Simondium (see Franschhoek map) • Est 1993 • 1stB 1994 • Tasting & sales Mon-Fri 8.30-5 Sat 10-4 (Nov-Mar) 10-2 (Apr-Oct) • Fee R20 (informal), R30 (tasting & tour) • Closed Christian hols • Tours by appt during tasting hours • Tour groups • Day conferencing for small groups (15 max) • Owner Distell • Cellarmaster/winemaker Niel Bester (Jan 1993) • Viticulturist Hannes van Rensburg • ±400ha (cab, merlot, shiraz, chard, sauv) • 800t/40 000cs own label 80% red 20% white • PO Box 121 Simondium 7670 • plaisirdemerletours@distell.co.za • www.plaisirdemerle.co.za

Proud of its natural and cultural heritage, this pristine mountainside spread now offers an historic wine tour (including a cellar visit, tasting and tour around the old mill, line house and farmstead). Also planned is a biodiversity tour, which will show off the farm's natural fynbos, buchu plantation, BEE trout farming project and historic wolf trap. Meanwhile, from his recently ISO 14000- and HACCP (BRC)-certified cellar, winemaker Niel Bester is thrilled to report that his Cab is a top seller in Scandinavia.

★★★★ **Cabernet Sauvignon** Cassis & violet-perfumed **04** expertly crafted to provide satisfying, tailored mouthful; oak tad dominant mid-2007 but should settle, harmonise, given time. ±16 mths oak, mainly Fr, 45% new. Continues step up in quality inaugurated with friendly but serious **03**.

★★★★☆ **Cabernet Franc** Mainly exported but limited quantities of this standout version available locally. Poised **05**, classically fine tannins, raspberry & tealeaf tones. Perhaps lacks sense of mystery of **04** (★★★★) & **03**, but shares their ethereal perfumes. WO Smnsberg-Paarl.

★★★★ **Merlot 02** & **03** were monovarietals, but **04** features smidgens petit v (10%), cab (5%). Textbook plumminess, lusciously ripe fruit, but oak slightly gruff, tail touch bitter. 12-16 mths Fr oak, mainly 2nd fill.

★★★★ **Shiraz 05** big & bold, brimming with red fruits, curryleaf nuances. Am oak vanilla scents, flavours. Alc (14%) & sugar (relatively) curtailed despite ripeness of the vintage. 60% new oak, mix Fr/Am 16 mths.

★★★★☆ **Grand Plaisir** Blend of Smnsberg-Paarl fruit, on upward path. **05** a treasure trove of intricate aromas/flavours & regal tannins. Mainly cab (40%), petit v, shiraz, cab f, malbec & merlot. 45% new oak, ±16 mths. **03** (★★★★), without shiraz, also impressive & delicious, deserving contemplation & ageing.

★★★★ **Sauvignon Blanc** Piercing acidity a thrilling counterpoint to **07**'s ripe fruit, leesy weight; attractive green-spectrum tones. 30% fruit ex-cool Lutzville & Groenekloof sites.

Chardonnay ★★★★★ Big step up for **06**; similar spicy brioche character to **05** plus vibrant citrus fruit, rich macadamia butter nuttiness. Pithy tail, courtesy lees stirring, most attractive. Fermented Fr oak, 50% new. Swiss gold. **05** (★★★★) similar but not quite as arresting. — *CvZ*

 Platinum *see Lyngrove*

 Podium *see Baarsma Wine Group*

 Poker Hill *see Somerbosch Wines*

Pongrácz

Popular and critically acclaimed brut-style cap classiques, named after the late Desiderius Pongrácz (pronounced Pon-grats), nobleman and refugee from the Hungarian uprising, who helped revitalise viticulture in the Cape. By Distell.

Desiderius ★★★★ Elegantly styled **00**, blend 60/40 chard/pinot with soft flavours & fine mousse; hints brioche, ripe apples & touch lemongrass on gd finish. **Pongrácz** ★★★ Pinot-driven (60%) MCC with chard has light floral bouquet, some green apple & citrus flavour - but fairly bland, though vibrantly refreshing. **NV**. Both off Sbosch vyds. — *JPf*

 Porcupine Ridge *see Boekenhoutskloof*

 Porter Mill Station *see Tulbagh Wine Cellars*

 Porterville Cellars *see Tulbagh Wine Cellars*

Post House Cellar

T 021-842-2409 • F 021-842-2409

Stellenbosch (see Helderberg map) ▪ Est/1stB 1997 ▪ Tasting & sales Mon-Fri 8.30-5 Sat by appt 8.30-1 ▪ Closed Easter Fri/Sun/Mon, Dec 25/26 & Jan 1 ▪ Owner/winemaker Nicholas Gebers ▪ 40ha (cab, merlot, petit v, pinotage, shiraz, chenin) ▪ ±200t/4 500cs own label ▪ PO Box 5635 Helderberg 7135 ▪ nick@posthousewines.co.za ▪ www.posthousewines.co.za

Owner/winemaker Nicholas Gebers has combined colour (his first love is painting) with the 'post house' theme in his 'Blueish' range - Blueish Black (a pinotage-based red blend) and Bluish White (a chenin-based white). His original offering, Penny Black (tints and stamps, again), so took a US customer that she when she died early last year, she asked to be buried with a bottle!

★★★★ **Penny Black** Serious red led by merlot, shiraz, with cab, petit v. Plush dark plums in **05**, with interwoven violet & savoury spice strands. 24 mths oaking shows in firm backbone, but tannins ripe, should develop with distinction.

★★★★★ **Chenin Blanc** Small crop from 24 yr old vines; native yeasts used, bottled unfiltered. Lovely complexity in **06**, citrus zest, almonds, roasted fennel, with an opulent, richly textured palate, but lack intensity, focus of pvs.

Cabernet Sauvignon ★★★★ Showing concentration of vintage, muscular **03** is dark-toned, with peppery spice & cedar. Its sturdy oak construction is already accessible, promises a further 4+ yr future. 24 mths barrelled, 30% new. **Merlot** ★★★★ Despite 24 mth oaking, **04** retains its charm & graceful lines. Scrub & mocha nuances accompany the berry tones, access is encouraged by supple tannins. Could age 4+ yrs. Native yeasts, unfiltered. Dabs cab, petit v. **Shiraz** ★★★★ Last available **03** had red-fruit lushness, white pepper/lily fragrance. Oak (16% new) rampant when previewed mid-2004; shd have mellowed by now. Provisional rating. **Blueish Black** ★★★★ Blend 4 varieties, tailored for earlier drinking. Shiraz, pinotage led in **06**, dictating wild berry, smoky, salty liquorice character, delicious suculence. **Blueish White** NEW ★★★ Easy drinking blend chenin, sauvignon (25%), **07** is packed with summer fruits flavours; fresh-toned & appetising. — *CR*

■ **Post Stones** *see False Bay Vineyards*

Premium Cape Wines
T 021-886-8515 • F 021-886-8515

Stellenbosch • Est 2003 • Closed to public • Owner Premium Trust • PO Box 12149 Die Boord 7613 • ansgar@gravitywine.com

This young negociant company supplies wines to supermarkets and direct sales companies in Germany, selecting the wines from various Cape cellars. Its brands include De Sonnenberg, Imvelo, Open Sky and Uhambo.

■ **Prince Imperial** *see The Stables*
■ **Private Collection** *see Saxenburg*

Prospect1870
T 082-878-2884 • F 0865 131 999

Est 1990 • 1stB 1998 • Closed to public (tasting at The Wine Boutique, Main Rd, Ashton) • Owner De Wet Family • Winemaker Chris de Wet • 35ha (cab, merlot, pinotage, shiraz, chard, sauv blanc, viognier) • 500cs • PO Box 141 Ashton 6715 • chris@prospectvineyards.co.za • www.prospectwines.com

The brothers De Wet are still concentrating 99% of their efforts on the US export market, under the Leatherwood label. At home, they make a tiny barrel selection called Prospect1870. 'It's only produced in very good years,' says Chris, 'and 2006, which is still in the barrel, looks like it will be a Prospect year.'

Prospect range
★★★★ Prospect Complex, heart-warming **06** revels in huge smoky bouquet of mocha, coffee & coconut. 100% new Fr oak, 15 mths. Country wine with class. Blend cab, merlot, shiraz (60/20/20).

Leatherwood range
Cabernet Sauvignon ★★★ Typical cab intro to **04**, blackberry, toasty oak wafts precede juicy, accessible fruit. **Shiraz-Viognier ★★★** Toasty, smoky notes followed by choc/toffee, **04** lifted by viognier's peachy fruitiness. Yr older oak. —*DB*

■ **Provenance** *see Saronsberg Cellar*
■ **Provin** *see Douglas Wine Cellar*

Pulpit Rock Winery
T 022-461-2025 • F 022-461-2025

Swartland • 1stB 2003 • Tasting & sales Mon-Fri 8-5 Sat 9-2 • Closed Easter Fri-Sun, Dec 25 & Jan 1 • BYO picnic • Tours by appt • Tour groups • Walks • Conservation area • Owner Brinkshof Wines (Pty) Ltd • Winemaker Piet Kleinhans (Dec 2003) • Viticulturist Koos van der Merwe (Aug 2005, consultant) • 400ha (cab, merlot, petit v, pinotage, roobernet, shiraz, chard, chenin, sauv) • 1 000t 60% red 40% white • PO Box 1 Riebeek West 7306 • info@pulpitrock.co.za • www.pulpitrock.co.za

Pulpit Rock's Brink Family range, mainly for export, has replaced Cape Haven locally. Viniman Piet Kleinhans reports a challenging harvest with heat waves causing high sugars and headaches but whites turned out well and reds, equally promising, are waiting in the wings. Vitiman Koos van der Merwe added petit verdot and mourvèdre to the previous year's vines – more spice for future blends.

Pulpit Rock Winery range
Cabernet Sauvignon ★★★ Early-drinking **04** last ed was a brooding giant, loaded with luscious mulberry fruit, supple tannins & cellar's standard ±15% alc. **Merlot ★★★** Idiosyncratic & chunky **04** was beginning to knit last time but full harmony's few yrs away. **Pinotage ★★★★** With cellar's trademark firm tannins needing time, **05**'s meaty, liquorice & spiced plum flavours will reward the wait. 15 mths all new Fr/Am, 70:30. **Shiraz ★★★** **04** balanced &

appealing last yr. Dry tannins matched by plum fruit, for smoother mouthfeel. 14 mths new oak, 30% Am. SAYWS gold. **Chardonnay** ★★★ Despite loads of flavour, sliced peaches, lemongrass, **05** has ultra-soft palate, lacks acid grip. Oaked 10 mths Fr, 80% new.

Pulpit Rock Brink Family range

Cabernet Sauvignon ★★ **06** dried herbs, plummy fruit, still tightly bound by robust tannins. **Merlot** ★★ **05** last ed showed similar ripe plummy intro as pvs; fat prune-like flavour with savoury centre. **Pinotage** ★★ **06** brambleberry & rhubarb typicity, with firm tannin foundation. **Shiraz** ★★ Smoky dark fruit appeals but **06**'s chunky youthful tannins not ready. **Chardonnay** ★★★ Shortbread, preserved lemon flavours on **06**; light-textured, friendly. Partially oaked. **Chenin Blanc** ★★★ Lees contact, 14% sauv addition perks up **07**'s appley fruit profile, adds mineral freshness. — *CR*

Pumlani [NEW]

T 021-903-5123 • F 021-903-3373

Est/1stB 2006 ▪ Tasting at Zevenwacht ▪ Owner Alfred Tsholoba & Nomsa Tiyo ▪ Winemaker Jacques Viljoen, with Pierre de Klerk ▪ 5 000cs 40% red 40% white 20% rosé ▪ info@ zevenwacht.co.za

Wine farm labourer to chairman of a 100% black-owned BEE wine venture was something Alfred Tshotoba never dreamed of, but assistance and mentorship from Zevenwacht and strategic industry players made it a reality. Pumlani ('Sit Down & Relax') mirrors their intention to bring wine culture to the SA market in the most hospitable way.

Pinotage ★★ Youthful, tobacco, sour cherry **05**. Spicy flavours, prominent acidity. **Cabernet Sauvignon-Pinotage** ★★ **05** blend oaked cab (60%) & unoaked pinotage. Plum fruit gripped by firm acidity. **Rosé** ★★★ **06** potpourri & raspberry from blend syrah, merlot & cab. Whoosh acidity minimises sweetness from 11g/l sugar. **Chenin Blanc** ★★ Third barrel-fermntd/mat 6 mths. **06** waxy, apple/guava aromas; brisk acidity to finish. **Chardonnay-Chenin Blanc** ★★★ 50:30 blend, remainder sauv in **06**. Leesy dimension, lime & pineapple flavours end on tart note. — *IM*

■ **Quagga Ridge** *see* Horse Mountain Wines

Quando 🍷

T 023-616-2752 • F 023-616-2752

Robertson ▪ Est/1stB 2001 ▪ Visits by appt ▪ Owner Irene Bruwer Family Trust ▪ Winemaker Fanus Bruwer ▪ Viticulturist Martin Bruwer ▪ 80ha ▪ 3 300cs own label 100% white ▪ EurepGAP certified ▪ PO Box 82 Bonnievale 6730 ▪ info@quando.co.za ▪ www.quando.co.za

'It's a lean, mean family business,' says winemaker Fanus Bruwer. He and brother Martin, officially the viti man, do 'just about everything'. Last year, that included harvesting chenin from 30-year-old vines planted by their father and blending with a minute portion of bought-in viognier. Their signature sauvignon is now selling well abroad, particularly in the UK.

★★★★ **Sauvignon Blanc** ▤ Gorgeous floral notes accompany grapefruit in **07**, crisp, refreshing & welcoming.
Chenin Blanc-Viognier [NEW] ▤ ★★★★ Venerable chenin, daubed with young-vines viognier. Maiden **07** shows lovely drinkability solo or with food: spicy cherry flavours, expert use of Hung oak staves adding flavour & structure, not grip. — *MM*

■ **Quantum** *see* Du Toitskloof Winery
■ **Queen of Sheba** *see* Eshkol Kosher Winery

Quest Wines [NEW]

T 023-342-5856/084-678-0322 • F 023-342-5856

Worcester ▪ Est/1stB 2006 ▪ Closed to public ▪ Owner Anja van Rijswijk & Hendrik Myburgh ▪ 100% red ▪ 12 Otto du Plessis Str, Worcester, 6850 ▪ admin@questwines.co.za ▪ www. questwines.co.za

Hendrik Myburgh and Anja van Rijswijk plan to have their own cellar and vineyards within the next 10 years. In the meantime, they've used their experience in viticulture and wholesale wine marketing to launch their own wine marketing company this year, and their own label, Cape Roots.

Cape Roots range

Cabernet Sauvignon ★★★ 06 same genes as stablemate. Ripe-fruited, eager to please but checked by lean, dry tannins. Here, 14.4% alc stands out. **Merlot ★★★** Similar bloodline to Cab (see note above); lower alc (13.8%) on this **06** more flattering. — *CvZ*

■ **Quiriga Reserve** *see* Rietrivier Winery
■ **Quiver Tree** *see* Oranjerivier Wine Cellars

Quoin Rock Winery
T 021-888-4740 • F 021-888-4744

Stellenbosch • Est 2000 • 1stB 2001 • Tasting & sales daily 9-5 • Fee R15, negated on purchase • Closed Easter Fri & Sun, Dec 25 & Jan 1 • Platters of fine cured meats & cheeses • Tours by appt • Owner Metlika Trading • Winemaker Carl van der Merwe (Jan 2002) • Viticulturist Doug Murdoch & Rossouw Theart • 60ha (cab, merlot, pinot, shiraz, chard, sauv) • 180t/5 000cs own label 70% red 30% white • PO Box 1193 Stellenbosch 7599 • wine@quoinrock.co.za • www.quoinrock.com

Truth-seeker Carl van der Merwe continues to swim against the mainstream by refining the organic, experimental and non-interventionist methods used at this striking Simonsberg farm and winery, with vineyards in the Agulhas area. Facets of his fine-tuning include two new 06 'estate reds' from home-farm vines; blending mourvèdre into the Syrah from the **06** vintage onwards; and taking advantage of the 'fantastic freshness' of their Agulhas fruit to create the area's first cap classique. The goal is 'wines that are awe-inspiring when opened after all the difficulties of market over-supply and competition ratings have been forgotten.'

Quoin Rock range

★★★★☆ **Syrah 05** TWS Trophy (as for **03**). Purposefully traditional, emphasising supple mouthfeel, oak (25% new) only a background enrichment. Sumptuous yet delicate spice, woodsmoke, savouriness, also lovely fragrant lilies. Exciting & sustained flavours. 14.5% alc.

★★★★☆ **Merlot** None since impressively structured **03**, showing power, elegance & freshness alleviating 14.5% alc. Smart Fr oaking (50% new). Smnsberg/Agulhas vyds.

★★★★ **Chardonnay 03**, from cool Agulhas vyds, still available. Pvsly we noted delicate lime/lemon purity, freshening acid & richness with few yrs potential. Fermented/aged yr Fr oak, 80% new.

★★★★ **Sauvignon Blanc** Cool Agulhas provenence eloquently expressed in **06** (sample last yr). Svelte, racy, with fine savoury acidity & minerals backing intense gooseberries & lemongrass.

★★★★ **Oculus** Flagship white growing in power & distinction. **05** customary tight-knit palate, vibrant & dry. Restrained tangerine & vanilla hints recur on broad, sustained tail. Few yrs ageing should be well rewarded. 100% sauv, fermented/yr Fr oak, 25% new.

Vine Dried Sauvignon Blanc ★★★★ Gorgeous barrel-fermented dessert from grapes dehydrated on the vine (no botrytis). **05** satiny succulence matched by concentrated fruit. Medium body, clean, delicious tangerine tang on lively finish. 164g/l RS; used Fr oak; natural ferment. **04 (★★★★)** & pvs under Glenhurst range.

Glenhurst range

Red Blend ★★★★ 02 similar shiraz, merlot, pinotage mix to maiden **01**; fruitier, with savoury spice extras; rounded, lively. Fr/Am oak, 50% new. WO W Cape. **Sauvignon Blanc-Viognier ★★★★** Distinctive yet refined apricot/honey fragrance from well controlled viognier (35%) in **06**; concentrated, lively, dry. Used Fr oak fermented/matured. Both ranges WO Smnsberg-Sbosch unless noted. — *AL*

■ **R62** *see* Joubert-Tradauw Private Cellar

Raats Family Wines
T 021-881-3078 · F 021-881-3078

Stellenbosch · Est/1stB 2000 · Visits by appt · Owner Bruwer & Jasper Raats Jnr · Winemaker Bruwer Raats · Viticulturist Jasper Raats Snr (2003) · 20ha (cab f, chenin) · 6000cs 15% red 85% white · PO Box 2068 Stellenbosch 7601 · braats@mweb.co.za · www.raats.co.za

It's all family hands on deck at the Raats boutique winery. Bruwer R is the winemaker/marketer; wife Janice handles the admin; and paterfamilias Jasper tends the 4ha owned and 21ha contracted vineyards, which now include new neighbourhood cab franc and chenin, plus Durbanville vines. Some 80% of their produce is exported – to Europe (all three Raats wines are listed by Sweden's government-owned liquor chain, Systembolaget) and the US, where their chenins, in particular, have received flattering reviews from the likes of the New York Times and Wine Spectator.

★★★★☆ **Cabernet Franc** Beautifully crafted & multifaceted red, stand out example in SA context. **05** (★★★★) as perfumed & darkly spiced yet more slender, understated than rich & velvety **04**; needs half a decade for latent berried fruit to harmonise with firmer tannins. Fr oak, ± 19 mths, ± 30% new.

★★★★ **Chenin Blanc** Promising wooded rendition now earning praise in US; rich & succulent **06** easily maintaining standard set by pvs vintages. Stewed quince, apple & honey flavours cut by sweet/sour acidity, 20% oak ferment/aged adds breadth & structure. Enjoy solo or with food.

★★★★ **Original Chenin Blanc** The unwooded version. **07** (★★★★) steely, subdued; leaner than pvs, dustier (perhaps courtesy touch Dville fruit?). Food, or yr aging, should temper is austerity.— *MW*

Racetrack   [NEW]
T 021-884-4304 · F 021-884-4304

Paarl · Est/1stB 2006 · Closed to public · Owner Agnes de Vos · Winemaker Carla Pauw (Jan 2006) · 19ha (cabs s/f, merlot, chenin) · 10t/650cs 50% red 50% white · PO Box 38 Elsenburg 7607

Damaraskloof, where grapes, olives, figs and roses are grown, has been in Agnes de Vos' family for over a century. The local racetrack, initially deemed viticulturally inferior because of its gravelly soils, gradually made way for vineyards – the 60-year-old chenin bushvines are still in production. With winemaker Carla Pauw, Agnes dV is reviving the family tradition by planting new vineyards and making handcrafted wines.

★★★★☆ **Damaraskloof Chenin Blanc** Intense spanspek, apricot compote aromas, sumptuous textures, rich, yet 06 dry on the finish, oak (barrel ferment, 2/3/4 fill) well hidden in developed, intense flavours.— *MF*

■ **Radford Dale** *see* The Winery of Good Hope
■ **Rainbow Nation Wines** *see* The Shosholoza Collection

Rainbow's End Estate
T 021-885-1719 · F 021-885-1722

Stellenbosch · Est 1978 · 1stB 2002 · Visits by appt · Fee R15 refundable on purchase of 4+ btls · Owner Malan Family · Cellarmaster Anton Malan · Winemaker Anton Malan assisted by Francois Malan · Viticulturist Francois Malan · 23ha (cabs s/f, malbec, merlot, petit v, shiraz) · 130t total 17t/950cs own label 100% red · PO Box 2253 Dennesig 7601 · info@rainbowsend. co.za · www.rainbowsend.co.za

With their Banghoek ward officially recognised and the vineyards fully planted, the Malans are now establishing a fynbos reserve at Rainbow's End. Spurred on by prestige listings locally, the success of their first exports to Sweden and an encouraging clutch of recent awards, they are set to increase their output.

Cabernet Sauvignon ★★★☆ Embryonic **07** tobacco & menthol notes in classic chalky mould, appealing leafy vein to ripe cassis fruit. Can't rate conclusively but seems an improvement on pvs. Combo new, 2nd/3rd fill Fr oak. Unfiltered/fined (as for all). **Cabernet Franc** ★★★★ Brooding, tightly wound **07**, previewed mid-2007 shows classic structure, well-managed tannins with tealeaf edge, floral notes covering generous layers of fruit. Too young for conclusive rating but appears notch up on **05** (★★★★), with lovely lifted fynbos character. Oak as for Cab. **Merlot** NEW Debut **07** barrel sample too unformed to rate but promises much: choc & ripe plum, serious structure & elegant fruit with hints fig, prune & exotic spice. New/2nd fill Fr oak. **Shiraz** ★★★★ Ex-single vyd; tasted from barrel, provisionally rated **07** a star in the making: opulent but balanced Christmas cake, dark cherry & bacon notes, fine texture & already seamless oaking (as for Cab). **Complexité** ★★★★ Aptly named bdx blend cab, merlot, cab f (39/31/30). Pvsly tasted **04** refined yet ripe berry flavours, plenty of cab's firmer tannins; harmonious; potential for ±5 yrs development. NE. — *RP*

Raka

T 028-341-0676 • F 028-341-0676

Kleinrivier (see Elgin/Walker Bay map) • Est/1stB 2002 • Tasting & sales Mon-Fri 9-5 Sat 10-3 during peak season otherwise by appt • Fee R10 for 4 wines • Closed Dec 25 • Tours by appt • BYO picnic • Walks • Nature conservancy • Owner Piet Dreyer • Winemaker Josef Dreyer 2007 • Vineyard Manager Piet Dreyer • 62ha (five Bdx reds, mourvèdre, pinotage, sangiovese, shiraz, sauvignon, viognier) • 15 000cs 75% red 17% white 8% rosé • PO Box 124 Caledon 7230 • info@rakawine.co.za • www.rakawine.co.za

It's been a period of consolidation for Piet Dreyer and family. While eldest son Gerhard has inherited dad's sea legs and taken charge of the squid fishing business, landlubber Josef is now manning the helm in the cellar following Danelle van Rensburg's departure to Van Loveren. 'He had just graduated from Elsenburg Agricultural College when she got the offer, so I was a bit nervous about him doing the 2007 vintage all by himself but I think the wines are marvellous!' says proud mom Elna. His confidence has also been bolstered by lots of positive comments about his early-release white wines.

★★★★ **Barrel Select Merlot** Imposing selection of best Fr casks. **06** in usual brooding style; chewy, muscular yet supple tannins cloak fresh black fruits backstage. As exciting as **05**; buchu-spiked game meat flavours in firm frame. Check from 2010.

★★★★★ **Biography Shiraz** Neither classic nor for the faint hearted, not short of character. **05** tingling white pepper & piercing pimento notes, mulberry fruits teem with finely poised components. **04** (★★★★★) stormed the shows - VDG, SAA, SAYWS, TWS - astounding; vanilla spice, dense fruit seamlessly integrated with & tethered by powder-fine tannins. Yr Fr oak.

★★★★ **Quinary** Less overt than above (no pinotage), carries cellar's stamp. **04** lush fruit rides on ribs of firm tannins hoping to emulate mineral **03**'s development - & trophy cupboard: MIWA Grand D'Or, SAA, VDG. Cabs s/f, merlot with dashes malbec, petit v. 14.5% alc. Not retasted.

★★★★★ **Figurehead Cape Blend** 14% pinotage joins Bdx quintet to add Cape flavour without distracting from finely tuned ensemble. Maiden **04** showed opulent plum/game tints with bramble fruits & pulpy red berries worked into incredibly fine tannic structure when reviewed last ed. MIWA DG. Yr 90% Fr oak, rest Am, mix new/used.

★★★★ **Sauvignon Blanc** ✓ Quintessential cool Stanford sauvignon; **07** retains heady flint focus, but more plump than pvs, penetrating finish bristles with freshness. **06** herby canned pea features held in shape by extended racy structure.

> **Rosé** ☺ ★★★ **07** slightly baked earthy fruit cut by tingling acidity, super truly dry tail. Blend ex 'all the reds in the cellar!' W Cape WO. No **06**.

Pinotage ★★★☆ **05** secures sweet fruit in puckering tannic stays, pvs ed noted time needed to allow softer plum features to emerge. **Sangiovese** ★★★ **06** redolent of oysters & peat, typical food-friendly tannins but in lighter style. WO W Cape. **Spliced** ★★★☆ 88% merlot dominance racks up clever blend with cab, ruby cab in **04**; succulent, meaty fullness within open-weave frame. Not revisited this ed. **Shannonea** ★★★★ Sauvignon (76%) joined by viognier & chard from **05**: perfumed, grippy lingering finish last ed. — *DS*

■ **R & De R-Fredericksburg** *see* Rupert & Rothschild Vignerons
■ **R&R** *see* Rupert & Rothschild Vignerons

Ravenswood

Budget wines made by Robertson Winery for Vinimark, now discontinued.

■ **Rawson's** *see* Cape Vineyards
■ **Ready Steady** *see* Southern Sky Wines
■ **Red Seal** *see* Fairview

Remhoogte Estate
T 021-889-5005 • F 021-889-6907

Stellenbosch ▪ Est 1994 ▪ 1stB 1995 ▪ Tasting & sales Mon-Fri 9-4 Sep-Apr, otherwise by appt ▪ Tours anytime by appt ▪ Guest cottage ▪ Olives & olive oil for sale ▪ Conservation area ▪ Exhibition of SA hunting trophies ▪ Game camp ▪ Owner Murray Boustred Trust ▪ Cellarmaster Murray Boustred ▪ Winemaker Chris Boustred, advised by Michel Rolland ▪ Viticulturist Jacques du Toit, advised by Andrew Teubes ▪ 30ha (cab, merlot, pinotage, shiraz, chenin) ▪ ±180t/6 500cs own label 95% red and 5% white ▪ PO Box 2032 Dennesig 7601 ▪ remhoogte@adept.co.za ▪ www.remhoogte.co.za

Chris Boustred, son of owner Murray B, last year took the winemaking helm at this mainly red wine estate on the Simonsberg. He's is ably advised by the quarterly visits of French partner and global oeno-consultant Michel Rolland, whose son-in-law, David Lesage, now sells Remhoogte in France as part of the Rolland Collection. Debuting is a Chenin from the only white-wine vines on the property. The well-stocked game reserve continues to bring a touch of 'wild Africa' to the winelands.

★★★★ **Bonne Nouvelle** Spearheads cellar's merlot-led 'Cape blend' trio, this with cab & dash pinotage. **04** (★★★★★) beautiful choc-mocha sheen to plush tannins, fresh acidity. Ripe **03** was cab-led, with merlot & pinotage (46:35:19). 20 mths 80% new Fr cask. EW.

★★★★ **Estate Wine** Pinotage (30%) at its zenith in 2nd of the red trios. Shows in perfumed **05**, more weighty, plummy; 15% alc growls in grippy finish. **04** more retiring, savoury rather than just fruity. Native yeasts, 50% new Fr oak 20 mths. EW.

Chenin Blanc NEW ☺ 🍷 ★★★ Full tropical fruits brushed with oak (15% fermented in new Fr), from 'Block No 6'. Best well chilled. EW.

Aigle Noir ★★★★ Juicy, chewy & brawny. **05** lots of red berries & smoked meats in sensibly modest oaking (14 mths seasoned Fr), fresh zip on exit. Half merlot, equal cab & pinotage. EW. Discontinued: **Cabernet Sauvignon, Merlot**. Smnsberg-Sbosch WOs. — *DS*

Re'Mogo Wine
T 082-638-6774, 082-253-5126, 072-030-5317 NEW

Swartland ▪ Est 2004 ▪ Closed to public (direct deliveries on request) ▪ Owner Re'Mogo Holdings (Pty) Limited ▪ 50% red 40% white 5% rosé 5% sparkling ▪ PO Box 1037 Stellenbosch 7599 ▪ remogo@webmail.co.za ▪ www.remogo.co.za

This BEE company is 'standing together' (the Setswana meaning of its name) to 'harness nature for a long life' via an agreement with a leading producer of branded wines. With confidence gained from exhibiting their wines at the Fancy Food Exhibition in Miami, among others, they aspire to make this a leading emerging lifestyle brand. Not finalised at press time, the line-up was to include a Cab-Merlot Reserve 05, Chenin **07**, and a Rosé and Sparkling, both **NV**.

■ **Renosterbos** *see* Hofstraat Winery

Retief Wines

T 021-872-9088 · F 021-872-9983

Paarl · Est 1747 · 1stB 2004 · Tasting & sales Mon-Fri 10-5 Sat/Sun by appt · Closed all pub hols · Owner Pearl Mountain Wines (Pty) Ltd · Winemaker Robert Frater (2004, De Zoete Inval) · 8.28 ha (cab, merlot, shiraz) · 67t/7 500litres 100% red · PO Box 709 Northern Paarl 7623 · retief@new.co.za

After four generations of table grape production, this prime piece of viticultural estate on the outskirts of suburban Paarl has partially converted to winegrowing. 'Our biggest strength is our long-standing table grape culture, which requires attention to detail,' believes MD Graham Retief. 'This allows us to produce a top-quality product.'

Above the Mist ★★★ Everyday mix merlot, shiraz & cab (60/30/10); **05** juicy dark plum & choc freshened by hint spicy oak (30% new), firm acid. **Yes It's Red** ★★ Ruby-hued **04**, very ripe strawberry features, 15% alc glow. 60/40 cab/shiraz. **Wagon Trail** ★★★ Spicy intro to **05** shiraz/merlot mix. Balanced, lively fruit enhanced by touch oak vanilla (30% new wood); ready. — *AL*

Reyneke Wines

T 021-881-3517/3451 · F 021-881 3285

Stellenbosch · Est 1863 · 1stB 1998 · Tasting & sales by appt · Uitzicht B&B · Owner Reyneke Family · Winemaker Johan Reyneke (2005/6) · Viticulturist Johan Reyneke (1992) · 20ha (cab, merlot, pinotage, shiraz, sauv) · 2 000cs own label 70% red 30% white · PO Box 61 Vlottenburg 7604 · wine@reynekewines.co.za · www.reynekewines.co.za

'We've moved out of the cowshed and into a proper winery for the first time,' smiles Johan Reyneke, 'which will enable us to make more wine for ourselves.' He's also decided to go 'the certification route', his vineyards now being organic and biodynamic to EU standards. Ian Engelbrecht (ex-Faure Farms) has brought 'some much needed level-headedness' to the viticulture, while Vinimark has taken over the marketing, sales and distribution. Another new team member is Tallulah Josephine Reyneke, born in August 2007.

★★★★ **Reyneke Reserve** ✿ Unshowy, elegant Rhône-like shiraz **05** from granite soils with perfumed clove, aniseed, dark plum, easily absorbing 16 mths 2nd fill Fr oak. Pure, supple fruit well-integrated with oak tannins & acidity. Enduring length.

Pinotage ✿ ★★★★ **05** previewed last ed from barrel. Unshowy elegance, appealing fruit purity, sufficiently ripe & dense to counter firm tannin & fine acidity. 16 mths older Fr oak, needing time before broaching. **Cornerstone** ✿ ★★★★ Youthful **05** previewed last ed; tannin & acid still assertive, checking rich blackcurrant fruit. Classic 60:40 cab/merlot blend. EW. **Sauvignon Blanc (Blanc Fumé)** ✿ ★★★★ Resembles wooded white rather than sauvignon; minerality rather than primary fruit. Quiet, with dimension with persistent finish. **Sauvignon Blanc** ✿ Unoaked **07** to young to rate, still dominated by peardrop ferment character, though fruit:acid components in balance. All wines biodynamic methods in vyd & cellar. All reds natural yeast fermentation. — *IM*

Rhebokskloof Private Cellar

T 021-869-8386 · F 021-869-8504

Paarl · 1stB 1989 · Tasting & sales daily 9-5 · Fee R25 (informal, incl bite-size foods); R45 (formal, booking essential); R75 (sunset tasting, booking required) · Tours by appt · Restaurant · Play area for children · Tour groups · Gifts · Conferences · Conservation area · Owner Rhebokskloof Wines · Winemaker Rolanie Lotz (Jan 2007) · Ops manager Daniël Langenhoven (May 1998) · Vineyard Manager TBA · ±40ha (cab, merlot, chard) · 240t/20 000cs 50% red 50% white · PO Box 2637 Paarl 7620 · info@rhebokskloof.co.za · www. rhebokskloof.co.za

With a revamped team, including ex-Simonsvlei winemaker Rolanie Lotz, Rhebokskloof has big plans. There's the new modern venue hall and upgrades to the cellar and vineyards. And to go with the overall good harvest, there's passion. Says Rolanie L: 'There's something magical about creating a product that's so complex yet so enjoyable.'

Private Cellar range

★★★★ **Cabernet Sauvignon** The flagship, ex-two vyds ±17 yrs old; only Fr oak, 20% new, 14 mths. **01** inviting toasty overlay to ripe blackberries & dark cherries, well-managed tannins fow now or keeping.

Shiraz ★★★★ Pleasing spicy nose & ripe, plummy fruit on **05**, underpinned by bracing tannin. 14 mths oak 25% new, 10% Am. **Chardonnay** ★★★ Now only chard in stable. **06** billowing vanilla biscuit & sweet melon, by clean lemony notes. 14 mths Fr oak, 20% new; 14% alc unobtrusive. **MCC** ★★ **04** unavailable. Maiden **03** MCC, tasted last ed, light-bodied & gently effervescent. Discontinued: **Merlot, Chardonnay Grande Reserve, Chardonnay Sur Lie/ Barrel Selection, Weisser Riesling, Weisser Riesling Special Late Harvest.**

Rhebok range

Pinotage ★★★ Warm, toasty **06**, wood (none new) well balanced with fruit & tannin. Could age few yrs. Pvsly under PC range. **Cabernet Sauvignon-Merlot** ★★★ Meaty, savoury notes, ripe blackberry fruit & clean, lingering finish on **05**. Usual 9 mths Fr oak, 10% new. **Chenin Blanc** ★★ Reported discontinued last ed, revives with clean, leafy **07**; crisp, dry, green-apple freshness. **Sauvignon Blanc** ★★ Grass & greenpeppers meet bright tropical fruit salad flavours in **07**. **Bouquet Blanc** ★★ Shy, understated **07** redeemed by some grassy sweetness for party pleasure. **Tamay Sparkling** ★★★ Pvsly in PC range. **06** clean floral wafts, crisp, dry apple fruit & lively mousse. Discontinued: **Dry Red, Chardonnay, Chardonnay-Sauvignon Blanc, Dry White.** — DB

▌ **Rhinofields Reserve** see Durbanville Hills

Rickety Bridge Winery
T 021-876-2129/3669 • F 021-876-3486

Franschhoek • Tasting & sales Mon-Fri 8-5 Sat & pub hols 9-5 • Closed Easter Fri, Dec 25/26 & Jan 1 • Fee R10 refundable on purchase • Cellar tours by appt • BYO picnic • Luxury accommodation & other attractions • Owner DS Sarnia (Pty) Ltd • Winemaker Wilhelm van Rooyen, with Dawid Gqirana (Jan 2001/Jun 1998) • Viticulturist Wilhelm van Rooyen • 16ha (cab, merlot, shiraz, chard, chenin, semillon) • 120t/5 000cs own label 65% red 35% white • PO Box 455 Franschhoek 7690 • sales@ricketybridgewinery.com • www.ricketybridgewinery.com

Their 'visitors welcome' message spread last year clearly was heard – weddings galore, the super-comfortable country house almost fully booked for a year ahead, and feet through the door of the tasting centre with its mountain views. Now they're also focusing intensively on countrywide marketing of the wines. 'We're getting the brand out there and securing distribution channels,' says marketing manager Izelle Bouwer.

★★★★☆ **Shiraz** Cellar's polished signature with hallmark concentrated black fruit, well-controlled spicy oak. **03** finer, less extrovert than pvs: rich, spicy/savoury palate, chewy tannins. 20-24 mths Fr brls, 20% new. Not retasted this ed, as for all except next wine.

★★★★ **Paulinas Reserve** Limited-release barrel selections honouring farm's founder. **04** (★★★) lacks generosity of **03** & pvs. Lean (100% cab, pvs incl merlot), with firm tannins, volatile whiff.

Cabernet Sauvignon ★★★★ Harmonious **02**, more savoury, less overt berry character than pvs, but food-friendly. 30 mths Fr oak, 25% new. **Merlot** ★★★ More body than fruit on **03**, tautish tannins, mint/mocha aromas with meaty hint. 2 yrs Fr oak, 25% new. **Duncan's Creek Classic Red** ★★★ Appealing, lightish & juicy **04**, shiraz (57%) with cab & dollop malbec. Gd fireside red, lightly chilled, summer picnic partner. ±13% alc. **Chardonnay** ★★★ Sinewy, elegant **05**, gd marmalade-toned fruit, smooth finish. 9 mths barrelled. **Chenin Blanc** ★★ **06** dry, with quick vegetal flavours. **Sauvignon Blanc** ★★★ **06** easy-drinker, light (12.7% alc), almost delicate, with unusual rosepetal hint. **Semillon** ★★★ Strongly barrel-influenced (9 mths Fr), **05** roasted nut overlay to variety's lanolin character, demure lemony finish. All these WO Fhoek or Coastal. *—JP*

Rico Suter Estate
T 023-355-1822 ▪ F 023-355-1822

Worcester ▪ Est 2004 ▪ 1stB 2006 ▪ Visits by appt only ▪ B&B (bookings: be.suter@breede.co.za) ▪ Table olives ▪ Walks ▪ Owner Rico Suter Family Trust ▪ Winemaker Carlo Suter, with Rico Suter (both Feb 2004) ▪ Viticulturist Bruno & Carlo Suter ▪ 55ha (cab, cinsaut, merlot, petit v, pinotage, shiraz, tannat, sauv, viognier) ▪ 600t ±2500cs own label 100% red ▪ PO Box 38 Breerivier 6858 ▪ ricosuterwines@breede.co.za

The close-knit clan on this estate is headed by Rico and Christine Suter, with son Carlo in the cellar, brother Bruno in the vineyards, nurturing fledgling rows of sauvignon and viognier. The new guesthouse, run by his wife Erika, offers splendid views of the Waaihoek Mountains.

Cabernet Sauvignon ★★★ Minty nose on **05** supported by plummy fruit, gd succulent flavours checked by firm tannins. Needs yr or so to soften. **Petit Verdot** NEW **04** not tasted. **Pinotage** NEW ★★★ **06** red berries & subtle oak; quite rich, creamy texture with lush fruit on attractive dry finish; firm tannin. **Shiraz** ★★★★ Old World fans will savour **05**'s bouquet of prune, dried fruit & shrubbery; coriander-spiced dark fruit & lovely long finish. Touch lighter (though still 14.8% alc) & more interesting than soft, mild-mannered **04** (★★★). **Cabernet Sauvignon-Petit Verdot** No new vintage. *— JP*

Ridder's Creek
T 021-873-7746 ▪ F 021-873-7746

Wellington (see Paarl map) ▪ Est 1999 ▪ 1stB 2002 ▪ Tasting by appt ▪ Owner George de Ridder & Jean Frick ▪ Winemaker Jeff Wedgwood (consultant) ▪ PO Box 72 Wellington 7654 ▪ ridders@iafrica.com ▪ www.ridderscreek.co.za

'We're refocusing on value for money,' advises negociant George de Ridder, adding that there's been some consolidation of the ranges. The Cape Red and White blends are the entry level, while the varietal Chenin and Shiraz represent the middle tier. 'All are in a friendly, easy-drinking style.'

Shiraz ★★★ Approachable **04** pvsly noted as offering ripe brambly fruit with hint of black pepper. **Cape Red** ★★ Quaffing-style **06**, preview reveals soft red fruit, mocha scents, chunky tannins. **Chenin Blanc** NEW ★★ Water-white **07** light textured, fresh & grassy. **Cape White** ★★ Sample **07** gently sweet sipper; shy tropical notes, moderate alc. *— CvZ*

Ridgeback Wines
T 021-869-8068 ▪ F 021-869-8068

Paarl ▪ Est 1997 ▪ 1stB 2001 ▪ Tasting & sales daily 10-5 (10-6 in peak season) ▪ Fee R15 for 5 wines ▪ Closed Easter Fri, Dec 25/26 & Jan 1 ▪ Light meals ▪ Guest house ▪ Tours by appt ▪ Owner Kilimanjaro Investments ▪ Winemaker Cathy Marshall (Jun 2000) & Toit Wessels ▪ Viticulturist Toit Wessels ▪ 35ha (cabs/f, grenache, merlot, mourvèdre, petit v, shiraz, chenin, sauv, viognier) ▪ 200t/16 000cs own label 70% red 30% white ▪ Eurogap certified ▪ PO Box 2076 Windmeul 7630 ▪ ridgeback@mweb.co.za ▪ www.ridgebackwines.co.za

Global warming or no, the Ridgeback team has identified the need to buffer the soil on their Paarl site against extreme heat. Neill Ferreira has taken on more responsibility in the vineyards, under longtimer Toit Wessels, who now also assists Cathy Marshall in the cellar and manages the farm, founder Jerry Parker having retired.

★★★★ **Merlot 04**, pvs ed, quieter & more refined than pvs. Medium bodied with dark plum & mocha tones. 80% new Fr oak.

★★★★★ **Shiraz** No follow up to this laudably consistent, expressive red. **04** layered notes of smoked meat, black pepper & hints of red fruits. Savoury length from 16 mths Burgundian barrels, 20% new.

★★★★ **Merlot-Cabernet Franc** No successor as yet to **04**. Merlot led (62%) sumptuous & big, though moderate 13.5% alc. Dark plum & cinnamon nuances with savoury finish. 10% new Fr oak.

Cabernet Sauvignon ★★★☆ Last-tasted **04** was sturdy with steak tartare/iron character, forceful dry tannins. **Vansha Dry Red** ▤ ★★★ **06**, newly bottled last ed, chunky shiraz (75%, rest cab) providing satisfying drinking. Unoaked. **His Master's Choice** ★★★★ Cassis & stewed dark ripe fruit on **05**; rich, well-made & balanced shiraz & mourvèdre (76/13), viognier adding fragrance. **Sauvignon Blanc** ★★ Grapefruit notes & sherbet texture with green apple crunch. **07** easy-drinking, where pvs more complex. **Viognier** ★★★★ Similar full-bore styling as pvs; **06** layered peach, floral, mineral notes; also variety's fatness, savoury dimension. Yeasty touch, noticeable acid add to singular character. **Vansha Dry White** ▤ ★★★ **07** chenin-led melange with sauv & splash viognier. Grapefruit & watermelon touches, light & easy. **Natural Sweet Viognier** ★★☆ Previewed as 'Sweet Viognier' last ed. Flinty/matchstick hints & variety's broad texture combine with unctuous sweetness on **06** — *MM*

Ridgemor Farm

T 021-842-2255 ▪ F 021-842-3393

Stellenbosch (see Helderberg map) ▪ Est 2003 ▪ 1stB 2005 ▪ Tasting & sales Mon-Fri 10-4 ▪ Discretionary tasting fee ▪ Guest villa (see Stay-over section) ▪ Owner Veronique Barge ▪ Viticulturist Johan Joubert (2003, consultant) ▪ 35.2ha (cab f, pinot, sangiovese, shiraz, chenin, sauv) ▪ 15t6/6 000 cs ▪ 77% red 12% white 11% rosé ▪ PO Box 3625 Somerset West 7129 ▪ info@ridgemorwines.com ▪ www.ridgemorwines.com

Ridgemor Farm now gives its name to the winery previously known as Weening & Barge. New wines, not ready for tasting, include a wooded Chenin and a follow-up release (06) of the characterful Pinot. Also new are the golf driving range and quad-bike track.

★★★★ **Cuvée Lynette Pinot Noir** No successor to **04**, last ed still to knit. Complexity incipient; forceful yet restrained palate, & fairly robust tannins receiving support from 14 mths 2nd/3rd fill barrels.

★★★★ **Cuvée Quint Shiraz** Ripe, creamy toffee nose on **04**; big, flavourful & dense (14.5% alc). When last tasted, a little unyielding, but plenty sweet red fruit to match the tannin & oak (14 mths, seasoned).

Cuvée Twister Cabernet Franc ★★★ Predilection for ripeness & sweetness (5.2gl sugar) last yr noted as juxtaposed in **05** with dry, food-inviting tannins. **Shiraz-Cabernet Franc** ★★★ Fynbos & red-fruited **05** (65/35), tamed by cab f & drier dusty tannins. Tight & touch rustic. **Pinot Noir-Shiraz-Cabernet Franc** ★★★ Dark spicy **05** with mocha notes harnessed by drier, dusty cab f notes & firm tannin. Unwooded. **Cuvée Terry Lynn Shiraz Rosé** ★★ Demure, light **06**, vaguely savoury, deep onion-skin colour. **Cuvée Blondie** ★★★ Bottled, **06** shows same cheery flavour profile as sample: zesty white peach tones, sugar-smoothed for easy quaffing. **Chenin Blanc-Viognier** ★★★ **06**, revisited, holding well with succulent fusion-food-friendly flavours, plump & fleshy at 14% alc. — *MW*

Riebeek Cellars

T 022-448-1213 ▪ F 022-448-1281

Swartland ▪ Est/1stB 1941 ▪ Tasting & sales Mon-Fri 8-5 Sat 9-2 Sun 10:30-3 ▪ Closed Easter Fri/Sun, Dec 25 & Jan 1 ▪ Tours strictly by appt ▪ BYO picnic ▪ Farm produce ▪ Owner 60 shareholders ▪ Cellarmaster Zakkie Bester (Dec 1999) ▪ Winemaker Eric Saayman & Alecia Hamman (Jan 1997/Dec 2004) ▪ Viticulturist Hanno van Schalkwyk (Sep 2000) ▪ 1 400 ha (cab, merlot, pinotage, shiraz, chard, chenin, colombard, sauv) ▪ 15 500t/45 000cs own labels + 40 000cs for customers, incl Rocheburg & Broken Rock (both UK) ▪ 40% red 50% white 10% rosé ▪ HACCP certification in progress ▪ PO Box 13 Riebeek Kasteel 7307 ▪ info@ riebeekcellars.co.za ▪ www.riebeekcellars.com

Elegant new labelling, a streamlined range and renewed focus on Riebeek Valley stars shiraz and chenin reflect this friendly winery's new lean, fresh, classic approach. Perfectly suited to burly winemaker Eric Saayman's unexpected skill with sushi (recipes and wine matches on the website). No such surprises from colleague Zakkie Bester, a potjiekos specialist.

Reserve Selection

Pinotage ★★★★ Fine typicity with savoury nuance, **05** last ed full of flavour & enough dry tannins for few yrs ageing. **Shiraz** ★★★★ Smoky, dark fruit, peppery nuances with firm ripe tannins giving (40% new oak) definition, ageability. **Shiraz-Cabernet Sauvignon** Warm, smoky, spicy fruit on 02, quarter cab supplies the stiffening for 4-5 yrs ageing. **Chenin Blanc** ★★★ Step up from pvs. **06** oaking (new small Fr) showcases melon fruit, doesn't overwhelm. Harmonious, tasty, long finish. Discontinued: **Chardonnay**.

Limited Releases

Pinotage ★★★★ **05** big whack wood greets you, then ripe fruit asserts itself attractively for bold but balanced appeal. **Tinta Barocca** ★★★★ Appealing & characterful **02**, touches pepper, game meat & savoury. Neither retasted.

Riebeek Collection

Chenin Blanc ☺ 🍷 ★★★ Bargain-priced dry charmer, **07** abounds with summer fruits.
Chardonnay 🍷 ☺ ★★★ Tropical-fruit toned **07**, partially oaked, harmonious.

Cabernet Sauvignon-Merlot ★★ Fruitier profile than pvs, berry mix, finishing with good friendly dryness. **Pinotage-Shiraz** NEW ★★ Dark fruit & salty liquorice styling, smoothly accessible, earlier drinking. **Shiraz-Cinsaut** ★★★ Unoaked, attractive equal blend, fruity, lively, perfect summertime red. **Pinotage Rosé** 🍷 ★★★ Drier than pvs, same light-textured red currant appeal. **Montino Petillant Light** 🍷 ★★ Grapey, lively white with perky petillance. Friendly 8.5% alc. **Sauvignon Blanc** 🍷 ★★ Leafy, appley freshness, ideal food partner. Following all **NV**: **Stein** 🍷 ★★ Grapey, rounded & sweet. **Kasteelberg MCC** NEW ★★★ Equal pinot blanc/noir touch chard. Appealing toasty & citrus richness. Drink soon. **Pieter Cruythoff Pinot2 Brut** ★★ Sherbet & apples add flavour to a brisk, sprightly sparkler. **Red Jerepiko** ★★★ Stewed fruit & English toffee richness, mouthfilling sweetness. **Cape Ruby** ★★★ Fruit the hero, youthful, harmoniously delicious. Discontinued: **Redneck**.

Cape Table range

Range of lowish-alc 1litre packs; all **NV**, untasted. Distributed by Riebeek Retail Brands, enquiries: Gerrit de Villiers T 083-463-4289, email gerrit@cape.co.za.– *CR*

■ **Riebeek Retail Brands** *see Riebeek Cellars*

Rietrivier Winery   🍷🍵🎋🎿

T 023-614-1705 · F 023-614-1705

Montagu (see Klein Karoo map) ▪ *Est 1965* ▪ *1stB 1990* ▪ *Tasting, sales & light meals Mon-Thu 8.30-4.30 Fri 8.30-3 Sat 9-1; or BYO picnic* ▪ *Closed pub hols* ▪ *Tours by appt* ▪ *Facilities for children* ▪ *Owner 46 members* ▪ *Winemaker Chris-Willem de Bod, with Petrus Bothma (Oct 1999/Jan 1994)* ▪ *Viticulturist Johannes Mellet (Aug 2005, consultant)* ▪ *300ha (merlot, shiraz, chard)* ▪ *5 000t/10 000cs own label + 4m litres bulk 20% red 80% white* ▪ *PO Box 144 Montagu 6720* ▪ *info@rietrivier.co.za* ▪ *www.rietrivier.co.za*

Every year Route 62 - that wonderfully scenic route through the Klein Karoo - sees increased tourism traffic, with spin-offs for this visitor-friendly winery near Montagu. Adding to Chris-Willem De Bod's quiet optimism is a record-breaking 2007 harvest: an additional 1000 tons picked - of remarkable quality, he adds.

Quiriga Reserve range

Merlot ★★★ **04** succulent red berry fruit supportively new-oaked (18 mths Fr), drinks well now, legs for another few yrs. **Shiraz** ★★★ Accessible, not-for-keeping **03**, pepper & mint touches, rich warm fruit. Oak as for Merlot. Neither this, range below, retasted this ed.

Rietrivier range

Merlot ★★ **05** promise of clean berried nose unfulfilled by lean, dry palate. **Pinotage** ★★ **04** cherry fruit, lightish tannins, medium body; 6 mths staves. **Shiraz** ★★★ **04** yard better than pvs; dark cherry, spice & char aromas/flavours, dry finish, integrated 14% alc. **Petite Rouge** ★★ Rustic, light bodied quick-quaff from equal parts pinotage & ruby cab; unwooded. **Route 62 Red** ★★ High-octane unwooded mix pinotage, merlot; over-ripe mulberry fruit on **03**. **Blanc de Noir** ★ Unsubtle **05** from red muscadel; eye-popping orange colour, sweet & soft.

Sauvignon Blanc ★ Semi-dry summer sipper; **06** v light & modestly fruited. **Colombar-Chardonnay** ★★ **04** tropically toned, fruity, smooth & ripe **Petite Blanc** ★★ Crisp, fruity, light bodied off-dry white; **NV**, 500ml screwcap. **Sparkling Vin Doux** ★ Light & sweet fizz in red & white versions, both **NV**. **Late Harvest** ★ Soft, sweet, straightforward chenin; **NV**; also in 500ml. **Rosé** ★ Natural Sweet style **NV** from pinotage; soft, sweet, barely vinous. **Montagu Hanepoot** ★★ **05** plump, distinctly sweet fortified with lemon zest flavours. **Montagu Red Muscadel** ★★★ Montagu-area speciality, here made jerepiko-style. **05** weighty raisined richness which the lovely, well fused spirit can't quite enliven. Also in 250 & 500ml. **Montagu White Muscadel** ★★ Barley sugar flavours, penetrating sweetness on **05**; alc a bit apart, perhaps needs time. **Montagu Ruby Port** ★★ From pinotage, **03** with idiosyncratic mulled wine character. — *IvH*

Rietvallei Estate

T 023-626-3596/4422 • F 023-626-4514

Robertson • Est 1864 • 1stB 1975 • Tasting & sales Mon-Fri 8.30-5 Sat 9.30-1 • Closed Easter Fri-Mon, Sep 24, Dec 25/26 & Jan 1 • Light lunches or BYO picnic • Facilities for children • Tour groups • Owner Johnny Burger • Winemaker Kobus Burger (2002) • Viticulturist Johnny Burger (1973) • 140ha (14 varieties r/w) • 2 000t/±40 000cs own label 40% red 45% white 15% fortified • Export brands: Wild Rush & Rushdale • PO Box 386 Robertson 6705 • info@rietvallei.co.za • www.rietvallei.co.za

'We're big, so we have a lot of wine to sell,' says Kobus Burger. Good news, then, that all the Burgers' markets are expanding, particularly the US, which analysts predict will become the world's biggest wine market this year. Even better tidings: the birth of a daughter last April, at the end of what Kobus B describes as a great harvest.

Single Vineyard Selection

★★★★☆ **Muscadel 1908** From vines planted in 1908. Opulent raisin & tealeaf aromas. Astounding surge of concentrated, complex flavours of morello cherry jam, raisins & spice gently gripped by tea-like tannins. Long, dry, savoury finish.(15% alc & 200g/l RS).
Special Select Cabernet Sauvignon ★★★★ Preview **05** cedar & violets overlay ripe black fruits, with firm spicy tannins from 24 mths Fr oak currently masking compact fruit flavours. Well-measured acidity to balance, finishing with sleek confidence. **Special Select Shiraz** ★★★★ Lush mulberry fruit & vanilla on preview **05**. Full-bodied & extracted with savoury meatiness a popular formula. 2yrs Fr/Am oak. **Juanita Cabernet Sauvignon Rosé** ★★★ Cherry pink **07** dry & seriously styled, with rose petal spiciness, decent palate weight & sweet-sour finish. **Special Select Chardonnay** ★★★★ Sample of very youthful barrel fermented & matured **07** (provisional rating) needing time to settle. Standout richness aided by 8g/l RS, but perfectly balanced by lemony acidity. Lingering finish. **Special Select Sauvignon Blanc** ★★★★ Half **07** (sample) oak fermented & matured 3 mths. Complex, concentrated primary fruit aromas & flavours, with lees contact and oak adding dimension. Taut, balanced acidity throughout contributing to resolutely firm finish. Range previously listed as 'Special Select'.

Classic Estate Range

Chenin Blanc NEW ☺ 🍴 ★★★ Richly tropical **07** flaunts sweet pineapple & citrus flavours, shot through by vibrant acidity to harmonious finish. **Red Muscadel** ☺ ✓ ★★★★ Fortified muscat **06** classic grapey rooibos tea aromas. Sweet entry, mid-palate grip countering 138g/l sugar & 15.6% alc.

Cabernet Sauvignon ★★★★ Sample **06** shows embracing, sweet, pure redcurrant aromas & elegantly styled, supple, ripe fruit with piquant finish. **Shiraz** ★★★ 15% cab f lifts ripe blackberry aromas in sample **06**. Fresh acidity & spicy tannins from yr in Fr/Am oak focuses richness. **Natural Chardonnay** ✓ 🍴 ★★★★ Unoaked sample **07** enchants with leesy complexity, melon & stonefruit aromas, zippy peach flavours & appetising acidity. **Rhine**

Riesling ▨ ★★★ Easy-going **07** with overt pineapple glacé & spicy aromas & flavours. Pleasantly light 11.5% alc. **Sauvignon Blanc** ▨ ★★★ Appealing, harmonious **07** balances fresh, grassy, flavourful apple & fig fruit with crisp acidity.

John B range

> **Cabernet Sauvignon-Tinta Barocca** ☺ ▨ ★★★ Sample **06** characterful 70:30 blend, staves adding smokiness to sweet rasberry, cranberry fruit. Easy, everyday quaffer.
> **Cabernet Sauvignon Rosé** NEW ☺ ▨ ★★★ Salmon pink, dry **07** pleases with delightful fruity, sour cherry flavours; some weight & seriousness, finishing sturdily.

Sauvignon Blanc-Colombar ▨ ★★★ Characterful, dry 60:40 **07** blend with light 12% alc & appetising acidity making perfect lunchtime partner.

Rietvallei range
Discontinued: **Chardonnay**. — IM

■ **Rijckbosch** see Mountain River Wines
■ **Rijckshof** see Kango Winery

Rijk's Private Cellar

T 023-230-1622 • F 023-230-1650

Tulbagh • Est 1996 • 1stB 2000 • Tasting & sales Mon-Fri 10-4 Sat 10-2 • Fee R5/wine • Closed Easter Fri-Mon, Dec 25 & Jan 1 • Tours during tasting hours • Country Hotel T 023-230-1006 • BYO picnic • Tour groups • Conferencing • Walks • Owner Neville Dorrington • Winemaker Pierre Wahl (Jan 2002) • Viticulturist Johan Wiese (Mar 1996, consultant) • 28ha (cab, merlot, pinotage, shiraz, chard, chenin, sauv, semillon) • ±180t/11 000cs own label 65% red 35% white • PO Box 400 Tulbagh 6820 • wine@rijks.co.za • www.rijks.co.za

Continuing refinement and focus on the cellar's strengths have led to 16ha of new southern Rhône vines, the first wines from these made in a new gravity-fed 'estate' cellar last year. These officially certified estate wines - a shiraz and shiraz-based blend - will be released in 2010. Pierre Wahl remains relaxed about continued award success, and bemused by the fact that the cellar team each lost an average of 7kg in the six-week harvest, then regained it within a week!

★★★★ **Cabernet Sauvignon** Cab doesn't come much bigger than these (from area once touted as white-wine country!); **03** with usual tannin fortress, ±15% alc, though ultra-ripe beefy/pruny fruit lacks focused thrill of **02** (★★★★★). Successful show entrant (TWS 2005 gold, Decanter ★★★★; Wine ★★★★, Winemakers Choice for **02**) though no track record to judge longevity. 18 mths Fr oak, 70% new.

★★★★★ **Shiraz** Robust high-toned style **03** opulent and big-boned, with layers of raspberry, nutmeg and vanilla, super-ripe slightly raisiny whiffs, sumptuous tannins, 15.1% alc less concentrated, intense than **02** Wine ★★★★.

★★★★ **Cabernet Sauvignon-Merlot** Seamlessly assembled **03** dark berry fruit notes; almond vanilla, cedary sweet spice; chunky yet savoury. 67% cab, 20 months oak ageing, **02** Swiss gold.

★★★★ **Bravado** Cab, shiraz, merlot blend (45/30/25); **02** improvement on maiden **01** (★★★) & admirable effort in difficult vintage. Elegant aromatic melange, choc/subtle mint highlights. Gd fleshy concentration, savoury minerality, balanced firm frame. Oaking complementary & refined (23 mths, 70% new Fr oak). **01** Winemakers' Choice.

★★★★ **Chenin Blanc** Bold-fruited honeyed style, with Loire-like zesty tang **06** showing oak, pronounced apricot and pear-drop character, fine citrus spice, angular at present, lacking restrained opulence of **05** TWS Trophy, now showing melon compote bottle aged notes.

★★★★ **Semillon** Authoritative and concentrated, with ripe lanolin, beeswax, and honeyed notes balanced by intense grapefruit freshness **05** seamlessly assembled, gooseberry tropical aromas harmoniously interwoven with thatchy herbaceous whiffs, restrained yet persistent. Fermented/11 mths Fr oak, 20% new.

Merlot ★★★ Characteristic minty thumbprint on **02**; sweet, simple fruit struggles against roughish dry tannins, alc. Drink up. 20 mths 60% new Fr oak. **Pinotage** ★★★★ Show circuit favourite. Latest **03** more simple red-wine flavours than overt varietal character, also generous coconut oak. Nicely tamed tannins; fresh, balanced. 16 mths largely new Am/Fr oak. **Iceberg Red** ▤ ★★★ Medley ripe dark fruits, firm tannin brace, hint 14.8% alc glow in tail. **03** shiraz (52%) with cabs s/f, merlot; Fr oak, none new, 14 mths. Winemakers' Choice. **The Crossing** NEW ★★★★ Precocious though still evolving red; **05** amply spiced, with bright floral hints ex-viognier lifting leathery, peppery shiraz/mourvèdre fruit, dry berry notes enhancing texture. **Chardonnay** ★★★ Sturdy, country-style **04**; last ed slight creamy lift alleviated strong oak & alc. Fermented/yr Fr oak, 70% new. **Sauvignon Blanc** ★★★ Herbal cut-grass notes on enticing, easy-drinking **06**, citrus fruit, steely crisp finish. **Iceberg White** ▤ ★★★★ Honeysuckle & peach aromas on **05**, apricot-pear flavours seamlessly intertwined, intriguing floral notes. **Semillon-Sauvignon Blanc** NEW ★★★★ Pungent gooseberry aromas, light thatch notes, funky & savoury, concentrated, mouthfilling, unshowy but food-friendly. — *MF*

■ **Rising River** see Wines of Cape Town
■ **River Grandeur** see Viljoensdrift Wines
■ **River's Edge** see Weltevrede Estate
■ **River's Tale** see Oranjerivier Wine Cellars

Riverstone Vineyards   🍶🍷🏠♿
T 023-349-1144 • **F** 023-349-1953

Breedekloof (see Worcester map) • Est 1963 • 1stB 1975 • Tasting & sales Mon-Fri 8-12.30; 1. 30-5 Sat 9-1 • Fee R10 refunded on purchase • Closed Easter Fri-Mon, Dec 25 & Jan 1 • Merwida Country Lodge T 023-349-1435 • Owner Schalk & Pierre van der Merwe • Cellarmaster/viticulturist Magnus Kriel • Winemaker Magnus Kriel (Dec 2000), with Sarel van Staden (Aug 1982) • 630ha (cab, merlot, shiraz, chard, chenin, sauv, semillon, viognier) • 10 000t/20 000cs own label 40% red 60% white • PO Box 4 Rawsonville 6845 • wines@merwida.com • www.merwida.com

For winemaker Magnus Kriel quality and longevity are the most important goals – he and owners, Schalk and Pierre van der Merwe, are proud that Merwida farm, home to the Riverstone brand, has joined the Biodiversity & Wine Initiative, striving for sustainable wine production.

Family Reserve range
Barbera ★★★ Mulberry nuances thread through crisp, food-friendly **06**; oak tad unknit at this stage, gives bitter hint on finish. 13 mths Fr barrels, 20% new. **Viognier** ★★★★ **06**, sample last yr, satisfying barrel-fermented offering, especially at palatable 14% alc. Generous white peach fruit, wafts oak-vanilla (3 mths Fr wood) & refreshing acidity. More appealing than unwooded **05** (★★★). No **07**.

Riverstone range
★★★★ **Chardonnay** Oak plays major role on unrated pre-bottling sample **07**: limy fruit currently hidden beneath toasty aromas, biscuit flavours. Firm acidity, gd mouthfeel suggest pvs rating within reach. Sensitively barrelled **06** exuded quiet confidence.

Cabernet Sauvignon ☺ ★★ Uncomplicated braai quaffer; **06** (sample) boiled sweets note, deft oak touches. **Sauvignon Blanc** ☺ ★★ Zippy, uncomplicated **07** strewn with khaki bush & hay, for early drinking.

Ruby Cabernet ★★★ Red-berried **05**, last ed lively, with typical thatch notes & steak-friendly tannins. **Shiraz** ★★★ Abundant wild berries & smoke on pvsly tasted **04** (sample), supple, well meshed & mouthfilling. 18 mths seasoned Fr oak. **Cuvée Brut** ★★★ Carbonated dry bubbly from sauvignon; plenty of varietal character, happy, frothy mouthfeel. **NV. Muscadel** ✓ ★★★★ Fortified white dessert, **07** bright & cheerful with juicy melon flavours, unusual white choc/apricot nuances. **Port** Not tasted. Discontinued: **Chardonnay-Viognier**. *— CvZ*

■ **Robert Alexander** *see Nico van der Merwe Wines*

Robertson Wide River Export Company

Joint venture between Robertson Winery and Vinimark, handling all Robertson Winery exports under brand names such as Kaapdal, Kleindal (mainly for Germany & UK), Silver Sands (chiefly UK), Sinnya (mainly Germany & Canada), The Veldt (primarily Scotland) and Vruchtbaar (The Netherlands). See Vinimark for contact details.

Robertson Winery   🍴🍷🎋📷
T 023-626-3059 • F 023-626-2926

Robertson • Est 1941 • 1stB 1987 • Tasting & sales Mon-Thu 8-5 Fri 8-5.30 Sat/Sun 9-3 • Closed Easter Fri, Dec 25 & Jan 1 • Tours by appt • BYO picnic • Gifts • Tour groups by appt • Small wine museum • Owner 43 members • Winemaker Bowen Botha, Lolly Louwrens, Francois Weich, Jacques Roux (Jan 1982/May 1995/Sep 1997/Jan 2000/Nov 2001) • Viticulturist Briaan Stipp (Jan 2005) • 1 900ha (cab, merlot, pinot, pinotage, ruby cab, shiraz, chard, chenin, sauv, viognier) • 29 000t 40% red 60% white • No 1 Constitution Rd Robertson 6705 • lolly@robertsonwinery.co.za • www.robertsonwinery.co.za

Barry Kok has recently joined Robertson Winery as the marketing manager, taking over the reins from Johann Meissenheimer who is now holding the fort in the US. Quality manager Johan Moolman is managing the Colour Project with Stellenbosch University, which aims to find a scientific manner of categorising vineyard quality. Viticulturist Briaan Stipp described the 2007 harvest as 'a dream'. The June 2006 Wacky Wine Weekend, a Robertson Valley initiative, was a runaway success and included the Robertson Winery's Miles of Smiles Half Marathon, a mountain biking event and the National Strong Man Competition. And the winery has laid claim to being the first in the southern hemisphere to achieve the highly sought after ISO 22000 stamp of approval.

Constitution Road range
★★★★☆ **No. 1 Constitution Road Shiraz** Concentrated red fruit & Karoo scrub in complex layers, interleaved with spicy, elegant & cedary fine-grained tannins on pvsly tasted **04**. Succulent, medium bodied, sweet spice & savoury nuances continuing on sustained finish. Gd potential.

Vineyard Selection
★★★★ **Prospect Hill Cabernet Sauvignon** Warm vintage shows with abundant ripe cassis on **05** (★★★★). Smooth, creamy mouthfeel & tannins. Long, spicy, sweet liqourice farewell. Accessible now & will hold 2-3yrs, but peak earlier due to warm vintage. **04** cemented higher general rating mooted by notch-up **03**.

★★★★ **Phanto Ridge Pinotage** ✓ Bold, confident **06** with plummy, mulberry & sweet tobacco spice. Sappy, juicy red fruit & savoury notes. Tight cedary tannins check pinotage's exuberant fruit for a sleek, well-muscled style.

★★★★ **Wolfkloof Shiraz** ✓ Seriously styled **05**, currently brooding with powerful case of dark ripe fruit & white pepper spice, restrained by tight tannins. Glimpses latent fruit augur well for development. Bold 14.8% alc.

★★★★ **Kings River Chardonnay** 🗐 Rich, spicy vanilla & toastiness on **06** (★★★★), dominated by oak mid-2007; some creamy breadth finishing with lovely limy twist. Needs time for fruit to shine through. **05** simialar vigorous new-barrel-fermented styling, but better balanced in youth.

★★★★☆ **Retreat Sauvignon Blanc** Clean-cut elegance on **07** (★★★★), abundant grassy nettles & fig leaf, refreshing racy acidity; long herbaceous finish. Understated but serious styling invites 2nd glass/bottle yet not in same class as vintage-boosted **06**, a real head-turner.

★★★★ **Almond Grove Weisser Riesling Noble Late Harvest** The original NLH in this line-up, from the eponymous farm, **06** pvsly tasted newly bottled & only hinting at future form; genteel, understated as pvs; again beautiful sugar/acid balance underpinning the tangy apricot fruit; ±10.5% alc as before. Unwooded.

Discontinued: **Wide River Reserve Noble Late Harvest**.

Robertson range

Cabernet Sauvignon ☺ ★★★ Mouthfilling berried fruit with sappy, firm tannin & bright acidity. **06** touch restrained with clean farewell. Very drinkable at 13.4% alc. **Pinot Noir** [NEW] ☺ 🖩 ★★★ Soft, earthy tones on **06** with smoky red fruits. Lively, bright acidity, medium bodied in a fresh & approachable yet food-friendly style. **Pinotage** ☺ ★★★ Jovial mulberries & spice balanced by firm, ripe tannins with a sappy, cinnamon-dusted farewell. **07** gutsy but approachable. Gd with robust food. **Ruby Cabernet** ☺ ★★★ Ripe-berried friendliness, soft tannins & refreshing tart finish. **06** juicy, medium-bodied everyday red. **Shiraz** ☺ ★★★ Soft & integrated with appealing balance of red fruit. Quaffable & friendly (13.4% alc). **06** for consumption in youth. **Chardonnay** ☺ ★★★ Soft ripe pear threaded with a hint of pithy, limy acidity. **07** shade less focus & fruit than pvs. For early consumption. **Chenin Blanc** ☺ ★★★ **07** crunchy Golden Delicious apple in refreshing & friendly, everyday quaffer style. **Viognier** ☺ 🖩 ★★★ **07** dusty dried yellow peach with almond nuance. Crisp & grippy, with tangy sweet/sour farewell. Gd fusion food match. **Beaukett** ☺ ★★★ Pretty & perfumed **07**, almost dances with bright balancing acidity. Chilled summer aperitif. 11.5% alc.

Merlot ★★★ Friendly blue-berried greeting cut short by spiky acidity & taut tannins. **06** needs food to coax into more amiable balance. **Cabernet Sauvignon-Shiraz** ✓ ★★★★ Rich & satisfying **06**, spicy dark fruit & savoury nuances throughout. Integrated, balanced & juicy. Trim but dapper. **Colombard** ★★ Shy floral notes on **07**, placid dry white with crisp farewell. **Gewürztraminer Special Late Harvest** ✓ ★★★★ Vivacious litchi & rose petal notes on **07**, lithe & light, with clean, crisp acidity. Delicious summer aperitif & fusion food match. Drink young. **Sauvignon Blanc** ★★ Lower alc (11.6%) & more restrained, lighter, than pvs. **07** grassy, herbaceous with zesty acidity & hint of minerality. **Muscadel** [NEW] ★★★ Billowing explosion of sweet honeysuckle & barley sugar, just checked by sherbety lemon-syrup acidity. **07** will delight sweetie fans. Drink in bloom of youth. **Port** ★★★ Rich ruby hues announce **04**, last ed dryish yet-undeveloped plum flavours with low but surprisingly active spirit (15.5%), needed time to settle.

Chapel range

Red ☺ ★★★ Spicy, plummy fruit, more savoury on palate with bright acidity & friendly tannins for easy everyday quaffing. **White** ☺ ★★★ Crisp, fleshy quaffer with hints of tropical & stonefruit, slight grip on finish. Lightish alc (11.9%). **Semi-Sweet White** ☺ ★★★ Passionfruit toned, fresh & uncloying; charming semi-sweet summer tipple. Low alc 10.9%.

Natural Sweet Rosé ★★ Light (7.6% alc) & simple, red-berried appeal with a tart tail. All **NV**, also in 500ml & 1.5litre bottles.

Natural Light range

Rosé ★★ Frivolity of strawberry & candyfloss; sweet & tangy, with low alc (8%). **NV**, as for all. **Dry Light** ★ Tight, light & dry; the dieter's delight (10% alc). **White** ★★ Billowing jasmine, gently sweet, low alc (8.3%), tweaked by tinge of acid on finish. **Red** ★ Muted plum flavours, softly sweet, innocuous & simple - barely vinous!

Two-Litre Certified Cask range

Shiraz ☺ ★★★ Smoky **06**, spiced fruit in rounded, accessible, appealing profile. **Chenin Blanc** ☺ ★★★ **07** fresh ripe apple tone in crisp effortless style.

Cabernet Sauvignon ★★★ Ripe & rounded **06**, dark fruit & smooth tannins. Foursquare, accesible & food-friendly. **Merlot** ★★★ **06** lively & nervy style, some smoky dark berry features. **Ruby Cabernet** ★★ Ruby on a diet! **06** lean fruit, thatchy note & brisk acid. **Chardonnay** ★★★ Ripe stonefruit & lime on **06**, gently rounded with crisp, refreshing finish. **Sauvignon Blanc** ★★ Shy, light, bone-dry & lean **07**, the slimmers friend. 11.7% alc.

Three-Litre Certified Cask range
Discontinued: **Cabernet Sauvignon**, **Shiraz**, **Chardonnay**, **Chenin Blanc**.

Three-Litre Cask range

Crisp Dry White ☺ ★★★ Light, fresh & floral, balanced everyday tipple.

Smooth Dry Red ★★ Shiraz, merlot & ruby cab in soft, red-berried mode; modest 13% alc. **Extra Light** ★ Scented off-dry sipper, with light 10.3% alc. **Johannisberger Semi-Sweet White** ★★ Cheerful tropical flavours for semi-sweet al fresco quaffing. 11% alc. **Natural Sweet Rosé** ★★ Sweet & light (7.8% alc) but lively, with crisp strawberry tones. **Johannisberger Semi-Sweet Red** ★★ Light, gently sweet & spicy red, guaranteed not to offend. **NV** for all.

Vinipak range
Smooth Dry Red ★★ Soft, red berried quaffer from shiraz, merlot & ruby cab, with modest 13% alc. **Dry White** ★★ Soft, tropical & light (12% alc), with upbeat conclusion. Effortless. **Extra Light White** ★ Off dry, light (10.3% alc), aromatic summer sipper. **Stein** ★★ Gently tropical easy-drinker, with zesty semi-sweet flavours. **Late Harvest** ★★ Ripe & jovial semi-sweet, offering dried fruit & tropical flavours. **Natural Sweet Rosé** ★★ Crisp strawberry tones with lively acidity. Sweet & light (7.8% alc). **Natural Sweet White** ★★ Crisp mango-infused semi-sweet, with lunch/picnic light 11% alc. **Smooth Sweet Red** ★★ Smoky ripe berries in gently sweet mode. 11.7% alc. Good-value anytime wines in 500ml & 1litre packs. All **NV**. – *MW*

■ **Robert's Rock** *see* KWV Limited
■ *Robusto* *see* Rudera Wines
■ *Rocco Bay* *see* Bottelary Winery

Roccorocco Wines   [NEW]

Closed to public ▪ *Owner Rocco de Villiers* ▪ *rrm@netactive.co.za*

Pianist Rocco de Villiers' wine range consists solely of one 2002 blend made at Beyerskloof, which turned out so well that winemaker Beyers Truter was actually loath to let it go. De Villiers' most probable encore is a pink bubbly to accompany his sparkling Liberace impressions.

■ **Rocheburg** *see* Arlington Beverage Group
■ *Rockfield* *see* Du Preez Estate
■ *Rocktail Bay* *see* Origin Wine
■ *Rodini* *see* Goudini Wines
■ *Roland's Reserve* *see* Seidelberg Estate
■ *Romansrivier Cellar* *see* Mountain Ridge Wines

Romond Vineyards
T 021-855-4566 ▪ F 021-855-0428

Stellenbosch (see Helderberg map) ▪ *Est 1993* ▪ *1stB 2003* ▪ *Visits by appt* ▪ *Walks* ▪ *Owner André & Rhona Liebenberg* ▪ *Winemaker André Liebenberg, advised by Marais de Villiers & Inus Muller (Jan 2003)* ▪ *Viticulturist De Wet Theron (Oct 2002)* ▪ *50t/3 000cs* ▪ *100% red* ▪ *PO Box 5634 Helderberg 7135* ▪ *romondwine@iafrica.com*

Filmmaker André Liebenberg is excited about the completion of his innovative cellar ('ideally suited for a 1½-man winemaking team') and the tasting room, with its enormous open fireplace where visitors can linger – perhaps over a glass of his 'really serious Rosé', due for release this year, and eventually the flagship Cab Franc.

Rebus ★★★ Quality grapes show in concentrated flavours on **03**, integrated oak (20 mths staves), though over-fresh finish noted in last review. Cab f (56%) & cab. —*IvH*

▊ **Rondebosch Cellar** *see Alvi's Drift Private Cellar*

▊ **Roodeberg** *see KWV Limited*

Roodezandt Wines & Vineyards
T 023-626-1160 ▪ F 023-626-5074

Robertson ▪ Est 1953 ▪ Tasting & sales Mon-Fri 8-5 Sat 9-12.30 Pub hols 9-5 ▪ Closed Easter Fri, Sun & Mon, May 1, Dec 16, 25 & 26, Jan 1 ▪ Tours by appt ▪ Owner 54 members ▪ Winemaker Christie Steytler & Elmo du Plessis, with Tiaan Blom (May 1980/Oct 1999/Oct 2005) ▪ Viticulturist Jaco Lategan (Dec 2006) ▪ 1 500ha (cab, merlot, pinotage, ruby cab, shiraz, chard, chenin, colombard, sauv) ▪ 23 000t ▪ PO Box 164 Robertson 6705 ▪ roodez@ intekom.co.za ▪ www.roodezandt.co.za

Coolest spot at last year's Wacky Wine Weekend in the Robertson district was Roodezandt's bubbling spa-bath filled with sauvignon; 'not the best, but certified', adds production manager Christie Steytler. He reports that last year's crop was the second biggest (up by 17%) in the winery's 54-year history; also up are sales to the US.

Balthazar range
Classic Cabernet Sauvignon ★★★★ Classy cedarwood & cigarbox scents introduce **02**'s rich, ripe, dark berry & prune flavours. V gd, & more complex, complete, than **01** (★★★★). Well-managed oak (yr new Fr); minimum filtration & no cold stabilization. **Wild Yeast Chardonnay** ★★★★ Occasional label. Last tasted **04** attractive honey & dried peach with savoury notes. Natural yeasts; unfiltered.

Roodezandt Wines & Vineyards range

> **Sauvignon Blanc** ☺ ★★★ **07** minerally, herby & flinty aromas give way to ripe pineapples & clean fresh finish. **Special Late Harvest** ☺ ★★★ Charming **07** evokes clean white linen; rosepetals & sun-warmed honey with crisp lingering finish.

Cabernet Sauvignon ★★★ **03** clean dusty vanilla with wood dominating; touch orange marmalade on finish. Yr 2nd fill Fr oak. **Syrah** ★★★ **05** tasted pvs ed showed textured plum & blackcurrant with sweet spices. Fermented with Am/Fr wood. **Red Muscadel** ✓ ★★★★ Raisins & all the earthy richness of Rbtson's sunshine (180g/l sugar) captured in **05**. Discontinued: **White Muscadel**.

Keizer's Creek range

> **The Rose** ☺ ★★★ Charming, light, dry rosé with loads of strawberry freshness.

The Red ★★ Easy-drinking unwooded red for poolside. Equal blend ruby cab, cab, merlot. **NV**, as are all these. **The White** ★★ Honest, flavourful, lightweight quaffer will please most palates. —*DB*

Rooiberg Winery
T 023-626-1663 ▪ F 023-626-3295

Robertson ▪ Est 1964 ▪ 1stB 1974 ▪ Tasting & sales Mon-Fri 8-5.30 Sat 9-3 ▪ Closed Easter Fri/ Sun, Dec 25 & Jan 1 ▪ Tours by appt ▪ Restaurant (see intro); also BYO picnic ▪ Facilities for children ▪ Tour groups ▪ 4×4 trail ▪ Audio-visual on video/CD ▪ Owner 30 members ▪ Cellarmaster André van Dyk (Oct 2002) ▪ Winemaker Eduard Malherbe (Oct 2002) ▪ Viticulturist

Newald Marais & Willem Botha (2002/2004, consultants) • 600ha (cab, merlot, pinotage, ruby cab, shiraz, chard, chenin, colombard, sauv) • 10 000t/75 000cs own labels 20% red 70% white 10% rosé • Export brands: African Collection, African Dawn, Amandalia, Goeie Tye, Oranje Straat, Signum, Tembana Valley & Zebra Collection • PO Box 358 Robertson 6705 • info@rooiberg.co.za • www.rooiberg.co.za

A bumper (and healthy) harvest had this team working round the clock, fuelled by delicious fresh breads and coffee from their popular bakery-deli, Bodega de Vinho. Also enticing are the roadside installations by landscape artist Strijdom van der Merwe – the most recent involved 50 giant red windsocks planted alongside the R60, where this winery is located.

Reserve range

Cabernet Sauvignon ★★★ **04** last ed was austere, slightly dried out character, very dry, earthy finish. These Rsv reds all 18 mths new Fr oak; alcs 14–14.5%. No **05**, **06** untasted. **Merlot** ★★★ Discreet oaking, classically dry & savoury **07**, cassis & dark choc flavours, good example of oft-maligned variety. **Pinotage** ★★★★ Latest **05** retains charm & appeal, though just misses **04**'s higher rating (★★★★). Warm baked plum, touches mocha, attractive oaking, slight sweetness not unwelcome. **Shiraz** ★★★★ Subtle oaking, understated charm in **05**, dark mulberry ruffled by some youthful tannin, but lots of life & enjoyment ahead. 100% new oak. **Chardonnay** ★★★ Peaches & custard, lots of oak (100% new) & creamy substance in **06**.

Rooiberg range

★★★★ **Red Muscadel** Latest **06** (★★★) still young & edgy, high-toned fruit pastille character, tart acidity, all need to come together. Maintains move to lighter texture. May rate higher after yr in bottle.

Pinotage ☺ ★★★ Attractive baked prune in **06**, warm & friendly, ripe tannins to match, just the thing for sipping around the braai or fire midwinter. **Shiraz** ☺ ★★★ Pleasing unoaked version; **06** welcoming, friendly. Roast beef, meaty charms, ripe tannins, slight sweetness. **Pinotage Rosé** ☺ ★★ Delicately fruity & dry **07**, nice tang of freshest raspberry. **Chardonnay** ☺ ★★★ Attractive peach invite on nose, creamy & dry **07**.

Cabernet Sauvignon ✓ ★★★ Attractive ripeness in **06**, extends to warm baked plum fruit & tannins, soft & approachable, raises the bar. This & all reds here ±50% yr barrel matured, used oak. **Merlot** ★★ Meaty, with dark choc heart, **07** (now bottled) pleasantly dry. **Cabernet Sauvignon-Merlot (Roodewyn)** ★★ **06** amiable everyday style, soft tannins, makes no demands, quick finish. **Selected Red** ★★ Soft, easy quick-quaff, trace of telltale pinotage bitterness on finish in **06**. **Chenin Blanc** ★★ Delicate melon & peach on **07**, dry & light textured. **Sauvignon Blanc** ★★ Less varietal punch in **07**, more of a quaffer; bone-dry. **Classic White** ★★ Lightly fruity, soft landing from 6 g/l sugar in **07**. **Cape White** ★★ Modest everyday quick quaff, off-dry **07** maintains style. **Brut Sparkling** ★★ Technically a brut, but tastes quite sweet thanks to ultra-soft acidity. All three bubblies **NV**. **Vin Doux Sparkling** ★★ Wafting muscat in this attractive version, nice interpretation of style. Balanced, with busy bubbles. **Flamingo Sparkling** ★★ Back with a flourish, subtle muscat, not oversweet at 44 g/l, attractive version. **Natural Sweet Red** ★ **05** last ed was thin, with ultra-soft acidity making for sweet flabbiness. **Natural Sweet Rosé** ★ Latest **06** less flavour, less of everything. **Natural Sweet Blanc** ★★ Delicate muscat invitation, better acidity & balace in **06**. **Vintage Port** ✓ ★★★★ Higher rating for **04**, getting closer to the Real Thing. Gd deep flavours, higher alc (18%) & dry meaty finish. Substantial wine, and best of all, a treat! Discontinued: **Rhine Riesling, Hanepoot, Red Jerepiko**. — *IvH*

Rose Garden Vineyards

🍾 🍷 ☕ 🎋

T 021-869-8211 • F 021-869-8211

Paarl • Est 1976 • 1stB 2003 • Visits by appt • Cheese platters by appt; or BYO picnic • Winemaker/viticulturist Nicolette Keyser ((2007) • 15ha (pinotage, merlot, ruby cab, shiraz, chenin) • 100t/8 000cs own label 80% red 15% white 5% rosé • PO Box 151 Wellington 7654 • epstein@polka.co.za • www.rosegardenvineyards.com

Good things come in threes, and at Rose Garden it's the appointment of Nicolette Keyser (ex-Durbanville Hills) as winemaker/viticulturist, the production of a maiden port, and an expansion of the farm's export market to the Czech Republic and Germany. Keyser and owner Shalom Epstein will also be doing personally supervised tastings by appointment.

Premium range
Cabernet Sauvignon Reserve 05 unready. **Merlot 05** available in 2008. **Pinotage** No new vintage. **Shiraz Reserve** Await new release. **Shiraz Limited Release** ★★ Ultra-ripe-styled **04**, last tasted, was intended as 'Italian coffee shop in liquid form'.

Rose Garden range
Merlot ★★★ **03** last ed was friendly braai sipper with ripe plummy fruit. **Pinot Noir** ★★ Fruity red cherry aromas on **05**, contrasting prominent tannins; edgier than perfumed **04**. **Pinotage** ★★ New blend of **03**; ripe plummy intro, savoury & stalky follow-through, needs food. **Shiraz** ★★★★ **05** definite notch up; fresh pepper, redcurrant & tangy red berry fruit. Elegant, balanced structure & refreshing acidity. **Chenin Blanc** ★★ Last reviewed **06** was light bodied, with combo bottle-age & apricot notes. **Shiraz Rosé Natural Sweet** Sold out. **Sweet Liaty Cape Ruby** NEW ★★★ Fruity & dense berry fruit, quite rich, with balanced sweetness though alc prominent (21%). **NV**. Discontinued: **Maya's Red, Chardonnay Reserve.** — *JP*

Rosendal Private Cellar
T 023-626-1570 • F 023-626-1571

Robertson • Est/1stB 2004 • Tasting Mon-Sat 8-5 • Restaurant (see Eat-out section) • Luxury guest house (see Stay-over section) • Conference facilities • Tour groups • Game drives • Owner Geir Tellefsen & Sissel Anderssen • Winemaker Alkie van der Merwe (consultant) • 60% red 30% white 10% rosé • PO Box Suite 128, Private Bag X3, Roggebaai 8012 • info@rosendalwinery.co.za • www.rosendalwinery.co.za

Wine has always been a hobby for IT entrepreneur Geir Tellefsen and spa expert Sissel Anderssen. 'Who would not want to make wine?' ask these Norwegian ex pats, doing precisely that on their 'little piece of Africa' with its well-established luxury wellness retreat. 'Our guests can now reminisce about their stay with a glass of Rosendal in hand.'

Cabernet Sauvignon ★★ Full-bore **05**, ripe, chewy & full-bodied (15%) with porty farewell. **Shiraz** ★★ Robust **06** over-ripe (noticeable VA), porty, with charry farewell. 15% alc. **Special Cuvée** ★★ **06** cab, merlot, shiraz blend, similar bold style to other reds, but less chunky. **Chardonnay** ★★★ Juicy, fresh & mouthfilling **06**, alive with ripe pear & citrus zest. Medium bodied & balanced despite 14.5 % alc. **Sauvignon Blanc** ★★ Tropical-fruited **06**, ripe, rounded easy-drinker with pithy acidity freshening finish. — *MW*

Ross Gower Wines
T 021-844-0197 • F 086-611-2179

Elgin (see Elgin/Walker Bay map) • Est 2003 • 1stB 2004 • Tasting & sales Mon-Fri 9-5 • Weekends & pub hols by appt • Tours by appt • Meals & picnic baskets by arrangement • Glen Stuart upmarket self-catering cottages (see Stay-over section) • Nature conservancy • Owner Gower family • Winemaker Ross Gower, with James Gower • Vineyard Manager Ross Gower • ±7ha (shiraz, sauv) • 3 000cs 40% red 45% white 15% MCC • PO Box 161 Elgin 7180 • rossgowerwines@worldonline.co.za

Ross Gower's decision to work only with varietal wines and only from Elgin vineyards has paid off, he believes, and he's thrilled with the quality of the fruit - mostly bought-in grapes. 'We hope to start developing our own vineyards with a honed sensitivity of our property's strengths, as well as a better developed awareness of which wine styles we want to achieve,' he says.

★★★★ **Sauvignon Blanc** Fabulous **07** cements quality rating after **06** consolidated trio of bottlings in earlier eds. Arresting pyrazines veritably gallop out of the glass, utterly delicious, highly reductive racy mouthful ends with super length.

★★★★ **Pinot Noir Brut** MCC sparkling deliberately 'slightly pink' as opposed to 'rosé', **06** offers zesty cherries in hugely refreshing, bracingly bone-dry send-off. Eminently drinkable, with a glance of tannin for table.

Rosé NEW ☺ ★★★ A vibrant treat for al fresco dining. **07** onion-skin hues herald flinty, sour-cherry tang in nice dry tail. More seriously styled than many of the burgeoning genre. 100% cab.

Merlot ★★★★ **05** dense colour/extract (but low alc) leavened by fragrant violets, red berry fruits tucked into fine tannins, promising when reviewed pvs ed. Yr 70% new Fr oak. **Shiraz** ★★★★ Chunkier red sibling, barrel sample **06** tightly wound mid-2007, less immediately open & approachable than **05**; yr seasoned Fr barrels. **Rhine Riesling** NEW ★★★★ Petal delicacy in youth, maiden **07** has sweet stonefruit ring to dry finish in enduring tail. Promises character with 1-3 yrs development in bottle. — *DS*

Rostrevor Farm   NEW
T 083-261-5747

Northern Cape • Est 2007 • Visits & amenities: phone ahead • Owner Herman Galama • Winemaker Ian Sieg (2007, consultant) • Viticulturist Vinpro consultants • ±45ha (cab, merlot, pinotage, chard, chenin, colombard, gewürz) • ±400t total 30% red 70% white • isieg@vodamail.co.za

Veteran upcountry winemaker Ian Sieg lauds Dutch engineer Herman Galama (married to local lass Louwdia) for his 'creativity, innovation, hard work and forward planning' in converting late mining magnate Sir Harry Oppenheimer's Rostrevor horse stud into a prize-winning grape supplier to Landzicht Winery. Vintage 2008 sees Rostrevor run its own race.

■ **Rotsvast** *see* Baarsma Wine Group
■ *Route 101* *see* Du Preez Estate
■ *Route 303* *see* Ultra Liquors
■ *Rowans Ridge* *see* Klein Constantia Estate
■ *Royle Family Vineyards* *see* Arra Vineyards

Rozendal
T 021-809-2621 • F 021-809-2640

Stellenbosch • 1stB 1983 • Tasting, sales & tours by appt • Luxury auberge with restaurant & amenities • Conference facilities • Walks • Owner Kurt & Lyne Ammann • Winemaker Kurt Ammann • 6ha (cabs s/f, merlot) • 2-3 000cs 100% red • PO Box 160 Stellenbosch 7599 • rozendal@mweb.co.za

The current release of the Ammann family's elegant Rozendal red is 02, but fans who appreciate more mature wines can also purchase vintages **99** to **01** from the Stellenbosch luxury auberge and wine farm, where biodynamic cultivation has been in place since 2001.

■ **Rozier Bay/Reef** *see* Mount Rozier Estate

Rudera Wines
T 021-852-1380 • F 021-852-1380

Stellenbosch • Est 1999 • 1stB 2001 • Closed to public • Owner Teddy & Riana Hall • Winemaker/viticulturist Teddy Hall • 18ha (cab, shiraz, chenin) • 3 400cs 45% red 50% white 5% NLH • PO Box 2868 Somerset West 7129 • info@rudera.co.za • www.rudera.co.za

Teddy Hall, owner of this boutique operation, continues to attract attention from competition judges and wine writers: Rudera was voted one of SA's top 20 wineries, the Robusto Chenin named among the top five local whites, and good reviews from US Wine Spectator, The International Wine Cellar and the New York Times. Planning yet another wine working holiday with the family abroad, Teddy H is delighted, at time of going to print, to be dashing off to Israel to make chenin there. Two years ago the family went to Spain, where he worked with albariño.

Samantha, Teddy and Riana's 11-year-old daughter, has completed her third successful vintage this year, making the Aubergine Chenin for restaurateur Harald Bresselschmidt under the close watch of her father. A true family affair!

★★★★☆ **Cabernet Sauvignon** Hard act to follow, but **04** manages well; a beefy, dark-fruited, pepper-spiced individual, requiring time to fully appreciate its many attributes. Elegant, with integrated tannins but structured for the longer haul.

★★★★☆ **CWG Auction Reserve Cabernet Sauvignon** Big, impressive wine, lots of depth, prospects, in last tasted **02**. Unfiltered; oak as for std Cab. Only ±60 cs. **04**, for 2006 Auction, not tasted.

★★★★ **Syrah** Carefully made, always elegant. In warm vintage, avoiding excess, **05** is impressively streamlined: berry coulis, whiffs smoke, roasted spice; harmonious & already delicious. As all these, good ageing potential.

★★★★ **Chenin Blanc** This & next from low-yielding old bushvines. Wonderful tropical richness in **06**, despite being dry; a savoury oak influence & usual invigorating acidity, both guarantees of food compatibility.

★★★★☆ **Robusto Chenin Blanc** Robust' but controlled, multiply gilded. Masterful **06** in same class as predecessors; dried peaches, citrus peel & nuts, a rich tangy mouthful that vibrates with intensity, flavours that won't let go.

★★★★☆ **Chenin Blanc Noble Late Harvest** Hand-selected botrytised berries; native yeast ferment in new Fr small oak. Each one a gem, **06** no different: mouthcoating molten peach & preserved quince, lifted by racy acidity, giving impressive length.

★★★★☆ **CWG Auction Reserve Chenin Blanc Noble Late Harvest** Same vinification as above for maiden **03**; pvd ed sumptuous aromas assailed the nose, mouthfilling honeyed sweetness was tempered by bracing acidity. Gd 5+ yr cellaring potential. 132g/l sugar. — *CR*

Rudi Schultz Wines
T 082-928-1841

Stellenbosch ▪ Est/1stB 2002 ▪ Closed to public ▪ Owner/winemaker Rudi Schultz ▪ Viticulturist Dirkie Morkel ▪ 800cs 100% red ▪ rudi@thelema.co.za

The tiny 800-case production of Rudi Schultz Syrah must now meet orders from Canada and the UK as well as the US and several Continental markets, testimony to Schultz's skills (honed through his day job as Thelema winemaker). The Syrah is now joined by a Viognier – in even more limited quantities.

★★★★☆ **Syrah** Hand crafted, in rich but classical style. Now bottled **05** in line with upgrade begun with sumptuous **04**. Thrilling white pepper nuance to fragrant, beautifully spiced mouthful; built for a decade. 20 mths Fr oak, 50% new.

★★★★☆ **Reserve Syrah** NEW The 'even better Syrah' promised last ed now in bottle: **05** deeply coloured, closed & brooding but all the promise of electric pepper & allspice; more detailed, finer wefts & warps in texture than sibling - terrific. 20 mths all new Fr oak, 15% alc well weighted. Only 110 cs.

Viognier NEW ★★★★ Barrel (3rd fill Fr) sample **07** billowing unambiguous flouncy peach-pip seduction at first review: can the opulence of this vinous catwalk translate into off-the-peg in-the-glass enjoyment? Time will tell… — *DS*

Ruitersvlei Wines
T 021-863-1517 ▪ F 021-863-1443

Paarl ▪ Est 1692 ▪ 1stB 1995 ▪ Tasting & sales Mon-Fri 9-5 Sat 9-3 Sun 11-3 ▪ Fee R10 (incl glass) ▪ Closed Easter Fri, Dec 25 & Jan 1 ▪ Tours by appt ▪ Farm produce ▪ Facilities for children ▪ Tour groups ▪ Gifts ▪ Reception/conference venue ▪ Conservation area ▪ Owner John Faure ▪ Winemaker Jurgen Siebritz (June 2007) ▪ Viticulturist Kobus Mostert (Nov 2001) ▪ 289ha (cab, merlot, pinotage, shiraz, chard, chenin, sauv) ▪ 1 400t/50 000cs own labels 70% red 29% white 1% rosé ▪ PO Box 532 Suider-Paarl 7624 ▪ sales@ruitersvlei.co.za ▪ www.ruitersvlei.co.za

New winemaker Jurgen Siebritz (ex-Boland) brings with him insights gained during two harvests in the US. 'Simplicity is paramount,' he says. 'You can make great wine by sticking to the basics and doing them well.' He aims to concentrate on the farm's shiraz, pinotage and cab.

Reserve range

Shiraz ★★★ When last tasted, **04** showed maturity, firmness & a sappy dry finish. Our advice was to enjoy soon. **Cabernet Sauvignon-Merlot ★★★ 04** showed forceful tannin/fruit structure when last tasted, & potential for few yrs ageing. Discontinued: **Cabernet Sauvignon, Merlot, Chardonnay, Four Sisters MCC, John Faure Port**.
Cabernet Sauvignon ★★★ 05 last ed succulent ripe blackberry flavours, inviting cedarwood nose & long, clean finish. **Merlot ★★** Robust, unwooded **05** campfire-compatible, though with modest 13% alc. Not retasted. **Pinotage ★★★** Fruit-driven, early drinking **05** generous bramble/banana, subtle oak (Am/Fr staves), youthful vibrancy noted last ed. **Shiraz ★★★ 05** everyday red with full, juicy red-fruit flavours. Tasted last ed. **Cinsaut-Cabernet Sauvignon ★★ 06** new to the guide, pvsly exported. Relaxed, juicy & uncomplicated wine. **Chardonnay** [NEW] **★★★** Maiden **05** has vanilla biscuit with lime & honey; well-managed oaking supports fruit. **Chenin Blanc ★★★** Sun-warmed hay on **07**, pleasant ripe pears & easy fruit/acid balance. **Sauvignon Blanc ★★** Fashionably green **07**: greenpepper nose, green apples, green grass & green figs. Discontinued: **Cabernet Sauvignon-Merlot**.

Mountainside range

Red ★★ Melange of red-fruit flavours from half-dozen red varieties in **05**, not retasted. Unwooded, spicy-dry & easily quaffable. **White ★★** Colombard/sauv pairing for pvs **06**, just-dry, light & delicately fruity. **Gold** No new vintage tasted. Discontinued: **Pink**. — *DB*

Rupert & Rothschild Vignerons
T 021-874-1648 • F 021-874-1802

Paarl • Est 1997 • 1stB 1998 • Visits only by appt Mon-Fri 9-4.30 • Fee R5/wine • Closed Easter Fri-Sun, Dec 25 • Owner Rupert family & Baron Benjamin de Rothschild • Cellarmaster Schalk-Willem Joubert (Jun 1997) • Winemaker Yvonne Lester, with Clive Radloff (Sep 2001/Jun 1997) • Viticulturist Renier Theron (Oct 2003) • 90ha (cab, merlot, chard) • 500t/35 000cs 95% red 5% white • ISO 14001 certified; HACCP accreditation in progress • PO Box 412 Franschhoek Valley 7690 • info@rupert-rothschildvignerons.com • www.rupert-rothschildvignerons.com

'I don't have anything exciting to report, it's all very basic here,' says cellarmaster Schalk-Willem Joubert. Then again, the wines emanating from this collaboration between two families of international standing – the Ruperts and the Rothschilds – can speak for themselves, having built an enviable reputation and serious following in the decade since their launch. Based at the historic French Huguenot farm, Fredericksburg, and advised by eminent French oenologist Michel Rolland, S-WJ and his team (winemakers Yvonne Lester and Clive Radloff, and viticulturist Renier Theron) work with 14 growers, separately vinifying fruit from 52 vineyards spread across the winelands, from Cape Point and Durbanville to the Langkloof.

★★★★☆ Baron Edmond After lesser 02 (★★★★), **03** impressive 76:24 cab-merlot blend, from Stbosch, Darling grapes. Last yr showed very ripe, bright fruit, extracted for power, richness, intensity; big, luscious tannins, showy oak (20 mths new Fr). 15.3% alc not graceful, but not unbalanced.

★★★★ Baroness Nadine Modern, elegant chard from Elgin, Cape Pt fruit. Usual lime notes on **05**'s fresh, well-textured & lightly forceful palate, not overpowered by toasty oak (30% new, yr). Should develop over a few yrs.

Classique ★★★★ After big, tannic 04 (★★★), **05** merlot-cab blend from widely-sourced grapes has more harmonious restraint: dark, ripe & serious, well structured & fresh; gd oaking (30% new). No hurry to drink. — *TJ*

■ **Rushdale** *see* Rietvallei Estate

Rustenberg Wines
T 021-809-1200 • **F** 021-809-1219

Stellenbosch • Est 1682 • 1stB 1892 • Tasting & sales Mon-Fri 9-4.30 Sat 10-1.30 Pub hols 9-4.30 • Closed Easter Fri, Dec 25 & Jan 1 • Owner Simon Barlow • Winemaker Adi Badenhorst, with Randolph Christians & Gareth le Grange (Dec 1999/Oct 1995/Jan 2003) • Viticulturist Nico Walters (Nov 1999) • 150ha (cabs s/f, grenache, merlot, mourvèdre, petit v, shiraz, chard, roussanne, sauv, semillon, viognier) • 1 800t/130 000cs 70% red 30% white • PO Box 33 Stellenbosch 7599 • wine@rustenberg.co.za • www.rustenberg.co.za

There is a strong commitment by the dynamic Rustenberg team to honouring the natural and historical heritage status (granted 2004) of this beautifully restored Stellenbosch farm in the Simonsberg foothills, with half of its 1200 hectares registered with the BWI. Successful with all their wines, they are proudest of their status as a producer of fine reds, with the 05 John X Merriman repeating the triumph of the **03** in winning the Calyon Trophy for best SA bordeaux blend. Their achievement with this and other critically lauded wines is to produce in significant quantities (14 500 cases for the **05** JXM) - something they're not credited for often enough. With stylish and sophisticated visitor facilities and a warm welcome, this 'first growth' is a compulsory stop on any winelands tour.

Single Vineyard range

★★★★☆ **Peter Barlow** Original, widely admired 'Rustenberg Cab', from nearly 20 yr old Smnsberg vyd. **04**, now bottled, still youthful. Protective tannin, fresh acid should allow full evolution of ultra ripe fruit given lengthy maturation. 15% alc. Native yeast, unfiltered. 20 mths Fr oak, 70% new. **05** not ready.

★★★★ **Five Soldiers** Indubitably New World chard: limy ripeness & spice/toast ex-new Fr oak (70%) are giveaways; difference/distinction achieved via subtle mineral/savoury nuances, esp notable in confident **05**. Powerful yet poised; usual maturation possibilities assured. Natural ferment, malo in barrel, 15 mths.

Stellenbosch Regional range

★★★★☆ **Syrah** NEW Delicious newcomer. **04** reveals Adi B's informed classic approach; aromatic breadth presented with great delicacy; lightness of touch evident in supple mouthfeel threaded with savoury freshening acid; very fine grip. All older Fr oak a subtle enrichment.

★★★★★ **John X Merriman** 'Modern classic' bdx-style blend; **03, 05** honoured as such, taking trophy on Calyon competition. Latter vintage a real charmer. Entices with fresh, ripe fruit perfume, silky sleekness, restraining ripe tannins. Merlot-led (54%), with cab s/f, petit v, malbec (33/4/6/3). Fr oaked, 50% new, 20 mths.

★★★★ **Chardonnay** 🍾 Usual decadent features - earthy overtones from native ferment, chewy texture - provide style consistency in **06**; lime/citrus purity, lighter, fresher feel introduce vintage difference. Complex but unintimidating. Oaked, yr Fr.

★★★★★ **The Last Straw 03**, from straw-dried chenin, last tasted. Next **07** from chenin, sauv, semillon, viognier, harvested ultra ripe, still fermenting at press time.

Roussanne 🍾 ★★★★ Silky **06** displays heady scents redolent of warm south (Cape rather than Rhône!); viscous texture enlivened by savoury acid & clean dry finish. Older oak ferment adds further dimension. **05** (★★★★) was slightly dumbed by oak.

Schoongezicht

★★★★ **Schoongezicht White 06** grenache bl, viognier, roussanne blend remains work in progress, not re-tasted.

Brampton range

★★★★ **QF** Weighty NLH; last **00** from sauvignon; next when botrytis obliges.

Cabernet Sauvignon 🍾 ★★★★ **05** another little giant among leviathans, one of only two cab golds at 2007 TWS. Over past yr has settled, highlighting bright fruit, easily handling 80% new oak; creamy mouthfeel, balanced freshness add to approachability with class. Step up on youthfully unsettled **04** (★★★☆). **Shiraz** ✓ 🍾 ★★★★ **05** realises last yr's sample's promise. Inviting, multi-faceted shiraz-led mix; mourvèdre, grenache, viognier important contributors to generous lifted spice. For current enjoyment, further few yrs. Fr/Am oak, 40% new. **04**

★★★★ (but IWC gold). **OVR** ✓ 🍷 ★★★★ (Old Vines Red pvs ed.) **05**, sampled last ed, offers tasty basket red fruits in friendly but firm wrapping. Fr oak rounded, 15% new. Cab-based. WO W Cape. **Rosé** ✓ 🍷 ★★★★ The Rhône meets Bordeaux in **07**'s most attractive varietal septet. Pretty cherry hue/flavours; light-toned, dry & lingering. For picnics but won't disappoint dinner table. Coastal vyds. **Unoaked Chardonnay** 🍷 ★★★★ Characterful example of genre. **06** fresh, steely & dry, broadened by leesy richness. Matured on/fined with pvs yr's Sbosch Chard lees. Not re-tasted. **Sauvignon Blanc** 🍷 ★★★★ **06** now quieter, more developed nuances; retains bounce, mouthwatering dryness noted in last yr's sample. W Cape WO. **Viognier** 🍷 ★★★★ Quiet though characterful **06** tasted last ed, starts & ends with dried apricot/honeysuckle notes. Oak (used Fr, fermented/matured 4 mths) well fused with full, rich body. Coastal WO. **Natural Sweet** ★★★★ Occasional label; none since **01**. **Port** ★★★ **NV** from Portuguese varieties; drier style still available. — AL

Rust en Vrede Estate

T 021-881-3881 · F 021-881-3000

Stellenbosch · Est 1694 · 1stB 1979 · Tasting & sales Mon-Fri 9-5 Sat: 9-4 Oct-Apr; 9-3 May-Sep; pub hols 9-4 · Closed Easter Fri, Dec 25 & Jan 1 · Restaurant (see Eat-out section) · Gifts · Walks · Owner Jean Engelbrecht · Winemaker Coenie Snyman (Dec 2006) · Vineyard Manager Wessel Combrink (Jun 1998) · 50ha (cab, merlot, shiraz) · ±300t/20 000cs 100% red · PO Box 473 Stellenbosch 7599 · info@rustenvrede.com · www.rustenvrede.com

Jean Engelbrecht (Ernie Els' partner-in-wine) has taken over the reins of this historic estate from his father Jannie, rationalised marketing and logistics, revamped the tasting area, added a fine-dining locale (where David Higgs, ex-Meerendal, will hold court), and brought in Coenie Snyman from the Els-Engelbrecht/Guardian Peak team to rejuvenate the cellar. Familiar with the area, known as Stellenbosch's 'Golden Triangle', Snyman says: 'I think Rust en Vrede is arguably the farm with the most potential in the Cape.' Where to from here? 'Only up, improving quality and making wines true to Rust en Vrede Estate.'

★★★★ **Estate Wine** Regular cab, shiraz, merlot ensemble (60/30/10) well fused in **04** to provide pleasant though lighter-toned vinosity, not overly disturbed by 18 mths all new oak. Few yrs cellaring will soften vintage's robustness, allow for balanced satisfaction if not grandeur of earlier bottlings.

★★★★ **Cabernet Sauvignon 03** excellent red vintage shows in savoury vinosity, creaminess, balanced freshness & grip; but probably not for long-term cellaring. **04** riper, more primary, lighter, will benefit from few more yrs rounding. Appropriately oaked; 60% new, 18 mths.

★★★★ **Merlot** Fresh, sumptuous fruit, anchored by firm, dry base signal compatible modern/traditional fusion in **05**. Needs further yr/2 for usual velvety breadth to fully emerge. Sensitively oaked, 25% new.

★★★★ **Shiraz** Hldrberg stalwart since maiden 79, making comeback with **04** after dip with now very advanced **03**, ready **02** (★★★★). Ripe, generously structured with balanced freshness. Quiet though well-defined red fruit enhanced by well-judged oak, 60% new, 18 mths. 15% alc. — AL

■ **Rusthof** see Mooiuitsig Wine Cellars

Rusticus Vintage Cellar

T 023-626-2033 · F 023-626-1277

Robertson · Est 2001 · 1stB 2002 · Tasting & sales Tue-Fri 9-4 Sat 10-4 Mon by appt · Closed Easter Fri & Dec 25 · Tours on request · BYO picnic · Pat Busch Private Nature Reserve - self-catering cottages & guest houses (see Stay-over section) · Tour groups · Conferences · Walks/hikes · Game drives & conservation area · 4×4 trail · Owner/winemaker/viticulturist Stephan Busch · 400t total, 3-5t own label, max 1 000cs · PO Box 579 Klaas Voogds West 6705 · info@rusticus.co.za · www.rusticus.co.za

Having tied the knot, Lindi Busch (née Broughton) partners husband Stephan in running this proudly low-tech winery, part of a splendid mountain reserve founded by Stephan's German-born parents, Pat and Karin, in the 1970s. The Busch seniors are thus granted some well-deserved rest from vintning, and are able to bask in the reflected glory of successes like the maiden Viognier, which has been snapped up by eager customers.

★★★★ **Cabernet Sauvignon Limited Release** NEW Only 3 barrels of bold, distinctive **04**. Blackberry leaps from glass, joined by Christmas pudding richness through to extended farewell. An individual, & great with roast venison.

★★★★ **Tilled Earth** Mainly cab (50%), equal merlot, shiraz; **05**, unready last ed, earthy, toasty prelude to palate-expanding layers black cherry & dark berry on well-managed tannin base. Rustic, but charming; satisfying; could gain elegance given time. Surprisingly low (for cellar) 13% alc.

★★★★ **Viognier** NEW Bold, spicy nose & huge, buttery, mouthfilling flavour make **06** a sit-up-and-take-notice wine; lingering textured finish. Wood fermented; only 2 barrels made. Like all these, WO Klaasvoogds.

Cabernet Sauvignon ★★★ Port-like concentration of blackberry & choc flavours on polished **03** last ed masked its vast 16% alc. **Merlot** ★★★ Last-tasted super-ripe **03** still in stock; massively fruited, intense plum character, expansive palate dominated by potent 15.5% alc. **Pinot Noir** Sold out. **Pinotage** ★★★ Cassis aromas noted last yr on atypical **03**; sweet impression (from supercharged 15.8% alc) not quite cushioning big dusty tannins. **Shiraz Limited Release** ★★☆ **04** showed some sophistication & typicity: full-ripe flavours, supple tannins, potential. **Shiraz** ★ Last-tasted **03** was porty, jammy & rustic. Discontinued: **Ruby Cabernet**. — *DB*

Saam Mountain Vineyards NEW
T 021-869-8244 • F 021-869-8245

Paarl • Est 2007 • Tasting at Perdeberg Winery • Owner Bibendum Wine Limited & Perdeberg Winery • Winemaker Pieter Carstens • Viticulturist Callie Coetzee • 37 000cs own label 80% red 20% white • BRC accredited • Ranges for UK customers: Jackleberry (Tesco) & J Sainsbury's • PO Box 214 Paarl 7620 • kirstie@saam-mountain.com • www.saam-mountain.com

The aptly named Saam ('Together') is a collaboration between independent London-based retailer Bibendum Wine Ltd, Perdeberg Winery and its 40 owner-growers tending naturally low-cropping vineyards around Perdeberg and Durbanville. The wines, including some novel blends, are exported to Europe, chiefly the UK. Locally, tastings are at Perdeberg.

Cabernet Sauvignon ★★★ Dried herbs, tobacco aromas lead to palate whose rather cloying sweetness struggles against, not with, dry tannins. All wines **06**, except as noted. All WO Paarl. **Leeuwenkuil Pinotage** ★★★★ Plum, dark berry notes; balanced freshness, succulent texture & juicy fruit, supported by oak, giving firm, savoury, sweet-fruit finish. **Pinotage** ★★☆ Ripe, friendly fruitiness leads to softly sweet flavours perked up by savoury tannins. **Koopmanskraal Shiraz** ★★★★ Spice & leather combine satisfactorily with boiled-sweet element; a firmly friendly grip from ripe tannin & oak supports gd finish. **Shiraz** ★★★ Characterful aromas lead to pleasant, sweet-savoury but fairly fresh flavours integrated with firm, ripe tannins. Sweetness less obvious than on other reds with simply varietal names (all ±5g/l RS). **Heldersig Pinotage-Viognier** ★★★★ Tiny white-grape addition gives perfumed touch to red berries & choc of fruity, fresh, medium-bodied wine. Like other 'named' reds, 12-18 mths oak, 80% new, well integrated. **Heldersig Shiraz-Viognier** ★★★★ Fragrant red/black berry aromas & flavours; easy-drinking charm, with some cooperative gently firm tannins; supportive oaking, some Am. **Chenin Blanc** ★★★★ Charming waxy, pineapple notes on unshowy but satisfying **06**. Lightly, freshly rich (just a little sugar); nice green bite on long dry finish. **Phisantekraal Sauvignon Blanc** ★★★★ Fig, gooseberry aromas presage unaggressive, well balanced mouthful; moderate 12.8% alc part of easy-going but characterful nature. **Sauvignon Blanc** ★★★ **07** light-feeling, restrained in blend of grass, tropicality. Softly bone-dry & easy, with crisp green edges. — *TJ*

Sadie Family
T 021-869-8349 • F 021-869-8101

Swartland • Est 1999 • 1stB 2000 • Tasting & sales by appt • Owner The Sadie Family (Pty) Ltd • Winemaker/viticulturist Eben & Niko Sadie • 10ha (grenache, mourvèdre, shiraz) • 900cs 70% red 30% white • PO Box 1019 Malmesbury 7299 • sadiefamily@mail.com

Eben Sadie left Spice Route in 2000 inspired by the Swartland, and travelled overseas to absorb some European winemaking philosophy. On his return he poured it all into just 17 barrels of his maiden Columella – an instant hit, and the 05 now notching the highest-ever Wine Spectator ranking for a Cape wine. A determination to never make a white wine soon evaporated and in 2002 an even smaller quantity of Palladius joined its sibling in the charts. Common to both are Sadie's belief in the value of blending, his relentless work in improving the best vineyards he can find, and the conclusion that Rhône and Mediterranean varieties are what work best here. See also Sequillo entry.

★★★★☆ **Columella** Usual stringent quality measures taken to extreme in **05**, resulting in 'controlled power & freshness, a paradox for the vintage'. Darkly ripe fruit, perfumed nutmeg spice & supple, savoury tannins beautifully integrated into textured sensation. Shiraz with 20% mourvèdre. 2 yrs Fr oak.

★★★★☆ **Palladius** Singular blend, 30% each viognier & chenin, rest chard, grenache bl. 'More structural than flavour sensation' says ES of **06**, & what a build! Waves of stonefruits woven into tingling minerality, bone-dry sensation to echoing length. Like pvs, should mature well. — DS

Sagila Wines
T 021-979-1719, 082-502-4562 · F 021-979-1719

Stellenbosch · Est 2004 · 1stB 2005 · Closed to public · Owner/winemaker Mzokhona Mvemve · 2000cs 100% white · PO Box 524 Stellenbosch 7599 · mgasela@iafrica.com

Young Madlozamahle may not yet be able to say 'Sagila' - but Swedes and Germans are happily managing, it seems: dad (and taster for this guide) Mzokhona Mvemve's wines are already known and enjoyed in their countries, and are moving into the US. Locally, they're available from select restaurants and boutique stores, and as production has increased to 1000 cases of each wine, there's more to go round.

Chenin Blanc ★★★ Light fruit richness enhanced by smidgen sugar, with tropical & dry-grass notes; **06** pleasing bounciness, but bit hard on finish. **Sauvignon Blanc** ★★★ Gd varietal character on **06**; fresh & dry, with savoury bright acidity. — TJ

Saltaré
T 021-883-9568

Stellenbosch · Est/1stB 2003 · Closed to public · Owner Christoff & Carla Pauw · Winemaker Carla Pauw · 5t/150cs · 30% red 30% white 40% MCC · PO Box 2290 Dennesig 7601 · ccpauw@gmail.com

Each January, wine-maker and -adviser Carla Pauw, husband Christoff and their friends pick and crush the first fruit for their private-label wines. The conviviality invariably includes song and dance, and in celebration of this time-honoured occasion the Pauws have named their brand Saltaré.

★★★★ **Cap Classique Brut** Impressive brioche aromas on 05 (★★★★★), toasty, creamy yet with zesty freshness, adding savoury food-friendly dimension, chard (60%, rest pinot) evident in fine citrus notes. 22 mths on lees. **03**, also 60/40, was full flavoured/bodied, rich & yeasty.

Syrah ★★★☆ Only 25 cs of **04**. Last ed was ultra-ripe, fruity & slightly porty aromas/flavours; 15% alc big but not brash, bright acidity & lovely smooth tannins. Fermented old oak; 18 mths 2nd fill Fr. — MF

Sanctum Wines
T 021- 849-8504 · F 021- 849-8504

Stellenbosch · Est/1stB 2002 · Closed to public · Owner Mike & Alice Dobrovic · Winemaker Mike Dobrovic · 3.2t/240cs 100% red · P. O. Box 110 Grabouw 7160 · info@sanctumwines.com · www.sanctumwines.com

'I must've been a farmer in a previous life,' says Alice Dobrovic, delighted with her move (ahead of husband Mike D, winemaker for Mulderbosch and for this, the family winery) to their spread in Elgin, and bandying farming terminology about like an old hand. New sauvignon vines are in the ground, and fixing the dam is her next project. Mike D meanwhile deadpans that he makes some wine for his wife's new venture.

★★★★ **Shiraz** Sumptuous **05** (★★★★★) amply fruited yet lithe & svelte, spicy pith stitched into upholstered tannins. Layers of flavour unfurl to up ante on demure **04**. Cool-climate edge ex-Stanford vyds. Supple 100% new Fr oak, 19 mths. — *DS*

■ **Sandy River** *see* Zandvliet Estate

Saronsberg Cellar
T 023-230-0707 • F 023-230-0709

Tulbagh ▪ Est 2002 ▪ 1stB 2004 ▪ Tasting & sales Mon-Fri 8.30-5 Sat 10-2 ▪ Closed Easter Fri-Mon, Dec 25/26 & Jan 1 ▪ BYO picnic ▪ Tours by appt ▪ Owner Saronsberg Cellar (Pty) Ltd ▪ Cellarmaster Kajo Malek (May 2006) ▪ Winemaker Dewaldt Heyns (Oct 2003) ▪ 37 ha (cabs s/f, grenache, malbec, merlot, mourvèdre, petit v, shiraz, chard, sauv, viognier) ▪ 65% red 35% white ▪ PO Box 361 Tulbagh 6820 ▪ info@saronsberg.com ▪ www.saronsberg.com

Pretoria property man Nick van Huyssteen saw a dream destroyed when fire swept through his newly-acquired farm early in 2003. A year later, he and new winemaker Dewaldt Heyns embarked on a development programme which ended last year, by which time Saronsberg was the Phoenix arisen of the Tulbagh Valley, with a slew of awards to its name. Dewaldt H rates vintage 2007 as almost as good as the 'amazing' 2004, his shiraz giving him particular pleasure and a maiden viognier awaiting release this year. A new range, labelled Provenance, aims (as the name implies) at better expression of the Saronsberg terroir.

★★★★ **Shiraz** Shiraz goes it alone in **05** (**04** had dashes mourvèdre, malbec, viognier). Sleek, perfumed, confident; power & allure without aggression. 18 mths Fr barriques, mostly new.

★★★★ **Full Circle** Opulent rhône-style blend led by shiraz, with mouvèdre & viognier seasonings (6%/4%). Like **04**, **05** (★★★★★) intoxicating floral notes to peppery/meaty cranberry bouquet, lovely seamless tannins. Touch sugar (3.8g/l) masks 15% alc, ensures approachability with potential of ageing. 18 mths new Fr oak.

★★★★ **Sauvignon Blanc** One of the racier versions; 3.7g/l RS certainly helps balance 7.2g/l acidity. Lightish (12.3% alc), light textured yet providing cocktail of crisp 'green' sauv aromas/flavours.

Seismic ★★★★ Claret-style red 85% cab, soupçons malbec & petit v. Understated **05** step up on charry **04** (★★★★). Mint & walnut fruit melded with regal tannins & 14.7% alc; 18 mths new Fr oak provides structure for gd few yrs ageing. **Chardonnay** ★★★★ **06** full flavoured, with enticing melange vanilla & citrus; 100% new Fr oak marries well with solid fruit core & 14.5% alc. **05** (★★★★) was delicious, slightly fresher. **Muscat de Frontignan** ★★★ No **06**; **07** a v sweet melon-brushed treat for cold winter evenings. 16.6% alc, 219g/l RS. 375ml.

Provenance range [NEW]

★★★★ **Rooi** Bdx-style red stand-out in the range; cab/merlot lead (39/36) with 18% malbec, dash petit v. Taut yet sleek cab tannins, brisk acidity on **05** give form to generous fruit, beautifully oak-spiced mouthful. 18 mths Fr oak, 35% new.

Shiraz Rosé ☺ ★★☆ **07** soft (6.5% sugar), well fleshed & easy-going; pleasant gentle tannins.

Shiraz ★★★ Uncomplicated dinner companion; **05** soft red fruit, accessible tannins courtesy 14 mths Fr oak, 35% new. **Mourvèdre-Viognier** ★★★ Playful labels adorn these seriously made wines. Mulberry-toned **05** has lifted peach notes ex 11% barrel-fermented viognier, zesty acidity; 15% alc really warming. 24 mths 2nd fill Fr oak. **Sauvignon Blanc** ★★★☆ Granny Smith apple acidity & persistent blackcurrant finish on charming **07**. Slender (12.6% alc) but well formed. **MCC Brut** Not tasted. — *CvZ*

Savanha

T 021-881-3690 • F 021-881-3699

Stellenbosch • Tasting, sales & tours at Spier • Owner Spier Wines Pty (Ltd) • Cellarmaster Frans Smit • Winemaker See Spier Wines • Viticulturist Johann Smit • 400 000cs 75% red 25% white • PO Box 99 Lynedoch 7603 • info@spierwines.co.za • www.spierwines.co.za

This premium quality brand, made by Spier Wines, has shown exponential growth. The success of the ranges – a Savanha Winemakers Selection now joining the Savanha Special Reserve and Savanha bottlings – lies in their fruit-driven, accessible style, a celebration of the abundant sunshine experienced in the Cape, says cellarmaster Frans Smit.

Savanha Special Reserve range

Cabernet Sauvignon ★★★★ **05** fruit-driven but not simple, underlying oak-spice, savoury firmness. Fr/Am barrel selection; few yrs ageing ability, as for all these reds. **Merlot** ★★★★ Voluptuous **05**, abounds with black cherries & violets, oak supplying underlying seriousness. **Shiraz** ★★★ Spiced red berries & plum compote ripeness fleshes out **05**'s firm frame. This, above reds, not revisited. **Sauvignon Blanc** Sample **07** difficult to rate: dusty, herbaceous & light, lean & steely profile. **Special Noble Late Harvest** NEW ★★★★ Unctuous **05** (sample) offers glacé pineapple, botrytis & toasted nuts (ex-18 mths Fr oak) melded with tangy marmalade acidity. 12.5% alc. Range for export only. Coastal & W Cape WOs.

Savanha Winemakers Selection NEW

Cabernet Sauvignon ★★★★ Understated but ripe **06**, smooth textured with supple dry tannins & dark fruit core. Lightly oaked, as are other reds. **Merlot** ★★★ Black cherries & blue berries in understated, balanced **06**. Dry, food-friendly tannins; 14.5% alc unobtrusive. **Shiraz** ★★★★ Savoury, black pepper & juicy red berries entice on **06**. Balanced, smooth (touch sugar) but dry, spicy farewell. 14.5% alc in sync. **Chardonnay** ★★★★ **07** (sample, rating tentative) shows zesty, friendly style. Ripe pear & tropical flavours, with brioche nuance (ex-lees maturation) adding breadth. Export range; all W Cape WOs.

Savanha range

Merlot ☺ ★★★ Abundance of dark ripe berries appeals on **07**. Cheerful, foursquare & friendly. **Pinotage** NEW ☺ ★★★ For export. Ripe & spicy **07**, mulberries in juicy, quaffable & smooth-textured mode. **Shiraz** ☺ ★★★ Ripe & spicy **07** in juicy, accessible & balanced style. Drink while young & fruity. **Rosé** NEW ☺ ★★ For export. Cranberry & strawberry notes on **07**, light-textured despite 14% alc, finishes dry. **Sauvignon Blanc** ☺ ★★ **07** light (12.6% alc) in leaner style with some asparagus notes.

Cabernet Sauvignon ★★★ Juicy & accessible **07** offers clean cassis flavours in a medium body (14% alc). Lightly oaked, as for all these reds. **Chardonnay** ★★★ **07** light toned, with crisp citrus & ripe pear flavours. For early drinking. All W Cape WOs. — *MW*

■ **SAVISA** *see African Terroir*
■ ***Saw Edge Peak*** *see Conradie Family Vineyards*

Saxenburg

T 021-903-6113 • F 021-903-3129

Stellenbosch • Est 1693 • 1stB 1990 • Tasting & sales Mon-Fri 9-5 Sat 9-4 Sun 10-4 (closed Sun-Tue in winter) Pub hols 10-4 (closed Easter Fri, Dec 25 & Jan 1) • Fee R3-6 • The Guinea Fowl Restaurant & 'Lapa' (see Eat-out section) • Farm produce • Conferencing • Miniature game park • Owner Adrian & Birgit Bührer • Winemaker Nico van der Merwe, with Edwin Grace (Nov 1990/Jan 2005) • Viticulturist Jan van der Merwe (Apr 2007) • 85ha (cab, merlot, pinotage, shiraz, chard, chenin, sauv) • 440t/50 000cs 80% red 20% white • Export brand: Bosman's Hill • PO Box 171 Kuils River 7580 • info@saxenburg.com • www.saxenburg.com

Nico van der Merwe celebrated his half-century last year with the release of a new Shiraz flagship. The winemaker says every cellar's long-term objective should be to create 'it's own taste, within a unique Cape style'. To this end he tries to balance his belief in traditional winemaking with the 'smart style' demanded by markets (and this means not adding pinotage or viognier to everything, he adds emphatically). And he looks increasingly at emerging markets in Asia and Russia, as 'the more easy style of SA wines is perfect for them.'

Saxenburg Limited Release

★★★★☆ **Saxenburg Shiraz Select** Pricey showpiece deserving many yrs ageing. Careful block selection, only free-run juice, best barrels chosen. Last-tasted **03** (★★★★★) assailed senses with cocoa bean richness, cream-textured body, fully integrated tannins. Smidgens cab, merlot. 2 yrs all-new wood, equal Fr/Am. **02** was a seductive combination plush velvet & fragrant vanilla bean, milk choc.

Private Collection

★★★★ **Cabernet Sauvignon** Always handsome, complex, gd ageing potential. **04** still hiding its talents, slow developer, as all these; herbaceous notes, cedar, brambleberries, refined tannins. A keeper.

★★★★ **Merlot** Always lush fruit in these, **04** no exception; full-ripe plums, dark choc, more amenable tannins than **03**, only 20% new. Silky, curvaceous, for drinking rather than keeping. 15.5% alc not intrusive.

★★★★ **Pinotage** Individual, stand-alone pinotage. Intriguing wild scrub, black pepper in **04** add further dimension to dark fruit; gd backbone ensures 6+ yr future. Fr/Am yr, half new. Worth cellaring.

★★★★☆ **Shiraz** Consistently excellent. Rhône-style **04**'s wild berries & scrub permeate, then further seduction awaits in silky structure, ultra-long savoury finish. Gorgeous. Ageworthy, but who'd want to? Yr Fr/Am, third new.

★★★★ **Sauvignon Blanc** Reductively made from combo riper style & early-picked fruit for max flavours. Sample **07** already bursting with lemongrass, asparagus intensity, enough zinging freshness to tackle a bucket of oysters.

Chardonnay ★★★★ Deservedly popular, always sells out. **06** offers peach slices & nuts, deliciously presented in smooth savoury-toned package. Perfect food partner. Ferm/matured yr Fr. **Le Phantom Brut Cap Classique** Not tasted. **Le Rêve de Saxenbourg Natural Sweet** Untasted this ed.

Guinea Fowl range

Red ★★★★ Muscular, dark-fruited merlot, shiraz, cab blend. Improvement on pvs, **05** has spice & scrubland layers, plenty fleshy power. Despite seasoned oak, tannins firm enough for few yrs cellaring. **Rosé** NEW ★★★ Enough lively charm in **07** to please all comers, with shiraz giving food-friendly savoury element. 20% pinotage. **White** ★★★ Predom chenin, ±third Wllngton viognier. Aromatic floral notes in just off-dry **07**, supported by chenin's juicy drinkability.

Concept range

Grand Vin Rouge ★★★ Bargain-priced 5-variety Fr/SA blend. Meaty, black plum core, nuances dried herbs, campfire smoke. Dry tannins call for food. **Grand Vin Blanc** ★★★ Predom chenin in latest, 20% semillon; light-textured, friendly, appley quaffer, belying name. Both **NV**.

Selection Famille

Named after Bührer children; available only from farm. Not retasted this ed: Gwendolyn (shiraz/cab) & Manuel (cab/merlot). Also wines ex-Ch Capion (Fr), so never tasted: Appollonia (white blend), Fiona & Adrianus (both red). — *CR*

Scali

T 021-869-8340 • F 021-869-8383

Voor Paardeberg (see Paarl map) ▪ Est/1stB 1999 ▪ Visits by appt ▪ Olive oil ▪ B&B guest accommodation ▪ Owner/winemaker Willie & Tania de Waal ▪ Viticulturist Willie de Waal ▪ 70ha (cab, merlot, pinotage, shiraz, chard, chenin, sauv, viognier) ▪ 1400cs 77% red 23% white ▪ PO Box 7143 Noorder-Paarl 7620 ▪ info@scali.co.za ▪ www.scali.co.za

Willie and Tania de Waal believe in long-term planning, and two of their aims for their vineyards are to go fully organic and to incorporate more Mediterranean varieties. A first step has been the planting of viognier and grafting of roussanne onto existing vines. Willie's 2007 harvest season produced 'wonderful ripeness at lower sugars'. Being named one of James Molesworth's top six SA producers in Wine Spectator was a high point, but, says Willie dW, the real prize is 'when people enjoy our wine'.

Scali range

★★★★ **Pinotage** Like pvs, **05**'s 13% shiraz adds perfume to red berry/meaty aromas which lightly recall variety. At 14.5% alc & gorgeously fruit-sweet (though dry), with big succulent tannins, not exactly elegant or refined - but close. Just 1 yr oak.

★★★★ **Syrah** Gracefully styled version, though strongly structured, with big but balanced 14.5% alc, & handsome, ripe fruit. Typical Pdberg-area character in fynbos & herbs aromas & fine tannins. Oak (2 yrs Fr, half new) better integrated than pvs. Native ferment.

★★★★ **Blanc** NEW Following fine maiden **05** blend 75% chenin, chard & a little viognier, oxidatively made, yellow-gold **06** (★★★★★) even more winning, with aromatic & flavour complexity, a richly fresh texture helped by yr in old oak, beautifully balanced. Both serious & delightful. — *TJ*

■ **Scarborough** see Cape Point Vineyards

Schalk Burger & Sons Winery
T 021-873-1877 · F 021-873-2877

Wellington (see Paarl map) ▪ 1stB 2003 ▪ Visits Mon-Fri 8.30-5 Sat 9-2 Sun by appt ▪ Fee R15 (incl glass) ▪ Closed Dec 25 & Jan 1 ▪ BYO picnic; also meals/refreshments for groups by appt ▪ Facilities for children ▪ Conferences, cricket pitch & other amenities ▪ Owner Schalk Burger Family Trust ▪ Winemaker Jacques Wentzel (Jul 2007), with Franco Lourens (Dec 2005) ▪ Vineyard Manager Tony Julies (Jan 2007) ▪ 140ha (cabs s/f, cinsaut, merlot, mourvèdre, petit v, pinotage, shiraz, chard, chenin, sauv, viognier, grenache) ▪ 1 200t total; 550t/cs 25 000 own label ▪ 75% red 25% white ▪ PO Box 51, Oakdene Rd, Wellington, 7654 ▪ wine@welbedacht.co.za ▪ www.welbedacht.co.za ▪ www.meerkatwines.co.za

Production is now almost six times that of the maiden 2005 vintage – and six is a magic number around here, hence the name of a new, soon-to-be-released wine: No. 6. 'Schalk Burger Jnr plays at number six for the Springboks, Schalk Snr made his provincial rugby debut at number six, and I also played number six provincial rugby,' explains younger son and marketing man Tiaan Burger. 'There are only six barrels, six cultivars and you can only buy six at a time.' That's probably all you'll be able to carry anyway, with an empty bottle weighing 1.1kg!

Schalk Burger & Sons range

★★★★ **The Cricket Pitch** Traditionally vinified (basket press, open fermenters et al). Last ed **03** made confident debut; 60/40 merlot-cab offering raspberry sweetness, savoury dryness. 18 mths small oak, new-3rd fill combo.

Welbedacht Wines range

Cabernet Sauvignon Barrique Select ★★★ **05** appealing forest floor wafts, whiffs cassis & oakspice. Confident, if uncomplex, fruit-oak marriage on palate; 30% new wood. No **04**. **Merlot Barrique Select** ★★ Mid-2007, **05** appears oak dominated, lacks much fruit profile: savoury, salty, charry on the palate; resinous on the nose. **Pinotage** NEW ★★★★ 'We are serious about pinotage', the Burger mantra; & the strict cellar regime pays dividends. Newcomer **05** restrained, elegantly seasoned with 45% new oak; attractive expression of the variety. **Syrah** ★★★ **05** pre-bottling sample reviewed mid-2006, now finished wine. Still red/black fruit cocktail with ripe tannins; decently dry, 14% alc integrated but oak a bit apart on finish. 45% new wood. **Chardonnay Barrel Fermented** 🍷 ★★★ As for Chenin, 65% new oak playing major but supportive role; brisk acidity cuts through variety's girth for a lively, juicy palate flavoured with lemons, limes & cashews. **Bush Vine Chenin Blanc Barrel Fermented** 🍷 ★★★ 60% new oak smartly handled, adds complexity, structure & weight; doesn't detract from lime & thatch notes. Zingy acidity ensures freshness, persistence.

Meerkat range

Pinotage 🗒 ★★★ **05** featured last yr as standalone wine, now part of the Meerkat 'family' (named for the friendly mongooses on the farm). **06** eminently drinkable, bright & cheery - just watch the 14% alc. **Burrow Blend** NEW 🗒 ★★ Wallet-pleasing, 'fun & funky' says Schalk Snr. **06** mixes merlot's plummy fruit with cab's hints of violets, firm backbone in 60/40 assemblage. Decently ripe & dry; tannins tad stalky. These reds lightly oaked. **Unwooded Chenin Blanc** 🗒 ★★★ **06** tasted last ed was for early drinking; grassy, with some old-vines intensity & weight. — *CvZ*

Schalkenbosch Wines
T 023-230-0654/1488 • F 023-230-0422/1488

Tulbagh ▪ Est 1792 ▪ 1stB 2002 ▪ Visits by appt ▪ Tours, meals & accommodation (B&B or self-catering) by appt ▪ Tour groups ▪ Walks ▪ Conservation area ▪ Mountain biking ▪ Owner Platinum Mile Investments ▪ Cellarmaster/winemaker Johan Delport (Jan 2005) ▪ Viticulturist Johan Wiese & Andrew Teubes (consultants) ▪ 35ha (cab s/f, merlot, mourvèdre, petit v, shiraz, chard, sauv, viognier, malbec) ▪ 180t/10 000cs 80% red 20% white ▪ PO Box 95 Tulbagh 6820 ▪ info@schalkenbosch.co.za ▪ www.schalkenbosch.co.za

The team is expanding: production is on the up, and the launch of their flagship range was imminent at press time. A BWI member, their next goal is Champion status. On a personal note, winemaker Johan Delport and wife Carlien became the proud parents of little Liza-Marié.

Schalkenbosch range

'Schalkenbosch' NEW ★★★★ Name undecided at press time. Mainly cab (86%), smidgens merlot & petit v. Serious intent signalled by all-new oak regimen (18 mths, Fr), adding coffee & cedar to **05**'s bitter choc & ripe black cherries. Youthfully introverted mid-2007, but potential shows. EW.

Edenhof range

> **Cabernet Sauvignon-Merlot** ☺ ★★★ **04**, tasted last ed, plush with sugared plums & creamy sweet oak, refreshing acidity. **Glen Rosa** ☺ ★★★ **05** warm woody notes & dark berries in appealing bdx-style blend. Complex wooding regime abets fresh dry finish. **Bin 409** ☺ ★★★ **06** (sample) slightly floral rhône-style red. Equal parts grenache, shiraz, mourvèdre, cinsaut. Soft, juicy & pleasant.

Cabernet Sauvignon ★★★ Inviting **05**, cherry & smoky spice; blackberries & toasted nuts plus cellar's signature firm tannins. **Pinotage** NEW ★★★ Initial juicy fruit of **06** kept under control by some quite stern tannins. Invites food or brief spell in cellar. 6 mths 2nd fill Fr oak. **Shiraz** ★★★ Last tasted **04** showed blackberry & savoury concentration; oaking allowing fruit to shine. **Cabernet Sauvignon-Shiraz** ★★ Pleasant smoky & spicy **04**, fruitiness held in check by bold tannins. **Sauvignon Blanc** ★★ **07** (sample) herbal & tight, with prominent acidity - tame with rich seafood. **Blanc de Blanc** ★★ Hint muscat grapiness adds friendly dimension to easy **07** quaffer. This, all above & below, mainly WO W Cape. Discontinued: **Viognier**.

Isis range

Dry Red ★★ New-thatch & molasses tones on **06** casual party quaffer. **Rosé** ★★ **07** gains deep blush from dashes mourvèdre & petit v; strawberry wafts & crisp dry flavours. **Dry White** ★★ As for Edenhof Blanc de Blanc. This trio sold in 1-litre bottles; marketed as 'Delichon' in Sweden. — *DB*

Schindler's Africa NEW
T 083-270-3449 • F 086-512-1306

Tasting by appt ▪ Fee R7p/p ▪ Owner/winemaker Klaus Schindler ▪ 250cs 100% red ▪ schindler@lando.co.za

Klaus Schindler, having sold and left Lemberg Estate (where the wines below were made), intends to continue making wine on a small scale, affording him more time to conduct hunting trips in the Karoo and guided game tours through the Kruger Park – a forestry scientist, he was based there in the 1980s. 'Pity that area's too warm for growing grapes, but what about transporting chilled grapes there?' he wonders.

Pinot Noir ★★★ Earthy, forest-floor nuances on **06**, followed by light, slightly savoury flavours & curious (not unattractive) citrus note on exit. **Pinotage ★★★** Ancestor pinot noir's truffle note evident on **06**, some warm mocha flavours; mouthfilling, unusual & interesting. Both organically grown. *— DB*

■ **Scholtzenhof** *see Ken Forrester Wines*

Schonenberg Wines
T 074-100-9769 · F 086-651-2485

Swartland ▪ Est 2005 ▪ 1stB 2006 ▪ Tasting by appt ▪ Farm produce ▪ BYO picnic ▪ Walking/hiking trails ▪ Owner Jaco & Yolande Marais ▪ Winemaker Jaco & Yolande Marais (2005) ▪ Viticulturist Jaco Marais (2005) ▪ 13ha (pinotage, shiraz) ▪ 46t/350cs 100% red ▪ European ISO 65 organic certification ▪ PO Box 67 Riebeek-Kasteel 7307 ▪ jaco.marais@gmail.com

The new wave of eco-friendly farming includes this picturesque family winery atop Porseleinberg Mountain in the Swartland. Jaco and Yolande Marais settled there in 2005 to realise their dream of raising children in a 'more natural, tranquil environment'. They've farmed biodynamically from the outset, and last year obtained organic certification through Control Union.

★★★★ Syrah These all **06**. Wonderfully delicate, but plenty of herbal, mineral red fruit, lightly touched by herbaceousness; fruit purity unblurred by oak - only older barrels used, 16 mths (racked once, 'on a full moon'). Fine tannins in appropriately modest support for lingering finish. Reasonable 13.1% alc.

Pinotage ★★★★ Exuberant, fragrant aromas; round, pure-fruited palate with herbal edge, gentle but dry tannins, & acceptable tiny bitter note. Oaking as for Syrah. These all spontaneous ferment, unfiltered/fined. **Cape Blend ★★★★** Syrah & pinotage equal partners, had an extra month in old oak together; a slightly awkward pawpaw note, but fruity charm, with lovely savoury tannin. *— TJ*

■ **Schoonberg** *see The Goose Wines*
■ *Schoone Gevel* *see La Motte*
■ *Schonenberg* *see Groupe LFE South Africa*
■ *Sebeka Wines* *see Swartland Winery*

Sedgwick's Old Brown Sherry

Blend jerepiko & dry sherry, launched in 1886 & still the fisherman's friend. By Distell.

Sedgwick's Old Brown Sherry 🍷 **★★** Richly sweet coffee & caramel flavours. Some less attractive volatile notes. **NV**. 750ml & 2-litre btls. *— MW*

Seidelberg Estate
T 021-863-5209 · F 021-863-3797

Paarl ▪ Est 1692 ▪ 1stB 1989 ▪ Tasting & sales Mon-Fri 9-6 Sat/Sun & pub hols 10-6 ▪ Fee R12 ▪ Closed Dec 25 ▪ Tours daily (by appt for groups of 5+) ▪ De Leuwen Jagt Restaurant ▪ Play area for children ▪ Farm produce ▪ Events/functions ▪ Tour groups ▪ Gifts ▪ Walks ▪ Hiking trail ▪ Conservation area ▪ Tractor rides ▪ Bronze-casting studio, glass blowing studio & artists lounge (with live demonstrations) ▪ Owner Roland Seidel ▪ Winemaker Cerina de Jongh (Jun 2002) ▪ Viticulturist Ian de Lange (Apr 2006) ▪ 110ha (cabs s/f, malbec merlot, mourvèdre, pinotage, shiraz, chard, chenin, sauv, viognier) ▪ ±500 tons ▪ 40 000cs 70% red 20% white 10% rosé ▪ PO Box 505 Suider-Paarl 7624 ▪ carol@seidelberg.co.za ▪ www.seidelberg.co.za

Roland Seidel's enhancement programme in the wine-tasting area done, he's started on a three-year extension project in the cellar and maturation area. Ever mindful of added value for visitors, he's partnered with Cape Malay cuisine expert Cass Abrahams in bringing the indigenous food of the region to South Africans who've forgotten about their heritage and diners from abroad who've never tasted it. Luxury accommodation is also now available on the farm.

Roland's Reserve range

Cabernet Sauvignon ★★★★ Red berry fruit with almond undertones on **05**, fine ripe tannins. 18 mths Fr oak, 70% new, with splash (10%) **07** vintage. **04** sold out before we could taste. **03** (★★★★) was classic, with gorgeous lead-pencil bouquet. **Merlot** ★★★★ **05** multi-layered with toffee, coffee, cassis & hints tobacco leaf; smooth entry, ripe jammy palate with fine tannins. 17 mths Fr oak. **Pinotage** ★★★★ After retiring **04**, **05** outgoing combo jammy ripe fruit, dust & lead pencil shavings. Tannins a little prominent, will soften over 2/3 yrs. **Syrah** ★★★ Sample **05** spicy & a bit stalky. Sweet oak notes with liquorice, friendly, juicy mouthfeel & soft, supple tannins.

Seidelberg range

★★★★ **Un Deux Trois** Still one-two-three part bdx-style red, with cassis & ripe blueberry in **04** showing cab (70%) dominance. Integrated, with ripe silky tannins; pleasant dry finish. 18 mths Fr oak.
Cabernet Sauvignon ★★★ **04** dark, rich blueberries with coffee hints; fruit follows through with ripe, juicy tannins. **Merlot** ★★★ **05** lifted by 10% cab from pvs vintage. Rich, ripe raisin notes & fine accommodating tannins. Combo staves & barrels. **Pinotage** ★★★ Minerality & subtle oak undertones on undemanding, friendly **06**, freshened by 15% from **07** vintage. Yr Fr oak. **Shiraz** ★★★ **05** in sedate style of pvs. Ripe black plums with white pepper undertones; warm stewed fruit, dry tannic departure. **Cabernet Sauvignon-Merlot** ★★★ Appealing **04**, 60/40 blend with classic cassis tone, juicy mid-palate & dry oak tannin. **Rosé** ★★ Off-dry, muscatty **07** appeals with rich honey & rosepetal fragrance & flavour. **Chardonnay** 🍷 ★★★★ Wooded this yr; food-styled **06** ripe Golden Delicious apple, hints watermelon & honey, disciplined oak, juicy, glowing finish. **Chenin Blanc** 🍷 ★★★ Off oldest producing vyd on estate; friendly **07** refreshes with tropical fruit flavours, hints grapefruit & light nutty nuance. **Sauvignon Blanc** ★★★ **07** grapefruit with passionfruit hints, full & round, high acid (7.1g/l) well-managed. Friendly 12.9% alc. **Viognier** ★★★ **07** not ready. Acidity in last-tasted opulent, fat & sweet-fruited **06** little too low for richness & 15% alc.

De Leuwen Jagt range

Cabernet Sauvignon ★★★ Lighter, trimmer-fruited **04** a departure from pvs hearty versions; dry chalky tannins add to leaner silhouette. **Merlot** ★★★ Green bean wafts on uncomplicated, easy-drinking **05**. Light, with fine tannins, braai-friendly. **Pinotage** ★★★★ Rich **07** upfront ground coffee on red-berry backdrop. Pleasant, well-structured (Hung/Fr oak-staved), juicy finish. **Shiraz** ★★ Raisined spiciness to over-ripe **04**. Not for keeping. **Cabernet Franc-Merlot** ★★★ Less exuberant partnership in pvsly tasted **04**, cab f's stalky minerals upfront, sturdy long-term tannins. **Leuwenrood** 🍷 ★★★ **05** not ready; **04** switched to shiraz (58%) merlot blend; full & fruity; v agreeable wild berry conclusion. **Rosé** 🍷 ★★ Rosepetals on attractive semi-dry **07**, mainly cab with dashes muscadel & pinotage. **Chardonnay** ★★★ Generous lime notes on **06**, some flintiness adds dimension, bit cloying solo - drink with zesty food. **Leuwenblanc** 🍷 ★★ Refreshing **07** smacks of grapefruit & green beans; acids juicy, finish long & clean. **Nuance** ★★ Jovial, pleasant **07** quaffer with prominent rosepetal bouquet. **Stein** 🍷 ★★ **07** appeals with opulent Turkish Delight, honey & lemon bouquet, off-dry fruit flavours. **Red Muscadel** ★★★ Inviting fortified dessert with molasses whiffs, rich & malty flavours & vg acid balance. Discontinued: **Sauvignon Blanc-Chenin Blanc**. Some in this range WO W Cape. Reds mainly unwooded. — *MM*

◼ **Selection Famille** *see* Saxenburg

◼ *Sénga* *see* MAN Vintners

◼ *Sensory Collection* *see* Stellar Winery

Sentinel
T 021-657-8100 • F 021-415-6385

Cape Town • Closed to public • PO Box 30 Constantia 7848 • wine@sentinel.co.za • www. cfwines.co.za

Things work a little differently at Sentinel, now owned by Wine of the Month, SA's leading mail-order wine club. 'Our aim is to source low-volume wines of award-winning standard,' explains Wendy Burridge. 'We visit as many wine cellars as possible and select special parcels that would often get blended away if the winemaker is unable to find a buyer.'

Sentinel range NEW

★★★★ **Cabernet Sauvignon-Cabernet Franc** Cab-dominated (85%) characterful blend with spicy oak & roast herb notes; **03** vivid ripe fruit complemented by supple tannins, giving serious edge. Balanced food partner.

Barrel Reserve Red ☺ ★★☆ From pinotage; **04** ripe mulberry mingles with toasty oak, rich cherry flavours, smoked ham meatiness.

Merlot ★★★☆ Minty, herbal **04** with lean but ripe fruit, light texture, sour cherry flavours & fresh acidity throughout. This, as all these, new to the guide. **Chenin Blanc** ★★ Shy **06**, muted melon & apple flavours & crisp, dry finish. **Sauvignon Blanc-Chenin Blanc** ★★☆ Incl dollop chard. **06** muted nose, sweet melon & peach flavours, spicy, off-dry finish. — *IM*

Sequillo Cellars
T 021-869-8349 • F 021-869-8101

Swartland • Est/1stB 2003 • Visits/amenities by appt only • Owner Eben Sadie & Cornel Spies • Winemaker Eben & Niko Sadie • 2 500cs 80% red 20% white • PO Box 1019 Malmesbury 7299 • info@sequillo.com • www.sequillo.com

Eben Sadie is convinced that warmer climates do best with varietal mixes. For some years he's been blending for all the complexity allowed by his beloved Swartland in the Sadie Family wines - whose own cellar also sees the making of Sequillo. But these are from quite different Swartland vineyards, and the Sequillo venture is in no way a 'second label'. But it now also has a pair of wines, with a new white based on the old-vine chenin which Sadie knows so well how to vinify and how to combine with other varieties, to local and international applause.

★★★★ **Sequillo Red** Delicious & lively **05** has pure, ripe red-fruit, spicy & dried herb notes, in opulent, subtly oaked, soft-tannined structure, with long finish. Gd example of emerging Swrtlnd shiraz-based red blend style, with 30% mourvèdre, 10% grenache.

★★★★★ **Sequillo White** NEW Richly, finely structured **06** from chenin, 20% grenache bl, 10% each roussanne, viognier, mostly fermented Fr oak, yr on lees. Intense aromas, persistent flavours (stone, fynbos, honeysuckle, citrus), but restrained & focused, with fresh acidity. Beautifully built to mature gd few yrs but approachable now. — *TJ*

■ Serengeti *see Leidersburg Vineyards*

Ses'Fikile
T 021-694-9840; 021-852-5052 • F 021-694-9840; 021-852-5085

Stellenbosch (see Helderberg map) • Est 2004 • 1stB 2006 • Tastings at Flagstone (see entry) • Owner Indlezane Investments • Winemaker Bruce Jack, with Wilhelm Coetzee • Viticulturist Bruce Jack • 5 500cs 70% red 30% white • PO Box 120 Guguletu 7750 • indlezane@mweb. co.za; sesfikile@gmail.com • www.sesfikile.co.za

Ses'Fikile, meaning 'We've Arrived in Style', did just that last year: on the dining tables of the SA High Commission in London for the Freedom Day celebrations, at the Prowein show in Germany, on the shelves of Marks & Spencer in the UK, and in the Netherlands and US markets. Proudly South African, their prime market is local: major retail stores and trendy township taverns including Wandis, Lehapa, Back of the Moon and Pistos Place.

Matriarch range

Cabernet Sauvignon Reserve NEW ★★★ Wide fruit selection & 24 mths oaking speak of serious intentions but **04** still incubating; lead pencils, brambleberry, dried herb nuances nudging through. Wine needs time to unfold. Provisional rating. **Shiraz Reserve** ★★★☆ Last tasted **04**, light yrs from version below in styling: raspberry compote, heaps of sweet spice. Voluptuous structure absorbed 15.6% alc & 24 mths Am oak. Gd cellaring potential.

Folklore range

Cabernet Franc-Cabernet Sauvignon NEW ★★★ Unlike siblings, **05** seriously oaked, 14 mths mainly new Am, hence vanilla spice shading to plum & berry flavours, backbone for few yrs ageing. **Pinot Blanc** NEW Not tasted.

Rainsong range

Pinotage ★★★ Previewed last ed, now finished wine, minimally oaked **05** focuses on freshness & quaffability, an honest tasty rendition of pinotage. **Shiraz** ★★★☆ Sample in last ed, now bottled. Capturing wild berry & salty liquorice tones of Rhône, lightly oaked **05**'s fresh juicy structure is a drinking delight. Not for long ageing. **Chardonnay** ★★★ Altogether better than pvs, unwooded **06** has fresher styling, citrus & freshly sliced peaches, with a friendly light-textured structure. **Chenin Blanc** ★★★ Last ed, **06** had pear-drop & melon typicity, attractive food-friendly minerality. **Sauvignon Blanc** ★★★ Previewed last ed, **06** more expressive yr later; fresh leafy green tones, food-friendly minerality on palate. *— CR*

Seven Oaks

T 083-639-0405 • F 086-617-8102

Worcester • *Est 2003* • *1stB 2004* • *Closed to public* • *Owner Farm Acres 27 (Pty) Ltd* • *Winemaker Francois Agenbag (Mountain Ridge)* • *Vineyard Manager Sindani Chibambo, assisted by consultant Dries Van Wyk* • *37ha (cab, cinsaut, pinotage, ruby cab, shiraz, chard, chenin, sauv)* • *345t/574cs own label* • *Customer brands: Villa Verde & United Bulk* • *PO Box 11 Breerivier 6858* • *jacqui@sevenoaks.co.za* • *www.sevenoaks.co.za*

On the cusp of greater things, with yet more plantings last year (10ha of chardonnay and chenin), the release of two new varietal labels, and a bigger thrust into organic wine. Besides making Padre Rednose SGS-approved grapes, grown on their farm in the Eilandia ward, the owners are in the process of having their cellar certified organic.

> **Chenin Blanc** ☺ ★★★ **07** great poolside quaffer with vivid tropical flavour, lemon twist in the finish. WO Breedekloof unless mentioned.

Padre Rednose Merlot-Cabernet-Sauvignon ★★★ **05** blueberry & choc-driven rich mouthful, with coconut notes from yr Fr/Am oak; gd structure. WO Rbtsn. **Cabernet Sauvignon-Shiraz** ★★★ Last tasted was easy-drinking, spicy-fruited **04**. **6+1 Cabernet Sauvignon-Shiraz** ★★★ Like Padre R, tasted ex-barrel last yr; **05** 60/40 partnership shows spicy fruit & obvious oak (18 mths Fr/Am), ending with mouth-drying tannins. **04** won Diners Club Young Winemaker award. Breede Rvr Vlly WO. **Pinotage Rosé** NEW ★ **07** sweet, strawberry-fruited pink. **Sauvignon Blanc** NEW ★☆ **07** just-dry & lean, with some green fig notes. *— JPf*

◼ **Seven Sisters** *see* African Roots Wine Brands

◼ **Shatot** *see* Slaley Estate

◼ **Shibula** *see* Freedom Hill Wines

Ship Sherry

Jerepiko-style **NV** fortified from two muscats & chenin by Distell.

Ship Sherry ▤ ★★ Plump raisins, mulled wine, caramel & mocha flavours slip down warmly (16.8% alc). *— MW*

Shoprite Checkers
T 021-980-4000 · **F** 021-980-4012

Enquiries: Stephanus Eksteen ▪ 30 000cs own labels 60% red 35% white 5% rosé ▪ PO Box 215, Brackenfell, 7561 ▪ seksteen@shoprite.co.za ▪ www.shoprite.co.za

National wine-buyer for Shoprite and Checkers Stephanus Eksteen convenes a panel of experts to select the national retail chains' in-house ranges. Two of the anonymous Oddbins wines, the Chardonnay Bin 221 and Cabernet Bin 219, were given best value awards by Wine last year. 'And we're selling over 80 wine estates in our Checkers Wine Route,' Stephanus E adds.

Oak Ridge range

Merlot ☺ ★★★ Cheerful ruby lights to **04**, not quite as jovial as pvs but still quaffable & appealing; dusty note & hint of dark choc. **Shiraz** ☺ ★★★ Warm, spicy notes on easy-drinking **04**, fleshed out with rich, plum & dark berry flavours.

Cabernet Sauvignon ★★★ When last tasted, **03** showed variety's sturdy structure & tannins, mellowed by vanilla oak. Vintages still selling, not retasted. **Cabernet Sauvignon-Merlot-Cabernet Franc** ★★ Partially oak matured **03** austere when tasted, with powerful tannins which should since have softened.

Oddbins range

★★★★ **Merlot-Cabernet Sauvignon-Pinotage Bin 217** ✓ Classy **04**, cedar, pencil shavings & cigarbox aromas complement dark choc, toasted nut, black cherry flavours; rich, lingering finish. Hearty, mouthfilling wine (15.28% alc) with ageing potential. Note: this range features limited editions sourced directly from estates & private cellars; bin numbers change as batches are replaced by new lots.

Pinotage Bin 220 ☺ ★★★ **03** earthy notes a reminder of pinot noir parentage; dark cherries well-balanced with crisp tannins, pleasant lingering finish. **Merlot Rosé Bin 224** ☺ ★★★ Pretty pink garb sets the tone for 'feminine' **07**, dusty rose & strawberry notes add appeal, finishes dry. **Chardonnay Bin 221** ☺ ★★★ Pretty floral/citrus intro, sweet jasmine flavours on debut **07**, clean lime finish. **Chenin Blanc Bin 225** ☺ ★★★ Pleasing pineapple aromas on **07** carry through to crisp tropical fruit salad flavours. **Sauvignon Blanc Bin 222** ☺ ★★★ **07** lunchtime charmer, redolent of greenpepper & musk, refreshingly crisp green melon notes. Friendly 12% alc. Sample tasted, as for most of these.

Cabernet Sauvignon Bin 219 ✓ ★★★★ **05** smoky cinnamon notes followed by big, juicy, dark plum fruit on well-managed tannin base. **Shiraz Bin 218** ✓ ★★★★ Spicy cloves & cinnamon in deliciously fruity maiden **06**. Lingering bone-dry finish. **Merlot-Cabernet Sauvignon Bin 209** ✓ ★★★★ Generous mocha nose & enticing mulberry flavours in maiden **05**'s carefully balanced trilogy of fruit, acid & tannin. — DB

■ **Short Tail** *see Groupe LFE South Africa*
■ **Sibeko** *see Daschbosch Wine Cellar*

Signal Hill

T 021-422-5206 · **F** 021-422-5238

Cape Town ▪ Est/1stB 1997 ▪ Open Mon-Sat 10-7 (also Sun in season) ▪ Luncheon restaurant ▪ Owner Ridon Family Vineyards ▪ Cellarmaster Jean-Vincent Ridon ▪ Winemaker Khulekani Laurence Buthelezi & Wade Metzer (1998/2005) ▪ Viticulturist Wade Metzer ▪ 5ha (cab, shiraz, pinot, muscat d'A) ▪ 45t/±3 000cs ▪ 70% red 27% white 3% rosé ▪ PO Box 12481 Mill Street 8010 ▪ info@winery.co.za ▪ www.winery.co.za

Now that his cellar in the heart of Cape Town is complete, the indefatigable Jean Vincent Ridon has a very stylish and central reception area for the grapes from his various urban and suburban vineyards, which now include Oranjezicht, Kalk Bay, Camps Bay and Rondebosch.

These join parcels from more traditional winelands locations to make up his exciting and diverse range. His success with 'extreme' winemaking, like the widely-lauded Eszencia, has only sharpened his resolve to refine the Cape's tradition of sweet wines and, generally, to encourage difference in his wines (witness his trials with vineyards planted on their own rootstocks, thumbing their noses at the spectre of phylloxera). The past year also saw the local launch of his Roussillon wines, Le Signal.

Signal Hill range

★★★★ **Malbec 04** last ed had exotic incense bouquet, lush cherry flavour, persistence. Follow-up not ready.

★★★★ **Petit Verdot** Extended barrelling (40 mths, 20% new) for preview **04** (★★★☆) required 'to tame this wild baby'. Tamed, maybe, but not obliterated intense violet scents, nor sharpish acid. Like rest of range, needs food to show best. **03** was more seductive though also firm.

★★★★☆ **Clos d'Oranje** Tiny shiraz vyd in central Cape Town; J-V Ridon's tribute to SA wine's origins. **05** persuasive varietal scents with Fr-style restraint. Last ed we noted needs yr/2 for flavours to grow. No successor.

★★★★★ **Empereur Rouge** NEW Delicious, but how to categorise? 'Very, very overripe' **05** Paarl cab (but uncertified), some raisins evident on nose; tiny botrytis portion less obvious. Somewhere between amarone & ruby port (but unfortified!); beautifully balanced, complex & lingering. Interesting ageing potential. Barrelled, 50% new. 375ml.

★★★★ **Crème de Tête Muscat d'Alexandrie NLH** Next is **06**, still in barrel. Judging from hedonistic **03**, worth the wait.

★★★★★ **Eszencia** Glorious & restorative elixir; mere 130 litres from 2ha furmint, chenin & sauv. Vastly sweet & rich, flavours electrified by nervy acid. Extreme stats: 480g/l sugar, 16g/l acid, 5.1% alc, latter recognised for wine in EU but not (yet) in SA. To date only **NV** (02).

★★★★ **Mathilde Aszú 6 Puttonyos** Still no follow up to **02** characterful Tokaji lookalike from botrytised Swtland furmint & Smnsberg sauv. Like many of Ridon's creations, a Cape first.

★★★★ **Vin de l'Empereur** Velvety yet fresh botrytised dessert from muscat d'A. **05** noble rot introduced cinnamon, baked apple notes to variety's vivid grapey tones. No **06**; **07** unready.

Olympia Cabernet Franc ★★★★ 'Cabernet Franc' last ed. Ex-Kalk Bay vyd near sea's edge; just 660 btls from 600 vines! **06** realises last yr's previewed promise with aromatic leafy spice, sweet fruit contained by lacy tannins. Carefully oaked for current drinking pleasure. **Pinot Noir** ★★★★ **05** still available. Last ed we noted clear cherry/forest floor fragrance, lively tannins, light texture. Will benefit from further yr/2. Older oak. WO Sbosch. **Syrah** ★★★☆ **06** (sample) mirrors **05** in its freshness & mint-embroidered spice, with slightly more fleshy amplitude. Current appeal should increase over next few yrs. **The Threesome** NEW ★★★★ None of trio sidelined in **05** 'gender mix' of le cabernet, la syrah (30% each) & le merlot. Fresh mint-lifted cassis; ripe pure fruit, gentle grip & minerality. Older Fr oak, 2 yrs. **Rosé de Saignée** ★★★☆ **06** mainly shiraz with pinot, cab f; 'light red' feel, generous savoury vinosity, lees enrichment & rounded dryness all suggest multitude al fresco food partners. **Tête Blanche** ★★★☆ Ridon's favoured mature chenin style. Last **03** partly oaked, from low-yield Smnsberg, Polkadraai vyds. Pvs notes incl melon & lemon fruit, cleansing acidity. No new bottling. **Viognier** ★★★ Restrained **05** still available, not re-assessed. Last time we noted suggestion bottle age to dainty apricot tones; best enjoyed soon. Some Fr oak. **Straw Wine** None since nutty, sherry-like **01** from unknown field blend, air-dried as traditional vin de paille demands. Discontinued: **Antica MM**, **Malwenn**, **Constantia**, **Vin de Glacière**.

La Siesta range

Grenache Noir ★★★☆ 'Grenache' pvs ed. Last **03** was a Southern Fr-style red. Next will be **06**. Discontinued: **Grenache Blanc**. —*AL*

■ **Signature Reserve** *see* Stettyn Winery

■ *Signatures* see Doolhof Estate
■ *Signature Series* see Jean Daneel Wines
■ *Signum* see Rooiberg Winery
■ *Silver Myn* see Zorgvliet Wines
■ *Silver Sands* see Robertson Wide River Export Company

Silverthorn Wines
T 021-712-7239

Robertson • Est 1998 • 1stB 2004 • Closed to public • Owner John & Karen Loubser • Winemaker/viticulturist John Loubser (1998) • 4ha (cab, shiraz, chard) • 50t/225cs 100% white • PO Box 381 Robertson 6705 • john@silverthornwines.co.za • www.silverthornwines.co.za

'Africa, sustainability, slow food and wine lifestyle' are the building blocks of winemaker John Loubser's philosophy, reflected in his The Green Man sparkling wine. The new release is from chardonnay, partly barrel fermented and matured on the lees for at least 20 months.

★★★★ The Green Man Blanc de Blancs NV (05) shows finesse of truly 'brut' MCC. Light, fresh; chard's citrus nuances meshed with pin-prick bubbles, enriched by 10% barrelled portion. Lovely development potential. 11.5% alc. — *AL*

■ *Simonay* see Simonsvlei International

Simonsig Estate

T 021-888-4900 • F 021-888-4909

Stellenbosch • Est 1953 • 1stB 1968 • Tasting & sales Mon-Fri 8.30-5 Sat 8.30-4 (T 021-888-4915) • Fee R15/R25 (incl glass) • Closed Easter Fri, Dec 25 & Jan 1 • Tours Mon-Fri 10 & 3; Sat 10 (min 5; booking essential for groups) • Cheese platters (R35) or BYO picnic • Play area for children • Tour groups by appt • Walking trail • Labyrinth vineyard • Owner Malan brothers • Cellarmaster Johan Malan • Winemaker Johan Malan (1981), with Van Zyl du Toit & Debbie Burden (Dec 97/Nov 99) • Viticulturist Francois Malan (1980), with Ludwig Uys advised by Johan Pienaar • 215ha (cab, merlot, pinotage, shiraz, chard, chenin, sauv) • 2 000t 57% red 25% white 18% MCC • PO Box 6 Koelenhof 7605 • wine@simonsig.co.za • www.simonsig.co.za

This year Simonsig celebrates the 40th anniversary of the launch of its first wines – and, baby, what a long way they've come! The tasting room has been upgraded; there's a new deli-restaurant; and the Kaapse Vonkel bar is set for opening. A South African first for the estate was the bottling of verdelho as a single variety (exclusive to Pick 'n Pay). And there's new packaging for the varietal range and a screwcap for the Sauvignon 07. Biggest seller Chenin – the only survivor of the first trio of wines Simonsig launched in 1968 – does exceptionally well on the estate's decomposed shale soils. 'To work with wine brings you close to nature and in a beautiful place such as Stellenbosch the passion comes naturally,' says winemaker Johan Malan. And, he adds, 'It's important to have fun in the process.'

★★★★★ Redhill Pinotage Regal **05** continues in vein set by standout **04**; elegant, restrained (despite 15% alc) & well-knit. Current version more red than black fruit (cranberry, strawberry) plus hints coconut from 30% Am oak (15 mths, 100% new).

★★★★★ CWG Auction Reserve Shiraz Sleek **05** (**★★★★**) brims with lily & cranberry nuances (viognier skins used to add perfume), spicy oak hints - perhaps too much oak, alc (15.2%) on finish mid-2007. Should mesh, improve in bottle. 18 mths new Fr oak. **04** was more balanced & elegant, with sheathed power.

★★★★★ Merindol Syrah Top-notch, single-vyd shiraz on poor sandy-loam soils. **05** iron fist in velvet glove; firm tannin, solid fruit core checks hefty 15.5% alc; vibrant acidity for freshness, 19 mths new Fr oak gives structure for long cellaring.

★★★★ Tiara Smartly oaked flagship, blend varies each yr in leading bdx-style. **05** (**★★★★**) currently in oak's grip (64% new, rest 2nd fill, mainly Fr), but so generously fruited you'd give it all the time needed to come around. Calyon gold. **04** was big boned & ripe.

★★★★ **Frans Malan Cape Blend** Pinotage-led blend with cab & merlot (32/9 in current version), named for visionary patriarch. **05** fruit in harmony with lemon acidity, confident oak detail; long, richly textured & flavoured. 16 mths Am/Fr barrels, 58/42, 83% new.

★★★★ **Chardonnay Reserve** 🔖 No **05**, only made in exceptional yrs.

★★★★ **Chenin Avec Chêne** Classy **06** (★★★★) gives elegant fruit centre-stage, sweet vanilla oak the suporting role. Full, (14.5% alc, 4.6g/l RS), with elderflowers & thatch notes, bracing acidity. 10 mths Fr oak, 30% new. **04** rounder (6g/l sugar) but lifted by variety's mouth-juicing acidity.

★★★★ **Gewürztraminer** ✓ **07** celebrates this Special Late Harvest's 30th anniversary (with 12% alc as opposed to usual 11%?). Alluring rosepetal aromas & delicious Turkish Delight palate. Always poised & delicate; a firm favourite.

★★★★ **Valentine Viognier** Sample **05** fine example of viognier with peach & apricot nose, oily & weighty palate. Charming & unforceful (as this variety can be), it needs ±yr for fruit to mesh with oak. 12 mths Fr.

★★★★ **Cuvée Royale** Prestige MCC made occasionally. **96** (50/50 chard/pinot) proved ageability of these. Tasted last ed, **99** (★★★★) was rich, with whiffs sugar-dusted croissants & cinnamon-spiced apple from unwooded chard (91%).

★★★★ **Encore** ✓ Unoaked sec-style MCC, 55/45 chard/pinot. **00** was first, no **99**, **98** tasted last ed debuted out of vintage sequence, showed highly attractive bottle maturity, honeycomb & candy apple characters.

★★★★ **Kaapse Vonkel** ✓ SA's first bottle-fermented bubbly; chard/pinot (55/41), splash pinot meunier; small oaked portion for richness. **06** delivers: vibrant & long, with Granny Smith apple freshness, anise finish.

★★★★☆ **Vin de Liza Sauvignon Blanc-Semillon Noble Late Harvest** Original salute to matriarch, from sauv (73%), semillon. **06** fruiter than chenin version; honeysuckle & pineapple brush against apricot botrytis tones. Bracing, uncloying finish. 12 mths Fr oak; 30% new, rest 4th fill.

★★★★☆ **Vin de Liza Chenin Blanc Noble Late Harvest** NEW **06** maiden NLH from chenin, aged 8 mths Fr oak (25% new, rest 3rd fill). Thrilling apricot, earthy tones to minerally yet rich & dense mouthful; built for decade+.

Adelberg ☺ 🔖 ★★☆ Loads of plummy fruit dusted with spicy oak on **05**. Under screwcap so opens easily, slips down easily too. Exported as 'Cabernet Sauvignon-Merlot'. This, many others, wearing smart new label. **Chenin Blanc** ☺ ★★★ Doing the family business for 40 yrs now! **07** our Superquaffer of the Year, floral, full-flavoured, balanced & bold. **Adelblanc** ☺ 🔖 ★★★ Zippy summer favourite, anytime, anywhere fun. **07** brims with grapefruit aromas/flavour. Exported as 'Sauvignon Blanc-Semillon'. **Franciskaner** ☺ ★★☆ Timeless Natural Sweet party-starter with thatch & blossom nose, aloe lift to tail in **06**. Mainly colombard & chenin, with morio muscat & hint semillon.

Labyrinth Cabernet Sauvignon ★★★☆ New name for hard-working member of the family's line (pvsly just 'Cabernet Sauvignon'), as for 'savage' white below. **04** well-balanced, loads of green herbs & licorice wrapped in creamy oak (16 mths, mainly Fr, some Am, mix old/new). **Pinotage** ★★★☆ **04** a celebration of unoaked pinotage, with abundant strawberry, wet earth & fennel snuggling against gentle fruit tannins. **Shiraz** ★★★☆ Lily scents flirt with soft & sasssy red fruits, grippy tannins, on crowd-pleasing **04**. 21 mths oak (seasoned Fr/Am 63/37). **Cabernet Sauvignon-Shiraz** ★★★ Now available in SA. **05** friendly partnership (52/48) delivers cassis fruit, broad tannins for early drinking. **Chardonnay** ★★★☆ Powerful barrel-fermented/matured version (10 mths, 20% new). **06** laden with ripe oranges, smothered with buttery oak. Acidity, oak rather unmeshed at present; should resolve in bottle. **Sunbird Sauvignon Blanc** 🔖 ★★★☆ Just 'Sauvignon Blanc' pvs ed. Cool feel to **07** is consistent with house style; zesty grapefruit palate, pithy texture, loads of flavour. **Mustique** ★★★ **05** tasted last ed was comfortingly sweet blend colombard, riesling & muscat d'Ottonel. **Brut Rosé** ★★★★ One of the moreish pink MCC sparklers available. Pinotage (88%) teams with dollops pinot m & n in charming strawberry & cream melange; long & luxurious. Discontinued: **Vin Fumé**. — *CvZ*

Simonsvlei International

T 021-863-3040 · F 021-863-1240

Paarl ▪ *Est/1stB 1947* ▪ *Tasting & sales: Mon-Fri 8-5 Sat 8.30-4.30 Sun 11-3* ▪ *Fee R15 for 5 tastings* ▪ *Closed Easter Fri & Dec 25* ▪ *Tours by appt* ▪ *Amenities & attractions see intro* ▪ *Owner 65 shareholders* ▪ *Cellarmaster Francois van Zyl (2000)* ▪ *Winemaker WS Visagie (2007)* ▪ *1 200ha (cab, shiraz, chard, chenin)* ▪ *10 000t/220 000cs own labels + 300 000cs for customers* ▪ *50% red 50% white* ▪ *PO Box 584 Suider-Paarl 7624* ▪ *info@simonsvlei.co.za* ▪ *www. simonsvlei.com*

'More than Wine', Simonsvlei's new slogan, encompasses its multi-faceted offerings: a three-tier wine range, the Paragon boutique cellar (for atmospheric tastings) and theatre, restaurant, conference and function facilities, gift and farm produce shop, loyalty programme and Simonsvlei Wetlands Trust rehabilitation programme. New on the vinous front is young winemaker WS Visagie (ex-Villiersdorp Cellar, seasons in America, Germany and France), whose objective is to produce estate-like wine which will compete favourably on quality, style and price.

Hercules Paragon range
Cabernet Sauvignon ★★★★ Mint & cherries on **04**; big, bold blackberries burst onto palate, well-managed underpinning of oak (yr). Step up from **03** (★★★★) classic cassis with dark choc & mint extras. **Shiraz** ★★★ Spicy, leathery, smoky aromas, followed by dark choc on **04**. Gd varietal character & structure for ageing few yrs. **Sauvignon Blanc** ★★★☆ Typical green, grassy nose, big pineapple & passionfruit zest, long, clean finish. **07** grapes again from Dbnvlle area.

Classic range
Cabernet Sauvignon ★★★ Last tasted **05** classic cassis & tealeaf character, gd frame of fruit & tannin, approachable but yr/2 to go. **Pinotage** ★★★ Light oaky nose from 6 mths staves contact, **06** easy, ripe, dark-berry fruit. Food-friendly. **Shiraz** ★★★ Old-World leather & spice, elegant soft ripe fruit. **05** comfortable fireside wine. **Cabernet Sauvignon-Merlot** ★★★★ Continuing successful style of pvs, **05** seamlessly integrates layers of fruit, mint & dark choc. Even better in 2/3 yrs. **Rosé** ★★ Pretty, playful party pink with pinotage's strawberry scents & flavours **07**. **Premier Bukettraube** ★★ **07** lightweight charmer with gentle honeysuckle tone. **Chardonnay** ★★☆ Vanilla biscuit from oak staves on **06**, followed by honey, lemon & clove. Finishes dry. **Premier Chenin Blanc** ★★★ Soft leaves introduce reliable, fresh & fruit-driven quaffer, **07** with crisp finish. **Sauvignon Blanc** ★★★ Green leafy **07**, wafts pepper & grapefruit. Long, clean finish. **Humbro Hanepoot** ★★★★ Full-sweet honey flavours & tang of marmalade combine in jerepiko-style bottled sunshine. **NV**. **Humbro Red Jerepigo** ★★☆ Sweet, pretty pink pudding wine from muscadel, with hints of fynbos, herbs & honey. **NV**.

Lifestyle range
Cabernet Sauvignon ★★★ **06** initial flintiness followed by well-balanced black cherry & youngberry on controlled tannin base. **Merlot** ★★★ Slightly austere **06** with flinty, minty nose & less pronounced fruit than pvs. **Pinotage** ★★★ **06** plum jam on the nose, but initial fruit overtaken by some tannic hardness. **Shiraz** ★★★ Spicy pencil shavings & juicy plum pudding richness contribute to big, friendly **06**. **Charming Red** In abeyance. **Simonsrood** ★★★ Popular friend of many years. Cinsaut fruit meets shiraz spice in comfortable, food-friendly blend. **Simonsblanc** ★★ Undemanding quaffer with waft of peardrop sweetness. **Stein** ★★ Easy, friendly, al fresco socialiser. **Extra Light** In abeyance. **Blanc de Blanc** ★★ From chenin. Lightish, hints of pear, firm acidic finish. **Natural Sweet Rosé** ★★ Perky pink by colour & nature, low alc (7.5%) & pleasing wafts of jasmine throughout. All above **NV** unless noted.

Simonay range
Classic Red ★★ 4-way casual quaffing blend with spicy touches & hefty 14.8% alc. **Blanc de Blanc** ★★ Refreshingly dry, well-made mix chenin, colombard & crouchen. **Johannisberger** In abeyance. **Stein** ★★ Signature soft, fruity crowd-pleaser with balanced sweetness. **Late Harvest** ★★ Lively fruit salad flavours, not over-sweet. None of above NVs retasted this edition. — *DB*

■ **Simply Red/White**   *see Hippo Creek*

■ *Sinnya*   *see Robertson Wide River Export Company*

Sir Lambert Wines
T 021-976-3361 • **F** 021-976-1810

Lambertsbaai (see Olifants River map) • Est 2004 • 1stB 2007 • Tasting Mon-Fri 9-5 Sat 9-3 at Diemersdal or by appt in Lambert's Bay • Closed Easter Fri/Sun, Dec 25 & Jan 1 • Xamarin Guest House & Restaurant • Conference facilities • Game drives • Golf course • Tour groups • BYO picnic • Conservation area • 4x4 trail • Facilities for children • Owner John Hayes, Johan Teubes & Thys Louw • Winemaker Thys Louw & Mari van der Merwe • Viticulturist Johan Teubes (2004) • 10ha (merlot, sauv) • 12t/700 cs 10% red, 90% white • PO Box 27 Durbanville 7551 • info@sirlambert.co.za • www.sirlambert.co.za

Thys Louw and Mari van der Merwe, winemakers at Diemersdal, are very excited about this new baby, hand-reared in joint-venture vineyards near the West Coast hamlet of Lamberts Bay. Just 3km from the Atlantic shoreline, the site produces pure, elegant sauvignon which – Louw is convinced – will put the new Lamberts Bay winegrowing ward on the map.

★★★★ **Sauvignon Blanc** Laudable cool-climate varietal expression in maiden **07**, nettles & grapefruit, pervading palate minerality. Minuscule yields. Look no further, perfect match for area's shellfish. — *CR*

■ **Six Generations**   *see Rietvallei Estate*

■ *1685*   *see Boschendal Wines*

Siyabonga
T 021-864-3155 • **F** 021-864-1744

Wellington • Est 1998 • 1stB 1999 • Closed to public • Owner H Investments #121 (Pty) Ltd/ Graham Knox • Winemaker Koos Bosman • Viticulturist Theo Brink (2003) • 15ha (cabs s/f, merlot, pinotage, chenin, semillon, viognier) • 3 000cs own label • PO Box 1209 Wellington 7654 • doolhof@mweb.co.za

In 2006 Siyabonga set out to rejuvenate the almost-lost variety semillon gris, or red semillon. About 350 new vines, from cuttings and grafts, have now been planted, and further bundles of fresh cuttings taken to Jacques Smit's Welvanpas nursery for grafting and rooting. 'We hope to plant another thousand vines this year, to produce enough juice to make three or four barrels that will probably be unique in the world,' says Graham Knox.

★★★★ **Pinotage** Unmistakably pinotage with plummy fruit in **03**, but dusty tannin keeps the opulence at bay. Classical (Fr oak-led) handling adds finesse. Low-yielding own vyd. Yr Fr barriques.

★★★★ **Cabernet Sauvignon-Merlot** Stylish, firm composition of concentrated blackcurrant fruit & ripe tannin on **03**, some dusky & tarry tones add intrigue. Young home vyd. 15 mths Fr oak.

★★★★ **Severney** 60/40 chenin/semillon blend, portion of former fermented in used casks. **04** (★★★) showing age; ready to drink. **03** was well-structured, firm & dry. Neither this, above, retasted for this ed. — *DS*

■ **Skilpaddop**   *see Skilpadvlei Wines*

Skilpadvlei Wines
T 021-881-3237 • **F** 021-881-3538

Stellenbosch • Est 2004 • Wine tasting, sales & restaurant hours daily 8-6 • Closed Dec 25/26 & Jan 1 • Tasting fee R10 • Six self-catering guest cottages • Country produce, facilities for children & other amenities • Tour groups • Owner/winemaker WD Joubert • Viticulturist JW Joubert • 62ha (cab, merlot, pinotage, shiraz, chard, chenin, sauv) • 652t/6 000cs own label 65% red 30% white 5% rosé • PO Box 17 Vlottenburg 7604 • info@skilpadvlei.co.za • www. skilpadvlei.co.za

The Jouberts continue to entice visitors, with a new tree-planting programme and a small chapel due for completion this year. Then there's the new Chenin, and the Skilpaddop Red wears its 'Best Value' badge with honour - like the rest of the range, both available only at local tasteroom or from the family-friendly farm.

Skilpadvlei Wines range

Cabernet Sauvignon-Merlot ★★★ No successor to **02**, equal blend showing herbal, cassis & gamey bouquet with big tannins. **Cabernet Sauvignon-Shiraz** ★★ Older-style **05**, reserved, with earthy, smoky & herbaceous notes; astringent finish inviting food. **Chenin Blanc** NEW 🍷 ★★★ Preview **07** ripe style with guava & grass; tasty melon/pineapple, refreshing acidity. **Sauvignon Blanc** ★★ Sample **07** shy grassy notes, simple but satisfying sauv character, easy drinking.

Skilpaddop range

Dry Red ★ Smoky & meaty **06**. Some berry fruit, but stalky & green tones detract. **Rosé** ★★ **06**, tasted pvs ed, from pinotage; mulberry & slight varnishy spice. **Dry White** ★★ Light, fruity **07**, guava & lemon tang; quaffable, with lively acidity. — JP

Slaley Estate

T 021-865-2123 • F 021-865-2798

Stellenbosch • Est 1957 • 1stB 1997 • Tasting & sales Mon-Sat & pub hols 10-4 • Fee R20 refunded with purchase • Closed Easter Fri, Dec 25/26 & Jan 1 • Tours by appt • Farm produce • Owner Hunting family • Winemaker Marius Malan (Oct 2005) • Viticulturist Jaco Mouton • 70ha (cab, merlot, pinotage, shiraz, chard, sauv) • 350t/12-15 000cs own label 90% red 9% white 1% rosé • EurepGAP certified • PO Box 119, Koelenhof 7605 • info@slaley.co.za • www. slaley.co.za

Jaguar car and history buff Lindsay Hunting gives Slaley winemaker Marius Malan a high degree of self-determination. 'I do not want to reduce the winemaker to the level of food technologist as is happening in many of the bigger corporates,' he says. 'It enables me to appoint winemakers of passion.'

Hunting Family range

★★★★ **Merlot** Dark choc & black cherry welcome to pvsly tasted **03** (★★★★), blackcurrant fruit, firm tannins. Highish acid but still some elegance. 18 mths new Fr oak. Lower alc (13.7%) than on big, softly ripe **02**.

★★★★ **Pinotage** From 50 yr old vyd. Juicy-fruited preview **04** (★★★) more barnyard, earthy character than **03**. Tannins chewy rather than ripe & supple, alc slightly higher (13.5%).

★★★★ **Shiraz** Components for ageing 3-7 yrs in youthful **03**. Subtle spice to meaty fruit, muscular & trim, with fine dry tannins on long, resonating finish. 18 mths Fr/Am oak, 50% new.

★★★★ **Chardonnay Noble Late Harvest** Rich & unctuous **06** from super ripe, vine-dried grapes. Now bottled, lemon marmalade waft, sugar (130 g/l) balanced by firm acidity, well-integrated oak (100% new, fermented/11 mths).

Cabernet Sauvignon-Merlot ★★★★ **03** light-textured 80/20 blend, modest 12.3% alc; last noted as having tart dry fruit, dry tannins but gd oak integration, long finish with acid tang. **Chardonnay** ★★★★ Last ed referred to **05** sample; was in fact **04**. Revisited, shows deep colour ex-11 mths oak (used Fr) & bottle age. Generous lemon cream & biscuit notes, tangerine core tighted by firm acid. For early drinking.

Broken Stone range

Cabernet Sauvignon ★★★ Dark-fruited, oak-matured **03** will please classicists with dry tannins, crisp acidity & light body. Not retasted, as for other reds. **Pinotage** ★★★ Yeast-extract whiffs to **03**, savoury & dry, with firm tannins. **Shiraz** ★★★★ Notch up on pvs, well-balanced **04** robust & savoury. Quite muscular, with baked plum, smoked beef aromas/flavours, tangy acid, dry finish. **Cabernet Sauvignon-Shiraz** ★★★★ Shows charm, grace. 10% pinotage imbues attractive, sweet plum character to **03**. Supple tannins, whiff vanilla; smooth juicy fruit. **Sauvignon Blanc** 🔲 Unrated but promising **07** sample complex grassy, gooseberry nose carrying to palate with addition of ripe passionfruit.

Shatot range

Lindsay's Whimsy ★★☆ Accessible **03** pinotage/cab blend last ed showed generosity of home variety. Plump & pleasing, warm plummy notes, nicely dry. **Planque** ★★ Everyday **03** blend cab/pinotage; modest fruit, dusty tannins, v dry. Not retasted. NE. **Plinque** ★★★ With **06**, pink Plinque graduates from fun wine to something little more serious. Characterful cherry/strawbery flavours ex-pinotage; don't over-chill. NE. — *JN*

Slanghoek Winery

T 023-344-3026/7/8 • F 023-344-3157

Slanghoek (see Worcester map) • Est 1951 • Tasting & sales Mon-Fri 8-5 Sat 10-1 • Open pub hols • Tours 11 & 3 by appt • Tour groups • Audio-visual presentation • Gifts • Walks • Conservation area • Owner 25 members • Cellarmaster Pieter Carstens (Aug 2002) • Senior winemaker Nicolaas Rust, with Nico Grundling & Jacques de Goede (Oct 2003/Dec 2002/Dec 2001) • Viticulturist Hennie Visser • 1 830ha (17 varieties, r/w) • 40 000cs own label + 14m litres bulk 20% red 60% white 10% rosé 10% fortified • Export brand: Zonneweelde • PO Box 75 Rawsonville 6845 • info@slanghoek.co.za • www.slanghoek.co.za

The commitment of all 25 farms to conservation was rewarded with BWI membership last year - only the third co-operative winery to achieve this. More feathers in caps for the recent spate of awards (including Swiss Air & Michelangelo golds) but Slanghoek continues to place value and quality conscious consumers before wine competition judges.

> **Cabernet Sauvignon** ☺ ★★★ Fresh, clean new-oak spice, lovely juicy fruit, dark berries on well-made easy-drinker. **06** previewed from (Fr) barrel. **Pinotage** ☺ ★★★ Appealing quaffer in easy ripe-fruit style. **06** (sample) aged 9 mths small oak. **Camerca** ☺ ★★ Cabmerlot blend misreported discontinued last ed. **06** juicy braai buddy with yeasty blackberry tones. Fr barriques. **Vin Doux** ☺ ★★☆ Cheerful, sweet **NV** bubbly with energetic mousse & muscat attractions.

Merlot ★★ Herbal, leafy tones on **06** make gd foil for rich food. **Shiraz** ★★★ **05** leathery, spicy nose leads to fruit-laden palate with dark cherry flavours. **Vinay Red** ★★ Berry-laden, sippable **NV** blend pinotage, malbec, petit v, with gd clean finish. **Vinay Rosé** ★★ Low-alc **NV** from muscadel. Turkish Delight on nose & sweetish palate. **Chardonnay** ★ Mere suggestion of pineapple on v shy **07**. Sample might perk up when bottled. Part barrel ferment. **Chenin Blanc** ★ Warm thatch tones to simple **07** quaffer. **Sauvignon Blanc** ★ Typical grassy nose on **07**, but lacks excitement. **Crème de Chenin** ★★★ Natural Sweet from botrytised chenin, with dollop hanepoot. **06** fragrant rosepetals on nose, aromatic honey flavours. Pure aphrodisiac. **Vinay White** ★★ Lightish, off-dry & easy-going **NV** quaffing blend. All the Vinays in 1 000ml bottles. **Cuvée Brut** ★ Undemanding **NV** celebration sparkler. Carbonated sauv, chenin, colombard. **Special Late Harvest** ★★★ From muscat d'A. **07** gorgeous potpourri of rosepetals & jasmine, clean acid balance. Try with curry. **Noble Late Harvest** ★★★★ Leap in quality. **05** delightful lavender & sun-dried apricots, perfect acid balance. Sweetness (121g/l RS) balanced by beautiful tangy acids. Mainly chenin with dollop muscat d'A, 11.5 % alc. 9 mths small Fr oak. **Sweet Hanepoot** ★★★ Honey & citrus nose, uncluttered sweetness, though **07** lacks freshness. **Red Muscadel** ★★★★ Unmistakable muscat perfume, lovely acid balance. **06** exactly what you expect in a muscadel. **Red Jerepiko** ★★★☆ Sweet fortified dessert from pinotage. **06** gentle raisin & dried pear nose introduces apricot & youngberry jam palate. Lingering aftertaste. **Cape Ruby** ★★ **05** appealing dried peach on nose but less convincing on palate. Discontinued: **Semillon**. — *DB*

Slowine

T 021-844-0605 • F 011-844-0150

Est 2005 • 1stB 1997 • Tasting & sales at Villiersdorp Cellar (see entry) • Winemaker WS Visagie • PO Box 48 Grabouw 7160 • info@slowine.co.za • www.cluver.com

Slowine is a 'collaboration between friends', namely Paul Cluver Estate, Villiersdorp Cellar, Beaumont Wines and Luddite Wines. 'Time becomes precious when life rushes by,' explains Villiersdorp's Ryan Puttick, who makes these happily affordable wines. 'The label tells people to take life a bit slower and enjoy it.' And they seem to be listening – sales are up 100% in a year.

Cabernet Sauvignon ★★★ Bold, balanced **05** ideal match for hearty dishes, has the overt fruit, grippy tannins to go the distance. ±15 mths oak, 3rd/4th fill. **Merlot** ★★★ Plush fruit, sweet choc-mocha nuances & persistent tannins on **05** demand a few mths in bottle to mesh, soften. Quite showy, but true to the variety. Oak as for Cab. **Shiraz** NEW ★★★ Youthful **06** tannins need to be tamed with food; rather spiritous (14.5%) but pleasing Christmas cake aromas & flavours. 12 mths, 3rd/4th fill. **Rosé** ★★★ **07**, like **06**, from pinot; dark salmon hue, strawberry aromas & flavours, sweet-sour tang; finishes dry despite 4.9g/l sweetness. **Chenin Blanc-Sauvignon Blanc** ★★★ Moderate 12.2% alc on flavoursome **07** makes perfect lunchtime sipping; appealing guava & blackcurrant leaf notes, diet-friendly 1.1g/l sugar. — CvZ

Smit Family Wines NEW

T 027-216-1407 ▪ F 027-216-1407

Olifants River ▪ Est/1stB 2007 ▪ Sales by appt Mon-Fri 8-5 ▪ Owner/viticulturist CJ & JJ Smit ▪ Winemaker Rudi Wium (2007, Meerhof) ▪ 60ha (cab, merlot, pinotage, ruby cab, shiraz, chard, chenin, colombard, hanepoot, semillon, riesling) ▪ 900t/250cs 50% red 25% white 25% muscadel ▪ PO Box 24 Klawer 8145 ▪ rudiwium@yahoo.com

Four generations of Smits have farmed on Uitkoms between Klawer and Vredendal, but it's the latest one – brothers Christie and Johan – who have finally realised a family dream to make wine from their own grapes. In-law and winemaker Rudi Wium believes that the finished product is a result of careful preparation in the vineyard. A tasting venue is on the cards.

Cabernet Sauvignon Warm, ripe **07** sample too unknit to rate. **Chenin Blanc 07** (unrated sample) restrained, light, tart & lean, with short lemony farewell. **Sweet Hanepoot** ★★ **07** unctuous fortified exudes honeysuckle & barley sugar charms, hint aniseed on finish. — MW

▪ **Smook Wines** see Anthony Smook Wines
▪ **Soek Die Geluk** see Goedverwacht Estate

SoetKaroo

T 023-541-1768 ▪ F 086-524-3801

Prince Albert (see Klein Karoo map) ▪ Est 2000 ▪ 1stB 2004 ▪ Visits Mon-Sat 8-6 ▪ Tours on request ▪ Closed Easter Sun, Dec 25 & Jan 1 ▪ Owner Herman & Susan Perold ▪ Winemaker Susan Perold ▪ Viticulturist Herman Perold ▪ 0.6ha (petit v, red muscat d'A, red muscat de F, touriga) ▪ 3.4 t/340cs (375/750ml) 100% fortified ▪ 56 Church Str Prince Albert 6930 ▪ perold@netactive.co.za ▪ www.soetkaroo.co.za

Susan Perold describes herself as 'an amateur in the Karoo', but her confidence is growing, and it shows. Besides her signature Red Muscat, she's made two new (as yet untasted) fortifieds: a carafe-bottled Reserve, and a petit verdot/touriga nacional blend; next year she'll experiment with port and 'learn faster!'

Red Muscat d'Alexandrie ★★★★ Sweet as honey but well balanced, retains slightly wild character of hanepoot. **06** again with smidgens touriga & muscat de F. V individual & characterful. — IvH

Solms-Delta

T 021-874-3937 ▪ F 021-874-1852

Franschhoek ▪ Est 1690 ▪ 1stB 2004 ▪ Visits daily 9-5 ▪ Closed Dec 25 & Jan 1 ▪ Picnics during opening hours ▪ Tour groups ▪ Gifts ▪ Walks ▪ Cultural museum & archaeological sites ▪ Owner Family trust ▪ Cellarmaster Fanie Karolus ▪ Winemaker Hilko Hegewisch (Mar 2003) ▪ Viticulturist Paul Wallace (Apr 2002, consultant) ▪ 16ha (mourvèdre, shiraz, viognier, grenache) ▪ 5 000cs ▪ 43% red 43% white 14% rosé ▪ PO Box 123 Groot Drakenstein 7680 ▪ info@solms-delta.co.za ▪ www.solms-delta.co.za

Painstaking restoration of the old buildings on the Solms family's farm has unearthed slave quarters in the old cellar, more or less intact. 'At one stage there were 40 slaves here,' explains owner and renowned neuroscientist Mark Solms, 'but alongside the horrors of the past – slavery and apartheid – there was a joyous tradition of music.' Hence his and new partner Richard Astor's decision to turn the old stables into a Cape musical heritage centre, where musical evenings will be held in the summer and where traditional musicians (David Kramer's helping to find them) and story-tellers will perform. Also planned, from this April, is a harvest festival for the farm workers of Franschhoek (and eventually a wider world), in thanks and celebration. Three new wines, based on Cape varieties and appropriately-named (how's 'Cape Jazz Shiraz'?) will launch with the first festival.

Solms-Wijn de Caab range

★★★★ Hiervandaan Shiraz-led blend settled into characterful, comfortable s-rhône style. **06** mimics **05**'s spice & mineral zestiness with greater focus & concentration; retains relaxed medium body, lightish texture. 80% new Fr oak beautifully absorbed.

★★★★ Lekkerwijn One of the best & most characterful dry Cape rosés. **06** reverts to more vinous, savoury style of maiden **04**; dry, firm, touch more concentration & red-wine length. Delicious & food friendly. Viognier, mourvèdre, grenache, fermented/10 mths used Fr barrels.

★★★★ Amalie Sexy, slightly decadent white blend; **06** (★★★★★) viognier & vine-dried grenache blanc (55/45), intriguing follow-up to maiden **05**. Savoury, oxidative, earth & mineral touches all seamlessly meshed & quite superb. New Fr oak, 5 mths.

Solms-Hegewisch range

★★★★ Africana Delicious & distinctive Amarone-inspired **05** from shiraz, not re-tasted. Perfumed wild strawberry & spice; full, flavoursome; analysis, oaking (100% new Fr, 16 mths) in remarkable feat of balance. 100% vine-dried fruit ex-Fhoek.

★★★★ Koloni Rich, spicy blend riesling (all vine-dried) & muscats d'A & F; **06** full bodied, sumptuous, with flavour-lenthening sweetness (8.6g/l). Fresh acid & influence from new oak (100%, Fr , 5 mths) add sophistication.

Fruit for all these widely sourced. — *AL*

Somerbosch Wines

T 021-855-3615 ▪ F 021-855-4457

Stellenbosch (see Helderberg map) ▪ Est 1950 ▪ 1stB 1995 ▪ Tasting & sales Mon-Sun 9-5 in season, otherwise Mon-Fri 9-5 Sat/Sun 10-3 ▪ Fee R10 refundable with purchase of any 6 btls ▪ Closed Easter Fri, Dec 25/26 & Jan 1 ▪ Tours by appt ▪ Somerbosch Bistro open daily 10-4 ▪ Child-friendly environment ▪ Small to medium function services ▪ Owner Somerbosch Wines cc ▪ Winemaker Marius, Japie & Wrensch Roux (1987/1995/2005) ▪ Viticulturist Marius Roux (1987) ▪ 80ha (cab, merlot, pinotage, shiraz, cinsaut, chard, chenin, sauv, semillon) ▪ 70% red 30% white ▪ PO Box 12181 Die Boord 7613 ▪ enquiries@somerbosch.co.za ▪ www.somerbosch.co.za

Die Fonteine has been the seat of the Roux family for over 50 years. Pop in for a case of well-priced wine (and strawberries in season) and you'll feel right at home too. Linger over lunch at the bistro (children welcome), and don't miss the annual harvest festival, foot-stomping fun for the whole family.

Somerbosch Wines range

★★★★ Chenin Blanc Natural Sweet Limited Release 【NEW】 Intriguing baked apple & biscuit savouriness on **05**, but palate pure hedonistic citrus peel, glacé fruits. Full-sweet (100g/l RS) but uncloying thanks to vein tangy acidity. A find.

Chenin Blanc ☺ **★★★** Tangy pineaple & peach fruit, **07** nicely rounded, refreshingly dry. Chenin with character, oomph!

Cabernet Sauvignon ★★★ 04 noted last ed as notch up on pvs: smoother, fruitier, tannins well meshed with fruit. Oak gives support for few yrs ageing. **Merlot ★★★ 04** exuberant red berries & light-textured structure ensure satisfying drinkability. Yr oaking well integrated.

Pinotage ★★★ Classic pinotage: **05** hedgerow fruit & rhubarb, juicy palate, yet backbone for few yrs. **Shiraz** ★★★ **04** brambleberries, black cherry flavours. Given firm foundation by yr mix age Fr/Am barrels. Drink now, 2/3 yrs. **Kylix** ★★★★ Name means 'Greek Drinking Cup'. **03** perfectly matured, remarkably drinkable, juicy, vibrant. 65/35 shiraz/cab. **02** (★★★★), lesser vintage, classy mineral character. **Chardonnay** ★★ **06** unwooded; gentle tropical tones, finishing in crisp, food-friendly style. **Sauvignon Blanc** ✓ ★★★★ Classic leafy, nettle nose & flavours, **07** tight acidity giving appetite appeal, ultra-long finish. **Late Bottled Vintage Port** ★★★ Sweet, luscious winter warmer from cab; plum-rich fruitcake & some savoury nuances on **NV** sample. Discontinued: **Chenin Blanc Barrel Fermented**

Poker Hill range
Shiraz-Merlot Sold out. **Semillon-Chenin Blanc** No newer vintage ready. — *CR*

■ **Somerlust** *see Viljoensdrift Wines*
■ **Sonop Organic** *see African Terroir*
■ **Soulo** *see Overhex Wines International*
■ **South African Premium Wines** *see Cape Coastal Vintners*

Southern Cape Vineyards
T 028-572-1012

Klein Karoo ▪ *gm@scv.co.za*
Three years after joining forces under the umbrella company Southern Cape Vineyards, Barrydale Cellar and Ladismith Cellar are returning to the status quo ante to avoid confusion in the market, and each winery's products are once again packaged under eponymous labels. See separate listings.

■ **Southern Lights** *see Bonnievale Wine Cellar*

Southern Right
T 028-312-3595 ▪ F 028-312-1797

Hemel-en-Aarde Valley (see Elgin/Walker Bay map) ▪ *Est 1994* ▪ *1stB 1995* ▪ *Tastings & sales Mon-Fri 9-5 Sat 9-1* ▪ *Tasting/sales of estate olive oil* ▪ *Closed Easter Fri/Sun, Dec 25/26 & Jan 1* ▪ *Tours by appt* ▪ *Conservation area* ▪ *Owner Mark Willcox, Mikki Xayiya & Anthony Hamilton Russell* ▪ *Winemaker Hannes Storm* ▪ *Viticulturist Johan Montgomery* ▪ *21ha (pinotage, sauv)* ▪ *225t/17 000cs 40% red 60% white* ▪ *PO Box 158 Hermanus 7200* ▪ *hrv@hermanus.co.za*

Named after the magnificent whales that cavort only a short distance away, these Walker Bay WO wines were previously made at Hamilton Russell Vineyards but have their own home from the 2008 harvest. The pretty Overberg farmhouses and historic brick factory on the property have been restored, and the olive trees produced a record crop in 2007, some of it to become new Southern Right Extra-Virgin Olive Oil. Meanwhile, the team continues to be encouraged by the sell-out response to the wines.

★★★★ **Pinotage** Appealingly forthcoming varietal character on **06**, now with small amounts roobernet, mourvèdre, cab. Ripe, sweet fruit on fresh palate, lightly dry tannins gentler, better balanced than pvs. 42% new Fr oak, 9 mths. Should develop 5+ yrs.

★★★★ **Sauvignon Blanc** Usual powerful pungent aromas/flavours of passionfruit, guava on **07**, with forceful greenness & hint of minerality. Gutsy, fresh; bone-dry finish. — *TJ*

Southern Sky Wines
T 021-871-1437 ▪ F 021-863-0444

Paarl ▪ *Est 2002* ▪ *Tasting & sales at I Love Wine (see entry)* ▪ *Owner Andrew Milne* ▪ *10 000cs* ▪ *80% red 20% white* ▪ *40A Main Street Paarl 7646* ▪ *sales@southernskywines.com* ▪ *www.southernskywines.com*

Through a targeted marketing approach Southern Sky Wines have exceeded their own growth expectations and show no signs of slowing down. Last year, exporter Andrew Milne had a dozen labels in South-East Asia, with 20 likely by the end of this year, and India's now in his sights. His firm belief: 'We're over-delivering on quality.'

Tara Hill range

Cabernet Sauvignon No new version ready for review. **Chardonnay** NEW ★★☆ **06** well-judged suggestion of vanilla oak (only 10% barrelled), adds to some orange marmalade flavour on the palate. **Sauvignon Blanc** Still selling out before we get to taste it.

Marimba range

Cabernet Sauvignon ✓ ★★★☆ **05** coffee & tobacco; forest-floor earthiness & crisp red berries; long clean finish. **Pinotage** ★★★☆ No follow up for **03**, combo banana, cherry, blackberry & savoury fruit; smooth tannins. **Shiraz** ✓ ★★★☆ Biscuity, spicy, vanilla nose on seriously styled, quintessential New World example. **05** entirely barrel-fermented, 30% new Fr oak. **Sauvignon Blanc** No new vintage ready.

Almara NEW

'Red Blend' ★★ Honest, cab-led uncomplicated red-berry quaffer, with fresh clean finish. **05** mainly unwooded.

Ready Steady range

Cape Red ★★☆ Not retasted; pvs offered spice, red berries & plums with savoury touch. **Cape White** ★★☆ Herbal sauv prelude to lush peachy chenin flavours, long dry finish. Both **NV**, for enjoying in youth. — *DB*

South Hill Vineyards
T 021-844-0888 • F 021-844-0959

Elgin (see Elgin/Walker Bay map) ▪ Est 2001 ▪ 1stB 2006 ▪ Visits by appt ▪ Displays of original artworks ▪ Guest house & function venue for conferences & weddings ▪ BYO picnic ▪ Conservation area ▪ Owner South Hill Vineyards (Pty) Ltd ▪ Winemaker Sean Skibbe (Jun 2005) ▪ Viticulturist Andrew Teubes (Mar 2006, consultant) ▪ 28ha (cab, shiraz, chard, sauv, semillon, riesling, viognier) ▪ 130t/4100cs 40% red 60% white ▪ PO Box 120 Elgin 7180 ▪ info@southhill.co.za ▪ www.southhill.co.za

This boutique farm now boasts a tasting room for its expanding range of wines (all under screwcap). Meanwhile, neighbouring farm Vuki - owned entirely by those who work on it - has been contracted to manage South Hill's farming activities. 'We believe this to be quite unique in SA,' says winemaker Sean Skibbe.

★★★★☆ **Cabernet Sauvignon** NEW ✓ 🍷 First vintage from young (4 yrs) but low-yielding vines. **07**'s complex black cherry, fennel, tobacco aromas/flavours, supple tannins, spotlight Elgin's red-wine credentials. Thrilling balance between ripeness, richness & elegance. Yr mainly seasoned Fr oak.

★★★★ **Sauvignon Blanc** ✓ 🍷 Maiden **06** mislabeled **'04'** last yr - but no error in rating - as **07** follow-up proves: vibrant green notes highlighted by sweaty hints, exciting edginess to mineral core; doesn't miss weight of small barrelled portion in **06**. Should show even better in ±12 mths.

Rosé NEW 🍷 ★★★★ Debut **07** an al fresco delight: light enough for lunchtime sipping (13%); dry, to suit most foods. Cab with splash muscat d'A for spice, zestiness. — *CvZ*

■ **South Point** *see Origin Wine*
■ **Spencer Bay** *see Namaqua Wines*

Spier Wines
T 021-881-3690 • F 021-881-3699

Stellenbosch ▪ Est 1692 ▪ Tasting & sales daily 9-4.30 at Wine Centre ▪ Tasting fees: R10 (Spier), R18 (Winelands Select), R30 (Wine Experience) ▪ Meals, refreshments & picnics ▪ Luxury hotel & wide variety of attractions/amenities ▪ Owner Spier Wines Pty (Ltd) ▪ Cellarmaster Frans Smit ▪ Winemaker Kobie Viljoen (red), Eleonor Visser (White) & Anton Swarts, Jacques Erasmus & Johan Jordaan ▪ Wine procurement Johan de Villiers ▪ Viticulturist Johann Smit ▪ 400ha (cab, merlot, mourvèdre, petit v, pinotage, shiraz, chard, chenin, sauv, viognier) ▪ 500 000cs 50% red 50% white ▪ PO Box 99 Lynedoch 7603 ▪ info@spierwines.co.za ▪ www.spierwines.co.za

A consolidation of their vinous assets sees core brands Spier and Savanha retained under the Spier Wines banner, and 'Taking our Wines to the World' their mantra. This operation looks set for its next successful decade: 'My vision is for Spier Wines to become the supplier of choice for premium SA wine brands in world markets,' says MD Neville Carew. Fitting, then, that Spier scored a double hat trick by winning three gold medals for the third consecutive year at the Concours Mondial (among several gilt-edged accolades). The Spier estate remains the HQ for the brands as well as a top tourist destination with a plenitude of attractions, including the popular cheetah and eagle encounters – although these may have a rival: Stoffel, cellarmaster Frans Smit's wine-quaffing dog, who ensures not a drop goes to waste when his master tastes in the cellar!

Private Collection

★★★★ **Cabernet Sauvignon** Multi-faceted wine for keeping. **05** ripe, sleek & muscular with ripe cassis core & hints leafiness. Supple fruit tannins & dusty nuance ex (65%new oak); warm glow on farewell (15%). Accessible now, with ageability.

★★★★ **Merlot 05** carries on the craftsmanship in elegant style. Blueberry, leafy flavours joined by moccha & sweet/spice in supple tannin structure & integrated oak (65% new). Poise & balance despite 14.8% alc & hint of afterglow.

★★★★ **Petit Verdot** NEW Supple tannins join blueberry & spice flavours in juicy **05**. Seamless oaking in balanced, food-styled partner (14% alc)

★★★★ **Pinotage** Powerful **05** notch up on pvs. Dense roasted spice & dark berried appeal; surprising balance for 15% alc with integrated oak (70% new). Excellent food-pairing partner with ageability.

★★★★ **Shiraz** More gutsy than pvs, **05** (ex warm vintage) ripe, smooth & powerful. Dark spicy fruit, dusty dry oak & 15.5% afterglow.

★★★★★ **Chenin Blanc** Voluptuous **06** shade less complex than pvs. Rich caramelized apple & toastiness, threaded with tangy acidity; brl fermentation 10 mths (60% new) absorbed by ripe fruit & touch R/S (4.7). Warm afterglow (14.7% alc).

★★★★★ **Sauvignon Blanc** ▤ Sample **07** too young to rate. Bold (14.2% alc) & gutsy, but shows mid-palate tussle between dusty ripe fig & tropical flavours, keen acidity & some minerality. **06** (★★★★) not showing usual palate punch; **05** combined intensity, brisk acidity.

★★★★ **Viognier** ▤ Rich, rounded **06** less floral than summery **04** & subdued, but peachy **05** (★★★★). Dried apricot & almonds flavours, clean acidity, some mid-palate grip & integrated oaking (14.3% alc).

Malbec ★★★★ No new vintage. Last tasted for 2006 ed, **03** showed ripe plump fruit for immediate pleasure, with few more yrs ahead. **Chardonnay** NEW ★★★★ **06** lime, toasted nuts & honey meld with richness ex lees & oak (40% new, 14 mths). Understated & food-styled (13.6% alc). Discontinued: **Noble Late Harvest**.

Vintage Selection

★★★★ **Shiraz** NEW Gutsy maiden **05** ripe with dark fruit, garrigue & black pepper. Firm oak (80% new), gd tannic structure, 14.7% afterglow.

★★★★ **Malbec-Cabernet Franc-Petit Verdot** Malbec-led **05**, blend in different proportions & restrained style leaner than pvs. Juicy dark fruit, dry tannins.

★★★★ **Cabernet Sauvignon** NEW Maiden **05** in bold but elegant style. Ripe cassis & leafy nuances; balanced, with 14.6% alc not obtrusive; judicious oaking (65% new) & ageability.

Pinotage NEW ★★★★ Pinotage's exuberant fruit tamed in **05** by dry wood tannins (80% new). Ripe (14.8%), but balanced, with dry, spicy farewell. **Shiraz-Mourvèdre-Viognier** ★★★★ **05** more robust than elegantly structured **04** charmer. Blend shiraz-dominated (91%), ripe & juicy, balancing oak (80% new) & dry, chalky tannins. 15% alc. **Sauvignon Blanc** ★★★★ Sample **07** in riper tropical style, plumper than pvs, & balanced with touch minerality. **Sauvignon Blanc-Chardonnay-Viognier** ★★★★ **06** peachy aromatic blend. Fleshy & balanced by tangy acidity & oak ex brl/fermentation chard & viognier.

Spier range

> **Pinotage** ☺ ★★★ Ripe, spicy & fruit driven (5.4 r/s) **06** in warm (14.5% alc) & amiable mode. Barbeque or curry styled quaffer.

Cabernet Sauvignon ★★★★ Bold **06** showcases cassis & moccha in firm tannnic frame. Ripe (dab R/S), with food-friendly finish & ageability. (Like other reds, all 10mths oak) **Merlot** ★★★★ **06** minted blueberries marry ripe, supple & dry tannins. Balanced, subtle oaking (10 mths) with fresh, juicy appeal. **Shiraz** ★★★★ Accessible **06** offers dense, dark fruit, roasted coffee & black pepper. Ripe (15% alc) & gutsy, with integrated, dry oak tannins. **Chardonnay** ★★★ Sweet-toned **07** (4.5 R/S) offsets ripe pear & soft, fleshy style with hint zestiness. Malay or Thai food partner. **Chenin Blanc** ★★★★ **07** clean glacé pineapple with tangy acidity & leesy breadth. Lithe 12.6% alc. Aperitif or food partner. **Sauvignon Blanc** ★★★★ **07** step up on pvs; balanced, fleshier. Vivacious fig, tropical & dusty flavour, with zesty fruit/acid focus. 13.3% alc. Also as 'Spier Inspire' for UK.

Discover range

> **Rosé** ☺ ★★ **07** Off dry, strawberry toned aperitif (14%). **Chenin Blanc** ☺ ★★ This & next, export only, not retasted. Melon & tropical ripeness on quaffing style **06**; softly rounded palate. **White** ☺ ★★★ Fruitful, crisp & dry summer quaffer. **07** thatchy chenin/ colomb blend, light 12.5% alc.

Merlot ★★★ **05** simple but tasty entry-level red, ripe plummy & smooth. **Pinotage-Shiraz** ★★★ No new vintage. Unwooded **05** showed piquant rhubarb & brambleberry aromas/flavours. Cut above usual quaffer. **Red** ★★★ **07** ripe & rustic savoury blend & barbeque partner. **Sauvignon Blanc** ★★ No new vintage. Gentle varietal character in **06**, whiffs lime, green fig. **Sweet** ★★★ Tasted pre-bottling, perfumed, light & delicate **07** a sweetie ex chenin, muscat & riesling.

Colours

> **Merlot** NEW ☺ ★★ Soft, ripe & accessible **07** with gentle blueberry flavours. **Rosé** NEW ☺ ★★ Gently flavoured **07** soft, with dilute strawberry tones. 14% alc.

Chenin Blanc-Sauvignon Blanc NEW **07** thatchy, soft & light (12.7%) dry white. Export only. — *MW*

▮ **Spitz** *see Bellingham*

▮ **Splendour** *see Villiersdorp Cellar*

Spookfontein Wines
T 021-461-6252 (MD); 082-265-1071 (CS) · F 021-461-9273

Upper Hemel-en-Aarde Valley (see Elgin/Walker Bay map) ▪ Est 2000 ▪ 1stB 2004 ▪ Visits by appt ▪ Self-catering cottage & farmhouse ▪ Walking, hiking, mountain biking ▪ Horse rides by appt only ▪ Owner Papermoon Properties cc (Mike Davis) ▪ Winemaker Craig Sheard (Feb 2006) ▪ Viticulturist Andries Gotze (2000) ▪ 10.4ha (cabs s&f, merlot, pinot) ▪ 35t/1000cs (rising to 6000) 83% red 15% rosé 2% MCC ▪ PO Box 12031 Mill Street Cape Town 8010 ▪ miked@dragons.co.za, cjswine@hotmail.com

Enthralled by Walker Bay wines, Mike Davis bought a farm with no infrastructure, vineyards or experience; 12 years later he and winemaker Craig Sheard are coming up trumps with a new 150-ton cellar, and combining Old-World techniques with New-Age attitude: Sheard 'senses' the vineyards, the better 'to understand their purpose, from dirt to glass'.

Cabernet Sauvignon ★★ Light-toned **06**, sweet fruit with variety's cassis uppermost, somewhat unlingering flavours. 18-20 mths Fr oak, as for other reds. **Cabernet Franc** ★★ Gd varietal expression - herbs, cut grass, hint of pepper - Old-World-style lean flavours & big dry tannins. **Merlot** ★★★ Appetising **04** has a savoury tone with tobacco & tealeaf glimpses, earthy/forest floor flavours; needs drinking soon though. **Rosé** ★★ From merlot; honey & lavender hints, **06** nice fruit concentration, pleasantly straightforward sweet flavours. — *MF*

Springfield Estate
T 023-626-3661 • F 023-626-3664

Robertson ▪ Est/1stB 1995 ▪ Tasting & sales Mon-Fri 8-5 Sat 9-4 ▪ Closed Easter Fri/Sun, Dec 25 & Jan 1 ▪ BYO picnic ▪ Owner Bruwer family ▪ Winemaker/viticulturist Abrie Bruwer, with Johan van Zyl (Jun 2000) ▪ 150ha (cabs s/f, merlot, petit v, chard, sauvignon) ▪ PO Box 770 Robertson 6705 ▪ info@springfieldestate.com ▪ www.springfieldestate.com

'They say you've arrived when you braai with cab and chardonnay wood!' quips Abrie Bruwer. But in fact he's referring to the serious business of replanting vineyards. 'Every year the vines got older and the wines went down a little in quality, so we finally decided to bite the bullet. We have replanted them in the same place, but in higher density, facing the sunset.' Another development has been revamping the white-wine cellar. 'Not to make more wine but to make things more comfortable. Now and again you have to invest money to make life easier otherwise your craft becomes a chore.' Nothing else new, insists Bruwer. 'We're quite happy doing the same thing every year; we just try to do it better.'

★★★★★ **Méthode Ancienne Cabernet Sauvignon** From steep mature vyd. 'Ancient' methods mean wild yeasts, all new Fr oak, no fining/filtration. Purity, balance & suppleness the hallmarks, as in delicious **01** (not retasted).

★★★★☆ **Whole Berry Cabernet Sauvignon** Fermentation of uncrushed berries with native yeasts makes for soft, friendly **05** (★★★☆), offering blackberry & tobacco, with creamy finish, but not concentration & focus of pvs. Yr oak, third new.

★★★★★ **The Work of Time 02** (★★★★) elegant blend of merlot/cab f/cab s/petit v (42/25/21/2), less fleshy & concentrated than maiden **01**. Pure cassis/cherry notes complicated by tobacco, finish marked by slightly dusty tannins. 18 mths oak, some new.

★★★★☆ **Méthode Ancienne Chardonnay** Extreme winemaking for this single-vyd, Burgundy-inspired version: night-picked, free-run juice fermented with wild yeast in oak, 50-80% new; yr on lees without sulphur; bottled un-everything (-filtered, -fined, -stabilised). Stunning **05** has intense lees/tropical flavours, finishing with complex minerality, uplifting acid twist.

★★★★ **Wild Yeast Chardonnay** Unwooded, characterful version, off 24 yr old vyd. 3 month alc ferment with native yeast gives complexity, depth. **05** has rich creamy palate (1 yr on lees), packed with tropical flavour, but finishes slightly bitter.

★★★★ **Life From Stone Sauvignon Blanc** From ±20 yr old vyd - the estate's stoniest, giving striking minerality; lightish 12.5% alc yet intense. **07** quintessence of sauvignon, with racy acidity, pungent lemongrass, zesty passionfruit; precise finish with gunpowder/stone notes.

★★★★ **Special Cuvée Sauvignon Blanc** From cool riverine vyd. More substantial, less precise than other version - probably needs more time (say 2 yrs). Stony undertone, mouth-filling flavours gooseberry/fruit salad, driven by cleansing acid. — *JPf*

Springfontein
T 028-341-0651 • F 028-341-0112

Walker Bay (see Elgin/Walker Bay map) ▪ Est 1998 ▪ 1stB 2005 ▪ Visits by appt ▪ BYO picnic ▪ Facilities for children ▪ Walks ▪ 4 self-catering cottages (B&B by appt) ▪ Owner Weber family & friends ▪ Winemaker Christo Versfeld (2007) ▪ Vineyard Manager Andre du Toit with Christo Versfeld ▪ 25ha (cab, merlot, mourvèdre, petit v, pinotage, shiraz, chard, chenin, sauvignon, semillon) ▪ 110t/±7 500cs ▪ 80% red 20% white ▪ PO Box 71 Stanford 7210 ▪ info@springfontein.co.za ▪ www.springfontein.co.za

A challenge last harvest for well-seasoned Christo Versfeld, now managing the farm with his wife Nikki: winemaking on a construction site, as building of a new cellar went hand in hand with the crush! But he and his 'German crew' (owners the Weber family, their friends the Schneiders and others) surpassed themselves, producing 100 tons of handcrafted wine.

Springfontein range

★★★★☆ **Jil's Dune Chenin Blanc** Unfiltered **05** sumptuous, with maritime-influenced refinement & enormous persistence. **07** ex-barrel mid-2007 promises similar attractions; confidently structured, deep flavours able to handle 80% new oak/11 mths. **06** untasted.

★★★★ **Ikhalezi Noble Late Harvest** 'Ikhalezi Chenin Blanc' pvs ed. NLH from chenin. Latest **06** (sample) botrytis with tangy peach/apricot fragrance, gorgeous fruity acid tension to sumptuous texture. Low 7% alc. 100% new oak, 14 mths. Likely (★★★★☆), step up from succulent **04**. No **05**.

Jonathan's Ridge Pinotage ★★★★ Fresh, sweet-fruited **06** with mineral elegance, fine tannins. Lightness of touch reflects grape's pinot parentage. All new Fr oak, 16 mths. Sample, tentative rating. Rung above **05** (★★★★). **Ulumbaza Shiraz** ★★★ Promising red fruit, spicy fragrance on medium-bodied **05**. Over-enthusiastic acid trims appeal. Fr oak, 30% new. EW. **Red** ★★★ **05** blend cab, merlot & p verdot (42/25/15%). Pure if simple cab-like fruit curbed by tense freshness. Fr oak, 40% new. EW. **White** Bdx-style white, 75% sauv with semillon. Noticable oak on previewed **07**, but showing clean sauvignon buzz underneath. Too young to rate. Both ranges WO W Bay.

Terroir Selection NEW

★★★★ **Pinotage** Well-tailored, modern **06**. Generous yet elegant red berry & plum flavours tucked into compact, mineral frame, polished tannins. Freshness, dry tail enhance cool-climate feel. Fr oak, 20% new, 10 mths. EW.

Chenin Blanc ★★★★ Neatly composed **07** (barrel sample) shows cool-provenance vibrancy, complementary florals, restrained oaking (only 10% new). Provisional rating. — *AL*

■ **Spring Grove** see Zorgvliet Wines

■ **Springtree** see The Springtree Wine Company

■ **Spring Valley** see Old Vines Cellars

■ **Spruitdrift** see Namaqua Wines

Stanford Hills Winery
T 028-341-0841 • F 028-341-0286

Walker Bay (see Elgin/Walker Bay map) ▪ Est 1856 ▪ 1stB 2002 ▪ Visits by appt ▪ 2 self-catering cottages ▪ Airstrip ▪ Trout fishing ▪ Hiking trail ▪ Owner Stanford Hills Estate (Pty) Ltd ▪ Winemaker Peter Kastner, with Niels Verburg (Luddite) ▪ Viticulturist Schalk du Toit (consultant, Jan 2002) ▪ 10ha (pinotage, sauvignon, shiraz, chard) ▪ 30t/1500cs own label 66% red 34% white ▪ PO Box 1052 Stanford 7210 ▪ peter@stanfordhills.co.za ▪ www.stanfordhills.co.za

White vines coming into production, and vinification still in the aeroplane hangar built by the previous owner, mean a cellar upgrade is needed. 'But the most important development on the farm,' beams Peter Kastner 'is the new addition in the form of our son, Jack Peter.'

★★★★ **Jacksons Pinotage 06** fresher, trimmer than **05** (14% cf 15% alc.) but similar distinctive curry leaf, red cherry, lavender profile. Light texture, sappy succulence, well-manicured tannins provide for current enjoyable drinking. Fr/Hungarian oak.

Jacksons Sauvignon Blanc NEW ▤ ★★★ Lively but unaggressive **06**, steely/grassy persistence to bone-dry finish. Vllrsdorp fruit. — *AL*

Stark-Condé Wines
T 021-887-3665 • F 021-887-4340

Stellenbosch ▪ Est/1stB 1998 ▪ Tasting & sales Fri 1-4.30 Sat 10-2 ▪ Owner Jonkershoek Cellars (Pty) Ltd ▪ Winemaker José Conde ▪ Viticulturist Pieter Smit ▪ 40ha (cabs s/f, merlot, petit v, shiraz) ▪ 60t/3 000cs 100% red ▪ PO Box 389 Stellenbosch 7599 ▪ info@stark-conde.co.za ▪ www.stark-conde.co.za

Stylishly minimal, the in-house designed labels reflect the new single brand identity for all the wines from this top-flight boutique producer. The grapes are mainly from vineyards on mountain slopes in Jonkershoek. More than 100ha are set aside for fynbos (BWI certification in progress), and a biodynamic vineyard experiment is underway. The first fruit for a new field blend of shiraz, cab and petit verdot on a nearby farm has been harvested, and a joint-venture parcel of pinot, overlooking the Palmiet River in Elgin, looks promising.

Stark-Condé Twin Peak Vineyards range

★★★★☆ **Jonkershoek Cabernet Sauvignon** Like below, from single Jnkrshk vyd. **05** in youth evidencing oak (22 mths, 70% new) with spice, cedar, though deep cassis fruit lurks, giving lingering finish. Dry, finely structured. Serious wine, but sophisticated more than characterful.

★★★★☆ **Jonkershoek Syrah** Touch of perfumed florality points to delicacy of this version, with pepper, smoke & spice too. Oak (30% new Fr) only supportive of fruit's elegantly rich intensity - balancing big tannins which need few yrs to soften & the 14.5% alc (in all these wines).

Stark-Condé Stellenbosch range

★★★★ **Syrah** A little less intense, tannic than senior version, but a fine alternative with elegant fruit, some dusty pepper & spice; lightly rich, silky texture; integrated Fr oak (third new).

Cabernet Sauvignon ★★★★ Enticing blackcurrant aromas on **05**, with herbal additions. Strongly built, with fruit enough for the power. Will benefit from few yrs. **Merlot** ★★★ After softer **04**, strong herbaceousness on powerful, seriously oaked (& perhaps over-serious) **05**, with lean astringency. Previously 'Stark' range. — *TJ*

■ St Clements *see David Frost Estate*

Steenberg Vineyards
T 021-713-2211 • F 021-713-2201

Constantia • Est 1990 • 1stB 1996 • Tasting & sales Mon-Fri 9-4.30 Sat & pub hols 9.30-1.30 • Closed Easter Sun/Mon, Dec 25/26 & Jan 1 • Fee R15 p/p for groups of 10+ • Tours by appt Mon-Fri 10 & 3 Sat 10 • Catharina's Restaurant; five-star Steenberg Hotel; championship golf course etc (see Stay-Over/Eat-out sections) • Owner Graham Beck • Cellarmaster John Loubser (Nov 2001) • Winemaker Ruth Penfold (2003) • Viticulturist Johann de Swardt (1990/1999) • 63ha (cabs s/f, merlot, nebbiolo, pinot, shiraz, chard, sauv, semillon) • 450t/50 000cs 40% red 60% white • PO Box 224 Steenberg 7947 • anetha@steenbrg.co.za • www.steenberg-vineyards.co.za

They'd be forgiven for resting on their laurels (among latest being named SA's leading wine estate at The World Travel Awards) but instead this historic Constantia property, guided by GM (previously cellarmaster) John Loubser, exudes a sense of renewal. Fresh-look labels accompany a change to screwcap closures, there's a new 'icon white' and a pinot MCC is in the making. That's just the cellar, now helmed by Ruth Penfold. In the vineyards, augmented by new blocks of sauvignon, semillon and nebbiolo, neutron probes have taken out any guesswork for viticulturist Johan de Swardt. A BWI member, Steenberg adheres to sustainable farming practices and is now almost 100% insecticide free, fighting pests and disease through biological control instead.

★★★★☆ **Merlot 06** classy: trademark minty hints very evident but mellowed by plum, red berry notes; restrained tannins cradling solid yet sappy fruit core. For cellaring 5+yrs. 14 mths new Fr oak. **04** was rich, with fresh acid backing.

★★★★ **Shiraz** Typically 'cool climate' as opposed to warm 'Aussie' style. **06** a tad awkward; has lots of lily, black pepper, red fruit aromas, but lacks shiraz's broad palate appeal. 12 mths 100% new oak, 60/40 Fr/Am.

★★★★ **Catharina** Flagship red (often merlot, shiraz, cabs s/f), for founder Catharina Ras. Complex **04** dash nebbiolo; **05** just trio merlot, cab, shiraz (43/33/24). Mid-**07** very woody; record suggests will knit in time. 20 mths new Fr oak.

★★★★ **CWG Auction Reserve Barrel Fermented Sauvignon Blanc** No new wine made, nor of CWG barrel fermented sauvignon-semillon below. Tasted last ed, **05** had great concentration & expanse of trademark dried grass, mineral, citrus flamboyance. Used Fr oak fermented/aged 4 wks.

★★★★ **Sauvignon Blanc** Typical cool climate sauvignon from Loire clone. **07** expertly crafted to showcase 'green' aromas/flavours; thrills with its long, wet stone finish.

★★★★☆ **Sauvignon Blanc Reserve** Standout among Cape versions, from 20 yr old vyd. Confident **07** in similar mould to ageworthy **06**; richer, more persistant than standard bottling. Poised, with bracing minerality, it has unrivalled elegance, presence.

★★★★★ **Semillon** With all the structure & weight to develop additional charm in bottle, **07** (★★★★☆) begs cellaring. Waxy high notes top 'struck match', elderflower & vanilla aromas; lemon acidity pierces oak richness. Barrel fermented in new Fr oak with weekly battonage, removed after 5 wks; 10% sauvignon for extra verve.

★★★★☆ **CWG Auction Reserve Barrel Fermented Sauvignon Blanc-Semillon** Tasted pvsly was sophisticated with fresh citrus peel/honey complexity, silky viscosity. 60/40 blend, fermented/aged 4 wks seasoned Fr barrels.

★★★★★ **Magna Carta** NEW **07** much anticipated sauv/semillon maiden; the latter barrel fermented in new Fr oak for 5 weeks prior to blending. Exquisite balance between oak richness, sauvignon raciness; honeyed-lemon semillon acting as the bridge. Fresh & enticing now but will reward cellaring 3yrs+. EW.

★★★★ **Steenberg 1682 Brut** Chard-based MCC, lightish (11.8% alc). Latest **NV** fresh & apply, smooth; lacking richness of pvs bottlings, nevertheless creamy.

★★★★ **Nebbiolo** One of only a few in SA. **06** could never be mistaken for Barolo but brims with honest sour cherry character and drying tannins. Like **05**, slips down easily, courtesy hint sugar; **04** more concentrated. ±14 mths used oak.

Discontinued: **Cabernet Sauvignon, Unwooded Chardonnay.** — *CvZ*

Stellar Winery
T 027-216-1310 • **F** 027-216-1537

Olifants River • Est 1998 • 1stB 2001 • Tasting & sales Mon-Fri 8-5 • Closed Easter Fri/Sun & Dec 25 • Tours by appt • Tour groups by appt • Owner Stellar Winery (Pty) Ltd • Winemaker Dudley Wilson (Jan 2002), with Berty Jones (2000) • Viticulturist Dudley Wilson • 100ha (merlot, pinotage, shiraz, chenin, colombard, sauv, muscat d'A) • 3 200t (organic) + 8m litres bulk (non-organic) + 130 000cs for clients, incl Peter Riegel (Ger), Lovian (Hol), Triton Export Exchange (USA), Masuda Co (Japan), Les Caves de la Riviera (Côte d'Ivoire), Ehrmanns (UK) • 58% red 31% white (incl sulphur-free) 7% rosé 4% organic juice • Fairtrade, Control Union (organic) & Eurepgap accredited; HACCP in progress • PO Box 4 Klawer 8145 • info@ stellarorganics.com • www.stellarorganics.com

Stellar is set to re-launch into the local market with a fresh look in labels and packaging, initially for the anchor Stellar Organics range. Markets abroad are well established and growing. The third vintage of no-sulphur-added wines has just been bottled, an indication of the viability of this method of winemaking. Fairtrade worker representatives have visited the UK, Germany and Holland, and one of the Stellar Joint Body members spent time in the UK on a wine industry educational sponsored by Stellar's UK agent.

The Sensory Collection
Cabernet Sauvignon � ★★★☆ Well-made **04**, medium bodied, dark berry-laced with good depth & fine tannins. Classy drinking, with touch of gd bottle-age. **Merlot** ☢ ★★★ Less varietal character on **04** than in rest of range, though still lush & inviting. Choc finish shows obvious oak (Am/Fr, none new). **Pinotage** ☢ ★★★★ Finely textured **04** backed by Fr & Am seasoned oak; cherry fruit offset by cinnamon & clove. **Shiraz** ☢ ★★★ Big, beefy **04**, less refined than siblings, powerful flavours with hints peppered fillet & fennel.

Stellar Organics range
Cabernet Sauvignon ☢ ★★ **06** attractive & varietally true, gd mint-tinged finish. **Merlot** ☢ ★★ Juicy, easy-textured **06** marred by dry, dull finish. **Pinotage** ☢ ★★ **06** pure banana-toned easy-drinker with gd grip. **Shiraz** ☢ ★ Sherbety **06** a little puckering & dry. **Chardonnay Reserve** 🖺 ☢ ★★★ Bruised apples & tinned pineapple to the fore in **07**; Fr oak adds caramel finish. **Chenin Blanc** NEW 🖺 ☢ ★★ **07** simple, juicy, pineappley quaffer. **Sauvignon Blanc**

🍴 🥂 ★★ **07** light & grassy with ultra-dry, steely finish. **Sauvignon Blanc Reserve** 🍴 🥂 ★★ Even more puckering than std version. **07** taut lime & minerals, needs food. **Colombard-Sauvignon Blanc** 🍴 🥂 ★★ Fun, lively blend, **07** richer than siblings. **Heaven on Earth Natural Sweet** NEW 🥂 ★★★★ Muscat, air-dried on bed of organic rooibos! **06** concentrated apricots & orange marmalade behind fresh waxy texture. Pvs listed as 'Heaven on Earth Vin de Paille'. Discontinued: **Colombar**.

Stellar Organics No-Sulphur-Added

Exclusively for Woolworths, see that entry.

Live-A-Little range

Really Ravishing Red 🍴 🥂 ★ **06** savoury, juicy shiraz flesh, yeasty finish detracts. **Rather Revealing Rosé** 🍴 🥂 ★ Perky strawberry-scented shiraz quaffer, **07** dry & best with food. **Wildly Wicked White** 🍴 🥂 ★★ Tangy melon touches to well-balanced, succulent **07** chenin/sauv blend. **Slightly Sweet & Shameless** NEW 🍴 🥂 ★★ Litchi heaven! Firm acid masks hanepoot sweetness (27.6g/l RS) on **06**.

Juhantha range

Cabernet Sauvignon 🥂 ★★★ Pine needles & mint on juicy-fruited **04**, soft but shortish finish. Not for keeping. All ranges WO W Cape. — *RP*

■ **Stellcape Vineyards** *see Stellenrust*

Stellekaya Winery

T 021-883-3873 · F 021-883-2536

Stellenbosch · Est/1stB 1999 · Tasting Mon-Fri 10-4 Sat 11-3 · Fee R10 (incl glass) · Sales Mon-Sat 9-4 · Closed pub hols · Meals by appt · Facilities for small tour groups · Owner Dave & Jane Lello · Winemaker Nontsikelelo Biyela, advised by Mark Carmichael-Green (2004/2005) · Viticulturist Paul Wallace · 100t 100% red · PO Box 12426 Die Boord 7613 · info@stellekaya.co.za · www.stellekaya.com

The original winery in booming Bosman's Crossing community village, Stellekaya is now part of a 'mini wine route' that includes Dalla Cia, Vilafonté and newest arrival The High Road. Winemaker Nontsikelelo Biyela, affectionately known as 'our Zulu queen', has completed her fourth vintage with Stellekaya and feels it's her best yet.

- ★★★★ **Cabernet Sauvignon** Minty, blackcurrant **05** with abundant rich, fresh fruit flavours needing time to integrate with oak (60% new). 15% alc contributes to sweet impression & warm finish.
- ★★★★ **Merlot 04** tasted last ed already showing maturity. Plum & blackcurrant flavours best enjoyed soon.
- ★★★★ **Shiraz** NEW Spicy cinnamon, peppery, floral **05** with softly textured, fresh red fruit & prosciutto flavours offer approachability now, with food. Half-new oak contributes supple well-integrated tannins.
- ★★★★★ **Orion** Classically styled flagship, bdx blend, elegant **04** tasted last ed. Vibrant, complex black fruit aromas, herb & spice tones complementing sinewy fruit; taut tannins & acid backbone offer cellaring potential.
- ★★★★ **Hercules** NEW Tuscan blend sangiovese, merlot, cab. **06** fresh food wine with sappy elegance, cured meat & chewy sour cherry flavours.

Cape Cross ★★★ **05** merlot, pinotage, cab blend offers raspberry & mint appeal, with pliant tannins checking vibrant, sweet plum fruit. **Boschetto Rosso Red** ★★★★ Consummate pizza wine with inclusion of juicy sangiovese, with cab, merlot & shiraz; previously reviewed **04** still available. — *IM*

■ **Stellenbosch Drive** *see Origin Wine*

Stellenbosch Hills

T 021-881-3828/9 · F 021-881-3357

Stellenbosch · Est 1945 · 1stB 1972 · Tasting & sales Mon-Fri 8-5 Sat 9-12.30 · Fee R10; R35 wine & biltong/nuts tasting · Closed Christian hols · Food & wine evenings · Owner 20 mem-

bers • Winemaker PG Slabbert, with Suzanne Miller (Jan 1997/Nov 2003) • Viticulturist PG Slabbert (Jan 1997), advised by Johan Pienaar • ±1 000ha (cab, merlot, pinotage, shiraz, chard, chenin, sauv, muscat de H) • 8 000t/20 000cs own label 65% red 35% white • PO Box 40 Vlottenburg 7604 • info@stellenbosch-hills.co.za • www.stellenbosch-hills.co.za

Stellenbosch Hills' value-for-money 1-litre range remains their biggest seller, along with their muscat de Hambourg – they're the only winery producing a wine from this variety. They've joined the move to screwcap (with the exception of their reserve). The Biltong & Wine tastings and, for vegetarians, Nuts about Wine, remain popular.

★★★★ **1707 Reserve** Huge whiff oak on **05** does not mask gorgeous, plumply ripe cassis fruit, disciplined by 18 mths all new Fr wood.

★★★★ **Muscat de Hambourg** Consistently delicious fortified dessert from unusual variety. Latest is **NV**, youthfully fresh & brash; tangy flavours, still edgy. Promising, needs time to integrate further, will delight fans.

> **Rouge** ☺ ★★★ Savoury, meaty version with pleasing dryness. Not the average fruit-bomb. **NV**.

Cabernet Sauvignon ✓ 🗐 ★★★★ **06** barrel sample shows classic Cape cab, mulberry fruit, lovely ripeness. Seriously oaked 16 mths Fr, 30% new. Could rate higher given time. No **05**. **Merlot** ★★★ **06** cool herbaceous notes, some green tannin to match. Barrel sample still grippy. No **04**, **05**. **Pinotage** ★★★ **06** preview shows cellar's savoury dryness. Mid-2007 varietal character still somewhat subdued. **Shiraz** ✓ ★★★★ Terrific dark plum, sprinkle of pepper, assertive oak on **06** sample. Taut leathery tones, dry but not austere. **Rosé** NEW ★★ Touch more acidity would add freshness to red berry favours. **NV**. **Chardonnay** ✓ 🗐 ★★★★ Big, luscious fruit on previewed **06**, balanced, lengthy finish. Could rate higher when bottled. Fermented/6 mths Fr barriques. **Sauvignon Blanc** ✓ ★★★★ Cape gooseberries, some nettle, green fig, lovely sweet/sour flavours, properly dry. **07** excellent varietal character, plus winery's hallmark soft acidity. **Blanc de Blanc** 🗐 ★★ Fresh grassy notes, ultra-soft acidity. Sauv/chenin, **NV**, 1-litre bttle. Discontinued: **Chenin Blanc**. — *IvH*

■ **Stellenbosch Regional** *see Rustenberg Wines*

Stellenbosch Wine & Country Estate
T 083-305-7332 • F 021-982-7925

Stellenbosch • Est 2004 • 1stB 2005 • Closed to public • Owner Stellenbosch Wine & Country Estate (Pty) Ltd • Winemaker Wynand Pienaar (Feb 2004), with Boschendal (James Farquharson) & Justin Hoy • Viticulturist Wynand Pienaar • 29.8 ha (cinsaut, pinotage, shiraz, chenin) • 31 tons 1 450 cs • 80% red 20% white • PO Box 158 Elsenburg 7607 • wynlpers@ iafrica.com

'A work in progress' sums up this lifestyle property development in the Muldersvlei area. Planning of the farm as a whole is in the early stages, and rezoning of some areas is still in process. But priorities are right: wine (made at Boschendal for the time being) is already flowing into shareholders' glasses (commercial bottlings to follow) and the vineyard rejuvenation programme is well underway.

Chenin Blanc ★★★ **05** last ed was robust & big-boned, oxidative style with sweet-ripe peach & prominent alc. Fr barriques, 6 mths. WO Smnsberg-Sbosch. — *IvH*

Stellendrift
T 021-887-6561, 082-372-5180 • F 021-887-6561

Stellenbosch • Est/1stB 1995 • Sales direct & through select retail outlets; also from Vredenheim • Owner Fanie Cilliers (SHZ Cilliers/Kuün Wines) • Winemaker Fanie Cilliers • Viticulturist Fanie Cilliers & Lindsy Cilliers • 20ha (cab, merlot, pinotage, shiraz, chenin , colombard, sauv) • ±5 000cs 90% red 10% white • PO Box 6340 Uniedal 7612 • fcilliers@ vodamail.co.za • www.stellendrift.co.za

'Like my Huguenot forefathers, I get ahead without land or cellar,' says Fanie Cilliers of Stellendrift, now in its 13th year. One of the winemakers at Vredenheim (where he rents cellar space), Fanie C also produces a Cilliers Cellars range 'in a slightly heavier style', and De Oude Opstal, earmarked for blends. Sample them all at Hudson's Coffee Shop at Vredenheim or - by prior appointment - at Fanie C's home.

Stellendrift range

Cabernet Sauvignon ★★★ Previewed **05** ripe, layered with friendly cassis fruit barely restrained by yr Fr oak, smooth tannins & velvety texture. **Klein Vredenburg Merlot** ★★★ Dense **05** (sample) step up from pvs. Ripe dark berries & eucalyptus checked by firm tannins; opulent fruit needs time to emerge. **Pinotage** ★★ Preview **05** rustic, with charry note & big 15.2% alc. **VOC Syrah** NEW ★★★ Spicy pepper & sweet/sour rhubarb fruit on rustic, chunky **05**, tempered by dry, dusty wood-chip treatment. **Merlot-Cabernet Sauvignon Blitz** ★★★ Shy fruitcake aromas with added marzipan nuance on pre-bottling **04**. Firm tannin structure & 14.6% alc balanced by pleasing dark fruit. **Rosasea Special Select Dry Red** ★★ Not retasted. Last ed **03** was affable & undemanding. Mainly cab, slugs pinotage/merlot, 3rd fill Fr oak. **Cape Huguenot Merlot-Pinotage** ★★★ Eucalyptus & mint on **05**'s richly fruited palate; 8 mths barrel maturation integrated with supportive dry tannins. May improve. **Cape White Savour** NEW ★★ Placid, easy-quaffing **07** from tropical-toned sauv.

Cilliers Cellars range

Cabernet Sauvignon ★★★ **03**, with dash merlot, last ed showed attractive ripe berry fruit & firm grip. **Merlot** ★★★ Polished leather on smooth & spicy **05**; dark fruit, dry, dusty tannins. Yr Fr oak.

De Oude Opstal range

Merlot-Cabernet Sauvignon NEW ★★★ Gentle fruitcake & hints marzipan on accessible **04** melded with ripe tannins & supportive oaking (18 mths, 40% new). — MW

StellenHills Wines
T 083-252-2020 • F 021-887-7745

Stellenbosch ▪ Est/1stB 2001 ▪ Visits by appt ▪ Owner/winemaker Johann Slazus ▪ ±700cs 36% red 64% white ▪ PO Box 415 Stellenbosch 7599 ▪ orders@stellenhills.co.za ▪ www. stellenhills.co.za

Ophthalmic surgeon and chardonnay specialist Johann Slazus produces two complementary styles of his chosen variety, plus a dry red.

Charade ★★★★ From shiraz (60%) & cab, yr new Fr oak. **01** soft & plump, plummy, powdery but harmonious tannins; modest 13% alc. **Barriques Nouveau** ★★★★ New Fr barrel fermented/aged chard ex-single Sbosch vyd. Toasty oak on **04**, intense & weighty but gd lively finish. **Chardonnay** ★★★★ Older oak for this (11 mths); vibrant & crisp **04**, melange of orange peel, apple & lemongrass. No newer vintage tasted for this, above. — MM

Stellenrust
T 021-880-2283 • F 021-880-2284, 021-865-2010

Stellenbosch ▪ 1stB 1928 ▪ Tasting, sales & tours Mon-Sat 10-5 ▪ Fee R20 for 7 wines (incl appetisers) ▪ Closed most pub hols ▪ Farm-style platters; or BYO picnic ▪ Grape 'stompings' ▪ Conferences/functions for 200+ ▪ Art gallery ▪ Owner Tertius Boshoff & Kobie van der Westhuizen ▪ Winemaker Tertius Boshoff ▪ Viticulturist Kobie van der Westhuizen ▪ 200ha (cab, merlot, pinotage, shiraz, chard, chenin, sauv) ▪ 1 700t total; 250t/15 000cs own label 70% red 30% white ▪ PO Box 26 Koelenhof 7605 ▪ info@stellenrust.co.za ▪ www.stellenrust. co.za

Not much 'rust' (rest) enjoyed here. Having performed an extreme makeover on the brand, confidence is running high, with a clutch of awards earned last year, a slew of new wines entering the Stellenrust stable, and the imminent relaunch of empowerment label StellCape.

Cabernet Sauvignon NEW ★★★★ A label to watch. Maiden **05** refreshing cranberry acidity enlivening sweet cassis/vanilla-oak palate, combining with grippy tannins to provide attractive dry finish. Open now or keep few yrs. **Shiraz** NEW ★★★★ Debut **05** modest &

unassuming; bright fruit cocooned in polished oak, hint of sweetness on finish courtesy 20% Am oak & dollop RS. 18 mths Fr/Am, 70% new. **Timeless** ★★★★ Tasted last ed, **04** was a showy, dense 60/40 blend with sweet vanilla whiffs; 16 mths Fr oak, mostly new. Much admired by Wine & Spirit Asia judges, WineX show-goers & others over the yrs. **Simplicity** ★★★ **06** appears less refined than much-awarded **05**. Shiraz picked full-ripe to promote jammy flavours, merlot/cab (39/28) earlier to retain natural acidity; mid-2007, the two styles not yet meshed. Still drinkable & wallet-friendly though. **Cabernet Franc Rosé** NEW ★★☆ Cask-fermented pink served in some of SA's leading hotels, rest exported. Brisk, lively, with leafy/meaty nuances. **Chenin Blanc** 🥂 ★★★ Harmonious, food-friendly **07** from venerable bushvines (±40 yrs); small botrytised portion adding luscious honeycomb element to zesty grapefruit flavour. **Sauvignon Blanc** 🥂 ★★★★ Step up for **07**, from 30 yr old bushvines. Blend early/later picked fruit yields more complex, weightier version, brimming with fresh-cut grass, capsicum & melon; persistant blackcurrant finish.

JJ Handmade Wines

Merlot ★★★★ Initially shy, **05** opens up to creamy oak, black plum & liquorice notes; approachable tannins, refreshing acidity provide immediate drinkability. 18 mths Fr oak, 80% new. **Picalot** NEW ★★★★ **05** named for its three components: pinotage, cab, merlot (52/26/22); the former adds lifted acetone notes to cab's stern backbone, merlot's density. 17 mths oak, 80% new. Drink or keep few yrs. Discontinued: **Cabernet Sauvignon**, **Shiraz**. — *CvZ*

■ **Stellenvale** *see* Ultra Liquors

Stellenzicht Vineyards
T 021-880-1103 • **F** 021-880-1107

Stellenbosch ▪ Tasting & sales Mon-Fri 9-5 Sat/Sun & pub hols 10-4 ▪ Fee R25 ▪ Owner Lusan Holdings ▪ Winemaker Guy Webber, with Samantha De Morney-Hughes ▪ Viticulturist Eben Archer ▪ 70% red 30% white ▪ PO Box 104 Stellenbosch 7599 ▪ info@stellenzicht.co.za ▪ www.stellenzicht.co.za

Winemaker Guy Webber's winemaking mantra is 'balance' - between wood, fruit and acid, and between vineyard and cellar. And this has certainly paid off in the Syrah, which was ranked top 10 in the world (and the only SA wine on the list) at the inaugural international Syrah du Monde Awards. This rhône-style wine was made from a single vineyard in the 'Golden Triangle' on the slopes of the Helderberg, known for blockbuster reds and some celebrated whites.

Stellenzicht Vineyards range

★★★★☆ **Syrah** Set Cape shiraz benchmark with standout **94**; subsequent vintages have maintained quality level. **03** offers fynbos highlights to dense black fruits, well supported oak (18 mths mostly Fr). Brooding mid-2007, will travel a decade.

★★★★ **Semillon Reserve** Intensely scented **04** true-toned & focused. Riper style gives waxy complexion to red apple flavours, 9 mths oak adds dimension. Pvs vintages have achieved admirable complexity; this, too, worthy of few yrs aging. **03** (★★★★) somewhat less striking.

Rhapsody ★★★★ **04**, tasted last ed, was intensely fruited, earthy 50/50 combo shiraz & pinotage; 16 mths mainly new oak, Fr/Am/Hung. Discontinued: **Stellenzicht**.

Cellarmaster's Release range

★★★★ **Cabernet Sauvignon 04** tasted pvs ed was well balanced, fruit driven; plushy textured wine with mint, blackcurrant & cedar notes. 100% new Fr oak, 16 mths.

★★★★ **Pinotage** NEW Fine tannins on **05** maiden combine with concentrated blackcurrant & a spicy edge, backbone for gd few yrs ageing courtesy 16 mths new oak.

★★★★ **Shiraz** Tasted pvs ed, **04** was showy & lush, showing forthright oak (mix Fr/Am/Hung), milled pepper & blackberry fruit. Good ageing potential.

Golden Triangle range

Cabernet Sauvignon ★★★☆ Mint, leather & plum on **02**, encased by soft tannins. 15% alc well hidden under ripe fruit, sweet-sour lift in tail more interesting than off-putting. **Merlot** ★★★ Choc-mint-laced **04** packed full of Christmas cake & ripe plums. Serious oaking (21 mths Am/Fr/Hung) shows in hefty tannin grip, slightly bitter farewell. **Pinotage** ★★★☆ Sweet-fruited, perfumed **06**, soft & fleshy, with mild espresso nuance to lively, balanced fruit. Sample reviewed, rating provisional. **Shiraz** ★★★☆ Notch-up **05**'s ripe & powerful pepper-infused mouthful balanced by fresh acidity & fine tannins. 16 mths oak. **Chardonnay** ★★★ Medium gold **04** quite developed mid-2007; citrus fruit overlain with honey bottle-age, acidity softening. Creamy backbone from oak fermentation/ageing & lees contact. Should be enjoyed soon. **Sauvignon Blanc** ★★★ Sample **07** medley of tropical fruits; crisp & fun, with ripe pineapple & melon notes. — *RP*

Sterhuis

T 083 411 0757 • F 021-906-1195

Stellenbosch • Est 1980 • 1stB 2002 • Visits by appt • Closed Christian holidays • Facilities for children • Conservation area • Owner Kruger family • Winemaker Johan Kruger • Viticulturist Hendrik de Beer • 48ha • 300t/6 000cs own label 25% red 75% white • PO Box 131 Koelenhof 7605 • johan@sterhuis.co.za

New stars at this Bottelary Hills winery are the Astra white and red blends which winemaker Johan Kruger calls 'Sterhuis terroir under a magnifying glass'. (Release date of the former unknown at press time.) Blessed with altitude, resulting cooler temperatures mean naturally lower alcohol levels and more elegant wines. But Johan insists that wine quality has as much to do with attitude and hard work as altitude. His motto: There is no easy way from the earth to the stars.

★★★★ **Cabernet Sauvignon** Classic rendition of a classic grape: **05** enticing cedar whiffs, seductive shiny cassis fruit, rippling, gently muscular frame. Classy wine. 18 mths Fr oak, 80% new.

★★★★★ **Sterhuis Astra** Finally, maiden **04** offers trip into orbit (mentioned as 'Red', the wine was unready last ed). Perfumed, packed with ripe brambly fruit & extract, yet balanced by fine structure; even manages 15% alc. Best 5 casks merlot & cab (60/40) selected at 16 mths, blend further matured 6 mths.

★★★★ **Barrel Selection Chardonnay** Generous yet elegant, in house style. **06** developed patina; depth of long all-natural ferment, integrated 100% new Fr oak.

Merlot ★★★★ Quieter than cellar siblings, no less refined. **05** folds fresh red berry fruits into smoked bacon, demurely tensioned finish. Fresh & manageable 13.5% alc. 40% new Fr oak, 16 mths. **Chenin Blanc** ✓ ★★★★ **06** ups ante: beautiful balance between peaches-&-cream girth & lively citrus acidity; lovely length. **05** (★★★☆) marmalade breadth was reined in by brisk acidity. 50% native yeast fermented/6 mths seasoned oak. **Sauvignon Blanc** 🗏 ★★★☆ Fullness of tropical fig & canned pea characters offset by bracing flint in **07**. Moderate 12.6% alc. — *DS*

Stettyn Winery

T 023-340-4220/4101 • F 023-340-4220/4101

Worcester • Est 1964 • 1stB ca 1984 • Tasting Mon-Fri 8-5 Sat 10-1 • Closed pub hols • Tours by appt • BYO picnic • Owner 4 major producers • Winemaker Albie Treurnicht (Nov 2000) • Viticulturist Pierre Snyman (VinPro consultant) • 310ha (12 varieties r/w) • ±6 000t/3 000cs own label + 4.7m litres bulk • 20% red 80% white • Export brand: FirstCape • PO Box 1520 Worcester 6849 • stettyncellar@breede.co.za • www.stettyncellar.co.za

It's all systems go, with volumes up by 30% in 2007. Besides feeding the insatiable FirstCape (still the fastest-growing SA brand in the UK), Albie Treurnicht is planting more pinot, a variety rare in the area, and hoping to harvest the first petit verdot and nouvelle this year.

Signature Reserve range

Cabernet Sauvignon ✓ ★★★☆ Attractive oak integration in **05**, with cellar's signature warm fruit, ripe tannins; 15% shiraz rounds out profile.   **Shiraz** NEW ★★ **05** soft & ripe, heading towards porty but freshened by 15% ex-**07** vintage. **Vin de Paille** ★★★ 3-vintage blend to imitate solera style. Air-dried muscat d'A; botrytis whiff enlivening marmalade & apricot richness. 2 yrs Fr/Am oak. 15% alc. 375ml, **NV**. Not retasted. Discontinued: **Chardonnay.**

Millstone range

Chenin Blanc ☺ 🗎 ★★★ Off 26 yr old vyd. Fresh-flavoured, tangy **07** suggests baked apples sprinkled with spice. Also in 3-litre 'fridgepack'. **Sauvignon Blanc** ☺ 🗎 ★★★ **07** dry quaffer with grassy notes & some style.

Merlot NEW 🗎 ★★ Easy-drinking **07**, everyday red rounded by dashes pinotage & shiraz. Discontinued: **Pinotage.** *— IvH*

▨ **Steytler** *see* Kaapzicht Estate

▨ **Stoep** *see* Main Street Winery

Stonehill
T 073-420-3300 • F 021-865-2740

Stellenbosch • Est 1990 • 1stB 2003 • Open by appt • Winemaker Mark Carmichael-Green • Viticulturist Lorna Hughes • 3.2 ha (cab, shiraz) • 100% red • PO Box 612 Stellenbosch 7599 • llhughes@telkomsa.net

Friday afternoons are for sundowners at the new Stonehill tasting room. Also new are a formalised partnership between Dave and Lorna Hughes (DH a taster for this guide), and winemaker Mark Carmichael-Green, called Bristle Wines; a name-change for the Cab (untasted this edition) from Yardstick to 4 Barrels -the former reminded Dave H too much of his parade-ground sergeant major; and a website. They're also rejuvenating a small block of 30-year-old shiraz.

Bristle Red ★★★★ Equal blend of gnarled-vine shiraz & younger cab. **05** last ed had savoury & spicy smoked meat flavours; gd structure & well integrated wood. **Dry Cabernet Sauvignon Rosé** 🗎 ★★★ Vivacious strawberry glints on **07**, soft & savoury with seasoned oak backing. Fleshy, a touch of sweetness carrying a long finish. *— RP*

Stonewall Wines
T 021-855-3675 • F 021-855-2206

Stellenbosch (see Helderberg map) • Est 1828 • 1stB 1997 • Visits by appt Mon-Fri 9-5 Sat 9-1 • Closed Easter Fri/Sun, Dec 25/26 & Jan 1 • Conferencing • Owner De Waal Koch • Viticulturist De Waal Koch • Vini consultant Ronell Wiid (May 2000) • 75ha (cabs s/f, merlot, pinotage, shiraz, chard, sauv) • 2 500cs own label 90% red 10% white • PO Box 5145 Helderberg 7135 • stonewall@mweb.co.za

A harvest with phenolic ripeness reached at lower sugars left De Waal Koch delighted and trying to decide on a name for his new fortified merlot. That's if there's any left - this experiment turned out so well he's afraid he may taste the whole barrel before bottling it!

★★★★ **Cabernet Sauvignon** Authoritative cab; ripe mulberry & cedar invite to **05**, follows onto palate with the variety's firmer tannins adding texture, dryness. Excellent typicity. 18 mths Fr oak, 80% new.

★★★★ **Rubér** Bdx blend cab/merlot, 50/50 in **05**; gorgeous cassis & lead pencils, densely fruity, lovely concentration dark-berried fruit, firm tannic grip. Needs & deserves time, say 3 yrs before opening. 50% new oak.

Chardonnay ★★★ **06** similarly soft & approachable to pvs. Tropical tones, slight sweetness on finish (4.6g/l RS). Oak fermented/aged 6 mths, 50% new. *— IvH*

Stoney Croft
T 021-865-2360 • F 021-865-2360

Stellenbosch • Est 2000 • 1stB 2001 • Visits by appt • Owner Excelebrate (Pty) Ltd • Winemaker Danie Steytler, with Charl Coetzee (Jan 2001/Mar 2003, Kaapzicht) • Viticulturist See intro • 3ha (shiraz) • 25t/2 000cs 100% red • PO Box 239 Koelenhof 7605 • margie@ excelebrate.co.za • www.frontierlifestyle.co.za/stoneycroft.htm

Stoney Croft's vineyard is maintained by a private viticulture company, and harvests 05 to **07** are still in barrel. 'They're works of art in progress,' says Margie Stone. The **04**, however, has now been released. The cellar's marketing focus remains the US.

★★★★★ **Shiraz** Well-extracted **04**, interesting & complex array of cedar, blackberry & earthiness; ripe, full-bodied, abundant berry, tobacco, spice flavours, seamlessly integrated oak, long rich finish. Yr Fr oak, 35% new. Back to superlative form of **01**, after blip in **03** (★★★). — *IM*

Stony Brook
T 021-876-2182 • F 021-876-2182

Franschhoek • Est 1995 • 1stB 1996 • Tasting & sales Sep-Mar: Mon-Fri 10-3 Sat 10-1; Apr-Aug Mon-Sat 10-1 or by appt • Closed Easter Fri/Sun/Mon, Dec 25/26, Jan 1 • Fee R20 (refunded on purchase of 6 btls/taster) • Owner Nigel & Joy McNaught • Winemaker Nigel McNaught • Viticulturist Paul Wallace (consultant) • 14ha • 80t/5 500cs 60% red 40% white • ISO 14001 certified • PO Box 22 Franschhoek 7690 • mcnaught@iafrica.com / info@ stonybrook.co.za • www.stonybrook.co.za

In an eventful year, the New York Times published a complimentary article that brought many American visitors to Stony Brook, and heavy winter rains cut off the house from the village. The new bordeaux blend is named 'The Max' after the McNaughts' Jack Russell, who has, says Joy McN, 'plenty of attitude'.

Stony Brook Reserve range

★★★★ **Cabernet Sauvignon** Greenpepper toned, serious & finely tuned **04** introverted & tight mid-2007, revealing only densley packed black fruits & taut tannic frame, but will repay patience.

★★★★★ **Syrah** 'Shiraz' pvs ed. Silky, long & serious **04** crammed with pure brambleberry & cracked pepper; elegant yet sumptuous with great flavour depth in a fresh, mid-weight package. Seasoned Fr oak; incl dollop mourvèdre. Similar to exceptionally concentred **02**, & notch up on earthy **03** (★★★★).

★★★★ **The Max** NEW 50/50 cab/merlot in **04**, delivering potently rich fennel-tinged fruit. Choc, plums & spice all in the mix, concluding with dry tannic flourish. Great now, excellent potential too.

★★★★ **SMV** NEW Shiraz, mourvèdre & viognier in appealing liquorice & bacon accented blend. House's Old-World savouriness evident here, plus sweet berry fruit & a lift from 12% co-fermented viognier.

★★★★ **Whispering Widow** NEW Flavourome & unusual **04** blend malbec/mourvèdre (60/40). Chewy tannins & lively acids underpin super-savoury, velvety cherry-berry fruit. Oodles of enjoyment, & much more outgoing than name suggests.

★★★★ **Semillon** NEW Lime & jasmine scented **06**, 100% new oak adds power though lively acidity mainains balance. Clean, neat, with waxy texture, ultra-persistent. Potential to age interestingly. Only 250cs.

Stony Brook range

★★★★★ **Ghost Gum** Ethereal cab with smidgen merlot & petit v. **04** matches class of **03** with classic cassis & pencil shavings, lovely fresh fruit layered with minerals. Fine crumbly tannins & fleshy core show super ageing potential. 100% new Fr oak.

★★★★ **V on A** NEW Gorgeous Natural Sweet style dessert from viognier; **06** brilliant glints, billowing peach & apricot with floral undertone. 100% new oak soaked up by intense, opulent fruit. Well controlled sugar, tastes almost dry. EW.

Cabernet Sauvignon 03 last ed flavours & dark-berried fruit all present & correct, as were strong tannins which might since have relented somewhat. 20 mths mixed oak. **Merlot** In abeyance while vyds are replanted. **Shiraz ★★★** Rhône styling with black fruit core secondary to dry savoury tannins. Hints farmyard & meat on **04**, mid-weight, tad short. **Camissa ★★★★** 62% merlot, rest cab & shiraz in **04**. Earth, prunes & leather in succulent mouthful, deep & classy. Firm acidity leads to dry tannic finish. Right profile for venison. **Rosé 🗎 ★★★** Dry rosé from cab & merlot (55/45); **06** last ed showed a buffed copper colour, sultry berry flavours in tangy tail. **Chardonnay ★★★★** Refined **04**'s delicate peach aromas last ed lead to firm, juicy, satisfying flavours. Bunch-pressed, fermented/4 mths oak. **Sauvignon Blanc 🗎 ★★★★** Perfumed **06** shows unusual yellow fruits, cool minerals & steely backbone. Well balanced & seamless. **Semillon ★★★★** Spicy vanilla & citrus on **06**. 60% new oak adds chunkiness to soft, pleasing lime finish. Not quite as exciting as **05** (★★★★), with deep flavour folded into waxy texture. Mostly Fr wood with Am & Hngrian. Some native yeasts. **Annie's Wine ★★★** Uncertified NLH-style dessert; Last was **02**, 80% sauv plus semillon. Orange marmalade character; lightly textured, doesn't cloy. 2 yrs new Fr oak — *RP*

Stormhoek

T 021-864-3155; +44-020-7802-5415 • **F** 021-864-1744; +44-020-7976-5376

Est 2003 • Visits by appt only • Owner SA and UK partnershhip • Cellarmaster Koos Bosman • Vineyard Manager Melvin Brown • 1209 Wellington South Africa 7654 • graham@stormhoek.co.za • http://www.stormhoek.com

Another year of superlatives for this Wellington upstart, as famous for its successful new-media-based advertising campaigns as its affordable, freshness-touting wines. An enviably long and varied list of awards and landmarks includes the IWSC trophy for best Pinotage; a rise to 1 million hits per day for the Stormhoek blog and associated websites; and a 50 Top award from the American Marketer's Association, placing Stormhoek in company of Apple, Sony and Disney. Sales in US, UK and Europe will be boosted by Orbital Wines' experienced new MD Mike Paul (ex-Kumala). The local team is equally upbeat about their new mourvèdre blend and viognier, embodying a 'fine wine at a good price' philosophy.

★★★★ **The Terraces Cabernet Sauvignon** NEW **04** has choc-mocha & cigarbox appeal; juicy & long, needs yr+ for fruit & oak tannins to knit, complement ripe cassis flavour. 24 mths Fr oak, 25% new. WO Wllgtn.

★★★★ **The Guava Pinotage** NEW Judiciously oaked **04** shows considerable complexity & poise. True-to-variety aroma of raspberry & hint acetone joined by nuts & cardamom, measured oak tannins rein in plush palate; 14.5% alc, 24 mths oak (30% new Am/10% new Fr/older Fr).

Cabernet Sauvignon 🗎 ★★★ Decent easy-drinker, **05** modest cassis fruit, hints oakspice & lemony acidity. Fermented with staves. **The Terraces Merlot** NEW **★★★★** Dark **04** a melange berries & fynbos, rounded & sustained; a complete if not overly complex wine. Fruit intensity obscures 14.5% alc, oak as for Cab. **Pinotage 🗎 ★★★** Pale-ish cherry hue, raspberry/tea leaf nose, ripe flavours; **06** not overly complex, has burly tannic grip. Fermented/5 mths on staves. 14.5% alc. Plummy **05** took 2006 IWSC trophy for variety. **Shiraz ★★★** Supple & persistent **06** from ripe Paarl fruit; friendly tannins, berry jam fruit. Oak staved. **Cabernet Sauvignon-Shiraz ★★★★** None since **03**, with blackcurrant, measured fruit/acid verve & aged portion (±8 mths, 20% new). **The Storm Mourvèdre-Shiraz** NEW 🗎 **★★★★** **06**'s 60% mourvèdre from Darling, 40% shiraz from Wllngtn. Big & forthright but supple tannin, lush fruit, scrubby whiffs. Oak staved. **Pinotage Rosé 🗎 ★★★** **07** leaner, drier, tad more alcoholic (13%) than stablemate; pleasant, soft-fruited al fresco tipple. From pinotage. **Couture Rosé on Ice** NEW 🗎 **★★★** Intense, full-throttle pink from cab, inspired by Graham K's wife who always adds ice to rosé. Maiden **07** brims with boiled sweets, lots of sugar (29.8g/l) but less alc (12%); serve chilled or over ice, like Di. **The Mountainside Chenin Blanc** NEW 🗎 **★★★★** **04** bold debut: while oak detail is enticing on bouquet, it's more powerful on palate; doesn't overwhelm juicy fruit but suggests a short spell in bottle will benefit evolution. Persistent if slightly warming (15% alc) farewell. **Pinot Grigio 🗎 ★★★** **06** step up; relatively slender (12.5% alc) but well formed nut, fennel & pear tones, dense fruit core; a lovely food wine.

. **Sauvignon Blanc** 🔳 ★★★ **07**, balanced, light-tripping (12% alc), also lightly flavoured (hints freshly cut grass & gooseberry) but charming. All WO W Cape, unless stated. **16-Barrel Semillon** 🔳 ★★★★ Characterful oaked version; tasted pvs ed, **05**'s lanolin/litchi combo brushed by sultry oak. 14.5% alc. Grapes off 35 yr old Wllngtn vyd; Fr barrels 8 mths, 50% new. **Viognier** NEW 🔳 ★★★★ **06** welcome addition to growing line-up a single-variety bottlings in SA. Broad without being flabby, pear, apricot & rose nuances. Half barrel fermented/6 mths, 10% new oak. Discontinued: **16-Barrel Chenin Blanc**, **African Storm Chenin Blanc**. — *CvZ*

■ **Stormy Cape** *see* Thelema Mountain Vineyards

Stoumann's Wines

T 027-213-2323 • F 027-213-2323

Vredendal (see Olifants River map) • Est 1997 • 1stB 1998 • Tasting & sales Mon-Fri 8-12; 2-5 Sat 9-11 • Fee R10 • Closed Easter Fri-Mon, Dec 25 & Jan 1 • Owner/winemaker/viticulturist Napoleon Stoumann • 112ha (cab, merlot, shiraz) • 8t 98% red 2% white • PO Box 307 Vredendal 8160 • stoumanns@kingsley.co.za

Napoleon Stoumann says bottling two Muscadels and a Hanepoot has little to do with developing a latent sweet tooth, and everything to do with 2007's top-quality grapes. The same holds for the range (untasted this ed), all still featuring the tortoise emblem - inspired by the 15 critters, now legal pets, saved when these virgin soils were first carved for vines.

Strandveld Vineyards

T 028-482-1902/6 • F 028-482-1902/6

Elim (see Southern Cape map) • Est 2002 • 1stB 2003 • Tasting & sales Mon-Fri 8-5 • BYO picnic • 2 self-catering guest cottages • Tours by appt • Tour groups by arrangement • Walks • Owner Strandveld Vineyards & Rietfontein Trust • Winemaker Conrad Vlok (Dec 2004) • Viticulturist Andrew Teubes (consultant) • 67ha (pinot, shiraz, chard, sauv, semillon) • 120t/8 600cs 45% red 55% white • PO Box 1020 Bredasdorp 7280 • sales@firstsighting.com • www.firstsighting.co.za

Formerly Agulhas Wines, Strandveld is now 'more proudly wine originating from the Elim ward and 100% from vines on the Albertyns' Uintjieskuil farm and Strandveld Vineyards', says winemaker Conrad Vlok. A Pinot debuts under the First Sighting label, and the flagship Strandveld label will soon include a wooded Sauvignon-Semillon and Shiraz-Viognier. Ever-maturing vines promise a capacity 350-ton harvest in 2009. All this only if local sea god Adamastor continues to guard over these maritime vineyards in one of SA's coolest winegrowing areas.

Strandveld Vineyards range NEW

★★★★ **Sauvignon Blanc** More sophisticated, intense of these sauvs. **07** full bodied, with touch of 'fumé' to its keen steely drive & mineral freshness. Ideal with area's fruits of the sea.

Shiraz 06 held over till next yr. **Adamastor 07** Fr oak fermented & matured blend sauv/sem not ready for tasting.

First Sighting range

Pinot Noir NEW ★★★★ **06** charms with limpid hues, purity of sweet fruit & supple, gentle mouthfeel. Wooding tad generous but pleasurable short-term drinking. Fr oak, 11 mths. **Shiraz** ★★★ Last yr **04** was full bodied but elegant; fruit mainly ex-Darling. No **05**; **06** unready. **Chardonnay** 🔳 ★★★ **05** unwooded version last ed offered generous, creamy pineapple & grapefruit zest flavours. **06** nearly sold out at press time; no **07**. **Sauvignon Blanc** 🔳 ★★★★ Cool-climate precision on inviting **07**. Medium body, firmly dry persistence makes for refreshing drinking; 8% sem adds breadth. Standout **06** (★★★★) had elegant 'sauvage' flavours. — *AL*

■ **Strata Series** *see* Flagstone Winery
■ *Sugar Bush Ridge* *see* Dominion Wine Company
■ *Suikerbosch* *see* Zidela Wines

Sumaridge Wines

T 028-312-1097 · F 028-312-2824

Hemel-en-Aarde Valley (see Elgin/Walker Bay map) · 1stB 2001 · Tasting & sales daily 10-3 · Fee R10 · Closed Easter Fri/Sun & Dec 25 · Light lunches daily 12-2.30 · Self-catering guest house (up to 6 people) · Conferencing · Walks · Owner Brenda Harcourt-Cook · Winemaker/ viticulturist Gavin Patterson · ±25ha (merlot, pinot, pinotage, shiraz, chard, sauv) · 120t/6 000cs own label 50% white 40% red 10% rosé · PO Box 1413 Hermanus 7200 · sumaridge@ itec.co.za · www.sumaridge.co.za

Previously marketed as a family destination with its lovely little restaurant, Sumaridge is repositioning itself with facilities for functions, and the restaurant is undergoing an upgrade with this in mind. There's revitalisation in the vineyards too, with new sauvignon, semillon, chardonnay and pinot to bolster older plantings.

- ★★★★ **Merlot 04**, tasted pvsly, achieved spicy richness & power at moderate alc (13.6%). 15 mths Fr oak, 40% new.
- ★★★★ **Syrah** Red fruit & pepper on juicy, tangy **05**. Firm tannins, understated cool-climate fruit waiting in the wings.
- ★★★★☆ **Chardonnay** Bold New-World style with attitude. **06** (★★★★), now bottled, rich buttered toast & marmalade, mineral notes & limy core. Full bodied, with succulence & zesty acidity. Standout **05** heralded new confidence & seriousness for this label.
- ★★★★ **Sauvignon Blanc** 🗎 Complex, classy sauv with clean, zesty grapefruit appeal; **07** dusty minerality & fig leaf tingle, refreshing acidity & sustained farewell. Back on form after **06** (★★★★), valiant effort from wind-reduced crop.

Pinot Noir ★★ Restrained, nervous **06** with sweet/sour red fruit & gripping dry tannins. **Pinotage** ★★ **06** edgy, leaner than **05** (which flew with SAA), smoky notes, tart mulberry flavours. **Dry Rosé** 🗎 ★★ From merlot; **07** herbaceous, fresh light style in pleasing cerise shade. — *MW*

- ■ **Sunny Day** *see Lutzville Cape Diamond Vineyards*
- ■ **Swallow** *see Natte Valleij*
- ■ **Swartberg Reserve** *see Kango Winery*

Swartland Winery

T 022-482-1134/5/6 · F 022-482-1750

Swartland · Est 1948 · Tasting & sales Mon-Fri 8-5 Sat 9-2 · Closed Mar 21, Easter Fri/Sun, Dec 25/26 & Jan 1 · Tours during tasting hours by appt · BYO picnic · Play area for children · Tour groups · Gifts · Farm produce · Conferences · Owner 60 producers · Cellarmaster Andries Blake · Winemaker Andries Eygelaar, Sean Nieuwoudt & Corrien Geleijnse · Viticulturist Klaas Coetzee (Jun 2006) · 3 200 ha (cab, merlot, pinotage, shiraz, tinta, chenin, chard, sauvignon) · 21 000 tons · 47% red 50% white 3% rosé · BRC, ISO 9001 & WIETA certified, IFS & SANS in progress · PO Box 95 Malmesbury 7299 · mkotze@swwines.co.za · www.swwines.co.za

Once a low-key co-op, this young public company's production has doubled over the past two years, leaving cellarmaster and keen angler Andries Blake little time to hang out the 'Gone fishing' sign. Exports increased by 60% to meet the challenge of supplying US wine giant E&J Gallo with a typically SA range under their Sebeka label. Responsibilities at home are, however, not forgotten: A portion of the proceeds of the Swartland Reserve (known overseas as Eagle Crest) goes to the Aquila Eagle Crest Conservation Fund, which focuses on the conservation of Black Eagles and other raptors.

Idelia range

Idelia ★★★☆ Enticing aromas on this seriously put together blend cab, shiraz, pinotage, with integrated oak & gd structure supporting sweet-fruited charm. A little hot from 14.5% alc, but clearly best of the lot here, pushing higher rating.

Indalo range

Cabernet Sauvignon ★★★★ Fresh, ripe, lightly fruity & spicy pleasantness, with smooth tannins. Like other reds here, big (14.5-ish % alc), well & harmoniously oaked (20% new). **Pinotage** ★★★ Attractive, forthright fruit aromas, but mix of alc power, robust tannin & quick-finishing lightweight fruit not entirely satisfactory. **Shiraz** ★★★ Very ripe aromas boiled sweets, herbs. Sweetly oaky palate (20% new barriques), decently built but not huge substance, warm finish. **Chenin Blanc** ★★★★ Promising 07 sample: well balanced, with some savoury richness complemented by gd oaking. **Sauvignon Blanc** ★★ Atypical ripe white plum character; **07** fresh & (oddly) flavourful.

Reserve range

Cabernet Sauvignon-Merlot ★★★ Dusty, light fruit & respectable structure give pleasant drinking. **06** modestly wooded, like next. **Shiraz-Cabernet Sauvignon** ✓ ★★★★ Rustic & satisfying, tasty & chewy, with savoury-sweet fruit, firm structure; **06** balanced except for hot high-alc finish. **Chenin Blanc-Sauvignon Blanc-Chardonnay** NEW ★★★ Successful, flavoursome blend, **07** with tropical & peach tones & zesty mildness. A little useful wooding. EW. Discontinued: **Chenin Blanc**, **Chenin Blanc-Chardonnay**. Known as 'Eagle Crest' in overseas markets.

Swartland range

Merlot ☺ ★★★ Juicy fresh cherries & plums, **06** with a little tannin to keep it well through the yr. **Shiraz** ☺ ★★★ Spicy elegance & pleasing herbaceous twist, **06** nicely balanced & firm. **Shiraz-Malbec** ☺ ★★★ Lovely party wine: **06** delicious sweet-edged juiciness, mildly structured, with minuscule oak influence. **Chardonnay** ☺ ★★★ Offers mild peach & citrus, well balanced acidity like most of these. **07** gd quaffer. **Chenin Blanc** ☺ ★★★ Easy-going, modestly flavourful, fresh & evanescent **07**. **Hanepoot** ☺ ★★★ Scented grapey aromas, deliciously sweet, lingering fortified, but lacking some bite. **NV**.

Cabernet Sauvignon ★★★ Ripe, baked aromas, savoury & mouthfilling, **06** with slightly tough core. These reds unwooded. **Pinotage** ★★ **06** rather grubby character, awkward dry tannins. **Tinta Barocca** ★★★ Port-like Christmas cake aromas; **06** sweet, quickly disappearing fruit, chunky dry tannin. **Dry Red** ★★ Ripely pleasant all-sorts red; not too trivial. **NV. Blanc de Noir** ★★★ Like other pink, from pinotage, with berry notes. **07** off-dry & fruitily tasty. **Rosé** ★★ Full, sweet (40g/l sugar) charm. **NV. Bukettraube** ★ 07 modest 12% alc, low flavour, high sugar. **Fernão Pires/Light** ★ Light but not quite dry; few other virtues. **NV. Sauvignon Blanc** ★★★ Mixes grass & tropicality; **07** green, crisp & dry. **Premier Grand Cru** ★★ Usual mildly fruity bone-dryness. **NV. Red Jerepiko** ✓ ★★★★ Latest **NV**, mostly from pinotage, bursting with undeniably delicious fruit pastille aromas/flavours, decently balanced & fresh. **White Jerepiko** ★★ Sweetly spiritous & soft. **NV. Port** ★★ Now vintaged, mostly ultra-ripe shiraz plus tinta. **06** nice enough but soft-centred. **Vintage Port** ★★★ From touriga (70%) & tinta, with gd fruitcake notes & just a touch too fiery - though only 17% alc; **05** satisfyingly dry conclusion. Discontinued: **Cabernet Sauvignon-Merlot**.

Sparkling range

Cuvée Brut ★★★ Customary apples-&-pears dryish bubbly from sauv. **Demi Sec** ★★ No party-pooper, this, especially for the sweeter-toothed. From buket. Both budget-priced carbonated sparklers are **NV**.

D'Vine range

Untasted this ed; 500ml; 750-litre glass, 2, 3 & 5-litre casks, all **NV**. Dry Red, Rosé, Dry White, Johannisberger/Semi Sweet & Light.

Cask range

2, 3 & 5-litre packs not reviewed; Shiraz-Cabernet, Grand Cru, Blanc de Blanc, Stein & Late Harvest, all **NV**. — *TJ*

■ **Sweetwell** *see* Terroir Wines of SA

Sylvanvale Vineyards
T 021-865-2012 • F 021-865-2610

Stellenbosch • Est 1997 • 1stB 1998 • Tasting & sales daily 11–7 • Fee R15 refundable with any purchase • Open pub hols • Tours by appt • Flavours Restaurant, Vineyard Terrace & Cedarwood Lounge (see Eat-out section) • Luxury 38-room Devon Valley Hotel (see Stay-over section) • Conferences • Tour groups • Play area for children • Walks • Owner LGI Hotels & Vineyards • Winemaker Mark Carmichael-Green (2002) • Viticulturist Lorna Hughes (1997) • 10ha • 4 600cs 80% red 10% white 10% rosé • PO Box 68 Stellenbosch 7599 • info@ sylvanvale.com • www.sylvanvale.co.za

The SylvanVale vineyards surround well-known Stellenbosch landmark, Devon Valley Hotel, which has been totally transformed over the past few years and now richly deserves its 2nd successive Great Wine Capitals Best of Wine Tourism accommodation award. The unirrigated south-east-facing vines provide a range of characterful wines for the hotel's tables and other local restaurants.

★★★★ **Pinotage** Wild herb & mint overtones characterise these. **04** (★★★★) quite opulent though variety's insistent tannin/nip of bitterness evident on finish last ed. Yr Fr wood, 70% new. Notch down on **03**, with unblemished fruity lushness & fine tannin. Above vintages inadvertently listed as 'Pinotage Reserve' last ed.

★★★★ **Pinotage Reserve** Still-available **02** pvsly noted as encapsulating the essence of pinotage: smoky mulberry bouquet, mouthcoating flavour packed with sweet berries, tannins & extract.

> **Dry Cabernet Sauvignon Rosé** ☺ ★★★ **06** now bottled, shows distinct bottle-age on nose, palate more lively, dry. Invites food.

Cabernet Sauvignon ★★★ Uncomplicated & approachable **04**; last ed offered nicely harmonised fruit/oak, well-managed tannin, simple yet tasty sweet mulberry/strawberry flavours. Fr oaked, 75% new. **Ghost Tree Pinotage** NEW ★★ Really dry & austere **05**, tannins awkward, gravelly finish. **Vine Dried Pinotage** In abeyance. **Ghost Tree Shiraz** NEW ★★★ **06** amiable, sweet-natured version, well-rounded personality backed by soft-ish tannins, nice dryness on finish. 40% oaked 2nd fill Fr. **Shiraz** NEW ★★★ **05** unshowy sweet red cherry fruit with eucalytus hint, pliant tannins, new Fr oak (40%) an understated backdrop. **Devon Valley Cape Blend** ★★★ Pinotage-led **04** pvs ed had house's wild herb/mint thumbprint; cab, shiraz (57/29/14) added extra spice & flesh. Harmonised by yr 100% new Fr oak. **Devon Valley Red** Current **04** untasted. **Ghost Tree Rosé** ★★★ For the sweeter-toothed. **05** generous ripe straw/raspberry tones; pleasant, if tad short on verve. Cab with chenin. **Old Vine Chenin Blanc** NEW ★★★ Gentle pear note on **07**, still very young & unformed, bone-dry, softish acidity but balanced. Needs time. 40% oak fermented, from 39 yr old vyd, one of oldest in Sbosch. **Jewel of the Valley** Sold out. All from Devon Vlly vyds. — *IvH*

■ **Table Bay** *see Ultra Liquors*

Table Mountain

Distell range celebrating 'SA's icon and welcoming symbol of Africa'. Ready-on-release, from selected Western Cape vineyards.

> **Chenin Blanc** ☺ ★★★ **07** zesty Granny Smith flavours & acidity enliven slightly plumper version than pvs; lowish 12.4% alc.

Cabernet Sauvignon ★★★ **06** fruit-driven, with spicy cassis & mocha notes; balanced, approachable & food friendly. **Merlot** ★★★ Warming, savoury **06**; dark fruits & mocha/choc; hint sweetness masks fairly robust tannins. **Chardonnay** ★★★ **05** last ed offered peach & tangerine aromas/flavours, complemented by careful oaking & brisk acidity. **Sauvignon**

Blanc ★★★ **07** pleasing varietal flavours of fig & nettle, ripe tropical flourish & hint of sweetness balanced by bright acidity. Enjoy young. — *MW*

■ **Talana Hill**   *see* Vriesenhof Vineyards

Tall Horse

DGB's 'critter brand', featuring a stylised giraffe in its colourful and awarded packaging. **Cabernet Sauvignon** ★★ Flattering dollops sugar a feature throughout this range; in **05**, the sweetness is balanced by flick tannin. **Merlot** ★★★ **05** mocha notes, dark choc, tad more serious than pvs. **Shiraz** ★★ **05** benefits from touch more austerity than unctuous **04**. **Pinotage Rosé** NEW ★★ Fruity, juicy **07**, picnic wine in typical easy style. **Chardonnay** ★★ Quaffability continues in **07**, fresh fruit salad flavours, easy summer drinking. **Sauvignon blanc** NEW ★★ **07** light, grassy, carefree fruity tipple. — *DB*

■ **Tamboerskloof**   *see* Kleinood

Tanagra Private Cellar

T 023-625-1780 • F 023-625-1847

McGregor (see Robertson map) ▪ Est 2000 ▪ Tasting & sales daily 10-4.30 ▪ Closed Dec 25 & Jan 1 ▪ BYO picnic ▪ Facilities for children ▪ Walks ▪ Conservation area ▪ Owner Christoph Reinhold & Felicia von der Schulenburg ▪ PO Box 92 McGregor 6708 ▪ tanagra@lando.co.za

The Reinhold/von der Schulenburg self-avowed 'family circus' has moved upcountry, where architect husband Christoph R is readying the Mpumalanga Stadium for the 2010 Soccer World Cup. Far from sliding into abeyance, winemaking is blooming at the McGregor farm under the aegis of new managers Alan and Cynthia Blain, who cheerfully remind email recipients that 'your GP recommends one or two glasses of red wine per day. Ours is all natural, unfiltered and quite heavenly'.

Felicity ★★ **06** ripe bdx blend, saturated sweet fruit, malt & oak flavours/textures. **Chardonnay** ★★ Flashy, oaky **07**, robust & spiritous (15% alc) with marked sweetness from 10g/l sugar. — *CvZ*

Tanzanite Wines   NEW
T 023-342-3529 • F 023-347-3895

Worcester ▪ Est 2006 ▪ Tasting by appt Mon-Sat (no pub hols) ▪ Owner Wentzel & Melanie van der Merwe ▪ Cellarmaster/winemaker Melanie van der Merwe (2006) ▪ 20-30t/600-1 200cs 100% MCC ▪ PO Box 5102 Worcester 6850 ▪ melanie.vdm@lando.co.za ▪ www. tanzanitewines.co.za

After 11 sparkling vintages at The House of JC le Roux, Melanie van der Merwe is creating her own cap classique. 'Small quantities made in the time-honoured, traditional way.' Tanzanite is her birthstone: 'It has all the qualities I want in my wine - rare, beautiful, delicate, high quality and highly sought after.'

Méthode Cap Classique ★★★★ Maiden chard (90%), pinot blend offers restrained mousse & brioche complexity, pleasant lemon freshness with lime juice finish. **NV**. — *IM*

■ **Tara Hill**   *see* Southern Sky Wines
■ **Tarentaal**   *see* Assegai Selection
■ **Tarentaal Farm**   *see* Terroir Wines of SA

Tassenberg

Enduring dry red affectionately known as 'Tassies'. Launched 1936, blend has varied over the years but not the affable persona. By Distell.

Tassenberg 🔲 ★★ Latest **NV** cheery cab/cinsaut mix, unoaked, with supple plummy flavours, moderate 12.5 % alc. Also in 5-litre packs. — *MW*

Taverna Rouge

Big-selling, off-dry (8g/l sugar), budget-priced red blend from Distell.

Taverna Rouge 🔲 ★☆ Latest **NV** cherry bouquet & flavours, bright acid & affable 12% alc. Also in 2 litres. — *MW*

Teddy Hall Wines
T 021-852-1380 • F 021 852 1380

Owner Rudera Wines • Cellarmaster/winemaker/viticulturist Teddy Hall • PO Box 2868 Somerset West 7129 • info@rudera.co.za • www.teddyhall.co.za

Acclaimed chenin exponent Teddy Hall vinifies a variety of top-end versions for his own Rudera brand (see separate entry) and for clients. The release below, under an eponymous label (and screwcap) is the one you'd most often find on Hall's table, accompanying lunch in the garden.

Chenin Blanc ✓ ★★★★ Always tasty but even better in **07**, a green-hued melon & lemongrass delight, crammed with tangy freshness. — *CR*

■ **Tembana Valley** *see Rooiberg Winery*

Tempel Wines
T 021-557-7312 • F 021-872-3883

Paarl • Est 2000 • 1stB 2003 • Closed to public • Owner Tuan Marais • Winemaker Neil Schnoor (2000, consultant) • Viticulturist DeWet Theron (2000, consultant) • 3ha (pinotage) • 11.8t/700cs 100% red • PO Box 7295 Noorder-Paarl 7623 • tempelwines@lantic.net • www.tempelwines.co.za

When Tuan Marais bought De Jooden Tempel on the Berg riverbanks in 1990, neither he nor the property had winemaking pedigree. But the history of the farm (early Jewish traders used it for religious purposes), the prospect of establishing tax-deductible vines, and consumer demand encouraged Marais to make SA's (and probably the world's) first kosher pinotage. A series of quality bottlings have helped elevate the reputation of kosher wine in general.

Pinotage ★★★★ MIWA gold for **04**, last ed noted as fruity, with red/black pastille succulence, firmly dry conclusion. Sympathetically oaked: 8 mths Fr, some new. — *CR*

■ **Terra del Capo** *see L'Ormarins Private Cellar*

Terroir Wines of SA
T 082-825-9001/ 082-452-7263 • F 021-842-2373

Stellenbosch • Est 2002 • 1stB 2003 • Closed to public • Owner/viticulturist Inus Muller & Bennie Diedericks • Winemaker Inus Muller (2002) • 8t/600cs 100% red • PO Box 5435 Helderberg 7135 • inusmuller@absamail.co.za

This is a one-stop winegrowing advisory service owned and run by Inus Muller and Bennie Diedericks, providing assistance to a new generation of artisan winemakers. Clients include Kelsey Farm, Kuikenvlei, Leeurivier Wines & Olives, Paul Wallace Wines, Romond, Sweetwell and Tarentaal Farm, some listed separately. Muller and Diedericks also make small quantities of wine for their own account under the brand name Karmosyn.

Karmosyn Cabernet Sauvignon NEW ★☆ **04** jammy & rather funky, with mouthdrying tannic finish. **Sweetwell Cabernet Sauvignon** ★★★ Cab's classic cassis/herbaceous notes on **04**, with fresh but somewhat dilute flavours, & integrated oak. **JWL Shiraz** ★★★ Last tasted **03**, ex-Hldrberg, had freshness & flavour. **Karmosyn Shiraz** ★★★ Extrovert **03** (not retasted) had smoky/meaty varietal flavours, big but unintimidating 14.5% alc. **Karmosyn Shimmer** NEW ★☆ **NV** blend shiraz (81%) & merlot tastes better than its aromas promise. — *JPf*

Teubes Family Wines
T 027-213-2377 • F 027-2133773

Olifants River • Est/1stB 2003 • Visits by appt (9-5.30 during wildflower season — Aug/Sep) • Closed pub hols • Self-catering/B&B guest house • Tour groups • Walking trails • Owner Johan & Ella Teubes • Winemaker Helene van der Westhuizen (Jan 2004) • Viticulturist Johan Teubes • 2 400cs own label 100% red • Also exported as Houmoed • PO Box 791 Vredendal 8160 • ella@teubeswines.co.za • www.teubeswines.co.za

With pristine soil, a dry climate and cleansing breezes, this area is perfect for organic farmers like the Teubes. Most of their SKAL-certified production goes overseas in bulk, and a little is bottled by wineries active in the relatively small SA organic market. Their biggest news is a joint venture with local physician John Hayes and Diemersdal Estate under the banner Sir Lambert Wines, separately listed.

Text

DGB-owned range launched late 2003 in packaging calculated to appeal to 'fashion-conscious trendsetters'. Last tasted were a non-vintage Ruby Cabernet-Merlot and Chenin; no further information available.

Thabani Wines
T 021-412-9302 • F 021-412-9305

Stellenbosch • Closed to public • Owner Jabulani Ntshangase • PO Box 1381 Stellenbosch 7599 • thabani@iafrica.com • www.thabani.co.za

After more than 30 years in the industry since starting as a wine shop assistant in New York, Jabulani Ntshangase sells his own-brand Thabani ('Joyful') wines through restaurants and from his elegant Grand World of Wine store in the ArabellaSheraton Grand Hotel, Cape Town. A pioneering mentor of winemaking talent and taster for this guide, Ntshangase is particularly joyful this year about the new Sauvignon vintage, from Durbanville vineyards. A Shiraz, Merlot and Cab-Merlot also available but unready for review.

▪ **Thandi Wines**   *see* The Company of Wine People
▪ **The Auction Crossing**   *see* Hex River Crossing Private Cellar
▪ **The Beach House**   *see* Douglas Green
▪ **The Berrio**   *see* Flagstone Winery
▪ **The Blends**   *see* Bellingham
▪ **The Centennial**   *see* Bovlei Winery

The Chase Vineyards
T 021-862-1489 • F 021-862-1489

Paarl • Est 2003 • 1stB 2006 • Tasting by appt • Owner Richard & Una West • Winemaker Nico Vermeulen with Rudi von Waltsleben (consultants, both Nov 2005) • 41ha (cab, merlot, pinot, shiraz, chenin) • ±400t/1 400cs 100% red • PO Box 11 Huguenot 7645 • rwest@kingsley.co.za

Former London-based civil engineer Richard West and wife Una found a piece of the old country in 1986 when they acquired part of the original Wildepaardejacht farm outside Paarl, renamed The Chase during early 20th century British occupation. Consultant Nico Vermeulen (Havana Hills) brings wide experience to the maiden Shiraz and still-maturing blend. Both were made in the new 50-ton red-wine cellar, small enough to prevent 'vocation' from becoming 'business', says 'semi-retired' West.

Shiraz ★★★ Appealing **06** greets with rasp/blackberry, lifted vanilla & coconut; velour-like tannins, lush sweet-fruited finish. Fr oak, 13 mths. EW. — *MF*

The Cheviot Winery
T 082-553-4771, 082-698-4315 · F 021-434-7249

Stellenbosch (see Helderberg map) · Est/1stB 2004 · Tasting & sales by appt Mon-Fri 9-12 · Fee R20 p/p, refundable on purchase · Closed pub hols & Christian religious days · Owner/ winemaker Elmari Swart & Jaap Scholten · Viticulturist John Arnold (2005) · 150cs 100% red · PO Box 5 Green Point 8051 · winesales@cheviot-wines.com · www.cheviot-wines.com

They've moved from the garage to a cellar between Stellenbosch and Somerset West, but that's the only change – even the grapes have been sourced from exactly the same five rows since 2005! 'Which we saw as an experimental vintage,' they hasten to add, explaining why the maiden 2004 was their only release until now.

★★★★ **Cheviot Syrah** Previewed ex barrel, **06** suggests will achieve similar elegance, silkiness to **04** (**05** untasted). Delicate aromas, fresh lingering flavours harmoniously oakenriched. Mix Fr/Hungarian/Am, 50% new. — *AL*

The Company of Wine People
T 021-881-3870 · F 021-881-3102

Stellenbosch · Est 2004 · Tasting at two venues: Helderberg Winery (see Helderberg map) Mon-Fri 9-5.30 Sat 9-5; Welmoed Winery Mon-Fri 9-5.30 Sat & pub hols 9-5 Sun 10-4 · Both venues closed Easter Fri, Dec 25 & Jan 1 · Meals: Helderberg Restaurant Mon-Sat during tasting hours (T 021-842-2012); Welmoed: Duck Pond Restaurant (see Eat-out section) daily during tasting hours (T 021·881·3310) · Both restaurants available for after-hours functions by appt · Play areas for children · Tour groups · Owner 200+ shareholders · Winemaker Nicky Versfeld, Morné van Rooyen, Stephan Smit, Danie van Tonder & Zahn Botha · Viticulturist Francois de Villiers & PD Koegelenberg · 15 000t/2.5m cs 60% red 40% white · ISO 9001, BRC, HACCP & WIETA certified · PO Box 465 Stellenbosch 7599 · info@ thecompanyofwinepeople.co.za · www.thecompanyofwinepeople.co.za

These 'people passionate about making wine for those who love wine' had their passion fuelled last year: They struck a deal with V&S Wine, biggest distributor in the Nordic region, one of the world's 10 biggest wine and spirits companies and owner of giant brand Absolut Vodka. According to CEO Hermann Böhmer, TCOWP will supply wines for V&S brands such as La Chasse and Chill Out, as well as its own brands. Among these are its flagship Kumkani (which took gold at the 2007 Concours Mondial for its Chardonnay-Viognier and at last year's Decanter awards for its Lanner Hill Sauvignon), export success Arniston Bay and Versus, now available in a 'pouch pack', with a convenient handle and leakproof tap.

Kumkani Reflections range
★★★★☆ **Triple J Shiraz 04** still available; concentration & elegance noted in last ed. Restrained spice/ripe berries in tailored lines, well judged tannins. Worth ageing further few yrs. 12 mths oaked.

★★★★ **Lanner Hill Single Vineyard Sauvignon Blanc** The richer, more sophisticated of this label's sauvs; **07** also more closed when sampled mid-2007; cool fruit intensity spliced by rapier-like acid. Powerhouse in the making. WO Groenekloof. **06** (★★★★) was delicious in lighter vein.

★★★★ **VVS** Innovative viognier, verdelho, sauv mix, headed by viognier's aromatic charms. **05** (★★★★) from riper yr, less focus, verve but attractive, flavourful. Not retasted; no **06**, **07** not ready.

Cradle Hill Cabernet Sauvignon NEW ▤ ★★★★ Handsome newcomer from Sbosch. **05** (ex-barrel) suave cab/cedar scents; fresh blackberry fruits infused with ripe tannins; classically dry. Malo/matured in Fr oak, 70% new. Provisional rating. This range Sbosch vyds unless noted.

Kumkani range
★★★★ **Shiraz-Viognier** ▤ **06** (sample) 95/5 co-fermented blend results in delicate, beguiling, shiraz-led fragrance. Delicately textured, too, with depth of sweet fruit, comfortable padding & build to improve over few yrs.

★★★★ **Sauvignon Blanc** ✓ 🗐 Previewed **07** true to variety in every respect: just-mown sweet grass scents, tingling fruity acids, bounce, concluding with broad persistence. Moderate 13% alc. WO Coastal.

★★★★☆ **Chardonnay-Viognier** 🗐 **06** vinified similarly to delicious **05** but, sampled mid-**07**, still too unsettled & oaky to assess definitively. Some lavender & peach intrigue, quite lush, possibly bit heavier, less fresh; maybe (★★★★).

Pinotage ★★★ **06** rather confected vanilla/banana nose; sturdily built with light fruit core, demonstrative tannins. Oaked 14 mths, 30% new. Coastal vyds. **Shiraz** 🗐 ★★★☆ Effusive **05** (sample) offering plenty Am oak & fruit spice; easy-going & supple but powerful too, probably better in youth. 30% new oak, 15 mths. **Shiraz-Cabernet Sauvignon** 🗐 ★★★★ Felicitous 60/40 mix for comfortable, rounded drinking. **05**'s gentle spice & savoury richness would complement wide range dishes. Fr oak, 30% new, yr. **Chenin Blanc** 🗐 ★★★★ **06** honeyed tropical tones, waxy quality accentuating fruit richness. A big, bold wine with terrific persistence; made for Thai dishes. **Viognier** 🗐 ★★★★ One of Cape's less showy versions. **06** dried apricot, peach & mineral scents; balance, concentration to flatter spiced fish dishes. 50% barrelled, 2 mths new Fr. This range Sbosch fruit unless noted.

Thandi Single Varietal range

Chardonnay ☺ ★★★☆ Cool lime/lemon fruit in spotlight on **06**. Soft, fleshy texture gently firmed by unobtrusive oak adds to satisfying drinkability. Fermented/8 mths Fr oak, 30% new.

Cabernet Sauvignon ★★★★ **05** still v young, restrained, but sweet fruit concentration should emerge after yr/2. Waiting recommended! Fr oak, 18 mths. **Pinot Noir** ★★★ **05** developed garnet hue, restrained cherry aromas, drying tannins suggest early drinking. **Rosé** NEW ★★ Vivid fuchsia pink as bright as shiraz spice on previewed **07** (provisional rating). Soft yet fresh & fruitily dry. WO Sbosch. These Elgin vyds unless noted.

Thandi Dual Varietal range

Cabernet Sauvignon-Merlot ☺ ★★★ Precocious **06**; pretty violets/plums fragrance, smooth & velvety; ripe tannins no hindrance to current pleasurable drinking. Portion oaked. **Shiraz-Cabernet Sauvignon** ☺ ★★★ Shiraz for fruit, suppleness; cab for structure, grip; **05** (60/40 blend) harmonious drinking, Fr/Am oak adding further subtle interest.

Merlot-Cabernet Sauvignon ★★★★ Elegant, accessible **04**, last ed had lush, ripe berry fruit plus stiffening for ±2 yrs. Older Fr oak, 14 mths. **Sauvignon Blanc-Semillon** ★★★ **07** tangy, succulent 75/25 mix with prominent tangerine & tropical fruit. Quite bold, weighty but whistle-clean, bone-dry.

Arniston Bay Reserve range

Bush Vine Pinotage NEW ★★★★ Impressive concentration from low-yielding bushvines on **05**. Built to age with firm but fine tannins & mineral acid. 60% older Fr oak, yr. **Bush Vine Chenin Blanc** NEW ✓ ★★★ Previewed **07** shows vivid fresh honey, canned pineapple concentration. Sumptuous fruit secured by big, firmly dry frame. Provisional rating. W Cape vyds unless noted.

Arniston Bay Single Varietal range

Rosé ☺ ★★★ Redcurrant freshness abounds throughout **07**; fruitily dry, moreish tang in tail.

Cabernet Sauvignon NEW ★★☆ This, Merlot, Pinotage & Shiraz all **06**, all previews (so ratings provisional). Similarly styled, dollops sugar highlighting nicely defined, juicy varietal fruit & rounded firm finish. All partially or wholly oaked. **Merlot** NEW ★★★ See under Cab. **Pinotage** NEW ★★★ See under Cab. **Shiraz** ★★★ See under Cab. **Chardonnay** NEW ★★☆ **07** (sample) bright limy notes, oak hint. Full body, balancing dash sugar. Provisional rating. W Cape vyds unless noted.

Arniston Bay Dual Varietal range

Chenin Blanc-Chardonnay ☺ ★★★ Ripe & generous floral & pear on **07** blend (80/20); rich & juicy, fruitily dry. 300 000cs of quality quaffing. **Sauvignon Blanc-Semillon** NEW ☺ ★★★ **07** food-friendly equal partnership. Quiet tropical/citrus tones; pleasantly weighty with cleansing minerals.

Cabernet Sauvignon-Shiraz NEW ★★★ **06** sample lightly oaked not to dampen spicy strawberry fruit. Incl flavour-enhancing 6g/l sugar. Tentative rating. **Ruby Cabernet-Merlot** ★★★ Unwooded **05**, last ed was generous with enough tannin for solo drinking or with food. **Shiraz-Pinotage** NEW ★★ Mildly fruity **06** sweetened more than softened by 8g/l RS. Oak influenced. **Shiraz-Merlot** ★★★ Last ed **05** noted as softly savoury with spice & juicy flesh. Unwooded & still available. W Cape vyds unless noted.

Arniston Bay Tides range

Cabernet Sauvignon NEW 🗏 ★★★ Fresh, ripe cab fruit on satisfying if straightforward **05**; dry finish & nip tannin make for gd food partner. Yr Fr oak. **Pinotage** NEW 🗏 ★★★ **06** introduced by limpid colour, well-tempered sweet fruit, rounded dry finish; dash tannin, older oak add to food-friendly nature. **Shiraz** NEW 🗏 ★★★ Whiffs coconut, white spice on **05**; light toned but ripe & flavoursome; dry tannins suggest best with food. **Barrel Fermented Chardonnay** NEW 🗏 ★★★★ Sample **07** styled for wide appeal. Balanced, bouncy; gentle lime marmalade/buttered toast freshness, clean dry finish. Fermented/8 mths older Fr oak. Tentative rating. **Barrel Fermented Chenin Blanc** NEW 🗏 ★★ Unobtrusively oaked **06**; bottle age adds honeyed layer to bruised apple bouquet. **Sauvignon Blanc** NEW 🗏 ★★★ Quiet yet telling tropical/fig aromas & flavours on **07**. Unaggressively fresh, dry, pleasing fruity length. W Cape vyds unless noted.

Arniston Bay range

The Shore White ☺ 🗏 ★★★ **07** preview offers ripe scents & flavours, easy-going vitality. Provisional rating.

The Shore Red 🗏 ★★★ Fragrant merlot/cab mix; previewed **06** uncluttered by oak, smooth, with agreeable bright fruit. **The Shore Rosé** NEW 🗏 ★★ Twinkling cherry pink **07**. Straighforward fruity sweetness; crisp, clean tail. **Méthode Cap Classique** ★★★ NV bottle-fermented bubbly, traditional varieties. Last yr offered fresh lemon & kiwifruit aromas; full, creamy, dryish flavours. 36 mths on lees. W Cape vyds unless noted.

Versus range

White ☺ ★★★ **07** packed with Granny Smith apple freshness, sweet juicy flavours; uncomplicated everyday pleasure. Convenient 1000ml & 500ml packaging.

Red ★★★ Quaffable merlot-based blend. **05** smooth, sweet flavours, firmed by dash oak. **Rosé** ★★ **07** flamboyant pink with candyfloss nose, flavours; unashamedly fruity sweet tail.

Welmoed range

Cabernet Sauvignon ☺ ★★★ Invitingly modern cab; **06** basket of fresh, juicy blackberries; twist tannin & oak-rounding are neat trimmings for current pleasure. **Shiraz** ☺ ★★★ Fruity but unshowy **06**, lively mulled-wine spice, fresh yet comfortably rich mouthfeel. Promotes sense of well-being. Portion Fr oaked. **Rosé** ☺ ★★★ Invigorating mouthful wild red berries & spice on dry, ultra-fresh **07**. Vividly hued pinotage/shiraz combo (85/15) in medium-bodied, pick-me-up style. **Chardonnay** ☺ ★★★ Some tropical, biscuity notes, initial juiciness, but **06** tiring, drink up. **Sauvignon Blanc** ☺ ★★★ Hint of sweat then cascade gooseberries, passionfruit & lemongrass on **07**. Lightish, plenty verve, but not too aggressive.

Merlot ★★☆ Cool minty/herbaceous fruit heightens **06**'s lively nature; firmness suggests early drinking with food. **Pinotage** ★★★ Sappy, refreshing, medium bodied **06**'s spirited mulberry fruit undimmed by partial oaking; can take slight chilling. **Chenin Blanc** ★★ **07** retiring honey/tropical aromas; lightish & short green-apple flavours. This range mainly WO Sbosch; all screwcapped.

Infiniti range

Brut ★★★ **03** MCC still available. Last ed toast, brioche & lemon peel flavours showed attractive honeyed development. Classic chard, pinot makeup. W Cape vyds. — AL

■ **The Edge** *see Edgebaston*

The Foundry
T 082-577-0491 • F 021-843-3274

Stellenbosch • Est 2000 • 1stB 2001 • Visits by appt • Owner Chris Williams & James Reid • Winemaker/viticulturist Chris Williams, with selected growers • 20t/1 000cs 90% red 10% white • PO Box 12423 Die Board 7613 • thefoundry@mweb.co.za • www.thefoundry.co.za

A small but faithful following in ten countries is what Meerlust winemaker Chris Williams' own project (with James Reid) now has. It's a creative outlet that allows him to 'find new ways to wrench individuality and class from our fruit'. He's after richness, suppleness, purity and litheness at lower sugar levels. Contentiously, he believes that chasing power and breadth in blockbuster styles is a dead-end for SA. On the personal side, as a Master of Wine student, Williams reckons he's given up trying to have interests outside of wine.

★★★★★ **Syrah** Now released as 3 yr old, which benefits **04**, a sensitive yet honest reflection of hot, dry yr. Touch firmer, more savoury than **03** but graceful & refined, as always. Structure, texture, harmonious oak all suggest future complexity. Incl usual splash viognier; Fr oak, 10% new 16 mths. Unfined/filtered.

★★★★ **Viognier 06** (★★★★★), previewed last ed, has developed into a beauty. Delicate yet convincing varietal perfume, flavours lifted by vibrant minerals; textured & dry. Ups ante on lovely **05**. Older Fr oak fermented/4 mths. — AL

The Goats do Roam Wine Company
T 021-863-2450 • F 021-863-2591

Paarl • Est/1stB 1998 • Tasting/sales at Fairview • 72% red 20% white 8% rosé • PO Box 583 Suider-Paarl 7624 • info@fairview.co.za

Taking their name from the goats which wander about Fairview farm, Paarl headquarters of wine (and cheese) entrepreneur Charles Back, these irreverently labelled wines are fun and easy to drink but far from frivolous. They have an enviable record at wine competitions and professional tastings (a 90-point rating by New York-based Wine Spectator for the Goat-Roti is one recent example), and their performance at point-of-sale has made them the biggest South African wine brand in the US. They're also swiftly eating into other markets including Canada, the UK and Scandinavia.

★★★★ **Bored Doe** Classic bdx blend 5 varieties. Cab, merlot dominant **05** reflects riper vintage; plush fruit, fine tannins, plums & cedar flavours. Streamlined, tailored for immediate enjoyment, enough backbone for 3/4 yrs ageing.

★★★★ **Goat-Roti** Northern Rhône-styled shiraz, with dash viognier. **05** packs punch in fruit concentration, broad-textured complexity, 15.5% alc but can't help liking the personality. Ultra-smooth, loads of flavour, celebrates variety at its bold best.

★★★★ **The Goatfather** No follow up yet for **05**, tasted pvs ed. Individual, powerful wine. Old World style with shiraz, cab, merlot, barbera, zinfandel/primitivo adding scrub & white pepper nuances.

Goats do Roam in Villages Red ★★★★ Creative blend, usually shiraz dominant. **05** dabs mourvèdre, pinotage, contributing dark brooding tones, beef extract, tobacco, liquorice. Accessible, medium-weight, not for long keeping. **Goats do Roam Red** ★★★★ Côtes-du-Rhône styled Mediterranean varieties plus pinotage. Scrub, prosciutto, wild berries only part of **06**'s appeal, this is drinkability personified: juicy, streamlined, just enough tannin. **Goats**

do Roam Rosé ★★★★ With the emphasis on appetite appeal, coral-hued, fresh-fruity multi-blend **07** delivers in lip-smacking style. **Goat Door Chardonnay** ★★★★ More than just a witty name & label, **06** shows classic styling with verve; lemon/lime & buttered toast, silky smooth texture, enough tangy freshness to awaken tastebuds. Paarl WO. **Goats do Roam in Villages White** ★★★★ Varying blend, usually chenin, some aromatic varieties. Viognier's dominance in **06** gives floral, peach fragrance. Characterful, tasty appeal. **Goats do Roam White** ★★★ **06** tasted pvs ed had more weight with addition of viognier & semillon to blend. All Goats WO W Cape or Coastal unless mentioned; most screwcapped. — *CR*

The Goose Wines
T 044-879-0020 • F 044-879-0700

Upper Langkloof (see Klein Karoo map) ▪ Est 2007 ▪ Visits by appt (T 082-653-6800) ▪ Walks ▪ Mountain biking ▪ 4×4 trail ▪ Owner Retief Goosen, Werner Roux & Morné Jonker ▪ Cellarmaster/viticulturist Morné Jonker ▪ Winemaker Alwyn Liebenberg (Uitvlucht) ▪ 17ha (cab) ▪ 200cs 100% red ▪ PO Box 1300 George 6530 ▪ info@thegoosewines.com ▪ www.thegoosewines.com

Having flown solo since 1994, literally (as a pilot) and figuratively (growing vines on Schoonberg, his wine farm high up in the Outeniqua Mountains near George) Morné Jonker has now paired off with investor and champion golf pro Retief Goosen to produce a range of wines known as – what else? – The Goose. 'The extremity and wildness of our valley, together with the extreme cold temperatures, caught his interest, and we share a passion for developing a wine brand with difference and rarity.' But don't expect much fanfare: 'He's quiet, we're quiet, our wine does the talking.' Farm workers produce their own wine too, called Kamanassie. 'We do this with love and involvement; the government apparently calls it BEE …

★★★★ **Cabernet Sauvignon 07** barrel sample shows promise; intense, concentrated yet pure fruit mingling with sweet oak vanilla/spice, tannins ripe but currently unfocused. Rating provisional.

★★★★ **Expression** 50/50 cab/shiraz blend from Bo-Langkloof vyds. Trio tasted: **04** abundant fruit/choc-mocha aromas/flavours, fresh acidity, but rather hard-worked tannins. In **05**, these better managed, resulting in more supple, rounded offering. Attractive bouquet repeated on **07** work-in-progress, showing potential to up the ante when bottled.

Shiraz Lovely mouthfeel, supple tannin & generous fruit, opulent nut/red berry/lily bouquet on barrel sample **07**, salty finish. Too unformed to rate but should impress when bottled. **Sauvignon Blanc** ★★★ Despite forthcoming mineral/nettle nose, **07**'s palate flavour shy; bracing grapefruit acidity does add interest, extend the finish. — *CvZ*

The High Road
T 021-425-4209 • F 021-418-2660

Stellenbosch ▪ Est/1stB 2003 ▪ Tasting by appt ▪ Boardroom facilities ▪ Owner Les Sweidan & Mike Church ▪ Winemaker Nontsikelelo Biyela (2004), advised by Mark Carmichael-Green (2005) ▪ 16t/1 000cs 100% red ▪ 7 Lower Dorp Str, Bosman's Crossing, Stellenbosch 7600 ▪ les@thehighroad.co.za ▪ www.thehighroad.co.za

Owners Les Sweidan and Mike Church speak hesitantly of 'a wine hobby entering a prospective business phase', but 2007 saw the release of The High Road's third vintage, and they vinify in illustrious company at Bosman's Crossing (Stellekaya, Vilafonté, Dalla Cia) with Mark Carmichael-Green consulting.

The High Road ★★★★ Stylish bdx blend (cab/merlot, touch cab f), lively, smooth-textured palate. **05** delicious. Yr Fr barriques, half new. — *CR*

▪ **The Hills** *see* Durbanville Hills

▪ **The House of Krone** *see* Twee Jonge Gezellen Estate/The House of Krone

▪ **The Juno Wine Company** *see* Juno Wine Company

Thelema Mountain Vineyards

T 021-885-1924 • **F** 021-885-1800

Stellenbosch • Est 1983 • 1stB 1988 • Tasting & sales Mon-Fri 9-5 Sat 10-3 • Closed pub hols • BYO picnic • Tour groups by appt • Owner McLean & Webb Family Trusts • Winemaker Gyles Webb & Rudi Schultz (1983, Dec 2000) • Viticulturist Conrad Schutte (since 2007) • Stellenbosch: 55ha (cab, merlot, shiraz, chard, muscat de frontignan, sauv, riesling). Elgin (Sutherland) 40ha (shiraz, sauv, chard, riesling) • 30 000cs 40% red 60% white • PO Box 2234 Dennesig Stellenbosch 7601 • wines@thelema.co.za • www.thelema.co.za

Sutherland, the Elgin fruit farm purchased in 2000, continues to infuse this stellar Stellenbosch team with fresh inspiration, with a fresh unwooded ('to retain the citrus character') Chardonnay and a slightly sweeter Rhine Riesling made from the vines planted there four years ago. Having also established small blocks of shiraz, cab, merlot, pinot and grenache, 'just to play around with', the plan is to slowly bring the Sutherland reds online from this year. Knowing how the vine rules the cellar, loyal subject Gyles Webb has been searching for a top viticulturist; last year he found one in Conrad Schutte (last port of call: Michigan State University) who'll help ensure that the new Elgin reds are worthy of the Thelema label. Come sample the results for yourself in the newly renovated tasting area, with lovely views of the Drakenstein Mountains.

★★★★☆ **Cabernet Sauvignon** Webb's flagship red a modern classic. Decadent cassis & scrub notes on **05** in harmony with perfectly proportioned mouthful; classy & assured. 20 mths Fr oak, 50% new. Follows distinctive & delicious **04**.

★★★★☆ **The Mint Cabernet Sauvignon** Name refers to 22-yr-old single clone vyd with distinctive mint character. **04**'s typical cab structure proved fair foil to its 'modern' fruit tone. **05** in similar vein; fine-grained tannins reveal dollops bright cassis, spearmint. 20 mths Fr oak, 100% new. For cellaring 5+ yrs.

★★★★★ **CWG Auction Reserve Cabernet Sauvignon** None since rich & beautifully proportioned **03**, barrel selection best cab, 20 mths new Fr oak.

★★★★ **Merlot** Very ripe **05** (★★★☆) opulent, seductive on nose; palate less so, tauter, given form/direction by tight tannins. Deserving of 3-8 yrs cellaring. 40% new Fr oak, 20 mths. On-form **04** was suave, creamy & rich, with fine, lively tannin.

★★★★★ **Merlot Reserve 05** (★★★★) plush black fruit, creamy texture similar to regular bottling; tannins, oak flavours more stand-out on this, need time for 20 mths new Fr oak to mesh. Authoritative, still one of SA's finest, yet seems to lacks the joie de vivre of 04, which more youthfully introverted but still seriously hedonistic.

★★★★ **Shiraz 05** lighter, more refreshing than 15% alc suggests thanks to clever acid/sugar balance, smart oak (20 mths 40% new, 90% Fr/Am). Most of its obvious charm in red fruits/scrub nose, accessability. **04** as pleasant, rounded.

★★★★ **Arumdale Shiraz 05** (★★★★) ebullient fruit & oak-driven, especially given warming 14.5% alc; more in line with sweetish **04** than intense **03**. Abundant red fruits, caramel nose (from 2nd fill Am oak) lead to broad palate. 18 mths oak, 90% Fr, 35% new.

★★★★ **CWG Auction Reserve Shiraz** NEW Maiden **05** no wallflower: with ebullient sweet red fruit, giddy lavender notes, solid tannins & beefy 15% alc , more likely the life & soul of the party. Barrel selection best shiraz, 20 mths new Fr oak; should high-kick for a decade or more.

★★★★ **Chardonnay** Relatively slender (13.3 alc) but well formed **06** lovely food wine; nutty & spicy, lemon-cream highlights, palate-cleansing acidity ex-partial malo. Fermented/ 11 mths Fr oak, 33% new. **05** had delicate hazelnut/lime hints.

★★★★ **Ed's Reserve Chardonnay** Barrel fermented chard named for late matriarch Edna McLean. Lemon peel, light dusting vanilla-oak spices, zesty acidity (50% malo) part of **06** (★★★★☆) appeal. Wine for you, a lazy afternoon & a book, or to share with your best friends.

★★★★ **Sauvignon Blanc** 🗐 Thrilling wet stone nuance to **07**'s green toned bouquet & blackberry leaf palate. Rapier acidity pierces ripe-fruit core, precedes steely, persistent finish. Certainly one of sauv fans' favourites.

★★★★ **Sutherland Sauvignon Blanc** ▤ Highland Elgin site giving cooler, more ethereal quality than the elevated Sbosch vyds. **07** (★★★★★) highly expressive, perfectly poised; exquisite cassis notes to nettle/greengage profile, delicate yet thrilling finish. 06 was concentrated, with mouthwatering fruity acids.

Arumdale Cabernet Sauvignon ★★★★ From neighbour's Elgin vyds, as is shiraz. **05** confident expression cooler climate cab: pure cassis/forest floor tones, mineral hints; tight tannins demand few yrs bottle age. **04** (★★★☆) claret-like if uncomplex. 20 mths Fr oak, 40% new.

Pinotage ★★★☆ No **05** made; **04** was friendly & juicy, for medium-term enjoyment with dark plum/blackcurrant nose, savoury tail. 18 mths Fr oak, 20% new. **Mountain Red** ▤ NEW ★★★ Maiden **05** includes cab/shiraz (45/13) not making it into farm's top wines, plus cab f (23%), petit v. For early drinking, yet fruity & flavoursome. 'Offers great value,' adds Webb. **Sutherland Chardonnay** NEW ▤ ★★★★ New addition to range; ex-Elgin. Unwooded **07** charismatic focused citrus fruit & thatch highlights bounce off mineral core. Variety's inherent richness shows in exceptionally long farewell. **Muscat de Frontignan** ✓ ▤ ★★★☆ Playful wallet-pleaser; dry wine pundits should not be put off by its 10g/l sugar, instead should give in to its kiwifruit, jasmine & grapey charms, vivacious acidity. **Rhine Riesling** ★★★☆ **06** full-flavoured, with floral & lime notes, whiffs terpene. Brisk, with barely noticeable 4.8g/l sugar, light on its feet (11.2% alc). Augurs well for ±5 yrs development. **04**, pvs bone-dry, with endearing edginess. **Sutherland Rhine Riesling** NEW ▤ ★★★★ Maiden, peppery **07** not showing much riesling character mid-2007 but eminently sippable, courtesy juicy lemon-sherbert flavours, sweet lilt in tail. **Rhine Riesling Late Harvest** ★★★★ Sweeter & richer than the Alsace style. 'Should become more complex with time,' says Webb. Lipsmacking lime acidity on **06** lifts 103g/l sugar, adds weight & texture to palate, affirming Webb's view. **Muscadel** ★★★☆ Still no new release of warming & luscious sweetie; fans of expressive 98 still waiting in hope. — *CvZ*

■ **The Marais Family** *see Wonderfontein*

■ **The Mask** *see Baarsma Wine Group*

The Mason's Winery 🍷
T 083-228-7855 • F 021-863-1601

Paarl ▪ Est/1stB 2001 ▪ Visits by appt; tasting/sales also at I Love Wine (see entry) ▪ Owner Mason's Hill Wines (Pty) Ltd ▪ Winemaker Derek Clift ▪ 10t/700cs 100% red ▪ PO Box 515 Suider-Paarl 7624 ▪ dehoop@mweb.co.za

'Some new developments are in the pipeline,' reveals stonemasonry owner and after-hours vintner Derek Clift, 'but it's too early to talk about them. Meanwhile, shiraz remains my single-minded focus.'

★★★★ **Shiraz** Hallmarks are Barossa-style flamboyance & power (14% alc). Previewed **05** in similar mode: voluptuous red fruit, well-judged oaking. Eminently drinkable but promises more delight with further ageing. 18 mths, 60% new.

★★★★ **Centenary Reserve Shiraz** Last-tasted **03** more elegant & svelte version of above. Rich cherries & raspberries, curvaceous body given 22 mths oak. Probably better prospects than std version but this so seductive, prognostications almost irrelevant — *CR*

■ **The Maverick** *see Bellingham*

The Observatory Cellars 🍶🍷
T 022-487-3023 • F 022-487-3023

Swartland ▪ 1stB 2000 ▪ Tasting by appt ▪ Owner Tom, Catherine, Elizabeth & André Lubbe ▪ Winemaker/viticulturist Tom Lubbe, with Catherine Lubbe (Jan 2000/Jun 2002) ▪ 15ha (pinotage, shiraz, chard, chenin) ▪ 17t/700cs 60% red 40% white ▪ PO Box 1098 Malmesbury 7299 ▪ syrah@netactive.co.za

Tom Lubbe has made wine in a Cape Town railway shed and at the biodynamic Domaine Gauby in southwest France. The latter's ethos is evident on the family farm: biodiversity is celebrated, and the vines are even treated to honey bush and various other teas to boost their immunity to disease. While Tom L is based on the Roussillon property he bought, in partnership with New Zealander Sam Harrop, sister Catherine and mother Elizabeth are the hands-on people in the Cape, bringing biodynamic methods, low yields, and the lightest of touches in the cellar to the search for wines which express their unique environment.

★★★★★ **Syrah** Low-yield granite vyd gives lovely perfumed purity; no swagger, but persistent, refined flavour. **06** floral edge to highly strung minerality. Like **04**, all in eminently drinkable balance. 17 mths used oak. 12.7% alc. No **05**.

★★★★ **Pinotage-Syrah** Elegantly exuberant **04** last reviewed mid-2005: scrub, herbs, minerals, with bright, sweetly cheerful fruit. Charming expression of pinotage (57%; biodynamically farmed).

★★★★ **Carignan-Syrah** Last **04** (67% carignan, 22% syrah, 11% cab) noted pvs ed as a pure-fruited terroir wine, miles from blockbusterism, delightfully herbal with blackcurrant aromas. **03** (★★★★★) reversed name, with 79% shiraz.

★★★★ **Chenin Blanc-Chardonnay** Most individual, with a nervous austerity in the Lubbe view of a European style. Capricious **06** (★★★) tense, piercing fennel features, bitingly dry. 80% chenin. More conventionally delicious **05** had fynbos aromas, lemon & anise in 50/50 blend. 12.5% alc. 17 mths old oak. — *DS*

▓ **The Pavillion** *see* Boschendal Wines
▓ **The Ruins** *see* Bon Cap Organic Winery
▓ **The Sadie Family** *see* Sadie Family

The Saints

DGB's range of 'heavenly' easy-drinkers not reviewed this edition; notes and ratings from previous guide. A petillant rosé was set to join the congregation at press time.

St Raphael ★★★ Light textured & soft dry red, last-tasted bottling from cinsaut & ruby cab. As all these, **NV**. **St Vincent** ★★ Refreshing & light-bodied dry white, uncomplex & inoffensive. **St Morand** ★★ Aromatic white blend, technically semi-sweet though some bottlings off-dry on taste. **St Claire** ★★ Appealing Natural Sweet rosé with low alc (8%) & balanced sweetness. **St Anna** ★★ Perfumed Natural Sweet white, with low alc (±8%). Blend of perfumed varieties including gewürz. **St Celine** ★★ Same blend as St R but with smoothing dollop sugar for extra quaffability. — *DH*

The Shosholoza Collection
T 021-674-7227 • **F** 021-671-6036

Closed to public • *Owner Rainbow Nation Wines* • *PO Box 44852 Claremont 7735* • *info@rainbownationwines.com* • *www.rainbownationwines.com*

'Shosholoza' is a uniquely South African rallying cry and now also a wine range intended to build 'Brand SA'. The three 'Collections' (none tasted) come from boutique to medium-sized producers; ultimately the brand will grow into a portfolio of complementary products.

The Spice Route Winery
T 021-863-2450, 022-485-7139 • **F** 022-485-7169

Swartland • *Est/1stB 1998* • *Tasting & sales at Fairview* • *Owner Charles Back* • *Winemaker Charl du Plessis (Dec 2001)* • *Viticulturist Andrew Teubes (consultant)* • *107ha (shiraz, mourvèdre)* • *700t/±12 000cs 60% red 40% white* • *PO Box 645 Malmesbury 7299* • *spiceroute@iafrica.com*

Winemaker Charl du Plessis has racked up several awards for his winery recently, including the Malabar and his Flagship Syrah. Not surprisingly, 'every wine I make - and drink - is memorable,' he believes. He's looking towards the US and Canada as emerging markets and is keeping up-to-date with eco-friendly practices. All the cellar and farm workers on this property, part of Charles Back of Fairview's burgeoning portfolio, own their own houses. And Charl's favourite hangover cure? 'On the first of January every year, I take a long, deep dive… I stay on the bottom of the sea and hide from everybody!'

★★★★ **Pinotage** Back on track, showing its class, **06** has svelte lines, smoothly integrated fine-grained tannins, inviting brambleberry & spice flavours. Quietly serious, has good cellaring future. 10 mths Am oak, half new. **05** (★★★☆) sacrificed some mid-palate definition to ripeness.

★★★★ **Flagship Syrah** New World style, seriously oaked. Spice-rich **04** entices with unfolding layers of campfire smoke, underbrush, dark fruit. Already accessible but structured for longer haul: 18 mnths Fr, half new. Concours Mondial gold.

★★★★ **Shiraz** From Swtland bushvines, unfiltered. Last ed, **05** had combo Old & New World smoke, tar, blackberries. 18 mths Fr, 30% new.

★★★★☆ **Malabar** Flagship blend, components dependent on vintage. **04** shiraz, mourvèdre, sprinkling petit syrah, grenache, melding in high-toned celebration of Rhône. Violets, black pepper, wild berries, with silky elegance cloaking firm backbone. Irresistible.

★★★★☆ **Chenin Blanc** 🗏 Ex 29 yr old Swtland bushvines. Ideal food fare, **06**'s intense fruit 6 mths barrel ferment/matured for extra layers of flavour, interest; savoury-citrus, seamed with lively acidity. Great maturation potential.

★★★★ **Viognier** Last tasted **06** went from floral towards fresh almonds, lavender biscotti perfume, luscious peach flavours. From low-yielding Swtland vyds; bunch pressed; fermented older Fr oak.

Mourvèdre ★★★★ Last tasted **05**, Rhône-like tarry, earthy, wild berry character from minuscule 2.7t/ha Swtland crop. Succulent & accessible despite Am oaking (yr used barriques). **Sauvignon Blanc** ★★★★☆ Given major vintage quality boost, **07** sample is a zesty, mouthfilling powerhouse of cut grass, lime & passionfruit, never-ending length. Gorgeous. Fruit ex-own Darling farm. **06** (★★★☆) was first from this source; appealing, with invigorating acidity. Discontinued: **Merlot**. — *CR*

The Springtree Wine Company   [NEW]
T 021-852-5052 ▪ F 021-852-5085

Est 2007 ▪ Closed to public ▪ Owner Springtree Wine Company ▪ Cellarmaster Wilhelm Coetzee ▪ Winemaker/viticulturist Bruce Jack ▪ PO Box 3636 Somerset West 7129 ▪ michellevanzyl@flagstonewinery.co.za ▪ www.springtreewines.com

Named after a 285-year-old olive tree on Waterbron farm in Riebeek-Kasteel, this joint venture between Flagstone Winery and Riebeek Cellars is the 'mother company' to several existing brands and some new ventures. There are big plans for the 300 000-case 'Fish Hoek phenomenon' in particular, reveals Flagstone's Bruce Jack: 'Our intention is to grow this into the biggest SA brand in the world.'

A Few Good Men

★★★★ **Chardonnay** Sample **06** same regime as step-up **05** (100% barrel-fermentation/6 mths Fr/Am oak (50/50). Could show same citrus/biscuit richness in time: building blocks in place.

Cabernet Sauvignon ★★★ Last-tasted **04** treated with ageing in mind, hence firm dry tannins holding fruit captive, needing few yrs. Yr Fr oak, some new, for these. **Merlot** ★★★ **05** full-ripe dark fruit, liquorice tones, enlivening acidity ensures satisfying drinkability. 9 mths 2nd fill oak, natural ferment. **Shiraz** ★★★★ Well-made, tasty **05**; savoury hedgerow fruit, dried herbs, food-friendly tannic firmness. Combo Am/Fr oak, third new.

Barbarossa range

Maria Cabernet Sauvignon ★★★ Dark plummy Swtland fruit given bold oak treatment, **05** is a serious wine. Broad shouldered, structured for 4+ yrs ageing; until then, will handle hearty stews, rich venison pie. Yr mix new, 2nd fill Fr.

Cellar Hand

Backchat ★★★ Mix 5 varieties led by tinta r, combo tank/oaked. Wild berries, touch liquorice in **06**, well-judged, light & friendly. **Chenin Blanc** ★★★ Last tasted **06** had crunchy apple & pear fruit salad, smooth textured drinkability its many fans expect.

Fish Hoek

> **Pinotage** ☺ ★★★ To hedgerow fruit & trademark smooth body of the range, sample **06** adds pinotage's juicy freshness. Unoaked. **Chenin Blanc** ☺ ★★★ 'For those who love picnics, eating fresh food', according to label, perfect casting for **07**'s melon/apple crunchy freshness.

Merlot ★★★ Lovely fruitcake aromas in charming **06**, light textured, juicy, enough tannin grip for food matching. **Shiraz** ★★★ Reining in pvs appealing typicity, ultra-smooth **06** epitomises uncomplicated drinkability: dark plums, touch of spice, palate-plumping sugar. **Shiraz Rosé** ★★★ 'Pink sweet' & strawberry aromas greet you in pale pink **07**, a softly rounded, friendly, just-dry quaffer. **Sauvignon Blanc** ★★★ Previewed last ed, **06** has integrated in interim; unaggressive gooseberry & leafy styling, fresh-fruity drinkability. *— CR*

The Stables
T 033-266-6781 • F 033-266-6252

KwaZulu-Natal • Est 2004 • 1stB 2005 • Tasting, sales & tours Mon-Thu by appt; Fri/Sat/Sun 10-6 (Oct-Apr) 10-4 (May-Sep) • Fee R20 • Closed Dec 25 & Jan 1 • Gourmet picnics in heated lapa or the herb garden • Farm-style produce • Harvest & jazz festivals (see website) • Tour groups • Owner Tiny & Judy van Niekerk • Winemaker Tiny van Niekerk • Viticulturist Diederik Le Grange • 23ha (cab, pinot, pinotage, shiraz, chard, nouvelle, sauv, riesling, viognier) • 100t/ 16 000cs 60% red 40% white • PO Box 159 Nottingham Road 3280 • info@stableswine.co.za • www.stableswine.co.za

Tiny van Niekerk, co-owner of South Africa's furthest-flung winery (in the midlands of Kwa-Zulu Natal), has to date processed almost 100 tons of his grapes and wryly observes 'he's now a winemaker to be reckoned with'. Their first sparkling wine is undergoing secondary fermentation and looking good - problem is they can't call it 'cap classique' but they promise a creative solution in due course. End of harvest was celebrated with a traditional grape-stomping party which allowed the enthusiastic locals 'to show the Cape how it should be done!' says spirited wife Judy. A tie-in with The Sharks rugby team has given the brand phenomenal exposure.

★★★★ **Reserve 1.618 Perfectly Proportioned** From KZN fruit, **05** shiraz-led (81%) blend with merlot & cab; last ed powerful bouquet & flavours, integrated, supple tannins & modest 13% alc. 15 mths new Fr oak.

KwaZulu-Natal range

Pinotage ★★★ When tasted last ed, dense, ripe fruit on easy-drinking **05** had already melded with 14 mths new Fr oak. **Pinotage Clairet** ★★★ Last visited coral-hued **06**, made blanc de noir style, showed drying & oaky tannins, lively acidity & cherry flavours. **Sauvignon Blanc** NEW ★★★ Cut-grass-toned **07** quiet but pure-fruited with mineral note; puckering acidity: will it integrate?

Nottingham Road range

Pinotage ★★★★ Last-tasted **05** was accessible, with ripe plums & cherries; lithe tannins & gd seasoned-oak support. **Shiraz** ★★★★ Well-muscled **05**, balanced 13.5% alc, gd tannins, robust fruit & healthy sprinkling spices. Should improve. **Time is Now** NEW ★★★ Smoke scents, forest floor notes on **05**. Dark fruits, mouthcoating chalky tannins, shortish. 60/40 cab/merlot blend, 27 mths seasoned oak well integrated. Sbosch fruit. **Ezintabeni** NEW ★★★ Ribena notes meld with fennel & buchu in inviting **05** blend shiraz, cab & merlot, let down by coarse finish. 14 mths 60% new Fr oak. **Chardonnay** ★★★ Last ed **05** showed inviting aromas & delicate vanilla oak, but was already advanced for its age. **Chenin Blanc** ★★★ Classically styled **06** delivers hints wet wool on limy palate. 3 mths new Fr wood gives some creaminess, but fruit tad faded mid-2007. **Sauvignon Blanc** Not tasted. **Drakensberg Tawny** Sold out.

The Sharks range
Raggie Red ★★ Friendly **05** proffers super-sweet fruits in agreeable package, soft & easy acidity. **Zambezi Pink** 🍷 ★★ Light-bodied quaffer from pinotage, **06** raspberry flavours kept lively by gd acidity. **Silver Tip** 🍷 ★ **06** chard & sauv with melon & strawberry hints. Simple & quite steely. — *RP*

■ The Tin Mine *see Zevenwacht*

Theuniskraal Estate 🍴🏕️♿

T 023-230-0687/88/89/90 • **F** 023-230-1504, 023-230-2284

Tulbagh • Est 1705 • 1stB 1947 • Tasting & sales Mon-Fri 9-12; 1-4 Sat 10-1 • Fee R5 refundable on purchase • Closed Easter Fri/Sun, Dec 25 & Jan 1 • BYO picnic • Tour groups • Owner Rennie & Kobus Jordaan • Winemaker Andries Jordaan (1991) • Viticulturist Jordaan brothers • 140ha (13 varieties, r/w) • ±1 800t/±40 000cs own label 10% red 90% white • PO Box 34 Tulbagh 6820 • tkraal@lando.co.za • www.theuniskraal.co.za

The whole Jordaan family is involved at this fourth-generation estate. 'From managing the vineyards, to making the wine, and even balancing the books, everyone has a job and that's what makes it a special place,' says winemaker Andries J, adding that both the Rosé and (untasted) export brand Ixia are selling well.

> **Prestige** ☺ ★★★ Appealing mint-scented blend ruby cab, cab, shiraz. **06** robust but pure strawberry & plum flavours, lightly oaked. **Semillon-Chardonnay** ☺ ★★★ Mouthfilling, minerally **07** softened with dollops citrus & pear. Super now, should keep yr/2. **Bouquet Blanc Natural Sweet** ☺ ★★★ Scented 60/40 gewürz/buket; **06** honeysuckle & lime loveliness, crisp despite sweetness, finishes clean.

Rosé ★★ **07** low-alc (10%) strawberry-laced off-dry pink, from a melange of grapes. **Riesling** ★★★ Enduring brand, launched 50+ yrs ago. Bright **07** with Granny Smith apple & mineral notes. Lean, crisp seafood partner. — *RP*

■ The Veldt *see Robertson Wide River Export Company*

The Winery of Good Hope 🍾🍷

T 021-855-5528 • **F** 021-855-5529

Stellenbosch (see Helderberg map) • Est/1stB 1998 • Open by appt • Owner Alex Dale, Andrew Openshaw, Yalumba, Edouard Labeye, Craig Smith, Ben Radford, Heather Whitman, Stephen Ludlam • Winemaker Edouard Labeye, Guillaume Nell (2006), with Tubby May (Feb 2003) • Viticulturist Guillaume Nell • ±120ha (cab, carignan, grenache, merlot, mourvèdre, pinot noir, shiraz, chard, chenin, sauv, viognier) • ±850t 50/50 red/white • Postnet Suite 124 Private Bag X15 Somerset West 7129 • thewineryofgoodhope@thewineryofgoodhope.co.za • www.thewineryofgoodhope.com

One of Australia's oldest and largest family-owned wine businesses, Yalumba Wine Company, has taken a 20% stake in this Helderberg winery, which gains among others access to capital for development, international markets and opportunities for staff development, says the local company's elated MD Alex Dale. He adds that Yalumba owner Robert Hill-Smith is a long-time friend who has been seeking opportunities in SA for over a decade. In addition, the winery team is excited about the imminent launch of new niche wines in its Radford Dale range. Among them are a pinot from Elgin, a single-vineyard Helderberg chenin and a vine-aged, single-vineyard viognier dessert.

Radford Dale range

★★★★ **Merlot** Previewed last ed, **05** since lost no silky elegance, complexity or charm. Template of variety's potential: violet & blackcurrant perfume, black pepper & scrub shading to the fine-grained tannins. Nudges next level.

★★★★ Shiraz Last ed **05** sashayed back to New World after glorious rhône-toned **04** (**★★★★☆**); showed plenty dark fruit, oak spices & smoky liquorice tones. Admirable definition in warm vintage, but for drinking, not keeping.

★★★★☆ Gravity Varying blend flagship red, shiraz-dominant in **05** (**★★★★★**). Wonderfully perfumed, spice, creamy dark fruit, tapenade, but there's power under the seductive appeal, good tannin backbone for a long, rewarding evolution. **03** impressed with pure savoury vinosity in soft frame; **04**, just bottled, provisionally rated (**★★★★**) last yr.

★★★★ Shiraz-Viognier Co-fermented, accounting for integration, harmony of **05** last ed. Brambleberries, earthy notes, with hovering fragrant lift from viognier. Unfined/filtered. 15% alc well assimilated.

★★★★ Shiraz-Merlot NEW Barrel sample **06** owes more to shiraz than merlot, but early days still; moorland scrub, brambleberries, pepper dusting, with firm tannins busy melding. Well constructed, great potential. Provisional rating. EW.

★★★★☆ Chardonnay Meticulous vyd selection & cellar care. Trademark deep-seated peach & citrus intensity in **06**'s intro but the palate is what distinguishes this chard: a fine-boned burgundian savouriness.

★★★★ Viognier Ex-barrel **07** already demanding attention with aromatic, floral bouquet, while oak works its magic on palate: savoury biscuit, peach pip austerity, perfect for food.

Pinot Noir 🍷 **★★★★** Last tasted **05** (sample, provisional rating) medicinal & slightly astringent, delicate redcurrant flavours; plenty of elegance. Dijon clone.

Black Rock range

★★★★☆ Red Blend 🍷 S. Rhône-inspired exotic blend, individual & compelling. Shiraz-led **06** doesn't falter: violets, dried herbs, campfire smoke & crushed blueberries. The trademark lithe tannins welcome participation; this is pure hedonism.

★★★★ White Blend 🍷 Majority blend 40 yr old bushvine chenin. With chard, dash viognier. **06** almost overpowers with a peach/preserved melon & citrus intensity. Gloriously tangy, food-friendly, thanks to enlivening acidity, oak influence.

Vinum range

★★★★ Cabernet Sauvignon 🍷 Showing confident New World styling, **05** is crammed with same delectable cassis, dark choc, sweet spice flavours as **04**, but is riper, reflecting vintage, for drinking sooner. No hardship here.

★★★★ Chenin Blanc 🍷 From old Hldrberg bushvines. Sample last ed, **06** shows how well gd chenin develops: citrus peel to the fore over tropical core, vein of acidity keeps everything fresh, lively. Potential for few yrs further cellaring.

The Winery of Good Hope range

Chenin Blanc ☺ 🍷 **★★★** Crammed with palate-awakening crunchy pear freshness, **07** is quaffability personified.

Pinot Noir 🍷 **★★★★** Pvsly ex-barrel, **06** delivers on early promise: underbrush & red berry flavours, hints of violets, captured in a fine-honed structure. Oak fully integrated. Elgin fruit. **Pinotage ★★★★** Previewed last ed, strikingly individual **06** is dark-fruited & savoury, cloves & black pepper spiced, with variety's trademark juicy palate. Tannins now well melded. Gd match with venison. **Granite Ridge Reserve** NEW 🍷 **★★★** Shiraz, cab, merlot blend **06** is a smooth-textured charmer: black pepper, smoked beef nuances to plummy fruit, aromatic lift from dash viognier. EW. **Chardonnay** 🍷 **★★★** Unoaked chard with character. Previewed last ed, **06** yr later has deepened peach & tropical tones, the same fresh-fruity mouthfeel. **Chenin Blanc-Chardonnay-Viognier** NEW 🍷 **★★★☆** Original blend, aromatic **06** focuses on juicy drinkability, showing the citrus & peach, buttered toast perfume, flavours of its admirably compatible partners. Discontinued: **Cabernet Sauvignon-Merlot**, **Sauvignon Blanc**.

New World range
Cabernet Sauvignon-Merlot 🍷 ★★★ Quaffability the key in **06**, all smooth edges, plum & black cherry flavours. 54/46 blend. **Sauvignon Blanc** NEW 🍷 ★★★ Cooler fruit source for **06** gives quality leap, exuberant gooseberry & lime freshness, friendly 12.5% alc. — *CR*

■ **Thierry's Wine Services** *see Cape Grace Wines*
■ *33 Degrees South* *see Wamakersvallei Winery*

Thokozani Wines

T 021-864-5050 • F 021-864-2095

Wellington • Est/1stB 2005 • Tasting & sales at Diemersfontein • Owner Diemersfontein employees, external investors & Diemersfontein Wines • Winemaker See Diemersfontein Wines • 1 000cs 40% red 40% white 20% rosé • PO Box 41 Wellington 7654 • info@ thokozani.co.za

'Diemersfontein's little infant is now teething,' is how marketer S'bangizwe Yekiso describes the status of this empowerment winery, having released a second vintage. Though only baby teeth, they've already been sunk into a few awards, so there clearly is a hunger to succeed at this Wellington start-up.

★★★★ **CV** NEW 🍷 **06** blend chenin/viognier. Restrained nose of white peach, honey & yellow apples; full-fruited palate with gd mineral grip & subtle, sappy apple finish. Coastal vyds.

Shiraz-Mourvèdre ★★★ Coffee, toasty obvious oak, on slightly reticent **06**. Gd, fresh fruit purity with attractive mourvèdre wildness to finish. **Rosé** ★★ Appealing scents of strawberry candyfloss & red cherry; sweetish juicy palate on **07**. Discontinued: **SCV**. — *JP*

■ **Thomas Kipling** *see Makro*
■ *Thornhill* *see Veenwouden Private Cellar*

Thorntree Wines
T 021-786-2487 • F 021-786-1476

Est/1stB 2001 • Closed to public • Owner/winemaker André Badenhorst • 50 000cs 50/50 red/ white • Suite 310, Private Bag X16, Constantia 7848 • andrebad@iafrica.com • www. thorntreewines.co.za

Seasoned exporter of affordable wines to the US, André Badenhorst is often called upon to do some fine tuning in other cellars. In return, he gains access to special parcels of wine, some of which have found their way into a new upmarket brand, Old Well House, after the historic Cape Point watering hole which houses his HQ.

Merlot ★★ **06** elegant, mint-scented, mulberry-laced sipper; delightfully fresh. Partly older-oaked. **Shiraz** ★★★ Floral **06** offers bacon & dark cherry in an elegant, finely-oaked shell. Fermented/aged 4 mths with staves. **Chardonnay** ★★ Appealing **07** (sample) has peach ice-cream flavours, smoothing 4g/l dash sugar. Fermented/4 mths with staves. **Sauvignon Blanc** ★★★ Racy, mineral, with lots of greenpepper perfume & flavour, **07** has super drinkability. All WO W-Cape. — *RP*

Thor Wines

T 082-393-8955

Walker Bay • Est 2006 • 1stB 2007 • Closed to public • Owner Emile Gentis & Renier Theron • Winemaker Emile Gentis & Renier Theron (Jan 2006/Jan 2007) • Viticulturist Renier Theron • 0.2ha (barbera, mourvèdre, sangiovese, shiraz, viognier) • 2t/150cs 90% red 10% white • PO Box 14 Vlottenburg 7604 • emilegentis@yahoo.com

A friendship between Emile Gentis, head winemaker for Long Mountain, and Rupert & Rothchild viticulturist Renier Theron was the spark that ignited this new garagiste endeavour that sees wine made at the edge of the Bot River Lagoon. They've been signing up other friends to join them. The name Hirondel, swallow in French, is a tribute to the nest in the garage where they made their first wine.

Hirondel range
Shiraz-Pinotage-Merlot ★★ Tobacco, tealeaf & cedarwood aromas, **06** rustic fruit compote, sweet-spice finish. — *MF*

■ **Three Peaks** *see Mount Vernon Farm*
■ **Three Rivers** *see Bon Courage Estate*

Tierhoek
T 022-921-3595 • F 022-921-3595

Citrusdal ▪ Est 2001 ▪ 1stB 2003 ▪ Closed to public ▪ Owner Tony & Shelley Sandell ▪ Winemaker Roger Burton ▪ Viticulturist Johan Viljoen ▪ 21ha (grenache, mourvèdre, shiraz, chard, chenin, sauv) ▪ ±2 000cs 5% red 95% white ▪ PO Box 53372 Kenilworth 7745 ▪ tierhoek@cybertrade.co.za

New winemaker Roger Burton has seen through the first vintage to be made on this high-altitude farm, and Adam Mason of Klein Constantia helped with the new straw wine. Plans for an expanded 200-ton cellar are moving ahead, and a full-time baboon-spotter has been employed to ensure the grapes make it there.

Grenache ★★ All new Fr oak for this unusual (in SA) varietal bottling. Sample **06**, strawberry milkshake flavours & strong tannins. **Wooded Chenin Blanc** ★★★ Missing wow factor of pvs, **06** honey & pineapple, coconut veneer from 50% new oak, fruit-sweet finish. **Unwooded Chenin Blanc** ★★★★ Last-tasted light, elegant & lingering **05** could still age few yrs. **Sauvignon Blanc** ★★★ Papaya & pineapple nuances on **07** preview, light but juicy with marmalade finish. **Straw Wine** NEW ★★★ Full-bodied, sticky, sweet & pleasing **06**, from chenin; enticing dried apricots & honey. All WO Piekenierskloof. — *MM*

■ **Timbili** *see Ernst & Co Wines*
■ **Tin Mine** *see Zevenwacht*
■ **TJ Wines** *see Twee Jonge Gezellen Estate/The House of Krone*
■ **TMV** *see Tulbagh Mountain Vineyards*

Tokara

T 021-808-5900 • F 021-808-5911

Stellenbosch ▪ Est/1stB 2000 ▪ Tasting & sales Mon-Fri 9-5; Sat, Sun & pub hols 10-3 ▪ Tokara Restaurant for lunch & dinner Tue-Sat (T 021-808-5959) ▪ Farm-grown varietal olive oils from The Olive Shed ▪ Art exhibits (enquiries: Julia Meintjes T 083-675-1825) ▪ Owner GT Ferreira ▪ Winemaker Miles Mossop (Jan 2000), with Dumisani Mathonsi (Jan 2004) ▪ Viticulturist Aidan Morton (Nov 2000) ▪ 110ha (cabs s/f, grenache, malbec, merlot, mourvèdre, petit v, shiraz, chard, chenin, sauv, semillon) ▪ 700t/50 000cs ▪ 40% red 60% white ▪ PO Box 662 Stellenbosch 7599 ▪ wine@tokara.com ▪ www.tokara.com

Tokara's Elgin vineyards, atop a sea-facing escarpment, came on-line and this year winemaker Miles Mossop & team will be releasing an Elgin Sauvignon to match the Walker Bay version. Also new, and available only from the cellar door, is the Zondernaam NLH from the Stellenbosch home-farm. And young Miles M is embracing technology. 'We're using multi-spectral photography to identify uniform portions within individual blocks to help with our picking, and are finding marked differences in the wines made from these portions,' he says. 'I'm also using phenolic ripeness analysis to help to decide when to harvest the reds and am beginning to develop a good understanding of when each block is optimally ripe.'

Tokara range
★★★★☆ **Red** Last tasted **04** was big, rich & dry. Needed yr/2 to round youthful tannin; possibly best within first 5 yrs. Cab-based with merlot, petit v & cab f (69/14/11/6); sensitively oaked (Fr, 78% new, 20 mths). **05** unready.

★★★★ **Stellenbosch Chardonnay** 'Chardonnay' last ed. Style consistency maintained in latest **06**: quiet hazelnut/limey façade; tight, sleek mineral structure. Creamy texture, flavour spectrum need yr-3 to develop fully. 10 mths Fr oak, 40% new; partial malo.

★★★★ **Walker Bay Sauvignon Blanc** 🬀 A sauv for every taste in GTF's portfolio! This raised in sea breeze-cooled Hemel-en-Aarde. As pvs, delicious **07** (sample) brimful tangily clean gooseberry & lemongrass flavours. Lovely verve, agility & weight. Listed as 'Sauvignon Blanc' pvs ed.

★★★★ **Elgin Sauvignon Blanc** NEW 🬀 Previewed **07** maiden big, very rich with steely core, quiet but pure varietal tones. Fish, poultry or pasta dishes great matches for this powerful style. 14.5% alc.

★★★★☆ **White** Switch to trendy but creditable sauv/semillon mix from **06** (★★★★). Less immediately scintillating than **05** or maiden **04**; edgy sauv (79%) yet to harmonise with semillon's honeyed texture. May gain more interesting depths given time. Fr oak, 20% new, 9 mths

Zondernaam range

★★★★ **Cabernet Sauvignon 04** follows in classy footsteps of **03**. Vividly fresh, compact & firm; charms with cassis, violets, spicy oak perfume. Juicily sweet fruit & medium body enhance accessibility, with further 3-4 yrs potential.

★★★★ **Shiraz** Last ed **04** had spice, red fruits & mocha resonance. Comfortably medium bodied with fruit-lifting savoury acid; quite pushy tannins needed yr/2. 18 mths Fr/Am casks, 30% new. WO Coastal. **05** unready.

★★★★ **Sauvignon Blanc** 🬀 **07** (sample) first from 100% own Sbosch, Elgin, Hermanus vyds. Wealth of tropical scents, ripe concentration. Balancing crisp fruity acids, greengage, mineral freshness ensure usual crowd-pleasing style.

★★★★ **Noble Late Harvest** NEW Attractive barrel-fermented semillon/sauv (51/49) dessert. **06** honey & apricot scents with moderate botrytis adding complexity. Tad light but has texture & balance to grow. 157g/l RS tempered by steely natural acid. 375ml.

Chardonnay ★★★★ **05** fresher, more succulent than **04** (★★★★), still big. Citrus aromas & flavours highlighted by bright acid; careful oaking (Fr, 15% new), lees stirring provide broader feel. **Chenin Blanc** 🬀 ★★★★ Modern, barrel-fermented/aged **06** beguiles with floral/honeyed subtlty; juicily ripe & full bodied but plenty freshening minerality &, like all Miles M's wines, very good length. 30+ yr dryland vyds. Fr oak, 19% new. Pvsly tasted **04** (★★★★) was sweetish, with alc kick. —AL

█ Tom Lubbe Wines *see* The Observatory Cellars

Topaz Wine
T 082-557-0826 • F 021-855-5086

Somerset West ▪ Est/1stB 2000 ▪ Visits by appt ▪ Owner Clive Torr ▪ Winemaker Clive Torr ▪ Viticulturist James Downes & Clive Torr ▪ 0.04ha 450cs 66% red 33% white ▪ 26 Topaz Str Heldervue Somerset West 7130 ▪ clivey@mweb.co.za

After studying styles of viognier in Condrieu in 2004, Clive Torr made one barrel in 2005, three the following year and six in 2007 - all natural ferments, using a biodynamic tincture to aid the process. 'It took a full nine months, just like a baby!' Speaking of which, Juliet Torr is now 3½. Her favourite drink? 'Pinot noir!'

★★★★ **Pinot Noir 06** (★★★★) has earthy red fruit (ex-Elgin), tangy acidity & tad less allure than pvs perfumed sipper. Moderate 13% alc appealing, in balance with leaner fruit, tauter tannins. Fr oak, 33% new. **04** had burgundian barnyard hints in tight tannin jacket.

★★★★ **Syrah** Last ed, poised **05** redolent of black pepper, ripe wild berries & spicy incense; palate enriched by savoury smoked meat & svelte, creamy texture. **03** (★★★★★) the Rhône-like standout, **04** (★★★★) was more New World (& shade less stunning).

Viognier NEW ★★★★ **06** maiden (& fashionable) white. Dried apricot, almond & peach in quieter, plump (14% alc) style. Smooth texture & clean acidity, with third new oak currently to the fore. —MW

■ **Towerkop** *see* Ladismith Cellar
■ **Tradouw** *see* Ladismith Cellar
■ **Tribal** *see* African Terroir
■ **Tricolore** *see* Weltevrede Estate

TTT Cellar
T 044-213-3 114 · F 044-213-3114

Calitzdorp (see Klein Karoo map) · Est/1stB 2000 · Visits Fri-Sun 8-5; daily during Christmas hols & Easter · Closed Dec 25 · Olives, olive oil & honey · BYO picnic · Self-catering flatlet - sleeps 4 · Owner Ashley & Pat Mason · Winemaker Ashley Mason (Feb 2000) · 0.5ha (souzão, tinta, touriga) · 3t/125cs 100% red · PO Box 7067 Newton Park 6055 · tttcellars@iafrica.com

'It began as a hobby,' laughs Ashley Mason, who helped the late Tony Mossop in nearby Axe Hill cellar. 'In 2000 Tony suggested we buy some grapes and make our own port. It turned out rather lovely - and the bug bit!' Having planted a vineyard, they've now built a cellar. 'The garage became too small…'

Cabernet Sauvignon ★★ Blackcurrant & thatch aromas, honeyed note, slight porty nuance on **06** conclusion. **Hanepoot ★★★** Rosepetals & raisiny spice, almond hint on unctuous **05** fortified dessert, sweetly persistent Turkish Delight flavours. **Cape Ruby ★★** A lighter-toned version; berry fruit, spicy-sweet finish with evident oak & alc. **NV. Cape Vintage ★★☆** Liqueur choc notes on **06**, some berries; v soft - more attack, grip, would up rating. *— MF*

Tukulu
T 021-809-8330 · F 021-809-8864

Groenekloof · Est 1998 · Tasting & sales by appt at Bergkelder · Owner Distell, Leopont 98 Properties, Maluti Groenekloof Community Trust · Viticulturist Hannes van Rensburg (1998) · 245ha (cab, pinotage, sangiovese, shiraz, chard, chenin, sauv, viognier) · 4 500cs own label · 60% red 40% white · PO Box 184 Stellenbosch 7599 · info@tukulu.co.za · www.tukulu.co.za

Tukulu's Pinotage continued gathering plaudits, and the 04 was selected for the ABSA Top 10 for the fourth time. The promised organic range, grown in the Darling district's deep, red, fertile soils and maritime climate, has now been launched.

- **★★★★ Pinotage** Seriously weighted **05** shows massive tannin grip, with classy cassis, nutmeg & wild mushroom replacing **04**'s plump, jammy fruit & soft tannins. Cranberry tartness contrasts with vanilla (from 45% Am oak) to balance ripeness.
- **★★★★ Shiraz** Peppery, blueberry-laced **06** still introverted mid-2007. Big yet fine tannins coat punchy red fruits, spice & smoke. Gd concentration. Pure but still rugged; needs yr/2's bottle-ageing.

Organic Sangiovese [NEW] **★★★** Vivid **06**, savoury fruits & florals, ripeness (15% alc) checked by extracted dry finish. Has potential; meanwhile, pasta please! **Organic Chardonnay** [NEW] **★★★** Quince layered with minerals, touch oak adds fullness, complexity to **07**. Still edgy mid-2007; might rate higher once settled. **Chenin Blanc ★★★★ 07** bolder & more mineral than pvs, lively citrus & green apple fruit, oak well guised in firm yet fleshy finish. *— RP*

Tulbagh Mountain Vineyards
T 023-231-1118 · F 023-231-1002

Tulbagh · Est 2000 · 1stB 2003 · Tasting, sales & tours by appt · Owner Jason Scott & George Austin · Winemaker/viticulturist Callie Louw (2007) · 16ha (cab, mourvèdre, shiraz) · 88t/90% red 6% white 4% straw wine · PO Box 19 Tulbagh 6820 · info@tmv.co.za · www.tmv.co.za

New winegrower Callie Louw brings premium international experience at Le Soula in the Roussillon and Cakebread in California with him, not to mention compost teas and a worm farm! 'With his fresh ideas, commitment to organic/biodynamic vineyard management and low-intervention cellar techniques, we really look forward to taking TMV to the next level,' says Jason Scott. Their eventual aim is holistic ecological balance across the whole farm, not just the vineyard. Hence a regime to replace 20% of their diesel with fuel recycled from cooking oil. 'And our conservation efforts go hand in hand with that.'

Tulbagh Mountain Vineyards range

★★★★ **Syrah-Mourvèdre** ☺ These two wines not retasted. Youthfully tight, powerful **04** with taut minerality & spicy Fr oak (22 mths, third new), lily & spice announcing shiraz (85%), & strong, rather dry tannins yet to soften into lurking sweet fruit. Like all from this cellar, native yeast fermentation.

Theta ☺ ★★★★ Ambitious, dark, ripe-fruited **03** from shiraz; spicy-tobacco oak (22 mths Fr, 50% new). One to watch. No **04**.

TMV range

★★★★☆ **Swartland Syrah 06** generous, engaging as ever, with Swtland's scrubby notes to shiraz's lilies & perfume. Smoothly firm tannins, balanced mineral freshness, fruit unblurred by subtle oaking (11 mths, scarcely any new). Lovely young, but will repay keeping few yrs.

★★★★ **Viktoria 05** (not retasted) half shiraz, with mourvèdre, cinsaut, cab. Ripe, forward fruit, richly flavourful; robust but restrained. Integrated oak - largely as above; also unfined/filtered.

★★★★ **White** Mid-gold chenin-based **06** (★★★★☆) has honeysuckle, herbs, plus florals from viognier (at 5%, as is clairette). Richer than **05** & technically off-dry, but clean, racy acidity balances beautifully. 11 mths older oak adds only breadth, roundness.

★★★★☆ **Vin Pi One NV** not retasted; no. to change each vintage. Puns on 'vin de paille'- chenin dried outdoors, naturally fermented in older oak. Fractional blending across 3 vintages allows slow oxidation. Unusual, but gorgeous & delicious: baked apple, burnt toffee elements. V sweet (298g/l sugar), but balanced with fresh acidity & light 11% alc. — *TJ*

Tulbagh Wine Cellars
T 023-230-1001; 022-931-2170 • F 023-230-1358; 022-931-2171

Tulbagh/Swartland (see Tulbagh map) • Est 1906/2006 • Tulbagh cellar: Tasting & sales Mon-Fri 8-5 Sat 9-1 • Closed pub hols except Easter Sat, May 1 & Sep 24 • Gift shop • Porterville cellar: Tasting & sales Mon-Fri 8-5 Sat 9-1 • Closed Easter Fri-Mon, Dec 25/26, Jan 1 • Tours by appt • Picnics/light meals by appt or BYO • Tour groups • Owner 126 members • Cellarmaster André Oberholzer (Porterville, Dec 1996) • Production manager Carl Allen (Aug 2002) • Winemaker Elsabé le Roux (Tulbagh, Dec 2002) • Viticulturist Juliana Claassen (Porterville, 2005) & Wedré Lourens (Tulbagh, Dec 2006) • 4 290ha • 15m litres; 20% red 70% white 10% other • PO Box 85 Tulbagh 6820; PO Box 52 Porterville 6810 • tkw@tulbaghwine.co.za • www.tulbaghwine.co.za

It's been two years since Tulbagh Winery and Porterville Cellars merged and it's been all systems go since, with a production capacity capping 15-million litres; a young and creative management team; and an intensive marketing programme to brand-build the ranges.

Klein Tulbagh Reserve range

Cabernet Sauvignon ★★★ Supple, classically styled **03**, showing tempting redcurrant & green olive notes. Note: No **04** vintages available for tasting; notes for **02** & all 03s from pvs ed. **Merlot** ★★★ Ripe, more extracted & unsubtle **03**, stewed plums, dried fruit & grainy tannins. **Pinotage** ★★★ Ripe **03** the most satisfying in range, with mulberry & sweet vanilla aromas from 47% Am oak. Pinotage Top Ten 2005. **Shiraz** ★★☆ Subtle strawberry & woodsmoke notes lift soft, quaffable **03**. **Vintage Port** ★★★ Packed with fruitcake flavour, **02** older-style with lower alc, highish sweetness; from pinotage.

Disa range

Cape Red ★★ Modestly flavoured, gently tannic vin ordinaire. **Rosé** ★ Off-dry sundowner with raspberry tones. **Cape White** ★☆ Unpretentious musky wallet-pleaser. All **NV**.

Porter Mill Station range

> **Chenin Blanc** ☺ ★★★ Food-friendly **07** with tantalising confectionery shop aromas, zippy acidity, perky tail. Lifts the bar on pvs. **Chenin Blanc-Chardonnay-Grenache Blanc** ☺ ★★★ Lightly staved **06**; appealing lunchtime sipper from equal portions chenin/chard plus grenache blanc & viognier (20/10). Floral & vibrant.

Cabernet Sauvignon ★★☆ Dry tealeaf tannins enhance **05**'s juicy black fruit palate, adding structure & length. Combo barrels/staves (50/50), same for all reds. **Pinotage** ★★ Tannin overpowers **05**'s strawberry fruit, but **04** sweet-sour zing retained. **Shiraz** ★★★ Oaky **06** lean & savoury. Pair with fatty boerewors sausage to cut acidity. **Sauvignon Blanc** ★★ Drink shy, slightly tired **06** soon, while some appley acidity remains. Discontinued: **Chardonnay**. 'Friendly & fruity drinking wines' is the goal for this eye-catching line-up. W Cape & Swtland WOs.

Porterville Unfiltered Reserve range

Cabernet Sauvignon ★★☆ **04** fairly easy red; soft & fruity, hints dried leaves, distinct dry tannins. Newer version of this, reds below, unready; notes for **03** & 04s from pvs ed. **Pinotage** ★★ Medium-bodied **04**'s savoury tone lifted by pleasant sweet-sour twist. **Shiraz** ★★★ Restrained fruit, modest alc (12.5%) characterise **04**. **Visage** ★★★ Blend shiraz (42%), pinotage, cab, grenache noir & merlot; **03** soft wild berry fruit yet strident tannins, modest 13% alc. Discontinued: **Chardonnay, Chenin Blanc Unfiltered, Chenin Blanc-Chardonnay-Grenache Blanc**. W Cape, Coastal & Swtlnd WOs for these.

Tulbagh range

Cabernet Sauvignon ★★ Slightly jammy **06** similar to pvs: earthy, muscular tannins, dry finish. **Merlot** ★★ Plum & leaf scents on **07**, with steak-taming tannins. **Pinotage** ★★ Organic hint & loads of strawberries are part of gluggable **06**'s charm. **Shiraz** ★★★ Vibrant fruit & acidity mask substantial 14% alc on **06**, stand up to raspy tannins. **Chardonnay** ★ Pineappletoned **07** very shy & insubstantial. **Chenin Blanc** ★ **07** water-white with scant melon scents, searing acidity. **Sauvignon Blanc** ★★ Despite reticent nose, **07**'s palate pleasantly weighted & flavoured. **Port** ★★ Spiritous **NV** from pinotage, lacks fruit concentration & substance; 95g/l sugar.

Village Collection

Classic Red ★★ Berry-rich, unwooded cab, shiraz & pinotage mix styled for easy quaffing. **Crispy White** ★★ Sauvignon & colombard deliver light (12% alc), racy sipper. **Extra Light** ★★ 9-variety demandingly dry dieter's friend (1.7g/l sugar, 10% alc). **Simply Sweet** ★★ Tropical blend hanepoot, chard & colombard with soft sweet charms. **Natural Sweet Rosé** ★★ Chenin, chard & cab party girl trips lightly (8.6% alc) to sweetish finish. All **NV**, in 750ml & 3litre packs. — *CvZ*

■ **Tulbagh Winery** *see Tulbagh Wine Cellars*
■ **Tutuka** *see Buthelezi Wines*

Twee Jonge Gezellen Estate/The House of Krone

T 023-230-0680 • F 023-230-0686

Tulbagh ▪ Est 1710 ▪ 1stB 1937 ▪ Tasting & sales Mon-Fri 9-4 Sat & pub hols 10-2 ▪ Casual tasting: no charge; formal tasting: fee on request ▪ Tours Mon-Fri 11 & 3; Sat & pub hols 11 ▪ Closed Easter Fri-Mon, Dec 25-26 & Jan 1 ▪ Owner/winemaker Nicky Krone ▪ 100ha (pinot, muscat de F, chard, chenin, riesling, sauv, semillon) ▪ 800t 8% red 80% white 12% rosé ▪ PO Box 16 Tulbagh 6820 ▪ tjg@mweb.co.za ▪ www.tjwines.co.za

Many remember NC Krone Snr, who died last year, as the pioneer of cold fermentation, the technology that changed the face of warmer-climate wines (NC's willing advice was sought by the likes of Robert Mondavi and Bryce Rankin). He was always a leader: at Stellenbosch University; as a sherry specialist; as a child during holidays he would even be 'touleiertjie' to a span of oxen carrying wine barrels. Son Nicky and daughter-in law Mary, assisted now by their sons Matthew and Luke have taken the wines to new heights, focusing on MCC style sparkling wines to the delight of innumerable fans locally and abroad. Raise your glass, observe the twinkle in the eye of the Krone Borealis, and know that the spirit of NC persists like the fine, spiralling bubbles.

Krone range

★★★★ **Borealis Brut** Exposition of classic consistency in composition (half each pinot/ chard), fine-boned styling (11.5% alc, 7.5-9.5 g/l sugar, no wood) & Krone quality in vertical array reviewed for this ed: preferences for freshness (current releases) or degrees of development (limited re-releases of earlier vintages) all catered for. Both **02** & **01** recently disgorged, penetrating vitality & rich toasty notes; **01** lighter & tighter; **99**, 5 yrs on lees, brioche-like warmth, still ends dry; **98** (disgorged 2003) textured, melted butter quality with caramel tints; **97** full 7 yrs on lees, still vibrant, remarkable finesse, pick of bunch. Venerable **93**, Diners Club winner 1995 (when disgorged), broad, golden & ready for contemplative pleasure.

★★★★ **Rosé Brut Cuvée** Exciting salmon-tinted MCC in accomplished house style, poised & elegantly balanced, delicate & refined. **01** lightly fruited, with ribbons of the finest bubbles in dry farewell. Like **00**, impressive 4.5 yrs on lees.

Syrah ★★★☆ **02** dusty berry & dried prune quality, dry earthy tannins; not retasted. **Engeltjipipi** Botrytised semillon, chenin & riesling melange. **01** was last tasted. **Balm of the Night** Fortified muscat de F; none since **99**.

TJ range

Thirty Nine ★★ Clone 39 riesling-dominated blend with sauv, chenin. Delicate, very soft **06** not retasted this ed. **Light** ★★★ Wafting muscat a signature: **07** jasmine sweetness to off-dry palate, 8% alc for anytime thirst. **Schanderl** ★★★ Fragrant honeysuckle on off-dry, assertive **06** from muscat de F, reviewed pvs ed. **The Rose** ★★★ Carbonated **NV**, deep rose-pink; meaty & assertive, from chenin, pinot, shiraz. Not retasted. **Night Nectar Natural Sweet** No new vintage. — *DS*

■ **Twin's Peak** *see Lateganskop Winery*

■ **Two Cubs** *see Knorhoek Wines*

Two Oceans

Good-value range by Distell mainly for export, though the Cab-Merlot and Sauvignon are distributed locally and available for tasting at Bergkelder Wine Centre (see entry).

Soft & Fruity Red ☺ ★★★ Mellow red for winter picnics or fireside quaffing. **06**'s hint of oak lends pleasing dry finish. **Rosé** ☺ ★★★ Shifts to pure shiraz ex-Sbosch & Mbury. **06** ripe, juicy red-berried appeal; off-dry, with fresh zesty finish. **Chardonnay** ☺ ★★★ Tangy, ripe lime, kumquat & marmalade flavours, with zesty lift. **06** medium body, dry finish from oaking. **Sauvignon Blanc** ☺ ★★★ Fresh **07** summertime easy-drinker gains extra grapefruit tang & clean-cut acidity this yr. **Chenin Blanc-Chardonnay** ☺ ★★★ Lively **06** medium-bodied blend (70/30) with subtle lemon flavours & oak-chip spice; clean finish. **Fresh & Fruity White** ☺ ★★★ Gentle, off-dry summer quaffer. **06** light (11.3% alc) with fresh acidity lifting ripe apple & fig flavours.

Pinotage ★★ Bright cherry & tart plum on **06**; Fr oak chips add spice. **Shiraz** ★★★ Ripe **06** has black pepper, bright acidity & fresh juicy appeal. Tannins firm but supple, sustained fruit & finish. **Cabernet Sauvignon-Merlot** ★★★ supple, juicy blend (cab 55%) in balanced, approachable style; pleasing dry 'tea-leaf' tannins. **Merlot-Shiraz** ★★★ Juicy, food-friendly **06**, dark-berried blend merlot & savoury shiraz (35%) with spicy oaking & assertive tannins. **Shiraz-Cabernet Sauvignon** NEW ★★★ Peppery dark fruit & liquorice in successful partnership. **06** firm but succulent tannins & some complexity, sustained dry conclusion. **Semillon-Chardonnay** ★★★ Quiet aromas to fresh, minimally oaked **06** 70/30 blend, but more action on palate & pithy, grippy grapefruit finish. All WO W Cape. Depending on country, available in 750ml/1.5-litre bottles & 3-litre casks. — *MW*

■ **277** *see* La Couronne
■ ***Tygerberg*** *see* Altydgedacht Estate
■ ***Ubuntu*** *see* Umkhulu Wines
■ ***Uhambo*** *see* Premium Cape Wines
■ ***Uiterwyk Estate*** *see* DeWaal Wines

Uitkyk Estate
T *021-884-4416* • **F** *021-884-4717*

Stellenbosch • *Tasting & sales Mon-Fri 9-5 Sat/Sun 10-4* • *Fee R20-R25 incl glass* • *Picnics in summer* • *Owner Lusan Holdings* • *Winemaker Estelle Lourens (2000)* • *Viticulturist Eben Archer* • *±870ha/20 000cs* • *PO Box 104 Stellenbosch 7599* • *info@uitkyk.co.za* • *www.uitkyk. co.za*

Uitkyk has had a busy year, particularly in the vineyards, with new viognier, sangiovese, mourvèdre and petit verdot vines. Big news is the launch of their second vintage of 10-year-old brandy (the last one was released in 1999), in new packaging. And the manor house, always a big attraction, is getting a facelift.

Carlonet ★★★★ 100% cab; **04** cool mintiness, cassis & cedar; ripe & elegant (13.5% alc) with sufficient tannin & acid to structure fleshy blackcurrant fruit. Fr oak, mostly new. More control, finesse, than last-tasted **01** (★★★★). **Cabernet Sauvignon-Shiraz** ★★★★ **04**, equal blend plus 7% merlot, offers Ribena flavours, firm tannins & savoury finish. 16 mths Fr/Am/ Hung oak. **Chardonnay** ★★★ Oak adds boldness, breadth & toastiness to citrus flavours of **05**, with pithy finish. Fermented/8 mths 70% Fr wood, 30% new. **Sauvignon Blanc** ★★★★ Pungent tinned pea & nettle aromas on previewed **07**, assertive green fig, passionfruit flavours & firm, slightly puckering finish. NE. — *IM*

Uitvlucht Wines
T *023-614-1340* • **F** *023-614-2113*

Montagu (see Klein Karoo map) • *Est 1941* • *Tasting & sales Mon-Fri 8-5.30 Sat 9-1.30 Sun 11-2 during high season* • *Light meals* • *Tour groups* • *Functions* • *Owner 41 members* • *Winemaker Alwyn Liebenberg (Aug 2006)* • *Viticulturist Alwyn Liebenberg (Aug 2006), with Johannes Mellet* • *382ha* • *5 100t/15 000cs 28% red 22% white 50% muscadel* • *PO Box 332 Montagu 6720* • *info@uitvlucht-wines.co.za* • *www.uitvlucht-wines.co.za*

Bulk wines are still the core business here but Alwyn Liebenberg is driving the Uitvlucht brand with niche products. Last year he bought 'the most expensive grapes money can buy'; replaced 60% of his barrels with new French oak; made signature wines for golfer Retief Goosen; and produced an impressive-sounding 'thick, black' port.

Montagu Wine Company range [NEW]

Chardonnay ☺ ★★★ Ripe apple & pear on **07**, supported by subtle oak; perfect easy drinking.

Cabernet Sauvignon Bo-Langkloof Preview **07**, enticing herbal red berry fruit & sophisticated structure. Too young too rate, but building blocks in place for fine debut. Upper Langkloof vyd, 60% new Fr oak. **Merlot** ★★★ Very ripe, New-World-style fruit. Rich choc, mulberry & woodspice yet slightly austere tannins on **07**. 25% new Fr oak. **Pinotage** ★★★ **07** sweet candy aromas rounded out by earthy notes. Juicy sour cherry & plum flavours, medium tannins. Oak as for Merlot. **Shiraz 07** unrated work-in-progress from Upper Langkloof still boarded shut; brooding spice & fruit, but lively redcurrant flavour shows promise. Oak as for Cab. **Chenin Blanc** ★★ **07** citrus & guava with a hint of tropical fruit; apricot finish & easy drinkability. **Red Muscadel** ★★★ Glacéd fruit & Christmas cake aromas on **07**, full-sweet & charming. Older oak aged. **White Muscadel** ★★★ Gorgeous candied orange-peel & blossoms on **07**, lush & well balanced, hint of minerality. **Port** ★★★ From touriga, **NV**. Upfront fruit

& charming brandy spirit touch. **Vintage Port Revolution** ★★★ Fortified prior to fermentation, no wood, aim being to 'bottle whole grape. All top ports will be made this way,' team predicts. **07** creamy blueberry fruit lifted by vibrant brandy spirit.

Sauvignon Blanc NEW ★★★ Vibrant cool-climate feel from Outeniqua fruit, 13% aged in Fr oak. **07** white pear & riper fig, melon; gently tart finish. **Muscat de Frontignan** ★★ 04 delicate white muscat aromas & huge (200g/l) lingering sweetness. Discontinued: **Derde Heuvel Rood**, **Rosé**, **Blanc de Blanc**, **Vin Sec Sparkling**, **Vin Doux Sparkling**. —JP

Ultra Liquors
T 021-797-4341 ▪ F 021-797-4341

marknorrish@ultraliquors.co.za

Leading independent discount liquor chain, sourcing value for money wines for its exclusive labels which include: Table Bay (Red, White and Rosé), Stellenvale (Cabernet Sauvignon, Merlot, Pinotage, Shiraz, Chardonnay and Sauvignon Blanc), Route 303 (Red and White) and Beaufort (5-litre cask range). See Specialist Wine Shops section for store locations and contact details.

■ **Umfiki** see Goudini Wines

Umkhulu Wines
T 021-874-2106 ▪ F 021-874-2106

Stellenbosch ▪ Est/1stB 2000 ▪ Closed to public ▪ Owner Fiona Phillips ▪ Winemaker Wilhelm Kritzinger ▪ 20 000cs 100% red ▪ PO Box 132 Simondium 7670 ▪ info@umkhulu.co.za ▪ www. umkhulu.com

Already enthusiastically received overseas, this range of reds (Sauvignon and Dry White discontinued) is now available locally to please demand. More excitement on the home front came just before harvest in the form of Jemima, the second daughter born to the Phillips family.

- ★★★★★ **Pinotage** New vintage not ready. Pvsly, **04** was bright & modern, with slightly sweet fruit hauled back by firmish tannins to add needed texture.
- ★★★★ **Tian** Bdx-style blend led by cab, with cab f, merlot, malbec, petit v. **02** extracted & modern, **03** (★★★★) on review shy & light-textured, dark berries checked by firm tannins. Yr Fr, 50% new. None tasted since.

Malbec ★★★ 05 a step up; leafy & savoury, some spicy notes, firm tannins countering exuberant mulberry fruit. Dry, moderate 13% alc. Fr oak, 25% new. **Shiraz** ★★★★ Sample **04** not retasted; rich & cordial-like, with sweet black cherry, hint mint & oak vanilla. Yr Fr oak, 50% new. **Ubuntu** ★★★ Pinotage leads this 'Cape blend' with 17% each merlot, petit v. Dark & powerful with concentrated berry/new oak aromas yet pliable, approachable tannins, fleshy core, attractive tarry hint. 14 mths new Fr wood. **Akira** ★★★★ 03 blend cab, pinotage, petit v (49/34/17), last ed was approachable; elegant tannins, pinotage sweetness added generosity & plumpness. Yr Fr/Am oak, 25% new. Next is **05**. **Njalo** ★★★ Last ed **05** was angular with bold tannins needing time or food. 60/20/20 combo merlot, shiraz, pinotage. Discontinued: **Dry Red**, **Sauvignon Blanc**, **Dry White**. — CvZ

Under Oaks

T 021-869-8045 ▪ F 021-872-5575

Paarl ▪ 1st B 2003 ▪ Tasting Tue-Sat 10-5 ▪ Fee R15, refundable on purchase ▪ Bistro Tue-Sat 10-5, Sun by appt for groups & occasions ▪ Art gallery ▪ Owner Hans & Theresa Britz ▪ Winemaker Theresa Britz ▪ Viticulturist Hans Britz ▪ 30ha (cab, chard, chenin, viognier) ▪ 2 000cs 50% red 50% white ▪ PO Box 777 Paarl 7620 ▪ info@underoaks.co.za ▪ www. underoaks.co.za

A bigger and bolder entrance mirrors the myriad improvements and additions to the farm buildings, and the recently replanted vines at Under Oaks. New in 2007 were a rustic bistro in the ancient cellar and an art gallery showing off some of SA's finest new talents, and there's a picnic/fishing deck and kids' area in the planning for summer 2007/8. The newly renovated tasting room is now open Tuesday to Saturday, making this even more of a magnet for tourists and locals.

Cabernet Sauvignon ★★★★ Typical older-style SA cab (& none worse for it!). **04** spicy redcurrants, hint caramel, herbaceous notes; firm, elegant & ready to drink. **Shiraz** NEW ★★★ Dark, brooding & spicy **05**, still tight & reserved mid-2007, gd ripe tannins need time to soften. **Chenin Blanc** Sold out. **Limited Release Sauvignon Blanc** 🗎 ★★★★ Reticent **07**, herbaceous, hints lime & lemon; zippy acid completes medium-bodied palate. Should fill out over next yr/2. — *JP*

United Nations of Wine NEW
T 011-884-3304 • F 011-883-0426

Stellenbosch • Est/1stB 2005 • Closed to public • Owner/winemaker David John Bate • 21 000cs 50% red 50% white • 8 Royal Ascot Lane, Sandown, Sandton 2196 • firstfrog@leopard-frog.com • www.unitednationsofwine.com

This is the prêt-à-porter range of Leopard Frog's David John Bate. Value, earth-friendly packaging and a zingy name ('Frisky Zebras') have established it as Canada's leading SA tetrapak wine brand. 'We want to leave the world a better place without sacrificing quality of lifestyle,' says Bate, 'and a good glass of wine.'

Frisky Zebras range
Seductive Shiraz ★★★ **05** easy yet characterful drinking with ripe red fruits & spice, rounded firm body, sound dryness. Fresh oakspice a pleasing extra. **Sensuous Sauvignon Blanc** ★★ For those who prefer quieter, slighter sauvs. **06** fresh but unaggressive, peep of tropical fruit, 12.5% alc. — *AL*

■ **Unity** *see* African Terroir
■ **uniWines** *see* WaverleyTBS/uniWines
■ **Upington** *see* Oranjerivier Wine Cellars

Upland Estate
T 082-731-4774 • F 021-873-5724

Wellington (see Paarl map) • Est/1stB 1998 • Visits by appt • Self-catering cottages • Distillery • Farm-grown/made olives & tapenade • Owner Edmund & Elsie Oettlé • Winemaker/viticulturist Edmund Oettlé • 12ha (cab, chenin, crouchen) • 30t/500cs 100% red • PO Box 152 Wellington 7654 • edmund@oettle.com • www.organicwine.co.za, http://oettle.com

This organic wine farm and distillery took a sabbatical last year, resting the vineyards and making no wine. Edmund Oettlé jokes that they did their bit to stem the world-wide tide of overproduction, instead turning attention to jobs that are often overlooked in the crush, like alien vegetation control and building maintenance.

Cabernet Sauvignon ✿ ★★★ **03** shows minty, dusty notes; spicy, warm, ripe & jammy fruit; quick dusty finish. **Pheasant Haven Cabernet Sauvignon** ✿ ★★★★ Maiden **03** last ed showed elegant 'claret' tone, supple fruit & spicy tannins; noted as repaying cellaring. **Equinox Port** ✿ ★★ Bottled version tad less appealing than last yr's preview: herbaceous & leathery, with woody molasses flavours. **NV**. — *MM*

Usana
T 082-896-3437, 083-625-2301 • F 021-865-2759

Stellenbosch • Est/1stB 2003 • Tasting by appt • Owner Naomi and Jennie Joubert • Winemaker Mike Dobrovic • Viticulturist Joubert brothers • PO Box 7087 Stellenbosch 7599 • usana@xsinet.co.za • www.usana.co.za

It took serious negotiation for sisters-in-law Jennie and Naomi Joubert to secure grapes from their vinegrower husbands for the maiden (03) white, made by Mulderbosch's Mike Dobrovic. It promptly sold out, encouraging them to add touches of rouge to the portfolio. The eventual aim is a two-wine range: the ever-popular Sauvignon and a single-varietal red.

★★★★ **Cabernet Sauvignon** Last-tasted **04** was bouncy & energetic, showing ripe fruit, touches choc & char from new oak well knit with youthful but pliable tannins. Would reward cellaring.

★★★★ **Sauvignon Blanc** ✓ Big & exciting **07** sustains upward trend. Pale green tinge & typical sauv notes herald concentrated greenpepper flavours & complexity from long lees-ageing. **05** stepped up, showed admirable depth & concentration. **06** untasted.

Merlot ★★★★ Last ed **04** was accessible, big on fruit & character. Choc/vanilla married with mellow berries, mint & herbs; 13.7% alc added glow. — *DB*

Uva Mira Vineyards

T 021-880-1683 • F 021-880-1682

Stellenbosch ▪ Est 1997 ▪ 1stB 1998 ▪ Tasting & sales Mon-Fri 8.30-4.30 Sat 9.30-1 ▪ Closed Christian holidays ▪ Owner Denise Weedon ▪ Winemaker Matthew van Heerden (May 2003) ▪ Viticulturist Matthew van Heerden (May 2003), advised by Kevin Watt ▪ 30ha ▪ 5 000cs 60% red 40% white ▪ PO Box 1511 Stellenbosch 7599 ▪ info@uvamira.co.za ▪ www.uvamira.co.za

'We've had an exceptional year,' reflects winemaker Matthew van Heerden, having been on the receiving end of numerous awards, particularly for the Chardonnay. Now, he says, the trick is to maintain the quality and momentum, and keep the wine drinker stimulated. 'We're not going to disappoint!' he assures, pronouncing the wines released mid-2007 as 'streets ahead, with a direct sense of place'. The opening of the high-altitude tasting room, surrounded by the most elevated vineyards (620 metres above sea level) on the Helderberg, coincided with the launch of their flagship Uva Mira Red.

Vineyard Selection

★★★★ **Uva Mira Red Blend** Delicious cab blend combining luscious cassis fruit with earthy, savoury tones courtesy dashes merlot, cab f, shiraz & oak (18 mths Fr, 30% new); 14.5% alc well hidden. Already drinking well, should improve 5-7 yrs.

★★★★★ **Single Vineyard Chardonnay** Single vyd origin now asserted on label (highest chard block on Hldrberg). Classy **06** shines with measured oak, refined lime fruit, refreshing minerality; has all the finesse of understated **05**, poise of harmonious **04**. 11 mths Fr oak.

Single Vineyard Shiraz NEW ★★★★ **06** still in 100% new barrels (so rating tentative) but already supple, lithe; lush but focussed fruit; hints leather, spice & cranberry in most promising debut; look forward to bottled version.

Cellar Selection

Merlot-Cabernet Sauvignon ★★★ Nearly equal portions merlot/cab in **05**. Intense leather & plum, following to fruit-dense palate, grainy tannins needing few yrs to settle. Yr Fr oak, 30% new. **Sauvignon Blanc** 🔲 ★★★★ Delicately balanced **07** ups ante: generous nettle & capsicum fruit pierced by zesty acidity, anchored by well-judged 13.5% alc. **06** (★★★☆) was softer & more curvaceous. — *CvZ*

Val de Vie Winelands Lifestyle Estate

T 021-863-4481 • F 021-863-2741

Paarl ▪ Est 2003 ▪ 1stB 2004 ▪ Tasting daily 10-5 ▪ Tours daily by appt only 10-4 ▪ Closed Easter Fri-Sun, Dec 25 & Jan 1 ▪ Restaurant ▪ Walks, hikes & mountain bike trails ▪ Proclaimed conservation area ▪ Owner Gatekeeper Asset Management Ltd. ▪ Winemaker Martin Fourie (Nov 2005) ▪ Viticulturist Tony Pretorius (Dec 2006) ▪ 24ha (carignan, cinsaut, grenache n/b, mourvèdre, shiraz, clairette, viognier) ▪ 75t/4 250cs 60% red 40% white ▪ Other export brand: Craftsman ▪ ISO 9001 & HACCP certification in progress ▪ PO Box 6223 Paarl 7620 ▪ wine@ valdevie.co.za ▪ www.valdevie.co.za

In Val de Vie's boutique cellar, it's the southern Rhône varieties that get attention. Small fermenters give winemaker Martin Fourie freedom to experiment, while an innovative approach to the oak-maturation process retains more of the natural characteristics of the grapes. This 'lifestyle estate' also boasts 550 residential plots and two world-class polo fields.

★★★★ **Shiraz 04** toasty oak & baked fruit - rather attractive. Ripe tannins to match, big & beefy, muscular, but charming. Not overripe at 14% alc. 60% new oak.

★★★★ **Val de Vie** Flagship label, **06** already approachable thanks to careful blending & loads new oak (15 mths). Creamy red & black fruits, smooth feel, slight sweetness on finish. Trendy blend mourvèdre 59%, shiraz 20%, grenache (noir) & carignan 7.5% each, dollop cinsaut.

Mourvèdre ★★★★ Individual **04** shows subtler side of variety, elegant red-berried fruits, silky feel, ultra-soft tannins, some earthiness on finish. MIWA DG. **Shiraz-Mourvèdre** ★★★★ **04** more grippy than varietal version, even more rhône-like, attractive dryness without sacrificing flesh & juice. 60% new oak. **Craftsman** ★★★★ **06** gutsier version of flagship above, some may prefer. Similar varietal mix, different proportions. Lovely richness & generosity but also more tannins; persistent. **Viognier** ★★★ Light touch with wood in **06** (10% oak fermented/aged), biggish build, slight earthiness. **GCV** ★★★★ Grenache bl, clairette & viognier. **06** loads of interest; complex blend floral, white peach & earthy notes. A breakaway from usual 'fresh & fruity', could do with better acidity to fight flab though. Unoaked. Mainly W Cape WOs for these. —*IvH*

■ **Vals Baai** *see* False Bay Vineyards

Van Loveren Private Cellar
T 023-615-1505 • F 023-615-1336

Robertson ▪ Est 1937 ▪ Tasting & sales Mon-Fri 8.30-5 Sat 9.30-1 ▪ Closed Easter Fri/Sun, Dec 25 & Jan 1 ▪ Tours on request ▪ Sweetcorn fritters available Sat 9.30-1 ▪ Tour groups ▪ Conference/function venue ▪ Self-catering Farm Cottage (see Stay-over section) ▪ Walks ▪ Owner Nico, Wynand, Phillip, Hennie, Bussell & Neil Retief ▪ Winemaker Bussell Retief with Danelle van Rensburg (since 2007) ▪ Viticulturist Neil & Hennie Retief ▪ 220ha (cab, red muscadel, sauv) ▪ 4000t/600 000cs 33% red 33% white 34% rosé ▪ PO Box 19 Klaasvoogds 6707 ▪ info@vanloveren.co.za ▪ www.vanloveren.co.za

One of SA's largest privately owned wine cellars continues to grow, with new vines of pinot gris/grigio (making them the biggest local grower of this variety), cape riesling, sauvignon and semillon, with more pinotage and shiraz coming soon. To help vinify this abundance, Van Loveren has broken with tradition and appointed its first non-family winemaker in the person of Danelle van Rensburg. Her portfolio includes the Van Loveren and Signature ranges, while cellarmaster Bussell Retief focuses on Four Cousins and Papillon. Not only is the cellar's capacity expanding to 600 000 cases, the Retief family is growing too: babies for Neil and Stephanie R, and Phillip and Charl-Mari, bring the number of grandchildren to ten. Upcoming developments include remodelling of the cellar, with smaller tanks and a new press.

Wolverine Creek Limited Releases

Cabernet Sauvignon ★★★☆ Sample **06** dark core, ripe mulberry fruit, soft & plushy textured. Juiciness held in check by well extracted tannins &12 mths oaking. **Shiraz** ★★★★ Peppery, classic **05**, lean, sinewy fruit underpinned by grip imparted from mix of Fr & Am oak (12 mths). Fresh, balanced & spicy. **Chardonnay** ✓ ★★★★ **06** toasty oak from well-judged 5 mths in new Fr; signalling more seriousness than **05** (★★); firm, some breadth from lees contact. Citrus & apple fruit lifted by lively acidity. TWS gold. **Noble Late Harvest** ★★★★ After skipping few yrs, lighter styled **06** varietally true. From riesling, with generous honeyed stonefruit flavours & clean, brisk acidity; lingering savoury finish. **03** (★★★) matured early. Range pvsly listed as 'Signature Series Limited Releases'.

Van Loveren range

Merlot ☺ ★★★ Ripe **06**, staved 6 mths adding grip & savouriness to plummy merlot fruit, pleasant early drinking. **Pinotage** ☺ ★★★ Juicily fruited & staved **06**, with little to detract from simple enjoyment. **Cabernet Sauvignon-Shiraz** ☺ ★★★ Unoaked cab (70%) shiraz blend, skins giving sufficient grip to bright fruit, otherwise easy-going **06**. **Red Muscadel** ☺ ★★★★ Fortified muscat (17% alc) with deceptively high 200g/l sugar. Abundant litchi with added spicy notes; acidity lifts finish & avoids cloying.

River Red ★★★ Popular unwooded blend shiraz, merlot, ruby cab in **06**. Bright, ripe fruit; spicy shiraz carries to finish. **Blanc de Noir Shiraz** ★★ **07** spicy red fruit aromas, pleasant, lively, perfect for picnics. **Blanc de Noir Red Muscadel** ★★ **07** unfortified muscat (11.5% alc); spicy litchi & rosepetal aromas. Clean & dry finish. **Chardonnay** ★★ Lightly staved **07** styled for popular appeal; buttery, crisp green apple & citrus flavours. **Colombard** ★☆ **07** fresh pineapple flavours, crisp acidity rounded by 13g/l. Pleasant quaffer. **Fernão Pires** ★★ **07** spicy pear-drop aromas, breezy, balanced; just off-dry. **Pinot Grigio** ★★ Preview **07** spicy baked apples, pleasantly dry & lively finish. **Cape Riesling** ★ **07** bone dry crisp & simple. From crouchen blanc. **Sauvignon Blanc** ★☆ **07** fresh pineapple; light & shy uncomplicated, easy, early drinking. **Light White** ★ **07** low in alc & kilojoules; dilute, perfect quaffing for the weight conscious. **Blanc de Blanc** ★★ **07** fresh, ideal easy lunchtime drink. Undemanding, light & simple. **Colombar-Chardonnay** ★★★ **07** soft lightly fruity, peachy, lunchtime quaffer (12.5% alc); area's trademark blend. **Special Late Harvest Gewürztraminer** ★★★ **07** abundant Turkish Delight. Balanced acidity gives clean, dry finish to delicate sweet & spicy flavours. **Ruby Port** ★★★ NV tasted pvs ed; delicious choc-laced prunes & berries with hints of coffee mocha. Discontinued: **Semillon**.

Four Cousins range

Dry Red ★★ Usual blend merlot, shiraz & ruby cab; unwooded pizza & party red. **Dry River White** ★★ Dry colombard chenin blend, easy quaffing party wine, zippy acidity. **Natural Sweet Red** ★★ Sweet & quaffable shiraz, ruby cab & grape juice blend. Light 9.5% alc; spicy grip. **Natural Sweet Rosé** ★★ Sweet red muscat & colombard blend, light 8% alc and spicy finish. **Natural Sweet White** ★★ Sweet (60g/l) muscat, light alc (7.5%) with simple clean finish. Serve well-chilled. All **NV**, uncertified handy party-size 1.5-litre bottles.

Five's Reserve range

Pinotage ☺ ★★★ Juicily fruited & staved **06**; little to detract from simple enjoyment.

Cabernet Sauvignon-Merlot ★★ Soft, juicy **06** blend; staved (Fr) 12 mths adding oaky spiciness. **Merlot Rosé** ★★ **06** tasted pvs ed blanc de noir in style with berry/candyfloss aromas. **Chenin Blanc** ★★ **07** very youthful; simple apple fruit but lavish acidity ensures clean dry finish. Name refers to Big 5 game featured on this BEE range's labels; some screwcapped.

Papillon Sparkling range

Brut ★★ From colombard & sauv; invigoratingly fruity with clean, fresh apple flavours. **Demi-Sec** ★★ Grapey muscat whiffs on semi-sweet sparkler, spicy mouthfeel with perky finish. **Vin Doux** ★★ Sweet red from muscat; piquant raspberry taking the edge off the sweetness. These are wallet-friendly, lowish alc (11-11.5%) **NV** carbonated bubblies; colour-coded butterfly labels depict style. — IM

■ **Vansha** *see Ridgeback Wines*

Van Zylshof Estate
T 023-616-2401 • F 023-616-3503

Robertson • Est 1993 • 1stB 1994 • Tasting & sales Mon-Fri 9-5 Sat 9-1 • Closed Easter Fri & Dec 25 • Tours by appt • Owner Van Zylshof Trust • Winemaker/viticulturist Andri van Zyl • 32ha (cab, merlot, chard, chenin, sauv) • 10 000cs 10% red 90% white • PO Box 64 Bonnievale 6730 • vanzylshof@lando.co.za

Andri van Zyl reports another harvest with not a single hiccup - not as big as the bumper 2006 but 'the quality was great!' After consultation, he decided to bottle a maiden Rosé, and the Chardonnay Riverain took Veritas gold for the third year running.

564 • VAUGHAN JOHNSON'S WINE & CIGAR SHOP

Van Zylshof Estate range

> **Rosé** NEW ☺ ★★★ Merlot-based pink **07**, fresh, fruity, with palate-cleansing acidity, fruit tannin tickle. Serve well-chilled. EW. **Chenin Blanc** ☺ ★★★ Vivacious **07** charms with usual ripe guava tone, lively acidity & long, friendly (12% alc) farewell. EW.

Cabernet Sauvignon-Merlot ★★★ Myriad flavours, aromas from blackberries to spearmint on **05**; confident, unpretentious & easy-drinking 70/30 mix. EW. **Chardonnay** ★★★ **06** soft orange/tangerine notes brushed by vanilla-cream from gentle oak; balanced 14% alc. EW. **Chardonnay Riverain** ★★★ Unwooded Rbtson chard. Pre-bottling sample **07** subdued, but does show signature lime minerality. EW. **Sauvignon Blanc** ★★ Pre-bottled **07** shows dusty green aromas & flavours, bracing lemon-drop acidity. EW. — *CvZ*

■ **Van Zylskloof** *see Johan van Zyl Wines*

Vaughan Johnson's Wine & Cigar Shop
T 021-419-2121 • F 021-419-0040

Est/1stB 1985 • Sales Mon-Fri 9-6 Sat 9-5 Sun 10-5 • Open pub hols • Gifts, souvenirs, spirits & beer available • Owner Vaughan Johnson • PO Box 50012 Waterfront 8002 • vjohnson@mweb.co.za • www.vaughanjohnson.com

'Producers have never been so generous with their samples,' notes Vaughan Johnson, owner of one of SA's busiest wine stores (on Cape Town's bustling V&A Waterfront), 'which proves my point that those with marketing and communication skills will succeed as overseas demand dwindles.' Demand from foreign tourists is for good value: 'They don't come here to pay Lafite prices!' Trends? Our world-class sweet wines, rosé, sauvignon and sparkling are on the up, but chardonnay and merlot are losing out, the latter because 'ours is underwhelming', says the trenchant retailer, whose own-brand housewines practise what their owner preaches.

> **Sunday Best Red** ☺ ★★★ Smoked meat & roasted herbs, spicy red fruit aromas from cab & merlot. Firm tannic grip invites food.

Good Everyday Cape Red ★★ Appealingly rustic blend; simple red cherry fruit with zippy acidity to finish. **Sunday Best White** ★★ Sauv & colombard mix, light bodied with lowish alc (12.5%). Undemanding. **Good Everyday Cape White** ★★ Apt moniker for uncomplicated, everyday quaffer from riesling, chenin, sauv. Both ranges **NV**, for current consumption.

Waterfront Collection

> **Captain's Claret** ☺ ★★★ Shiraz led, with dollop merlot; generous ripe mulberry fruit. Soft tannins & sweet spicy finish.

Great White ★★ From chenin; simple fresh apple aromas with racy acidity throughout. Nautical labels distinguish this value-priced, quaffable duo. — *IM*

■ **Veelplesier** *see Baarsma Wine Group*
■ **Veelverjaaght** *see Beau Joubert Vineyards & Winery*

Veenwouden Private Cellar
T 021-872-6806 • F 021-872-1384

Paarl • Est 1989 • 1stB 1993 • Sales & tasting by appt Mon-Fri 9-4.30 • Fee R100/btl if no purchase made • Closed pub hols • Tours by appt • Owner Deon van der Walt Trust • Winemaker Marcel van der Walt, with Faried Williams (Jan 1994/1995) • Viticulturist Marcel van der Walt, with Sias Louw (Jan 1994/1995) • 14ha (cabs s/f, malbec, merlot) • ±100t/5 500cs own labels 99% red 1% white • PO Box 7086 Northern Paarl 7623 • admin@veenwouden.com • www.veenwouden.com

Sometime professional golfer Marcel van der Walt and wine colleague Faried Williams both marked 15 years of winemaking last year, and celebrated their 13-year partnership at this upscale Paarl property with, among others, a new people-friendly photon sterilisation system. In addition to still lower yields of higher-grade grapes, recently planted malbec and petit verdot are opening up new areas of play – the latter already earmarked for blending.

Veenwouden Private Cellar range

★★★★☆ **Merlot** A Cape 'celebrity' wine. **04** (90% merlot & equal mix cabs s/f) reverts to fuller style of **02**. No longer single vyd but still Rubenesque showing lots of fleshy fruit & firm yet rounded tannins from 2 yrs 80% new Fr oak. **03** was more fine-toned.

★★★★☆ **Veenwouden Classic** Highly regarded bdx blend cabs s/f, merlot & soupçon malbec; 50% barrel fermented. Just bottled, **04** (★★★★) dark fruits gripped by powerful tannins; needs cellaring ±5yrs to soften, gain complexity. Aged as merlot below.

★★★★ **Vivat Bacchus** No new vintage. Last ed, **03** was firm yet pliable with lingering finish. 60% merlot, with malbec, cabs f/s. 50% new Fr oak, 2 yrs.

★★★★☆ **Chardonnay Special Reserve** Stand-out version, neither merely opulent nor just elegant. Meursault-like **04** had apple pie with a tangerine twist, moderate 13% alc. New Fr oak fermented, sur lie ageing 9 mths. Tasted last ed, **05** not ready.

Thornhill range

★★★★ **Shiraz** Stylish, bold & dramatic **04** more perfumed & spicy, less chunky than **03**. 14 mths seasoned Fr oak, 8% unwooded viognier replaced cab of pvs. Not retasted.

Tempranillo-Cabernet Sauvignon ★★★★ Tangy **05** has sour cherry, scrub notes & refreshing acidity boosted by licorice tones, linear tannins of 40% cab. 14 mths used Fr oak. **Viognier-Chenin Blanc** NEW ★★★★ **06**'s tropical fruit braced by acid. Unwooded, 13% alc. — *CvZ*

Vendôme

T 021-863-3905 · F 021-863-0094

Paarl · Est 1692 · 1stB 1999 · Tasting & sales Mon-Fri 9.30-1 Sat 9.30-12.30 · Fee R5 refunded on purchase · Closed pub hols · Tours on request · Conferencing/functions for up to 60 · Owner Jannie le Roux Snr · Winemaker Jannie le Roux Jnr · Viticulturist Jannie le Roux Snr & Jnr · 40ha (cabs s/f, merlot, shiraz, chard, chenin, colombard, sauv, semillon) · 20t/1 400cs own label 70% red 30% white · PO Box 36 Paarl 7645 · lerouxjg@icon.co.za · www.vendome.co.za

Winemaker Jannie le Roux Jnr, whose philosophy centres on 'no adding or subtracting; just straightforward, honest winemaking', aims to focus on one white blend and two red blends in the future. 'I'm trying to keep it as simple and natural as possible at all times,' he says.

Classique ★★★★ **03** last ed was promising New-World-styled bdx red with layered fruit, brisk acidity & touches savoury & minerals. Yr oak; unfiltered. **Sans Barrique** ★★★★ Yellow fruit enhanced with lemon freshness; zippy acidity & mineral finish. **06** blend chard, semillon, sauv. Super food wine. Discontinued: **Merlot-Cabernet Sauvignon**. — *JP*

Vera Cruz Estate *see Delheim*

Vergelegen

T 021-847-1334 · F 021-847-1608

Stellenbosch (see Helderberg map) · Est 1700 · 1stB 1992 · Tasting daily 9.30-4.30 (sales close at 5) · Entrance fee R10 p/p · Closed Dec 25, May 1 & Easter Fri · Lady Phillips Restaurant: à la carte lunches daily; Rose Terrace: al fresco restaurant Nov-Apr; picnics Nov-Apr (see Eat-out section) · Guided winery tours daily 10.15, 11.30 & 3 Fee R2-R10/wine · 'Interpretive Centre' depicting farm's history; also self-guided tour to the homestead · Gifts · Tour groups · Owner Anglo American plc · Winemaker André van Rensburg (Jan 1998) · Viticulturist Niel Rossouw, with Petrie Dippenaar & Dwayne Lottering · 112ha (cabs s/f, merlot, shiraz, chard, sauv, semillon) · 47 000cs 60% red 40% white · ISO 9001/140001 & BRC certified · PO Box 17 Somerset West 7129 · vergelegen@vergelegen.co.za · www.vergelegen.co.za

Here, at one of the Cape's most respected and historic properties, the winemaking team is going back to its roots to ensure that the tradition of excellence continues. André van Rensburg completed his tenth vintage in 2007 and is looking forward to the farm being completely replanted to virus-free vines within the next year - leaf-roll virus having been identified as a major quality inhibitor. Another milestone, as this BWI Champion farm steadily becomes more eco-integrated, is the introduction of a small herd of bontebok. Meanwhile eradication of alien vegetation has vastly improved dam levels thanks to better run-off. Van Rensburg is also particularly proud of the 2 million injury-free hours that Vergelegen has logged.

Flagship range

★★★★☆ **Vergelegen** Cape bdx-style blend immaculate fruit, alluring texture, suave tannins. Cab from relatively warmer Rondekop vyd, with 18% merlot & drop cab f in superb **03** (not retasted); beguiling, incipiently complex; showy oak (2 yrs new) shd integrate, if given the time deserved.

★★★★★ **Vergelegen V** Expensive, usually dramatic - like **03**; **04** tends more to classic bdx model. Single vyd cab with total 7% cab f, merlot. V young, showing superb oaking (100% new), but deep, dark reserves of fruit & rich tannins will triumph - already giving v long, fresh finish with fine, subtle note of black choc. Needs min 5 yrs.

★★★★★ **Vergelegen White** Much-praised semillon-sauv blend (now ±70/30), with proven possibilities for maturing well over 5+ yrs. **06** (TWS trophy) shows usual early reticence, spicy oak (50% new) over citrus & ripe tropical hints - but finely concentrated & subtle vinosity rather than overt fruit. Silky, light tannic grip. Immaculate.

★★★★☆ **Auction Reserve White** NEW Just 4 barrels from the best semillon, touched up by 7% sauv, as André van R raises the stakes again. Successfully so: showy - yes, with power on **07** that is all from intense fruit (just 13% alc) & allows rich elegance. 50% new oak for 16 mths a subtle presence. Long, long finish with tangerine piquancy. Shd develop splendidly.

Reserve range

★★★★☆ **Cabernet Sauvignon** Always serious wine, needing time to unmask rich, sweet cassis flavours lurking under oak (2 yrs, 70% new). Ripe, sombre **04** perhaps even tougher in youth than usual, but promising: big, forthright, quite thickly textured. Some dry tannin on end. Hold 5 yrs min.

★★★★★ **Merlot** After showy, savoury **04**, **05** (★★★★) offers more minty herbaceousness along with bright red fruit. Some sweet notes, but a little ungracious & hard, big bones rather gawky (14.5% alc shows); drying tannic finish.

★★★★☆ **Shiraz 04** refined, despite blockbusterish 15% alc. **05** (★★★★) a bit less powerful, but also easy appeal, with red/blackcurrant fruit; chewy, fleshy & succulent, plus gd tannic support. Usually the most early approachable of all these reds. 13 mths oak, 30% new.

★★★★☆ **Chardonnay Reserve** From Lower Schaapenberg vyds. **06** already has complexity, with oatmeal, hazelnut, citrus notes, along with spicy toast from oak (fermented, 14 mths, half new; partial malo). Lightly creamy, with tannic undertone & fine lemony freshness.

★★★★★ **Sauvignon Blanc Reserve** Wind-swept Schaapenberg site the single vyd origin for this fine wine, where variety seems almost secondary to the subtle vinous complexity. **06** concentrated & intense, with a range of ripe flavours & an earthy bass-note. Well balanced, with modest 12.8% alc & tangy freshness; persistent, dry finish.

★★★★ **Semillon** Only occasionally made, in small volume in gd yrs. **06** has floral notes along with citrus, supported by subtle oak (fermented/10 mths, 50% new); firm, generous, savoury mouthful with modest 13% alc, dry finish. Has few yrs to go.

★★★★ **Weisser Riesling Noble Late Harvest** Lashings of pineapple & marmalade, some honey & raisins on **05** (tasted last ed). Low 10% alc & high acidity invigorating 160g/l sugar sweetness. Delectably lingering.

Premium range

★★★★ **Chardonnay** As usual **06** has unshowy but substantial presence supporting beguiling aromas oatmeal, citrus, toast. Fresh, well balanced; fruit not concentrated, but elegant. Some oak fermented (25% new), all 10 mths on lees.

★★★★ **Sauvignon Blanc** Just a touch of semillon on **07**. Grassy green edge to ripe gooseberry, passionfruit character; mouthfilling, with succulent acid enlivening almost rich texture.

Mill Race Red ★★★★ Sturdy **05** blend cab/merlot, with some malbec, cab f. Spicy, herbal aromas. Serious rather than easy, with gd tannins, evident alc (14.5%) & oak (20 mths, 30% new); herbaceous finish. No hurry. **Vin de Florence** ★★★ No longer chenin based, **06** adds a little hanepoot to sauv & semillon for light flowery, fruity charm; softly off-dry, fresh. — *TJ*

Vergenoegd Estate

T 021-843-3248 • F 021-843-3118

Stellenbosch • Est 1773 • 1stB 1972 • Tasting & sales Mon-Fri 8.30-5 Sat 9.30-12.30; tasting also during restaurant hours: Tue-Sat lunch & (booking essential) dinner; Sun & pub hols lunch only; breakfast for groups by appt only • Tours by appt • Owner Vergenoegd Trust • Winemaker John Faure (1984) • Vineyard Manager Chris van Niekerk (May 2003), advised by Drikus van der Westhuizen • 90ha (cabs s/f, merlot, shiraz) • 500t/10 000cs own label 95% red 5% port • PO Box 1 Faure 7131 • enquiries@vergenoegd.co.za • www.vergenoegd.co.za

Vergenoegd's first-ever malbec and new cab franc block will soon be adding further dimension to their blends. Meanwhile, diners at Mike Israel's Pomegranate, which has found a home on the estate, continue to enjoy the sight of the Indian Runners returning home from the vineyard - John Faure is also a prize-winning duck breeder.

★★★★ **Cabernet Sauvignon** Richly textured red with estate's signature restraint & elegance. **04** cassis; leather & cedar spice from combo Fr, Russ & Am oak. Persistent juicy finish, unobtrusive 14.5% alc. Should reward 3 yrs+ cellaring. EW.

★★★★ **Shiraz 04** less burly than pvs, shows sappy red fruit, estate's dry, elegant tannins, salty lick on finish. 18-14 mths Fr oak, 30% new. **03** more 'masculine' with leathery, smoky notes. EW.

★★★★☆ **Vergenoegd Estate Blend** Imposing yet elegant médoc styled blend cab/merlot/cab f. **04** savoury & succulent; complex, with seaspray hints, leather & cedar. Alc (14.5%) & 22 mths oak (87% new) balanced by fruit. Accessible, food-friendly & cellar-worthy as was more medicinal, sturdy **03**. EW.

★★★★ **Old Cape Colony Vintage Port** Classically profiled (around 85g/l sugar, 20% alc), fermented in open kuipe, matured 18 mths in old oak. **03** (★★★★) equal parts tinta & touriga; has prune, choc & Friars Balsam hints; chunky tannins, peppery, spirity bite. **01** (★★★★☆) was the standout vintage, **02** (★★★) in a lighter style, tinta-only **00** very pleasing. EW.

Merlot ★★★★ Blackcurrant & leafy notes to **04**, juicy with bright, food-friendly acidity, firm tannins from 22 mths Fr oak, 33% new. EW. **Terrace Bay** ★★★★ 'Second label' blending 5 of farm's 6 varieties into savory tipple. **04** more supple, less serious minded than pvs; 14.5% alc in sync, pleasant, dry farewell. EW. — *MW*

Versailles

T 021-898-9314 • F 021-873-2608

Wellington • Est 2003 • 1stB 2004 • Visits by appt • Conservation area • Owner Tienie Malan & Annareen de Reuck • Winemaker Loftie Ellis • 116ha (cab, merlot, shiraz, chenin) • 1 200t/ ±700cs own label 100% red • Export brand: Malan de Versailles • PO Box 597 Wellington 7654 • adereuck@ezinet.co.za

This year sees the introduction of an easy-drinking Versailles 'housewine', but Annareen de Reuck (neé Malan) remains most passionate about keeping her family name alive through the boutique Malan de Versailles range. 'Otherwise our 160-year-old history on this farm would have ended when my brother died 16 years ago.'

Malan de Versailles Shiraz ★★ Pleasant oak & black pepper notes, refreshing acidity on **04**, slightly dull fruit the only caveat. — *CvZ*

■ **Versus** *see* The Company of Wine People
■ **Vertex** *see* Bonnievale Wine Cellar
■ **Victoria Peak** *see* Daschbosch Wine Cellar

Vilafonté

T 021-886-4083 • F 021-883-8231

Stellenbosch • Est 1996 • 1stB 2003 • Tasting & tours by appt • Italian bistro serving light meals; Lavazza coffee shop • Retail gift shop • Local produce • Wine & Cigar Experience • Cellar tours & tour groups by appt • Function room for special occasions • Owner Mike Ratcliffe, Zelma Long & Phil Freese • Winemaker Bernard le Roux • Viticulturist Phil Freese • 15ha (cabs s/f, malbec, merlot) • ±80t/3 000cs 100% red • 7C Lower Dorp Street; Bosman's Crossing; Stellenbosch; 7600 • info@ vilafonte.com • www.vilafonte.com; www.vilafonte.blogspot.com

This high-profile collaboration between the US's Zelma Long and Phil Freese, and Warwick's Mike Ratcliffe now has a home at Bosman's Crossing in Stellenbosch. The 'winemaking studio' has Zelma L enthusing: 'Its design supports the best winemaking I have ever done, anywhere'. Alongside is a 'winetasting studio' where visitors can enjoy the Vilafonté Sensory Experience, which encompasses food and wine pairing, by appointment. New members of the team include vineyard manager Edward Pietersen and relationship manager Pippa Wordie. Extensive marketing travel has made the year a whirlwind, says Mike R, but an auspicious one, as the brand is 'going from strength to strength'.

Vilafonté range

★★★★☆ **Series C** Mostly cab, as name implies (66%, with 22% merlot, 6% each malbec & cab f), in this powerful but seamless & polished red; **05** rich, scented; resolute but ripe tannins, harmonious oaking (90% new Fr).

★★★★★ **Series M** Merlot-headlined blend - hence name - with cab & malbec (31/15). **05**, from concentrated yr, appropriately deeply perfumed, opulent & sweet-fruited; accessible but well-structured for longer term cellaring. Fr oak, 34% new. — *AL*

Viljoensdrift Wines

T 023-615-1901 • F 023-615-3417

Robertson • Est/1stB 1998 • Tasting & sales Mon-Fri 8.30-5 (cellar); Cruises @ Riverside tasting area open Sep-Apr Wed-Sat & 1st Sun/mnth 10.30-5; May-Aug Wed & Sat 10.30-2; Dec & Jan Mon-Sun 10.30-2. Closed Easter Fri, Dec 25, Jan 1 • Create your own picnic from the deli • Tours by appt • Owner Fred & Manie Viljoen • Winemaker Fred Viljoen • Viticulturist Manie Viljoen • 120 ha (cab, pinotage, shiraz, chard, chenin, sauv) • 1 200t/±80 000cs 50% red 48% white 2% rosé • Export brands: Die Rivierkloof, Elandsberg, Keurfontein, River Grandeur & Somerlust • PO Box 653 Robertson 6705 • wines@viljoensdrift.co.za • www. viljoensdrift.co.za

The Viljoens' all-seasons 'theatre-style' tasting room, boasting old-fashioned 'bioscope' armchairs, is now complete. Visitors can view art movies here, or DVDs on the life of a working wine farm. With its lovely locale on the banks of the Breede River, it also promises to be a big draw for weddings and conferences. Hot favourites remain winter fireside wine tastings and, in summer, a deli with foods for a DIY picnic… and, of course, river cruises aboard 'Uncle Ben'. The standard range is now screwcapped and the maiden MCC is ready for lift-off.

River Grandeur range

Chenin Blanc ☺ ★★★ Golden delicious aromas in **07** with crisp, balanced flavours & moderate 12.5% alc, ideal lunchtime quaffer.

Cabernet Sauvignon ★★★ **05** high-toned, ripe blackberry aromas; very ripe, juicy fruit kept firmly in check by firm tannins & acidity. Yr Fr oak. **Pinotage** ★★★★ Appealing violet & plum aromas, soft, juicy marello cherry flavours. Well-integrated, smooth tannins from yr Fr oak.

Shiraz ★★ Enticing lily, ripe mulberry, aniseed aromas let down by harsh tannin & acid, warm 15% alc & salty finish. Yr Fr/Am oak. **Chardonnay** ★★★ Crowd-pleasing **07** with vibrant stone fruit flavours & zingy acidity. Well-judged 3 mths Fr oak plays supporting role. **Sauvignon Blanc** ★★★ Both herbaceous & tropical **07** in light, delicate style. Crisp, soft finish.

Viljoensdrift range

★★★★ **Serenity** Bdx-style blend cab, merlot, cab f & petit v with serious ambitions. Classic medicinal, blackcurrant, cedar aromas; furry tannins from all new Fr oak currently masking rich, compact fruit. Needs time to soften.

Rosé ☺ 🍽 ★★★ Popular & appealing simple rosé from shiraz. 14g/l sugar on **07** softens & balanced acidity ensuring clean, dry finish.

Cape Blend NEW ★★★ **06** blend shiraz, pinotage, cab & merlot spent yr in oak. Assertive tannin & acid mask blackberry fruit. Dry, savoury finish. **Wine on the Water Sweet Rosé** NEW New wine, currently out of stock. **Colombar-Chenin Blanc** 🍽 ★★ Light, balanced, floral **07** pleasant daytime quaffer. 12.5% alc. **Cape Vintage Reserve** ★★★★ Spicy 2nd vintage **04** from souzão in unwooded, lighter style (16% alc) with decent grip from grape tannins. 110g/l RS. Discontinued: **Merlot-Shiraz**. — *IM*

■ **Village Collection** *see* Tulbagh Wine Cellars
■ ***Villa Verde*** *see* Seven Oaks

Villiera Wines
T 021-865-2002/3 • F 021-865-2314

Stellenbosch ▪ Est/1stB 1983 ▪ Tasting & sales Mon-Fri 8.30-5 Sat 8.30-3 ▪ Closed Easter Fri/ Sun, Dec 25, Jan 1 ▪ Self-guided tours anytime during tasting hours; guided tours by appt ▪ Annual St Vincent's Day dinner (closest Sat to Jan 22) ▪ BYO picnic in summer ▪ Owner Grier family ▪ Cellarmaster Jeff Grier ▪ Winemaker Jeff Grier, with Anton Smal (Oct 1992) ▪ Viticulturist Simon Grier ▪ 260ha (13 varieties, r/w) ▪ 2 000t/100 000cs own label + 16 000cs for Woolworths + 9 000cs for Marks & Spencer (UK) ▪ 38% white 33% red 4% rosé 25% sparkling ▪ PO Box 66 Koelenhof 7605 ▪ wine@villiera.com ▪ www.villiera.com

'We're in a consolidation phase,' says Jeff Grier, referring to local operations. But that doesn't equate to any slacking off at this enterprising family-run winery. Taking advantage of growth in the sparkling wine market, they've expanded cap classique production and upgraded their cellar facilities to include a new bottling, labelling and disgorging line. Further afield, their boutique winery in southern France released its first wines, including a number of blends under the Côtes du Rousillon appellation, as the guide went to press. Other projects include a mentorship brand, M'hudi, with neighbours the Rangaka family, and Jeff G's involvement with Elgin Vintners as sauvignon-maker (in exchange for cool-climate fruit). Committed to fair labour practices, Villiera is WIETA accredited.

Villiera Wines range

★★★★ **Monro** Merlot/cab, straddles conservative/modern divide. Thoroughbred, improved **04** misleads with its sinuous body but there's sheathed power. Complex layers red berries, cigarbox, choc confirm its stature, appeal.

★★★★ **Traditional Bush Vine Sauvignon Blanc** ✓ Single-vyd wine, more Loire than New World. Terroir reflects in **07**'s steely minerality, nettle & gunflint tones. Racy acidity & modest alc perfect foil for styling, hold flavours long after glass is empty.

★★★★★ **Brut Natural** Notably dry & refined MCC from chard. No dosage, sulphur; uses native yeast. Lemon zest & savoury baked apple in **04**, accompanying the fine bead, palate-awakening liveliness. Perfect aperitif for fine dining.

★★★★ **Monro Brut** Chard/pinot, former barrel fermented; released after 5 yrs on lees. Latest **01** loads of character, delicious: toasted brioche, citrus peel richness, long lingering flavours. Potential to age few yrs.

★★★★ **Tradition Rosé Brut** Salmon-pink **NV** MCC. Colour from pinotage (majority) added to pinot n & m, chard juice. Latest charms with perfumed, bright fruitiness but palate is pure sophistication: earthy, tastebud-awakening dryness.

★★★★ **Inspiration** Barrel-fermented chenin NLH. Always impressive, **06** (★★★★☆) even better: barley sugar, liquidised apricots, velvety richness, with tangy 9.5g/l acidity making it go down oh-so-deliciously-easy. 10 mths oaking. 375ml. **05** was also decadently delicious & tangy.

Shiraz-Touriga Nacional-Carignan NEW ☺ ★★★ **05** offers wild berries, scrubland perfume, juicy vibrancy. An unusual blend, designed & priced for drinking pleasure.

Cabernet Sauvignon ★★★★ Always textbook varietal expression, well-structured, honest & good. Deliciously juicy cassis, sweet spice rewards the **05** drinker. Yr oaking well judged, fully integrated. **Merlot** ★★★ With smooth drinkability down pat, **05**'s mint & fresh berry charm will delight merlot fans. Partly oaked. **Pinotage** ★★★ Reflecting vintage, **05**'s ripe plummy fruit, fleshy smooth-drinking structure will appeal widely. Yr oaking, portion new, fully integrated. **Shiraz** ★★★★ Last ed, delicious **04** had high-toned brambleberries, mulberries shot through with roasted spice; fleshy richness from gd vyd care. **Chenin Blanc** ✓ ★★★★ Quality, quintessential chenin at bargain price. Melon, pear richness on **07** sample, while palate's limy tang wakens the tastebuds. With touch oak. **Gewürztraminer** ✓ ★★★★ Designed for hedonists, **07**'s wafting rosepetal perfume, softly curvaceous body is pure drinking pleasure. Just off-dry. **Muscat Ottonel** ★★★ Name change from 'Sonnet'. Last tasted **06**, aromatically grapey, off-dry, light (12.5% alc) & perfectly charming. **Rhine Riesling** ★★★★ Just off-dry, retaining freshness & food compatability, **07**'s passionfruit & glacé pineapple tones beautifully reflect variety's aromatic appeal. **Sauvignon Blanc** ★★★★ With leafy nuanced, sliced pear/apple freshness, zesty palate, **07** would love food, also gd solo. With 22% Elgin grapes. **Sauvignon Blanc-Chenin Blanc** ★★★ Sample last ed, **06**'s light-textured (13.2% alc) drinkability, crisp pear & apple fruit tones, make it tasty summertime fare. **Brut Special Dosage** ★★★★ Friendly **NV** MCC with dosage to brut limit; uses same base wine as Tradition. Plumper, richer, without being sweet, for those who prefer their celebrations less dry. **Tradition Brut** ★★★★ Popular **NV** MCC from chard, pinot, pinotage, splash pinot meunier. Satifying drinkability woven throughout; tiny festive bubbles, fruit perfectly balanced by vibrant acidity, lively finish. **Fired Earth** ★★★★ In LBV port style, last-available **01** from 48% shiraz with touriga, pinotage, tinta. Deliciously ready (but will keep ages), with mocha, pruney spicy notes; grip more from acid than tannin. 3 yrs in older oak. WO Coastal. Discontinued: **Merlot-Shiraz-Pinotage**.

Cellar Door range

★★★★ **Chenin Blanc** Characterful example fermented/matured on lees, Fr oak 8 mths. Gd ageing potential, as all these. Previewed **07** had tropical fruit, peach kernel perfume, flavours, sinuous elegance, ultra-long finish.

★★★★ **Rhine Riesling Noble Late Harvest** Last-tasted **05** showed lingering tinned pineapple & marmalade notes, integrated acidity on light, fine richness. 500ml.

Discontinued: **Merlot**.

Down to Earth range

White ☺ ★★★ Reliably tasty quaffer, sauv, portion semillon, **07** sparks with greenpepper vibrancy, juicy flavours.

Red ★★★ 5 varieties consorted in safe, pleasant **05**. Last time showed toasty baked aromas, warmly friendly palate. Yr oaked. **Rosé** ★★★ Mainly pinotage, some gamay, pinot, giving **06** refreshingly dry, earthy, berry flavours. Perfect for al fresco meals or solo enjoyment. — *CR*

Villiersdorp Cellar
T 028-840-1120 • F 028-840-1833

Worcester • Est 1922 • 1stB 1980 • Tasting & sales Mon-Sat 8-5 • Fee R10 for groups of 7+ • Closed Easter Fri & Dec 25 • Fully licensed restaurant, farm stall, wine boutique & gift shop (hours as above + Sun & pub hols 9-3) • Owner 50 growers • Winemaker Ryan Puttick • Viticulturist Leon Dippenaar (Vinpro consultant) • 400ha • 4600t/10 000cs own label 40% red 60% white 6% rosé 14% fortified • PO Box 14 Villiersdorp 6848 • info@vilko.co.za • www.vilko.co.za

Now making the wine as well as overseeing the vineyards, Ryan Puttick is upbeat about sales prospects: 'We keep our producers happy and our prices don't put people off.' He's as delighted as partners Luddite, Paul Cluver and Beaumont with the high-performing Slowine range, whose Shiraz 06 attracted much attention at last year's London IW&S Fair.

Villiersdorp Cellar range

Chenin Blanc ☺ 🍽 **★★★** Vibrant acidity, lemon & peardrop flavours provide attractive early drinking in **07**. WO Overberg. **Sauvignon Blanc** ☺ 🍽 **★★★ 07** (sample) for those partial to sauv's wild side (cat's pee & khaki bush), oyster-friendly acidity. WO Overberg.

Cabernet Sauvignon ★★ Tasted pvs ed, **05** needed time for lusty Fr oak to marry fruit. **Merlot ★★★ 05** last ed paired big oak & alc with delicate fruit; possibly better meshed now. **Shiraz ★★ 05** when last tasted, subtle fruit played second fiddle to vanilla-oak. **Rosé ★★** Slender, sweet **07**, from muscat de F; serve well chilled. Low 7.5% alc. **Late Vintage 🍽 ★★ 07** floral, light, ending gently sweet. Tasted pre-bottling. **Hanepoot Jerepigo 🍽 ★★★** Full-sweet fortified dessert. Tasted last ed, muscat/barley sugar flavoured **06** was fuller, sweeter than pvs. **Port 06** last yr too unformed to rate; pvs were fruity & jammy, from tinta & pontac. Discontinued: **Chardonnay**. Both ranges WO W Cape unless mentioned.

Splendour range
Classic Red 🍽 ★★★ 05 lively, generous, equal cab/merlot, last time combined ripe berry fruit with hint oak. **Blanc de Blanc 🍽 ★★ 07** ex-tank light-textured colombard/chenin sipper, with tart tail; Overberg fruit. — *CvZ*

■ **Vine Collection** see Oranjerivier Wine Cellars
■ **Vineyard Selection** see Blaauwklippen Agricultural Estate

Vinimark
T 021-883-8043/4 • F 021-886-4708

Stellenbosch • Closed to public • Directors Tim Rands, Cindy Jordaan, Geoff Harvey & Gys Naudé • Exports: Ross Rutherfoord • rossr@vinimark.co.za • PO Box 441 Stellenbosch 7599 • www.vinimark.co.za

Wine merchants marketing, selling and distributing various ranges with local partners, including, Kleindal, Long Beach, Silver Sands and Zomerlust, some listed separately.

Vins d'Orrance
T 021-683-7479 • F 021-683-7489

Cape Town • Est/1stB 2001 • Tastings by appt 8.30-4.30 • Owner/winemaker Christophe Durand • 840cs 70% red 30% white • 10 Squirrels Way, Newlands, 7735 • christophe@vinum.co.za

Hands-on winemaking and marketing pay off, Frenchman Christophe Durand believes. His Syrah recently received US honours (91 points in Wine Spectator) and was voted one of SA's best by a French wine magazine. It's currently vinified in Hidden Valley's cellar in the Helderberg; the Chardonnay is made in true garagiste fashion in suburban Cape Town.

★★★★ Syrah Cuvée Ameena Compelling & graceful **05** (**★★★★★**) has the delicacy of the N Rhône; fragrance & savoury vinosity are deep & wide ranging; harmonious wood injects extra spice. Supple & fresh, its 14.5% alc carried with ease allowing gd few yrs beneficial development. Fr oak, 60% new, 14 mths.

★★★★ **Chardonnay Cuvée Anaïs** Attractive varietal notes introduce genteel **06** (★★★). Touch more oak, apparent sweetness (3.5g/l), detract from usual classic styling. Possibly less long-lived than **05** & pvs. Fermented/11 mths 80% new Fr barriques. — *AL*

Vintage International Brands
T 021-762-5975 · F 021-761-8536

Cape Town ▪ Closed to public ▪ PO Box 19049 Wynberg 7824 ▪ info@vib.co.za

Independent producing-wholesaler based in Cape Town, importing wines and spirits for the retail trade and producing their own-label wines, Hippo Creek and Simply Red & White (see Hippo Creek).

■ **Vintage Selection** see Spier Wines
■ **Vinum** see The Winery of Good Hope

Vinus Via
T 27 21-855-5244 · F 27 866 184089

Stellenbosch ▪ Est/1stB 2004 ▪ Closed to public ▪ Owner/cellarmaster Richard Hilton ▪ 5000 cs 50/50 red/white ▪ 21 Topaz Street, Heldervue, Somerset West 7130 ▪ info@vinusvia.co.za ▪ www.vinusvia.co.za

Richard Hilton focuses this negociant side of his wine business on bespoke entry-level wines for large customers who wish to share joint ownership of a brand in any given territory. No wines tasted for this edition. See also Pax Verbatim.

Vin-X-Port South Africa
T 021-872-0850 · F 021-872-0849

Paarl ▪ Est 2001 ▪ Closed to public ▪ Directors Hennie van der Merwe & Maretha Waso ▪ 191 Main Rd, Paarl 7646 ▪ marketing@x-port.co.za ▪ www.x-port.co.za

Negociant house specialising in procuring, producing and shipping quality wines, and in creating and marketing new brands. Its extensive portfolio includes African Treasure, Cape Circle and BunduStar, exported to various countries.

Virgin Earth
T 021-972-1110 · F 021-972-1105

Klein Karoo ▪ Tasting by appt ▪ Postnet Suite 57, Pvt Bag X18, Milnerton 7435 ▪ sales@ havanahills.co.za

A new maturation dam is being built on this unique farm in the new Langeberg-Garcia ward. Yes, you read correctly: underwater ageing started with owner Kobus du Plessis' innovative solution to insufficient power to run a cooling system. Easier-to-use tweaks include a track system which will transport barrels into the water and winch them up when required. New Klein Karoo-born and -bred farm manager Hendrik Otto oversees the vineyards, now cooled by a fine overhead water spray, as well as the undeveloped portion of 14 000ha spread, given over to conservation.

Pinotage ★★★ **04**, tasted pvs ed, had unequivocal estery hints, sweet plum fruit & vanilla highlights from yr Fr oak, 30% new. Pdberg grapes. **High 5ive** ★★★★ No follow-up as yet to **05**. Bdx combo cab s/f, merlot & petit v, blending creamy berry fruit with scrubby spice. Oak as for Pinotage. **Chenin Blanc** ★★★ **06** last ed was off-dry, had spun-sugar bouquet & pleasantly sweet-fruited palate. **Sauvignon Blanc** 🔖 ★★★ Slender (12.5% alc) **07** flinty & peppery, racy acidity & hints lemongrass & fynbos. Langeberg-Garcia WO. — *RP*

Virginia

Enduring big-volume white by Distell.

Virginia range
Virginia ★ Equal chenin/colombard; semi-dry, lightish (11% alc), slips down easily. 2 & 4. 5litre versions. W Cape. **NV**. — *MW*

Vleiland Wines

T 027-213-2525 · F 027-213-2825

Vredendal (see Olifants River map) · Est 2004 · 1stB 2005 · Visits Mon-Fri 8-5 Sat 8-12 · Closed Easter Fri-Mon, Dec 25 & Jan 1 · BYO picnic · Gift shop · Farm produce · Walks, hikes, 4x4/mountain bike trails · Owner Nico Laubscher Snr, Alette Laubscher, Nico Laubscher Jnr · Winemaker/viticulturist Nico Laubscher · 48ha (cab, pinotage, shiraz, chard, chenin, colombard, sauv) · 790t/280cs own label 100% red · PO Box 627 Vredendal 8160 · alzanne@kingsley.co.za

Cucumber farming is the full-time family occupation, but Stellenbosch graduate Nico Laubscher Jnr finds time to make wine for family, friends and a growing local following. 'It's lekker to produce and enjoy your own wine, especially if it turns out well.' Any success he'll no doubt attribute partly to a couple of years at Diemersdal under well-seasoned Tienie Louw.

Two of the Best ★★★ Sweet blackberry fruit on **05**, peppery, plum notes, savoury, sumptuous mid-palate, harmoniously oaked, (90% Fr/Hung) easy drinking. — *MF*

■ **Vlottenburg Winery** *see Stellenbosch Hills*

■ **Volmaak** *see Baarsma Wine Group*

Vondeling

T 021-869-8595 · F 021-869-8219

Voor Paardeberg (see Paarl map) · Est 2001 · 1stB 2005 · Visits by appt · Owner Armajaro Holdings UK · Winemaker Matthew Copeland · Viticulturist Julian Johnston · 40ha (cab, carignan, grenache, merlot, mourvèdre, shiraz, muscadel, chard, chenin, sauv, viognier) · 160t/10 000cs 45% red 55% white · PO Box 57 Wellington 7654 · winery@armajaro.co.za · www.armajaro.com

UK financial services group Armajaro own this 1704 property, whose original name, Vondeling, has moved to the bottle label. Englishman Julian Johnston says his biological vineyard management is showing returns, and he has recently been joined by winemaker Matthew Copeland from Welbedacht/Schalk Burger. The winery is designed for gentle treatment, aimed at elegance and finesse rather than extract, and travelling Atlantic breezes reach to some now nicely mature vineyard blocks.

Erica Shiraz NEW **★★★** Very ripe, soft-tannined **05** with dollops mourvèdre, carignan; pleasant, though a touch bitter; balanced oak (third new). **Cabernet Sauvignon-Merlot ★★★★** Cab-merlot blend (64/36) **05**; tobacco, dry herb aromas. Plenty of gd berry fruit to taste, but rather dryly tannic finish mid-2006. Ex-barrel, rating provisional. **Baldrick** NEW ▤ **★★★** Aromas best show ripe, delicious fruit on lightly wooded, easy-drinking if short **06**; shiraz-based blend with mourvèdre, splash viognier; for UK gastropub market. **Sauvignon Blanc** ▤ **★★★** Greenpepper, tropical aromas on **07**, with big, green flavours; a touch too tart. **Semillon** ▤ **★★★ 06**'s light lemony fruit supported by ferment/11 mths in oak giving nice tannic edge. Dry, lowish 11.5% alc; gd fresh bite. WO Swtlnd. **Babiana noctiflora** ▤ **★★★★** Spicy wood (11 mths, 40% new) shows on attractive **06** chenin-based blend (with viognier, chard, sauv, muscadel), with lemon, dry herb notes. Pushes higher rating - a label to watch. **Petit Blanc** NEW ▤ **★★★★** Not tasted. **Sweet Carolyn** NEW **★★** Straw-dried grapes for raisiny dessert wine; **05** oddly off-flavoured, but silky & richly balanced. All WO Voor Pdberg unless noted. — *TJ*

Von Ortloff

T 021-876-3432 · F 021-876-4313

Franschhoek · 1stB 1994 · Tasting, sales & tours by appt · Owner/winemaker Georg & Eve Schlichtmann · Viticulturist Eduard du Toit (2005) · 13ha (cab, merlot, shiraz, chard, sauv) · 5 000cs own label 60% red 40% white · PO Box 341 Franschhoek 7690 · vortloff@mweb.co.za

When we catch up with Georg Schlichtmann, it's between trips to Germany - he and wife Evi spent much of last year there, preparing their new shop in Münster, where they sell a select range of top-end SA goods. Needless to say this includes their new Quintessence Chardonnay, a once-off release, from 6 barrels they'd virtually forgotten!

★★★★ **No. 7** From merlot; **05** (★★★★) beckons with warm toffee & coffee; tad bitter entry masked by choc & juicy ripe tannins. Inch off **04**, bursting with dark fruit.

★★★★ **Cabernet Sauvignon-Merlot** Style & presence, showing attention to detail; last-tasted **01** blend 76% cab, 24% merlot; ripe cassis fruit, less taut than pvs, continues trend to easier accessibility.

★★★★★ **Quintessence** Cab-led (64%) blend with merlot, from selected barrels, in classic Old-World style. None reviewed since **00**. The Von O reds commendably cellar-aged & released when ready, though enough structure & substance for gd few yrs.

★★★★ **Chardonnay** Elegant barrel-fermented example since **93**. **03** (★★★★) last ed noted as more commercial, missing some of the restrained classicism of **02** & earlier vintages.

Quintessence Chardonnay NEW ★★★ Waxy, hints citrus & wood; sweet oak & honey flavours showing food-friendliness now & over next few yrs. **NV** (blend **02/03**). **No. 3** ★★★ Unwooded chard. Now bottled, **06** uncomplicated & light, with orange-peel, lemongrass & slightly nutty tail. **No. 5** ★★ From sauvignon. **06**, pvs ed a sample, more mineral/earth notes than fruit, still fresh but needs drinking. *— MW,MM*

■ **Voorspoed**   *see Baarsma Wine Group*

Vooruitsig
T 082-566-4700, 082-564-3231 • F 021-855-3028

Paarl • Est 1998 • 1stB 2002 • Closed to public • Owner Mozelle Holdings (Pty) Ltd • Viticulturist Vini consultant Jean-Vincent Ridon (Signal Hill, 2002) • 3ha (merlot) • 500cs 100% red • PO Box 6080 Uniedal 7612 • vooruitsig@prime-invest.co.za • www.prime-invest.co.za/ vooruitsig.htm

Vooruitsig, which specialises in merlot, has branched out into olives, with three hectares of trees planted and production of their own cold-pressed oil. Wine-wise, the 2003 vintage, held back until deemed ready, is now available; succeeding bottlings are undergoing further maturation.

Merlot Limited Release ★★ Foursquare **04** not up to std of pvs: some volatility, sour prune notes, prominent, slightly drying tannins. *— JP*

■ **Vrede**   *see Vrede Wine Farm*

Vrede en Lust Wine Farm
T 021-874-1611 • F 021-874-1859

Paarl • Est 1996 • 1stB 2002 • Tasting & sales daily 10-5 • Closed Dec 25 & Jan 1 • Tours 10-4 by appt • Cotage Fromage Deli & Restaurant • Guest accommodation in three cottages & Manor House • Tour groups by appt • Conferences & functions • Play area for children • Owner Dana & Etienne Buys • Winemaker Susan Wessels • Viticulturist Etienne Buys (Jun 1998) • Vrede en Lust: 38ha (cab, malbec, merlot, petit v, shiraz, chard); Casey's Ridge, Elgin: 32ha (pinot gris, shiraz, chard, chenin, sauv, semillon, viognier) • 20 000cs own label • ISO 14001 certified • PO Box 171 Groot Drakenstein 7680 • info@vnl.co.za • www.vnl.co.za

Susan Wessels, winner of the 2007 Landbou Weekblad Woman Winemaker of the Year trophy, now heads up the cellar. The Cotage Fromage has been revamped to a 160-seater restaurant. And the property was the winner of the 2006 Wine Capitals of the World competition in the Weddings, Meetings and Conventions category.

Shiraz NEW ▤ ★★★★ Appealing maiden **06**, characteristic shiraz nose, firm palate with gd fruit/spice balance - but looking forward to more depth in future. **Reserve** ★★★★ Bdx blend cab, merlot & petit v (47/43/10) in **03**, plusher, riper than **02** (★★★★). Choc & plum fruit enrich complex nose; sappy freshness followed by gd ripe tannins on firm finish. **Classic** ★★★★ Bdx blend mainly cab & merlot, dollops petit v & malbec (50/35/8/7) in **04**. Rich choc nose balanced by herbal & woodspice notes; focused palate with gd ripe fruit & classic finish. Better fleshed & more accessible than **03** (★★★). **Cara** ★★★ Red blend with mainly cab & shiraz, with merlot (39/37/24); robust **03** not retasted; had less new oak than earlier versions (10% vs. ±25). **Simond** ★★★ Early-drinking version of above cab, merlot, shiraz. **04** fruity, with just enough oak to add definition. Not retasted. **Jess** ▤ ★★★ Dry rosé; lovely pinkish partridge eye **07**, shy red berry nose, hint spice; elegant lingering flavours. **Marguerite** ★★★★ Chard, showing restrained lemon notes fleshed out with butter & oak; **06** ripe, rich-fruited palate; gd wood integration. Ready to enjoy. **Karien** 🗖 ★★★★ From chenin; spicy, apple-pip & refreshing lime nose on **07**; broad palate with ripe apples, tropical fruit & hint pineapple balanced by refined acid. **06** (★★★) more savoury, food compatible. **Sauvignon Blanc** NEW ★★★★ **07** grassy, cool nose complemented by melon & fig; attractive acidity rounds off palate with herbal & tropical fruit balance. Vyds in Dbnville/Sir Lowry's Pass. **Viognier** NEW 🗖 ★★★ Prominent new-oak character masks white peach, spice & apple-pip nose on **07**; sweet, rich palate. Gd curry partner. — *JP*

▉ Vredendal Winery *see Namaqua Wines*

Vredenheim Wines
T 021-881-3637 • F 021-881-3296

Stellenbosch • Tasting & sales Mon-Fri 9-5 Sat 9.30-2 (Dec 9-5) • Fee R2/tasting • Closed Easter Fri, Dec 25 & Jan 1 • Barrique Restaurant T 021-881-3001 • Hudson's Coffee Shop T 021-881-3590 • Other amenities: see intro • Owner Bezuidenhout family • Winemaker Fanie Cilliers advised by Elzabé Bezuidenhout • 80ha • 10 000cs 60% red 40% white • PO Box 369 Stellenbosch 7599 • trendsetter@vredenheim.co.za • www.vredenheim.co.za

As the guide went to press, a new label was being readied for launch: Oryx, featuring one of the antelope species that roam the grounds of this tourist-friendly winery, which also boasts a collection of vintage Jaguar motorcars, some for hire. The coffee shop and restaurant have been upgraded, and more rooms are planned for stay-over visitors.

Cabernet Sauvignon NEW ★ Yr oak imparts dusty note to **04**, light berry flavours touched with earth. **Merlot** NEW 🗖 ★★ Plummy **05**, touches earth & spice, gd dry tannins. Small portion oaked. **Pinotage** 🗖 ★★ Savoury/salty **05**, amenable tannins for early drinking. **Shiraz** ★★ Smoked meat intro, **05** juicy elegant fruit; incl dashes merlot & cab. **Reserve 214** ★★ **03** mature caramel notes, v soft, boneless, enjoy soonest. Yr oak. **Rosé** ★★ Sexy wine in sexy bottle, say winemakers; **06** scented muscat tones, charming honeyed sweetness. **Vredenvonkel** ★★ Sweetish any-occasion sparkling with delicate apple notes, refreshing crisp bubbles. NV. **Angel's Natural Sweet** NEW 🗖 ★ Chenin & colombard, prettified by muscat; **07** sweet but fleeting tropical flavours. — *JP*

Vrede Wine Farm NEW
T 021-865-2440/2815 • F 021-865 2440

Stellenbosch • 1stB 1998 • Tasting & sales Mon-Thu 9-5 Fri 9-4 Sat 10-1 • Closed Easter Fri & Sun, Ascension Day (Jun 5), Dec 25/26 & Jan 1 • BYO picnic • Owner Duplenia Plase/Kleintjie Bellingan Family Trust • Winemaker Willhelm de Vries & Martin Stevens (Koelenhof Winery) • Viticulturist Herman du Preez (Koelenhof Winery) • 99 ha (cab, merlot, shiraz, chard) • 890 tons/7000 cs 60% red 40% white • Export brands: Vrede, Koelenbosch • Brands for customers: Karuwa & October Red • PO Box 7271 Stellenbosch 7599 • lorman@yebo.co.za • www.vredewines.co.za

Good wine shouldn't be available only to those with fat wallets, is the credo at this heretofore low-key winery, now looking to make a bigger splash. Their wines are grown on three Stellenbosch farms (Vrede, San Michelle and Koelenbosch), and vinified and matured at Koelenhof Winery. A link-up with the Michelangelo and Woman Winemaker of the Year competitions enables visitors to taste and buy Vrede wines alongside award winning bottlings from across the winelands.

Shiraz ★★★ Smoky **06**, herb & tobacco aromas, raspberry black cherry flavours, ample tannin and spice. **Charmé Merlot-Cabernet Sauvignon** ★★★ Winegum blackcurrant aromas, **03** surprisingly sweet-fruited, sumptuously textured, supple & persistent. **Classic Red** ★★ **03** greengage plum, savoury notes, grippy, austere tannins. **Charmé Chardonnay** ★★★ Toffee, vanilla aromas, sweet, **04** creamy butterscotch notes, uncomplicated. **Sauvignon Blanc** ★★ Lean-fruited capsicum whiffs, **06** brisk & over-crisp. — *MF*

■ **Vreughvol** *see* Baarsma Wine Group

Vriesenhof Vineyards
T 021-880-0284 · F 021-880-1503

Stellenbosch · Est 1980 · 1stB 1981 · Tasting Mon-Thu 10-4 Fri 10-3.30 Sat 10-2 (groups of 10+ by appt only) · Tours & meals/refreshments by appt · Owner Landgoed Vriesenhof (Pty) Ltd · Winemaker Jan Coetzee, with Richard Phillips (2001) · Viticulturist Hannes Coetzee · 37ha (cabs s/f, merlot, pinot, pinotage, chard) · ±350t 85% red 15% white · PO Box 155 Stellenbosch 7599 · info@vriesenhof.co.za · www.vriesenhof.co.za

This is arguably the best-kept secret on the Stellenbosch wine route, with a lush mountain setting, gracious grounds, delicious wines and nary a tourist bus in sight. Even the entry-level Paradyskloof range, with trademark peacock on the label, struts its stuff. 'Yes, it's all moving along nicely,' admits equally laid-back marketer Eddie Smit, though there may be some fanfare when they release the 05 Kallista (either next year or 2010), and celebrate 25 years of producing one of the Cape's most rated blends.

Vriesenhof range
- ★★★★ **Cabernet Sauvignon** Out of sequence **01** (★★★★★, in magnum only) nicely old-fashioned & modest; rather like Jan B himself. Claret-like bouquet & mouthfeel: cassis, forest floor give way to well-muscled palate. **03** & **02** tasted together last ed, hints dry scrub & forest floor, fresh acidity, astringent tannins, all set for the long haul.
- ★★★★ **Pinot Noir 05**, tasted pvs ed as preview, initially subdued: takes time to open to lifted sour cherry fruit, undergrowth nuances. Harmonious, silken, this is a wine that 'just is', rather than being a sum of its parts.
- ★★★★★ **Kallista** Oft cab-led flagship; **02/03** cab f & merlot in majority. **03** ★★★★ (31/35/34), retasted (sample pvs ed), spearmint & cassis aromas overlain with well-worn leather, tobacco; smooth tannins in sync with 14% alc, fruit a tad lean. ±24 mths Fr oak, some new.
- ★★★★ **Enthopio** Greek for 'truly indigenous', so pinotage leads; in sample **04**, it's 79%, with dollop merlot & drops cab f/shiraz for complexity. Tannins too brusque to broach now, need ±3yrs to mesh with exuberant mulberry & fennel fruit.

Melelo ✓ ★★★★ Unoaked red muscat d'A from 50 yr vines: fortified to 15.2% alc, dash touriga for colour. **06** less sweet than pvs, now only 146g/l RS. Ginger & watermelon aromas to tickle your fancy. Drink well chilled.

Talana Hill range
- ★★★★ **Royale** Pre-bottling sample **03** (★★★★) continues trend to merlot/cab f blend started by **02**, shows similar characteristics: wet biltong, fynbos & iodine. Tannins firm, but approachable. Usually 8 mths Fr oak, new/2nd fill.

Chardonnay ★★★★ Bunch fermented in barrel, aged ±10 mths 2nd fill Fr. Full-bodied & flavoursome **05** step up; rich, with orange blossom/spice highlights to usual lemon-lime aromas/flavours.

Paradyskloof range
Pinot Noir ★★★★ Even at 14% alc, **06** light on its feet, balanced. Cherry fruit quite high-toned, also showing wet earth characters. No new oak. **Pinotage** ✓ ★★★★ **05** reminiscent of strawberry-centred chocolates; older Fr oak (15 mths) supporting juicy fruit core, not adding many vanilla, toasty notes. Modest ±13% alc. **Cabernet Sauvignon-Merlot** ✓ ★★★★ **06** slips down easily courtesy gentle tannins, 2nd/3rd fill Fr oak ±15 mths; brisk acidity adds lively notes to rich fruit. **Chardonnay** ★★★★ Unwooded **06** ripe & delicious with vibrant lemon zest core. — *CvZ*

■ **Vruchtbaar** *see* Robertson Wide River Export Company

Vruchtbaar Boutique Winery
T 023-626-2334 · F 023-626-4081

Robertson · Est/1stB 2001 · Visits by appt · BYO picnic · Tour groups · Guest house · Owner Alwyn & Francois Bruwer · Winemaker Francois Bruwer · Viticulturist Briaan Stipp (2005, adviser) · 35ha (cab, pinotage, merlot, ruby cab, chenin, chard, colombard, sauv) • 400t/100cs own label • 75% red 25% white • PO Box 872 Robertson 6705 • vruchtbaar@mweb.co.za

'The only new planting at Vruchtbaar is our baby Meg,' jokes Francois Bruwer. Wine wise, he's sticking to the same timeless approach: getting it right in the vineyard, if not organically, then with minimal interference. Marketing is still the big challenge: 'It's a price war, and we're competing against big guns.'

★★★★ **Cabernet Sauvignon 04** stylish combo restrained fruit/fine tannins & sweet Am oak coconut. Will reward cellaring. Single vyd block. 18 mths, 50/50 Fr/Am oak.

Island Red ★★★ Light-hearted, early-ready red from young vines; mainly cab & pinotage. **05** bursts with fruit & flowers. **Sauvignon Blanc** ★★★ Sample **05** super-fresh, green fig & greenpepper notes, racy lime palate, undaunting 13.5% alc. Not retasted, as for all these. —AL

Vukani Wines
T 044-534-8007 • F 044-534-8007

Plettenberg Bay • Est 2005 • Tasting/sales/winemakers as for Bramon Wines (see entry) • Fee R20 for 4 wines • ±1 400cs 56% red 44% white • PO Box 1606 Plettenberg Bay 6600 • peter@ vukaniwines.com • www.vukaniwines.com

Vukani means 'Wake up', which seems appropriate given that this winegrowing empowerment of previously disadvantaged local farmers has inspired quite a few other people to establish vineyards in the mountainous Crags area around Plettenberg Bay. 'We're getting nice results from our vines,' explains Vukani Trust member Peter Thorpe. 'The area is taking off.'

Shiraz ★★★ Drink-early **04**, pepper & spice, dark berries plus slight porty notes. **Shiraz-Cabernet Sauvignon** ★★★ Straightforward but tasty **04**; melange choc, spice, red fruits smoothly meshed, savoury finish. Yr Fr/Am oak, none new. **Chardonnay** ★★★ **05** unoaked, juicy, smooth, fruit bolstered by touch sugar. **Sauvignon Blanc** ★★★★ Delightfully fresh **05** captures variety's gooseberry & lemongrass purity; gentle yet well defined flavours. This, all above, WO W Cape, not retasted. —AL

Vunani Wines NEW
T 083-318-3237 • F 086-502-5079

Wellington (see Paarl map) • Est/1stB 2004 • Tasting & sales Mon-Fri 10-4.30 • Cellar tours 10-4 • Closed pub hols • Refreshments Mon-Fri 12.30-2 • Conservation area • Owner Nkewu family, with workers trust • Winemaker Jaco Potgieter, with Niël Groenewald (Feb 2004/ 2005, consultants) • Viticulturist Jaco Potgieter (Feb 2004) • 80ha under management (cab, pinotage, chard, chenin, colombard, muscadel) • ±2 300t/150 000cs 60% red 40% white • ISO 9002 & BRC accredited • PO Box 8021 Mbekweni Paarl 7626 • vumilen@vunaniwines.co.za • www.vunaniwines.co.za

Vumile Nkewu has had ties with the wine industry all his life. As a schoolboy he worked in the vineyards and later, at Customs & Excise. Today, he and his family are the drivers behind Vunani ('Harvest'), an empowerment initiative established in 2004, with three main labels being available locally and exported successfully to Europe.

Sizwe range
Cabernet Sauvignon-Shiraz-Merlot ★★★ **05**'s complex cigarbox, black fruit, white pepper notes lead to restrained palate with attractively austere tannins.

Isilimela range
Cabernet Sauvignon ★★ Dry-tannined **04** sample has herbal notes, lean centre. **Pinotage** ★★★ Bright, black cherry whiffs on **05**; rustic tannins v food-friendly. **Cabernet Sauvignon-Merlot** No tasted. **Chardonnay** ★★ **06** has subtle citrus notes, is light-fruited & brisk. **Chenin Blanc** ★★ **06** zesty, with super-fresh appley aromas, understated flavours.

Ekasi range
Cabernet Sauvignon-Merlot ★ Vegetal hints on **05**, racy acidity & somewhat unknit structure. **Chardonnay-Colombard** ★★ Lime-grapefruit notes, succulent pear-drop flavours &

zesty freshness on **06** easy-drinker. **Ntombi Sweet** ★★ Bright rosepetal aromas, honeyed overlay, concludes on a tangy note. **NV**. — *MF*

Vuurberg
T 021-885-2334 • **F** 086-689-3792

Stellenbosch • Est 2000 • 1stB 2003 • Visits by appt • Owner Sebastiaan Klaassen • Winemaker Miles Mossop, with Sebastiaan Klaassen (both 2003) • Viticulturist Aidan Morton (2002, consultant) • 10ha (cab s/f, malbec, merlot, petit v, chenin, grenache bl, roussanne, viognier) • 1 500cs 100% red • PO Box 449 Stellenbosch 7599 • helshoogte@mweb.co.za • www.vuurberg.com

Though Sebastiaan Klaassen jokes that his kitesurfing is still being interrupted by the harvest, he and partner Anna Poll are serious about creating a new flagship red. After much experimentation with clones, harvest times, wood types and vinification techniques, they believe the result from the 06 harvest might finally become their long hoped-for 'Vuurberg One', replacing both current reds.

★★★★ **Vuurberg Reserve** Fynbos reigns in **05**, seems to be cellar signature. Classic bdx blend merlot, cab, petit v 66/32/2. Hints mocha, toast to ample dark-berried fruits, clever tannins allow early drinking & cellaring. Fr oak, 60% new.

Vuurberg ★★★★ Bdx blend merlot, cab, petit v, 18 mths Fr oak, 35% new. Pushy, plummy fruits abound in **05**, quite showy. Warm spice, approachable tannins, plump & amiable, will find many friends. **White** NEW ★★★★ **06** blended with 7% each sauv & viognier. Intriguing dried herb, fynbos notes; full-bodied & satiny, glides across the palate. Portion discreetly oaked, all Fr, some new. Discontinued: **Chenin Blanc**. — *IvH*

Waarburg Wines [NEW]
T 021-880-0535 • **F** 021-880-0326

Paarl • Est 2005 • 1stB 2007 • Sales Mon-Fri 8-5 • Owner Martin & Lizemarie Versfeld, Iain Brodie • Winemaker Nico van der Merwe (Jan 2005, consultant) • Viticulturist Paul Wallace (Jan 2005, consultant) • 10.45 ha (cabs s/f, pinotage, shiraz) • ±66t/2900cs 100% red • 23 Quantum Rd, Rhino House, Technopark, Stellenbosch 7600 • info@waarburgwines.co.za • www.waarburgwines.co.za

The first vintage of this Paarl producer, a shiraz blend, was bottled last year, the result of a guiding principle to 'work hard at what we aim for', according to Lizemarie Versfeld, one of the owners with Martin Versfeld and Iain Brodie. The current focus is broadening the distribution network locally and abroad, mainly in the UK, Sweden and Canada.

★★★★ **Waarburg** Shiraz, with 30% cab & 15% cab f, in impressive debut **05**; Red fruit core with notes of dried herbs, finely honed body, serious oaking (18 mths Fr, 10% new), but not a harsh note in sight. With lots to show over 3+ yrs. — *CR*

■ **Waboomsrivier Co-op** *see Overhex Wines International*

Wamakersvallei Winery

T 021-873-1582 • **F** 021-873-3194

Wellington (see Paarl map) • Est 1941 • Tasting & sales Mon-Fri 8-5 Sat 8.30-12.30 • Closed pub hols except May 1 • Tours by appt • BYO picnic • Conferences • Owner 40 members • Cellarmaster Christiaan Visser • Winemaker Hugo Truter • Viticulturist Koos van der Merwe • 1 400ha • 55% red 45% white • PO Box 509 Wellington 7654 • sales@wamakersvallei.co.za • www.wamakersvallei.co.za

The friendly tasting room at this Wellington stalwart was busier than usual with the first Wellington Wine Harvest Festival last March. In the past year, visitors were also treated to the opportunity of tasting older vintages of their awarded La Cave range. On the new side, West Coast winemaker Christiaan Visser joined the cellar in time for the harvest, and the viticultural team was proud of landing first prize in the regional Grower's Competition – for the third year in a row.

La Cave range

Cabernet Sauvignon ★★★ With alc down to 14%, **05** more restrained, better balanced than lauded pvs. Banana & coconut oak aromas from yr new wood. **Merlot** ★★★ Last ed, ripe **04** was easy to drink; tangy background freshness warding off potential brawniness of 15.5% alc. **Pinotage** ★★★ Despite ebullient raspberry & toffee bouquet, **05**'s tealeaf tannins & astringent finish are sturdy rather than scintillating. Oak as for cab above. **Shiraz** ★★★ With slightly more Am oak than reds above, **05** gives sweeter impression, balancing 15% alc. Fennel & caraway spice up fruit profile.

Bain's Way range

Cabernet Sauvignon ☺ ★★★ Boisterous **06** melange red fruits & lifted cassis; weighty 15% alc masked by firm tannins. 9/12 mths seasoned oak; same for all these reds. **Pinotage** ☺ ★★★ Cheery **06** has characteristic banana & raspberry tones; soft, easily accessible tannins. Glides down. **Chardonnay** ☺ 🍴 ★★★ Unwooded **07**'s bouquet somewhat subdued, mere hints lemon blossom & white peach. Palate shows more assertive chard weight, texture, length. **Sauvignon Blanc** ☺ 🍴 ★★★ Crisp & dry **07** has interesting thatch & matchstick top notes to its green aromas/flavours.

Merlot ★★ **06** unready for tasting; unpretentious **05** last ed was berried & punchy. **Shiraz** ★★ Ripe, fruitcake **06** lacks sufficient tannin & fruit to hide beefy 15.5% alc. **Chenin Blanc** 🍴 ★★ Faint bruised apple aromas/flavours, brisk acidity on wallet-pleasing **07**. **Viognier** ✓ 🍴 ★★★★ Quality leap: appealing varietal peach kernel, wax notes on **07**; fresh yet rounded spicy palate. Quite precise, not sprawling as viognier can be. **Sparkling Brut** NEW ★★★ Frothy & lightish new **NV** sauv sparkler finishes appealingly dry. Discontinued: **Sparkling Vin Sec**.

33 Degrees South range

Semi Sweet ☺ 🍴 ★★★ Cheerful semi-sweet sipper from chenin with brisk, cleansing acidity, lovely floral & thatch aromas. Both **NV**, for drinking soonest after purchase.

Rosé 🍴 ★★ From pinotage; crisp, dry yet laden with fruity charm. Discontinued: **Dry Red**, **Dry White**.

Dessert range

Fishermans Jerepigo ★★★ Fortifying salty sea dogs since 1941; **NV** from hanepoot; very sweet & supple. **Jagters Port** ★★★ 'Hunter's Port', **NV** from ruby cab. Suave rather than rustic & earthy. Neither retasted. — *CvZ*

Wandsbeck Wines 🍷 ♿

T 023-626-1103 • **F** 023-626-3329

Robertson ▪ Est 1965 ▪ 1stB 1986 ▪ Tasting & sales Mon-Fri 8-5 ▪ Closed Easter Fri-Mon, May 1, Dec 25/26 & Jan 1 ▪ Tours by appt ▪ Owner 22 members ▪ Winemaker Helmard Hanekom (Jan 1986), with Zonia de Kock ▪ Viticulturist Willem Botha (consultant) ▪ 448ha (cab, cinsaut, merlot, pinotage, semillon) ▪ 6 440t/±10 000cs own label 50% red 50% white ▪ PO Box 267 Robertson 6705 ▪ wandsbeck@breede.co.za

Vinifying at Wandsbeck last harvest took a sideways step when winemaker Helmard Hanekom tore his Achilles tendon and found himself on crutches for the duration. Fortunately, recently appointed assistant Zonia de Kock was on hand with stair-climbing capability and encouragement. The biggest crush in 41 years is prompting plans for new storage capacity.

Cabernet Sauvignon ★★ **02** BBQ-amenable quaffer with dark berry fruit, vanilla hint, low tannins & sensible 13.4% alc. Yr Fr oak; extra yr bottle-aged. Not retasted, as for all. **Ruby Cabernet** ★★ **04** cheery & distinctive thatch & plum whiffs, rounded (via dollop sugar) but dry finish thanks to combo brisk acidity & fruit tannins (unwooded). **Shiraz** ★ Powerful & unsubtle **04**, in youth had gruff tannins which might since have smoothed. **Sauvignon Blanc** ★★ **05** light (12.5% alc), with restrained lime & lemon aromas, crisp acidity. **Muscadel** ★★ Sweet fortified red, **04** pleasant muscat scent, syrupy finish — could do with splash more acidity. Discontinued: **Chenin Blanc**. *— DH*

Warwick Estate

T 021-884-4410 · *F 021-884-4025*

Stellenbosch • Est 1964 • 1stB 1984 • Tasting & sales Mon-Fri 10-5 Sat/Sun 10-4 • Closed Easter Sun, Dec 25 & Jan 1 • Tours by appt • Mediterranean picnic baskets by appt, or BYO • 'Wedding Cup' demonstrations • Gifts • Walks/hikes • Owner Ratcliffe family • Winemaker Louis Nel (Jun 2001) • Viticulturist Ronald Spies (Aug 2001), advised by Phil Freese • 55ha (cabs s/f, merlot, pinotage, shiraz, chard, sauv) • 250t/23 000cs 60% red 40% white • PO Box 2 Elsenburg 7607 • info@warwickwine.com • www.warwickwine.com

The momentum at this critically acclaimed family-run winery continues to be high. There's been expansion into China, Russia and the former Soviet republics, while the UK and particularly the US markets keep growing. The Three Cape Ladies blend now accounts for almost a third of the estate's total production, and the Professor Black Sauvignon is now 100% screwcapped (the Old Bush Vines Pinotage to follow from the 06 vintage). Materfamilias and 'Chairman of the Board' Norma Ratcliffe completed a cross-England tour, presenting 20 Years of Trilogy with the UK Wine Society; and daughter Jenny's wine book, Spit or Swallow, received enthusiastic reviews. Son and GM Mike R contentedly proclaims: 'It's been the best year in the history of Warwick.'

★★★★ Cabernet Franc Latest **05** a little bigger, sterner, in ripe, concentrated vintage. Vivid spice/leaf scents plus lots of cedary oak (70% new); sweet fruit currently contained by mouthcoating tannins. Best give 2-3 yrs to settle. 14.6% alc.

★★★★ CWG Auction Reserve Similar cab s & f, merlot mix as Trilogy, selection best vyds; **05** presents plush new-oak aromas, some underlying spice from larger cab f component (33%); shortish, with dry, forceful grip. 2 yrs tight-grain Fr oak, 70% new.

★★★★☆ Trilogy (Estate Reserve) Flagship bdx blend, recognised for well-tailored proportions. Cab-led **05** (**★★★★**) unusually insistent, dry tannins dominate fresh, dark berried tones. May soften with few yrs ageing. Fr oak, 70% new, 2 yrs. 59% cab with 21/20 cab f/merlot. **04**, though also taut, touch more yielding on release.

★★★★ Three Cape Ladies Last-tasted **04** (with four 'ladies' involved: pinotage, cab, merlot & shiraz), modern, well oaked, sumptuous but homogenous. 2 yrs Fr wood, 20% new. **05** unready.

★★★★ Chardonnay Elegantly expressive style. **06** follows in quiet, confident tracks of **05**: gently pure pear/citrus freshness layered on lees-enriched base, subtle wood embellishment. Fr oak fermented/8 mths, 25% new.

Old Bush Vines Pinotage ★★★★ 05 last ed showed typical tart red-fruit, mint/acetone character. Contrasting juicy/tangy flavours with bitter nip in tail. Fr oaked, 20% new. **06** unready. NE. **Professor Black Sauvignon Blanc** 🗎 **★★★★** Vivid tropical, fresh green pea, lemongrass intensity leap from glass of **07**. Replicates minerally drive, concentration, bounce of **06** but with more polish, snappier finish. WO Sbosch. NE. Discontinued: **Stansfield**. All above WO Smnsberg-Sbosch unless noted. *— AL*

Waterford Estate

T 021-880-0496 · *F 021-880-1007*

Stellenbosch • Est/1stB 1998 • Visits Mon-Fri 9-5 Sat 10-3 • Fee R20-35 • Closed Easter Fri, Dec 25 & Jan 1 • Wine & Chocolate Experience (bookings recommended) • Owner Jeremy & Leigh Ord, Kevin Arnold • Winemaker Kevin Arnold & Francois Haasbroek • Viticulturist Lombard Loubser • 50ha (barbera, cabs s/f, grenache, malbec, merlot, mourvèdre, petit v, sangiovese, shiraz, tempranillo, chard, sauv) • 400t/30 000cs 80% red 20% white • PO Box 635 Stellenbosch 7599 • info@waterfordestate.co.za • www.waterfordestate.co.za

Co-created in 1998 by the Ord and Arnold families, Waterford has 50ha under vines. Senior winemaker and partner Kevin Arnold registered Waterford as an estate in 2004 'to give integrity to our intentions', and while Waterford's Cab and Kevin Arnold Shiraz are well respected, Arnold remained convinced that a blend would deliver the best expression of the Waterford vineyards. 2007 therefore sees the release of the estate's flagship red blend, named 'The

Jem' after owner Jeremy O. The estate continues to hone its award-winning welcome, adding a Private Reserve tasting experience to its other attractions.

★★★★☆ **Cabernet Sauvignon** Accomplished **04** with equal portions cab f/merlot (total 10%). Undergrowth, tomato cocktail top notes to cassis-laden bouquet/palate, 13.5% alc, taut tannin all very claret-like; structured for ageing. Powerful yet restrained, as was spicy/choc **03**. 90% Fr/Am oak, 25% new.

★★★★☆ **Kevin Arnold Shiraz** Dash mourvèdre (6%) usually spices up this confident rhône-style red. **04** (★★★★) wet earth & scrub scents mingle with wines's trademark leather tone (love it or hate it); round tannins approachable yet with life for 5+ yrs. 16 mths oak, Am portion down again to 20%. **03** was heady with spice & lavender whiffs. NE.

★★★★☆ **The Jem** NEW The flagship, 7 yrs in the making (perfectionist Arnold content to wait); takes moniker of co-owner Jeremy Ord. 8-variety mix reflects estate's red plantings. Proverbial iron fist in velvet glove; all the opulence of main components cab s/f, whiffs leather signature of shiraz. Crafted for cellaring; expect hefty price tag on release.

★★★★☆ **CWG Auction Reserve Red 04** bdx red for 2007 Auction departure from usual mourvèdre, petit v, barbera & shiraz blend. If fruit tone is wedded with cassis/menthol scents, structure is pure bdx: tight & fresh, with firm but ripe tannins. Cabs s & f lead (50/35) with equal drops petit v, merlot, malbec. NE.

★★★★☆ **Chardonnay** Satin-textured **06** as charming, understated as zingy **05** (★★★★★). Poised acidity highlights lemon-lime fruit, dances through buttery oak richness. Could keep few yrs. Fermented/aged briefly Fr oak, 40% new, no malo; incl tank-fermented portion.

★★★★ **Sauvignon Blanc 07** poised & elegant with all the minerality & edginess the variety can offer. Restrained & taut, has myriad green-toned aromas, memorable juicy finish. 4 mths lees contact up from 3 of step-up **06**.

★★★★ **Heatherleigh Noble Late Harvest** Complex, luxuriously botrytised dessert from equal parts chard, hanepoot & semillon; showing (mid-2006) apricots, almonds, clotted cream; sweet (95g/l RS) with fresh acidity & pithy lift to tail. 50% barrel fermented/yr 2nd fill Fr. 15% alc. 375ml. NE.

Pecan Stream range

Pebble Hill ▤ ★★★★ New name for modest sipper (pvsly 'Cabernet Sauvignon-Shiraz'), blend varies with each vintage. **05** a flourish of cabs f/s, sangiovese, barbera & shiraz; gd tannin tug; 6 mths old oak. NE. **Chenin Blanc** ★★★★ **07** fuller, fatter than pvs thanks to 10% wooded portion from **06** vintage. Still floral/thatch scented, still slips down easily. From Bottly bushvines. NE. **Sauvignon Blanc** ★★★ Dusty fynbos, white asparagus & zesty acidity are part of **07**'s appealing persona. Combo Darling/SBosch fruit. NE. Stylish & well priced '2nd label'. — *CvZ*

▪ **Waterfront Collection** *see* Vaughan Johnson's Wine & Cigar Shop

Waterkloof 🍷 NEW
T 021-873-2418/2639 ▪ **F** 021-873-7580

Somerset West (see Helderberg map) ▪ *Est 2004* ▪ *1stB 2005* ▪ *Visits by appt only* ▪ *Owner Paul Boutinot* ▪ *Winemaker Werner Engelbrecht (Jun 2004)* ▪ *Viticulturist Werner Engelbrecht, advised by Johan Pienaar* ▪ *47ha (cabs s/f, grenache, merlot, mourvèdre, shiraz, chard, sauv)* ▪ *120-140t/11 000cs 30% red 70% white* ▪ *Other export brands: Circumstance & Peacock Ridge* ▪ *PO Box 1286 Wellington 7654* ▪ *ceo@boutinotsa.co.za*

MD Jean du Toit's expectations of their Schapenberg site haven't been disappointed: 'Features like the natural cropping by the south-easter, the cool sea breeze, the altitude and its cool slopes facing south and south-west combine so well with the two main soil types. Natural winemaking techniques - natural fermentation for most of the wines, whole-bunch pressing, extended lees contact and the use of open-top wooden fermenters for the quality reds - are core to the production team's 'little intervention is best' philosophy.

Sauvignon Blanc ★★★★☆ Wines from windswept Schapenberg tend to thrill with their minerality, steeliness. Invigorating **06** no exception. Oak (30% fermented in barrel) barely detectable, adds weight & texture rather than aroma or flavour. Leap up from maiden **05** (★★★).

Circumstance range
Merlot ★★★★ Maiden **05** exciting, but needs time for strident tannins to mesh with plummy fruit. Friendly & broad-beamed, with meaty nuance. 18 mths oak, 60% new. **Cape Coral Mourvedre** ★★★ Pre-bottling sample **07** delicately flavoured, gently spiced. Lively, satisfying but not very long. **Chardonnay** 🍷 ★★★★ Impressive newcomer with potential to improve further. **06** charming partially wooded (40% barrel ferment) version with luscious lime, rich oak notes; lovely length & balance. 9mth lees contact for additional complexity. **Sauvignon Blanc** ★★★ **06** first bottling another expression of this variety from this producer: tropical, 14.5% alc rounding out the palate. Fatter, zestier than cellarmate, should suit foodies.

Peacock Ridge range
★★★★ **Merlot** 🍷 Plenty juicy fruit, zingy acidity give dark plum/choc-toned **06** freshness, verve. 20% new oak plays supportive role, yet adds nice dry touch to finish.
★★★★ **Chardonnay** 🍷 Clever oak detail (30% barrel ferment) allows vibrant fruit to take center stage in harmonious, invigorating **06**. No malo.
Sauvignon Blanc ★★★★ **07** more 'green' toned than the other versions. Leaner, too; taut yet balanced, with lemon finish. — *CvZ*

Waterstone Wines
T 021-842-2942 ▪ F 086-505-8691

Stellenbosch (see Helderberg map) ▪ Est 2007 ▪ Visits by appt ▪ Self-catering facilities ▪ Owner Pim de Lijster & Reino Kruger ▪ Winemaker Reino Kruger (April, 2007) ▪ 20 000cs 75% red 25% white ▪ PO Box 7094 Stellenbosch 7599 ▪ reino@waterstonewines.co.za ▪ www. waterstonewines.co.za
Big changes at this Helderberg property, most notably new branding: the original 'Waterhof' is now the name of the flagship label. From a modest start of a shiraz in 2006, owner Pim de Lijster and partner Reino Kruger have developed an impressive 34 (none tasted), including the Africa range, profits of which are ploughed into social upliftment projects.

Waverley Hills Organic Wines
T 023-231-0003 ▪ F 023-231-0004

Tulbagh ▪ 1stB 2004 ▪ Tasting & sales Mon-Sat 10-4 ▪ Closed Easter Fri, Dec 25 & Jan 1 ▪ Cellar tours by appt ▪ Organic Bistro Tue-Sat 10-4 Sun 11-3 ▪ Hiking trail ▪ Facilities for children ▪ Owner Du Toit family ▪ Winemaker Theuns Botha, advised by Mark Carmichael-Green ▪ 24ha ▪ Export brand: Dixon's Peak ▪ PO Box 71 Wolseley 6830 ▪ info@waverleyhills.co.za ▪ www. waverleyhills.co.za
Organically certified and a member of the Biodiversity & Wine Initiative, this wine-and-olive property last year completed a gravity-fed cellar in time for their third vintage. Tastings, a short botanist-designed hiking trail, lunch at the Organic Bistro and lovely valley views are all part of the experience – and children are welcome.
Cabernet Sauvignon ★★★★ **05**,tasted pvs ed, more intense & complex than **04** (★★★). Ripe fruit to balance oaking (30% new Fr) with gd few yrs ahead. **Shiraz** ★★★ No successor tasted to **05**, pvsly showcased light fruit & spice with earthy vanilla-wood flavours from mix Fr/Am (15% new). **Cabernet Sauvignon-Shiraz** [NEW] Not ready. **Semillon-Chardonnay** ★★★★ **06** on pvs review showed tropical- & stone-fruit, vanilla & butterscotch from 4 mths new Fr wood. **Semillon-Sauvignon Blanc** [NEW] 🍷 ★★★ Dry, fleshy **07** blend sem, sauv, chard (70/20/10). Waxy & nutty aromas; lively acidity & pithy citrus farewell. Gd summer quaffer or seafood partner. — *MW*

WaverleyTBS/uniWines
T 023-349-1017; 09-44-1442-206800 ▪ F 023-349-1012; 09-44-1442-206888

Est 2002 ▪ Closed to public ▪ Owner UK-based WaverleyTBS ▪ WaverleyTBS, Punchbowl Park Cherry Tree Lane Hemel Hempstead Hertfordshire, HP2 7EU ▪ elaine.dickie@waverleytbs.co. uk ▪ www.waverleytbs.co.uk

The allure of the Cape continues to be promoted by the Cape Promise brand in Europe, with the inviting advertising slogan 'Have you been there yet?' Both partners in the brand, the UK's WaverleyTBS & SA's uniWines, are upbeat about the Fairtrade accreditation for their Isabelo range.

Cape Promise

Pinotage NEW ★★★ Deeper than pvs easy-sipper, **07** brims with ruddy colour, earthy nuances, plummy ripeness - & 14.5% alc. **Cabernet Sauvignon-Merlot** ★★ Herbal nose & almost porty ripeness to **06**. Enjoy soon. **Ruby Cabernet-Pinotage** NEW ★★★ Mocha & dark choc combine with pudding richness in **07**'s warming 65/35 blend. **Shiraz Rosé** NEW ★★★ Cheerful dry charmer mixing strawberries & spice in inviting, fruit-sweet **07**. **Oaked Chardonnay** ★★★ 'Chardonnay' pvs ed. Creamy vanilla notes on **07**, interesting peppery touch adding zing to clean citrus. **Oaked Chenin Blanc** NEW ★★★ Oak influence gives extra depth to pleasantly biscuity **07**, boosted with 10% chard. **Chenin Blanc** ★★ Waft dusty grass & soft, ripe fruits on gentle, understated **07**. **Sauvignon Blanc** NEW ★★★ Dry, grassy nose on quiet **07** introduces soft pineapple & melon fruitiness with gentle finish. **Noble Late Harvest** ★★★★ Delicious **06** adds 50% muscadel to pvs solo chenin. Honeyed dried apricot & citrus undertones; gd acid/sweetness balance ensures long, clean parting.

Isabelo range

Merlot NEW ★★★ Light oak hardly discernable in friendly, fruit-driven, quaffing **06**. **Semillon** NEW ★★ **07** frisky lunchtime white with lively hints of lemon zest. Fairtrade wines. — DB

Webersburg Wines 🍷🏛📷
T 021-881-3636 • F 021-881-3217

Stellenbosch • Est/1stB 1996 • Tasting & sales Mon-Fri 9-5 Sat 10-4 • Closed pub hols • Luxury guest house & function venue • Owner Fred Weber • PO Box 3428 Somerset West 7129 • wine@webersburg.co.za • www.webersburg.co.za

Visitors to the elegantly restored 18th-century property, with an idyllic lakeside setting below the Helderberg Mountains, may now enjoy the elegant reds at a new tasting facility. Also new are a function venue for up to 200 guests, and a production cellar set to come online this year.

★★★★ **Cabernet Sauvignon 03** (★★★★) shifts stylistic gears to more open, easy & accessible, richly fruited; lacks complexity of last-tasted classic **01** which needed time to unfurl. **00**, not revisited this ed, still available.

★★★★ **Webersburg** Made at Meerlust, maturing at Webersburg, **03** slated for release in 2008; handsome in open-faced, full-fruited, gentler-tannin styling. **02** had more austere, piquant savoury edges. Cab s & f with merlot (46/29/24). — DS

Wedderwill Estate Wines 🍾🍸🎋📷♿
T 021-858-1558 • F 021-858-1558

Stellenbosch (see Helderberg map) • Est 1992 • 1stB 1997 • Visits incl tours by appt Mon-Sat 9-6 • BYO picnic • Walks/hikes • Game reserve • Owner Georg Ludwig von Loeper & Neil Ian Jowell • Winemaker Nico Vermeulen • Viticulturist Dawie le Roux • 42ha (cabs s/f, malbec, merlot, mourvèdre, petit v, shiraz, chard, chenin, sauv, semillon, viognier) • 40t/3 200cs 80% red 20% white • PO Box 75 Sir Lowry's Pass 7133 • contact@wedderwill.co.za • www.wedderwill.co.za

Wedderwill has joined prestigious neighbour Vergelegen in becoming a Biodiversity & Wine Initiative champion. 'Our focus is the long-term health of the land,' says GM Wolfgang von Loeper. 'Let the soil live again!' Winemaker Nico Vermeulen endorses this win-win approach wholeheartedly: 'Great grapes make great wine, not the winemaker.'

Shiraz ★★★★ **04**, a sample last ed, ultra-ripe (15% alc) & powerful yet balanced, accessible thanks to rounded tannins, freshness, careful Fr/Am oaking. **'Bordeaux Blend'** NEW ★★★★ Fragrant cab-led blend with merlot/cab f (55/36/9); judicious oak, fine structure, to complement light though tasty ripe flavours. **04** Fr oaked, 30% new, 14 mths. **Sauvignon Blanc** ★★★★ European-styled **06**. Medium bodied, clean chalk/mineral tension; fresh, unabrasive savoury acid; bone-dry. An individual; perfect with oysters. — AL

Wederom Boutique Winery

T 023-626-4139 • F 023-626-3306

Robertson • Est 2002 • 1stB 2003 • Tasting & tours by appt only • Facilities for children • Conference facilities • Hiking/biking trails • Guest house • Function venue • Owner Philip & Almien du Toit • Winemaker Newald Marais (consultant), with Philip du Toit • Viticulturist Philip du Toit • ±20ha (merlot, shiraz, chenin) • ±120t/1 320cs 100% red • PO Box 60 Robertson 6705 • wederom@myisp.co.za • www.wederom.co.za

We want to keep the Italian connection, affirm Philip and Almien du Toit, referring to the Italian POWs who worked on the farm during WWII. A restaurant, housed in three converted cement tanks in the old cellar (dating back to 1933), is now open for functions. Expect an Italian flavour matched with suitably Old-World-styled wine.

Shiraz NEW ★★★★ **05** more serious than stablemate, denser fruit & tauter tannins, given 50% new Fr oak. Deserves ±2 yrs to show best. **Salvadori Vino Rosso Shiraz** ★★★ Vanilla notes, tight tannins on **05** flatter red berry nose & palate. Enjoy soon, & note active 14.7% alc. 18 mths old Fr oak. — *CvZ*

Wedgeview Wines

NEW

T 021-881-3525 • F 021-851-3749

Stellenbosch • Est 2005 • 1stB 2004 • Tasting & sales by appt • Facilities for children, tourgroups • Conference facilities • Wedgeview Country House & Spa • Owner Travis Braithwaite, Matthew Spicer & Patrick Gardner • 300 cs • 100% red • wine@wedgeview.co. za, travisbraithwaite@yahoo.co.uk • www.wedgeview.co.za

Travis Braithwaite and Matthew Spicer tripped and fell into winemaking. 'After consuming slightly too much of our favourite blend, we decided that making a quality bordeaux-style blend couldn't be THAT difficult...' The result is Chronology, so named because 'timing really is everything' in winemaking. New partner Patrick Gardner shares their vision: 'Total production is only 3000 bottles, of which we intend to drink half ourselves!'

★★★★ **Chronology** Impressive red led by merlot (70%) with 25% cab, dash cab f; unusually, **NV.** Claret-like, with black fruits, cigarbox, hint forest floor; refreshing cab acidity & regal tannins; dry & persistent, moderate 13.5% alc. A complete wine. — *CvZ*

Wedgewood Wines

 NEW

T 023-626-3202 / 083-285-5354 • F 023-626-1031

Swartland • Est 2007 • Tasting Mon-Sat 9-5 Sun 10-5 • Closed Easter Fri, Dec 25 & Jan 1 • Meals by appt or BYO picnic • Conference facilities • Guest house & self-catering accommodation • Owner Wiggo Andersen & Peter Tillman • Winemaker Consultants • PO Box 896 Robertson 6705 • breedevalleywines@xpoint.co.za • www.wedgewoodguestfarm.co.za

Wedgewood Guest Wine Farm between Paarl and Malmesbury is HQ for Peter Tillman and Norwegian Wiggo Andersen's wine and lifestyle ventures, which include luxury accommodation in a renovated Cape Dutch manor house dating from 1795. Wine-wise, restorations to the historic cellar are complete, and tastings now take place there as well as at the Breede Valley Wines Wine Boutique in Robertson. The Wedgewood property's grapes are mostly sold to neighbouring wineries, but increasing quantities will be channelled into the own-brand as facilities and markets come on-line.

Cabernet Sauvignon-Merlot Directors Choice ★★ Nutty black fruit, raisin whiffs & fine tannins on **06**, 15% alc evident. Fr oak. **Shiraz-Cabernet Sauvignon** ★★ Ripe-style **05**, fruit compote & raisin notes, bold flavours & matching tannins. 15% alc. **Sauvignon Blanc-Chardonnay** ★★★ Lime & grapefruit aromas, pear-drop & tropical hints, **07** fresh, crisp, easy-drinker. — *MF*

■ **Weening & Barge Winery** *see Ridgemor Farm*

Welgegund Farm

T 082-554-7871 • F 021-873-2683

Wellington (see Paarl map) • Est 1800s • 1stB 1997 • Tasting & sales by appt • B&B • Owner Alex & Sheila Camerer • Winemaker Corlea Fourie • Viticulturist Johann Smit (Winecorp,

2004) • 30ha (cab, carignan, grenache, merlot, shiraz, viognier) • 100% red • PO Box 683 Wellington 7655 • rac@icon.co.za • www.welgegund.co.za

Alex Camerer is delighted with his discovery of carignan's ability to make a drier rosé wine. The grape's Spanish origins were celebrated at the successful inaugural Wellington Wine Harvest Festival, hosted with tapas under the oaks at Welgegund. He's also thrilled with the 04 Cab's 4-star Wine magazine rating.

Cabernet Sauvignon ★★★ Last ed mint-seamed **04** showed choc flavours & firm tannic texture despite cushioning of 4.4g/l sugar. No **05**. **Carignan** ★★★ **04** more Old World than New as leather & game hints take centre stage; soft tannins indicate early drinking. **Merlot** ★★★ **04** last ed offered dark fruit aromas with savoury edge, tight 'green leaf' tannins. No **05**. **Carignan Rosé** ★★★ Rare-in-SA variety vinified as dry rosé, ex-27 yr old bushvines; juicy, raspberry-toned **07**, balanced, light & persistent. Discontinued: **Cinsaut Noir**. — CvZ

Welgeleë Vineyards

T 021-875-5726 • F 021-875-5726

Paarl • Est 1999 • 1stB 2003 • Visits daily 9-5 • Picnics by appt • Owner/viticulturist Liris Trust (Chris & Lidea Meyer) • Winemaker Chris Meyer • 3ha (shiraz) • 300cs 100% red • PO Box 439 Klapmuts 7625 • welgelee@absamail.co.za

Making wine, say Chris and Lidea Meyer, is all about 'enjoying the best of what the Boland offers'. They comment that the smaller-than-expected 2007 harvest was due to 'Mom Nature doing her lady-like best to make life interesting'. Their ever-expanding boerboel family also kept them on their toes.

Cabernet Sauvignon ★★★ **04** ripe fruit tannins & abundant blackcurrant fruit, but powerful oak needs time. **Shiraz Reserve** ★★★★ Elegant **03** nutmeg aromas, black berry flavours, fine tannins & unobtrusive oak support (9 mths Fr). **Petlou Shiraz** ★★★★ Balanced & refined; alluring choc-mocha & liquorice tones complement juicy fruit & black pepper flavours. **NV**. None above retasted. — IvH

Welgemeend Estate

T 021-875-5210 • F 021-875-5239

Paarl • 1stB 1979 • Tasting & Sales Mon - Fri 10-4 Sat 10-2.30 • Tours by app • Closed pub hols • Owner Welgemeend Estate Pty Ltd (8 shareholders) • Winemaker Lizette Steyn-James • Viticulturist Lizette Steyn-James with Schalk du Toit • ±11ha (cab s/f, grenache, malbec, merlot, 'petit mystery', pinotage, shiraz) • 3 500cs 100% red • PO Box 1408 Suider-Paarl 7624 • welgemeend@worldonline.co.za • www.welgemeend.co.za

This boutique winery, which made significant contributions to the Cape's vinous history, has started a new chapter, the Hofmeyrs having sold the farm to a Gauteng-based consortium. Fans of the restrained and elegant house style will be reassured to hear that incoming winemaker Lizette Steyn-James, ensconced mid-harvest and herself a long-time lover of Welgemeend's wines, has no plans to reinvent the wheel. Expect tweaks, though, including the replanting of old blocks.

★★★★★ **Estate Reserve** First Cape bdx blend, with loyal following around the wine world for over 25 yrs. Sample **02** (★★★★) revised since pvs review: less (63%) cab & f, more merlot; light, but hallmark polished restraint. Gentle 13% alc. Might be rebranded.

★★★★ **Douelle** A fragrant, alternative nod to Bdx. **02** mostly malbec with merlot, cab & splash cab f, 18 mths oaked; supple tannins & sweet fruit when last tasted. **03** (more cab & less merlot) not ready for review this ed.

Soopjeshoogte ★★★★ Cabs s/f with merlot; for earlier drinking than Reserve. **02** retasted: mellowing tar/asphalt notes, delicately fruited, slightly porty. Enjoy at table or lightly cooled. **Amadé** ★★★★ Idiosyncratic Cape interpretation of rhône-style blend; roughly third each shiraz, grenache & pinotage. **02** last had smoky, earthy, baked pudding features. Untasted **03** bottled after press-time. — DS

Welgevallen Wines
T 021-883-8627 · **F** 021-883-8627

Stellenbosch · Est/1stB 2000 · Visits Mon-Fri 10-2 · Closed pub & school hols · Owner Paul Roos Gymnasium Old Boys Union · Viticulturist Wouter Pienaar & Tinnie Momberg (consultants) · 10t/450c 100% red · oldboys@prg.wcape.school.za · www.paulroos.co.za

Paul Roos Gymnasium nurtures future winemakers with an original fundraising scheme. Every year the Old Boys Union vinifies 10 tons grown by ex-pupils. The winemakers (Wouter Pienaar and Middelvlei's Tinnie Momberg) are also old boys, as are many of the consumers. Public tastings are at the OBU office in Stellenbosch.

Cabernet Sauvignon ★★★ Herbal redpepper notes to dark fruits; **03** attractively lean & structured, showing gd touch of maturity - ready to enjoy. — *JP*

■ **Welgevonden** *see Vrede Wine Farm*

Wellington Cooperative Cellar
T 021-873-1163 · **F** 021-873-2423

Wellington (see Paarl map) · Est/1stB 1934 · Tasting & sales Mon-Fri 8-1, 2-5 · Owner 46 members · Winemaker Gert Boerssen, Koos Carstens & Chris Smit (1980/1990/2005) · Viticulturist Koos van der Merwe (Sep 2005) · 1 600ha (cinsaut, pinotage, chard, chenin, sauv) · 12 000t/±6 500cs own label · PO Box 520 Wellington 7654 · info@wellingtoncellars.co.za · www.wellingtoncellar.co.za

No talk of tasting facilities or visitor tours here; the focus is very much on making wine, and, talking of which, the team last year had a bumper crop to vinify, and was looking at purchasing a new 'flush machine' to ferment off the skin. This would aid the lighter, early-drinking styles demanded by overseas customers.

Reserve range
Cabernet Sauvignon ★★ **03** wooding last ed masked rich cassis fruit, needed ±3 yrs to integrate. **Pinotage** Sold out. **Shiraz** ★★ Heavy oak influence on **03** dominating ethereal ripe plum fruit. **Chenin Blanc** ★★ Chunky **04** sheathed in wood; lurking fruit still to emerge.

Wellington range

> **Chenin Blanc** ☺ ★★★ **07** forthcoming tropical nose; ripe supporting palate with gd grip & richness. Only this wine tasted this ed, all others reviewed pvsly.

Cabernet Sauvignon ★★★ Wood-powered **03** (9 mths Fr) needed time to settle. **Merlot** Sold out. **Pinotage** ★★ Gd red berry & cherry aromas on **04**, palate less ripe & gripped by stern tannins. **Shiraz** ★★★ Less fruit concentration in **04**, 9 mths oak influence still to integrate. **Classic Cape Red** ★★★★ Maiden **04** promising debut; gulpable gd fruit concentration & deft oaking. **Cinsaut-Ruby Cabernet** Out of stock. **Pinotage Rosé** Sold out. **Chardonnay** No successor in sight. **Sauvignon Blanc** No newer vintage ready. **Late Harvest** ★★★ **04** semi-sweet chenin; pear tones & tangerine hint, not too sweet; light 12% alc. **Hanepoot Jerepiko** ★★★ Steely streak to **05** out of line with delicate floral aromas & cloying sweetness. **Port** No new stock. — *JP*

■ **Welmoed** *see The Company of Wine People*

Weltevrede Estate
T 023-616-2141 · **F** 023-616-2460

Robertson · Est 1912 · 1stB 1975 · Tasting & sales Mon-Fri 8-5 Sat 9-3.30 · Tours by appt · Café on Weltevrede Tue-Sat (closed Jun/Jul) · Guest cottages · Conservation area · Walks · 4×4/mountain bike trail · Owner Lourens Jonker · Winemaker Philip Jonker (1997) · Viticulturist Philip Jonker, advised by Francois Viljoen · 100ha (cab, merlot, shiraz, chard, colombard, sauv) · 1500t/25 000cs own label 15% red 75% white 10% other · PO Box 6 Bonnievale 6730 · info@weltevrede.com · www.weltevrede.com

BWI registration is proceeding for the area of renosterveld vegetation which flourishes in the farm's complex and varied soils. Soil diversity is also reflected in the names and characteristics of the quartet of chardonnays produced by this family-run estate. The Place of Rocks bottling was recently lauded as 'burgundy at half the price' by the Beaujolais Restaurant in Canada. Still talking chardonnay, the Jonkers were preparing to unwrap a new range of cap classique sparklings as the guide went to press.

★★★★☆ **Poet's Prayer Chardonnay** An oenological artwork born of attention to detail: slow wild yeast ferment, 19 mths Fr oak, further yr in bottle - all lavished on a single cask. **04** (★★★★) last ed a symphony from both the 'Rocks' & 'Rusted Soil' sites, in complex mineral style of pvs, but whisper short of their finesse. **03** rich yet tight, elegantly crafted.

★★★★ **Rusted Soil Chardonnay** If above projects cellarmaster's persona, this & chard duo below reflect the nature of their terroir. Limestone vyd origin gives **06** plush, tropical girth hauled in by orange peel twist. **04** as lush. No **05**. 10 mths Fr oak.

★★★★ **Place of Rocks Chardonnay** From shale soils, taut, less exuberant: Melted butter aromas of **06** belie flinty mineral seam, a foil for hazelnut core. Excellent amongst pacy peers. Oaked 10 mths. EW.

★★★★ **The Travelling Stone Sauvignon Blanc** ✓ Hand-cropped vine selection from vyd on quartzite stone which originally 'rolled down the surrounding hills'. **07** fig fullness to racy spine & penetrating finish. Should fill out over yr/2.

Bedrock Black Syrah ★★★★ Leads trio of reds in otherwise white-wine country. **06** fuller than last-tasted **04** (★★★★); dark choc mulberry fruit gives substance to still bracing pepper frame. All Fr oak. **05** not reviewed. EW. **Gewürztraminer** ★★★★ Developed **06**, aromatic jasmine tones to litchi flesh, Turkish Delight viscosity in off-dry finish. **Ovation Rhine Riesling** ★★★ Natural Sweet in crossover style: rich botrytis but drier than NLH. **99** well-developed at last review mid-2005. **Ouma se Wyn** ★★★ Single white muscat de F vyd; **06** grapey, full sweet & viscous, clean finish. 375ml. **Philip Jonker Brut** ★★★★ Critically acclaimed (Cap Classique Challenge, Diners' Club runner up), MCC from chard. **04** rich mouthfeel, persistent finish; enjoy on release. Not revisited this ed. EW. **Oupa se Wyn** ★★★ From red muscadel & muscat de H, partly ex-octogenarian bushvines. **06** more complex than just grapey, roast nut interest in fresh tail. 375ml. Discontinued: **Rhine Riesling**.

River's Edge range

Chardonnay ☺ ★★★ Fourth in Jonker's terroir series, from alluvial soils. Lip-smacking, tongue-clucking refreshment of **07**; summer melon focused by lime freshness. No wood.

Shiraz NEW ★★★ First red in this range; in the groove: **05** offers spicy grip & a sappy texture, confident enough for winter hotpots. **Sauvignon Blanc** ★★★ Fresh grassy notes in sample **07**, for easy drinking.

Tricolore range

Red ★★★ Chunky red, the carnivore's wine. **05** merlot, cab & shiraz; tangy berries tucked into soft oak tannins. Satisfying 14.5% alc send-off. **White** ★★★ Tank sample **07** vibrant medley sauv, colombard filled out with semillon; penetrating grassiness followed by enough girth for the picnic. — DS

Welvanpas
T 021-864-1238 • F 021-864-1239

Wellington (see Paarl map) • Tasting & sales Mon-Fri 9-12.15; 1-5 Sat 9-1 • Owner D Retief & Son Cellars • Winemaker/viticulturist Dan Retief Jnr • ±500t total; 15-30t own label 75% red 25% white • PO Box 75 Wellington 7654 • welvanpas@xsinet.co.za

'Nothing's changed...' on this Wellington family farm, which dates back to 1705, according to Dan Retief Snr. A tasting with this raconteur may bring the past to life with fascinating tales of their forebears, which include Voortrekker leader Piet Retief.

Cabernet Sauvignon ✭ Artisinal **03** with smoky, savoury aromas & flavours, chewy tannin. **Pinotage** ✭ Rustic & reticent **03**, 15% alc gives sweet impression to lifted finish. **Revival Red** ✭✭ Uncomplicated **03** quaffer with fruit pastille flavours & grainy tannins. **De Krakeelhoek Rooi** ✭ Equal shiraz/merlot blend; **03** touch rustic, for early consumption. **Chenin Blanc** ✭ **04** tropical, with caramel notes. This, all above, not retasted. — *MM*

■ Weskus *see Winkelshoek Wine Cellar*

Westbridge Vineyards
T 021-884-4433 • F 021-884-4324

Stellenbosch • Est 1998 • 1stB 1999 • Tasting & sales Mon-Sat 8-6 (phone ahead T 083·631·2229) • B&B guest accommodation • Chapel/wedding venue • Owner JC Starke & Muldersvlei Estates • Winemaker Ian Starke • Viticulturist Julian Starke • 17ha (cab, chenin) • 60t/4 000cs 85% red 15% white • PO Box 66 Muldersvlei 7607 • wine@muldersvlei.co.za

Westbridge have downscaled production to 15 000 bottles, from vineyards now only 40% of their previous size. All production is sold at the farm or served at their flagship events venue. The Starkes meanwhile continue with several successful businesses, including wine blending, fruit export, a beef herd and tourist accommodation.

★★★★ Pinotage Reserve Two vintages to date: **99** characterful & full-flavoured with pronounced savoury edge; **00** attractively rustic.

Merlot 03 too young to rate but shows extraordinary concentration. **Pinotage ★★★☆ 03** individually styled, tropical fruit & hints tobacco & earth, tannins less daunting than pvs. Oak chip fermented/aged. **Shiraz ★★★ 02** characteristic shiraz spice, plus house's earthy touches, firm tannins. **Juliette ★★★☆** Blend changes with vintage; **03**, with smidgen pinotage, fruitier, more satisfying than pvs. This, above, not retasted. — *DH*

■ Western Wines South Africa *see Kumala/Constellation South Africa*

Whalehaven Wines
T 028-316-1633 • F 028-316-1640

Hemel-en-Aarde Valley (see Elgin/Walker Bay map) • Est/1stB 1995 • Tasting & sales Apr-Nov (incl) Mon-Fri 9.30-5 Sat & non-religious hols 10.30-4.30; Dec-Mar (incl) Mon-Fri 9.30-5 Sat, Sun & non-religious hols 10.30-4.30 • Fee R10 pp for groups of 5+ • Closed Easter Fri/Sun, Dec 25 & Jan 1 • Tours by appt • BYO picnic • Owner Bottega family • Winemaker Reino Thiart (Jul 2007) • Vineyard Manager Tim Clark • 120t capacity • Private Bag X14 Hermanus 7200 • wine@whalehavenwines.co.za • www.whalehaven.co.za

An apt whaletail-inspired 'W' insignia will replace the ship on the new releases this year, but the Bottega family remains at the helm. All their ranges – including Idiom and Enoteca Bottega, listed separately in the guide – are offered at the upgraded cellar tasting facilities at the gateway to the Hemel-en-Aarde Valley. The fruit for all but the Pinot and Chardonnay is sourced from the family's Da Capo Vineyards in the Helderberg.

★★★★ Pinot Noir 06 follows on from last-tasted **00**, in burgundian style, laced with cherry fruit. Savoury layers contrast toasty oak (40% new), yet to integrate.

Old Harbour Red ☺ **★★★** Now vintage-dated. **05** dusty eucalyptus tones with firm backbone. Merlot-led blend (74%), sweet fruited. Delicious now & for few yrs.

Cabernet Franc ★★★★ Leafy, perfumed **05**, rounder & riper than **04** (**★★★★**). Excellent balance of opulent fruit & 50% new Fr oak. One for the cellar. **Merlot ★★★☆** Marmite & underbrush notes contrast with sour cherry flavours & compact tannins on **06**. Fleshy fruit core & sturdy structure of will allow few yrs ageing. **Bord de Mer ★★★** Rustic edge does not hide touch of sweetness on **04**. Fine tannins give elegance to firmly oaked blend merlot & shiraz (76/24). **Rosé ★★★** Mulberry-infused **06** drier than pvs, crisp & fun. Gd pure flavours from kaleidoscope of grapes. **Chardonnay ★★★** Bold styling continues in **05**, heavily oaked (80% new Fr), so sweet pear fruit a tad overwhelmed mid-2007. Might simply need time.

Viognier-Chardonnay ★★★☆ Upfront styling with melon, kiwi & aromatic notes from 85% viognier; **06** full off-dry flavours with some grip; unoaked; great with rich Asian food. — *RP*

■ **What? Wines** *see* Woolworths

■ *White River* *see* Bergsig Estate

■ *Wide River* *see* Robertson Winery

Wildekrans Estate

T 028-284-9829 • F 028-284-9902

Walker Bay (see Elgin/Walker Bay map) • Est/1stB 1993 • Tasting & sales: Farm cellar Mon-Fri 9-5 Sat-Sun 11-3 (May-Aug open by appt); Wildekrans Wine Shop & Art Gallery at Orchard Farmstall, Grabouw (T/F 021-859-5587), Mon-Sun 9-5.30 (closed Dec 25) • Cellar tours on request • BYO picnic to farm by appt, picnics available by appt • Bird watching/walks on farm by appt • Play area for children • Conservation area • Owner Wildekrans Trust • Winemaker William Wilkinson (2006) • Viticulturist Kobus Jordaan • 40ha (cabs s/f, merlot, pinotage, shiraz, chenin, sauv, semillon) • 240t/10 000cs own label 50% red 50% white • PO Box 31 Botrivier 7185 • wines@wildekrans.com • www.wildekrans.com

This previously family-owned property on the Green Mountain Eco Route has been bought by a group of entrepreneurs, including Gavin Varejes, CEO of Richmark Holdings, Mark and Brett Levy and Gary Harlow of Blue Label Investments. Co-investor and project co-ordinator David Marais says their goal is 'to create a premium brand and make Wildekrans even more special'. Seasoned Kobus Jordaan (ex-Klein Constantia) has been brought on board to help drive the renewal in the vineyard; William Wilkinson continues to helm the cellar.

Cabernet Sauvignon ★★★ **06** herbal, blackcurrant aromas, light bodied, red fruit flavours, firm but ripe tannins, with firm acidity needing food. **Pinotage** ★★★ Light-textured **05** gripped by firm acidity & lean, austere tannins. Yr 60% new oak. **Pinotage Barrel Select** ★★★ **06** richer than standard release; spicy vanilla from yr 70% new Fr & Am oak. Fine cured meat & bright cherry flavours presently dominated by tannins & firm acidity. **Shiraz** ★★★★ Sample **06** spicy, with pure, focused red berry compôte flavours in balance with firm acidity & moderate tannins. Fr & Am oak. **Cabernet Franc-Merlot** ★★★ **05** tasted mid-2006 lean, earthy fruit & dry tannins. 89/11 blend, 9 mths older Fr oak. **Warrant** ★★★★ Bdx blend led by merlot; sweet plum & cassis on **02**; sour cherry & roasted spice flavours well-integrated with oak tannins from yr new barrels. Light, fresh, elegant structure. **Chenin Blanc** 🍷 ★★ Pale gold **07** (sample) with apple & lanolin aromas & racy acidity. **Sauvignon Blanc** 🍷 ★★★ Upfront grassy **07**, breezy & fresh green fig aromas with more restrained acidity than pvs. **Méthode Cap Classique** ★★ Characterful **02** brut from chard, 3 yrs on lees; appley/lactic aromas, clean dry mousse noted last ed. NE. Discontinued: **Chardonnay**, **Semillon**.

Caresse Marine range

Merlot 🍷 ★★ Light cranberry-toned **06** with piquant acidity, yr oak softens tight fruit; calls for pasta. **Cape Red Blend** ★★★ Shiraz leads pinotage & merlot in characterful **05**, pvsly tasted; savoury tannins from 20% new Fr oak. NE. **Dry White** 🍷 ★★ **06** chenin/semillon blend; fresh, zippy Granny Smith apple flavours; bracing acidity to cut through rich shellfish dishes. **White** 🍷 ★★ Floral, spicy apricot **06**, semi-sweet style for easy drinking with lightly spiced Asian dishes. — *IM*

■ **Wildfire** *see* Cape Vineyards

■ *Wild Olive Farm* *see* Buck's Ridge Wines & Olives

■ *Wild Rush* *see* Rietvallei Estate

■ *Wild Tales* *see* Baarsma Wine Group

■ *Wilhelmshof* *see* Nico van der Merwe Wines

William Everson Wines
T 082-554-6357 • F 021-851-2205

Paarl • Est/1stB 2001 • Visits by appt • BYO picnic • Owner/winemaker William Everson • 300cs 80% red 20% white • 7 Prospect Street Somerset West 7130 • we@intekom.co.za

Still fully occupied in the transport business, William Everson is slowly starting to think about establishing his own boutique cellar. 'There are now only three of us left sharing facilities in Paarl's Main Street – and still enjoying each others' company! But I am looking to set up my own space soon.'

Shiraz-Mourvèdre NEW ★★★ **05** intriguing hedgerow fruit, asphalt tones, elegant Old-World style but not for ageing. Incl Mbury fruit. **04**, labelled 'Shiraz', had small dash mourvèdre. **Chardonnay** ★★★★ **06** makes bold statement with powerful toastiness, more citrus intensity than pvs. Long, refreshing finish. Yr oaking, some new. WO W Bay. **Semillon** NEW 🗐 ★★ **06** waxy biscuit overlay to tropical fruit; light textured, easy. — *CR*

Windmeul Cooperative Cellar
T 021-869-8043/8100 • F 021-869-8614

Paarl • Est 1944 • Tasting & sales Mon-Fri 8-5 Sat 9-1 • Closed pub hols • Tours during tasting hours by appt • Owner 48 members • Cellarmaster Danie Marais • Winemaker Francois van Niekerk (Dec 1999/Dec 2004), with Pierre Vienings (Dec 2005) • Viticulturist Paul Malan (Dec 2001) • 1 700ha (cab, merlot, shiraz, chard, chenin, sauv) • 11 013t/6 000cs own label 55% red 45% white • PO Box 2013 Windmeul 7630 • windmeul@info.com • www. windmeulwinery.co.za

Quality is what differentiates the survivors, the Windmeul team believe, which is why they're extending their top-end Reserve range with a Pinotage (a variety they see as a major growth opportunity for SA wine). They're working on improving perceptions too: the Reserve range is now presented in stylish black packaging.

Reserve range
Cabernet Sauvignon ★★★★ **05** well-managed Fr oak (80% new); berry fruits almost dominated by firm tannin, needing some time to settle. No **04**. **Pinotage** NEW ★★★★ No retreating violet. **06** toasty oak, mocha/choc notes on firm tannin background. Fr barriques, 18 mths. **Shiraz** ★★★★ **03** last ed offered creamy vanilla flavours with a sweet/sour twist. Yr oak, 45% Am.

Windmeul range
Cabernet Sauvignon ★★ Flinty/mineral **05**, slightly austere, needs food. Combo staves/barrels. No **04**. **Merlot 05** sold out before tasting. **06** unready. **Pinotage** ★★ **05** not ready; last tasted **04** dusty, acetone notes, astringent tannins. **Shiraz** ★★ **05** not ready; **04** last ed was rustic & robust. **Cabernet Sauvignon-Merlot** ★★★★ **05** more serious than pvs. Dark choc, bold black cherry & ripe plum flavours. **Chardonnay** NEW ★★★ Lightly wooded **06**, soft butterscotch, citrus & tropical fruit, crisp acidity. **Chenin Blanc** ★★★ Appley **07** charms with crisp flavours, invitingly clean melon finish. **Sauvignon Blanc** ★★★ **07** classic grassy intro, delicious ripe gooseberry, brisk finish. **Port** ★★★★ Friendly **04** pretty ruby colour, plum pudding notes, rich plummy flavours & elegant dry finish. — *DB*

■ **Winds of Change** *see African Terroir*

Wine Concepts
T 021-671-9030 • F 021-671-9031

Cape Town • Tasting & sales Mon-Fri 9-7 Sat 9-5 • • Cardiff Castle, cnr Kildare & Main St, Newlands 7700 • sales@wineconcepts.co.za • www.wineconcepts.co.za

The limited release Lollapalooza, a Cab 05 made by Murray Giggins, partner with Mike Bampfield-Duggan in this wine retail and garagiste business, has seen the light of day and is being be sold from their shops in Newlands and Gardens. Keeping up the momentum, Murray G has plans to make a Shiraz soon, squeezing in a garagiste winemaking course too.

■ **Winecorp** *see Spier Wines*

■ *Winemaker's Selection* see Cloverfield Private Cellar

Wine of the Month Club
T 021-657-8100 ▪ F 021-415-6385

Est 1986 ▪ Founder Colin Collard ▪ MD Tai Collard ▪ Private Bag X2 Glosderry 7702 ▪ wineclub@wineofthemonth.co.za ▪ www.wineofthemonth.co.za

The Collard clan runs Good Taste magazine and the pioneering Wine of the Month Club wine subscription business, now in its 21st year. In the latter, Colin Collard has been joined by sons Gis and Tai, and over the past year, sourced wines from among others Villiera, Flagstone, Meerendal and Steenberg. Colin's daughter, Natalie, is involved in purchasing, with Wendy Burridge.

Wine of the Month Club range [NEW]

★★★★ **Kirkwood Cabernet Sauvignon** Inviting **05**, herbal, spicy cherry tobacco & black-currant fruit, vanilla flavours & savoury, flavoursome finish. By Klein Constantia, from Sbosch fruit.

★★★★ **Jakkalskloof Cabernet Sauvignon 05** spicy clove & cinnamon, cherry tobacco aromas; dense structure filled out by fleshy red berry fruit; high 15% alc in balance. Tannins & richness to cellar, but drinking well now. By Klein Constantia, from Sbosch fruit.

★★★★ **Forrest Hill Cabernet Sauvignon-Shiraz-Merlot** Modern, confident & plush **05**, almost equal blend cab, shiraz, splash merlot. Densely coloured, ultra-rich & well-structured; opulent sweet red fruit checked by soft tannins & balancing savoury acidity. 10 mths Fr & Am oak. By Guardian Peak.

Barrington Merlot ★★★★ Wafts plum & roast herbs on **05**, leather/tobacco notes; lean fruit, tight acidity & dry, elegant finish. By Klein Constantia. **Khayamandi Shiraz** ★★★ Overtly New World **05** with sweet red fruit, chocolate, mocha & vanilla. Soft, supple, balanced & ready for early drinking. By Cape Classics. **Blackwood Shiraz** ★★★ **05** redolent of roasted spice & ripe blackberry. Soft & sweet (5.7g/l RS) held in check by pliable tannins. By Cape Classics. **Martindale Shiraz-Cabernet Sauvignon** ★★★★ Spice, roasted herbs & leather aromas in **04** blend shiraz/cab with splashes merlot, malbec. Grippy tannins well-integrated; spicy finish. By Vrede & Lust. **Delia Sauvignon Blanc** ★★★ **06** more tropical than herbaceous, balanced, not overtly fruity, but quietly drinkable & vinous, versatile with food. **Caimanskloof Sauvignon Blanc** ★★★ Gooseberry & nettle on **06** with fresh peach flavours & lively acidity. Well-balanced for easy enjoyment. By Villiera. **Willowbrook Semillon-Chenin Blanc** ★★ **06** restrained citrus & waxy semillon aromas, nougat flavours, balanced acidity. By Franschhoek Cellars. **Jakkalskloof Riesling-Chenin Blanc** ★★★ Appealing sweet, spicy aromatics in **06**, rich apricot & melon flavours, fruity, spice-laden finish. By Flagstone.

Select Winemakers Collection Limited Release [NEW]

★★★★ **Etienne le Riche Cabernet Sauvignon** Elegant, classic-style **04**, as ecpected from E le R: blackcurrant, well-harmonised spicy cedar wood, lightly textured sweet fruit; thread of acidity throughout.

★★★★ **Charles Hopkins Shiraz-Mourvèdre** Splash viognier in **06**. Bright, spicy shiraz aromas, sour cherry flavours. Melded toasty tannins add pleasant savouriness to balanced, concentrated fruit. Firm, spice-laden finish; Third Am oak. Dbnvlle vyds.

Hempies du Toit Shiraz ★★★★ **03** showing maturity. Almost porty, with aniseed aromas; sweet, v ripe mulberry fruit; robust alc & big tannins. 3 yrs Fr wood. — *IM*

■ **Winery of Good Hope** see The Winery of Good Hope

Wines of Cape Town
T 021-863-1471 ▪ F 021-863-3059

Paarl ▪ Tasting & sales daily 9-5 ▪ Deli/bistro & other attractions ▪ Owner DS Sarnia (Pty) Ltd ▪ Winemaker Nico Vermeulen ▪ Viticulturist Wilhelm van Rooyen ▪ PO Box 1317 Southern Paarl 7624 ▪ sales@winesofcapetown.com ▪ www.winesofcapetown.com

Having purchased all trademarks from Cru Wines and renamed the holding company last year, a new winemaker has been appointed: the experienced Nico Vermeulen, whose task is to create 'exceptional wines for each price point and taste profile'. With exports to 30 countries (and growing), Nico V certainly has his work cut out, but he has his sleeves rolled up and MD Mike Byers is relishing the challenge too.

Alphen Hill range

Cabernet Sauvignon ★★★ **04** food friendly in leaner, savoury style. **Merlot** ★★★ Easy-drinking **06**, gentle black fruit with mocha hints, subtle oaking. **Pinotage** In abeyance. **Shiraz** ★★ Pvsly tasted **04** ultra-soft acidity & tannins; sweet, spice-dusted fruit. **Chardonnay** NEW ★★ Clean, crisp **07**, understated lemon & lime flavours untouched by oak. **Chenin Blanc** ★★ Clean, crisp & shy, **07** with nuance of apples. **Sauvignon Blanc** ★★ Shy, lean & tart **07**, tad nervous & lacking fruit.

Bushman's Creek range

Cabernet Sauvignon ★★★ Maiden **04** last ed was light textured & soft, for early enjoyment. Wine Best Value Award. **Shiraz** ★★★ Smoke, spice & bright red fruit on **05**, lively tannins need time or food. **Cabernet Sauvignon-Merlot** ★★★ Clean-cut **05**, restrained, with dark fruit & integrated oak; medium bodied. **Chardonnay** ★★★ Lime marmalade & hints of lees butteriness on **06**, gentle rounded drinkability. **Sauvignon Blanc** ★★ **06** soft, understated, with clean passionfruit appeal. **07** unready.

Dolphin Bay range

Cabernet Sauvignon NEW ★★★ Bright berry-fruited attractions in friendly, approachable **05**. For early drinking. **Pinotage Rosé** ★★ No new vintage. Last tasted **06** semi-dry sunset sipper. **Chenin Blanc** ★★ **07** slender summer quaffer. **Semi Sweet** NEW ★★ Floral, off-dry & fresh **07** with tangy sherbety appeal. **Sparkling Brut** Not tasted. **Sparkling Vin Doux** NEW Unready for review. Discontinued: **Pinotage-Ruby Cabernet**. Mainly WO W Cape for all ranges. — MW

▋ **Wines of Charles Back** *see* Fairview

Wine Village-Hermanus
T 028-316-3988 ▪ F 028-316-3989

Walker Bay (see Elgin/Walker Bay map) ▪ Est 1998 ▪ 1stB 2004 ▪ Open Mon-Fri 9-6 Sat 9-5 Sun 10-3 ▪ Closed Easter Fri & Dec 25 ▪ Owner Paul & Cathy du Toit ▪ ±1 000cs 50% red 50% white ▪ PO Box 465 Hermanus 7200 ▪ wine@hermanus.co.za ▪ www.wine-village.co.za

Paul and Cathy du Toit's delightful country wine shop is situated at the gateway to both the Hemel-en-Aarde Valley and Hermanus, a favourite destination for whale- and wine-lovers. A feature is a library-style layout which makes it easy to find varietal and blend categories. Available are a Dry Red and Dry White under the owners' own label, neither tasted.

Winkelshoek Wine Cellar
T 022-913-1092 ▪ F 022-913-1095

Swartland ▪ Tasting & sales Mon-Fri 9-4 Sat 9-12 ▪ Fee R5 ▪ Gifts ▪ Owner Hennie Hanekom & Jurgens Brand ▪ Winemaker Hennie Hanekom (1984) ▪ PO Box 395 Piketberg 7320 ▪ info@ winkelshoek.co.za

This cellar's easy-drinkers are available for tasting and sale from the visitor centre near the intersection of the N7 and R44 roads outside Piketberg. The wines, untasted for this edition, include the Weskus Dry Red, Grand Cru, Blanc de Blanc and Late Harvest; and the Cap Vino Red (unwooded) and White (chenin).

Withington
T 021-865-2108 ▪ F 088-021-865-2108

Stellenbosch ▪ Est 1999 ▪ 1stB 2002 ▪ Tasting & sales by appt ▪ Closed pub hols ▪ Owner Withington family ▪ ±4 000cs own label 67% red 33% white ▪ Export brand: Livingstone (UK) ▪ PO Box 236 Darling 7345 ▪ mail@withington.co.za ▪ www.withington.co.za

A military heritage spawned the Withingtons' 'guerilla' strategy of focusing on underexploited market niches, and they've been quietly developing a loyal following with a friendly range of wines. The Shiraz-Cab in particular has proved popular, both in the UK mail order market and locally with the likes of V&A Waterfront retailer Vaughan Johnson.

Merlot ★★★★ More structured **04** a step up; smoked meat & fynbos notes, ripe fruit, gd tight tannins. **Shiraz-Cabernet Sauvignon ★★★** Enticing St Joseph's lily hints to **05**'s tea & leather bouquet; fruit/acid palate tango, woody tail. Yr new Fr/Am oak. **Chardonnay** 📖 **★★** Slender, fruit-shy **07** drops baton: some pear & lemondrops, gravelly finish. **Sauvignon Blanc** NEW **07** not ready. Discontinued: **Cabernet Sauvignon**. — *CvZ*

Withoek
T 044-213-3639 · F 044-213-3639

Calitzdorp (see Klein Karoo map) · Est/1stB 1996 · Tasting & sales Mon-Fri 9-4 · Closed Mar 21, Easter Fri, Apr 27, May 1, Jun 16, Aug 9, Sep 24 · Tours by appt · Self-catering cottages · Farm produce · Walks · Conservation area · Owner/winemaker/viticulturist Fanie Geyser · 20ha (cab, petit v, ruby cab, shiraz, tinta, touriga, chenin, colombard, hanepoot, muscadel) · ±300t/400cs own label 50% red 50% fortified · PO Box 181 Calitzdorp 6660 · withoek@telkomsa.net

After several months of trying to straddle two cellars 350km apart, Fanie Geyser has opted to settle full-time on the family farm. (He was until September last year also winemaker at Landskroon.) It's not just the distance, he says, but the vines planted by his late father are now coming into fruit, and prospects are good. Note: no wines tasted this edition.

■ **Withof** *see* Wines of Cape Town

■ **Witteboomen** *see* Thorntree Wines

■ **Wolvenbosch Family Vineyards** *see* Jason's Hill Private Cellar

---

Wolvendrift Private Cellar
T 023-616-2890 · F 023-616-2396

Robertson · Est 1903 · 1stB 2002 · Tasting & sales Mon-Fri 9-4.30 Sat 10-1 · Closed Easter Fri-Sun, Dec 25/26 & Jan 1 · Tours by appt · BYO picnic · Farm produce · Walks · Owner Michael Klue · Winemaker Michael & Jan Klue (Jan 1973/Jan 2003) · Viticulturist Jan Swart (Jan 2000) · 120ha (cab, merlot, chard, chenin, colombard, sauv) · 45% red 45% white 10% fortified · Box 24 Robertson 6705 · wolvendrift@lando.co.za · www.wolvendriftwines.co.za

Carlin Klue has joined father Michael and brother Jan, and the enlarged team say they are expecting even bigger and better things of their white-walled winery on the Breede River banks. Last year the winemakers experimented with different yeast strains and ferment temperatures, while Carlin K took over the administration and ran the wine tastings.

Cabernet Sauvignon-Merlot ★★★ 04 mentioned pvs ed was 60/40 blend; red berry fruit with some toasty oak. **Chardonnay ★★** Easy-drinking **06** unready last ed; now showing ripe yellow peach & hint of honey, inviting early consumption. **Riverstone Sauvignon Blanc ★★** Sample **07** grass, gooseberry & ripe guava; light & rather tart, best enjoyed ice-cold. **Muscadel ★★★** Fortified red muscadel; **06** pvs ed brimmed with Turkish Delight & raisins; sweet yet tangy; mellow 17% alc. — *JP*

Women in Wine NEW
T 021-887-3375 · F 021-887-3423

Stellenbosch · PO Box 6225 Uniedal Stellenbosch 7612 · women@wine.co.za · www.womeninwine.co.za

Women in Wine is one of the first entirely women-owned and -run empowerment companies in the SA wine industry. It aims to give women, who have made immeasurable contributions to the Cape's wine industry without receiving recognition or benefiting from business opportunities along the way, an overdue share in the profits.

Eden's Vineyards range
Cabernet Sauvignon-Shiraz ★★ 02's toasty dark-fruit nose balances pleasant, earthy & light-bodied palate. **Pinotage Rosé ★★★** Subtle strawberry fruit on **06**; medium-full red-

berry palate with light, playful finish. **Chardonnay-Chenin Blanc** ★★ Bottle age character dominates **05**'s creamy, food-friendly palate & soft acidity. —JP

Wonderboom *see* Groupe LFE South Africa

Wonderfontein
T 023-626-2212 • F 023-626-2669

Robertson • Est ca 1884 • Tasting & sales Mon-Fri 8.30-6 Sat 8.30-1 • Tour groups • Conference & picnic facilities, 4×4 trail & other attractions • Owner Paul René Marais • Winemaker Stefan Bruwer (2002) • Viticulturist Gert Visser, advised by Anton Laas (Jan 1997/Jan 2005) • 240 ha (cab, merlot, pinotage, ruby cab, shiraz, chard, chenin, sauv, viognier) • 5 500t/3 000cs own label • 10% red 80% white 1% rosé 9% fortified • PO Box 4 Robertson 6705 • law@lando.co.za • www.wonderfonteinestate.co.za

For the first time, the public have an open invitation to visit this old family farm, for tastings as well as functions like weddings and their latest draw, musical recitals. Or visit their first-time website! Family changes saw all the farm cats move, with youngest daughter, Jeanne Marais, into her grandmother's house.

La Bonne Vigne Sauvignon Blanc ☺ ★★★ Zesty & lively **07**, lots of salad greens & herbal notes, zippy acid will put a spring in your step.

Merlot ★★★ Shyish **06**, pleasing lighter style at 12% alc. Attractive dryness, earthy finish.
Wonderfontein Red Muscadel ★★★ Hedonistic sweet fortified; **06** last ed showed gentle perfumes, slight raisined character; at 229g/l sugar, a dessert in a glass. —IvH

Woodhill *see* Grangehurst Winery

Woolworths
F 021-407-2777

Category manager William Fakude T 021·407·3683 • Technologist Warren Dam T 021·407·2714 • Wine trainee Eric Botha T 021·407·3107 • Selection manager Allan Mullins T 021·407·2777 AllanMullins@woolworths.co.za • Buying manager Ivan Oertle T 021·407·2762 IvanOertle@woolworths.co.za • AllanMullins@woolworths.co.za

'The pace is relentless,' says Ivan Oertle about working at Woolies (as the upmarket retail chain is affectionately known), from new product launches and large-scale packaging upgrades to the Good Food & Good Business Journey, which encompasses environmental sustainability and ethical practices. Bubbly is the star performing category at the moment, from 'friendly organic' and blush to own-brand champagne and sparkling Italian pinot grigio. When it comes to this trendy Italian grape, Oertle believes Woolies now has the most comprehensive range in SA retail by far. Rosé has also seen 'explosive development in virtually all the ranges, from R20 to R365'. But he's most excited about the new True to Terroir range: created, sourced, blended and bottled exclusively for Woolworths by Spier (unfortunately not ready for review). 'A high point in our development initiatives.'

Reserve range
★★★★ **Cabernet Sauvignon** Pvsly bottled as 'Founder's Reserve'. Last tasted **03** (★★★) less showy than racy **06**: lifted spearmint/peppermint whiffs waft over dense cassis/scrub bouquet, lively acidity cuts through sappy core. Showstopper… not for classicists. Ex-Diemersfontein.
★★★★ **Merlot** NEW Inky hue; intense plum & leafy nose cradled by creamy oak in **05**. Big & bold (14.4%) yet with refined tannins. Buy now but cellar ±3 yrs. 20 mths Fr oak, 35% new. From Morgenhof.
★★★★ **Groenekloof Shiraz** ✓ Expressive **04** ripe yet elegant with refined tannins & restrained fruit, velvety & mushroom characters. **05** (★★★★★) in similar vein but shorter oaked (8 vs 12 mths) & less alc (14.3 vs 14.5%), intense dark berries add complexity. Lovely now, should improve 5+ yrs.

★★★★ **Cabernet Sauvignon-Merlot** Neil Ellis' classic approach ensures his wines reflect vintage variations, as this wine has shown over the yrs. **05** no exception; warmer & riper but beautifully crafted, lush fruit melding with well-judged oak. **04** (★★★☆) was a shorter-term wine. ±17 mths Fr oak, 25% new.

★★★★☆ **The W Reserve** NEW Newcomer to Woolworths' range from relatively new but acclaimed Tulbagh Mountain Vineyards. **05** accomplished, a little flashy, different. Red, floral-toned shiraz fruit accentuated by 13% mouvèdre's spice; balanced, integrated. 22 mths Fr oak, 25% new.

★★★★☆ **Chardonnay** **05** exquisite wooded version in which oak plays seasoning role, allowing bright citrus fruit to take centre stage. Tangerine & spice melange provide lift & flavours; seemingly endless nutty finish. By Dewetshof.

★★★★ **Barrel Chenin Blanc** ✓ Pre-bottling sample **07** back on form, lifts the ante on tasty **05** (★★★☆) (no **06** tasted) with intense thatch aromas; piercing chenin acidity fattened by touch RS & dusted with oak spices. For keeping few yrs.

★★★★☆ **Sauvignon Blanc** Composed & elegant cool-climate version ex-Groote Post. **07** as refined as maiden **06**: enticing green fig/khaki bush nuances washed by sweaty suggestion, zesty lemon acidity & long capsicum finish; impressive weight from fruit & 3 mths lees contact. Drink now, or in yr/2's time.

★★★★ **Noble Late Harvest Chenin Blanc Barrel Reserve** Barrel-fermented NLH. **06** mid-2005 was sumptuous & complex, vibrant interplay between honey, apricot & lemon, tangy acidity.

Pinotage ★★★☆ **05** not retasted, mid-2006 juicy fruit was swamped by creamy Am oak (100%), should have integrated by now. By Bellevue. **Cabernet Sauvignon-Shiraz** ✓ ★★★★ Step up for **06** (★★★★), its bold & forthright red/black fruit notes marrying with mocha-coffee oak, bouncing off refreshing acidity. 15 mths, 20% new oak. Needs ±12 mths to show at best. Last tasted **04** was charry, with black fruit. Ex-La Motte. Discontinued: **Chardonnay (Neil Ellis)**.

Limited Release range

★★★★☆ **Cabernet Franc** NEW **05** top-notch maiden from Diemersfontein/Raats Family; Bruwer R fast earning a reputation as the cab f maestro. Leafy, with oakspice & mint nuances; long liquorice conclusion. Grippy tannins (18 mths Fr oak, 25% new) need some time mesh.

★★★★ **Malbec** Fruitful **05** by Bellevue. Fresh rosemary, thyme & pepper notes engage with new leather & mulberry. Supple tannins, soft fleshy centre ensure immediate gratification but has structure from yr 100% new Fr oak to improve.

★★★★ **Pinot Noir** Quintessential pinot undergrowth & sour cherry notes in **06** offering from Catherine Marshall; cool-climate Elgin/Darling grapes providing firm yet approachable tannins, great length & vibrant fruit core in a warmer vintage. 20% new oak, 12 mths.

★★★★ **Shiraz-Grenache** Ken Forrester supplies exuberant **04** mouthful; ultra-ripe palate, soft tannins for juicy quaffability, alc a tad obvious on finish.

★★★★ **Chardonnay Sur Lie** ✓ **07** all an unoaked, serious chard should be: vivacious & focused with lively citrus fruit, creamy highlights from less contact (4 mths), seemingly endless conclusion.

★★★★☆ **Gewürztraminer** Intense roses, lime, honeysuckle billow from succulent but zesty **07** (★★★★) tank sample; 11g/l sugar softening, lifting the finish. Not as complex as pvs **05**, but welcome alternative to more mainstream white varieties. By Paul Cluver.

★★★★★ **Sauvignon Blanc (Cape Point Vineyards)** One of SA's best examples; ample 'green' aromas & flavours, pulsating flavours, pinpoint poise & seemingly endless length the cornerstones on which its reputation is built. **07** finely fruited, delicately crafted, mineral. From Cape Point Vineyards.

★★★★ **Sauvignon Blanc (Nitida)** Ripe yet cool, another superb example. Ex-Nitida in Dbnville, from what is a SA classic sauv area. **07** more tropical than above, but also fine: explosive palate, gd length sure to attract many fans; smidgen semillon adds lemon hint.

★★★★ **Semillon** Winemaker Bernhard Veller (Nitida) shows he is just as adept at crafting top-notch semillon as he is its bdx blending partner, sauv. **07** rather subdued, waxy & floral; opens to nettle, blackcurrant pastille, finishes with pithy texture, zesty acidity.

Merlot ★★★★ Ex-Jordan Winery; judiciously oaked & classic. **05** brims with forest floor, black plum & leafy notes, exudes confidence. 17 mths Fr oak, 40% new. **Pinotage ★★★** 100% new Fr staves account for woody nuance to **07**'s mulberry fruit. Juicy, uncomplicated; only slight tar note, very ripe, confected finish. By Diemersfontein. **Shiraz ★★★★** Toasty coffee-choc oak leads **06**, from producer known for this style, Diemersfontein. Bright acidity cuts through fruit/oak richness, extends palate. Of its style, vg; 90% new oak, mainly Am staves. **Cabernet Sauvignon-Merlot ★★★★** New wine not ready for tasting; cab-led **03** (85%) reviewed last ed featured merlot & splash petit v, was classically styled & flavoured with firm tannins, lead pencil & cassis. Ex-De Wetshof. **Weisser Riesling ★★★★** Rosepetals & lime of young riesling spring from glass of sample **07**, pepper & spice are top notes. Classy sipper, with palate-broadening 11.56g/l sugar. From Paul Cluver, Elgin grapes.

Organic range

> **Shiraz** ☺ **★★★** This ex-African Terroir. Moreish red berry/meaty notes on **07** pre-bottling sample lifted by sour cranberry, firm tannins; slightly bitter twist not off-putting. **Sauvignon Blanc** ☺ **★★★** Enchanting dusty greenpepper nuances on easy-drinking **07** charmer. Subtle nutty finish.

Cabernet Sauvignon No-Sulphur-Added ★★★ By Stellar Winery unless noted. **06** tasted last ed had firm tannins, interesting meat/baked fruit & bread pudding aromas. Fr/Am oak chips used for flavour, act as anti-oxidant. **Merlot No-Sulphur-Added ★★** Gorgeous inky carmine hue caps supple plum & creamy **07** sipper; fermented with Fr/Am chips. **Chardonnay ★★★** Lovely partially Fr chipped version; **07** has nut/oatmeal & tangerine nuances, vibrant finish. Well-balanced if uncomplex. Discontinued: **Chenin Blanc Sulphur Free**.

Classic range

★★★★ **Cabernet Sauvignon** Decent claret tones of elegant yet earthy **05** would add panache to any meal; approachable tannins now or cellaring few yrs. Yr Fr/Am oak. By Villiera.

★★★★ **Merlot 06** offering ex-La Motte quite focused: exuberant fruit topped by leafy notes, spicy oak, fresh & vibrant conclusion. 12 mths 2nd fill oak.

★★★★ **Cabernet Sauvignon-Merlot** By Delheim; cab-led maiden 05 shows class of this venerable Sbosch property. Plum & cassis dusted with dried tobacco; soupçon ruby cab adds softness to lengthy finish. 14 mths Fr oak, none new.

★★★★★ **Cobblers Hill** Classy cab-dominated bdx blend; **03** not retasted for this ed, last was concentrated & long with impeccably managed tannins, poise. Merlot 30%, petit v 15%. 23 mths Fr oak. Ex-Jordan Winery.

★★★★ **Chardonnay Lightly Wooded** Beguiling vanilla, butter & cream notes mingle with tangerine & lemon flavours on **06**, by Jordan Winery. Long & balanced, supple. 9 mths sur lie, 40% new.

★★★★★ **Limestone Hill Chardonnay** Unwooded version from chardonnay master Danie de Wet. **07** chalky/mineral, fruit in confident balance with acidity/alc; deserves ± yr cellaring to build even more character. 06 (★★★★) was atypically subdued, had tad noticeable 14.9% alc.

★★★★ **Wild Yeast Chardonnay** Vibrant yellow hue, intense tangerine & lime aromas/flavours on **05** tell how ripe this unwooded Rtbson sipper is; fruit intensity more than sufficient to mask 14.5% alc. Finishes round & rich. By Springfield Estate.

Merlot ★★★★ Best-seller by Villiera. **05** soft, rounded; sugar-dusted red fruit meshes with firm, slightly bitter oak. 40% new Fr oak. **Shiraz ★★★** Pre-bottling sample **06** well seasoned with combo barrels, staves & chips yet ripe, almost raisined, red fruit shines through. Slips down easily, so note nearly 15% alc. Ex-Rooiberg. **Syrah ★★★★** Pepper, lily & spice on this well-fruited, slightly spiritous (14% alc) **05** sipper from Bon Cap. Super with lamb or beef (preferably organic). 14 mths oak, 20% new. **Grand Rouge ★★★★** Regal bdx blend led by cab, with 30% merlot, 12% cab f. Inky blackness on **06** hints at concentration to come; leafy, slightly raisined finish. 12 mths, 2nd fill oak. Drink soon after purchase. By La Motte. **The Ladybird** ★★★☆ Laibach delivers a winner: **06** brims with plum/herbaceous notes; reined-in tannin provides solid structure from which hangs plush fruit. Merlot led, with cabs s & f, malbec & petit v; 13 mths 30% new oak. **Goshawk Chant** ★★★★ Five-way blend led by merlot with cabs s/f, shiraz & petit v; all matured separately yr in Fr oak. Tasted mid-2006, expansive **04** had sprawling ultra-ripe red & black fruits with tannins to match. By Diemersfontein. **Shiraz-Cabernet Sauvignon** ★★★☆ Popular combo revved up by dash petit v; **06** confident, modest & assured, lovely vanilla oak detail from 14 mths Fr oak, 50% new. By Diemersfontein. **Chenin blanc Spier** NEW **06** not tasted. **Rhine Riesling** ★★★ Subtle rose/lime, faint terpene of young riesling provide ideal foil for slightly sweet (7g/l), cleansing 5.9g/l acidity. **06** neat package by Villiera. **Sauvignon Blanc Bush Vine** ✓ ★★★★ Slender form (11.5% alc) belies **07** bushvine sauvignon's serious intent; herbaceous/figgy on nose & palate, has racy acidity & gd ecent fruit weight, lengthy conclusion. By Darling Cellars. **Viognier** ☙ ★★★★ No new vintage; last ed lightly oaked **06** was charming, had exotic apricot perfume & buttery texture. By Bon Cap. **Chardonnay-Pinot Noir** ★★★★ Versatile white from chard/pinot (60/40) courtesy moderate 12.5% alc. **07** charming: smooth lime & strawberry flavours lifted by well-judged 6g/l sugar. By Cabrière, as is Tranquille. **Pierre Jourdan Tranquille** ★★★ **06** super al fresco sipper from 60% pinot & chard. Berry flavours & aromas zipped up by 6g/l sugar. Lighter (11.5% alc) but not as silky as stablemate. Discontinued: **Nature in Concert**, **Pinotage**, **Cabernet Sauvignon-Merlot**.

House Wines

Red ★★ Staved **06** has oodles charry, jammy charm; if slightly rustic goodbye. Blend shiraz, cab, merlot & ruby cab (42/27/15/10) ex-Franschhoek Vineyards, as is White. **House Rosé Delheim** NEW ★★ By Delheim; **07** a pretty pink with refreshing strawberry tones, zippy acidity hiding 5.7g/l sugar. Mostly pinotage with splash gamay. **White** ★★ **07** marries chard, chenin, sauv, colombar & semillon (40/24/17/14/5) for a crisp, dryish (4.2g/l sugar) sipper; ideal for lazy Sunday brunches. **Sweet** ★★ **07** from chenin; supple, uncomplicated thatch tones, sip well chilled. Pvsly bottled as 'Late Harvest'. Ex -Simonsvlei. **Bel Rosso Sweet Red** ★★ 100% tinta in medium-bodied **06**; **05** featured soupçon merlot. Smooth early drinker with pepper & herby notes. Despite 36.7g/l sugar, not as sweet as you'd expect. By Bergsig.

What? range

Pinotage ☺ ★★★ Quintessential pinotage but reserved rather than flamboyant. Some tar, strawberry on **06**, nicely dry & taut. **Chenin Blanc** ☺ ★★★ Unwooded **07** complex, with citrus/tropical nuances, crisp refreshing acidity. Sip well chilled, watch the 14% alc. A Ken Forrester wine, as are Pinotage & Shiraz. **Sauvignon Blanc** ☺ ★★★ **07** grassy with tropical nuances, passionfruit finish. Slightly more alc than pvs (12.4% vs 11.7%). From Bergsig.

Cabernet Sauvignon ★★★ **04** tasted pvs ed; had firm tannin backbone & hint of spice from 18 mths ageing in older Fr barrels, New World eucalyptus/classic cassis bouquet. **Merlot** ★★★ **05** very ripe, with black plums, meaty aromas/flavours; gently cushioned by smooth oak, supple tannins from 8 mths in oak. Franschoek Vineyards is the supplier. **Shiraz** ★★★ Rampant coconut oak with smoky cherry/plum fruit, friendly tannins make **05** an enticing quaffer. **Chardonnay** ★★★ **07** bursting with tropical/citrus notes; pineapple, melon & lemon/lime. Rich & long, satisfying. Ex-Weltevrede.

Longmarket range

Merlot ☺ ★★★ **06** deep & dark powerhouse from Simonsvlei. Spicy plums, sweet tannins & 5g/l sugar lift ensure early drinkability. 30% new Fr oak. **Merlot-Cabernet Franc** ☺ ★★★ Also from Simonsvlei; **06**'s 40% cab f providing extra leafiness, firmer tannins than on single variety bottling, yet still very plush & ripe. Same oaking.

Cabernet Sauvignon ★★ 80% new oak (Fr/Am combo for 12 mths) gives structure to **05** ripe fruited palate. Rustic, will stand up to hearty stews; not for keeping. By Bergsig. **Pinotage** ★★ Rooiberg Winery's **06** is woody, spiritous, courtesy combo staves/chips/

barrels & 14.3% alc. Already showing signs of age - enjoy soon. **Shiraz** ★★ Sweet vanilla, jammy fruit on **06**, from Swartland Winery. Dense, grippy, with warmish finish. **Shiraz-Pinotage** NEW ★★ By Spier, as is Chard-Viognier. 40% pinotage finds a niche in shiraz's comfortable, broad palate on **06**; hints tar & acetone are nuanced not overbearing - slightly bitter, 14.7% warm goodbye. 8-10 mths Fr/Am oak. **Blanc de Noir** ★★ Swartland Winery delivers modest strawberry hued/toned easy-drinker with 7.2g/l sweetness; **07** from pinotage. **Rosé** ★★★ **07** from Villiera; spicy high notes from 30% muscat ottonel add complexity to red & black berry aromas/flavours. Very sippable. **Chardonnay** ★★ **07** has subdued lemon & biscuit notes, finishes with ripe tangerine flavours, brisk grapefruit acidity. By Robertson Winery. **Chenin Blanc** ★★ Subtle thatch & floral notes on fruit-shy **07**; revved up by racy acidity. Ex-Rooiberg Winery. **Gewürztraminer** ★★★ Supplied by Bergsig in **05**, not retasted for this ed. Lightish everyday quaffer with appealing if slightly confected roses & lime character, sweetish finish. **Pinot Grigio** ★★ **07** cheerful poolside sipper by Van Louveren with endless nutty, zesty appeal; dry finish. **Sauvignon Blanc** ★★ Slender (11.7% alc) but flavoursome **07**; oodles capsicum & grapfruit acidity. Robertson Winery is the supplier. **Wet Rocks Sauvignon Blanc** ★★★ Step up for this Bergsig contribution; **07** a super al fresco white, bracing acidity & pungent herby/herbaceous tones really quite charming. **Chardonnay-Semillon** ★★★ **07**'s 62/34 blend zipped up with 4% sauv. Complex, refreshing & long; an amiable & wallet-friendly companion. **Blanc de Blanc** ★★★ Dusty fynbos & forthcoming greenness star in this pleasant sipper; **07** with just hint of sugar for plumpness. 63/37 sauv/chenin, from Villiera. **Sauvignon Blanc-Semillon** ★★★ Spier makes this & chardonnay-viognier below. **07** tumbles sauv's grassy green tones with semillon's waxy, weight; racy & flavoursome. **Chardonnay Viognier** NEW ★★★ Barrel fermented/aged viognier (12 mths, Fr) adds floral & spice highlights to mainly (82%) chardonnay **06** maiden. Complex, with interesting nutty notes, should be welcomed by shoppers.

Lite range

Bianca Light ★★ Staple ex-Delheim. **07** combo colombar/pinot blanc/muscat d'F/morio muscat combine to deliver musky, light & sweetish tipple; 9.5% alc & 9g/l sugar revved up by cleansing, 7.6g/l acidity.

Zesties

Juicy Red ★★ These all by Bergsig. **05** tasted pvs ed was mix tinta/merlot, spicy & dry with supple tannins. **Perky Pink** ★★ **07** a gently sweet quaffer blending whites colombar/chenin with reds tinta/merlot. Will brighten any picnic basket. **Sassy Sweet** ★★ Flirtacious **07** chard/chenin/colombard has lilting 20.2g/l goodbye; not much aroma/flavour. **Zesty White** ★★ **06** chenin/colombar combo lived up to its name tasted last ed; racy acidity, zesty green apple fruit gave flavour & length.

Concept range

Reckless Red ★★ Forthcoming berry melange from quartet reds (40% merlot, 30% shiraz, 20% cinsaut, 10% cab) in **06**, has just a hint of tannin for interest courtesy 20% staved portion. **Hint of Red** ★★ New label has put new life back into retailer's stalwart rosé. Glorious sunset hue on **07**, perky berry flavours thanks generous mix cab/merlot (85/15). Short but fun. **Wild White** ★★ **06** from 6 white varieties, mostly cruchen bl, chenin. Tasted mid-2006 was balanced & light.

Cap classique sparklers

★★★★ **Brut** Enchanting **NV** from pinotage, pinot & chard; the former playing greater role (63%) than pvs. Tad brassy hue belies fine character: balanced & long, satisfying weight/richness from inclusion of red varieties. By Villiera.

★★★★ **Brut Natural** New name; pvsly 'Brut Zero'. Tiny bubbles hint at **05**'s finesse; mouthfilling mousse gives way to delicate brioche & cream notes, crisp lemon acidity, long & balanced conclusion. From chard.

★★★★★ **Vintage Reserve Brut** Distinguished pinot/chard (60/40) sparkler, traditionally made & matured: 6 yrs on lees, further 12 mths on cork. Luxurious **99** rich & creamy; honey accents to refined citrus/red berry fruit, invigorating acidity. Latest not retasted this ed. All by Villiera.

Blanc de Blanc Brut Chardonnay ★★★☆ Last ed, 04's leesy creaminess, apple compote ripeness was countered by lively acidity, had fine, melting bubbles, fresh finish. 8g/l RS. **Brut Rosé** ★★★★ Lastest NV similar to onion-skin-hued pvs, in which pinotage (56%) played leading role supported by near-equal splashes pinot & chard. Latest meaty, slightly metallic, but with soft red berries; enters fruit-sweet but finishes softly dry, long. Minimum 18 mths on lees, 6 on cork.

Basic sparklers

Brut ★★ Semi-dry rather than brut (14.6g/l RS); slips down easily with pleasing grassy tones. All **NV** by Rooiberg, unless noted. **Spumante** ★★ White muscadel stars in this frothy crowd pleaser with pleasant grapey charm. **Organic Vin Sec Bon Cap** NEW ★★ By Bon Cap: 100% colombard; fresh, sea spray bouquet & gently sweet farewell. **Spumante Rosé** ★★ Berry flavoured sweetish sparkler oozes party-fun. From red muscadel.

Cask wines/'Flexibles'

Cabernet Sauvignon-Merlot ☺ ★★★ Firm but friendly tannic handshake goodbye on well-flavoured 06; berries, meat & smoke do the business. Not for keeping. **Dry Red** ☺ ★★★ Another user-friendly red from this range. 06 has enticing berry/cinnamon/oak spice middle & decent, dry & savory tail. **Semi-Sweet** ☺ ★★★ Melon, tangerine & citronella abound on gently sweet 07; fulfilling mouthfeel from fruit weight & 12.9% alc. Not for keeping. **Stein** ☺ ★★★ Late Harvest-style 07 blossoms with tropical/citrus aromas/flavours, has pleasant sweet lift in its tail. Drink up.

Merlot ★★★ 06 bounds up the quality; powerful nose & palate of spicy plums suggest a hearty tswe its best companion but sweet tannins & 5g/l sugar lift in its tail ensure early drinkability. **Light Rose Simonsvlei** NEW Maiden 07 not available for tasting this ed. **Chardonnay** ★★ Ex-Robertson Winery, 07 rather shy on the nose but very refreshing courtesy zesty tangerine flavours, grapefruit acidity. **Sauvignon Blanc** ★★ Ex-Robertson Winery. 07 has vibrant capsicum aromas, grapefruit acidity; light on its feet 11.7% alc. **Blanc de Blanc** ★★ 07 balanced, rounded with fresh lime/lemon & biscuity notes for immediate sipping. **Crisp White** ★★ 07 lightly flavoured, delicately scented with citrus/bready notes for uncomplicated summer fun. **Light White** ★★ Just 10% alc in 07, light-bodied yet fullsome; zesty green apple acidity jostles with grass/lemon flavours. Discontinued: **Selected Cape Red**. — *CvZ*

■ **Wozani** *see* Oranjerivier Wine Cellars

■ **Wyma Vineyard** *see* Cape Hutton

■ **Y** *see* Yonder Hill Wine Farm

■ **Yamme** *see* Overhex Wines International

Yonder Hill Wine Farm ▮❦&
T 021-855-1008 • F 021-855-1006

Stellenbosch (see Helderberg map) ▪ Est 1989 ▪ 1stB 1993 ▪ Visits Mon-Fri 9-4 ▪ Closed pub hols ▪ Owner Naudé family ▪ Winemaker/viticulturist David Lockley (Jul 1998) ▪ 10ha (cabs s/f, merlot) ▪ 85t/±12 600cs 100% red ▪ PO Box 914 Stellenbosch 7599 ▪ wines@yonderhill.co.za ▪ www.yonderhill.co.za

'It's all in the grape,' says a modest David Lockley, maker of last edition's Superquaffer of the Year, the Y Merlot 06. 'But it pays to put the same energy into all your wines.' Of verve there's no lack, even after 20 vintages, nor enjoyment of the rewards of experience. A vertical tasting of the flagship Merlot confirmed David L's belief that 'we're on the right track. Each vintage is an experiment. But the experiments get easier and more interesting.' A recent example is a non-commercial 'Merlot Light', from nascent vines which in time will feed the flagships.

★★★★ **Merlot** Complex 05 (★★★★☆) raises the bar: poised, confident & elegant. Alluring choc, dark berries, polished leather & hint of mint; firm ripe tannins & integrated (all-new) Fr oak. Confident, as was 04, with structure for cellaring.

★★★★ **Inanda 05** bdx blend brims with abundant dark fruit, cedar & leather; threaded with chalky dry tannins & creamy nuances from 90% new oak. 14.7% alc not obtrusive; all augur well for gd ageing. **04** (★★★★☆) was richly textured & classy.

Cabernet Sauvignon ★★★ No successor yet to herbal **02**. Discontinued: **Shiraz-Merlot**.

Y range

Merlot ★★★ Exuberant juicy berry fruits & frisky acidity on **07**; friendly, smooth, with dry spicy finish. **Shiraz** ★★★ Ripe, spicy dark fruits & liquorice on **06**. Mid-palate appears tad hollow, 14.9% alc warming, slightly out of kilter. **Muscadel** ★★★★☆ **04** barrel sample ups the ante, grapey muscat de F aromas, spicy old oak & dry nutty appeal, integrated spirit.
— MW

■ **Z** *see* Neil Ellis Meyer-Näkel

Zanddrift Vineyards
T 021-863-2076 • F 021-863-2081

Paarl • Est 1995 • Closed to public • Owner Windsharp Trading 23 (Singapore) • PO Box 1302 Suider-Paarl 7624 • zanddrift@xsinet.co.za

Christo Jacobs is the SA point man for the Singaporean group of owners, who visit twice a year. The rehabilitated vineyards yielded their third vintage of cab and shiraz in 2006. The Shiraz will be released this year and the Cab in 2009.

Zandvliet Estate   🍾 🍷 🎋 ♿
T 023-615-1146 • F 023-615-1327

Robertson • Est 1867 • 1stB 1975 • Tasting & sales Mon-Fri 9-5 Sat & pub hols 10-2 • Closed Dec 25 • BYO picnic • Owner Paul & Dan de Wet • Winemaker Johan van Wyk (Apr 2000), advised by Paul de Wet • Viticulturist Dan de Wet, advised by Francois Viljoen • 150ha (cab, shiraz, chard) • 1 350t/60 000cs own label 50% red 45% white 5% rosé • Export brands: Enon, Cogmans/Kogmans Kloof, Cogmans River & Sandy River • PO Box 36 Ashton 6715 • info@zandvliet.co.za • www.zandvliet.co.za

Zandvliet's shiraz focus paid off handsomely when their top-of-the-line Kalkveld Hill of Enon brought home gold from the Syrah du Monde competition in France. Somewhat ironically, this berry selection appears in a high-shouldered bordeaux container; the new wide-bottomed bottle traditionally associated with rhône-style syrah encloses what used to be the Kalkveld French Oak Matured incarnation. Other changes include a fresh-look Le Bistro range (with stelvin twist-off caps) replacing the old Astonvale label, and a semi-sweet Chenin joining the commercially successful My Best Friend range, also under screwcap.

Zandvliet Estate range

★★★★ **Kalkveld 'Hill of Enon' Shiraz** Literally, berry selection from this famed, if unofficial, single vineyard (thus ridiculously small yield: 2t/ha), matured new Am oak 14 mths. Tasted mid-2005, **03**'s oak vanilla set off fragrant allspice features, had textured grip, concentrated mineral finish.

★★★★ **Kalkveld Shiraz** NEW Separate Fr & Am oak aged versions from this unofficial single vineyard discontinued. **03** sample powerful; has lashings brooding fruit, purposeful tannins & 14% alc warming the goodbye. Needs few yrs to show at best. Fr oak, all new.

★★★★ **Shiraz** Less demanding but satisfying version. **05** (★★★★☆) peppery fruit brushed with oak char & fynbos; concludes dry & savoury yet has jammy nuances on entry & mid-palate. ±20 mths combo older oak. **04** continued pacier trend set by **03**.

★★★★ **Chardonnay** Deftly handled oak (30% barrel fermented/3 mths) marries with bright citrus fruit in poised **06**; lively acidity corrals oak/fruit richness, abets seemingly endless finish.

Discontinued: **Kalkveld Shiraz American Oak Matured**, **Cabernet Sauvignon-Shiraz**.

Astonvale range

Discontinued: **Ruby Cabernet**, **Shiraz**, **Unwooded Chardonnay**, **Sauvignon Blanc**, **Crème**.

Le Bistro range

> **Crème**  ☺ 🍽 ★★★ Good every day drinking delivered by lithe & fresh colombard/sauvignon **07** combo (80/20). NE.

Cabernet Sauvignon NEW 🍽 ★★★ Worth trying if you prefer classic savoury tones to New World-ish fruit bombs. Sample **05** has ripe fruit, cigarbox, smoky bacon (from 15% dollop shiraz) & no-nonsense tannins; only older oak. NE. **Chardonnay Unwooded** NEW ✓ 🍽 ★★★★ **07** a welcome addition to unwooded ranks. Sample's intense orange/lemon/lime bouquet promises full citrus palate… & doesn't disappoint; pleasing weight & texture from several mths lees ageing. 13.5% alc. NE. **Sauvignon Blanc** NEW 🍽 ★★★ **07** sample flavoursome, balanced; slips down easily. Cheery summer's day companion with forthright grassy nuances. NE.

My Best Friend range

> **White** ☺ ★★★ As usual, combo chard, chenin & colombard provides vibrant, fruity charm; nicely balanced with 4.9g/l sugar adding roundness. NE.

Red 🍽 ★★★ Tasted last ed, **04** had chunky fruit, food-friendly tannins for pizza/pasta. NE. **Shiraz Rosé** ★★ Tangy acidity drives **07**; shy nose, subdued palate with subtle red-berry fruit salad hints. Friendly 12.5% alc. NE. **Semi-Sweet** NEW 🍽 ★★ **07** maiden semi-sweet from chenin; uncomplicated sipper with muted aromas & flavours. NE. *— CvZ*

■ **Zandwijk** *see* Kleine Draken

■ **Zantsi** *see* Darling Cellars

■ **Zaràfa** *see* Mountain River Wines

■ **Zebra Collection** *see* Rooiberg Winery

■ **Zellerhof** *see* Huguenot Wine Farmers

Zevenwacht
T 021-903-5123 ▪ F 021-903-3373

Stellenbosch ▪ Est 1800 ▪ 1stB 1983 ▪ Tasting & sales Mon-Fri 8.30-5 Sat/Sun 9.30-5 ▪ Fee R17 ▪ Closed Dec 25 ▪ Cellar tours ▪ Manor House Restaurant & picnics daily (see Eat-out section) ▪ Luxury country inn, vineyard cottages & self-catering chalet (see Stay-over section) ▪ Conferences/banqueting ▪ Chef school ▪ Spa ▪ Tour groups ▪ Children's play park ▪ Farm produce ▪ Conservation area ▪ 4×4 trail ▪ Owner Harold Johnson ▪ Winemaker Jacques Viljoen (Jan 2002), with Pierre de Klerk (Sept 2004) ▪ Viticulturist Kevin Watt (Jan 2001, consultant) ▪ 200ha (cab, merlot, pinotage, shiraz, mourvèdre, zinfandel/primitivo, chenin, sauv, viognier, semillon) ▪ ±1 000t/65 000cs 50% red 50% white ▪ PO Box 387 Kuils River 7579 ▪ info@ zevenwacht.co.za ▪ www.zevenwacht.co.za

'A great sauvignon year,' Jacques Viljoen enthuses, yet another winemaker rooting for 2007. Ideal timing, as this popular variety is scaling new sales heights. 'We're now making two versions, our normal flagship Sauvignon and the 360 Degrees, which we've named after the views from this very special block, is a stunner'. Two new high-end blends – a mere 4 barrels of each – have been released. These are best sampled on-site, judging from the results of the latest international Best of Wine Tourism Awards, which placed Zevenwacht first in the Significant Wine Tourism Experiences category.

Zevenwacht range

★★★★ **Syrah 05** not ready. Focused fruit expression in **04** (tasted mid-2006); spicy intensity honed by splash viognier, fine tannins echoed in length of finish. 10% new Am, rest used Fr casks.

★★★★ **Primitivo** Exotic sandalwood, vanilla spiciness to **05**, black cherry flavours. Seriously structured, balanced, with intense acid thread to finish. Tannins currently masking compact mulberry fruit - deserves time. WO Coastal.

★★★★ **Gewürztraminer** Dry, seriously-styled **06** with distinctive, layered aromas litchi, Turkish Delight. Broad, spicy flavours shot through by vibrant acidity, Fr oak ferment/lees contact provide texture & complexity.

Rosé NEW ☺ 🍸 ★★★ Maiden **07** bled from cabs s/f & shiraz; strawberry & raspberry flavours, ending with long, dry finish softened by smidgen sugar (5g/l). **Chenin Blanc** ☺ 🍸 ★★★ Honeyed, waxy **06** offers simple apple flavours, crisp acidity & concluding lime twist. Half oak ferment/6 mths ageing adds dimension. **Bouquet Blanc** ☺ 🍸 ★★☆ Aromatic **07** riesling/gewürz blend overflows with spicy honeysuckle, litchi. Zippy acidity diminishes 11g/l sugar to finish bone-dry.

Cabernet Sauvignon ★★★★ **05** (★★★★) first since lesser, leafy **01**; cool & minty with pronounced blackcurrant aromas. Classically styled & structured with ample supple, ripe berry fruit to balance firm tannins & acidity. Half new Fr oak 13 mths. **Merlot** ★★★★ Ripe plum **05** with minty tones & savoury scrub spice; taut tannins & savoury acid yield refreshing food wine. **Pinotage** ★★★★ **05** popular recipe: toasty mocha, aniseed, choc, vanilla; firm tannins & acidity restraining ripe red fruit, clean finish. **Zevenrood** 🍸 ★★★ **05** merlot/shiraz driven blend, 70% oaked. Chewy tannin & tight acid dominate shy fruit in **05** tank sample. WO Coastal. **Sauvignon Blanc** 🍸 ★★★★ Flinty, cool **07** with sugar-snap pea & fig aromas, citrus & apple flavours balanced by lemony acidity. **Zevenblanc** ✓ 🍸 ★★★ Pedestrian no more, thanks to serious signals from cool **07** capsicum aromas. Crisp apple flavours with long, structured finish. **Semillon Natural Sweet** ★★★★ Made by crushing bunch stems to allow raisining on vine. Arresting **06** pronounced orange blossom & honey scents, light 11% alc. 146g/l sugar lifted by fresh acidity, giving sweet-sour, pineapple finish. Delicious! Fr oak ferment.

The Tin Mine range

★★★★ **White** 🍸 **06** barrel-fermented blend sauv, chard & viognier; vinified seperately. Gunflint aromas & almond toastiness, needs time to reveal its honey & apricot charms; presently unyielding. Up to speed of pvs, after less complex **05** (★★★★).

Red ★★★★ **05** not yet ready for tasting. **04** shiraz, merlot, cab, zin combo tasted last ed less gauche, more concentrated than pvs. 70/30 Fr/Am oak. Celebrates enterprise of early 20th century miners on the property. — *IM*

Zidela Wines
T 021-880-2936 • **F** 021-880-2937

Stellenbosch • Est 2001 • 1stB 2002 • Closed to public • Owner Danie Kritzinger, Herman Nell & Jaco Kritzinger • Winemaker Jaco Kritzinger (May 2002) • 80% red 15% white 5% rosé • Other brands: Suikerbosch & Gordon's Bay • PO Box 3021 Matieland 7602 • info@zidelawines.co.za • www.zidelawines.co.za

A few small tweaks to the wine line-up (petit verdot added to the cab-merlot blend; new Suikerbosch semi-sweet and red blend), but last year the main focus was on marketing. Besides creating a new website, the owners appointed a consultant with wide experience in the central African market and are in conversation with experts on the East.

Zidela Wines range

Cabernet Sauvignon-Merlot-Petit Verdot ☺ ★★★ Lighter-styled bdx blend with smoky, toasty allures; **05** fresh, accessible blackberry fruit. **Chenin Blanc** ☺ ★★★ Real character & appeal at a giveaway price; **07** clean, leafy, fresh fruit salad notes, great value quaffing. **Sauvignon Blanc** ☺ ★★★ **07** grassy intro, crisp pineapple flavour, refreshingly light bodied.

Merlot ★★ Pvsly-tasted **04** wild berried & light bodied for uncomplicated quaffing. **Shiraz** ★★★ **04** inviting smoky note, light & fruity, friendly outdoor wine.

Gordon's Bay range

Shiraz ★★★ Zesty fruit, firm tannins & dry finish noted on vibrant **04** last time. **Sauvignon Blanc** ★★★ Dry grass & bright acidity on **07**, perfect for seafood. Discontinued: **Chardonnay**.

Suikerbosch range

> **Chenin Blanc** ☺ ★★★ **07** cheerful white with fresh herbal nose, summer fruits & crisp, dry finish.

Shiraz-Merlot NEW ★★ 'Kaapse Rooi' in new garb. **06** easy-drinker with shy spice notes, raisin undertone. **Kaapse Rosé** ★ **07** simple, undemanding off-dry poolside quaffer. **Golden Nectar Semi-Sweet** NEW ★ **07** straightforwardly sweet white with warm hay nuance. — DB

Ziggurat Vineyards
T 021-863-3494 • F 021-863-1804

Paarl • Est 1692 • 1stB 2003 • Tasting & sales Mon-Sat 9-5 (Oct to Apr); otherwise call ahead T 021-863-3494 • Tours by appt • B&B/self-catering cottage • Owner Louw family • Winemaker Anton Louw (Jan 2005) • Viticulturist Dawid Gerstner (Jul 1999) • 174ha (cab, merlot, shiraz, chard, sauv) • 1 080t total • 11t/500cs own label 65% red 35% white • PO Box 2 Simondium 7670 • ziggurat@mweb.co.za • www.zigguratwines.co.za

The winery, tasting venue and most of the farm Babylons Toren have been sold, but the Louw family retains the Ziggurat brand and the prime vineyards, and the wines listed below can still be bought from them directly. Winemaker Anton L reluctantly chose not to make wine last year: after completing a Wine Business Management course, he took time off to travel and research. 'But I won't hang up my cellar boots for long!'

★★★★ **Shiraz** Debut **04** abundant red-fruit melange, floral nuances from 5% viognier add gloss. Balanced, enduring fleshy flavours & polished tannins. 18 mths 2nd fill Fr wood. Should improve few yrs. Not retasted, as for all.

Cabernet Sauvignon-Merlot ★★★★ Upbeat, early-drinking 50/50 blend in **04**, impressive fruit weight, supple tannins, vanilla finish. 18 mths combo new-4th fill Fr oak. **Rosé** ★★★★ Rather sophisticated **06**, herb & red-fruit scents, zesty acidity, firm fruit tannins & bone-dry tail. **Wild Card Chardonnay** ★★★ pvsly noted as 'wild' & unmeshed - should since have melded. Bouquet a riot of oak-influenced aromas, palate thick with lime & ripe tangerine. Acidity cuts richness short on finish. 6 mths 1st fill Fr oak. **Sauvignon Blanc** ★★★★ **06** attractive cut grass, tropical fruit & 'wet pebble' notes, racy yet flavoursome unfinished sample. — CvZ

Zoetendal Wines
T 028-482-1717 • F 028-482-1720

Elim (see Southern Cape map) • Est/1stB 2004 • Visits Mon-Fri 9-5 Sat 9-1 • Closed Easter Sun, Dec 25 & Jan 1 • Meals for groups of 10+ by appt; picnics • Walks • Conservation area • Owner Johan & Elizan de Kock • Winemaker/viticulturist Johan de Kock • 8.5 ha (shiraz, sauv) • 2 480 cs 35% red 65% white • PO Box 22 Elim 7284 • zoetendal@telkomsa.net

The new self-catering guesthouse will be sure to please nature lovers wishing to linger longer at this boutique Elim cellar, fringed by SA's biggest wetland ecosystem. A BWI member and long committed to conservation, Zoetendal was recently registered with BirdLife South Africa as a birder-friendly establishment. Owner, viticulturist and now winemaker Johan de Kock is pleased with the vinous addition to the flock: a bordeaux-style blend named Milè ('Elim' spelt backwards).

Shiraz ★★★★ Juicy ripeness gives luscious charm (if not complexity) to previewed **06**, & balances big 14.5% alc, gentle tannins. Moderate oaking (none new) leaves pure fruit in charge.

Milè Cabernet Sauvignon-Cabernet Franc-Petit Verdot NEW 06 cab-led (64%) blend shows fragrant fruit-pastille aromas but, tasted from barrel mid-2007, dominated by big dry tannin & 15% alc; too unready to rate. **Sauvignon Blanc** 📖 ★★★★ With dry, grassy delicacy of pvs **06** (★★★★), **07** (tasted ex-tank) adds round ripeness; full flavours & lovely savoury acid. Rating provisional. — TJ

Zomerlust

Carefree quaffers in 2- and 5-litre packs, by Robertson Winery for Vinimark.

Dry Red ★★ Trio of reds in soft, red-berried mode, modest 13% alc perfect for quaffing. **Blanc de Blanc** ★ Scented off-dry white with light 10.3% alc. **Stein** ★★ Gentle semi-sweet easy-drinker, with zesty tropical flavours. **Late Harvest** ★★ Ripe & amiable semi-sweet, tropical flavours with tangy hint of dried fruit. — MW

■ **Zondernaam** see Tokara

Zonnebloem
T 021-808-7911 • F 021-883-2603

Stellenbosch ▪ *Owner Distell* ▪ *Group cellar manager Callie van Niekerk (Dec 2005)* ▪ *Cellar manager (Adam Tas facility) Michael Bucholz (Jan 2006)* ▪ *Winemaker Deon Boshoff (whites, Dec 2001), with Elize Coetzee (née Wessels); reds - TBA* ▪ *Viticulturist Henk van Graan (Jan 1996)* ▪ *9 000t ±220 000cs 59% red 41% white* ▪ *PO Box 46 Stellenbosch 7599* ▪ *mbucholz@ distell.co.za* ▪ *www.zonnebloem.co.za*

This popular stalwart, with roots in the 18th century, began 2007 with a revamp of its labels to enhance and update – but not tamper with – the tradition that the bottle celebrates. Plans for the coming year are the launch of two new wines, a viognier and a rhône blend. The team is soon to be joined by a new red-wine maker, while assistant white-wine maker, Elize Wessels, married Flagstone's Wilhelm Coetzee. Meanwhile Michael Bucholz, cellar manager at the Adam Tas winery, is involved in a winemaking project in two-harvests-per-year Tanzania.

Limited Editions NEW
★★★★ **Pinotage 05** similar aromas/flavours to std bottling, also biltong & scrub nuances. Finely tuned tannins, lively acidity, bright fruit plus moderate 12.6% alc make for a v agreeable drink. 100% new oak.

Sauvignon Blanc ★★★★ **07** has the most distinctive & pungent greenpepper aroma imaginable, contrasting with water-white appearance & relatively delicate flavours. Gd juicy acidity, rounded mouthfeel. WO Coastal. **Semillon** ★★★★ Unoaked semillon from coastal vyds. **07** dusty sauv-like nose; balanced, sustained & vinous but mid-2007 quite bland, needs time to develop more character in bottle.

Zonnebloem range
★★★★ **Shiraz** Dense but fresh fruit, lily & black pepper are part of **05**'s appeal. Fine tannins, reined-in alc (13.9%), brisk dry finish complete the package. Mix new/older barrels. Back up to speed after slight dip in **04** (★★★★).

★★★★ **Lauréat** The flagship; more generously oaked than rest of range. **05** (★★★★) combines cab (55%) & merlot (30%) with smidgens malbec, petit v. Modern fruit tone yet classic styling, with gripping dry tannins; marked acidity a detraction this vintage, whereas **04** was sumptuous & internationally hailed (incl IWC, IWSC golds).

Cabernet Sauvignon ★★★ Wanting fruit flavours & weight of pvs; brisk acidity stands apart, yet **05** does have some sweet/sour cranberry notes, form-giving tannins. 25% new oak. **Merlot** ★★★★ Decently dry, leafy **05**, medium-bodied despite substantial 14.2% alc; modest prune flavours with creamy oak hint. **Pinotage** ★★★ Raspberry & tar tones on **05**, lively, finishes with firm but friendly tannic hug. Mix new, older oak. **'Rhône-Style Blend'** NEW ★★★★ Fine tannin structure, generous fruit on maiden **06** led by wooded shiraz, splashes unoaked cinsaut, mourvèdre, viognier. Appealingly dry; some scrub character. Reds all WO Sbosch. **Chardonnay** ★★★ Reticent **06** mainly oak-fermented (equal mix new, 1st & 2nd fill plus 10%

tank). Vibrant acidity, 14% alc, creamy wood all in balance, yet v fruit-shy. **Sauvignon Blanc** ★★★ Minerality, rapier acidity, greenpepper, lemon pithiness the cornerstones of pleasant **07** sipper. **Viognier** NEW ★★★ Debut **07** has all the apricot, litchi, fruit kernel charm of this variety, none of the blowsiness. Tad short, though, with warming 14% alc. **Blanc de Blanc** ★★★ Invariably a lightish (±12% alc), easy-drinking blend. **07** chenin & sauv mix (80/20); fresh, dry, with Granny Smith apple & thatch notes. Whites all WO W Cape unless noted. **Premier Grand Cru** ★★★ Unshowy but sound everyday white. Zesty freshness on tropical **07**, pleasantly undemanding 11.5% alc. 50/50 chenin/colombard. — *CvZ*

■ **Zonneweelde** *see Slanghoek Winery*

Zorgvliet Wines

T 021-885-1049 • F 021-885-1290

Stellenbosch ▪ Est/1stB 2000 ▪ Tasting & sales Nov-Apr: Mon-Thu 9-5 Fri 9-6 Sat 10-7 Sun 10-5 May-Oct: Mon-Fri 9-5 Sat/Sun 11-5 Pub hols Jan-Dec 10-3 ▪ Closed Easter Fri & Dec 25 ▪ Fee R15 p/p ▪ Herenhuis 1692 Restaurant Mon-Sat 12-9.30 Sun 12-3.30; Le Pommier Restaurant: daily 8am-9.30pm ▪ Zorgvliet Deli: Tue-Sun 9-6 weather permitting ▪ Cellar tours by appt ▪ Facilities for children ▪ Gifts ▪ Conferencing ▪ Vineyard Lodge & Spa (see Stay-over section) ▪ Owner Mac & Marietjie van der Merwe ▪ Winemaker Neil Moorhouse (Jan 2003) ▪ Viticulturist Rudolf Jansen van Vuuren (Jun 1999) ▪ Viti adviser Kevin Watt (Aug 2002) ▪ 57ha (cabs s/f, merlot, shiraz, chard, sauv, semillon, viognier) ▪ 500t/25 000cs own label 60% red 40% white ▪ PO Box 1595 Stellenbosch 7599 ▪ winecellar@zorgvliet.com ▪ www.zorgvlietwines.com / www.zorgvliet.com

'Another breakthrough year for Zorgvliet wines,' says Neil Moorhouse, winemaker at this Banhoek Valley farm. He reveals vineyard holiday packages are now attracting visitors from as far afield as India (where the Silver Myn Viognier has proved exceptionally popular, perhaps as a good match for spicy cuisine). Meanwhile, client demand has resulted in the introduction of a wine club 'with benefits not previously been seen in the industry'. But Moorhouse's focus remains on the quality of the final product, right down to the closures: 'Screwcaps are now established as part of the brand positioning.'

Zorgvliet range

★★★★ **Cabernet Sauvignon** Powerful yet elegant **05** has polished leather, dark spicy fruit, fine grainy tannins, structure for cellaring 5 yrs+ courtesy well-judged oaking (18 mths 48% new Fr).

★★★★☆ **Richelle** Flagship bdx-style blend features mainly cab plus 4 other traditional varieties. **05** juicy, complex; cassis, cedar & exotic note of clove; expansive 15% alc & serious oaking (22 mths, 90% Fr, 80% new) well integrated. Firm, fine tannins suggest gd few yrs development.

★★★★☆ **Sauvignon Blanc** Herbal & tropical **07**, plumper, riper than pvs yet with signature citrus tone. Unrated early preview also shows less somewhat less gravitas, verve, than richly concentrated & mouthfilling **06**.

Shiraz ★★★☆ **04** last ed had spicy nuance, brisk acidity, dry tannic finish; needed few yrs to mesh with soft, smoky, red-berried fruit.

Silver Myn range

★★★★ **Cabernet Franc** Restrained, perfumed **06** (sample) has impressive core red fruit, powdery dry tannins which should reward few yrs ageing. Mainly Fr oak, 40% new.

★★★★ **Petit Verdot** Tasted pvs ed, **05** was tight, with fine tannins, well hidden 15% alc, usual smidgen merlot adding violet lift to mineral nose/palate. 10% Am oak forgone for Russ, remainder Fr.

★★★★ **Chardonnay 07** (★★★) not as complex, intense as last-reviewed **05**. Muted lime aromas/flavours tinged with creamy coconut (ex 8% oaked portion). Crisp, for early drinking.

> **White** ☺ ★★★☆ Crisp & fruity **07** sauv/semillon duo (77/23). Appealing dusty grapefruit pith nuance for food pairing.

Cabernet Sauvignon ★★★☆ Bold & brooding **05** sample chalky & dry. Cassis, choc & liquorice flavours integrated, as are oak tannins ex-mainly Fr, 35% new barrels. **Pinot Noir** NEW ★★★☆ Maiden **07** (sample, rating provisional) shows elegance, restraint. Cranberry & earthy flavours; supple, firm tannins & supportive oak (86% Fr, 43% new). **Shiraz** ★★★ Uncomplicated **04** offered sweet, spicy nose & tutti-frutti palate mid-2006. **Merlot-Cabernet Franc** ★★★☆ Courtesy the warm vintage, merlot-led **05** very ripe, less well structured than **04** (★★★★), needs time to integrate with insistent dry tannins. Oaked 16 mths, mainly Fr, 30% new. **Dry Rosé** ★★★ Pinot joined **05** mix last ed; this plus lower alc (12%) made for refreshing aperitif with cranberry piquancy, savoury highlights. **Sauvignon Blanc** ★★★☆ After stellar **05** (★★★★), **06** went straight to Germany, was not reviewed. While showing **05**'s tropical & fig tones, **07** quieter, softer; more aperitif than main course. **Viognier** ★★★☆ Inviting **07** balanced, cleverly oaked (around 50% fermented/5 mths). Foral & dried apricot tones, clean, crisp & just off-dry.

Le Pommier range

> **Sauvignon Blanc** ☺ ★★★ **07**, with 14% semillon, less fruit-filled than pvs, but still appealing & fresh for summer quaffing.

Cabernet Sauvignon ★★★☆ **04** fruit-driven, touch spicy from 14 mths older oak. No new vintage of this, reds following; none retasted. **Cabernet Sauvignon Reserve** ★★★☆ 10% 1st fill oak (16 mths) added vanilla/cedar notes, fine wood tannins to generously fruited **04**. **Cabernet Franc** ★★★ Pvsly visited **04** was earthy, brooding & savoury; may now have opened up to show more aromatic, flavoursome fruit. **Shiraz** ★★★ Restrained fruit on **04** dominated by resinous oak mid-2006; 14 mths oak, third new. **Semillon** NEW ★★★ **07** back-to-guide in refreshing summer style; quietly herbaceous with cool, green flavours, lightish (12.5%), some waxy breadth. All screwcapped.

Spring Grove range

Cabernet Sauvignon ★★★ Garnet-hued **04** showed cassis hints, sour cherry flavours & judicious oaking last ed. Neither in range retasted. **Shiraz** ★★★ Lightly oaked **03**; jelly-baby aromas followed by red fruit miscellany, short finish. — *MW*

■ **Zwalu** *see* Neil Ellis Meyer-Näkel

Introducing the tasters for this edition

MICHAEL FRIDJHON

Widely consulted liquor industry authority and leading wine writer, Michael is chairman of the Trophy Wine Show and has judged in wine competitions in several countries. Visiting professor at the University of Cape Town Graduate School of Business, he is a chevalier of the French Ordre du Mérite Agricole, writes for Business Day, The Weekender, Wine, Fine Wine and Decanter. He has also written or contributed to over 30 books and has been a taster for the guide since the early 1980s.

ANGELA LLOYD

During her 24 years' professional involvement with wine, Angela has lectured and broadcast about and 'even made' wine. She's pursued her love of travel, exploring the world's winelands, on occasions as a judge, a role also regularly fulfilled in SA. As a wine writer, commissions come from local and international publications; she's also associate editor of Grape. Her longest association is with this guide; the 2008 edition is her 22nd as a taster and scribe.

CATHY VAN ZYL

Cathy is SA's only resident Master of Wine. A relative newcomer to the wine industry, over the past few years she has judged at the Trophy Wine Show, Diner's Club Winemaker of the Year, for Grapeworx and has started judging internationally. She is a co-founder of Grape, and still a regular contributor. Cathy also lectures for the CWA on tasting. Her online wine diary, Cathy's Blog, is an SA pioneer of this increasingly popular genre.

TIM JAMES

Tim has a PhD in English literature but 'no proper ambitions' or full-time job – leaving more time for wine matters. His biggest involvement is with the Grape website (www.grape.co.za) but he also writes for local and international publications. Other activities have included lecturing on wine and studying it (he is a Cape Wine Master). He confines his wine judging to smaller events, mostly for Grape, but also some restricted competitions. Tim has tasted for this guide for several years now.

CHRISTINE RUDMAN

Christine started out in FMCG marketing in Johannesburg. Accepting a job at SFW and needing to learn about wine she enrolled with the CWA. Her Cape Wine Masters qualification was earned in 1988; she ran the CWA for seven years, and has since been occupied with consultancy work, professional tastings, wine judging and writing. She's travelled widely, tasted on international panels, written A Guide to the Winelands of the Cape; and says there's no retirement in sight, she's 'having too much fun'.

IRINA VON HOLDT

After qualifying as a Cape Wine Master and writing for numerous publications, Irina decided that it was time to get her hands dirty. Concerned that SA chenin blanc was not getting the attention she felt it deserved, she set about making her own and started the Chenin Blanc Association to refocus and elevate the status of SA's most widely planted variety. She is a regular judge at industry tastings and internationally for chenin blanc.

MERYL WEAVER

Meryl swapped her legal career in Gauteng for one in wine when she moved to the Cape a decade ago. She's now a Cape Wine Master, lectures for the Cape Wine Academy, and, as a registered wine tourguide, conducts many tours for international wine-journalists and -judges on behalf of Wines of South Africa. Meryl tasted with many of the Platter team during her previous role as coordinator and as an official panel member and contributor since 2006.